Reports of Cases in the Court of Exchequer From 1685 to 1714

English Law Reports of the Early Modern Period

Volume One: *Equity Cases in the Court of Exchequer, 1660–1714*, Edited by W. H. Bryson, 2007. [This volume can be cited as Eq. Cases Exch.]

Volume Two: *Robert Paynell's Exchequer Reports (1627–1631)*, Edited by W. H. Bryson, 2009. [This volume can be cited as Paynell Exch.]

Volume Three: *Robert Paynell's King's Bench Reports (1625–1627)*, Edited by W. H. Bryson, 2010. [This volume can be cited as Paynell K.B.]

Volume Four: *Reports of Cases in the Court of Exchequer in the Time of King George I (1714–1727)*, Edited by W. H. Bryson, 2013. [This volume can be cited as Exch. Cases *temp.* Geo. I.]

Volume Five: *Reports of Cases in the Court of Exchequer in the Time of King Charles II*, Edited by W. H. Bryson, 2017. [This volume can be cited as Exch. Cases *temp.* Char. II.]

Volume Six: *Reports of Cases in the Court of Chancery in the Time of King George I*, Edited by W. H. Bryson, 2019. [This volume can be cited as Chan. Cases *temp.* Geo. I.]

Volume Seven: *Paul Jodrell's Chancery Reports (1737 to 1751)*, Edited by W. H. Bryson, 2020. [This volume can be cited as Jodrell.]

Volume Eight: *Reports of Cases in the Court of Chancery in the Time of Queen Anne*, Edited by W. H. Bryson, 2021. [This volume can be cited as Chan. Cases *temp.* Anne.]

Volume Nine: *Reports of Cases in the Court of Chancery 1660 to 1673*, Edited by W. H. Bryson, 2022. [This volume can be cited as Chan. Cases 1660–1673]

Medieval and Renaissance
Texts and Studies

Volume 585

Center for Law Reporting

Volume 10

Reports of Cases in the Court of Exchequer From 1685 to 1714

EDITED BY

W. H. BRYSON

ACMRS PRESS

Tempe, Arizona

2024

ACMRS PRESS

Published by ACMRS Press
Tempe, Arizona

ISBN 978-0-86698-646-5

∞
This book is set in Adobe Caslon Pro.
Printed in the United States of America.

Introduction

This collection of reports of cases in the Court of Exchequer attempts to publish all of the reports, whether in manuscript or in print, from this court from 1685 to 1714. However, it does not reprint the cases from this period of time that are to be found in W. H. Bryson, ed., *Equity Cases in the Court of Exchequer 1660 to 1714* (2007) nor the official decrees in tithes cases in the Court of Exchequer that are published in H. Wood, ed., *A Collection of Decrees by the Court of Exchequer* (1798). (Some of Wood's decrees are copied in F. K. Eagle and E. Younge, edd., *A Collection of the Reports . . . Relating to Tithes.*) This book is the companion volume for common law and revenue cases to *Equity Cases in the Court of Exchequer 1660 to 1714* (2007), volume 1 of this series, and is the sequel volume to *Reports of Cases in the Court of Exchequer in the Time of King Charles II* (2017), volume 5 of this series.

It is to be noted that the collection of Exchequer reports by Thomas Hardres ends in 1669. Thereafter, until the eighteenth-century Exchequer reports by William Bunbury, which begin systematically in 1714, the only cases from this court that were in print are a very few reports scattered among the general English law reports, which concentrate on the Court of King's Bench.

The manuscript law reports of Edward Ward (1638-1714) include some miscellaneous cases and notes from all of the high courts of England during his professional life, but the vast majority of them are from the Court of Exchequer. This was where his law practice was centered and where he later sat as the Chief Baron. Ward's manuscript reports, which are the foundation of this edition, are presently in Lincoln's Inn; they are catalogued as Misc. 557 to Misc. 559 and Misc. 531 to Misc. 539. There is an eighteenth-century copy at the Georgetown University Law School Library, Brown MSS. B88-7 to B88-10. Kudos to Lincoln's Inn and the Georgetown Law School for acquiring, preserving, and making available these legal manuscripts.

Edward Ward reported law cases beginning with his days as a law student and continuing throughout his very successful and long legal career, including his lengthy tenure as Chief Baron of the Court of Exchequer, from 1695 to 1714. His successor Chief Baron, Samuel Dodd (1652-1716), at the end of his own law reports, noted Ward's final days. '[On] 16 July 1714, Friday, Lord Chief Baron Ward died at his house in Essex Street. He sickened the Monday before he was to have gone on circuit on the Tuesday, but sickness and death prevented him, *multum deploratus*. He said the disease was a fever of the nerves, but I [Samuel Dodd] think it was a general decay of nature at once. He was always very strong and healthful, but was very far in years, *viz.* seventy-seven.'

Table of Cases Reported

[These references are to case numbers, not page numbers.]

Reports of Cases in the Court of Exchequer From 1685 to 1714

1

Earl of Derby's Case

(Ex. 1685)

In this case, a rent claimed by the crown was discharged, having been released by a grant from the crown.

Lincoln's Inn MS. Misc. 557, f. 74, pl. 1

23 January, Hilary term 36 & 37 Car. II, 1684/5. Office of the Treasurer's Remembrancer.

King Edward IV granted to the then earl of Derby in tail male Salterford and five other parcels of land in Macclesfield forest in Cheshire under the annual rent of £5 payable at the Exchequer of Chester. Afterwards, Queen Elizabeth granted the reversion of Salterford to one to whom the then earl of Derby agreed to sell. But it was under and liable to all rents issuing and chargeable upon it. The purchaser took upon himself to pay all the rent of £5 *per annum*, and his estate was defeasible upon non-payment. Afterwards, in 16 Car. I [1640 × 1641], William, then earl of Derby, accepted a grant and confirmation from the crown of all the lands in the first grant except Salterford, and there was a reservation of £5 *per annum* upon them *unacum omnibus aliis redditibus solubilis seu reservatis pro praemissis*. And then there was a clause immediately following this reservation to such effect, that *rex voluit et concessit* that the premises granted and confirmed by those letters patent nor any part of it will be liable or charged or chargeable with any double rent otherwise reserved for the premises or any part of them *aliquo in praesentibus [?] contentis in contraria non obstante*. And, in truth, this grant was only a grant of confirmation and to avoid a commission of concealments and defective titles.

And, inasmuch as one £5 only was paid to the crown and one rent of £5 *per annum* certified and sold by trustees for the sale of fee farm rents (and this was the rent reserved upon the first grant of Edward IV), the court, upon the consideration of this clause in the grant of 16 [Car. II] for exempting the lands from a double rent and the circumstances of the payment and no other rent in charge with the Auditor, discharged the process of the Pipe [Office] that lately issued for twenty-four years arrears, and ordered no other process to issue for the times past for this last £5 *per annum*.

I [*Edward Ward* was] for the earl.

[Other copies of this report: Georgetown Univ. Law Sch. MS. B88–7, p. 548.]

2

Shaw v. Hinckley

(Ex. 1685)

A suit for mortuaries lies in the common law courts, and not in the ecclesiastical courts.

Lincoln's Inn MS. Misc. 557, f. 74, pl. 2

Saunders cited these cases against the prohibition, Sidderfin 263; Deg. 354, Jeffreys and Wood, Deg. 355; Cro. Car. 237; Halsey and Halsey, Jones rep.[1]

[Other copies of this report: Georgetown Univ. Law Sch. MS. B88–7, p. 550.]

Lincoln's Inn MS. Misc. 557, f. 80

Hilary 1684/85. In prohibition.

The defendant here libeled in the ecclesiastical court of Worcester against the plaintiff here for a mortuary. The plaintiff obtained a [writ of] prohibition upon a suggestion of the Statute of 21 Hen. VIII, ca. 6,[2] by which it is enacted that no mortuary will be paid where it was not paid by custom before this Statute. And he averred that nothing was paid or due by custom and that he pleaded it in the ecclesiastical court, which refused to admit this plea.

Somers prayed a [writ of] consultation be granted that a suit for mortuaries is proper in an ecclesiastical court being an ecclesiastical duty and that this court will try the custom as an incident to the jurisdiction of the principal and, for this, he cited 2 Inst. 491, upon the Statute *De Circumspecte Agatis*, where it is said that mortuaries are only due by custom and not within the Statute *De Circumspecte Agatis*, which speaks only of tithes, 2 Hen. V, 10, and that the Statute of Hen.

---

[1] *Marke v. Gilbert* (1665), 1 Siderfin 263, 82 E.R. 1095, also 1 Keble 919, 83 E.R. 1320; *Jeoffries v. Wood* (K.B. 1671), S. Degge, *Parson's Counsellor*, p. 349; *Hinde v. Bishop of Chester* (1631), Croke Car. 237, 79 E.R. 808; *Halsey v. Halsey* (1631), W. Jones 230, 82 E.R. 121, 2 Gwillim 468, 1 Eagle & Younge 371.

[2] Stat. 21 Hen. VIII, c. 6 (*SR*, III, 288–289).

VIII gives jurisdiction by the liberty that it gives to the suit in the ecclesiastical court.[1]

Response: Mortuaries were due before by a provincial constitution made 1294. Linwood, *de Sepulturis*, cap. *Quia inter Rectores etc.*, li. 3, fo. 134,[2] another constitution 1366, which two constitutions were made by archbishops Winchelsea and Langham in Canterbury province.

As to the jurisdiction given by 21 Hen. VIII to the ecclesiastical court, it is only when the suit is according to this Act *in omnibus* and [there is] no doubt or question between the parties, because it is only a jurisdiction by implication.

But this Statute is a settlement of the right of mortuaries, *vide* the preamble, the enacting clauses, and the last clause and the penalties imposed for a suit against this Statute. And, by this Statute, as well the right as the quantum is settled and in what cases.

The custom here alleged, to be exempt or not to pay, certainly will be tried by the common law.

First, this Statute is now all the foundation that mortuaries have by any law. And the words and penalties are plain. And a suit will not be determined there if they will try the custom because what will become of the penalties imposed for suing against this Statute if the ecclesiastical court will judge of the custom?

Second, it is a rule that the exposition of statutes belongs to the common law.

Third, it is another rule that prescriptions also will be tried at common law. 2 Inst. 491. A pension is suable in the ecclesiastical court by the Statute *De Circumspecte Agatis*. But, if it is claimed by prescription, it is not suable there, inasmuch as prescriptions will be tried by the common law. The canon law and the common law differ in this. 2 Inst. 491, *in terminis*.

Fourth, a *modus decimando*, if it is admitted by both parties, the suit can be tried in an ecclesiastical court. But, if the defendant denies the *modus*, the trial of it will be at common law. And this is an apt and parallel case, and determines, in effect, this question.

Objection: Siderfin 263, Marke and Gilbert.[3]

Solution: This is not to our purpose because it was a contention between a parson and a vicar, which the ecclesiastical court can determine. And, there, it was admitted that a mortuary was due by custom, but the difference was only to which person. And there, it is said that the statute took away those which were not due by custom. So that this case maintains the jurisdiction of the common law when the custom is in question, though it did not award [a writ of] prohibition as to a competition between ecclesiastical persons.

---

[1] E. Coke, *Second Institute* (1642), p. 491; Stat. 13 Edw. I, *Circumspecte Agatis* (*SR*, I, 101–102); YB Trin. 2 Hen. V, f. 10, pl. 9 (1414); Stat. 21 Hen. VIII, c. 6 (*SR*, III, 288–289).

[2] W. Lindwood, *Provinciale* (J. V. Bullard & H. C. Bell, edd., 1929), p. 70.

[3] *Marke v. Gilbert* (1665), *ut supra*.

Objection: Jeffreys and Wood's Case, Deg. 354.

Solution: This case says that [a writ of] prohibition will not be awarded unless they proceed contrary to the Statute, which is a vehement implication that it will be awarded when proceedings are made against the Statute, which they are here when they sue for mortuaries when nothing is due.

Objection: Cro. Car. 237, Hind and the bishop of Chester.

Solution: First, this case is out of the Statute of 21 Hen. VIII, being for mortuaries due to the archdeacon of Chester, which is excepted out of the Statute, and the suit for it directed as before, and thus is nothing to our case. Second, in this case, two judges were against two, and to determine the question, it was directed that the defendant should demur, and then the court will give judgment upon the record. But nothing more was done, as Deg 355.[1] Thus, it is no authority in the case.

Objection: Halsey and Halsey's Case, Jones 230, that a court Christian has cognisance of common ways for carrying tithes, and [a writ of] prohibition was denied.

Solution: This does not relate to the matter in question, but the reason is there given and plain that it is given by the Statute of 2 Edw. VI [*blank*] and Fitzherbert, *Natura Brevium*, in consultation.[2]

The [writ of] prohibition between Clobery and Shaw was obtained in [the Court of] Common Bench in a Herefordshire case, Hilary 33 & 34 Car. II, rot. 1975, upon a similar suggestion. And the constant practice, as the practisers say, was upon the reasons first mentioned of the statutes and prescription, that they should be expounded and tried by the common law.

And the Chief Baron [Montagu] said that a case in [a writ of] error depended before the justices of the Common Bench and barons of the Exchequer upon a prohibition granted in the King's Bench in a case of mortuaries. *Vide* 13 Rep. 9, where *Doctor and Student*, l. 2, ca. 55, fo. 105,[3] was cited, that [a writ of] prohibition lies where mortuaries are sued for otherwise than the Statute of 21 Hen. VIII directs.

And, in the principal case, [a writ of] consultation was denied upon the reasons aforesaid.

I [*Edward Ward* was] for the prohibition.

And afterwards in the Common Bench [. . .] 1700 or 1701, [there was a] similar resolution against some in the King's Bench.

[Other copies of this report: Georgetown Univ. Law Sch. MS. B88–7, p. 562.]

---

[1] *Hinde v. Bishop of Chester* (1631), *ut supra*.

[2] Stat. 2 & 3 Edw. VI, c. 13 (*SR*, IV, 55–58); A. Fitzherbert, *Natura Brevium*.

[3] *Rochester v. Porter* (1608), 13 Coke Rep. 4, 9, 77 E.R. 1416, 1421, also Noy 152, 74 E.R. 1114; C. St. German, *Doctor and Student* (T. F. T. Plucknet & J. L. Barton, edd., 1974), 91 Selden Soc. 313.

3

Villiers v. Jesson

(Ex. 1685)

Where lands have been seized upon several executions of judgments, the holder of the first lease has priority over creditors who have prior outlawries and inquisitions.

Lincoln's Inn MS. Misc. 557, f. 76, pl. 2

23 and 28 January 1684/85. Sir William Villiers and Bowater upon the outlawry of Sir William Jesson.

Sir William Jesson was outlawed at the suit of Bowater in [an action of] trespass and an inquisition was taken of his lands, and they were seized into the hands of the king. And, afterwards, he was outlawed at the suit of Gisborne in [an action of] debt and another inquisition was taken, which seized the same lands with others. Gisborne obtained a lease and assigned it to Sir William Villiers. Process issued for the levying of the profits upon Bowater's outlawry. And several sums were levied upon it, which, upon a motion for Sir William Villiers, were by order of the court ordered to be paid to him because, although Bowater had the first inquisition and outlawry, yet not having any lease, the court must order the money levied by the process of this court to be paid to him who had the lease although it was granted upon the later outlawry and inquisition. And thus was the judgment of this court in Mr. Brudenell's Case, which see Liber J, 42 and 67.[1] And the court cannot deny the money to him who had the lease, though upon a junior outlawry and inquisition in expectation that he who had the first outlawry and inquisition could afterward obtain a lease or grant. And *non refert* that the lease is *quamdiu in manibus nostris vacand' utlagar' praedict' remanere debeant*. And, in truth, the lands are in the hands of the king by the first inquisition because neither the inquisition not the lease gives possession but only pernancy of the profits by the process of this court that are governed by the lease granted and not by the first inquisition until the lease is granted upon it.

[Other copies of this report: Georgetown Univ. Law Sch. MS. B88–7, p. 554.]

4

Pettit v. Wood

(Ex. 1685)

A vicar who is a denizen, though born abroad, can receive tithes.

---

[1] *Brudenell v. Norwood* (Ex. 1681–1682), Exch. Cases *tempore* Car. II, 489.

Lincoln's Inn MS. Misc. 557, f. 83, pl. 2

13 February.

The plaintiff, a Frenchman denizened, vicar of Collumstock, Devonshire, sued for tithes. The defendants insisted upon the Statute of 1 Hen. V, ca. 7, which confirms the statutes of 25 Edw. III, ca. 23, and 13 Ric. II, ca. 3, which disabled Frenchmen to be ministers.[1]

[It was said] for the plaintiff the statutes confirmed did not extend to a denizen, though 1 Hen. V seemed to disable them, but this is not an enacting but a confirming law.

It seems these statutes are obsolete, and thus the Statute 1 Hen. V is marked by Keble, Roll's, *Presentment*, fo. 348, L, 4; Hobart 148; 4 Inst. 338.[2] And [a writ of] prohibition in the Court of King's Bench was denied.

And the cause here was referred to the bishop, and his award was to be decreed. And the plaintiff was held to be capable, and a decree passed. But see 4 Inst. 338, which seems contrary, but consider in this case.

[Other copies of this report: Georgetown Univ. Law Sch. MS. B88–7, p. 569.]

5

Chuseman v. Pierce

(Ex. 1685)

Where goods are seized for non-payment of import duties and sold, the goods go to the bidder and the money goes to the informer and to the crown.

Lincoln's Inn MS. Misc. 557, f. 84, pl. 3

20 February 1684/85.

Chuseman and Lucas, Custom House officers, seized upon the water in a ship a parcel of Roman gloves,[3] being prohibited to be imported by the Statute of 3 Edw. IV.[4] The goods were afterwards appraised, and the defendant claimed the property, and, upon a proclamation in the court, one Cary offered to give £100 more than the appraised value, which was accepted by the court. And, notwithstanding the claim entered by the defendant, the court ordered the goods to be delivered to the bidder upon bringing his money bid into the court *nisi causa* such a day in the last term.

---

[1] Stat. 1 Hen. V, c. 7 (*SR*, II, 172–173); Stat. 25 Edw. III, stat. 4 (*SR*, I, 316–318); Stat. 13 Ric. II, stat. 2, c. 2 (*SR*, II, 69–74).

[2] 2 Rolle, Abr., *Presentment*, pl. L, 4, p. 348; *Colt v. Bishop of Coventry* (1612), Hobart 140, 148, 80 E.R. 290, 297; E. Coke, *Fourth Institute* (1644), p. 338.

[3] Sic in MS., perhaps for cloves.

[4] Stat. 3 Edw. IV, c. 4 (*SR*, II, 397) (re gloves).

At which day, I [*Edward Ward*], for the defendant, insisted that the goods cannot be sold where there is a claim entered, because the claim opposes a forfeiture and, before a trial, whether forfeited or not, there cannot be any sale without consent at least, which there is not in this case. And there is not any precedent of such a sale where a claim is entered.

But the court overruled it, supposing that, in this case, the claim was entered purely for delay, inasmuch as it was observed that the defendant himself had bid for the goods £20 more than Cary, but it was refused.

And, in this case, the goods being of a perishable nature and decaying in their scent, which is a great part of the value, before the next term, the court ordered the sale notwithstanding the claim. But the court declared that the informer's moiety cannot be sold inasmuch as it is his property vested in him by the law and is not taken away by the proclamation or bidding, which extends only to the moiety of the king, according to the resolution in Michaelmas term last, which see above, fo. 67.[1]

But at this day, *Sawyer*, Attorney General, opposed it, notwithstanding this resolution by his opinion above, 67, upon the reason that the bidding, as he thought for his client, the bidder, in this case, goes to all the goods. And, thus, he said, the precedents were.

But I [*Edward Ward*], for the officers, showed to the court the said first resolution and opinion and the reason of it which is founded upon the property that the law vests in the informer by the seizure, which is a moiety of the goods and not of the value. And it is plain that the words of the proclamation do not respect more than the interest of the king in the goods, which is only a moiety, because they are, 'if any[one] will give any more for the goods than so much [which is the appraised value], let him come forth and he shall be heard or else the goods shall be recovered and the king answered the price', which must be understood the price of his moiety, inasmuch as he had nothing to do with the informer's.

With which the court agreed.

But then, it was urged by the Attorney General [*Sawyer*] that the seizure was fraudulent and with the assent of the defendant, in which case, as he supposed, all belongs to the king.

And, upon this, the court ordered the goods to be delivered to Cary, the bidder, bringing a moiety of the money into the court to be disposed according to the event of the case, either to the king or to the informer. *Quod nota.*

And note that, afterwards, the informer had his moiety of it as to the bidding, *vide ante*, fo. 67, and as afterwards.

And, upon the whole matter, it seems to me [*Edward Ward*] that the bidder will have all the goods, because he bid for all and not for the moiety and the

---

1 *Russell's Case* (1684), Lincoln's Inn MS. Misc. 557, f. 67, pl. 2.

judgment upon the bidding is that the bidder *oneratur* to the king for one moiety of the appraised value and to the informer for the other moiety of it.

[Other copies of this report: Georgetown Univ. Law Sch. MS. B88–7, p. 572.]

6

Attorney General v. Lownds

(Ex. 1685)

An assignment of a note to pay a debt does not create a debt.

Lincoln's Inn MS. Misc. 557, f. 90, pl. 1

Easter [term] 1685.

In evidence at the Guildhall upon a trial there after Easter term [1685] between the Attorney General, plaintiff, and Lounds, defendant, upon an inquisition that found Younge indebted to the king, Nelthorp indebted to Young, and Lounds indebted to Nelthrop. And, upon a *scire facias* against Lounds, he pleaded that he was not indebted to Nelthorp.

And it was ruled by the Chief Baron [Montagu] as a plain case that, though Lounds gave a note to pay £53 to Corbee for serges sold and Corbee assigned this note to Nelthorp, yet this assignment did not make Lounds such a debtor to Nelthorp that this sum could be found and seized into the hands of the king as a debt in aid or otherwise and this upon the reason of Mountney and Royden's Case, L. 1, 467, and L. 2, 13b, and Broune and London's Case, L. 2, 178; Modlene and Sporth [?], 285; and Bruen's Case, L. 1, 262,[1] by which it was resolved that such a debt cannot be seized and that [an action of] *indebitatus assumpsit* does not lie upon a bill of exchange. And the verdict was for the defendant.

I [*Edward Ward* was] for the defendant.

[Other copies of this report: Georgetown Univ. Law Sch. MS. B88–7, p. 581, pl. 1.]

7

Attorney General v. Farrin

(Ex. 1685)

Fees of customs officers cannot be established by mere usage.

---

[1] *Mountney v. Royden* (Ex. 1668–1669), Exch. Cases *tempore* Car. II, p. 137; *Brown v. London* (1670), Lincoln's Inn MS. Misc. 500, p. 178, also 1 Levinz 298, 83 E.R. 416, 1 Ventris 152, 86 E.R. 104, 2 Keble 695, 713, 758, 822, 84 E.R. 438, 450, 479, 520, 1 Freeman 14, 89 E.R. 11, 1 Modern 285, 86 E.R. 889, Hardres 485, 145 E.R. 560; *Brewen's Case* (Ex. 1666), Exch. Cases *tempore* Car. II, p. 91.

Lincoln's Inn MS. Misc. 557, f. 90, pl. 2

Upon the trial, the case was thus. Farrin was a clerk to Kent, who was a Receiver of the Customs, and [he was] appointed by the Commissioners of the Customs to make the repayments in the case of exportation within the second rule of the Book of Rates[1] though and notwithstanding that Sir John Shaw, the collector and a patent officer, was the proper and legal officer and against whom only the action lay for the non-repayment. Farrin demanded and received of divers merchants 12d. upon each debenture that he paid within the month after a demand in the said second rule mentioned, be the debenture for more or less.

And upon an information brought against him in the name of the Attorney General grounded upon the twenty-fourth rule in the Book of Rates to disable him to have any office in the Custom House and upon his defense that he took this sum only for a gratuity for the payment of the money within the month and not after, yet it was not held a good excuse to take anything for the payment of the money of the king. And it was plain that he demanded it as a fee inasmuch as he did not make a difference between a debenture for £1000 and 20s., but for each debenture. And he was held clearly to be a person within the rule who is subject to the disability. And there was a verdict for the plaintiff.

But the Attorney General [*Sawyer*] consented that judgment will not be entered inasmuch as this information was brought more to settle the right than to disable Farrin and, though such payments have been paid for many years, yet, inasmuch as there was no such fee in the Book of Rates, it was held that the usual taking of it cannot establish any fee.

And, in this case, it was held also that, though the offense particularly lay in the information for taking of 10s. of Cary, it was before the time in the information laid and, there being a general charge that he took divers other sums of others, that the proof of the taking of others generally alleged was good. And the particular offense lay in the nature of trespass, which is sufficient if at any time before the action though not within the time in the information.

I [*Edward Ward* was] for the plaintiff.

[Other copies of this report: Georgetown Univ. Law Sch. MS. B88–7, p. 581, pl. 2.]

8

Attorney General v. Clarke

(Ex. 1685)

A court can require special bail to be given by a defendant in a case of the crown upon a simple allegation of a debt.

---

[1] Stat. 12 Car. II, c. 4, app. (*SR*, V, 184–205).

Lincoln's Inn MS. Misc. 557, f. 99, pl. 1

Trinity [term] 1685. Touching special bail.

Clarke, the father, and Clarke, the son, having been stewards to Lord Gray,[1] attained of high treason by outlawry, and thought to have great sums in their hands of the estate of Lord Gray, forfeited to the king, were arrested by [a writ of] *capias* issuing out of the Office of the King's Remembrancer, in the County of Northumberland, upon a surmise that they were indebted to the king in great sums. And the writ was marked for special bail for £10,000. And for fault of bail, [they were] committed to jail, and removed by [a writ of] *habeas corpus*. And the last day of Trinity term, [they were] brought to the bar of the Exchequer Court and, there, charged with an information in the name of the Attorney General charging them to be indebted to the king in £10,000 for so much money received to the use of the king.

And I [*Edward Ward*], for the Clarkes, moved to have them discharged upon an appearance entered without any special bail, inasmuch as no debt to the king appeared upon record or otherwise but by a nude surmise only in the information, in which case, no special bail should be compelled in a case of the king, nor ever was it done in the case of a subject without an oath of the debt or duty. And though, in the Case of Hector Philips (*q.v.* L. 2, fo. 141), it was ruled that [a writ of] *capias* lies in the first process by virtue of the Statute of 33 Hen. VIII, ca. 39,[2] which gives any process at the discretion of the court and that special bail will be given in [an action of] debt upon an escape, yet this case, as to bail, greatly differs inasmuch as, in Philips's Case, the debt for which the [writs of] process and extent went and upon which the escape was, appeared by record, being a judgment against Sir Michael Livesay that was given to the king by the Act of Attainder, 12 Car. II, ca. 30.[3] But here nothing of a debt appears except by a surmise and nude suggestion, and no oath is made.

But, by the award of the court, the parties must give special bail for £10,000, and they were sent back to the Fleet [Prison] for the default of it.

And, afterwards, in the vacation, they were forced to give special bail to the value demanded or to lie in prison. *Quod nota et quaere* whether [it was] ever done before in such a case. It seems that [an action of] account and not *indebitatus* lies and, if *indebitatus* lies, it is not [an action of] debt, but [an action of] case.

Vide Whitacre's Case, 1701, Exchequer.[4]

[Other copies of this report: Georgetown Univ. Law Sch. MS. B88–7, p. 604.]

---

[1] R. L. Greaves, 'Grey, Ford, earl of Tankerville (bap. 1655, d. 1701)', *Oxford Dictionary of National Biography*, vol. 23, pp. 834–836.

[2] *Attorney General v. Philips* (Ex. 1671), Exch. Cases *tempore* Car. II, p. 220; Stat. 33 Hen. VIII, c. 39, s. 37 (*SR*, III, 886–887).

[3] Stat. 12 Car. II, c. 30 (*SR*, V, 288–290).

[4] *Whitacre's Case* (Ex. 1701), Lincoln's Inn MS. Misc. 532, f. [123].

9

Winter v. Jones

(Ex. 1685)

The question in this case was whether alluvion belongs to the lord of the manor adjacent to the water or to the leasehold held of that manor.

Lincoln's Inn MS. Misc. 557, f. 105, pl. 1

Michaelmas [term] 1685. In [an action of] ejectment.

In a trial at the bar by a Gloucestershire jury, the question was whether 100 acres of land derelict by the Severn River belonged to the plaintiff as lord of the manor of Lidney or to the defendant as owner of the manor or farm of Nass in Lidney parish held of the manor of Lidney by rent and services. And the plaintiff's title was as lord of the manor, and the defendant's as owner of the land next adjoining to the Severn, by which he claimed these derelict lands *per consuetudinem patriae*. And it was proved that the custom of the country for derelict lands went as well to the owners of the land fronting the sea not being lords of the manors as to the lords of the manors who have land adjoining. And divers instances were given in evidence of this custom for owners not lords of manors.

And it seems the custom is grounded upon natural reason that those who have land adjoining to the sea or a royal navigable river, as the Severn, that can and sometimes is washed away by the water will have the benefit of the dereliction because *qui sentit onus sentire debet et commodum*.

And the jury, being of knights and esquires of great estates, gave a private verdict for the defendant that, by the mistake of the attorney who took this private verdict, when the jury appeared at the bar, disclosed the verdict before the plaintiff was called, and, on account of this, the plaintiff became nonsuited.

I [*Edward Ward*, was] for the defendant.

And, in this case, there was not any special or common rule entered for confessing a lease, entry, and ouster, and, the declaration being for 400 acres, the defendant's counsel will confess only for 100 acres, he not having title or possession of more, and whether he can thus do was the question. And *Winston*, Protonotary of the Common Bench, and *Clarke*, Secondary of the King's Bench, informed the court that the common rule in such a case is only for the tenements in the defendant's possession or of his tenants. And thus here.

[Other copies of this report: Georgetown Univ. Law Sch. MS. B88–7, p. 613.]

10

Fagg v. Trevor

(Ex. 1685)

In this case, the land in issue passed by the devise in issue.

Lincoln's Inn MS. Misc. 557, f. 105, pl. 4

Sir John Fagg and his wife vs. John Trevor, Esq., and his wife, upon a trial at the bar of the Exchequer in [an action of] ejectment for lands in Sussex.

The wife of Sir John Fagg was heir at law to Mr. Morley, and the defendants were devisees by the will of Mr. Morley. And the question arose upon the words of the will, which were thus:

> I devise all my manors of A., B., C., and D. with all those my messuages, lands, tenements, and hereditaments with their and every of their appurtenances thereunto belonging, situate, lying, and being in the parishes of A., B., C., and D., County of Sussex, to [his] faithful wife.

And whether this devise passed the lands in those parishes that were not parcel or held of those manors was the question, because, as to those that did not pass by the will, the plaintiffs have title as heirs at law.

And for this, the plaintiffs' counsel will have the words so construed that the last words 'thereunto belonging' tie up and restrain all of the devise to the manors and lands parcel of the manors, because the principal devise is of the manors and the words 'with my messuages etc. with their appurentances thereunto belonging' are only explanatory of his interest that nothing passes unless belonging to the manors or to the lands part of the manors. And for such exposition, the Case of Pratt and Moon, Yelverton 82, was urged, *vide* also 6 Rep. 39, Hughes' Case, and Hobt. 175.[1]

But all of the court were of the opinion that all of the lands in those parishes, as well parcels as not parcels of the manors, passed by the devise. And, upon this, the plaintiffs were nonsuited.

I [*Edward Ward* was] for the plaintiffs and think it to be for the plaintiffs, notwithstanding this opinion of the court.

Note, by the opinion of Serjeant Pemberton, the lands not parcel of the manors did not pass by the will. And this opinion made the principal cause of the suit though, at the trial, Pemberton was of counsel with the defendant against his opinion.

---

[1] *Pratt v. Moon* (1605), Yelverton 82, 80 E.R. 56, 6 Coke Rep. 39, 77 E.R. 310, also 1 Brownlow & Goldesborough 184, 123 E.R. 744; *Stukeley v. Butler* (1615), Hobart 168, 175, 80 E.R. 316, 322.

And, afterwards, MONTAGU, Chief Baron, and GREGORY, Baron, Levinz and Dolben being displaced, gave their opinions against this judgment under their hands.

11

Earl of Macclesfield, qui tam v. Starkey

(Ex. 1685)

Special bail cannot be demanded as a matter of right.

A member of a grand jury cannot be sued for defamation for anything contained in a presentment.

3 Modern 41, 87 E.R. 25

The plaintiff brought an action upon the Statute *de Scandalis Magnatum*[1] against Sir Thomas Grosvenor, for that he, being the foreman of the grand jury in Cheshire, spoke these words of the plaintiff, 'He is a tedious man, and a promoter of sedition and tedious addresses.'

The plaintiff desired that the defendant might put in special bail.

But the court would not grant it, and said it was a discretionary thing, and not to be demanded of right. It was denied to the duke of Norfolk unless oath be made of the words spoken. The court, therefore, ordered common bail to be filed.

Dodd 56

The plaintiff declared upon the Statute of *Scandalum Magnatum* and that the defendant by conspiracy with others etc. prepared and presented and published a paper, which was the presentment of the jury in Cheshire, which had scandalous things in it.

The defendant justified as a grand juryman, upon which the plaintiff demurred.

[It was argued] by the plaintiff: first, the presentment ought to be of a fact of which the court has cognizance and of which the plaintiff has some means to clear himself, otherwise it is inconvenient and contrary to the rules of justice; second, if the grand jury presents anything of which it had no jurisdiction, as J.S. [is] unfit for such an office etc., an action lies; third, [it] amounts to [a plea of] the general issue only; see Cr. Car. 157.[2]

---

1 Stat. 2 Ric. II, stat. 1, c. 5 (*SR*, II, 9); note also Stat. 3 Edw. I, Westminster I, c. 34 (*SR*, I, 35).

2 *Lynner v. Wood* (1629), Croke Car. 157, 79 E.R. 737.

[It was argued] by the defendant [that] the action does not lie for the matter [because]: first, this presentment is before proper judges; Dr. 285; second, it is by proper persons. 21 Edw. III, 17; 8 Hen. IV, 6; third, for good causes. Dalton 79.[1]

See Dr. 285; 4 Rep. 4. The jury is not answerable for any matter before they are empaneled if empaneled after. N.B. 115 D; Stamford 173; 12 Rep. 23; Bridge. 130.[2] No action against a grand jury ever had success.

[It was] objected to the objection of the general issue [that] a man can plead specially in two things: first, where he admits to color for the action but avoids it specially; second, where it is matter of law.

And a color [is] given and color implied: first, for color given, 10 Rep. 88;[3] second, for color implied, as in trespass, the defendant justifies by it that the tenth part set out and severed from the ninth is good because it implies that the plaintiff has a cause of action in everything unless the defendant has specially avoided it. 9 Hen. VI, 64, Brooke and Fitzherbert, tit. *Mayntenance*;[4] thus Rastall, same title, as also where a man pleads a collateral warranty and release. See, for all these [points], the books 21 Edw. III, 17; 22 Ass. 12; Moo. 600; 3 Cr. 871, 900; 2 Cr. 130; Kelway 81; Dr. 285; Bridgman 130; Rastall 123.[5]

In Hilary [term] following [1685], [it was] adjudged by all of the barons that the action did not lie.

See 32 Hen. VIII, ch. 43; 33 Hen. VIII, 13; 27 Hen. VIII, 5; 3 Hen. VII, 12; 9 Hen. VII, 12; 12 Edw. IV, 16; 4 Rep. 94; 1 Inst. 303, 309; 2 Cr. 357; Rastall 123; 2 Cr. 582 and 20; Dr. 69b, 115; 3 Cr. 434; Kelway 26; Spelman 145;

---

[1] *Lord Beauchamps v. Croft* (1497), 2 Dyer 285, 73 E.R. 639, also Keilwey 26, 72 E.R. 182, 115 Selden Soc. 349; YB Hil. 21 Edw. III, f. 17, pl. 19 (1347); YB Mich. 8 Hen. IV, f. 6, pl. [8] (1406); perhaps M. Dalton, *Country Justice* (1619), p. 97.

[2] *Lord Beauchamps v. Croft* (1569), *ut supra*; *Cutler v. Dixon* (1585), 4 Coke Rep. 14, 76 E.R. 886, also *sub nom. Cutter v. Dixwell*, 3 Leonard 123, 74 E.R. 581, 4 Leonard 35, 74 E.R. 711; *Natura Brevium*; W. Staunford, *Plees del Coron* (1557), 'Conspiracie'; *Floyd v. Barker* (1607), 12 Coke Rep. 23, 77 E.R. 1305; *Agard v. Wilde* (1617), J. Bridgman 130, 123 E.R. 1251.

[3] *Leyfield's Case* (1611), 10 Coke Rep. 88, 77 E.R. 1057, also 1 Bulstrode 154, 80 E.R. 846, Croke Jac. 317, 79 E.R. 272.

[4] *Rothewel v. Pewer* (1431), YB Hil. 9 Hen. VI, f. 64, pl. 17; Brooke, Abr., *Maintenance*, pl. 3; Fitzherbert, Abr., *Maintenaunce*, pl. 4.

[5] YB Hil. 21 Edw. III, f. 17, pl. 19 (1347); YB 22 Edw. III, Lib. Ass., p. 88, pl. 12 (1348); *Varrell v. Wilson* (1594), Moore K.B. 600, 72 E.R. 785; *Pain v. Rochester* (1602), Croke Eliz. 871, 78 E.R. 1096; *Chambers v. Taylor* (1602), Croke Eliz. 900, 78 E.R. 1123; *Marham v. Pescod* (1606), Croke Jac. 130, 79 E.R. 113, also *sub nom. Pescod v. Marsam*, Noy 116, 74 E.R. 1081; *Anonymous* (1506), Keilwey 81, 72 E.R. 243; *Lord Beauchamps v. Croft* (1569), *ut supra*; *Agard v. Wilde* (1617), J. Bridgman 130, 123 E.R. 1251.

Bridgeman 130; Moo. 143; Stamford 97; Hob., Warneford and Warner;[1] these authorities [were] cited for and against.

Folger Shakespeare Library MS. V.b.151, f. 93

Thursday, 12 January 1684[/85] in the Court of Exchequer, in Hilary Term, 1 Jac. II. Earl of Macclesfield v. Starkey. This day being appointed for the judgment of the court in this cause, the Lord Chief Baron and the other three barons delivered their opinions *seriatim*, beginning at the puisne, whose respective arguments as near as could be taken [down] were as follows.

Mr. Baron Wright: Charles, earl of Macclesfield,[2] who prosecutes as well for our sovereign lord the king as for himself upon the Statute of *Scandalum Magnatum*, is plaintiff, and John Starkey is defendant.

The plaintiff in his declaration sets forth that he was for thirty years last past and still is one of the peers and great men of this kingdom and had his seat in Parliament and [is] a gentleman of the king's bedchamber and in those places and offices had behaved himself with great honor and fidelity, yet the defendant Starkey falsely and maliciously intending to disgrace the plaintiff and to render him as one suspected that were disaffected to the government and a disturber of the peace, being in conspiracy with Sir Thomas Grosvenor and others, did invent and write a certain scandalous libel of the plaintiff and that libel so invented and written at Wantage in the County of Berks did publish and cause to be published, which writing is set forth verbatim in the declaration, when in truth he never was disaffected to the government nor a disturber of the king's peace nor guilty of any of the things in the said libel, by which he lost his reputation and honor and was out of favor with his Majesty and discords may arise and have arisen between the king's subjects and this he lays to be against the Statute to the damage of the plaintiff £10,000.

To this, Starkey, the defendant, comes and pleads that at the sessions of Chester held at Chester in the Common Hall of Pleas there [on the] 17th of September in the 35th year of the late king [1683] before Sir George Jeffreys and John Warren, justices there, he the said Starkey with Sir Thomas Grosvenor and others were duly empaneled to be of the grand inquest and sworn and charged

---

[1] Stat. 32 Hen. VIII, c. 43 (*SR*, III, 796); Stat. 33 Hen. VIII, c. 13 (*SR*, III, 849); Stat. 27 Hen. VIII, c. 5 (*SR*, III, 534–535); *Lovet v. Fawkner* (1614), Croke Jac. 357, 79 E.R. 306, also 2 Bulstrode 270, 80 E.R. 1114, 1 Rolle Rep. 109, 81 E.R. 364; *Fitz-William's Case* (1603), Croke Jac. 19, 79 E.R. 17; *Buckler's Case* (1551), 1 Dyer 68, 73 E.R. 145; *Lord Beauchamps v. Croft* (1569), *ut supra*; *Agard v. Wilde* (1617), J. Bridgman 130, 123 E.R. 1251; *Broughton's Case* (1583), Moore K.B. 141, 72 E.R. 493; *Warner v. Wainsford* (1615), Hobart 127, 80 E.R. 276, *sub nom. Wainford v. Warner*, 1 Brownlow & Goldesborough 80, 123 E.R. 679.

[2] R. Hutton, 'Gerard, Charles, first earl of Macclesfield (c. 1618–1694)', *Oxford Dictionary of National Biography*, vol. 21, pp. 932–936.

to enquire for our sovereign lord the king and the body of that county upon certain articles there delivered to them by the said justices and that he and they did according to their oaths and upon evidence and testimony there given concerning the earl, the plaintiff, make the presentment set forth in the declaration, and then he traverses that he, the said John Starkey, is guilty of the premises in the County of Berks or elsewhere out of the County of Chester or otherwise than as is by the plea set forth.

Upon which, there is a demurrer.

Thus, stands the case upon the pleadings, and the case of the country at the time of making this presentment was not much unlike it. In the year 1683, these gentlemen being empaneled to be of the grand jury for the County of Chester and a villainous and damnable plot being lately discovered against the lives of our late sovereign of blessed memory and our now dread sovereign, his sacred Majesty, whom God long preserve, as by his late Majesty's declaration read in open court was manifested and declared, this gentleman and the rest of the grand jury considering of the same and weighing the consequences of that horrid conspiracy, if it had taken effect, and the articles given them in charge to enquire of and remembering the late tumults that had been made in many parts of that county and the disorderly, riotous processions of the duke of Monmouth and other disaffected persons with him and the seditious address made to Mr. Booth and Sir Robert Cotton at their election for knights of the shire promising to stand by them in procuring the Bill of Exclusion and such other irregular things, thought it expedient for the preservation of the peace and security of the government to present that such as they there named to the number of about thirty should find security for the[ir] good behavior, and, to this presentment, these loyal gentlemen put their hands. And upon this presentment thus made, this noble peer has grounded this action.

And the single question is whether this action be maintainable or not. And I hold that this action thus brought by the noble plaintiff against the defendant for making this presentment, being brought against a grand juryman for what he did as a grand juryman, is not maintainable.

I confess those gentlemen that were of counsel for this noble lord, the plaintiff, have in their arguments taken no small pains to support this action, which has been as learnedly and ingeniously answered by the gentlemen that were of counsel for the defendant. I have looked into all the cases that have been cited on the one side and on the other and do not find one case which can be of any authority to support this action nor any one case where ever a grand juryman was subject to an action for doing his duty, being upon his oath to do it.

But I shall take up so much of your time as to show some authorities and reasons for what I say in this case. We, all of us, know that the public peace is preserved by the execution of the public justice, in which the grand juries have so great a part. For, by the rules of law, no offender can be brought to judgment without the enquiry of juries nor be put to answer without presentment before justices according to the old law of the land says the Statute of 42 Edw. III, c. 3.[1] The judges of the land cannot proceed to judgment upon their own private knowledge but must proceed in the course that the law prescribes, which has put the first key in criminal matters in the hands of the grand jury, and by their finding facts offered to them [find] *billa vera* or *ignoramus*. The courts do proceed or stop their hands. Their oath shows their duty and their power. They are sworn diligently to enquire and true presentment make of all such matters and things as shall be given them in charge and of all other matters and things which shall come to their knowledge touching the[ir] present service, so that they may present upon their own knowledge without evidence. But here it is stronger, for it is said to be *secundum evidentiam de eodem comite etc.*

I shall here cite a passage out of a book that may be of great authority with some people. It was printed within these few years and written, I suppose, to another purpose. It is called *The Security of Englishmen's Lives, of the Trust, Power, and Duty of the Grand Juries of England.*[2] It has no name indeed to it, but I suppose there is no one here but has seen it, and it may with some be a very good authority, I say. There in folio [*blank*] we have this passage: 'It is the joint interest of England . . . .'[3]

There is a difference, I must confess, between a presentment and an indictment, and that makes, perhaps, the best part of the question in this case. An indictment comes to a jury by the presentment of others. A presentment is what the grand jury do of their own heads; it is their own act, as Mr. Lambart says in his book called *Eirenarcha*, lib. 4, c. 5.

And there is also a great difference between a grand jury and a petit jury. The petit convict or acquit of the crime. The grand jury do only *crimen imponere*, and their presentment or indictment does imply but a bare supposition of a crime.

Now that for such a thing as this, no action lies against an officer for doing his duty. I would put this ordinary, common case. Suppose a felony be committed and one informs the constable that A. did the felony and thereupon he takes A. and there is no other evidence against A., who is discharged. No action lies against the constable for this. Or, say that no felony were committed; but upon information of one, the constable takes A., yet no action lies against him, for he did no more than what he was bound to do by law, and yet here was no cause to take A. and he had injury by it, for though the information were false, yet his office will protect him for what he does in execution of it.

So it is in this case before us. Though there were no reason to accuse my lord, the plaintiff, of any of the things in the presentment, yet, if they do think it fit to

---

[1] Stat. 42 Edw. III, c. 3 (*SR*, I, 388).

[2] This was written by John Somers (1651–1716) and first published in London in 1681. W. L. Sachse, *Lord Somers: a Political Portrait* (1975), pp. 18–19.

[3] The rest of the passage is not copied in the manuscript though a large blank space is left for it.

present and are sworn to present, either upon their own knowledge or evidence from others, they shall not sure be chargeable with an action for presenting.

Next, a juror is compellable to serve in that office, and therefore it is but reason he should be protected for doing that which the law forces him to undertake.

Besides, presentments are but only a way of offering matters to the court to be by them put into a methodical proceeding. And the grand juries are but in the nature of relators who are not subject to actions for what they do in a legal course.

This person here justifies as a juryman that, being summoned and sworn of this grand jury, he according to his oath and conscience and upon evidence did what a grand juryman is to do, i.e. present what he might present and traverses that he did it anywhere else or in any other manner. This must certainly be a good justification.

If this action should prevail, it would be the first time that ever a grand juror or indictor was made liable to an action and would be against all precedents and rules of law. For I take it to be a standing rule in law that, where one is indicted, though the party be acquitted, yet no conspiracy does lie against the indictors. The law will not suppose any to be not indifferent jurors that are duly sworn to try or enquire. That I take to be the sense of all the books that have been cited on the one side and on the other.

It has been said in defenses of this action that it is a case of great consideration. It is so, and I conceive the Oath of Allegiance is worth consideration too, which every man that comes to the bar has taken and should always remember. We must not favor or countenance anything that may bring the government in[to] danger. And, if these actions do prevail, I am sure we must do that or something very like it. We shall hinder the course of law and methods of justice; for there is no man [that] can safely or will heartily and cheerfully serve his king and country in such an office, if he is liable to an action for doing his duty in it.

As to what has been said of danger on the other side of juries' extravagances, this I have to say, they are liable to the correction of the court if they exceed their bounds. If they are negligent to present, they break their oaths. If they mistake in [a] matter of law, their proceedings are void, so that there can be danger from their extravagance on the one side or their remissness on the other while the law protects them from irregular prosecutions.

It has been likewise said that this is an action brought as well for the king as the party and, the king having an interest in it, it ought to be favored. It is true the king has his name used in it, but whether with his own consent is a question, for this is not the first time the king's name has been used against himself. And the using of the king's name is not to defend an action that harasses his loyal subjects for doing their duty. It is something like the rebellious army in the late times that very religiously protested to fight for king and Parliament against the king's person and friends.

I shall conclude all with delivering my opinion shortly in so plain a case. I take the law to be clearly for the defendant, that this is a very good justification and that the plaintiff's action cannot be maintained. Therefore, judgment ought to be given for the defendant.

Mr. Baron Gregory: Charles, earl of Macclesfield, is plaintiff, and John Starkey is defendant, and this is an action of *scandalum magnatum* upon the Statute of 2 Ric. II, wherein the plaintiff declares and recites the Statute and then says he is and for many years past has been a peer of this realm and [a] gentleman of the king's bedchamber and has always behaved himself with great faithfulness and honor, that the defendant maliciously intending and designing to take away his honor and reputation and to make him to be reputed disaffected to the government etc. [on the] 17th of September in the 35th year of the late king at Wantage in the County of Berks by conspiracy between him and Sir Thomas Grosvenor and others a scandalous and malicious libel against the plaintiff did write or cause to be written and the same did publish and then he repeats this libel *in haec verba*. My brother Wright has opened the contents of it and therefore to save the time of the court, I shall not trouble you any further with it now. Then he avers that he never was disaffected to the government nor a disturber of the peace nor guilty of any of the things mentioned in the paper, by reason of which libel, he is scandalized and hurt in his honor and many discords do and may arise and false rumors spread of him, which he lays to his damage of £10,000.

The defendant, he comes in and pleads that at the sessions of Chester held at Chester in the County of Chester in the Common Hall of Pleas there for that county before Sir George Jeffreys, chief justice there, and John Warren, another justice for that county, he was duly and according to law empaneled and sworn to be of the grand inquest at that sessions and sworn and charged to enquire for the king and the body of the county upon certain articles to them delivered by the justices and that he and the rest of the jurors according to their oaths and conscience and according to evidence of the plaintiff to them given for the preservation of the king's peace in the said County of Chester at the same sessions did duly present in the English words in the declaration mentioned, as was lawful for them to do, and then [he] traverses *absque hoc* that he is guilty of the premises in the declaration specified in the County of Berks or elsewhere out of the County of Chester in manner and form as the plaintiff complains *vel aliter vel alio modo quam* the plaintiff[1] *per placitum suum praedictum allegavit*.

To this plea, the earl of Macclesfield, the plaintiff, has demurred.

I confess here is a case before us where both parties claim the favor of the law. The plaintiff's action ought to be favored for [the] preservation of the honor of the great peers of the realm and for avoiding the inconveniences mentioned in the Statute. On the other hand, the defendant, he claims the favor of the law, because what he did was but in execution of the law. It was his duty to do it, and, therefore, he says he ought to be protected for it [so] that the justice of the nation

[1] defendant *MS.*

be not intimidated, that persons may not be afraid to do their duty upon their oaths for being liable to actions and trouble for so doing. So that on both hands, the favor of the law is claimed, and it is indeed due to both as their cases and circumstances may be.

Upon the pleadings, these questions have been started by the counsel at the bar.

First, whether the matter here pleaded by the defendant be a sufficient justification in point of law to excuse the defendant from this action.

Secondly, whether that matter be well pleaded or not; that is, whether this matter of justification and the traverse joined to it do answer the whole declaration.

But before I speak to these points, I shall only say this and observe that because our books do some of them speak of actions of conspiracy brought against jurors and others of such actions against witnesses, I shall, therefore, take some difference between them. And I do truly think that greater favor in law is to be given to jurors than to prosecutors, for a grand juryman is returned by process of law, is compellable to come in and do that service, is sworn to enquire and present, and has thereupon many obligations upon him, which should excuse him in what he does from being liable to an action. A prosecutor, too, if there be not malice in the case ought to have the protection of the law, because all that he does is in the execution of justice. But in regard [that] prosecutors are many times stirred up by hatred, malice, or revenge to prosecute, for that reason, a less matter will make the malice of such an one to appear in his prosecution than of a juror in indicting, who comes involuntarily and compelled into that service.

Now, as to the first point, the matter here that is pleaded by the defendant, whether that be a sufficient justification, I do conceive it is, because I do not conceive that the defendant has done anything more than what was his duty to do as a grand juryman and where a man does not exceed his duty, though the thing done turn to the prejudice of another, he ought not to be punished for it. And I build my judgment in this point upon these considerations.

First, what I said before, that the jury come not in voluntarily but by compulsion, they serve by the command of the king and of the law. They are compelled and enjoined to appear and do their duty. Now, when a man is not willing to do a thing, does not put himself officiously forward into such work, but comes by command of superiors, he shall be presumed to be upright in what he does unless the contrary do appear, especially where he himself is no way concerned in point of interest, but only the public is concerned.

Secondly, jurymen are not only compelled to serve, but, as my brother did observe, they are upon their oaths; they are sworn to be indifferent and neither for fear, favor, nor upon any account to deviate from the truth. And, if men are sworn to present offenses according as they shall be satisfied of the truth upon oath and then be exposed to be liable to actions if they do present, that will be very hard upon them to have them open to trouble for what the necessity of their office and their oaths require from them, especially, too, considering that we are not by any law or reason to presume a thing to be done by them maliciously by those whom the law calls to such a work as indifferent, unless by some plain, overt act, they express that malice and by contrivance came into the office out of design.

21 Edw. III.[1] It was much debated whether or no, if a man gets himself returned of a jury and is sworn and makes presentments and indicts a third person, though it be out of malice, whether that be actionable, for it is said when a man upon an inquest is sworn to make true inquiry and presentment, those presentments and indictments that he makes shall never be intended to be by conspiracy. But it is there agreed by all, if a juror does nothing but what the law says is his office and duty to do, he shall not be liable to an action for so doing. The same case is cited in Stamford, *Plees del Coron*, 173, which book was cited by Mr. Solicitor [General].

Then, let us come and look into the presentment itself. And there we are to consider whether in making this presentment, they have observed their duty and done what the law requires of them. Now there:

First, I must take notice that the several offenses mentioned in the (I know not what to call it) preface or preamble of this presentment are offenses that grand jurors are bound by their oaths to enquire of and present to the court. For:

First, here is mention made of an address to the members of Parliament in order to the altering of the succession of the crown. That I take to be an offense against the peace. Several persons have been elsewhere indicted and some fined for it. In last Michaelmas Term, there was a gentleman of Northamptonshire, one Mr. Butler, I think was his name, [who] was indicted for publishing such an address as that which is mentioned in the preface of this presentment and, being found guilty upon his trial, was fined 500 marks for that offense, in the King's Bench. So that by the judgment of that court, it was a finable offense, and, therefore, the jury in presenting it did not exceed their bounds.

So, great numbers riding armed up and down the country to the terror of the people is an offense, and a great one, against many statutes and, therefore, presentable as a great breach of the peace.

The meeting of great numbers in a seditious manner in conventicles is an offense that is presentable too.

These, indeed, are offenses that are not charged directly upon this noble lord, the plaintiff, or any of the rest, but those are set down to be the ground of their fears, for they do not present these as the particular crimes of the plaintiff or the other gentlemen that are named but as reasons for them to fear the peace of the kingdom may be in danger, and, therefore, they desire the court to take care in the way they mention to provide for the security of the peace.

---

[1] YB Hil. 21 Edw. III, f. 17, pl. 19 (1347).

I confess this presentment is not so formal as it might have been made, and, truly, I cannot remember well that ever I saw any English presentment of this nature was so formally drawn up, but, if exceptions had been taken to it, it must have been too weak to support itself. But this I must say withal that this is as other presentments of this like kind are and, being no direct charge, no exceptions I conceive can be taken to it. They are no indictments, for then it would be a good exception to them that they are in English and [they] should be in Latin. But they are a kind of warrants to the clerk to draw up indictments by, and they are evidence to another grand jury to find those indictments upon when drawn. And that is the usual method at the assizes and sessions. Jurymen need not be solicitous of the form of their presentments so as they be careful of the substance not to exceed their bounds but keep within the compass of their duty.

Now, what is the end of this presentment here before us? Only that the persons therein named may give security for the peace. And what injury or reflection is that upon any man? A private man shall come before a justice of peace and, swearing he is afraid of his life or some bodily hurt, shall have process issue out against the party he fears to put him under security of the peace. Then, if a private man swearing he is afraid such an one will do him harm shall require the peace to be secured to him, may not the body of the county that is represented by the grand jury, who are upon their oaths to take care of the peace, present their fears of danger and pray the peace against particular persons? I think they may upon the same reason. Nay, I take it to be a much stronger case.

Third, 20 Hen. VI, f. 33.[1] It is said if a commission be directed to some persons to enquire of all trespasses in such a county, they swear a jury and charge them to enquire of all felonies as well as trespasses and accordingly they do and indict J.S. of felony, which indictment not being taken by a lawful authority, it was there held that the jurors shall be excused from an action of conspiracy. And the reason is because they were compelled by process made by the commissioners to do it, which is to them the authority of the law. Those are the very works of that book.

So that a jury are to be excused if they mistake the authority of the court they serve in, shall not then a juryman be excused too when he mistakes the style of the court only, if it were so, in this case, for that was one of the instances Mr. Williams gave of fault in this presentment and urged that the usual methods of law and forms might be observed.

A juryman, I conceive, is not liable to an action if he mistake the law in what he does as a juryman, for if a bill of indictment be presented to a grand jury of felony for stealing of wood or pieces of timber and they find this bill and it appears afterwards upon the trial that it was not felony but only a trespass and the indictment fail, shall a grand jury for mistaking the law in such a case be liable to

[1] YB Trin. 20 Hen. VI, f. 33, pl. 3 (1442).

an action of conspiracy? That would be hard. So oftentimes a grand jury indict a man of grand larceny, upon which the man's life is in danger and, upon the trial, the petit jury find it only petit larceny because of the small value; shall a grand jury be liable to an action of conspiracy for such indictment? There is no color in it in the world.

So here, if the grand jury have mistaken the law and presented the plaintiff and the rest for these offenses as endangering the peace, though, in truth, there were no such terror nor any breach of the peace did ensue, but yet they had, as they thought, probable cause for their apprehensions of danger. Shall they be punished for such conceptions, though mistaken ones, nay, though they should have mistaken the form of law? No, I think not truly by any means.

For although this Statute *de Scandalis Magnatum* does upon very good grounds give this action to a peer and forbids any slighting, disrespectful words to be spoken of the great men of the kingdom, because of the quality of their persons, the honor of the peerage, and those great dangers and mischiefs which the Statute does enumerate that may arise upon such offenses, and, therefore, the law does make that actionable for a peer that it does not for another person. Yet, in the case of doing justice, where a man has that that will justify him[self] against a commoner, the same will justify him against a peer. Where a commoner shall not have an action of conspiracy, the peer shall not have a *scandalum magnatum*. That which is a justification in one case, is a justification in the other too.

And this appears very fully in Kelway 26, that has been cited at the bar, my lord Beauchamp's Case, which is likewise reported in Dyer 285,[1] but much more largely in Kelway; where the case was an action of *scandalum magnatum* was brought by my lord Beauchamp for that the defendant sued out against the plaintiff a writ of forger de faux faits and, before that action was tried, my lord Beauchamp brought this suit supposing himself scandalized and the defendant justified that he was now sued only for using the course of law. The book says that by the better opinion of the court, upon a demurrer to this justification, the plea was held good.

If a man slander a lord either by word or writing without cause and have no authority for what he does, he shall be punished by [an] action at the lord's suit upon this Statute. But although a man have no cause, yet if he sue a writ of appeal or lawful action for any crime or wrong against a peer, he shall not be punished by [an] action upon this suit, for the law restrains not any man from having a lawful action against a peer as well as against a commoner. And Kelway 29 in that case says that this Statute does not intend to oust a man from suing any action but only to punish those that slander lords when they have not any cause to meddle with them by the law. He likewise puts a case there: if a lord recover by false verdict, yet the defendant may have an attaint, and yet there, he must allege

1 *Lord Beauchamps v. Croft* (1569), *ut supra*.

that the lord recovered by false oath, which is no scandal, being in a course of law. And, if a lord were one of the jurors against whom he brings the attaint and thereby calls him a false juror, yet the matter being still in a course of law, there is not, during the pendency of this action against him, any slander in anything he does in preferment of the action, and much more to the same purpose, we have in that book.

So, in Hobart 266, Waterer and Freeman's Case,[1] it is held if a man brings an action upon a false surmise in a proper court, the defendant cannot bring an action against him and charge him with it as a fault directly and *ex diametro* as if the suit itself were a wrongful act, for *executio juris non habet injuriam*. And this case of my lord Beauchamp, 11 Eliz., there is cited.

If, then, one that is a party concerned in interest who sues a peer for his own interest voluntarily, and it may be sometimes without a cause, shall be free from an action for so doing because it is in a course of law and execution of justice, how much more shall a man be protected who comes in by process of law to serve the king and the country, who is a person indifferent and no way particularly interested as to himself in the matter presented and is upon his oath obliged to present?

[In] 12 Coke, fo. 23,[2] the case cited by my brother, it was resolved by the Lord Chancellor, two chief justices, [the] Chief Baron, and all the Court of Star Chamber that, when a grand inquest indicts one of felony and after the party is acquitted, yet [action of] no conspiracy lies for him against the indictors, because they are returned by the sheriff by process of law to make enquiry (and so also to make presentments) upon their oath and it is for the service of the king and commonwealth. And, there, all the reasons and authorities are cited and alleged for it. And so is the book of 20 Hen. VI and Stamford, *Plees del Coron*, 173, not there cited.

Therefore, I am of opinion in this case that the matter of the justification is good in point of law.

But in the next place, it has been objected that in this justification, the presentment is said to be made according to evidence and testimony given and they do not show what that evidence and testimony was [so] that the court here may judge of it. And, truly, I think they need not do it. For:

First, it is against their oaths. They are sworn to keep secret the king's counsel, their fellows, and their own and not to disclose it but in court.

In the next place, it is a misdemeanor or misprision punishable by fine and imprisonment for any of the grand inquest to discover any of the persons indicted or evidence, as appears in my lord Hale's, *Pleas of the Crown*, 131, so that such an action as this were by a side wind to compel grand jurymen, before the fact be

---

[1] *Waterer v. Freeman* (1617), Hobart 205, 266, 80 E.R. 352, 412, also Noy 23, 74 E.R. 994.

[2] *Floyd v. Barker* (1607), 12 Coke Rep. 23, 77 E.R. 1305.

tried that is presented, to discover the king's evidence, which is not only against their oaths, but a very mischievous offense. It is to make them to disobey the law and to draw them into the guilt of misprision. Again:

Thirdly, grand juries may, if they please, nay, and their oaths oblige them to it, present upon their own knowledge. And how can that be shown or tried or judged upon in such an action as this? Or one of them may inform the others, and that is sufficient to them, nay, and is by experience frequently done, and to discover it, you see, is misprision.

But if it had been set forth particularly, as the plaintiff's counsel would have it, what would it avail as to this action? How can the court judge whether it were sufficient evidence to find the bill or make such presentment or not?

As in Bushel's Case in my lord Vaughan's reports,[1] which has been several times cited by the plaintiff's counsel as an authority for them, in page 142, he observes that the verdict of a jury and the evidence of a witness are very different things in the truth and falsehood of them, for a witness swears but to what he has heard or seen or what generally or more largely comes under the knowledge of his senses. But in what a juryman presents upon his oath, he swears to what he can infer and conclude from the testimony of such witnesses, so that he does not swear the thing directly and positively to be so and so done, but in my apprehension according to my understanding and what I can collect upon this evidence, I find so and so, so that there is a great difference in that.

For this cause, juries are returned of the vicinage as being presumed to have some knowledge of themselves of the fact they are to try and may be able to give a true verdict, though no evidence else be given them. And if there be several pieces of evidence, the jury may all agree to give the same verdict and yet upon several reasons, some upon such a part of the evidence and others upon [an]other part of it. They may agree in the end though not in the way.

We come then to consider the second great point in the case, whether this be well pleaded and whether the traverse joined to the justification do answer the whole of the declaration. And the main question lying upon the traverse, I think it is well enough in the manner as it is pleaded and does answer the whole charge in the declaration.

As to that objection that was made and which is assigned upon record as a special cause of demurrer, that this plea amounts to the general issue, it has been fully answered by the defendant's counsel and particularly by the authority cited of Warner and Wainsford in Hobart 127,[2] which as to the matter of special pleading is an express case. The defendant, being sued as administrator,

---

1 *Bushell's Case* (1670), Vaughan 135, 124 E.R. 1006, also T. Jones 13, 84 E.R. 1123, 1 Modern 119, 86 E.R. 777, 1 Freeman 1, 89 E.R. 2, *State Trials* (Cobbett, ed., 1810), vol. 6, col. 999, Lincoln's Inn MS. Misc. 500, f. 177, pl. 3; note also *Bushel v. Starling* (1674), 3 Keble 322, 84 E.R. 744; *Bushel v. Howel* (1674), 3 Keble 358, 84 E.R. 765.

2 *Warner v. Wainsford* (1615), *ut supra.*

pleaded that the intestate owed him fourscore pounds by bond and no assets beyond that sum came to his hands and that he detained that for his [own] debt; there, it was demurred to, because the plea amounted to the general issue, fully administered,[1] and that he might have pleaded. But the court said that was but a matter of discretion in the court to make them plead the general issue to avoid prolixity of pleading upon the record, and, therefore, the plaintiff ought not to have demurred for that reason but moved the court that the general issue might be pleaded. Nay, that book says further that it, being a matter in law, has always been allowed to be pleaded specially.

And the truth is I do not see how it could be pleaded otherwise, for, by pleading not guilty, they would have confessed the fact, if proved, to be a fault. But here is a confession of the fact that they did in such a manner publish such a paper, but that will not be actionable in law, not as a libel maliciously to scandalize the plaintiff, but we did draw such a paper up and presented it upon our oaths according to our duty as jurymen, so that, if they had pleaded not guilty, they must have been gone, for if a man pleads not guilty to an action of trespass and gives a license in evidence, that will not maintain the plea or issue.

There is a case in Moor 600, Varrell against Wilson,[2] an action of conspiracy against the prosecutor of an indictment of felony, to which action, the defendant pleads that his goods were feloniously taken away and he found them in the possession of the plaintiff and thereupon he indicted the plaintiff and gave evidence to the jury that found the bill and upon trial gave evidence to the petit jury, who acquitted the plaintiff and traverses that he did not conspire *aliter vel alio modo*. The plaintiff demurred. But it was adjudged [that] no action lay, but it was a good justification for the finding the goods in the plaintiff's possession was sufficient cause of suspicion. Now here, the jury upon oath present the cause of their suspicion or apprehension, therefore sure they shall not be liable to an action.

In the beforementioned book of Kelway 27b, it is said, if the matter be confessed, by intendment of law, there needs no traverse, as in trespass. Suppose the trespass is the first of May and the defendant pleads he did it the same day by license, it needs no traverse, for it answers the action in point. And, there, in the principal case, was no traverse at all, because it was said to be for prosecuting a writ of forger *de faux faits* against my lord Beauchamp and it did appear that writ was still depending and so he needed not to traverse that he did it at any time after for the suit was still depending, and so he might justify giving evidence or instructions to counsel for proceeding in the cause and all under justification of bringing the action.

But in this case, here is a traverse taken that he is not guilty of the premises in Berkshire or elsewhere out of the County of Chester, which goes to all England but Chester, in which county, the presentment is made by a grand jury. And

---

1 *I.e. plene administravit.*

2 *Varrell v. Wilson* (1594), Moore K.B. 600, 72 E.R. 785.

then it goes on and says that he did not do it *aliter vel alio modo* than as in the plea is alleged, which I think is as comprehensive as may be.

As to the style of the court, I take that to be no exception at all, it being a presentment in English and it being the clerk's office to correct any such error. It is in a county palatine and therefore such a court as the courts in Westminster Hall are bound to take notice of of course.

Therefore, upon the whole, I am of opinion that the matter pleaded is a sufficient justification in point of law and, next, that the justification and traverse comprehend the whole matter in the declaration, and the same are well pleaded. And, therefore, the plaintiff's demurrer ought to be overruled.

Mr. Baron Atkyns: The earl of Macclesfield is plaintiff and John Starkey is the defendant, and this is an action of *scandalum magnatum* grounded upon the Statute of 2 Ric. II, c. 5. I mention not the particulars of the Statute; they are so well known. The plaintiff sets forth that he is and has been for divers years past one of the peers of this kingdom and gentleman of his majesty's bedchamber and in those offices and dignities has behaved himself with great honor and fidelity and that the defendant not weighing the penalty of the law in that Statute but maliciously designing to scandalize the plaintiff in his honor and reputation and to bring him into displeasure with the king and to make him to be looked upon as a person disaffected to the government and a disturber of the king's peace 17th of September in the 35th year of the late king at Wantage in the County of Berks by conspiracy between him and Sir Thomas Grosvenor and others did invent, write, and publish a certain libel against the plaintiff and cause the same to be written and published, which libel is set forth *in haec verba*, whereas in truth, he never was disaffected to the government nor any ways a disturber of the peace nor guilty of any of the things charged in the libel, by reason of which he is greatly injured in his honor and reputation, has lost that grace and esteem which he had with his majesty and other persons, and false rumors have arisen and may arise and discords, and this he says [is] to his damage of £10,000.

To this, the defendant has pleaded specially that at the session of Chester for the County of Chester held at Chester in the Common Hall of Pleas there the said 17th of September before Sir George Jeffreys, justice of our lord the king for that county, and John Warren, another justice of that county, the defendant and the rest named in the declaration were duly empaneled and summoned to serve on the grand inquest and sworn and charged to enquire for our sovereign lord the king as well as the body of that county upon certain articles then and there delivered to them by the said justices and that they according to their oaths and according to evidence and testimony to them given concerning the earl, the plaintiff, and according to their consciences and to keep the king's peace did present in the English words set forth in the declaration and then he says 'as was lawful for them to do' and traverses 'without that that the defendant is guilty of the premises in the said County of Berks or elsewhere out of the said County of

Chester *vel aliter vel alio modo* than as the defendant has by his plea alleged and so prays the judgment of the court *si actio*'.

To this plea, the plaintiff has demurred specially and assigned several causes of demurrer, and the defendant has joined in demurrer, and so the case comes now before us for judgment.

Upon this record, the general question is whether this action as it stands before us does lie or not. And I am of opinion the action does not lie but that judgment ought to be given for the defendant.

And I shall first speak to this that is the general question and then I shall speak to those exceptions that have been made by Mr. Williams and Mr. Ward, who argued for the plaintiff.

First, I say as to the general question whether this action does lie in this case or not, I conceive it does not. And in proving it, I must a little make use of the method which was taken up at the bar, and so:

First, I shall consider the court and the jurisdiction of that court in which this presentment was made.

Secondly, I shall consider the persons who did make the presentment, and:

Thirdly, I shall consider whether this presentment does contain matter in itself proper to be presented. Only, indeed, I shall invert the order of these points and begin with the last first, to wit whether this presentment does contain in it matter presentable.

The presentment is long. As to the first part of it, it takes notice of the king's declaration concerning a treasonable conspiracy against his person and government and does contain only a dutiful and loyal presentment of their apprehension about it and speaks only their opinion of the extensiveness of it and the dreadful consequences of it had it taken effect. And as to that part of the presentment, I only say this, that the defendant and the rest of his companions only say what all or most of the grand juries of England throughout all the counties and places did about that time present.

The next thing is a material part indeed. They say they had apprehensions of danger from a disaffected party in that county who had shown their defection by an address to the knights of the shire for that county, which address was tending to alter the succession of the crown and divers other seditious purports, and by their several meetings and cabals since administering suspicion from their provision of arms and by their riding armed and assembling with schismatics and disaffected persons in a riotous reception of the duke of Monmouth, which was an occasion of great terror to the king's good subjects and thereupon, says the presentment, they conceive it expedient that such as had any hand in these matters should give security for the peace, and then come and mention particular persons, among others, the plaintiff.

Now that these are things proper to be presented by a grand jury, I think no person will deny. They are things of a public nature. An address tending to alter the succession of the crown, providing of arms, meetings tending to the disturbance of the peace, and riotous assemblies are certainly matters of a public nature and proper to be enquired into and presented. And I do not well see how offenses of this nature can receive a judicial determination unless it be in the method of presentment by a grand jury.

These offenses are mentioned in all commissions of oyer and terminer. They are part of the articles that are constantly given in charge by the court to the juries. And if these are not proper for a jury to enquire of, I see not what is proper.

But my second reason for my opinion this; I take this for a rule [that] where a man speaks words or does any act which is in a court of justice, though those words, perhaps, are false and those matters and things in themselves actionable, yet being, I say, spoken and done in the way of administration of justice, the law is always tender and careful that such person be protected from all action or damage for such things. For this, I might cite many cases, but I shall only mention two, the one for words spoken, the other for something done.

The case for words was Clapham and Moulton's Case, Easter term, 15 Car. I, in the King's Bench,[1] upon reading an affidavit of the plaintiff, the defendant said in court that it was false and the plaintiff forsworn and that he would prove [it] by forty witnesses. It was held [that] these words were not actionable, because the defendant spoke them in a course of justice in his own cause.

Then for an act done, there is the case of Cutler and [*blank*], 4 Co. 14. If a man does exhibit articles [*blank*] no action does lie against him for exhibiting such articles, and the reason is because it is done in a course of justice. And so is Buckley and Wood's Case that was cited at the bar.[2]

Now, that which is the great consideration of the case and those that are the forcible words in the declaration are three, *viz.* that this is laid to be done by conspiracy *falso et malitiose*, and it is those that are the emphatical words that must season all actions of this nature to make them hold water.

And yet notwithstanding these words are here put in this declaration, yet I take it this action will not lie. It is true, I must grant, that the matters laid in the declaration abstracted from the circumstances set forth in the plea in their own nature would bear an action, but the circumstances that attend the fact of this case do alter it in that point. I remember my lord Coke had this observation that every particular case has and must have a different judgment upon those particular reasons that arise from the variety of circumstances that attend it. Therefore, that which is actionable in itself, by the addition of circumstances, may become not actionable.

---

1 *Molton v. Clapham* (1639), March N.R. 20, 82 E.R. 393.

2 *Cutler v. Dixon* (1585), *ut supra*; *Buckley v. Wood* (1591), 4 Coke Rep. 14, 76 E.R. 888, Croke Eliz. 230, 248, 78 E.R. 486, 503, 2 Anderson 28, 123 E.R. 528, 2 Brownlow & Goldesborough 100, 123 E.R. 838, *sub nom. Wood v. Buckley*, Moore K.B. 705, 72 E.R. 853.

To this purpose, I may cite one case that was adjudged in this court, and it is a case that I must confess as to the reason of it, I cannot difference from the case here at the bar. I do not know whether Mr. Ward was an attendant at this bar when this case was adjudged, but some here may remember it. My Lord Chief Justice Hale was then Chief Baron, and it was the case of Vandeburgh v. Blague;[1] it was [in] Trinity term, 13 Car. II, in this court. The case was thus. An action of the case was brought. The plaintiff declared that he was a merchant denizen and such a day and year was possessed of a pack of linen cloth to the value of [*blank*] as of his own proper goods and merchandise, for which he had duly paid the custom and that the defendant without just cause did seize this pack of linen cloth as goods of merchants unknown and [*blank*] in the name of merchants denizen though he well knew the plaintiff's proper goods and that he was a merchant denizen and had duly paid the custom. It goes on further that the defendant had put in an information into this court upon that seizure to have the goods condemned, and it does allege all this to be done *falso et malitiose.* Upon not guilty pleaded, the jury find a special verdict to the same effect that the plaintiff had declared and that it was done falsely and maliciously. But then they find further that the defendant at that time was one of the surveyors of the customs and by letters patent duly constituted and employed to seize all goods shipped or unshipped which had not [*blank*]. And then they come and pray the advice of the court whether the action lay or not. It was argued by the plaintiff's counsel that the jury having found that the information was preferred falsely and maliciously, though it was exhibited in a course of justice and in a regular court, yet in respect of falsity and malice found by the jury, in that case, the action would lie. But my Lord Chief Justice Hale, who was then Chief Baron at the time of arguing that case, was of opinion that the action did not lie. And his reason was that the action and information being in a legal way and in a proper court whereto the plaintiff might pleaded and defended his goods from forfeiture if he had cause, the action would not lie, as he thought, though those words were alleged and found by the jury, and that this was his opinion, his words show, which I have set down in a report of that case, which I have by me, which words are 'and I think it has been so adjudged'.

There was, indeed, another exception taken in that case to the declaration (for I would give every case its right), but I find the judgment upon the whole is *quod querens nil capiat per billam.*

Now, I do not well see, I say, how the case in question differs from this case, only, if there be a difference, that case goes a great deal further, for there, the jury do find that all was prosecuted falsely and maliciously, yet being done in course of justice and a legal way to which he might answer and defend himself, there was no room left for any such averment that it was done falsely and maliciously.

---

[1] *Vandebergh v. Blake* (1661), Hardres 191, 194, 145 E.R. 446, 447.

It was a long time a question whether an action did lie against one for suing another though the matter were false and vexatious. And that appears by the case so often cited, my lord Beauchamp's Case in Dyer and Kelway. And, there, it was held there was no punishment appointed for a suit in law, it being a legal thing. And, indeed, there is a very strong case, 11 Jac. I, Rolle's *Abridgment*, 1st part, tit. 'Barretors', f. 355.[1] There it is held if a man did prosecute an infinite number of actions, if they were all his own suits, though the matter were false and vexatious and malicious, no action would lie for such prosecution, because if the matter were false, he must pay costs; and that was one Soam's Case.

It is true this point is now settled that an action does lie in such a case, but we must be careful how we enlarge our interpretation in favor of such actions, for otherwise, it may tend to the interruption of all justice, for we see how these actions have improved from actions for malicious and vexatious prosecutions. The next step we see is to bring actions for indictments and presentments against grand jurors, and this will, if countenanced, tend very much to the hindrance and obstruction of justice. For as private persons will be afraid to accuse any offenders for fear of actions, so will grand juries be afraid to indict and present them for fear of vexatious suits for it. And I do not well see but with a parity of reason, it may extend to the judges of the courts of justice.

It was observed by Mr. Williams in his argument as an inconvenience of countenancing extravagant presentments that grand juries, if they have such impunity by their office, may extend their presentments against courts of justice themselves, and I say with as much reason these actions under correction may at length, if countenanced, extend to courts of justice and the judges there.

I agree that actions upon this Statute are not to be measured by ordinary actions of slander, for that which is not actionable in the last case may be in the first, as my brother Gregory has observed. The dignity of the peers and their nearness to the king may justly make a difference between them. But yet, I cannot see but that that which is a plea to one action is a plea to another.

It is true the boldness and intemperance of men's tongues and actions is not to be allowed in the least to asperse the honor and dignity of a nobleman and that having of late grown very exorbitant has awakened the penalty of this Statute according to that which is said in my Lord Townsend's Case, in a book called Modern Reports, f. 234,[2] that for 120 years after the making of that Statute, rarely if ever any action was brought upon it. It is, I say, the folly and imprudence of men that awakened this sleeping law, and it were to be wished that the prudence and sobriety of men now would let this Statute take such another sleep.

There is one thing more which I would observe upon the reading of this record, which, though I make not any use of it as a cogent reason or argument, yet

---

1 *Soam's Case* (1613), 1 Rolle, Abr., *Barretors*, pl. A, 1, p. 355.

2 *Lord Townsend v. Hughes* (1677), 1 Modern 232, 86 E.R. 850, also 2 Modern 150, 86 E.R. 994, 1 Freeman 217, 220, 222, 89 E.R. 155, 157, 159.

I would thus far offer it in this case. It is a maxim of law that multiplicity of actions is to be avoided as much as possible. Now, here it does appear that nine of this grand jury are named to be in this conspiracy to present, and there are some twenty-eight or thirty presented. What is the consequence of this but that if this action hold good, then all these twenty-eight have actions and will probable bring them against all those nine jurors, so that possibly there may be a creation of 250 actions, for thought only one or two be peers in it, yet all will have the same reason, if this be a libel, and so we shall have a kind of riot of actions as well as there has been a riot of the persons. This I say, though it be no cogent reason, yet is observable in the consequence of it.

And so, I do upon this point conclude that this presentment does contain in itself matter proper to be presented.

Secondly, then, I come to consider whether this presentment be made in a proper court, for if it be made in a proper court and made of matters proper to be presented, then, it is admitted, no action will lie against the maker of it. And I conceive it is made in a proper court that had jurisdiction of the matter presented. And under this head, I will speak to the objections made by Mr. Williams that is to the defendant's plea, the justification contained in it, and the traverse joined to it.

His first exception, if I took him right, was that the defendant pleaded that this was made at the session of Chester, and it does not appear that this *sessio Cestrie* was any court, for as to the word *sessio*, it is an ambiguous word and admits of several interpretations; it is in general any meeting or assembly. That, I think, was his exception.

Now, as to this, if there had been another word used, and that is *curia*, which he would have to be wanting *ad curiam*, etc., the same objection might have been made, for that admits of divers significations. Sometimes, it signifies a senate, sometimes a nobleman's seat, and the like. But that sure[ly] is too nice an exception to hold, for, in legal proceedings, we must take words according to their legal acceptation. And here, I would further take notice that the defendant in his plea has proceeded very warily, for he has followed the very words of the Statutes of 32 and 33 Hen. VIII,[1] for they call it not by the word court but session of Chester and appoint the times wherein it shall be held. It is not a creation of a new court, but only ordering of the time of it, so that it appears to be the true name of the court.

His second objection was this. If it be taken for a court, yet what court is it? Says he, you must set forth by what authority they did sit, whether it were the sessions of the peace or sessions of oyer and terminer or of gaol delivery. And he

[1] Stat. 32 Hen. VIII, c. 43 (*SR*, III, 796); Stat. 33 Hen. VIII, c. 13 (*SR*, III, 849).

did cite a case he thought was pat to the purpose, and that was Sir Christopher Heydon's Case.[1]

Now as to this, in 4 Inst. 21,[2] my lord Coke observes that the county palatine of Chester 'is the most ancient and honorable county palatine . . . in England', and, indeed, all the other counties palatine were shaped according to that.

What was anciently the *comes palatinus* is to be gathered from what we have in Spelman's *Glossary*, f. 143,[3] where he says '*Transiisse autem videtur huius comitis officium in capitalis justitiarii cancellarii et aliorum.*' He had the same jurisdiction as those great officers had.

And the Statutes of 2 and 3 Edw. VI[4] calls him the high justice of Chester, so that it appears he had an original jurisdiction.

And as to what was said, that the defendant ought to have set forth the particular commission upon which the jury was sworn, whether that of the peace or oyer and terminer or gaol delivery, therein I doubt Mr. Williams does mistake, for I have endeavored to learn as much as I could in this short time allotted for this matter and to be informed of the truth of the fact as to this court, and I do find they sit not by virtue of any particular commission of oyer and terminer or the like but by the letters patent of the king, which do constitute the justice of Chester, who had an ancient jurisdiction in matters criminal, not erected, as Mr. Ward thought, by the Statutes of 32 and 33 of Hen. VIII. But of which, of course, the courts of Westminster Hall always took cognizance as original jurisdictions, and the Statute of 32 or 33 of Hen. VIII does not make a new court but only alters the time of sitting for the old one, when the frequent session became the grievance of the county. And, therefore, the defendant need not set forth any particular commission, because they do not sit by any particular commission.

A third objection that he made was this. Supposing this was a court and had jurisdiction, yet here is nothing presented upon which that court can proceed nor [is anything] formally drawn up.

Now, as to this, the declaration calls it *quoddam scandalosum famosum et malitiosum libellum contra ipsum comitem falso et malitiose machinatum*, that is positive. And truly, the defendant's plea is as positive, that he with the rest *secundum juramenti sui debitum ac secundum evidentiam et testimonium eis ibidem exhibitam de prefato comite* did present so and so in the English words in the declaration. But we are to consider whether this be a proper presentment in a proper place, especially when we see the design of it, which is good, the security of the government

---

1 *Heydon's Case* (1614), Godbolt 247, 78 E.R. 144, *sub nom. Haydon v. Godsale*, Palmer 150, 280, 81 E.R. 1022, 1083, Croke Jac. 334, 341, 79 E.R. 285, 291, 2 Bulstrode 159, 237, 80 E.R. 1032, 1088, *sub nom. Heydon v. Shepherd*, Moore K.B. 834, 72 E.R. 936, *sub nom. Godsol v. Heydon*, 1 Rolle Rep. 14, 78, 81 E.R. 293, 340.

2 E. Coke, *Fourth Institute* (1644), p. 211.

3 H. Spelman, *Glossarium* (1664), p. 143.

4 Stat. 2 & 3 Edw. VI, c. 28 (*SR*, IV, 71).

and the peace, which was under their consideration, though it be not so very formally drawn up as it ought to be in the case of an indictment, which the clerk is to take care of that it have far greater formality than a presentment needs.

It is true I do not argue with Mr. Solicitor in his distinction that he made, that either here is a positive charge upon the plaintiff or there is not. If it is positive, then no action lies, because it is in a legal way and course of justice. If it is not, then here is nothing of aspersion that the plaintiff can complain of, for I take it clearly that words in themselves will bear an action, though they do not positively allege a charge or accusation.

As, if a felony be committed, and J.S. shall say of J.N. 'you did not steal such a man's goods', that in the literal construction is not a charge but a discharge and no accusation at all. And yet being spoken in such a manner they carry in them the force of an affirmative accusation and an action will lie. But truly, I take it in this case, there is enough positively alleged and, therefore, [is] a good matter of justification.

Then, I came to consider the traverse, and, there, the objection lies thus, as I take it, that there is matter in the declaration that is not justified in the plea nor answered in the traverse. The declaration lays the fact in Berkshire. The justification goes only to the Common Hall of Pleas in Chester, and the traverse only saying not guilty out of the County of Chester, the defendant may be guilty of this matter in some other place than the Common Hall of Pleas even within the County of Chester, and so the traverse is not full enough; it is too narrow for the declaration.

Now, as to this, pray let us consider what the defendant says in his plea. He justifies that at the sessions of Chester in such a place, he did so and so. That, perhaps, had not been full enough of itself, but then, the traverse takes all in that was out of the justification, without that that the defendant was guilty *de premissis* (which refers to all the parts of the declaration) *in predicto comitatu Berks* (which goes to the place mentioned in the declaration) *vel alibi extra comitatu Cestrie vel aliter vel alio modo* than as in the plea, so that, take all together, it is perfect in the justification and the traverse. What one wants, the other supplies.

Then the third main question is whether this presentment be made by proper persons. But this I shall spend very little time in, for there is no doubt of it, but it is they were a grand jury. Their very title declares their office, and their office makes it plain to be their duty. They are called the grand inquest, grand, because they represent the body of the county, and inquest, *ab inquirendo*, which shows what they are to do, to enquire of and then present offenses.

So, I think I have done now with the main question of the case. I shall, therefore, speak very shortly to the exceptions taken by Mr. Ward to the pleading.

First, says he, it is said to be *secundum evidentiam et testimonium eis exhibitam de eodem comite*, but they do not set forth what the evidence was [so] that the court may judge of it. And for that purpose, Bushell's Case in my lord Vaughan was cited.

Now, as to that, I take it that grand juries are not bound to discover, nay, in some sort, they are obliged to conceal their evidence. I must needs say, in Vaughan, that was an exception in that case, but I find he was the only judge that gave the opinion of all the court. But the reason and ground of the judgment was thus. They did hold that let the evidence be what it would, a jury were not properly finable in that case, if they had gone against their evidence merely considered, so that had the return been general or special, they held that the jury were not punishable for such a verdict unless some particular matter of contempt to the court were alleged.

Secondly, says Mr. Ward, the plea does not conclude and say *prout patet per recordum*, as it ought. And, truly, I think it had been naught, if it had been so, for there was no record at all to refer to.

Thirdly, it was said this plea was ill because it amounts to the general issue. And, no doubt, he might have pleaded the general issue and given this special matter in evidence. And it is true also in some cases where a man pleads specially what does amount to the general issue, that is faulty.

But then that does not arise from any insufficiency in the special plea that it is not good but because the law does not care to have long, tedious, prolix records where there is no cause for them, and it is a matter discretionary in many cases for the court to make them plead the general issue.

But besides this, as to our purpose and case, I would only mention my lord Cromwell's Case, which is a case of a *scandalum magnatum* too, in 4 Co. 12,[1] where this objection was started. And there, it was resolved that a man shall not be bound to plead the general issue in two cases.

First, where he does confess the words and justifies them to be true.

Secondly, where he confesses the words and by matter specially pleaded shows that they are not actionable, which I take to be the very case of the now defendant.

So that I shall trouble you no longer with any long argument of this case, but I take it that the court here was such an one as had proper jurisdiction of the matter, that the things presented were presented by proper persons, and that the matter presented was properly presentable. And upon the whole matter, I conceive the plaintiff has no cause of action. But judgment ought to be given for the defendant.

Lord Chief Baron [Montagu]: The earl of Macclesfield is plaintiff, and John Starkey is the defendant. The record has been put so fully by my brothers that I need not open it but very shortly.

---

[1] *Lord Cromwell's Case* (1578–1581), 4 Coke Rep. 12, 76 E.R. 877.

It is an action brought by the earl as well for the king as for himself upon the Statute of Ric. II of *Scandalum Magnatum*,[1] reciting the Statute and that he is a peer of great honor and clear in his reputation and then declares that Starkey, the defendant, nor regarding the Statute of Ric. II nor the penalty of the Statute of Westminster I,[2] which is inflicted by the Statute of Ric. II but maliciously intending to bring this noble earl into disfavor with the king and disesteem of others [on the] 17th September in the 35th year of the late king at Wantage in the County of Berks by conspiracy between the defendant and seven or eight more that are named in the declaration did a certain scandalous and malicious libel against the plaintiff falsely and maliciously invent, write, and publish and cause to be written and published in such English words and sets forth the tenor of the writing verbatim and then the declaration goes on 'Whereas the said earl was a person free from all the offenses described and mentioned in that libel which he is injured by in his honor and dignity' and lays it to his damage of £10,000.

To this, the defendant pleads that at the session of Chester in the Common Hall of Pleas there before Sir George Jeffreys and John Warren, justices for that county, he the said Starkey and the rest named in the declaration were empaneled and returned to be of the grant inquest for that county and sworn to enquire for the king and the body of the county upon certain articles to them delivered by the said justices and that the said Starkey and the rest of that inquest according to their oath and according to evidence and testimony there given them *de praefato comite* according to their consciences and to preserve the peace of the county did present in the English words in the declaration mentioned, as lawfully they might, and so they confess and justify the writing. And then comes the traverse *absque hoc* that the defendant is guilty in Berkshire or out of the County of Chester or otherwise than as in the plea is alleged.

Upon this plea, there is a demurrer joined, and upon this demurrer the case has been twice argued at the bar on both sides and now stands for the judgment of the court wherein my brothers have delivered themselves so fully and accurately, taking off all the objections and speaking likewise to the matter in law, that, truly, I must needs confess I can say very little or nothing more. They have prevented me in what I had designed to say in the case, and I shall but repeat what has been said. But yet it is my duty to deliver my own thoughts in the series wherein I had laid them, which may vary from my brothers' arguments in the method they have observed, though in substance they will conclude in the same opinion. And so in short upon this case, I declare I do hold with my brothers that the defendant's plea to this action, as it is upon this record, is a good plea both for matter and form and that judgment is to be given for the defendant.

The matter in law, as it makes a question in this case, I shall consider last, and to keep my own method that I have proposed to myself, I shall go upon the

---

[1] Stat. 2 Ric. II, stat. 1, c. 5 (*SR*, II, 9).

[2] Stat. 3 Edw. I, c. 34 (*SR*, I, 35).

objections first and answer them, though my brother Atkyns, I conceive, has done it very fully already.

I observe that the plaintiff's counsel have made their chief objections and batteries against the form of the pleadings here, but, as to the matter in law, they have said little against the authorities alleged by the counsel for the defendant.

I, likewise, observe that Mr. Williams made diverse objections of his own but ingenuously as well as respectfully to the court to save their time in this argument did not repeat again what was objected before by Mr. Ward, who argued on the same side but withal did in faithfulness to his client not waive those other objections but reserved the advantage of them without troubling the court with the repetition, so that what has been said both times at the bar, I shall as near as I can remember and recollect and upon the whole give you my reasons why I am of this opinion.

First, it is true as has been said this is an action brought as well for the king as for this noble lord, the plaintiff. But withal, I would take notice that the king's being made a party to the suit will contribute nothing to the maintenance of the action, if it be not maintainable by law.

Secondly, it is likewise clear that this noble lord, my lord of Macclesfield, is a person of great honor and dignity and in a great office of trust and so apparently within the benefit of the Statute. And the Statute has ever been interpreted in favor of the peers, so that an action of *scandalum magnatum* lies upon slighter words and upon less occasion of slander to a peer than will to a commoner. But yet as has been often said and is most clear also when the subject matter is alike actionable, the action of a peer is subject to the like bar as the action of any ordinary person is. Now, presentments and indictments are no more the subject matter of an action upon the case allowed to peers than to commoners and, therefore, the peers' actions upon such matters are subject to the like bars.

As to the bar to this action by the plea of the defendant, there has been much excepted to it.

First, they say it is naught, because it is not alleged that they did present upon oath. But that has been likewise answered, and I cannot but think, satisfactorily to all here. If they were sworn to enquire and according to their oaths did present as is set forth, if this be not a presentment upon oath without those express words *super sacramentum suum presentant*, I cannot see what is a presentment upon oath.

The other objections have been fully answered by my brother Atkyns and my other brothers too and by the defendant's counsel at the bar as particularly that this presentment is such an one as ought not to be taken by the court, because it wants form and is not positive either as to things or persons. But I think it was mentioned by my brother that it is said to be *secundum evidentiam et testimonium de prefato comite* and there, sure[ly], the person is sufficiently described.

Then, as to the form, they object that it is no positive charge because it only says 'we conceive and hold it our duty to present', but that is no presentment. I say that is no objection, for, if a presentment have substance, that is matter presentable in a proper place; though it be informal, that want of form is intended to be supplied by the skill of the clerks, who are to draw it up. But jurymen are not conversant in forms of law and, as was observed by my brother Gregory, what would become of all the presentments of grand juries, which are usually made at the rising of the assizes, when there is not time to put them into form? They are the desires of the country expressed by their representatives and lie with the clerk as matter for indictments to be preferred to another grand jury when drawn up in form by the clerk.

It was likewise objected that here is mention made of certain articles given them by the justices upon which they were to enquire, but these articles are not set forth what they were. I think that is not necessary at all, for we all know what articles they have given them to enquire upon. The charge grand juries commonly have is by the judge, but yet they are not confined to make inquisition only upon what is given them in the charge, but they have a larger field and have liberty to make presentment of things within their own knowledge.

It was also further objected that, though it is said to be according to evidence, yet it does not appear, neither what that evidence was. And Bushell's Case in my lord Vaughan was much insisted upon to maintain the objection that my brothers and so Mr. Holt, too, in his argument gave a full answer to, that it was a return from a court after open evidence given, but a grand jury whatever evidence they have to found their bills and make their presentments upon, those are matters given in secret in the jury chamber, and it is that which they ought to conceal and not to divulge, being the king's evidence. And that case of Bushell, which was so relied upon as a pattern for this case, my brother said right, that all the law that is upon the matter to be collected out of that case is that very rarely and difficulty scarce, if at all, a jury is to be fined for going contrary to evidence and direction of the court. And that rather furnishes the other side with an argument against this action, that it ought not to be brought because of the tenderness the law expresses to jurors to protect them from fines and vexations for what they do upon their oaths and in their office.

These were the objections made by Mr. Ward. I come now to those that were made by Mr. Williams.

First, he says this *sessio Cestriae* is not sufficient, but it ought to be called a court and tell what court it is. But the vanity of that has been shown by my brother Atkyns, for he does follow the very words of the Statute, which I have looked upon, and there at least five times in that short Statute, it is called the sessions of Chester. Nay, and I observe further that all the precedents in Coke, *Intrationum*, tit. 'Error',[1] of records removed by writ of error out of Chester, as the two or three first cases are, it is the very stile as is used here.

[1] *Regina v. Chester Justices* (1596), E. Coke, *Book of Entries* (1614), 'Error', pl. 1, f. 225b.

He did next object that it is not hinted what commission the court sat by, whether as justices of peace or of oyer and terminer etc. And yet Mr. Williams confesses there are great and ancient courts there. And I must acknowledge my brother Atkyns has given me much light into what I had not so much leisure as to enquire, that they sit by letters patent of the justice's place and not by any particular commission. And, then, there can be no doubt in the world but that this court has an ancient usual name and style which we are to take to be this here used, because we know no other. And though there is a Statute that does erect a court, which is 27 Hen. VIII,[1] yet that Statute does not name the courts nor does the Statute of 32 [Hen. VIII] give any name. Therefore, must not we take notice of it by the style given it time out of mind?

But the greatest objection to the form of this plea was its amounting to the general issue. And that was made not so much an objection by the counsel as one of the causes of demurrer, which makes it to be the more considered for its being so assigned. But this has likewise received a plain answer both from the counsel and my brothers. And I can but repeat what they have said. It was answered by the authority of Warner and Wainsford's Case in Hobart 123, that where there is a matter in law to be pleaded, that is always allowed to be pleaded specially though it amount to the general issue, for matters in law are not to be left to a jury upon an issue. And there was also another answer given to it, and, I think, a very clear one from Dr. Leyfield's Case, 10 Co.,[2] whether it is a rule that where the defendant by plea admits some color of action in the plaintiff and pleads [in order] to bar it a matter in law, there such pleading specially is good and not to be avoided because it amounts to the general issue. So, here is color given to my lord Macclesfield and an admission that this action by confession of the fact would be against every man but a juryman, which is the protection he pleads for himself.

Then, for the exceptions that were taken to the traverse, they were two.

The first was by Mr. Ward that it answers only to the presentment but not to the conspiracy. But that, I think, was fully answered thus. That when the presentment is said to be upon oath, the conspiracy is purged (and so were the authorities cited) so that he needed not to plead it to all and every part.

But then the other objections my brothers have taken notice of and answered, and I can add nothing but only repeat their words. It is defective, says Mr. Williams, for it takes not in the whole matter charged in the declaration. It justifies only by a presentment made in the Sessions Hall at Chester and traverses the County of Berks and elsewhere out of the County of Chester and yet does confine the presentment to the Common Hall of Pleas and so it might be done elsewhere in the County of Chester and so the *aliter vel alio modo* will not help the defect of the place.

---

[1] Stat. 27 Hen. VIII, c. 5 (*SR*, III, 534–535).

[2] *Leyfield's Case* (1611), 10 Coke Rep. 88, 77 E.R. 1057, also 1 Bulstrode 154, 80 E.R. 846, Croke Jac. 317, 79 E.R. 272.

This objection is grounded certainly upon a mistake, for the declaration is not for writing or publishing in Cheshire, but it is for doing it in the County of Berks, and, if the declaration indeed had been of a fact in Cheshire, the owning of the doing it at the Sessions Hall and not elsewhere out of the County of Chester *nec aliter* etc. had been short and defective. But then, the defendant would never have put in *nec alibi extra Comitatu Cestriae* surely if it had been laid in Cheshire. But the plaintiff's alleging it to be done at Wantage in Berkshire made the *nec alibi extra Comitatu Cestriae* necessary, which, being pleaded, covers all places but where the presentment was made, to wit in Cheshire, and the *nec aliter vel alio modo* etc. completes the traverse and covers the whole matter alleged, so that for the form of the plea, I conceive it is very well.

Now, for the matter in law of this plea, I shall speak but shortly to it, because it has been so fully debated and spoken to by my brothers. That now depends upon this question, whether upon this record, as it is set forth upon this demurrer, this action lies. And I conceive it does not lie. And, therefore, judgment ought to be given for the defendant. My reasons for this opinion are these.

First, because it is an action against a grand juryman for what he does as a grand juryman.

Secondly, as was urged by the counsel for the defendant in answer to the objections made by the counsel for the plaintiff, because the matters contained within the presentment were matters within the defendant's conusance in that office and presentable by him. And

Thirdly, because this presentment was made before proper judges that had sufficient jurisdiction of the cause.

Now, first, that this action lies not against a grand juryman for what he does as a grand juryman, the books and authorities are many and full. They have been truly cited, and so Mr. Williams acknowledged they were.

Fitzherbert, *Natura Brevium*, 115. If jurors are sworn to enquire and, after any of them is discharged by the judges, he shall not be punished for that which he did when he was sworn.

Lib. Ass., 30, pl. 21.[1] It is held to be a good plea in conspiracy that the defendants were indictors and so what they did was upon their oaths.

There are old books cited in Brooke, *Abridgment*, tit. 'Conspiracy', nos. 1, 9, 11, 12,[2] out of the year books, and two or three more out of Edw. III, all to the same purpose, were mentioned.

That case of Lloyd and Barker in 12 Co. 23[3] was fully opened by my brother Gregory and is very pertinent to the case. And, therefore, I shall not stay to repeat the particulars of these authorities but only take up so much of your time as

---

1 YB 30 Edw. III, Lib. Ass., p. 177, pl. 21 (1356).

2 YB Mich. 20 Hen. VI, f. 5, pl. 15 (1441); YB Mich. 47 Edw. III, f. 16, pl. 30 (1373); YB Mich. 7 Hen. IV, f. 31, pl. 15 (1405).

3 *Floyd v. Barker* (1607), 12 Coke Rep. 23, 77 E.R. 1305.

to speak to that case in Bridgman, f. 131, because it is so pat to our purpose; it is Agard and Wild's Case.[1]

An action is brought by Agard against Wild for slander and maliciously intending to make him reputed a common barretor and thereupon procuring him to be indicted for barretry. Wild pleads that he and others were empaneled upon the grand inquest and sworn in court to enquire upon their oaths of all felonies, trespasses, and misdemeanors and, being so sworn, having evidence by good men, did indict the plaintiff, as lawfully they might do. There was a demurrer and judgment for the defendant. And this is the reason for the judgment given. Forasmuch as the defendant was sworn upon the inquest, it cannot be presumed that he did it of malice but that it was done in zeal to justice by reason of his oath, and most of the books cited in this case are there cited, and, particularly, the saying of Thorp is there put down, 21 Edw. III, 17a,[2] that conspirators are always in fault, but when one is of the inquest and sworn to speak the truth, that which he then says is upon his oath and not of conspiracy and there is no reason to accuse one of conspiracy where he does nothing. And there is another precedent alleged where, in the same action, there was the same plea and the same judgment given. And there are likewise cited several precedents out of Rastall's *Entries* 122; Fitzherbert, [*Abridgment*] 'Conspiracy', nos. 3, 4, and 5,[3] which are all cases of actions brought against indictors. The same bar [was] pleaded, and judgment [was] for the defendant.

These books being so full and express in the point that, what they do as jurymen, they are not subject to actions for. It thereby appears how careful the law is to encourage jurors to do their duty and, if in doing that, they do not act so formally and prudently as they might, yet they are not to be subjected easily to actions, for, when they are commanded, as they are upon summons and impanelled to serve, which they cannot refuse, and when they act upon so sacred an obligation as an oath, that does purge and excuse all former conspiracies and malicious intentions.

And as my brother Atkyns truly cited it, there was that case which he mentioned in this court. I remember it very well; I was then a reporter here and as far as I remember, though I did not look upon it before I came, it was as he says. Though it were found by the jury to be done falsely and maliciously, yet it was adjudged by the court [that] no action lay for it, which goes further than our case, because of the jury's finding it to be done falsely and maliciously, and so [it] is a fuller case in point than ours.

Now, I shall only add one authority more that has not yet been mentioned at all, because it is suitable to this very case, it being an action brought by a very

1 *Agard v. Wilde* (1617), J. Bridgman 130, 123 E.R. 1251.

2 YB Hil. 21 Edw. III, f. 17, pl. 19 (1347).

3 YB Pas. 22 Hen. VI, f. 49, pl. 9 (1444); YB Hil. 33 Hen. VI, f. 1, pl. 6 (1455); YB Mich. 35 Hen. VI, f. 14, pl. 24 (1456).

honorable and noble peer, to show that, even as to their actions against jurors, the law defends jurors and they cannot prevail against them.

It is my lord Coke, 2 Inst., f. 228,[1] in his comment upon the Statute of Westminster I, c. 34, which is one of the statutes that gives this action and penalty, for 2 Ric. II, c. 5, only refers for the penalty to this. There, my lord Coke says 'it is to be understood that although this Statute and the Act of 2 Ric. II be general in the negative, yet do they not extend to all manner of false news or horrible and false scandals . . . but only to [such as are] extrajudicial', for if they be in a way of judicial proceedings, though the charge be false, no action lies. These are the words of that book which brings all the other cases, as to the reason of them, home to the case at bar and shows that such a course of law is a bar to a peer's action as well as it is to a commoner's, it being a judicial proceeding.

Now, to these authorities, I must observe there has been very little if anything at all alleged on the other side to answer them but only what rests in bare imagination of something that Mr. Williams would have us conceive to be in the Table of Titles to my lord Hale's commonplace book, where he finds cited 9 Edw. II and 8 Edw. III and says he had not time to look into the book itself, which is in Lincoln's Inn Library. But what we must imagine thence, I cannot conceive, nor, indeed, can he tell us. I believe, rather, his imagination that there was nothing in those quotations that could be opposed to these authorities that have been so fully opened and urged and, therefore, chose to leave it in a cloud for amusement's sake that he might say something to the point that might have a shadow of authority for his client's cause.

As for the wording of the titles conspiracy versus coroners and versus jurors, whether it lies or not is just but the same that is in Ashe's tables,[2] and, if Mr. Williams look there, he will find all the cases and all the references of this nature in the old books.

There remains, then, no authority of any case that has been objected to these numerous authorities on the other side but that Case of Bushell in my lord Vaughan, which yet has been fully shown by the reason of the case and the authority of the opinion and judgment there given to support the defendant's case, for it is an argument of the tenderness of the law in the case of jurors. And I may very well infer thence that there ought to be the like tenderness not to give way to actions brought against grand jurors for doing what their oath and office obliges them to.

The books of Dyer and Kelway which are both reports of one case, my lord Beauchamp's Case, do make mightily for this assertion that we go upon, *viz.* whatsoever is done in a way of judicial proceedings excuses from an action, even in the case of a peer. And this assertion is at least three times repeated in Kelway.

---

1 E. Coke, *Second Institute* (1642), p. 228.

2 T. Ashe, *Promptuarie* (1614).

As for the Case of Smith and Crashaw in Palmer, f. 315, and 1 Cro. 15,[1] and the Poulterers' Case, 9 Co. 55,[2] they all warrant but this that conspiracy does lie for causing and procuring one to be indicted falsely and maliciously, but that comes not home to this point, for it cannot be thence inferred that it does lie against indictors. He that is not under the obligation of an oath and an office which he is compelled to take upon him[self] by law is not to expect the same protection for his actions as he that is thus obliged.

So that for that first reason, I do conclude this action does not lie, because it is brought against a grand juryman for what he did as a grand juryman.

Secondly, I say the matters mentioned within this presentment are such as were within their conusance to present and grounds for their defense in it. Not to mention the particulars at large, they observe there was a treasonable conspiracy discovered; they take notice of factions and seditious practices of some in that county; they speak of dangerous assemblies and tumults and unlawful meetings and conventicles.

But I must observe, by the way, nothing is asserted in it against my lord of Macclesfield and, therefore, to call it a scandalous libel and charge upon him is strange. And as Mr. Holt, in his argument, truly said, if this action be supported, it is with a *subintelligitur*, for nothing is expressed so in it.

Yet withal, I would say, certainly the things they here speak of were good grounds for them upon their fears and apprehensions about them to desire that the peace of the country might be preserved and, therefore, that all from whom they did apprehend danger might give security to preserve it. Then

Thirdly, that this was a presentment before proper judges is as clear as anything else and has been as fully shown by my brothers. The style is *sessio Cestriae*, and Chester is a county palatine and, as my lord Coke says in this *Fourth Institute*, the ancientest county palatine. And we that are judges in Westminster Hall are, of course, to take notice of their courts. They have a large jurisdiction and that jurisdiction of theirs is to be by law supported.

Now, when a court has jurisdiction of a cause, as this court of Chester certainly had of the offenses mentioned in this presentment, if they had any jurisdiction at all, the case of [*blank*], Moor 143,[3] has ruled it that for proceeding in a legal way in such a court, no action will lie.

---

1 *Smith v. Cranshaw* (1622), Palmer 315, 81 E.R. 1100, Croke Car. 15, 79 E.R. 618, also 2 Rolle Rep. 258, 81 E.R. 785, W. Jones 93, 82 E.R. 48, Gilbert Cas. 179, 93 E.R. 298, Benloe 152, 73 E.R. 1019.

2 *The Poulterers' Case*, 9 Coke Rep. 55, 77 E.R. 813, also *sub nom. Stone v. Walter*, Moore K.B. 813, 72 E.R. 923.

3 *The Case of Lord C.* cited in *Broughton's Case*, Moore K.B. 141, 143, 72 E.R. 493, 494.

As for the cases in 4 Co. [14], Bulckley and Wood's Case, and Moor 705 and 3 Cro. 348,[1] which are all one and the same case, if they are any authority as to this case at all, they are authorities for our opinion that, for proceedings in a judicial way in a proper court, no action will lie. But when the star chamber or any other court proceeds for matters that are without their jurisdiction and conusance, there an action will lie, but for that reason only, because it was not a proceeding in a proper court and no legal proceeding at all. But now, it is my opinion as well as it is the opinion of all my brothers that all things are proper, the presentors, the presentment, and the court it is made in.

And, therefore, for these reasons, because it is an action brought against a grand juryman for what he did as a grand juryman, because the matters contained in the presentment were within the grand jury's conusance and good ground for their desire in it and because it is made in a proper court that had jurisdiction of the cause, I am clear of opinion the matter of the plea is good to bar the plaintiff's action. And as for the form, I think it is well enough, notwithstanding all the objections upon the reasons that have been given. And so, I conceive judgment ought to be given for the overruling of the demurrer.

Mr. Berrisford: Do you order judgment for the defendant?

Lord Chief Baron [Montagu]: Yes, we are all of one opinion, and let judgment be entered for the defendant.

Judicium: *Quod querens nil capiat per billam.*

[Other reports of this case: British Library MS. Hargrave 370, f. 6v, State Trials (Cobbett, ed., 1811), vol. 10, col. 1413.]

[Appeal denied: Dodd 330.]

12

Bristow v. Cooper

(Ex. 1686–1687)

A taxpayer can arrange his business affairs so as to avoid the payment of taxes.

Lincoln's Inn MS. Misc. 557, f. 110, pl. 3

Hilary [term] 1685/86. Touching tobacco imported in the ship *Jeffreys* the 23 June 1685.

In [an action of] trover for a great quantity of tobacco upon a trial at the bar by a Middlesex jury of great quality, the question was whether tobacco imported and entered in the port of Sandwich the 23rd day of June 1685 and the duty then due to the king paid and secured to the officer of the king at Sandwich for part of the goods landed the same day but the other and far the greater part afterwards,

[1] *Buckley v. Wood* (1591), *ut supra.*

the 24 of June 1685 will be liable to the 3d. per pound imposed by the Statute of 1 Jac. II, ca. [*blank*],[1] upon all tobaccos imported after the 24th of June 1685.

And, upon the trial, these matters and questions arose, first, whether the entry of the ship by the merchant with the officer in the port of Sandwich can be proved by witnesses without producing and proving a copy of the entry.

And it was urged by the plaintiff's counsel that it could, being only a matter of fact and not of record. Copies of such entries out of the Custom House or of church books being proved are evidences of their own of the things that they contain. But the facts themselves which these copies contain can be proved, and copies of the entries are not necessary. A man can prove the death or christening of another without a copy out of the church book.

But the whole court delivered their opinion *seriatim* that the entry in the Custom House cannot be proved without a copy of it, though it was admitted that the entry itself was not a record. And the court directed the jury accordingly.

But the jury did not observe the direction, but found the entry as proved, for which [there was a] new trial.

Second, another question was whether the plaintiff here was guilty of fraud against the king inasmuch as the ship was originally ordered and intended to be brought into the port of London. But as it was held that the 3d. per pound took place after the 24th of June, before which time, this ship could not arrive into the port of London, upon which new orders were given to make for the first port in England and enter before the 24th of June and the plaintiff had arrived and entered in Sandwich accordingly, it was urged for the plaintiff that it was only a prudent and discrete act and no fraud or deceit to the king because no duty attached or vested in the king, and, on account of this, [it was] no fraud.

And of such opinion was the court. And the jury gave a general verdict for the plaintiff.

[Other copies of this report: Georgetown Univ. Law Sch. MS. B88–7, p. 625.]

Lincoln's Inn MS. Misc. 557, f. 147, pl. 3

Hilary [term] 1686[/87]. See above 110. Entered in the Office of Pleas, Hilary [term] 1 & 2 Jac. II.

The special verdict was this term argued by myself [*Edward Ward*], for the plaintiffs, and *Roger North*, one of the King's Counsel, for the defendant. And judgment was for the plaintiff in Michaelmas 1687 by the whole court.

And note that this special verdict was found upon a second trial at the bar. The jury that tried the cause at first having given a general verdict for the plaintiff and 40s. damages, and, it being entered, the counsel for the plaintiff refused to find[2] the matter specially, upon which the court granted a new trial upon pay-

[1] Stat. 1 Jac. II, c. 4 (*SR*, VI, 3–7).

[2] Sic in MS.

ment of costs. But the plaintiff's refusing costs, the order was to have a new trial generally, and [there was] no mention of costs *nisi causa* such a day. And, at this day, the court ordered a new trial without costs, there being a rule for a new trial and no mention of costs.

[Other copies of this report: Georgetown Univ. Law Sch. MS. B88–8, p. 12, pl. 1.]

Lincoln's Inn MS. Misc. 558, f. 14, pl. 3

Michaelmas [term] 1687.

Touching the importation of a ship with tobacco, whether the coming into the port and entering and securing the duty for all and landing a small part at Sandwich before the 24 June 1685, the greater part not being unloaded until after the 24th June 1685, be an importation to prevent payment of the 3d. per pound imposed by the Statute 1 Jac. II, ca. 4, judgment [was given] for the plaintiff that it is a good importation and this duty is not due.

I [*Edward Ward* was] for the plaintiff.

[Other copies of this report: Georgetown Univ. Law Sch. MS. B88–8, p. 113, pl. 3.]

13

Newbery, qui tam v. Pym

(Ex. 1686)

Rattines are cloths, not stuffs, and are prohibited import items.

Lincoln's Inn MS. Misc. 557, f. 111, pl. 2

Hilary [term] 1685/86.

Note, upon a trial at Middlesex this term [Hilary 1686], the question was whether a sort of clothes called rattines, which are not woven or made as cloth, but as stuffs, and commonly called and known by the name of stuffs or rattines, which is the peculiar name, and have been imported for twenty years from ports beyond the sea, are prohibited to be imported under the statutes that prohibit importation of foreign cloth or not or whether they as well as other stuffs can be imported.

And the jury found rattines to be cloth and not stuffs. And this trial was to settle the question without a forfeiture.

I [*Edward Ward*] was for the defendant.

[Other copies of this report: Georgetown Univ. Law Sch. MS. B88–7, p. 627.]

14

Wyberd, qui tam v. Doughty

(Ex. 1686)

Even though aulnage duties have been paid for cloth, if that cloth is later dyed so that its value is greatly increased, then additional aulnage duties are payable.

Lincoln's Inn MS. Misc. 557, f. 118

Upon a seizure of fifteen pieces of scarlet or bowdyed shalloones dyed ingrain, in the office of the King's Remembrancer upon a Latin information and a trial at law, the sole question was whether clothes, when alb, are sealed with the seal of the collector of the subsidy of the aulnage and this duty is paid, will pay another aulnage as clothes dyed ingrain under the Statute of 27 Edw. III, ca. 4,[1] being scarlet or bowdyed, which is a resemblance to scarlet, and the tincture of it proceeds from cochineal. And notwithstanding that it was objected that nothing is called color ingrain under the Statute for the increase or enlarging of the duty of aulnage except scarlet and that the dye called bowdye, or clothes dyed with cochineal, are not scarlet and that the practice has not been to take this duty within the time that the true scarlet dye ceased and the bowdye began, which was *circa* forty or fifty years past, and notwithstanding that the scarlet dye is used at the making of the Statute, it was extremely dear, ten times the price of bowdye or cochineal colors and, in respect of the color, adds so much to the price of the cloth. And, for this reason and cause, the aulnage for such clothes was increased.

Yet, upon the examination of several witnesses, as well of the part of the king as of the defendant, it was clearly proved that the colors of bowdye and [that] given by cochineal are commonly called colors ingrain and the clothes thus dyed called clothes ingrained and that, at this day, no other colors are called colors ingrain and these colors adding to the value of the cloth, and the intent of the Statute was to give revenue to the crown for all clothes ingrain of what nature soever, the thing was that gives the tincture called ingrain. And, inasmuch as it appears by a decree in this court 33 Eliz. that all clothes ingrained with any sort of art, seed, grain, fly, or matter whatever either reputed or sold for cloth ingrained will pay the rates for clothes ingrained expressed in the said Statute and that by another order or decree made in the court 11 Jac. I, the merchants and drapers were ordered to pay for these scarlets of assize 2d. and for half cloth 1d. for each cloth of assize half ingrained and each cloth of assize dyed with cochineal carrying the name of ingrained cloth 1d. and for half such cloth ½d., and thus after this rate for all kerseys and other clothes beyond the subsidy of 4d. payable in the country and inasmuch as cochineal is expressly mentioned in the latter decree and, by implication, in the decree of 33 Eliz., it being a fly.

---

[1] Stat. 27 Edw. III, stat. 1, c. 4 (*SR*, I, 330–331).

The jury, by direction, as a clear case, found for the plaintiff, but, by consent, the forfeiture to be waived, this trial being intended to settle the duty. And, though the full duty as to alb was paid, yet the subsequent accession of the grain gives a new duty, that is to say to make alb the duty paid as to all to amount to the duty upon clothes ingrained.

I [*Edward Ward* was] for the king.

[Other copies of this report: Georgetown Univ. Law Sch. MS. B88–7, p. 635.]

15

Langly, qui tam v. Gooday

(Ex. 1686)

A plaintiff can traverse a plea in abatement, and the issue will be tried by a jury, and a verdict on the merits can be found.

Lincoln's Inn MS. Misc. 557, f. 119, pl. 1

Upon a seizure of brandies, the defendant pleaded in abatement that Langly was not an officer of the customs nor had the power to make a seizure and, on account of this, he pleaded the clause in the Act against Frauds, 14 Car. II, ca. 11,[1] which restrains seizures to the custom officers, and he prayed judgment of the information.

The Attorney General [*Sawyer*] replied that the defendant *respondere debet quia dicet [?] quod* Langly was an officer of the customs at the time of the seizure, *viz.* at Ratcliff etc. *et hoc petit quod inquiratur per patriam, et praedictus defendens similiter.*

And, at the trial, the evidence was that Langly was the searcher of Ipswich by a patent in the time of Charles II *durante bene placito* that ended with the death of the king, which was thus agreed, and he had not any other patent.

But it was insisted by the Attorney General [*Sawyer*], and allowed by the Chief Baron [Atkyns], that the proclamation of the now king immediately after the death of King Charles II that all officers will continue in their offices until further order had continued him a good officer under the Statute of Frauds to make seizures. And there was a verdict for the plaintiff upon the trial.

I [*Edward Ward* was] for the defendant.

And, afterwards, the plaintiff had judgment entered for himself and the king in chief, *viz.* for the forfeiture of the goods though the plea was in abatement, because, in such a case, it was peremptory, *quod nota et quaere* whether it was because the defendant would not pursue a writ of error.

---

1 Stat. 14 Car. II, c. 11 (*SR*, V, 393–400).

Vide Cro. Car. 566,[1] the difference, when the matter in abatement is pleaded in bar after an imparlance there is a general judgment, by which it seems that *respondeas ouster* is to be awarded when it is purely in abatement.

[Other copies of this report: Georgetown Univ. Law Sch. MS. B88–7, p. 637.]

16

Attorney General v. Santeen

(Ex. 1686)

The crime of perjury can be prosecuted in the Court of Exchequer.

Lincoln's Inn MS. Misc. 557, f. 119, pl. 2

In an information for perjury in the Exchequer in the office of the King's Remembrancer, by a Michaelmas record 1 Jac. II, the case was that three pieces of silk were seized as forfeited for non-payment of duties.

The defendant averred them to be imported at Dover and there to have paid the duties. And he made an oath of it before Mr. Nicholas, the Surveyor of the Custom House. And, upon this oath, they were discharged of the seizure.

And the fact sworn by the defendant being false, this information was exhibited, and the defendant was found guilty by a London jury at the sitting after this term.

But the defendant moved in arrest of judgment by *Williams et al.*:

First, that the information for perjury did not lie in this court, but it should be in the King's Bench, being merely a criminal thing.

But, to this, it was said that this matter concerns the king in his customs, the jurisdiction of which belongs to this court, and, on account of this, the information contains a deceit as well as perjury, and the perjury is only a consequent of the deceit, and, on account of this, it is well cognizable here. And there are precedents of informations for forgery in this court by the Attorney General, as it was in the Case of Watts of Gray's Inn touching Coke's will in the time of Chief Baron Hale, *circa* 1663, Hardres, fo. [*blank*].[2] And the king can elect his court. And the court here can well fine and imprison for an offense at common law, and *vide* Statute 33 Hen. VIII, ca. 39,[3] with which the court agreed.

The second exception was that Nicholas, the Surveyor, had not any power to administer this oath, it not relating to any of these things of which he with oth-

[1] *Dawson v. Lee* (1640), Croke Car. 566, 79 E.R. 1086.

[2] *Attorney General v. Watts* (Ex. 1663), Hardres 331, 145 E.R. 483, also Exch. Cases *tempore* Car. II, p. 7.

[3] Stat. 33 Hen. VIII, c. 39, s. 37 (*SR*, III, 886–887).

ers or he alone had power by the Act of Tonnage and Poundage Book of Rates[1] and acts against frauds to administer any oath, because the oath in question was only to satisfy the doubts of the Commissioners of Customs whether the goods seized had paid customs, which is not within the acts. And the Surveyor, notwithstanding the practice by him, did not have any power by his letters patent of the grant of his office for life to administer any oath and, this being a new office created and erected only sixty years ago, no power by prescription or usage could be urged.

And it seems to me [Edward Ward] that this was a material and fatal exception if the defendant's counsel had insisted upon it upon the trial, but now the jury has found the defendant guilty of the information. And, in this, it was alleged that Nicholas had a lawful power to administer this oath, and, on account of this power, it was found by the jury and nothing to the contrary appeared to the court. And for this reason, the court cannot take notice of any defect of power in Nicholas but that he had power to administer this oath. And, for this reason, the exception is worth nothing.

The third exception was that, admitting that the matter of the oath was false, yet that the defendant is not punishable here neither for perjury nor for a false oath at common law by indictment or information inasmuch as the oath was not made in any court of record nor in any court in a thing judicially there pending. And, for this, was cited Roll's Abridgment, tit. *Perjury*, fo. 257, no. 40, etc., and Stile's rep. 336, Howell Gwyn's Case, and 3d Inst.[2]

But, to this, it was answered that the false oath here tends to the deceit of the king. See 1, 2, 6, 11 articles of the Book of Rates and the clause for goods paying duty *ad valorem* and 3 Inst. 166 and Gwyn's Case, *supra*. And, if this distinction will hold, no merchant who forswears himself upon any of these articles could be punished, inasmuch as, when those oaths are made, there is not any cause judicially depending in any court nor are the oaths made in any court of record when they are made before the officers of the customs.

And the court held this to be a considerable thing, but gave no resolution upon it.

The fourth exception was that, in truth, there is not any perjury assigned, because, in truth, here, there were two oaths made by the defendant, the first of which was that (*prout sibi videbatur*) three pieces of silk were seized by one of the searchers of wool and (*ut informatur*) brought into the warehouse of the king and (as the defendant *credebat*) were the same pieces that he sent to the chapman. *Et signatus fuerit* by such marks and *exoneratur* at such a day by one Eaton at Dover in the name of one Noymer. Which oath not being positive, the commissioners refused and, afterward, the defendant made another oath before Nicholas at the

---

[1] Stat. 12 Car. II, c. 4, app. (*SR*, V, 184–205).

[2] 2 Rolle, Abr., *Perjurie*, pl. A, 3, p. 257; *Custodes v. Gwinn* (1652), Style 336, 362, 82 E.R. 756, 779; E. Coke, *Third Institute* (1644), pp. 163–167.

Custom House, by which he swore that the three pieces of silk that were brought to the warehouse were the same pieces of silk that paid customs at Dover at the same time by Eaton and the perjury was assigned in it, *ubi revera et in facto* the three pieces of silk *non exoneratus fuerunt* the said day by Eaton in Noymer's name. And, thus, the defendant committed a corrupt perjury in displeasure of God, in contempt of the laws, and against the peace of the crown and dignity of the king, for which the Attorney General prayed the advice of the court and process against the defendant, who pleaded *non culpabilis*.

And it was held by the court after several motions that the assignment of the perjury was not good and, in truth, no perjury was assigned even though it was endeavored to make the perjury plain by comparison and inference if it will avail in a criminal thing. But the court stayed judgment until further order.

I [*Edward Ward* was] for the king.

But the information was drawn by an unskillful hand and never perused by counsel for the king and prosecuted against the opinion of the Attorney General and myself, and nothing further was done in the cause.

For the jurisdiction of the court to hear a plea and give judgment and inflict a fine or other punishment for frauds, false swearing, or similar, [see] Statute 33 Hen. VIII, ca. 39, §§ 9 and 11; Watt's Case, *ubi supra*, incident to each jurisdiction to punish offenders by a fine etc., *vide* Solicitor General v. Wemes *et al.*, in the King's Remembrancer's Office in the Exchequer, entered Easter 7 Queen Anne, *anno* 1708, and my argument upon it.

[Other copies of this report: Georgetown Univ. Law Sch. MS. B88–7, p. 638.]

17

Attorney General, ex rel. Moore v. Capel

(Ex. 1686)

Where a bankrupt's assets are seized by the crown before they are assigned to commissioners of bankrupts, the crown has priority over the bankrupt's other creditors.

Lincoln's Inn MS. Misc. 557, f. 123, pl. 2

Attorney General, *pro* Moor and Thomas v. Sir Henry Capell *et al.* upon a plea to a *scire facias* touching a debt in aid.

The case was thus. 29 September last, Moor and Thomas were bound by a bond to the king in £1250. A [writ of] extent issued upon this bond against the obligors *quoad bona et catalla debita, credita, etc.* returnable 23 January *tunc proxime*. And, by the inquisition upon this extent 23 December last, it was found that White and Mercer, at this time, were indebted to Moor and Thomas in £450 for money lent. And this debt was seized into the hands of the king. 24 December last, a [writ of] immediate extent (upon oath) issued against White and Mercer, *quoad* body, goods, and lands to the Sheriff of London. And, on 22 January last, an inquisition was taken upon this extent which found White possessed of 800 barrels of anchovies of the value of £360 and seized them into the hands of the king. 4 February last, Sir Henry Capell, Daynes, and Woodford, assignees of the commissioners of bankrupts upon a commission prosecuted against White and Mercer, pleaded to this extent their property in the anchovies. And for title, they showed that, 12 September last, White and Mercer became bankrupts and that, 3 October last, a commission issued and that, 26 December last, the commission was renewed and that, 2d February last, which was after the inquisition seizing the anchovies into the hands of the king, the commissioners of bankrupts assigned the anchovies to the pleaders for themselves and in trust for other creditors of White and Mercer.

Upon which plea, the Attorney General demurred, and the defendants joined.

And, upon argument, there was a judgment for the king, because, though White and Mercer were bankrupts before Moor and Thomas became debtors to the king, yet, inasmuch as the bankrupts' goods were by due course extended and seized into the hands of the king before any assignment by the commissioners of bankrupts, the king had the better title and the defendant's title was insufficient.

And this was upon the reason of Stringfellow's Case, Dyer 67; Roy v. Crump, Pas. 22do Car. II, in this court, L. 2, 89; and Muncke and Clayton's Case, King's Bench, in Keble's 3d part of his reports, fo. [*blank*]; and L. G, 59; and Attorney General, *pro* Surry v. Thomas, butcher, *et al.*, *supra*, fo. 44, 67.[1]

I [*Edward Ward* was] for the king; *Pollexfen* was for the defendants.

[Other copies of this report: Georgetown Univ. Law Sch. MS. B88–7, p. 645.]

2 Shower K.B. 480, 89 E.R. 1053

The [writ of] extent, reciting that Moore and Thomas, by bond, became indebted to the king the twenty-ninth of September, in the first year of James II, in £1000, and that, by inquisition taken the twenty-third of December, it is found that John White and Benjamin Mercer were indebted to the said Thomas in £450, and, thereupon, it is commanded that inquiry be made of White and Mercer's estate on the twenty-third of December, *teste* the twenty-fourth of December, returnable the twenty-third of January following. The inquisition found that, on the twenty-third of December, they had eighty barrels of anchovies.

[1] *Stringfellow v. Brownesoppe* (1549), 1 Dyer 67, 73 E.R. 142; *Rex v. Crump and Hanbury* (Ex. 1668–1670), Exch. Cases *tempore* Car. II, p. 134; *Monke v. Clayton* (1668), 3 Keble 1, 68, 84 E.R. 560, 598; *Attorney General v. Lambert* (Ex. 1675), Lincoln's Inn MS. Misc. 555, f. 59; *Attorney General v. Thomas* (Ex. 1684), Exch. Cases *tempore* Car. II, p. 588; *Shish v. Attorney General* (Ex. 1684), Equity Cases Exch. 212.

The defendants, thereupon, come in and plead that, long before White and Mercer were bankrupts, that commissions issued out against them and that, on the second of February, the commissioners made an assignment of those barrels of anchovies.

The Attorney General demurs.

The question is whether the extent be good, the party being a bankrupt before.

I [*Shower*] argued that, at the time of the bankruptcy committed, the creditors, *viz.* Moore and Thomas, are entitled but to their ratable part and, then, afterwards, the king shall have but what he has a title to. In case the creditor be debtor to the king before, then he was a creditor for and entitled to his whole part, and the king should have the benefit of the whole, and no act of bankruptcy shall afterwards oust the king of his remedy for his debt, for, he, not being bound by any of the Statutes of Bankruptcy,[1] shall not be in the least prejudiced by them. But, here, Moore and Thomas were not indebted to the king at the time of the bankruptcy, by which White and Mercer became as dead in law, and could not do any act. Now, the king's right to this remedy commences but from the first debt to the king, and, therefore, as to the quantity, the king can have but the right of his debtor, though, as to the manner of execution, he has a prerogative. '*Nemo enim plus juris potest transferre quam habet.*' '*Potestas derivativa non major quam primitiva.*' At the same rate, they may after an assignment become debtors to the king, and so make an extent in aid the same with an extent original. And, now, suppose White and Mercer had after an act of bankruptcy and becoming bankrupts contracted a debt to the king etc. By the party's becoming a bankrupt, every man that was creditor to him becomes entitled to his share. And, all that time, the condition and interest of every creditor is fixed and cannot be bettered by any act of his or the bankrupt's. Now, there was no debt of record to the king before that. And, in the case of an executor, if, after the death of the testator, a creditor by bond assign to the king, the executor may pay a judgment before it, because it was not a debt of record to the king at the time of the testator's death. And [it was] so resolved in Trinity term, in the eighteenth year of James I, in the Exchequer.[2] Here is the same reason.

But it was answered that, if the extent come before the assignment, it shall and must be preferred. See the like case in the twentieth year of Charles II, in the Exchequer, as to executors etc. Edward Lewis was indebted to the king by bond on the third of March, in the nineteenth year of Charles II; an extent issued on that bond, dated twenty-first March; the inquisition finds Lewis possessed on the fifteenth of April, and then Captain Handbury pleads his title, that Lewis, on the fifth of March, became a bankrupt, that, the fifth of March, a commission issued, that, the sixth of March, the commissioners found that Lewis

---

[1] Stat. 21 Jac. I, c. 19 (*SR*, IV, 1227–1229).

[2] *Anonymous* (1610), 2 Rolle, Abr., *Prerogative le Roy*, pl. H, 8, p. 159.

was a bankrupt before the date of the commission, that, the twelfth of March, the goods in question were seized by warrant from the commissioners, that, the twenty-first of March, the commissioners of bankrupt assigned to the creditors, and, thereby, they became possessed.[1]

To this plea, the Attorney General demurs generally.

And judgment is given for the king. And, although the goods were actually *in custodia legis*, yet, because the extent came before the property was vested by an assignment, it was held a good extent.

Extents have been held good that have been made upon goods actually levied by virtue of a [writ of] *fieri facias* and in the sheriff's custody, the extent coming before a bill of sale made, so as the property was not altered. *Nota.*

18

Attorney General v. Hart

(Ex. 1686)

An administrator must pay the debts of the decedent's estate that are due to the crown before paying debts due to private persons.

Lincoln's Inn MS. Misc. 557, f. 126

22 June Trinity [term] 1686.

Upon a *scire facias* touching a debt in aid, the case upon the pleading was thus. In October 1685, one Charles Gregory, merchant, was bound to the king in a recognizance of £180 for the payment of money and, before it became due, that is to say 23 December 1685, an inquisition was found upon [a writ of] extent against Gregory *quoad bona et catalla, debita, credita, et specialitates* returnable in Hilary term next, by which it was found that one John Hart, deceased, at the time of his death, which was in December 1684, was indebted to Gregory in £105 for goods sold and delivered, which debt was seized into the hands of the king by this inquisition, after which, that is to say 24 December 1685, another inquisition was found upon a *diem clausit extremum* against John Hart, returnable Hilary term next, by which it was found that Hart died December 1684 possessed of goods to the value of £1100 and £313 more and that, in January 1684[/85], administration was committed to the defendant, who possessed those goods.

And upon this, a *scire facias* issued against the defendant to show cause why the king's execution against him of the goods and chattels of the said John Hart (omitting in his hands *administrandum*) for the said debt of £105 *habere non debeat.*

[1] *Rex v. Crump and Hanbury* (Ex. 1668–1670), 2 Shower K.B. 481, 89 E.R. 1054, Lincoln's Inn MS. Misc. 500, f. 89, pl. 1, Exch. Cases *tempore* Car. II, 134.

The defendant pleaded two several judgments against him as administrator upon debts upon two bonds to two several persons for a £300 true debt due by the intestate in his lifetime, and also he pleaded another bond of £1800 entered into by the intestate to Firebrass for a true debt and to have these debts upon judgments for the said £1800 bond to be for just debts and to be in force not reversed or falsified. And thus he pleaded *plene administravit* and that, at the time of the extent that seized this debt into the hands of the king or ever afterwards and he never had any goods or chattels of the intestate at the time of his death in his hands to be administered except goods and chattels of the value of £10 which did not suffice to satisfy the said two judgments and £1800 bond, and that, at the time of the extent, they were chargeable and bound to the payment of these judgments and bond, *et hoc paratus etc.* And he prayed judgment whether the king should have execution against him and to be dismissed with proper averments to be the same persons and things.

The Attorney General demurred to this plea, and the defendant joined.

And the court gave judgment for the king notwithstanding the case in Roll's, *Prerogative*, 159,[1] that an executor can pay a judgment to a private person before such a debt to the king, because, in this case, none of the judgments were paid and this judgment was against the testator, but this was against the administrator. And the king will be preferred in his debts and this upon the Statute 33 Hen. VIII, ca. 39, § 25.[2]

But I [*Edward Ward*] go upon this rule that the plea is entire of two judgments and one obligation and, as to the obligation, certainly the plea is not good inasmuch as the debt seized will be preferred before the obligation, and, in this case, there is time to plead the special matter against the obligation that process cannot be to the judgment if it not be upon a *scire facias*, and then the case is a plain case that, when the administrator pleads three things in bar and one is insufficient, the plaintiff will recover all his debt though the other two things would swallow up all the assets, because he should not plead any matter that is not good and sufficient. And this is the common practice. L. 2, Hancock v. Prowd, 60; and fo. 4b and 73.[3]

And the court held it a plain case and gave judgment upon this reason. And that the debt to the king will be preferred before the obligation.

I [Edward Ward] relied upon the Case of Attorney General v. Knowles, Easter [term] 1683, L. J, 100,[4] and the common observation that debts to the king of whatever nature will be paid before debts to subjects of a superior nature

[1] *Anonymous* (Ex. 1610), 2 Rolle Abr., *Prerogative le Roy*, pl. H, 8, p. 159.

[2] Stat. 33 Hen. VIII, c. 39, s. 37 (*SR*, III, 886–887).

[3] *Hancock v. Prowd* (1669), Lincoln's Inn MS. Misc. 500, p. 60, also 1 Siderfin 429, 82 E.R. 1198; *Perkins v. Morfield* (1669), Lincoln's Inn MS. Misc. 500, f. 4v, pl. 1; *Tretheway v. Atland* (1670), Lincoln's Inn MS. Misc. 500, f. 73v, pl. 1.

[4] *Attorney General v. Knowles* (Ex. 1683), Exch. Repts. *tempore* Car. II, p. 541.

according to the reasons given in Burnett's Case, which see among my arguments.[1]

Judgment [was given] for the king.

I [*Edward Ward* was] for the plaintiff, and *Ettrick* and *Pollexfen* were for the defendant.

Vide after 129; 33 Hen. VIII, ca. 39, § 25; and Li. L, 17, and L. J, 100, L. H, *diem clausit extremum* condemned, 129.[2]

[Other copies of this report: Georgetown Univ. Law Sch. MS. B88–7, p. 648.]

19

Canham, qui tam v. Balderston

(Ex. 1686)

The subsidy of aulnage is payable for cloth made partly of worsted and partly of silk pro rata.

Lincoln's Inn MS. Misc. 557, f. 129, pl. 1

Trinity [term] 1686.

Upon a seizure, it was ruled upon evidence that the subsidy of aulnage will be paid for Norwich stuffs made partly of worsted and partly of silk *pro rata, scil.* one-fourth a piece, according to the reason of the payment of aulnage for dornix and linsey woolsey, etc., which has been adjudged beforehand.

[Other copies of this report: Georgetown Univ. Law Sch. MS. B88–7, p. 656.]

20

Attorney General v. Hartford

(Ex. 1686)

Where a decedent was never a debtor to the crown, the retainer by an administrator is not liable to the crown by process of diem clausit extremum.

Lincoln's Inn MS. Misc. 557, f. 129, pl. 2

The case was thus. Surry and Stevenson were bound to the king by a bond in July 1680 for £200. In July 1685, a [writ of] extent issued against them, upon which it was found by an inquisition that one Arey, at the time of his death, was indebted

---

[1] *Rex v. Burnett* (Ex. 1682), Lincoln's Inn MS. Misc. 510, f. [125], Public Record Office E.159/522, Hil. 31 & 32 Car. II, recorda, rot. 86.

[2] *Attorney General v. Hartford* (Ex. 1686), see below, Case No. 20; *Attorney General, ex rel. Carlton v. Allanson* (Ex. 1687–1688), see below, Case No. 29.

to them for goods sold £90 and that Arey died in June 1685 and that the defendant [Heritage Hartford] was his administrator, which debt was seized into the hands of the king, upon which a *diem clausit extremum* issued against Arey to enquire what goods and chattels etc. Arey had at the time of his death and of what value and to seize them into the hands of the king with a proviso not to sell without a further command until the king will be satisfied his debt. In August 1685, an inquest was found, by which it was found that Arey, at the time of his death, was possessed of such goods, mentioning them, to the value of £90 which came to the defendant's hands. And the sheriff seized them into the hands of the king.

The defendant came in and claimed property to the goods. And he pleaded that, 1 April 1685, Arey became bound to the defendant in a £400 bond for the payment of £203, being a just debt, and thus died this debt not satisfied and that inasmuch as no relation came to claim administration, the defendant, as the principal creditor, took administration the 10th of June 1685 and that it was before the first extent that seized the debt into the hands of the king, and so, as administrator, *adtunc et ibidem* he took these goods into his possession and *eundem retinet erga* satisfaction of his debt. And he prayed judgment and [a writ of] *amoveas manus* and restitution of the goods and that the inquisition will be quashed and the pleader dismissed.

Upon which plea, the Attorney General demurred.

And judgment was given for the king without any argument, because the parties, that is to say Surry and Hartford agreed.

But it seems that the matter of the plea, *scil.* the retainer, was good, because, in truth, no *diem clausit extremum* in this case as to enquire and seize the goods and chattels of the intestate lies, nor are the goods bound in such a case, inasmuch as the intestate never was a debtor to the king. And, on account of this, his goods, at his death, were never liable to the debt of the king, but they are assets in the hands of the administrator, which is held after the seizure of the debt by simple contract into the hands of the king to pay this debt (thus become a debt to the king) before any other debt unpaid. And, thus, it will be bound upon a *scire facias* against him. But the goods themselves are not liable, but the administrator in respect of them, *vide* Magna Carta, ca. 18,[1] which is the foundation of the [writ of] *diem clausit extremum* and it respects only the debt of the testator or intestate only to the king and thus subjects his goods. But, here, the intestate never was a debtor to the king. And, in truth, a *scire facias* and not a *diem clausit extremum* to seize the goods should have issued. And this was by the ignorance of the clerk and solicitor in the case.

And Surry and Stevenson being advised in the case, they took less than their debt, and the defendant, not being appraised of the law, agreed and paid them the major part of their debt.

---

[1] Stat. 25 Edw. I, Magna Carta, c. 18 (*SR*, I, 116).

And this was the first case of this nature that I [*Edward Ward*] ever heard was practiced and brought into judgment, that is to say as to a *diem clausit extremum* against one who never was a debtor to the king. And it seems to be utterly void and groundless and not the practice of the court. And if there are any precedents *sub silentio* and by the ignorance of the clerks and surprises upon the barons for their warrants for such writs and if the goods *quare non* the lands of the dead person who never was a debtor to the king will be liable which is *res inaudita*, and there is no difference between goods and lands in such a case.

In the principal case, I [*Edward Ward*] was of counsel with Surry and Stevenson and condemned the practice. And by my advice, they compounded the debt *ut supra*.

But a *scire facias* should be brought and no seizure. L. J, 100, Trinity 24 Car. I, Roy v. Knowles, *scire facias*; *vide* after, 138.[1]

[Other copies of this report: Georgetown Univ. Law Sch. MS. B88–7, p. 657.]

21

Attorney General, ex rel. Starke v. Moline

(Ex. 1686)

A writ can be executed upon a person's goods on the day of his death, though it be done after his death.

The Statute of Frauds does not apply to the crown.

Lincoln's Inn MS. Misc. 557, f. 138, pl. 2

Upon a debt in aid, a [writ of] extent issued against Starke, debtor to the king by bond, in May last, upon which an inquisition was found the 4 September 1686 that Moline was indebted to Starke by bonds and simple contract in more than £1000, which debts were seized by this inquisition into the hands of the king. And, upon an oath made and a warrant of a Baron, a [writ of] immediate extent issued against Moline *quoad* goods and chattels etc. *teste* the 9th of September last. And this writ was sued out and delivered to the Sheriffs of London the same day of the *teste* and in the lifetime of Moline. But Moline died the same day before sunset and before any entry or seizure of the goods by the officers. And, in the evening of the same day, after the death of Moline, the officers seized the goods of Moline upon this immediate extent.

And, upon the motion of *Williams* for the executrix of Moline and other creditors and several days' debate, it was held and resolved by the court that this execution upon the extent was legally executed notwithstanding the death of

[1] *Attorney General v. Knowles* (Ex. 1683), Exch. Repts. *tempore* Car. II, p. 541; *Rex v. Cross* (Ex. 1686), see below, Case No. 22.

Moline, because, being the same day as the *teste* and suing out of the writ and the writ being delivered to the sheriff in the lifetime of Moline, his goods and chattels were bound by the *teste* of the extent as well as in a similar case they were as well in the case of the king as a common person before the Statute of Frauds and Perjuries, 29 Car. II.[1]

And it was also resolved that the case of the king is not within this Statute so that the goods will not be bound before the delivery of the writ to the sheriff, but that, in the case of the king, the *teste* binds the goods as at common law before the Statute of Frauds, except the method of proceeding in the vacation and the immediate extent.

I [*Edward Ward* was] for the king and Starke.

[Other copies of this report: Georgetown Univ. Law Sch. MS. B88–7, p. 670, pl. 2.]

22

Rex v. Cross

(Ex. 1686)

The crown cannot seize the goods in an executor's hands of a testator who was never a debtor of the crown.

Lincoln's Inn MS. Misc. 557, f. 138, pl. 3

Rex, *pro* Renew and Lewin v. Cross, executor of Taylor, for a debt in aid and a *diem clausit extremum.*

The case was thus. Taylor, being indebted to Renew and Lewin by a simple contract, made his will 6 September last, and he made Cross and Basely executors, to whom he was indebted by bond at his death. And he died the 8th of September, after whose death and that the executors had inventoried the goods of the testator and paid some debts, but before probate, a [writ of] extent issued against Kent, who was indebted to the king by bond *quoad bona et catalla etc.*, upon which, the 18th of September last, it was found by inquisition that Renew and Lewin were indebted to Kent by a bond of £800, which bond and debt were seized into the hands of the king. After that, another extent issued against Renew and Lewin *quoad bona et catalla etc.* upon which, the 20 September, an inquisition was taken which found that Taylor, who then was dead, was at this time indebted by simple contract to Renew and Lewin in £414 17s. 6d., which debt was seized into the hands of the king, upon which a writ of *diem clausit extremum* issued after the death of Taylor, upon which it was found by an inquisition taken the 4th of October last that Taylor died the 8th of September last and that, at the time of his death, he was possessed of such goods of such values, amounting to

[1] Stat. 29 Car. II, c. 3 (*SR*, V, 839–842).

£416, which were seized into the hands of the king. And the writ commanded an enquiry and seizure of the goods and chattels that Taylor had at the day of his death and what lands he had the 20th of September last, when he first became a debtor to the king.

And these writs were all made, executed, and returned in the vacation by warrants of a baron and upon oath. And the goods of Taylor in the executors' hands, by color of this last writ, being an immediate extent, were seized and taken out of the possession of the executors.

And I [*Edward Ward*] moved for a [writ of] *supersedeas* to this writ, which was granted upon the reason that such a writ does not lie to levy the goods of one who never was a debtor to the king and who was dead before any extent or inquisition, and, an account of that, [there is] no color to seize the goods, though within a year past by the ignorance and practice of any junior and inferior clerk any such writs have issued, because it is impossible that this writ could be executed upon the goods of one who was dead and never a debtor to the king. But the sole remedy is to have a *scire facias* upon the second inquisition and extent against the executors, and, then, they have the opportunity to plead in discharge. But it is utterly erroneous and novel to take the goods of the testator who never was a debtor to the king out of the executor's hands.

And for this, a *supersedeas* was awarded.

I [*Edward Ward* was] for the executors.

See above 129.[1]

[Other copies of this report: Georgetown Univ. Law Sch. MS. B88–7, p. 671.]

23

Lechmere v. Shepeard

(Ex. 1686–1688)

Where goods are seized by a levy upon a writ of fieri facias, the ownership of the goods is transferred.

Lincoln's Inn MS. Misc. 557, f. 139

Michaelmas 1686; touching an execution and a debt in aid.

Cherrington was indebted to Lechmere by a judgment in £400, upon which a [writ of] *fieri facias* was prosecuted *teste* the 17th and delivered to the Sheriff of Middlesex the 18th of November this term. And, upon this, the Sheriff of Middlesex seized the goods of Cherrington and inventoried them the same 18th day, after which, on the same day, Shepheard, who was indebted to the king by a bond and to whom Cherrington was indebted by simple contract, prosecuted

[1] *Attorney General v. Hartford* (Ex. 1686), see above, Case No. 20.

a [writ of] extent against himself. And the inquisition found the same 18th day (the extent being returnable the 19th) the debt by simple contract to Shepheard [which] was seized into the hands of the king by a [writ of] immediate extent by the warrant of a baron (though in term time) was awarded *teste* the 19th. And, upon this, the Sheriff took the goods of Cherrington (seized and inventoried upon the *fieri facias*) in execution.

And, upon a motion to the court for redress against the extent and execution, the court seemed to incline that the seizure and inventorying upon the *fieri facias* amounted to an alteration of the property and that the extent came too late, because, in truth, there was not any bill of sale upon the *scire facias* until the 19th, except this, because it seems against Stringfellow's Case, Dyer 67, and Crump's Case, L. 2, 89,[1] and the common experience that [a writ of] extent of the king binds the goods from the *teste* and that, if the seizure is before a sale upon a *fieri facias*, it alters the property. The court declared the sale upon the *fieri facias* before the *teste* of the extent, though the *fieri facias* is not returned, is a good alteration and prevents the extent.

And, in the principal case, the goods were ordered to remain with Lechmere, who gave his security to abide by the order of the court upon a plea to be pleaded by prosecution of the extent in the name of the Attorney General.

I [*Edward Ward* was] for Lechmere.

[Other copies of this report: Georgetown Univ. Law Sch. MS. B88–7, p. 673.]

Lincoln's Inn MS. Misc. 558, f. 19, pl. 4

Lechmere, Disbrow, *et al.* v. Shepheard, in a case of debt in aid touching goods of Hyde.

Hyde, a vintner in London, was indebted to the plaintiffs and the defendant, his creditors, in divers sums, some to the plaintiffs by judgment and bond and to the defendant by simple contract. The defendant being in debt to the king by a Custom House bond for the duties of wines, the said Hyde discovered his inability to pay to the plaintiffs, and they to the defendant, who offered to take proportionally with the plaintiffs and other creditors and in person came and appointed and agreed to the appraisal of the goods of Hyde. But, at the same time, he prosecuted a [writ of] extent in aid against the goods of Hyde and took them in execution, having seized his debt due to him by Hyde and also Hyde's goods in execution by two extents and inquisitions the same day.

And, upon the motion for the creditors and an oath of the truth of the thing, the court superseded the extents and inquisitions upon them as erroneously and improvidently awarded and taken as well upon the reason of Shepheard's agreement to come in as a creditor proportionally with the others as for the irregular

---

[1] *Stringfellow v. Brownesoppe* (1549), 1 Dyer 67, 73 E.R. 142; *Rex v. Crump and Hanbury* (Ex. 1668–1670), Exch. Repts. *tempore* Car. II, p. 134.

obtaining of the extents and inquisitions the same day and upon the surprise against the Chief Baron, who gave the warrant for the last immediate extent.

I [*Edward Ward* was] for the plaintiffs.

Note that, in this case, the said Shepheard was privy and agreed to the bill of sale of all the goods of the said Hyde made to the plaintiffs for the benefit of all of his creditors, and still he prosecuted the extent.

[Other copies of this report: Georgetown Univ. Law Sch. MS. B88–8, p. 122.]

Lincoln's Inn MS. Misc. 558, f. 44

Michaelmas 1688. Touching a debt in aid, entered Michaelmas 2 Jac. II, *ex parte Rememeratoris Regis in Scaccario.*

Shepheard being bound to the king by a bond dated in January 1 Jac. II [1686] for the payment of £210 to the king for customs, a [writ of] extent in aid upon this bond *teste* 4 November 2 Jac. II [1686] issued against Shepheard *quoad bona, debita, credita, etc.* returnable 19 November 2 Jac. II [1686], upon which extent there was an inquisition taken the 18th of the same November, by which it was found that one Sherrington was indebted to Shepheard in £137 for goods sold. And this debt was on account of it seized into the hands of the king. Another extent *teste* the said 18 November 2 Jac. II [1686] grounded upon this inquisition issued against Sherrington *quoad* body, goods, etc. returnable the 22nd of the same November, upon which last extent, there was an inquisition taken the 20th of the same November, by which it was found that Sherrington at the time of the awarding and *teste* of the last extent was possessed of divers goods, mentioning them, *ut de bonis et catallis suis propriis.* And these were seized into the hands of the king towards the payment of Shepheard's debt due to the king upon the said bond.

Lechmere came in and claimed ownership of these goods. And he pleaded that this extent against Sherrington actually issued the 19th of this November. And, also, he pleaded that, before the actual issuing of this extent or the caption of the inquisition upon it, the goods thus seized were his own goods and in his actual possession, *viz.* in such a place.

And he took two traverses:

First, *absque hoc quod* the said extent against Sherrington actually *emanavit ex hac curia praedicta 18 die Novembris anno secundo supradicto vel ante praedictum 19um diem Novembris eodem anno*; and also

Second, *absque hoc quod* the said Sherrington, the said 20 November *anno secundo supradicto* or at the time of the issuing of this extent against Sherrington *vel unquam postea* was possessed of these goods or any of them *modo et forma prout per inquisitionem praedictam superius supponitur, et hoc paratus etc.*

The Attorney General and Shepheard replied that the said extent against Sherrington *actualiter emanavit ex hac curia ante praedictum 19um diem Novembris, scil.* the 18th of November 2 Jac. II, *et hoc petit quod inquiratur per patriam.*

Lechmere demurred upon the replication inasmuch as there is not any answer to the second traverse because, admitting that the extent *actualiter emanavit* the 18th, yet, inasmuch as Lechmere made a title to himself to the said goods before the issuing of the extent and traversed the title of Sherrington at the time of the issuing of this extent *vel unquam postea*, this traverse must be answered. And for the default of answer, it is a cause to demur.

No further proceedings were after.

[Other copies of this report: Georgetown Univ. Law Sch. MS. B88–8, p. 179.]

24

Attorney General v. Penn

(Ex. 1686)

A grant that fails as a conveyance can nevertheless be a revocation by implication.

Dodd 61

Upon a special verdict, the point was [there was a] grant for life with a power of revocation; the tenant for life grants, bargains, and sells to J.S., but it is not enrolled nor [is] livery executed nor will it operate as any conveyance. And whether this will be a revocation by implication (because it is not an express revocation) is the query.

Hill: Yes. If a tenant for life has granted the reversion with attornment, this grant before attornment will be a revocation, because otherwise the attornment will pass an estate for life only because it relates. [It is] also [?] of the feoffment because, if he does not revoke before livery, it is a forfeiture.

Ward: No. No estate will be revoked by implication but by such a deed that passes an estate. There is a difference between powers upon their penning.

First, a declaration or intention to revoke.

Second, an actual revocation.

Raym. 295, Guy and Dormer's Case[1]: [There was] a power of revocation by express words; [there was] a revocation by implication by a deed; they are express words, but the power was 'shall declare his intention by express words to revoke' and he devised the land to another person; [it was a] good execution of the power. Raym. 295.

Powers may be suspended in part but not conditions. Snipe and Thornton, Cr. Car. 472, Jones 392.[2]

---

[1] *Guy v. Dormer* (1679), T. Raymond 295, 83 E.R. 152.

[2] *Snape v. Turton* (1637), Croke Car. 472, 79 E.R. 1008, W. Jones 392, 82 E.R. 206.

A tenant for life with a power to revoke by a deed covenants to levy a fine; this is not a revocation before the fine [is] levied because the deed is the ceremony but does not have substance. Wickson and Garrett's Case,[1] *juncta juvant*.

Dodd 63

[It was] argued by *Finch* that:

First, it is a revocation because the intentions of the parties govern revocations. If the party had declared by a deed etc. that 'I will that this estate shall be to me and my heirs', this will be a revocation and yet not pass any estate. Thus, this deed by consequence will have this effect, that the party will be seised in fee etc.

Second, the other point that the issue is that he is not seised in fee and a wrongful seisin is found, this is a seisin within the issue. The diversity is, if you traverse, you must falsify,[2] but, if you will confess and avoid, then you must aver showing the right.

Pollexfen, contra: As to the second point, first, see 3 Cr. 431, Moo. 359, Hob. 72, that intention without a deed will not revoke as in the case of the will. Kobbett and Lee, Hob.,[3] the will is not a revocation until it is a will, *viz.* until the death of the testator. Thus [it is] of a feoffment before livery.

A deed to levy a fine is not a revocation until the fine [is] levied, which proves that it must be a complete conveyance before it will be a revocation by implication.

Dodd 66

This case was adjudged for the plaintiff, being argued by all in the Exchequer.

Milton, Baron: The point is whether he revoked.

First, [it] seems to be in the way [of] the lease for years, but that will not extinguish the power. Also, it is a lease in trust for him.

Second, the deed recites all and declares etc.; [it is a] good revocation notwithstanding nothing passes; the intention of the parties seems not material if by words or by deed the owner has power and [sees] not fit to restrain, circumstances are pursued.

If [it was] no revocation, yet it shows the right.

Heath, Baron: It is a revocation [. . .]:

1 *Wigson v. Garret* (1676), 2 Levinz 149, 83 E.R. 492, T. Raymond 239, 83 E.R. 124, 3 Keble 366, 489, 510, 536, 572, 84 E.R. 769, 837, 850, 865, 886, 1 Ventris 278, 86 E.R. 186, 1 Freeman 407, 411, 89 E.R. 303, 305, Lincoln's Inn MS. Misc. 500, f. 267 (Edward Ward's reports).

2 *I.e.* deny.

3 *Stone v. Newman* (1635), Croke Car. 427, 431, 79 E.R. 971, 974; *Sherly v. Wood*, Hobart 71, 72, 80 E.R. 220, 221; *Kibbet v. Lee* (1619), Hobart 312, 80 E.R. 455.

First, the lease for 1000 years [is] no revocation for [it is] derived out of the estate for life and meddles not with the remainder.

Second, it is a power of revocation and not a new limitation.

Third, [it is] not a [. . .] power but a power derived out of the fee and so ought to be favorably construed. A deed makes a revocation without taking notice of the power.

This pursues all circumstances; it is a plain evidence of an intention to revoke and an execution of that revocation.

Objection: No estate passes.

Answer: The power does not require an estate to pass. This deed is a revocation of the old uses and a limitation of new uses. Fitzwilliam's Case and Dr. 147; Rolle, *Powers*, 261,[1] second power [is] good. A power to make a lease for life [is] good without livery.

Jenner:

First, the lease [was] no suspension.

Second, if [it was a] revocation, then the king has title.

Powers of revocation came first in upon knavish accounts, a badge of fraud upon 27 Eliz.,[2] [and] are of no great estimation and have but little countenance so that a revoking has been construed liberally.

Objection: No execution.

Response: A deed [is] sufficient to declare her intention. Moo. 735.[3]

In Dormer and Dormer's Case,[4] the power was in express words, 'shall signify his mind to revoke'; a revocation by construction or implication [is] good.

A *monstrance de droit* [or an] office of inquisition may be traversed. Savile 43. Traverse and *monstrance de droit* differ only in words. 34 Edw. III, 14; 36 Edw. III, 13; 2 Edw. VI[5] [are] statutes [which] concern it.

Chief Baron Atkyns: One point differs: no revocation. A revocation in pursuance of a power must be either express or implied. It is no express revocation. Nor is it a revocation by implication, for then it ought to be inconsistent with the first uses. But it is not inconsistent, for though it has words enough, yet it wants execution by enrollment etc. Seymor and Nosworthy's Case, 16 Car. II, in the

---

[1] *Fitzwilliam's Case* (1604), 6 Coke Rep. 32, 77 E.R. 300, Moore K.B. 681, 72 E.R. 836; *Villers v. Beamont* (1557), 2 Dyer 146, 73 E.R. 319; 2 Rolle, Abr., *Powers*, pl. A, 7, p. 261.

[2] Stat. 27 Eliz. I, c. 4 (*SR*, IV, 709–711).

[3] *Frampton v. Frampton* (1604), Moore K.B. 735, 72 E.R. 872.

[4] *Guy v. Dormer* (1679), T. Raymond 295, 83 E.R. 152.

[5] Stat. 34 Edw. III, c. 14 (*SR*, I, 368); Stat. 36 Edw. III, stat. 1, c. 13 (*SR*, I, 374–375); Stat. 2 & 3 Edw. VI, c. 8 (*SR*, IV, 47–48).

Exchequer,[1] a first and last will may stand and the subsequent is no revocation unless by express words or [they are] inconsistent.

If a revocation, it must be by the intention, but that intention or a declaration of the intention to revoke is no revocation; it must be a legal intention. It was intended to revoke by a conveyance, but it proves [to be] no conveyance.

[As for the] second point, [it is] a wrongful fee and so within the issue. Mayn[ar]d's Reports 45.

Judgment [was given] for the king.

25

Bryan and Browne, qui tam v. Hookeboat

(Ex. 1686)

The question in this case was whether a ship is forfeited for importing contraband where the master of the ship did not know of the illegal contents of the casks on board and where they were landed against his will.

Dodd 64

An information [was brought] upon [the Statute] 20 Car. II[2] for importing hams. Upon [a plea of] not guilty, a special verdict [was] found that the hams were imported in the *Hookeboat* but that the master did not know that there were any hams in the cask etc. until the plaintiffs came on board and seized them and carried them off the ship against the master's will to the land and put on shore the hams. And whether this fact makes a forfeiture of the ship was the doubt.

Pollexfen: Yes.

First, that the master did not know [that] there was bacon in his ship.

Second, they were put on shore against his will.

First, importation forfeits though [it is] not put on shore. It shall be presumed he does know what is in his ship; if a deceit were put upon him, it ought to have had another sort of finding, and he has his action against the deceiver.

Second, against his will is not issuable nor can the law try what the will or mind of a man is.

Ward: No. [It is] a penal law and not to be helped by intendment.

First, 'he did not know': [He] is not bound to know whether he can or no, for if he were obliged to know, then he should have a means to know, *viz.* by breaking open, which he cannot do; his bills are signed inside and [the] contents [are] unknown.

---

[1] *Seymour v. Noseworthy* (Ex. 1664–1665), Hardres 374, 145 E.R. 504, Lincoln's Inn MS. Misc. 499, p. 113, Order of 22 November 1666: Public Record Office E.126/9, f. 164, Exch. Cases *tempore* Car. II, 49, Equity Cases Exch. 1.

[2] Stat. 19 & 20 Car. II, c. 12 (*SR*, V, 641–642).

Second, 'against his will': Words of a law broken by compulsion is no breach of the law, [thus there is] no forfeiture unless [the goods are] landed.

[It was] objected to the pleadings:

First, the forfeiture is given to the informer and [the] poor of the parish where [the goods are] landed and here [it is] said to be the precinct of St. Catherine's and no parish [is] named; now a precinct is not in law a parish; the goods [are] forfeited to [a] parish precinct etc., but the ship forfeited is tied up to the poor of the parish. The informer's demand ought to be good and certain. The king is not concerned. Moo. 564; Cr. Car. 311; Hob. 245.[1]

Second, it is found imported from Amsterdam but not added *a partibus transmarinis*, so Amsterdam may be in England. It is right in the information but not in the verdict.

Third, upon the Acts of Parliament, 18 Car.[2] was a temporary law, 20 Car. seems perpetual in words but in truth is but additional to the temporary law and so determines with the temporary law. Otherwise, it was once lawful to import bacon etc. but forfeits the ship, therefore [it is] but relative.

32 Car.[3] revives the [Statute of] 18 Car. but ties itself in words to that Act, and so [it] cannot revive 20 Car.

Attorney General [*Sawyer*]: Notice [is] not material [to] a plain ignorance by a gross negligence; by the Tonnage Act,[4] [the] importer [is] to enter [the] quantities and qualities of his goods. Spices imported from Holland in casks [are] forfeited without notice.

Contra voluntatem: Goods [are] forfeited if seized on shipboard and so [it is] justifiable to bring them on shore and, when on shore, they forfeit the ship.

By the court: the Chief Baron [Atkyns]: One clause [makes a] forfeiture upon landing.

Jenner: [It is] forfeited upon the importation; [it] might take the goods but not bring in the ship. Query the acts.

Adjornatur.

---

[1] *Agar v. Cavendish* (1594), Moore K.B. 564, 72 E.R. 761, also Croke Eliz. 327, 78 E.R. 576, Savile 134, 123 E.R. 1055, 2 Anderson 127, 123 E.R. 581; *Rex v. Talbot* (1633), Croke Car. 311, 79 E.R. 871, also W. Jones 320, 82 E.R. 169; *Pie v. Westly* (1618), Hobart 245, 80 E.R. 390.

[2] Stat. 18 & 19 Car. II, c. 2 (*SR*, V, 597).

[3] Stat. 32 Car. II, c. 2 (*SR*, V, 941–942).

[4] Stat. 12 Car. II, c. 4 (*SR*, V, 181–205).

Lincoln's Inn MS. Misc. 557, f. 138, pl. 1

Bryan *et al.*, *qui tam* v. Hookeboat.

Upon a seizure of a ship for importing bacon, [there was a] special verdict. [It was] argued this term by *Pollexfen*, for the plaintiffs, and me [*Edward Ward*], for the defendant.

[Other copies of this report: Georgetown Univ. Law Sch. MS. B88–7, p. 670, pl. 1.]

26

Attorney General v. St. Lin

(Ex. 1686)

A false oath that is extra-judicial does not constitute the crime of perjury.

Dodd 65

No information of perjury at common law or [by] statute [lies] upon an extra-judicial oath. 3 Inst. 164, 165, 167; Bagg's Case, 11 Rep. 166; Dr. 242, 243.[1] No information for perjury in the court does lie at common law. See Cr. Eliz. 428; Savile 43.[2] The court doubted and adjourned.

27

Crossman v. Goodridge

(Ex. 1687)

In this case, where the defendant was in default, by consent, the damages were agreed to be proved by the oath of the plaintiff.

1 Rayner 66, 2 Gwillim 534

Upon payment of the costs, the value of the tithes was ascertained by the oath of the plaintiff himself, by consent, the bill for tithes being taken *pro confesso*, the defendant having stood out until a [writ of] sequestration.

[Order of 24 February 1688: 1 Wood 254, 1 Eagle & Younge 554.]

[1] E. Coke, *Third Institute* (1644), pp. 164, 165, 167; *Bagg's Case* (1615), 11 Coke Rep. 93, 77 E.R. 1271, also 1 Rolle Rep. 224, 81 E.R. 448; *Onslowe's Case* (1565), 2 Dyer 242, 73 E.R. 537.

[2] *Regina v. Bowles* (1595), Croke Eliz. 428, 78 E.R. 668; *Anonymous* (1582), Savile 41, 123 E.R. 1001.

28

Guavas v. Fountain

(Ex. 1687)

A writ of sequestration lies to enforce a final decree in equity.

2 Freeman 99, 22 E.R. 1083, Dodd 327

The question was whether the Court of Exchequer could grant a [writ of] sequestration after a decree for a personal duty.

It was admitted that, in process for appearance, a sequestration was always grantable by this court, but, for a personal duty after a decree, there were many instances in my Lord Chief Baron Hale's time and in the Lord Montagu's time where it had been denied. And these precedents that had been produced for it were most of them where it was the suit of the king, which was admitted on all hands that, where the king was plaintiff, it might be granted.

But, by the opinion of barons Jenner, Heath, and Powell, it ought to be granted, for they thought that, if it might be granted in mesne process, where it did not appear whether there was any duty or not, *a fortiori* after a decree, where the duty was adjudged and ascertained. And it being always the practice of the Chancery, it ought much more in this court, where the plaintiff was supposed to be a debtor to the king. And they thought that the jurisdiction of the court of equity would be to little purpose if the court had not sufficient authority to see their decrees executed.

The Lord Chief Baron [Atkyns] doubted, because the Lord Chief Baron Hale could never be prevailed upon to grant it, nor the Lord Montagu, to whose learning he said he must greatly subscribe.

But, by the opinion of the other three, it was granted.

[Other copies of this report: 2 Eq. Cas. Abr. 710, 22 E.R. 597.]

2 Eq. Cas. Abr. 281, 22 E.R. 237

A [writ of] sequestration may be granted in the Exchequer, as it has been always practiced in Chancery, where a decree is for a personal duty. Otherwise, the jurisdiction of the court of equity would be to little purpose if it had not sufficient authority to see its decrees executed, [which was held] by three barons.

But the Lord Chief Baron [Atkyns] doubted, because Hale nor Montagu could never be prevailed upon to grant it.

But, by the opinion of the other three, it was granted.

[Other reports of this case: Equity Cases Exch. 262.]

[Orders of 1 and 8 February 1687: Public Record Office E.127/16, ff. [47v], [63v].]

[Affirmed on appeal: Lords' Journal, vol. 14, pp. 407, 425, 473.]

29

Attorney General, ex rel. Carlton v. Allanson

(Ex. 1687–1688)

A debt by simple contract seized into the king's hands is to be preferred to bonds not paid before seizure, but payment of bonds by an administrator, before seizure or notice of the king's debt, may be well pleaded against the king.

Judgment creditors have priority over bond creditors.

Lincoln's Inn MS. Misc. 558, f. 17, pl. 4

Attorney General *pro* Carlton in a debt in aid v. Allanson, administratrix of Allanson, deceased.

The intestate was in debt in his lifetime to Carlton by a single contract and to three others by obligations. And he died. After whose death, Carlton being indebted to the king by an obligation, a [writ of] extent issued upon it. And the debt by simple contract was seized into the hands of the king by an inquisition. And upon it, a [writ of] *scire facias* issued against the defendant to show cause why the king should not have execution against him for this debt on the goods of the intestate in her hands to be administered.

The defendant pleaded in bar the three bonds for true debts and all [were] in force and that *plene administravit* and *riens en mains* the day of the inquisition except £10, which was bound and charged in her hands to the payment of the three bonds.

And the Attorney General demurred generally.

And upon the argument of *Browne* for the king[1] and *Ward* for the defendant, the court was of the opinion that judgment will be [given] for the king and that the seizure by the inquisition of the simple contract preferred it before the bonds not paid before the seizure because it is a debt to the king and there is no difference between it when found and an original debt to the king. But the court held that, if the bonds had been paid before the inquisition (and they seemed to incline before notice upon the *scire facias*) that the payment of them had been good against the king.

And the Case of Attorney General v. Knowles, *q.v.* L. J, 100, was remembered where the very case in question was adjudged for the king and Dashwood.[2] And I [*Edward Ward*] relied upon the case in Rolls, *Prerogative*, 159, and Lane 65,[3] and the mischief that executors incur and the payment of debts in the order as they stand at the time of the death of the testator's in [. . .].

---

1 Ruer *MS.*

2 *Attorney General v. Knowles* (Ex. 1683), Exch. Cases *tempore* Car. II, p. 541.

3 *Anonymous* (Ex. 1610), 2 Rolle Abr., *Prerogative le Roy*, pl. H, 8, p. 159; *Dimock's Case* (1609), Lane 60, 65, 145 E.R. 299, 303.

But the court held that the seizure into the hands of the king is a good plea to the debt upon an obligation, which query. And judgment [was given] for the king *nisi causa* within the term and, afterwards, absolutely. L. K, 126–129; Statute 33 Hen. VIII, ca. 39, § 25.[1]

Note there are several judgments in similar cases for debts in aid against executors and administrators whose testators or intestates never were debtors to the king, as this, as well before as after this resolution. But it seems to me a harsh case and not according to the ancient practice to have such [writs of] extent, inquisitions, and proceedings in aid of subjects against executors and administrators and by them such a preference of simple contracts before debts by a specialty.

[Other copies of this report: Georgetown Univ. Law Sch. MS. B88–8, p. 116, pl. 2.]

Parker 260, 145 E.R. 774, Dodd 328

The intestate [Allanson] was indebted in his lifetime to Carlton by simple contract and to three other persons by bond, and [he] died. After his death, Carlton, being indebted to the king by bond, an extent issued thereupon, and the debt by simple contract was seized by the inquisition into the king's hands, and upon this, a *scire facias* issued against the defendant to show cause why the king should not have execution against him for this debt of the goods of the intestate remaining in his hands to be administered.

The defendant pleaded in bar the three bonds for true debts and all [were] in force and that he had fully administered and had nothing in his hands on the day of the inquisition besides ten pounds, which are bound and charged in his hands with the payment of the three bonds.

The attorney general demurred, and the case of The King and Knowles (1683) was cited as in point for the king. And Rolle's, Abr., *Prerogative*, 159, and Lane 65[2] were relied on by the defendant's counsel.

But the court gave judgment for the king and held that the seizure by the inquisition of the simple contract debt into the king's hands preferred it to the bonds not paid before the seizure and would be a good plea to actions on such bonds because it is thereby become a debt to the king upon record and implies notice. But they also held that if the bonds had been paid before the inquisition or before the administrator had actual notice of the debt to the king, such payment would have been good against the king, because there was no debt upon record and the administrator had no means to discover whether there were any or what debts to the king, and the inconvenience would be infinite, if, in such cases, executors or administrators should, notwithstanding their utmost care, be

[1] *Attorney General v. Hart* (Ex. 1686), see above, Case No. 18; Stat. 33 Hen. VIII, c. 39, s. 37 (*SR*, III, 886–887).

[2] *Anonymous* (1610), 2 Rolle, Abr., *Prerogative le Roy*, pl. H, 8, p. 159; *Dimock's Case* (1606), Lane 31, 35, 60, 65, 145 E.R. 275, 278, 299, 303.

charged with the misapplication of assets out of their own estates. And the court held accordingly.

Dodd 71

[It was] resolved that a debt due by simple contract to J.S., who is a debtor to the king, and by inquisition seized into the king's hands and [there is a writ of] *scire facias* upon it brought against the executor of the debtor, it is not a good plea by the executor to plead bonds in bar, because now it is a debt upon a record. And it [was] by the court several times resolved thus. See Lane 65; 2 Rolle 159, which seems to the contrary; see below, Burnet's Case or Rex against the executors of A. and Attorney General and Dickinson.[1]

30

Attorney General, ex rel. Verdon v. Baspoole

(Ex. 1687)

An officer of the crown has the right to cross-examine witnesses who allege his misfeasance in office.

Lincoln's Inn MS. Misc. 557, f. 151

Attorney General, by the prosecution of Samuel Verdon v. Baspoole, Under Sheriff of Norfolk, touching concealments and misdemeanors in his accounts to the king.

In Trinity vacation last, by a warrant of the Lord Treasurer, a commission out of the Treasurer's Remembrancer's Office in the Exchequer issued directed to divers gentlemen of estates and credit and some of Verdon's friends giving to them power to examine and take the depositions of witnesses in the country for the purpose of discovering all or any sums of money which have been received or levied by three sheriffs of Norfolk, to all of whom Baspoole was an under sheriff, and not answered to the king upon account. And the commissioners having received from Verdon catalogues of divers sums so levied and received and not answered upon account, they took the affidavits of divers persons to prove such levies and receipts. But the affidavits were drawn by Verdon, and the commission was executed in the absence and without the privity of the sheriffs or Baspool. And the affidavits were annexed to the commission by which the particulars and certainties of the sums and the causes for which [they were] levied or received. And all were returned into the Exchequer, upon the motion of Baspoole's coun-

---

[1] *Rex v. Burnett* (Ex. 1682), Lincoln's Inn MS. Misc. 510, f. [125] (Edward Ward's Reports), Public Record Office E.159/522, Hil. 31 & 32 Car. II, recorda, rot. 86; *Rex v. Executors of A.* (1689), see below, Case No. 78; *Attorney General v. Dickenson* (1692), see below, Case No. 88.

sel, in Michaelmas term, the return being expired. And this commission was in the nature of it grounded upon the Statute of 6 Hen. IV, ca. 3, *q.v.*, and 4 Inst. 117.[1] And the levies and receipts being charged to be actually made by Baspool, he gave security by a recognizance (after some of the affidavits were read) to attend the court *de die in diem* and not to depart without license.

And this recognizance, as all others that relate to anything in the Office of the Treasurer's Remembrancer, was taken in the Office of the King's Remembrancer. And, by the affidavits, it appeared that Baspool and his bailiffs, by his privity, had levied and received by virtue of the process of this court divers sums which he had not answered for upon his apposals or account. And this matter was examined in open court several days this term.

And the Attorney General [*Sawyer*] and others were for the king and the prosecutor, who either had or executed a reward, and I [*Edward Ward*] and others were of counsel with Baspool, who gave some good answers to several of the matters alleged against him. But, as to others, the matter by him alleged was not so clear, but took further time.

And Baspoole, by order of the court, had copies of the commission and affidavits against him. And the charge against him was by the records of the court, *scil.* the process and his return and response to and upon them. But Verdon dying in the next vacation, there was not any further proceeding against Baspool.

And the Case of Michael Knight, under sheriff of Kent, in the time of Chief Baron Hale was remembered, where there was such a prosecution, though no commission, and examination of the matter in open court, and the misdemeanors proved by affidavits or oath in court and by the records themselves. And he was fined and censured.

But I [*Edward Ward*], for Baspool, alleged that this commission should not have issued out of the Exchequer but under the great seal, because thus is the opinion of Lord Coke, 4 Inst. 117.

To which the Attorney General [*Sawyer*] answered that this commission did not issue upon the Statute of 6 Hen. IV, but it issued at the discretion of the court or the Lord Treasurer to enquire into misdemeanors and concealments done to the prejudice of the revenue of the king, of which this court has original jurisdiction to enquire by any way whatever.

Second, I [*Edward Ward*] objected that the affidavits are not such examinations of the witnesses that the commission respects, but these affidavits were taken in the absence and without the privity of Baspool and were dressed up by Verdon or his means. And Baspool, by this means lost the opportunity to cross-examine the witnesses. And, on account of this, these affidavits should not be conclusive against him. And as the commission is for the examination of witnesses, cross-examination by the adverse party is implied, which was lost here.

---

[1] Stat. 6 Hen. IV, c. 3 (*SR*, II, 149–150); E. Coke, *Fourth Institute* (1644), p. 117.

And this objection seemed reasonable to the court and, on account of this, to give time to Baspool for cross-examination by affidavit if he wished.

Third, I [*Edward Ward*] objected that the court should not proceed to give any judgment by fine or otherwise upon these affidavits and proceedings, but possibly these affidavits could be a ground for the Attorney General to exhibit an information against Baspool, to which he could plead and have a trial, and, if convicted, could be punished by a fine or otherwise, because, though in some of the things where the truth of the matter appears by the records of the court, there [is] no use of other proofs or proceeding. But, in others, there are divers matters of fact some of which tend to the excuse or justification of Baspool and some others are necessary to be proved before any crime is duly proved against him. And [there can be] no proof in such a case without a trial.

Fourth, that this objection is more reasonable inasmuch as divers of the affidavits contain matters of which the commissioners do not have any power to administer oaths, *viz.* divers things that contain circumstances solely and inducements of arguments to prove the crime's objects, but not the crime themselves. And the commission is restrained to certain things and further or more than these commissioners could not or should not administer oaths.

And the court did not give any positive resolution to it. But, for the cause *supra*, there was no further prosecution.

Query whether the sheriff had a *quietus* and four years passed if, by virtue of the Statute of 21 Jac. I and 14 Car. II, they are not discharged.[1]

[Other copies of this report: Georgetown Univ. Law Sch. MS. B88–8, p. 24.]

31

Attorney General, ex rel. v. Palmer

(Ex. 1687)

The crown has a right to aulnage duties for wool caps.

Lincoln's Inn MS. Misc. 557, f. 153, pl. 1

Hilary 1686[/87]. Attorney General for the Aulnagers v. Palmer *et al.* for aulnage of knit caps made of wool, at the setting down of causes after this term.

It was ruled and decreed in this case that there is a duty of subsidy of aulnage, that is to say according to the rate of 4d. for 64 pound weight due to the king and his farmers of aulnage for knit caps made of wool at Bewdly in Worcestershire. And it stands upon the same reason as the decrees for knit stockings, which yield such a duty, and for which there are divers decrees of this court, that is to say 4 Jac. I, for Norwich stockings; 6 Car. I, for Richmond stockings; and,

[1] Stat. 21 Jac. I, c. 5, s. 1 (*SR*, IV, 1215); Stat. 14 Car. II, c. 21, s. 7 (*SR*, V, 416).

in the year 1678, another decree between the Attorney General and Sanderson, for Yorkshire stockings. And this duty for stockings is commonly answered at this day in all parts of England. And, though the defendants by their answer insist that no such duty is due nor was it ever paid and they also insist upon the Statute of 21 Jac. I, ca. [*blank*],[1] for the quiet of subjects and that time of which [memory does not run] such knit caps were made and no duty paid nor ever in charge nor demanded until recent times, yet the defendants having confessed the number and weight of the caps made by them, the court decreed *ut supra* without any proof of any party.

I [*Edward Ward* was] for the plaintiff.

Note, in this case, nothing was decreed for the aulnager's fee, but only for the subsidy of aulnage.

[Other copies of this report: Georgetown Univ. Law Sch. MS. B88–8, p. 29.]

32

Backwell's Case

(Ex. 1687)

The crown cannot seize lands in an heir's hands of an ancestor who was never a debtor of the crown.

Lincoln's Inn MS. Misc. 557, f. 153, pl. 2

Upon a motion at the setting down of causes after Michaelmas term 1686 touching an extent etc.

John Ball being one of the Governors and Commissioners of the Excise in 1671 and 1672, a *super* was put upon all of these Governors and Commissioners in their account of £1637 due to the king. Alderman Backwell[2] was indebted to Ball in £407 5s. 10d. for that he had a note under Backwell's servant's hand payable upon demand. And, after this note, the Exchequer Stop immediately followed so that the debt was not paid. And Ball refused an assignment for a proportional part of the annual interest granted by King Charles II to the bankers. Alderman Backwell died in 1683, after which, that is to say in 1684, Ball prosecuted against himself a [writ of] extent in aid upon this *super*, and, upon it, he procured this debt by simple contract due to him from Backwell to be found and seized into the hands of the king, after which a [writ of] *scire facias* issued against the executors etc. and the heir and terre tenants of the lands of Backwell *tempore mortis suae* to show cause *quare* the king will not have execution against them for

1 Stat. 21 Jac. I, c. 18 (*SR*, IV, 1224–1226).

2 G. E. Aylmer, 'Backwell, Edward (c. 1619–1683)', *Oxford Dictionary of National Biography*, vol. 3, pp. 113–116.

this £407 5s. 10d. And a *scire feci* was returned to one Stoakes, tenant of Garrowaie's Coffee House, of which Backwell was seized in fee *tempore mortis suae*, after which, for default of a plea, there issued [a writ of] *capias in manus* of the king of the said tenement. And it was executed. And afterwards, an inquisition was found that seized it into the hands of the king at the yearly value of £150. And process of *levari facias* issued for this value.

And I [*Edward Ward*] moved for Mr. Backwell, son and heir of the alderman, to set aside all of the proceedings as utterly illegal and irregular, which was done accordingly and a stop put to all further proceedings because it is impossible to affect the lands of Alderman Backwell with a debt due from him to Ball by a simple contract at the time of his death. And, though this debt is afterwards seized into the hands of the king, yet it being after the death of the Alderman, it cannot affect his lands at his death who never was a debtor to the king, but his lands descended to the heir not affected with the debt, because neither the Alderman nor the heir ever were debtors to the king. And, on account of this, these lands were never liable.

And of this opinion was the court, and they ordered as *supra*. And a writ of *supersedeas* to all of the proceedings was awarded, and, as I [*Edward Ward*] think, they were all quashed.

[Other copies of this report: Georgetown Univ. Law Sch. MS. B88–8, p. 30.]

33

Dashwood v. Soan

(Ex. 1687)

A writ of extent to enforce a debt cannot be issued upon a bond for a debt that is not yet due and payable.

Lincoln's Inn MS. Misc. 557, f. 155, pl. 1

19 or 20 April, Easter [term] 1687. Touching an extent in aid.

The case was that one Proby borrowed of Soan £800. And, on account of this, he made a lease of lands for divers years to Soan under a peppercorn rent. And, two days afterwards, Soane re-demised the premises to Proby for twenty-one years rendering to Soane £88 *per annum* with a covenant for the payment of the £88 and other collateral covenants. And Proby gave a bond of £1600 for the performance of the covenants in the re-demise.

[Sir Robert] Dashwood, by a prior mortgage, evicted Soan's title. Soan, being indebted as a surety for Starke to the king by three bonds, took [a writ of] extent against himself, and, upon it, seized the bond of £1600 into the hands of the king. And he made an oath that the £1600 was a true debt and that Proby had failed in his estate and the debt was in danger. And, upon this, by a warrant of Baron Jenner, [a writ of] immediate extent issued which seized divers goods of Proby pretended to be sold to Dashwood.

And, upon all of the matter, the court set aside the [writ of] immediate extent inasmuch as the bond was only for the performance of covenants none of which appeared to be broken, because the quarterly payment of the £88 *per annum* was paid for Christmas before the extent, which was taken in January last. And it was held that no immediate extent should issue upon a bond for the performance of covenants unless it was one for the payment of a certain sum. 2 Leon. 55, Beaumont's Case.[1]

But the court would not set aside the inquisitions that found the matter and seized the debt into the hands of the king but left them to be proceeded upon by a *scire facias*, if Dashwood please.

Vide L. 1, 480, Mosely's Case.[2]

[Other copies of this report: Georgetown Univ. Law Sch. MS. B88–8, p. 35.]

34

Anonymous

(Ex. 1687)

Where a modus is payable in lieu of tithes in kind, it is irrelevant whether it is payable to the impropriator, parson, or vicar.

Lincoln's Inn MS. Misc. 557, f. 155, pl. 3

[A writ of] prohibition was awarded after a sentence for tithes in kind in the ecclesiastical court upon a suggestion that the defendant in the ecclesiastical court should not pay tithes in kind but a *modus* of 2s. to the vicar in lieu of all tithes of his farm. And the suit was by the impropriator.

And it was held that there is not any difference when a *modus* is alleged by a parishioner against an impropriator or parson; the same is payable to himself or payable to the vicar.

Afterwards 158.[3]

[Other copies of this report: Georgetown Univ. Law Sch. MS. B88–8, p. 36.]

---

1 *Beaumont's Case* (Ex. 1587), 2 Leonard 55, 74 E.R. 353, also Owen 46, 74 E.R. 889.

2 *Rex v. Mosely* (Ex. 1668), Exch. Cases *tempore* Car. II, p. 140.

3 *Newton v. Lucy* (Ex. 1687), see below, Case No. 36.

35

Rex v. Lile

(Ex. 1687)

The Court of Exchequer can find a witness in contempt of court for refusing to testify as to a debt upon a writ of extent in aid.

Lincoln's Inn MS. Misc. 557, f. 155, pl. 4

Note he [Lile] was summoned to be a witness upon an extent in aid against Wood before the Secondary of London. He refused to discover the debts though he acknowledged he knew them, by which the extent was lost. And the debts [were] assigned by commissioners of bankrupts.

And, upon [a writ of] attachment and an examination of the party, the contempt appeared. And he was committed to the Fleet [Prison] for this contempt. And the first attachment was awarded upon the certificate of the Secondary and an oath of the truth of it.

I [*Edward Ward* was] for the king and the debtor in aid.

[Other copies of this report: Georgetown Univ. Law Sch. MS. B88–8, p. 37.]

36

Newton v. Lucy

(Ex. 1687)

The ecclesiastical courts have jurisdiction over tithes but not a modus decimandi.

Lincoln's Inn. MS. Misc. 557, f. 158, pl. 1

[A writ of] prohibition was granted to the ecclesiastical court to stay a suit there for tithes by an impropriator, lessee of the bishop of St. David's, upon a suggestion of a *modus* of 4d. *per annum* paid to the vicar.

And it was held that prohibition well lay though spiritual persons were concerned inasmuch as a court Christian will not determine the *modus* though it can the right of the tithes themselves.

Roll's, *Prohibition*, 310; 3 Bulstr. 220; 1 Leon. 94.[1]

I [*Edward Ward* was] for the defendant.

Note the diversity between the tithes themselves and a *modus*. Before 155.[2]

[1] *Anonymous v. Buller* (1632), 2 Rolle, Abr., *Prohibition*, pl. Z, 3, p. 310; *Savel v. Wood* (1588), 1 Leonard 94, 74 E.R. 787, also Croke Eliz. 71, 78 E.R. 331, Moore K.B. 908, 72 E.R. 989.

[2] *Anonymous* (Ex. 1687), see above, Case No. 34.

[Other copies of this report: Georgetown Univ. Law Sch. MS. B88–8, p. 42.]

[Related cases: Lucy v. Newton (Ex. 1687), Equity Cases Exch. 276.]

37

Gawden, qui tam v. King

(Ex. 1687)

The quality of cloth, not its provenance, determines the rate of import duties.

Lincoln's Inn MS. Misc. 557, f. 158, pl. 2

The question upon a seizure and trial at Middlesex was whether linen cloth made at Minster will pay as Minster's rate in the Book of Rates[1] at 56s. 8d. the roll though this cloth in question was more fine and better than the ordinary minsters imported from such place at the time of the making of the Book of Rates and at all times afterwards until the importation of the cloth in question.

And it was declared by the Chief Baron [Atkyns] and found by the jury that the cloth was forfeited for the non-payment of a greater duty, because, though it was made at Minster and thus within the denomination of the place, yet, inasmuch as the Minster rate and, before importation, they were course and not worth 9d. per ell and this cloth was fine and worth more than 2s. per ell, this cloth in question will not be said minsters within the meaning of this law though made there. But it will pay as Holland cloth of the same breadth and fineness.

I [*Edward Ward* was] for the defendant.

[Other copies of this report: Georgetown Univ. Law Sch. MS. B88–8, p. 43.]

38

Southwick, qui tam v. Philpe

(Ex. 1687)

The quality of cloth, not its provenance, determines the rate of import duties.

Lincoln's Inn MS. Misc. 557, f. 158, pl. 3

Upon a seizure and trial touching linen cloth called hinterlands and so rated in the Book of Rates[2] at a certain duty of 2s. 8d. per 100 ells, the plaintiff for the king endeavored to make it pay as narrow East Country cloth the duty of 4s. per 100 ells. And a coarser sort was insisted for the king to be the hinterlands, which pays the lesser duty.

---

1 Stat. 12 Car. II, c. 4, app. (*SR*, V, 184–205).

2 Stat. 12 Car. II, c. 4, app. (*SR*, V, 184–205).

But, upon proof that the very sort of cloth in question had been imported and paid the lesser duty at all times after the making of the Act of Tonnage and Poundage 1660[1] and before and that this cloth in question was not finer or broader, the jury found for the defendant and that the lesser duty only was due.

I [*Edward Ward* was] for the defendant.

[Other copies of this report: Georgetown Univ. Law Sch. MS. B88–8, p. 44, pl. 1.]

39

Sherman, qui tam v. Procter

(Ex. 1687)

A jury can determine the quality of imported goods in order to determine which rate of import duties applies.

Lincoln's Inn MS. Misc. 557, f. 159, pl. 1

Upon a seizure and trial touching a thin sort of copper plates, round and square, being only wrought or forged at the mill by a hammer there and being some small and some large and of the thickness of a kettle, the question was whether a custom will be paid for them *ad valorem* or according to the rate of 6d. per hundred according to the Book of Rates[2] as unwrought bricks or plates, round or square.

The counsel for the king insisted that these are wrought and not unwrought plates and that they are fit for use without any other hammering or manufacture except bending and nailing.

But it being fully in proof that this sort of thin copper plates have been imported before and at all times after the Act of Tonnage and Poundage 1660[3] and during all the times had paid only the duty of 6d. per hundred weight according to the Book of Rates and that, in truth, these plates are not fit for service without more hammering and operation in the fire without which they will not resist the fire nor contain the liquor, the jury found them unwrought copper plates within the meaning of the Act. And the verdict was for the defendant.

I [*Edward Ward* was] for the defendant.

[Other copies of this report: Georgetown Univ. Law Sch. MS. B88–8, p. 44, pl. 2.]

---

[1] Stat. 12 Car. II, c. 4 (*SR*, V, 181–205).

[2] Stat. 12 Car. II, c. 4, app. (*SR*, V, 184–205).

[3] Stat. 12 Car. II, c. 4 (*SR*, V, 181–205).

40

Attorney General v. Foxcroft

(Ex. 1687)

An innkeeper is liable to the king where the king's servant was robbed in his inn. A party cannot argue against his own pleading.

Lincoln's Inn MS. Misc. 557, f. 163

Trinity [term] 1687, by a Michaelmas record 2 Jac. II [1686], ex parte Rememeratoris Regis.

The Attorney General exhibited a Latin information against the defendant showing that, by the law and custom of the realm, *hospitatores qui hospitia communia tenent ad hospitandum homines per partes ubi huiusmodi hospitia existunt transeuntes et in eisdem hospitantes eorum bona et catalla infra hospita illa existente absque substractione et amissione custodire die et nocte teneantur ita quod per defectu dictorum hospitatorum vel servientium suorum huiusmodi hospitibus dampnum non eveniat ullo modo.*

And also, he showed that the defendant such a day and before and after was a *communis hospitator* and held a common inn with such a sign in the City of Lancaster and, the same day, *hospitavit* in the said inn one Joseph Holden, one of the servants of the now king, *viz.* a collector of the revenue of the hearth money *debire constitute ut hospitatem suum*, and that the said Holden *adhuc et ibidem quodem bagam cum £41 in pecuniam numeratum* of moneys of the now king contained in it into the said inn imported and under the custody of the defendant and his servants *adtunc et ibidem existentem per defectu* [?] of the defendant and his servants *adtunc et ibidem amissit* against the law and custom aforesaid and to the damage of the king £60 *unde* the Attorney General for the said king prayed the advice of the court in the premises and that the defendant will come to answer the king in the premises.

The defendant pleaded not guilty.

And the plaintiff's attorney, in entering the plea, entered the plea in such form, that the defendant *non est culpabilis de praemissis ei superius imposit contra formam statuti praedicti modo et forma prout per informationem praedictam superius supponitur et de hoc ponit se super patriam, et praedictus Attornatus Generalis pro eodem domino rege petit etiam quod inquiratur per patriam.*

And, upon the trial, a verdict was [given] for the king and damages £41.

And it was moved in arrest of judgment by *Williams* of Gray's Inn and others:

First, that the information for the king did not lie in this case inasmuch as the king *propter* his dignity will not be understood to lodge at an inn or to be a guest at an inn, and the words of the writ are strictly to be accepted and confined to guests in a common inn *ibidem hospitantes* and this writ or action, being grounded upon the custom of the realm, does not admit any variance from the strict words of it. And, if there can be any suit, the servant and not the king must bring it. Also, in the information, it is not said that the guest was *transeuns*, which he must be. And, for the reasons of these exceptions, they relied upon the Case of Caly, 8 rep., fo. 32, etc.[1]

Second, they object that, if the action and information lies for the king, yet there is not any issue joined, because the issue joined is upon the defendant's plea, which is *non culpabilis contra formam statuti etc.* and there is not any statute in this case.

And, for this, divers authorities as to the joinder of issue were cited, as 2 Cro. 579; 2 Sanders 279; Moor 47; Dy. 243; Hobt. 113, Kent and Hall; 2 Cro. 90 and 93.[2]

But it was answered by me [*Edward Ward*], for the king, that, as to the first exception, this suit and information well lies for the king in this case, because it is not a question but that the master can bring the action when the servant is robbed in the inn, as well as in the case and upon the Statute of Hue and Cry,[3] which is the common practice. And the Case of Bedle and Morris, 7 Jac., Yelverton 162, Co. Entr. 347, 2 Cro. 224, and Drone and Chair's Case, 1 Car. I, in Latch 126,[4] are full authorities that a master can bring the action when his servant is robbed of his master's money in an inn or lost it there by the default of the hostler or his servants. And the exception there was taken that the word '*transeuntes*' was omitted and the answer to it was that perhaps the guest was at the end of his journey, and, on account of this, it is no exception.

And, if this action lies for a master, *quare non* for the king when his servant is robbed or he loses the money in an inn by the default of the hostler, and what reason is it that the king will not have a remedy for his money or a writ as well as any of his subjects? And he will be in a worse condition, because, though the king does not commonly lodge in an inn, though sometime he lodge there, yet his servants constantly lodge in inns, and it is not any sense that a hostler will not be liable to the king as well as a subject for a robbery in an inn.

---

1 *Calye's Case* (1584), 8 Coke Rep. 32, 77 E.R. 520, also *sub nom. Windham v. Mead*, 4 Leonard 96, 74 E.R. 753.

2 *Aldrich v. Walthall* (1620), Croke Jac. 579, 79 E.R. 495, also 2 Rolle Rep. 186, 204, 209, 81 E.R. 740, 752, 755; *Wood v. Aldrich* (1671), 2 William Saunders 261, 85 E.R. 1051, also 2 Keble 730, 740, 84 E.R. 461, 468; *Anonymous* (1563), Moore K.B. 47, 72 E.R. 431; *Anonymous* (1565), 2 Dyer 243, 73 E.R. 538; *Kent v. Hall* (1600), Hobart 113, 80 E.R. 262; *Brook v. Montague* (1605), Croke Jac. 90, 79 E.R. 77; *Lancaster v. Lowe* (1605), Croke Jac. 92, 79 E.R. 79.

3 Stat. 27 Eliz. I, c. 13 (*SR*, IV, 720–722).

4 *Bedle v. Morris* (1609), Yelverton 162, 80 E.R. 108, E. Coke, *A Booke of Entries* (1614), 'Hosteler', pl. 2, f. 347, Croke Jac. 224, 79 E.R. 194; *Drope v. Thaire* (1626), Latch 126, 82 E.R. 307, also Benloe 173, 73 E.R. 1034, Noy 79, 74 E.R. 1046, Popham 178, 79 E.R. 1274, Paynell K.B. 102.

And of such opinion upon these reasons was all of the court.

Second, as to the exception to the issue, I [*Edward Ward*] answered that the substance of the defendant's plea is *non culpabilis* and this part that respects the statute is solely surplusage. And the defendant will not take advantage of the impertinency or insufficiency of his own plea.

And this was the opinion of all of the court. And judgment was entered for the king in such manner, *consideratum est per easdem barones quod dictus dominus rex recuperet versus praefatum Georgium Foxcroft dampna sua praedicta ad £41 per juratores praedictas in forma praedicta assessata et quod quoad misses et custagiis praedictis Georgius Foxcroft eat inde sine die.*

And this remitter of the costs was entered by advice, inasmuch as the king, in this case, will not recover costs.

I [*Edward Ward* was] for the king.

[Other copies of this report: Georgetown Univ. Law Sch. MS. B88–8, p. 52.]

41

Cawly v. Bishop of Lincoln

(Ex. 1687)

A prescriptive right that exists only between ecclesiastical persons is within the jurisdiction of the ecclesiastical courts.

Lincoln's Inn MS. Misc. 557, f. 166, pl. 1

The defendant sued the plaintiff in the [Court of] Arches for the subtraction of a pension called prestations, which is due to the bishop from [Dr. Cawly,] the archdeacon [of Lincoln], for his exterior jurisdiction and procurations that he receives at visitations. And the defendant, though he had a bull from the pope for it *circa* 250 years ago, yet, according to the form, he claimed this pension by prescription.

And, on account of this, [a writ of] prohibition was prayed inasmuch as all prescriptions will be tried by the common law, according to 2 Inst. 491; Sidderfin 146; and Mod. Rep. 218.[1]

But the prohibition was denied inasmuch as the thing is purely ecclesiastical and between ecclesiastical persons.

Vide L. G, fo. 105.[2]

[Other copies of this report: Georgetown Univ. Law Sch. MS. B88–8, p. 59, p. 2.]

---

[1] E. Coke, *Second Institute* (1642), p. 491; *Anonymous* (1663), 1 Siderfin 146, 82 E.R. 1023; *Barry v. Trebeswycke* (1676), 1 Modern 218, 86 E.R. 840.

[2] *Bround v. Archbishop of York* (Ex. 1676), Exch. Cases *tempore* Car. II, p. 300.

42

Attorney General v. Earl of Anglesey

(Ex. 1687)

In this case, the court refused to allow an amendment to the defendant's plea based on newly discovered facts.

Lincoln's Inn MS. Misc. 557, f. 169, pl. 2

The earl of Anglesey's case as heir to his father upon [a writ of] *distringas ad computandum.*

In Trinity term last [1686], a writ of *distringas* issued out of the Exchequer to the sheriff of Oxford against the executors, administrators, occupiers of the goods, heir, and terre tenants of Arthur, earl of Anglesey, deceased, formerly called Arthur Annesly, Esq., to render an account to the king of £20,000 *ei soluta* by Nelthorp and Lawson, formerly receivers general of the assessments for the Army and treasurers to the war between the 2d day of February 1659 and 1 April 1662 upon account *pro solutione exercitata in Hibernia unde nondum computaverit.*

The sheriff returned James, earl of Anglesey, to be the son and heir to Earl Arthur and others to be terre tenants of divers terms, no executors, administrators, or occupiers of the goods of the former earl. After divers delays, the Earl James, as son and heir to Earl Arthur, in Easter term last, put in his plea as of Michaelmas term before, when the *distringas* was returnable, *protestando* that the writ of *distringas* was insufficient and that the now earl did not have any lands or tenements by descent from his father. *Pro placito*, he said that Earl Arthur, his father, in his lifetime, *scil.* between the 2d February 1659 and 20 April 1665, in the Exchequer of the king in Dublin in Ireland, *plene et debita juris forma computavit cum dicto nuper Rege Carolo secondo de et pro praedicto* £20,000 and that his account was duly declared and allowed in the said court of record *prout patet per recordum.* And he averred his plea *per recordum.* And he prayed judgment whether *ipse, ut filius et haeres* of his father, should be compelled to render an account to the now king for the said £20,000, *et quod ipse quoad praemissa dimittatur.*

In the latter end of Easter term, the Attorney General replied *nul tiel record.* And he gave a rule in Trinity term for rejoinder.

And, upon this, the defendant rejoined *quod habetur talem recordum.*

But, before a rule was given for the defendant's producing the record and during the time that all was in paper and no record made, the defendant's agents discovered that the Earl Arthur, who was vice-treasurer for Ireland and had received divers great sums there, for which he had accounted in Ireland before the commissioners duly constituted, and the accounts were declared and allowed and among which accounts £19,500 of the £20,000 in the *distringas* was contained and an account was given for it. The defendant's counsel moved to amend his plea in this particular and to plead *plene computavit* for £19,500 and an allowance of the other £500 for a return of the money out of England into Ireland, it being the truth of the case and not discovered before, the fact being that this £19,500, part of the £20,000 in the *distringas*, was part of £39,000 contained in the account of the said late earl from 4 April 1660 until 20 March following for money received out of England of one William Smithier against the payment of the Army in Ireland and the other £500 allowed for the return *ut supra*.

And this being the truth and not discovered nor could it be discovered before, the now earl not being privy to his father's affairs and the account relating to things more than twenty-six years past and in a foreign kingdom and the prosecution and demand being quick upon an heir and the ancestor lately dead, the court was moved to give leave to amend the plea in these particulars. And the books and certificates mentioning the matter to be thus were produced, some of which were newly gained out of the hands of the late Lord Treasurer, who and also the former Commissioners of the Treasury, were satisfied with the truth of the fact, as *supra*. The counsel further urged that the alteration is solely in the form of the plea and the substance and conclusion of it and also the reply and rejoinder remain not altered.

Yet the court refused to give leave to amend and made a peremptory order that, if the pleader not produce the record according to his plea by the setting down of causes after this term, which at this time was not three weeks, to procure a [writ of] *certiorari* out of the Chancery here and the transmission of the record out of Ireland into the Chancery and out of the Chancery into this court, judgment will be entered for the king that the defendant *computet* with the king for the said £20,000. And they refused to give a longer time.

And, at the said setting down of causes, which was too short a time to procure those things to be done, notwithstanding the motion made for a longer time, judgment *quod computet* was entered and auditors were assigned to take the account.

Quod nota and that the greater part of all that will be recovered was granted, as it was said, to Bernard Howard and Colonel Philips, Chancellor of the Duchy.

I [*Edward Ward*], Mr. *Finch*, Mr. *Lechmere*, and others were for the defendant.

Note, afterwards, it fully appeared and the auditors, having the account transmitted to them, certified that the earl had accounted for the money in question and thus the matter was acquiesced, and no further prosecution was made.

[Other copies of this report: Georgetown Univ. Law Sch. MS. B88–8, p. 69.]

43

Attorney General v. Charlton

Charlton v. Hall

(Ex. 1687)

Parties to litigation will not be prejudiced by the misfeasance of the officers of the court.

Lincoln's Inn MS. Misc. 558, f. 1

23 October 1687. Charlton and Bennett ads. Attorney General and *versus* Mr. Hall, one of the attorneys in the office of the King's Remembrancer, who was the attorney in this cause for the king.

Mr. Francis Charlton being attainted of high treason by an outlawry, a commission was awarded under the Exchequer seal to enquire of the real and personal estate of the said Mr. Charlton. And the commissioners returned several inquisitions, by which the particulars and values of the real and personal estate were found. And these inquisitions were returned into the court around the beginning of May last. And Mr. John Charlton, son and heir of Charlton, attainted, who had a settlement upon a marriage several years before the treason was committed, and Master Bennet, to whom the said Charlton, attainted, before the treason, had conveyed the residue of his real and personal estate for the payment of his debts and the raising of portions for younger children, upon my [*Edward Ward*'s] motion, were admitted to plead to these inquisitions and to have security until the middle of Trinity term last.

And these orders for the pleas that contained the particulars of the things to which the pleas extended were drawn and delivered by Buggin, the defendants' attorney, to Hall, attorney for the king. And he detained them in his hands, though called for, until the time for putting in the pleas was passed and, without which orders, neither the pleas which were prepared in paper nor the security could be perfected. And Hall was every day acquainted that the pleas were ready and the orders demanded to be returned for entry. But he deferred until the setting down of the causes for Trinity term was passed so that no opportunity remained to move the court. And then, he said that he could not accept the pleas, the time being passed.

And, upon an inquiry into the matter, it was found that the same Hall, who knew all the matter before the time allowed by the court to put in the pleas and give security was expired, had made a particular upon which a commission by order of the Commissioners of the Treasury was awarded to collect and levy the rents of the real [estate] and to sell the personal estate, which amounted to great sums, upon which an application was made in the vacation to the Chief Baron [Atkyns], who excused his intermeddling, being after the setting down of causes and, principally, the commission being made by the warrant of the Commissioners of the Treasury. And, on account of this, he advised for an application to the Treasury, which was done by a petition.

But nothing was done, the Treasury saying that it was the commission of the court, though by their warrant.

But, in the vacation, a petition was made. And the first day this term, I [*Edward Ward*] moved to have the pleas accepted and security given and the process stayed and the commissions and all the proceedings upon it superseded, which was ordered accordingly upon hearing of the Attorney General and others for the king, being a plain case, that the default was not in the pleaders but in Mr. Hall. And query the form and justice of such commission, inasmuch as [writs of] *venditioni exponas* and *levare* [*facias*] and not a commission should in such a case issue.

[Other copies of this report: Georgetown Univ. Law Sch. MS. B88–8, p. 76.]

44

Dudding v. Denman

(Ex. 1687)

Whether certain lands are part of a manor or part of a rectory is not a matter within the jurisdiction of the ecclesiastical courts.

Lincoln's Inn MS. Misc. 558, f. 3, pl. 1

Michaelmas term 1687. In prohibition to the archdeacon's court of Stow in Lincolnshire.

The defendant, being a tenant to Magdalene College in Cambridge of certain lands in Aulkebarrow, Lincolnshire, was sued in the ecclesiastical court to repair the chancel of the church there, surmising that the messuage and lands were the parsonage house and glebe belonging to the rectory. The defendant there and plaintiff here prayed [a writ of] prohibition upon a suggestion that the said house and lands were not any part of the rectory but part of the manor of Aulkebarrow and contributory to the repairs of the nave of the church and not of the chancel, which is a thing solely determinable at common law, whether part of the manor or the rectory.

And upon my [*Edward Ward*'s] motion the last term, a rule was granted for a [writ of] prohibition *nisi causa* the first day of this term. And no cause being shown, the prohibition went, the proceedings in the meantime being stayed by the rule of the last term.

[Other copies of this report: Georgetown Univ. Law Sch. MS. B88–8, p. 81, pl. 1.]

45

Mitchell v. Clerke

(Ex. 1687)

A verdict will not be arrested because of the infancy of a defendant unless the defendant moves the court for a stay.

The infancy of a party and a parol demurrer must be affirmatively pleaded.

Lincoln's Inn MS. Misc. 558, f. 4, pl. 2

Hilary [term] 2 & 3 Jac. II, in the Office of Pleas in the Exchequer.

The plaintiff brought [an action of] debt upon two bonds of Ralph Thorne in which he bound himself and his heirs, one for £360, the other for £120, 13 & 14 Car. II [1662] against Matthew Clerke and Elizabeth, his wife, Nicholas Exton and Mary, his wife, Henry Blowes and Anne, his wife, which wives were the daughters and heirs of the obligor. And the plaintiff declared against the defendants as present in court, *viz.* all the defendants except Anne by their attorney and against the said Anne, *quae infra aetatem 21 annorum existit*, by her guardian. All the defendants, except the said Anne, by their attorney and the said Anne, being under age, by her guardian, defended the force etc. and prayed *oyer* of the bonds, which being for the payment of money at days passed, the defendants pleaded payment of the sums by their father at the days in the conditions.

And, upon a trial, the verdict was for the plaintiff.

And *Sir John Holt*, king's serjeant, for the defendants, moved in arrest of judgment inasmuch as the parol in this case should have demurred until the full age of Anne, the infant, because, in all cases when an heir is in by descent, he must have his age and all of the three daughters are only one heir, and, for the infancy of one, the parol demurs, as Marshall's Case, 6 rep. 3, and Rolle, *Age*, fo. 140 and 146, and this title throughout.[1]

And it was admitted in the case that the parol should have demurred if the defendants had prayed it. But the sole question was whether it will demur without a prayer though it appeared by the declaration and the plea that one of the heirs is under age.

And, *Holt* argued yes, inasmuch as the infancy appeared upon the record and the court should *ex officio* award that the parol will demur as well as if infancy had been pleaded. And, for this, he relied on the case of 8 Edw. III, fo. 10,[2] cited in Marshall's Case, fo. 5, and upon the reason that infancy is under the care and protection of the court and that laches will not prejudice an infant according to 8

---

1 *Markal's Case* (1593), 6 Coke Rep. 3, 77 E.R. 258; 1 Rolle, Abr., *Age*, sections C and N, pp. 140–141, 146–147.

2 YB Hil. 8 Edw. III, f. 10, pl. 28 (1334).

rep., Sir Richard Lechford's Case, and 2 Cro. 464, Holford v. Plat.[1] And, in this case, the infant, if she had had her full age, could have pleaded *reins per descent* or any other plea.

But I [*Edward Ward*], for the plaintiff, argued that infancy in this case should have been pleaded though it appears by the declaration and plea because, it being a dilatory [plea], it must come out of the mouth of the defendant. And all of the precedents are that the parol demurs at the prayer of the defendant for the infancy of the defendant. And thus are the precedents. Rastall 209, 360; Aston 209, 239, etc.; see also Rolle, tit. *Age*, 146, L, the case of 11 Hen. VI, 10b.[2] And the reason that it must be pleaded is that it must appear of what age the infant is, because he pleads that he is of such an age and no more, so that it can appear upon the record when he will have a resummons or that he can counterplead the age pleaded. And the case of 8 Edw. III, in Marshall's Case, where the court awarded the parol to demur without a plea inasmuch as it was for the infancy of the demandant and not of the tenant which made the difference. Also, here, this is a case after a verdict.

And, upon these reasons and authorities urged by myself [*Edward Ward*], the court gave judgment for the plaintiff.

But the defendants brought a writ of error by the advice of Serjeant Holt. And, afterwards, the parties agreed among themselves, the plaintiff receiving satisfaction for his debt.

[Other copies of this report: Georgetown Univ. Law Sch. MS. B88–8, p. 84.]

Dodd 70

In [an action of] debt upon an obligation, [the case was thus]. The ancestor had two coheirs, one is of full age, the other appears by guardian and is a minor and pleads only *ad diem*. And after a verdict for the plaintiff, Serjeant *Holt* moved in arrest of judgment because it appears by the record that he is a minor and that the court should *ex officio* award that the parol demur and this without a prayer of the party because the nonpaying is only a laches that will not be imputed to the minor. And he cited 6 Rep. 5, Marshall's Case; and 8 Edw. III, 10; 8 Rep., Rochford's Case; 2 Cr. 464.[3]

Ward [argued] *contra*, that the party must pray that the parol demur and the form of the pleading is that [he is] under age [being] of the age of seventeen and

---

1 *Undrell v. Elsey* (1610), 6 Coke Rep. 99, 77 E.R. 627, also *sub nom. Underhill v. Kelsey*, Croke Jac. 226, 79 E.R. 195; *Holford v. Platt* (1618), Croke Jac. 464, 79 E.R. 397, also 2 Rolle Rep. 14, 22, 81 E.R. 628, 633.

2 W. Rastell, *Colleccion of Entrees*; R. Aston, *Placita Latine Rediviva; a Book of Entries*; YB Mich. 11 Hen. VI, f. 10, pl. 21, 1 Rolle, Abr., *Age*, pl. L, 1, p. 146 (1432).

3 *Markal's Case* (1593), 6 Coke Rep. 3, 77 E.R. 258; YB Hil. 8 Edw. III, f. 10, pl. 28 (1334); *Lechford's Case* (1610), 8 Coke Rep. 99, 77 E.R. 627, also *sub nom. Underhill v. Kelsey*, Croke Jac. 226, 79 E.R. 195; *Holford v. Platt* (1618), Croke Jac. 464, 79 E.R. 397.

not more, and thus the plaintiff had the opportunity to contest it or to pursue a resummons out of the roll when he comes of age, which advantages the plaintiff is deprived of if judgment will be arrested after verdict, as above. See 11 Hen. VIII, 10b.

The court [agreed] with Ward and gave judgment for the plaintiff. Note.

46

Scott v. Grove

(Ex. 1687)

The right to a seat in a church is not within the jurisdiction of the ecclesiastical courts, but should be litigated in the common law courts.

Lincoln's Inn MS. Misc. 558, f. 5, pl. 1

A suit was prosecuted in the consistory court of Lichfield touching a disturbance of sitting in a seat in the church. And the suit was for the reformation of manners and *salute animae*. But, in the proceedings, examinations were made that went to the right of the seat, but no good prescription as to the right of the repairs was alleged.

Scott, against whom the sentence was probable to go, prayed [a writ of] prohibition, suggesting a right to the seat as appurtenant to the messuage and a prescription to repair. And it was granted *nisi*.

And I [*Edward Ward*] moved against the prohibition inasmuch as the principal cause was only a disturbance, and not the right of the seat, which is proper for their jurisdiction, and no title at law was alleged by the plaintiff here in this court.

But the court granted the prohibition notwithstanding upon this suggestion, that it should be tried at [common] law and not in the ecclesiastical court, not regarding that no good right or title to the seat or obligation to repair appeared in the ecclesiastical proceedings but that it appeared upon the suggestion, upon which the defendant can take issue. And, inasmuch as the matter suggested is properly and solely determinable at common law and not in the ecclesiastical court, a prohibition issued, because, perhaps, the court Christian will proceed upon the examinations.

[Other copies of this report: Georgetown Univ. Law Sch. MS. B88–8, p. 86.]

47

Fulwood's Case

(Ex. 1687)

A writ of execution that was based upon false information will be set aside.

Lincoln's Inn MS. Misc. 558, f. 5, pl. 2

Martell with Fulwood and Collins, his sureties, though not so mentioned, became bound to the king in the Custom House for the payment of several sums for customs of wines at several days for three payments. After one of the payments [was] passed and before the others were due, Fulwood declined in his estate. And he was in debt to Martell in divers sums, for the recovery of which, Martell, upon an oath of Fulwood's declining and not discovering[1] that the debt due to the king was for Martell's wines, procured [a writ of] extent against Fulwood's estate, notwithstanding that Martell was sufficient.[2]

Against which practice, I [*Edward Ward*] moved for Fulwood.

And the court condemned Martell's proceedings, but, for this reason, they would not set them aside, though they declared that, upon the payment of all due to the king, Fulwood will have the process against Martell. But, upon perusal of the extents against Fulwood, the dates and sums of the bonds in which Fulwood was bound were mistaken. And, for this reason, [writs of] *supersedeas* and restitution were awarded.

[Other copies of this report: Georgetown Univ. Law Sch. MS. B88–8, p. 87.]

48

Williams and Bowers' Case

(Ex. 1687)

Writs of process can be issued and returned before the return date is expired.

Lincoln's Inn MS. Misc. 558, f. 5, pl. 3

The case was thus. Williams and others were bound to the king for customs [duties] in a bond for payment at three days. One being passed, a [writ of] extent in aid issued against Williams, upon which it was found that Bowers was in debt to Williams in such a sum for goods sold. And this debt was seized into the hands of the king. And this extent was *teste* 15 October returnable *tres Michaelis*. Before the return of which writ, that is to say 19 October, a [writ of] *scire facias* returnable the 24 October issued against Bowers to show cause why the king will not

[1] *I.e.* disclosing.

[2] *I.e.* credit worthy.

have execution against him for the debt seized. On 20 October, Bowers died. And a *mortuus* being returned the 21 October, being before the return of the *scire facias*, upon an affidavit made of Bowers' death and that his doors were shut up, by a warrant of the Chief Baron, a [writ of] extent in the nature of a *diem clausit extremum* issued against his lands and goods and [was] executed to the value of £97 returnable the 31 October.

And, in this case, inasmuch as Bowers, in his lifetime, was found a debtor to the debtor of the king and this debt was seized into the hands of the king so that Bowers was in truth debtor to the king at his death notwithstanding that the *scire facias* issued before the return of the extent and the *diem clausit extremum* issued before the return of the *scire facias*, the court refused to set aside those proceedings touching those good in such a case, but offered to admit the defendant to plead if he wished to Bowers' debt, the defendant being administrator to Bowers.

I [*Edward Ward* was] for the defendant.

Query the right of such a practice as to the issuing and returning of process before the return is expired, because the usage is only of recent times and the first opinion that it was good, and, as I remember, the first practice was in Surry and Thomas and Hinton's Case, in 1684, which see, L. K, 44.[1]

[Other copies of this report: Georgetown Univ. Law Sch. MS. B88–8, p. 88.]

49

Bliss and Smith's Case

(Ex. 1687)

In this case, the debt due to the crown's debtor was not paid, and an agreement to pay it over time did not defeat the execution on behalf of the crown.

Lincoln's Inn MS. Misc. 558, f. 6, pl. 1

Bliss was a debtor to the king by a bond for wine license money received. Smith was a debtor to Bliss by a bond for the payment of the gross sum at a day now passed. Upon the usual oath of the insufficiency and failer of Smith, a [writ of] immediate extent was awarded [and] Smith's bond was seized into the hands of the king upon [a writ of] extent against Bliss, and execution was had.

And it was now moved to set aside this execution inasmuch as Bliss had given a defeasance under his hand and seal to take his debt by £40 *per annum*.

But it appeared to the court that the money was not paid for the first bond or according to the defeasance and that the bond became broken if it had not been conditioned. The court would not discharge the proceedings.

I [*Edward Ward* was] for Bliss.

[1] *Attorney General v. Thomas* (Ex. 1684), Exch. Cases *tempore* Car. II, p. 588.

[Other copies of this report: Georgetown Univ. Law Sch. MS. B88–8, p. 90, pl. 1.]

50

Robinson and Huntly's Case

(Ex. 1687)

In this case, a writ of extent was set aside by the court, having being procured through fraud.

Lincoln's Inn MS. Misc. 558, f. 6, pl. 2

Robinson and Asgill, as sureties for Wagstaff, became bound to the king by a bond 2nd July last for the payment of money for customs at a time to come. Huntly being indebted to Robinson in £500 and more and being in a failing condition, Robinson procured a [writ of] extent against himself the same day that the bond is dated and an inquisition upon it the same day that found and seized Huntly's debt to Robinson into the hands of the king. And this extent was returnable *tres Michaelis*, before which return and two days after the said bond and inquisition taken, upon an oath of the insufficiency and failure of Huntly, Baron Heath made a warrant for [a writ of] immediate extent against Huntly and his estate. And Huntly living at Newcastle and being taken in execution for debt at another three weeks after awarding the immediate extent, Huntly's goods were seized in execution in aid of Robinson.

And upon a motion of Huntly's creditors, who have prosecuted a commission of bankrupts and an oath made that Robinson sought afterwards and endeavored to procure himself to be a surety with Wagstaff to the purpose to make himself a debtor to the king and thus to have aid to recover his debt against Huntly and considering that the bond to the king and the inquisition were the same day and the immediate extent but two days after, the court held it to be a bad practice and dangerous to countenance such proceedings. And on account of this, they set aside all the proceedings and awarded [writs of] *supersedeas* and restitution.

Sawyer, Attorney General, *et alii* [were] for Robinson.

[Other copies of this report: Georgetown Univ. Law Sch. MS. B88–8, p. 90, pl. 2.]

51

Stanlake v. Bewly

(Ex. 1687)

Where a debtor is sued upon a scire facias and is in default as to a response thereto, he cannot afterwards assert defenses to the alleged underlying debt.

Lincoln's Inn MS. Misc. 558, f. 6, pl. 3

Stanlake was indebted to the king by bond for the payment of money. And, upon [a writ of] extent against him, it was found that Hind and Toplady were indebted to Stanlake in £530 for money received for him and this debt was seized into the hands of the king, upon which another extent issued against Hind and Toplady to enquire and seize their estate into the hands of the king, upon which it was found by inquisition that Bewly was indebted to Hind by a bond of such a date and penalty for the payment of such a sum, which bond and debt were seized into the hands of the king, upon which [a writ of] *scire facias* issued against Bewly. And upon two *nichils* returned, Bewly was taken in execution.

And now, he moved to set aside this inquisition, alleging that the bond given by him was for money lost at play and, on account of this, void. And Hind [was] only a trustee for another, and no debt [was] truly due to Hind.

But, inasmuch as those proceedings were regular and two *nichils* returned upon a *scire facias*, which, in law, amount to a *scire feci*, the court refused to discharge the proceedings.

I [*Edward Ward* was] for Stanlake.

[Other copies of this report: Georgetown Univ. Law Sch. MS. B88–8, p. 92, pl. 1.]

52

Taylor v. Brookes

(Ex. 1687–1688)

Several mariners may sue jointly for their wages in the Court of Admiralty, but they cannot sue jointly in a common law court.

Lincoln's Inn MS. Misc. 558, f. 7

The defendants, being mariners in the ship *Greyhound alias Richard and Elizabeth*, libeled in the Admiralty Court against the ship only for their wages due from 2 July 1684 until 26 May 1685, of which ship, one Wood was master and Trig owner, who afterwards sold the ship to Tudor. And the wages were incurred for the most part in the time of Trigg, who had entered into a charter party with Wood, the master, who continued master after Tudor became owner. And the defendants were many, that is to say twenty-four, and their wages were small, that is to say many were under 40s. and some but 14s.

And the plaintiff here prayed [a writ of] prohibition upon a suggestion, first, that the contract was *super terram*, second, that the ship never was at sea, but remained at Ratcliff *super terram* all the time that the defendants sued for their wages.

And, upon this suggestion, the court made a rule for a prohibition *nisi* and to stay in the meantime, the defendants being ready for a sentence and the rule not served until the day before the showing of cause and two days before the day for sentence.

And I [*Edward Ward*], for the defendants, moved to discharge the rule for the prohibition, the suggestion not containing good matter for a prohibition, because, as to mariner's wages, it is the practice in Westminster Hall not to grant a prohibition inasmuch as in the Admiralty several [parties] can join in one suit, who cannot in a suit at common law. Also, the suit here is only against the ship and not against the master. And this court, if it will grant a prohibition cannot give relief to the mariners against the ship, and, if their suit in the Admiralty will be prohibited, the mariners are without a remedy against the ship, which without doubt is liable by their law for the mariners' wages. Cro. Car. 296; Hayn's Case, 22 & 23 Car. II, L. [*blank*]; and Wilmot and Shaw, in this court, Pas. 1681, L. J, 28, in the point that no prohibition will be granted in this case.[1]

And, as to this point, that the ship never was at sea and, on account of this, not liable, this is a matter proper for the jurisdiction of the [Court of] Admiralty, which is of high consideration and erudite judges. And, if it belongs to their jurisdiction, the courts here will give faith and credit to their judges.

Also it is a common and usual thing that mariners are entitled to wages or at least to demi-wages during [the time] the ship is in the river. And it will be unreasonable to compel each mariner to bring a distinct suit for his wages or to try the matter upon the prohibition where no costs will be recovered.

But the court, thinking that this suit was prosecuted by the master to charge the wages upon the ship, which is mortgaged to the plaintiff, though no such thing was in the suggestion, continued the rule until the first day of the next term, when counsel of both sides will be heard upon the matter.

I [*Edward Ward* was] for the defendants.

Vide L. H, 35, Potts and Green,[2] a prohibition was denied upon the reason that the suit was against the ship.

Nota for calling a woman a whore generally will not carry an action, but an action lies in London, and, if it be removed by [a writ of] *habeas corpus*, there will be [a writ of] *procedendo* upon the reason that there should not be a failer of justice, because the courts at Westminster, in such a case, will not restrain any jurisdiction where they could not give relief for the same thing.

And afterwards, in Hilary term next [1688], the rule for the prohibition was discharged upon my [*Edward Ward*'s] argument for the defendants for the reasons and causes before urged. And, if there was any fraud, the Court of Admiralty, who had the jurisdiction of the principal, will do justice as to all incidents.

Baron JENNER seemed to dissent as to the fraud, that this is triable here. But the other three barons were clear in this point, and the rule was discharged.

[Other copies of this report: Georgetown Univ. Law Sch. MS. B88–8, p. 92, pl. 2.]

---

1 *Wilmot v. Shaw* (Ex. 1681), Georgetown Univ. Law Sch. MS B88–7, p. 249.

2 *Potts v. Green* (Ex. 1679), Exch. Cases *tempore* Car. II, p. 399.

53

Bertie, qui tam v. Bickham

(Ex. 1687)

In this case, a party was forced to abandon his claim for fear of being arrested on another matter if he appeared in court.

Lincoln's Inn MS. Misc. 558, f. 8, pl. 2

The plaintiff, in the last vacation, seized two tuns of French wines [at Bristol] as forfeited for not paying the custom [duty], though, in truth, the custom was paid. Mr. Gardner, a merchant in London, advised touching the case and seizure with a counsel who was retained by him. But there being another personal information against the defendant for other supposed offenses, the plaintiff employed two several attorneys in the office, one for the seizure and the other for the personal information. Gardner employed an attorney for all for the defendant. And he, thinking that the plaintiff had only one attorney, expected information in all from him so that he did not enter the claim, but recovery passed, and a debit was made for the plaintiff to pay in the Receipt [Office] the moiety of the appraised value. But, before any payment was made, Bickham moved the court to have his claim admitted upon oath made of the truth of the matter, which the court held a thing just and reasonable. And, in truth, it was never denied. And an order was made for receiving the claim, and the claim was admitted and the fees of the recovery were paid to the plaintiff's clerk in court and a stop was put to the payment of the money in the Exchequer. And this was the 14th of November.

The next day, the plaintiff's counsel without notice, at the side bar, obtained an order to show cause against the receiving of the claim. And the 18th and the 22nd, the plaintiff's counsel showed for cause that the defendant was in contempt and absconded from the serjeant or messenger of the Commissioners of the Treasury, who was sent by those Commissioners to take the defendant into custody upon a suggestion of certain misdemeanors alleged to be committed by the defendant in defrauding the king of his customs and bribing the Custom House officers, for which offenses, informations were pending in this court.

And, on account of this, *North*, counsel of the king, prayed that the defendant's claim should not be admitted (being, as he alleged, a favor) *nisi* the defendant shall render himself to the serjeant or officer of the Commissioners of the Treasury, which, at first, the court thought as a harsh thing, but, afterwards, the court ordered this *nisi* the defendant by Saturday next will appear in person in this court and make his claim, that his claim will not be admitted, and it discharged the first order for the admission of it.

And the defendant, thinking that, if he appeared, he will be taken into custody, did not appear, and his claim was rejected. And recovery passed.

I [*Edward Ward* was] for the defendant.

Query well of this case because it seems extraordinary to put these things on the defendant, because it is held to be the common course and justice of the court to admit claims in such cases in the same term before payment of the money upon any reasonable cause shown. And here, the defendant had great reason and was in no default, but it was a mere mistake, which was testified to the court. And it seems to me there was no reason to restrain the defendant from his claim *nisi* he, in effect, will render himself into the custody of the officers of the Commissioners of the Treasury, who is not an officer of this court, *quod nota et quaere bene.*

And query also the right of such proceedings by a warrant of the Commissioners of the Treasury to take a person into custody without legal proceedings or prosecution in a court of justice, because what remedy will the party have if he is not guilty, and, if he is guilty, the law has appointed a prosecution and a penalty and not imprisonment. And informations for the supposed offenses were pending, and, on account of this, no other prosecutions should be [had].

[Other copies of this report: Georgetown Univ. Law Sch. MS. B88–8, p. 96.]

54

Mosely, ex dem. Arundel v. Shorter

(Ex. 1687)

Where a plaintiff in an action of ejectment prevails in any small part, though he fails for the greater part of his claim, he will be given court costs for the entire litigation.

Lincoln's Inn MS. Misc. 558, f. 9

Mosely, lessee of Colonel Arundel, plaintiff; Sir John Shorter [1625–1688], Mayor of London, defendant.

The plaintiff brought [an action of] ejectment for divers lands and houses in and near Southwark in the County of Surrey, thinking them to be part of the manor of Kennington in Lambeth and part of the duchy of Cornwall, of which the plaintiff's lessor was lessee under the Exchequer lease made 25 Car. II, in which lease there was also a demise of certain land containing sixty-two pees in front and twenty-five pees in breadth where formerly the old barge houses of the kings of England stood and to which land the title of the crown was under a long lease made by the same person under whom the defendant claims. The defendant's title was as part of the manor of Paris Garden, formerly part of the possessions of the Knights Templars, and well derived under the crown and an ancient prior's lease

And this cause having two or three times before been tried at law, in all which trials as also in this one in question, which was tried at the bar, the sole question was whether the things in question were part of the manor of Kennington or part of the manor of Paris Garden. And the verdicts or nonsuits upon a view and full evidence always were for the defendant and his title. And [there was] constant possession accordingly and enjoyment for 120 years without other interruptions except these, which the plaintiff's lessor gave by these actions.

And now, upon long and full evidence given by the defendant and no evidence except one mistaken pretended survey supposed to be made *circa* fifty or sixty years past by the steward and jury of the Kennington court without notice to any other and no possession or enjoyment according to it but it was always with the defendant and those under whom he claimed, there was a verdict for the defendant for all except the barge house soil, and for this, [there was] a verdict for the plaintiff.

And the defendant, having by mistake and without advice, taken upon himself the defense of all of the land in the declaration without distinction and confessed the lease, entry, and ouster for all in his possession, as he had at a former trial where the plaintiff was nonsuited after a view and full evidence at the bar of this court, in which there was no notice of the barge house, and though he did not have any title to the barge house land nor meant to defend the title to it nor did he acquaint his counsel that he had any possession of it, yet it being proved that the defendant's timber and boards, he being a timber merchant, were laid upon this land and notwithstanding that his counsel at the trial disclaimed all title and possession to it, yet this verdict, for the plaintiff for this little thing, not only barred the defendant from his costs of the trial at the bar, which was granted upon the defendant's motion and solely intended to try the title to these lands, for which the verdict was for the defendant, but it also subjected the defendant to pay all of the costs of the trial at the bar to the plaintiff, which were taxed at £60 and, notwithstanding, the court refused to moderate them.

The Chief Baron [Atkyns] inclined to some moderation as a mere mistake and oversight, but the other three barons refused.

I [*Edward Ward* was] for the defendant.

[Other copies of this report: Georgetown Univ. Law Sch. MS. B88–8, p. 98.]

55

Merefield's Case

(Ex. 1687)

A customary compromise for aulnage duties, though reasonable, is not legally enforceable.

Lincoln's Inn MS. Misc. 558, f. 10, pl. 2

The plaintiff, being a large dealer in worsted stockings in Somersetshire and sent by him to London to be sold, complained of a seizure made of several of his parcels for refusing to pay the duty and subsidy of aulnage according to 1d. for a score of men's stockings notwithstanding that he had tendered and offered to pay according to the rate of 4½d. for each sixty-four pounds of stockings, which, as the plaintiff's counsel alleged, was the rate settled by the decree of this court [*blank*] Car. II. And, on account of this, he prayed relief and delivery.

For the aunalgers, it was shown that these stockings, coming to London between boards, could not be taken out of them and weighed without great trouble and prejudice to the owners and, on account of that, as an accommodation, 1d. per score had always been paid for the aulnage. And the plaintiff himself and others had paid it constantly, and the practice was thus *tempore* Charles I, as appears by affidavits. And as to the decree mentioned, truly it is there was such an order, but it concerned only course woolen stockings made at Richmond and not fine worsted throughout the realm.

And the court held the 1d. per score reasonable and convenient for the traders. But, if the plaintiff refused to pay it, the court left the aulnagers to proceed upon informations of seizure. And, if he would try them according to the rules of the court, no delivery will be granted.

I [*Edward Ward* was] for the aulnagers.

[Other copies of this report: Georgetown Univ. Law Sch. MS. B88–8, p. 101.]

56

Hayne, qui tam v. Mason

(Ex. 1687)

In this case, the sugar that was imported was found to be brown sugar and thus liable to a lower import duty than refined sugar.

Lincoln's Inn MS. Misc. 558, f. 11, pl. 2

Upon an information of seizure of one hogshead of sugar for non-payment of the duties and customs to the king upon the Statute 1 Jac. II, ca. 4,[1] the case upon the trial at the bar by a Middlesex jury was thus. By the Statute of Tonnage and Poundage and the Book of Rates enacted 12 Car. II[2] and revived 1 Jac. II, the duty imposed upon brown sugars and muscoradoes from the English plantations was 18d. the hundredweight. And, by the Statute 25 Car. II, ca. [*blank*],[3] for securing the plantation trade, a duty is imposed upon brown and muscoradoes sugars, among others, if carried and loaded in ships and a bond not given to carry to England, Wales, or Berwick. And, by the Statute of 1 Jac. II, ca. 4, it was enacted that, for all sorts of sugars and tobaccos imported into England, Wales,

---

[1] Stat. 1 Jac. II, c. 4 (*SR*, VI, 3–7).

[2] Stat. 12 Car. II, c. 4, app. (*SR*, V, 184–205).

[3] Stat. 25 Car. II, c. 7 (*SR*, V, 792–793).

or Berwick after the 24th of June 1685, there will be paid to His Majesty the further rates and duties following, *viz.* for all sorts of tobacco of the growth and production of His Majesty's plantations, islands, or territories in America such rates mentioned there, and then follows the clause upon which the case arose:

> And, for all muscorade sugar of the aforesaid plantations, islands, lands, or territories, one farthing the pound weight above what it now pays and, for every pound weight of sugar of the English plantations made fit for common use or spending, three farthings above what it now pays and, for every pound weight of muscorade sugar of Brazil or any other foreign part not of English plantations, one half penny above what it now pays and, for all panela sugar, one half penny the pound above what it now pays and for every pound of foreign white powder sugar, one farthing above what it now pays, and, for all foreign sugar imported in the loaf, 3d. the pound above what it now pays.

The defendant and divers other Jamaica merchants, the last vacation, imported divers great quantities of muscorade sugar from Jamaica, and paid the duty imposed by the Statute of Tonnage and Poundage and the farthing per pound imposed by the Statute of 1 Jac. II upon muscorade sugars from the English plantations. But Sir Dudley North and the others of the Commissioners of the Customs, thinking that these sugars that the merchants imported and entered as muscorade sugars were sugars 'made fit for common use or spending', demanded and insisted to have three farthings per pound for them and, for the non-payment, they caused the sugars to be stayed until the merchants give the security to pay this duty if, upon a trial of this hogshead in question, it will be found and adjudged sugar made fit for common use or spending.

And it was agreed that this hogshead will be the standard for all those imported. And some of the merchants bringing [actions of] trespass in London for seizing their sugars against the officers of the customs, which actions were removed by the officers into the Office of Pleas of this court by [writs of] *habeas corpus* and bail given in this court to the action, as it was in London and the plaintiff declared in trespass in London and the Attorney General and others for the king moved to change the venue into Middlesex, though the trespass was committed in London, the action not being local in nature and London ot being an indifferent place for trial, inasmuch as the merchants and traders live there who will favor the matter against the king. And the court, upon the hearing of the counsel of both parts, altered the venue accordingly for the aforesaid reasons. After which, it was agreed that these actions will abide by the event and fate of this case upon the information.

And, in the debate of this case, the counsel for the king endeavored to have the fact found specially, that is to say that the sugars in question were sugars fit for common use or spending and called by the name of muscorade sugars and thus to leave the matter of law to the court whether those sugars will pay only the farthing as muscorades or the three farthings as sugars made fit for common use or spending.

But the defendant's counsel totally opposed any special verdict, the matter in question being a mere matter in fact whether the sugars were muscoradoes or not.

And the counsel for the king insisted that, though there are sugars called muscorade sugars that pay only the farthing per pound, yet they are only those sugars that are not fit for common use or spending. But, when any sugars are fit for common use or spending, though they are known by the name of muscorades, they must pay the three farthings because the duty is given in regard of the use and not of the name. And they produced divers persons, cooks, grocers, and others in London, who proved that this sugar called muscorade sugar is and always has been sold by grocers to their customers and frequently used by cooks and other trades in making their small commodities and for the use of poor persons.

But it was agreed by all that, for one pound of this sort so spent without further improvement, ten pounds of the other sorts of sugar were consumed. And, on account of this, the defendant's counsel urged that such little expense and by poor persons cannot give a denomination to sugar 'fit for common use or spending' because every *denominatio est ex majori.* And the defendant's counsel, by divers witnesses and arguments, proved to the court that the sugar in question is and always was called muscorade sugar and never by another name (perhaps sometime as brown) and that there is not nor ever was any other sort of sugar that was or was called muscorado sugar but only this in question, so that this is muscorade in name and nature also. And the Act of Parliament plainly distinguishes between muscorade sugar and sugar made fit for common use or spending, and it is impossible to make these terms one, so that this sugar which is and should pay as muscorade cannot be intended to be the sugar made fit for common use and spending, because the Parliament distinguished between them in name and duty also, which things cannot be confounded. And the farthing for the muscorade further rate is proportionable to the three farthings for sugar made fit for common use or spending and with respect to the first duties before the Statute 1 Jac. II.

Also, it was urged for the defendant that the three farthings are not imposed upon sugar fit but 'made' fit for common use or spending so that there must be a manufacture after which it is sugar, which here it is not, because the sugar in question is the first and original sugar and never had anything done to it after which it was sugar, because, after the juice of the cane is boiled to the consistency and put into pots to be dried, these pots are emptied into casks and thus imported into England. And all this is called and esteemed muscorade sugar not having undergone any operation after which it becomes sugar. But the sugar in the Act for which the three farthings must be paid must be first sugar and, afterwards, this sugar must be 'made fit' for common use and spending. And it is either by claying, baking, or other refining that commonly takes two parts out of three. And, though it is true that the muscorade sugar after it is in the cask in the voyage into England and after, in lying still, will purge and ferment and the dregs descend lower in the vessel, so that this at the top or perhaps a third part down can be purged and dried and, on account of this, sold for 4d. per pound and used in ordinary things, yet, as the rest of the cask is not of any use unless it is refined and all this, as well the purged as the unpurged sugar, is called muscorade. And, in truth, three casks of muscorades only equals one cask of sugar made fit for common use or spending. And, for this reason, the king had his full duty. And thus it seems clear to be the intention of the Parliament to lay treble the duty upon refined sugars than upon muscorades, inasmuch as three casks of muscorades make only one cask of refined sugar.

Another argument for the defendant was urged out of the construction and consideration of the Act itself, which, in all cases, imposes a greater duty upon foreign than upon English plantations. But, if these muscorade sugars of the English plantations will pay three farthings, it would be a greater duty than is imposed by the same Act upon muscorade sugar of Brazil or other foreign plantations, which certainly never was the intent of the Act, nor could it be the reasonable construction of it.

Also, it is unreasonable to think that the king will have two distinct duties for the same cask of sugar, the one as sugar fit for use, the other solely for muscorade, and in what manner and in what proportions there will be such distinct duties levied and in what manner should the merchant enter his casks of sugar, because perhaps one cask has purged more or less than another has so that it is impossible as well as unreasonable to compel the merchant to make distinct entries and to pay distinct duties for the sugars in the same cask, because it was admitted by all that the greater part of each cask is only this sort of sugar that the counsel of the king admits to pay the farthing as muscorade.

And after a long trial, the jury, which was of knights and gentlemen, having a view of the hogshead which was brought into court at the request of the defendant, and upon a view of samples taken from the top, middle, and bottom of the cask, gave a general verdict for the defendant, intending by it that the sugar in question was all muscorade sugar within the Act and liable solely to one farthing per pound and not sugar 'made fit for common use or spending'.

I [*Edward Ward* was] for the defendant.

Note, in this case, no exception was taken to the information of seizure, though it did not appear by the Act that a seizure is warranted by this Act, but a duty only is given by it to the king without a remedy by a seizure. And, on account of this, an information in the nature of an action of debt lies. But the defendant, relying on the merits of his case, did not take advantage of this exception. And it seems that a seizure is not given, inasmuch as, in the great case of Bristol v. Cooper,[1] in this court lately for tobacco imported, upon the same Act,

---

[1] *Bristow v. Cooper* (Ex. 1685–1687), see above, Case No. 12.

the merchant was chased to his action of trover, it being objected by Sawyer, Attorney General, that a seizure did not lie.

[Other copies of this report: Georgetown Univ. Law Sch. MS. B88–8, p. 103.]

57

LeNeve, qui tam v. Cox

(Ex. 1687)

In this case, an exporter of imported goods who mistakenly certified the quantity of the goods at issue was found liable to the crown.

Lincoln's Inn MS. Misc. 558, f. 13

Upon a *devenerunt* touching drawbacks, the plaintiff brought his information *tam quam* grounded upon the Statute of 14 Car. II, ca. 11,[1] for procuring a certificate from the officers of the customs within the port of London for exporting into parts beyond the sea 41,016 pounds weight of tobacco *ubi revera* he fraudulently shipped out less tobacco in quantity and value than was expressed in this certificate in deceit of the king in his customs and against the Statute, by which the defendant forfeited the value, which was laid at £1025. *Et unde* the informer prayed a moiety.

The defendant pleaded *non culpabilis*.

And, upon the trial, it appeared that the defendant had imported tobaccos at three several times and made three entries of them in the Custom House, that is to say the 7th, the 10th, and 21st of February 1686[/87]. This entry of the 10th of February was of 42,000 pounds weight of Virginia tobacco out of the *Susanna*, Thomas Dell, master, and other quantities were entered the other two days out of other ships. And the certificate for exportation was dated and made the 22nd of February 1686[/87] for exporting 41,016 pounds weight of tobacco, part of a greater parcel that he imported the 10th and paid duties for. And upon this certificate, he procured a cocket for shipping out the said tobacco, upon which he endorsed the marks, numbers, and contents of 109 hogsheads and carried them to the searcher to be executed for shipping out in the same hogsheads, which was done accordingly. And, by this certificate and shipping out, the defendant was entitled to demand and to have a repayment by way of a drawback of 4½d. per pound. After which exportation, it was discovered that only 71 hogsheads of the 109 were part of the entry of the 10th of February and that the other 38 hogsheads containing 13,866 pounds weight were not part of this entry, but were of other entries. And this appeared by the marks, numbers, and weights of the casks. And the truth was thus.

[1] Stat. 14 Car. II, c. 11 (*SR*, V, 393–400).

And it was admitted that the defendant exported the full quantity of the tobacco contained in his certificate and that he was in no default in anything touching the exportation of the tobacco and drawing back the duty, but only that he confined the tobacco in his certificate to be part of the tobacco in his entry of the 10th of February that the 38 hogsheads containing the quantity before mentioned were not but part of his entries of the 7th and 21st February. And for this thing and default only, the defendant was found guilty of the offense in the information, because, although the defendant exported all the quantity of tobacco mentioned in the certificate, yet he did not export the same tobacco there mentioned, because the tobacco there mentioned to be exported is all of the entry of the 10th and here 38 hogsheads were not part of it. And, on account of this, 13,866 pounds weight of tobacco was exported that was not mentioned in the certificate, and, by consequence, so much less exported than was contained in his certificate because the certificate can justify the exportation only of the tobacco that the defendant had entered the 10th of February.

And it was proved to be the constant practice that the verity and certainty of the tobacco and as entered inwards was and should be contained in the certificate procured for exportation outwards and without confinement to the particular and certain entry inwards, the king is certainly subject to be defrauded, because his officers cannot in such a case know what tobacco and when imported is to be exported *nisi* the true time of the importation and the true entry inwards are ascertained in the certificate for exportation. And this ascertainment is to be made by the party, who exports at his peril, because, by such certainty in the certificate, the officers are guided and instructed for inspecting these entries inwards to see if those entries inwards were within the year or nine months before the exportation or certificate for exportation, after which no exportation for drawing back a duty according to the second rule in the Book of Rates[1] can be, and to see whether the quantity imported will warrant the quantity to be exported.

And for this mistake only, the Chief Baron [Atkyns], the trial being before him at *nisi prius*, directed the jury, as a plain case, to find for the king. And the verdict was accordingly. But the jury found the value only at £200 in favor of the defendant, who, beyond these damages, lost the benefit of drawing back the 4½d. per pound upon exportation, which amounted to £600 or £700.

The Attorney General [*Sawyer*], the Solicitor General [*Powys*], Mr. *North*, and myself [*Edward Ward*, were] for the king, and Mr. *Heneage Finch* and Mr. *William Williams* and others [were] for the defendant.

But afterwards, the Commissioners of the Customs, upon recommendations to them by the court and payment of the £200, admitted the defendant to the benefit of his debenture for a drawback.

Vide afterwards 19.[2]

---

1 Stat. 12 Car. II, c. 4, app. (*SR*, V, 184–205).

2 *Bates, qui tam v. Barret* (Ex. 1688), see below, Case No. 67.

[Other copies of this report: Georgetown Univ. Law Sch. MS. B88–8, p. 110.]

58

Carpenter, qui tam v. Dansie

(Ex. 1687)

It is illegal to transfer freight from one ship to another ship without official permission.

Lincoln's Inn MS. Misc. 558, f. 14, pl. 1

Michaelmas [term] 1687.

Upon the seizure of a ship for the taking of goods in it out of the ship's boat, which took them out of another ship coming inwards without a warrant or presence of officers, contrary to the Statute 14 Car. II, ca. 11,[1] judgment [was given] for the king. But [a writ of] error was brought.

See the special verdict and arguments and reasons among my arguments.

I [*Edward Ward* was] for the king.

[Other copies of this report: Georgetown Univ. Law Sch. MS. B88–8, p. 113, pl. 1.]

59

Attorney General, ex rel. Shepheard v. Goldesbrough

(Ex. 1687)

A writ of extent does not lie against one who never was a debtor to the king.

Lincoln's Inn MS. Misc. 558, f. 14, pl. 2

Michaelmas 1687.

Touching a debt in aid seized and charging one to the king as *occupator bonorum* of one who never was a debtor to the king or any other who was in his lifetime debtor to the king, judgment [was given] for the king. But [a writ of] error was brought.

See the demurrer, arguments, and reasons among my arguments.

I [*Edward Ward* was] for the defendant.

And, afterwards, that is to say, *circa* 1694, this judgment was reversed.

[Other copies of this report: Georgetown Univ. Law Sch. MS. B88–8, p. 113, pl. 2.]

---

[1] Stat. 14 Car. II, c. 11 (*SR*, V, 393–400).

60

Ellis, qui tam v. Martin

(Ex. 1687)

An alien can practice a trade in England.
Service alone is sufficient evidence of an apprenticeship.

Dodd 67

Information [was sued] upon [the Statute] 1 Jac., ch. 17,[1] for £5 *per mensem* for using the trade of a felt maker. The defendant was a Frenchman. And upon a special verdict, [it was] found that he was an alien and that he had served seven years beyond the sea according to the usage there but there was not any indenture of apprenticeship.

First, at common law, any foreigner can use a trade; then comes the Statute 1 Ric. III, ch. 19, which is the first restraining law of foreign artificers, and then 21 Hen. VIII, ch. 16, and afterwards 32 Hen. VIII, ch. 16, after [that] 5 Eliz., ch. 4, and 8 Eliz., ch. [*blank*], and then this Act of 1 Jac., and the express resolution, Hutton 132,[2] that an alien born cannot use a trade etc.

Second, there must be a retainer by a deed: Crompton 84; Dalton 95; 5 Eliz., ch. 4, sect. 41.[3]

[*blank*] *contra*:

First, the resolution in Hutton [is] nothing because there [it was] said that Finch and Denham [were] present when they were not in town, as appears [in] Cr. Car. 466.[4] Neither Croke nor Jones report any such resolution. See 11 Rep. 53; Hob. 211, an express authority; and 8 Rep. 126b.[5] 5 Eliz. repeals prior laws as to artificers, but it does not extend to aliens. 1 Jac. has two clauses: (1) 'no man may make' etc. who has not been an apprentice and it is general, (2) 'No man shall set strangers to work' etc.

Second, service or retainer without a deed [is] good; [if] an Englishman is an apprentice beyond the sea for seven years, he can set up in England.

---

[1] Stat. 1 Jac. I, c. 17 (*SR*, IV, 1035).

[2] Stat. 1 Ric. III, c. 12 (*SR*, II, 495–496); Stat. 21 Hen. VIII, c. 16 (*SR*, III, 297–301); Stat. 32 Hen. VIII, c. 16 (*SR*, III, 765–766); Stat. 5 Eliz. I, c. 4 (*SR*, IV, 414–422); Note (1614), Hutton 132, 123 E.R. 1152.

[3] A. Fitzherbert and R. Crompton, *Justice of Peace* (1584), ff. 144, 145; M. Dalton, *Country Justice* (1619), pp. 69–74; Stat. 5 Eliz. I, c. 4 (*SR*, IV, 414–422).

[4] Memorandum (1636), Croke Car. 466, 79 E.R. 1003.

[5] *Ipswich Tailors' Case* (1614), 11 Coke Rep. 53, 77 E.R. 1218, also Godbolt 252, 78 E.R. 147, 1 Rolle Rep. 4, 81 E.R. 285; *Norris v. Staps* (1616), Hobart 210, 80 E.R. 357, also Hutton 5, 123 E.R. 1060; *Case of the City of London* (1610), 8 Coke Rep. 121, 77 E.R. 658, also *sub nom. Waggoner v. Fish*, 2 Brownlow & Goldesborough 278, 284, 123 E.R. 941, 944.

[It was held by the] court [that a] retainer without a deed [is] good because upon evidence [one] never produces the indenture of apprenticeship, but service is an evidence as to an apprenticeship.

As to the point if an alien can set up a trade, the court, doubting, adjourned.

Lincoln's Inn MS. Misc. 558, f. 14, pl. 4

Michaelmas 1687.

Upon an [action of] debt *qui tam* against an alien hatmaker upon the Statute 1 Jac. I, ca. 17,[1] [it was] adjudged that an alien cannot be a hatmaker.

I [*Edward Ward* was] for the plaintiff.

[Other copies of this report: Georgetown Univ. Law Sch. MS. B88–8, p. 114.]

61

Grascomb v. Jeffreys

(Ex. 1687)

In this case, tithes for marshland were ordered to be paid in kind because the alleged modus was void as too large.

2 Vesey Sen. 515, 28 E.R. 329

17 November 1687.

This was a Kentish cause. And the plaintiff demanded tithe in kind for marshland. The defendant alleged a *modus* or custom time out of mind to pay 12d. per acre for all marshland within the parish in lieu of all tithes. Proof was made of this payment for forty or fifty years. And, upon this and as there was no proof of payment of tithe in kind, a trial was prayed to be directed.

But the court denied the trial, and declared the pretended *modus* or custom to be void, as it was proved that the marshland was rented at so much per acre, that it was not possible nor could a reasonable intendment be made that the *modus* or custom time of mind could be. And, therefore, the court overruled the *modus*, and said that the court usually overruled a *modus* which seemed too great and which did not seem reasonable to the value.

[Lord Hardwicke:] But note this cause was reheard upon the defendant's motion, and the *modus* was sent to a trial at law by a Middlesex jury. But it does not appear what was done afterward.

[Other reports of this case: Eq. Cases Exch. 285.]

[1] Stat. 1 Jac. I, c. 17 (*SR*, IV, 1035).

62

Martin, qui tam v. Powell

(Ex. 1688)

A person who sells wine to be consumed on the premises must have a wine license.

Lincoln's Inn MS. Misc. 558, f. 17, pl. 2

Hilary term 3 & 4 Jac. II, 1687/88.

Upon an information for selling wine consumed in his mansion house in Canterbury without a license of the commissioners of the king for wine licenses, [it was] argued the first of February, and judgment [was given] for the king without better cause [shown]. And, afterwards, the same term, judgment [was given] for the king absolutely. And, afterwards, in the same term and in Easter and Trinity [terms] after, [there were] several judgments for the king upon the same point without formal argument.

I [*Edward Ward*] was in all [of them] for the king.

And the judgment was affirmed in a writ of error by the Commissioners [To Hold] the Great Seal by the advice of Holt and Pollexfen.

[Other copies of this report: Georgetown Univ. Law Sch. MS. B88–8, p. 115, pl. 2.]

Dodd 71

An information upon 12 Car., ch. 25, for selling wine without a license; the defendant pleads the Statute 7 Edw. VI, ch. 5,[1] that he is one of the four persons licensed in Canterbury and he has a license for keeping a tavern. And thus he justified selling wine in the tavern.

And the court, upon argument of *Ward*, for Martin, and *Randall*, for the defendant, adjudged that the power upon this Act is solely for selling wine outside of the house and not in the house, because there is an express clause in the Act against it. And they said that it had been thus adjudged before.

63

Hayne, qui tam v. Dagnall

(Ex. 1688)

The question in this case was whether an informer upon a penal statute must make an affidavit of the venue of the alleged offense.

[1] Stat. 12 Car. II, c. 25 (*SR*, V, 266–268); Stat. 7 Edw. VI, c. 5, s. 3 (*SR*, IV, 169).

Lincoln's Inn MS. Misc. 558, f. 17, pl. 3

Upon the Statute 4 Jac. I, ca. 6, for selling leather by weight, and upon the Statute 1 Jac. I, ca. 22, for buying and selling leather not made into made wares.[1]

Note an exception was taken that no affidavit was made that the offenses were made in the proper county where the information was laid, *viz.* the first in Hertfordshire, the second in London, according to the Statute 21 Jac. I, ca. 4.[2]

And the court was in doubt whether such an affidavit was necessary. But the plaintiff informer made an affidavit, and the trials proceeded.

Query the usage as to the courts at Westminster or whether this clause extends only to causes which can be tried before justices of the peace etc. in the country.

[Other copies of this report: Georgetown Univ. Law Sch. MS. B88–8, p. 116, pl. 1.]

64

Cottell v. Masters

(Ex. 1688)

An ecclesiastical court has jurisdiction to decide the right to a seat in a church where there are no common law questions involved.

Lincoln's Inn MS. Misc. 558, f. 18, pl. 1

Cottell and Roll and Dr. Masters *et al.*; prohibition.

The plaintiff having a fair estate in a vill called Marham Church in the County of Cornwall and not having any convenient seat in the church there suitable to his quality and there being a vacant space in the nave of the church, the plaintiff procured a certificate from the minister, church wardens, and several of the parishioners that no particular person had any particular right to this vacant space. And they gave their consent that the plaintiff could erect a seat there for the use of himself and his family, upon which the bishop of Exeter, the diocesan, by a writing under his episcopal seal gave a license to the plaintiff to erect a seat there. And the seat thus erected, the bishop, by his episcopal authority, confirmed to the plaintiff and the occupiers of his house there called Rattenbury *in perpetuum* to be enjoyed always quietly, by virtue of which instrument and in pursuance of it, the plaintiff at his own charges erected the seat, and he sat there for a year.

And, afterwards, upon the promotion of Sir John Roll and others before the Chancellor of the same bishop who granted the faculty, a suit was prosecuted to revoke the faculty as unduly obtained.

---

[1] Stat. 4 Jac. I, c. 6 (*SR*, IV, 1143); Stat. 1 Jac. I, c. 22 (*SR*, IV, 1039–1048).

[2] Stat. 21 Jac. I, c. 4 (*SR*, IV, 1214–1215).

And, upon this, the plaintiff prayed a [writ of] prohibition. And he had a rule for it the last term and to stay in the meantime.

But this day, upon the hearing of the counsel of both parts, the court discharged the rule, denying any prohibition upon the ground that the matter is purely and solely examinable and determinable in the spiritual court and that no title appears at common law, which is solely by prescription, as appurtenant to the ancient house time of which [memory does not run] and in the repairing of it, none of which were in this case.

And though I [*Edward Ward*] objected that this was a faculty, if it gives an interest to the plaintiff, it cannot be recalled, and, if it was only an authority in the bishop *disponere sedes in nave ecclesiae* and he, by this faculty, had executed this authority, by this reason also, it was not revocable.

But the court held as *supra* and declared that they would not hinder the bishop to proceed as it pleased him in this case of which the temporal court did not have any jurisdiction by prescription for repairs or otherwise.

I [*Edward Ward* was] for the plaintiff.

[Other copies of this report: Georgetown Univ. Law Sch. MS. B88–8, p. 118.]

65

Attorney General v. Smith

(Ex. 1688)

A writ of diem clausit extremum will not be issued before a mortuus be returned upon an antecedent writ.

Lincoln's Inn MS. Misc. 558, f. 19, pl. 2

In a case of a debt in aid, the defendant Jonas Smith with others were bound to the king as farmers of the hearth money[1] divers years past. And Hanscomb, who was bound and partner with them for security of a debt due to him in the name of Hackshaw, prosecuted a *diem clausit extremum* against the executors of Smith upon oath that he was dead and greatly incumbered, as he heard and believed. And, upon a motion, this writ of *diem clausit extremum* was awarded against the executors and heirs of Smith without cause such a day.

And, for the executors, I [*Edward Ward*] moved that the affidavit was uncertain and concluded nothing.

And, inasmuch as there was not a *mortuus* returned upon an antecedent writ, though an oath was made of the death, the court refused to grant the *diem clausit extremum, quod nota*.

[Other copies of this report: Georgetown Univ. Law Sch. MS. B88–8, p. 120.]

---

[1] Stat. 14 Car. II, c. 10 (*SR*, V, 390–393); Stat. 15 Car. II, c. 13 (*SR*, V, 493–495).

66

Heber v. Meadows

(Ex. 1688)

Calf skins that were not well tanned cannot be seized as forfeited under the statute unless they are made into wares.

Lincoln's Inn MS. Misc. 558, f. 19, pl. 3

[There was an action of] trespass for taking and carrying away calf skins and a justification upon the Statute 1 Jac. I, ca. 22,[1] where the question was whether the Curriers' Company had the power to seize calf skins and dispose of them by reason that they were not well curried, and the action [*blank*].

[Other copies of this report: Georgetown Univ. Law Sch. MS. B88–8, p. 121.]

Lincoln's Inn MS. Misc. 558, f. 48, pl. 1

In [an action of] trespass, upon a demurrer, *in Officio Placitorum Scaccarii.*

In this case, it was adjudged by the three barons against the opinion of the Chief Baron [Atkyns] that the Master and Wardens of the Curriers' Company did not have power to search and seize calf skins or any unwrought leather under the pretense that it is not sufficiently tanned or curried under the Statute of 1 Jac. I, ca. 22, but that their power to search, to seize, and to sell goes only to boots, shoes, and other made wares.

And judgment was [given] for the plaintiff, and the defendants' justification was ruled not good.

I [*Edward Ward* was] for the plaintiff.

And afterwards, in 1689, this judgment was affirmed in a writ of error.

[Other copies of this report: Georgetown Univ. Law Sch. MS. B88–8, p. 191.]

Dodd 73

[In an action] in trespass, the defendants justified as master and wardens of [*blank*] upon the Statute of 1 Jac. I, ch. 22, sect. 29,[2] etc. The point was that the plaintiff had calf skins not well tanned and the defendants seized them.

[It was] adjudged by the three puisne [barons] against the Chief Baron [Atkyns] that he [sic] could not unless [they were] made into wares. But the Chief Baron [Atkyns held] *contra.*

---

[1] Stat. 1 Jac. I, c. 22 (*SR*, IV, 1039–1048).

[2] Stat. 1 Jac. I, c. 22, s. 29 (*SR*, IV, 1044).

67

Bates, qui tam v. Barret

(Ex. 1688)

An import and export merchant is liable for the errors and omissions of his brokers and agents.

Lincoln's Inn MS. Misc. 558, f. 19, pl. 5

[The case was] upon the Statute of 12 Car. II, ca. 11, against frauds for shipping out less than was expressed and contained in his certificate.[1]

Note the defendant obtained a certificate for the exportation of 21,000 pounds weight of tobacco imported in April last in 125 hogsheads bought of Starke. And he endorsed his contents of sixty of these hogsheads to be 20,696 pounds, part of the 21,000 pounds, and the sixty hogsheads were put in a lighter to be carried to shipboard, in which lighter, they were seized inasmuch as the contents of the sixty hogsheads upon weight were only 20,395 pounds without allowance also for 4 pounds weight for the draught of each hogshead inwards allowed to the merchant importer and 195 for damaged tobacco, which damaged tobacco was not within the information.

And, even though it was proved by the oath of the defendant's broker, Jills, that the mistake of the quantity of the sixty hogsheads was only and merely by the fault of Jills and not by the defendant's fault nor known to him and that Jills and not the defendant managed the entire matter and the defendant gave direction to Jills not to prejudice the king and Jills swore that the mistake was in the 300 weight by the involuntary mistake of him in the figures endorsed without the privity of the defendant and the words of the Act are fraudulently to ship out less in quantity than is contained in the certificate and though defendant's counsel alleged the mistake of the defendant's agent cannot conclude the defendant to be guilty of fraud, yet it was declared by the Chief Baron [ATKYNS] that the mistake of the defendant's agent and broker was the same thing as if the matter had been managed by the defendant and the defendant is liable for it.

The jury found the defendant guilty, by which the goods to the value of £600 were forfeited and the benefit of the drawback was lost.

But it was referred to the Chief Baron [ATKYNS] to moderate as it pleased him, who seemed perturbed for the defendant, notwithstanding his direction. And he recommended the matter to the Commissioners of the Customs and reserved the power to reduce the penalty as he pleases.

I [*Edward Ward* was] for the plaintiff.

See above, 13, 14.[2]

---

[1] Stat. 14 Car. II, c. 11 (*SR*, V, 393–400).

[2] *LeNeve, qui tam v. Cox* (Ex. 1687), see above, Case No. 57.

And, afterwards, upon the mediation of the Chief Baron [Atkyns], the defendant, upon the payment of £80 to the informer for costs, was admitted to the composition for a small sum, and he had the benefit of his debentures for drawing back.

[Other copies of this report: Georgetown Univ. Law Sch. MS. B88–8, p. 123.]

68

Deering v. Firebrace

(Ex. 1688)

A bond to save harmless from another bond for the payment of money is not a counterbond, but it is a bond for the payment of money.

A court can order a mistake in the record made by a clerk of court to be amended.

Lincoln's Inn MS. Misc. 558, f. 20

Sir Henry Deering v. Sir Basil Firebrass; touching a debt in aid.

The case was thus. Both of the parties were debtors to the king, the said Sir Henry Deering as farmer and manager of the revenue of the wine licenses and the defendant by a bond to the Custom House for duties of wines. And one Finch, deceased, a merchant, was indebted to Sir Henry Deering by a bond in £6000 and more for the payment of £3000 or £4000 real money and debt, and he was also bound by a bond to Sir Basil Firebrace [1652–1724] to save him harmless from such bonds and debts in certain and mentioning which, for which he was bound for the said Finch.

Finch died. Sir Basil Firebrace prosecuted the executrix upon an extent which seized those counterbonds into the hands of the king in aid of Sir Basil Firebrace, after which Sir Henry Deering procured his bond, in which Finch was bound to him, to be seized into the hands of the king, and he prosecuted a *scire facias* against the executrix. And he prayed that the proceedings for Sir Basil Firebrace will be stayed inasmuch as, by the Rules of the Court 1639, no extent or seizure in aid will be [had] upon a counterbond to save harmless or a bond for the performance of covenants. And, in truth, the rules are to the same purpose.

But the court, upon an oath made that Sir Basil Firebrace had paid such a sum upon the bonds in which he was bound as a surety for Finch and did not have any satisfaction for the money so paid, refused to stay the proceedings, holding that such a bond to save harmless from another bond for the payment of money is not such a counterbond that is within the Rules in 1639, but it is in a similar nature as a bond for the payment of money, *quod nota et quaere*.

Upon which, I [*Edward Ward*] moved that the seizure of the counterbond into the hands of the king was not good inasmuch as the extent upon which the inquisition that found and seized this counterbond was returnable *tres Michaelis* and the inquisition was returned to be taken the 29th of October, which was six days after the return of the writ. And, in truth, the inquisition returned was so.

But, upon an oath made that the original inquisition found by the jury and subscribed with their hands was the 19th and not the 29th of October and so before the return and upon the production of this original and that it was only a mistake of the clerk, the court ordered it to be amended. And it was amended accordingly. But before this amendment was made, the parties agreed between themselves.

I [*Edward Ward* was] for Sir Henry Deering.

[Other copies of this report: Georgetown Univ. Law Sch. MS. B88–8, p. 124.]

69

Queen Dowager v. Earl of Clarendon

(Ex. 1688)

The issue in this case was whether the agents of the queen dowager could declare accounts in the Exchequer.

Dodd 75

The commissioners of the queen dowager's council board caused the deputy auditor of her Majesty to make up my Lord Clarendon's account, who was receiver general to her Majesty and direct him to receive and remit into the treasurer's remembrancer's office a *super* of the account. And thereupon a *scire facias* (as upon a record) issues to show cause *quare non solveret*, upon which the earl demurs in abatement for that it is no sufficient record to charge him. And [it was] argued by Levinz for the earl and afterwards by Lechmere, Winnington, and Ward for the earl and by Attorney General Powys, Solicitor [General] Williams, and others for the queen etc.

For the earl, [it was argued] by *Ward* that the queen's council [are] not officers of this court; the writ [is] not well founded; the *constat* [was] made by the deputy auditor, and he [is] no officer of the court.

The auditors of the court are first the two auditors of the imprest and the seven auditors of the revenue by 27 Hen. VIII, ch. 27,[1] and these yet continue auditors although the fee farm rents are sold. The articles and usage is for an accountant to swear his accounts and the auditor delivers them signed by the chancellor and barons or one of them and then process goes. All receivers' accounts [are] sworn to and declared before a baron and then, and not before, process [issues]. The auditor is but the baron's clerk. 4 Inst. 106.[2] And the baron is really

[1] Stat. 27 Hen. VIII, c. 27 (*SR*, III, 569–574).

[2] E. Coke, *Fourth Institute* (1644), p. 106.

the auditor. The course of the Exchequer is that no one officer can charge or discharge alone for foreign accounts. See 14 Car. II, ch. 21[1]: of lands seized by extent and inquisition or outlawry.

This account consists of several items *in pones* and not for estates that stand in charge upon record in this court as part of the revenue.

The king's auditor could never make any *constat* for process but upon accounts declared before a baron or debts standing upon record. The queen in all things has not the same prerogative as the king. A bond to her must be sued as other bonds. The statutes 5 Ric. II, ch. 9; 33 Hen. VIII, 39; 34 & 35 Hen. VIII, ch. 2; 7 Edw. VI, 1; 13 Eliz., 4, are all for getting in the king's debts.[2]

The queen [is] not within [the Statute] 33 Hen. VIII for remedy or relief. Bonds to her do not affect the real estate.

The king can have but a [writ of] *distringas ad compotum* or may sue by information. There are precedents *quod domina regina queritur.* 20 Edw. III, rot. 1; 27 Edw. III.

If the auditor had undercharged my Lord Clarendon, it would not have been a discharge for him against the queen. Thus here. The estreats of the justices are by 3 Edw. I, 45; 9 Edw. III, 5; 14 Ric. II, 11; 13 Eliz. 9, for sewers.[3] Transcript of an outlawry by the attorney general's clerk no objection for the office of record, the seizure of record before and the proceedings all of record, and this only to award a [writ of] *levari* [*facias*].

Lincoln's Inn MS. Misc. 558, f. 21

20, 21, and 22 February 1687[/88]. Earl of Clarendon v. Queen Dowager.

The case was touching an account with the queen dowager and an amendment of a *scire facias* after *scire feci* returned and filed in another term.

Henry, earl of Clarendon,[4] having been Treasurer and Receiver General to Queen Catherine for a year ended at Michaelmas 1685, part of which year was when she was the consort to King Charles II and another part of which when she was queen dowager, and for divers years before, but after the discharge from this office, his account for the said year was made by William Aldworthy, the deputy auditor of the queen dowager and declared by the lords and others of the Council of the said queen, in which declaration, divers allowances usually made to his predecessors and himself, as for New Year's gifts, poundage, etc., were denied

---

[1] Stat. 14 Car. II, c. 21 (*SR*, V, 414–416).

[2] Stat. 5 Ric. II, stat. 1, c. 9 (*SR*, II, 21); Stat. 33 Hen. VIII, c. 39 (*SR*, III, 879–892); Stat. 34 & 35 Hen. VIII, c. 2 (*SR*, III, 898–899); Stat. 7 Edw. VI, c. 1 (*SR*, IV, 161–164); Stat. 13 Eliz. I, c. 4 (*SR*, IV, 535–537).

[3] Stat. 3 Edw. I, c. 45 (*SR*, I, 37–38); Stat. 9 Edw. III, stat. 1, c. 5 (*SR*, I, 272); Stat. 14 Ric. II, c. 11 (*SR*, II, 77); Stat. 13 Eliz. I, c. 9 (*SR*, IV, 543–544).

[4] W. A. Speck, 'Hyde, Henry, second earl of Clarendon (1638–1709)', *Oxford Dictionary of National Biography*, vol. 29, pp. 140–144.

to be made to him in this account, for the reason of which disallowance, he became a debtor to the queen for £4000 and odd pounds. And inasmuch as these allowances were denied, he disapproved of the said account and did not sign it, which sum with £2000 and odd pounds further, which he admitted to be due to the queen and which, after this account was declared, he paid to the use of the queen, making £6998 5s. 5d. in total, was returned *in super* for the said account upon the said earl. And, in order to have this *super* levied and recovered against the said earl by the prerogative process made in such cases for the king, the said deputy auditor, that is to say William Aldworth, delivered into the Treasurer's Remembrancer's Office in this Court a writing in English signed with his own hand of the effect following.

In the declaration of the account of the Rt. Hon. Henry, earl of Clarendon, late Treasurer and Receiver General to Her Majesty the queen dowager for one year ended at the feast of St. Michael, the archangel, in the first year of the reign of his now Majesty, King James II *Annoque Domini* 1685, amongst other things, is contained as follows, *viz.* upon the said earl himself for so much remaining in His Lordship's hands at the end and determination of the above mentioned account due and payable to Her said Majesty the sum of £6998 5s. 5d., I have made forth this *constat* by order of the right honorable the lords and others of Her Majesty's said Council, bearing date the 9th of May 1687, 22 May 1687, estreated by W. Aldworth, Lord Auditor of the lady queen dowager of England.

Upon which, a writ of *scire facias* issued out of the Treasurer's Remembrancer's Office directed to the sheriff of Berkshire reciting *quod cum* the said earl was indebted to the said queen dowager in the said £6998 5s. 5d. *pro tantis denariis in manibus eiusdem comitatis remanen' super determinationem compoti sui* for the aforesaid year *prout in declarationem compoti eiusdem comitis* for the said year *plenius patet*, the sheriff was commanded *scire facere* to the said earl to be before the Barons of the Exchequer *mensem Michaelis proxime* to show *quare ipse praedictum summam* £998 5s. 5d., omitting the £6000, *eidem domine regine solvere et satisfacere non debet.*

And this writ not being returned into the office until after the end of Michaelmas term, a motion was made by the counsel of the earl at the setting down of causes after this term for time to plead or say anything against the said writ until the first day of this Hilary term, which was granted accordingly, at which time and divers times after the same term, it was moved by the counsel of the earl that this writ should be quashed being *primae impressionae* and without precedent and not grounded upon any record of this court, because there is not anything to warrant it except this English certificate of the deputy auditor and it is not any record, not being in Latin, nor made by any officer of this court nor any account in the office to warrant it, because, in truth, the account itself remained with the council of the queen and never was sent into this court. And nothing was urged for the earl against the method and legality of this proceeding. And it was touched [upon] and insisted that neither the queen for herself if she was a consort, *a fortiori* being only a dowager, nor the king for the queen had such a prerogative to charge the earl in this case with the said pretended debt and to make his person and estate liable for it as if it was in the case of the king.

But the court, upon the hearing of counsel of both parts several day did not think it reasonable to quash this writ upon a motion only, but allowed the earl time to plead or to demur to this writ as he will be advised until the first day of the next term.

And because the reason, precedents, and authorities urged on both sides upon this debate were for the most part the same that were urged in the argument upon the plea and demurrer after and coming more aptly at this time to be reported, I omit them here.

But note that after the time given by the court to plead or demur to this writ, the counsel for the queen spied the said omission of £6000 in the said *scire facias*, and, on account of that, he moved to have it amended by the court, being, as they alleged, merely the fault and omission of the clerk and the writ would be sufficient if the sum in this case had been totally omitted, being mentioned before.

But this amendment was opposed by the counsel of the earl, the sheriff having returned that he *scire fecit* to the said earl *prout interius sibi praescripebatur.* And this was to show cause *quare* the said earl should not pay the said sum of £998 5s. 5d., and, on account of this, the writ is totally insufficient. And by the amending of the writ, the return of the sheriff was altered and falsified, because, in truth, he never *scire fecit* to the earl to show cause *quare* he should not pay the said £6998 5s. 5d. And to amend the writ that falsifies the return of it cannot be.

But the court ordered the amendment, and it was amended accordingly.

I [*Edward Ward* was] for the earl.

[Other copies of this report: Georgetown Univ. Law Sch. MS. B88–8, p. 126.]

70

Nash, qui tam v. Potter

(Ex. 1688)

Tobacco stalks are tobacco for the purposes of the revenue Statute 14 Car. II, c. 11.

Lincoln's Inn MS. Misc. 558, f. 24, pl. 2

Easter [term] 1688. By an information touching tobacco stalks imported from Holland; entered Michaelmas [term] 2 Jac. II [1686] ex parte Rememeratoris Regis Scaccario.

In a special verdict upon a seizure of a parcel of tobacco stalks imported from the Netherlands, the jury found the clause in the Act against Frauds in the

Customs, 14 Car. II, ca. 11,[1] by which it was enacted that no sorts of tobacco, *inter alia*, be imported from the Netherlands or Germany upon any pretense whatsoever under forfeiture of ship and goods. And the doubt of the jury was whether the tobacco stalks imported are tobacco within this clause or not. If it is, then [they find] for the plaintiff; if not, then for the defendants.

And, by all of the court, upon the first argument, judgment was given for the plaintiff that tobacco stalks are tobacco within this clause upon the ground that, it being a restraining law, it is to be liberally interpreted to restrain all things within the mischief of it, that tobacco stalks are being (as it was urged but not found) put to the same use that tobaccos are, that is to say smoked in pipes, and, because the stalks of tobaccos are part of the tobacco usually imported, and the stalks and leaves are the substance of tobacco, and the stalk is a sort of tobacco and the leaf another sort, notwithstanding that it was argued and objected by me [*Edward Ward*], for the defendants, that tobacco stalks, generally speaking, are not tobacco but distinguished in stalks, and a contract for such a quantity of tobacco is not satisfied with stalks, and the words of the Act are general, that is to say 'tobacco' and, if tobacco stalks, generally speaking, are not tobaccos, then stalks are not within the Act, and the duty given to the king upon importation is under the general denomination of tobacco without any addition or denomination, and, if a man imports a parcel of tobacco stalks, they will not pay the duty of tobacco, and, if the duty of tobacco will be paid for them, they will withdraw the duty upon exportation as tobaccos, and the word 'tobacco' is here general in the Act of Frauds and means the same thing as the word tobacco in the Book of Rates,[2] and, if tobacco stalks are tobacco upon importing, they are tobacco upon exporting, and, if not tobacco upon exporting, they are not tobacco upon importing from the Netherlands, and it seems to me the stalks of tobacco are no more tobacco than the stalks of beans are beans when the cods are avelled or wheat straw is wheat when threshed. Also, I objected the custom at the Custom House not to allow repayments for tobacco stalks upon exportation. And [it was] so ruled in Trinity term 1682 between Beauvoir and Charlton, *qui tam versus* Alderman Booth,[3] where repayment for tobacco stalks was not only denied but adjudged to be forfeited for shipping out less in value than was contained in the certificate, the certificate in this case being tobacco and the thing shipped out stalks. And it is plain that the king has a duty for stalks with the leaves when imported and the drawback is proportional to the duty inwards. And repayments are for the encouragement of importation. And, by the same reason that the stalks do not draw back, the leaves severed from the stalks will not draw back, which would be against reason and justice. And, if tobacco stalks are not tobacco

---

1 Stat. 14 Car. II, c. 11 (*SR*, V, 393–400).

2 Stat. 12 Car. II, c. 4, app. (*SR*, V, 184–205).

3 *Beauvoir, qui tam v. Booth* (Ex. 1682), Exch. Cases *tempore* Car. II, p. 520.

to draw back, they are not tobacco at all, and, if not tobacco, then it is not within this Act against Frauds.

And, as to the objection that the word in this Act is no sort of tobacco and the stalks are a sort of tobacco, I [*Edward Ward*] responded and observed that this word 'sort' is to be understood in such a case to the intent to include all sorts of tobaccos, as Spanish, Virginia, Barbados, etc. and not to distinguish between stalks and leaves.

But, notwithstanding, judgment was [given] for the king and the informer.

It is notable that the duty upon tobaccos is by the weight and certainly the stalks of tobacco contribute to the weight, and it is reasonable and within the intention of the acts which give a benefit of a drawback upon exportation that allowance of it will be made for the thing imported.

[Other copies of this report: Georgetown Univ. Law Sch. MS. B88–8, p. 133.]

71

Nelms, qui tam v. Spooner

(Ex. 1688)

A judge can allow an amendment in order to substitute the correct plaintiff's name.

Lincoln's Inn MS. Misc. 558, f. 25, pl. 2

19 May.

The plaintiff seized a ship at Yarmouth in December under the pretense that it was forfeited for having wool aboard to be transported with the privity of the owners. And the ship, being ready for the voyage, gave a bond to the plaintiff entered in the name of the king to answer for the value if it be condemned. And, afterwards, the ship returned in February, and the plaintiff seized it again and procured an appraisal and exhibited his information. And the defendant, claiming ownership, entered his plea.

And the court refused a writ of delivery if the plaintiff will try the cause this term though it was in a case of a ship and it was bound by a charter party to the voyage immediately.

And, afterwards, the plaintiff declared that he will not try the cause but that the defendant could have a writ of delivery. But he moved that the name of Nelms could be struck out of the information and proceedings and the name of another person, *viz.* one Bathurst, inserted in the place of Nelms, who he said was the true seizer and he was only a witness, which motion was made without notice.

But it was opposed by myself [*Edward Ward*] as a strange and unreasonable thing and so urged.

But the court, without giving any reason, ordered it to be done accordingly, *quod nota et quaere*, even though it could be by law, because it is not any amendment but a new information, because the first was the information of Nelms, but, now, it is the information of another, which are two distinct informations.

And, afterwards, the defendant was aided.

[Other copies of this report: Georgetown Univ. Law Sch. MS. B88–8, p. 136.]

72

Herne, qui tam v. Trinquand

(Ex. 1688)

Imperial size paper pays the same import duties as royal size paper.

Lincoln's Inn MS. Misc. 558, f. 26, pl. 1

The plaintiff seized a parcel of paper commonly called and known by the name of imperial paper as forfeited for the nonpayment of the duty *ad valorem*, not being any of the sorts of paper rated by the Book of Rates[1] and, on account of this, as thought, it should pay *ad valorem*, according to the clause in the end of the Book of Rates for this purpose, the sorts of paper there enumerated not extending to this sort in words, but the next to it was royal paper, which pays 12d. per pound. And this duty was paid as royal pays for the paper in question.

And it was argued in this case that the paper in question was worth 55s. or £3 per ream, which is double the value of royal paper.

But, upon proof by the defendant that this sort of imperial paper had been imported for more than forty years and that it had paid duty only as royal paper and that some royal paper is not worth more than 10s. per ream and some imperial paper is not worth more than 15s. per ream and that some royal paper not for printing pays less than 12d. per pound and that the word 'royal' includes royal, superroyal, and imperial or imparoyal, as the defendant's counsel said, the jury gave a verdict for the defendant.

The Attorney General [*Powys*] and I [*Edward Ward* were] for the plaintiff; *Sir Robert Sawyer* and others were for the defendants. And this trial was only to settle the question and duty.

[Other copies of this report: Georgetown Univ. Law Sch. MS. B88–8, p. 139.]

[1] Stat. 12 Car. II, c. 4, app. (*SR*, V, 184–205).

73

Hutchest v. Packe

(Ex. 1688)

In an action for defamation, an allegation of foreswearing is a allegation of perjury.

Lincoln's Inn MS. Misc. 558, f. 32, pl. 1

Trinity 1688; [an action] in slander.

The plaintiff brought an action for these words, 'Charles Hutchest is an old foresworn rogue, and foreswore himself at the Lord Mayor's Sessions held the 27th of June last, and he foamed at the mouth when he took his oath.'

And the verdict [was] for the plaintiff and damages £5.

And, in arrest [of judgment], it was moved that the action did not lie, inasmuch as it was not shown what court the Lord Mayor's Sessions was, nor that such a court was held, and, on account of this, to say on one hand generally that he is forsworn is not actionable if it is not shown that he was forsworn in a court that had power to administer an oath, which is not here. And 'Lord Mayor's Sessions' without saying which lord mayor or which sessions or averring such sessions were held is utterly uncertain. And the difference is between the manner of the expressions forsworn and perjured; the latter word implies perjury in a proper court. The first could be in common communication. And, on account of this, it is necessary to be shown to be in a court. And, for this, [see] the authorities of Marche's rep., fo. 7; 2 Leon. 98, Cro. El. 168; and several authorities in Roll's Abridgment, *action sur le case*, fo. 40, etc.[1]

But, for the plaintiff, it was answered that, necessarily, it must be understood that the foreswearing must be in this case in a court and in the manner of administering oaths, inasmuch as it is said he foamed at the mouth when he took his oath, so that it is not to be understood to be foreswearing in a common communication because it is not said a taking an oath.

And of this opinion was the entire court. And the plaintiff had judgment.

See Roll's Abridgment, *action sur le case*, 40, Gilbertin and Row, 1 Car.; and Shaw and Thompson, 40 Eliz.[2]

I [*Edward Ward* was] for the plaintiff.

[Other copies of this report: Georgetown Univ. Law Sch. MS. B88–8, p. 149.]

---

[1] *Smith v. Anonymous* (1598), March 7, 82 E.R. 387; *Rymersly v. Cooper* (1589–1590), 2 Leonard 98, 74 E.R. 389, Croke Eliz. 168, 78 E.R. 426; *Gilbertine v. Rowe* (1625), 1 Rolle, Abr., *Action sur Case*, pl. F, 8, p. 40.

[2] *Shaw v. Tompson* (1598), Croke Eliz. 609, 78 E.R. 851.

74

Rogers, qui tam v. Ingram

(Ex. 1688–1689)

Cloth made partly of English wool must pay aulnage duty proportional to the amount of the English wool.

Lincoln's Inn MS. Misc. 558, f. 38, pl. 1

5 July. Rogers, Deputy Aulnager, *qui tam* v. Ingram upon a seizure of hats called felts in Warwickshire for being exposed for sale before the subsidy of aulnage was paid.

The question upon the trial was whether felts made partly of English wool and partly of cony wool, Spanish wool, etc. will be liable to the payment of the subsidy of aulnage in a proportional manner for the English wool in them or not.

And it seemed to the Chief Baron [Atkyns], before whom the trial was, that they are upon the same reason as Bewdly caps, crepes, stockings, linsey woolsey, Norwich stuffs mixed with silk or hair are, all which have been decreed in this court. And the duty is not strictly confined to clothes, though all garments are clothing. And there was a probable evidence given that the fourth or sixth part of the materials that made the felts were English wool.

But the jury gave a verdict for the defendant for lack of sufficient evidence that English wool was used in the making of these felts.

After which verdict, the defendant prosecuted an action of trespass *quare* the plaintiff Rogers *vi et armis* broke into his house at Alchester, Warwickshire, and entered and took away the felts and the linings of them to such a number and value etc. to the damage of £40.

And the court, upon motion, removed the action and changed the venue and bound the plaintiff in it to lay his action at Westminster in the County of Middlesex, though the cause of it arose in Warwickshire and notwithstanding that the breach and entry of the house was local and also notwithstanding that the action was against the officer who seized and the constable who assisted, and by the Statute [*blank*],[1] in such a case, the action is directed to be laid in the proper county; otherwise, the defendants would be found not guilty, the court directing that the defendants in the action should not take advantage of it. *Quaere de ceo.*

I [*Edward Ward* was] for the officers.

But afterwards, in 1689, the court discharged the order for laying the venue in Middlesex, and the plaintiff tried his action in Warwickshire, and he recovered his damages for more than the value of the hats.

[Other copies of this report: Georgetown Univ. Law Sch. MS. B88–8, p. 169.]

---

[1] Stat. 21 Jac. I, c. 4 (*SR*, IV, 1214–1215).

75

Gwyn's Case

(Ex. 1688)

Bevan and Jevons are not idem sonans, but are different names.

A return by commissioners will be quashed for a misnomer of the commissioners.

Lincoln's Inn MS. Misc. 558, f. 47

Sir Rowland Gwyn, being nominated sheriff of the County of Brecon in Wales and being in Holland, did not take upon himself the office nor was any commission sued out for him. And, notwithstanding this, Serjeant Wynne and Serjeant Geers, judges in Wales at the [Court of] Great Sessions held for this county, imposed a fine of £3000 upon him for non-attending this office though he never had any commission nor was he sworn into it. And this fine was estreated into the Exchequer. And process was issued for the levying of it of his goods and chattels, which the sheriff levied on the tenants' goods, which was a mistake and rectified.

And, in April 1688, Sir Rowland was served in Holland with a [writ of] privy seal to return into England within fourteen days after service, he having worked in Holland with the license of the king.

And, upon an oath made before a Master of the Chancery of this service the 24 July last, the 26th of the same July upon an allegation made in Chancery by the Attorney General [Powys] that he was not returned, a writ issued out of the Petty Bag [Office] directed to the Barons of the Exchequer to seize his lands etc. into the hands of the king *ita quod* the king will be answered for the issues and profits of them, upon which a commission issued out of the Office of the King's Remembrancer in the Exchequer directed to Anthony Gwyn, Charles Bevan, William Thomas, David Thomas, Edward Carne, and William Basset, or any of them or several of them to enquire and seize the lands of Sir Rowland that he had in divers counties in Wales enumerated in this commission. Upon which commission, William Thomas and Charles Jevans made a return of the seizure of divers lands in these counties. And this commission and return were filed in the Exchequer.

And I [*Edward Ward*], for Sir Rowland Gwyn's creditors and mortgagees, who were held to plead a superior title to the contempt and seizure, moved to quash this return and to stay the issuing of all process upon it because the return was not made by two of the commissioners, but, in truth, only by one, *scil.* by William Thomas, because Charles Bevan in the commission and Charles Jevons in the return cannot be understood to be the same person but separate, Bevan and Jevans being district names, as well in Wales as in England.

And of such opinion the entire court thought, and stayed all proceedings until further order.

And note, in the first part of the case, it seemed to be a great mistake in the judges to impose a fine upon Sir Rowland for not attending the Great Sessions as sheriff, as, in truth, he was not the sheriff. But, if Sir Rowland had been convicted upon an information for not taking upon himself the office of sheriff, being duly nominated and appointed to it and having notice of it, the court, before there was such a conviction, could have imposed a fine upon him for this neglect, as was done in Sir John Read's Case, which see among my arguments.[1]

[Other copies of this report: Georgetown Univ. Law Sch. MS. B88–8, p. 189.]

76

Fremoult, qui tam v. Curtis

(Ex. 1688)

In this case, the defendant was convicted of intending to violate a penal statute.

Lincoln's Inn MS. Misc. 558, f. 48, pl. 2

Upon an information of seizure of wool lying in a house near the shore or coast of the sea with intent to transport it beyond the sea, the case upon the trial was that the defendant, having purchased the wool, laid it in a house of his brother-in-law in Wilsborow [Kent] a mile and a half distant from Ashford, where the defendant lived and exercised the trade of woolen draper. And, in truth, Wilsborow is distant from the next part of the sea ten miles. And the wool had been packed for land carriage, but not for transportation. And it was not combed, but in the fleece. And when it came to Wilsborow, it was unpacked and lay loose and the packing clothes lying by when the seizure was made.

And no evidence was given of any intention to transport it, nor was the defendant any person who ever transported wool.

And, because the defendant did not give any account of what became of the other part of the wool that was laid at the same house, Baron LECHMERE thought it presumable, and the jury without any evidence presumed, that this wool so seized was intended to be transported, though I [*Edward Ward*] for the defendant, strongly insisted that, without any evidence, the defendant cannot be thought guilty. And it is against law, especially upon a penal statute,[2] which this in question is, to forfeit any person's goods by a presumption. Also, I insisted that the defendant was not guilty upon this information for laying the wool next to the seacoast or shore, it being ten miles distant.

---

[1] *Attorney General v. Read* (Ex. 1671), Exch. Cases *tempore* Car. II, 229, also *Attorney General v. Read* (Ex. 1676), 1 Freeman 327, 89 E.R. 242, 2 Modern 299, 86 E.R. 1083, Dodd 256.

[2] Stat. 14 Car. II, c. 18 (*SR*, V, 410–412); Stat. 1 Will. & Mar., c. 32 (*SR*, VI, 86–98).

But the Chief Baron [Atkyns] overruled this also, saying that, if it was more distant, if there was an intention to transport the wool, it is within this clause, notwithstanding that I [*Edward Ward*] objected the inconvenience that could ensue to all persons having wool and living in a maritime county if such a construction and presumption should prevail. And it seems to me [*Edward Ward*] to be a hard case and against law.

[Other copies of this report: Georgetown Univ. Law Sch. MS. B88–8, p. 192.]

77

Kinvin, qui tam v. Biggs

(Ex. 1688)

Molasses are sugar, and not a product manufactured from sugar.

Lincoln's Inn MS. Misc. 558, f. 49, pl. 1

In this case upon an information, upon a trial, the question was whether molasses drawn and made in France out of sugars imported into France out of the French plantations in America can be imported into England in any ships or are totally restrained by the clause in the Act for Navigation, 12 Car. II, ca. 18,[1] which makes a forfeiture of all goods imported into England from any place not being the place of growth, production, or manufacture nor where they were or could be first shipped for navigation.

And it was held that they were so restrained by this Statute. And [there was a] verdict accordingly for the plaintiff and the king. And the reason seemed [to be] that these molasses are part of the sugars and they were thus part in America and, without doubt, French sugars, that is to say sugars of the French plantations in America, cannot be imported into England from France, France not being the place of growth, production, manufacturing, or first shipping of them. And the molasses, as to this Act, are of the same nature with the sugars out of which the molasses were extracted. And, of account of this, if the molasses are not restrained, the sugars themselves that were refined will be pretended not to be restrained also.

I [*Edward Ward* was] for the plaintiff.

[Other copies of this report: Georgetown Univ. Law Sch. MS. B88–8, p. 193.]

---

[1] Stat. 12 Car. II, c. 18 (*SR*, V, 246–250).

78

Samon v. Jones

(Ex. 1688)

The issue in this case was whether the grant in issue would operate as a covenant to stand seised.

Dodd 72

Upon a special verdict upon a deed by A. in which he gives, grants, bargains, and sells a reversion to Robert, his son, and his heirs, *habendum* to him and his heirs to the uses following, *viz.* to himself for life, remainder to his wife during the minority of Robert for the maintenance of the younger children and afterwards to R[obert] in tail with warranty and covenants that Robert and his heirs shall enjoy etc.

Ward [argued] that it amounts to a covenant to stand seised and the habendum [is] void. See Beddell's Case; Crossing and Scudamore's Case; and Trinity [term] 28 Car. [1676] in the Exchequer, Walker and Hale,[1] in consideration of a contract of marriage, he gives, grants, enfeoffs, and confirms to Margaret, the intended wife, and her heirs to the uses following viz. etc. and a letter of attorney in the deed but a blank for the attorney's name and a memorandum of the livery made with blanks. Yet [it was] adjudged a covenant to stand seised. See Rolle's [Abr.], Uses, 786, 787, and it is not a use upon a use; see Sid. 25, 82.[2]

Winnington, contra: The question is not whether [there was] an intention to give the land but whether to make this conveyance. The court upon current authorities have construed covenants to stand seised upon implied considerations but not upon express considerations as where money is mentioned; this is not ever intended to be a covenant to stand seised because he intends the uses to arise out of the legal estate. Sid. 25; Plow. Qr. 305; 2 Cr. 127.[3]

Adjornatur.

---

[1] *Bedell's Case* (1607), 7 Coke Rep. 40, 77 E.R. 470; *Crossing v. Scudamore* (1671), 1 Ventris 137, 86 E.R. 94, 1 Modern 175, 86 E.R. 810, 1 Freeman 368, 89 E.R. 274, 2 Levinz 9, 83 E.R. 428, 2 Keble 754, 784, 84 E.R. 476, 495, Lincoln's Inn MS. Misc. 500, ff. 149, 155; *Walker v. Hall* (1677), 2 Levinz 213, 83 E.R. 524.

[2] 2 Rolle, Abr., *Uses*, pp. 786–787; *Hore v. Dix* (1661), 1 Siderfin 25, 82 E.R. 948; *Foster v. Foster* (1662), 1 Siderfin 82, 82 E.R. 983, also 1 Levinz 55, 83 E.R. 294, T. Raymond 43, 83 E.R. 24, 1 Keble 160, 225, 274, 319, 83 E.R. 874, 913, 942, 970.

[3] *Hore v. Dix* (1661), 1 Siderfin 25, 82 E.R. 948; Plowden, Quaeries, 58, 75 E.R. 939; *Osborn v. Churchman* (1606), Croke Jac. 127, 79 E.R. 111.

Dodd 73

Pollexfen: No use [is] executed to the cestui que use [where] the plain intention is for this deed to convey to Robert and his heirs such an estate that the subsequent uses may arise out of and not being executed by attornment etc. it cannot. [He] agreed clearly that it cannot be a use upon a use. The Case of Crossing and Scudamore was a strain, as appears by 2 Cr. 127; 2 Rolle 589; Syd. 82; 3 Cr. 394; 7 Rep. 40; and Crossing's Case. And also Walker and Hall's Case[1] [is] different from this case, because in those cases, no use is limited to anyone but the covenantee or grantee, because it is to the use of them and their heirs. See Poph. 49; 4 Rep. 81; and an express case, Syd. 25, Hoare and Dix.[2]

Note: The Chief Baron [Atkyns] afterwards agreed it to be the same case but said that Crossing's Case was subsequent.

Rotheram, Baron: We must make void and reject the words in the habendum. It is a difference between the considerations of love and money because, in consideration of love to my son, I cannot give to a stranger, but, in consideration of £10 paid by A., I may grant to B. and [it is] good, because the owner had a consideration for the land. The grant to Robert and his heirs is an agreement or declaration of his mind that the land shall be to the uses in the deed. Pibus and Mitford[3] creates an estate by implication by way and cites Hale who did grant it operates as a future use; there it is a descendible quality in the meantime. But where [there is] no mediate descent, there it is a present estate; in Pibus' Case, [it was] not properly created but qualified an estate; a covenant to stand seised in consideration of money can be a bargain and sale if enrolled; thus, a bargain and sale for love can be a covenant to stand seised if not enrolled. See Bedell's Case.[4]

Ingolby and Heath, barons, *ad idem*; Chief Baron Atkyns *ad idem*.

---

[1] *Crossing v. Scudamore* (1671), *ut supra*; *Osborn v. Churchman* (1606), Croke Jac. 127, 79 E.R. 111; 2 Rolle, Abr., *Uses*, p. 789; *Foster v. Foster* (1662), 1 Siderfin 82, 82 E.R. 983, also 1 Levinz 55, 83 E.R. 294, T. Raymond 43, 83 E.R. 24, 1 Keble 160, 225, 274, 319, 83 E.R. 874, 913, 942, 970; *Ward v. Lambert* (1595), Croke Eliz. 394, 78 E.R. 639; *Bedell's Case* (1607), 7 Coke Rep. 40, 77 E.R. 470; *Walker v. Hall* (1677), 2 Levinz 213, 83 E.R. 524.

[2] *Collard v. Collard*, Popham 47, 79 E.R. 1165; *Corbet's Case* (1599), 4 Coke Rep. 81, 76 E.R. 1058; *Hore v. Dix* (1661), 1 Siderfin 25, 82 E.R. 948.

[3] *Pibus v. Mitford* (1673–1674), 3 Keble 239, 316, 338, 84 E.R. 697, 741, 754, 1 Ventris 372, 86 E.R. 239, 3 Salkeld 337, 91 E.R. 859, T. Raymond 228, 83 E.R. 119, 2 Levinz 75, 83 E.R. 456, 1 Modern 98, 121, 159, 86 E.R. 761, 780, 800, 1 Freeman 351, 369, 89 E.R. 262, 275, Lincoln's Inn MS. Misc. 500, ff. 214, 224, 236 (Edward Ward's reports).

[4] *Bedell's Case* (1607), 7 Coke Rep. 40, 77 E.R. 470.

In Coleman and Stenhouse's Case, Hilary 1679[/80],[1] in the end of a deed was these words that the son did agree that if he died without issue, then he did give, grant, release, and confirm to his mother and [it was] resolved that [it is a] good consideration between the son and the mother and that it might futurely arise.

A. bargains and sells for a year dated 2nd July and releases in fee dated 20 July and he is outlawed [in the] mean [time], yet [it was] held that the release is good and [it is] but one conveyance notwithstanding in strictness the term is forfeited by the outlawry.

In case there had been a power to the grantee for life to make leases, it would have been a stronger case, because the construing it a covenant to stand seised had been a destruction of the power. Hore and Dix is the same case but precedent to Crossing and Scudamore. The conveyance by way of lease and release was invented by Sir Francis Moore [1558–1621].

Judgment [was given] by the whole court for the plaintiff.

[In] Trinity [term] 1690, 2 W. & M., [it was] reversed by the opinion of the two chief justices, Holt and Pollexfen, because the party intended that the estate would grow out of the seisin of the grantee and not out of his own seisin, and ideo not enure as a covenant to stand seised.

Upon argument, it was affirmed in the House of Lords. 2 Ventr. 318.[2]

79

Rex v. Executor of A.

(Ex. 1689)

A debt due to the crown is not prior to debts due upon bonds to private persons until the crown's debt is reduced to a judgment.

Dodd 85

The testator gave a note under his hand to such an effect, 'received of B. (a collector of chimney money) £10 which I promise to repay for his Majesty's use'. And A. was also indebted to other subjects by bond. The executor before notice of this suit applied the assets to the bond creditors. And [it was a] good administration because it was not a debt upon record nor had he any means to discover it. But if he had notice before payment of the assets, then it is otherwise.

---

[1] *Coleman v. Stenhouse* (1680), Dodd 32, *sub nom. Colton v. Senhouse*, 2 Shower K.B. 11, 89 E.R. 762, *sub nom. Coltman v. Senhouse*, Pollexfen 523, 86 E.R. 633, 2 Levinz 225, 83 E.R. 530, T. Jones 105, 84 E.R. 1169, *sub nom. Coldham v. Senhouse*, 3 Keble 855, 84 E.R. 1051.

[2] *Samon v. Jones* (1690), 2 Ventris 318, 86 E.R. 463.

Second, it was held that an executor who is a creditor by a bond cannot retain in such a case against such a note because the retainer does not operate [as] a *devastavit*, and thus the executor must pay the king. But in the other case, if the king will be paid, it is by implication that the payment of the bond will be a *devastavit*.

See above Rex v. Executor of Alanson and below Attorney General and Dickinson.[1]

In Burnett's Case in the Exchequer, W. Burnett died in debt to the king by a simple contract [for] £100 and indebted to Thomas Burnett by a bond. Thomas took administration, and an information [was] brought against him for the £100; he pleaded the bond and [that] he did not have assets beyond £5 to satisfy the bond, and upon a demurrer, [it was] adjudged for the king. Hilary [term] 31 & 32 Car. II, rot. 86.[2]

80

Paine v. Tape

(Ex. 1690)

Where a person is indebted to the king and also to a private person, the king has priority in payment.

No act of a bankrupt subsequent to his bankruptcy can defeat the interests that his creditors have in his estate.

The voluntary permitting by a bankrupt to be outlawed does not prejudice his creditors.

1 Salkeld 108, 91 E.R. 99, Conroy 138

Upon an English bill in the Exchequer, the Barons prayed the opinion of the judges of the [Court of] Common Bench. The case was H. becomes bankrupt, and, long after, was outlawed. The king made a lease of the profits of his lands and also a grant of his chattels. Afterwards, a commission of bankruptcy was taken out. And the question was whether or how far this outlawry, lease, and grant should prejudice the creditors of the bankrupt.

And, first, it was taken for certain that, where a person is indebted to the king and also to a subject, the king shall have preference in payment;

Secondly, that no subsequent act of the bankrupt can defeat the interest his creditors have by his bankruptcy in his estate;

Thirdly, that the king has by common law such a power to require his subjects to answer all demands of law and justice that not appearing upon process is such a contempt of law that the person guilty is put out of the law [and] forfeits

---

1 *Attorney General, ex rel. Carlton v. Allanson* (Ex. 1687–1688), see above, Case No. 29; *Attorney General v. Dickenson* (1692), see below, Case No. 88.

2 *Rex v. Burnett* (Ex. 1682), Lincoln's Inn MS. Misc. 510, f. [125] (Edward Ward's Reports), Public Record Office E.159/522, Hil. 31 & 32 Car. II, recorda, rot. 86.

his goods and chattels, 11 Hen. VI, 17, his leases for years, 9 Hen. VI, 21, and his trust in such leases, 2 Ro. 807; Hob. 214, and the profits of his lands of freehold; 9 Hen. VI, 20; 21 Hen. VII, 7.[1]

[It was] resolved, therefore, first, that the creditors are not hurt by the outlawry, for that was his own act and by his own default, and the voluntary permitting himself to be outlawed shall not prejudice them. 2 Sid. 115.[2] Secondly, that the assignee of the king's lease, having paid £37 for it, is a purchaser within the 21 Jac. I, c. 19,[3] not to be impeached by the commission sued out five years after the bankruptcy.

[Other reports of this case: Equity Cases Exch. 324.]

81

Dummer v. Wingfield

(Ex. 1690)

As to tithe of wool, the year ends at shearing day.

The parson has pasturage tithe for such sheep as are kept after shearing day and sold afterwards out of the parish.

Dodd 94, 1 Eagle & Younge 566

The plaintiff was rector of Hardwick cum Weedon in Buckinghamshire and brought his bill against the defendant for tithes. And upon other points, the court resolved (1) that the year ends at shear day for sheep, (2) that for such sheep as were kept after shear day and sold away afterwards out of the parish, the parson should have a pasturage tithe for them. And those two points were affirmed again upon a rehearing.

Note: The parishioner had a *modus* for tithe sheep from Candlemas [2 February] until shear time *ut sequitur, viz.* the sheep to be told at Candlemas and the parson to have the tenth fleece or the value thereof for all [of] them at shear time, but for such as are bought in after Candlemas, the parson is to have 4d. per score *per mensem.*

Note: The sheep for which the court decreed a pasturage tithe were bought in after Candlemas and sold out after shear time, but no profit was made of them.

---

[1] *Andrew v. Harlwyn* (1433), YB Hil. 11 Hen. VI, f. 16, pl. 9; YB Trin. 9 Hen. VI, f. 20, pl. 15 (1431); *Rex v. Lamot* (1632), 2 Rolle, Abr., *Utlagarie*, pl. B, 11, p. [807]; *Earl of Somerset's Case* (Ex. 1618), Hobart 214, 80 E.R. 361, also Exchequer Repts. 1604 to 1648, p. 195; YB Hil. 21 Hen. VI, f. 7, pl. 6 (1506).

[2] *Radford v. Bludworth* (1658–1659), 2 Siderfin 69, 114, 176, 82 E.R. 1262, 1286, 1319, also 1 Levinz 13, 83 E.R. 273, 1 Keble 11, 83 E.R. 779.

[3] Stat. 21 Jac. I, c. 19 (*SR*, IV, 1227–1229).

See Brooke, [Abr.], *Dismes*, 18; Fitzherbert, *Natura Brevium*, 1029, a; [S. Degge], *Parson's Counsellor*, 246, 256; 1 Rolle, [Abr., *Dismes*], 640, 641, 642.

Note: A bill of review was brought and the case debated at length and the Chancellor of the Exchequer was there and was against the decree. But the other barons affirmed it and allowed the demurrer to the said bill of review. 1 Pas. 3 Will. & Mar.; Hil. 3 Will. & Mar., 1691. The court decreed the full tithes in kind of wool although the sheep had been but two months in the parish where sheared, between Perne and Swaine of Liverington in Ely,[1] because wool is tithed in kind, *per curiam*.

[Other reports of this case: Equity Cases Exch. 328.]

[The order of 10 February 1690, Public Record Office E.126/15, f. 302v, is printed at 1 Wood 273.]

82

Leach v. Hibbett

(Ex. 1690)

The issue in this case was whether a judgment creditor can redeem a prior mortgage made by his debtor without payment of a later mortgage which was taken without notice of the judgment.

1 Freeman 331, 22 E.R. 1237, 89 E.R. 246

A. mortgages to B. in trust for C. and then confesses a judgment to D. And, afterwards, C. lends him more money and takes another mortgage of the same estate in his own name.

D., the creditor by judgment having extended the lands, preferred his bill to be let in to redeem upon payment of the money due upon the first mortgage. And the sole question was whether he should be let in without paying off both the mortgages.

And [it was held] by Atkyns, Nevill, and Lechmere he shall redeem upon payment of what was due upon the first mortgage only. For, when the judgment was acknowledged, he had a right to the equity of redemption prior to the second mortgagee, which could not be taken from him by any act of the mortgagor.

But [it was held] by Turton *e contra* that he shall not redeem but upon payment of both. And it is the common practice for the last mortgagee to take in the first mortgage and, by that means, to protect himself against all subsequent mortgages. And it was admitted by the counsel of the other side that, if a purchaser takes in the first mortgage, that shall protect him in his purchase. But

[1] *Swaine v. Pern* (1695), 1 Wood 341, 1 Eagle & Younge 607.

they distinguished where it is a security only and not an absolute purchase, that they shall there take place according to their priority in time.

Query of the resolution of the court in this case, because it seems against the constant practice in Chancery, and a mortgagee is a purchaser *pro tanto* to the value of his debt as much as an absolute purchaser.

[Other reports of this case: Dodd 97, Equity Cases Exch. 327.]

83

Bonner's Case

(Ex. 1691)

The crown, by its prerogative, can assign or grant a chose in action.

The Court Exchequer has the power to compromise claims by the crown.

Lincoln's Inn MS. Misc. 558, f. 105

In the Treasurer's Remembrancer's Office in the Exchequer.

Upon a recognizance estreated and granted to him by two privy seals, the recognizance was afterwards compounded without the permission of the grantee, 15 May 1691, *quod nota*.

And afterwards, upon motion, the composition money amounting to £120 was by the order of the court paid to the grantee of the privy seal and his acquittance was to be as good a discharge as a tally of payment. And it seemed to be founded upon the privy seals usually granted to the court to make compositions and discharges. Otherwise, the court has not the power to do it (as it seemed to some).

But note that, though the king can grant a recognizance before or after it is estreated and it, by the grant, is vested in the grantee, notwithstanding that it is a chose in action, which the king, by prerogative can grant, yet, by this resolution and in the cases after-mentioned, the court thought it to be in their power to discharge or compound it. And thus is the practice in all liberties granted by the crown to the subject with a grant of fines and forfeitures arising in it, which certainly pass all future fines and forfeitures, yet the court, without any regard to such grant, constantly discharges or compounds such fines and forfeitures and the Greenwax grants without permission and against the desire of the lords of such liberties, because the grantees take such fines and Greenwax by the judgment of the court, but if there is not any composition or discharge, the grantee of the liberty is entitled and receives the benefit of such fines and Greenwax.

And for this, note the power of the court against the grants of the king and that whether it be of the original jurisdiction or by the Statute of 5 Ric. II, ca.

[*blank*], or by the Statute 33 Hen. VIII, ca. 39,[1] or by all of them together, or by virtue of a privy seal. But upon all or any of them, it is certainly void. 1 Inst. 131b; *vide* Hardress 334, 376; 2 Cro. 180; Savil 133 and 213; Dy. 30b; L. H, 38.[2]

And it seems that the court has jurisdiction in these cases either original or by statute, 5 Ric. II or by the Stat. 33 Hen. VIII, ca. 39, the clause of equity in it. *Vide* African Company's Case in the Exchequer, Easter 1710.[3]

[Other copies of this report: Georgetown Univ. Law Sch. MS. B88–8, p. 211.]

84

Queen Dowager v. Tenants of Richmond

(Ex. 1691)

In this case, manorial lands owned by the king were granted to the queen for her life, and, when the king died, no customary payments upon the death of the lord of the manor were due, because the queen lived on.

Lincoln's Inn MS. 558, f. 107

20 May, Queen Dowager v. Tenants of Richmond and Marquis fee in the Barony of Kendal, County of Westmoreland, upon a [writ of] extent.

The tenants of this fee being in number *circa* 300, each by himself held their tenements by the northern customary tenant right to them and their heirs paying annual rents and a gressume or fine at the death of their lord and upon the death of each tenant, *viz.* upon the death of the lord three years' rent and upon the death of the tenant two years' rent, and, if the tenant leaves a wife, then a heriot in respect of which the wife will enjoy the tenement during her life. King Charles II settled this barony in 1665 upon Queen Catherine, his consort, now Queen Dowager, for her life, and the tenants held their estate under her at the time of the death of King Charles II. And it was alleged that a gressume or fine of three years' rent from each tenant became due to the Queen Dowager upon the demise of King Charles II in 1684 and it was not paid.

Aldworth, the auditor of the queen, in the declaration of the particular receiver's account for the year ended at Michaelmas 1689 put a *super* in this manner, *viz. super seperales tenentes de Richmond et Marquiss fee in Baronia de Kendal*

---

[1] Stat. 5 Ric. II, stat. 1, cc. 9–16 (*SR*, II, 21–23); Stat. 33 Hen. VIII, c. 39, s. 55 (*SR*, III, 891–892).

[2] E. Coke, *First Institute* (1628), f. 131b; *Ashe's Case* (1663), Hardres 334, 145 E.R. 484; *Howard v. Lenthall* (Ex. 1664), Hardres 376, 145 E.R. 505; *Rex v. Twine* (Ex. 1607), Croke Jac. 179, 180, 145 E.R. 156, 157, Exch. Repts. 1604–1648, p. 34; *York v. Allen* (1583), Savile 133, 123 E.R. 1054; *Breverton's Case* (1537), 1 Dyer 30, 73 E.R. 67; *Angell's Case* (Ex. 1679), Exch. Repts. *tempore* Car. II, p. 400.

[3] *Knapp and Garway v. The African Company* (Ex. 1710), see below, Case No. 358.

pro quodam fine sive gressum dictae dominae reginae debet per mortem domini nuper regis Caroli II summa £299 11s. 1½d., being in truth the sum total of all the fines of each tenant together. And for the recovery of it upon a constat made of this sum in the Office of the Treasurer's Remembrancer, the long writ issued (but query by what authority), and, upon this, the sheriff of Westmoreland took in execution the goods of each of the 300 tenants for their part of this fine with charges.

And upon this I [*Edward Ward*], for the tenants, moved against the *super* and process as utterly irregular, first inasmuch as the *super* is joint upon all of the tenants and yet their fines (if due) were several; secondly, inasmuch as the long writ in this case should not issue, nor in truth, any process out of this court upon such *constat* of the Auditor, there not being any debt of record nor he any officer of record in this court. And, in the Earl of Clarendon's Case,[1] the right of setting such a *super* was contested and not determined. And, in this case, a *scire facias* at most and not an extent can by the order of the court issue.

And the court in the case in question awarded a *supersedeas* to the writ and restitution and to show cause why the prosecutor should not pay costs, there being a great disturbance among the tenants.

And the tenants insisted that the fine is not due in this case, there being the same lord and tenant at the death of King Charles II and no alteration of them in estate.

And afterwards in the term, an order was made that the Queen Dowager will pay the costs. But, afterwards, at the setting down of causes, upon an affidavit that William Aldworth, auditor to the Queen Dowager, who set the entire *super*, did not attend upon the queen's Council at law to be directed in this matter according to the order of the Board, the court ordered the said Aldworth to pay the tenants' costs as taxed, *quod nota*.

And it seems no fine or gressume was due upon the death of King Charles II for the reasons *supra*.

[Other copies of this report: Georgetown Univ. Law Sch. MS. B88–8, p. 212.]

85

Attorney General v. Earl of Castlemain

(Ex. 1691)

In this case, a gift from the king was found to have been truly and timely made.

Lincoln's Inn MS. Misc. 558, f. 108

Easter [term] 1691.

---

[1] *Queen Dowager v. Earl of Clarendon* (Ex. 1688), see above, Case No. 69.

The Attorney General brought an information of trover and conversion against the earl [of Castlemain] for 1050 ounces of wrought and 7000 ounces of plain plate delivered to him in the time of the reign of the former King James when he went upon his embassy to Rome and for which he gave a receipt in the Jewel Office and bound himself to restore the plate back to the Jewel Office, which not being done. The information was brought, suggesting that King James abdicated the government and that the now king and queen succeeded on the throne and that the said plate belongs to them, but that the defendant refused to deliver it, but converted it to his use to the damage etc. £10,000.

And the defendant pleaded *non culpabilis*. And, for his defense, he gave in evidence a privy seal dated the 8th of December 1688, which was three days before the abdication, by which the plate was given to the defendant to his own use.

And the sole question was whether this privy seal was sealed the day of the date or at some other time before the 11th December, which was the day of the abdication. And the party who had the custody of the privy seal, being one of the clerks there, swore that he knew it was done at the time of the date or before the abdication. But he could not be confident of it.

And another witness swore that he had seen it under the seal two or three days before the privy seal was delivered to King James. But he could not be confident that it was before the 11th.

And upon this evidence, though the defendant's counsel insisted strongly that the privy seal, being a thing of record, proved itself and that all deeds will be presumed to be made the day of their dates without proof to the contrary, yet the Chief Baron Atkyns referred it to the jury when this privy seal was sealed, whether before or after the abdication and, if it was before, then it was a good grant; otherwise, not.

And the jury found against the defendant. But, afterwards, in the same term, upon an affidavit made by Lord Arundell of Wardour, who was then Lord Privy Seal, that he delivered the privy seal to King James the 10th of December 1688 and that, before this, the grant under the privy seal in question was sealed, the court awarded a new trial upon payment of costs.

I [*Edward Ward* was] for the defendant. But note that there was no new trial, inasmuch as the Attorney General did not prosecute after[wards], and the Lord Castlemain retained the plate to his own use, as I think and heard.

[Other copies of this report: Georgetown Univ. Law Sch. MS. B88–8, p. 214.]

86

Williamson v. Regem

(The Bankers' Case)
(Ex. 1691–1692)

The issues in this case were whether an annuity granted by the king out of the hereditary revenue of the excise is a personal matter that ends upon the death of the king that made the grant and what are the remedies against the crown if such an annuity is not paid.

The judges who hear arguments on a writ of error from the court of Exchequer sit only as advisers to the Lord Chancellor, who is the sole judge.

Dodd 98

Upon a petition of right in the Exchequer, [the case was thus]. Sir Robert Viner[1] had £2503 *per annum* granted to him by King Charles II out of the hereditary revenue of the excise. Sir Robert grants £60 *per annum* thereof unto Robert Williamson in fee and, this being in arrears from Christmas 1683, he brought a petition setting forth the letters patent to Viner and the grant to him and prayed that it will be allowed and that he could have the arrears paid and a future payment of it according to the precedent of Nevil's Case and Wroth's Case[2] in the *Commentaries*. And upon this petition and also upon several others brought by Smith and also by Hornby, who was an original patentee, the attorney general demurred in law. And now it was argued by *Trevor* for the king and by *Ward* for Williamson.

Trevor:

First, it is a personal inheritance in the king and nothing of the realty. If the king grants an annuity out of an incorporeal inheritance, it is not a good charge because it is only a personal duty and [one] should apply to the person of the king for it; the letters patent contain many powers in them to officers, but they are only authorities without interest and thus end by the death of the king or they are revocable notwithstanding [they are] under the great seal.

Second, [if you] admit it [is] an interest, yet it is not a proper remedy. The king's treasury cannot issue but by authority under the great or privy seal. But if the petition prevail, then he will have their money upon a judgment of this court. [There were] never any precedents since Nevill and Wroth's cases, and they are charges upon realty.

Third, they have prayed judgment for the growing duty and that cannot be because they are precedent charges as management of the revenue etc. and therefore [they] ought to bring constant petitions.

---

[1] G. E. Aylmer, 'Vyner [Viner], Sir Robert (1631–1688)', *Oxford Dictionary of National Biography*, vol. 56, pp. 616–619.

[2] *Nevil's Case* (1570), 1 Plowden 377, 75 E.R. 572; *Wroth's Case* (1573), 2 Plowden 452, 75 E.R. 678.

Fourth, how far the plaintiff [is] entitled as assignee, the words of the patent are 'in trust for all creditors that shall come in within a year' and a covenant from Sir Robert that he will grant it to them. But it appears that the plaintiff's grant is three years after.

Fifth, they have pleaded that [they are] seised of this rent *ut de feodo et jure*, but if [it is] a rent in the realty and not a personal duty, then they should plead *in dominico suo ut de feodo.*

Ward: The king [was] a purchaser of the excise because he released wardship etc. for it upon the Act.[1] It is a good inheritance and issues and of that which furnishes the crown to pay this, for the excise has an existence, and the difference between a personal and real inheritance is nothing to this purpose. A grant of an annuity out of the money payable at the Exchequer [is] good. Here is an authority coupled with an interest, and then [it is] not revocable.

To the objection that he did not come within the year, it is to no purpose because [they are] not negative words, besides Viner might grant after for he had it in fee and the interest remains notwithstanding the trust [is] discharged.

To the objection [as to] *ut de feodo et jure*, it ought to be so in all incorporeal inheritances; [it is] otherwise of corporeal inheritances.

First, the king had a good interest to grant.

Second, it is well granted to Viner in fee.

Third, Viner had a power to grant and has well granted [it].

First, the king's honor must be preferred before his profit, and it is the greatest honor to pay debts. See 9 Rep., Bewley's Case.[2]

Second, the grant of the king should be construed to the advantage of the subject. Sir John Mollins' Case, 6 Rep.[3]

Third, the court has an original jurisdiction in this cause. The two cases in the *Commentaries* and the writ of *liberate* in this court are full authorities. In Nevil's Case, there was an annuity granted by a subject out of the land, which came to the king by attainder. They are the treasurers of England, and this is by the tradition[4] of the baton. He is the treasurer of the Exchequer, and this is by patent to the same party. And there is an undertreasurer of the Exchequer, and this is to another by patent also. A judicial writ sealed with the Exchequer seal is a good authority to issue to the treasury of the king without the great or privy seal. The writ is directed to the Treasurer and Chamberlain of the Exchequer. And thus is the *liberate* to deliver of the king's treasury to A.B. such sums for necessaries *teste* the Chief Baron, and money [is] paid constantly accordingly.

---

[1] Stat. 12 Car. II, c. 24 (*SR*, V, 259–266).

[2] *Bewley's Case* (1611), 9 Coke Rep. 130, 77 E.R. 918.

[3] *Molyn's Case* (1598), 6 Coke Rep. 5, 77 E.R. 261.

[4] *I.e.* delivery, whereby a Lord Treasurer is installed in office.

Fourth, it is plain [that] this court had a jurisdiction, by the precedents in Plowden, and if they once had it, then the adverse party must show how it has lost it.

The court [said] a tally of prest is an interest and [is] not countermandable.

Adjornatur.

Dodd 103

Mr. Solicitor [General, *Somers*]: It is an express trust in the grant, *viz.* for such of the creditors as should accept; therefore, he should have averred who has given notice, because a trust *in casu regis* is a condition.

(But [it was said] by *Finch*, thus, it goes of the other part and it is a condition subsequent and performance should not be averred.)

This duty of the excise was in lieu of purveyance, which was inalienable, and thus it was held in general although to a particular person of a particular estate, otherwise it was; this is an incorporeal inheritance *in prendre*. [If] a man grants £5 *per annum* out of a piscary, common, or such like, nothing passes; a rent cannot be reserved out of them. Also, it is a chose in action and not assignable by the grantee. It is a personal demand which should be to the person of the king by petition. The Earl of Devonshire's Case[1] shows how and by what powers the money of the king can be disposed. See 2 Ric. II, ch. 9.[2] The *liberate* in the Exchequer is but for usual allowances; all others are under the great seal and have writs of allowances with them.

Finch: The questions are, first, if a right; second if in a proper way.

First, [it is] true it is incorporeal, but the king may grant a rent out of all or any of his revenues. It is assignable over like an annuity to a man and his assigns is assignable. If the revenue of the crown is not grantable, that overturns all grants.

Second, in a proper way: Stanford cites an ancient *praecipe* [. . .] and Edward I instituted it to be by petition as more mannerly. This patent is under the great seal.

The court [held] the authorities in Plowden are great. Also 1 Hen. VII, Br., *Tally*, 65,[3] is a case to [this] purpose.

Adjornatur.

Dodd 104

Mr. Attorney General [*Treby*]: [There are] two points:

First, that this is a void grant; second, yet that this is not an apt remedy. It is in lieu of purveyance, which was not alienable. Moo. 833; 4 Inst. 202, 203; 2

---

[1] *Earl of Devonshire's Case* (1607), 11 Coke Rep. 89, 77 E.R. 1266.

[2] Stat. 5 Ric. II, stat. 1, c. 9 (*SR*, II, 21).

[3] YB Hil. 1 Hen. VII, f. 8, pl. 5 (1486), Brooke, Abr., *Taile dexchequer*, pl. 5.

Rolle 163; Rot. Parl. 40 Edw. III; Fleta 183.[1] The treasury of the crown is not alienable no more than the gates and walls of a city. Grotius, lib. 2, ch. 6, sect. 11, f. 174.[2] What is granted? It is either a rent or a sum of money. If [it is] a rent, it is void, for it is out of an incorporeal inheritance. 9 Hen. VI, 12a; Fitz., *Annuity*, 4, 5; Br., *Grant*, 3;[3] Hob. 140, 248; Moo. 249. The king ought to have the election. 5 Rep. 56a.[4] If the debts in the patent be not discharged, then the grant is void and the king deceived. It is not averred that they are satisfied nor can the grant be an extinguishment of them and then the king is doubly charged. 1 Leo. 30, 118; 3 Leo. 212, 258; Cr. Eliz. 292, 304; Hob. 41, 42; 2 Saunders 350;[5] Fitz. [Abr.], *Account*, 79; Br., *Contract*, 20. 'In consideration that I am indebted to you, I do bargain and sell' [is] bad because the debt remains and is not by this satisfied or discharged. The king cannot be estopped. A tally is a debt of record. Br., *Tally, toto*; Plowd. 186; Br., *Contract*, 10, 40; Hob. 223, 224; Lane 74, 102, 1 Rolle 411; Hob. 204, 223; 21 Edw. IV, f. 48, by Bryan; Moo. 295.[6] Something in the Act that looks unalienable, proviso for the leases, the king may grant it; he may release it to the people. Therefore:

Second, it is not a proper remedy, and it should be by petition to the person of the king. Stam., *Prerog.*, title 'petition'; Br., [Abr.], *Reseisor pro Rege*, 13; Fitz.,

---

1 *Walter v. Hanger* (1611), Moore K.B. 832, 72 E.R. 935, also 2 Bulstrode 134, 261, 80 E.R. 1011, 1107; E. Coke, *Fourth Institute* (1644), pp. 202, 203; 2 Rolle, Abr., *Prerogative le Roy*, pl. S, 1, p. 163; see *Rotuli Parliamentorum*, vol. 2, p. 62 (5 Edw. III), p. 377 (8 Edw. III); *Fleta* (H. G. Richardson and G. O. Sayles, edd., 1972), vol. 3, 89 Selden Soc. 12.

2 H. Grotius, *De Jure Belli ac Pacis* (1646).

3 *Parker v. The Queen* (1430), YB Trin. 9 Hen. VI, f. 12, pl. 1; Fitzherbert, Abr., *Annuitie*, pl. 5; YB Mich. 9 Hen. VI, f. 53, pl. 36 (1430), Fitzherbert, Abr., *Annuitie*, pl. 4; *Pole v. Ardren* (1424), YB Mich. 3 Hen. VI, f. 20, pl. 34, Brooke, Abr., *Grauntes*, pl. 3.

4 *Knight's Case* (1588), 5 Coke Rep. 54, 77 E.R. 137, also 1 Anderson 173, 123 E.R. 414, 3 Leonard 124, 74 E.R. 582, Moore K.B. 199, 72 E.R. 530, Gouldsborough 15, 75 E.R. 965.

5 *Hungerford's Case* (1585), 1 Leonard 30, 74 E.R. 28; *Cowper v. Andrews* (1614), Hobart 39, 40, 80 E.R. 189, 191, also Moore K.B. 863, 72 E.R. 957; *Peeters v. Opie* (1671), 2 Williams Saunders 346, 85 E.R. 1141, also 2 Levinz 23, 83 E.R. 435, 1 Ventris 177, 214, 86 E.R. 120, 144, 2 Keble 811, 837, 3 Keble 45, 84 E.R. 512, 529, 586.

6 Brooke, Abr., *Taile dexchequer*; *Woodward v. Lord Darcy* (1558), 1 Plowden 184, 186, 75 E.R. 282, 286; YB Mich. 11 Hen. IV, f. 28, pl. 53 (1409), Brooke, Abr., *Contract*, pl. 10 and pl. 40; *Needler v. Bishop of Winchester* (1615), Hobart 220, 80 E.R. 367, also 1 Brownlow & Goldesborough 162, 123 E.R. 730; *Sawier v. East* (1609), Lane 74, 108, 145 E.R. 311, 339, 1 Rolle, Abr., *Condition*, pl. K, 4, p. 411; *Swaine v. Holman* (1616), Hobart 203, 80 E.R. 350; YB Mich. 21 Edw. IV, ff. 44, 48, pl. 6 (1481); *Finch v. Throckmorton* (1590), Moore K.B. 291, 295, 72 E.R. 587, 589, also Croke Eliz. 221, 78 E.R. 477.

Petition 18, 19; Kelw. 178; Rastall and Coke, *Entry*, title 'Petition'; 3 Hen. VII, 13, 14.[1]

[For the] objection [of the] difference between lands and debts, [I] respond [there is] no difference. Long Quinto 5 Edw. IV, 307, 108; Fitz., [Abr.], *Petition*, 8; 1 Anderson 281; Stam., *Prerogative*, ch. 22; Ryley 52, 251, 253; 2 Edw. III, 50, pl. 6.[2]

[For the] objection [as to] the two precedents in Plowden, [I] respond [there are] only two, and those [were] at one time and without any precedent. Moo. 338; 1 Leo. 151; 2 Leo. 194; 4 Inst. 214.[3] Wroth's Case was for a pension out of the augmentation and, upon the dissolution of this court, the parliament provided that it will be paid.[4] It is a defeasible title or a mortgage, and the mortgagee must demand it at the Exchequer. Moo. 558. It is a condition. 1 Inst. 204a; Br., [Abr.], *Patent*, 29; one ought to aver that [it is] a debt; 21 Edw. IV, 49a,[5] and that tallies and orders delivered up [or] else the king is not discharged and thus deceived because it is in satisfaction etc.

[There is] no writ of error in criminals without a petition to the king. Moo, 338; 4 Inst. 314, 315; see 5 Ric. II, ch. 10,[6] [which] declares the law.

Sir Robert Sawyer contra: The points are: first, whether this grant transfers a right; second, if we have well disclosed this right; third, if we have pursued a proper remedy.

The petition is in [the] nature of a *monstrans de droit* and not a petition of right. See Rolle, [Abr.], *Prerogative*, 198; *Register* 292;[7] 2 Ric. III. First, at common law, there was no petition of right where the party claims from or under the crown, because it affirms the title of the crown. 2 Hen. VII, 8, 9; Long Quinto

---

[1] W. Staunford, *Exposition of the King's Prerogative* (1567), ff. 72–75; Brooke, Abr., *Reseiser pro Rege*, pl. 13; Fitzherbert, Abr., *Peticion*, pl. 18, 19; *Anonymous* (1515), Keilwey 178, 72 E.R. 354; *Wingfield's Case* (1487), YB Mich. 3 Hen. VII, f. 13, pl. 19.

[2] YB Mich. 5 Edw. IV, Long Quinto, ff. 107, 108 (1465); YB Trin. 34 Hen. VI, f. 50, pl. 18 (1456), Fitzherbert, Abr., *Peticion*, pl. 8; *Blofield v. Havers* (1592), 1 Anderson 280, 281, 123 E.R. 473; W. Ryley, *Pleadings in Parliament* (1661).

[3] *Mordant's Case*, Moore K.B. 338, 72 E.R. 615; *Regina v. Buckberd* (1594), 1 Leonard 149, 151, 74 E.R. 138, 140; *Hurlston's Case* (1587), 2 Leonard 194, 74 E.R. 471; E. Coke, *Fourth Institute* (1644), pp. 214–215.

[4] *Wroth's Case* (1573), 2 Plowden 452, 75 E.R. 678; Stat. 1 Mar. I, stat. 2, c. 10 (*SR*, IV, 208–209).

[5] E. Coke, *First Institute* (1628), f. 204; *Rex v. Abbess of Sion* (1460), YB Trin. 38 Hen. VI, f. 33, pl. 2, Brooke, Abr., *Patentes*, pl. 29; YB Mich. 21 Edw. IV, ff. 44, 49, pl. 6 (1481).

[6] *Mordant's Case*, Moore K.B. 338, 72 E.R. 615; E. Coke, *Fourth Institute* (1644), pp. 214–215; Stat. 5 Ric. II, c. 10 (*SR*, II, 21–22).

[7] 2 Rolle, Abr., *Prerogative le Roy*; *Registrum Brevium*.

Edw. IV, 131b; 13 Edw. IV, 5; Dr. 269.[1] The court always has the power to allow original accounts if in surplusage out of other monies and the Stat. 5 Ric. II, ch. 10, extends it to imprest accounts. The Act 33 Hen. VIII, ch. 39 or 9,[2] has a clause that gives jurisdiction in that case, and [it is] probable the resolutions in Plowden are pursuant to it.

[It was] adjourned to Michaelmas term.

It was argued by the Attorney [General, *Treby*] and *Sawyer* again.

Sawyer insisted that annuities have been granted out of the Exchequer and cited *Register* 193, 196; J. Selden's *Titles of Honour*, chapter on earls; this duty was given generally and [there is] nothing to restrain the king. Thus [it is in] his pleasure.

But (it was said) by Lechmere 27 Hen. VIII, ch. 28,[3] says 'the king and his assigns' (which means) to do with at his pleasure.

The king is not deceived, because the consideration is passed and therefore not to be averred. Acceptance of letters patent is a bar to the order tally. Query. St. Savior's Case, 11 Rep.,[4] [is not] a petition of right where the title is from the king, but only where the subject sets up a title; no petition of grace [lies] where [one] had a right. This patent is [under] the great seal. What can you expect? The privy seal [is] a better warrant, and the king has done all he can. 26 Car. II, in the pipe roll, Earl of Pembroke's Case, a liberate will charge the officer [and] his executors. 2 Hen. VII, 8; see Register, 193; Selden, Titles, 538.[5] The subject's remedy was in chancery before the Statute 33 Hen. VIII and the annexing [of] the augmentation court. If this be a legal charge, the court by 33 Hen. VIII can give relief. There are several precedents in the point, as 1 Eliz., rot. 108, Pomeroy's Case; Easter [term] 4 Eliz., rot. 151, Tudman's Case; Easter [term] 6 Eliz., rot. 145; Trinity [term] 11 Eliz., rot. 147, Nevill's Case; Hilary [term] 13 Eliz., rot. 143; Trinity [term] 23 Eliz., rot. 148, Sir Thomas Heddy's Case;[6] Davies' Case, Michaelmas [term] 1656, all in the King's Remembrancer's [office], some for

---

1 *Emthorp v. Elrington* (1487), YB Hil. 2 Hen. VII, f. 8, pl. 1; YB Mich. 5 Edw. IV, Long Quinto, f. 131 (1465); YB Mich. 13 Edw. IV, f. 5, pl. 15 (1473); *Anonymous* (1566), 3 Dyer 268, 269, 73 E.R. 596, 597.

2 Stat. 33 Hen. VIII, c. 39 (*SR*, III, 879–892).

3 Stat. 27 Hen. VIII, c. 28, s. 1 (*SR*, III, 575).

4 *St. Saviour's Case* (1613), 10 Coke Rep. 66, 77 E.R. 1025, Exch. Repts. 1604–1648, p. 116, also Lane 21, 145 E.R. 266.

5 *Emthorp v. Elrington* (1487), YB Hil. 2 Hen. VII, f. 8, pl. 1; *Registrum Brevium*; J. Selden, *Titles of Honor*.

6 *Tyrwhytt's Case* (1562), Public Record Office E.159/344, Pas. 4 Eliz. I, recorda, rot. 151; *Martin's Case* (1564), Public Record Office E.159/347, Pas. 6 Eliz. I, recorda, rot. 145; *Nowell's Case* (1570), Public Record Office E.159/360, Trin. 12 Eliz. I, recorda, rot. 147 (re vicar of Tamworth); *Long's Case* (1571), Public Record Office E.159/361/1, Hil. 13 Eliz. I, recorda, rot. 143; *Sir Thomas Hennage's Case* (1581), Public Record Office E.159/381, Trin. 23 Eliz. I, recorda, rot. 143.

repayment where [money was] paid by mistake (as Hilary [term] 13 Eliz.), others [are] judgments to be paid by [a] receiver or bailiff of a manor or [the] treasurer and chamberlain [of the Exchequer].

Adjornatur.

Dodd 111

[This case] was argued by the court this term [Hilary 4 W. & M., 1692]. And the three puisne [barons] argued in one day, and Powell and Turton [held] for the petitioners, the plaintiffs, and Lechmere [held] against them and for the king.

[It was argued] by the petitioners (1) it is a good grant and (2) [it is] a proper remedy.

[As] to the first, it is good notwithstanding it is an annuity of the inheritance. The crown may and has aliened the ancient demesne lands, land entered in Domesday [Book].[1] Thus, he can charge. [As to the] objection [of] King John's grant to the pope [as] bad, as 4 Inst. 13,[2] [it is] responded the intent was to hold of the pope in feudal [tenure]; also the pope was an alien and not capable. 5 Rep. 56.[3] Ireland [is] not alienable. [It is] responded it is a dominion of the crown, but the Isle of Man [was] obtained by conquest and [is] alienable. 4 Inst. 283; 7 Rep. 21; see Cr. Jac. 78; *Natura Brevium* 152, K; Dyer 92; Hob. 248; 9 Hen. VI, 12,[4] 52. And [there is] no difference in the case of the king between a rent and an annuity.

Secondly, it is good in respect of the revenue being given by act of Parliament. The *magna et antiqua custuma* was given to King Edward I and his heirs by Act of Parliament[5] and [it is] not an ancient inheritance. 2 Inst. 58, 59; Vaughan 161, 163. Yet [it is] chargeable. Dyer 92; 9 Hen. VI, 12. In Edward III's time, the custom of the wool abated and clothing began and then a subsidy of aulnage which had been always made, charged, and granted without question. See Br., *Quisne*, 7; 2 Rolle 198; 19 Hen. VI, 62; 4 Inst. 126. The king may discharge of taxes before [they are] granted [and] *a fortiori* may grant [them] after. 2 Hen. IV, no. 15; 2 Rolle 176.[6]

---

[1] Public Record Office E.31.

[2] E. Coke, *Fourth Institute* (1644), pp. 13–14.

[3] *Knight's Case* (1588), 5 Coke Rep. 54, 77 E.R. 137, also 1 Anderson 173, 123 E.R. 414, 3 Leonard 124, 74 E.R. 582, Moore K.B. 199, 72 E.R. 530, Gouldsborough 15, 75 E.R. 965.

[4] E. Coke, *Fourth Institute* (1644), p. 283; *Lord Anderson's Case* (1597), 7 Coke Rep. 21, 77 E.R. 443; *Anonymous* (1553), 1 Dyer 92, 73 E.R. 200, also Jenkins 208, 145 E.R. 141; *Parker v. The Queen* (1430), YB Trin. 9 Hen. VI, f. 12, pl. 1.

[5] Referred to in the *Confirmatio Cartarum*, Stat. 25 Edw. I, c. 7 (*SR*, I, 124).

[6] E. Coke, *Second Institute* (1642), pp. 58–59; *Sheppard v. Gosnold* (1672), Vaughan 159, 124 E.R. 1018; *Anonymous* (1553), 1 Dyer 92, 73 E.R. 200, also Jenkins 208, 145 E.R. 141; *Parker v. The Queen* (1430), YB Trin. 9 Hen. VI, f. 12, pl. 1; YB Hil. 1 Hen.

Thirdly, the king is not deceived in the consideration. All considerations [are] personal [and] executory, and they should be averred. But personal considerations executed should not. Lane's Reports 76; 10 Rep., St. Saviour's Case; Br., *Patent*, 4; 10 Rep. 47b; Com. 455.[1]

[As] to the second point, the form of the petition of right, see Fitz., Petition, 34; Kelw. 178; Stam. 71, 73; 4 Rep. 55.[2] It is said to be only for a freehold in 1 Hen. VII, 3, but denied by Stamf. 75, 76; 34 Hen. VI, 5; Br., Patent, 3; Fitz., Petition, 4.[3] But it is also a remedy for a petitioner to the barons without going to the person of the king. And it is like a matter of right or title. The authorities of Nevill's Case and Wroth's Case in the Commentaries[4] [are] unanswerable; they are no new, but ancient, laws. The authority of the court did not commence by 37 Hen. VIII, but before, as [is] 9 Hen. VI, 13; Fitz., Annuitie, 5.[5] Error in proceedings in the lord's court must be examined by petition to the lord, thus to the person of the king or lord. Yet [it was] adjudged good to the barons. 1 Rolle 539;[6] Lane 88. Thus, the writ of liberate is a disposition of the treasury by this court, 2 Inst. 496, and [there is] no difference between an annuity for life and by inheritance. See 5 Ric. II, ch. 12; 1 Eliz., rot. 108, in the King's Remembrancer's [memoranda roll], Richard Pomroy's Case; 12 Eliz., Vicar of Tamworth's Case; 13 Eliz. Long's Case;[7] Michaelmas [term] 1658, Davie's Case, all in the Exche-

---

VII, f. 8, pl. 5 (1486), Brooke, Abr., *Quinzime*, pl. 7; 2 Rolle, Abr., *Prerogative le Roy*, pl. I, 2, p. 198; YB Pas. 19 Hen. VI, f. 62, pl. 1 (1441); E. Coke, *Fourth Institute* (1644), p. 126; 2 Rolle, Abr., *Prerogative le Roy*, pl. G, 7, p. 176.

[1] *Sawier v. East* (1609), *ut supra*; *St. Saviour's Case* (1613), *ut supra*; YB Trin. 9 Hen. VI, f. 27, pl. 30 (1431), Brooke, Abr., *Patentes*, pl. 4; *Lampet's Case* (1612), 10 Coke Rep. 46, 77 E.R. 994, also *sub nom. Lampit v. Starkey*, 2 Brownlow & Goldesborough 172, 123 E.R. 880; *Wroth's Case* (1573), 2 Plowden 452, 75 E.R. 678.

[2] YB Pas. 22 Edw. III, f. 5, pl. 12 (1348), Fitzherbert, Abr., *Peticion*, pl. 3; YB Pas. 10 Edw. III, f. 26, pl. 48 (1336), Fitzherbert, Abr., *Peticion*, pl. 4; *Anonymous* (1515), Keilwey 178, 72 E.R. 354; W. Staunford, *Exposition of the King's Prerogative* (1567), ff. 71, 73; *The Sadlers' Case* (1588), 4 Coke Rep. 54, 76 E.R. 1012, also 1 Anderson 180, 123 E.R. 418.

[3] YB Mich. 1 Hen. VII, f. 3, pl. 3 (1485); W. Staunford, *Exposition of the King's Prerogative* (1567), ff. 75, 76; YB Trin. 34 Hen. VI, f. 50, pl. 18 (1456); YB Trin. 9 Hen. VI, f. 20, pl. 15 (1431), Brooke, Abr., *Patentes*, pl. 3; YB Pas. 10 Edw. III, f. 26, pl. 48 (1336), Fitzherbert, Abr., *Peticion*, pl. 4.

[4] *Nevil's Case* (1570), 1 Plowden 377, 75 E.R. 572; *Wroth's Case* (1573), 2 Plowden 452, 75 E.R. 678.

[5] *Parker v. The Queen* (1430), YB Trin. 9 Hen. VI, f. 12, pl. 1; Fitzherbert, Abr., *Annuitie*, pl. 5.

[6] *Edwards' Case* (1611), 1 Rolle, Abr., *Court*, pl. Q, 8, p. 539.

[7] *Nowell's Case* (1570), Public Record Office E.159/360, Trin. 12 Eliz. I, recorda, rot. 147 (re vicar of Tamworth); *Long's Case* (1571), Public Record Office E.159/361/1, Hil. 13 Eliz. I, recorda, rot. 143.

quer. Monastery lands [were] granted away by the crown; thus of this revenue £24,000 [went] to the duke of York and £12,000 to the dowager queen.

The Lord Chief Baron [Atkyns] said to the objection that the assignment was not within the year that notice does not appear nor will it avoid the assignment; to the objection that it was not averred sufficiently, he responded that he will have judgment first. To the objection that the king [was] deceived, he responded that [it] must appear either by plea or by verdict or in the grant. Aldmond's Case; Berwick's Case; Lane 3, 108; Hob. 230.[1]

Lechmere, *contra*: (1) no good right; (2) no power to relieve.

[As] to the first, this excise of inheritance is not grantable nor can [the king] bind the successor in regard to the things for which it was granted. And upon the affirmative clauses in the Act which imply a negative, Hobart 298,[2] the monastery lands are clauses in the acts which show the king might do it and that the Parliament meant so as to dispose at his will and by 27 Hen. VIII and by 31 Hen. VIII confirm all grants that were or should be made in three years and that the king and his patentees may hold discharged of tithes, 32 Hen. VIII, to use and enjoy, 1 Edw. VI, all grants [are] good etc. the recompense ought to remain to the crown as long as the exemption remains to the subject, but at this rate, the crown is to have no support, yet the subject is to bear the burden. If the recompense is gone, it will be a reason and temptation to resume tenures and purveyance.

This patent is void against a successor. The Parliament has set a mark upon it by the words of the law and by restraining contracts other than for three years. To the point of the Duke of York's Case, [it] is by Act of Parliament. And the dowager queen's [case] is not an alienation but a dower or jointure, and so it is allowed. Thus, a tenant in tail against the Statute *De Donis*, as tenancy by curtesy, dower, etc. See the Prince's Case, 8 Rep. 22.[3]

[As] to the second point, what can the court do? They can only send writs *teste* Robert Atkyns to do [a thing]. But the patent always is under the great seal, *teste me ipso*, which is stronger. In the Black Book[4] in the Exchequer, the chief justiciar of England sat in this court, and he had the disposal of the treasury. But that officer vanished in Edward I's time. See Spelman's *Glossary* 331. From Ed-

---

1 *Barwick's Case* (1595), 5 Coke Rep. 93, 77 E.R. 199, Moore K.B. 393, 72 E.R. 649; *Bret v. Johnson* (1605), Lane 1, 145 E.R. 249; *Sawier v. East* (1609), *ut supra*; *Needler v. Bishop of Winchester* (1615), Hobart 220, 230, 80 E.R. 367, 376, also 1 Brownlow & Goldesborough 162, 123 E.R. 730.

2 *Slade v. Drake* (1617–1620), Hobart 295, 298, 80 E.R. 439, 442, 1 Gwillim 385, 1 Eagle & Younge 314, also Noy 97, 74 E.R. 1063, W. Jones 6, 82 E.R. 5, 2 Rolle Rep. 250, 81 E.R. 780, Merefield 12.

3 Stat. 13 Edw. I, c. 1 (*SR*, I, 71–72); *The Prince's Case* (1606), 8 Coke Rep. 1, 77 E.R. 481.

4 Public Record Office E.36/266, E.36/267, transcribed by F. S. Thomas, in *Ancient Exchequer* (1848).

ward I's time until Queen Mary's time, this court never disposed the treasury nor even the middle of Queen Elizabeth's time until now. The true reason of Wroth's Case was that it was a pension payable in the augmentation [court] and that court was by [Statute of] 1 Mary[1] annexed to the Exchequer and [there was] a clause that the Exchequer will pay the pensions and, upon this, Wroth grounded his petition and the court gave judgment, and most of the subsequent cases then were upon the same ground.

At another day, the Chief Baron [Atkyns] concurred with Powell and Turton for the petitioners and in all things against the king. He said that in the time of the Saxons, the kings could not dispose, but [it was] otherwise in the time of the Normans, because then kings were absolute, that it is true anciently the crown grants were in Parliament but not necessarily. This grant is an interest and not a bare authority; therefore, [it is] not revokable. Dr. 176 B, 223 B; Com. 457; Palmer 71, 72; Dr. 49. The clause in the Act restrains the lord treasurer, not the king. This is a good grant. 2 Hen. VII, 8; Br., *Tally*, 4, 5; *Register* 266, 307, 192, 193; 2 Inst. 116; 21 Edw. III, 47; Selden, *Honours*, 637, 637; 1 Edw. IV, ca. 1; Cotton's *Records* 159, no. 58; 439, no. 23; 423, no. 16; 431, no. 48, 17; Cr. Jac. 78.[2] Notwithstanding that it is granted out of the excise, however, the judgment is general. Thus [is] Wroth's Case. Second, the court [is] proper, and the barons only are judges. 9 Hen. VI, 13.[3]

Judgment [was] for the petitioners.

Dodd 168

Attorney General v. Hornby (Ex. Cham. 1696).

In the great cases of Hornby, Williamson, Sir Jeremy Snow, *et al.*, upon the patent to them and the goldsmiths made by King Charles II, upon a petition preferred in the Exchequer, they had judgment by three against Lechmere, upon which the Attorney [General] brought [a writ of] error in the Exchequer [Chamber] upon the Statute 27 Edw. III[4] etc. And there, by the opinion of all of the judges, except Treby, the judgment should be affirmed. But the [Lord] Keeper [Somers] was of the opinion that it should be reversed. And upon this, debate arose who was the judge in this case, whether the [Lord] Keeper should give judgment according to his opinion and thus consider the judges as advisors or as-

[1] Stat. 1 Mar. I, stat. 2, c. 10 (*SR*, IV, 208–209).

[2] *Wroth's Case* (1573), 2 Plowden 452, 75 E.R. 678; *Web v. Paternoster* (1619), Palmer 71, 81 E.R. 983, also Popham 151, 79 E.R. 1250; *Emthorp v. Elrington* (1487), YB Hil. 2 Hen. VII, f. 8, pl. 1; Brooke, Abr., *Taile dexchequer*, pl. 4; YB Hil. 1 Hen. VII, f. 8, pl. 5 (1486), Brooke, Abr., *Taile dexchequer*, pl. 5; *Registrum Brevium*; *Earl of Kent's Case* (1347), YB Hil. 21 Edw. III, f. 47, pl. 68; J. Selden, *Titles of Honor*; Stat. 1 Edw. IV, c. 1 (*SR*, II, 380); R. B. Cotton, *Records*; *York v. Twine* (1605), Croke Jac. 78, 79 E.R. 67.

[3] *Parker v. The Queen* (1430), YB Trin. 9 Hen. VI, f. 12, pl. 1.

[4] Stat. 31 Edw. III, stat. 1, c. 12 (*SR*, I, 351–352).

sistants only or should give judgment according to the opinion of the majority of the judges and thus consider them as in conjunction with himself. And upon this point, the [Lord] Keeper desired the judges to meet and consider. And a case was stated in writing to this purpose.

And afterwards, the judges met and spoke among themselves. And the last Tuesday of this term, the [Lord] Keeper and they sat in the Exchequer chamber, and there the [Lord] Keeper reported before them and read it out of a paper that HOLT, POWELL, and EYRE were of the opinion that the [Lord] Keeper must give judgment according to the majority of the opinions and that TREBY, WARD, NEVILL, ROKEBY, LECHMERE, TURTON, and POWYS were of the contrary opinion and that the [Lord] Keeper was the judge and the judges only advisors or assistants. And thus the [Lord] Keeper [SOMERS] said it was his own opinion, and accordingly, he gave judgment that the prior judgments will be reversed.

1 Freeman 331, 89 E.R. 246

King Charles II, having taken up great sums of money of the petitioners or their testator, who were bankers, in consideration thereof granted to them and their heirs several annuities chargeable upon the hereditary revenue of excise, given to the king by the Statute of 12 Car. II, cap. 24.

The said annuity being for many years arrear, the petitioners exhibited their petition to the Barons of the Exchequer for the said arrears, whereupon two questions did arise:

First question, whether this grant of the king were good to bind the successor so as to continue a charge upon the said revenue;

Second question, whether the petitioners had taken their proper remedies for recovery of the said arrears.

To the first question, ATKYNS, TURTON and POWELL, were of opinion that the grant was good to charge the successor. It was admitted, that the king could not grant away his kingdom, nor put it in vassalage or subjection to the pope or any other, as is said in 4 Inst. 13, 14, 83, 202, 357; that the king may grant an annuity or charge his revenue; 2 Cro. 78; 5 Co. 56; 7 Co. 21; 9 Hen. VII, 12; 2 Inst. 58; Vaugh. 161; 4 Inst. 29; Dyer 92; 9 Hen. VI, 12; Bro., *Quinz.*, 7; 2 Rolle 176, 198; 19 Hen. VI, 6; 4 Inst. 126; 6 Co. 73; 2 Rolle 98; Moor 833; 2 Hen. VII, 8; Reg. Orig. 193, 266, 307; 21 Edw. III, 47. But it must be said of whose hands to be received, or else it is not good, for he cannot charge his person. *Natura Brevium* 52; Dy. 92; Hob. 148.

Objection: That it was out of an incorporeal inheritance.

Answer: It is good notwithstanding. 1 Inst. 47.

Objection: It was pretended that the king was deceived in his grant as to the consideration.

Answer: If the king be deceived in a consideration real executory, it will void the grant, but not in a consideration personal executed. Plow. 454; Lane, 3, 76, 108; 10 Co. 47; 6 Co. 56; 1 Co. 43; Yelv. 1; 11 Co. 90; Hob. 230. That there have been acts of resumption shows that the grants were good, because they could not be avoided but by act of Parliament.

Objection: This is but an authority, and so void by death, because revocable.

Answer: It is an interest, and a licence coupled with an interest is irrevocable. Dy. 176; Natura Brevium 223; Plow. 457; Palm. Rep. 171, 172; Dyer 49.

To the second question, all the barons held that the remedy by petition to the barons was a proper remedy and that it was in their power to relieve the petitioners and give judgment for them. Keilw. 178; Stamf. 73, 75.

A petition of right lies as well for a personal, as a real, due. Plow. 377, 434, Wroth's Case, and Nevill's Case, 9 Hen. VI, 13; 1 Rolle 539; Lane 38; 4 Inst. 415.

Baron LECHMERE *e contra*: That the king could not alien or charge this revenue. Fleta, 183, 3, 549; Selden; Grotius; Prynne, 9, 390, *Vindication of the Liberties of English Freemen*.

First, it was given in lieu of a revenue unalienable but by act of Parliament, *viz.* the Court of Wards.

Second, if the king may alien part, he may alien all, and then the subjects will bear the burden, for they must grant new supplies to support the crown.

Third, this charge was granted by the king at a time when he had no occasion for money, but merely for to gratify his prodigality, being at a time when the Parliament rained golden showers into his lap. It appears by the answer Edward III gave the pope that it is not in the power of the king to alien his kingdoms etc. 4 Inst. 13, 14.

Fourth, the very words of the act of Parliament show that it was the intent of the Parliament it should continue in the crown unalienable, there being the words 'forever hereafter to remain to the king and his successors' several times in the Act.

Fifth, a power in the Act to enable the king to let to farm for three years shows the Parliament never intended he should have power to alien as he pleased.

Sixth, where the Parliament intended a power in the king to alien, it is otherwise worded, as in the acts that give monasteries to the crown, it is said 'to do therewith as he pleased'.

But judgment was given for the petitioners upon the opinion of the other three judges.

[Reversed on appeal: 5 Modern 29, 87 E.R. 500, Skinner 601, 90 E.R. 270, Comberbach 270, 90 E.R. 472, Carthew 388, 90 E.R. 825, State Trials (Howell, ed., 1816), vol. 14, cols. 1–114, Harvard Law Sch. MS. 1052, f. 63v, pl. 2.]

87
Poulston v. Clapham
(Ex. 1691)

Contraband goods that have been condemned to be destroyed are not saved by a subsequent general pardon.

Dodd 102

Upon an information to destroy goods upon the French Act,[1] [the case was thus]. These goods were French goods and taken and condemned as prize after the first French Act for destroying French goods, and afterwards came the General Pardon.[2] The main question was whether this had enfranchised the goods etc.

And [it was] adjudged upon a special verdict not.

Note: This case was before the second act of the 2d of January 1690[/91].[3]

Leak and How's Case, Cr. Eliz. 533, prize goods shall pay customs. See the Act 3 Edw. IV, for foreign manufacturers; [it was] adjudged that after they are condemned, they are always afterwards free. Harlem and Canon's Case.[4] But the court differenced the cases because they said that in the case of French goods, they are, as it were, infected and carry their death's wound in them and are to be destroyed, but, in [the] case of other goods, [they are] only to be forfeited.

Note this judgment was reversed for other points.

88
Attorney General v. Dickenson
(Ex. 1692)

A precedent judgment obtained by a bond creditor shall be preferred to the king by the Statute 33 Hen. VIII, c. 39, but a subsequent judgment shall not. But a plea by an executor of several judgments is entire, and, if one of them fails, judgment shall be against him.

Dodd 109, Parker 262, 145 E.R. 774

Attorney General v. Dickenson, executor of Holcroft.

---

[1] Stat. 1 Will. & Mar., c. 34 (*SR*, VI, 98–103).

[2] Stat. 2 Will. & Mar., c. 10 (*SR*, VI, 174–179).

[3] Stat. 2 Will. & Mar., c. 14 (*SR*, VI, 247).

[4] *Leak v. Howel* (1596), Croke Eliz. 533, 78 E.R. 780, also Noy 55, 74 E.R. 1023; Stat. 3 Edw. IV, cc. 1–3 (*SR*, II, 392–398); *Harling v. Cannon* (1674), 1 Freeman 325, 89 E.R. 241, Exch. Cases *tempore* Car. II, p. 260.

The point was A. was indebted by judgment to B. and by bonds to C. and D. and by simple contract to E. and died. E., being a debtor to the king, caused the debt due to him to be seized into the king's hands; and upon this a *scire facias* issued against Dickenson, the executor of A. and before the return of it C. and D., the bond creditors, obtained judgment; and then Dickenson pleaded to the said *scire facias*, the judgment prior, and the subsequent judgments. And the attorney general demurred.

The points argued [in Hilary 1691/92] were, first, whether the subsequent judgments should be preferred against the king, for it was admitted that the precedent judgment should be preferred? Secondly, if the subsequent judgments should not be preferred, and the precedent judgment should be preferred, then if pleading them all in one entire plea, judgment should be against the defendant; or if the Attorney [General] ought to have replied assets beyond the first judgment?

As to the first point, Burnet's case, entered Hilary, 31 & 32 Car. II, roll 86, and The King and Knowles, in 1683, and The King against Allanson, in 1687,[1] were cited; where it was adjudged, that a debt by simple contract and then seized into the king's hands should be preferred and paid before a debt to the subject by bond. Secondly, [it was held in] Attorney [General] and Knowles' Case such a debt to the king will be preferred before a bond again, and thus the court inclined.

As to the second point, was cited the opinion of Chief Justice Vaughan, in Edgcumbe and Dee (in his Reports 104),[2] that so long as one judgment [is] good, you should not have judgment on such a plea. But on the contrary was cited the current opinion, and Hancocke and Prowde's case in 1 Saund. 337, 2 Saunders 50, 51,[3] and that the plea was entire, to which the court inclined. But Baron Powell said that Hale was never satisfied with it and cited Atwood's Case in Rolle to the contrary.

[This case] was adjourned. After Easter [term] 1692, it was adjudged for the king that the debt of the king should be preferred before the subsequent judgments, viz. before any bond, Hardr. 23,[4] but a precedent judgment should be preferred before the subsequent judgments, viz. before any bond. But a precedent

[1] *Rex v. Burnett* (Ex. 1682), Lincoln's Inn MS. Misc. 510, f. [125] (Edward Ward's Reports), Public Record Office E.159/522, Hil. 31 & 32 Car. II, recorda, rot. 86; *Attorney General v. Knowles* (Ex. 1683), Exch. Repts. *tempore* Car. II, 541; *Attorney General, ex rel. Carlton v. Allanson* (Ex. 1687–1688), see above, Case No. 29.

[2] *Edgcomb v. Dee* (1670), Vaughan 89, 124 E.R. 984.

[3] *Hancocke v. Prowd* (1669), 1 Williams Saunders 328, 336, 85 E.R. 475, 485, also 1 Siderfin 429, 82 E.R. 1198, 2 Keble 535, 542, 562, 568, 84 E.R. 335, 339, 353, 357.

[4] *Attorney General v. Andrew* (Ex. 1655), Hardres 23, 145 E.R. 360.

judgment will be preferred before it, upon the words of the 26th section of the Statute of the 33 Hen. VIII, c. 39.[1] So as the subject had not judgment before etc.

Secondly, it was adjudged, that the plea was entire and that it was not necessary for the plaintiff to reply assets beyond the first judgment.

See 2 Rolle 104; 1 Lev. 16; Salk. 298, Carth. 429, Lord Raym. 263.[2]

89

Edge v. Oglander

(Ex. 1692)

In this case, a modus decimandi was found to be valid.

Dodd 115, 1 Eagle & Younge 628

[It was] resolved that £8 was a legal *modus* for a farm in Pancras in Sussex; the farm was [worth] about £80 *per annum* [and] the tithe about £16 *per annum* but sometimes not so much.

Note: The *modus* was decreed by the consent of the parson seeing the opinion of the court. But LECHMERE said that it was too big. The other barons said that the *modus* may be better than the tithe and yet good.

See below, Browne and Chaplin.[3]

[Other reports of this case: 1 Rayner 71, 2 Gwillim 536.]

[The decree of 4 February 1691/92, Public Record Office E.126/15, f. 462, is printed at 1 Wood 288.]

90

Attorney General v. Duke of Beaufort

(Ex. 1692–1697)

A court cannot adjourn for a part of a day.

A court can take two privy verdicts in the same case.

In this case, the lease in issue was found to be a fraudulent conveyance.

---

[1] Stat. 33 Hen. VIII, c. 39, s. 51 (*SR*, III, 891).

[2] *Blockley v. Skinner* (1639), 2 Rolle, Abr., *Judgment*, pl. M, 10, p. 104; *Tompson v. Noel* (1661), 1 Levinz 16, 83 E.R. 274; *Ashton v. Sherman* (1697), 1 Salkeld 298, 91 E.R. 265, Carthew 429, 90 E.R. 849, 1 Lord Raymond 263, 91 E.R. 1072, also 12 Modern 153, 88 E.R. 1229, Comberbach 444, 449, 90 E.R. 581, 584, Holt K.B. 308, 90 E.R. 1070.

[3] *Browne v. Chaplin* (Ex. 1696), see below, Case No. 138.

When a fraudulent conveyance is set aside, the plaintiff can recover the mesne profits without any deductions for expenses.

Dodd 115

In the Exchequer, in an issue tried at the bar about My Lord Powys's[1] estate forfeited for treason and a deed pleaded, the trial was on Wednesday and, that night, a privy verdict [was reached] and the next day, the court rose out of the Exchequer chamber and went into the other court to take the verdict, and then the jury disagreed, and the court returned and at one [o'clock] adjourned until four [o'clock] to take the verdict if the jury by this time agreed. And afterwards, a dispute arose whether they could adjourn [for] part of a day, and [it was held] by the major part no; second, whether they could take two privy verdicts in the same case, and [it was held] by the major part yes, and thus it was done.

Note, because *alia aliter* they thought especially to the first point.

Note: A new trial at the bar [was] granted. And thus was [the case of] Michaelmas [term] 25 Car. [1673], Alter and Rukely.

Dodd 122

The king, at the trial at bar, challenged two persons, and then several are sworn, and then the defendant challenged one and thus it lacked twelve, upon which, the attorney general insisted that the defendant show his cause and the defendant insisted that the king show his cause first. And he agreed, if the defendant had challenged the entire panel, that the king must show his cause.

But, by the three puisne [barons] against the Chief Baron, [it was] resolved now not, but that the defendants shall show cause first, because now the king and the subject [are] in equal right.

Note 2 R.R. 394.[2]

Dodd 169

For the marquess of Powys's estate, [the case was thus]. The marquess being attainted for outlawry for high treason and his estate in Wales seized by a commission into the king's hands, the duke of Beaufort, earl of Pembroke, Sir Edward Wiseman, and Hughes pleaded a lease for twenty-one years for payment of debts in a schedule and gave security upon the plea (as usual), upon which process was stayed, as in like cases. And afterwards, the attorney [general] replied to this plea *per fraudem*. And upon a trial at bar, it was found fraudulent. And upon this, the court was moved for an order to pay the mesne profits in order to sue the recognizance. And a question arose and was greatly debated whether the mesne profits

1 V. Slater, 'Herbert, William, styled first marquess of Powis (c. 1626–1696)', *Oxford Dictionary of National Biography*, vol. 26, pp. 746–747.

2 *Stewer v. Stewer* (1623), 2 Rolle Rep. 394, 81 E.R. 874.

should be computed according as the value was found in the inquisition or that the value found should stand only as a charge and deductions should be made out of it for taxes, repairs, bailiff's salaries, annuities, rents [that] will issue out of it, and other matters.

And the court held clearly that no deduction will be for repairs, collections, etc., because the inquisition is of such a value beyond reprises. But for taxes subsequently granted by parliament, the court hesitated. But, finally, upon debate and precedents produced, the court referred it to the Deputy [Remembrancer] to compute the mesne rates, which amounted to £13,000 where the security given was only £8000 and it [was] computed according to the inquisition without deduction.

And the first day of this term, it was moved that the report will be confirmed and that the court will make an order for payment of them or that process should go upon the security. And upon debate again of counsel and praying a direction to the deputy for an allowance etc., the court confirmed the report and made such order as was desired and said that there was no other rule to go by but the value in the inquisition in regard the pleaders saw the value and took upon them[selves] to give security and to keep the possession and thus [were] cognizant of fact and kept the king, upon this security, out of possession.

Note: Two precedents were produced accordingly, *viz.* one between the Attorney General and Penn in King James II's time and the other between the Attorney General and Baden, in 1693 or around then,[1] in both [of] which, I [Samuel Dodd] was counsel.

Note, in this case, it was said that the taxes were the same at the time of the inquisition as now, but the court did not much regard it.

Lincoln's Inn MS. Misc. 559, f. 83

Michaelmas [term] 1696. Between the Attorney General of the Lord King, plaintiff, [and] Henry, duke of Beaufort, Thomas, earl of Pembroke, Edmund Wiseman, knight, Richard Hughes, gentleman, defendants, upon a plea to an inquisition seizing the late marquess of Powis's estate in Montgomeryshire into the king's hands upon an attainder for high treason, ex parte Rememeratoris Regis in Scaccario.

Upon a trial at the bar in the Exchequer by a special jury of the County of Middlesex the last day of this term save one, the case was this. At the sessions of oyer and terminer held at the Old Bailey the 9th of October 1689, William, lord marquess of Powis, was indicted of high treason for compassing and imagining the death of his now Majesty and the late Queen Mary and for levying war against them in Ireland. And this treason was laid in the indictment to be done

[1] *Attorney General v. Penn* (Ex. 1686), see above, Case No. 24; *Rex v. Baden* (Ex. 1693), see below, Case No. 101.

the 1st of May 1689, and, upon this indictment the said marquess was outlawed on Monday next before the feast of St. Valentine, which is in February 1689. And, thereupon the said marquess was attainted of high treason, and all his real estate whereof he was seised at the time of the treason committed became forfeited to His Majesty and the late queen. And, in order to find the estate so forfeited that the king might be ascertained of the same (though by the statutes of 26 and 33 Hen. VIII,[1] the crown, in such a case, is in possession without an office), a commission issued under the great seal of England (though under the seal of the Exchequer had been sufficient, it being but an office of instruction and not of instituting) to divers commissioners therein named to inquire and seize into His Majesty's hands the castles, lordships, lands, tenements, and hereditaments whereof the said marquess was seized at the time of the treason committed or after, whereupon an inquisition was taken upon the oaths of twelve good and lawful men of the County of Montgomery whereby it was found that the marquess, at the time of the treason committed, was seised in fee of Powis Castle and of divers manors, lands, and tenements in the County of Montgomery therein particularly mentioned of the several yearly values therein also set down, *in omnibus exitibus ultra reprisas*, amounting in the whole to about £4000 *per annum*, all which were said thereby to be seized into His Majesty's hands.

To this inquisition, the now defendants as terre tenants to all, except the lordship of Strata Marcella, came in and pleaded in discharge of the said forfeiture a lease for twenty-one years made by the said marquess, who by the plea was alleged to be seised in fee, and by the Lord Montgomery, his oldest son and heir apparent unto the defendants at the parish of St. Giles in the Fields in the County of Middlesex by a deed dated the 8th of December 1688, which was precedent in time to the treason in the indictment, whereby the said marquess and Lord Montgomery, taking notice that the marquess was justly indebted to several persons in the schedule to the said deed annexed and also in the plea particularly named in several sums of money, showing what, making in all £10,000, did grant and demise the said premises to the defendants and their assigns for the term of twenty-one years from the date in trust that they should pay and satisfy by and out of the rents, issues, and profits of the premises the said several debts and that, by virtue thereof, they entered and were possessed until ousted by the said inquisition and seizure. And they aver that the debts are not satisfied but that a great part thereof, naming a sum, yet remains unpaid. And they pray to be restored to the possession of the premises for the residue of the term.

The Attorney General prays *oyer* of the deed and has it *in haec verba*, which is entered of record, whereby it appears that the deed was made upon these trusts: first, to discharge the charges of the trustees; secondly, to pay the scheduled debts of £10,000 with interest and damages; thirdly, that, if the marquess or

[1] Stat. 26 Hen. VIII, c. 13 (*SR*, III, 508–509); Stat. 33 Hen. VIII, c. 20 (*SR*, III, 855–857).

Lord Montgomery or the trustees raise and pay the debts, then to be a trust for such as pay those debts; fourthly, after that done, to pay and dispose the rents as the marquess and Lord Montgomery or the survivor shall direct by deed or will; fifthly, in default of such appointment, then to such as shall have the freehold expectant upon that term. Then follows a clause which exempts the defendants from being answerable the one for the other or for any steward or agent employed or empowered by the marquess or Lord Montgomery.

And, then, the Attorney General replies that the said demise was made by the marquess by fraud and collusion of the marquess with a design to avoid the forfeiture of the premises during the term for the treason aforesaid.

The defendants rejoin that the said demise was made for good and valuable considerations therein mentioned, and traverse the fraud and collusion. And, thereupon, issue was joined.

And, to make out the issue as far as concerns the defendants, they produced the deed, which was confessed to be dated and executed by the pleading *prout* and rested it there, it carrying a consideration in it and fraud not being to be presumed but proved. But, upon the producing of it, it appeared (as also it did upon the *oyer*), that there was a blank left for the Christian name of the earl of Pembroke.

The counsel for the king laid it down for a rule, which was not opposed by the defendants' counsel, that whatsoever deed would be fraudulent as against a purchaser and to defraud him of his purchase would be so as against the king to defraud him of his forfeiture for treason or otherwise and that by the Statute of 13 Eliz., ca. 5.[1] And it was further insisted on on the behalf of the king that, though the deed be confessed in pleading, yet, upon the question of fraud, it may be very proper for the pleaders to avoid all suspicion to prove not only the sealing and delivery but the time when the deed was sealed and where, because the date of the deed was but three days before the abdication of King James, with whom or shortly after the marquess went, and the four witnesses to it are all Frenchmen and absent and the [*blank*] for the earl of Pembroke's Christian name renders it very suspicious, they being a near relation, but the defendant's counsel did not think fit to do any more as to those matters save to prove that all the witnesses to the marquess's sealing were in France and went thither about the 10th of December 1688 and proved their hands and that, in June or July 1689, it was sealed by the Lord Montgomery, then in the Tower [of London] the marquess's seal being then to it. And yet the same witness proved that Lord Montgomery was in London the 9th of December 1688, and was acquainted with the earl of Pembroke and was his kinsman. And no reason was given why the Lord Montgomery did not then seal it nor why a blank was left for the Christian name of the earl of Pembroke, a trustee named by the said marquess and Lord Montgomery, upon

[1] Stat. 13 Eliz. I, c. 5 (*SR*, IV, 537–538).

which matters the King's Counsel laid some stress as evidences of fraud, as they did also upon the frame and nature of the deed and upon the concealment of it from the creditors a considerable time after it was made, for none of them knew of it until 1692 and then it was produced by Lord Montgomery for the creditors' satisfaction. And [. . .] insisted upon the clause in the deed that the trustees, the defendants, should not be chargeable or accountable for any steward or agent employed or empowered by the marquess or Lord Montgomery that that clause amounted in effect to a power of revocation, at least to an overthrow of the trust for the creditors, for, by virtue of that, the marquess and his son by their agents might receive all to their own use and the creditors nothing so that it was a trust or not a trust for the creditors at the pleasure of the marquess and his son, which the King's Counsel insisted was a badge of fraud and would make such a deed void as against a purchaser and, by parity of law and reason, against the king.

And it was proved in the cause that, after the date of this deed, *viz.* 1 January 1688[/89], the marquess and his lady made a letter of attorney to the Lord Montgomery in their names and to their uses to receive, sue for, and recover all debts, rents, etc. in England or Wales and to call to account any receivers or bailiffs etc. which needed not nor ought to have been in case this deed was then executed.

And it was proved by several witnesses that, all along after this deed, the courts of the manors were kept and rents received as belonging to the marquess until the taking of the inquisition September 1691 and that the defendant Hughes, between the deed and the inquisition, acted as agent for the marquess and never claimed as trustee and that, when the trust deed was discovered, then, Hughes took up the receipts he had given to the tenants for rents as for the marquess, and he gave them other receipts instead thereof, and that Hughes acted as the marquess's agent and not as trustee nor for the creditors until about two years since and, all along until that time, managed the whole estate for the marquess and owned him as lord thereof and was steward of several of the manors, which he could not be if the deed was good and known, for, then, he was one of the *domini pro tempore*, which is inconsistent with being steward.

The defendants, with whom the creditors joined, made a probable proof of many of the debts in the schedule, but were defective in the proof of some. And it appeared that the Lord Montgomery was bound for most of the debts, and, being so bound, had received a great part of the rents and profits to enable him to pay (and he had paid) some part of the debts and kept the trust up for reimbursing himself what he had paid and not received and to enable him to pay the residue and discharge his engagements, they being all originally the marquess's debts.

And the defendant's counsel insisted upon these things:

First, that the marquess, long before the making of this deed, *viz.* 1687, did declare his intention to make provision for the payment of his debts, and this was at a time when he was in great splendor and favor, and this was proved by Sir Peter Pet;

Secondly, that, by the execution of this deed in question, he had made provision accordingly, which was both a just and honorable thing and what became him to do;

Thirdly, that this deed being made for the payment of debts, many of which are proved to be just and unpaid, it cannot be called a fraudulent deed, being made upon so great and just a consideration and though possibly the rents and profits have not been so strictly and constantly applied to the paying off of the scheduled debts to the respective creditors themselves, yet the Lord Montgomery, who was bound for them and having received some of the rents and paid and given further security for some of the debts and lying at stake for them all, having had the custody of the deed and upon occasion, though not so early as might have been, acquainted the creditors with it and they acquiescing under his management, it ought not to invalidate the intent and deed of the marquess, which was for the payment of his debts, nor can it be thought that a deed that was good in its creation should become fraudulent by the subsequent using or acting under it not so strictly and precisely as might have been done;

Thirdly,[1] that the deed being confessed in the pleading, the date and time of execution must be taken to be as they appear in the pleading until the contrary be proved;

Fourthly, that, as to the blank for the Christian name of the earl of Pembroke, it was a time of hurry and confusion and it might not be readily in the mind of the marquess at that time and, after he had sealed it, it could not be put in by Lord Montgomery when he came to seal it, which was not until June or July 1689, as above, but gave no answer why he did not seal it sooner, being (as their own witness Milot [?] proved) in London the 9th of December 1688, which was the day after the date of the deed, and London being the place where they would have it understood to be sealed;

Fifthly, that, as to possession, receipt of rents, and pretense of ownership until the inquisition September 1691, it may be reasonably supposed that, until then, no notice was taken of the attainder not any prosecution had upon it and, therefore, it was natural for the first owner to receive the profits until the crown took a course to assert its own title and presently, after the return of the inquisition, the defendants put in their plea;

(But it was proved in the cause by one of the defendants' witnesses that the Lord Montgomery was pressed for money to pay one of the debts and yet he never acquainted the party with this deed or the provision made by it which might have satisfied the pressure.).

Sixthly, it was desired by the defendants' counsel that the earl of Pembroke (present in court) might be examined whether the marquess of Powis ever desired he might use his name in the trust (which, as they said, would answer the blank

[1] Sic in MS.

and supposed secrecy of the deed) and urged that, being but a trustee, he might be a witness for that purpose. But that was opposed by the King's Counsel and refused by the court as a strange motion, being a defendant in the very trial and concerned to answer for the mesne rates, if [there be] a verdict for the king, and though courts of equity sometimes allow trustees to be witnesses, yet never in such a case as this, nor at a trial at law, where he is named plaintiff or defendant or may be concerned in consequence;

Seventhly, the defendants urged that the premises seized by the inquisition were granted in fee to the earl of Rochford.[1] But there was no such grant nor copy of record, nor other thing than the Lord Keeper's receipt, to prove it, and the court could not allow less proof of such a grant than a copy of the enrollment. And the granting out varies not the case one jot as to the making of the deed fraudulent or not fraudulent, for if it would be fraudulent against the king if not granted out, it will be no less fraudulent against the grantee when it is granted out nor was there any evidence given that any such grant had passed the seal.

Mr. Attorney [General *Trevor*] replied that, though these debts should be real ones, yet this deed will be fraudulent unless these debts were really and absolutely secured by it and made with such intent and not to be ambulatory or arbitrary to be used or not used for the payment of the debts at the pleasure of any other [person] besides the creditors, who, as also the trustees, the defendants, were not for some years after the date of it so much as acquainted with it. And it is not material how the trustees or Lord Montgomery would use the deed after the forfeiture incurred, for, possibly, they may rather prefer the creditors than the king. But how it was used for some years after the date and that was not to the payment of the creditors, which shows the original intent was not for the payment of debts but at will and pleasure which is a badge of fraud.

And upon the whole evidence on both sides strictly and impartially summed up with all the observations and objections on both sides and left to the jury, they found for the king, that is, that the deed was fraudulent.

The trial lasted until near ten o'clock at night.

Note there was another deed of the same date, tenor, and effect with this and for the payment of the same debts of the marquess of the Middlesex and Northamptonshire estates. And, upon a trial at the bar of the court upon the like issue for the Middlesex estate in February 1691 and a verdict passed in favor of the deed, yet, upon a trial at the same bar by a Northamptonshire jury in May 1692 and upon a new trial granted for the Middlesex estate and tried June 1692, there were verdicts for the king and against that deed in both those trials upon the same issues with this now tried. And so the deed in effect stands impeached by three verdicts at the bar. But none of these verdicts were offered in evidence.

[1] H. Dunthorne, 'Nassau van Zuylestein, William Frederick van, first earl of Rochford (1649–1708)', *Oxford Dictionary of National Biography*, vol. 40, pp. 258–259.

Note that, at the setting down of causes after this term, the judgment in the cause above being entered, Mr. Attorney [General *Trevor*] and Mr. Solicitor [General *Hawles*] moved for an order of court to be made touching the mesne rates from Michaelmas 1691, which was after the inquisition and also long after the forfeiture by the attainder, which in the judgment of the law relates to the first of May 1689 and, from that time, the king is entitled to the profits, until the judgment, which was a determination of the defendant's plea, and that the defendants, according to the condition of the recognizance given, upon putting in of the said plea by Sir Edmund Wiseman and three others of the penalty of £8000 that the defendant should perform and abide such order as the court should make touching the mesne rates of the premises might be ordered forthwith to pay the mesne rates according to the values found in the inquisition, which are therein mentioned to be above all reprises, the court referred it to the Deputy Remembrancer to compute the same, which he did according to the said values without regard to any taxes or other reprises. And, the first day of Hilary term following, that report was confirmed, thereby it appearing that, after such computation, the mesne rates, as above, came to above £13,000 and the penalty of the security was but £8000. And, notwithstanding it was much insisted on by the defendant's counsel that the taxes of 4s. in the pound granted by Parliament after the inquisition were not in the prospect of the jury that found the inquisition, being such as happened since by act of Parliament and the double of them in respect of not taking the oaths have been paid, yet there ought to be an abatement of such taxes out of these mesne rates, yet, in regard the court had nothing before them but the inquisition nor could those taxes or the payment of them be taken notice of upon any order for the mesne rates or by him that computed them nor any examination made therein, and, in regard by the constant practice of the court, the rates and values in the inquisition are and have been such by which the party as well as the king have been bound and have been and are the measure and proportion by which the security of mesne rates is always taken upon putting in the plea and thereby submitted to by the pleaders to be the values that must be answered to the crown; in case the pleader's title prevails not, the court could not, for what appeared judicially before than take notice of any other values than those in the inquisition nor of any abatement to be made out of them being found upon oath upon the inquisition to be the annual values above all reprises.

And, therefore, the court confirmed the report and ordered payment forthwith to be made or else process of *scire facias* to issue upon the recognizance of £8000, which indeed is not sufficient to pay the annual value of the premises in case there was or should be an abatement made for the taxes, and, in case there ought to be a deduction of taxes, it must be had in another manner and not upon a parol allegation at the bar.

And, after this, an English bill was exhibited against the Attorney General and the earl of Rochford, whose grant (and not until there) appeared to the court.

Afterwards, fo. 97; *vide* residuum.

[Other copies of this report: Georgetown Univ. Law Sch. MS. B88–8, p. 463.]

Lincoln's Inn MS. Misc. 559, f. 97, pl. 2

And, for authority and precedent that the mesne rates are to be computed according to the values in the inquisition without abatement for taxes, the cases of the Attorney General and Baden, in this court about two years ago, and of Waller and Lord Jeffreys,[1] about Dudley Ruse's estate, about the year 1686 or 1687, were remembered in which cases the mesne rates were answered according to the inquisition, though in Baden's Case, which was upon debate in court, it was made out by affidavits that the annual profits or values of the lands were not so much.

And, after judgment was entered for the king in the principal case, it was moved that an injunction should issue to the sheriff to put the king or his assignee in possession.

But, upon inquiry, the sworn clerks did all inform the court that the practice was first to award an injunction to the tenants and parties to quit the possession of the premises. And, if they did not do so, then to award an injunction to the sheriff, as above, which was observed in this case, though, afterwards, upon a search and enquiry, it appeared that, sometimes, the injunction to the sheriff was at first awarded without any to the parties as well in such a case as this as upon a judgment in [an action of] intrusion.

And at the setting down of causes after Hilary term, the Attorney General having regard to the defendants' English bill to be relieved by a deduction of taxes, it was prayed that the Lord Rochford, who had a grant by a privy seal of the arrears and had answered, might be ordered to rejoin likewise, which the court could not do without consent. But it left the plaintiffs in that bill to proceed by the rules of the court. And, thereupon, they prayed that they might be at liberty to proceed at present against the Attorney General alone without prejudice, which was allowed as a common and usual motion and that they might proceed afterwards against the earl of Rochford as they thought fit, which was allowed. But nothing was done further. Afterwards 125. See Lane 42, 48, 108.[2]

[Other copies of this report: Georgetown Univ. Law Sch. MS. B88–8, p. 510.]

Lincoln's Inn MS. Misc. 559, f. 124

After the injunction had been granted to the defendants to quit the possession, judgment being entered for the king, and the possession of Powis Castle and some other lands, part of the premises, not being delivered, as appeared by affidavit, a writ of injunction was awarded to the sheriff of the County of Montgomery to put the king or his assigns into possession and Mr. Attorney General hav-

---

1 *Lord Jeffries v. Herbert* (Ex. 1699), see below, Case No. 193.

2 *Rex v. Earl of Nottingham* (Ex. 1609), Lane 42, 145 E.R. 284; *Sawyer v. East* (Ex. 1611), Lane 74, 108, 145 E.R. 311, 339.

ing endorsed upon the writ that he directed the possession should be delivered to the earl of Rochfort, the king's grantee, or to such as he should appoint and the earl, by writing under hand and seal, having appointed two persons or either of them to receive the possession and this writ and authority from the earl being showed both to the sheriff and under sheriff at two several times long enough before the return of the writ, and they [were] required to execute it and deliver the possession accordingly, but did not, upon an affidavit made thereof (and that £40 was tendered them to do it, though no known fee is allowed for such service, especially in the king's case), the court awarded a Messenger to fetch up both sheriff and under sheriff for their contempt.

But this matter came no more before the court because the parties came to an agreement or accommodation between themselves.

[Other copies of this report: Georgetown Univ. Law Sch. MS. B88–8, p. 601.]

Lincoln's Inn MS. Misc. 559, f. 125

Attorney General v. Sir Edmund Wiseman and three others in a *scire facias*. Hilary term 8 Will. III [1697]; Easter term 1697. King's Remembrancer's [Office].

The defendant, Sir Edmund Wiseman, who was one of the schedule creditors of the late marquess of Powis, and three others, the 5th of March 5 Will. & Mar. [1693], entered into a recognizance of £8000 penalty jointly an severally to the king and queen. And upon this, there goes a *scire facias, teste* the 29th of January and returnable the next day, reciting the recognizance and that the money was payable at a day past but that the defendants had not paid it *prout per inspectionem rotulorum de Scaccario nostro praedicto nobis constat* directed to the sheriff of Middlesex to make known to the defendants what they had to say why the king should not have execution against the defendants for the said £8000. The sheriff returned a *scire feci* to all the defendants, who all appeared. And, after *oyer* of the recognizance and of the condition thereof, which was that, whereas by an inquisition taken the 2d of September last past before the date before such persons (naming them), His Majesty's commissioners under the great seal to inquire of and seize the manors, lands, and tenements of William, marquess of Powis, outlawed for high treason, the barony and castle called Powis Castle and other lands therein mentioned were seized into His Majesty's hands as the said marquess's lands, in discharge of which seizure, the duke of Beaufort and others there named put in their plea in this court. If, therefore, the said duke of Beaufort and the other pleaders of whom the defendant Sir Edmund Wiseman was one or any of them, their or any of their heirs, executors, or administrators shall stand to perform and abide such order as shall be made by this court upon the determination of this plea or otherwise concerning the mesne rates and profits of the said extended premises by them pleaded unto as aforesaid and for the arrears of the rents thereof and shall prosecute an end of their said plea with effect, then the recognizance to be void, else etc.

The defendants pleaded *quod ipsi de praedictis £8000 ergo dominum regem nunc onerari non debent quia dicunt* that the duke of Beaufort and others the pleaders in discharge of the seizure *perimpleverunt, performaverunt, et observaverunt omnia et singula in conditione recognitionis de eorum parte perimplendum, performandum, et observandum secundum conditionem recognitionis praedictis juxta formam conditionis praedictis, et hoc parati sunt verificare unde petunt judicium si dictus dominus rex nunc executionem versus ipsos pro praedicta £8000 habere debeat aut valeat.*

To this plea, the Attorney General demurred specially, and showed for cause that the plea was *duplex, incertum, insufficiens, et caret formam* and prayed judgment *et quod* the defendants *onerentur erga dominum regem* with the £8000 *et eidem domino regi satisfaciant.* And the defendants joined in demurrer.

And, though, upon the first arguing of this demurrer, there appeared no difficulty but that the plea was naught, yet, at the desire of the defendant's counsel (rather as was thought to gain time than out of any hopes to make the plea good), they were permitted to argue it a second time in this term.

And then the court *una voce* gave judgment for the king upon the insufficiency of the defendants' plea upon these grounds:

First, because, where there are particular acts to be done which are or are to be done upon record, there, those acts must be particularly and specially pleaded and showed to be done, and a plea of general performance in such a case is clearly bad. And here are two acts to be done upon record which are performance of an order of this court (which the condition mentions and which was made by the court, though the defendants take no notice of it) and the prosecuting the plea with effect. And this is yet stronger, being in the case of a condition of a recognizance, which is a matter of record, than in the case of a condition of a obligation which is not of record. And yet the law is so in the last case and in the case of a subject. And, for this purpose, these cases were cited, 2 Hen. VII, fo. 14; 1 Instit. 303b, Lre. A.; Cro. Jac. 559, Lee and Luttrell's Case;[1]

Secondly, where acts are to be done by a stranger, they are to be particularly pleaded. And, here, all are strangers (except Wiseman), and, if he might (which nevertheless for the reasons above, he could not) plead generally, yet the other strangers joining with him in this general plea makes it bad. Lamb's Case, 5 rep.; 1 Instit. 209;[2]

Thirdly, it is not held good pleading in the case of the king where the condition of a bond is for the doing of several things particularly expressed to plead a general performance, though they be all in the affirmative. And this was adjudged in this court Easter term 24 Car. II, between the King and Morgan and others, *q.v.*, L. 2, fo. 193b, which is a much stronger case, and more reasonable to

---

[1] YB Hil. 2 Hen. VII, f. 14, pl. 20 (1487); E. Coke, *First Institute* (1628), f. 303; *Lea v. Luthell* (1620), Croke Jac. 559, 79 E.R. 480, also 2 Rolle Rep. 159, 81 E.R. 724.

[2] *Lamb v. Brownwent* (1599), 5 Coke Rep. 23, 77 E.R. 85, also Croke Eliz. 716, 78 E.R. 950; E. Coke, *First Institute* (1628), f. 209.

have been allowed than this; and Cro. Eliz. 749; nor the same book 2, 81, were neither the case of the king.[1]

The defendant's counsel did not go about to maintain the plea to be good, but took these exceptions to the *scire facias*:

First, that it appears it was returnable the next day after the *teste*, which is not a reasonable time.

But, to that, it was answered the sheriff returned a *scire feci*, and all the defendants have appeared and pleaded, and so all of that objection, if it had been any, vanished.

Secondly, it does not appear where the recognizance was taken, for, if it was taken at Lechmere's chamber in the Middle Temple, that was in London, then the *scire facias* ought to have gone thither.

But, to that, it was answered, if it was taken in London, yet the enrollment and record being in Middlesex, that was well warranted the *scire facias* there. But there is nothing here within this record that mentions London, but the record is all in Middlesex. *Vide* Hall and Wingfield's Case, Hobt. 195, 196, and L. 2, 111,[2] where it was thought that it appearing upon the record that the recognizance was acknowledged in London though enrolled in Middlesex the *scire facias* might well be in London. But there is nothing of that in this case; nothing of London appears.

Thirdly, it is recited in the *scire facias* that the four defendants have not paid the £8000 and does not say that they nor any of them had not paid it and, being joint and several, the payment by any one was sufficient.

[This] was allowed to be so if, in truth, any of them had paid the money. But the defendants have not made that their case by the plea. And, if it had been so, they might well have pleaded it and had the advantage of it. But that is put into the *scire facias* by way of inducement and the money was not otherwise to be paid than as the defendants failed in performing the condition which they took upon them to plead they have done, but failed therein.

So, upon the whole matter, the objections made by the defendants' counsel did not seem to have any weight, but judgment was entered for the king.

Attorney General [*Trevor*] and *Dodd* were for the king; *Winnington* and *Powis* and *Browne* were for the defendants.

[There was a] like judgment as to this third point 27 November 1705, between the Attorney General and St. John *et al.* For the same reasons.[3]

[Other copies of this report: Georgetown Univ. Law Sch. MS. B88–8, p. 602.]

[1] *Attorney General v. Morgan* (Ex. 1672), Exch. Repts. *tempore* Car. II, 239; *Mints v. Bethil* (1600), Croke Eliz. 749, 78 E.R. 981; *Farnham v. Watkins* (1670), Lincoln's Inn MS. Misc. 500, f. 81, pl. 4.

[2] *Hall v. Wingfield* (1617), Hobart 195, 80 E.R. 342, also Moore K.B. 883, 72 E.R. 973, 1 Brownlow & Goldesborough 69, 123 E.R. 671; *Wynne v. Taylor* (Ex. 1670), Exch. Repts. *tempore* Car. II, 169.

[3] *Attorney General v. St. John* (Ex. 1705–1706), see below, Case No. 254.

91

Saunders v. Ryall

(Ex. 1692)

An endowment of a glebe carries all of the profits of the land with it.

Dodd 116, 1 Rayner 71, 1 Eagle & Younge 570

Ryall [was the] lessee of the preceding vicar. The vicar was endowed of all small tithes within the parish and of four acres of the glebe, and the parson or impropriator had all of the great tithes. The vicar leased the glebe to A., who sowed it with corn, and then the vicar died, and B. was instituted and inducted, and A. carried off the corn, and B. sued him for the tithes.

And [it was] held by all that A. should pay the tithe. But the great point was to whom because it was objected that, now it is a great tithe, it should go to the parson and not to the vicar because he was not endowed with great tithes.

But LECHMERE and POWELL [said] that the vicar should have [it] because the endowment of the glebe carries all of the profits of the land with it.

But TURTON [held] *contra* and that the parson should have [it] because the land was only discharged of the great tithes in the hands of the vicar, but he could not have them *en prendre* because the parson had all of the great tithes.

In the absence of the Chief Baron, it was decreed for the vicar.

See Cr. Eliz. 579, Grisley's Case, cited in Blencowe and Barksdale's Case,[1] to the contrary. But this case was not cited to the court nor by them, notwithstanding [that the] court took two days to consider [the case]. See below, Hawkins and Chittle.[2]

2 Gwillim 537

Hilary term 3 & 4 Will. & Mar., 1692.

A vicar endowed with the glebe has a right to the great tithes growing thereof although he has no right to the great tithes in general in the parish. [It was] so held.

N.B., in this case, the vicar had let his glebe which was sowed with corn, and he then died. The court decreed that the next vicar should have the tithe of the corn, and not the impropriator.

---

[1] *Blinco v. Backsdale* (1597), Croke Eliz. 579, 78 E.R. 822, 1 Gwillim 197, 1 Eagle & Younge 134.

[2] *Hawkins v. Chittle* (Ex. 1696), see below, Case No. 136.

92

Gray's Case

(Ex. 1692)

Grants of public offices that contain new and unusual clauses and requirements are void, such as that a deputy to an Auditor in the Exchequer be approved by the Lord Treasurer.

Dodd 117

He [Mr. Gray, the Auditor of Wales] had a patent for this office (at pleasure) to exercise by himself or his sufficient deputy, as usual. But then followed this unusual clause in relation to the deputy, *viz.* 'to be approved of by the Commissioners of the Treasury or Lord Treasurer for the time being'. And the court refused to swear Mr. Gray upon this patent because the approbation and sufficiency of the deputy appertains to the Court of Exchequer and this clause looks like an encroachment upon the jurisdiction of the court. And notwithstanding that it was answered by one that the clause was but *in majorem cautelam* and that after the Treasury had approved, yet [he] must come to court to be sworn and then the court can refuse, to which barons LECHMERE and TURTON inclined and agreed; however, the Chief Baron and POWELL refused to swear Mr. Gray and said that it is a void grant and would not permit an unusual clause in any patents of ancient offices, and thus Mr. Gray cannot be sworn.

POWELL said that if a *custos brevium* be granted in the [Court of] Common Pleas to be exercised by himself or his sufficient deputy to be approved by the Lord Chancellor, it will be void.

These books were cited: 4 Inst. 109; Dr. 211; 2 Hen. VI, c. 10; 4 Inst. 115;[1] Maynard's *Memorandum Scaccario*, 3, 6, 7, 16, 17. All moneys must be accounted for in the Exchequer. No deputy can act until sworn and allowed by the court by the Chief Baron. *Clausula inconsueta.*[2]

LECHMERE said that, in Squibb and Lovell's Case, it was resolved that he was an officer before [being] sworn. (This was the office of one of the tellers. Query.) [In] Harris and Stewkley[3] in this court, [it] was adjudged that a grant of an office that appertained to the customs for life was good notwithstanding many acts of Parliament [were] against it, because those acts are only a direction to the grant, but the king is not tied up by them.

---

[1] E. Coke, *Fourth Institute* (1644), f. 109; *Chester's Case* (1562), 2 Dyer 210, 73 E.R. 465; Stat. 2 Hen. VI, c. 13 (*SR*, II, 222); E. Coke, *Fourth Institute* (1644), f. 115.

[2] *Clausulae inconsuetae semper inducunt suspicionem*; unusual clauses always induce suspicion; see *Twyne's Case* (1601), 3 Coke Rep. 80, 81, 76 E.R. 809, 814.

[3] *Arris v. Stukely* (1677), Exch. Repts. *tempore* Car. II, 314.

Note: There was a *non obstante* [clause] in the grant. Query. Afterwards, a new grant was procured by Mr. Gray without the clause, and he was sworn by the Chief Baron at his house upon it [on] 24 May 1692.

93

Pettit v. Churley

(Ex. 1692)

The issue in this case was whether an alien can sue for tithes.

Dodd 122, 1 Rayner 72,

2 Gwillim 536, 1 Eagle & Younge 569

After the close of Trinity term, upon a plea to a tithe bill that the party was a Frenchman and not capable of the benefice by the acts of Ric. II and Hen. V,[1] the court doubted. See Rolle, *Presentment*, 348,[2] etc.

Note: The acts are printed in Rastall, [*Statutes*].

94

Stump v. Ayliffe

(Ex. 1692)

The king's books are conclusive evidence of the value of an ecclesiastical living.

Dodd 123, 1 Eagle & Younge 567

Upon an English bill for tithes in the Exchequer, the defendant set out and proved that the plaintiff had taken a second benefice which, by the proofs, was above £8 in value, etc. But in the king's books, it was below the value etc. And the court doubted whether the value should be determined by the king's books conclusively or whether it should be according to the real value. *Adjornatur.*

See Dy. 237, Cro. Eliz. 853, Cro. Car. 456, Degge 29.[3]

Afterwards, 5th December 1692, at Serjeants' Inn, it was resolved upon debate that it should be according to the king's books, and the defendant was decreed to account.

I [*Samuel Dodd*] was of counsel with the plaintiff.

---

[1] Stat. 3 Ric. II, c. 3 (*SR*, II, 14–15); Stat. 7 Ric. II, c. 12 (*SR*, II, 34–35); Stat. 13 Ric. II, stat. 2, c. 2 (*SR*, II, 69–74); Stat. 1 Hen. V, c. 7 (*SR*, II, 172–173).

[2] 2 Rolle, Abr., *Presentment*, pl. L, 4 and 5, p. 348.

[3] *Anonymous* (1565), 2 Dyer 237, 73 E.R. 524; *Bond v. Tricket* (1601), Croke Eliz. 853, 78 E.R. 1079, also Noy 38, 74 E.R. 1008; *Humphreys v. Knight* (1636), Croke Car. 455, 79 E.R. 994, also W. Jones 387, 82 E.R. 203; S. Degge, *Parson's Counsellor.*

[Other reports of this case: 1 Rayner 72, 2 Gwillim 536.]

[The order of 21 June 1692, Public Record Office E.126/16, f. 29, is printed at 1 Wood 294.]

95

Berwick v. Swanton

(Ex. 1692)

A sequestrator of tithes lacks standing to sue for tithes.

Dodd 123, 1 Eagle & Younge 574

The plaintiff brought a bill for tithes as sequestrator of the tithes of Stamford in Norfolk, and upon the hearing the court dismissed the bill, because a sequestrator is like a bailiff and accountable [to the bishop] and has no interest, and so it was before resolved in November 1686 in the Exchequer between Banks and Roy.[1]

Note: The plaintiff was a parson and served the cure by appointment of the bishop and had a sequestration of the tithes.

Note: See below, Bishop of Norwich and Eachard against Bucklea.[2]

[Other reports of this case: 1 Rayner 72, 2 Gwillim 537.]

[The order of 22 June 1692, Public Record Office E.126/16, f. 31v, is printed at 1 Wood 295.]

96

Grove's Case

(Ex. 1692)

An oral contract to retain tithes is valid.

Dodd 124, 1 Eagle & Younge 575

In a prohibition in the Exchequer, the case of Thornton and Cremer[3] was cited, which was resolved in the time of Chief Baron Hale that an agreement by parol to retain tithes was good and within the Statute of Edw. VI[4] notwithstanding it

---

[1] *Banks v. Rye* (Ex. 1686), Equity Cases Exch. 247.

[2] *Bishop of Norwich v. Bucklea* (Ex. 1713), see below, Case No. 432.

[3] *Breamer v. Thornton* (1661), Hardres 203, 145 E.R. 453, 1 Rayner 33, 1 Eagle & Younge 436.

[4] Stat. 2 & 3 Edw. VI, c. 13 (*SR*, IV, 55–58).

was for more than one year, and so it was resolved in Web and Beal's case in the Exchequer, 28 Car., that it was good for three years by way of retainer.

And it was said by LECHMERE and POWELL, barons, that it was resolved in Jelus Case upon a prohibition:

First, that for one year an agreement by parol was good and unavoidable;

Second, that an agreement was good for more years and only avoidable by election, but if the years incur, the parson cannot after the years make it void, but it ought to be avoided within the time for suing for the tithes, and compared it to a tenancy at will which cannot be determined a few days before the rent becomes due, etc.

Note: In the present case, the libel was for three years. The defendant insisted upon the agreement for the first year and said that he set out the tithes the second, etc. And afterwards, [he] moved for a prohibition suggesting this agreement. And, by the court, it appears the agreement is waived by the setting out of the tithes, and no prohibition was granted.

97

LeNeve, qui tam v. Sweetapple

(Ex. 1692)

The issues in this case were whether a person can melt down foreign silver and whether a duty is payable on it when it is exported.

Dodd 125

[Upon] an information upon the Statute of Tonnage etc.[1] for shipping six ingots of silver, the custom not paid, upon the general issue, a special verdict [was] found, *viz.* that it was Spanish plate and Irish silver and by the defendant melted into ingots and shipped. And whether this was legal upon [the Statute] 15 Car. II, c. 7, s. 12,[2] was the doubt.

The court inclined that one could not melt foreign silver and that it should be continued in the same case[3] as it was when imported.

Query, because it seems to me to the contrary.

Another point was stirred by the defendant, that if it is prohibited, yet it will not pay a duty and thus the information [is] bad. And the court doubted upon this but inclined that no duty will be paid if prohibited and adjourned for both points.

---

1 Stat. 12 Car. II, c. 4 (*SR*, V, 181, 195).

2 Stat. 15 Car. II, c. 7, s. 9 (*SR*, V, 451).

3 placita *MS*.

98

Barecroft v. Hundreds of Stock and Burnham

(Ex. 1693)

A pleading cannot be amended to cure a claim after the period of the statute of limitations has expired.

Dodd 127

Barecroft was the receiver of the money of the king in Worcester and he sent up by his servants along with the carrier £2400, and the carrier and servants were robbed near Beconsfield in these hundreds [Stock and Burnham in Buckinghamshire]. And he brought an action in the Exchequer against the hundreds and declared that he was assaulted and robbed and had made oath etc. And upon the issue joined, the jury appeared at the bar, and [the court] adjourned to another day because of the trial of lord Mohun.[1] And before the day, the plaintiff saw the faults in his count and that it was his servant that had been assaulted and robbed and that the servant should make the oath etc., because Barecroft was in London. And he prayed to amend, because if he could not amend, then the action was gone because [it was] above one year and a day since.

And upon debate [it was held] he is not to amend.

And a precedent [was] vouched out of the Common Pleas in the Case of Christie and Beckett of Bedford, that upon an action brought against him for making a false return of the burgess upon the Act of Hen. VI[2] etc. and he was mistaken in several points as he declared who [was] elected 'by burgesses' where it was elected 'by the freemen, inhabitants, and burgesses' and several other faults. And [it was] resolved that [he could] amend, otherwise his action was lost, because [it was] above three months etc.

Note: This [was] in a case in the Common Pleas [in] 2 W. & M. [1690 × 1691].

3 Levinz 347, 83 E.R. 723

Bearecroft v. Hundreds of Burnham and Stone.

Bearecroft, being receiver general of taxes for the County of Worcester, sent towards London by the Worcester carrier £4000 and sent divers servants with the wagon to guard it. The wagon was robbed in divers hundreds of Burnham and Stone, for which Bearecroft brought his action against the hundreds and declares of an assault and robbery done to himself, he being then at Worcester fifty miles from the place where the robbery was committed, and declared that he made oath that he did not know any of the persons. And the trial being ready

1 *Rex v. Lord Mohun* (1692), *State Trials* (Hargrave ed. 1777), vol. 4, p. 510.

2 Stat. 6 Hen. VI, c. 4; Stat. 8 Hen. VI, c. 7 (*SR*, II, 235–236, 243–244).

to be at bar, the jury appeared at the day. But for other business, it was adjourned to another day. And before the day to which the adjournment was, the mistake in the declaration being espied, the court was moved to amend the mistake, and to declare of a robbery on the servants and of oath made by the servants who had also made oaths of the robbery etc.

And upon great debate and hearing counsel on both sides at several days and view of two precedents, the one between Chisly and Becket, in the King's Bench, *intrato* Hil. 2 W. & M. rot. 432, in an action for false return of a member to Parliament on the Stat. of Hen. VI, where the plaintiff declared on a custom of Bedford to elect *per majorem ballivos et burgenses*, and the issue was joined and brought to the Assizes to be tried, but there it being discovered that the custom was to elect *per majorem ballivos, burgenses, et liberos homines*, the plaintiff withdrew the record, and, although the issue was entered of record in court, the plaintiff moved to amend his declaration, and, upon great deliberation and hearing of counsel, seeing that the time limited by the Statute for bringing the action was elapsed and so the action [was] lost if it were not amended, the court ruled it should be amended, and so it was, notwithstanding the great erasures, obliterations, and interlineations it made in the record, as it would also do in this case, the year for bringing the action being now passed.

And the Court here, *viz.* Sir Robert Atkyns, Lechmere, Turton, and Powys ruled the declaration should be amended, notwithstanding the opposition of the defendant. The other precedent produced was [from] Trin. 16 Car. II [1664], in the Common Pleas, where in an [action of] *quare impedit*, after issue joined, the replication was amended.

99

Rex v. Parry

(Ex. 1693)

A former sheriff can be ordered to amend a return after his term of office has ended.

Dodd 128

[Upon] an extent to enquire what lands Parry had at the time of the entering into a bond to the king and to seize into the king's hands, the sheriff took an inquisition that Parry [was] seised of such land. But he did not return that he had seized in[to the king's] hands. And, upon debate, [it was] amended.

Note: The court ordered the sheriff to amend notwithstanding [that he was] out of his office two years before. 10 Hen. VII, 23; 3 Keble 313; Syd. 259; 2 Cr. 534; Littleton's *Reports* 279; Palmer 408.[1]

---

[1] YB Pas. 10 Hen. VII, f. 23, pl. 27 (1495); *Hopkins v. Wood* (1674), 3 Keble 313, 84 E.R. 739; *Rex v. Glover* (1665), 1 Siderfin 259, 82 E.R. 1092, also 1 Keble 907, 83 E.R.

100

Chetmel, qui tam v. Shackle

(Ex. 1693)

In this case, the duties claimed were held due under a statute that was repealed, and the case was dismissed.

Dodd 129

Upon a special verdict in the Exchequer, the point was upon a clause in 1 Eliz.,[1] for selling native goods on shipboard after they were entered and before they arrived beyond [the] sea. And the court doubted the meaning of the clause but inclined that it was to prevent clearing alien's goods. But 25 Car. II,[2] having taken off alien's duties from native commodities and having altered the reason of the first law, has by consequence and implicitly repealed it. [It was] adjudged for the defendant.

I [*Samuel Dodd*] argued this [case].

101

Rex v. Baden

(Ex. 1693)

An inquisition upon an outlawry gives to the crown a title that is superior to a subsequent title by elegit.

Dodd 129

Baden had a judgment against Clarke and, after his judgment, Clarke is outlawed at the suit of P. in debt etc., and, upon the outlawry, an inquisition is taken and the land seized, as usual, and then Baden took [a writ of] *elegit* and, upon it, had a moiety delivered to him, and then he came into the Exchequer and pleaded as terre tenant to remove the hands of the king. And the court doubted.

But it seems clear that he cannot, because he who pleads of the king's hands ought to have a legal title to the estate before the inquisition.

In this case, it was agreed that the lessee upon an outlawry can neither plow nor sow, for the king has a mere perception of profits. Secondly, it was agreed that the *elegit* was well executed, because by the same reason that the conveyance

---

1313; *Moor v. Blackwel* (1619), Croke Jac. 534, 79 E.R. 458; *Anonymous* (1629), Littleton 279, 124 E.R. 246; *Plumme's Case* (1627), Palmer 480, 81 E.R. 1181, also Latch 210, 82 E.R. 350.

[1] Stat. 1 Eliz. I, c. 11 (*SR*, IV, 372–374).

[2] Stat. 25 Car. II, c. 6 (*SR*, V, 791–792).

of the party will be good, thus the conveyance of the law. Thus [it was] adjudged in Viner's and Massam's Case. But no ejectment lies, nor can the party enter upon the king against his grantee.

See 9 Hen. VI, 20; Br., Outlawry, 36b; 45 Dower; Hob. 122; Hardr. 23; Dr. 67; Hardr. 106; 1 Keble 57, 74, 76; Godb. 181.[1]

Dodd 133

[The case was] argued again and [it was] adjudged not to remove the hands of the king. And it was said and agreed that the inquisition made the title and not the outlawry, because if a man is outlawed and then sells or acknowledges a judgment etc. before an inquisition [be] taken upon the outlawry and the judgment is extended before the inquisition upon the outlawry, it is good. [And it was] affirmed in a writ of error coram Lord Keeper Somers, Holt and Treby, chief justices, after several arguments and great debates [in] Easter [term] 1694. And [in] February afterwards, error [was] brought in the House of Lords, and, upon argument, the judgment [was] affirmed.[2]

Parker 136, 145 E.R. 737

Baden had a judgment against Clarke; and, after his judgment, Clarke is outlawed at the suit of Allen. And, upon the outlawry, an inquisition is taken, and the lands seized into the king's hands. And, then, Baden takes out a [writ of] *elegit*, and has a moiety delivered to him. And then, he comes into this court, and pleads as terre tenant to remove the king's hands.

But judgment was given for the king, and affirmed in the Exchequer Chamber and, afterwards in the House of Lords, 20th February 1694, upon this particular reason that he who pleads off the king's hands ought to have a legal title prior to the estate found by the inquisition, and it was his own laches and default that he did not perfect his title by suing out an *elegit* and extending the lands before the taking of the inquisition upon the outlawry, for then he would have had a good title against the crown.

2 Salkeld 495, 91 E.R. 424

A. owes money to B. on a judgment, and to C. on a bond; A. is outlawed at the suit of the obligee, and his lands seized on the outlawry. And the question was whether the conusee of the judgment could extend these lands. And it was held the outlawry should be preferred and that the king's hands should not be

---

[1] YB Trin. 9 Hen. VI, f. 20, pl. 15 (1431); Brooke, Abr., *Utlagary*, pl. 36; *Attorney General v. Andrew* (1655), Hardres 23, 145 E.R. 360; *Stringfellow v. Brownesoppe* (1549), 1 Dyer 67, 73 E.R. 142; *Master v. Whitefield* (1657), Hardres 106, 145 E.R. 404; *Windsor v. Saywell* (1661), 1 Keble 57, 74, 76, 83 E.R. 809, 820, 821, also T. Raymond 17, 83 E.R. 10, 1 Levinz 33, 83 E.R. 283; *Anonymous* (1611), Godbolt 181, 78 E.R. 110.

[2] *Lords' Journal*, vol. 15, p. 501, Shower P.C. 72, 1 E.R. 50.

amoved, unless the conusee could show covin and practice between the obligor and obligee.

8 Price 326, 146 E.R. 1218

Baden had a judgment against Clarke. Clarke was outlawed at the suit of another person. And, on an inquisition taken thereon, the land was seized into the king's hands. Then Baden takes out a [writ of] *elegit*, and he has a moiety delivered to him, and he pleaded as terre tenant to amove the king's hands.

It was held certainly there that the [writ of] extent should be preferred. But it is also said that, if he had not been guilty of laches and neglect, but had sued out his *elegit* and extended the lands before the taking of the inquisition on the outlawry, he would then have had a good title against the crown.

[On appeal: Rex v. Baden (1694), Shower P.C. 72, 1 E.R. 50.]

102

Attorney General, ex rel. Lee v. Thorncroft

(Ex. 1693)

Governors of schools are required to take the oaths of supremacy and allegiance.

Dodd 130

Upon solemn argument, [it was] resolved by three against Powell that the governors of Macclesfield School, founded by Edward VI, are [in] a place of trust and within 25 Car.[1] to take the oaths, etc.

POWELL [held] *contra* and that it extends only to public trusts and not to governors of schools, fellows of colleges, or similar.

The bill was brought by the Attorney [General] *ex relatione* Lee and others to quiet Dobson in the place of schoolmaster and those in the place of governors. And an issue [was] directed whether Dobson was duly elected, and [it was] found yes. But Powell, who took the verdict, saved the point of law, whether the governors were bound to take the oaths to their present Majesties and the oaths upon 25 Car. And upon argument and debate, [it was] resolved as above.

103

Buckle v. Vanacre

(Ex. 1693)

Billets and faggots of wood pay tithes.

---

[1] Stat. 25 Car. II, c. 2 (*SR*, V, 782–785).

Dodd 131, 1 Eagle & Younge 570,
Bunbury 99, n., 145 E.R. 609, n.

20 February 1692[/93].

Upon a tithe bill for tithe wood in Erith in Kent at Serjeants' Inn, the 20th February 1692[/93], [it was] resolved that if [trees] above twenty years growth be felled and part of them used for timber and part made into billets, faggots, etc., that tithe shall be paid for this part so made into faggots, billets, etc. And it was said that it is not the thing but the use which exempts from tithes, and, notwithstanding [they were] above twenty years growth, it shall not avail etc. Acton and Smith in Hampshire, adjudged upon hearing, rehearing, and review; so in Watts and Wendown. Query the law. See Franklyn and Jones, 1687, and reports confirmed 1690; Cowper and Layfield of Burraton in Hampshire [and] Taswell and Athill, below.[1]

1 Rayner 73

Upon a bill for tithe wood in Erith in Kent about twenty years growth, part used for timber and part made into billets and faggots, [it was] resolved that the last shall pay tithes, for the trees being above twenty years growth alone will not privilege them, but the use [will].

104

Wild v. Acton

(Ex. 1693)

Vicars are entitled to tithes only through their endowments.

Chaplains and curates are not entitled to tithes.

Dodd 132, 1 Rayner 74, 1 Eagle & Younge 575

Wild was lessee of the impropriation and manor of Kempsey in Worcestershire, in which there is a vicar endowed. Stoulton is a vill therein and has a chapel of ease, and the inhabitants hire a curate or chaplain to say prayers and give him a salary. Wild brings his bill for tithe hay in this vill. [The defendants,] the inhabitants, insisted that the chaplain had the tithe hay and that they had agreed with him for their tithes. And upon debate, [it was] resolved:

First, that tithe hay is payable in this case, and it [was] admitted by the defendants;

---

[1] *Acton v. Smith* (Ex. 1687), Equity Cases Exch. 277; *Watts v. Melden* (Ex. 1666–1669), 1 Wood 77, 103; *Franklyn v. Jones* (Ex. 1686), Equity Cases Exch. 237; *Layfield v. Cowper* (Ex. 1694), 1 Wood 330, 1 Eagle & Younge 591; *Taswell v. Athill* (Ex. 1695), see below, Case No. 117.

Second, that either the parson or vicar must have it; the vicar does not pretend to be endowed [of it], and the common right is with the parson;

Third, that the chaplain is too uncertain a person and has too uncertain an estate to be capable of it, for he is put in and removed at pleasure.

[Orders of 4 May and 5 December 1693: Public Record Office E.126/16, ff. 104, 148v.]

105

Daniel v. Tuffnal

(Ex. 1693)

If turnips are sold or any profit is gained from them, they are liable for tithes, even though sown on fallow ground.

Dodd 134, 1 Rayner 75,
2 Gwillim 537, 1 Eagle & Younge 578

[It was] resolved that if the occupant sow turnips and then agist the sheep of a stranger or fattens his own sheep and sell them, he shall pay tithe for such herbage or agistment, notwithstanding they are sown upon the fallow ground (as this case was) and meliorate the land for corn. So here [is it also] if the turnips be sold or any profit made of them.

106

Shaftoe v. Hooke

(Ex. 1693)

A judgment creditor has priority over a bond creditor.

Dodd 134

Upon a rehearing, the point formerly resolved 9 February 1692[/93] and now resolved again upon a rehearing was [that] Shaftoe had a decree for a sum certain upon an account against Powell, and it was signed and enrolled. Powell died, having made his will and an executor, who renounced. And then Hooke, being a creditor by a bond took administration *cum testamento annexo*, and Shaftoe brought a bill against him to discover assets and [to] subject them to his decree.

And [it was] resolved that Hooke should not retain [the assets] against him but that the decree should be performed before the bonds. Thus, here it was resolved upon a hearing in chancery in Searle and Lane, 5 March 4 Jac. II [1688],[1]

[1] *Searle v. Lane* (1688), 2 Freeman 103, 22 E.R. 1086, 2 Vernon 37, 88, 23 E.R. 634, 667, *sub nom. Searle v. Hale*, pl. 4, 1 Eq. Cas. Abr. 332, 21 E.R. 1082, Chancery Cases *tempore* Jac. II, p. 419.

and affirmed upon a rehearing 24 November afterwards. There the point was [that] the administrator had paid away his assets to the bond creditors before notice, and yet [it was] resolved that he should take notice at his peril and should pay the decree first.

Note: In Shaftoe's Case there was another point that Hooke entered an attachment against the arch[deacon] and took the goods under color of it and then [became] administrator; [the point was] whether he would not be executor *de son tort*. And the court did not resolve this but determined [the case] upon the other point, Powell doubting.

1 Freeman 333, 22 E.R. 1237, 89 E.R. 248

Stasby v. Powell.

A decree was had against the defendant's intestate by the plaintiff for £400 for the profits of lands received by him, and the intestate, before the said decree, was indebted to the defendant by bond. The intestate dying, the defendant got administration. And the question was whether the defendant could retain to satisfy his own bond against this decree, there being not assets to satisfy both.

And [it was] held by Atkyns, Turton, and Lechmere that he might. And [it was] thereupon decreed that the defendant should pay the plaintiff, in case he had assets, in the first place.

Powell doubted, for that in case the party was sued at law for debt upon a bond, he could not plead nor give this decree in evidence at law to bar the plaintiff, and so it would be one way at law and another way here. But for that, it was answered that the party might be relieved by his bill in equity and have an injunction.

3 Levinz 355, 83 E.R. 727

Shafto v. Powell.

[There was] a *scire facias* against the defendant, executor of J.S., upon a decree in the Exchequer against J.S. for money. The defendant pleads that the testator was indebted to him upon an obligation and that he had paid himself before the scire facias [was] brought or any notice of the decree.

This case having been heard before, it was ruled by Lechmere and Turton, barons, against the opinion of Baron Powell that it was no bar. And now, upon a rehearing before all the barons, Atkyns, Chief Baron, agreed with Lechmere and Turton against Powell that it was no bar and that a decree in equity obliges an executor in equal degree, at least, with a judgment at common law.

[Order of 15 May 1693: Public Record Office E.126/16, f. 99.]

107

Molineux's Case

(Ex. 1693)

In alleging that a person is a Roman Catholic recusant, the words of the Statute, 'popish recusant convict', must be used.

Dodd 135

A man brought an action as executor; the defendant pleaded that the plaintiff was a Roman Catholic, *anglice* a papist convert *prout* by certification of the record here etc.

And the court resolved that [the plea was] bad, because it should be a 'popish recusant convict' which are the words of the Statute,[1] and so here. [It was] adjudged in the king's bench in the Lady Portland's Case,[2] here it was held that the plea *prout per certificationem recordi* etc. in this court is good.

108

Westby v. Stanley

(Ex. 1693)

A person who is both heir and executor and who is sued for the same debt of his ancestor in two separate actions in his two separate capacities cannot plead auter action pendent in both cases.

Dodd 135

An action of debt upon an obligation [was brought] against the heir and the same action against the executor the same day and term. (Note the heir and executor were the same party.) And he pleaded severally in abatement to both of the counts the pendency of the other plea.

And the court thought it bad, and thus here [it was] resolved in the Common Pleas [in] 2 W. & M. [1690 × 1691]. And thus was the resolution in the Common Pleas in Cooper and Langhorne's Case, Hilary [term] 2 W. & M. [1691], rot. 445, 446.

---

[1] Stat. 3 Jac. I, c. 5 (*SR*, IV, 1077–1082).

[2] *Countess of Portland v. Cole* (1681), 3 Levinz 2, 11, 83 E.R. 546, 551.

109

Knowles, qui tam v. Merrick

(Ex. 1693)

The issue in this case was whether an information of seizure can be amended and post-dated.

Dodd 135

Upon an information of seizure of a parcel of tobacco, [the case was thus]. Knowles made a seizure the 11th of October and preferred an information the 12th of October upon it, and a writ of appraisement issued and was returned. Afterwards, Knowles, finding he could not prove the seizure, made a second seizure the 30th of October, and then in Easter term last and this term [Trinity term 5 Will. & Mar., 1693] moved to amend his information and postdate it to comply with the second seizure.

And upon several debates, the court made an order to amend *nisi causa*, Powell dissenting. And afterwards, the court was divided because Lechmere changed his opinion and agreed with Powell, but the prior order stood, and the information was amended this term. And these precedents were produced: Lib. 7, 28 May 24 Eliz.; Lib. 11, Jac. 114; *ibidem* fo. 219; Lib. 10, fo. 308, 14 June 27 Eliz., in the Exchequer in the King's Remembrancer's Office; see below Layton and Pierce.[1]

110

Watts v. Watkins

(Ex. 1693)

In this case, the amount of the tithes due was proved in general terms by the testimony of witnesses to their value.

Dodd 136, 1 Eagle & Younge 578

[In a tithe bill concerning Sir John Hopkins, Thursday, 29 June 1693], the decree was to account for the tithes or the value thereof. The plaintiff examined the defendants upon interrogatories, who, as far as they could, set out their corn, hay, wool, lamb, etc. The plaintiff also examined two or three witnesses, who swore

[1] *Attorney General, ex rel. Wilson v. Penythorpe* (Ex. 1582), Public Record Office E.123/7, f. 236v; *Bedow v. Waters* (Ex. 1610), Public Record Office E.124/11, f. 114v; *Dawson v. Anonymous* (Ex. 1610), Public Record Office E.124/11, f. 219v; *Avery v. Fynch* (Ex. 1585), Public Record Office E.123/10, f. 307v; *Layton, qui tam v. Pierce* (Ex. 1705), see below, Case No. 257.

they knew the premises and that the lands were worth so much and that they believed the tithes were yearly worth two shillings in the pound, without specifying any particulars, etc. And upon this, the deputy [King's Remembrancer] reported, and the defendants excepted, and *per curiam* the report [was] confirmed. *Quod mirum.*

[An earlier order of 22 June 1692, Public Record Office E.126/16, f. 36, is printed at 1 Wood 296.]

111

Ward v. Hilder

(Ex. 1693)

In this case, the defendant was ordered to pay tithes at the correct amount in spite of long usage at a lesser amount.

4 Price 83, 146 E.R. 401

The defendant admitted having paid tithes at a rate of £1 16s. assessed upon him for his premises.

But, when he brought the question of his liability to pay so much before the court, the court decreed that, notwithstanding he had paid at that rate for a long period, that, of right, he ought to have paid at the rate of 2s. 9d. in the pound on the yearly rent or annual value of the premises, which was proved to be £40.

The plaintiffs, it seems, having thus established their right, submitted to continue to accept the former payment of £1 16s. if the defendant would continue to pay it.

But, he having refused to do so, the court made a decree:

> that he should pay the tithes after the rate of 2s. 9d. in the pound rent or value of the premises, the same to be rated at and after the rate of £30 *per annum* for the yearly rent or value of the said house and premises, which amounted at that rate to £4 2s. 6d.

And that sum he was decreed to pay.

[Other reports of this case: Equity Cases Exch. 336, 2 Gwillim 538, Western 103.]

112

Hough v. Greeves and Sheldon

(Ex. 1694)

If there is one defendant and he plead to part of the declaration, all is discontinued.

Where there are two defendants and one pleads and the other does not, this is a discontinuance in all.

Repleader is not allowed after a demurrer.

Dodd 140

[In an action of] trespass for taking away a £100 worth of hair, the defendants as to the *vi et armis* [allegation] plead not guilty and at to the residue plead *actio non*, because Sheldon says 'and so he alone tells an idle story', and then both aver it and demand judgment whether the action [etc.]. The plaintiff replies impertinently and both defendants demur.

And [it was] adjudged by three against Lechmere that it is a discontinuance and that the plaintiff cannot have judgment.

First, if [there is] one defendant and he plead to part, all is discontinued. 7 Hen. VI, 5; 27 Hen. VIII, 1; 11 Rep. 6; 1 R.R. 135, 176, 216, 406; 1 Rolle 487, 488,[1] which settles the law.

Second, where [there are] two defendants and one pleads and the other does not, this is a discontinuance in all. 30 Ass. 36; Plow. 138; 7 Hen. VI, 27; 39 Hen. VI, 1; Cro. Eliz. 762, [are] in point, Yelv. 5, 6; Rastall 221; Coke, *Entries*, 142, 325, 619.[2]

But Lechmere said that a discontinuance is either in the process or in the dies datus or where the matter is out of the court, but here the matter was never out of court. See Cr. Jac. 239, 288; Cr. Car. 594,[3] etc.

Second, all [of the court] held the count [to be] good although [it was] for £100 worth of hair [in] general without showing what hair.

---

[1] YB Mich. 7 Hen. VI, f. 5, pl. 8 (1428); YB Pas. 27 Hen. VIII, f. 1, pl. 4 (1536); *Heydon's Case* (1612), 11 Coke Rep. 5, 77 E.R. 1150; *Wilson v. Dod* (1615), 1 Rolle Rep. 135, 176, 81 E.R. 383, 412; *Carpenter v. Weltch* (1615), 1 Rolle Rep. 216, 81 E.R. 442; *Dense v. Dense* (1616), 1 Rolle Rep. 406, 81 E.R. 569; *Wilson v. Dodd*, 1 Rolle, Abr., *Continuance & Discontinuance*, pl. E, 10, p. 487.

[2] YB 30 Edw. III, Lib. Ass., p. 179, pl. 36 (1356); *Browning v. Beston* (1552), 1 Plowden 131, 138, 75 E.R. 202, 213; YB Pas. 7 Hen. VI, f. 27, pl. 19 (1429); YB Mich. 39 Hen. VI, f. 1, pl. 1 (1460); *Green v. Charnock* (1600), Croke Eliz. 762, 78 E.R. 994; *Crumpton v. Smith* (1602), Yelverton 5, 80 E.R. 4, also Noy 44, 74 E.R. 1014; *Johnson v. Turner* (1602), Yelverton 6, 80 E.R. 5, also 1 Brownlow & Goldesborough 192, 123 E.R. 748; *Marshal v. Wilkinson* (1565), E. Coke, *Book of Entries* (1614), 'Det', pl. 21, f. 142, also 2 Dyer 247, 73 E.R. 546; *Crowther v. Crowther* (1566), E. Coke, *Book of Entries* (1614), 'Formedon', pl. 8, f. 325; *Gilling v. Hunt* (1602), E. Coke, *Book of Entries* (1614), 'Scire facias', pl. 6, f. 619.

[3] *Watson v. Thorpe* (1610), Croke Jac. 239, 79 E.R. 206; *Tampion v. Newson* (1611), Croke Jac. 288, 79 E.R. 247, also Yelverton 210, 80 E.R. 138; *Watkinson v. Turnor* (1640), Croke Car. 594, 79 E.R. 1110.

Third, all [of the court] agreed that no repleader [is allowed] after a demurrer, [as] in Ridgway's Case, 3 Rep. 52.[1]

I [*Samuel Dodd*] was of counsel for the plaintiff, and [was] not satisfied with such a judgment.

113

Martin v. Wilsford

(Ex. 1694–1695)

After a condemnation of goods in the Court of Exchequer, no further action at common law lies to challenge the recovery. The condemnation is res judicata.

After judgment upon an information for a seizure of goods forfeited, the property of such goods is divested from the right owner.

Dodd 152

Martin v. Winford.

The plaintiff declares in [an action of] trespass for the taking of two pieces of cloth at Tavestock in Devonshire. The defendant justifies for it that he is deputy collector of the aulnage in Devonshire and that the two pieces were put to sale at Ratcliffe in Middlesex before [being] sealed by which they were forfeited and that he as much for himself as for the king seized and afterwards exhibited an information in the Exchequer and pleaded it and [had] judgment and payment of the king's moiety and [the] goods [were] delivered and so [. . .] which is *eadem* trans[action] etc. There was a replication that the goods were not sold before [they were] sealed, and [there was] a demurrer upon it.

And upon debate, the court held clearly that after a condemnation, an [action of] trespass or trover does not lie and that the party [may] not falsify the recovery.

And Ward, Chief Baron, cited Smith and Eaton's Case[2] and Cole and Powell's Case to be so resolved in [a writ of] error out of the King's Bench before the judges of the Common Pleas and barons of the Exchequer and the judgments given in the King's Bench [were] reversed at the bar. Also was cited Roe and Huntington Brewers' Case accordingly and Hardres 194, 195.[3]

But the doubt here was upon the pleading:

First, he alleged himself an officer in Devonshire and yet seized in Middlesex;

Second, he did not justify in Devonshire nor traverse the place etc.

---

1 *Rigeway's Case* (1594), 3 Coke Rep. 52, 76 E.R. 753.

2 *Smith v. Ekins* (Ex. 1679–1680), Exch. Cases *tempore* Car. II, 448.

3 *Vanderbergh v. Blake* (1661), Hardres 191, 194, 145 E.R. 446, 447.

To the first, it was said that the deed was in Devonshire, but 21 Jac.[1] does not extend to the information for aulnage and so he had the election to lay it where the informer pleases and being laid in Middlesex, his justification must be there, and if he had traversed, it will be against the pleader, for the seizure was in Devonshire, and thus his informations for customs etc. But it was said that if those two points were other points than in the information, query how and where by this plea it shall be tried.

Adjornatur.

[It was] argued [in] Hilary [term] again.

And LECHMERE [held] that alleging himself an officer in Devonshire will be void because anyone can seize because [it is] forfeited notwithstanding the Statute 27 Edw. III,[2] that it will be seized by an aulnager or his deputy but [there are] no negative words and then if it had been omitted, all had been good.

But [it was held] by the Chief Baron [WARD] that it should be, and thus are all of the precedents, that he seized them at Tavestock and afterwards preferred an information and alleged the forfeiture in Middlesex, and thus he pleaded the condemnation and then traversed *absque hoc* that [he] is guilty of any other taking or at any other time or place, and it will be good.

Gould, who argued for the plaintiff, took exception to the conclusion of the plea, that there should be judgment if it will; [he] responded no judgment *si actio*; 1 Leo. 313; 2 Leo. 160;[3] also judgment *si actio* he relied upon any particular.

Adjornatur.

After Easter [term, it was] adjudged by three against Lechmere for the plaintiff upon the Chief Baron's [WARD's] reason.

LECHMERE cited Burchier v. Hamett, 20 Car. II [1668 × 1669], an information for a false report and laid all to be in the port of London, and upon the trial it was [found to have been] in the port of Bristol, and [it was] good.

Carthew 323, 90 E.R. 790

Martin brought an action of trespass in the Court of Exchequer against Wilsford and one Nicholls and laid his action in Devonshire and declared that the defendants at Tavistock in the County of Devon, 5 April *anno* 6 Will. & Mar. [1694] had taken and carried away two pieces of cloth, called kersies, of him the plaintiff to the value of £30 and had converted them to his own use.

The defendant pleaded in bar that the two pieces of cloth in the bill mentioned, being goods and merchandize for which a subsidy was due to the king and queen, were between the first of October 5 W. & M. [1693] and the 30th of August then next following exposed to sale at Ratcliffe in the County of Middlesex, before they were sealed with the seal of the collector of the said subsidy,

---

[1] Stat. 21 Jac. I, c. 4 (*SR*, IV, 1214–1215).

[2] Stat. 27 Edw. III, stat. 1, c. 4 (*SR*, I, 330–331).

[3] *Kempton v. Cooper* (1589), 1 Leonard 313, 74 E.R. 285; *Borough v. Holcroft* (1578 × 1579), 2 Leonard 160, 74 E.R. 442.

according to the true intent of a certain Act of Parliament in that part made and provided against the form of the same statute, by reason whereof, he the said Wilsford, then and yet being one of the deputy aulnagers and collectors of the subsidy of woollen cloth vendible in the several counties of Devon and Cornwall, lawfully constituted and authorized, did according to the duty of his office and the defendant Nicholls as his servant and by his command, between the said first day of October *anno* 5, and the said 30th of August following at Ratcliffe in the county of Middlesex within the port of London, *bona praedicta ob causas praedictas seisiverunt et ad opus dictorum domini regis et dominae reginae tanquam forisfacta arrestaverunt*; and the said Wilsford *tunc officiarius praedictus ut praefertur existens* afterwards, *viz.* the same 30 August by the name of Thomas Wilsford, gent., one of the deputy aulnagers and collectors of the subsidy of woollen cloth vendible in the several counties of Devon and Cornwall, *qui pro eisdem domino rege et domina regina sequebatur dedit curiae hujus scaccarii intelligi et informari*, that be between the 1st of October *anno* 5 and the 30th of August next following at Ratcliffe in the county of Middlesex, had seised and arrested, to the king and queen's use, as forfeited, two pieces of woollen cloth, called kersies, *de bonis et catallis personae ignotae*, for that the said two pieces of cloth being made and wrought to sell and utter, for which subsidy was due, were within the time aforesaid, at Ratcliffe aforesaid in the County of Middlesex, exposed to sale before they had been sealed with the seal of the collector of the subsidy aforesaid, *contra formam statuti in ea parte editi et provisi et petit advisamentum curiae*, etc. and that the cloth might remain forfeited according to the form of the statute aforesaid.

Et superinde taliter processum fuit etc. that afterwards, *viz.* 23 October *anno* 6 [1694], it was adjudged by the barons of the Exchequer that the goods aforesaid for the cause aforesaid should remain forfeited and that Wilsford should be charged with and satisfy to the king and queen £20, being the value of the said goods, *prout per recordum inde plenius apparet.*

And that he the said Wilsford afterwards *viz.* 8 November *anno* 6 Will. [1694] paid the said twenty pounds into the Exchequer, *prout patet per recordum praedictum per quod* the said Wilsford and the said Nicholls as his servant etc. upon the day last mentioned at Ratcliffe aforesaid in the said county of Middlesex *praedicto duas pecias panni lanei* in informations *et judicio praedicto existento duas pecias panni lanei in billa ipsius* (the plaintiff) *superius mentionatus in usum ipsius Thomasi Wilsford converterunt et disposuerunt prout eis bene licuit quae sunt eadem captio, asportatio, conversio, et dispositio praedicto duarum peciarum panni lanei unde* (the plaintiff) *superius se modo queritur et hoc*, etc.

To this, the plaintiff replied, *protestando non cognoscendo aliqua, etc. pro placito dicit quod praedictae duae peciae panni lanei in billa ipsius* (the plaintiff) *superius mentionatus non expositus fuerunt venditioni antequam sigillatus fuerunt sigillo collectoris subsidiorum praedictis modo et forma prout et hoc petit quod inquiratur per patriam*, etc.

And upon a general demurrer to this replication, it was insisted that it was naught, for that the validity of the seizure (after it appears on record that the goods were condemned) cannot be put in issue but that the plaintiff in this action was concluded as to that matter by the judgment and condemnation upon the information, for he had time to have appeared and pleaded to the information; and upon issue joined the legality of the seizure might have been tried, *viz.* whether the cloth was exposed to sale or not before it was sealed, but he having slipped that opportunity, he is now foreclosed from trying the merits.

Besides, it had been always held, that after judgment upon an information for a seizure of goods for the king, the property of those goods are altered thereby, so as neither trover nor trespass will lie for him who was the owner; and it is not reasonable that a judgment should be subverted by a collateral action.

To which all the barons agreed and declared it to be the standing rule of the court.

But then it was insisted for the plaintiff, that the plea was ill, for the reasons following:

First, for that by the Statute,[1] which gives the forfeiture of the cloths exposed to sale before they are sealed with the seal of the collector of the subsidies, it is appointed, that such forfeited cloths shall be seised for the king by the collector or aulnager or by the deputy of one of them or else by the bailiffs of the town where the cloths were exposed to sale, so that no other person has power to seize but those named in this Statute.

And it appears by the plea that the defendant Wilsford was only a deputy aulnager and collector for cloths vendible in the counties of Devon and Cornwall and by consequence had no power to seize elsewhere out of those two counties, and yet by his own showing it appears that he seized etc. at Ratcliffe in the County of Middlesex, which was out of his deputation and where he had no manner of power.

The same matter likewise appeared in the body of the information pleaded, so the judgment therein was *ipso facto* void, because the information was *felo de se* showing that the very informer had no power to seize, and then by consequence the court would not condemn goods upon a seizure which appeared on record to be void and illegal.

Second, the plea is likewise ill for another reason, *viz.* because it was at large without respect to the time or place laid in the declaration and this being a transitory action, the defendant by his plea ought to have followed the plaintiff both in time and place, since his justification was not local, or at least he ought to have added a traverse, *viz. absque hoc* that he was guilty *aliter vel alio modo*, etc.

So that the plaintiff might have an opportunity of taking issue upon such traverse and so to maintain his declaration.

---

[1] Stat. 27 Edw. III, stat. 1, c. 4 (*SR*, I, 330–331).

Third, the plaintiff has laid the conversion etc. to the use of both the defendants and they have confessed a conversion, but to the use of one of them alone, which does not meet with the plaintiff's declaration.

The Court gave their opinions *seriatim*.

POWYS, TURTON, and WARD, Chief Baron, [held] that the plea was ill for the first two reasons *supra*, for they held that no person has authority to seize the cloth forfeited by the Statute 27 Edw. III, aforesaid, but only those very officers expressed in that statute, and it appears that the defendant had no authority to seize at Ratcliffe, for by his own showing, his deputation extended only to Devonshire and Cornwall.

They also held that the defendants in this case ought to have added a traverse to their plea, *viz. absque hoc* that they were guilty *aliter vel alio modo.*

And the Chief Baron WARD added that it was a certain rule in pleading that where the action is transitory, the defendant in his plea must follow the plaintiff, unless his justification is local, and then he must traverse *absque hoc* that he is guilty *extra.*

But in this case, the action is transitory and the justification is not local and yet the defendant has neither followed the plaintiff nor added any traverse wherefore the plaintiff remains unanswered.

Now if the defendant had pleaded well, he should have set forth that he seized the cloth at Tavistock upon the day mentioned in the declaration, and thereupon he informed this court as upon a seizure at Ratcliffe, with the necessary averments that all was the same, and then have added a traverse *absque hoc* that he was guilty *aliter vel alio modo*, which would have been sufficient without adding *vel alio tempore.*

And so it was adjudged in a case of a seizure made at Salisbury,[1] and thereupon an information and condemnation, as upon a seizure in Middlesex, and in an action of trespass the matter was pleaded specially, with the like traverse, *ut supra.*

And the like special justification and judgment in another case between Cole and Powell; and he said he could not find any precedent in this court to warrant such a form of pleading as in the principal case, and farther, that in those collateral actions, after a condemnation upon a seizure, the rule is, *viz.* if the action is trover, the condemnation may be given in evidence upon the general issue, because thereby the property is divested out of the party, but if the action is trespass, then the matter may be specially pleaded, and though, if well pleaded, it might have been a good bar to the action, yet now it is ill pleaded, the court cannot take any notice of the matter itself but must give judgment upon the insufficiency of the pleading.

---

1 *Smith v. Ekins* (Ex. 1679–1680), *ut supra.*

Lastly, where a statute makes a forfeiture and gives power to seize generally without naming any persons who shall seize, in such case, any person, though he is no officer, may seize for the king, but here the Statute names the persons by their offices, who shall seize for him upon this forfeiture, and though there are no negative words, *viz.* that no other person shall seize, yet, in this case, *expressum facit cessare tacitum,*[1] and the negative is implied by the express affirmative.

But Baron LECHMERE was of opinion for the defendants for no other reason but because a condemnation did appear on record and the defendant charged with the value, and therefore no action will lie by the first proprietor after such condemnation, and the defendant, being an officer, ought to be favored in matters concerning his office, and, in this plea, it is said that the cloth in the declaration and in the information are the same and that is sufficient. But he could not cite any precedent of the court for such sort of pleading.

The plaintiff had judgment by the opinion of three barons.

114

Rex v. Portington

(Ex. 1694)

The Statute of Frauds does not apply to the king.

The king can re-direct a trust for a superstitious use to a proper charitable purpose.

1 Salkeld 162, 91 E.R. 151

On a traverse to an inquisition *post mortem* of Ann Barlow, the jury found for the king, by reason the said Ann had devised her land to superstitious uses; but a case was made as follows.

Ann Barlow devised to the Lady Portington and her heirs, absolutely without any trust, that she did it for the good of her soul, and that the devisee owned that this estate was not her's, but belonged to God and His saints. The question was, whether this devise could be averred to be in trust to a superstitious use?

And the Court of King's Bench held[2] it could not, and that both from the Statute of Frauds[3] and from the nature of the thing. Supposing the devisee was a nun, it was considered how the law was then; and the court held that a monk now might purchase, because that part of the canon law whereby his disability arose is now abolished and the common law takes no notice of him.

After this, *viz.* 26 May 1693, an information was preferred in the Exchequer for a discovery and an application of the devise to an use truly charitable.

---

[1] E. Coke, *First Institute* (1628), ff. 183b, 210a.

[2] *Rex v. Portington* (K.B. 1692), 3 Salkeld 334, 91 E.R. 856, 12 Modern 31, 88 E.R. 1145.

[3] Stat. 29 Car. II, c. 3 (*SR*, V, 839–842).

And it was held:

First, that the Statute of Frauds did not bind the king, but took place only between party and party;

Secondly, that the king, as head of the commonwealth, is obliged by the common law and for that purpose entrusted and empowered to see that nothing be done to the disherison of the crown or the propagation of a false religion and to that end entitled to pray a discovery of a trust to a superstitious use;

Thirdly, this use, being superstitious, is merely void, and for that reason the king cannot have it; yet, however, it is not so far void as that it shall result to the heir, and, therefore, the king shall order it to be applied to a proper use.

[Other reports of this case: 1 Eq. Cas. Abr. 96, 21 E.R. 906, Dodd 137, Equity Cases Exch. 338.]

115

Gwinne v. Poole

(Ex. 1695)

The court of the mayor of Hereford has jurisdiction to hear personal actions.

An action at law does not lie against a judge or an officer of a court for official actions.

Dodd 144

[The case] upon a special verdict [was thus]. A. brought [an action of] trespass *vi et armis* [for] assault, battery, and false imprisonment against B., C., and D., who pleaded that the City of Hereford is an ancient city, that time out of mind, a court of record has been held there before the mayor for personal actions, that at a court held [on] such a day before B., the mayor, C., administrator of E., entered a plaint for £20 and prayed process, and thereupon an attachment was awarded directed to the sergeant at mace [returnable to the court], that D.[1], being one of the sergeants, arrested A.[2] and imprisoned him by default of bail, which is according to [?] etc. The plaintiff replies and traverses that the cause of action did not arise within the jurisdiction. And the defendants demur.

And [it was] adjudged that an action does not lie, by Turton and Powell against Lechmere.

Lechmere [held] that it lies: first, it is a *capias* as first process without a summons, which is void; second, it is a return to the next court, which is bad; third, it is out of the jurisdiction.

---

[1] C. *MS.*

[2] B. *MS.*

But the others [held] *contra*: first, it is error in the process; second, it is good by prescription etc.; third, trespass does not lie against a judge. An officer [is] not a party.

See the book and my argument, and Ch. J. Jones 214; 1 Ventr. 369.[1]

[Other reports of this case: 2 Lutwyche 935, 1560, 125 E.R. 522, 858.]

116

Smelton v. Bridges

(Ex. 1695)

Tithes are not due to a vicar as a matter of common right, but only by endowment.

Usage is evidence of an endowment of tithes.

In this case, the modus decimandi was held to be good.

Dodd 145, 1 Eagle & Younge 590

[To] a tithe bill brought by the vicar of A. in Kent, the defendant says that four pence an acre is payable for every acre of marshland in discharge of all small tithes due to the vicar for marshland and upland. And upon debate, the court held:

First, that tithes are not due of common right to the vicar, but only by endowment.

Second, that usage is the evidence of his endowment, and where he has had no small tithes, it is an evidence that he was not endowed; and in this case, it appears that he has but a groat an acre, but in this point the court doubted, because the four pence is in discharge of small tithes, so he is admitted to have them, if the *modus* do not discharge them.

Third, that this is a good custom and not part of tithe in discharge of other tithe, as four pence a hogshead in discharge of tithes of apples, which is naught; but money answers all tithe in this case, and the number of acres is but to ascertain the quantum of the money. And the parson has no wrong, if one have one acre of marsh and all the upland, for though this party pays but one four pence, yet the rest of the parish pay for the rest of the marshland.

Note: [It was] resolved, and the bill [was] dismissed. Sir John Banks and Sir Eliah Harvey [were the] owners of the land.

[The order of 7 February 1695, Public Record Office E.126/26, f. 247, is printed at 1 Wood 337, sub nom. Smelter v. Bridges.]

---

[1] *Olliet v. Bessey* (1682), T. Jones 214, 84 E.R. 1223, also Dodd 33, 2 Shower K.B. 148, 204, 89 E.R. 851, 892, *sub nom.* Lambert v. Bessey, T. Raymond 421, 467, 83 E.R. 220, 244, *sub nom.* Elliot v. Besey, Skinner 49, 90 E.R. 24; *Hodson v. Cooke* (1683), 1 Ventris 369, 86 E.R. 237, also 2 Shower K.B. 328, 89 E.R. 968, Skinner 131, 90 E.R. 61.

117

Taswell v. Athill

(Ex. 1695)

Toppings and loppings of trees are not tithable by the person who sold them uncut. Toppings and loppings of trees are not tithable in the absence of a custom.

Dodd 147, 1 Rayner 75,
2 Gwillim 537, 1 Eagle & Younge 590

Upon an English bill for tithe wood, the case was thus. Athill sold the toppings and loppings of oak, ash, and elm to Cressey, standing. Cressey cuts them, and Taswell brings a bill against both. And [it was] resolved:

First, that is does not lie against Athill, because he sold them uncut, notwithstanding in Franklyn and Jones's case from Monmouthshire [it was] resolved *contra*, 2 Jac. II.[1]

Second, it was resolved that, without a custom, they are not tithable.

Third, [it was] resolved that notwithstanding the Statute of *Silva Caedua*,[2] they may be tithable by custom, and accordingly an issue [was] directed to try the custom.

Note: The plaintiff was parson of Wood Morton in Norfolk.

Note: Athill was dismissed with costs, notwithstanding Franklyn and Jones's case, which was the mother [was] tenant for life of underwood, remainder to the son in fee, both joined in a sale to A., who felled them, and B., the parson, brought a bill against the son (the mother being dead) for tithes, and [it was] resolved that he should pay them, and [he was] decreed to account accordingly. See above, Buckle and Vanacker.[3]

[Order of 11 February 1695: Public Record Office E.126/16, f. 236.]

118

Pocock v. Cole

(Ex. 1695)

In this case, two moduses in lieu of tithes were held to be valid.

---

[1] *Franklyn v. Jones* (Ex. 1686), Equity Cases Exch. 237.

[2] Stat. 45 Edw. III, c. 3 (*SR*, I, 393).

[3] *Buckle v. Vanacker* (Ex. 1693), see above, Case No. 103.

Dodd 147, 1 Eagle & Younge 583

In a tithe bill brought by the plaintiff, being rector [of a parish] in Devonshire, the defendant set forth two customs in bar of the plaintiff's bill, which was *inter alia* for tithe clover grass eaten and for apples, *viz.* 2d. an acre payable for all tithe hay, and secondly, 1d. for all apples growing in a garden or orchard of the party.

As to the first, [it was] resolved that [it was a] good custom, notwithstanding clover is a new grass, because the *modus* is not laid for meadow ground, but for hay, so that if upland or arable, by being sown with clover, bear hay, the *modus* extends to it. And the case of Stanfast and Hughes, which concerned Dr. James, head of Queen's College, in the time of Montagu, Chief Baron, was cited, which was [that] arable land pays tithes in kind to the impropriator, cinquefoil was sown upon it, and it stood to seed, and the profit was in the seed not in the stalk, and there was a custom for 2d. an acre for hay, payable to the vicar, and [it was] resolved: first, that notwithstanding that the stalk and seed was in the nature of corn, yet it should be looked upon as grass and shall be paid accordingly; second, that the *modus* was good.

As to the second custom, it was resolved that 1d. for all apples in the garden or orchard was good. Query if it extends to new orchards; it seems if it be laid for all apples upon the farm, that [it would be] good; otherwise, it should be intended ancient orchards. The penny was apple garden penny, yet it does not alter it, for in Sparks and Manwood, a penny called a hearth penny was a good *modus* for woad sold.

[The order of 20 February 1695 is printed at 1 Wood 336.]

119

Wilbraham v. Saunders

(Ex. 1695)

Tithes are not due for agistment of trespassing cattle.

Dodd 149, 1 Rayner 76,
2 Gwillim 544, 1 Eagle & Younge 607

In this case, A. had a farm adjoining to a farm called B. in another parish, the fences of B. were down, the cattle of A. went into the said farm of B. by defect of the fences, and ate there for four months. And [it was] resolved that the parson should not have tithe of the herbage, for they were as trespassers, and a trespasser, or he whose beasts stray through the defect of fences, shall not pay tithes.

Lechmere cited the Parson of Bangor's Case, that tithes shall not be paid for cattle which go by reason of vicinage.

But Powell [held] *contra* and that in the principal case, A. was but a disseisor and should pay tithes, for it was not an accidental trespass but a continued act.

It seemed to me clearly to the contrary.

[The order of 6 December 1694, sub nom. Wilbraham v. Kingsman, Public Record Office E.126/16, f. 221v, is printed at 1 Wood 328.]

120

Ansell v. Adman

(Ex. 1695)

Tithes are not due for ancient mills.

Dodd 150, 1 Rayner 76, 1 Eagle & Younge 610

Upon an English bill in the Exchequer Chamber, it was resolved that of an ancient mill, tithes shall not be paid, for the Statute *Articuli super Chartas*[1] implies this.

Note: The bill [was] dismissed. I was of counsel with the complainant. Query; see 2 Inst. 621; 1 Rolle 656; 2 Rolle Rep. 84; Cro. Jac. 523.[2]

[The order of 6 June 1695, Public Record Office E.126/16, f. 288, is printed at 1 Wood 352.]

121

Newbury, qui tam v. Colgate

(Ex. 1695)

Vessels having neither midship beam nor deck are not within the Tonnage Act of 12 Car. II.

Dodd 150

In the Exchequer upon a special verdict upon the late Act of Tonnage,[3] [it was] resolved that a vessel that carries wood, etc., from Feversham to London, being thirty tons but had no midship beam nor deck is not within this law because the description of ships and vessels to be charged are those that have decks and midship beams notwithstanding it was objected in Banbridge and Bates' Case[4]

---

1 Stat. 9 Edw. II, *Articuli Cleri*, stat. 1, c. 5 (*SR*, I, 172).

2 E. Coke, *Second Institute* (1642), p. 621; 1 Rolle, Abr., *Dismes*, pl. M, 3 and 4, p. 656; *Anonymous* (1619), 2 Rolle Rep. 84, 81 E.R. 674; *Danderidge v. Johnson* (1619), Croke Jac. 523, 79 E.R. 448.

3 Stat. 12 Car. II, c. 4 (*SR*, V, 181–205).

4 *Bambridge v. Bates* (Ex. 1679), T. Raymond 305, 328, 337, 83 E.R. 158, 170, 175, Dodd 276, Exch. Cases *tempore* Car. II, 442.

where the words of the Act were [. . .] ten yards of foreign materials shall pay etc., yet those made of molasses[1] made in England should pay; thus steel mirrors [are] chargeable as looking glasses, callico as linen. Thus 27 Edw. III and 17 Ric. II[2] give aulnage of measurable cloths, yet aulnage [is] due for stockings and caps which are not measurable etc.

I [*Samuel Dodd*] was of counsel with the defendant.

122

Jones v. Soames

(Ex. 1695)

A patent officer in reversion is, upon the death of the possessor, presently in possession before admittance or being sworn so as to have an action for the profits.

Dodd 153

Upon an issue at the Guildhall and a verdict for the plaintiff after term and motion for a new trial, [it was] resolved:

First, that a patent officer in reversion is, upon the death of the possessor, presently in possession before admittance or being sworn so as to bring an action for the profits. [It was] so resolved in Squibb's Case, and afterwards in the time of Charles II in the Exchequer between Arris and Stewkely[3] for a customer's office depending upon a life and [it was] affirmed in error.

Note: [It was] there held that the offices of the customs can be granted for life with a *non obstante* [clause] and thus [it was] then resolved.

Second, that the damages, being the total allowance, were well given without a deduction for the defendant for service and goods.

Note: The plaintiff was by patent apothecary to the household at an establishment of £160 *per annum* for a salary (before £40) and bill money, and the defendant procured the lord chamberlain to admit him and receive the £160.

Lincoln's Inn MS. Misc. 559, f. 15

The plaintiff [William Jones] brought an [action of] *indebitatus assumpsit* against the defendant for £160 had and received to his use. And, upon a trial before me [Edward Ward] at *nisi prius* in London after the [Michaelmas] term, the plaintiff, to maintain his action, made his case to be this, that, in 1677, King Charles

---

1 Sic in MS.

2 Stat. 27 Edw. III, st. 1, c. 4 (*SR*, I, 330–331); Stat. 17 Ric. II, c. 2 (*SR*, II, 88).

3 *Rex v. Squibb* (Ch. 1668), Lincoln's Inn MS. Misc. 499, pp. 445, 466, Chan. Repts. 1660–1673, p. 341, note also *Dennis v. Loving* (Ex. 1667), Exch. Repts. *tempore* Car. II, 97, Hardres 424, 145 E.R. 529; *Arris v. Stukley* (Ex. 1677), Exch. Repts. *tempore* Car. II, 314.

II granted to John Jones, the plaintiff's father, by letters patents under the great seal the office or place of apothecary to the household of the king, his heirs, and successors for his life under an annual salary of £40 payable at the Exchequer with a grant of all profits, allowances, etc. belonging to that place. And, in the same letters patents, the king, for him, his heirs, and successors, granted the same office to the plaintiff after the death of his father with the same salary and profits. And the plaintiff proved his father's death in January 1693 and that the defendant received £160 due for that place of apothecary to the king's household from the Treasurer of the Chamber for a year ended at Christmas 1694, for which the action is brought by the plaintiff as belonging to him and received for his use.

The defendant, at first, stood upon it, that the office was grantable by the Lord Chamberlain of the Household and not by the king. And he produced an admission, but no grant, under the now Lord Chamberlain, the earl of Dorset's, hand and seal of the defendant into that office and that he was sworn into it. And he further insisted that, if the office was in the grant of the king, yet it was not grantable in reversion nor was the plaintiff ever admitted or sworn. But the defendant's counsel, afterwards, admitted that the office of Apothecary to the Household was in the king's grant and that the plaintiff may recover his salary of £40 *per annum* at the Exchequer. But, as to the £160, the counsel urged that the plaintiff had no right to that, because it wholly subsisted by virtue of a new establishment made by his now Majesty and signed by him and the Commissioners of the Treasury 1690 whereby, indeed, there is appointed to be paid to the Apothecary of the Household by the Treasurer of the Chamber for salary and bill money £160 *per annum* to begin from the time of the officer's being admitted or sworn into his place and that, for that reason, because this is a new establishment and not the salary and profits in being at the time of the plaintiff's grant, it was urged that this £160 did not belong to the plainitff. But, it being proved in the cause that this £160 was for all salary and profits formerly due and payable to the apothecary of the Household and that it was made for so much because the king or his officers should not be troubled to pay the apothecary's bills for medicaments furnished to the Household as was formerly done and that this £160 was looked upon to come in lieu of the £40 and profits and that, after the establishment, it was paid to the plaintiff's father whilst he lived and the arrears which incurred during his life and not paid to his executors since his death in virtue of his right by the letters patents and that it cannot be thought the king should pay the £160 and the £40 *per annum* also and because the £160 was to be paid to the Apothecary of the Household, which the defendant was not by good constitution, but the plaintiff was by his grant. And such grant is an admission of itself into the office when it falls, and [there is] no need of any other [. . .] and no title the plaintiff to bring an action and that there is nothing in law against the crown's granting such offices in reversion.

And it no way appearing that the defendant had done anything for this £160, no not so much as paid taxes for it or furnished any medicaments, the defendant's own counsel was satisfied that the defendant had no right but that the money belonged to the plaintiff, who had a verdict for the same.

But, afterwards, the defendant, upon a motion to the court for a new trial, setting forth that he had done and paid something not proved at the trial, the plaintiff by agreement allowed him something. And so it was settled with the plaintiff, which had it appeared upon the trial would have been considered in damages. And, indeed, the plaintiff laid his action short, for another year was due to him, which, if the defendant had insisted on a new trial, he would have had liberty to have put into his declaration. And, for that reason, he, the defendant, accepted what really he had paid. And the verdict stood.

[Other copies of this report: Georgetown Univ. Law Sch. MS. B88–8, p. 273.]

123

Anonymous

(Ex. 1695)

The king cannot be personally charged for an annuity, but the royal revenue can be.

1 Salkeld 58, 91 E.R. 56

Trinity 7 Will. III.

The king cannot grant an annuity, for his person is not chargeable, as [is] the person of a subject. But, if he grant it out of his excise or any branch of his revenue, it is good, for there is somewhat therewith chargeable.

124

Pritchard, qui tam v. Boyle

(Ex. 1695–1697)

A new trial can be granted in an action on a penal revenue statute where the jury disregarded the instructions of the court.

In cases of pecuniary forfeitures upon penal statutes, the court can grant a new trial after a verdict for the defendant.

Parker 69, 145 E.R. 716

27 November 1695; Richard and Boyle.

A claimer was admitted to enter his claim after a recovery. And [it was] presumed that it was a regular recovery, because the court put terms on the claimer to plead to issue forthwith, to take short notice of trial, to bring no writ of error, and, in case of a verdict for the king, the judgment to stand as a security; otherwise, the recovery was not to be vacated.

Dodd 167

In this case upon an information for shipping goods without a cocket, the verdict was, two or three terms ago, for the defendant against the opinion and direction of the Chief Baron [Ward]. And upon several motions for a new trial, it was ordered to search [for] precedents for a new trial upon penal laws. And upon a search in the Exchequer, these [were] found, viz. 23 Car. II, Burleigh, qui tam and Walker; 27 Car. II, Welsh, qui tam against Fellowes; 26 Car. II, Williamson et al., qui tam against Sir Thomas Littleton, Papilian, et al., a notable precedent. See 2 Keble 266;[1] see Easter [term] 27 Car. II, in the Exchequer, Harrison, qui tam and Steuard, upon a seizure of wool, a new trial was granted to the plaintiff upon [a] suggestion that discovered several material witnesses.

Afterwards, [on] 12 February 1696[/97], a new trial [was] granted.

Lincoln's Inn MS. Misc. 559, f. 97, pl. 3

Hilary term 1696[/97].

Upon an information brought by the plaintiff against the defendant grounded upon the Act against Fraud in the Customs, 14 Car. II, ca. 11,[2] he declared upon a seizure of a cask or barrel with money in it to the value of about £400 for that the same was shipped on board a certain ship or vessel to be carried forth to the open sea from one port to another in England without a coquet or entry as that Act directs whereby the goods became forfeited.

Upon the general issue pleaded, the matter came to trial before me [Edward Ward] as Chief Baron in Middlesex after the end of [*blank*] term last, where the case appeared to be that the defendant brought the money on horseback out of Wales to Swansea with an intent (as sworn) to carry the same on horseback to Bristol but that, the horse tiring, it was resolved to carry the same from Swansea to Bristol by water and that, thereupon, at an inn, a cask being ready, the money was put into the cask and there being two vessels lying ready for Bristol called the *Happy Return* and the *Hopewell*, a man was sent to the Custom House officer to make an entry and take out a coquet, and, thereupon an entry was made by one Bachelor aboard the *Happy Return* of one small hooped cask of butter, not taking any notice of money. The cask was seized aboard the *Hopewell*.

And I [Ward] told the jury that the law seemed to be plain that this was not such an entry as the Act requires, for the end of the law is that the particular good carried coastwise must be expressed in the entry; otherwise, the bond, which the Act directs to be in the value of the goods, can never be complied with to be delivered up, as that Act directs, and, without such bond and certainty of the goods carried coastwise being described, it cannot be known whether they are carried coastwise or beyond the seas. If the latter, then the king is cheated in

1 *Rex v. Anonymous* (1667), 2 Keble 226, 84 E.R. 142.
2 Stat. 14 Car. II, c. 11 (*SR*, V, 393–400).

the customs or [they] may be goods prohibited to go beyond the seas, and both those cases this Act provides against, so that I thought it was plain that the entry of a cask of butter would not justify a cask full of silver coin and that, therefore, it seemed plain that the money was forfeited within the Act.

But the jury, contrary to expectation, found for the defendant. And, being asked the reason, they said they believed it to be a mistake only in the defendant and persisted in their verdict.

Mr. Attorney General [*Trevor*] and others, for the plaintiff, prayed a new trial as being a verdict directly against the evidence in a point of law and against the direction of the court.

The court, being informed by me of the nature of the case, inclined to [grant] a new trial. But because new trials upon penal laws where the defendant has been acquitted have been often denied and [it was] questioned if [they be] grantable, the court took time to advise, and directed a search to be made for precedents where new trials upon penal laws have been granted where, upon the evidence, verdicts have passed for the defendants.

And these precedents in the office of the King's Remembrancer in the Exchequer were produced, *viz.* Easter 3 June 23 Car. II, between Burleigh, *qui tam* against Waller, upon the Statute for taking in a new store of wines before he had given an account to the commissioners; a verdict was for the defendant and [there was] a new trial upon the payment of costs. Another was Michaelmas 26 Car. II, 13 November, between Ralph Williamson and others, *qui tam*, plaintiffs, and Sir Thomas Littleton, Josiah Child, and Thomas Papillon, Esq., defendants, upon a seizure of beef and pork as forfeited, where a verdict was for the defendants, and, though the court did not think fit in that case, under the nature and circumstances of it, to grant a new trial, but ordered judgment to be entered for the defendants, yet the court did declare (and it is so mentioned in the order) that new trials may be had upon just and reasonable grounds in informations upon seizures and other pecuniary forfeitures and penal laws as well at the desire of the informer as His Majesty's Attorney General as of the defendants in such informations. And another was 21 April 27 Car. II, Easter *recorda* between Walsh, *qui tam* against Fellows in a seizure of a parcel of faggots, there was a verdict for the defendants; a new trial was granted. And another was 26 October 27 Car. II, between Harrison, *qui tam* against Stewart, upon a seizure of wool; there was a verdict for the defendant, and a new trial was granted unless cause [be shown], and it was made absolute the 19th of November following. There was a case remembered by myself which was between Temple, *qui tam* against Gold, upon a seizure of wine, and there was a verdict for the defendant, and, the 19th of June 1678, a new trial was granted upon affidavits made that the plaintiff wanted a material witness (naming him). But, in Strudwick and Foster's Case, 5

May 1680, L. H, 83, upon a seizure of silks upon the French Act,[1] then in force, and a verdict for the defendant, the court denied a new trial, principally upon the ground that the jury had the view of the silks, which is one part of the evidence by the Act, though, in this case, the court seemed to incline against all new trials when verdicts have passed for defendants upon penal statutes *prout ante*, fo. 64, unless where there is practice or corruption in the jury or witnesses or the jury find against directions of law, which seems to be a good distinction. And the causes why the aforesaid new trials were granted did not appear, and they might be because of such practice or corruption.

But, in this case, Baron LECHMERE and Baron POWYS were for a new trial, and Baron BLENCOWE (upon a mistake) was against it. So, there being two barons against one for the new trial, it was granted.

And, in this case, a distinction was taken between criminal cases and pecuniary forfeitures upon penal laws. In the first, there are no new trials against defendants once acquitted as have been against defendants in the others. *Vide* L. 1, 465, Rex v. Payton and Parsons, and 468, Rex v. Merchant; *vide* also L. 2, 262, Rex v. Cornelius, Michaelmas 27 Car. II, where Chief Justice Hale said that it is as proper to grant new trials in criminal cases as in civil and that it is possible there may be a reason to grant a new trial where the party is acquitted.[2]

Vide ante fo. 64.[3]

Note that, afterwards, upon the new trial in the principal case, it appeared by the evidence for the king that it was a design laid beforehand to put this money into a cask and send it by sea and to have it concealed what it was from the officers of the customs and, for that reason, it was entered as butter. And a verdict passed for the king.

Note in this case, the words of that Act of Parliament are 'goods, wares, and merchandise to be shipped and all such wares and merchandise forfeited', which *per curiam*, include money. Raym. 414 accord.[4]

[Other copies of this report: Georgetown Univ. Law Sch. MS. B88–8, p. 512.]

---

[1] *Strudwick v. Foster* (Ex. 1680), Exch. Repts. *tempore* Car. II, 456; Stat. 29 & 30 Car. II, c. 1, ss. 70–76 (*SR*, V, 862–864).

[2] *Rex v. Payton and Parsons* (K.B. 1668), Lincoln's Inn MS. Misc. 499, p. 465, pl. 5; *Rex v. Merchant* (K.B. 1668), Lincoln's Inn MS. Misc. 499, p. 468, pl. 1; *Rex v. Cornelius* (K.B. 1675), Lincoln's Inn MS. Misc. 500, p. 462, pl. 1.

[3] Note (1696), Lincoln's Inn MS. Misc. 559, f. 64.

[4] *Osborn v. Wandel* (1680), T. Raymond 414, 83 E.R. 217.

125

Parkinson, qui tam v. Tildesly

(Ex. 1695)

False Latin in a pleading cannot be objected to after a verdict has been rendered.

Lincoln's Inn MS. Misc. 559, f. 3, pl. 1

Trinity [term] 1695.

In an action of debt *qui tam* brought by the plaintiff against the defendant upon the Statute of Recusancy[1] for £20 a month for not coming to church, it was laid in the declaration *quod defendens non accedit nec conavit se accidere* to any church *prout* the Statute. And there was a verdict for the plaintiff for three month's absence.

And it was moved by *Dormer* in arrest of judgment because of the false and improper Latin words *conavit* and *accidere*, there being no such Latin words as *conavit*, but it ought to have been *conatus fuit* and ought to have been *accedere* and not *accidere*. And many cases were cited where advantage had been taken of the impropriety of Latin words, as *destricto* for *destructo*, etc.

But it was answered and resolved by the court that neither of these two words vitiated the declaration, for false Latin, as *conavit* here is, will not hurt no more than *billa verra* for *billa vera* will, which, in Crone's Case, it was resolved it did not. Besides, it is after the verdict, and it plainly appears the party did not come to church. And, though the Statute says 'shall endeavor to come', yet this word *conavit*, though not proper, yet must be intended to signify the same thing and, being but false Latin only, does not vitiate. And for the word *accidere*, upon the perusal of the dictionaries, the word *accido* signifies to come to as well as the word *accedo*.

And the plaintiff had judgment.

Vide Mod. Rep., fo. 43.[2] *Mitto* signifies to forbear as well as send. *Mitto me quaeso* (in Terence); pray let me alone.

[Other copies of this report: Georgetown Univ. Law Sch. MS. B88–8, p. 234.]

126

Attorney General v. North

(Ex. 1695)

Money due to a person who has been outlawed is forfeited as of the date of the outlawry, not the date of the inquisition.

---

[1] Stat. 29 Eliz. I, c. 6, s. 4 (*SR*, IV, 771).

[2] *Buckly v. Turnor* (1670), 1 Modern 43, 86 E.R. 718, also 1 Siderfin 446, 82 E.R. 1209.

Dodd 174

Wansett and Plummer were outlawed *die Lune proxime ante festum Sancti Marcii evangeli sexto Will. & Mar.* at the suit of Maria Milbourne in debt 6 October after it is found by inquisition that £68 *in pecunia numerata* was in the hands of Hugh North, of the outlaws at the time of the promulgation of the outlawry, upon which a [writ of] *scire facias* issues against North, who appears and prays *oyer* of the inquisition, by which it is found that Wansett, at the day of the outlawry and at the taking of the inquisition, was possessed of £68 *in pecunia numerata et de bonis et catallis suis propriis* in the hands and custody of Hugh North and so seizes the same into the king's hands; and then [he] pleads that the day of taking the inquisition or at any time after [the inquisition], the said Wansett was not possessed of the said £68 *aut de aliqua inde parcella* in the hands or custody of the said Hugh North.

And upon which the Attorney General demurred, and [upon argument, it was] resolved clearly that the money was forfeited by the outlawry before the inquisition and judgment for the king in regard he does not answer to the day of the outlawry but only to the day of the inquisition.

Note: It was resolved thus about two years ago although I took no note of it until now, but it was not a resolution of this term.

127

Acton v. Lawton

(Ex. 1695)

The Court of Exchequer at Chester cannot take jurisdiction over anyone that lives outside of its jurisdiction for matters in equity involving an in personam remedy.

Lincoln's Inn MS. Misc. 559, f. 3, pl. 2

Upon a motion for a [writ of] prohibition to the Court of Exchequer at Chester, the case was thus. There was a suit by English bill in that court against five persons relating to an equity about salt works in the County Palatine of Chester, who all sued at law in Chester for the lands and works. Four of the persons lived in and the fifth lived out of the jurisdiction of the County Palatine, but the fifth as well as the others answered there. And the plaintiff proceeded against him and them. And thereupon, a [writ of] prohibition was prayed and granted to stay the suit against the fifth person because that court cannot proceed against any who are out of its jurisdiction for matters relating to equity where *agitur* only *in personam*, for which purpose Egerton's Case, 4th Inst., fo. 213,[1] was cited, where

[1] *Egerton v. Earl of Derby* (Ch. 1614), E. Coke, *Fourth Institute* (1644), p. 213, also 1 Eq. Cas. Abr. 137, 21 E.R. 940.

it was resolved that, if a defendant dwell out of the County Palatine and there be cause to sue him for lands or goods which are within the County Palatine, the plaintiff may (which is to be interpreted 'must') complain to the Chancery of England because he has no means to bring him to answer and there is to be no failer of justice. And, there, it is said that the court of equity binds only the person. And the Case of Lord Ward against Lady Ann Brereton,[1] which was the same in effect with this, one of the defendants living in Staffordshire, was remembered, and the law was taken to be as here that the Court of Exchequer at Chester could not proceed against any that lived out of their jurisdiction for a matter of equity. And though the defendant below that now prays the prohibition did answer, yet that will not give the court below a jurisdiction, for the matter and person both ought to be within the jurisdiction. And Grigg's Case, Hutton's reports 59,[2] was cited, and it is a full case in the point, *quod vide*.

And the [writ of] prohibition was awarded in the principal case.

And as to the comparison of the case with gildable and demesne etc., these cases were cited, 8 Hen. VI, 31; 20 Hen. VI, 23; 2 Hen. IV, 25; 7 Hen. VI, 40; 49 Edw. III, 9; Plo., Queries, 116.[3] *Vide* Ward and Brereton's Case, L. G, 104, a full case in point, and several prohibitions before and also after this case have been granted in this court upon the same grounds and reasons.

[Other copies of this report: Georgetown Univ. Law Sch. MS. B88–8, p. 235.]

128

Powell, qui tam v. Baritteau

(Ex. 1695–1696)

An information for not paying customs dues can be sued in the County of Middlesex though the offense occurred in another county.

Lincoln's Inn MS. Misc. 559, f. 4

Easter term 1695. Entered Easter 6 Will. & Mar. [1694] in the Office of the King and Queen's Remembrancer.

The plaintiff exhibited an information against the defendant grounded upon that part of the act for continuing certain acts and charging joint stocks made 4 & 5 Will. & Mar., ca. 15,[4] that relates to undertakers and insurers of uncustomed

---

[1] *Lord Ward v. Lady Brereton* (Ex. 1676), Exch. Repts. *tempore* Car. II, 299.

[2] *Grigg's Case*, Hutton 59, 123 E.R. 1100.

[3] *Falk v. Burley* (1430), YB Hil. 8 Hen. VI, f. 30, pl. 26; *Darcy v. Condrey* (1442), YB Trin. 20 Hen. VI, ff. 32, 33, pl. 2; YB Trin. 7 Hen. VI, f. 40, pl. 7 (1429); *Barneston v. Mounter* (1375), YB Pas. 49 Edw. III, f. 9, pl. 1; Quaery No. 116, Plowden Qu. 18, 75 E.R. 883.

[4] Stat. 4 Will. & Mar., c. 15 (*SR*, VI, 401–404).

and prohibited goods and causing them to be delivered without payment of duties etc., which information set forth that, between such days, divers packets of French silks were imported into England, *viz.* at Ratcliffe in Middlesex, by persons unknown from beyond the seas against the form of the Statute and that the defendant, between the said days at Ratcliffe aforesaid in the county aforesaid agreed with one Richard Read to pay him 45s. 6d. for conveying those goods to the parish of Chaulke in the County of Kent, the said defendant then and there, knowing them to be prohibited goods, contrary to the form of the Statute, and prays that the defendant may forfeit £500 and that he may have a moiety thereof according to the form of the Statute.

Upon not guilty pleaded, a special verdict was found that the goods were French and imported into England within the time in the information and that the defendant, at Chaulk in the County of Kent, agreed with Read for conveying the goods to Chaulk knowing them to be prohibited goods and then and there gave to Read 45s. 6d. to convey those goods to the parish of Chaulke in Kent and that those goods were according to that agreement conveyed and delivered by Read at Chaulke in the County of Kent and that no agreement touching the premises was made between the defendant and Read in Middlesex or elsewhere out of the County of Kent, and whether the defendant be guilty or not within this information was the doubt of the jury and referred to the court, and, if it is seen to the court that he is guilty, then they find him guilty; if not, then they find him not guilty.

This case was argued several times at the bar. And the only question was whether the agreement by the information alleged to be made at Ratcliffe in Middlesex but, by the jury, found to be at Chalke in Kent was local or not. If the agreement was local, then the information is ill founded, for a jury of Middlesex cannot enquire of a thing that is local in Kent. There was no doubt made but that the importation of the goods which was alleged by the information to be at Ratcliffe in Middlesex was well though the fact was that they were really imported in Kent, for that was looked upon to be within the excepting clause of 21 Jac., ca. 4, the last proviso.[1] But the question arose upon the agreement which is collateral to the importation and the case upon which the information is founded and so insisted to be local where the agreement was really made.

But all the barons were of opinion and so gave judgment that the importation being rightly alleged as to place, the agreement which was a consequent and a thing depending upon it might well be alleged to be at the same place and not to be restrained to the very place where it really was made, it being of a transitory nature.

[Other copies of this report: Georgetown Univ. Law Sch. MS. B88–8, p. 236.]

---

[1] Stat. 21 Jac. I, c. 4 (*SR*, IV, 1214–1215).

Dodd 162

Powell, *qui tam* v. Borrellian.

[It was] resolved upon a special verdict in an information exhibited for £500 on the Joint Stocks Act, 4 & 5 W. & M. 389, that the information well lay in Middlesex though the offense was in Kent, [and it was so] resolved in Easter [term] 1695 in the Exchequer, and yet this was for prohibited goods and not customable goods.

129

Hayward v. Dyson

(Ex. 1695)

A person who might have an interest in the outcome of a lawsuit is not a disinterested witness and is incompetent to testify.

Lincoln's Inn MS. Misc. 559, f. 6, pl. 1

30 October 1695.

Note in a trial at the bar this day by a Middlesex jury, upon two issues directed out of the Duchy Court, the first whether by custom within the wapentake of Wirkesworth in the County of Derby, the quarter cord in a pipework is to be measured from the spindle of the stones or from the outskirts of the mine;

Secondly, whether, by the like custom, where there is sufficient water in the mine wherewith the ore can be washed and buddled, the miners may wash and buddle the ore gotten out of such mine or not.

And a verdict was for the plaintiff in the affirmative for both, that is to say that the quarter cord is to be from the outskirts of the mine and that the miners may wash and buddle with the water in the mine.

And, in this case, it was held by the court upon evidence that none that have land in that wapentake could be witnesses against the custom though it did not appear there were any mines in their land, for their land is subject to the custom and, though no mines appear at present, yet inasmuch as there may be mines discovered upon search to be made, no owner of lands can be indifferent but seems to be an interested person.

[Other copies of this report: Georgetown Univ. Law Sch. MS. B88–8, p. 242.]

130

Harrison v. Isaackson

(Ex. 1695)

A statute should be construed so as not to create a repugnancy with other statutes that are in force.

Lincoln's Inn MS. Misc. 559, f. 13, pl. 2

The question, upon a trial before me [Edward Ward] at *nisi prius* in an action of trover brought by the plaintiff against the defendant, a Custom House officer, was this, what duties were due to the crown for French prunes taken prize and condemned as such. And this question depended upon the consideration of several acts of Parliament, first by the Statute 1 Will. & Mar., ca. 24,[1] the importation of all French goods is prohibited and, if imported, to be destroyed as the Act directs, which Act took effect from the 24th of August 1689 and was to continue for three years and thence to the end of the next session of Parliament; secondly, by the Statute made 2 Will. & Mar., ca. 4, second session,[2] for a further supply to the king and for the reducing of Ireland, an additional imposition was granted upon East India and other goods imported between the 25th December 1690 and the 10th November 1695, where in fo. 203, there is a <charge> duty of £10 percent to the crown given for all grocery ware, which prunes are, and this over and above all impositions, duties, charges already imposed and payable for the same, but no notice or mention is taken or made in the Act of French goods, and, in the same session, ca. 14, French goods taken prize are enacted to be destroyed and, in default, the officer to incur penalties. Then came the Statute of 4 & 5 Will. & Mar., ca. 5,[3] which gave several additional impositions to the crown upon divers goods and merchandises between the 1st of March 1692 and the 1st of March 1696, amongst which divers French goods by name are enumerated, and then, fo. 264, there is a general charge of £25 percent upon all French goods above what is charged by the Book of Rates,[4] and then, in the same session, ca. 25, the two former acts prohibiting the importation of French goods, except what [was] altered by that Act, are continued for three years longer. But, in that Act, there is a provision that French goods taken prize and condemned should be sold by inch of candle, and, out of the money arising by such sale, the subsidy of tonnage and poundage and all other duties and impositions payable to Their Majesties for such goods should be deducted and the rest answered as that Act directs.

[1] Stat. 1 Will. & Mar., sess. 1, c. 34 (*SR*, VI, 98–103).
[2] Stat. 2 Will. & Mar., sess. 2, c. 4 (*SR*, VI, 221–225).
[3] Stat. 4 Will. & Mar., c. 5 (*SR*, VI, 380–387).
[4] Stat. 12 Car. II, c. 4, app. (*SR*, V, 184–198).

And the question was whether all the three duties, *viz.* tonnage and poundage and the £10 percent and £25 percent, were all to be answered out of French prizes or only the tonnage etc. and the £25 percent omitting the £10 percent. And it was agreed that a case should be made and left to my opinion.

And I [Edward Ward], advising with the three other barons, Lechmere, Turton, and Powys, we all were of opinion that the other two duties, but not the £10 percent, were payable, for it could not be thought that that duty could be intended by the Parliament to be given or paid to the king for French goods, which then stood prohibited to be imported, and, though the words be generally upon all goods, yet such a construction must be made as may consist with other acts of Parliament and not make a repugnancy between them. And, if the Parliament had intended French goods should have been liable to the £10 percent, they must have expressed it as well in that as they did in the subsequent acts and that the Parliament did not intend French goods should be brought in and pay duty, *viz.* the Act 2 Will. & Mar., ca. 5, for continuing the duties upon wines etc., there is a provision, fo. 226, that that act should not alter the French prohibition act made 1 Will. & Mar. and *vide* the acts made 2 Will. & Mar., fo. 311, 312, 318, and, more particularly, the Statute 5 Will. & Mar., ca. 2,[1] which recites the Act 4 & 5 Will. & Mar., ca. 4, of their grant of a duty upon brandies etc., and that the said grant contrary to the intent of the said commissioners became ineffectual by reason of the first prohibiting French Act. And see the clause about bacon there, all which evince that the Parliament at the time of the grant of the £10 percent did not intend to charge French goods with that duty which then stood prohibited to be imported.

And with this opinion, the Attorney General [Trevor] was satisfied. And the goods were delivered upon payment of the tonnage and poundage and the £25 percent, but not the £10 percent.

[Other copies of this report: Georgetown Univ. Law Sch. MS. B88–8, p. 267.]

131

Allen, qui tam v. Brittiss

(Ex. 1695)

In this case, the plaintiff suffered a nonsuit during the trial of the action.

Lincoln's Inn MS. Misc. 559, f. 14, pl. 1

Michaelmas 1695.

Upon a trial at *nisi prius* before me [Edward Ward] after the term, the case was this. An information was exhibited in the Attorney General's name as of

[1] Stat. 5 Will. & Mar., c. 2 (*SR*, VI, 442–443).

Hilary term 1693[/94] against the three defendants, being sea captains, for embezzling French prizes taken at sea, grounded upon the Act of Parliament called the Privateer Act, 4 & 5 Will. & Mar., ca. 25,[1] by which Act, every officer offender forfeits £500 and is disabled from serving Their Majesties in any office or employment for seven years.

The plaintiff Allen, in April 1694, exhibited an information *tam quam* in the [Court of] Exchequer for the same offense in the Attorney General's name. The information mentioned and prayed a moiety of the money forfeitures, the Act giving a moiety to the king, the other to the informer. Shortly after this last information was exhibited, the king ordered the Attorney General to *non pros* all informations or suits either in the King's Attorney's name or in the *tam quam*s as far as the king was concerned in them. And, thereupon, Allen's information as to the king was *non pross*ed, but he proceeded, as by law he might, for his moiety as informer, to which the three captains pleaded the pendency of the Attorney General's information for the same offense, to which plea Allen replied that the information in the Attorney General's name was exhibited *per fraudem et covinam inter* the three captains to deceive the king and all others that were or might be entitled to those forfeitures of their respective parts thereof, to which replication the defendants rejoined that the Attorney General's information was exhibited *bona fide*, and they traversed the fraud. And, thereupon, issue was joined.

But the plaintiff was not able to make out any fraud or give the least color of evidence of it, but only endeavored by a paper book that lies open in the King's Remembrancer's Office wherein the attorneys and underclerks promiscuously enter at their pleasures the times of the coming in of informations to make it out by an entry therein that Allen's information was first entered therein, endeavoring thereby to make it out that his information was first and that such priority was a badge of fraud.

But no proof being made of any fact and there being only a bare entry in the book, not of any record nor for necessity, but for some reasons of convenience in the office, and the

entries in it being promiscuously made by sworn and unsworn clerks, it was not thought conclusive to say that the king's information, which was filed of record as of Hilary term before, should be falsified by such an entry.

And the Attorney General [*Trevor*] offered to demur upon that evidence if they insisted upon it and offered no other.

But the plaintiff's counsel not having other evidence at that time submitted to have the plaintiff called nonsuit, which was done accordingly

[Other copies of this report: Georgetown Univ. Law Sch. MS. B88–8, p. 270.]

[1] Stat. 4 Will. & Mar., c. 25 (*SR*, VI, 419–423).

132

Attorney General v. Elton

(Ex. 1695)

The question in this case was whether the goods in issue should pay import duty as bay yarn or as worsted yarn.

Lincoln's Inn MS. Misc. 559, f. 14, pl. 2

Upon a trial at *nisi prius* before me [EDWARD WARD] of a seizure of worsted yarn imported from Ireland, wherein the forfeiture of the goods was waived, the only question was whether the yarn seized was to pay the duty of 3s. 4d. a hundred [weight] as woolen or bay yarn according to the Book of Rates[1] or as worsted yarn, which is *ad valorem*, no certain rate being set upon it.

The witnesses for the king, who was to have it pay *ad valorem*, said the yarn was made of combed wool called worsted and, for that reason, they thought it was worsted yarn. But the defendants' witnesses proved that, for divers years and indeed all along, this sort of yarn has been called bay yarn and that bays cannot be made without it, that it is the chain that holds all together and by that chain and the short [?] carded wool that fills it up, bays are made, that it was always at Bristol, where this seizure was, entered and paid duty as bays yarn. And about ten years since, being questioned by an officer, the Commissioners of the Customs, upon consideration, let it go.

And there was a verdict for the defendant in this case that it was bay yarn.

[Other copies of this report: Georgetown Univ. Law Sch. MS. B88–8, p. 272.]

133

In re Shales

(Ex. 1695)

An Auditor of the Exchequer must be appointed to his office under the great seal.

An Auditor of the Exchequer is not a judicial officer.

Lincoln's Inn MS. Misc. 559, f. 129

Henry Shale's case about an auditorship.

Note that, upon the death of John Shales, the Auditorship of His Majesty's Revenues in Kent, Surrey, Sussex, Oxfordshire, Berkshire, Bedfordshire, Buckinghamshire, Durham, and Northumberland became void. And, in September 1695, the Lords Commissioners of the Treasury taking notice thereof and that Henry Shales was willing to undertake the execution of the said office without

[1] Stat. 12 Car. II, c. 4, app. (*SR*, V, 198).

any further or other charge to the crown than the present allowances, which only defray clerks' salaries and the incidental expenses to the performance of the office, Their Lordships, by a writing under their hands and seals dated 13 September 1695, did constitute and appoint the said Henry Shales to the said office of Auditor to take the accounts of His Majesty's revenue in those counties and to perform that office as fully as Stephens and John Shales or any of their predecessors had done and to take into his custody all books, records, and writings touching or concerning that office, requiring all mayors, sheriffs, reeves, bailiffs, fee farmers, receivers, and tenants of His Majesty's revenue and all of His Majesty's loving subjects to be aiding and assisting to the said Henry Shales in the due execution of the said office whereof all officers of the Exchequer are desired to take notice with a proviso that the salary of £200 *per annum* shall cease and determine.

Mr. Shales brought this instrument to me [Edward Ward], as Chief Baron, and desired that he might be admitted and sworn Auditor accordingly. But I conceiving that this was not a proper or legal constitution of an Auditor, but that he must, as anciently, be made under the great seal and advising with the ancient officers who never knew any Auditor otherwise made than under the great seal and solemnly sworn an officer of the court and into his place, I deliberated upon the swearing of him. And I attended the Lords Commissioners of the Treasury, and gave them my reasons, as aforesaid, why I did not swear him.

And Their Lordships were very well satisfied therewith, and directed Mr. Shales to pass a patent in the usual manner for that office under the great seal, which he did accordingly. And, then, he was admitted and sworn Auditor.

Note this was about a year before Aldworth's Case came in question and was a good ground for my proceeding therein.

And, afterwards, when Auditor of the Revenue died and the counties in his assignment appointed to any other that survived, such survivor was constituted Auditor of these counties by letters patent under the great seal. And it so fell out that, upon the death of William Aldworth 1700, Auditor Shales, to whom his counties were assigned, passed new letters patent under the great seal for that office, and he was sworn Auditor accordingly. And he held his auditorship of the several counties by his several grants under the great seal.

And it is to be observed that an Auditor, though he be an officer of record and in a court of record, yet he is no judge, nor can he of himself determine any account, for, in all accounts that are declared, the Auditor is styled *clericus*, and the Baron that declares the account, he is styled auditor. And that is the authority for making any *super*, charge, or *ipsum* to be a record and warrant for process upon it.

[Other copies of this report: Georgetown Univ. Law Sch. MS. B88–8, p. 612.]

134

Pile v. Aldworth

(Ex. 1696)

Where a person sues on a bond to perform an arbitral award, he cannot later sue on the award itself.

Lincoln's Inn MS. Misc. 559, f. 27

Hilary 1695[/96]; George Pile, plaintiff; William Aldworth, defendant; Office of Pleas, entered Trinity [term] 5 Will. & Mar.

The plaintiff brings [an action of] trespass upon the case against the defendant. And he declares that the plaintiff and defendant, 22 May 3 Will. & Mar. [1691], at such a place, *posuerunt se in arbitrium etc.* of one Mannie Emmet concerning all actions, claims, and demands before that time between them so that the award be made in writing ready to be delivered to such of them as should require it upon or before the 8th of June following. And he shows that Emmet the 5th of June following, by his award under hand and seal ready to be delivered etc. did, *inter alia*, award that the defendant should pay the plaintiff £541 3s. 5d. upon the 28th of August following in full satisfaction of all demands, *per quod* the defendant became indebted to the plaintiff in that sum. And being so indebted, he assumed and promised to pay it, but has refused *licet saepius requisitus ad damnum* £300.

The defendant pleads that the same time that the plaintiff and defendant put themselves to the award of Emmet, *scil.* such a day the defendant became bound by bond to the plaintiff of the same date in £500 conditioned to abide the award of Emmet. And then he shows the award made by Emmet *prout* the declaration, and that the plaintiff, the 23rd October 1691, put that £500 bond in suit in this court against him for non-performance of the award and obtained judgment thereupon in Michaelmas term 4 Will. & Mar. [1692], *prout per recordum*, for £500 debt and £21 00s. 02d. costs, *et hoc paratus est verificare*, and he prays judgment if the plaintiff shall maintain this action against him.

To this plea, the plaintiff demurred generally, and the defendant joined.

And, after several arguments in the case, the whole court this term gave judgment for the defendant that this action did not lie for the £41 3s. 5d. over and above the £500 recovered by the bond and judgment, the plaintiff in this action not pleading or standing upon it to recover more than the overplus. And the principal ground that the court went upon was that the submission to the award was by bond and the penalty of that bond was the stated sum which each party agreed to pay to the other in case the award was not performed and, though the arbitrator thought fit to award more than the penalty, yet that cannot enlarge the submission or agreement of the parties or make either of them liable beyond the sum of the bond, which was the measure of the submission, for each party was willing to trust the arbitrator as far as such a sum but not beyond it. And, when that sum submitted is recovered, there is an end of all demands by reason of the submission. It is a rare thing to have the sum or duty awarded to exceed the penalty of the submission, but there is an instance of it in the Case of Veale and Warner, 1 Saunders 326, 327,[1] where the bond of submission was £2000 and the sum awarded £3100. But, in that case, the suit for non-performance of that award was brought upon the bond, and there was no pretense or demand for the £1100, which was the sum awarded beyond the penalty of the bond. And that was too great a sum to be lost in case it had been thought it could have been recovered.

It was thought the plaintiff here might have had a more probable case to have recovered the sum awarded in case he had at first brought his action upon the award instead of bringing it upon the bond. And the difference was observed between submissions by specialty and by parol. In the first case, if the arbitrator, in writing under seal, awards a sum in such case upon a suit for that sum, the defendant cannot wage his law, as he may do upon such award made upon a parol submission, 2 Saunders 65, Hodgson and Harridge, Rolls, *Ley Gager*, 107, though that is not within the Statute of Limitations,[2] because the award is in the nature of a specialty. And the reason why an [action of] *indebitatus assumpsit* lies not in this case is because there is nothing that the plaintiff can recover but what he can obtain either upon the bond or upon the award, which the first is, and the other is in the nature of a specialty, and each destroys the *assumpsit* as much as a specialty once taken for a debt by simple contract does forever destroy an *indebitatus* for that debt. And, in this case, there is no promise precedent to the bond; if there was, the bond has destroyed it, and the plaintiff has determined his election by suing the bond and obtaining judgment upon it, which judgment destroys all remedies by *assumpsit*s though there be no execution sued upon it. 40 Edw. III, 27, and Brome and Wootton's Case, Yelverton [*blank*].[3]

And, if that judgment upon the bond be not a bar, there may and will be a double recovery and the defendant [will have] no remedy to plead the first in bar of the other which, for the reasons above, determines the plaintiff's whole demands upon that submission. And how can the plaintiff here divide the sum awarded, which is an entire sum, and take two several and distinct remedies for

---

[1] *Veale v. Warner* (1669), 1 Williams Saunders 323, 85 E.R. 463, also 2 Keble 568, 84 E.R. 357, 1 Modern 20, 86 E.R. 699.

[2] *Hodsden v. Harridge* (1670), 2 Williams Saunders 61, 85 E.R. 672, also 1 Levinz 273, 83 E.R. 403, 1 Siderfin 415, 82 E.R. 1189, 2 Keble 462, 497, 533, 536, 84 E.R. 290, 312, 334, 337; 2 Rolle, Abr., *Ley Gager*, pl. C, 3, p. 107; Stat. 21 Jac. I, c. 16 (*SR*, IV, 1222–1223).

[3] YB Trin. 40 Edw. III, f. 26, pl. [2] (1366); *Broome v. Wooton* (1605), Yelverton 67, 80 E.R. 47.

one and the same sum? *Vide* Bro., *Det*, 23, the Case of 33 Hen. VI, fo. 2;[1] and the reason of the book.

And there was a fault in the plaintiff's declaration in setting forth the award, which, in this case, is the foundation of his demand, for he says that Emmet did, *inter alia*, award, and that is not good in a declaration, for the whole award ought to have been set forth, the same being a judgment, which must not be pleaded with an *inter alia*.

The cases cited for maintenance of the action were 1 Roll's rep. 11, Child and Durant, 2 Cro. 237, Yelverton 217; Cro. Car. 214; 1 Roll's Abr., fo. 9; Jones 337, 364; 2 Saunders 73.[2] But none of those cases or the reasons of them came up to this point.

And judgment was given for the defendant.

[Other copies of this report: Georgetown Univ. Law Sch. MS. B88–8, p. 305.]

Dodd 154

[In an action of] *assumpsit*, the plaintiff declared that the defendant and himself put themselves to the arbitration of Emett, that Emett made his award and, *inter alia*, awarded the plaintiff £540 and the defendant, thus being in debt, promised to pay. The defendant pleads that he entered into a bond of £500 penalty to perform the award of Emett and that Emett made such award *prout* in the count and, for the nonpayment of the money, the plaintiff sued the bond and recovered. The plaintiff demurred.

And upon argument, [it was] adjudged that the £500 was the measure of the submission and [the defendant] will not be charged beyond the bond.

Note: There were divers exceptions taken by the defendant:

First, that [an action of] general *assumpsit* does not lie;

Second, that the count set forth the award, *inter alia*, that it was nought, because it is a judgment and entire, that the submission it is by a specialty and the award is a specialty and then *assumpsit* does not lie, the action upon an award ought to set out material promises [or] else no consideration [is shown]. 1 Rolle 7.[3] It is like wagers or money lost at play.

---

1 YB Hil. 33 Hen. VI, f. 2, pl. 8 (1455), Brooke, Abr., *Dett*, pl. 23.

2 *Childe v. Durrant* (1614), 1 Rolle Rep. 11, 81 E.R. 290, Croke Jac. 337, 79 E.R. 287, Yelverton 217, 80 E.R. 142, also 1 Brownlow & Goldesborough 221, 123 E.R. 766, 1 Bulstrode 157, 80 E.R. 849; *Flower v. Elgar* (1631), Croke Car. 214, 79 E.R. 787, also W. Jones 238, 82 E.R. 125; *Acton v. Symons* (1635), 1 Rolle, Abr., *Action sur Case*, pl. O, 10, p. 8, W. Jones 364, 82 E.R. 190, also Croke Car. 414, 79 E.R. 960; *Rex v. Priest* (1634), W. Jones 334, 82 E.R. 176; *Roberts v. Mariett* (1670), 2 Williams Saunders 73, 183, 188, 85 E.R. 742, 938, 954, also 1 Modern 42, 289, 86 E.R. 718, 891, 2 Keble 614, 618, 702, 84 E.R. 386, 388, 442, 1 Levinz 300, 83 E.R. 417.

3 *Freeman v. Sheene* (1614), 1 Rolle Rep. 7, 81 E.R. 288, also Croke Jac. 339, 79 E.R. 290, 2 Bulstrode 93, 80 E.R. 286.

And by the plaintiff, [it was] insisted that if a bar will be pleaded by estoppel and presumption that all but the £500 [was] paid, and then it should be relied upon or he had an election and had sued the bond.

See my argument for the defendant, for whom judgment [was] given.

TURTON said that [an action of] debt lies upon an award, as [in] 2 Saunders 73; 3 Keble 566; 1 Bro. 55. Query Litt. Rep. 312, that an award set out in the count, *inter alia*, [is] good. Mod. 36.[1]

135

Attorney General v. Gronen

(Ex. 1696)

An agent who makes a contract is personally bound thereby even though he later claims he was acting for an undisclosed principal.

Lincoln's Inn MS. Misc. 559, f. 38

Easter 1696. In case.

Mr. Attorney [General] having formerly exhibited a Latin information in the nature of an *indebitatus assumpsit* and *quantum meruit* against the defendant [Frederick Gronen] for a parcel of prize wines sold by the Commissioners of Prizes unto the defendant for £2900 and odd pounds and the same coming at the sitting after Hilary term to be tried before me [EDWARD WARD] at the Guildhall, the case appeared to be thus. One Toune, a common broker in London, bought the said parcel of wines of the Commissioners of Prizes for £2900 and odd pounds, as he swore, for and upon the account of the defendant and entered into a contract in his own name for the payment thereof under his hand and seal, but did not then nor for some days after mention to the Commissioners of Prizes or any other that the same were bought for the defendant or any other person in certain. But some few days after the sealing the contract, he told the Commissioners that the wines were bought for the defendant. And, upon the trial, he swore that the defendant gave him an order to buy them for him whatever they cost or to that effect.

It appeared at the trial that, four or five days after the contract was sealed, the defendant was sent to for to fetch away the wines and pay for them and that he denied that he ever gave the said Toune an order to buy them (which never-

[1] *Roberts v. Mariett* (1670), 2 Williams Saunders 73, 183, 188, 85 E.R. 742, 938, 954, also 1 Modern 42, 289, 86 E.R. 718, 891, 2 Keble 614, 618, 702, 84 E.R. 386, 388, 442, 1 Levinz 300, 83 E.R. 417; *Jenkinson v. Allenson* (1675), 3 Keble 513, 556, 84 E.R. 852, 877, also 1 Freeman 415, 89 E.R. 308; *Gage v. Gilbert* (1594), 1 Brownlow & Goldesborough 54, 123 E.R. 661; *Leake v. Butler* (1629), Littleton 312, 124 E.R. 262; *Leach v. Morris* (1670), 1 Modern 36, 86 E.R. 713, also 2 Keble 601, 84 E.R. 378.

theless was sworn by Toune) and that the wines were about four or five days after the contract sold by consent of the Commissioners of the Prizes and of the defendant for the best price that could be got for the same, which amounted only to £1300 and odd pounds, which was above £1400 less than was to be given by the contract.

And in order to recover damages for that lesser sum was the action brought. Upon the trial, two questions were moved by the defendant's counsel: first, whether the contract of Toune, the broker, was the contract of the defendant in regard the defendant's name was never used nor did the Commissioners know for whom the wines were bought, whether for the defendant or any other and who; secondly, if it should be said to be the contract of the party for whom the broker buys without mentioning his name, yet, when the broker in his own name seals the contract, whether that does not so far alter the case as to make it wholly the contract of the broker and not to oblige the party for whom bought in regard the contract is passed into a specialty upon which the remedy and recovery must be had and not upon the parol agreement which was had at first.

As to the first of these, it depends much upon the custom of London how far the common broker's contract obliges the principal whose name is not mentioned nor known at the time of the contract. Indeed, if the principal fetches away the goods and owns the contract, that may be well. But, if it shall rest wholly in the power and upon the evidence of a common broker who shall be charged by the contracts that he shall make without other proof than his own oath of being employed by his principal, he may swear any merchant into a great loss and damage by his own oath, and yet, when he likes the bargain, making the contract in his own name and the vendor not knowing who is the buyer besides the broker, he may take advantage of good bargains and put bad ones upon others.

And, therefore, I [Edward Ward] left it to the jury upon that evidence whether, by the custom and usage of London, this was the contract of the defendant by Toune, the broker. And they found that it was.

As to the second, I [Edward Ward] directed the jury that, if they found the contract by Toune was made in his own name and was put into writing and sealed by him, as Toune swore it was, and as in truth it was, though not produced by the plaintiff's counsel, that then it should be found specially how far that contract did bind the defendant in point of law. And the jury did not find that such contract was sealed, though sworn so by Toune, so that they believed Toune in one part but not in another part of his evidence.

And the verdict was not given for the king. But enquiring what damages they found, they said they had not considered that, though they were expressly and particularly charged with it, that, if they found for the king, they should find what damage, it appearing that the contract was for above £2900 and the sale but for a little above £1300, whereby the king had less for the wines by above £1400 there contracted for.

And, thereupon, the jury went out and, after some time, returned their verdict for the king and £80 damages.

And, this term, the Commissioners of the Prizes moved by Mr. Attorney General [*Trevor*] and others for a new trial by reason of the smallness of the damages. And, upon an affidavit of a discourse with two of the jury, who said they meant to £80 for interest. And, upon producing a writing under the hand and seal of the defendant which recites that Toune had charged him with a contract under hand and seal for wines which he never gave him an order to buy, the defendant thereby agreed that the wines should be sold for the best price that could be got and that he would make good the loss to the king according to law or reference.

I [EDWARD WARD] gave the barons [of the Exchequer] a particular account of the trial, *ut supra*. And they were to judge of the new matter offered for a new trial, and, with all that, it seemed to me the jury had full consideration of the matter, but, if they had not, then I thought a new trial might be had. And I observed that, after the cause upon the trial was opened, that Mr. Attorney [General] was desirous that a juror might be withdrawn, which the defendant opposed, and that, when the jury brought in a verdict for the king but not what damages, that then the defendant was desirous to have a juror withdrawn, which the plaintiff's counsel refused.

And, upon this whole matter, Baron POWYS inclined to a new trial, but LECHMERE and TURTON, barons, were against it as this being [?] the plaintiff had good luck to get a verdict and that it would be hard to put the defendant upon a new trial in order to pay greater damages, having neither directly nor indirectly had a [. . .] advantage in the matter but has lost his costs and pays £80. And, as to the defendant's agreement to pay the loss, it is under hand and seal, and a remedy may be had upon it as far as it will extend, and it ought not to be extended further. And, though the king has not so much as his first contract, yet he has all that the wines were worth or could be sold for by the Commissioners within four or five days after the first contract. And it is strange they should really be so much less worth than they were four or five days before, which shows the first contract was not very sincere or right. And, upon the occasion of asking a new trial, the defendant made oath that he never employed or gave an order to the said Toune, the broker, or any other to buy the wines for him.

So, no new trial was granted.

[Other copies of this report: Georgetown Univ. Law Sch. MS. B88–8, p. 331.]

136

Hawkins v. Chittle

(Ex. 1696)

The lessee of a glebe pays tithes for it unless the vicar's endowment discharges it of tithes.

Dodd 156, 1 Eagle & Younge 616

The lessee leased his glebe; the lessee sowed it with corn; the impropriator brought a bill for his tithes; and, upon debate, the court resolved:

First, that *prima facie* the lessee of the vicar should pay tithes, because the vicar himself is privileged in respect of his person. Query by me [Samuel Dodd], because an ecclesiastical person may prescribe in *non decimando* for himself and his tenants. Bishop of Winchester's case;[1]

Second, that, if the glebe had been heretofore leased and the lessee had not paid tithes, it was an evidence that the land by the endowment was discharged, and this was the case in question, and the bill [was] dismissed.

See above Saunders v. Ryall; Cro. Eliz. 579; Hob. 188; Cro. Eliz. 479; and a case cited by Chief Baron Ward of Greenwood v. Grainger, 1684,[2] where it was resolved that the court would presume an endowment upon non-payment. See Degge 200.[3]

[Other reports of this case: 1 Rayner 77, Equity Cases Exch. 358.]

[The order of 20 February 1696, Public Record Office E.126/16, f. 316v, is printed at 1 Wood 356.]

137

Stevens v. Martin

(Ex. 1696)

In this case, the tithes of turnips and green peas were found to belong to the vicar.

---

[1] *Wright v. Wright* (1596), 2 Coke Rep. 38, 76 E.R. 501, Moore K.B. 425, 72 E.R. 672, Croke Eliz. 475, 511, 78 E.R. 726, 760.

[2] *Saunders v. Ryall* (Ex. 1692), see above, Case No. 91; *Blinco v. Barksdale* (1597), Croke Eliz. 578, 78 E.R. 821, 1 Gwillim 197, 1 Eagle & Younge 134, also Moore K.B. 910, 72 E.R. 990; *Harris v. Cotton*, Hobart 188, 80 E.R. 335, also 1 Brownlow & Goldesborough 69, 123 E.R. 671; *Blinco v. Marston* (1596), Croke Eliz. 479, 78 E.R. 730, also Moore K.B. 457, 72 E.R. 692; *Greenwood v. Grainger* (Ex. 1684), Equity Cases Exch. 209.

[3] S. Degge, *Parson's Counsellor.*

Dodd 157, 1 Eagle & Younge 616

In the Exchequer chamber, upon an English bill brought by the plaintiff as vicar of Linton in Cambridgeshire, [it was] resolved that the vicar shall have the tithes of turnips and of hasting[1] or green peas growing in the field and managed with a hoe.

Note: The land was field land and plowed, but there was evidence that, until thirty years last, the vicar had them and that then the quantity increased and the impropriator took them.

The decree [was] affirmed in the House of Lords.[2]

[Other reports of this case: 1 Rayner 82, 2 Gwillim 549, Equity Cases Exch. 362.]

[The order of 20 February 1694, Public Record Office E.126/16, f. 326, is printed at 1 Wood 357.]

138

Browne v. Chaplin

(Ex. 1696)

In this case, a modus decimandi was held to be good.

Dodd 157, 1 Eagle & Younge 617

[Upon a] tithe bill, [it was] resolved that a *modus* of 20s. *per annum* for the small tithe of land worth £26 *per annum* was good, because the *modus* may be better than the tithe in kind and the value of small tithes uncertain. The cases of Dodderidge and Startup and Edge and Oglander, above, were cited.[3] But the case of Vicaridge and Goodier of Heathorp in Oxfordshire[4] was also cited, where £30 for all the small tithes was adjudged too great a *modus*.

[Other reports of this case: Equity Cases Exch. 360.]

---

1 hasty *MS*.

2 *Lords' Journal*, vol. 16, pp. 104–105.

3 *Doddridge v. Startop* (Ex. 1690), Eq. Cases Exch. 324; *Edge v. Oglander* (Ex. 1692), see above, Case No. 89

4 *Viccaris v. Goodere* (Ex. 1681), Public Record Office E.126/13, f. 307v.

139

Wilkinson v. Newson
Bobbot v. Seager

(Ex. 1696)

In these cases, the issues involved the method of proof of the value of tithes.

Dodd 158, 1 Eagle & Younge 618

The first [case was] for the tithes of Langthorpe in Yorkshire of the possessions of the priory of Newburgh, and the second for the tithes of Michael Creech in Somerset, part of the possessions of the priory of Montacute. The court inclined:

First, that, notwithstanding a surrender produced of them to the crown 30 Hen. VIII, it shall be intended that they came by 27 Hen. VIII[1] if the value be not proved;

Second, that a minister's accounts of annual and casual profits should not be evidence of the value;

Third, that these religious houses seldom or never had partial discharges, because in the case of Bobbot, they always paid great tithes, but never paid small tithes.

Note: As to the first, it appeared to me, that the law is clearly to the contrary, because the Statute 27 Hen. VIII gives only those under £200 *per annum*, and then came the Statute 31 Hen. VIII,[2] which did not give the greater abbeys only, but the words of the Act are rather a confirmation of what had been given to the crown, and though exemption is extended to all lands which from and after the 4th of February 27 Hen. VIII came to the crown, and the surrender in 30 Hen. VIII is an evidence that they came to the crown after the 27 Hen. VIII especially with the usage of non-payment.

As to the second, that a minister's account is good evidence of the value, because many of the surveys are lost.

[As to the] third, as well as they may be discharged of the whole, it appears to me clear that they may be discharged partially, or for some part, because their discharges were infinite, and non-payment is the best evidence in such cases, but Chief Baron Ward held the contrary as to this point, although not absolutely.

[Other reports of this case: Equity Cases Exch. 361.]

[An order in Wilkinson v. Newsom of 20 February 1695, Public Record Office E.126/16, f. 316, is printed at 1 Wood 355.]

---

[1] Stat. 27 Hen. VIII, c. 28 (*SR*, III, 575–578).

[2] Stat. 31 Hen. VIII, c. 13 (*SR*, III, 733–739).

140

Attorney General v. Webster

(Ex. 1696)

A share in a corporation is real estate and is taxable.

A super in the pipe roll for a tax is a debt to the crown.

Dodd 163

Upon a *super* in Middlesex in the great roll of A., B., and [Margaret] Webster and others, proprietors of the New River [Water] £1800 upon the Poll Act,[1] which charges each share with 2s. in the pound, she pleads that she has three parts in thirty-six parts and that she lived in London and was there taxed and paid all [that was] upon her assessed, to which the attorney general demurs.

And after argument, the court resolved:

First, that her plea that she was assessed in London and paid all upon her assessed, to which the attorney general demurs, for that she did set out that she was assessed for these shares, signifies nothing.

Note: The Act appoints that each person shall be assessed for his personal estate where he [is] resident.

Second, this is well set in Middlesex for it is not merely personal but is a real estate although charged in the Poll Act where no other real estate is charged.

Third, that this *super* is not so void as that she is to be discharged of all of it, for although she ought not to be charged with the whole, yet it is a ground for the king to demand her share. It is a debt due to the crown, the parliament giving the duty that owners [are] chargeable for 2s. in the pound. It is rather the judgment of the commissioners that £1800 is due from all than a joint charge. In 35 Car. II [1683], a *super* of the bishop of Gloucester *vel W.W. sicat executor utriusque eorum* [was] held good upon the argument; by the report of the Chief Baron [Ward], who in this case delivered the opinion of the court.

Judgment [was] *quod onerabilitur*, but the court [will] consider before process shall issue and what process shall go.

Skinner 642, 90 E.R. 287

In the Exchequer, upon a *super*, the question upon the Statute[2] for imposing the tax of 4s. in the pound arose upon the clause in one of the first acts, for taxing the shares in the Company of the New River Water, which ordains that the shares in this company should be taxed in the county where the owners inhabit. And in the principal case, the defendant [Margaret Webster] inhabited in one county and was taxed in another, and therefore she refused to pay.

---

[1] Stat. 5 & 6 Will. & Mar., c. 14 (*SR*, VI, 472–479).

[2] Stat. 5 & 6 Will. & Mar., c. 14 (*SR*, VI, 472–479).

And the court was clear that she ought to pay, for there is an interest vested in the king by the Act and if the remedy for collecting it or the method for assessing it prove impracticable, the duty being vested in the king, this shall be levied by the aid and assistance of this court. And it was adjudged accordingly. But insomuch that there was £1800 and more returned upon the *super*, the court declared that the defendant shall not be charged for the whole, but only for her own proportion.

141

Medly v. Talmy

(Ex. 1696)

In this case, the lands in question were found to be discharged of the payment of tithes.

Dodd 164, 1 Rayner 81

In an English bill, the plaintiff as lessee of the provost etc. of Eton of the rectory impropriate of Leominster in Sussex demands tithes of corn and hay. The defendant insists that [his lands], by some lawful ways, [are] discharged and that in 1652 he bought the lands and all tithes thereon.

Upon [the] hearing of the cause, the court declared that, though the tenant could not prescribe in *non decimando*, yet that, against a lay impropriator, they would presume the tithes granted to the terre tenant, no tithes having ever been paid, but the land (as sworn) [was] looked upon as tithe free; and though the occupier could not show the grant nor any perception of tithes, yet non-payment would presume a grant and although the defendant had insisted that the lands were free or discharged from tithes, yet the court would intend the freedom or discharge to be upon the non payment, that the tithes were formerly granted away.

Query. Note the cases of Sir John Hoskins, Dean and Chapter of Litchfield, Dr. Hickeringill, and several others, which *semble contra*. But, in this case, the bill [was] dismissed by the Chief Baron [Ward] and Powys.

2 Gwillim 559, 1 Eagle & Younge 620

[In a] bill for tithes generally, [the] defendant states that, in 1652, his father purchased the lands whereof the tithes are claimed and, by the purchase deed, they are mentioned to be tithe free and are conveyed as such, that defendant is owner and occupier of the said lands, which contain eighty acres and are of only £30 a year value, that all the said lands are and will appear to be free and by lawful means discharged from the payment of tithes of corn and grain and other predial tithes or any customary rate in lieu thereof, that the ancient deeds relating to the said estate are lost or mislaid so that he cannot particularly set forth by what ways or means the said lands are exempt or discharged from tithes. He discovers quantities and values.

Upon long debate of the matter, the court did not think fit to decree for the plaintiff without a trial at law but proposed that he should bring his action on the Statute,[1] which the plaintiff declining, the bill was by his consent dismissed without prejudice and without costs.

[Order of 9 July 1696: Public Record Office E.126/16, f. 360.]

142

Ustick, qui tam v. Timbrell

(Ex. 1696)

A ship that comes into a port through distress does not import her cargo for the purposes of forfeitures or duties.

Dodd 167

The ship *Eagle*, foreign built but taken and condemned as prize and made free and navigated by an English master and mariners, loaded currents at Zant in the dominions of Venice and [was] bound for London but [was] taken at sea as prize by the French and afterwards rescued herself and put in at the port of Bideford. The plaintiff preferred an information against her upon the Act of Navigation.[2]

And upon the trial, the Chief Baron [Ward] inclined that the words in the Act 'That no currants or Turkish commodities shall be imported' etc. extend generally to all currants, Turkish or non-Turkish. Query. Secondly, that coming into port is sufficient to forfeit without entry or breaking bulk. But if it be to entitle the king to the duty there should be entry made or bulk broken. But in the principal case, the jury found that [she] put in by distress and fear of enemies, and thus it prevents a special verdict.

143

Portman v. Snow

(Ex. 1696)

Where several parishioners sue to establish separate moduses, they cannot join in one suit.

[1] Stat. 2 & 3 Edw. VI, c. 13 (*SR*, IV, 55–58).

[2] Stat. 12 Car. II, c. 18, s. 8 (*SR*, V, 248).

Dodd 168, 1 Eagle & Younge 620

Upon hearing, it appeared that the bill was brought for establishing *modus*es in the parish, but each party claimed a distinct *modus* for his farm and not any general *modus* throughout the parish. And the court dismissed the bill without prejudice, because [it is] not possible to try forty-two several *modus*es, for the infinite vexation and multiplicity of them, besides they were in their nature forty-two several suits or causes.

[Other reports of this case: Equity Cases Exch. 407.]

144

Macarty, qui tam v. Romices

(Ex. 1696)

The jury are the judges of the credibility of the witnesses.

A verdict will not be set aside where there was some substantial evidence to support it.

Lincoln's Inn MS. Misc. 559, f. 40

Easter term. Macarty and Radford, *qui tam* v. Romices and Gastling, upon an information of seizure of French goods, *viz.* rosin, kid skins, prunes, and cork.

The information was grounded upon the statutes restraining the importation of any goods of the growth, production, or manufacture of France or of any of the territories or dominions of the French king. By the first act made 1 Will. & Mar.,[1] the *onus probandi* is put upon the claimer and, for default of proof, they are to be condemned and burnt. But by the Statute of 4 & 5 Will. & Mar.,[2] if they be seized by an officer of the customs and prosecuted in the Exchequer as that Act directs, they are not to be burnt, but the king, upon the condemnation, shall have two-thirds and the informer the other third.

And upon this trial, the defendants took upon them the proof that the goods were Spanish and not French. And, for that purpose, they produced divers Spaniards for witnesses, who swore by their interpreter that these goods were all laden aboard the ship, the *Francisco*, off St. Sebastian's and that they came over with them in the said ship from St. Sebastian's in Spain where they were laden aboard. And some of them spoke to the buying of the goods at St. Sebastian's and that some of them were brought upon mules' backs from the mountainous parts of the Spanish Navarre and bought of merchants by name, living at Saragossa in Aragon in Spain, and that that country usually produces goods of the same kind and natures for sale, especially since the prohibition from France. And one of the wit-

1 Stat. 1 Will. & Mar., c. 34, s. 2 (*SR*, VI, 100–101).
2 Stat. 4 Will. & Mar., c. 35 (*SR*, VI, 419–423).

nesses said he saw some of the rosin made in the Spanish mountains of Aragon twenty leagues from France and brought on mules' backs from thence and that no part of the dominions of the French king where any such goods are made are within divers leagues of St. Sebastian's.

But, it [was] proved on the king's behalf that there is of late a trade set up of bringing French goods from St. Sebastian's into England, and, divers witnesses being examined, they swore they had dealt or did deal in those commodities for many years and that they had skill therein and could very well and easily distinguish between French and Spanish and that they verily believed these were all French, and they showed their reasons for such their knowledges and distinctions. And Mr. Garret, a witness for the defendant, said, if he was to buy the prunes, he would buy them for Spanish and sell them for French.

And there being few or no goods of this kind brought from St. Sebastian's to England until of late, the jury found for the king.

And a new trial was denied by the court, the jury having evidence on both sides and being a substantial jury and [it being] wholly a matter of fact whether Spanish or French and the credit of the witnesses on both sides was left to the jury, whereof they are the proper judges.

[Other copies of this report: Georgetown Univ. Law Sch. MS. B88–8, p. 336.]

145

Whitehall, qui tam v. Cagnoni

(Ex. 1696)

A special verdict as to the facts of a case will not be set aside as inadequate where there was evidence to support it.

Lincoln's Inn MS. Misc. 559, f. 41

Easter term 1696. Whitehall, *qui tam* v. Cagnoni and Magnoni, for importing wine from Leghorn in shipping not duly navigated according to the Act of Navigation, 12 Car. II, ca. 18.[1]

The information was by way of *devenerunt* for wines imported in ships not duly navigated whereby they became forfeited and being so forfeited came to the defendants' hands. And it laid their values to be very great, which were sought by that information, one moiety for the king, the other for the informer.

And, upon the trial, it appeared that the wines were imported in a ship not duly navigated and so, by law, the wines were forfeited. But it also appeared that the merchant made his entries and paid his duties publicly and the navigation was not strictly looked after in regard it was a time of war and that the ship was

[1] Stat. 12 Car. II, c. 18 (*SR*, V, 246–250).

gone and no seizure made and that this information of *devenerunt* was prosecuted by the plaintiff some time after the ship was gone, the plaintiff being turned out from being a Custom House officer. And, upon the trial, it seemed to me [Edward Ward] that the wines, above all charges and payments of customs and by the decay of the wines in quantity and quality, were worth £4 or £5 a tun and that fifty tuns came to the defendants' hands. But the jury, though they found for the king and the informer, found the value to be but £25 in the whole, which is 10s. a tun, which I [Edward Ward] thought was a strange verdict, though the jury said they found fifty tuns.

And, upon a motion for a new trial by Whitehall, the King's Attorney having entered a *nolle prosequi* as to the king's moiety after the verdict, a new trial was denied by the court, the values of the wines being mere matter of fact, it was a substantial jury, and [the verdict being] specially returned. But it seemed strange as to the values.

[Other copies of this report: Georgetown Univ. Law Sch. MS. B88–8, p. 338.]

146

Whitehall, qui tam v. Riggs

(Ex. 1696)

Where a party could have postponed a trial because his witnesses failed to appear at the trial, but did not, the verdict will not be set aside.

Lincoln's Inn MS. Misc. 559, f. 42, pl. 1

Easter term 1696.

Upon an information of *devenerunt* for the goods grounded upon the Act of Navigation[1] for importing naval stores from Norway in a Dutch built ship and not duly navigated, the evidence upon the trial was strong that the ship was unqualified and not duly navigated. But there was no proof that the goods came to the defendant's hands. It was only proved by the officer of the customs that the defendant gave him a paper containing the particular of the goods in order to [make] the entry and that this was before the goods were unladen.

And, upon this evidence, the jury found for the defendant.

And the informer prayed a new trial upon an affidavit that he served two or three witnesses with a subpoena in order to give evidence at the trial who could have proved that the goods came to the defendant's hands but that they appeared not.

But the court denied a new trial upon that ground, for, without his witnesses, he needed not to have tried the cause and the jury, not having evidence that

[1] Stat. 12 Car. II, c. 18 (*SR*, V, 246–250).

the goods came to the defendant's hands, have not misdemeaned themselves in their verdict, it not being just that the defendant should answer for the value of the goods not proved to have come to his hands.

[Other copies of this report: Georgetown Univ. Law Sch. MS. B88–8, p. 339.]

147

Jeffreys, qui tam v. Lowe

(Ex. 1696–1697)

Where a penal statute puts a penalty on a seller, the penalty cannot be levied against the seller's agent.

Lincoln's Inn MS. Misc. 559, f. 42, pl. 2

Easter term 1696.

An information [was] grounded upon the Statute of 15 Car. II, ca. 8,[1] for preventing the selling of live fat cattle by butchers. And, upon the trial, it was proved that the defendant was a butcher and, within the times of the information, did sell in Smithfield three fat oxen valued £9 each and exposed several others to sale, the Statute reciting that of the 3 & 4 Edw. VI, ca. 19,[2] whereby the penalty was laid upon butchers buying and selling fat cattle alive, and this Statute, reciting the difficulty of proving the buying of them, enacts that no person using the trade of a butcher should after Michaelmas following sell, offer, or expose to sale in any market or elsewhere, either by himself or any servant or agent whatsoever, any fat oxen, steers, runts, kine, heifers, calves, sheep, or lambs alive upon pain to forfeit the double value of the cattle so sold or offered or exposed to sale, one moiety to the king, the other to the informer.

It was proved on the defendant's behalf by one Wingfield, a butcher, that he was employed by one Mr. Hale, a gentleman of Buckinghamshire, to sell some live fat cattle for him in Smithfield and that he, meeting the defendant as he was going into Smithfield to sell them and having other business, desired the defendant to sell the same for him and for such as the defendant sold [. . .] proved that he ordered the buyers to pay the money to the said Wingfield at The Rose in Smithfield, which was Wingfield's inn, which was done accordingly, as was also proved by the plaintiff's witnesses, to whom the defendant sold the three oxen, that they paid the money to Wingfield accordingly.

And I [Edward Ward] was in doubt in this case whether the defendant was a butcher and his sale as such within the words or meaning of the Statute, for, though the defendant was a butcher and did sell and expose to sale, yet, in

[1] Stat. 15 Car. II, c. 8 (*SR*, V, 452).

[2] Stat. 3 & 4 Edw. VI, c. 19 (*SR*, IV, 119).

regard Wingfield, who was a butcher, employed him, whether he can be said to be other than the servant or agent of the butcher Wingfield and so Wingfield and not the defendant (otherwise than as Wingfield's servant or agent) can be deemed the seller within that law, which lays the penalty upon the butcher that by himself or servant or agent sells and not upon the servant or agent that sells. And, therefore, I [EDWARD WARD] was willing to have the matter found specially if the jury found the sale by the defendant and the value of the cattle sold, which they did and the value to be £27, which doubled is £54. But the parties, by their counsel, being desirous to save the pains and charge of a special verdict, agreed to have a case made of it and to attend me [EDWARD WARD] for my opinion in point of law and, accordingly, judgment to be entered or not entered as I should direct. But the informer, being apprehensive that it was against him, compounded with the defendant, and nothing more was done upon it.

And had that case been brought to me, I should have inclined (as so advised) for the defendant that he was not the person punishable by this Act but that Wingfield was, the sale made by the defendant being merely as servant or agent for Wingfield, whose sale it was by the defendant as his servant or agent.

[Other copies of this report: Georgetown Univ. Law Sch. MS. B88–8, p. 340.]

Lincoln's Inn MS. Misc. 559, f. 99, pl. 1

Hilary term 1696[/97].

Upon an information grounded upon the Statute 15 Car. II, ca. 8, restraining butchers from selling or offering or exposing to sale any live fat cattle under the penalty of forfeiting double their value, the defendant was convicted by a verdict for selling three live fat oxen, several others being laid in the information. And the endorsement upon the [writ of] *distringas* was the defendant '*culpabilis quoad tres boves*', and nothing was said as to the rest. The *postea* was returned, the trial being at the Guildhall, that the jury found the defendant guilty *quoad venditionem trium bovum parcellam etc.* in the information and not guilty *quoad venditionem residuum in informatione.*

Serjeant *Levinz* moved in arrest of judgment, first, because the information was laid in the disjunctive for selling or offering or exposing to sale, whereas he would have it that the offense ought to have been certain, *viz.* either selling or exposing to sale expressly laid.

But, to that, the court answered it was well enough in the reason of the thing, for the jury must ascertain and had in this case ascertained the crime to be in selling. And the precedents in this court are and always have been disjunctive, as this is where the law upon which the information is grounded is in the disjunctive for the disjunctive matters are all equally criminous and the defendant can be found guilty but of one of them.

Then, he moved that the verdict was uncertain and that no judgment could be given upon it, for, though the first part that found the defendant guilty as to the sale of three was certain enough, yet there was nothing endorsed upon the *distringas* to warrant any judgment for the residue, and, then, if the verdict do not cover the whole information, it is void for the whole. And, if anything might be entered for the residue, yet what was entered on the *postea* was not sufficient, for that goes only to the sale and not to the offering or exposing to sale.

The court stayed entry of judgment at present. But, afterwards, in the term, the plaintiff's counsel showed that it is the practice amongst the clerks of assize, associates, and marshalls many times to enter what the jury find the defendant guilty of and to say nothing of the rest, and that is sufficient for entry of judgment for the defendant for the residue. And, upon enquiry, the practice was found to be so. And the entry being *quoad venditionem residuum etc.* without saying anything of offering or exposing to sale, it being made out to the court that the word '*venditionem*' in that case was interlined by a mistake of the marshall, it was ordered by the court that the endorsement of the *postea* should be amended in that particular and that the word so interlined should be put out, and then it [. . .] *quoad residuum* for the defendant, whereby the defendant was fully acquitted of all that he was not found guilty of before and made a complete verdict.

[Other copies of this report: Georgetown Univ. Law Sch. MS. B88–8, p. 517.]

148

Roberts v. Lee

(Ex. 1696)

The question in this case was whether a proctor for a married woman in a case in an ecclesiastical court can sue for his unpaid legal fees.

Lincoln's Inn MS. Misc. 559, f. 50

Trinity term 1696; Office of Pleas of the Exchequer.

The plaintiff here, being a married woman but separated from cohabitation with her husband by a sentence in the ecclesiastical court and being sued by the defendant Lee, her proctor in the ecclesiastical court, for his fees and money laid out by him in that suit for the now plaintiff against her husband, prayed a [writ of] prohibition to Lee's suit in the [Court of] Arches for his said fees and money laid out in that court and in that suit upon a suggestion that the plaintiff here being defendant below was a married woman and ought not to be sued without her husband and, secondly, that the Arches ought not to hold a plea for proctor's fees or money laid out by any proctor for his client in a suit in that court, thirdly, nor can they try the custom whereby the defendant here and plaintiff below endeavors to entitle himself to the fees in regard of the difference that is between our law and theirs what a custom is, forty years there making a prescription but, at common law, it must be time of which [memory does not run] etc.

And a day being given to show cause why a [writ of] prohibition should not be awarded, *Chesshyre*, for the defendant, showed that it was allowed by the courts in Westminster Hall for proctors to sue for their fees in the ecclesiastical court. And he cited and relied upon the judgment of the whole court of Exchequer, Hilary 1683[/84] in the like case with this between Skelton, plaintiff, and the now defendant Lee, defendant, *q.v.* L. K, 41,[1] where the same objections were made to that suit below as are here, and yet the court, upon argument, denied the prohibition because such suits for fees have been constantly allowed and they are the best judges whether they are due or not. And though a married woman may have no estate of her own to pay the fees, yet, where she sues as plaintiff without her husband, as there she did, the suit against her there is good, and she must either procure her husband to pay the fees, that being a cause of defamation against the wife, or else undergo the sentence. And it was urged that this cause is stronger because the wife's suit was proper against her husband and the sentence of separation obtained thereupon so as in some sense she is to be looked upon as an unmarried woman. And it looks hard to compel the husband, who was the defendant to his wife's suit and against whom the sentence was, to pay the charges of the wife's suit. Cro. Car. 16.[2] And, where the spiritual court allows the wife to sue without her husband, it is but reasonable to make the wife, without her husband, to be answerable for the costs, the rather because the husband's release of the suit is no bar. As Cro. Car. 222 (but there it seems to be good for the costs), and the Case of Huelson and Chamberlain, lately in the King's Bench,[3] was cited where it is said it was resolved that the husband's release of the costs of his wife's suit without him in a cause of defamation was no bar. And here it is more strong, being after a sentence of separation *a mensa et thoro*. And the case 1 Ventris 165[4] was cited, where it is said than an apparitor may sue in the ecclesiastical court for his due and customary fees.

But, for the [writ of] prohibition, it was urged that, in that case, a prohibition was granted upon a suggestion that no such fees were due by custom. And, by that and also 1 Ventris 274,[5] it was resolved that the custom for fees or duties in the ecclesiastical court shall be tried at common law. And it was said that the question whether a proctor can sue in the ecclesiastical court for his fees is now depending in the King's Bench in a case of a prohibition between Johnson,

---

[1] *Shelton v. Lee* (Ex. 1684), Exch. Repts. *tempore* Car. II, 585.

[2] *Green's Case* (1625), Croke Car. 16, 79 E.R. 619.

[3] *Anonymous* (1631), Croke Car. 222, 79 E.R. 794; *Chamberlaine v. Hewson* (1695–1696), 5 Modern 69, 87 E.R. 524, Holt K.B. 99, 90 E.R. 953, 1 Salkeld 115, 91 E.R. 107, 1 Lord Raymond 73, 91 E.R. 945, 12 Modern 89, 88 E.R. 1184.

[4] *Anonymous* (1671), 1 Ventris 165, 86 E.R. 112.

[5] *Anonymous* (1675) 1 Ventris 274, 86 E.R. 183.

plaintiff, and the now defendant Lee, defendant,[1] and that the court seemed to incline for a prohibition, and therefore, *curia advisare vult* until next term, the parties here agreeing to stay all in the ecclesiastical court in the meantime saving liberty for the plaintiff there to call for an answer in order to examine witnesses, but not to go to sentence.

The title that Lee makes to his fees and sums of money contained in a schedule annexed to his libel is *de communi usu in dicta curia tempore unmemorato*. And yet, in that schedule, there are divers sums which are not fees, as so much for waterage under the title of *expensum aquaticis*, so much for attending and instructing doctors and so much for other things which are not fees and the suit title and custom goes to all by the libel.

But it was again urged that, if a prohibition shall go here, Lee is without a remedy at [common] law, for he cannot sue the husband at common law for the fees or money, they not being due or laid out for the use or at request of the husband, but the contrary and that may distinguish this case from others where the husband may be liable at law.

But to that, it may be answered that Lee was not bound to be the woman's proctor but might have refused or else he might have taken security for them before he meddled but now he did it at this peril and it is his own fault if he loses them and such a distinction will not give a jurisdiction to the ecclesiastical court to try a custom for fees, which is only determinable by the common law.

But one of the parties dying, the matter fell without the opinion of the court. But, it being if fees may be sued for in the ecclesiastical court, nothing but bare [?] stated fees can be sued for there and then prohibition *quoad*.

[Other copies of this report: Georgetown Univ. Law Sch. MS. B88–8, p. 360.]

149

Helyng v. Jennings

(Ex. 1696)

False Latin in a plaintiff's pleading will not defeat a verdict for the plaintiff.

Lincoln's Inn MS. Misc. 559, f. 65, pl. 1

Michaelmas term 1696, 8 Will. III.

A verdict was had in [an action of] trover, and entire damages were given for divers particular things and, amongst which, one was '*pro una chirographa, Anglice*, a muff'. And it was moved by *Turner* in arrest of judgment because, in the propriety or etymology of that word, if it signified anything, it signified a

[1] *Johnson v. Lee* (1696), 5 Modern 231, 87 E.R. 627, Skinner 589, 90 E.R. 264, Holt K.B. 656, 90 E.R. 1262, 1 Comyns 18, 92 E.R. 937.

handwriting. And it not being shown what it was and damages being given for it for which none ought to be, not being anything shown to be under any party's hand or seal and so no action lay for it, or damages ought to have been given and, here, the damages being entire and the jury not having distinguished this from the rest, no judgment ought to be entered, for it cannot be understood that damages should be given for a muff, there being no Latin word for it. And the *anglice* will not help it without some expression of Latin, because all pleadings must by the Statute of Edw. III[1] be enrolled in Latin, and, according to the reason of Osborn's Case, 10 Rep. 130,[2] where there is a proper Latin word, there it must be used and there needs no *anglice*, but, where there is no proper Latin word, there, a word may be framed and the *anglice* will help and explain it. And, here, *chirotheca*, though not *chirographa*, is proper Latin for a muff.

But, on the other side, to which the court agreed, it was answered that there is no proper Latin word (at least, at the time of the Statute of Edw. III, there was not) for a muff. And, though some dictionaries now do say that *chirotheca* is Latin for a muff, yet, in this case, it shall be intended that that is not proper and genuine Latin. And, therefore *chirographa* with an *anglice* may very well express it, there being in truth no such Latin word as *chirographa*, though there is *chirographia*. So either the *anglice* with that improper Latin word of *chirographa* shall make it plain to the jury and upon the record to signify a muff, for which the jury gave damages, or else, if it signifies nothing, the jury shall be intended not to give any damages for it. And so *quacumque via*, the plaintiff shall have his judgment, which he had accordingly.

In this case, the cases of Siderfin 445, Taylor and Wells, and the cases in Style's there cited were remembered and considered,[3] and so was the Case of Osborne, 10 rep. 130.

And in this case, '*uno vestimentum pro puero, Anglice* a suit of child bed linen' was held good.

Query if [an action of] trover lies de duobus pecii auri, not saying what nor the value, be good. [It was] held not by a Common Bench judgment. But de duobus catulis was held good, not saying what sort of whelp, whether lions, bears, bitches, etc. And in Michaelmas [term] 1700, in an [action of] trover for una imagine, anglice a maid to dry clothes on, was held bad for the uncertainty of the word 'imago', which ought to have been more particular.

[Other copies of this report: Georgetown Univ. Law Sch. MS. B88–8, p. 402.]

---

1 Stat. 36 Edw. III, stat. 1, c. 15 (*SR*, I, 375–376).

2 *Osborn v. Middleton* (1613), 10 Coke Rep. 130, 77 E.R. 1123, also Jenkins 270, 145 E.R. 194.

3 *Taylor v. Wells* (1670), 1 Siderfin 445, 82 E.R. 1208, also Lincoln's Inn MS. Misc. 500, f. 81, pl. 2, 1 Modern 46, 86 E.R. 721, 1 Ventris 71, 86 E.R. 50, 2 Keble 623, 640, 663, 84 E.R. 392, 403, 417, 2 Williams Saunders 74, 85 E.R. 743; *Cremer v. Brunet* (1651), Style 266, 82 E.R. 698; *Iles v. Windsor* (1654), Style 419, 82 E.R. 827.

1 Lord Raymond 133, 91 E.R. 985, Dodd 348

[In an action of] trover '*pro uno vestimento lineario pro pueris, Anglice* a suit of child bed linen, *pro uno chirographo, Anglice* a muff', [there was a] verdict for the plaintiff and judgment, after a motion in arrest.

Ex relatione magistri Mather.

150

Easly v. Philpot

(Ex. 1696)

A municipal corporation cannot arbitrarily tax its inhabitants.

Lincoln's Inn MS. Misc. 559, f. 69, pl. 2

Office of Pleas, Exchequer, entered Michaelmas term 4 Will. & Mar., Kent.

The plaintiff [Dennis Easly] brings an action of trespass against the defendant [John Philpot] for breaking his house and close and taking his goods, showing what, at Feversham, and lays it to his damage of £10.

The defendant, as to the force and arms and to all the trespass besides entering the house and close of the plaintiff and taking and carrying away the goods in the declaration, pleads not guilty. And, thereupon, issue is joined. And, as to the entering of the house and close and taking and carrying away goods, [he pleads] *actio non*, for that the Town of Feversham is and time out of mind has been an ancient town *olim incorporata* by the name of the Barons of Feversham and, afterwards, by the name of the Mayor, Barons, and Commonalty of Feversham and now and by the space of 140 years last past and more incorporated by the name of the Mayor, Jurats, and Commonalty of the Town of Feversham and that, for the maintenance, continuance, and preservation of all and singular their ancient customs, liberties, and franchises in that town and for the good order and wholesome government of the said town and of the burgesses and freemen thereof, the magistrates, chief burgesses, and commonalty for the time being, that is to say, the barons of the said town for the time being in their time and after their time, the Mayor, Barons, and Commonalty of the said town for the time being in their time and after their time, the Mayor, Jurats, and Commonalty of the said town, for the time being in their time for all time whereof the memory of man is not to the contrary, have used to assemble and from time to time to hold a certain Court of Wardmote and there make and establish just, reasonable, and necessary laws and orders for that purpose and, time out of mind, to impose reasonable and moderate sum and sums by way of a penalty or forfeiture upon the transgressors of such laws or orders to be paid for the use of the said town, whether the transgressors were foreigners or freemen of the town if they should commit anything against the said laws or orders within the town or the liberties thereof and that, by virtue of the customs, franchises, and liberties of the said town and of divers charters as well before as after the time of King Henry VIII by divers progenitors of the now king and queen to the said town and burgesses thereof and their successors made and granted the Mayor, Jurats, and Commonalty of the said town for the time being, the 18 November 4 Eliz. [1561] assembled at Feversham in a Court of Wardmote according to the use and custom aforesaid, then and there held by them, did, *inter alia*, establish, confirm, and enact that, whereas by the laudable custom of the town, time out of mind, the freemen commoners being twenty-four persons who represented the whole state of the commons and commonalty of the said town or the major part of those twenty-four were used to assemble together at such a day, place, and time as the Mayor of the said town for the time being had used to appoint to offer and assess upon all men being inhabitants in that town and not free thereof such moderate fines in respect of the privileges, emoluments, and commonalties which they enjoyed *ratione habitationis et residentiae eorum ibidem* as to the same twenty-four persons or the major part of them for the time being from time to time shall seem reasonable, which sums so imposed were usually paid to the Chamberlain of the said town for the time being or his deputy without any contradiction of the parties upon whom they were imposed until of late.

Therefore, by the said Mayor, Jurats, and Commonalty of the said town then being, it was ordained and enacted that, if any person should afterwards deny to pay the fine imposed upon him, that, upon such denial, it should be lawful for the Chamberlain to distrain his goods and chattels distrainable by law, provided that no widows of freemen dwelling within the said town during their widowhoods should be liable to any such fines.

Then, he sets forth that, afterwards, *scil.* 4 September 27 Eliz. [1585], the Mayor, Jurats, and Commonalty of Feversham assembled in the Court of Wardmote there, according to use and custom, did, *inter alia*, ordain that the sums and fines upon the inhabitants of that town not free should be yearly imposed and taxed by the commons of the Common Council of the said town time out of mind used should thenceforth be yearly imposed and taxed upon every Easter Monday.

The 29 September 3 Will. & Mar. [1691], the Mayor, Jurats, and Commonalty of the said town assembled there in the Wardmote Court according to use and custom did, *inter alia*, order that the Serjeant at Mace of the said town should be authorized to collect for the use of the said town the fines for gutters and foreigner's fines and others usually put in the Chamberlain's rolls which there were or afterwards should be due to the town.

Then, he shows that the plaintiff, by the space of five years past, had been and then was an inhabitant in the town of Feversham and exercised the occupation of a collarmaker and was not free of the town and that the commons of Feversham, upon every Easter Monday in the years 1689, 1690, [and] 1691, did tax the plaintiff 18d. a year, amounting to 4s. 6d. for his foreigner's fines, and that the defendant was the Serjeant at Mace there and that, the 31st of March 4 Will. & Mar. [1692], the Mayor, Jurats, and Commonalty, assembled in a Wardmote Court according to custom, did *inter alia*, ordain that the defendant, being the Serjeant at Mace, should collect for the use of the said town or should distrain for the said sum of 4s. 6d. upon the plaintiff for his said foreigner's fines, and, because the plaintiff did not pay the same upon request, but refused to pay, then the defendant, by virtue of the order aforesaid, entered into the plaintiff's house and close, the doors being open, *eodem tempore quo etc.* and distrained the goods in the declaration and carried them away and yet detains them in his custody for the said 4s. 6d. yet unpaid, *prout ei bene licuit, quae sunt eadem intrato domus et clausum et capto et asportato* of the goods *unde* the plaintiff *se modo queritur, et hoc paratus etc., unde petit judicium* if the plaintiff *actionem suam praedictam versus eum habere seu manutenere debet.*

To this plea, the plaintiff put in a special demurrer, and assigned for cause that the plea was repugnant, uncertain, and wanted form. And the defendant joined.

The exceptions taken to this plea were both to the substance and validity of the bylaw of 4 Eliz. and to the other ordinances and also to the form of the pleading of them.

As to the bylaw itself of 4 Eliz., it was objected that it was void as being against (1) the common law, (2) the statute law, (3) reason.

First, the common law allows living and exercising of trades anywhere, *vide* preamble to Statute 13 & 14 Car. II, for the poor, ca. 12, § 1,[1] which restrains peoples going from one parish to another, which, before and at common law, was lawful.

Second, against statute law, Magna Charta, ca. 29; 19 Hen. VII, ca. [. . .].[2]

Third, against reason. It is unreasonable that a man should pay a fine for nothing, for, though it is said *ea ratione privilegiorum* that he enjoys by living in Feversham, yet there is not any special or particular privilege shown that he enjoys, nor in truth does he enjoy any but the breathing in that air, which is none of the best. And such a bylaw as subjects a man to pay a fine arbitrary at the will of the Mayor and twenty-four for nothing but living in his own house is very unreasonable and against that liberty and property which the law of England allows to the people. It is not so much as a *quid pro quo*, and it is against the public good, for to restrain inhabitancy is as bad and stands upon the same foot and reason which restraint of trade does according to the authorities of Davenant and Hurdis, in Moore, and Second Institute, and the Tailor of Ipswich's Case, 11 rep.; 2

[1] Stat. 14 Car. II, c. 12, s. 1 (*SR*, V, 401).

[2] Stat. 25 Edw. I, Magna Carta, c. 25 (*SR*, I, 117); Stat. 19 Hen. VII, c. 12 (*SR*, II, 656–657).

Brownl. 179–180; Bridgman's rep. 139.[1] Had there been special privileges shown that the inhabitants of that town by reason of being inhabitants there only had enjoyed, it might have been otherwise. Besides, this bylaw cannot, in the nature of it, subsist by any custom or prescription, the matter of it being unreasonable. Cro. Car. 259; Li. Ass. 44, pl. 8; Moor 580.[2]

And, though the fine here set is but 18d. a year, yet the smallness of it will not justify the power to set it, for the Mayor and twenty-four may alter it when they please.

And, for these reasons, nothing material being offered on the other side, and without regards to the defects in pleading, which were many, the court unanimously gave judgment for the plaintiff.

[Other copies of this report: Georgetown Univ. Law Sch. MS. B88–8, p. 418.]

151

Anonymous

(Ex. 1696)

There must be a return made of the first writ of scire facias before a second such writ can be issued.

Before the return of a second writ of scire facias, a principal debtor may surrender himself in discharge of his bail.

Lincoln's Inn MS. Misc. 559, f. 71

Michaelmas term 1696.

It was prayed last term that the defendant in the action might surrender himself in discharge of his bail, which was opposed by the plaintiff in the action in regard it was said that there was a second [writ of] *scire facias* returned against the bail. But, upon enquiry, it was found that indeed there was never a *scire facias* returned at the time the principal offered to surrender himself, nor was there any *scire facias* to be found at the sheriff's office. But, after the offer of surrendering, there were two [writ of] *scire facias* brought to the sheriff's office which were also made and sealed after the offer.

And the matter appearing as above upon examination, the court allowed the principal to surrender himself in discharge of his bail, and disapproved that way

---

1 *Davenant v. Hurdis* (1599), Moore K.B. 576, 72 E.R. 769; E. Coke, *Second Institute* (1642), pp. 741–743; *Tailors of Ipswich's Case* (1614), 11 Coke Rep. 53, 77 E.R. 1218, also Godbolt 252, 78 E.R. 147, 1 Rolle Rep. 4, 81 E.R. 285; *Borough of Gravesend v. Edmunds* (1612), 2 Brownlow & Goldesborough 177, 123 E.R. 883; *Wood v. Searl* (1618), J. Bridgman 139, 123 E.R. 1257.

2 *Tredymmock v. Perryman* (1632), Croke Car. 259, 79 E.R. 826; YB 15 Edw. III, Lib. Ass., f. 43, pl. 8 (1341); *Davenant v. Hurdis* (1599), *ut supra*.

of getting [writs of] *scire facias* returned after the time of their returns were out, which grows to a practice, the end of the law, which is to give notice to the party that he be not surprised, being thereby eluded, for, in truth, there ought to be a return made of the first *scire facias* before a second be sued forth and, before the return of the second *scire facias,* the principal may surrender himself in discharge of his bail.

[Other copies of this report: Georgetown Univ. Law Sch. MS. B88–8, p. 425.]

152

Hunt v. Silvester

(Ex. 1696)

A general plea of performance is allowed where the setting forth of the particulars would tend to multifariousness or prolixity.

The parties to an action can agree to have a trial on an issue that was not properly pleaded.

Lincoln's Inn MS. Misc. 559, f. 72

Michaelmas [term] 1696. Martha Hunt, administratrix of William Hunt, plaintiff; John Silvester, defendant; entered in the Office of Pleas, Michaelmas term, 7 Will. III [1695].

The plaintiff brings an action of debt upon a bond of £100 penalty dated the 24th of March 25 Car. II [1673] entered into by the defendant to the plaintiff's intestate conditioned that:

> whereas the said William Hunt, present cook of His Majesty's Ship *Royal Charles,* has by order of His Royal Highness, the duke of York, constituted and in his place put the said John Silvester to be his deputy cook in the said ship, if, therefore, the said Silvester, his heirs, executors, etc. shall and do well and truly pay or cause to be paid to the said William Hunt, his executors, etc. the sum of 25s. of lawful money per month and so after that rate for every month as the said ship shall be and continue in full or sea pay and 8s. per month for so long time as the said ship shall lie in harbor or be continued upon petty warrant, and also, if the said John Silvester shall and do by any means or procurement whatsoever procure, obtain, or get the grand or principal warrant to be cook of the said ship, if then the said John Silvester, his executors, etc. shall and do well and truly pay or cause to be paid to the said William Hunt, his executors, etc. the full sum of £30 over and besides the several sums of money before mentioned within one month next and immediately after the procuring, obtaining, or getting of the said grand or principal warrant, then this obligation to be void.

The defendant after *oyer* of this condition pleads *action non quia dicit* that the said ship in the condition mentioned was not nor did continue in full or sea pay nor lay in port nor was or continued upon petty warrant beyond the 16th day of September 1689, and that he, the defendant, paid to the intestate in his lifetime, *viz.* the 17th of September 1689, at London etc. *secundum ratam* 25s. for every month when the said ship was or continued in full or sea pay and 8s. for every month when the said ship lay in port or was continued upon petty warrant *secundum formam et effectum conditionis scripti obligatoris praedicti*, and that he, the defendant, *nullis modis aut procurationibus quibuscunque* did procure, obtain, or get the great or principal warrant to be cook of the said ship of the said King Charles II called the *Royal Charles, et hoc paratus est verificare.*

The plaintiff replies and says *praecludi non,* because he, the defendant, *post confectionem* of that bond, *scil.* the 30th of June 1689 at London etc. *quibusdam modis et procurationem* did procure, obtain, and get the great or principal warrant to be cook of the said ship of the said King Charles II called the *Royal Charles tempore confectionis scripti obligatoris praedicti* and did not pay to the intestate in his life nor to the plaintiff afterwards the said sum of £30 above and besides the several sums of money in the condition aforesaid mentioned within one month next after the procuring of the said warrant *secundum formam et effectum conditionis praedicti, et hoc paratus est verificare.* And she prays judgment with her debt and damages.

The defendant rejoins and demurs specially to this replication and assigns for cause that the replication contains matter disjunctively pleaded where it ought to be absolute and particular; secondly, that the replication contains new matters which ought not to be pleaded, *viz.* '*non solvit summam £30*' and '*tempore confectionis scripti obligatoris praedicti*'; thirdly, that the replication concludes by averment where it ought to conclude to the country; fourthly, that it is double, uncertain, vagous, and wants form.

The plaintiff joins in demurrer.

And, upon this sort of pleading, I [Edward Ward] was of opinion that judgment could not be given for the plaintiff to recover his debt by bond, for, though the defendant's plea that the ship was not nor did continue in full or sea pay nor lay in port or was or continued upon petty warrant beyond the 16th of September 1689 and that the defendant had paid to the intestate after the rate of 25s. and 8s. per month *prout* the plea might have been better pleaded, that is to say more particularly and distinctly by saying it lay so long under full or sea pay and so long upon petty warrant and that he had paid those particular sums, yet that plea does contain a competent certainty upon which the plaintiff, if she thought fit, might have assigned a breach if payment had not been duly made and such sort of general pleading has been formerly and at this day allowed in the cases between subjects, as in the cases of Mints and Bethell, Cro. Eliz. 749, and Acton and Hill, same book 253, and the same book 916, and 1 Siderfin 334,

Church and Brunswick,[1] by which books, it appears that a general plea of performance of the particular things where the setting them forth would tend to multifariousness or prolixity has been allowed. And there is no mischief in it, for the plaintiff is at liberty to assign a breach in any particular thing. And a demurrer to such a plea ought to be special and not general.

But, in this case, where the plaintiff has passed over that part of the condition and, by replication, has assigned his breach in another thing, *viz.* the obtaining of the warrant to be cook of the ship, that seems to have cured the imperfection of the defendant's plea as to the generality of it. And, then, the party, by his replication, having set forth new matter, *viz.* first, that the ship was called so *tempore confectionis scripti praedicti* and, secondly, that the defendant had not paid the £30 within a month, as the condition is, it was not possible for the defendant to take issue upon that replication, especially as to the non-payment of the £30, which is part of the replication and must be rejoined to, for, if he should have rejoined to that replication, it must have been in the nature of a contradiction, for, to the first part, it must have been that he did not obtain and, to the second part, it must have been (to have made an issue to it) that he had paid the £30 within the month, the putting in of which non-payment of the £30 spoils all, for the defendant having pleaded that he did not obtain the warrant and the plaintiff having replied that he did obtain the warrant, that was the complete issue, and, if the warrant was obtained, then, upon this pleading, the bond was forfeited and the penalty lost. And the non-payment of the £30 was no breach of the bond, for that was not to be paid unless the defendant had obtained a warrant, which he says he did not. And then to rejoin to issue to all this replication was in effect to have said thus, I have not obtained the warrant and yet I have paid you the £30, which in effect is a contradiction.

This case was twice argued, but I [EDWARD WARD] taking these exceptions, the parties, upon the court's recommendation, agreed the plaintiff might discontinue and try the merits of the case whether the defendant obtained the warrant or not or paid the monthly sum according to the condition of the bond at the plaintiff's election.

Note, afterwards, by consent, the parties descended to the issue whether the defendant did procure the warrant to be cook of the said ship or not. And it was found for the plaintiff that he did.

[Other copies of this report: Georgetown Univ. Law Sch. MS. B88–8, p. 426.]

[1] *Mints v. Bethil* (1600), Croke Eliz. 749, 78 E.R. 981; *Acton v. Hill* (1591), Croke Eliz. 253, 78 E.R. 509; *Braban v. Bacon* (1603), Croke Eliz. 916, 78 E.R. 1137; *Church v. Brownewick* (1667), 1 Siderfin 334, 82 E.R. 1140, also 2 Keble 220, 221, 84 E.R. 137, 138.

153

Lilburne v. Carr

(Ex. 1697)

Where a judgment by confession is set aside on procedural grounds, a second judgment can be confessed pursuant to the same power of attorney.

Lincoln's Inn MS. Misc. 559, f. 94

Hilary term 1696[/97]. Newcastle upon Tyne.

The plaintiffs [the mother and daughter] gave a warrant of attorney directed to all or any of the attorneys in the [Court of] King's Bench, Common Pleas, or Exchequer to enter one or more judgment or judgments upon a bond which they had given to the defendant for the payment of a just debt of £400 due to the defendant. And Douglass, the defendant's attorney caused a judgment to be entered in the [Court of] Common Pleas. But neglecting to file an original and there being no release of errors, the now plaintiffs, there defendants, brought a writ of error and reversed that judgment, after which Douglass caused another judgment to be entered by virtue of that warrant of attorney in the Office of Pleas of this Court [of Exchequer]. And by execution thereupon, the now plaintiffs, who were discharged out of execution upon the former judgment in the Common Pleas, were taken in execution.

And *Wright*, the King's Serjeant (made so the last vacation) moved to have the judgment in this court set aside and a [writ of] *supersedeas* to the execution. And he also complained against Douglass for causing two judgments to be entered in two distinct courts upon one and the same warrant of attorney.

The court caused it to be examined by the master of the office how the judgment in this court came to be entered, who reported that Owen, one of the attorneys, affirmed to him that he had a good warrant for doing it and would be answerable for it in any action to be brought and that he knew nothing of the judgment in the Common Pleas, but that Douglass brought him the warrant and that all was regularly done.

It was insisted upon by the plaintiffs' counsel that the authority given by the warrant of attorney for entering up one or more judgments was executed by the entry of the judgment in the Common Pleas and, if so, that the second judgment in this court was without warrant and so to be set aside; at least, Douglass to be punished for a misdemeanor.

But, upon debate, the court did not think fit to set aside this judgment, for, if the judgment in this court had been entered by virtue of the same warrant by which that in the Common Pleas was, which nevertheless was not made out to the court, yet this being for a just debt and it was intended by the plaintiffs that the defendant should have a judgment for her security and it being a slip only not to take a release of errors and the warrant being to enter up one or more judgments and Douglass proceeding by advice to get this second judgment and the warrant to enter up the judgment not being a naked authority only but carrying an interest and by the reversal of the first judgment as the bond revived, so it is but reasonable to revive the authority for the judgment.

The court did not think fit either to set aside the judgment or punish the attorney. And this being put to Chief Justice Treby and Justice Turton, they thought it just, before we gave our opinions.

Vide Latch 8; Raymond 69; 21 Ass. 17, 21 Edw. III, 61b; 2 Ventris 114, Trippet and Eyres; 3 Cro. 7; 18 Edw. IV, 18 and 20; 1 Cro. 219.[1]

[Other copies of this report: Georgetown Univ. Law Sch. MS. B88–8, p. 500.]

154

Carpenter, qui tam v. Anonymous

(Ex. 1697)

Where the court finds that the plaintiff's failure to proceed to trial was in bad faith, the court can discharge the defendant's special bail.

Lincoln's Inn MS. Misc. 559, f. 98

At the setting down of causes.

The plaintiff exhibited a personal information against the defendant, being an alien and living at Bruges, in Flanders, but then happened to be in London, for entering alien's goods in a denizen's name. And [the court] held the defendant to £1100 bail. The plaintiff gave notice of a trial to be within this term, which the defendant attended, but the plaintiff did not proceed. And, therefore, the defendant had costs. The plaintiff might also have tried it the sitting after the term, but he did not, pretending that he could not try the cause for the want of a witness (naming him).

The defendant, being obliged to return to his habitation at Bruges but could not, being hindered by his bail until after the trial, moved the court that the bail might be discharged, else he should be ruined. And he made an affidavit of his innocence as to the crime suggested against him and that the person which the plaintiff named to be his witness and absent was seen upon the Exchange at the time and in the plaintiff's company.

[1] *Anonymous* (1625), Latch 8, 82 E.R. 247; *Manser v. Shelley* (1663), T. Raymond 69, 83 E.R. 38; *Burnel v. Burnel* (1347), YB 21 Edw. III, Lib. Ass., f. 81, pl. 17, YB Mich. 21 Edw. III, f. 60, pl. 8; *Trippet v. Eyre* (1689–1690), 2 Ventris 110, 113, 86 E.R. 338, 340, also 3 Levinz 263, 83 E.R. 681, 1 Shower K.B. 76, 89 E.R. 459, 5 Modern 457, 87 E.R. 762; *Arscott v. Heale* (1625), Croke Car. 6, 79 E.R. 611; YB Mich. 18 Edw. IV, ff. 18, 20 (1478); *Bind v. Plain* (1591), Croke Eliz. 218, 301, 78 E.R. 474, 553, also Moore K.B. 596, 72 E.R. 781.

Two or three several days were given to Mr. Attorney [General Trevor] and the plaintiff to show cause why the bail should not be discharged.

And, upon hearing Mr. Attorney [General, *Trevor*] and counsel for the plaintiff, Mr. Attorney [General] not opposing the discharge of the bail, it was discharged, by the opinion of the court, Mr. Attorney [General] not opposing it made it more reasonable. Otherwise, query.

[Other copies of this report: Georgetown Univ. Law Sch. MS. B88–8, p. 516.]

155

Attorney General v. Crofts

(Ex. 1697)

A court can take judicial notice of what ecclesiastical province a parcel of land lies in.

Dodd 172

An inquisition upon the attainder of Sir Roger Strickland[1] for high treason was taken at York Castle, whereby it was found that Sir Roger, at the time of the attainder, [was seised in fee] of Blackacre in Caterett in the County of York. Crofts, the defendant comes in and pleads a lease for years of this estate, long before the treason, to A., who assigned to B., who died intestate and administration [was] granted to C. by the archbishop of Canterbury, and that C. assigned to Crofts, the pleader, and so prays the king's hands to be removed.

Upon this, the Attorney General demurs. And I [*Samuel Dodd*], for the Attorney [General], show the cause to be that it appears the pleader claims a lease for years of lands in the County of York and makes title by an administration granted by the archbishop of Canterbury where it should be the archbishop of York and that the administration granted by the archbishop of Canterbury was totally void.

And upon argument last term, judgment *nisi* was given for the king.

This term, the objection made by Serjeant *Levinz* was that [the archbishop of] Canterbury had general jurisdiction and that the court cannot take notice that Dale in Yorkshire was within the province of York.

But the court resolved that they were distinct provinces and distinct original jurisdictions and that the court took notice that Yorkshire is within the province of York and not presume it to be a peculiar within Canterbury, especially it not being alleged in the plea that the archbishop of Canterbury was *loci illius ordinarii.*

---

[1] J. D. Davies, 'Strickland, Sir Roger (bap. 1640, d. 1717)', *Oxford Dictionary of National Biography*, vol. 53, pp. 78–79.

See 3 Cr.; Byron's Case, Noy 54; Hetley 68; Hardr. 216; 2 Rolle 390; Dyer 327; Co. Entr. 496; Cr. Car. 342, Jones 330; Palmer 470; R. Reps. 14 Jac. Starling's Case, 1 Rolle 884.[1]

The old grants of the clergy were severally as to the provinces. The court writes to the bishop; he certifies a writ of excommunication upon a recovery in *quare impedit* goes in all that the court takes notice of the dioceses and provinces as well as of counties.

Note: *Levinz* took exceptions to the inquisition, but the court told him he could not do it if he had no title, for it matters not what the faults are if the pleader has no title. Also, he said that this was for treason in Ireland, and the party was indicted at the Old Bailey and outlawed in the King's Bench, and in such a case, all the proceedings should be in one place. But the answer was that this must be questioned by writ of error upon the attainder.

Judgment [was made] absolute.

Lincoln's Inn MS. Misc. 559, f. 95

Hilary term 1696[/97]; Attorney General vs. Crofts and Woodcock.

Sir Roger Strickland, in the first year of His Majesty's reign, was attainted of high treason by outlawry. And, upon a commission and inquisition thereupon, the manor of Catterick in the County of York and divers farms and lands in Catterick were found and returned to be part of his estate at the time of the treason and outlawry and he was seised in fee thereof and they were thereby seized into His Majesty's hands as forfeited by the treason. The defendants as terre tenants of the premises come in and plead in discharge of the said forfeiture and allege a seisin in fee in Sir Stafford Brathwait long before the treason and that he mortgaged the said manor and premises in 1674 for 1000 years to Sir Henry Hunlock for securing the payment of £1000 and interest at a time then shortly to come, and they derive a title at law to themselves under the mortgage by divers mesne assignments and conveyances during the residue of the term charged with further sums of money. And they lay the immediate assignment to the defendants to be made by Mary Maddison, relict and administratrix of Christopher Maddison,

[1] *Byron v. Byron* (1596), Croke Eliz. 472, 78 E.R. 709; *Byron's Case*, Noy 54, 74 E.R. 1023; *Harvey v. Fitton* (1628), Hetley 68, 124 E.R. 348; *Allison v. Dickenson* (1661), Hardres 216, 145 E.R. 460; *Bray v. Fisher* (1623), 2 Rolle Rep. 390, 81 E.R. 871; *Archbishop of York and Willock's Case* (1573), 3 Dyer 327, 73 E.R. 740; *Salusburie v. Bishop of Lincoln* (1601), E. Coke, *Book of Entries* (1614), 'Quare impedit', pl. 13, f. 296; *Cort v. Bishop of St. David's* (1634), Croke Car. 341, 348, 79 E.R. 899, 905, also *sub nom. Lort v. Bishop of St. David's*, W. Jones 330, 82 E.R. 174; *Evans v. Ascuithe* (1627), Palmer 457, 470, 81 E.R. 1169, 1176, also Latch 31, 233, 82 E.R. 259, 362, W. Jones 158, 82 E.R. 84, Noy 93, 74 E.R. 1060, Benloe 187, 73 E.R. 1045, Exch. K.B. 127, 168, 264, 292; *Starling's Case* (1616), 1 Rolle Rep. 174, 434, 81 E.R. 411, 589, 1 Rolle, Abr., *Excommengement*, pl. E, 1, p. 884.

and lays the title to the administratrix to be by an administration granted by the archbishop of Canterbury at Catterick aforesaid the 24th of December 1687 with a *profert in curia* of the letters of administration. And they plead that, by virtue of that assignment by the said administratrix, the pleaders entered and were possessed for the residue of the 1000 years until [it was] seized into the king's hands *colore commissionis et inquisitionis praedictis* and so pray the king's hands may be amoved from the possession of the premises during the residue of the said term of years.

To which plea, the Attorney General demurred generally, and the defendants joined.

And, upon the arguing of this demurrer the last day but two in the term, the Attorney General [*Trevor*] and *Dodd*, for the king, showed the cause of the demurrer to be that the defendants made title to the term by the administration granted to Maddison by the archbishop of Canterbury of a term of years in lands lying in Catterick in the County of York, which is out of the province of Canterbury and in the province of York. And so the administration is void, and not voidable only, being of a chattel interest that lies in another province wherein the archbishop of Canterbury has nothing to do, for the provinces are of distinct and independent jurisdictions and the archbishop of Canterbury has no more to do in the province of York, though he be *primas et metropolitanus totius Angliae*, than the archbishop of York, who is but *primas et metropolitanus Angliae*,.has to do in the Province of Canterbury. And the books seem to be clear, especially of the later times, that, where there are *bona notabilia* in both provinces, there ought to be administration in both provinces. Hardress 216; Hetly 68, etc.[1]

Serjeant *Levinz*, for the defendants, did not much contest the point of law as to the administration being void if granted by the archbishop of Canterbury of a chattel lying in the province of York. But he insisted that it did not here judicially appear to the court that Catterick, though mentioned to be in the County of York, is in the Province of York, for it may, for aught appears to the court, be in the jurisdiction of the archbishop of Canterbury, and the Attorney General, if he would avoid the defendants' title by that administration, ought to show that Catterick is in the Province of York before he can take advantage of it, for this court does not judicially take notice of the extent or limits either of provinces or dioceses, but those ought to appear in pleading, being issuable and triable *per pais* if contested.

To this it was answered by the King's Counsel that it must be intended that Yorkshire is in the Province of York. And it appears plainly within the record that Catterick, where the chattel lies, is in the County of York and, by consequence, in the Province of York. And it is reasonable so to understand it unless the defendants had made it appear to be otherwise.

---

[1] *Allison v. Dickenson* (1661), Hardres 216, 145 E.R. 460; *Harvey v. Fitton* (1628), Hetley 68, 124 E.R. 348.

Per curiam: The defendants here being pleaders to avoid the king's title must make an unquestionable and unexceptionable title to themselves, which they do not if Catterick be in the Province of York. And it is possible that, in such a case as this, the defendants ought to have shown that the archbishop of Canterbury had a power to grant this administration for lands lying in Yorkshire. The court judicially takes notice that there are two provinces, the one of Canterbury, the other of York. And this appears by their distinct grants of subsidies and aids in Parliament.

And they gave judgment for the king *nisi causa* the last day of term.

And, then, the defendants insisting that this was made a [. . .] but two days ago and that the limits or extent of the provinces do not appear to the court, the court continued the rule for judgment for the king *nisi* better cause [be shown] first Friday next term. But, in regard the court was informed that the security given upon the plea was not sufficient for the mesne profits become due, the defendants were either to give further security for them or the court would order the rents due and to be due at Lady Day [25 March] next to be brought into court, which was ordered accordingly at the setting down of causes after the term.

And, afterwards, upon the first Friday in Easter term 1697, Serjeant *Levinz* came to show cause why judgment should not be entered for the king. And touching maintaining the defendants' plea, he urged no more but his doubt whether administration granted by the archbishop of Canterbury of a chattel lying in the Province of York was void or voidable only. And, by the authority cited by himself, Hetly 68 and Hardress 216 and other books, it appeared to be plain that such an administration is not voidable only, but plainly void.

And the he [*Levinz*] took exceptions to the matter of the king's title appearing by record that it was not sufficiently found nor did *constare* to the court, but he grounded himself principally that, by the commission and inquisition returned, there did not appear to be a good seizure of the lands into the king's hands, for, as he would have it to be, the king's title wholly depended upon this commission and inquisition, against which he took these exceptions, first, that it is not said the outlawry was *per judicium coronatorum*, secondly, that there was one Stephen Rudsdale, by whom as one of the jury the inquisition is taken, that has not signed the return, thirdly, that the commission was to inquire of the estate of Sir Thomas Strickland in Yorkshire and the inquisition which found it is taken *apud Castrum Eborici* which does not appear to be in Yorkshire, fourthly, that the commission is said to be dated *apud Westmonasterium*, not saying *in Comitatu Middlesexiae*, as in pleading it ought to be, fifthly, that the commission is, *inter alia*, directed to John Cattrell, senior, and John Cattrell, junior, and the inquisition is returned to be taken, *inter alia, coram Johanne* Cattrell, junior, but his subscription to it is 'John Cattrell', which, in legal understanding is intended to be the elder, sixthly, that the commission is for enquiry of foreign treasons directed to the Mayor of London, judge *et al.* at the Old Bailey and the indictment thereupon found and then removed into the King's Bench by [a writ of] *certio-*

rari and then the outlawry thereupon, which he supposes erroneous. And so, for these faults, he urged that the title of the king is defective.

But to this, it was answered by the King's Counsel and resolved by the court that these exceptions affect not this case, but, if they be faults, they are such as advantage may be taken of by writ of error to reverse the outlawry and not otherwise, for it is plain in law that the king's title is without office by 26 and 33 Hen. VIII and that this commission and inquisition is but instructive and not instituting. Page's Case, 5 rep.[1]

Secondly, the defendant must not take any advantage of the king's defect of title without making a good title to himself and thereby avoiding the king's title, which the defendant had not done.

And, therefore, judgment was given absolutely for the king.

But note, afterwards, Dixwell Hungerford, having obtained an administration in the Province of York, pleaded the same title and had judgment, which was affirmed in the Exchequer, but an English bill was exhibited by the Attorney General[2] to discover trusts for Sir Roger; see the judgment Michaelmas term 1707.

[Other copies of this report: Georgetown Univ. Law Sch. MS. B88–8, p. 502.]

[Related cases: Attorney General v. Earl of Fauconberg (Ex. 1697), see below, Case No. 159; Rex v. Hungerford (1704), 2 Lutwyche 996, 125 E.R. 555; Allibon v. Attorney General (1707), Colles 393, 1 E.R. 341; Attorney General v. Croft (Ex. 1707), Equity Cases Exch. 567; Attorney General v. Crofts (1708), 4 Brown P.C. 136, 2 E.R. 91, Lords' Journal, vol. 18, pp. 614, 629.]

156

Hull v. Kennet

(Ex. 1697)

A surety for an undersheriff will not be preferred over the creditors of a bankrupt.

Dodd 175

The plaintiff was surety for the high sheriff, being the undersheriff, in a recognizance of £120 and prosecutes a [writ of] extent in aid against Hooke,[3] who was a bankrupt. And upon debate, the court superseded the extent, and held that a

---

1 Stat. 26 Hen. VIII, c. 13 (*SR*, III, 508–509); Stat. 33 Hen. VIII, c. 20 (*SR*, III, 855–857); *Attorney General v. Page* (Ex. 1587), 5 Coke Rep. 52, 77 E.R. 133.

2 *Attorney General v. Croft* (Ex. 1707), Equity Cases Exch. 567, Order of 13 November 1707: Public Record Office E.126/18, f. 678(b).

3 The defendants were creditors of Hooke.

man by being security for an undersheriff is not entitled to aid. He was the sheriff of Devonshire.

157

Poole v. Draper

(Ex. 1697)

In this case where two separate defendants were sued for tithes in one bill, the court awarded the court costs for the entire suit against one of the defendants.

Dodd 175, 1 Eagle & Younge 627

A tithe bill [was filed] wherein the plaintiff sues both defendants for all tithes. Draper answers and insists upon a *non decimando* for tithe herbage in the hundred. Osborne answers by herself and says she had no unprofitable cattle, but if she had, yet there is a *non decimando* in the hundred; and [she] says she had a plot of meadow, which [was] compounded with the plaintiff for 6s. The plaintiff replies and takes out a commission, and both defendants join in the interrogatories and examinations, that [they were] not tithable in the hundred, etc. The court condemned Draper in tithe herbage and Osborne in 8s. for hay only. And £90 costs [were] taxed. And Osborne only [was] served.

I [*Samuel Dodd*] moved the court to separate the costs, for they were several causes and different duties [were] decreed and, though Osborne had insisted that no tithe herbage was due by the custom etc., yet that she had no herbage.

But the court, upon debate, would not separate the costs, though I cited them Lister v. Cape and Salmon,[1] where it was so done, Friday, 25th November 4 Will. & Mar. [1692] in this court, but the court notwithstanding would not do it. Query.

2 Gwillim 560

Michaelmas term 8 Will. III, 1697.

In a bill for tithes against two, the defendants make two separate defenses. And [there is a] decree against them both with £90 costs taxed. It was moved that the costs might be separated, being several causes in effect and different dues decreed. And so [it was] said to be done 25th November 1693 in the Case of Lister v. Captain.

But the court would not now do it.

[Other reports of this case: 1 Rayner 83, Equity Cases Exch. 398.]

[Order of 19 May 1679: Public Record Office E.126/16, f. 411v.]

---

[1] *Lister v. Cane* (1692), 1 Wood 293, 1 Eagle & Younge 572.

158

Eyres v. Smith

(Ex. 1697)

The Court of Exchequer can release fines that were placed upon a bailiff for not executing writs where the parties to the suit later settled the case out of court.

1 Salkeld 54, 91 E.R. 53

Mich. 9 Will. III, at Serjeants' Inn.

Eyres sued a writ out of the Common Bench *versus* Smith, directed to the Sheriff of York, who sent a warrant to Simpson, the bailiff of the liberty of Pomfret, who did not return the writ, upon which he was amerced £50, *viz.* time after time. And that was estreated into the Exchequer.

Afterwards, Eyres and Smith agreed, and, upon producing a certificate from the attorney for the plaintiff that the debt was satisfied, these amercements were discharged upon a motion to the barons.

Note there ought to be a *constat* of the estreats, and, as the clerks said, the court uses not to discharge the amercements, but allow you to compound them.

159

Attorney General v. Earl of Fauconberg

(Ex. 1697)

In this case, the conveyance in issue was found to have been fraudulent.

Lincoln's Inn MS. Misc. 559, f. 116

7 May 1697. Attorney General, plaintiff v. Earl of Falconberge, Lord Viscount Lonsdale, and Sir Bryan Stapleton, defendants, *in Officio Rememeratoris Regis in Scaccario.*

Upon a trial at the bar by a Yorkshire jury, the question and issue was whether a deed dated the 10th of January 1688[/89] made by Sir Roger Strickland[1] to the defendants and pleaded by the defendants in avoidance of the king's title to the manor of Thornton Bridge and other lands in the County of York, seized into the king's hands as forfeited by the attainder of Sir Roger Strickland by outlawry for high treason, was made by fraud and collusion to avoid the forfeiture of the lands in question for the said high treason or not. The treason was laid to be the 1st of May 1689; the indictment the 9th of October 1689; the outlawry in February 1689[/90]; the commission to enquire of the estate the 23rd of October 1690;

[1] J. D. Davies, 'Strickland, Sir Roger (bap. 1640, d. 1717)', *Oxford Dictionary of National Biography*, vol. 53, pp. 78–79.

and the inquisition thereupon the 20 December 1690. And the deed expressed that Sir Roger, for securing the payment of the debts and yearly sums in a schedule annexed and the interest thereof, being five several debts in all, the one to his sister, Dorothy Strickland, of £1200, another to one John Taylor, a tailor, of £55, and the other three to three other persons, amounting in all to £3611, did demise the premises to the pleaders and others since deceased for 1000 years from Michaelmas before the date of the deed, without waste, at a peppercorn rent upon trust and confidence that the lessees by and out of the rents of the premises should pay all the debts in the schedule and, after that, then to permit such persons to receive the same as Sir Roger by deed or will with two witnesses should appoint and, in default of such deed or will, then to such as should have the freehold of the premises. And, in the deed, there is a clause which expresses it to be the intent of the deed, and Sir Roger declares and agrees, that the trustees shall not be chargeable with the acts, deeds, or omissions, one of the other, 'nor with the receipts, payments, acts, deeds, or omission of any steward, receiver, bailiff, or other person employed by or with the consent of the said Sir Roger Strickland in or about the managing of the premises or about receiving or paying of any rents or profits thereof' but only be accountable for their own actual receipts etc. And a provision was in the deed for the trustees deducting their own charges.

In order to make out the fraudulence of this deed, the King's Counsel made observations, first, from the time of the date of it, which was after the abdication and withdrawing of King James, with whom Sir Roger went, or presently afterward, went to him by the erasure of the month, *viz.* January, which made it suspicious, and, though the deed be confessed in the pleading to be the deed of Sir Roger and to bear that date and so *prima facie* to be then executed and it being produced in court and having the names of three witnesses endorsed, who are all alive (and one was said to be present in court), yet the defendant's counsel, who appeared to defend for the creditors, the trustees not concerning themselves further than to let their names be used in the defense, utterly refused to produce any of the witnesses or to give any other evidence for supporting the credit of the deed than its being confessed by pleading;

Secondly, from that unusual clause in the deed which exempts the trustees from being answerable for any whom Sir Roger should appoint to manage the estate and receive and pay the rents and profits, which in effect makes a trust for Sir Roger and destroys that whole design and intent of the deed for real and honest payment of debts and makes it wholly to be in the power of Sir Roger whether any of the debts should be thereby paid or not, and such a clause as that in a deed would make the deed fraudulent against a purchaser and, by parity of reason and law, it must be so against the king for a forfeiture within the Statute of 13 Eliz.;[1]

[1] Stat. 13 Eliz. I, c. 5 (*SR*, IV, 537–538).

Thirdly, that it was proved in the cause that the estate was all along, after the deed and until the inquisition, managed, let, and disposed as the estate of Sir Roger Strickland and the rents and profits received to his use without any respect had to the payment of the debts;

Fourthly, that, though, after the inquisition, there was some pretense made by one Mr. Walters, one of the trustees, that the estate was demised for the payment of the scheduled debts, yet it was proved that it was reputed and esteemed the estate of Sir Roger Strickland and, as such, paid double taxes to which Mr. Walters, being one of the commissioners, was privy and signed the warrants, for, had this been the trustee's estate for the payment of debts, it would not nor ought to have paid double taxes. And there was not the least proof that any part of the debts in the schedule, principal or interest, was ever paid by or out of the rents or profits of the premises or demanded so to be;

Fifthly, that there was not any satisfactory proof made of either of the two debts due to Mrs. Strickland or Taylor. And, as to the other three debts, there was not the least evidence offered to make it appear that they were ever due or had been paid;

Sixthly, it was proved that one of the endorsements upon Mrs. Strickland's bond for six month's interest in 1688 was but freshly done and when produced at the taking of the inquisition in December 1690, the ink was fresh and would have blotted.

All which things with several other circumstances concurring being observed and left to the jury (being a jury of great quality), they found the deed fraudulent.

Vide ante, a similar case, fo. 83 etc.[1]

[Other copies of this report: Georgetown Univ. Law Sch. MS. B88–8, p. 569.]

[Related cases: Attorney General v. Crofts (Ex. 1697), see above, Case No. 155; Rex v. Hungerford (1704), 2 Lutwyche 996, 125 E.R. 555; Allibon v. Attorney General (1707), Colles 393, 1 E.R. 341; Attorney General v. Crofts (1708), 4 Brown P.C. 136, 2 E.R. 91.]

160

Tussingham v. Swayle

(Ex. 1697)

Where a defendant who is insolvent requests a new trial after a verdict, he may be required to give security to pay court costs.

[1] *Attorney General v. Duke of Beaufort* (Ex. 1692–1697), see above, Case No. 90.

Lincoln's Inn MS. Misc. 559, f. 127, pl. 1

Easter [term] 1697. Tussingham and his lessee, plaintiffs vs. Sir Solomon Swale, defendant. In the Office of Pleas.

There having been a verdict at the last York Assizes in an [action of] ejectment for lead mines in Yorkshire in favor of the title of the crown, under which the plaintiff here claimed, against the defendant Sir Solomon [Swayle] and Justice Turton having certified the court that it was a fair and full trial on both parts, the court did incline against the defendant's motion for granting any new trial, it being in ejectment and the defendant having the liberty by law to try his title as often as he pleased. But in regard the possession had been long with the defendant and his ancestors and that the thing in question was of about £100 *per annum* and of some length and difficulty, it was thought it might be proper to have a trial at the bar. And the plaintiff and defendant did upon terms agree to a trial at the bar the next term wherein Sir Solomon was to be the plaintiff and to bring no writ of error if judgment [went] for the plaintiff, but the possession was to remain with Sir Solomon until after the trial at the bar and then to go according to the success of that trial. And other matters were settled between them by consent. But, it being made out by affidavits that Sir Solomon was much in debt and a prisoner in the Fleet [Prison] and his estate incumbered, it was insisted on that, in regard he desired the trial to be at the bar, he ought to give security to pay the costs in case he was nonsuited in it or that a verdict passed against him. And whether security for costs in such a case as this or indeed in any case where an insolvent person desires a trial at the bar which, either for value or difficulty, may be proper to be tried at the bar ought or was proper to be given was the question.

And, because there were strenuous allegations *pro* and *con* touching the practice in such cases, we [the court] directed Marriott, the Master of the Office of Pleas, to certify to us the usage in other courts. And he, having attended Chief Justice Holt and some other judges and informed himself of the principal officers of both courts of King's Bench and Common Pleas, reported to us that, where it was made out to the court that the party that desires the trial at the bar is not of the ability to pay the costs if the cause goes against him, that, in such a case, the court in its discretion, noes not grant a trial at the bar without some security for costs and withal reported to us that he had put this very case in question to them and that it was their opinion that some security should be given in this case.

And, thereupon, by consent, Sir Solomon gave his own and two other persons' security by a recognizance of £200 for payment of £100 in part of the costs of the trial at the bar in case he was either nonsuited or had a verdict against him in it.

And, afterwards, in Trinity term (afterwards, fo. [*blank*]), there was a trial at the Exchequer bar by a special jury of knights, esquires, and gentlemen of the County of York. And, upon a full and long evidence which began about nine in the forenoon and lasted until past twelve at night, a verdict was given for the plaintiff's title, which was derived under the crown.

Vide also Easter [term] 1708, a trial at the bar between the Attorney General and the Earl of Wharton.[1]

[Other copies of this report: Georgetown Univ. Law Sch. MS. B88–8, p. 608.]

161

In re Aldworth

(Ex. 1697)

An Auditor in the Exchequer must be appointed to his office under the great seal.

Lincoln's Inn MS. Misc. 559, f. 127, pl. 2

Easter term 1697. William Aldworth's Case touching the office of Auditor and the constitution of the Auditors of the Exchequer.

King Charles II, in the 35th year of his reign, thinking it necessary to his service that an officer should be appointed for the taking of the accounts of all such casual revenues as should arise to His Majesty, his heirs, and successors, by reason of any penal laws and of all such other accounts as are after mentioned by the advice of the then Commissioners of the Treasury, by his letters patent under the great seal of England, erected, created, and constituted an office called the Office of the Auditor of all such casual revenues as should arise or grow due to His Majesty, his heirs, or successors for or by reason of any penal laws and of such other accounts as should be referred unto such auditor by the Commissioners of the Treasury or the Lord Treasurer for the time being so that the same interfered not with the right of any auditor then constituted. And he thereby gave such Auditor power to examine, state, hear, and (with the allowance of the Treasury) to determine the accounts of such persons who had or should receive any money arisen or to grow due to His Majesty, his heirs, or successors for or by reason of any penal laws and also all such other accounts (*prout supra*) so as the same interfere not with the right of any auditor already constituted and to act and do all things to the office of an auditor in relation to the said accounts appertaining. And, by the same letters patent, he created William Aldworth such Auditor, and granted to him the said office during pleasure with the yearly fee or allowance of £100 together with all other fees and profits to such office of Auditor belonging. And he authorized and commanded the Commissioners of the Treasury, Lord Treasurer, Chancellor, Undertreasurer, and Barons of the Exchequer and all oth-

---

[1] *Attorney General, ex rel. Marriot v. Lord Wharton* (Ex. 1706–1708), Equity Cases Exch. 536, T. Gates, ed., *'The Great Trial' A Swaledale Lead Mining Dispute in the Court of Exchequer, 1705–1708* (2012).

er of the officers of him, his heirs, and successors to admit and receive him into the said office and to treat him as such officer and to allow and give unto him all allowances, rights, protections, and privileges as are justly due and ought to be given to any such auditor or clerk within the view of the Exchequer.

By the demise of King Charles II, that grant to Aldworth determined, being only during pleasure. In the first year of King William and Queen Mary, that grant in the like terms was renewed to the said Aldworth under the great seal. And, in regard to the offices of the six Auditors of the Revenue (Wales not included), by and since the sale of the fee farm rents in 1671, were become of little value and business, King Charles II, in consideration thereof, granted to each of them an annuity of £200 *per annum*, making in all £1200 *per annum* to those six auditors. Now, upon the death of Mr. Morice and Mr. Phelips, two of those six auditors, the said Aldworth obtained from the Lords of the Treasury two writings under their hands, whereby they referred the taking of the accounts within those two assignments to Aldworth. And, after Morice's death, Aldworth took upon him[self] under color of the said letters patent and of those writings from the Lords of the Treasury to make up the accounts of the receivers general of taxes and assessments within that assignment, and procured those accounts to be sworn and declared before some of the Barons, who, never enquiring into or looking after the authority of Aldworth to be Auditor (nor was he ever admitted or took the oath of an Auditor) some accounts were declared.

And since I [Edward Ward] came to be Chief Baron, Mr. Phelips dying and Aldworth having obtained the like instrument from the Treasury, he pretended to make up the accounts of the receivers general within that assignment without ever taking any oath or being admitted by or in the court, whereof I, taking notice, enquired into the matter and found his pretenses to the auditorship of those two assignments to be as above. And I, not being satisfied therewith that he was legally constituted an auditor of those two assignments, refused to declare any of those accounts within those two assignments, nor, indeed, could he be a legal auditor to make up and determine accounts with the allowance of the Treasury exclusive to the barons.

And the other barons being acquainted therewith by me and of my doubt and stop therein, we, all of us, considered of the matter and were of the opinion that Aldworth was not a legal auditor to make up and pass those accounts, for an auditor of the Exchequer, such as Morrice and Phelips were, is an officer of record constantly made by a particular grant under the great seal of England by special words and terms proper for that purpose and always sworn and for whom there is a particular prescribed form of an oath. And we all thought that neither the words nor the meaning of the letters patent of the king and queen of making Aldworth auditor of such accounts as should be referred to him by the Treasury did or could extend to make him an auditor for passing receivers general's accounts within any of the assignments of the six Auditors of the Revenue, and the rather because of the exception so as the said accounts did not interfere with the right of any Auditor then constituted, which was thought to be a full explanation of the grant, that it should not extend to any accounts which any others had a right to make up, which the then Auditors of the Revenue had, but it was a grant only of making up and passing accounts of penal statutes and other casual matters which were not within the province of any other Auditor, nor could they neither be legally determined or any legal *super* or charge set but what must by judgment of the court. Nor could we justify the allowing any man to be an Auditor otherwise than by the usual letters patent under the great seal whereby Auditors of the Revenue were anciently constituted with and by enrolling those letters patent and administering the usual oath to the Auditor and that it would be of dangerous consequence to do otherwise.

And, thereupon, I acquainted several of the Lords Commissioners of the Treasury therewith. And they directed that Aldworth should pass a grant of the auditorship of those two assignments under the great seal and be sworn and make his deputy upon record as other auditors of the Revenue anciently did, all which was done accordingly.

And, though the business of the Auditors of the Revenue be greatly sunk since and by the sale of fee farm rents so that it was hardly worth the while to pass a grant of them, the king resuming the £200 *per annum* granted by King Charles II, yet, in regard matters of record must be transacted by officers of record by grant, it was thought necessary that letters patent should pass accordingly, which, at length, Aldworth did unwillingly. And, thereupon and not until then, he and his deputy were sworn, and the accounts were made up by them declared, which were stopped until that time.

[Other copies of this report: Georgetown Univ. Law Sch. MS. B88–8, p. 610.]

162

Lougher v. Llewellin

(Ex. 1697)

The question in this case was whether Welsh words that were allegedly defamatory should have been translated into English in a libel in an ecclesiastical court.

Lincoln's Inn MS. Misc. 559, f. 132, pl. 1

5 June.

The defendant [Ap Evan], *ad instantiam* of Florence Lougher of Llantriessent in the County of Glamorgan, widow, exhibits two libels in the Consistory Court of the bishop of Llandaff against the two plaintiffs in two causes or instances of defamation *pro reformatione morum*. And the words of defamation are laid all in the Welsh language without any explanation of them.

The two plaintiffs here pray two several [writs of] prohibition upon two suggestions that the words in the libel are not defamatory nor intelligible nor any ways pertaining to the ecclesiastical jurisdiction.

And, this day [5 June], the defendant showed for cause against the prohibition that the words are Welsh words and well understood in Glamorganshire, which is in Wales, where they were spoken, and that they are the common and known language of the country and, to all that understand them, are very defamatory and proper for the ecclesiastical jurisdiction *pro reformatione morum*. And, as *Sir William Williams*, counsel for the defendant and, by country, a Welshman, urged and interpreted them, they appeared to be very scandalous and defamatory and proper for the reformation of manners in that court.

And the court, being desirous to have the Welsh words Englished, proposed that an interpreter should be sworn, who was to interpret the words to the court, which did not understand the Welsh tongue, whereby they might attain to the knowledge whether those Welsh words were defamatory or not.

But this was opposed at first by the plaintiffs' counsel, who stood upon it that the words were not intelligible but that, as the libel and suggestion sets them out, they are unintelligible. And, upon that point, it principally was that they prayed the prohibition as they said and it did not appear by the libel that the words were Welsh or any other language that was or could be understood and that it was not fit that the ecclesiastical court should hold a plea of unintelligible words.

But the court, for their own satisfaction thought fit to be informed what sense and meaning those words bore. And it being affirmed they were Welsh, there needed no explanation of them in the libel, which was in the court where Welsh is well understood. And to say that, because the court did not understand what language the words were, that, therefore, they must prohibit the ecclesiastical court in Wales, where the words were understood and spoken in the presence of those that understood Welsh and prohibit the proper language of the country under pretense that the words are not intelligible is not fit. And there is no reason assigned to prohibit the ecclesiastical court but either because the words are senseless and unintelligible or because they are not defamatory, and it is not possible to know either of these unless the court be assisted by some person skillful in that language.

And, thereupon, one present in court looked upon the libel, and, being skillful in Welsh, said it was that language, and, being sworn, he interpreted it. And, as he rendered it in English upon his oath, the words appeared very defamatory, but such for which and action at law would not lie for damages. But it was fit to be proceeded in the ecclesiastical court *pro reformatione morum*. And, thereupon, the rule for a prohibition was discharged *nisi*, and, afterwards, absolutely.

[Other copies of this report: Georgetown Univ. Law Sch. MS. B88–8, p. 613.]

Dodd 174

[In a case] at instance, [there was] a libel for words exhibited before the vicar general of the bishop of Llandaff for words spoken in Glamorganshire, but, in the libel, the words were not Englished nor laid to be Welsh words, nor in the British language, but to us altogether unintelligible and might be Dutch [or] Arabic etc. And upon a motion in the Exchequer for a [writ of] prohibition because [the words were] not intelligible nor defamatory and upon information by the counsel against the prohibition that they were Welsh words and defamatory, the court examined one upon his oath to render the sense of them in English in court *instanter.* And upon this, they appeared to be defamatory and a prohibition [was] denied.

Query this matter etc., because it seemed to me it should be [made] to appear in the libel what the English of them was or else at least they should be averred in the libel to be Welsh words.

163

Attorney General v. Connoway

(Ex. 1697–1698)

Importation occurs where the goods imported were unloaded, not where the vessel carrying them first arrived.

Lincoln's Inn MS. Misc. 559, f. 133, pl. 3

Trinity term 1697.

In an information in the nature of an action of debt for the duty of the tonnage of a ship from the East Indies, this cause coming before me [EDWARD WARD] to trial at *nisi prius* after Hilary term last, I desired there might be a special verdict in it. But the counsel on both sides, to avoid the charge, rather desired that a case should be made of it and referred to my opinion. And a verdict was agreed to be taken for the king *de bene esse* but to be controlled if my opinion happened to be for the defendant.

And the case was this. By the Act made 5 & 6 W. & M., ca. 20, for granting to Their Majesties several rates and duties upon tonnage of ships and vessels etc.,[1] it is enacted that, for four years from the 24th of June 1694, there shall be throughout England, Wales, and Berwick raised, levied, collected, and paid to the use of Their Majesties, their heirs, and successors for and upon the tonnage of all ships and vessels wherein at any time or times and for every time during the said term of four years there shall be imported any goods or merchandises into the kingdom of England, dominion of Wales, or town of Berwick upon Tweed

[1] Stat. 5 & 6 Will. & Mar., c. 20 (*SR*, VI, 483–495).

from any the parts, places, or countries in that Act mentioned or carried coastwise as in that Act is mentioned the several rates, impositions, duties, and sums of money in that Act mentioned, *viz., inter alia*, for every ton of the burden or contents of any ship or vessel importing goods, wares, or merchandises from the East Indies or any parts southward or eastward of Cabo Bona Speranza the sum of 30s. Then, the Act appoints that the rates and duties so imposed shall be accounted, taken, and paid according to the measure of such ships or vessels which shall be made and taken by Their Majesties' officers in the respective ports or places where they shall arrive and that the masters, owners, or freighters of all such ships importing goods inwards or carrying goods coastwise shall upon the arrival of such ships or vessels at the port or place of their discharge or unloading in England, Wales, or Berwick cause such ships or vessels to be entered in the Custom House of or belonging to such port or place and, at the time of such entry and before any goods be unloaded thereout, pay or secure the duty of tonnage by that Act granted, and, if any goods be unloaded before the duty be paid or secured, the ship or vessel with all her guns etc. shall be forfeited, one moiety to the king, the other to the informer, and, moreover, the master, owner, and freighter to be liable to Their Majesties for the said duty. And then the Act directs in what parts and proportions the said duty shall be borne between the masters and owners or freighters, and then prescribes a way and method how the ships and vessels shall be measured and gauged, and then follows these words 'according to which method and rule all ships and vessels shall be measured and the duty of tonnage thereby be computed and collected accordingly, any custom, practice, or usage to the contrary notwithstanding'.

Now, the case made and agreed upon by the counsel, both for the king and the defendant, and signed by them was this. The ship called the *Nassau* of London loaded with goods and merchandises from the East Indies did arrive in the port of Scilly within the kingdom of England, not being the port or place of her discharge, between the first day of January 1695 and the 17th of May 1696. The said ship loaded with the said goods did after the 17th of May 1696 arrive at the port of London, being the port of her discharge. The goods and merchandises were so in manner as aforesaid imported in the said ship from the Indies into England by the defendant [John Connoway] master, owner, and freighter of the said ship.

The question was whether the defendant ought to pay for the tonnage of the said ship the duty granted to His Majesty by the Act of Parliament before mentioned.

Note that, by a subsequent Act of Parliament both of them precedent to the fact of this cause, the first made 6 & 7 Will. III, ca. 12, fo. 395,[1] the manner of measuring and gauging of ships in order to the payment of the duty is after the

[1] Stat. 6 & 7 Will. III, c. 12 (*SR*, VI, 592–593).

24th of June 1695 altered to the method therein prescribed and the other Act was made 7 & 8 Will. III, ca. 31,[1] for continuing to His Majesty certain duties upon salt etc. and establishing a land bank and taking of the duties upon tonnage of ships etc., by which last Act, all the rates and duties for tonnage of ships etc. are made to continue until the 17th of May 1696 and then to cease and determine, so that, upon this record and case, the only question is whether the arrival of the ship the *Nassau* from the East Indies after the 24th of June 1695 and before the 17th of May 1696 at Scilly, which the case is agreed to be a port within the kingdom of England, which nevertheless (to me at least) is doubtful whether, in truth and fact, it be so or no be such an importation into England though the ship did not arrive at the port of London, which is found and agreed to be the port of her discharge until after the 17th of May 1696, as shall subject that ship or the master of owners thereof to pay the duty of 30s. a ton for the said ship nor were any goods unloaded nor was the ship measured before the 17th of May 1696, so that whether the tonnage duty was due upon the arrival of the ship at Scilly or not due until after her arrival in the port of discharge where the Act directs the ship to be entered and measured, the Act expiring before such arrival, is the question.

And cases being carried to the other barons, whose opinion I [Edward Ward] desired, some doubt was conceived whether it was due or no. And, afterwards, *viz.* 30 June 1697, I put the case to the judges assembled (upon other occasions) at Serjeants' Inn in Chancery Lane. And, by the opinion of Chief Justice Treby, Justice Neville, Justice Rokeby, Justice Turton, and Justice Powell (Chief Justice Holt and Justice Eyre not being present), they all were unanimous upon perusal of the Act that the duty was not due, and so were the other three Barons, for they held that the duty was not due by the ship's arrival at Scilly nor that any duty by that Act from beyond the seas was due until the ship's arrival at the port of discharge and, the Act determining the duty before the ship's arrival at London, the port of her discharge, which was not until after the 17th of May 1696, the duty for this ship did not by the words or intent of the Act become due at all.

And, upon this advice of the judges, I [Edward Ward] declared my opinion that the duty for which the action was brought was not due.

But this not being done publicly, nor any order drawn up, the Solicitor of the Customs said he had retained the King's Solicitor to argue the case again if I pleased, which being granted was so done the 2d of November 1697 at my chamber before myself and the three other Barons and by *Ettrick*, for the defendant, upon which the three Barons retained their former opinions.

And the Commissioners of the Customs or [the Commissioners] of the Treasury, having notice thereof, desired that Mr. Attorney General might be heard before I delivered my opinion, which was granted.

---

[1] Stat. 7 & 8 Will. III, c. 31 (*SR*, VII, 130–148).

And he [*Trevor*], for the king, and *Ettrick*, for the defendant, argued the case openly in court in Easter term 1698 and on 12 July 1698, being in Trinity term, the court *seriatim* delivered their opinions that the duty was not due, neither within the words nor intent of the Act, for, though it was objected by the Attorney General [*Trevor*] that the duty is given for all the ships importing goods into England and this ship did import goods into England within the time, *viz.* before the 17th of May 1696, though not to the port of discharge by that time, that the duty in point of right attached upon the ship's arrival in any port of England, though it was not to be paid until it came to the port of discharge; so it is a *debitum in praesenti* but *solvendum in futuro*. And the subsequent clauses for measuring the ship and paying the duty at the port of discharge do not take away or abridge the duty which grew due upon the importation any more than if the ship had arrived at the port of her discharge before the 17th of May 1696 but had not been measured until after, in which case, he thought it clear the duty was payable, which was not denied.

But the court conceived that there was no such importation as the Act intended into England until the ship came to the port of her discharge, for it is not the bare coming into a port which, in the judgment of the law, makes an importation without something more, as an entry or breaking bulk, even in the case of customs upon the Act of Tonnage and Poundage, *prout* the opinion of Chief Baron Hale in Raworth's Case, in Hardress, fo. 362,[1] and for the reasons there. And the Case of Cooper and Jeffries, in this court in 1686,[2] was remembered, where the like opinion was as to importation not complete so as to pay duties until entry etc.

And the Attorney General [*Trevor*] did not deny that distinction between customable and prohibited goods, in the first of which coming into port, though with good will, is no importation to oblige payment of duties without entry or the breaking of bulk, but, in the case of prohibited goods, it is an importation without an entry or breaking bulk if it come in with good will, though not if by stress of weather or other necessary, involuntary, or unavoidable occasion so as not willfully to stay after that occasion [was] removed. And the Case of Newbury and Colgate, in this court four or five years ago,[3] was remembered, wherein it was resolved that a vessel that had no midship beam, though otherwise within the charging words of the Act, should not pay tonnage because it could not be measured as the Act directed, which shows that the measuring is to be before the duty attaches and, where no measuring was had according to the Act, no duty [was due]. And the Act expressly directs the measuring to be in the port of discharge.

[1] Stat. 12 Car. II, c. 4 (*SR*, V, 181–205); *Holton v. Raworth* (Ex. 1664), Hardres 358, 145 E.R. 496, also *sub nom. Alton, qui tam v. Raworth*, Exch. Cases *tempore* Car. II, 22.

[2] *Bristow v. Cooper* (Ex. 1686–1687), see above, Case No. 12

[3] *Newbury, qui tam v. Colgate* (Ex. 1695), see above, Case No. 121.

And it was by me [Edward Ward] further observed that, though, in the former part of the clause, fo. 327, it is said the duty shall be paid according to the measure of such ships which shall be made and taken by the king's officers in the ports where they shall arrive, which might give color to think that to be at the first port of arrival, yet, afterwards, in the same clause, such port of arrival is mentioned to be the port of discharge and must so be understood and not to make a fraction in the same clause and so the measurage not being to be until the port of discharge and the Act determining the duty before it came to the port of discharge, nothing became due. Consider the reverse of this case and the mischief that otherwise might ensue if a foreign or English ship comes in to port for water or orders and then goes towards the port of discharge and the foreign ship goes to foreign places or the English ship perish before arrival at the port of discharge, surely no duty be due, which by the other construction must be.

[Other copies of this report: Georgetown Univ. Law Sch. MS. B88–8, p. 620.]

164

Attorney General v. Adrian

(Ex. 1697)

A statute that refers to England, Wales, and Berwick will be construed to include the Channel Islands.

Lincoln's Inn MS. Misc. 559, f. 135

Trinity [term] 1697.

In an information in the nature of an action of debt for the tonnage of a ship that imported French goods taken as prize, upon the like trial before me [Edward Ward] at the same time with the last cause of the Attorney General and Connoway and upon the same Act of Parliament for the tonnage of ships and a like agreement to have a case.[1] The case agreed and subscribed by the counsel of both sides was this. The ship called the *Magdalen* of Dartmouth did arrive at the port of Dartmouth between the 1st of July 1694 and the 28th of November following. The ship came from the Isle of Guernsey and was laden with several goods and merchandises of the growth, production, or manufacture of the kingdom of France, which had been taken and condemned as prize at Guernsey and sold as the law directs, and with no other goods or merchandises, and that the goods were shipped at Guernsey and unloaded at Dartmouth by the defendant master, owner, and freighter of the ship. Then, it sets forth the title of the Act for tonnage of ships etc. whereby a duty is laid upon all ships or vessels arriving in

1 *Attorney General v. Connoway* (Ex. 1697–1698), see above, Case No. 163; Stat. 5 & 6 Will. & Mar., c. 20 (*SR*, VI, 483–495).

any port of England *prout* the Act and that the ship in question is of the burden of thirty tons. And the question is thereby made whether the duty of tonnage pursuant to the said Act of Parliament is due to the king for ships laden with French prize goods imported into England from Guernsey, and, if the said duty be due, then what such duty is.

Note there is a clause in that Act which provides that, if a peace be made between Their Majesties and the French king at any time during the continuance of the duty by that Act, that, in such case, all ships and vessels importing any goods from the French king's territories in Europe without the Straits [of Gibraltar] shall pay like tonnage as if imported from Portugal over and above all other duties payable for such ships.

It is observable that Guernsey is neither a port of England nor in or part of England nor in France or any other country, but it is a place belonging to the king of England, 4 Inst. 286,[1] nor is it a territory of the French king, nor is there in the Act any mention made of Guernsey so that, if any duty of tonnage can be claimed, it must be either as a French duty and that takes not place until after the war, which still continues, nor will it then, because Guernsey is not any of the French king's territories and there is no duty laid by the Act, but it is said from what place the ship must come, either by name or description, which is not in this case by the Act, or else the duty must be a coast duty. And that is objected against in regard the words of the Act that give the coast duty is for ships used or employed in the coasting trade from port to port in England, Wales, or Berwick upon Tweed, none of which Guernsey is. So, as the defendant's counsel urged, this of Guernsey was a *casus omissus* in the Act, and, upon consideration of the Act, it does seem to be so.

And of that opinion were the three barons. And I [Edward Ward] declared my opinion accordingly. And, in this opinion, the King's Counsel rested satisfied and did not desire to stir this case anymore, as they did the last case of the tonnage between the king and Connoway.

And so judgment was entered in this case for the defendant.

[Other copies of this report: Georgetown Univ. Law Sch. MS. B88–8, p. 628.]

165

Jones, ex dem. Griffith v. Lloyd

(Ex. 1697)

Possession is a good title where a better title does not appear.

[1] E. Coke, *Fourth Institute* (1644), p. 286.

Lincoln's Inn MS. Misc. 559, f. 139, pl. 1

In a special verdict in [an action of] ejectment entered in the Exchequer Office of Pleas 7 Will. III, upon an ejectment lease made by Johanna Griffith, widow, to the plaintiff for lands in the County of Denbigh, there was a long special verdict, finding the plaintiff's title, which did not seem to be very good. But there was no manner of title found for the defendant, but the jury, in the special verdict, after the plaintiff's title, found also that the plaintiff's lessor, before the time of the trespass and ejectment, entered into the lands in question and was thereof seised and that, being seised, she made the lease to the plaintiff *prout* to hold to the plaintiff from the last of February for seven years, that, by virtue thereof, the plaintiff entered and was possessed until the defendants, afterwards, the first of March, *vi et armis*, entered upon him and ejected him, but whether, upon the whole matter, the defendant is guilty of the trespass and ejectment or not, they know not, but pray the advisement of the court, and they conclude, if, for the plaintiff, for the plaintiff, if for the defendant, for the defendant.

And, in this case, the whole court gave judgment for the plaintiff without regard had to the title found by the special verdict, but upon this point only that here is a prior possession expressly found for the plaintiff and his lessor and no title at all for the defendant nor any special conclusion or other thing to help or alter the case, as it was in Goodale's Case, in the 5th report, fo. 97a,[1] where the not finding of a title for the defendant was helped by the special conclusion, without which the judgment must have been for the plaintiff in the case, which was also the case of an ejectment. And, upon that point also, was the like resolution in the Case of Worledge and Benbury, 2 Cro. 436, 437,[2] and upon the reason and authorities of those two cases and for that it is found that, when the plaintiff's lessor entered and was seised [. . .] it be supposed that it was by disseisin, yet she thereby gained a fee and had the power to lease to the plaintiff for the seven years and, then, when the plaintiff entered, as it is found, by virtue of that lease, he was in possession by a title, and, then, the defendant ought not to have entered upon him and ousted him without making out to himself a better title than the plaintiff had, which he has not done nor, indeed, made out any title at all. And this is the difference between evidence and matter upon record, for it is true, if the plaintiff makes not out upon evidence a good title to his lessor, the defendant is not guilty to him and, thereupon, he must be nonsuited, yet, when, upon record, here is a prior possession found which makes a title and no title is found for the defendant and though in evidence the former rule holds, yet, when the court comes judicially to give judgment, they must do it upon the record be-

---

1 *Goodall v. Wyat* (1597), 5 Coke Rep. 95, 77 E.R. 202, also Jenkins 261, 145 E.R. 187, Gouldsborough 176, 75 E.R. 1076, Moore K.B. 708, 72 E.R. 855, Croke Eliz. 383, 78 E.R. 629, Popham 99, 79 E.R. 1209.

2 *Worledge v. Benbury* (1617), Croke Jac. 436, 79 E.R. 373.

fore them and for one who has a title found and cannot do it for the defendant who appears not to have any title at all, and a prior possession is a title where a better [one] does not appear.

[Other copies of this report: Georgetown Univ. Law Sch. MS. B88–8, p. 640.]

166

Anonymous

(Ex. 1697)

A Scotsman is not required to give special bail upon an information in the Court of Exchequer.

Lincoln's Inn MS. Misc. 559, f. 142, pl. 1

Michaelmas [term] 1697.

A Scotsman's case about special bail to an information upon a motion by *Browne*, of counsel with the defendant, praying that the defendant, being a Scotsman, may be admitted to enter his appearance to an information upon a penal law exhibited against him in the King's Remembrancer's Office and not be bound to give special bail which aliens are held to, it was resolved by the court that a Scotsman is not to be understood to be an alien so as to be held to special bail, for, before the Statute of 29 Eliz., ca. 5, § 21,[1] it was, as the Act mentions, often stood upon to have special bail upon such informations, and, thereupon, that Statute discharges the demands of special bail in all such cases and enacts that all persons sued upon penal laws may appear by an attorney and shall not be obliged to give special bail, any law, custom, or usage to the contrary notwithstanding so that, by the generality of the words of this law, aliens as well as natives were to have the benefit of it and not to give bail.

And the subsequent Statute of 31 Eliz., ca. 10, § 20,[2] explains the other to extend only to the natural subjects born or to be born within the dominions of the queen, her heirs, and successors and to persons made free denizens and to no other, so that, though, at that time of the making of those laws, Scotland was not under the dominion of the crown of England and so, by consequence, the subjects were then aliens to England, yet the words of this last Statute 'born or to be born within the dominions of the queen, her heir, and successors' do entitle a Scotsman born there after the union of the two crowns of England and Scotland to have the benefit of the Statute of 29 Eliz., for the defendant is a natural born subject of the king of England, who is the heir and successor of Queen Elizabeth, being born in Scotland after the union of the two crowns. And so he is a subject

---

[1] Stat. 29 Eliz. I, c. 5, s. 4 (*SR*, IV, 770).

[2] Stat. 31 Eliz. I, c. 10, s. 3 (*SR*, IV, 809).

born within the dominions of the heirs and successors of Queen Elizabeth. And so he is not liable to give bail.

[Other copies of this report: Georgetown Univ. Law Sch. MS. B88–8, p. 653.]

167

Beverton, qui tam v. Russell

(Ex. 1697)

In this case, no good cause was shown for the court to order a new trial.

Lincoln's Inn MS. Misc. 559, f. 143

23 November 1697.

The plaintiff having exhibited an information against the defendant for transporting or causing 2000 weight of wool to be transported between two certain days mentioned in the information *anno* 1695 into parts beyond the seas contrary to the statutes, whereby he forfeited 3s. for every pound of the said wool, upon not guilty pleaded, it came to trial before me [Edward Ward] at *nisi prius* in Middlesex after Easter term last. And, upon the evidence of one Burwash, who fully proved the fact, the defendant having two counsel there, who cross-examined the king's witness but produced none for the defendant, there was a verdict for the king and the informer. And the defendant was found guilty of transporting so much wool as came to about £300 for the penalty.

The prosecutor did not procure the *postea* to be returned until this term. And, then, the defendant, by his counsel, moved for a new trial upon these reasons.

First, the verdict was obtained upon the single evidence of Burwash, who, as they endeavored to prove by affidavits, was an ill man and had been tampered with. But nothing of this last was made out.

Secondly, that the defendant had made affidavits that he was altogether innocent of what he was charged with and that he never transported or assisted in the transporting of any wool at any time. And he brought some affidavits of his neighbors in Romney Marsh, where the offense was committed, testifying their belief that the defendant was innocent and how he disposed of his wool in that year.

But upon hearing the Attorney General [*Trevor*] and others for the king, it being admitted that the trial was upon due notice and the defendant not at all surprised in it nor showing any reason or cause at all why he did not make any fuller or better defense or that he wanted any witnesses at the trial and the information containing the offense particularly, which gave the defendant an opportunity of showing how he had disposed his wool in that year, which he neglected or did not think fit to do and it being made out by several affidavits that the defendant was a common transporter of wool and had transported in that very year 1695 great quantities of wool to France and that, if occasion had required, there were other witnesses in court at the trial that could have proved the defendant guilty within the information and considering the great inconvenience and ill precedent in such a case to set aside a trial duly and regularly obtained upon a defense made by cross-examining the plaintiff's witnesses and merely because the defendant pretends that, had he known who had been the witness against him, he could have brought witnesses against his credibility, this being no reason for new trials in cases where the defendant is not first made acquainted with the plaintiff's witnesses, which may have a dangerous consequence of preventing or disappointing the king's evidence, especially in such a case as this is too commonly practiced in that place, and the defendant's affidavits being much fuller against the plaintiff than the plaintiff's were to induce a new trial, the court delivered their opinions *seriatim* that, in the course of justice, there was not sufficient [matter] offered by the plaintiff to set aside the former trial and to grant another upon payment of costs. And better it was to suffer a mischief, if it should be one, against the plaintiff than an inconvenience to grant new trials without any other ground than because the defendant apprehends that, if he had known who would have been a witness against him, he doubts not but he could have had testimony to have disparaged his credit, for this may be objected in all cases and then it must become necessary for the king to discover his witnesses beforehand, which in all probability will defeat all prosecutions of this kind.

And Mr. Attorney General [*Trevor*] refusing to consent to a new trial, though moved thereunto, the court denied to grant a new trial for the reasons above, nor was anything made out to the satisfaction of the court against the credit or evidence of Burwash.

[Other copies of this report: Georgetown Univ. Law Sch. MS. B88–8, p. 655, pl. 2.]

168

Sherrington v. Andrews

(Ex. 1698)

The land tax is payable only for the net income that the taxpayer receives from the land.

12 Modern 171, 88 E.R. 1242

A., seised of a rectory of £120 *per annum*, charged with a fee farm rent of £26 *per annum*, was taxed for all the rectory only according to the rate of £25 *per annum* for taxes. He retains 4s. per pound for the fee farm rent, which was much more than he really paid.

The whole matter appearing in the Exchequer, where a bill was brought, it was decreed that the owner of the fee farm rent should allow only in proportion to what was paid.

Comberbach 483, 90 E.R. 605

Note Mr. Mynshul informs me that, in this case, it was at first decreed that, whereas a tenant was easily assessed to the king's tax, he should deduct with his landlord only *pro rata* for what he actually paid. But, afterwards, in the Exchequer, between Sir John Werden and Pickering,[1] the defendant demurred to the plaintiff's bill in the like case, and the demurrer was allowed, for it should not be intended that the tenant paid less than the 4s. per pound according to the Act of Parliament.[2]

Mr. Chesshyre likewise acquainted me of these cases, and he said he conceived, for the same reason that the demurrer was allowed in the latter case, the court ought not to have permitted such an examination in the former case.

169

In re Pelham

(Ex. 1698)

The Exchequer office of Clerk of the Pells must be granted to a person for life. This office is granted by the Lord Treasurer.

Public offices must be granted according to the customary usage.

Dodd 177

This term [Hilary 1698, 9 Will. III], Wardour, Clerk of the Pells, died. And Colonel Strangeways, who had a grant under the great seal in reversion, tendered himself to be sworn, and Mr. Henry Pelham [c. 1661–1721] procured a grant from the Commissioners of the Treasury of this office during their pleasure and tendered himself to be sworn. But against this, after the court had refused Colonel Strangeways, I [*Samuel Dodd*] objected that the commissioners had a commission not to execute the [office] of Lord Treasurer but only of the Treasurer of the Exchequer, and, therefore, could not grant this office, supposing it in the gift of the Lord Treasurer, which was an ancient office and had been always granted for life (as it appears) and, therefore, a grant at pleasure and at the pleasure of particular persons was void, because ancient offices must be granted as usual.

And upon search [of the records], it appeared that Wardour was an officer by the gift of the lord Cottington, Lord Treasurer, at Oxford in 1644 and sworn in the Exchequer in 1660 upon this grant, and took a grant afterwards from the

---

[1] *Werden v. Pickering* (Ex. 1695), Equity Cases Exch. 345.

[2] Stat. 5 & 6 Will. & Mar., c. 1, ss. 3, 4 (*SR*, VI, 427).

crown in confirmation. And, in the Black Book in the Exchequer,[1] there were several entries of the disposal of this office [by the Lord Treasurer].

And, therefore, the court took the possession to have gone along with those grants and so refused to swear the king's grantee but agreed to swear the grantee of the treasury but not upon the present grant, it being void in respect [that] it was at will.

And, afterwards, Mr. Pelham procured a new grant for life, and was this term sworn and admitted by the court upon it. And a record was made thereof, and his patent was enrolled, as had been done upon Mr. Wardour's grant July 1660 in this court.

170

Layfield v. Enticknap

(Ex. 1698)

In this case, an alleged modus decimandi of lambs was found to be too large and thus void.

Dodd 178, 1 Rayner 83, 1 Eagle & Younge 627

The plaintiff, as rector of Chiddingfield in Surrey brought his bill against the defendant for tithe lambs. The defendant insists that there was a *modus* for all lambs sold before St. Mark's Day [25 April] of 3d. a lamb and tithe lambs in kind for the rest. And upon rehearing, the court were of opinion that 3d. was too great a sum and therefore could not be a *modus*, for anciently a lamb could not be worth 2s. 6d., and then the 3d. is at least tithe in kind, and [they] decreed tithe in kind, which to me seemed hard.

Note: The custom was not very clearly proved, but the court would not direct an issue, for they said it was a void *modus*. Also, the Chief Baron [Ward] said that is was odd to have tithe in kind after St. Mark's Day and a *modus* for lambs sold before. But it seems to me that there is clear reason for it and also that the *modus* is good.

2 Gwillim 560

Hilary term 9 Will. III, 1697.

The rector of Chiddinfold, in the County of Surrey, claimed tithes of sheep and lambs.

The defendant insisted on a custom to pay 3d. apiece for all lambs yeaned and fallen before the feast of St. Mark that were sold before the said feast day and to pay tithe in kind for such as were not sold before that day. But, in case there

[1] Public Record Office E.36/266, E.36/267.

were but seven, then to pay the seventh. But, where there were under seven, then to pay 3d. apiece.

The cause was heard on the 18th of November last, and an issue was directed to try the custom. But the plaintiff, being unwilling to try the same, moved on the 30th of November for a rehearing, which came on this day, when the court unanimously agreed that the said custom was not a good one and that there ought to be no trial at law.

[Other reports of this case: Equity Cases Exch. 457.]

[The decree of 3 February 1698, Public Record Office E.126/17, f. 11, is printed in 1 Wood 383; see also the order of 7 July 1698: Public Record Office E.126/17, f. 36.]

171

Eachard v. Brown

(Ex. 1698)

Turnips that are harvested and fed to livestock are tithable but not unharvested turnips.

Dodd 179, 1 Rayner 84, 1 Eagle & Younge 623

The plaintiff was vicar of [Boaly] in Sussex and bought his bill for small tithes and amongst others demands, tithes for turnips against A. and B. And upon the proof, it appeared that A. had ten roods of turnips, which he plucked up and carried into another field and there fed his cattle and hogs upon them, and B. had ten roods of turnips growing and did not sever them. And [it was] decreed that A. should pay tithes for the turnips severed and that B. should pay no tithes for his turnips, because [they were] not severed. Note, 24 February 1697[/98].

172

Attorney General v. Buckley

(Ex. 1698)

An information for a penalty abates by the death of the defendant after trial and before judgment, and this may be taken advantage of by suggestion of the death upon the roll confessed by the Attorney General without a writ of error.

In an information for the crown, there is a discontinuance if the defendant dies after the verdict but before the day the judgment is to be entered in court.

Dodd 181

Upon an information upon the French Act,[1] for having in his custody French lace and silk, etc., whereby he forfeited such a sum, *viz.* so much per pound; the defendant pleaded not guilty and was found guilty to the value of £2000 at *nisi prius* after Trinity term last, and then he died before Michaelmas term. And his executor moved, upon an affidavit of the death, that judgment should not be entered, because the information was abated. And upon debate, the court doubted whether this matter could appear by affidavit and not put the party to [bring a writ of] error. But then it was insisted, that it was remedied by the Act [of] 16 & 17 Car. II, c. 8,[2] which helps this point in common cases; and the doubt was whether this case of the king for a forfeiture upon an information was within it. The words are, 'In all actions real, personal, or mixed, the death of either party shall not be alleged for error'. These books were cited: 1 Rolle 768; Cro. Car. 507; 3 Keb. 292; Hardr. 161; 1 Sid. 131; 2 Sid. 34, 40.[3]

Et adjornatur.

The information was a *devenerunt.* Afterwards in Hilary term [it was] adjudged by the Chief Baron [Ward], Powys, and Hatsell that judgment will not be entered.

Note: The death was suggested upon the roll, and Mr. Attorney [General], upon the roll, confessed it [a] profert.

Dodd 182, Parker 264, 145 E.R. 775

This motion was made in Michaelmas term 10 Will. III, and adjourned to Monday 13th of February 1698[/99], when it was resolved by Lord Chief Baron Ward, barons Powys and Hatsell that judgment should be stayed, for they thought, first, that it was not an action real, personal, or mixed; secondly, that the king was not properly said a party; thirdly, that it was a penalty, not a duty, nor in lieu of customs or any revenue of the crown; fourthly, that 'actions' does not comprehend informations; 'between party and party', does not include the king. 3 Leon. 215.[4]

Note: The court were in doubt whether the death might be shown to the court by affidavit; and, by consent, to avoid this question, it was suggested upon the roll and confessed by the Attorney General.

---

1 Stat. 4 Will. & Mar., c. 25, s. 23 (*SR*, VI, 423).

2 Stat. 16 & 17 Car. II, c. 8 (*SR*, V, 556–557).

3 *Hide v. Marker* (1617), 1 Rolle, Abr., *Error*, 'En Judgments', pl. A, 2, p. 768; *Bartrop v. Gwillim* (1674), 3 Keble 292, 84 E.R. 727; *Harris v. Philips* (1659), Hardres 161, 145 E.R. 431; *Morby v. Urlin* (1659), Hardres 161, 145 E.R. 432; *Pershall v. Smith* (1663), 1 Siderfin 131, 82 E.R. 1013; *Waldern v. Ward* (1657), 2 Siderfin 34, 82 E.R. 1242.

4 *Baxter's Case* (1587), 3 Leonard 214, 74 E.R. 641.

12 Modern 228, 88 E.R. 1281, Dodd 349

[There was] an information in the Exchequer by the Attorney General against the defendant, and a verdict was given against the defendant. After verdict and before the day in bank, the defendant died.

And the question was whether this information was within the Statute 17 Car. II, c. 8, which enacts 'that in all actions real and personal or mixed, the death of either party between verdict and judgment shall not be alleged for error, so as such judgment be entered within two terms after such verdict'.[1]

And upon solemn argument by Ward, Powys, and Hatsell (Lechmere absent), it was held that an information was not within the word 'action', nor the king within the word 'party', and that it was never said 'the death', but 'the demise' of the king.

And [it was] adjudged that the information should be discontinued.

Lincoln's Inn MS. Misc. 532, f. [11v]

The defendant, at *nisi prius* after last term, was convicted upon an information in the Attorney General's name for above £2000 penalty for French goods come to his hands within the time of the information.

The defendant died after the *nisi prius* and before the day in bank, which was this term.

And it was moved on the behalf of the executors of the defendant upon affidavits of five persons read in court of such death that no judgment might be entered up:

First, because, by the death before the day in bank when judgment should be given, the suit was actually abated, and then no judgment ought to be entered against a dead man and in a suit actually abated, and, for that, some authorities were cited *prout* another paper;

Secondly, because the Statute of 17 Car. II, ca. 8, for Avoiding Unnecessary Suits and Delays, whereby it is enacted that, in all actions real, personal, or mixed, the death of either party between the verdict and judgment shall not be alleged for error, so as such judgment be entered within two terms after such verdict, does not extend to this case, for it is neither an action real, personal, or mixed, but an information grounded upon a penal law;

Thirdly, that the affidavits proving such death is a sufficient proof and satisfaction to the court to believe such death;

Fourthly, that it would be very unreasonable to enter judgment and drive the defendant's executors to a writ of error, especially where the error is only an error in fact and cannot be assigned for error in the [Court of] Exchequer Chamber upon error brought, because it cannot be any ways tried.

[Other copies of this report: Georgetown Univ. Law Sch. MS. B88–9, f. 7v.]

---

[1] Stat. 17 Car. II, c. 8 (*SR*, V, 580).

Lincoln's Inn MS. Misc. 532, f. [13v]

26 November [1698].

Mr. Attorney [General *Trevor*]: There are two things considerable in this case: first, whether the Statute of 17 Car. II extends to this case upon the information; second, whether the judgment is to be arrested upon a motion grounded upon an affidavit without anything appearing upon the record as a suggestion and the fact of death either confessed or denied.

First, this information and case is within both the words and meaning of 17 Car. II. An information is either an action real or mixed. These words extend to all actions or suits the general expression [?] is *inter placita coronae et placita civilis*, the last are comprehended under real, personal, or mixed. The first [is] capital and criminal; 1 Inst. 285 warrants this distinction. This information is a civil suit and so without the words of actions real, personal, or mixed. They are not said [to be] pleas of the crown because the king is a party, for the king may prosecute civil actions, but it is the subject matter that makes it civil, and this information is the king's trover and conversion, which is a civil suit, and it is a personal information, which is a personal action and this is wholly parallel to the subject's [action of] trover, and this is personal and to recover damages only and seeks no punishment for crimes.

He agrees *placita coronae* are neither actions real, personal, or mixed and this is not real because that *agit in rem*, but this is personal and *agitur in personam*. *Placita coronae* extends only to indictments for crimes, not informations for recovery of civil rights. If a [writ of] *quare impedit* is brought, surely that is within the Act in the king's case. And the words of the Act are 'actions real, personal or mixed' and distinguishes not between the king and a subject, but the king is as much within the Statute as the subject and [it is] a suit of the same nature.

This is not a criminal prosecution though grounded upon a penal law, for it is a suit of property and not for a crime.

So he concludes it is within the words [of the Statute].

Second, it is within the intention of the Act and that appears by the distinction between this and former acts of jeofails which generally except prosecutions upon penal laws and that omission here proves the parliamentary intention that this is within the law, for, had they not intended it, they would have excepted it, as in the jeofails statues. In the Statute 32 Hen. VIII, ca. [*blank*], [there is] no exception of criminal prosecutions. The second Statute, 18 Eliz., ca. 13, extends to all actions, suits, plaints, bills, and demands in any court of record, which would have reached this case and there is an exception [of] pleas of the crown and the prosecution upon penal laws, which exception proves that prosecutions upon general statutes were within the purview of the Act, else [there would be] no need of the exception. 1 Inst. 287; an appeal of murder is a personal action and releasable by those words and yet that is looked upon as a plea of the crown.

Third, the Statute 27 Eliz., ca 13, has the like exception and stands upon the like reason.

Fourth, 21 Jac. I, ca. 16, has the same exception and the like reason.

But this Statute of 17 Car. II, ca. 8, has no exception. The words here are as large as in the purview of the statutes where there are exceptions, which shows the Parliament did not intend to except penal statutes in this 17 Car. II [act].

There is no reason why the king should be in a worse condition than a subject or to distinguish between the king and a subject in such a thing as this, where a personal duty [. . .] partly single this is a remedial law. And why is the king not within it as well as a subject? Why should the king lose his right or abate his suit by a death more than in a subject's case where the reason of each is equal?

Objection: The words in the [Statute of] 17 [Car. II] mention the death of either party not to be [. . .] and the king is not said to be a party to a suit and so it must be intended to hold only between subjects.

Solution: the king is a party to a suit. 7 rep., case of discontinuance of process [*blank*]. In that case, it is said the Statute 1 Edw. VI, for discontinuance of process between party and party extends not to the king. He agrees it is so said there. But he distinguishes between the words of suits between party and party and the words of this Statute, which does not say between party and party, which must be intended between subject and subject. But this is the death of either party, which is not so strong.

Objection: This statute must be intended to be mutual where the death of either party abates the suit. But, in this case, the death of the king does not abate the suit.

Solution: He agrees all abates by the king's demise but the information itself. And, therefore, Parliament prevents the mischief by carrying in the verdict without an abatement.

As to the precedents, none [?] are for the defendant. The order is [. . .] for the king, which possibly might pass *sub silentio.*

[As to the] second point, if [the Statute of] 17 [Car. II] extends not to this case, yet the affidavit of the death of the party is in no ground to arrest the judgment, for such a cause of arrest must appear upon the record and, in all such arrests, there must be a judgment given, which is examinable upon [a writ of] error and must be affirmed upon [a writ of] error or reversed. Upon a matter of fact, no judgment can be arrested upon an affidavit, for that appears not upon the record nor determined by a jury. And, here, fact and law are both in question. The fact is not proved. The law is not to be after[wards] questioned upon [a writ of] error if no judgment be given, for here can be no judgment. The death ought at least to be suggested upon the roll, and then all is upon the record.

Objection: Error in matter of fact is not triable.

Solution: All is answered if the death is suggested upon the roll.

As to the cases cited of [. . .] taking notice of the death by an affidavit, 1 Siderfin 34 observes the [. . .] but [gives] no resolution. Other cases were upon a suggestion on the record.

Objection: Dy. 353, a case upon an intrusion.

Solution: It is only a query, and the judgment was not reversed upon that point.

8 Rep., Blackmore's case; Coke says that 32 Hen. VIII extends not to *placita coronae*. He agrees with it, but this is not *inter placita coronae*.

Mr. Solicitor General [*Hawles*] *pro rege*: First, there is no reason to arrest [the judgment]; second, there is no good method taken in order to arrest.

He follows the Attorney [General's] method, and repeats the same. 1 Inst. 286, 287; an appeal of mayhem is an action personal. [He notes] the distinction between the king and a subject. [. . .] 5 rep., a perjury indictment is not within 5 Eliz., that word not being in the Statute. He observes 8 Hen. VI excepts appeals etc., but 32 Hen. VIII has no exceptions. He observes the putting in and leaving out exceptions in the statutes of jeofails *prout* the Attorney [General's] opinion the case of 353 in Dyer and that judgment was reversed for another reason.

Hardress 169; that proceedings in a *scire facias* for the Protector [Cromwell] were within the Statute of 32 Hen. VIII, for the judgment was for the Protector but without notice of that objection which could not have been warranted unless [. . .] of process.

Objection: Blackman's Case [. . .] pleas of the crown are not within [the Statute of] Hen. VIII. Indictments are not within the Statute.

Solution: Being mentioned [?] but an information may, because it is only for damages.

The second point [was it is] no proper way to arrest [a judgment] by an affidavit. The cases cited by the defendant were only dis[. . .], and the court was not obliged. It is mischievous to the party for whom the verdict [was because there was] no [writ of] error upon it.

Mr. *Newport*, for the king, [argued to the] same effect. All informations for the king's debt or forfeiture are but civil and personal actions. There is no negative in the Act upon the king.

Mr. *Phipps*, for the king: The sole question is whether this information be an action or not. An action is defined in *Mirror*, 2nd chapter, 15; a lawful demand of [*blank*]. *Fleta*, 1st book, 16 cap.; *actio nihil aliud quam jus prosequendum in judicio quod alicui debetur et [. . .] nescitur ex maleficio vel quasi quod provenit ex delicto vel injuria*. This information comes within those definitions as being a right of prosecution and demand though it does *provenire ex delicto*, as *Fleta* says.

The query in Dyer is the ground of the exceptions in the statutes of Eliz., Jac., and Car.

Objection: If either party die.

Solution: 7 rep.

An action is as large as a suit. The first is the right; the second is the prosecution of that right. [It is the] first case upon the Act, and it is not to be determined.

The suggestion of death is on the roll and the fact will be admitted.

Mr. *Bridges*: Cro. Jac. 481, Parker and Webb's Case, and Dr. Foster's Case.

Mr. *Ettrick*, for the defendant: The words of the statutes in and after 18 Eliz. are larger than these were, and, therefore, the exceptions are necessary. These are actions popular as well as real, personal, and mixed.

How can informations upon seizures be called personal, real, or mixed? Yet there are persons that are concerned in them.

The Parliament did not intend the king should be, in this case, within the Act when [the statute of] jeofails excluded [him]. [Actions between] party and party do not properly include the king.

As to the suggestion upon the roll, how can it be? It must be as *amicus curiae* and not otherwise. Error in fact is not triable. There is no precedent of an entry for such a judgment.

This is only a remedy for a penalty, not a debt, originally, and the Statute respects suits between party and party only.

Four other of the defendant's counsel desire to be heard the first Tuesday next term, which is agreed to. But the court must give a judgment so as, if a judgment is to be entered, it may be entered within the next term. Otherwise, the Statute of 17 Car. II will not extend to the case which directs that judgment must be entered within two terms next after the verdict.

32 Hen. VIII, ca. 30, for mispleadings and jeofails; the recital of the Act respects plaintiffs and demandants, defendants and tenants in all manner of actions and suits real and personal and, therefore, it makes provision under those terms in any manner of action or suit at common law in any of the king's courts of record. There is no exception of criminal causes or actions popular in this Act.

18 Eliz., ca. 13, for the reformation of jeofails, extends to all actions, suits, bills, plaints, or demands in any court of record. There is a proviso in this Act which excepts, first, all writs, declarations, and suits of appeals of felony and murder, second, indictments or presentments of felony, murder, treason, or other matter nor to any process upon any of them, third, all writs, bills, actions, or informations upon any popular or penal law.

21 Jac. I, ca. 13, an Act for the further reformation of jeofails, which recites the two former acts and provides a further remedy. And this extends to cases wherein a verdict of twelve men or more should be given for the plaintiff or demandant or for the defendant or tenant, bailiff in assize, vouchee, prayee in aid, or tenant by receipt in any action, suit, bill, plaint, or demand in any court of record. In this, there is a proviso of exceptions in the same words with 18 Eliz.

16 & 17 Car. II, ca. 8, for preventing arrests of judgments and superseding executions, extends to cases wherein a verdict of twelve men should be given in any action, suit, bill, or demand. There is the like exception in effect with 18 Eliz., but it adds in informations concerning customs and subsidies of tonnage

and poundage. And the clause in the Act which concerns writs of error extends to verdicts and judgments in any action personal whatsoever. But there is an exception of actions popular and upon penal laws (except tithes), and of indictments, presentments, inquisitions, informations, or appeals.

17 Car. II, ca. 8, for avoiding unnecessary suits and delays (upon which the case in questions depends) that, in all actions personal and real or mixed, the death of either party between the verdict and the judgment shall not hereafter be alleged for error, so as such judgment be entered within the two terms after such verdict.

[Other copies of this report: Georgetown Univ. Law Sch. MS. B88–9, f. 8.]

173

Anonymous

(Ex. 1698)

In this case, the court adjudicated various rights of tithes relating to hops, wood, and corn.

1 Freeman 334, 22 E.R. 1237, 89 E.R. 249,
2 Gwillim 562, 1 Rayner 85, Dodd 348

In a cause where a person preferred a bill for tithes, these points were held by the judges:

Where the parson had tithe hops, no tithes should be paid for the poles which were used in the hop yard. And a question arose whether the parson should have tithes of the bark of the poles, the bark being sold. And [it was held] by LECHMERE he should. But the Chief Baron [WARD] and the others [held] *e contra*, for the poles being privileged, the bark shall be so too.

That for fuel spent in fire to dry the hops, tithes should be paid, because the parson had no benefit by that, the tithes being paid before they were dried.

That tithes ought to be paid as soon as the tenth part can be well severed from the nine, if there be no custom to the contrary. And so it is for corn and hay as soon as it is made into shocks or cocks.

That for wood employed to hedge or fence corn, where the parson had tithe corn, no tithe shall be paid. And it was said to be a general rule that no tithe shall be paid for anything *per quod decimae fiunt uberiores*.

Whether tithes shall be paid for fuel spent in the house, where there is no custom, they said they should not determine, it being no point in this case and there being opinions both ways. 1 Cro. 113[1] was cited at the bar that such fuel shall not be discharged without a custom.

[1] *Norton v. Fermer* (1628), Croke Car. 113, 79 E.R. 699.

That land where wood grew and was stocked up and converted into tillage is not such barren land as ought to be exempted from payment of tithe, but only such is intended barren land, which, before the ploughing, produced no profit to the owner.

That for rakings of corn, no tithe was payable if they were involuntary, but, if there was any fraud in leaving more than was necessary, that tithe should be paid.

That the parson could not justify his coming to set out tithes without the consent of the owner, because by the Statute [2 & 3] Edw. VI, [c. 13],[1] the owner is to set out his tithes and, if he do not, he is liable to the penalty of the Statute.

174

Anonymous

(Ex. 1698)

A defendant from Jersey is not required to give special bail upon an information in the Court of Exchequer.

Lincoln's Inn MS. Misc. 559, f. 142, pl. 2

Michaelmas term 1698.

It was likewise so ruled in the case of a man born in Jersey that he should not give [special] bail upon a like information as being a subject born within the king's dominions and inheritable to lands in England. 7 rep., Calvin's Case, fo. 20 and 21.[2]

Vide Act of Parliament 3 *Annae Reginae*, ca. 7, fo. 166.[3]

[Other copies of this report: Georgetown Univ. Law Sch. MS. B88–8, p. 655, pl. 1.]

175

Lady Gerard v. Duke of Hamilton

(Ex. 1698–1699)

Whether to require special bail at the beginning of a lawsuit rests in the sound discretion of the court.

In this case, special bail was required but not in a certain sum, but generally to pay any judgment.

[1] Stat. 2 & 3 Edw. VI, c. 13 (*SR*, IV, 55–58).

[2] *Calvin's Case* (1608), 7 Coke Rep. 1, 77 E.R. 377, also Moore K.B. 790, 72 E.R. 908, *State Trials* (Cobbett, ed., 1809), vol. 2, p. 559.

[3] Stat. 3 & 4 Ann., c. 7 (*SR*, VIII, 351–352).

When something is to be done after an event, the day of the event is not included in the computation of the time for it to be done.

Harvard Law Sch. MS. 1052, f. 58v, pl. 162

Michaelmas term 10 Will. III.

The defendant[1] had covenanted to give a release within two days after marriage. And, in the same deed, he had obliged himself to do it in the penal sum of £10,000. He did not release.

And the plaintiff brings her action of debt for the £10,000.

It was strongly debated whether special bail was to be given in regard the damages by not giving the release were altogether uncertain and no affidavit had been made how much the plaintiff had been damaged.

When the count came to give their opinion, all the four barons agreed *i.e.* that an affidavit was not necessary, because an affidavit is made of damages sustained in the preter tense, which, in this case, could not be in regard that such damages as may be to the plaintiff for want of the release relate to the future and may be more or less as things may happen, second, that the defendant being of the first quality in Scotland and the first peer of that kingdom and his estate, seat, and residence is there, in case he should withdraw out of this kingdom to his own proper habitation, this court could not extend their authority to him whatever occasion should be.

And Hatsell, puisne baron, compared this cause to the case of an inferior jurisdiction where, though the cause of suit be under 40s., yet if the defendant be taken within the jurisdiction, they make him put in special bail, for, if he remove out of the jurisdiction, the plaintiff cannot be relieved.

Third, whereas it had been strongly urged for the defendant that special bail ought not to be required because the damages are altogether uncertain.

The Chief Baron [Ward] said that, though the breach of a covenant seems to sound in the uncertainty, yet, where there is a penalty annexed, that reduces it to a certainty. And he compared this case to the Case of the East India Company in My Lord Bridgeman's time.[2] That company had caused all the captains and masters of ships employed by them to covenant with a penalty not to import any East India goods for themselves or their own separate profit. And it was adjudged that, though the damages which that company might sustain by such importation was altogether uncertain, perhaps little or nothing, yet such damages were really and in effect settled to the quantum of the penalty.

For these reasons, the barons, who had advised with the other judges, who were all of the opinion that bailing is discretionary, resolved that the defendant

[1] R. K. Marshall, 'Hamilton, James, fourth duke of Hamilton (1658–1712)', *Oxford Dictionary of National Biography*, vol. 24, pp. 848–852.

[2] *East India Co. v. Blake* (1673–1674), Reports *tempore* Finch 117, 23 E.R. 64, 2 Chancery Cases 198, 22 E.R. 909, 73 Selden Soc. 59.

ought to give special bail, which, accordingly, he did, procuring two rich householders in Westminster. But they were obliged in no express sum, but, generally, to produce the defendant's body or pay the condemnation money in case the cause go against him.

Lincoln's Inn MS. Misc. 531, f. [144v], pl. 3

Saturday, 11 February, Hilary [term] 1698[/99].

[There was an action of] debt upon a writing under the defendant's hand and seal for £10,000 whereby the defendant, having agreed to marry the plaintiff's daughter, did before that marriage, *viz.* 15th July 1698, by that writing, declare and agree that the plaintiff had fully accounted for, paid, and satisfied all the personal estate of the young lady's father left to her and the rents of her real estate to that time, and, therefore, he did by that writing covenant and agree within two days next following the solemnization of that marriage to seal and execute such release of the said personal estate and rents of the real estate of the young lady coming to her from her father, the late lord Gerard of Bromley, deceased, as he should be advised by Sir Thomas Powys, counsellor at law. And to the performance of this, the said duke by the said writing did bind himself, his heirs, executors, and administrators in the penal sum of £10,000, for which this action of debt is brought.

And, upon the trial, it appeared that the marriage was solemnized between the duke and the young lady upon Sunday the 17th of July 1698 at seven in the evening and that the release dated the 18th of July 1698 was advised by Sir Thomas Powys before the marriage and was tendered to the duke to be executed on Tuesday the 19th of July 1698 at four in the afternoon by the plaintiff, who then told the defendant that it was advised by Sir Thomas Powys.

And the issue being whether the duke had notice within two days next following the marriage that Sir Thomas Powys had advised that writing which being proved that he had notice at four on Tuesday the 19th in the afternoon, it came to be the question whether that was within the two days next following the marriage or not.

And *Hawles*, the king's Solicitor [General], and *Wright*, the King's Serjeant, and *Sir Francis Wynnington* and others of counsel with the defendant strenuously insisting that it was not within the two days demanded it to be found specially for that, as they insisted, the day of the marriage must be taken to be one of those two days and, then, Tuesday could not be within the two days. and they cited Clayton's Case, 5 rep., fo. 1,[1] that a lease made to take effect from the time of the making is from the sealing that day and includes that day.

And *Wright* affirmed that it was lately adjudged in the Court of Common Bench that, where one had promised to pay a sum within ten days next after a

[1] *Clayton v. Presenham* (1585), 5 Coke Rep. 1, 77 E.R. 48.

demand that the day of the demand was held to be one of the ten days. And, if my [Edward Ward] opinion was otherwise, they prayed it might be specially found.

And I [Edward Ward] declared my opinion to be that it was within the two days and that the Sunday on which the marriage was had could not be taken to be one of the two days, for the law not admitting of fractions of days in the computation of time, it must be understood that the day of marriage could not be one of the two days after marriage, for to argue so is to maintain that that Sunday was the day before the marriage and the day of the marriage, and the day after the marriage, which I held to be incongruous and, indeed, in effect, nonsense and by no means the intent of the parties nor within the ordinary and regular computation of time in a legal sense.

And so I directed the jury with great clearness for the plaintiff. But the defendant's counsel being very pressing and urgent to have it found specially, declaring upon their learning and reputation that they took [. . .] and oft times urging the judgment of the Common Bench in the case of the demand, as above, which, if so, seemed to be a parallel case.

I did (though against my own opinion) yield to have it found specially, being demanded by counsel of so great places and stations. But it being a special jury of London (the two foremen whereof were knights and the rest were substantial citizens) they refused to find it specially, but gave a general verdict for the plaintiff.

And the defendant, being in Chancery to be relieved against the penalty,[1] submitted to it, though I told the jury the peril they ran in case the law should be as the defendant's counsel urged. But they said they would venture that, being, as they said, a case of common sense to reckon two days from the marriage, which they took clearly to comprehend Tuesday. *Et sic finivit.*

[Related cases: Duke of Hamilton v. Lady Gerrard (Ch. 1699), Precedents in Chancery 92, 24 E.R. 44; Lord Mohun v. Duke of Hamilton (H.L. 1704), 2 Brown P.C. 239, 1 E.R. 916.]

176

Attorney General v. Wells

(Ex. 1698)

The question in this case was whether the administrator of a deceased alleged debtor to a debtor of the crown was liable to the crown upon a particular fidelity bond that was forfeited.

---

[1] *Duke of Hamilton v. Lord Mohun* (Ch. 1710), 2 Vernon 652, 23 E.R. 1025, 1 Peere Williams 118, 24 E.R. 319, 1 Salkeld 272, 91 E.R. 147, 1 Eq. Cas. Abr. 90, 21 E.R. 901, 2 Eq. Cas. Abr. 387, 22 E.R. 330, Chan. Repts. *tempore* Anne, 18.

Lincoln's Inn MS. Misc. 532, f. [8]

In a scire facias entered in the Office of the King's Remembrancer Michaelmas [term] 8 Will. III, the case upon the pleadings was this. 8 March 7 Will. III [1696], Mr. Richards and Mr. Gape became bound to the king by bond of the penalty of £19,000 for Richards' well demeaning himself in the office of receiver general of the taxes in the County of Hertford and his due answering and accounting for the same.

Richards failing therein, 27 April 1696, a [writ of] extent issued to the sheriff of London upon that bond against the said Richards to enquire *quae debita, credita, et specialitates* Richards then had and to seize them into the king's hands.

29th of April 1696, 8 Will. III, an inquisition is taken upon the extent, whereby it was found that Giles Groom, late of Watford in Hertfordshire, then deceased, was indebted at the time of his death (not finding when that was) unto the said Richards in divers sums of money therein mentioned upon simple contract, which debts were thereby seized into the king's hands (but does not find they were then due and unpaid).

1 July 1696, a [writ of] *scire facias*, reciting that extent and inquisition, issues to the sheriff of the County of Hertford commanding him to make known to the executors of the last will of the said Groome and to the administrators and occupiers of the goods and chattels which were the said Groome's the 29th of April 1696, being the time of taking the inquisition and mentioned in the writ to be the time when Groome first became debtor, though, in truth, Groome himself never was a debtor to the king, to show cause *tres Michaelis proxime* why the king should not have execution against them, *de bonis et catallis terris et tenamentis praedictis* for the said debts and sums so seized into the king's hands.

A *scire feci* is returned against the defendant Wells as administrator and occupier of the goods and chattels of Groom generally *ad ostendum* as the writ required.

Wells appeared, and, after *oyer* of the writ, pleads *quod dominus rex executionem suum adversus ipsum* for the debts seized or any part thereof *habere non debet quia dicit quod ipse non est nec unquam fuit administrator seu occupator aliquorum bonorum seu catallorum quae fuerunt dicti Egidii Groom dicto 29 Aprilis 1696, quae die* the said Groome is by the writ alleged to become first debtor to the king or at any time after, *et hoc paratus est verificare etc.* and prays judgment whether the king ought to have any execution against him and to be dismissed.

The Attorney General replies that the king *executio suum praedictum de bonis et catallis dicti Groome defuncti habere debeat,* because he says that the defendant, at the time of issuing the *scire facias, scil.* 1 July 1696, *fuit administrator bonorum et catallorum quae fuerunt dicti Egidii Groome tempore mortis suae, viz. apud St. Albans etc., et hoc petit quod inquiratur per patriam, et praedictus defendens similiter.*

Upon this, there was a trial and verdict for the king.

And it was moved in arrest of judgment that, in this case, there ought to be no judgment (at least but a repleader) in regard there was no proper issue joined, only for that Groome, at the time of the inquisition, was dead and then at best and soonest Groome's administrator in respect of Groome's goods then in his hands unadministered became first liable and not in respect of any goods of Groome that were his at the time of his death and so the *scire facias* is. And the defendant's plea is that he is not nor ever was administrator of any of Groome's goods at the time of the inquisition or at any time after.

And Mr. Attorney [General's] replication does neither maintain the *scire facias* nor answer the defendant's plea as to the defendant's being administrator of any goods of Groome at the time of the inquisition, but maintains that Groome at the time of the issuing of the *scire facias* (which indeed is after the inquisition) was the administrator of the goods and chattels of Groome at the time of his death (which death was never mentioned before). And so he concludes to the country and makes up the record, and tries it, so that there is a trial but no issue joined between the parties.

[It was said] by me [Edward Ward] there seem these things are considerable:

First, that it does not appear upon this record when Groome died, for aught appears to the court, it might be twenty years ago;

Second, that it ought to have been found by the inquisition when Groom died and that at Groome's death and after[wards] at the time of the inquisition, the debts alleged to be due from Groome to Richards were due and unpaid, for it is only found that Groome, at his death (*non constat* when) was indebted to Richards and, for aught appears, they might be paid, for it is not said they remain due or were so at the time of the inquisition;

Third, the *scire facias* should have been against the defendant as administrator of Groome to show cause why the king should not have execution for the debts seized *de bonis* of Groome at his death remaining unadministered in the hands of the defendant at the time of the inquisition, for then and not until then did the defendant become liable to the king's debt and in respect only of such goods as were then or afterwards in his hands, and not for or in respect of any goods of Groome which were administered or disposed after the death of Groome and before the inquisition, for, put the case the defendant, as administrator, had goods of Groome at his death in his hands, after the death of Groome and before the inquisition, which he had aliened or disposed and were come again to him or which remained in his hands after the inquisition but were retained before the inquisition to satisfy a debt due to the defendant or that the defendant had paid Groome's debts before the inquisition to any other and retained these goods for his satisfaction, which, by law, he might, yet, as Mr. Attorney [General's] replication is, these goods were Groome's at his death, but being retained before the inquisition were never liable to the king's debts. And yet they are within the words of Mr. Attorney [General's] replication. And so, if judgment should be entered here upon this pleading, the defendant may become liable for those goods to which he had good title before the inquisition, whereas, by law, he can be liable for none but what were remaining unadministered in his hands of Groome's goods at the time of the inquisition or after.

So, it is one thing to say the defendant was administrator of Groome's goods at his death in the defendant's hands after the inquisition remaining and to say that Groome's goods, at the time of his death unadministered by the defendant at the time of the inquisition or after, remained in the defendant's hands.

[Other copies of this report: Georgetown Univ. Law Sch. MS. B88–9, f. 2.]

Lincoln's Inn MS. Misc. 532, f. [16v]

After the setting down of causes, [it was] agreed by counsel to try it upon this issue, whether Groome, at the time of his death, was indebted to Richards in any of the sums in the inquisition or any part of them and, if any be found, then to enquire what assets of Groome's estate Wells [had] in his hands upon or after the 1st July 1696. This is to be tried upon a feigned issue at the Hertford Assizes and judgment to be entered upon the same record for the plaintiff for security of what shall be found for assets with a release of errors and, if the defendant dies before the trial, judgment to be vacated.

[Other copies of this report: Georgetown Univ. Law Sch. MS. B88–9, f. 4.]

177

Atkyns v. Lord Lechmere

(Ex. 1698)

A court cannot take judicial notice of a privilege unless it be pleaded or a writ of privilege be brought under the great seal.

Lincoln's Inn MS. Misc. 532, f. [12]

15 November 1698. Sir Robert Atkyns v. Baron Lechmere.

Mr. *Sloan* moves that the defendant may plead to the plaintiff's declaration filed in this court against him the last day of Trinity term last, whereby the plaintiff demands £5989 against the defendant.

Sir Francis Winnington and Mr. *Ettrick* enquire of Sloan why he makes this motion, for that rules in the office are always used to be given in such a case and the court is not to interpose. And it is the fault of the plaintiff's attorney if he will not give such rules.

Sloan replies that Mr. Arden, the plaintiff's attorney, refuses to make give a rule because the defendant insists upon the privilege of Parliament. And Mr. Arden says he has been served with the defendant's writ under the great seal whereby the defendant is summoned to attend in this Parliament which has been under prorogations and is to meet the 29th instant. And so he says he dares not to give a rule lest it should be a breach of privilege.

Sloan desired of Winnington to know whether his client stood upon the privilege.

He said he did by his advice.

Then, *Sloan* said that being declared was what he desired and he now knew what to advise his client or to that effect. And he seemed to hint that the Parliament would be petitioned when it met.

The court said rules for pleading were proper and the constant practice of the office and withal hinted to the plaintiff's attorney that he had best be sure there was a privilege in the case, for that this court could not take notice of a privilege unless pleaded or a writ of privilege be brought under the great seal, neither of which was done in this case. And they told Mr. Sloan that it was a strange thing for him to move the court to go out of all method of practice when his client's attorney retained by him might do the thing regularly, and, if he did not, an action would lie.

And so no more was said or prayed by the plaintiff's counsel but that an application must be made in Parliament, besides the plaintiff, if he pleases, may change his attorney and give rules, and, if no attorney will undertake it, the court will assign one.

26 November 1698, the defendant having yesterday waived his privilege and there not being time to give a rule this term to plead, *Sloan*, for the plaintiff, moved that the defendant might plead an issuable plea as of this term, though, by the standing rules not obliged without a special order. [There was] no reason for the motion but the delay by the privilege. By the standing rules, no plea can be [filed] until eight days in the next term by a rule given. And it was the plaintiff's attorney's fault not to have given a rule of eight days this term. But that [can be] omitted; if [there be a] just cause of a privilege, then [there is] no delay. If not just cause, why [was] no rule given? The court sees no default in the defendant to forfeit the loss of the ordinary rules, being by the rules bound to plead an issuable plea within eight days of next term and that the defendant go forward as if pleaded [. . .].

[Other copies of this report: Georgetown Univ. Law Sch. MS. B88–9, f. 5v.]

[Related cases: Lord Lechmere v. Atkyns (Ex. 1698), see below, Case No. 180.]

178

Garnins v. Gwillim

(Ex. 1698)

Where a writ of consultation is moved, proof of the suggestion in issue must be made within six months.

Lincoln's Inn MS. Misc. 532, f. [24v]

Pauncefort moves for [a writ of] consultation because no proof of the suggestion that the lands whereof the tithes were sued for lay not in the parson's parish but in the parish of Dale was not proved in six months.

Price [argued] against the consultation. There was no need of proof of the suggestion; this case is not within the Statute.[1] The suggestion that ousts the ecclesiastical court of jurisdiction is that it is not in the parson's parish, being in the negative and, though an affirmative that it is in the parish of Dale be added, yet that alters not the case, the whole question to be tried being whether it is in the parson's parish or not. That it is in the parish of Dale is rather evidence than an issue, for, though it should not be in Dale, yet, if it be not in the parson's parish, the issue will be against the parson or, at least, the prohibition continue or a new one granted.

Authorities [cited were] 2 Inst. 662, in point, and so is Gawdy and Smith, King's Bench, Hilary term 19 & 20 Car. II, L. 1, 384, and 2 Keble 311.[2]

Where the suggestion was that the lands lay in the parish of B., whereof the plaintiff was not the parson without saying 'and not in the plaintiff's parish', as ought to have been, yet a [writ of] consultation was denied for want of a proof of the suggestion in six months.

[Other copies of this report: Georgetown Univ. Law Sch. MS. B88–9, f. 25.]

179

Harris v. Adge

(Ex. 1698–1699)

In this case, the rector was entitled to the tithes, having acted as rector though his title was slightly defective.

1 Rayner 84, 2 Gwillim 560

Trinity term, 9 Will. III.

The court presumed that the plaintiff had read the articles where tithe had been paid, though this was the defendant's defense.

Dodd 183, 1 Eagle & Younge 624

Between John Harris, clerk, rector of Easton Gray in Wiltshire, plaintiff, and Joseph Adge, defendant, [the case was thus].

---

1 Stat. 32 Hen. VIII, c. 7 (*SR*, III, 751–752).

2 E. Coke, *Second Institute* (1642), p. 662; *Gaudy v. Smith* (1668), Lincoln's Inn MS. Misc. 499, f. 384, 2 Keble 401, 430, 84 E.R. 251, 270, also 1 Levinz 250, 83 E.R. 392, 1 Siderfin 376, 82 E.R. 1167.

The plaintiff in a tithe bill set out that he was presented, instituted, and inducted in 1683, and ever since continued lawful rector and that the defendant had occupied twenty acres ever since, etc. Upon hearing the cause, it appeared that the plaintiff had ever since officiated and all persons had paid their tithes except the defendant, who had paid for two years and then forbore under pretence the defendant did not read the articles, etc. The defendant in 1697 got a new presentation and had induction and now brought his bill without taking any notice of his new title, and [it was] resolved:

First, that, having done the work, he ought to have the wages in such a case and that the court will presume very much for him and his having read the articles in such a suit, although he had not proved it, but on the contrary there was proof that he had confessed that he had not read the articles;

Second, at least that his new title would entitle him to all arrears notwithstanding he had not mentioned his title in his bill, for it appears to the court; here is the parson entitled one way or another.

[The defendant was] decreed to account.

[Order of 26 January 1699: Public Record Office E.126/17, f. 72.]

180

Lord Lechmere v. Atkyns

(Ex. 1699)

The question in this case was whether the defendant should give special bail.

Lincoln's Inn MS. Misc. 532, f. [31]

3 February 1698[/99].

The plaintiff sued out a *capias* in privilege against the defendant [Sir Robert Atkyns[1] and] caused it to be marked for special bail for £2500. The defendant gave bail to the sheriff. And, at the return of the writ, he entered his appearance, but insisted that no special bail was to be given, making an affidavit he owed not the plaintiff a penny, but that, on the contrary, the plaintiff owed him a great deal of money.

The plaintiff insisted on special bail, and amerced the sheriff of Gloucestershire [for] not having the defendant's body at the day. And he endeavored to have an assignment of the bail bond.

And, thereupon, Serjeant *Levinz* and Mr. *Dobbins*, for the defendant, moved the court for a stay of the plaintiff's proceedings and that he might accept of common bail.

---

[1] J. Greenberg, 'Atkyns, Sir Robert', *Oxford Dictionary of National Biography*, vol. 2, pp. 857–860.

The plaintiff made an affidavit that the defendant had gotten into his hands above £2000 of the plaintiff's money and yet refused to perform the agreement upon which he received it.

And the case appeared to be this. The plaintiff bought a manor in Gloucestershire of the defendant for which he was to pay him £6000, and, thinking it too dear, was willing not to have proceeded. But, in order to compel him to perform the articles and go on with the purchase, the defendant last term filed a bill in the Office of Pleas against him upon which some proceedings were had *prout* last term's [. . .] and the now plaintiff filed a bill in Chancery to be relieved against that action and articles, which bill and the answer to it were afterwards, at both parties' petition to the Lord Chancellor, taken off the file and delivered to the now defendant. And then the now plaintiff agreed to go on with his purchase and paid the now defendant £2000 in [part] thereof for which the defendant gave a receipt under his hand and seal and released the plaintiff of so much of the purchase money [. . .] agreement the defendant was to convey the manor to the plaintiff, and he presently to mortgage it to the defendant for securing the residue of the money [. . .] not being done through some misunderstandings between them, this action was brought.

And the sole question was whether the defendant, considering the case and the plaintiff's and his own affidavits, should be held to special bail or not.

For the plaintiff, it was insisted he should have special bail, if not from the [. . .] of the demand, yet, in regard of the plaintiff's privilege as one of the barons of the Exchequer, it being the practice that all officers [. . .] have privilege to sue shall have special bail let their [. . .] be for a sum for which others should not have special bail [. . .] is allowed by the Statute of 13 Car. II, ca. 2, § 4.[1]

The defendant's counsel agree that attorneys who sue for their fees shall give such special bail. But, if they or any other privileged persons sue for other things besides fees, they shall have no privilege of bail but where others not privileged shall. And, in case of privilege, they must show a cause of action ere they can have bail.

And the court inclined against special bail.

And, afterwards, the parties agreed [out of court].

[Related cases: Atkyns v. Lord Lechmere (Ex. 1698), see above, Case No. 177.]

181

Owen v. Anonymous

(1699)

The words spoken in this case were held to be defamatory and actionable.

[1] Stat. 13 Car. II, stat. 2, c. 2, s. 4 (*SR*, V, 324).

Dodd 182

In [an action of] case for these words 'Arthur Owen is a traitor and not fit to sit in the Parliament', after a verdict, [it was] adjudged in arrest of judgment [to be] actionable. Judgment *nisi* [was given in] Hilary term, and then upon debate judgment absolutely.

182

Capon v. Coke

(Ex. 1699)

The correct venue for an action for a false seizure of goods is where the information of seizure was laid not where the seizure was made.

Dodd 183

[There was] a seizure of goods for non-payment of customs. And upon a trial, the plaintiff, Capon was acquitted. And afterwards, he brought his action against Coke, the informer, and laid it in Suffolk where the seizure was made, although the information was laid in Middlesex. And upon debate:

First, the action was removed out of the Common Pleas;

Second, the venue was changed into Middlesex.

Note the Case of Degraves was cited to be thus; thus [it was] resolved. Query.

183

Perch v. Gee

(Ex. 1699)

Tithes of hops are measured by the bushel or by weight when they are picked.

Dodd 184, 1 Eagle & Younge 633

[One was] decreed to account for tithes in Michaelmas term preceding. And upon debate now to settle the order, [it was] resolved that tithe hops shall not be paid by the parcel nor by the hill, but by the bushel or weight of them when picked, because, [as held] by the court, then alone are they severable.

Note: Upon debate, this is of common right where there is no usage in the manner of setting out. Query whether a *modus* may be for hops or whether a *modus* of setting out may be, and it seems not, and thus afterwards [it was] resolved in the case of Conald v. Spratling.[1]

[1] *Conald v. Conald* (Ex. 1703), see below, Case No. 236.

Note: In the case before, a *modus* of 10s. an acre was insisted upon, and the court held it was not good for hops that are a new plantation. 1 Rolle 648.[1]

1 Rayner 87

Now, upon settling the order, [it was] resolved, first, that tithe hops shall not be paid by poll or hill, but by bushels etc. weight when picked, second, that no *modus* can be for hops, being a late thing. 1 Roll. Abr. 648.

[Order of 17 November 1698, sub nom. Gee v. Perch, Public Record Office E.126/17, f. 67v, is printed at 1 Wood 386, 2 Gwillim 563.]

184

Anonymous

(Ex. 1699)

This case explains the system of priorities among proceedings upon outlawries.

Dodd 184

Upon a debate touching outlawries, the Chief Baron [Ward] cited these differences.

Where there are two outlawries at different times, the first inquisition shall prevail. This was Brudenell's Case.[2]

Where there are two inquisitions on one day, the first outlawry will be preferred.

Where there are two outlawries on one day, the first inquisition shall be preferred. This was Payn and Lewis' Case.[3]

But where there are two outlawries on one day and both inquisitions are on one day, there, the first lease will be preferred.

185

Cooke v. Attorney General

(Ex. 1699)

No drawback for pepper is due unless it is exported within a year or the exportation is prevented by accident.

Where goods are imported by one person, exported by another, who sells to a third, the drawback is lost.

---

1 1 Rolle, Abr., *Dismes*, p. 648.

2 *Brudenell v. Norwood* (Ex. 1681–1682), Exch. Cases *tempore* Car. II, 489.

3 *Payne v. Dewy* (Ex. 1669), Exch. Repts. *tempore* Car. II, 157.

Dodd 185, Parker 266, 145 E.R. 775

Upon an English bill for a drawback for pepper exported or to have new debentures, the first being cancelled by the advice of the commissioners of the customs, it was resolved:

First, that if goods are imported by an Englishman [on] 23 October 1697 and shipped on board for exportation [on] 1 October 1698 and the endorsed to another ship and so did not go out of port until 1 November 1698, that no drawback is due for it is now out of time and they must be actually out of port within the year if not prevented by [some] accident;

Second, that if goods are imported by one and shipped for exportation by another and then they are on shipboard, the second person sells to J.S. reserving for the drawback, in this case, the drawback is lost, for the property must not be changed after the shipping or exportation.

Note the second rate in the Book of Rates.[1]

[Affirmed: Lords' Journal, vol. 16, p. 556.]

186

Attorney General v. Weeden and Shales

(Ex. 1699)

Choses in action belonging to an alien enemy are forfeited to the crown, but there must be a commission and inquisition to entitle the king.

A peace before the inquisition discharges the cause of forfeiture by an enemy alien.

Dodd 186, Parker 267, 145 E.R. 776

One Peter La Store, who was a Frenchman naturalized, made his will during the war and gave several legacies to Frenchmen living in Bordeaux and died. Some of the legacies were payable presently, others at age, etc. A commission issued to find this matter, and then the peace was made, and ten days after an inquisition was found and returned. And upon long debate, it was resolved:

First, that choses in action which belonged to an alien enemy are forfeitable to the crown;

Second, that this ought to be found by inquisition to make a title to the king; and that this was an inquisition of entitling, and not of informing;

Third, that the peace being concluded before the inquisition was taken discharged the cause of the forfeiture;

Fourth, that the inquisition taken afterwards, did not relate to set up this forfeiture, for the cause was but temporary, and that cause being removed before the king's title is found, the finding after shall not relate.

[1] Stat. 12 Car. II, c. 4, app. (*SR*, V, 184–205).

Note these cases were cited: 19 Edw. IV, 6; Br., [Abr.], *Det*, 119; Rolle, [Abr.], title *Alien*; 1 Saund. 361; Rastal's *Entries* 605; 2 Rolle's Abr. 399; 8 Rep. 170; 1 Inst. 118; Magna Charta, c. 30: 2 Inst. 58; 5 Hen. VI, ch. 7; 4 Edw. III, c. 1; 14 Edw. III, c. 2; 7 Edw. IV, 14; 2 Ric. III, 2; 1 Rolle's Rep. 175; 3 Bulstr. 27; [The King against Williamson, since published in Freeman's Rep. 39]; 1 Inst. 129; Moo. 431; Mich. 18 Car. II, C.P.[1]

Note also great stress was laid upon the articles of peace.

[Order of 14 February 1699: Public Record Office E.126/17, f. 75.]

187

Brown v. Franklyn

(Ex. 1699)

The issue of prize or no prize is within the jurisdiction of the Court of Admiralty.

Carthew 474, 90 E.R. 873, Dodd 350

[A writ of] prohibition to the Court of Admiralty [was prayed], suggesting the Statute of Ric. II[2] and that pleas of trespass on the case for the conversion of any goods or merchandise, as also the trial of the property of any goods, etc. and the cognisance thereof belongs to the king and his crown and not to be tried before the admiral, etc. that nevertheless the defendant, being the king's proctor, had libelled against the plaintiffs in the Admiralty concerning the property of a certain ship called the *Francis* and her furniture as also of 6000 chequins of foreign money, 200 elephant's teeth, 300 pieces of muslin, 300 pieces of calico, etc. *Ubi revera navis praedictis fuit wrecca maris* in the East Indies, out of the king's dominions *ac ubi revera navis praedictis* and her loading were not the goods of the French king or of any of his subjects, enemies to our king, but did belong to the subjects of the king of Portugal, who is in amity with us; *ac ubi revera* all the said foreign money and the goods and merchandise aforesaid came to the hands of the plaintiffs *super terram* in the East Indies and, there, were by them sold, etc.

---

[1] *Esterling's Case* (1480), YB Hil. 19 Edw. IV, f. 6, pl. 4 and 6; *Reynolde v. Knott* (1459), YB Hil. 37 Hen. VI, f. 13, pl. 3, 51 Selden Soc. 147, Brooke, Abr., *Dett*, pl. 119; 1 Rolle, Abr., *Alien*, sect. B, p. 195; *Toomes v. Etherington* (1669), 1 Williams Saunders 361, 85 E.R. 520; 2 Rolle, Abr., *Relation*, p. 399; *Tourson's Case* (1610), 8 Coke Rep. 170, 77 E.R. 730; E. Coke, *First Institute* (1628), f. 118; E. Coke, *Second Institute* (1642), p. 58; Stat. 5 Hen. IV, c. 7 (*SR*, II, 145); Stat. 4 Edw. III, c. 1 (*SR*, I, 261); Stat. 14 Edw. III, stat. 2, c. 2 (*SR*, I, 290); YB Trin. 7 Edw. IV, f. 14, pl. 8 (1467); YB Mich. 2 Ric. III, f. 2, pl. 4 (1484); *Marsh's Case* (1615), 1 Rolle Rep. 175, 81 E.R. 411, 3 Bulstrode 27, 81 E.R. 23; *Rex v. Williamson* (1672), 1 Freeman 39, 89 E.R. 31; E. Coke, *First Institute* (1628), f. 129; *Watford v. Masham* (1596), Moore K.B. 431, 72 E.R. 676.

[2] Stat. 15 Ric. II, c. 3 (*SR*, II, 78–79).

Upon opening this case, the fact appeared to be thus. The plaintiffs [Brown and Burton] were masters of two ships belonging to the East India Company, and, being in a port there, they had intelligence that about the island Joanna there was a rich French ship which might easily be surprised, and accordingly, they sailed thither and found the ship whole but stranded near the shore, and the ship's crew were at land; that the plaintiffs landed their men and surprised the enemy on shore and found the chequins quilted in their clothes about their bodies and the rest of the goods were in the ship, where the plaintiffs took it, and brought all away, but left the ship behind, being stranded.

The news whereof coming to England, it being in the time of war between the English and the French, the defendant by libel pursues for the king in the Court of Admiralty to have the ship, money, and goods condemned as lawful prize (as a perquisite of the Admiralty) and accordingly after general admonitions on the Exchange, as usual in such cases, and no person coming in to claim property, there was a sentence, whereby all the said things were condemned as lawful prize.

And upon that sentence, this libel was founded against the plaintiffs, charging them that all came to their hands and that they had embezzled it and converted the same to their own use and that they might account for the value.

And now it was insisted for a prohibition, that it was unreasonable the plaintiffs should be concluded by the sentence upon the general libel to which they were not parties, neither had they any notice thereof, for, at that time, they were in the Indies. And, therefore, it was moved that the plaintiffs might still have an opportunity upon a prohibition to try their property and to controvert their right against the said sentence, if prize or not and whether the capture was at land or on the sea.

And the court inclined that the plaintiffs ought to have an opportunity to be heard and to controvert the matter of fact. And, thereupon, a day was appointed to hear a civilian upon this question, *scil.* whether the plaintiffs, upon this libel depending against them in the Court of Admiralty, might controvert their property there against the tenor of the first sentence.

And at another day, Dr. *Lane* acquainted the court that it was the constant practice amongst them to admit of appeals from such general sentences for prize and that the appellants were always let in to controvert their right and to disprove the prize, notwithstanding the sentence, because, upon an appeal, their method was to exhibit new allegations and, thereupon, to receive new and farther proofs so that the cause was many times another thing before the [court of] delegates than what it was at the time of the first sentence.

And it was then made appear to the court that the plaintiffs had actually appealed from this sentence of condemnation for prize and so were in the proper method to controvert their right. Wherefore, and for that the court apprehended (as it was insisted upon on the other side) that prize or no prize was a matter not triable at common law but altogether appropriated to the jurisdiction of the Admiralty, the prohibition was denied.

188

Davis v. Price

(Ex. 1699)

Court costs for witnesses can be had where the plaintiff puts off the trial after the witnesses have come to the place of trial.

Lincoln's Inn MS. Misc. 532, f. [33]

9 May, Easter term 1699, 11 Will. III, ejectment.

There being [a] rule of court last term, a trial at the bar [was] appointed to be the 5th of this month [May] by a Herefordshire jury for lands in Cardiganshire late the estate of Sir Carbery Price.

The plaintiff, upon the death of one Corbett, admitted and sworn to be a material witness for him, who died the 15th of April last, did give notice of that death to his clerk in court, Owen, who, thereupon, the 22nd of the same April (being also one Ashe had notice of it) entered in the office book a diswarning of the trial and gave notice to the [. . .] which was completely thirteen days before the day of trial appointed, but it happened that, before the defendant in the country had notice of that diswarning, he and some of his witnesses living about 150 miles from London were come towards London and were there three or four days before the day of trial appointed and some of the jury were also come up, not being diswarned. And whether the plaintiff in this case should pay any and what costs for not proceeding to trial was the question, the same being moved for by the defendant and opposed by the plaintiff.

And, in this case, the court resolved that such of the jury as came up before diswarned should have their costs, to which the plaintiff agreed. But, as to the defendant's having any costs for himself or witnesses, it was opposed upon these grounds: first, that diswarning a trial at the bar in due time is a good cause to be excused of any costs; secondly, that this diswarning was in due and convenient time, being given in the office book, which is the standard both of warning and diswarning of trials in the office without other notice to the clients, as was affirmed by the Master of the Office and sworn clerks, and thirteen days is sufficient time for diswarning a trial at the bar be it never so distant, the written rules of the Office being that four days' diswarning for London and Middlesex and eight days where country causes is held sufficient for *nisi prius*, and the day of diswarning was upon a post day and notice was sent that night. But the plaintiff and witnesses happened to be come out two days before to be early in town, *viz.* four days, before the trial for preparation.

It was admitted that there was no rule in the office or precedent in the like case. But, for the defendant, it was insisted that he was in no fault in his early preparations, and, though it was the plaintiff's misfortune to lose his witness, which might be a good cause why he did not go on, yet that is no reason to make the defendant lose his costs, being come out before notice of diswarning.

The court informed themselves what was usual in other courts, and were told there were never any diswarning of trials at the bar but in the late trials between the Earl of Bath and Mountagu,[1] but it was by them thought reasonable that what the costs the defendant had been unavoidably at in coming up of himself and witnesses to the trial should be paid, which was ordered accordingly to be taxed with moderation.

[Other copies of this report: Georgetown Univ. Law Sch. MS. B88–9, f. 35.]

189

Everard, qui tam v. Elliot

(Ex. 1699)

A criminal information cannot be amended so as to increase the amount of the penalty.

Lincoln's Inn MS. Misc. 532, f. [34], pl. 2

[Everard] informed against the defendant as captain of a ship upon the Privateer Act 5 W. & M.,[2] for embezzling prize goods whereby the offender loses his share; secondly, forfeits £500; and, thirdly, disabled to serve His Majesty.

The cause was twice brought down to be tried before me [Edward Ward] at *nisi prius*. But the plaintiff went not on, the king's part *non pross*ed.

And now, after notice of trial this term, the plaintiff prayed leave to put into his information some other goods taken and embezzled by the defendant in the same ship. But the court thought that of dangerous consequence, for the plaintiff has enumerated in his information a great mulcture [?] and if he proves but any, the penalties run upon the defendant so that to put the defendant to make a defense against the new charge and not give him time for it would be hard and, indeed, in such a penal case, it is hard that any amendment should be at all.

So the plaintiff waived that part of his motion and agreed to go in to trial, only that he might amend this particular, that, whereas in the information it is laid, *inter alia*, that the defendant embezzled 3000 golden pieces of eight of the value of £3000 that the [word] 'golden' might be put out and the value and the pieces expressed to be silver, and that the king's officers at the Admiralty and belonging to the Admiralty Court, who had the papers relating to these prizes,

1 *Earl of Montagu v. Earl of Bath* (1693), 3 Chancery Cases 96, 22 E.R. 988.
2 Stat. 4 Will. & Mar., c. 4, s. 7 (*SR*, VI, 421).

might attend at the trial with them for their charges to be paid, both which were ordered unless cause [be shown to the contrary].

[Other copies of this report: Georgetown Univ. Law Sch. MS. B88–9, f. 36v.]

190

Calthorpe's Case

(Ex. 1699)

The Court of Exchequer cannot review the assessments of the tax assessors, but it can review charges in the Pipe Office.

Lincoln's Inn MS. Misc. 532, f. [49v], pl. 1

10 November 1699.

Ettrick moved the court that a *super* set upon Sir Christopher Calthorpe of about £20 as a double charge upon him for lands in Norfolk because he did not take the oaths to the [. . .] and, therefore, by the acts for the 4s. in the pound to be doubly taxed might be discharged upon an affidavit produced of one of the assessors and collectors that he was not taxed double when the assessment was delivered in to the commissioners but, afterwards, the double was put in by the other assessor by the direction of one of the commissioners only.

But the motion was not granted in regard that the *super* was duly returned by the receiver general and duly put in charge and drawn down into the Pipe [Office]. And this court cannot enquire into the regularity or irregularity of the assessors in putting in the double nor how it came to pass. But he ought to have appealed to the commissioners, and, if this court could and should enquire into the methods of levying each man's tax and set aside *super*s duly set for aught appears to the contrary by the receiver general upon such an affidavit, it might open a gap to unravel the proceedings of the commissioners for all the taxes and make them and the assessors and receivers general to appear here, which ought not to be done, the appeal to the commissioners being final by the acts. And, if he conceived he was relievable, he might put in his plea to the charge and have the judgment of the court.

[Other copies of this report: Georgetown Univ. Law Sch. MS. B88–9, f. 42v.]

191

Ward, qui tam v. Willet

(Ex. 1699–1700)

It lies in the sound discretion of the court to allow the use of depositions de bene esse of witnesses who live abroad.

Lincoln's Inn MS. Misc. 532, f. [49v], pl. 2

The plaintiff having seized a parcel of linen of the defendant for non-payment of duties supposing it to be French, whereas the duty paid was only for Germany linen, which is very much less than the French duty and notice being given of a trial for this term, the defendant exhibited his English bill against the Attorney General and Ward in order to have a commission to have his witnesses at Hamburg examined, which he alleges he cannot get over, swearing them to be material witnesses, the suggestion being that the linen was made in Saxony by the French refugees lately planted there after the manner of French linen and, therefore, the more necessary to have the manufacturing in Germany proved.

This was opposed by Mr. Attorney [General *Trevor*] as dangerous to have such commissions so as to delay the cause and set those examinations up as legal evidence when the witnesses may be had *viva voce*.

The court observed:

First, that this is not a seizure upon the Act of Navigation, in which case, the Act 14 Car. II, ca. 11, against Frauds,[1] allows a commission out of Chancery and stays the trial and makes the depositions legal evidence as if present *viva voce*. But this is upon the Act for Tonnage and Poundage,[2] in which case, it is true the *onus probandi* lies upon the claimer, but that Act makes no provision for such a commission.

And I [Edward Ward] observed that though such commissions have sometimes of late been executed and the depositions of persons beyond the sea read upon the trials as legal evidence, yet it has been observed that there have and may for the future be great inconvenience in that way, for it is observable that the depositions are generally thorough slick against the king and informer. And there is more regard to be given to one witness examined *viva voce* than to three or four examined beyond the sea where either no proper commissioner can or will attend for the king, and the witnesses well know they are not punishable if they forswear themselves.

Nor is it considered whether they hold themselves obliged by any oath administered to them by a foreign authority, and there may seem a partiality for the advancement of the trade of their own country. And it is not unreasonable to think that the Parliament, when they gave the commission upon the Act of Navigation[3] and gave the directions above, did not intend they should be extended [. . .] and the Act and case wherein they gave them and yet at the same time could not but observe that the mischief which they sought to remedy was as extensive [. . .] upon the acts of tonnage and poundage and the Act against Frauds and other cases of seizures of foreign goods as that upon the Navigation

[1] Stat. 14 Car. II, c. 11 (*SR*, V, 393–400).

[2] Stat. 12 Car. II, c. 4 (*SR*, V, 181–205).

[3] Stat. 12 Car. II, c. 18 (*SR*, V, 246–250).

Act. And, if the depositions taken upon such a commission were to be read at law, there needed not such a clause for their establishment. And in regard (by all probability) there is a confederacy to import French linen under the pretense of Germany, which will defraud the king of a great part of his customs and not only so but will continue the French king in a temper never to establish a trade between the two kingdoms and it being a common and easy thing to get French linen to Hamburg and thence to England and, it appearing by Ward [. . .] that the now defendant's father owned to him that the linens came from France and that his son traded hither and that he would allow him a certain sum upon every ship to [. . .] them at the Custom House and offered him gold to quit this seizure, the court declared themselves unwilling to have such examinations made use of as legal evidence and [. . .] told the defendant he must get his witnesses to London and may well do it by the next term, to which time (by Mr. Attorney [General's] consent) the trial was put off.

And yet, nevertheless, in regard some of the defendant's witnesses might die before the trial and that there could be no commission beyond the seas without a motion and order, the court ordered that the defendant might take out a commission to Hamburg if he pleased, returnable next term, but cautioned him to bring his witnesses *viva voce* to the trial, giving him no encouragement to expect the depositions of any of them should be read which were not proved to be dead.

However, I did observe that, in the case of merchandising, such examinations may be necessary to be had and allowed for distant places and upon great emergencies and where the proof rises properly beyond the seas and lies upon the merchant and where the merchant cannot procure their witnesses to come over and has no means to compel them by process so that this matter of examination of witnesses beyond the seas to be used as legal evidence is not to be confined to any certain rule, but must expect the nature of each case. And the court, upon consideration of the circumstances of the case, may either allow or disallow of them as evidence at law and may or may not put off the trial until the return of such a commission.

Note, afterwards, in Easter term 1700, the cause being ready for trial, the defendant withdrew his claim, and suffered to goods to be recovered, notwithstanding the pretenses above, *quod nota*.

And it was said that all the defendant's pretenses were untrue.

[Other copies of this report: Georgetown Univ. Law Sch. MS. B88–9, f. 43.]

2 Price 178, 146 E.R. 60

11 November 1699.

Upon the motion of Mr. *Bernard*, of counsel with the plaintiff in the said English cause, informing the court that all the linen in question in these causes are all of the manufacture of Germany and imported into England from thence and that the same were seized by the said John Ward, the plaintiff in the said information, as goods and merchandize of the manufacture of some of the dominions of the French king and the said Francis Willet having thereupon filed his said bill in order to obtain a commission to examine his witnesses beyond the seas, to which bill his Majesty's Attorney General and the said John Ward had put in their answers, to which answers the said Francis Willet had replied, and his Majesty's said Attorney General and the said John Ward had rejoined, it was, therefore, now prayed by the said *William Bernard* that the trial of the cause in the said Ward's information may be put off until next term and that the said plaintiff, Willett, may in the meantime have a commission for examination of his witnesses beyond sea and that the same may be read and made use of as evidence upon the trial of the said Ward's information.

And, upon reading the affidavits of Humphry Willet and Francis Burgois and upon hearing Mr. *Ettrick* and Mr. *Browne*, on behalf of the said Willet and of his Majesty's Attorney General [*Trevor*], Mr. *Dodd*, and Mr. *Bridges*, on behalf of his Majesty and the said Ward, it is this day ordered by this court, that the trial on the said plaintiff Ward's information shall be put off until the last sitting of the next term; and that, in the meantime, the said Francis Willet, the plaintiff in the said English cause, may take forth a commission for examination of his witnesses in parts beyond the seas, wherein his Majesty's Attorney General and the said Ward may join if they think fit, but, in case they will not join therein, within a week after the term, the said Willet may take forth a commission *ex parte* and publication of the said depositions shall pass upon return of the said commission.

6 February 1699[/70].

Upon the motion of Mr. *Turner*, for the defendant, to put off the trial until next term, he, having a commission, having gone into Germany to examine witnesses, which is not returned, and reading the affidavits of Francis Willet, Mr. *Ettrick*, Mr. *Browne*, and Mr. *Barnard*, of the same side, Mr. Attorney [General *Trevor*], Mr. *Dodd*, and Mr. *Bridges, pro querente*, it was ordered by consent of Mr. *Ward* and at the desire of the defendant Willett that the plaintiff have his costs taxed this afternoon and paid him tomorrow morning and then the cause to be put off until next term to be tried; otherwise, the cause is not put off.

7 April 1700.

Upon the motion of Mr. *Turner*, it is ordered that publication pass on Saturday, unless cause [be shown] on Friday and the depositions, being returned in High Dutch, to be translated by a public notary upon oath.

192

Collet v. Lawton

(Ex. 1699–1700)

Words that were uttered in passion and anger can be actionable defamation.

Court costs are paid by a defendant in a writ of prohibition where judgment is given against him upon a demurrer.

Lincoln's Inn MS. Misc. 532, f. [50v], pl. 1

[In] Collet and Lawton, [a writ of] prohibition for want of showing cause [was] granted for the stay of a suit in the ecclesiastical court for *reformatio morum* only for these words, 'go take to your [. . .] whore and bastard', *innuendo* A.B. and her child.

And the court inclined for a [writ of] consultation. But, the plaintiff in the prohibition offering to declare upon it and the other side accepting it, it was ordered accordingly.

Vide Trinity term 1700 for the judgment of the court.

[Other copies of this report: Georgetown Univ. Law Sch. MS. B88–9, f. 44v.]

Lincoln's Inn MS. Misc. 532, f. [87v]

The plaintiff here had a [writ of] prohibition to the ecclesiastical court to stay a suit there for slanderous words *pro reformatione morum.*

And, upon debate, a [writ of] consultation was granted, there being a demurrer to the plaintiff's declaration upon the prohibition. And the defendant prayed costs to be taxed for him in this case upon the new Statute 8 & 9 Will. III, ca. 11, fo. 206,[1] whereby, after a judgment upon a demurrer given against the plaintiff in any action, plaint, or suit in any court of record, the defendant is to have his costs. And, fo. 207, it is further enacted that, where, in suits upon prohibitions, the plaintiff obtains judgment on a demurrer etc., he shall have his costs and, if the plaintiff became nonsuited or discontinue or have a verdict against him, the defendant is to have costs.

But, in this case of prohibition, there is no provision made for the plaintiff's paying costs in case judgment passes against him upon a demurrer. And whether the defendant in a prohibition where judgment is given against him upon a demurrer shall pay costs is the question.

[*blank*] urged that he shall within the first clause, fo. 206, which is general, to give costs against plaintiffs upon demurrers.

But [it was] objected that the case of a prohibition is not within the words of that clause but specially provided for as to costs by the second clause, fo. 207, which does not extend to this case of giving costs to a defendant upon a prohibition and, if a prohibition was not within the first clause, then all that is done for costs therein goes only upon the second clause, which extends not costs against but for plaintiffs. And so this is a *casus omissus* as to costs in prohibition against plaintiffs upon demurrers.

[1] Stat. 8 & 9 Will. III, c. 11 (*SR*, VII, 201–203).

But now, it being certified by Baron Hatsell, that upon enquiry, save Chief Justice Holt and the judges of the King's Bench and Common Pleas of Serjeants' Inn in Chancery Lane, that they allowed the defendant costs upon a demurrer in a prohibition by virtue of the first clause, fo. 206, under the general words of 'action, plaint, or suit' which, as they said, comprehended a prohibition, though not expressed, as it is in the second clause.

The rule here was for costs, *quod nota et quaere.*

[Other copies of this report: Georgetown Univ. Law Sch. MS. B88–9, f. 74v.]

Dodd 195

[There was a] libel in the spiritual court for these words 'Go take to your whore and bastard', *innuendo* etc. And upon a prohibition and a demurrer, after argument, a [writ of] consultation [was] granted by Hatsell and Powys against Chief Baron Ward, because he held these words [were] of heat and anger and not suable in the spiritual court.

193

Lord Jeffries v. Herbert

(Ex. 1699)

In this case, a material fact that was not included in the special verdict could not be added later, though it must necessarily have been found and thus implied in the verdict.

Lincoln's Inn MS. Misc. 532, f. [53v]

28 November 1699.

There was a special verdict found upon a trial at the Exchequer bar in the year 1684 concerning the estate of one Penn and Dudley Rewse, which both parties claimed under the crown. And the defendant made part of his title under letters patent of King Charles II made *anno* 1679 wherein there was a proviso that they should be enrolled before the Auditor of the County of Buckingham within six months after the date. And, in the notes of the special verdict, the patent was found *prout* and the enrollment of it within six months after the date was attested by Rabe [?], the then Auditor's deputy of Buckinghamshire, and the jury, in express words, found all other things necessary to bring the matter in question. And, because it was not expressly found in the notes that this patent was enrolled within six months after the date, the plaintiff's counsel refused to let it be found in the special verdict.

And upon a motion to have it found, Powys and Hatsell, barons, were of the opinion that it ought not to be put in the special verdict, not being expressed in the notes in regard it is a matter of fact whether it was enrolled in six months or not, notwithstanding the Deputy Auditor's endorsement, which is not a matter of record, and, therefore, ought expressly to have been found by the jury and to have been mentioned in the notes.

But I [Edward Ward] was of the opinion that the finding of the enrollment to have been within six months ought to be put into the special verdict as drawn at large, for that patent being the very foundation of the defendant's title and which makes the question between the parties and it appearing that it was read at the trial, if it had not appeared at the trial to have been enrolled within the six months, it would never have been found in the special verdict, in regard, otherwise, nothing could pass by it. And it was fruitless and in vain to find a patent *in haec verba* which was void and passed nothing. And it appeared that the date of the patent was above four years before the trial in which it was found, at which time, if the enrollment had not been proved to the court, it could never have come into the cause. And the Deputy Auditor's entry of the enrollment is as much evidence that it was enrolled in six months as the endorsement of the officer in the Chancery upon a deed is that it was so enrolled, which never was denied nor further proof made of it. Besides, the general finding of the jury of things necessary to bring the matter in question answers the objections of being matter of fact, for if it be such a thing as is necessary to bring the matter in question, then, without doubt, the jury have found it, for so is their express finding.

But, by the opinion of the other two barons, the finding was rejected, *quod query*.

[Other copies of this report: Georgetown Univ. Law Sch. MS. B88–9, f. 47v.]

194

In re Morrison

(Ex. 1699)

A court can set aside fraudulent proceedings that appear upon its records.

Lincoln's Inn MS. Misc. 532, f. [54]

The Remembrancer's entering clerk of this court, bound by a recognizance in Easter term last and so continued to the last day of this term, in order to be prosecuted for great misdemeanors in fraudulently procuring about thirty informations for uncustomed goods and other offenses to be exhibited and licenses and compositions for 20s. each upon them as far as the Chancellor's and Baron Lechmere's names were obtained, but then stayed, he acting on both sides for the plaintiff and the defendant and in the names but without the privity of any of the sworn clerks of the office, they all disowning their names used in the proceedings, and he carried on the proceedings without entering the licenses, as was lately ordered, and the examination of this irregularity being referred to the Deputy [Remembrancer] and certified by him and owned in court by [George]

Morrison, the court set aside all the informations, licenses, compositions, and proceedings as fraudulent and irregular and done with an intent to deceive the king and prevent any other informations by the Attorney General or any other [person] for the same offenses, after which or during which proceedings other informations were exhibited.

But there was not any prosecution on the behalf of the king against Morrison, as was expected and directed by the court, which appeared strange.

[Other copies of this report: Georgetown Univ. Law Sch. MS. B88–9, f. 48v.]

195

Griffith, ex dem. v. Vogle

(Ex. 1700)

It lies in the sound discretion of a court to set aside a default judgment.

Who seeks equity must do equity.

Lincoln's Inn MS. Misc. 532, f. [73]

12 November. Ejectment.

The lessor of the plaintiff was the widow of Sir [*blank*], and claimed the residue of a term under an assignment by her husband in consideration of a marriage and a portion he had with her of £2000. The defendant's title was by a mortgage of the same term for £500 made by the husband but puisne to the jointure. But the defendant was in possession of the leased premises, which were houses in London, and had also the original lease (from a company in London) and the assignment of that lease to the husband which enabled him to make both the jointure to the wife, which was after the marriage, and also the mortgage to the defendant.

And to recover the possession, the plaintiff brought her [action of] ejectment in the Office of Pleas, and moved the first day of this term for judgment against the casual ejector, which was granted, as usual, unless the tenants in possession should appear and plead within a fortnight.

The defendants retained an under clerk in the office to appear for them and plead and this before the term. But he did not cause any appearance to be entered, but the [. . .] was out upon a Monday, and the plaintiff did not sign the judgment until Thursday, which was then done. And the tenants thereupon attorned to the plaintiff without execution.

Whereupon, the defendant moved the court to set aside the judgment, offering to pay costs and to try it this term, which was opposed by the plaintiff unless the defendant would at the trial produce the original lease and the assignment to the husband, under which both parties claimed, without which the plaintiff could not make out her title, the defendant having gotten them into his hands, and equity would not compel them out in regard he was a mortgagee for a valuable consideration without notice of the plaintiff's title, which the defendant refused to do [. . .] so that the mere right could not be tried.

And, therefore, the court did not think fit to set aside the judgment which was fairly and duly obtained. The rule being fairly entered in the book and was very long, contained the names of many tenants, and could not well be overlooked, though the clerk made an oath he searched the book, but did not see it.

And though it is a usual thing to set aside judgments upon an offer to plead and try the same term or next assizes, yet, in this case, where it is apparent that the plaintiff must fail unless the original lease and assignment be produced or confessed (which was refused) and the court could not compel either to be done, therefore, the plaintiff having legally obtained the judgment and the defendant desiring equity, he must do equity, which, he refusing, the judgment stood. But, upon the defendant's offer to be the plaintiff if the now plaintiff would appear and plead and try this term, a rule for that purpose was entered.

[Other copies of this report: Georgetown Univ. Law Sch. MS. B88–9, f. 62.]

196

Pugh v. Pascall

(Ex. 1700)

In this case, there was a question whether an institution to a rectory sine cura is void.

It was also in issue in this case whether tithes can be withheld by a patron from a vicar where the patron has received the services of the vicar even though the vicar was not properly in office.

Dodd 191, 1 Rayner 92, 1 Eagle & Younge 637

The plaintiff prefers his bill for tithes as vicar of Much Baddow in Essex. The defendant says that it is a vicarage with cure of above £8 value and that the defendant, before the time in demand, was instituted and inducted into the rectory of Snoweham within the parish of Latchington in Essex, being a benefice with cure without any qualification. And upon hearing this cause, it appeared that the bishop of London had instituted the plaintiff into this rectory *sine cura*, etc. The court resolved that the plaintiff had not accepted a rectory with cure and that, in case it be a rectory with cure, then the institution was null and void.

Query, because it appears to me that the institution is good and the adding the words *sine cura* null and void.

As to the second point, [it was] resolved, that the defendant in this suit (as the plaintiff had done the work and this was but in the nature of wages) should not take advantage of it; and the court said that in *nil debet* on the Statute[1] he should not take advantage in such case.

Query, because it appears to me contrary.

Note: The defendant was patron, and therefore the court said he ought rather to try the point in a new presentation or by [an action of] *quare impedit* than in this suit.

[Order of 28 June 1700: Public Record Office E.126/17, f. 160.]

197

Hunt v. Codrington

(Ex. 1700)

Teasels are small tithes.

Dodd 192, 1 Rayner 94, 1 Eagle & Younge 636

In a tithe bill by the farmer of the impropriation for the tithe of teasels that are planted and afterwards used by clothiers (note they were first planted in the parish of Congresbury in Somerset about forty-five years ago although immemorially in other places) and the tithes always since paid to the impropriator, and four successive vicars in this time never demanded or received the same, but now, because it appeared that the vicar was endowed of all small tithes, the court adjudged this a small tithe and to belong to him, in regard the time of planting it was known, and dismissed the bill.

[The order of 26 June 1700, Public Record Office E.126/17, f. 150, is printed at 1 Wood 391, 2 Gwillim 564.]

198

Thorngate v. Wallop

(Ex. 1700)

In this case, a custom of not paying tithes for hay and wood was held to be valid.

Dodd 192, 1 Rayner 93, 1 Eagle & Younge 636

The plaintiff exhibited his bill as farmer of the rectory of Hursburn Priors and St. Mary Brame in Southampton for the tithes of hay and wood. The defendant answered that the bishop of Winchester had the first mowth of four acres in Honey Mead in discharge of the tithe of hay arising upon Honey Mead and other meadows in the parish occupied by the defendant and that no tithes in kind were ever

[1] Stat. 21 Hen. VIII, c. 13, s. 9 (*SR*, III, 293).

paid; and as to the wood, he never heard that any tithes were paid for that and said that it formerly belonged to the priory of Hursburn and, being so vested in the church, is exempt from payment of any tithes.

Upon the hearing, it appeared that these woods and meadows belonged to the hospital of St. Swithin's in Winchester and came to the crown, 30 Hen. VIII.[1] And though the defendant had not by answer so set it forth and for the meadow had made another defence, yet no tithe having ever been paid, the court dismissed the bill.

[The order of 26 June 1700, Public Record Office E.126/17, f. 167, is printed at 1 Wood 396.]

199

Dowdeswell v. Harker

(Ex. 1700)

A custom of not paying tithes for wood or furze burned in the house is valid.

Dodd 193, 1 Eagle & Younge 637

The plaintiff brought his bill, amongst other things, as rector of Kingham in Oxfordshire for the tithe of furze or wood. Upon the defendant's answer and hearing the cause, it appeared to be burned in the house; and the defendant having said generally that no tithe of furze or wood burned in the house was payable by the custom of the parish, the court resolved accordingly and said that, generally speaking, tithe of wood burned shall be paid, but if there be a custom in the parish to the contrary, *viz.* in *non decimando*, it is good, and so the books shall be intended. See Moo. 909; Cro. Car. 113; 1 Sid. 447; 1 Rolle, Abr., 644.[2] And [the court] dismissed the bill as to that demand.

[Order of 29 June 1700: Public Record Office E.126/17, f. 170.]

200

Goldsborough v. Evans

(Ex. 1700)

A final judgment at common law is res judicata as to a subsequent suit in a court of equity.

---

[1] This hospital was dissolved by Stat. 37 Hen. VIII, c. 4 (*SR*, III, 988–993).

[2] *Austin v. Lucas* (1598), Moore K.B. 909, 72 E.R. 990, 1 Rolle, Abr., *Dismes*, pl. Z, 3, p. 644; *Norton v. Fermer* (1628), Croke Car. 113, 79 E.R. 699; *Tilden v. Walter* (1670), 1 Siderfin 447, 82 E.R. 1209, Lincoln's Inn MS. Misc. 500, f. 83; *Ellis v. Drake* (1616), 1 Rolle, Abr., *Dismes*, pl. Z, 1, p. 644.

Harvard Law Sch. MS. 1052, p. 69, pl. 182

Michaelmas term.

The complainant's bill appearing to be for relief against a trial at law not long before and that he did endeavor to try the same over again in equity after a verdict and judgment entered, My Lord Chief Baron [Ward] would not hear of it nor admit a thing of that nature after a verdict by any means.

Vide Siderfin, p. 463, King and Standish,[1] where it is said that to sue in Chancery for relief against a judgment given at common law incurs a praemunire; yet see Moor, fo. 828, n. 1114; see also 3 Inst., fo. 122, 123; Cro. Ja., p. 335, Heath and Ridley's Case.[2]

201

Thomas v. City of London

(Ex. 1701–1702)

The older debts and obligations of the City of London that were in issue in this case were discharged by the Act of 5 & 6 Will. & Mar., c. 10.

Lincoln's Inn MS. Misc. 532, f. [107]

31 October 1701, 13 Will. III.

[In an action of] debt upon a bond of £2500 dated the 1 August 1643 whereby the Mayor, commonalty, and citizens of London became bound to Robert Campion, deceased, who left James Campion, deceased, his executor, and to whom the plaintiff is executor, in that sum, the condition was for payment of £1040 to the said Robert Campion the 3d of February next after the date, which was in 1643.

The defendants plead the Statute made 5 & 6 Will. & Mar.,[3] whereby provision is made for the paying and discharging of the City debts to the orphans of London and other of the City creditors, and insist that that Act has discharged the plaintiff's bond absolutely by the express words, *prout* fo. 206. To this plea, the plaintiff has demurred, and the defendant joined.

There are two questions: first, whether this bond and debt be within the provision of the Act; secondly, if it be, whether the defendants should not have

[1] *King v. Standish* (1670), 1 Siderfin 463, 82 E.R. 1218, also 1 Levinz 241, 83 E.R. 387, 1 Modern 59, 86 E.R. 730, 1 Keble 927, 83 E.R. 1324, 2 Keble 402, 661, 84 E.R. 251, 415.

[2] The Lord Chancellor's Speech, Moore K.B. 826, 72 E.R. 931; E Coke, *Third Institute* (1644), pp. 122, 123; *Heath v. Rydley* (1614), Croke Jac. 335, 73 E.R. 286, also 2 Bulstrode 194, 80 E.R. 1062.

[3] Stat. 5 & 6 Will. & Mar., c. 10 (*SR*, VI, 464–470).

[. . .] thence; thirdly, [. . .] plaintiff has or might [. . .] the benefit of the Act's [. . .].

Mr. *Stephens*, for the plaintiff, thinks this bond and debt is not within the provision of the Act, being made in 1643 and the first provision for payment of interest rises not until 1655 and so the bond or debt is not touched by the Act. And so the plea is not to the purpose. If it be within the Act, yet the defendants ought to have shown that they have allowed the plaintiff the benefit of the provision made by the Act before the bond can be thought to be discharged by the Act or shown they had been ready to do it.

Mr. *Dee*, Common Serjeant, for the defendants, holds the orphans' debt has discharged this bond by the words and intent of the Act, being for the relief of creditors. And it is discharged. Though it does not appear in the record to have the benefit of the interest provided by that law, [it] states the different interests in the Act; the creditors by bond etc. [are] distinct from orphans.

The 14th paragraph [was] compared with former clauses, and it appears that this debt by bond to the plaintiff is one of the debts for which the interest is provided notwithstanding the first period of time for computing interest is but 1665 and this bond is elder. He holds the money due before 25 December 1655 and 25 December 1683 are within the reason of the Act, though possibly the interest before 25 December 1655 is not within the Act, then the 15th paragraph wholly discharged the debt in words and the party must pursue [. . .] as the be advised [. . .] and, by the custom of London, the party must appear and do the [. . .] Act and acknowledge satisfaction and, when that [is] done, then and not until then he is entitled to the 4 percent and [. . .] be let into the remedy by the Act for interest of 4 percent by the Act.

[Other copies of this report: Georgetown Univ. Law Sch. MS. B88–9, f. 85.]

Lincoln's Inn MS. Misc. 532, f. [109v]

Easter Term 13 Will. III.

The plaintiff [William Thomas], as executor of James Campion, who was executor of Robert Campion, brings an action of debt against the mayor, commonalty, and citizens of London upon a bond under the common seal of the City of London dated the first of August 1643, whereby the said mayor, commonalty, and citizens of London bound themselves and their successors to the said Robert Campion in the penalty of £2500 conditioned for paying to him, his executors, etc. the sum of £1040 on the 3d of February then next following.

The defendants, after oyer of the bond and condition, pleaded that, by a certain Act in Parliament (not saying made) held by prorogation at Westminster, County of Middlesex, 7th day of November 5 Will. & Mar. (not mentioning any title of the Act nor what statute) *inter alia enactitatus fuit authoritate eiusdem Parliamenti quod provisio facta per eundem actum pro solutione interesse, anglice* interest money, *inperpetuo in dicto actu mentionato foret et per eundem actum declaratus fuit fore in plena satisfactione et exoneratione de et pro debitis a praefato majore, communitate, et civibus dictae Civitatis Londinis debita orphanis ac etiam aliorum creditorum et de et ab omni interesse debitae vel fore debit' pro eisdem usque 25 diem Decembris anno domini 1693, quodque [. . .] et quilibet dictorum orphanorum et aliorum creditorum sive eorum respective executorum, administratorum, vel assignatorum secundum usual' consuetud' cognoscerent satisfactionem de respectivis debitis praedictis (solvent' officiar' concep' tal' feod' tantum modo qual' major et curia aldermanorum pro tempore existente dirigerent et appunctuar' non excedendum 13s. 4d. pro qualibet £1000).* And they say that the said mayor, commonalty, and citizens and their successors were and, by that Act, are acquitted and discharged of and from the said debts and interest. And, then, they further show the clause in that Act, fo. 219, that says that that Act should be taken and reputed to be a general act and all judges in all courts are to take notice of it as a public act of Parliament. *Et sic*, the defendants say, *quod ipsi a scripto obligator' praedict' et a denar' superinde debitus acquietatus et exoneratus existunt scil. apud Westmonasterium praedictum, et hoc paratus sunt verificare*, and they pray judgment if the plaintiff against them this action ought to maintain.

To this plea, the plaintiff says that the plea aforesaid and the matter therein contained *provision' praedict' eidem Williamo satisfation' praedict' eodem Williamo libent' recognitur' non adhibit' existens* are insufficient in the law, and so demurs and prays judgment and that the defendants *de debita super scriptum obligatorem praedictum convincantur [?]*. And, for cause of demurrer, he shows that the defendants' plea *non respondet materiis eis in hoc parte object' nec tendit ad exit' unde [. . .] habeatur prout cur' in hac parte ordinavitur.*

The defendants join in demurrer, and say that the matter in law by them pleaded is sufficient to bar the plaintiff, and pray judgment.

The Act in the pleadings mentioned is that of 5 Will. & Mar., ca. 10, entitled an Act for Relief of the Orphans and Other Creditors of the City of London, which, though to be taken as a general law, ought to have been more particularly referred to not as an act referring to the crown but the [. . .] kingdom.

The questions upon the pleadings are these:

First, whether this debt due by bond from the City is a debt to the payment and satisfaction of which the provisions made by that Act do extend;

Secondly, if they do, yet whether that Act absolutely discharges that debt and obliges the plaintiff to acknowledge satisfaction for his debt, though it does not appear in the pleadings that the defendants have or have offered or are ready or willing to let the plaintiff in to the benefit of the provision made by that Act for the payment of the plaintiff's debt; nay, though they shall absolutely refuse to do the same;

Thirdly, whether the plaintiff has any and what remedy to compel the defendants to let him into the benefit of that provision before or after he has acknowledged satisfaction, as aforesaid, and whether he must acknowledge satisfaction of his debt before he can be entitled to the provision by the Act;

Fourthly, whether there be any and what imperfections in the pleadings which may influence the judgment of the court.

It seems plain both by the title, preamble, and purview of the act that the Parliament did intend to have a fund raised and appropriated for the payment of the City's debts to the orphans and other their creditors generally without omitting any; that the same were to be paid and satisfied in this manner; that each orphan's and creditor's principal and interest for the same to the 25th of December 1693 was to be computed; the orphan's interest to the 25th of December 1683 at 5 percent and thence to the 25 December 1693 at 3 percent, fo. 192; the other creditors' interest between the 25th of December 1655 and the 25 December 1693 at £4 percent, fo. 193.

But here rises an objection that, because this Act does not provide for the payment for the payment of interest of any creditor's debt (not being an orphan's) but from the 25th of December 1655, that, therefore, the provision by that Act does not extend to any creditor's debt (not being an orphan's), which grew due or was contracted before the 25th of December 1655 and, by consequence, not to the now plaintiff's debt, which was contracted and secured long before, *viz.* in 1643.

The consequence of which objection must be this, that, if the court shall be of the opinion that the plaintiff's debt is provided for by that Act, then some way or other, he must be let into the benefit provided by the Act. And, then, it must be a question what judgment the court shall give.

But, if the court shall be of the opinion that the plaintiff's debt is not within the provision of the Act, then the judgment must be general that the plaintiff do recover against the Mayor, commonalty, and citizens his debt. And, by such judgment, the real and personal estate of the City in their corporate capacity not otherwise appropriated by the Act must and will be made liable so that hereupon it seems the great question will be between the orphans, who are said to defend this suit, and the City of London.

Now, to answer the objection above and to make it out that all debts from the City before the making of that Act and to the 25th of December 1693 are provided for by it, it is to be considered:

First, the title of the Act is for Relief of the Orphans and Other Creditors of the City of London, which, being general, must include all;

Second, the preamble of the Act that the City was indebted to the orphans and other creditors for principal and interest in more than they were able to pay without assistance, this, also being general, does not exclude any, but enables the payment of all;

Third, the Act provides that towards the raising a fund for paying interest at £4 percent:

First, of the principal and interest due to the orphans etc. to the 25 December 1693;

Second, such interest to be computed from the time it was first payable to the 25 December 1683 at £5 percent and thence to the 25 December 1693 at £3 percent;

Third, and also to pay the like yearly interest of 4 percent of the principal and interest thereof to be computed as aforesaid, due upon bond, bill, or note liable to pay interest between the 25th of December 1655 and the 25th of December 1693 'or any other the creditors of the City on the 25th of December 1693 from the Chamber of the City or from the City' and so proportionally for greater or lesser sums. Here also, no distinction or exclusion is made of any principal debts but only computation of interest;

Fourth, all the City lands and revenues, except the bridge and hospital lands, are by that Act charged from 24 June 1694 for satisfying and paying £8000 *per annum* free from all deductions.

And other particulars in the Act are together with that £8000 *per annum* and £6000 *per annum* more issuing out of the City revenues after the determination of a duty of 6d. per chald or tun are (fo. 204) made the fund and appointed to be employed by the City for the payment.

Either, first, of the 4 percent for the orphans' debts and the interest thereof due or the 25 December 1693, second the like yearly interest of £4 percent and the interest thereof to be computed as aforesaid due at any time between the 25th of December 1655 and 25 December 1693 upon bond, bill, or note liable to pay interest from the City to any person whatsoever or to so much thereof only as the funds shall amount to to satisfy and pay towards the said interest to the said orphans and other the creditors of the City equally in proportion according to their respective interests.

Fo. 205: To be paid at St. Thomas and Midsummer [24 June] or in fourteen days yearly, the first payment to be made at St. Thomas 1699. And then it makes the fund unapplicable to any other uses.

Fo. 206: Enacted that the provision thereby made for that perpetual interest shall be and is thereby declared to be in full satisfaction and discharge of and for the debts due from the City to the orphans and other their said creditors and of and from all interest due or to be due for the same to the 25th of December 1693. And all the said orphans and creditors, their executors, etc., shall according to the usual custom acknowledge satisfaction of their debts, paying the fees settled. And the City and their successors are and shall be hereby acquitted and discharged of and from the same.

207: Then it appoints the Chamberlain to keep books of entry of receipts and payments whereto all persons may have recourse, and it appoints who shall audit the accounts;

208 appoints a forfeiture on the Chamberlain etc. for misemployment.

It directs the Chamberlain and the Common Serjeant on request to give the orphans and creditors, their etc., a note in writing of the principal and interest owing to such orphan and creditor, who have power to assign and so *toties quoties* and to be irrevocable.

210: If the City or any of their officers or persons employed by them misapply the money, the City revenue is to be chargeable.

213: The orphans' debts sold are redeemable in three years.

214: The like in case of solicitor's contracts etc.

219: The Act is to be taken notice of as a general law.

It takes notice that the residue of the City revenue above what is appointed to the orphans and creditors is not sufficient until farther improvements to support the City government and charges.

A provision is made for taking £2000 *per annum* for seven years out of the funds and, if, at the seven years' end, there is a deficiency in paying all that is due to the orphans and creditors during that time, such deficiency is to be charged upon the City revenue.

How could the Parliament think the residue of the City revenue should be applied to pay the City old debts before 1655 when they take notice it would not support the City revenue? And it must not be thought that the Parliament should wholly omit a provision for the payment of old honest debts and provide for later.

14 November 1701.

Serjeant *Jenner*, for the plaintiff: First, whether the bond in question is within the Act; second, whether the defendants' plea, as pleaded, be a bar to the plaintiff's demand.

He holds this bond is not within the Act or the provision of it, because there is no provision for payment of any interest for any debt by bond before the 25th of December 1655 and this bond in in 1643, which is before 1655, and so it is not within the Act and, by consequence [it is] recoverable against the City's estate not subjected to the orphans' fund.

[There is] no provision of interest from 1643 to Christmas 1655, and Parliament could not intend to lose all that interest and the principal too.

The words 'due in 1655' will not help the matter and, because the Parliament provided not payment of the interest, it is an argument they intended the principal money before 1655 should not be paid after that time; the second part if the debt be within that Act, yet the plea as pleaded is not good because [it was] not shown that the plaintiff is let in to the provision of the Act.

Objection: The note was upon request and, therefore, the request was necessary, and that is a condition precedent, and, that request is not laid to be made.

Solution: A provision however made, which are the words in the Act, must be understood to have a benefit by it, and that ought to have been shown by the defendants.

Serjeant *Lovell*, Recorder, for the defendants: The question is only whether the plea is good or not.

Objection: The plaintiff's debt is not within the Act.

Solution: It is a debt within the Act, and that appears by, first, the preamble [which] is general and extensive to all creditors, second, the interest of the principal and of the interest to be the stated debt, third, the computation of interest only and not the principal goes between 25th December 1655 and 25th December 1693, though the principal grew due before.

And this shuts out all interest from precedent debts to the 25th December 1655, but, from thence, lets interest unpaid between 1655 and 1693 into the principal and then £4 percent for principal and that interest is from 25 December 1693.

He observed the particulars of the funds *prout* in the Act, and fo. 206 the provision by this Act in satisfaction of the debts.

It is not necessary to say in the plea that the plaintiff is entitled to the benefit of the provision. The plaintiff is bound to acknowledge satisfaction of his debt in the Orphans Court beforehand, that being the custom of the City

(*Per me* [Edward Ward] if the orphan when he was of age did acknowledge satisfaction of his debt before he had or could receive any money.)

And this Act directs satisfaction to be acknowledged according to custom and, if that is not the custom before this Act, it cannot be so here, and it is a strange custom to [. . .] to acknowledge satisfaction before the debt be paid, *non constat* satisfaction is acknowledged on this record, but he may do it when the plaintiff pleases.

An honest satisfaction is given by the Act. The provision is really 70 or 80 percent for all the orphans and creditors.

4th February 1702.

Mr. Attorney General *Northey*, for the plaintiff, states the Act: first, the title of the Act; second, he takes notice of the City being debtors to orphans and others; third, then follow the enacting clauses *prout* (1) he considers that part which provides for orphans; (2) that which provides for interest for other debts; (3) the funds given; (4) the provision for £2000 *per annum*.

The single question is whether there is any provision for the payment of any debts by bond grown due before the 25th of December 1655. He thinks not.

First, it is notorious that the City in late times had contracted debts in the times of the late wars.

Second, first and, indeed, all effectual application for the Act by and for the orphans who became creditors by the constitution of the City, and it being taken notice of that orphans' money had paid the City's debt, they were to be first served. And it was the settled opinion of all in the obtaining of the Act not to take care of any debt before 1655.

And this question, being started, whether the debts before 1655 should be within the provision and petition, [was] rejected.

But query how the court in this case shall take notice of this [. . .] first provision is distinct for the orphans and their interest provided for under a double consideration of distinct interests.

He understands the provision for debts does not extend to debts before 25 December 1655, because [there is] no provision for payment of interest until that time as to the debtors [?] provision for bond, bill, or note. The word 'due' goes as well to the principal as the interest, and not to the interest only and then, if that be so, the clause must be construed that the provision shall go for all orphans and for such debts as were contracted by the City after the 25th of December 1655.

But query how the word 'due' in that time must be construed to be contracted in that time.

The City practiced this way and intended no further all debts before that time contracted not to be considered in regard they were taken up to be lent by the City to the Parliament upon the public faith or other uses against the then king.

Query how that appears.

Mr. Serjeant *Lovell*, Recorder of London, for the defendants: Whether the City be discharged of all debts, both to orphans and others, before 1693 by this Act subject to the provisions by it. He holds they are and that this debt being before 1655 is discharged and nothing is to be paid him, *quod mirum*.

First, the intent of the Parliament was so, by this fund, for it is in full satisfaction of all debts due from the City to the orphans and the said creditors. Second, this provision is an adequate provision, the 4 percent being worth £100. This is to be in full satisfaction and discharge of all the City debts *prout* the words, fo. 206 of the Act. And he lays stress upon that.

But note the words 'said creditors'.

The City allows finding money. But no interest is due by the custom of London for orphan's money. And what Parliament calls interest for orphans was really but finding money.

The words 'to be computed' cannot be applied to principal; it must be only to interest.

By *Dodd*: It seems to be agreed that the bond is not discharged. He holds it is a subsisting debt at this time from the City and not discharged by the Act.

9 May 1702.

Chief Baron [WARD's] opinion: The plaintiff, as executor to an obligee from the City of London by a bond from the City which bound themselves and their successors in £2500 in 1643 to pay to the plaintiff's testator £1040 in six months after the date, brings an action of debt against the City upon that bond, who plead thereto, and [there is] a demurrer thereupon.

And the main question in this case is whether the Statute of 5 Will. & Mar., in the pleading referred to, has made a provision for the payment of the debt due upon that bond or not.

If it has, then the plaintiff must be content with that provision and not recover upon the bond. And if it has not, then the plaintiff must recover against the City, the defendants, and take such execution and thereby such benefit as the law will allow.

It must be observed and owned that the defendants by their plea do acknowledge and submit that the plaintiff's debt is within the provision by the Act, but the plaintiff does not agree thereto by his demurring to the defendant's plea.

And whether this bond and debt be within the provision of that Act or not depends upon the consideration and construction of that Act.

And notwithstanding what has been offered to the contrary, I am of the opinion that the provision made by that Act of Parliament does extend to this debt in question. In order to make this Act, I shall consider these things:

First, the title of the Act; it is an Act for the Relief of the Orphans and Other Creditors of the City of London; this is general, and must go to all creditors, and the word 'other' makes the orphans to be considered but as creditors;

Second, the preamble of the Act recites the City to be chargeable with the orphans' money from time to time paid into the Chamber of London, and by reason of sundry accidents and public calamities are became indebted to the said orphans and other creditors in more than they are able to satisfy and pay unless assistance be given them for the same. This preamble as fully respects creditors as orphans and considers them both as such, fo. 192.

Third, then the purview of the Act comes for raising a perpetual fund for the payment of £4 percent interest for principal and interest thereof due to any orphan, his etc., unto the 25th of December 1693. The interest is to be computed, first, from the time first payable to Christmas 1683 at 5 percent, second, from thence to Christmas 1693 at 3 percent. Then follows the words upon which the question rises 'and also to pay the like yearly interest of 4 percent for principal and interest thereof to be computed as aforesaid, due upon bond, bill, or note liable to pay interest between Christmas 1655 and Christmas 1693 or any other the creditor or creditors of the City or the executors or assigns of such creditor on Christmas Day 1693 from the City or Chamber. And by the purview of this Act, all the City lands and revenues, except the bridge and hospital lands, are by that Act charged.

Now, upon the frame and contexture of this whole Act, I cannot conceive, at least it does not appear to me, that it was the Parliament's intention or meaning to shut out all principal debts upon bond from the City borrowed and secured before the 25th of December 1655.

First, the Act, neither in the title nor preamble, looks towards it, but both speak of creditors generally without distinction of time when the debts were contracted.

Second, I cannot but think that the Parliament intended to set the City free from all orphans and other creditors by the provision they made by the Act. And, if there had been any debts they were liable to and for which no provision was made, they would have expressed it more fully and clearly than to leave it upon a doubtful construction subsisting wholly upon an imagination that, because there is not provision made for the interest of debts contracted before 1655, though then and after subsisting debts, that, therefore, the principal must be lost, for there is no doubt that this debt in question was a just and legal demand against the City which they could not gainsay to pay had they been able. Now this Act comes to enable the City to pay their debts.

Third, if this Act and provision should not extend to this debt, then, in effect, it must be lost and that by the means of the Parliament who have by this Act taken away the estates which would be liable to the satisfaction of that debt, and the Act takes notice, fo. 219, that the remainder of the City revenue above the payment to the orphans and creditors is not sufficient to defray the charges of the government.

Now, can it be reasonably thought that the Parliament that took notice of the inability of the City to pay their debts without assistance should give them an assistance to pay some only and to leave others unpaid and so deliver them up to be torn in pieces by suits and to deprive the City of a support for their government, which is recited to be already not sufficient, or, in justice, to deprive the creditors before 1655 of the fruit and benefit of the law upon recoveries upon their bonds by taking away the estates and applying them to other uses?

Fourth, this Act is an act for relief and therefore liberally to be expounded, especially when another construction seems not only harsh but very injurious and prejudicial to creditors, who are favorites in the law.

Fifth, the great argument used is this debt or any other before Christmas 1655 is not provided for by the Act, because there is no provision made for the payment of any interest until or before Christmas 1655 and that is enforced by the words 'to be computed as aforesaid'.

Now, though that be true that there is no provision for the payment of interest before Christmas 1655, that does not make it but that the principal were due upon bond between the 25 of December 1655 and 25 of December 1693 and the word 'computed' can go only to the interest and possibly the Parliament might discharge the precedent interest but not the principal. There are no words or sense for that.

Again, fo. 193, there are these additional words [. . .] to what went before relating to debts between Christmas 1655 and Christmas 1693 or any other the creditor or creditors of the City or the executors or assigns of such creditors on the 25th of December 1693 from the Chamber or City and so proportionably for any greater or lesser sums.

Now this general clause which seems to make that provision extend to all sums and debts due or payable from the City Christmas 1693 without any respect or limitation of time as to the commencement or time of contracting such debt is not, in my apprehension, to be slighted but, by such general words, the Parliament seemed to signify their mind and intent that the provision by that Act should extend to the payment and satisfaction of all the debts which the City owed the 25th of December 1693.

Objection first: That, if the City debts before 1655 be let in, it will defeat the provision made by the Act for the orphans and other creditors after Christmas 1655, there being many debts before [. . .], which the Parliament respected not.

Solution first: That does not appear to this court nor that there are any other debts besides this £2500 bond before 1655. But, if it did, it seems the Parliament made no distinction between them before and those after Christmas 1655 except only in the computation of interest before 1655. And fo. 205; it is expressed that the orphans and creditors are to come in proportionably in that fund. There is no distinction there between orphans and creditors, nor is there in the reason of the thing. *Ubi lex non distinguit nec nos distinguere debemus.*

Objection second: That the Parliament rejected the petition of the creditors whose debts were before 1655 as not thinking them well contracted nor upon just cause. And much more has been urged of that nature, which was matter of fact before the committees etc. or the houses of Parliament before the Act passed.

Solution: Nothing of that can be taken notice of here. We must not take upon us to know mental intentions; the Parliament have declared their meaning by their words in the Act, and, upon those words, we must put a legal construction, such as judges ought and have used to do.

My sense and understanding leads me to think by what the Parliament have expressed by their words and by that frame and contexture of the whole Act that they intended that the provision made by that Act should go to all principal debts, at least before 1655 and to all principal debts and interest for them contracted after Christmas 1655 and to the interest of the principal debts incurred after Christmas 1655 for the principal moneys secured before that time.

And that I delivered as my judgment.

But the other three barons were of an opinion that this debt, being contracted and secured before 1655, was not within the provision of the new Act, nor was discharged, but remained a debt demandable against the City. And so they gave judgment for the plaintiff.

9 May 1702.

Baron Bury opens the case at large. The question is whether this be a bond or debt within the provision of the Act or not. If it be, then this bond and debt is discharged by the Act; otherwise, it is in force and suable against the City. He lays it down that the clause of discharge extends only to those debts for which provision is made by the Act. And he holds this is not a debt within the provision of the Act, first, because no provision is made by that Act for the interest of any debt before Christmas 1655. Parliament did not reject interest for the long standing, but rather left it and the principal out of the Act that a remedy might be had against the City for the whole.

The clause that makes the provision is of two parts, first, for the orphans, secondly, for the creditors. And the creditors' clause is different from the orphans'. He holds the word 'due' relates to the principal and interest. [. . .] due more applicable to interest but instead of due became better [?].

Second, the creditors' clause is wholly tied up to debts after Christmas 1655. Otherwise, the Parliament would have used [. . .] words.

And, therefore, he concludes for the plaintiff, that he must recover against the City and this is not a debt within that Act.

Baron Tracy was of the same opinion for the same reasons. The doubt rises upon the provision for creditors. He considers the objections, title, preamble, and purview; 'other creditors' do not include all (*quod quaere*).

Objection: What was not due before was due between the times.

Solution: That is not so.

Objection: Debts before 1655 are not provided for.

Solution: It was said at the bar the bonds before 1655 were not due or good. Then there is no judgment for them.

(But query how the court may take notice of what was rejected by Parliament.)

Parliament intended 4 percent for the orphans, and that must be secured, which will not be if all creditors came in.

(Query how that appears.)

Baron Hatsell was of the same opinion for these reasons: first, this bond carries interest from 1643; second, the Act of Parliament was not pleaded truly, for the creditors must be said creditors, but that [. . .]; third, it is not provided for by the Act, 'other creditors' is not all; fourth, from what time interest is payable for debts before Christmas 1655, and, therefore, because there was no provision for such interest, therefore, it not within the Act.

So, they three conclude for the plaintiff to have judgment against the City, not being a debt within the provision of the Act, but it must be satisfied some other way.

Note this judgment given by the three barons against my opinion was reversed upon [a writ of] error by the opinion of the two justices, Tuesday, 9 February 1702, upon the point that the bond was within the provision of the Act to be paid as other of the City debts by bond were, though it was entered into before 1655, but the computation of interest was to commence only from 1655. And, therefore, the City was discharged of that debt, and the plaintiff to be let in with the City's other creditors and the orphans.

[Other copies of this report: Georgetown Univ. Law Sch. MS. B88–9, f. 88v.]

Harvard Law Sch. MS. 1052, p. 72, pl. 187

4 July, Trinity term 13 Will. III, 1701.

A statute was pleaded *in Parliamento tento* such a day.

Chief Baron Ward: The pleading is naught, for it should have been either *in Parliamento inchoato et tento* such a day or *in sessione Parliamenti tento per prorogationem* such a day.

202

Camell v. Clavering

(Ex. 1701–1702)

An action in ejectment lies for small tithes if they are pleaded with particularity.

Lincoln's Inn MS. Misc. 532, f. [121v]

25 November. Ejectment for small tithes.

Chief Baron [Ward] delivers it [the opinion of the court] at the request of the other barons, being all of one opinion.

The questions that have been made in this case have been three:

First, whether a [writ of] *ejectione firmae* lies of small tithes, *viz.* wool, flax, hemp, lambs, and calves, being mentioned particularly in such two vills;

Second, whether the adding after them *et omnes alias decimas minutas quascunque* in the same two vills makes the declaration and title uncertain so that the plaintiff cannot have any judgment;

Third, whether the verdict which finds the defendant guilty as to the tithes in Kiloe, being one of the two vills and not saying what those tithes are, whether any of those particularly enumerated and specified in the declaration or such as may fall under the general term of 'all other small tithes' makes the matter so uncertain as that the plaintiff cannot have judgment for any of the small tithes in Kiloe.

First, we are of opinion that an [action of] ejectment well lies for all sorts of tithes, as well great as small, being distinguished and particularized under their proper names, kinds, and certainties for these reasons: first, they are things capable of being demised and, by consequence of the lessee's being ousted of them, as well as of anything else; second, by parity of reason with other things whereof ejectments are adjudged to lie, as (1) of a pasture for an ox, Register 227; Plo. 228; (2) of a bulliary of salts, 2 Cro. 150; Sidderfin 161; (3) of a coal mine, and the like, which are frequent in the books.[1]

Third, by express words of an act of Parliament and by authorities of law in point: first, the Statute of 32 Hen. VIII, ca. 7, gives a like remedy for recovery of possession of tithes, great and small, as for lands, and there is no distinction whether in gross or part of a rectory or belonging to a chapel; second, Henry Harper's Case, 11 rep. 25, and the same case is reported by Moor, fo. 837, and the cases in Dyer.[2] And, indeed, it is the constant experience.

---

[1] *Willion v. Berkley* (1562), 1 Plowden 223, 75 E.R. 339; *Comyn v. Kyneto* (1607), Croke Jac. 150, 161, 79 E.R. 131, 141; *Smith v. Barrett* (1663), 1 Siderfin 161, 82 E.R. 1032.

[2] Stat. 32 Hen. VIII, c. 7 (*SR*, III, 751–752); *Harpur's Case* (1614), 11 Coke Rep. 23, 77 E.R. 1173, also *sub nom. Worrall v. Harper*, Moore K.B. 837, 72 E.R. 938, 1 Rolle

But, by those and other the books and authorities, the natures and kinds of the tithes must be set forth, for it will not lie by the general term *de omnibus decimis* in Dale and, upon that exception taken by Lord Coke in Harpur's Case, for that purpose and for that reason, it was ruled bad, being too general. And how he says it ought to have been expressed *de omnibus decimis garbarum, feni, lane, agnellorum* or other certainty of the nature etc., which shows by the way that an *ejectione firmae* lies *de decimis lanae et agnellorum*. And, if of them, why not of all other small tithes?

Nay, the Statute 32 Hen. VIII, ca. 7, gives the remedy at law for oblations also, carrying them all along with tithes and though the subsequent Statute of 2 & 3 Edw. VI extends a remedy for them in the ecclesiastical court and for tithes also, yet that Act, being affirmative, takes not away the remedy by the first, which is where the title, not the duty, is in question.[1]

Fourth, as to the uncertainty, it had been better to have mentioned the tithes in each of the two vills, laying them distinctly, but we think it is well as it is laid for the wool, flax, hemp, lambs, and calves, which are particularized. But it is not good for any other small tithes in either of the two vills, none being particularly expressed, for it seems clear that the enumerated tithes go to both the vills, and so do the general words of all other small tithes too. And, though the plaintiff cannot recover for them not expressed, yet that will not vitiate what is certain and legal in the declaration. *Utile per inutile non vitiatur.*

Fifth, as to the verdict, it finds for the plaintiff as to all the tithes in Kiloe, not saying what they are.

Now, we are of the opinion it must be understood that this verdict finds for all tithes of wool, flax, hemp, lambs, and calves and all other small tithes in Kiloe, for it is all tithes in each vill without restraint as to the person or other restriction whatsoever. And, if it be so, then here is a verdict for those that are expressly mentioned and also for the other small tithes in Kiloe.

And the first being good, why should the uncertainty of the last make the first that are good void? *Utile per inutile non vitiatur*, as before.

It is said it does not appear that there are any of the enumerated tithes that lie in Kiloe but it may be that only the other small tithes not enumerated lie there.

But that is a harsh construction and not to be intended in this case, for it must be understood that the plaintiff made out a title as well to the enumerated as the other small tithes in Kiloe. And, if the plaintiff take execution of the enumerated tithes in Kiloe, it is no more than what the jury have found, and he takes execution at his peril.

Vide Yelverton, the last case, Deuce and Deuce,[2] ejectment for eight acres of land, four of meadow, four of pasture in B. and C. in the County of Kent. The

---

Rep. 65, 81 E.R. 331.

[1] Stat. 2 & 3 Edw. VI, c. 13 (*SR*, IV, 55–58).

[2] *Deuce v. Deuce* (1613), Yelverton 228, 80 E.R. 149.

jury finds the defendant guilty as to a third part of four acres and not guilty for the residue. [It was] moved in arrest [of judgment] for the uncertainty for that *non constat* in which of the vills that third part lay. *Sed non allocatur per curiam* for it shall be intended that each acre of land named in the declaration lies in both vills, for so much is presumed by the declaration and by the [writ of] *venire facias* of both vills.

Quod nota, per totam curiam. And judgment [was given] accordingly.

So, here, let the plaintiff take his judgment and enter it up as his case will warrant. And that was the award of the court. I [Edward Ward] delivered my opinion, [that] of the whole court.

[Other copies of this report: Georgetown Univ. Law Sch. MS. B88–9, f. 100.]

Dodd 195

[In an action] in the office of pleas in ejectment, the plaintiff declares that William Chatts by indenture etc. did demise unto him *lana, lini, canibi, agnorum, et vitulorum et omnes alias decimas minutas quasqunque annuatim crescendum, provenienendum, seu renovandum in A. et B. in parochia de C.* And upon [a plea of] not guilty, the jury found as to the tithes in A. *parcella decimarum in exitu mentionatur* that the defendant is guilty [of] damages 1s. [and] costs 40d. and as to the rest that the defendant is not guilty. And upon this, it was moved in arrest of judgment:

First, that ejectment does not lie for small tithes at all;

Second, that if it lie for *lini, canibi etc.*, yet it is nought for *omnes alias decimas* without mentioning them;

Third, entire damages are given, and so [it is] bad;

Fourth, the release of them will not help and take judgment for the *lini, canibi* for perhaps those arose all in B., for which the defendant is found not guilty and the *omnes alias decimas* were in A., of which the defendant is found guilty.

To which, it was answered and resolved upon argument, by the court:

First, that an ejectment does lie of all manner of small tithes if particularized. So [it was held] in Harper's Case;[1]

Second, that the plaintiff may release his damages and take his judgment for the tithes particularized, and it will be good;

Third, it shall be intended that his *lana, lini, canibi etc.* did arise in both vills and that the *omnes alias decimas* goes to both also.

11 Rep. 25; Dyer 84; 32 Hen. VIII, ch. 7, sect. 7; Cr. Car. 301; it lies for a bulliary of salt, Cr. Jac. yet last case; 3 Cr., Pulman's Case, was cited; Dy. 34,

[1] *Harpur's Case* (1614), 11 Coke Rep. 23, 77 E.R. 1173, also *sub nom. Worrall v. Harper*, Moore K.B. 837, 72 E.R. 938, 1 Rolle Rep. 65, 81 E.R. 331.

for the defendant, 2 Cr. 146; 3 Keble 364; Yelv. 143; Hard. 57; Dy. 116; 15 Hen. VII, 8; Sty. 30, 364.[1]

2 Lord Raymond 789, 92 E.R. 26, Dodd 352

An [an action of] ejectment was brought in the Exchequer *de minutis decimis*. And upon not guilty pleaded, [there was a] verdict for the plaintiff. And Mr. *Chesshyre* about five or six years ago moved in arrest of judgment that an ejectment would not lie for small tithes:

First, because eggs are small tithes and it is absurd to say that an ejectment would lie of an egg.

Second, because the sheriff does not know of what he is to deliver possession upon a [writ of] *habere facias possessionem*.

But it was not allowed because it has been adjudged that an ejectment lies of wool, being tithe, and by the same reason for an egg. And, therefore, by all the barons, judgment was given for the plaintiff.

11 Co. 25.[2]

Ex relatione magistri Chesshyre.

203

Anderson, qui tam v. Selby

(Ex. 1701)

It lies in the sound discretion of the court to set aside a judgment and to grant a new trial where the defendant's witnesses failed to appear at the trial.

Lincoln's Inn MS. Misc. 532, f. [107v]

Two informations were prosecuted distinctly against the defendants [Selby and Alder] for loading wool upon horses to be carried out of England into Scotland, which gives a forfeiture of 3s. in the pound against the offenders, grounded upon the statutes 12 and 14 Car. II.[3] The fact of both cases arose and was done in Northumberland within seven or eight miles of Scotland. But the law allows the

---

[1] *Harpur's Case*, *ut supra*; *Dean of Bristol v. Clerke* (1553), 1 Dyer 83, 73 E.R. 181; Stat. 32 Hen. VIII, c. 7 (*SR*, III, 751–752); *Baldwin v. Wine* (1633), Croke Car. 301, 79 E.R. 863, also W. Jones 321, 82 E.R. 170; *Molineux v. Molineux* (1607), Croke Jac. 144, 145, 79 E.R. 126, 128; *Aston v. Lyder* (1674), 3 Keble 364, 84 E.R. 768; *Challenor v. Thomas* (1608), Yelverton 143, 80 E.R. 96, also 1 Brownlow & Goldesborough 142, 123 E.R. 718; *Hancock v. Price* (1656), Hardres 57, 145 E.R. 379; *Ibgrave v. Lee* (1556), 2 Dyer 116, 73 E.R. 256; YB Trin. 15 Hen. VII, f. 8, pl. 1 (1500); *Anonymous* (1647), Style 30, 82 E.R. 506; *Ashworth v. Stanley* (1652), Style 364, 82 E.R. 780.

[2] *Harpur's Case* (1614), *ut supra*.

[3] Stat. 12 Car. II, c. 18 (*SR*, V, 246–250); Stat. 14 Car. II, c. 18 (*SR*, V, 410–412).

informations to be laid where the informer pleases. And they were brought and tried in Middlesex at the sitting after last term, being 12 July 1701.

And, upon the trials, one James Hunter was the only witness that was produced for the informers, and he positively swore the loading and carrying away of the wool in Northumberland into Scotland upon the defendant's horses respectively and with their privity and direction and in their presence. And he named others that were there and that Mr. Selby's offense was in April 1700 and Alder's offense was 11 September 1700.

And no defense being made by either of the defendants, there were verdicts against the defendants, *viz.* against Mr. Selby, a gentleman of good estate of £800 *per annum* and a justice of the peace, for 4672 pounds weight of wool and against Alder for 1168 pounds of wool.

And now, it was moved by Mr. *Dodd* and others, of counsel with the defendants, that there might be a new trial in each cause for these reasons:

First, that, though there was in strictness above ten days notice of the trial, which is the rule in the two short terms, yet by reason of the distance of the place, 250 miles off, it was impossible for the defendants to get up their witnesses. And, though they did move the court to put off the trials, yet the affidavits not being full and naming none as witnesses, the court did not think fit to put them off and the affidavit that did name the witnesses came not until the last day of term and so too late, so that they did not nor could make any defense at the trials.

Secondly, the penalties are too great to be forfeited upon trials behind the defendants' backs and upon the single evidence of one man, against whose credit and the credibility of his evidence and testimony, they produced divers affidavits and also for the defendants' innocence.

But the new trials were vehemently opposed by *Northey* and *Hawles*, Attorney General and Solicitor General, and others:

First, because the court was moved and refused to put off the trials and that justly, because it did not appear there were any evidences for the defendants;

Secondly, because the defendants' counsel and agents attended the trials and took notes of the king's evidence and it would be of dangerous consequence to grant new trials after the king's evidence is discovered;

Thirdly, because it was the defendants' own fault why they had not their witnesses, having legal notice, and it does not appear by any of the affidavits that the defendants had used diligence to get their witnesses and were frustrated;

Fourthly, because the affidavits that speak to the merits of the case, *viz.* the defendants' innocence and impeachment of the credit of the king's witnesses or contradicting his testimony are not to be regarded at this time nor ought by law to be any evidence for a new trial.

Baron BURY was for a new trial.

Baron TRACY proposing that the defendants might indict the king's witness of perjury if they pleased and, if he was convicted, there would be reason to stay the entry of any judgment, whereto Mr. Attorney General [*Northey*], for the king, and the defendants' counsel agreeing, it was so ordered by consent and an information to be brought in this court forthwith, which was done accordingly. And the king's witnesses [were] found guilty of perjury.

In case that had not been so consented to, I [Edward Ward] should have been for a new trial upon payment of costs as this case was, for, though the defendants in strictness had notice of the trial and though it was reasonable for the court not to put off the trial for want of sufficient affidavits at that time, yet, when it now appears the defendants could not get their witnesses nor make any defense, it is too hard to fix so great penalties upon them without being heard.

Note, afterwards, upon Tuesday the 17th of February 1701[/02], there were two informations of perjury tried before me [Edward Ward] at the *nisi prius* [sittings] at Westminster against James Hunter, the only witness for the king in the two former trials. And he was acquitted in both by two special juries returned.

[Other copies of this report: Georgetown Univ. Law Sch. MS. B88–9, f. 85v.]

204

Pacy v. Lady Rich

(Ex. 1701)

It lies in the sound discretion of the court to allow a defendant to plead de novo.

Lincoln's Inn MS. Misc. 532, f. [120v]

[There was] a debt in aid for Pacy, and, upon an inquisition, [it was] found Sir Robert Rich, deceased, at the time of his death, was indebted to Pacy, receiver general of taxes in Suffolk, in £800, and that debt was seized. And there was a *scire facias* against the defendant as administratrix.

And she pleads that Sir Robert, at the time of his death, was bound to the king by bond of £34,000, that debt not satisfied.

Pending that plea, the king was satisfied all that was due, which, *puis darrein continuance*, was replied by the Attorney General.

And now, the defendant prays she may plead *de novo* a *super* in the Pipe [Office] and an imprest debt upon Sir Robert.

It was granted by the court as reasonable, because the former plea was good and is avoided by the act of the king.

The parties agreed [out of court].

[Other copies of this report: Georgetown Univ. Law Sch. MS. B88–9, f. 99, pl. 1.]

205

Kemish v. Howells

(Ex. 1702)

A verdict cannot cure a pleading that is faulty because insufficient and defective.

Lincoln's Inn MS. Misc. 532, f. [123v]

Glamorgan.

The plaintiff [Sir Charles Keamish] brings an action of debt against the defendant [George Howells] for £50 grounded upon the Act of Parliament for the 2s. aid, 11 & 12 Will. III, fo. 139–40,[1] which provides that no attorney etc. or any receiver general or collector of any aid granted to His Majesty shall be capable of acting as a commissioner in the execution of that Act. And, if any person intended by that Act to be disabled for any of the causes aforesaid shall nevertheless presume to act as a commissioner in the execution of that Act or any of the powers therein contained, every such person for such offense shall forfeit £50 to be recovered by any person or persons that will inform or sue for the same in any court of record at Westminster by an action of debt etc.

The plaintiff declared that the defendant, the 13th of May 1700 did act as a commissioner of the tax by that Act in the County of Glamorgan being nominated a commissioner by that Act and the defendant, when he so acted and before being receiver general of divers acts before granted to the king, *contra formam statuti*.

Nil debet [was] pleaded. And [there was a] verdict for the plaintiff. A new trial was prayed, because the defendant had not at the trial his *quietus* for the former years, whereof he was receiver, they being then at his house distant from Hereford.

But that was not allowed because, in truth, the defendant had not his *quietus* for 1699, when he was receiver nor since similar to former records of former aids disabled to act as commissioners in this Act in case they have not a *quietus* for such former aids but, if he had *quietus*es, that such former receivers *qua* such are not disabled to act as commissioners in this Act after they have their *quietus*es for all precedent aids for which they were receivers. Otherwise, all precedent receivers and collectors of any precedent aids will stand perpetually disabled from acting about the aid granted by the Act in question and in all future aids if that clause be continued.

Afterwards, a motion was made in my [Edward Ward's] absence in arrest of judgment, and time was given to speak to it until next term. Query the objections.

---

[1] Stat. 11 Will. III, c. 2 (*SR*, VII, 545–581).

Note, in truth, the defendant had passed his account for the years in question, and had it declared before the Cursitor Baron, but it lay in the King's Remembrancer's Office and gone no farther. And all this was before he acted as commissioner for the last tax, for which the action was brought.

[Other copies of this report: Georgetown Univ. Law Sch. MS. B88–9, f. 102.]

Lincoln's Inn MS. Misc. 532, f. [148]

Sir Charles Keymish, baronet, plaintiff; George Howell, esq., defendant. Office of Pleas, Exchequer, entered Hilary [term] 12 Will. III.

In an action of debt grounded upon the Statute of 11 & 12 Will. III, ca. 2, for granting an aid [. . .] of the forfeited estates in Ireland and by a land [. . .] whereby (fo. 139), it is provided that no attorney, solicitor, or person practicing as such or any receiver general or collector or any aid granted to His Majesty shall be capable of acting as a [. . .] in the execution of that Act. And, then (fo. 140), it is enacted that, if any person intended by that Act to be [. . .] for any of the causes aforesaid shall nevertheless [. . .] to act as a commissioner in the execution of that Act [. . .] the powers therein contained every such [. . .] for such offense shall forfeit the sum of £50 [. . .] person or persons that will inform or sue for the [. . .] to be recovered in any of His Majesty's courts of record by action of debt or upon the case, bill, suit, or information. And the plaintiff declares in [an action of] debt for £50 [. . .] against the defendant, for that the defendant, the 13th of May [. . .] Will. III at Neath in Glamorganshire, did act as [. . .] for the said County of Glamorgan *in executionem [. . .] Actus Parliamenti incepti apud Westmonasterium [. . .] die Augusti anno Domini 1698, 10 Will. III, et [. . .] continuati per diversas prorogationes et adjornamenta usque ad 16tum diem Novembris anno Domini* [. . .] entitled an Act (setting forth the title of [. . .] save the word 'sale' was written 'saile') [. . .] the defendant *existen' nominatus unus commissionem [. . .] Actus praedictus et dicto tempore quo agebat'* commissisoner in the execution of that Act and before [. . .] receiver general *diversarum taxationum, anglice* [. . .] before that time granted to the king *contra formam statuti actus praedicti et quod actio accrevit* to the plaintiff for [. . .] of £50 against the defendant according to the form and [. . .] of the said Act.

The defendant pleads *nil debet.* And, upon a trial at the Assizes for the County of [*blank*] there was a verdict for the plaintiff.

And it was the last term, moved in arrest of judgment and appointed to be argued on both sides this term, which was done accordingly by *Grove, Dodd, Price*, and *Lechmere*, for the defendant, and *Harcourt, Bannister, Bridges*, and *Lloyd*, for the plaintiff.

And the judgment was arrested by the opinion of the whole court for these reasons and causes:

First, because the plaintiff has mistaken in his declaration the commencement of the Parliament, and there is no such act as is there mentioned, for the

Parliament that made that Act was summoned [. . .] to meet the 24th of August but that meeting was [by a] writ of adjournment put off to the 27th of September and thence by a like writ to the 27th of October, thence by a like writ to the 29th of November and [. . .] by a like writ to the 6th of December in the same year, by which several writs under the great seal, His Majesty being then in Holland, directed to the prelates, nobles, and peers of the realm and to the knights, citizens, and burgesses chosen to the Parliament to [. . .] at Westminster the 24th of August it is [. . .] that the king, the said Parliament to the 27th of September *duxit prorogandum* and thereby discharged their attendance [. . .] that day but commanded their appearance the 27th of September and so each successive writ reciting the former enjoined the same thing. And, upon the 6th of December, the king, lords, and commons met at Westminster, and the king opened the Parliament by a speech. And then, not until then, the Parliament, in judgment of law began, all which proceedings appear upon record in the Lords' House and whereof the judges take notice, as they do of the commencement and determination of [. . .] Parliament. And this way of adjourning the meeting of Parliament is no new thing, but has been frequently used. In all times, the Parliament is not said in judgment of law to commence until that day to which the last adjournment is made and when the king or queen, either in person or by commission, open the Parliament. And for that purpose, Dyer 203 and 4 Inst., fo. 7, are in point and so is Hetly 119.[1] And it is a principle of our law and constitution that the king, lords, commons make the Parliament and that there can be no Parliament begun unless the king be there in person or a representation by a commission under the great seal.

And *Lechmere* cited these precedents of Parliament so continued 5 Eliz. [. . .] of a precedent date to the [. . .] the summons returnable 11 January and by writ adjourned to the 12th, the like in 28 Eliz. from the 15th to the 27th of October and after to the 29th and then by commission prorogued to a further day and a memorandum in the margin of the roll that the 29th of October was the first day of Parliament; the like adjournment 21 Jac. I from the 12th to the 19th of February; and three other instances in that reign; and 1 Anderson 294,[2] warrants [. . .] upon the occasion of Englesfield's attainder which was confirmed by Parliament.

[. . .] that though the Act in the declaration is a public [. . .] yet when misrecited, it is fatal. Partridge's Case, Plowd., f. 84.[3]

And for these reasons and authorities, the whole court was of the opinion that the Parliament did not in the judgment of the law begin until the 6th of December and so the declaration [is] mistaken [. . .] that it is insensible to say an

[1] *Walgrave's Case* (1561), 2 Dyer 203, 73 E.R. 448; E. Coke, *Fourth Institute* (1644), p. 7; *Jenkin's Case* (1628), Hetley 119, 124 E.R. 389.

[2] *Englefield's Case*, 1 Anderson 294, 123 E.R. 480.

[3] *Partridge v. Strange* (1553), 1 Plowden 77, 75 E.R. 123, also 1 Dyer 74, 73 E.R. 159.

act of Parliament [. . .] at such a day. It ought to have said the Act was made at a Parliament begun such a day, for as [. . .] it is uncertain whether it was the Act or the Parliament begun such a day.

[. . .] because it is not shown what act the defendant did [. . .] which ought to have been set forth, being [. . .]able and the defendant disabled to defend himself at [. . .] trial not knowing with what he shall be charged.

The declaration has not brought the defendant to [. . .] offender against that Act, for though it is said that the [. . .] acted as a commissioner for the County of Glamorgan, yet [. . .] not said that he was named a commissioner for that county.

[. . .] that it is no good pleading to say by [. . .] prorogation and adjournment, for every act of Parliament when pleaded must be pleaded to be made *ad Parliamentum inchoatum et tentum* such a day or *ad [. . .] Parliamentum tentum per prorogationem* such a day.

It ought to have been shown what the aids [. . .] were whereof he was the receiver, which being issuable, ought particularly to have been set forth.

There were other lesser faults found in the declaration [. . .] for those above and, principally, for the first, judgment was arrested, the verdict not curing [. . .] and some other of the faults above. Nor did the plaintiff's counsel offer anything material to answer those exceptions.

And so judgment was given by the court *quod querens nil capit per billam.*

[Other copies of this report: Georgetown Univ. Law Sch. MS. B88–9, f. 124.]

206

Attorney General v. Mainwaring
Attorney General v. Biddulph

(Ex. 1702)

In this case, the court found that the rejoinder was not a departure in pleading.

Lincoln's Inn MS. Misc. 532, f. [132v]

In a *scire facias* upon a bond to the king wherein the case is this. 9 July 1698, Morgan Whitley, Esq., and the such defendant, Sir John Mainwaring, and several others became bound to the king in £19,000 with conditions reciting that the said Whitley was appointed to be a receiver general within the County of Chester and the City and County of the City of Chester and of several counties by name in Wales of the moneys granted to His Majesty by an Act of Parliament[1] entitled An Act for Granting to His Majesty the sum of £1,484,015 1s. 11d. 3qu. for disbanding forces, paying seamen, and other uses therein mentioned, that, if

[1] Stat. 10 Will. III, c. 1 (*SR*, VII, 452–453).

the said Whitley, his heirs, executors, and administrators shall truly satisfy, content, and pay or cause to be satisfied, contented, or paid to the use of the king's Majesty, his heirs, or successors into His Majesty's Receipt of the Exchequer at Westminster at the several days and years limited and appointed in and by the said Act of Parliament all such sums of money which he or his deputy or deputies or any other by his appointment shall at any time collect or receive by virtue of the power to him granted as aforesaid and also, if he, the said Whitley, his heirs, etc., from time to time as often as he or they shall be required by the Lords Commissioners of the Treasury for the time being or any three or more of them or by the Lord Treasurer of England for the time being, Chancellor, or Under Treasurer of the Exchequer for the time being or by such person or persons who are or shall be appointed by the Commissioners of the Treasury, Treasurer, Chancellor, or Under Treasurer of the Exchequer for the time being to have an inspection and care of that affair or any of them shall make up and render a true and just account of all moneys which the said Whitley, his deputies, or any other by his appointment, shall at any time have collected or received by virtue of the power granted to him as aforesaid and of the execution of the said office of receiver general for the said counties and of all moneys, as well collected as uncollected and in arrear, of every payment of the said rates, duties, and assessments, and, if he, his heirs, etc. on or before the 20th of May 1699 shall enter into and make a true and faithful account to the king, his heirs, etc. of all such moneys as Whitley, his deputies, or any other by his appointment shall have collected or received or lawfully might have collected or received by virtue of his said office and shall finish the same account before the last day of Trinity term then next following and all the money so due to the king upon the determination of that account shall pay to the king or otherwise sufficiently discharge himself thereof, then the bond to be void; otherwise, remain in force.

The defendant, after *oyer* of the bond and condition, pleads that Whitley has well and truly observed, performed, fulfilled, and paid all and singular the articles, clauses, agreements, orders, rules, directions, payments, and sums of money which, on his part, ought to be observed, performed, fulfilled, and paid according to the condition of the bond, *viz.* at St. Margaret's, Westminster, in the County of Middlesex and so prays judgment and the bond to be delivered up and cancelled.

The Attorney General replies that, by virtue of that Act of Parliament, great sums of money were granted and made payable to the king in and upon the said several counties and, *inter alia*, in and upon the County of Chester £20,261 4s. 2d., which Whitley and his deputies or others appointed by him had received or might and ought to have received by virtue of his said office and whereof he ought to have made a faithful account to the king and to have entered upon it at or before the 20th of May 1699 and to have finished it by the end of Trinity term following according to the said condition which account he did not enter into and perfect according to the said condition, and, therefore, he prays execution for the £19,000 upon the bond.

The defendant rejoins that neither Whitley or any of his deputies or any other by him appointed did or ought or lawfully might receive by virtue of his office the said £20,261 4s. 2d. in and by the said Act charged upon the said County of Chester or any other sum by that Act charged upon the said County of Chester over and besides the sum of £17,301 15s. 3d., which he paid to the king at the receipt of the Exchequer upon the 20th of May 1699, according to the condition.

(Note he does not plead payment *prout patet recordum.*)

And [he rejoins] that said Whitley, upon the said 20th of May 1699 and divers other times before that, offered to enter into, render, and make to the king a true and faithful account of all moneys which he or any of his deputies or others by him appointed did or could receive by virtue of his said office, but there was no person duly appointed or authorized nor yet are auditors to take that account and that the said Whitley always was and still is ready to enter into and make the said account to the king and to finish it according to the condition of the bond. *Et hoc paratus est verificare etc.*

(Note no place was laid where these things were offered to be done.)

To this rejoinder, the Attorney General demurs generally. And the defendant joins.

The like *scire facias*, pleadings, and demurrer [were filed] between the Attorney General and Sir Michael Biddulph, another obligor in the same bond.

3 February 1701[/02].

Northey, Attorney General, assigns for cause of demurrer that the defendant's rejoinder is a departure, for when, by his plea, he says he has performed the condition of the bond generally, which is that he has done all the particular things therein mentioned, among which one is that he has accounted and paid *prout* the condition, which Mr. Attorney General replies he has not done, it lies not in the defendant's mouth to say afterwards he was ready to account, but there was no auditor to take it, which is a plain departure.

Dodd, the defendant's counsel, at first insisted the *scire facias* was not good, because it is set forth therein that, three being bound, they did not pay, and does not say that none of them paid.

But that the court held was well enough in the *scire facias* and, if either or any of them paid, it might have been pleaded. But payment is not the point, for, after *oyer* of the condition, they severally plead performance and the allegation in the *scire facias* of not paying is but inducement and not the foundation of the suit but to bring in the defendants to say what they can why the king should not have execution for the penalty of the bond.

Another exception was taken that, upon *oyer* prayed by the defendant of the bond, the same is set forth to be a bond by three jointly and severally. And the conclusion is *sub sigillo meo sigillatus*, which makes it uncertain, being in the singular number, which of the obligor's seal it was.

But, as to that, it was said by the court that that was no fault appearing in the *scire facias*, but it arose upon the *oyer*, and the defendant ought to have taken what advantage he could of it in pleading. But he has not said anything to it, for, if he thought fit, he might have pleaded *non est factum*, but, pleading conditions performed, he has admitted it to be his bond, and the *scire facias* is brought severally against all the obligors, so each of them, in judgment of law, may be said *sigillo suo sigillare*.

Then, it was objected that there is no departure in the case, because Whitley was not obliged to account but upon request and no request was made.

But it was held by the court that the breach assigned by the Attorney General in the replication for not entering upon his account on or before the 20th of May 1699 and finishing it by the end of Trinity term was a substantive and distinct part of the condition independent upon any request, and, the breach being assigned in that part, the defendant ought to have showed how he had performed it, for he has taken upon him to do it without a request, no such word request being here used. Judgment [was given] *pro rege nisi* better cause be showed this day sennight, which was afterwards put off to the last day of the term.

The same in the Case of Sir Michael Biddolph, who was bound in the same bond and pleaded the like plea and made the like rejoinder and demurrer to it.

And no cause being showed the last day of the term, judgment was given absolutely for the king against them both.

[Other copies of this report: Georgetown Univ. Law Sch. MS. B88–9, f. 109v.]

207

Masson, qui tam v. Anonymous

(Ex. 1702)

Security need not be given by claimers upon seizures for alledged illegally imported silks.

Lincoln's Inn MS. Misc. 532, f. [135]

The plaintiff made a seizure of a parcel of black alamodes and lustrings at Ratcliff in Middlesex between the first of December 1700 and the 7th of November 1701 in the custody of an unknown person, for that they were there found not being marked and sealed with the mark and seal of the Custom House or marked and sealed with the mark or seal used by the Royal Lustring Company contrary to the form of the statute. Therefore, he prays that the goods may remain forfeited and that the said Masson may have one third part thereof, according to the form of the statute.

The defendant comes in and claims property without giving any security to answer any of the penalties or forfeitures imposed by any of the statutes relating to lustrings or alamodes, which claim being entered without the privity of the informer's clerk in court, the informer's counsel move that the claim may be set aside because no security was given for the purposes aforesaid.

And whether, in this case and upon this information, security ought to be given is the question, the same being opposed by the defendant's counsel. And, because there are many acts of Parliament to be considered, the court took time to peruse the same, which appear to be as follows.

4 & 5 W. & M., ca. 5,[1] for granting certain impositions etc. to Their Majesties, fo. 273, no alamodes and lustrings are to be imported after 25 March 1693 but upon notice to the Commissioners of the Customs of the quantities, qualities, marks, numbers, and package of them intended to be imported with the name of the ship and of the master and place where they are intended to be imported and license from the commissioners for their landing and, if imported without notice and license as aforesaid, to be forfeited, one moiety to the king and queen the other to such as seize or sue for the same in any of Their Majesties' courts of record at Westminster.

Second, 5 & 6 W. & M., ca. 20,[2] for granting a duty upon tonnage of ships, fo. 372, reciting the benefits arising by the Lustring Company, enacted that the Commissioners of the Customs after the end of that session of Parliament shall mark and seal all lustrings and alamodes then imported and in the hands of any persons and such as shall thereafter be imported and keep an entry and register of them, what already imported to be sealed and registered in twenty days, and what after to be imported to be sealed and registered before delivered out of the warehouse. And all lustrings and alamodes imported after the 15th of May 1694 and not so sealed and marked [are] to be forfeited and the importers or possessors to be subject to like penalties and forfeitures as importers of French goods by the Statute 1 W. & M. for prohibiting trade and commerce with France. If any alter or counterfeit the mark or seal used for the purposes aforesaid, [he is] to forfeit £500 to anyone that will sue for the same in any of Their Majesties' courts of record at Westminster.

Third, 6 & 7 Will. III, ca. 18,[3] for granting a duty upon glass, stone, and earthen wares, fol. 470, reciting the fraudulent importation of French alamodes and lustrings, notwithstanding former laws, and the exportation of wool and money out of England, enacted that none shall deal or sell or buy or sell again or send beyond the seas any black alamodes or lustrings unless they have the seals used for foreign goods at the Custom House of the seal used by the Lustring Company for goods manufactured by them in England under [penalty of]

---

[1] Stat. 4 Will. & Mar., c. 5, s. 12 (*SR*, VI, 385).
[2] Stat. 5 & 6 Will. & Mar., c. 2, s. 44 (*SR*, VI, 494).
[3] Stat. 6 & 7 Will. & Mar., c. 18, s. 24 (*SR*, VI, 606).

forfeiture of the goods and £100 for every offense, one moiety to the king, the other to the person that sues for the same in any of His Majesty's courts of record at Westminster. If the buyer of the goods not sealed within twelve months discover the person of whom he bought them, he shall not only be discharged of the penalty but have a moiety of the sum imposed upon the seller or disposer. If any person alter, counterfeit, or misapply any seals or marks used or required to be used, he shall forfeit £100 to such person as shall sue for the same to be recovered as aforesaid.

Fourth, 8 & 9 Will. III, ca. 36,[1] for the further encouragement of lustrings and alamodes etc., fol. 659 etc., enacted that the importers of those silks and do not pay the king's duties or import any prohibited to be imported or by way of insurance or otherwise undertake or agree to deliver or in pursuance of any undertaking or agreement deliver the said goods or who agree to pay any sum etc. for insuring or conveying any such goods or knowingly receive or take the same into his house, custody, or possession shall and may be prosecuted for such offense by a *capias* in the first process and give bail to answer and pay all the forfeitures and penalties incurred for such offense or yield himself to prison. All black alamodes and lustrings wheresoever manufactured found in any person's custody or possession not sealed with the seal of the Custom House or Lustring Company are to be forfeited, and he in whose custody found to incur all the penalties relating to alamodes and lustrings in the Act above, 6 & 7 W. & M., which is £100.

Upon this clause, the information is brought.

For alamodes and lustrings seized and forfeited by any law now in force to be exported and what of those exported not to be allowed any drawback. Alamodes and lustrings manufactured in England before the 10th of April 1697 are to be sealed by the Company *gratis*. Weavers are to give an account to the Company weekly to whom they sold their goods under forfeiture of the double value.

Fifth, 9 & 10 Will. III, ca. 43, fo. 695,[2] for the better encouragement of the Lustring Company etc., taking notice that, notwithstanding the laws made for the encouragement of that manufacture, those silks have been imported without payment of the duties for the due encouragement for the Company to proceed in so good a work, enacted that no lustrings or alamodes be imported into any other than the port of London and that the Commissioners of the Customs there have notice given them of the quality, quantity, etc. of the silks intended to be imported with the name of the importer, name of the ship, and the master wherein to be imported, and where to be taken aboard, and a license from the Commissioners of the Customs for their importation. The silks, when imported, are to be sealed and entered before being delivered from the Custom House, and, if any imported into any other port or without a license or not sealed, they are to be forfeited. The importers of those silks contrary to that Act and the receivers of them [taken] into

[1] Stat. 8 & 9 Will. & Mar., c. 36 (*SR*, VII, 289–290).

[2] Stat. 9 Will. III, c. 43 (*SR*, VII, 426–429).

custody and the sellers etc. to forfeit £500. Then there are several penalties and disabilities laid upon commanders of ships, mariners, Custom House, and other officers that shall act contrary to that Act. Then, it lays penalties upon the alterers and counterfeiters of the Custom House or Company seals. And it enables the search for and the seizing of silks so fraudulently imported or not sealed according to that Act or sealed with counterfeit seals by a writ of assistance out of the Exchequer etc. And, if a question arises about the silks, whether manufactured beyond the seas or imported against the Act, the *onus probandi* is to lie upon the importer, claimer, owner, proprietor, or seller in whose custody they are found.

[There is a] penalty upon customs officers conniving at any fraudulent importation, receiving, buying, or selling of any of the said silks contrary to that Act and upon the seizers and prosecutors upon that or any other act delaying prosecution by fraud etc. Second or oftener offenders are to forfeit double. A *capias* is in the first process, and bail is to be awarded and given upon all prosecutions upon that or any other the said acts. The king is to have two-thirds and the officer one-third of the penalties, and the king is to bear the charge.

Trials upon seizures or other prosecutions for alamodes and lustrings upon that or any other law may be had as in customs cases.

To avoid vexatious claims, no claim is to be admitted until security before the barons etc. to pay the penalties and forfeitures incurred by virtue of that law and, for want of security to be condemned.

Upon this clause, it is that security is required.

And that is a general law, and treble costs [are given] against him that molests the prosecutors upon that or any other law if there is a verdict, judgment, or discontinuance, suits are to be brought upon that Act in two years after an offense be committed.

Note, for these reasons, no bail [is allowed] upon this information.

First, this last Act, which only stays claims without security or seizures gives no penalty for that offense for which this information is brought; therefore, there is no need or reason for security.

Second, the Act gives bail in personal informations. But this is a seizure.

Third, the last Act, upon which this information is brought uses the words 'black alamodes' etc., but the word 'black' is not in this information. [It was] amended.

And, thereupon, Mr. *Browne*, the counsel for the plaintiff, agrees not to insist upon security in this case. But he prays the word 'black' may be put into the information, which was done, and to try the merits of the case this term, which is whether the goods seized be alamodes and lustrings or sort of silks called rasty janes.

It is agreed, whatever they be, they were manufactured in England. So the motion for bail or security ended.

[Other copies of this report: Georgetown Univ. Law Sch. MS. B88–9, f. 112v.]

208
Williams v. Harris

(Ex. 1702)

The issue in this case was the validity of a sheriff's bail bond given at the beginning of the action.

Lincoln's Inn MS. Misc. 532, f. [137v]

Michaelmas [term] 12 Will. III. In Officio Placitorum Scaccarii. Nicholas Williams, former sheriff of Carmarthen, plaintiff vs. Hector Harries, defendant, in [an action of] debt upon a sheriff's bond.

The plaintiff brings [an action of debt] against the defendant, and declares upon a bail bond entered into by the defendant of £100 to the plaintiff conditioned that, if John Swymer, who was also severally bound on the same bond, should personally appear before the barons of His Majesty's Court of Exchequer at Westminster on the 13th day of July next ensuing the date of the bond, which was dated the 27th of June 10 Will. III, to answer Lewis Magget in an action of debt of £100, then the bond to be void.

The defendant pleads that he ought not to be charged by virtue of that bond, and he pleads the Statute of 23 Hen. VI,[1] setting forth the clause in the Statute touching sheriffs' letting to bail prisoners etc. And then he pleads further that, at the time of the taking of the bond, the plaintiff was the sheriff of the County of Carmarthen and that, in Easter term 10th [year] of the king, the said Magget sued forth of the Court of Exchequer at Westminster a writ of *quo minus* directed to the sheriff of the said County of Carmarthen whereby he was commanded to take the body of the said Swymer and him safely to keep so as to have his body before the barons of the Exchequer of our lord the king at Westminster *in octabis Sanctis Trinitatis tunc proxime sequente* to answer the said Megget *in placito transgressionis* and that the plaintiff, by virtue of that writ and before the return of it, *scil. dicto 27mo die Junii anno 10mo supradicti* at such a place in the said county, did arrest the said Swymer and detained him in his custody until the defendant together with the said Swymer and one Powell afterwards, that is to say *praedicto tempore confectionis scripti obligatoris praedictis* entered into the said bond and thereby became bound to the plaintiff in the said £100 with the condition aforesaid *pro easiamento et favore eidem Johanni Swymer de imprisonamento suo praedicto per eundem*, the plaintiff *demonstration' et pro deliberatione sua abind', habend', et obtinend'*, which said bond was taken by the plaintiff *colore officii sui praedicti contra formam statuti praedicti*. And so he says that the said bond in form and for the cause aforesaid made and taken by virtue of the Statute aforesaid is void in law.

[1] Stat. 23 Hen. VI, c. 9 (*SR*, II, 334–336).

Et hoc paratus est verificare. And he prays judgment if he ought to be charged by virtue of the said bond.

The plaintiff replies *praecludi non etc.* because he says that the said Megget, the 9th of June in the 10th year of the king, sued out a writ of *quo minus* against the said Swymer to the then sheriff of the said County of Carmarthen directed, whereby the said sheriff was commanded to take the said Swymer and him to detain so as he should have his body before the barons of the Exchequer at Westminster *dicto 13tio die Julii tunc proxime sequente* to answer Megget *de placito transgressionis quo minus etc.*, by virtue of which writ, he was arrested the 25th day of June *anno decimo supradicto* and detained until the bond above was entered into *modo et forma* as the plaintiff above has declared, *prout ei bene licuit.*

And he traverses that the said bond was taken from the defendant *modo et forma prout* the defendant has pleaded. *Et hoc paratus est verificare.* And he prays judgment and his debt.

To this replication, the defendant has demurred generally. And the plaintiff has joined.

[Other copies of this report: Georgetown Univ. Law Sch. MS. B88–9, f. 115.]

209

Attorney General v. Newton

(Ex. 1702)

The question in this case was whether an excise duty on paper applied to books that were made of paper.

Lincoln's Inn MS. Misc. 532, f. [143v]

Per informationem ex parte Rememeratoris Regis in Scaccario intratur Michaelis 11 Williami tertii.

The information charges that the defendant [James Newton, Doctor in Physic (1639–1718)],[1] the first of March 1696 at Clerkenwell in Middlesex, had in his possession seventy reams of paper for his own use and benefit for sale, a particular or the value whereof he neglected to give to the proper officer appointed by Act of Parliament in that case made and provided. And the same paper, the 5th of March 1696 and for divers days after, then and there, concealed, His Majesty's duties for the same not being paid or secured, contrary to the form of the statute, whereby he forfeited to the king £50, which is demanded by that information.

The defendant pleads not guilty.

---

[1] A. McConnell, 'Newton, James (c. 1664–1750)', *Oxford Dictionary of National Biography*, vol. 40, p. 724.

And, upon the trial by *nisi prius* at Westminster, there is a special verdict found to this effect. The jury find that the defendant for eleven years past designed to print a herbal[1] and that then he bought the paper in the information to print the said herbal and took subscriptions for printing it and that the defendant had the said paper in his custody the first of March 1696 for sale and to be sold when the same should be printed with the impression of the said herbal and not otherwise, the particular or value of which paper the defendant neglected to give to the king's officer appointed according to the Act the fifth of March 1696 or at any other time according to the provision of the said Act. They further find that the defendant is a doctor in physic and is not otherwise a dealer in paper except for his said herbal and that divers specimens of the said herbal are printed but none of the book of the said herbal are yet printed or sold. And so they conclude that, if it seems to the court upon the matter aforesaid found that the defendant is guilty, then they find him so; otherwise, not guilty.

This information is grounded upon the Act of Parliament made 8 & 9 Will. III, ca. 7,[2] for granting to His Majesty several duties upon paper etc., whereby (fo. 155) it is recited that several merchants, stationers, wholesale sellers, retailers, and other persons, bodies politic or corporate, have or may have on the first of March 1696 several stocks or quantities of paper etc. to be sold, it is enacted that all such merchants etc., repeating the same words again having on the said first of March in his or their custody or possession or in the custody or possession of any other for his or their use, benefit, or account any stock or quantity of paper etc. in England, Wales, or Berwick, 'being for sale', shall pay the king a duty of £17 10s. *per centum* of the true and real value of such paper etc. within ten days after the said first of March. And then (fo. 157) the merchants etc. are required to deliver to the king's officers a particular in writing of the quantities and values of the said paper etc. and the said officer is authorized to search and view and, if refused, the offender to forfeit £20. And, if the duty be not paid or secured by the 11th of March 1696, then the officer is to levy by distress etc. And then (fo. 160) follows a clause that, if the merchants etc. shall neglect to give such particular or valuations, then the offender is to forfeit £50, *viz.* one moiety to the king, the other to the suer. And the paper etc. is to be forfeit and liable to be seized for the king's use.

Vide Everingham and Allen's Case, Trinity [term] 1697, L. M, 139.[3]

Martis 5 May 1702, [it was] argued by *Squibb*, for the king, and *Ettrick*, for the defendant.

Squibb, for the king, observed the clauses in the Act, *prout ante*, first, that the defendant here is a person within the Act, second, that the defendant gave no particular *prout* the Act [. . .] this second matter to be clear and uncontested.

---

[1] J. Newton, *Enchiridion Universale Plantarum* (1695).

[2] Stat. 8 & 9 Will. III, c. 7 (*SR*, VII, 189–196).

[3] *Everingham v. Allen* (1697), Lincoln's Inn MS. Misc. 559, f. 139.

As to the first, the jury have found the use of the paper previous to the sale to be for printing a herbal, which, when printed, it is to be sold. The denomination is from the final cause and principal thing. Hobt. 123, Smith and James, the hospital there was within the Statute of 1 Edw. VI; Dy. 255, spiritual persons extends to Trinity College.[1] And so it is paper within that Act.

Second, printing alters not the property. It is only an addition. 5 Hen. VII, 15, leather made into shoes; Dy. 121, pl. 70, it does not alter the property for cloth.[2]

Third, acts of Parliament of revenue are liberally expounded. Though it be said goods by way of merchandise, yet, if sold, that is tantamount. Vaugh. 165, 166.[3] He cites and relies upon Everingham and Allen's Case, Trinity [term] 1697, supra.

The second point is the jury's finding the design of the defendant and the providing the paper so long beforehand alters not the case. And, where the law has not distinguished, nor must the court.

Thirdly, as to the quality of the person, though a doctor, yet he is within the general term of 'all persons' and, if the paper be for sale, no person that had it can be excused.

Fourth, though the defendant had not good success, yet that alters not the case. 12 rep., fo. 7, about goods imported;[4] salt in port changed from ship to ship carried beyond the sea is unshipped to be laid on land and liable to pay duty.

And so he concludes for the queen.

Mr. *Ettrick*, for the defendant, considers the clause *prout*. As this verdict is found, it is not found to be paper to be sold, but more properly books. A lawyer or attorney having a quantity by him and written upon and then sold is not liable. The value is not as paper, but when sold, and it is not sold until printed, and then it is books not paper. He differences this case from Everingham and Allen, first, those were persons that were traders and got a living by it, but, here, the defendant is no trader nor ever had any other paper, and this was six years before the Act; second, the duty never incurred, for it is not payable until the sale; here, it was found the duty was not payable until the sale; here, there was a length of time and no fraud, as might be supposed in Everingham's Case.

[Other copies of this report: Georgetown Univ. Law Sch. MS. B88–9, f. 119.]

---

[1] *Pits v. James* (1614), Hobart 121, 80 E.R. 271, also 1 Rolle Rep. 417, 81 E.R. 576, Moore K.B. 865, 72 E.R. 959, 1 Brownlow & Goldesborough 178, 123 E.R. 740; Stat. 1 Edw. VI, c. 14 (*SR*, IV, 24–33); *Trinity College's Case* (1566), 3 Dyer 255, 73 E.R. 566.

[2] YB Hil. 5 Hen. VII, f. 15, pl. 6 (1490); *Lord Mounteagle v. Countess of Worcester* (1555), 2 Dyer 121, 73 E.R. 265.

[3] *Sheppard v. Gosnold* (1672), Vaughan 159, 124 E.R. 1018.

[4] *Case of Customs* (1582), 12 Coke Rep. 18, 77 E.R. 1299.

Lincoln's Inn MS. 532, f. [150]

9 June 1702.

Sir John Hawles, for the queen: First, the Act intended to lay the duty upon all paper made after 1 March 1686 and of another duty upon all imported after that time and a third duty, which is £17 10s. per cent upon all paper in stock 1st of March 1696, and discovery under a penalty of £50. It being for sale, the defendant is a person within the words 'any other person having paper for sale', and as such ought to have discovered. The defendant had this for sale, for the sale after printing is paper sold, though it be printed [upon]. The defendant here is within the reason of the case of Everingham and Allen. And the defendant here is a printer for sale, though not so great a printer as they in the other case. The Act 11 & 12 Will. III, ca. [*blank*],[1] for laying an imposition upon wrought silk, there is a proviso for Dr. Alix, who had a liberty to import 5000 reams of paper to print the [. . .] upon [. . .] within the reason of the Act and, without that proviso, that must have paid the duty.

Mr. *Dodd*, for the defendant: As to Everingham and Allen's Case, it is not to be a precedent nor conclusive, being between strangers. As to Alix's Case, the greatness of the quantity must have made it liable to [pay the] duty. The Act here intended only to hold in a case of trade, not for scholars' private learning, [nor is it] like for paper to make fans of, attorneys or solicitors or scriveners having paper for private uses and writing sermons and after printing them.

Second, the jury found this paper for sale to be sold when printed and not otherwise. And they found it is not yet printed.

Third, the herbal in not yet printed.

Objection: Crown revenue is favorable.

Solution: [It is] not a duty, but a penalty sued for.

The words of the Act 'stock or quantity of paper' must intend of merchandise for sale. Stationers and booksellers are merchants, and their goods are merchandise. In Everingham's Case, it was a fraud to buy up paper to defraud the king. Here, it is none such. The defendant is no trader, but a private scholar, so he is not within the Act. He has a particular purpose. Paper *qua* paper is not chargeable, but the purpose and design makes it so or not.

The objections to the finding of the verdict [are]:

First, by the Act, a particular is to be in writing signed by the party, and the jury found not that, and, if the defendant be acquitted or convicted, yet he is liable to be fined again for not giving a particular in writing signed by the party;

Second, the proper officer in this case ought to have been named, being but a private duty, and it differs from custom and excise officers whose commissions are upon record, and this he insisted on;

---

[1] Stat. 11 Will. III, c. 3 (*SR*, VII, 582–586).

Third, that the Act, the information and verdict as to giving the particular by the 5th of March;

Fourth, the verdict that the defendant concealed the paper the 5th of March and several days after which might be, for the defendant had time for payment until the 11th of March.

Curia advisare vult.

210

Paul v. Cooke

(Ex. 1702–1704)

In this case, the question was whether prisage wines pay import duties.

Lincoln's Inn MS. Misc. 532, f. [158v]

Entered Trinity [term] 13 Will. III, 1701.

The plaintiff [William Paul, Esq.] brings an [action of] *indebitatus assumpsit* against the defendant [Thomas Cooke, Esq.] for £50 for so much had and received to the plaintiff's use by the defendant. And he lays the promise to be the 1st of February 12 Will. III [1701] at Westminster in the County of Middlesex.

Upon a trial at *nisi prius* at Westminster, there is a special verdict found to this effect. They find that King James I, under the great seal dated 26th of June 9 Jac. I [1611] [granted] to Sir Thomas Waller in reversion after the expiration of a former lease for ninety-nine years if three lives or any of them lived so long for the term of forty years under the yearly rent of £500. And then they find that the forty years lease is by mesne assignments and means in the law come to the plaintiff and that the former lease for ninety-nine years if three lives lived so long determined upon the 29th of September 1668 and then the forty-year lease began. Then they find that the defendant is a collector of duties due and payable to the crown upon wines imported into the port of London and that the £50 in the declaration were deposited by the plaintiff in the defendant's hands on account of the new subsidy of tonnage required by the defendant for a certain parcel of prisage wines imported from beyond the seas into the port of London to be paid to the use of the king if the subsidy of tonnage was due and payable for the wines so imported and, if not due, then the £50 to be paid to the plaintiff. Then they find that the plaintiff paid for those wines these duties following, *viz.*, first, the old impost, being a duty laid by the Statute 1 Jac. II,[1] for granting His Majesty an imposition upon all wines and vinegar imported between the 24th of June 1685 and the 24th of June 1693; secondly, another duty called the additional imposts by the Act 4 & 5 Will. & Mar., entitled an Act for Granting to Their Majesties Certain Additional Impositions upon Several Goods and Merchandises for

[1] Stat. 1 Jac. II, c. 3 (*SR*, VI, 2–3).

Prosecuting the Present War against France;[1] thirdly, another duty of £25 per tun upon French wines by an Act 7 Will. III, for granting to His Majesty an additional duty upon all French goods.[2] Then they find that the new subsidy, for which the said £50 was deposited, is a duty imposed *super vina praedicta* by an Act made 9 & 10 Will. III,[3] for granting to His Majesty a further subsidy of poundage and tonnage towards raising the yearly sum of £700,000 for the service of His Majesty's household and other uses therein mentioned during His Majesty's life. And then they find that the same subsidy of tonnage was before granted to the king for the term of two years and three quarters in and by an Act made 8 & 9 Will. III,[4] for granting to His Majesty a farther subsidy of tonnage and poundage upon merchandises imported for the term of two years and three quarters and an additional land tax for a year for carrying on the war against France. And they find that, during all the time the last Act continued, the new subsidy of the said tonnage for prisage wines was not paid to the collector of the subsidy. Then they find the Act of Tonnage and Poundage made 12 Car. II,[5] whereby it is *inter alia* declared and enacted that prisage of wines or prize wines ought not to pay tonnage or custom and shall not be charged with the payment of any subsidy or customs or any sum of money imposed upon wines by that Act. But whether it shall appear to the court upon the whole matter that the plaintiff ought to pay the new subsidy of tonnage aforesaid for the general prisage of wines or not, the jury know not and thereof pray the advice of the court. And if the court be of the opinion that the plaintiff ought not to pay the said new subsidy, then the jury find the defendant made the promise *modo et forma prout* in the declaration and assess damages to £50 and costs to 40s. And, if the plaintiff be liable to pay that new subsidy, then they find the defendant did not assume *modo et forma* as he has pleaded.

12 May 1702.

Mr. *Browne*, for the plaintiff: The only question is whether prisage wines shall pay the duties imposed by the [Statute] 9 & 10 Will. III. He considers these things:

First, whether any duty, by law be due for prisage wines before any of these acts in question. Prisage is defined in 1 Rolle's rep. 139; 4 Inst. 30. Aids and subsidies are additions to the crown, but prisage is the king's own by common law, and, therefore, not to be under the terms of aids etc., nor any aid or subsidy to be granted to the king out of what belongs to the king. Lane 15. [It is] not liable to [pay] customs and prisage. The like reason goes for wrecked goods. Vaughan

[1] Stat. 4 Will. & Mar., c. 5 (*SR*, VI, 380–387).
[2] Stat. 7 & 8 Will. III, c. 20 (*SR*, VII, 97–98).
[3] Stat. 9 Will. III, c. 23 (*SR*, VII, 382–385).
[4] Stat. 8 & 9 Will. III, c. 24 (*SR*, VII, 259–266).
[5] Stat. 12 Car. II, c. 4 (*SR*, V, 181–205).

rep., fo. [*blank*], and a late judgment in the Common Bench and affirmed in [a writ of] error that wreck goods are not liable to customs. In these cases, the whole was the king's and [there is] no reason to give the king a duty for his own goods or out of them;[1]

Second, if it could be thought otherwise that prisage wines should be liable to customs, yet the Statute of 12 Car. II wholly ousts the question by the last section, whereby it is declared and enacted that the prisage of wines or prize wines ought not to pay tonnage or customs and shall not be charged to the payment of any subsidy or money by that Act;

Third, prisage wines are not within the [Statutes] 8 & 9 nor 9 & 10 Will. III, because, as he observed, the words are 'wines imported by way of merchandise', but prisage wines are not imported by way of merchandise, and, therefore, not within those Acts;

Fourthly, prisage wines did pay the duty by [the Statutes] 1 Jac. II and 4 & 5 Will. III and 7 Will. III for two reason; first, because, in those three laws, the duty is laid generally upon wines imported and it does not say by way of merchandise; now it must be admitted that prisage wines are imported, though not by way of merchandise; secondly, because, in 1 Jac. II, there is an express clause to subject them to that duty (§ 7) at the latter end whereby it is appointed that the merchant shall not pay the duty for prisage wines, but he that enjoys the benefit of the prisage;

Fifthly, because, by 8 & 9 Will. III, the duty laid upon wines is general upon wines imported, and it is not said upon wines imported by way of merchandise, and it is found that, during the time of this Act, prisage wines paid not that duty;

Sixthly, upon which this question rises, the Statute of 9 & 10 [Will. III], being the same in words and by reference to and with the last law, the same reason that the wines were not liable to pay nor did pay duty in the law, not liable by this. He observes the exception, fo. [*blank*].

And he concludes upon the reasons above for the plaintiff.

Mr. *Phipps*, for the defendant, holds the prisage wines are imported by way of merchandize, and, therefore, are liable to the duty. He agrees the clause of exemption of prisage wines in 12 Car. II, last section, but he infers from thence that, without that clause, they would have been liable. But he insists that that clause extends only to the duties that arise by that particular Act, and not to any other duties granted by any other law. He reads the proviso 1 Jac. II, fo. 16, which makes the farmer of prisage wines liable for them; that is the merchants' case, but this here is the farmer. The farmer here receives the benefit of guarding the seas equally with the merchant. It is like the case of a parson leasing the glebe;

---

[1] *Waller v. Hanger* (1615), 1 Rolle Rep. 138, 81 E.R. 386, also Calthrop 33, 80 E.R. 656, Moore K.B. 832, 72 E.R. 935, 2 Bulstrode 134, 261, 80 E.R. 1011, 1107, 117 Selden Soc. 356; E. Coke, *Fourth Institute* (1644), p. 30; *Anonymous* (1607), Lane 15, 145 E.R. 261; *Sheppard v. Gosnold* (1672), Vaughan 159, 124 E.R. 1018.

the lessee pays tithes. [This] exposition is best for the king. By all statutes since 12 Will. III, prisage wines have paid the duties, and usage is the best exposition.

But query that, for it is a mistake.

Wednesday, 22 November 1704.

Mr. *Dodd*, for the plaintiff: The only question is whether prisage wines in the hands of a lessee or farmer of the prisage be liable to the new subsidy given by 9 & 10 Will. III. He considers prisage.

First, it is an ancient duty to the crown, and the crown does not pay prisage to itself nor a duty for it. It is a purveyance. 4 Inst. 30; Davis [*blank*]; 2 Rolle, *Prerogative*, 162.[1] And whether it be due by Parliament or prescription is all one. Customs are given ever since Edward I.

Second, whether the king's farmer shall pay customs or duty for prisage wines, he holds not. The farmer has the same privilege against a third person that the crown has, as in possessions etc. The crown cannot have the whole and part of the whole. Rent for prisage wines is all one with prisage. It is not like the case of a parson having tithes of his own glebe leased. Tithes are collateral to the land, but rent is the prisage.

Third, he considers the Act that lays the duty. The words of 9 & 10 [Will. III] do not charge prisage wines but only all wines imported by way of merchandize, which prisage wines are not. The farmers are not liable to bankruptcy.

Parliament did not give a duty to the crown out of the crown's own wines. There is no drawback because there is no oath to be made by the exporter or importer. A farmer is no importer. The prisage farmer takes them in specie. The former acts under which prisage wines are paid are differently penned. And 8 & 9 [Will. III] never paid, as found, and 9 & 10 [Will. III] is the same with that.

Fourth, the Act of 9 & 10 [Will. III] is relative to 12 Car. II in the term of the subsidy. And in this Act, fo. 452 etc., there are the relative words annexing the duty and remedies to 12 Car. II. And by express words in that law, prisage wines pay no duty, and that declarative clause is not enactive. And that clause was revived by general words of this law as well as the remedy for the collecting and managing of that duty.

Fifth, he answers the objections.

Objection one: Prisage wines must have paid a subsidy if not for the proviso of exemption.

Solution one: This is only a declarative, not an enacting clause.

Objection two: If this prisage is not payable, other duties are lost.

Solution: These are to be considered by themselves.

Objection three: That tonnage was granted to James I before the farm was granted.

[1] *Attorney General v. Mayor of Waterford* (1607), Davis 7, 80 E.R. 496; 2 Rolle, Abr., *Prerogative le Roy*, 'Prisage', pl. R, p. 162.

Solution: Subsequent acts of Parliament gave it to Charles I after the farm.

(The Attorney General [*Northey*] says there was no grant by Parliament to Charles I until 1641. Query that, for it is a mistake.)

Waller and Hanger's Case[1] mentions precedent leases and never any payment or demand of a duty.

So, he prays judgment for the plaintiff.

Attorney General *Northey*, for the defendant: This is a case of the revenue, and it influences divers grants of 25 per cent and 8 per cent. And it is of great consequence to the revenue. He insists that prisage wines are liable to all duties except 12 Car. II, which he agrees exempts.

[As to the] omission in the special verdict that any covenant from the crown that the wines should be free, he agrees [it is an] omission, but it may be supplied by letters patent which [. . .].

No title is found by the special verdict for the plaintiff for the lease for forty years which commence.

Brudenell's Case, 5 rep.[2]

Mr. Attorney General [*Northey*] insists that the special verdict ought to be amended according to the letters patent and the plaintiff amend also, as the lessees for life.

And that was agreed to, and it was amended accordingly.

[Other copies of this report: Georgetown Univ. Law Sch. MS. B88–9, f. 137.]

211

Attorney General v. Queens' College, Cambridge

(Ex. 1702–1703)

Colleges in universities are not required to pay any tax on beer that was brewed and consumed on their own premises by their members.

Lincoln's Inn MS. Misc. 532, f. [164]

Entered in the Office of the King's Remembrancer in the Exchequer Hilary [term] 12 Will. III.

Thomas Trevor, knight, Attorney General to the king, exhibited a Latin information against the defendants in the nature of an action of debt thereby charging the defendants that they [. . .] and unjustly detained from the king £136 2s. 7½d. for that the defendants between the 10th of February 9 Will. III [1698] and the 20th of January 12 *eiusdem regis* [1700] at Westminster, County of Middlesex, did brew 469 barrels and a half of beer, each barrel not exceeding

1 *Waller v. Hanger* (1615), *ut supra*.

2 *Brudnel v. Skidmore* (1592), 5 Coke Rep. 9, 77 E.R. 61.

in value 6s. and 394 barrels of beer, each barrel not exceeding the value of 6s. And all the aforesaid several barrels of beer did sell out to several persons to the Attorney General unknown, whereby the £136 2s. 7½d. became due to the king from the defendants for the said barrels of beer so sold as aforesaid. But they have refused and still refuse to pay the same to the king or the Commissioners of Excise or other officers of the king appointed to receive the same or to any other to the use of the king, *per quod actio accrevit* to the king to have and exact from the defendants the said moneys which, though often requested, they have refused and still refuse to pay or any ways to satisfy to the king, and, thereupon, the Attorney General prays the advice of the court in the premises and due process of law against the defendants to answer the king in the premises.

The defendants come in and plead *nil debent*.

And a trial at *nisi prius* is had at Westminster 13 July 13 Will. III [1701]. And a special verdict is found to this effect: that Queens' College in the University of Cambridge at and long before the making of the Statutes for Excise, 12 Car. II,[1] was one of the colleges of the University and that the defendants, the President and Scholars of the College, brewed all the beer in the information mentioned within the time in the information and that the several duties of excise payable by the several acts of Parliament in that case made and provided for the same quantity of beer at the respective times of the brewing thereof *si forent solubil' in hac casu* did attain to £118 and not more and that all the beer in the information was brewed in the said college brew house, being within the precinct of the said college and not elsewhere; that, within the time in the information, no beer or ale was brewed in that brew house *praeterquam pro usu Praesidentis et Sociorum Collegii praedicti in collegio praedicto potom'*; that the said brew house is an ancient brew house and was the brew house of that college and used for the service of that college only and not otherwise until the year 1651 and that, until that time, all the beer and ale of that college was brewed in that brew house and that no beer or ale before that time was brewed in that brew house for any person but for the college; that, from the year 1651 unto the year 1659, that brew house was a common brew house and, by that time, a common brewer of beer, then undertenant to the said college, did brew beer and ale in that brew house and sold it to such as would buy it; that the several quantities of beer in the information were brewed by the defendants in that brew house for the use of the President and fellows of that college and were sized out and sold to the respective members of that college within the precincts of the said college only; and that, from the year 1659 until the year 1697, that brew house was not used as a brew house and, within that time, the defendants did not brew any beer or ale for themselves or otherwise; that, in the year 1697 and thence to the time of the information, the defendants did brew in that brew house that the beer in the information was all

[1] Stat. 12 Car. II, c. 23 (*SR*, V, 255–259).

brewed within the time of the information by the defendants in the said brew house within the precincts of the college for the use of the defendants and were sized out to the respective members of the said college within the precinct of the college and to them only sold; but whether, upon the whole matter aforesaid found, the several duties of excise be due and payable for the beer in the information to the king or not, they know not, and thereof pray the advice of the court; and, if the court shall be of the opinion that they are due, then they find that the defendants do owe to the king £118, parcel of the sum of £136 2s. 7½d. in the information mentioned in form as by the information is supposed; and, if the court shall be of the opinion that the said several duties of excise be not due to the king, then the jury says that the defendants do not owe to the king the said £118 in the information mentioned nor any penny thereof *modo et forma* as in the information aforesaid *interius [. . .] supponuntur*; and that £10 2s. 7½d. of the aforesaid £136 2s. 7½d. residue the jurors say that the defendants do not owe the same or any penny thereof to the king *modo et forma* as by the information is aforesaid.

Note [this is] by the Statute 15 Car. II, ca. 11, § 21.[1]

And it is hereby further declared that every college and hall in either of the universities which before the duty of excise was imposed did brew their own beer and ale within their own precincts and size it out to their respective members within their own precincts only are not liable to the payment of any duty of excise for the same, either by this or any of the aforementioned acts.

May 1702.

Mr. *Ettrick*, for the queen, opens the special verdict *prout ante*. Whether there be any duty of excise that charges the colleges by the Statute 12 Car. II, ca. [*blank*], for excise. What exemption arises by the Act of 15 Car. II, ca. 11, § 21, *prout ante*. Whether the subsequent acts to 15th charge the college with those subsequent duties of excise.

For the first, he considers the statutes 12 [Car. II] and that generally of the words that charge that duty and he holds that the words reach the college and make that and all other colleges liable to the duty of excise, for he holds that sizing out beer by colleges is selling, and so he concludes the college is charged by that Act.

The words of exemption by 15 [Car. II] reach not this case.

First, the words before the duty of excise imposed are not [. . .] for it is found, from 1651 in effect to 1697, [there was] no brewing in that brew house; therefore, though there might [be] brewing before 1651, yet none was brewed there by the college from that time to the Act 12 [Car. II].

---

[1] Stat. 15 Car. II, c. 11, s. 21 (*SR*, V, 492).

Second, the construction upon this Act [is] liberal for the crown, it being in effect a purchaser of half in 12 [Car. II] by the [Court of] Wards and Liveries and the subsequent duties given for the public good.

Third, the statutes of 12 [Car. II] fully charge colleges and, was it not for the 15th clause, [there would be] no question, and, therefore, the words are to be considered. And the word 'before' must have a reasonable construction to be in a short time before. And this is considerable that the Statute gives the duty for half a year before the Act was made. And, therefore, that explains and satisfies the word 'before', which must be in a small time before otherwise of any brewing 100 or 200 years before would be before and intended. Dy. 362, Roll's, *Prerog.*, 186, Lord of Leicester's Case. As to the words *ante hac* reasonably restrained; Co. Entr., 384; Imber and Wilkins' Case, where the last separation or period is regarded, not the former; the case put in the reasons of a double title precedent and subsequent; and the Abbot of St. Albans Case, and bishops' liberties; the case of a pardon to a sheriff, there put the like.[1] This case here upon 15 [Car. II] is only an exception, which must be strictly interpreted.

Third,[2] the clause in 15 [Car. II] extends not to exempt from excise by subsequent laws, for those two acts which follow, *viz.* 4 & 5 Will. & Mar., ca. [*blank*]; 5 & 6 Will. & Mar., ca. [*blank*].[3] In both these acts, the charging clauses are the same, and are new acts and charges, and not discharged by any words in either of them.

The same clauses for levying and collecting the excise *prout* the Statutes 12 and 15 [Car. II] and to be done in the same manner. This clause exempts no duty but only communicates the recovering power of the duties by those two last acts by the same ways and means as the two former acts directs. He cites and relies upon the Case of Sands and Shaw in this court *prout* the judgment of this court as a parallel case. He puts it upon those acts, and depends upon it that there is as strong a relation in this case as there was in that.

And, so, he prays judgment for the queen.

Mr. *James Montagu*, for the defendants: He agrees the question to be whether the defendants be chargeable with the duties of excise given by the several statutes. Three things are to be considered: first, whether any duty of excise be charged upon the college for beer brewed and sized out within the words or meaning of the statutes of 12 Car.; second, whether the clause in 15 [Car. II]

---

[1] *Earl of Leicester's Case* (1578), 3 Dyer 362, 73 E.R. 812, also 1 Leonard 15, 74 E.R. 14, 2 Rolle, Abr., *Prerogative le Roy*, pl. L, 3, p. 186, E. Coke, *A Booke of Entries* (1614), 'Information', pl. 13, f. 381; *Rex v. Imber and Wilking* (Ex. 1579), 2 Rolle, Abr., *Prerogative le Roy*, pl. L, 4, 5, p. 186, E. Coke, *A Booke of Entries* (1614), 'Information', pl. 12, f. 378.

[2] Sic in MS.

[3] Stat. 4 Will. & Mar., c. 3 (*SR*, VI, 372–378); Stat. 5 & 6 Will. & Mar., c. 20 (*SR*, VI, 483–495).

makes any distinction between the colleges; third, if colleges be liable and a distinction between them, yet whether this college be not discharged.

As to the first, he considers the charging words in the several acts which, as he says, fall under two denominations, first, either common brewers or, secondly, persons brewing and selling or tapping out beer or ale. As to these, none think colleges that did brew their own beer are common brewers and [*blank*].

As to the second denomination, first, the word 'persons' do not extend to bodies politic (query that), secondly, the sizing out of beer cannot be understood to be selling it within that law, for that law respects sellers and tappers out of beer for profit only. And here is neither gaining nor losing by the sizing out of beer. The consumption is among themselves, and no profit is raised to the college. The buyers and sellers here are the same persons and there is no alteration of property *prout* as joint tenants, 1 Inst. 185, and there [he] agreed they cannot sell one to another.

And the clause in 15 [Car. II] is full as to all beer before that Act brewed and sized out to the college members.

[As to] the distinction between colleges that did or did not before the first acts brew their own beer, he see not any.

The words of the Act 15 [Car. II] and the circumstances of this case exempts the defendants from excise. He reads the clause in 15 [Car. II]. It is found that, before 1651, the brew house was used for brewing that college beer; so [it is] within the words.

Objection: There was a discontinuance from 1651 to 1659, and then it became a common brew house.

Objection: From 1659 to 1697, there was a further discontinuance and note that, at or for eight years before 1660, this college did not brew their own beer.

Solution: The defendants [are] within the words of the clause of 15 [Car. II], for they did before the first acts brew for themselves, though not within eight years, yet within ten years, as found by the jury.

And so he concludes: first, colleges generally are not chargeable; second, this college, in particular, is not charged; third, the clause in 15 Car. II exempts it from all excise.

Wherein note by me [Edward Ward]:

First, it is a harsh construction of the two first acts of excise to bring colleges that brewed and sized out their beer to the members of it within the precincts to be intended under the terms of common brewers, such as sell or tap out beer or ale publicly or privately.

Secondly, the clause 15 Car. II, ca. 11, § 21, fully exempts every college that before the imposing of the excise did brew their own beer in their precincts and therein sized it out to their members.

Thirdly, the defendant, the college, is within those words literally for it is found by the verdict they did so before and until 1651 though not immediately before the imposing of the excise, for, if it was before, it is enough. It is not necessary to be immediately before.

Fourth, subsequent acts to 15 [Car. II] are relative to 12 [Car. II], and, if 15 [Car. II] discharges 12 [Car. II], then the subsequent acts of the same reason with 12 [Car. II] in regard they refer to and are governed by them.

Fifth, if the acts of excise subsequent to 15 [Car. II] create a new substantive and independent duty and are not liable to the construction under the first head as not within the words or intention of being common brewers or persons publicly or privately selling or tapping out of beer nor to the exemption by 15 [Car. II] for the acts after, then, it must follow that for all the beer and ale brewed by all or any of the colleges in both universities after the statutes of the 4th & 5th of King William and Queen Mary must pay also the [. . .] of excise imposed by the statutes subsequent to 15 [Car. II]. And that I [Edward Ward] think has never yet been pleaded to.

Sixth, if the rates of excise subsequent to 15 [Car. II] be due or payable and yet the excises by 12 [Car. II] and 15 [Car. II] be not payable by reason of the exemptions in 15 [Car. II], then I [Edward Ward] cannot see what judgment can be given in this case as this verdict is found, for the excise given both by 12 [Car. II] and 15 [Car. II] and also those after are comprehended in the 118 without any distinction so that, unless all be due both by, before, and after 15 [Car. II], there is no separation or distinction of duties found. And, then, if some be due and not others, what judgment can the court give here but such as in that case must either wrong the crown or the defendants, which I take to be a fault in the drawing up of this special verdict what there ought to have been found the quantities of the several duties of excise as they arose and grew due according to the several rates imposed by 12 [Car. II] and 15 [Car. II] and by the subsequent statutes.

Wednesday, 25 November 1702.

Northey, Attorney General, for the queen: First, he observes the words of the first statute, 12 Car. II, for every barrel of ale etc. sold or laid out; second, the exempting clause in 15 [Car. II].

Montagu, for the defendant: There are two questions: first, whether 12 [Car. II] charges; secondly if 15 [Car. II] discharges; third, whether excise is due by the laws subsequent to 15 [Car. II].

First, as to the first, the words are plain, 'every person', which includes a corporation. 2 Inst. 737,[1] upon cottages, 'person' includes corporations. 25 Car. II, in the Common Bench, corporation under the word 'person'.

Second, the sizing here is selling and a corporation may sell to a member. Bro., *Corporation*, 4, instances in several things which a corporation may do to a member and *vice versa*.[2]

---

[1] E. Coke, *Second Institute* (1642), p. 737.

[2] YB Pas. 3 Hen. VI, f. 43, pl. 16 (1425), 1 Brooke, Abr., *Corporation*, pl. 4.

The second point and difficulty of the case is whether 15 [Car. II] extends to this case by the proviso of exempting colleges.

Objection: That clause is declaratory that 12 [Car. II] did not charge.

Solution: The word 'declare' here must be understood enact.

He instances that 15 [Car. II] creates a new duty and remedy in divers cases. And he observes the words. And it was for supplying defects and relief of people. The colleges in being at that time that brewed are exempt from excise, but no other. The words 'who before the Statute of 12 [Car. II] brewed' must be taken strictly and reasonable certainty and within a reasonable term.

The mischief upon the colleges that in 12 [Car. II] did brew should be charged and the remedy by 12 [Car. II] can extend to no more than where the mischief was, and that was only to the colleges in being that brewed their own beer, and not to extend to nor exempt any other colleges that did not then brew their beer. And this construction agrees with the rules and cases put in Dy. 362; Co. Entr. 384; Imber and Wilkins, general and relative words restrained to some reasonable certainty.

Thirdly, if 15 [Car. II] exempts this college, yet [it is] liable to pay all subsequent excises. And this is justified by the resolution in Sands and Shaw's Case, in this court, since affirmed in error. *Vide* [. . .] Case. The ward's advantages in that case are understood to be only advantages of the collection and no other advantages which might be to merchants.

And so he prays judgment for the queen.

Mr. *Dodd*, for the defendants, insists upon the finding of the jury that, if all the duties be due, then for the plaintiff. First, they are not liable by 12 [Car. II]; second, if they are charged by that, yet it is taken off by 15 [Car. II]; third, the circumstances of the exemption by [15 Car. II]; fourth, subsequent acts to 12 [Car. II] charge none that was not chargeable before or exempt by 15 [Car. II].

First, the college is not chargeable under the words of 12 [Car. II]. First, [they are] no common brewer, for he is obliged to sell if any would buy, and surely the college is not compellable to sell. And a common brewer is well charged. Second, and the words 'any other person' [. . .] sell or tap out to others reach not the college and the scholars; no man than boarders can be called vendees of beer. A college is a school of learning, as boarding of instruction. Selling and tapping out must be a trade and for gain and profit. But nothing of that is here, either of trade or gain, only a dividing the beer between themselves; and the brewing charge of the brew house [. . .] and other materials are at the equal charge of all the members. All here are but one house and do not sell one to another. [It was an] agreement between persons. No college that brewed their own beer between 12 [Car. II] and 15 [Car. II] paid excise.

The second point [is] if [they are] charged by 12 [Car. II], yet they are discharged by 15 [Car. II], which complains of officers for undue [. . .] and then the words follow 'be it declared' [. . .] are not introductory but only declaratory that [they were] never chargeable by 12 [Car. II].

It was enacted and declared as to the brewing vessels were, in truth, only declaratory, because by law liable. And he says that the Court of King's Bench in the Case of Mecke [?].

Thirdly, the circumstances found in the case bring this college under the full privilege of 15 [Car. II], for it is true in fact and so found that this college did before the Statute brew their own beer and what shall be understood by the word 'before' is the doubt. A lessee by tenants in tail and in the right of the church must reserve the rent before usually reserved. Lands once demised, though out of lease for a great while, yet may be leased again. The time must be in view or easily provable. Possibly, no new building within this Act may gain the privilege, but here was then a brew house always in being. Here, the college is within all the words of the proviso, and is not to be construed out.

Fourth, [it is] not chargeable by the subsequent acts, for they are, first, additional duties and pay[able] over and above all other duties payable or imposed by Parliament; second, [there is] nothing of charging anything new but adding; third, the remedies are to be the same with the former. The colleges are favorites. And, if this college be distinguished from the rest, [it would be a] discouragement and hindrance to scholars.

Mr. Attorney [General *Northey*] replies. The college must submit to the law. The quantity of drink brewed was found, and the court should judicially take notice of all the particular duties, and it may be ascertained. It was expressly found that the college sold. The word 'before' must have a reasonable construction and that [is] not considered as a brew house for the college but another sort of use. He thinks subsequent acts create new duties and participate not of the old ones.

[Other copies of this report: Georgetown Univ. Law Sch. MS. B88–9, f. 141.]

Lincoln's Inn MS. Misc. 533, f. [149], pl. 1

In Officio Rememeratoris Reginae in Scaccario.

The court gave judgment this term in the case between the Attorney General and Queens' College in Cambridge, the points wherein were:

First, whether the College that brewed and sized out their drink to their own members in and before 1651 and then let their brew house to a tenant who left it in 1659 and it was not made use of as a brew house until 1698 and then used by the College to brew their own beer only, which was sized out to their own members within the precincts of the College only, was to enjoy the benefit of the clause in the Act 15 Car. II, ca. [*blank*], whereby it is declared that such colleges in the universities which before the duty of excise imposed, which in fact was first imposed 12 Car. II, did brew and size out their own drink in their precincts and to their own members only should not be liable to the duties granted by that or any other former act;

Secondly, if Queens' College should be within that clause, yet whether they should be liable to the excise granted by subsequent acts.

And it was adjudged by the Chief Baron [Ward] and barons Bury and Smith, against the opinion of Baron Price, that Queens' College was within the benefit and privilege granted by the Statute 15 Car. II and so not liable and that it was not liable to the excises granted by the subsequent acts.

[Other copies of this report: Georgetown Univ. Law Sch. MS. B88–9, f. 215.]

212

Keach and Rawlins v. Molineux

(Ex. 1702)

The question in this case was whether the contract in issue concerning a maritime voyage was enforceable in the Court of Admiralty or not.

Lincoln's Inn MS. Misc. 532, f. [174]

Trinity [term] 1 Ann., 1702. In [a writ of] prohibition to the Admiralty.

The case was this, as it appeared to the court here. The 29 February 1699[/1700], *quaedam materia controversiae sive querella de et concernente proprietat' et interesse ad mare emission'* of the ship the *Pelican* then in the river of Thames between Brooking, the master, and his partners, proprietors of five-eighths of that ship, by virtue of several bills of sale to them made at land, *viz.* at London etc. and Molineux and Bredgar and others, proprietors of the other three-eighths of that ship, by virtue of several other bills of sale to them made at land, *viz.* at London etc., upon which said matter of controversy, it was agreed by the parties voluntarily to go into the said Court of Admiralty and there give a stipulation or recognizance from the plaintiffs here with others containing the agreement of the said parties, which stipulation the Court of Admiralty took. And it was this, that the 29th of February 1699[/1700] before Dr. Bridges, surrogate etc., in Doctors' Commons Hall has in the presence of Tillet, notary public, Boheme, a proctor, produced *in fide jussores* the two plaintiffs and one Nichol, who bound themselves, their heirs, executors, and administrators for the proprietors of the five-eights of the ship in £246 to the defendants Molineux and Bredgar, each of them proprietors of one-eighth, to bring back the said ship, designed for a voyage from London to and from the Mediterranean, into the river of Thames within two years and to restore those two-eighths to the defendants if extant in specie or else to pay the true value of them according to the appraisement taken by the authority of the Court of Admiralty extending in the whole to £492 11s. 8d. in case the said ship shall perish in the meantime or not be brought back into the river of Thames in that time and the said two-eighths not restored to the defendants *et nisi etc.*, which caution the said Surrogate, by the relation of the Marshall, receives.

This stipulation is put in suit in the Admiralty Court against the plaintiffs. And they pray a [writ of] prohibition, suggesting the Statute of 15 Ric. II,[1] restraining the Admiralty from meddling with any contracts, pleas, or quarrels had within the body of any county and that all such ought to be tried and determined by the laws of the land and not before the Admiral and further suggests that all pleas for non-performance of contracts and agreements made at London between any persons and the taking of stipulations and recognizances of debts for the performance of any such contract or agreement where the recognitors bound themselves and their heirs, executors, and administrators for the performance of such agreements or contracts or for the payment of any money for the value or in the satisfaction of the property or interest of any ships, the said property and interests arising by any contract or bill of sale made at land within the body of the county and such ships then being within the body of the county and not at sea nor within the Admiralty jurisdiction, and the prosecutions of such stipulations and recognizances for recovery of any money therein and the conusances of all pleas, stipulations, and recognizances belong to the queen's courts, and not the Admiralty. And they suggest all to be made and done at land within the body of the county and not within the Admiral's jurisdiction and that they have alleged all this in the Admiralty Court, but the judge refuses to admit it. And so they pray [a writ of] prohibition.

Note nothing was moved in this case this term though, to me [EDWARD WARD], it seemed a probable cause for a prohibition *prout* the authorities of Godbolt 260; Hardress 473, and my reports, L. 1, 391; Raymond 78; and Noy 24.[2]

[Other copies of this report: Georgetown Univ. Law Sch. MS. B88–9, f. 150v.]

213

Davison v. Baker

(Ex. 1702–1703)

The venue of a case can be changed to one that is more convenient to the defendant than the venue chosen by the plaintiff.

Lincoln's Inn MS. Misc. 532, f. [176v], pl. 1

6 June. Davison, Under Sheriff of Newcastle upon Tyne, plaintiff; Michael Baker, Marshall of the Exchequer, defendant.

---

[1] Stat. 15 Ric. II, c. 3 (*SR*, II, 78–79).

[2] *Greenway v. Barker* (1612), Godbolt 193, 260, 78 E.R. 117, 151; *Justice v. Brown* (1668), Hardres 473, 145 E.R. 554, Exch. Cases *tempore* Car. II, 128; *Par v. Evans* (1663), T. Raymond 78, 83 E.R. 43, also 1 Keble 489, 500, 515, 542, 552, 83 E.R. 1069, 1076, 1086, 1101, 1108; *Record v. Jobson*, Noy 24, 74 E.R. 994.

The plaintiff brings [an action of] trespass and false imprisonment against the defendant and for detaining him in custody until he paid him £10 and gave a bond of £200 to appear and be apposed upon the process of the Exchequer, and laid the action at Newcastle upon Tyne.

And, upon the motion of *Browne* and *Phipps*, for the defendant, and hearing *Dodd*, for the plaintiff, the court changed the venue into Middlesex in regard it appeared that the defendant's justification would be as an officer of the Exchequer and by virtue of an order of the court for taking the sheriffs into custody for not being apposed upon their process in the term after the return thereof. And this was held reasonable as well as usual to change such a venue in a cause not local, but transitory, for, if every officer of a court that executes the process of it shall be compelled to defend his cause at such a distance from London, it will be discouraging to any officer to do his duty. And the reason of his privilege, which is his continual residence, will be frustrated; besides, the justification rising by matter of record in Middlesex made it more reasonable to change the venue in this case.

But the defendant was not to delay the cause upon the special plea of justification by the order of this court beyond the usual rules of the court for the trying of the cause.

[Other copies of this report: Georgetown Univ. Law Sch. MS. B88–9, f. 152v.]

Lincoln's Inn MS. Misc. 533, f. [184]

In [an action of] trespass and false imprisonment, entered Easter term 1 Queen Anne [1702] in the Office of Pleas in the Exchequer, the plaintiff [Thomas Davison] declares against the defendant [Michael Baker], who, with Michael Baker, senior, are Marshal of the Marshalsea [Prison] of the queen's Exchequer in proper person of a plea of trespass for assault and imprisonment, for that the defendant, the 17th September 13 Will. III [1701], *vi et armis*, the said plaintiff at Newcastle upon Tyne, in the county of that name, made an assault and him did beat, wound, evil entreat, take, and imprison and, in prison, did detain by the space of twenty-four hours without any reasonable cause and against the laws and customs of England did detain *quousque finem pro* £10, which the defendant and a certain writing obligatory of £200 to his late Majesty did make for his delivery *et alia enormia etc. ad damnum* £300.

The defendant, in proper person, comes and pleads *quoad venire vi et armis et quiquid quod est contra pacem etc. necnon vulnerationem praedictum fieri supponit* and, thereupon, issue. *Et quoad residuum transgressionum, insultum, et imprisonamenti superius fieri supponit actio non*, because *tempore quo et* long before the supposed trespass etc., *scil.* by the space of ten years last past and continually after *usque tempus quo etc.*, the defendant and the other Michael Baker were Marshal of the Marshalsea [Prison] of the Exchequer of the late king and now queen and yet so are in that office lawfully and duly constituted, admitted, and sworn, *viz.*

at Westminster in Middlesex and that, *ante praedictam tempus quo etc. scil. termino Paschae 5 Williami et Mariae* [1693] in and by the Court of Exchequer of the said late king and queen *hic apud Westmonasterium quidam ordo fuit habitus et recordatus fuit et adhuc ordo huius curiae existit* in the same court *habere de recordo* among the orders of this Court of Exchequer *ex parte Rememeratoris Thesaurarii* entered and remaining, by which said order, reciting that, whereas divers writs and process of that court against accountants and other debtors of the said late king and queen bearing *teste* in Hilary term then last past [*blank*][1]

[Other copies of this report: Georgetown Univ. Law Sch. MS. B88–9, f. 198.]

214

Bellamy, qui tam v. Hannet

(Ex. 1702)

A common informer cannot compel the production of the documents in the Custom House in order to prove his case.

Lincoln's Inn MS. Misc. 532, f. [177v]

Tuesday, 16 June.

The plaintiff exhibited several informations *tam quam* etc. of *devenerunt* for wines forfeited for non-payment of duties and come to the defendant's hands. The supposition was that French wines imported into England from St. Sebastians in Spain were landed at Ratcliff in Middlesex within the time in the information and had paid only the Spanish duties, which ought to have paid the French duties, being above a third part more than the Spanish duties.

And it was agreed by all as very clear and so all along admitted in all causes that, if any wines or other goods be imported and pay a duty less than the law imposes, though the same be accepted by the king's officers of the customs, yet such acceptance does not hinder or deprive the informer or, in his default, the Attorney General for the king, to recover the forfeiture and value of the goods in regard the true and full duties due and payable by law for those goods have not been paid. But in such case, the duties that have been paid, though not the full, have been considered and allowed by the jury out of the value of the forfeiture.

And the informer in this case prosecuted the causes. And, in some of them before brought to trial and in one at the trial, the Attorney General entered *noli prosequis*, the king having made compositions and received satisfaction for all such pretense of forfeitures upon subsequent informations exhibited by officers of the customs for the like pretense of forfeiture with the now plaintiff.

[1] This report end here in mid-sentence.

And the plaintiff, having tried one cause after such *noli prosequi* entered, was not able to prove the goods to come to the defendant's hands otherwise than by the help of the defendant's entries and warrants in the searchers' [?] office in the Custom House where the originals are filed and kept. And, for want of the producing of the same by the proper officers in the Custom House or a true copy thereof of any sufficient evidence that the goods came to the defendant's hands, a verdict passed for the defendant.

To prevent which for the future in the other causes, the plaintiffs, the 5th of May 1702, moved the court by *Sir Simon Harcourt*, Solicitor General, and Mr. *Conners* that were of the queen's counsel, the causes being now only between the informer and defendants, that in the succeeding trials in those cases and to prevent the failer of evidence therein that the court would order that the queen's officers of the Customs might attend the court at the trials of those causes with the original bills of entry or warrants touching such supposed forfeited goods, whereupon the court ordered that precedents should be searched whether any could be found that, in causes touching the forfeiture of goods wherein the crown was not interested, any such order for such attendance as is desired was or had been made. That order by another of the 8th of May 1702 was continued to this term.

And the plaintiff's counsel, [. . .]ening to the court that no such precedents could be found, desired that the plaintiff might have liberty to proceed to trial against the defendants Hannet and Thomas upon such other evidence as he should be able to give upon the said trials, which was ordered accordingly.

But the plaintiff did not think fit to proceed in any such trial, but by one [. . .], of the queen's counsel, and others he moved the court this term for an order for the queen's officers to attend at the trials of these causes this term with the said entries and warrants. And whether that motion should be granted or no, the court appointed to hear counsel this day [16 June] on each side, which were heard accordingly, *viz. Harcourt*, Solicitor General, and *Coniers*, of the queen's counsel, and *Phipps*, for the plaintiff, *Northey*, Attorney General, and *Cooper*, one of the queen's counsel, and *Ettrick, Dodd*, and *Browne*, for the queen and the officers of the customs.

And it was urged on the plaintiff's behalf that such an order ought to be made as is desired from the nature of the thing and justice of the cause, though it was confessed no precedents in the like case could be produced, in regard the plaintiff founding his demand upon an Act of Parliament, *viz.* 12 Car. II, of Tonnage and Poundage,[1] which is a public law and for the good of the crown and kingdom to have the legal duties upon goods imported to be paid, all due assistance and encouragement ought to be given to him, especially he having discovered the mystery of an iniquity so long concealed and practiced in im-

[1] Stat. 12 Car. II, c. 4 (*SR*, V, 181–205).

porting French wines from St. Sebastians which paid only Spanish duties to the great defrauding of the crown and kingdom and though *noli prosequis* have been entered, the defendant's having compounded with the crown upon subsequent informations upon the plaintiff's discovery of the offenses in such subsequent informations, yet the plaintiff's services thereby to the crown are meritorious and the wrongdoers ought to be liable to him for his part of the forfeiture. And, in regard it will evidently appear by such entries and warrants that the goods came to the defendants' hands, which otherwise the informer cannot prove, it is but just he should be assisted by them or true copies to be allowed at the trial and the rather because, if this assistance be denied, it will inevitably deter all prosecutions by *devenerunt* brought by any persons besides Custom House officers and the law being already that none can seize goods but Custom House officers, it will unavoidably follow that neither *devenerunts* nor seizures can be brought for unlawful importations or exportations by any other but Custom House officers. And, if all such prosecutions be confined to those officers only, it may prove a great prejudice and mischief to the public.

On the other side, on the behalf of the queen and the officers, it was insisted that the plaintiff, who prosecutes only for a forfeiture and not for any duty, is not entitled to such assistance as is desired, for the coming of the wines to the defendants' hands is pure matter of fact and may well be proved *in pais* and the officers of the customs are neither parties nor privies in this suit, nor is the crown concerned. And though the entries and warrants may be evidence for the plaintiff if produced, yet the plaintiff has no right in law or justice to compel the officers to produce or attend with them, no more than, if A. and B. be at law and C. has a deed of his own which, if produced, might be an evidence for either of them touching the matter in variance, yet, inasmuch as neither of them has any right to that deed, they cannot compel C. to produce or attend with such deed. And this is not like the case of a lord or steward of a manor who has the custody of the court rolls who may be compelled to produce them in regard they are the evidences as well for the tenants as for the lord. But it is not so here. A common informer must stand and fall by his own strength. And, if this way of compelling of entries and warrants in the offices and hands of the Custom House officers to be produced for the sake of a common informer only should be countenanced, it may become a thing of dangerous consequence, for a common informer may in such a case exhibit an information at an adventure and then hunt for evidence and compel the officers of the customs to search, discover, and produce all such entries and warrants as the informer shall think proper or necessary to make out his cause of suit and thereby give great trouble and disquiet as well to the officers of the customs as the merchants without any just or probable grounds. And the *devenerunt* being only in the nature of trover and conversion, it is enough for the informer to prove that such wines were imported and that they came to the defendant's hands or use or were taken up by his servants or agents, for the *onus probandi* of paying the duties lies upon the defendant, which, if he cannot do, the cause must go against him.

Upon which arguments and debates, the court took time to consider.

And, afterwards, *viz.* The 23rd of June [. . .] by order of Tracy and Bury that [. . .] declared the opinion of the court to be that, as this case is, they cannot by the rules of the law and justice order the officers of the customs to attend the trials which the plaintiff shall think fit to proceed in wherein there are *noli prosequis* entered for the reasons and causes alleged by the Attorney General and others on the behalf of the queen and her officers, who, it is true, are third persons and not parties nor interested in the cause, but the queen is concerned not to have her customs books, warrants, and entries exposed nor her officers troubled without just reason and cause. And the Attorney General having declared in court that he has directions to oppose this motion, the crown being satisfied all its dues in these cases, and it being considered by the plaintiff's counsel that there is no precedent for such an order as is desired, the court, considering what has been offered on both sides an the circumstances of this case, cannot think themselves enabled to make the order desired by the rules of law and justice in this unprecedented case. And the plaintiff may have evidence of the importation and landing and who took up the wines and to whose hands they came without the help of these warrants and entries.

Suppose A. brings [an actions of] trover and conversion against B. for goods (and a *devenerunt* is such an action) and he cannot prove either the coming to the hands of the conversion by B. but by a book, letter, or writing in the hands of C. which wholly belongs to C., can any court of justice make an order that C. shall attend at a trial at law with that writing to make out such coming to have or conversion? Surely no.

Yet, in such a case, there is interest and property concerned and here only a seeking for a penalty by a common informer and that after such time as the duty for which the penalty was imposed has been paid and satisfied to the crown to which only the injury was done and which had power to have discharged the offense before the information was preferred.

The exhibiting of an information in this case into this court gives the court no more authority or jurisdiction to make the order desired than the bringing of an [action of] trover and conversion would do in the case before put, which is agreed cannot be nor ever was done.

Here, nobody goes about to deprive the plaintiff of his right or remedy or of any evidence that belongs to him or which he can produce.

[Other copies of this report: Georgetown Univ. Law Sch. MS. B88–9, f. 154.]

215

Williams v. Smith

(Ex. 1702)

In this case, a solicitor agreed to have his fees taxed by the court and then refused to pay what was so taxed, and he was held in contempt of court.

Lincoln's Inn MS. Misc. 532, f. [180]

14 June 1702.

It having been formerly complained of that the plaintiff [Ambrose Williams] having employed the defendant [Matthew Smith] for and as his solicitor in prosecuting two several prohibitions to the Admiralty in this court, which were argued and debated in court and allowed to stand, the defendant had brought to and demanded from the plaintiff several bills of costs and charges amounting to above £153 15s. 6d., which being apprehended to be very unreasonable, were upon the motion of the plaintiff's counsel referred to the Master of the Office of Pleas to inspect the said bills and to tax what was reasonable and just, the plaintiff submitting to pay what should be so taxed. And, upon the report of Marriott, the Master of the Office of Pleas, this day made to the court that, upon examination of the matter he found and it was made out to him that the plaintiff had actually paid to the defendant as his solicitor in and for those causes £153 15s. 6d., of which he allowed £56 15s. 4d. only, and reported that the plaintiff had overpaid to the defendant £97 00s. 2d., which report, upon hearing counsel both for the plaintiff and the defendant, was approved of by the court. And the defendant refusing to repay to the plaintiff the said £97 00s. 2d. so overpaid upon the account of the said suits in this court was immediately by the judgment of the court committed to the Fleet [Prison], and his recognizance formerly given to appear *de die in diem* was upon the said commitment discharged, this being held to be a great misdemeanor and contempt to the court and the justice thereof and the proceedings therein to exact and receive from the plaintiff so great a sum above the ordinary, just, and usual fees and allowances in like cases.

[Other copies of this report: Georgetown Univ. Law Sch. MS. B88–9, f. 157v.]

216

Dear v. Duke of St. Albans

(Ex. 1702)

Interest is payable for an unpaid debt from the date the debt was payable.

Lincoln's Inn MS. Misc. 532, f. [180v]

19 June 1702.

The plaintiff brought an action of debt against the defendant for £40 upon a bill under the defendant's hand and seal whereby he promised to pay to the plaintiff the said £40 at such a time, which not being paid, the plaintiff brought his action upon that bill, and the defendant suffered judgment to pass by default. And whether the plaintiff should recover judgment for damages besides costs for non-payment of the money at the day or not, there not being any penalty or writ of enquiry executed, was the question.

And it was urged by *Raymond* that he should, the measure of which damages was to be computed according to the rate of interest which was the rule and practice both of the King's Bench and the Common Pleas, for which he cited the Case of Holdipp against Otway, 2 Sanders, fo. 106, 107,[1] a full authority in the point; nay, a stronger case, for that was against an executor that had no assets and the entry of the judgment must be and constantly is *ex assensu* of the defendant for the debt and so much for damages. And it is there resolved to be the constant course and practice of both those courts and that it is at the election of the plaintiff whether he will take a writ of enquiry of damages or his damages in such a case of delaying of a certain debt during a certain time to be taxed by the officer that signs the judgment.

And, in the principal case, Marriott, the Clerk of the Pleas, declared that he would sign a judgment for damages and costs according to the duty of his place and the practice and usage of the other courts, which was left to him to do accordingly.

[Other copies of this report: Georgetown Univ. Law Sch. MS. B88–9, f. 158.]

217

Harding v. Earl of Peterborough

(Ex. 1702)

In this case, a motion to set aside a default judgment was denied.

Lincoln's Inn MS. Misc. 532, f. [181]

[An action of] debt was brought upon a bond for the payment of money. [A writ of] *venire facias* was awarded against the defendant, and a summons was returned by the sheriff after that for a year together [with] several [writs of] *distringas* issued and returned with issues, which were estreated. And, then, this term, the earl appeared. And, upon his appearance and for want of a plea in ten days, judg-

[1] *Holdipp v. Otway* (1670), 2 Williams Saunders 102, 85 E.R. 802, also 2 Keble 624, 84 E.R. 393, 2 Modern 266, 86 E.R. 1064.

ment was entered, against which the earl's counsel moved for two things, first, that the earl was entitled to an imparlance until next term in regard there was no appearance until this term, which is the common proceedings in all courts.

But it was answered that, whenever a defendant comes in upon a process which imports a contempt, such defendant is not entitled to any imparlance, but must plead presently, and, if he do not so do within ten days and take notice of trial, the plaintiff may enter his judgment. And that is the written rule and practice in the office, as was reported by Marriott, Clerk of the Pleas, and agreed to by the attorneys and clerks in that office.

And, then, the defendant's counsel insisted that the judgment was entered before the ten days were out. And that depended upon this question whether the leaving of the declaration upon the defendant's attorney's desk in the office at half an hour past seven in the evening when that attorney was just gone out of the office, but the master of the office and several clerks were in the office and stayed until nine, was a good leaving or delivery of the declaration or not, it being admitted that leaving declarations in office hours upon the attorney's desks even in the absence of such attorney is a good delivery by the constant course of the office.

And upon hearing the master of the office and clerks not concerned [in] the causes, it was held to be a good delivery at such house and in such absence, that being held by all in the office, except the defendant's attorney, to be an office hour, after which the defendant's counsel desired that His Lordship might be admitted to plead *solvit ad diem* and try it after the term, which, to avoid questions, the plaintiff's counsel agreed to, so as, if the verdict went for the plaintiff, the present judgment by consent might stand, and he have execution upon it, which the defendant's counsel not assenting to, the court, in justice, could not set aside the judgment, which, upon examination and report, was entered regularly.

And, thereupon, the defendant's agents forthwith produced a writ of error, which was allowed.

[Other copies of this report: Georgetown Univ. Law Sch. MS. B88–9, f. 158v.]

218

Carus v. Carus

(Ex. 1702)

In this case, a penal bond to enforce an arbitral award was enforced.

Lincoln's Inn MS. Misc. 532, f. [193]

Michaelmas [term] 1702. George Carus, plaintiff; Thomas Carus, defendant. Intratur in Officio Placitorum, Paschae, 13 Will. III.

The plaintiff brings [an action of] debt upon a bond of £200 penalty dated the 2d of August 10 Will. III [1698] against the defendant conditioned for the performance of an award made between them by arbitrators chosen by them, *viz.* Charles Rigby, Esq., and Thomas Wither, to whom they mutually submitted the determination of all actions, suits, bills, bonds, writings obligatory, accounts, reckonings, trespasses, quarrels, damages, and demands whatsoever had, moved, and depending between the said parties so as they made their award in writing under their hands and seals ready to be delivered to either of the parties requiring the same at or before the 24th of September next.

The defendant prays *oyer* of the bond and condition and pleads *quod arbitratores praedictis nullum fecerent arbitrium in scriptis sub manibus et sigillis suis de et super praemissis in eadem conditione specificata ad vel ante praedictum 24tus diem Septembris in eadem conditione specificata, et hoc paratus etc.*

The plaintiff replies, and sets forth an award made in writing by the arbitrators under their hands and seals the said 24th day of September in the condition of the bond mentioned thereby reciting that, by a deed of settlement made and dated upon or about the 14th of February 13 Car. II [1638] between Thomas Carus, Esq., then deceased, grandfather of the plaintiff and defendant of the one part, Sir John Middleton, then also deceased, Richard Butler, Edward Tildesley, and Thomas Stanley, Esquires, all afterwards deceased, of the other part, it was provided and established to and for the plaintiff and his assigns for his life an annuity or rent charge of £20 *per annum* issuing out of all those several messuages, lands, tenements, and hereditaments in Halton or elsewhere in that writing mentioned to commence after the death of Christopher Carus, then deceased, father of the plaintiff and defendant payable as in that writing is mentioned, and reciting also that, by a deed of settlement of the 4th of May 4 Jac. II [1688] made between the said Christopher Carus, of the one part, and Robert Dalton, Richard Butler, Thomas Stanley, and Henry Blundell, of the other part, the said annuity or rent charge of £20 *per annum* was confirmed to the plaintiff and his assigns according to the purport of the first recited deed and that in the said last recited writing, it was provided and established to and for the now plaintiff and his assigns for and during his life another additional annuity or rent charge of £10 *per annum* to commence after the death of the said Christopher Carus and to issue out of the same lands with the other and referring to the last deed.

The arbitrators did order and arbitrate, first, that as well the said two annuities or rent charges of £20 and £10 as the said two writings and every clause therein contained, notwithstanding that that award should continue and remain and be due and payable according to the purport thereof as if that award had never been made. Nevertheless so as the plaintiff and defendant should mutually seal and execute each to the other at or before the first of October next after the award one pair of indentures of demise and grant affixed to the award having the arbitrators' hands in the margin, that then and during the joint lives of the plaintiff and the defendant and Mary Carus and not longer, the said two annuities should continue and be in suspense and quiet enjoyment by the plaintiff and his assigns of the lands and premises by the said indentures of demise and grant shall be taken, adjudged, and esteemed to be not only in lieu, satisfaction, and full discharge of all arrears of the said two annuities become due since the death of Christopher Carus but also in satisfaction and discharge of all future dues and duties upon account of those two annuities that thenceforth should become due at any time during such quiet enjoyment by the plaintiff and his assigns as aforesaid; second, that the defendant, his heirs, executors, or assigns shall pay or cause to be paid to the plaintiff or his executors, administrators, or assigns the several sums of money at the several days and places after mentioned, *viz.* £15 upon the 16th of November next following between one and three in the afternoon within the porch in the south side of the parish church of Lancer called Lancer; the further sum of £50 on the 1st of June 1699 at the same hours and place, and the further sum of £50 on the 16th of November 1699 at the said place and between the said hours; third, that, upon payment of those three sums in the manner aforesaid, the plaintiff or his assigns shall deliver to the defendant or to Richard Stanley, Esq., or to one of them, their, or one of their, heirs to be cancelled a writing obligatory dated the 1st of May 1688 wherein the said Richard Stanley and Thomas Stanley's father, deceased, stood bound in the sum of £400 to the said Christopher Carus conditioned for the payment of £200 the 2d of February 1689, which bond was then in the plaintiff's custody as executor of Christopher; fourth, that the defendant upon the 1st of October next after the award should seal and deliver as his absolute deed to the plaintiff or his use a general release of all actions, causes of actions, debts, duties, accounts, controversies, trespasses, damages, and demands from the beginning of the world to the date of that writing; fifth, and that the plaintiff at the same time should execute the like release to the defendant to the day of the writing obligatory aforesaid, except out of the plaintiff's release all right, title, claim, and interest of the plaintiff, his heirs, executors, and administrators to the said two annuities of, in, and to all other messuages, lands, and tenements in or by virtue of the said two in part recited deeds of settlement mentioned etc. comprised by virtue of any limitation, use or trust, power, or provision therein contained or otherwise howsoever *prout* the award.

Then, the plaintiff avers that he and the defendant did not seal and execute each to the other at or before the said 1st of October the said pair of indentures annexed to the award. *Ac protestando* that the defendant has not performed anything in that award or his part to be performed, the plaintiff in fact says that, though he, on the said 16th of November 1699, did attend at the time and place appointed and was ready to receive from the defendant the said £50, yet the defendant did not pay it, but refused so to do and the same is still unpaid contrary to the form of the said award. And so he prays judgment and his debt.

To this replication, the defendant has demurred generally. And the plaintiff has joined [in the demurrer].

Note the defendant not attending to maintain his demurrer, the plaintiff had judgment *nisi causa* such a day and, afterwards, absolutely. There was no argument in the case.

[Other copies of this report: Georgetown Univ. Law Sch. MS. B88–9, f. 163v.]

219

Attorney General v. Lawton

(Ex. 1702)

A plea that is argumentative is bad and cannot be cured by a verdict.

Dodd 197

[In an action of] *scire facias* upon a bond entered into by the defendant for the duty of salt to the king conditioned for payment of £1000 on the 25th September following, the defendant pleads payment before the aforesaid 25th September *secundum formam et effectum et veram intentionem eiusdem conditionis.*

Mr. Attorney [General] replied *non solvit secundum tenorem et effectum conditionis eiusdem scripti obligationis modo et forma prout in* plaintiff's etc. And upon the trial, the jury found *quod non solvit secundum tenorem et effectum conditionis scripti obligatoris praedictis.*

And upon a motion in arrest of judgment, the court resolved:

First, that it was a bad plea and could be demurred unto, for it is but argumentative;

Second, that the verdict has not helped it.

And they awarded a repleader and reply upon [it]. Cr. Jac. 434 and 288; Cro. Eliz. 144.[1]

220

Attorney General v. Orpheur

(Ex. 1702)

Scotland is not beyond sea within the meaning of the Salt Acts to discharge a debenture or drawback.

---

[1] *Holms v. Broket* (1617), Croke Jac. 434, 79 E.R. 371; *Tampion v. Newson* (1611), Croke Jac. 288, 79 E.R. 247, also Yelverton 210, 80 E.R. 138; *Long v. Woodliffe* (1589), Croke Eliz. 144, 78 E.R. 401.

Dodd 197, Parker 269, 145 E.R. 776

[It was] resolved upon a demurrer to a plea [to a writ of *scire facias*] upon a salt bond that Scotland is not in that case beyond the sea, or within the meaning of the Salt Acts[1] to discharge a debenture or drawback of the duty upon exporting the salt into Scotland.

221

Ashe v. Harding

(Ex. 1703)

In this case, a verdict was amended many years after it had been entered.

Lincoln's Inn MS. Misc. 533, f. [111]

Hilary [term] 1702[/03].

In [an action of] ejectment, upon a long special verdict depending in this court where the late Lord Jeffreys *et al.* were lessors of the plaintiff and Mr. James Herbert, the defendant, each party claiming the estate of Dudley Rewse by a title under the crown. And the only doubt with the jury made as now entered up and argued was whether the defendant's entry upon the plaintiff's possession was lawful or not. If [it was] not lawful, then they find the defendants guilty; if lawful, then they find the defendants not guilty.

This cause was tried at the bar in [*blank*] term. And it lay a considerable time before the special verdict was drawn up. At last, it was drawn up by the plaintiff and great struggling there were, and many motions and debates in court were had about the settling of it.

And, in Easter term 1700, books were delivered on both sides. And the court appointed several days for argument in Trinity, Michaelmas, and Hilary terms 1700. But it was put off at the desire of the counsel on both sides. And in Easter term 1701, it was argued by counsel on each side; the like in Trinity [term] 1701, and also in Hilary term 1701[/02]. And the court appointed to deliver their judgments in Easter term 1702. But, by the change of judges in the court, it could not be. And, in Michaelmas term 1702, after the court was settled, it was appointed to be again argued. But something being started from the court whether there was any estate in fee found to be in Dudley Rewse or only in others in trust for him, it was deliberated upon by both sides.

And now, this term [Hilary 1702/03], *Northey*, the queen's Attorney General, for the defendant, objected against the drawing up of the special verdict as to the special conclusion by making it the only doubt of the jury and, by conse-

[1] Stat. 9 Will. III, c. 44 (*SR*, VII, 429–446); Stat. 10 Will. III, c. 11 (*SR*, VII, 508–511).

quence, laying the whole stress of the case upon the lawfulness or unlawfulness of the defendant's entry without any respect had to the plaintiff's title, inverting thereby the known and constant rule that the plaintiff must recover by the strength and goodness of his own title, and, if he make not out a good one, the defendant is not guilty to him. And he said this sort of drawing up a special verdict in an [action of] ejectment to put the defendant to make a title against the plaintiff is unprecedented and there is nothing to warrant it by the notes of the special verdict, which make the usual and general conclusion '*si pro querente, pro querente; si pro defendente, pro defendente*.' And it must be contrivance in the plaintiff's counsel and an inadvertency in the defendants to have such a special conclusion. And, therefore, he prayed it might be amended, and the doubt of the jury to be upon the whole matter and the conclusion to be general, as in other special verdicts, there being neither reason nor interest or agreement of the defendant or his counsel to have it otherwise. And that amendments may be made, where there is good reason for it, he cited Rawlins's Case, 4 rep. 54,[1] where, in an [action of] ejectment, the demise found in the special verdict was found to be by a deed, omitting the word 'indented', and, though the verdict had been entered on the roll three terms past, yet, upon the view of the notes whereby the demise was found *prout etc.* and so referred to by the notes, it was amended.

And it is frequent in the books as well as practice to have amendments made even after judgment and writs of error brought, 2 Cro. 185, and even in the judgment of the court. 2 Cro. 631, 632; Higgins and Smith, 1695, which see L. M, 9,[2] where after error was brought and judgment pronounced for the reversal *nisi*, upon an application to the King's Bench, the record was amended, as found by the special verdict, which was wrongly entered, and, by that amendment and a [writ of] *certiorari* awarded, the first judgment was affirmed. And this was upon a wrong conclusion which the jury had made. Cro. Eliz. 677, 866, and Blackmore's Case, 8 rep.[3]

Note it is a rule in Goodale's Case, 5 rep. 97,[4] that the court shall not doubt of more than the jurors have and so if no title in [an action of] ejectment be found for the defendant, yet, if the jury make a special conclusion, that supplies it.

---

[1] *Rawlyns v. Somerford* (1587), 4 Coke Rep. 52, 76 E.R. 1007, also 4 Leonard 116, 74 E.R. 767, Gouldsborough 89, 93, 75 E.R. 1015, 1018, Jenkins 254, 145 E.R. 180.

[2] *Harrison v. Fulstowe* (1607), Croke Jac. 185, 79 E.R. 161, also Yelverton 108, 80 E.R. 74, 1 Brownlow & Goldesborough 96, 123 E.R. 689; *Mason v. Fox* (1622), Croke Jac. 632, 79 E.R. 544; *Higgins v. Smith* (1695), Lincoln's Inn MS. Misc. 559, f. 9.

[3] *Lewson v. Redleston* (1599), Croke Eliz. 677, 709, 78 E.R. 914, 944; *Gramvel v. Rhobotham* (1601), Croke Eliz. 865, 866, 78 E.R. 1092; *Blackamore v. Franke* (1610), 8 Coke Rep. 156, 77 E.R. 710.

[4] *Goodall v. Wyat* (1597), 5 Coke Rep. 95, 77 E.R. 202, also Jenkins 261, 145 E.R. 187, Gouldsborough 176, 75 E.R. 1076, Moore K.B. 708, 72 E.R. 855, Croke Eliz. 383, 78 E.R. 629, Popham 99, 79 E.R. 1209.

But note, in Seymor's Case, 10 rep. 96,[1] in [an action of] ejectment and thereafter a title on both sides is found, the jury *super totam materiam praedictam* doubted whether the defendant *legitime intravit necne* and pray the advice of the court etc. and conclude upon the lawfulness or not lawfulness of the defendant's entry, as here, but that must be intended where the parties agreed to such special conclusion.

A special verdict [was] amended after judgment [in] Bold and Walter, 12 Jac., 1 Rolle, tit. *Amendment*, 207, 15, by the notes.[2]

The counsel for the defendant in this case, *viz. Powys*, the queen's First Serjeant, *Browne*, and *Phipps* insist against the amendment after so long a time and such proceedings and the rules of court for the plaintiff to bring in objections against the special verdict as drawn with the special conclusion to it and the lawfulness of the defendant's entry upon the plaintiff being a great part argued for the defendant as a main point, and these things were never questioned until now. And, therefore, they think the amendment unreasonable and not fit to be made.

And the court took time to advise until the last day of this term [Hilary 1702/03]. And then the court *seriatim* delivered their opinions that the amendment should be made as desired: First, because, by the notes of the special verdict, which are always the ground and rule to draw up the special verdict by, the jury made no such special conclusion, but concluded generally, if for the plaintiff, for the plaintiff; if for the defendant, for the defendant, and, therefore, they left it to the court to judge upon the whole matter without restraining or confining it to the lawfulness or unlawfulness of the defendant's entry, which is only one single point and, indeed, is but the consequence of the title found on either side. And there is no reason nor warrant to conclude upon one special matter when the court is to judge upon the whole matter found;

Secondly, because there does not appear nor, upon examination, could be made out (nor was the truth so) that the plaintiff or his counsel or attorney ever agreed to nor was made acquainted with (otherwise than by having the special verdict delivered to them) this special conclusion, and, as to the passing it so, it was wholly an act of inadvertency, not looking into it nor thinking it to be otherwise than a general conclusion;

Thirdly, that this special conclusion inverts the method of the law that puts the plaintiff to recover by his own title and not by the defendant's weakness; but, here, the defendant makes not out his title, though the plaintiff has none, the defendant must lose his estate, which ought not to be without his consent to such a conclusion;

Fourthly, that the length of time and proceedings upon this special verdict so far as to a third argument is not too late to set the special verdict right, accord-

[1] *Heywood, ex dem. Seymor v. Smith* (1612), 10 Coke Rep. 95, 77 E.R. 1070, also 1 Bulstrode 162, 80 E.R. 853.

[2] *Bowlde v. Walter* (1614), 1 Rolle, Abr., *Amendment*, pl. F, 15, p. 207.

ing to the notes upon the reasons and authorities urged by Mr. Attorney General etc. and before cited, where such amendments have been made after arguments, nay, even after judgments.

And a rule was given to make the amendment accordingly by altering the special conclusion into the general conclusion according to the notes of the special verdict signed by counsel on both sides. And the amendment was made, and the case after that [was] several times argued by counsel.

[Other copies of this report: Georgetown Univ. Law Sch. MS. B88–9, f. 173v.]

Dodd 199

In a special verdict concerning My Lord Jeffreys and Mr. Herbert at Chalfont in Buckinghamshire, the notes had a general conclusion but the verdict drawn up had a special conclusion, *viz.* 'if the defendant's entry upon the plaintiff were not lawful, then for the plaintiff'. And notwithstanding the verdict found at the bar six or eight years before and many motions about settling it in other matters and that it had been long since entered and four or five times argued and stood for the judgment of the court, yet this matter being now discovered and found to turn the case (although notice in that argument had been once taken of it), yet the court upon debate this term [Hilary, 1 Anne, 1703] amended the verdict and made the conclusion general according to the notes.

Note that, upon the verdict as found, it is supposed that neither plaintiff nor defendant had any title but as now found; if the plaintiff have none, then the defendant is safe, as being in possession. Rawlins's Case, 4 Rep.; Rolle, [Abr.], *Amendment*, 207,[1] etc. Note.

222

Evans v. Powell

(Ex. 1703)

In this case, the arbitral award in issue was valid and enforceable.

Lincoln's Inn MS. Misc. 533, f. [110]

Hilary [term] 1702[/03] 1 Anne.

[To an action of] debt upon a bond to perform an award, *nullum fecit arbitrium* [was] pleaded. The plaintiff replies, and sets forth the award *de et super praemissis modo et forma sequente.* And then he shows the arbitrators awarded that the defendant should pay the plaintiff such a sum at such a day and that J.S., who

[1] *Rawlyns v. Somerford* (1587), 4 Coke Rep. 52, 76 E.R. 1007, also 4 Leonard 116, 74 E.R. 767, Gouldsborough 89, 93, 75 E.R. 1015, 1018, Jenkins 254, 145 E.R. 180; 1 Rolle, Abr., *Amendment*, pl. F, 15, p. 207.

also submitted himself to the award and was [. . .] to the defendant in the action submitted with the now defendant, should also pay the plaintiff such a sum at such a day and that, upon payment of those sums, the plaintiff should give releases to each defendant. The defendant demurs generally.

And, now, *Grove*, for the defendant, alleges that the award is not good, being of one side only and not certain, for he ought not to have set forth the award *modo et forma sequente* but absolutely. And he relied upon the case in Roll's Abr. 254, 11, and Hobt. 49,[1] and that it appears to be of one side only is because the now defendants, if he should have paid the sum he was awarded to pay, yet should not have any release until J.S. had paid his money also [which] does not appear to be paid and possibly may never be paid. And so, in effect, he is awarded to pay the money only, and [there is] nothing effectual for his discharge.

To which it was answered and resolved by the court that this was a good award on both sides, for it must be understood *reddendo singula singulis* as to the releases and upon the defendant's payment to have a release. And were it not so but that the defendant was to stay for a release until J.S. had paid, yet it is an award of both sides. And the plaintiff had judgment.

The award being made *de et super praemissis* is good without any release to be had. 1 Roll's Abr. 153, b, 11.[2]

Judgment [was given] by all of the court for the plaintiff.

[Other copies of this report: Georgetown Univ. Law Sch. MS. B88–9, f. 172.]

223

Patterson, qui tam v. Keyler

(Ex. 1703)

An error of Latin in a nisi prius record that is obvious will not prevent a judgment to be entered.

Lincoln's Inn MS. Misc. 533, f. [110v], pl. 2

Hilary [term] 1702[/03].

In an information for loading aboard *qingent libratis ponderis lanae* for transportation contrary to the statutes, [it] so prays that the defendant may forfeit £75, *viz.* 3s. per pound for the wool aforesaid. The record of *nisi prius* was a Q. 3. *minnomus et gent'* as above. I [Edward Ward] took notice of it at the trial, and the Attorney General [*Northey*] said he would go on and, if the jury found for the

[1] *Nicholls v. Grunwin* (1616), 1 Rolle, Abr., *Arbitrement*, pl. K, 11, p. 254, Hobart 49, 80 E.R. 199.

[2] *Nicholls v. Grunwin* (1616), *ut supra.*

plaintiff, the defendant should have the advantage of it in [a motion for] arrest [of judgment] or move for a new trial.

And so the jury, according to the evidence, found for 500 pounds weight, which, by a true computation after 3s. per pound, comes to £75.

The defendant's counsel, at the trial, as soon as I took notice of the doubtfulness of the word, declared they would give no evidence nor make any defense, but rely upon that defect. It did not seem they had any witnesses. But full proof was for the plaintiff.

And now *Dodd* and *Turner* move in arrest of judgment for the uncertainty and insignificance of that word '*qingent*', for, if that word be so uncertain that it can signify nothing, then no judgment ought to be entered, for the jury had no quantity to try. In a bond, if the word for the sum be improper or does not denote a certain sum, yet, when the plaintiff sues that bond, he must make use of a proper and significant word in his declaration, and the court must judge whether the improper word is rightly expressed by the proper word made use of, as if the word in the bond is '*sessanta*', which he understands to be sixty, yet he must declare the word of *sexaginta*. So are all the cases. Roll's, *Obl.* etc.[1] And the case of a bond mightily differs from this case, for many times the sum in the condition illustrates the meaning of the improper word in the obligation. But, here, this word stands by itself, and the recovery must be in virtue of this word or nothing. Now, nobody can say that '*qingent*' signifies anything, for, if it be read *qingent*, it is utterly uncertain and void. And to supply a 'u' after the 'q' and so to read it '*quingent*' is without reason or authority. These very letters that make up '*qingent*' are to be considered. They are no abbreviation but an entire word. What authority is there to supply a 'u' next after the 'q'? That is to amend in a penal case, which is not allowable, as it is said in Blackamore's Case, 8 rep.[2]

Mr. Attorney [General, *Northey*], Mr. Solicitor [General, *Harcourt*], Mr. *Ward*, and *Bridges*, for the plaintiff, insist, first, that there is no instance that ever any letter in any language followed a 'q' but a 'u' and so in pronunciation, though not in letters, it is '*quingent*' and to supply a 'u' next after the 'q' when no letter can follow next is but reasonable. And, as it is written, it must be looked upon but as an abbreviation of '*quingenti*', and that seems best to agree with the intent of the parties and to be so understood in regard 500 3s. makes just £75, which is the sum demanded. *Qd.* stand indifferently for '*quid*' or '*quod*', and the 'u' is supplied in both cases; *vide* Osborn's Case, 10 rep. 133.[3] But it was objected that that was an abbreviation, which this is not by any dash[4] etc.

---

[1] *Parker v. Kennedy*, 2 Rolle, Abr., *Obligation*, pl. C, 12, p. 147, also Hobart 19, 80 E.R. 171.

[2] *Blackamore v. Franke* (1610), 8 Coke Rep. 156, 77 E.R. 710.

[3] *Osborn v. Middleton* (1613), 10 Coke Rep. 130, 133, 77 E.R. 1123, 1129, also Jenkins 270, 145 E.R. 194.

[4] *I.e.* a tilde.

Note both the information itself and the entry upon the roll are both '*quingenti*'. Only the *nisi prius* roll is mistaken, as above.

And, afterwards, Easter [term] 1703, the court gave a judgment for the queen and the informer, for that word, 'qingent', as it is written is to be taken rather for an abbreviation of 'quingentis' than, to read it 'qingentis' and so to make it wholly insignificant. And this construction is made upon the same ground that an insignificant word in a bond is many times made good by the same in the condition, as the case Roll's, Obligations, mentions, for here, the demand of 3s. in the pound for 500 pound weight of wool comes just to £75, which is the sum demanded by the information. And, then, the original information and the plea roll, being 'quingentis' sufficiently evidences what was intended by the word in the nisi prius roll, which wants only a 'u', which always in writing and pronunciation does and must follow a 'q', and so makes the abbreviation the more probable and easy. Besides, as it is written, it may be well pronounced 'qingent' in omitting the sound of the 'u', which is often omitted in the pronunciation.

And, then, the jury, upon the evidence, having found that the defendant exported 500 pound weight of wool in the time of the information, all these things considered, they well warrant giving judgment for the plaintiff.

The Chief Baron [WARD] delivered the opinion of the whole court for the plaintiff at the desire of the other three barons, being all of one opinion.

[Other copies of this report: Georgetown Univ. Law Sch. MS. B88–9, f. 172v.]

224

Attorney General v. Shallet

(Ex. 1703)

Goods in execution can be sold where no security has been given for the protection of the creditor.

Lincoln's Inn MS. Misc. 533, f. [113], pl. 1

20 February 1702[/03].

Several parts in ships [were] seized upon [writs of] extent, and rules [were made] for [a writ of] *venditioni exponas*, and [it was] awarded but not executed. Others, claiming under Shallet, came in to claim and plead, which [was] ordered. But, upon security not coming in until after *venditioni* awarded and no difference in reason why security should be given in the case of a seizure of lands upon putting in a plea, after a *levari* [*facias*] and no [. . .] in the case of a plea to stop a *venditioni exponas*, those to be different, the like order in the Case of Mr. Pawlet that claimed live cattle seized for Cobb's debt, which being chargeable to keep, the defendant agreed the goods should be sold and the money brought into court.

Note it seems, notwithstanding the practice in the office to allow pleas upon such seizures without security, that there is no reason for it.

[Other copies of this report: Georgetown Univ. Law Sch. MS. B88–9, f. 176.]

225

Anonymous

(Ex. 1703)

Writs of assistance for former sheriffs are not enforceable by their successors in office until after the successor is chargeable.

Lincoln's Inn MS. Misc. 533, f. [113], pl. 2

Note, in the cases of two writs of assistance for the late sheriffs to assist them to levy forfeited issues, fines, or amercements at sessions of the peace, they were laid aside in regard they issued before the sheriffs had charged themselves or were chargeable by the court for them, for the writ is to assist such a late sheriff to levy such sums which are due from the parties to the said late sheriffs, which cannot be said to be due to them until the sheriffs have charged themselves with them which, in these cases, they had not nor, indeed, could in regard the estreats of the sessions are not by the Statute 22 Car. II[1] returnable but in Michaelmas term and though the sheriff, by the estreat delivered to him by the Clerk of the Peace at the end of every sessions so is enabled to levy what he can within his year, yet he is not entitled to any assistance from the Exchequer until after the court is possessed of the estreat from the Clerk of the Peace and charged himself upon his apposals with those sums, which, in these cases, they neither did nor could, their apposals not being then come, and so the writs of assistance are set aside and not to be executed by the succeeding sheriff, who, thereby, would be deprived of the levying of those unlevied and lose his fees for them.

226

Williams v. Mytton

(Ex. 1703)

It is lawful to forcibly remove a person who is disturbing the peace and disturbing a church service.

Lincoln's Inn MS. Misc. 533, f. [118v]

Easter [term] 2 Anne, 1703.

---

[1] Stat. 22 & 23 Car. II, c. 22 (*SR*, V, 739–741).

[An action of] assault and battery and wounding was brought by the plaintiff [Lumly Williams]. The defendants [Mytton and his wife] plead *son assault demesne*. The plaintiff replies his father was to be buried and his grave dug in the chancel, and the defendant's wife, one of the defendants, filled up the grave and disturbed the divine service and disturbed the people so within, scolding and brawling, so that they could not proceed to the solemnizing of the funeral and therefore to preserve the peace and that the funeral of his father might be solemnized, he laid his hands upon the defendant's wife and put her out of the church. The defendants rejoin *de injuria sua propria absque causa*. And, thereupon, issue was joined.

The jury found the defendants guilty of the wounding and that the plaintiff *verberare, vulnerare, seu maletractare* the defendant's wife *non voluit*, damages £5.

And it was moved by *Grove* in arrest of judgment that the plaintiff's excuse to the *son assault demesne* as to the defendant's wife's filling up the grave and scolding and disturbing the funeral was not sufficient to lay his hand upon the woman and put her out, for it does not appear that there was any right to bury the plaintiff's father in the chancel, and it might be that there was no right so to do. And, if there was a right, he ought to have shown it; else [it is] to be intended it was not lawful, nor did or could avoid the effect of the defendants' plea of *son assault demesne*, the fact of which is admitted but not justified by the replication.

But the plaintiff had judgment upon the wounding, and the cause of laying hands and putting the wife out from disturbing the funeral was a good and justifiable act. Sanders [*blank*]. And it is lawful for any at the funeral to turn out such a disturber, as that case and reason both well warrant.

[Other copies of this report: Georgetown Univ. Law Sch. MS. B88–9, f. 181v.]

227

Wells v. Kennett

(Ex. 1703)

An ecclesiastical court can determine the validity of a license to preach where it does not involve the right of a curacy of a church.

Lincoln's Inn MS. Misc. 533, f. [131]

Zachary Wells, clerk, plaintiff; White Kennett, D.D., defendant.

In [an action for] a [writ of] prohibition, it being a question whether the plaintiff or the defendant[1] has the right to be curate or chaplain of the parish church of St. Buttolph without Aldgate, the plaintiff claiming under the crown's

[1] L. Okie, 'Kennett, White (1660–1728), historian and bishop of Peterborough', *Oxford Dictionary of National Biography*, vol. 31, pp. 283–287.

title by letters patent and the defendant under the impropriator of Aldgate by an instrument under his hand and seal. The defendant having obtained a license from the bishop of London to preach in the church, and the plaintiff applying to the bishop for the like license, the defendant opposed him, but, the bishop granting the license to the plaintiff, the defendant appealed to the [Court of] Arches from the bishop's act of granting that license, supposing he had not right nor, in justice, ought to grant such a license. And to stop the proceedings upon that appeal, the plaintiff prayed a [writ of] prohibition upon a suggestion that the right of appointing a curate in that church was drawn in question in that appeal, which ought not to be in regard that court ought not to take upon them the determination of the validity of the queen's letters patents, but that they ought to be determined in this court or at common law.

But the court, upon consideration of the appeal and suggestion denied to grant the prohibition in regard there was not in these proceedings any questions upon the right of making the curate, but only whether the bishop of London had done well or not in granting the plaintiff a license, which is a matter wholly spiritual and of ecclesiastical cognizance, the license in this case not tending one way or the other towards the determining the title of the curacy. L. 2, 52, accord.

Attorney General [*Northey*] *et al., pro querente; Ettrick et al., pro defendente.*

[Other copies of this report: Georgetown Univ. Law Sch. MS. B88–9, f. 203v.]

[Related cases: Hollingworth v. Umfreville (Ex. 1694), 1 Wood 332; Attorney General, *ex rel.* Wells v. Brewster (Ex. 1703–1705), Equity Cases Exch. 476, 1 Wood 455.]

228

Crispe's Creditors v. Molineux

(Ex. 1703)

Writs of immediate extent can only be granted upon motion in open court.

Lincoln's Inn MS. Misc. 533, f. [131v]

12 November 1703. Pleasant Crispe's creditors v. Molineux, in a debt in aid.

Benson, a collector of the excise, entered into a bond to the late king of £2000, and, by order of the court, leave was given to find debts due to him. And a [writ of] extent *teste* 13 March 1 *Annae Reginae* [1702] was thereupon awarded returnable in Easter term next. And, by an inquisition thereupon taken 27th of the same March, it was found that Molineux was then indebted to Benson in £1676 12s. 03d. for so much had and received to Benson's use and that debt was thereby seized into the queen's hands. And, by Baron Hatsell's warrant, a [writ of] immediate extent was awarded against Molineux (but what was done upon that *non constat*) but, by an order of the 23 April 1703, mentioning that extent and that there was occasion to prosecute one Browne, a debtor to Molineux, a new extent was awarded against Molineux, which, the 16th of June 1703, issued accordingly *quoad debita, credita, et specialitates* of Molineux for satisfaction of the said debt of £1676 17s. 3d. returnable *tres Michaelis proxime* and by inquisition thereupon taken 17 August 1703, [Pleasant] Crispe was found debtor to Molineux in £1075 11s. 6d. upon a stated account, which was seized into the queen's hands the same day. And, the same day, Molineux made an affidavit that the debt due from him to Benson was for money received by him of the duty of excise to be returned to London for the late king's uses and was still unpaid and that he was not able to pay it unless the debt due from Crispe to him was recovered, which he swore was a just debt *bona fide* due and Crispe decayed in his estate and broke and absconds and Her Majesty in danger of losing the debt so seized, and the same day, being vacation time, the Chancellor of the Exchequer made a warrant for a [writ of] immediate extent against Crispe's body, lands, and goods which was executed both in London and Surrey and houses and goods seized returnable *tres Michaelis*. And, upon a motion to the court on the behalf of the assignees of the commissioners of bankrupts that Crispe making it appear by affidavit that the stated account was a mere fraud and trick to get a stock jobbing bargain preferred before all other the creditors, the court referred it to have the whole case stated by the Deputy [Queen's] Remembrancer, which appearing to be as above, the court set aside the inquisition that seized the debt of Crispe and all process and proceedings thereupon as utterly irregular in these things:

First, the court, by their order of the 23rd of April intended only to renew the extent against Molineux for Browne's debt;

Second, that this was only in aid of Molineux and, for aught appears, Benson has paid all to the crown and that Molineux makes these proceedings only as a handle to get in his private debts to the prejudice of the other creditors;

Third, that here the last immediate extent is awarded before the return of that of the 16th June, which was not returnable until *tres Michaelis* and this granted in August returnable the same time, which is always held bad in cases of debts merely in aid and where the crown debt is not in danger, as here it is not;

Fourth, by the Rules of 1639, [writs of] immediate extent must be upon motion in open court, which was not here and the oaths were not regular.

[Other copies of this report: Georgetown Univ. Law Sch. MS. B88–9, f. 204.]

229

Reynolds v. Lloyd

(Ex. 1703–1704)

In this case of an accidental mayhem, the court refused to increase the damages awarded by the jury to the plaintiff.

Lincoln's Inn MS. Misc. 533, f. [133v]

Last day of [Michaelmas] term.

The plaintiff brought [an action of] trespass for assault and battery and mayhem, generally, against the defendant. The defendant pleads not guilty as to force and arms and, for the residue, *son assault demesne*. The issue was found for the plaintiff generally and damages of £12. And this was tried before Baron Bury at the Shrewsbury Assize. And the plaintiff's counsel producing the plaintiff in court who had lost his right eye by the defendant's beating him, prayed he might be inspected and the damages increased.

But Baron Bury not being prepared to give the court a particular account as to the mayhem, the court inspected the plaintiff and left it to be further considered until the first day next term when they should be informed how it was at the trial, as was done last term in the King's Bench in a like case, 1 Siderfin 108, Angell and Shatterton.[1]

There these things seem to be clear: first, that, upon a general *mayhemavit* and justification, damages may be increased; second, but, in such a general case not increased unless the judge that tried the cause certify the particulars of the mayhem. Burford *et ux.* v. Dadwell, Sid. 433, L. 2, 64.[2] The court was of opinion that they might increase the damages where it appears by the declaration and the fact found was that three fingers were lost, though the word *mayhemavit* was not in the declaration. But it is true the court, in that case, did not see reason upon inspection to increase them.

[Other copies of this report: Georgetown Univ. Law Sch. MS. B88–9, f. 206.]

Lincoln's Inn MS. Misc. 536, f. [18], pl. 2

The court having been formerly moved to increase £12 damages given by the jury for a mayhem by the defendant's striking out one of the plaintiff's eyes, for which purpose, the plaintiff was inspected by the court heretofore *de bene esse*, Baron Bury, who tried the cause, giving the court an account of the trial that the plaintiff was present at it and it was by a special jury and upon a drunken fit between the plaintiff and the defendant and that it did not appear to be willfully and maliciously done and the defendant being a poor man, though *son assault demesne* was pleaded and found against the defendant, yet being rather an accident, as it was in Angell and Shatterdon's Case, 1 Siderfin 85, the court there, as also the court here, did not think fit to increase the damages.

[Other copies of this report: Georgetown Univ. Law Sch. MS. B88–9, f. 237v, pl. 1.]

---

[1] *Angell v. Shatterton* (1663), 1 Siderfin 108, 82 E.R. 1000, also 1 Keble 472, 83 E.R. 1060.

[2] *Burford v. Dadwell* (1669), 1 Siderfin 433, 82 E.R. 1201, Lincoln's Inn MS. Misc. 500, f. 64.

230

Attorney General v. Tristram

(Ex. 1703)

An inquisition found for the crown as to land cannot defeat a private person's statutory possessory rights.

Lincoln's Inn MS. Misc. 533, f. [134]

An information of intrusion was exhibited against the defendants who, upon the usual oath made according to the Statute 21 Jac. I, ca. [*blank*],[1] that the crown or any claiming under the crown nor any claiming under the same title by which the crown claims had been in possession or received any of the rents or profits of the lands in question within the space of twenty years before the exhibiting of this information, had leave to plead the general issue of not guilty and to retain the possession. And he did so plead. And issue being thereupon taken, it came to be tried before Chief Justice Trevor of the Common Bench at the Hereford Assizes last.

And the counsel for the queen, instead of giving any evidence for the crown, produced a copy of an inquisition formerly taken upon a commission under the great seal returned into the Chancery and transcribed and sent by a [writ of] *mittimus* into this court to have proceeding thereupon according to law, by which inquisition, it was found that the lands in question were the lands of J.S., who died without an heir and that they belonged to the crown *tanquam eschaeta sua*, but it found no tenure of them of the crown nor of any manner belonging to the crown. And the lands by the inquisition were seized into the late king's hands *tanquam eschaeta sua*. And it was at the assize insisted upon that the defendant should not nor could give in evidence any title to the lands upon that issue, it appearing by the said inquisition that they were in the king's hands, and, therefore, the defendants must first discharge that inquisition before any of their title could be admitted and, for that reason, there was a verdict for the plaintiff. The defendants prayed a new trial or that, at least, things might stay upon that verdict until the former inquisition was traversed, which was opposed by the Attorney [General, *Northey*] and the Solicitor General [*Harcourt*] and others, who insisted upon it that the judgment should be entered upon this verdict and the defendants might be left to do what they pleased as to the traversing the former inquisition.

But I [Edward Ward] observed that this was a way and matter which, if allowed, must needs defeat the subject of the benefit intended by the Statute of 7 Jac.,[2] for this inquisition is the only record by which the crown's title appears and upon which the very information of intrusion is grounded and unless upon such

[1] Stat. 21 Jac. I, c. 14 (*SR*, IV, 1221).

[2] Stat. 7 Jac. I, c. 15 (*SR*, IV, 1171).

oath that, for twenty years before, the crown had no possession or perception of profits, such plea of not guilty shall be allowed, that Statute must signify nothing, which was plainly intended that, in such case, for want of such possession, the subject should not upon an information of intrusion be put specially to plead off the crown's title, but should have the advantage of making out a title against everything under which the crown claims, for, if the title of the crown, which must always be upon record and, in most cases is, by inquisitions upon commissions, must be pleaded off, then there will remain no title for the crown to ground an information of intrusion upon. And, then, there can be no such information. But that Statute supposed that, where any information of intrusion upon any of the crown's title whatsoever should be brought and wherein the crown had not had any possession or profits within twenty years before, that the subject should have the benefit of pleading not guilty and retaining the possession, and it particularly directs that, where an information of intrusion can fitly be brought, that so *scire facias* etc. should be brought to deprive the subject of the benefit of that Statute.

Note it is harsh that a defendant that is allowed by law to plead not guilty to an intrusion and to make out his title upon the trial should be denied so to do and thereupon be subjected to lose the possession and answer for the mesne rates and pay a fine for his intrusion.

Harcourt, Solicitor General, said this way was practiced in that circuit before Justice Giles Eyre and allowed and the crown had judgment in like intrusions, for that only reason, because lands are by record in the king's hands.

But note there was no such oath nor order for pleading not guilty as here nor, indeed, could be made, because, for lands given to superstitious uses, the crown claimed under them that were owners and had the possession all along.

And the true difference is, where a subject is plaintiff, he cannot maintain an [action of] ejectment where lands are in the king's hands. But, where the subject is defendant, he may upon oath and order, as above, defend his title.

[Other copies of this report: Georgetown Univ. Law Sch. MS. B88–9, f. 206v.]

231

Anonymous

(Ex. 1703)

A new trial can be ordered where the verdict was contrary to the evidence, but not a second new trial.

Lincoln's Inn MS. Misc. 533, f. [135]

In a prohibition to the Admiralty, issue was joined whether the goods in question being French brandies were wreck or not. And, upon the trial, which was before Justice Tracy of the Common Bench at the last Sussex Assizes, the great and, indeed, the only question was whether a Frenchman that was found to lie upon plowed lands a good distance from the seaside and where no sea comes nor can [. . .] within a great number of yards at the highest tides and was proved to belong to that ship which was alleged to be wrecked, did come or was brought ashore alive or not, for, if he escaped alive out of the ship and came or was brought alive ashore, then it was no wreck. Otherwise, it was a wreck, and, in such case of a wreck, the goods belonged to the plaintiff as lord of the manor or else to Prince George, Lord High Admiral of England,[1] as a perquisite of the Admiralty, the jury, being a special one of Sussex, found it to be a wreck by consequence that that man did not escape or come ashore alive out of the ship.

The judge, being spoke withal in order to a new trial, declared himself not fully satisfied with the verdict and that, if he had been upon the jury, he should not have given that verdict, but he would not certify directly that he thought it fit to be tried again. But he left that to the court.

And, upon hearing divers counsel on both sides and considering the judge's dissatisfaction so far as it went and that he certified the circumstances by which it did probably appear that the man was alive after he was upon the plowed lands in regard where he lay, it appeared that there were scratchings of the earth and earth was found between his fingers when clutched which very probably and, indeed, almost necessarily implied he was there alive. And it appearing by affidavits of another person that was not nor could be at the trial being then and long before and after at sea that he saw that man as he lay upon the lands move his hands and thighs and that life was then in him.

The Chief Baron [Ward], barons Bury and Price (*dissentiente* Smith) thought upon the whole matter that it was fit to be tried again upon the payment of full costs and not taking away the benefit of giving that verdict in evidence, which was ordered accordingly.

And note that, at the Lent Assizes following, another trial was had, and a verdict [was found] the same way, and, in Easter term following, the goods were delivered.

[Other copies of this report: Georgetown Univ. Law Sch. MS. B88–9, f. 208.]

[1] W. A. Speck, 'George, prince of Denmark (1653–1708)', *Oxford Dictionary of National Biography*, vol. 21, pp. 795–799.

232

Smith v. Weale

(Ex. 1703)

In this case, the rent in issue was due on certain days of the year regardless of whether the year was past.

Lincoln's Inn MS. Misc. 533, f. [137]

29 November, by a Michaelmas record 2 Queen Anne [1703]. Radnor.

The plaintiff declares in an action of debt for rent against the defendants upon a demise made 2nd April 1698 of a moiety of a messuage and lands by the plaintiff to the defendants *habendum* from the 2d of February last before for a year *ex tunc proxime sequente et plenar' complend' et finiente* and so from year to year so long as both parties shall please, *reddendo inde* to the plaintiff *annuatim et quolibet anno* that the defendants should hold and enjoy the premises by virtue of that demise the yearly rent of £6 at the two feasts of St. Philip and Jacob [1 May] and St. Michael, the archangel, [29 September] by equal portions, by virtue of which demise, the defendants entered and were possessed and held the premises until the feast of St. Michael, the archangel, *anno primo reginae*, which was 1702, *et postea* [. . .] by virtue of that demise, did hold and enjoy, and [. . .] of that rent for five years due and payable at that feast of St. Michael were behind and yet remain unpaid, *per quod actio accrevit* to the plaintiff to recover it.

To this declaration, the defendants demurred generally.

And *Jansens*, of their counsel, showed the cause to be that the plaintiff had mistaken his action, having brought it for five years' rent when it appears there can be but four years and a half due, for the reservation is for so many years as the defendants shall hold the lands and there is of that time but four years and a half past at Michaelmas last from the time of the demise.

But it was resolved by the court and so adjudged that the rent being payable at two certain days by name in the year as also as those days did incur during the time the defendants held the lands so many half years' rents did incur and the words 'yearly and every year' that the defendants should hold and enjoy the premises by virtue of that demise do not contradict the express reservation of the rent to be paid on the certain feast days happening in the year, though the complete year for holding them is not fully expired.

[Other copies of this report: Georgetown Univ. Law Sch. MS. B88–9, f. 210v.]

233

Cope v. Tilley

(Ex. 1703)

Specification of debts is not necessary for debts that do not bear interest.
Writs of error can be allowed only by the Chief Baron unless that office is vacant.

Lincoln's Inn MS. Misc. 533, f. [137v]

At *nisi prius* at the Guildhall.

The plaintiff brought [an action of] debt upon a bond against the defendant, who pleaded that it was sealed and left in the hands of Dr. Evans as an escrow to be delivered as his deed when one Bromhall, who is mentioned to be bound in the same bond should seal and execute it and not before nor otherwise. And then he shows that Bromhall had not yet sealed and executed that bond. And so he pleads it was not his deed.

The defendant's counsel opened the cause, the issue lying on his side to prove, after which they called for a specification of the debt and saying, without that, the bond could not be given in evidence.

The plaintiff's counsel said they did not think a specification necessary in this case upon these pleading, for the defendant had taken upon himself the proof of his pleas as much as if he had pleaded *solvit ad diem*, in which case, nobody ever pretended that a specification, according to the late acts for taxes was necessary to be produced, in regard the plaintiff does not in that case give the bond in evidence nor does the plaintiff upon this issue do it. But the defendant to make out his plea and to defend himself called for it. And he shall not object against his own evidence, for the plaintiff, upon this plea, need not give the bond in evidence. But, when the defendant uses it, he may offer proof to it and, if [it is] not produced and the plea is proved, the verdict must be against the defendant, wherewith the defendant's counsel rested satisfied.

And the trial proceeded, and a verdict was for the plaintiff.

A new trial was moved for by Mr. Solicitor [General *Harcourt*], both upon the evidence and the point of the specification.

But the court, upon my [Edward Ward] giving them an account of the matter, did not think fit to grant it. Besides, the condition was for payment of such a sum at a certain time without interest and a specification is not to be made but in case of debts at interest, which this is not.

[Other copies of this report: Georgetown Univ. Law Sch. MS. B88–9, f. 211.]

Lincoln's Inn MS. Misc. 533, f. [139]

Michaelmas [term] 1703. Touching the allowance of writs of error in the Exchequer.

Note that, after this term [Michaelmas 1703], Tilly brought a writ of error upon a judgment obtained against him upon a bond by one Cope, the trial being in term time by *nisi prius*. Richard Lloyd, one of the attorneys in the Office of Pleas, at the instigation of Tilly, as he affirmed, was prevailed upon to let Tilly carry the writ of error to Baron Price to be allowed, who, at first, scrupled it, but, upon false suggestions made to him by Tilly's solicitor that puisne judges allow writs of errors, he wrote '*allocatur*' upon it and put his name to it. And, upon bail taken by the said baron after the said allowance, Tilly and his attorney and solicitor carried a writ of *supersedeas* to Marriott, Clerk of the Pleas, to be signed and allowed, and they showed him the writ of error allowed, as above. But he refused to allowed the *supersedeas*, telling them the writ of error was not duly allowed, for none but the Chief Baron could allow it. And, thereupon, he was summoned before Baron Price to show cause why he did not allow the *supersedeas*, who gave him the reason above.

The Baron [PRICE] told him he would advise with the other two puisne barons. But he said no more to him nor took any notice that he ever spoke with them.

And I [EDWARD WARD] hearing of this by chance, sent for Marriott and told him I insisted upon my right, which was that all writs of error in the Exchequer, which are directed indeed *thesaurario et baronibus*, have in all times been allowed by the Chief Baron and no other, as the writs of error in the King's Bench and Common Pleas are in those courts, unless in the vacancy of a Chief Baron, and, then, by the senior Baron, in whose name the process of that court is *teste*.

Marriott assured me he would not make any [writ of] *supersedeas* unless the writ of error was allowed by me. And I sent for Mr. Lloyd, the attorney, and demanded of him how he dared invade the rights of my place and carry any writ of error to be allowed by anybody else. He endeavored to excuse it by saying it was wholly Tilly and his solicitor's doings. I assured him I would assert my right against any encroachers and encroachment. He owned it was my right and that this was a mistake. And, thereupon, the writ of error was brought to me, and I signed and allowed it. Marriott assured me that he had searched through the office and found that all writs of error were allowed by the Chief Baron when there was one and by no other.

It is also the right of the Chief Baron to take all recognizances and securities upon all writs of error in the Exchequer and the bail taken upon that writ of error by Price, not being approved, was rejected. And, afterwards, [it was taken] before me.

[Other copies of this report: Georgetown Univ. Law Sch. MS. B88–9, f. 213.]

234

Edwards v. Male

(Ex. 1703)

The question in this case how to plead an obligation where the written contract has been altered without the agreement of the plaintiff.

Lincoln's Inn MS. Misc. 533, f. [149], pl. 2

In Officio Placitorum in Scaccario upon a demurrer to the plaintiff's replication.

The plaintiff declares upon articles under hand and seal whereby the defendant covenanted to carry up the chimneys of the plaintiff's house in a workmanlike manner to the equal height of the defendant's own.

The defendant prays *oyer* of the articles. And thereby, as interlined, it appears that the covenant runs to carry up the tops of the plaintiff's chimneys in equal height with the defendant's. And, thereupon, he pleads that he did carry up the tops of the plaintiff's chimneys in equal height with his own *et hoc paratus est verificare etc.*

The plaintiff replies that, at the time of the sealing of the articles, the words 'tops of the' which are now interlined were not interlined nor inserted in the articles, but were interlined and inserted after the sealing and delivery of them, *scil.* at such a day and place by one William Nuttall, having those articles in his custody, at the request and assent of the defendant as they are now inserted and interlined and that the said interlineation and insertion was done without the privity and assent of the plaintiff, *et hoc paratus est verificare prout etc.*

To this replication, the defendant put in a general demurrer.

And, after argument of counsel on both sides, the three barons were of opinion that judgment should be given for the defendant because of the apparent variance between the covenant in the declaration and that which appears upon the *oyer*, for the covenant in the declaration is to carry up the chimneys, but that upon the *oyer* appears to be the tops of the chimneys only, which is a manifest variance, and the articles set forth upon the *oyer* is part of the plaintiff's own declaration. And so it makes the declaration inconsistent with itself. And, for that reason, as they held, judgment was to be against the plaintiff. And they held the replication to be departure.

But I [Edward Ward] was doubtful in that point upon the whole pleadings in the case, for, if the law be so and the truth of the fact alleged in this replication, which was really thought to be as thereby set forth, it cannot be come at by pleading, as many such like cases are in Piggot's Case, 11 rep. 26b.[1] Then, it must follow that, if a man gets his deed which he made to me into his own or

[1] *Winchcombe v. Pigot* (1614), 11 Coke Rep. 26, 77 E.R. 1177, also 1 Rolle Rep. 39, 81 E.R. 311, Moore K.B. 835, 72 E.R. 937, 2 Bulstrode 246, 80 E.R. 1096.

a stranger's hands and, by himself or a stranger without my privity, interlines or inserts anything into it or vitiates it, I can never sue my deed unless I first erase out that which was interlined or inserted after the execution of it, for, otherwise, upon *oyer*, which cannot be denied, it must and will appear to be different from the case set forth in my count, which I must truly set forth therein, though different from the interlineation to the end the truth of the fact as to the interlineation may come in question. And it can no otherwise come in question than by pleading, and to erase out the interlineation may be hazardous to avoid the whole deed. And, had the defendant in this case taken issue upon the fact alleged in the replication, the truth and justice of the cause would have appeared. And it is to be considered how the plaintiff could have refused to give *oyer*, as, then, it was in regard the court could not be satisfied of the truth of the fact by affidavits one way or the other nor otherwise than by a trial, which cannot be attained otherwise. *Vide* several cases in Pigot's Case, *supra*, leading the reason of this. And query the danger of the plaintiff's erasing out the interlineation.

But the honesty of the case seeming to be for the plaintiff, the court gave him leave to discontinue, paying costs.

Query how he shall amend his case so long as the interlined words which vary the cause of action remain in force.

[Other copies of this report: Georgetown Univ. Law Sch. MS. B88–9, f. 215v.]

235

Soper v. Widmere

(Ex. 1703)

In this case, after the death of one joint tenant, the property vested entirely in the other to the exclusion of their issue.

Dodd 200

[There was a] trust of a term to A. and B. and the issue of the body of A. on B., if any issue between them, and, in default etc., then to C. etc. [It was] resolved that A., after the death of B., had the entirety and it did not vest in the issue. See the case etc.

[Orders of 11 May and 17 June 1703: Public Record Office E.126/17, ff. 325, 343; order of 11 November 1703: Public Record Office E.126/18, f. 284.]

236

Conald v. Conald

(Ex. 1703)

Hops are small tithes.

Dodd 201, 1 Eagle & Younge 654

The plaintiff Conald was vicar, and the plaintiff Spencer [was] lessee of the impropriation of Boughton under the Bleane in Kent; the rest [were] occupiers. The vicar brought his bill for tithe hops, and the impropriator likewise. Hops had not been planted above twenty or twenty-five years; the vicar had all or most of the small tithes.

And [it was] decreed by the court that hops are a small tithe; that where the vicar has generally endowment of small tithes, he shall have them; that grass in new orchards, and so of beans in new gardens, etc. (which were the small tithes the impropriator had received) belongs to the impropriator; and when the vicar has them, it is intended ancient. The impropriator had once taken woad, flax, etc., yet [it was] decreed for the vicar, for the court thought, upon the proof, he had all the small tithes.

[Order sub nom. Conald v. Sprakling, 29 June 1703: Public Record Office E.126/17, f. 342v.]

237

Stringer v. Hundred of Candleshaw

(Ex. 1703)

If one co-plaintiff dies pendente lite, the action abates.

Lincoln's Inn MS. Misc. 533, f. [115]

Hilary term 1702[/03].

[There was a motion] in arrest of judgment, there being a verdict for the plaintiff Stringer.

Ettrick, for the defendant: First, the hundred was not liable under the Statute 7 & 8 Will. III, ca. 28, unless [it was] carried through the hundred and there exported. Here, the exportation is laid to be from Ratcliff in the County of Middlesex.

Objection: It is only at Ratcliff, County of Middlesex, to comply with the clause in the Act for trying the cause in any county.

Solution: The Act warrants the *venire* out of any county, and it ought not to have been laid in the information that the exportation was from Ratcliff, but that the exportation was out of the hundred in Lincolnshire, according to the truth of the fact, *vide* the Act, fo. 577. And, then, to have entered a prayer upon the roll that the cause might be tried by a Middlesex jury and to have prayed a *venire facias* accordingly.

Second, this information was exhibited in the names of the plaintiff and of one Clarke, which Clarke died, and his death was suggested on the record, but, by his death, the information abated. And this is not a case within 8 & 9 Will. III. That Act extends only where [there is] a precedent right and that might survive. But this is no action, but an information. And, in Buckley's Case, the difference was observed between an information and an action and that an information was not under the word 'action'.

Dodd, to the same effect; so by *Turner* and *Parker.* And they say as to the first objection that, since there ought to have been a suggestion upon the roll that the plaintiff desired to have the cause to have been tried by a jury of Middlesex and, then, the trial might well proceed in Middlesex. The case is like the surmise upon the fact in the Cinque Ports; the Statute gives not leave to lay it out of the hundred, but only to try it out of the county. The like as to the abatement, *ut supra.* This is not an action, but an information.

Per curiam: Stay until next term *quousque* the plaintiff move the court.

Note the words of the Act 7 & 8 Will. III, upon which this information is grounded, fo. 574, after the first of May 1696, no wool is to be loaded or carried within five miles of the seacoast but between sunrising and sunsetting under forfeiture of the wool, horses, and carriages and no ship or vessel shall export the same into parts beyond the seas under forfeiture of the wool, ship, and vessel and treble the value thereof with treble costs of suit. And the inhabitants of the hundred, port, or place exempt next adjoining to the seacoasts out of or through which any wool etc., shall be so carried or exported shall forfeit £20 if the wool be under the value of £10; if above, then treble the value thereof so exported or carried out of the kingdom as also treble costs of suit. The penalties and costs [are] to be recovered by an action of debt, bill, plaint, or information by him or them that shall sue for the same against the inhabitants of the hundred etc. out of or through which the said wool shall be exported in any of the king's courts of record at Westminster.

Fo. 576: The inhabitants of the hundred in the name of the Clerk of the Peace [are] to recover treble the value of all forfeitures they shall be liable to or charged with against the owners of the wool and the aiders to the exportation or carrying to be recovered in the courts at Westminster.

Fo. 577: And for the better and more impartial trials of all such actions and informations prosecuted by virtue of that Act, it is enacted that such actions and informations shall be tried in any of his majesty's courts of record by a jury of good and lawful freeholders to be summoned out of any other county than that where the fact shall be committed.

Note this Act distinguishes between actions of debt and informations. And, therefore, they are two distinct remedies. And, where the plaintiff has chosen to bring an information and not an action of debt, he cannot properly call his information an action within the Statute 8 & 9 Will. III so as to have that benefit of that Statute as an action. And, if it is not an action within that Statute, then, at common law, the information is abated by the death of one informer.

20 April 1703.

Browne, for the plaintiff, answers the objection in arrest [of judgment].

First objection: [It was] improper [to have the] trial in Middlesex; [it] ought to be in Lincolnshire.

Solution: First, the Act of 7 & 8 [Will. III] allows the trial to be in any county, and that he relies on the matter is tried and well tried in Middlesex. Second, this is not a local information. The matter is not made so by 21 Jac. I, but allowed by that Act to be laid anywhere it concerns the transportation of wool. Third, the information is a contradiction when it supposes the carriage to be through the hundred of Candleshaw and yet it is said it was carried from Ratcliff in Middlesex. And, therefore, fourth, there ought to have been a special surmise upon the roll praying a summons of a jury from Middlesex.

Solution: The Act directing the trial to be in any county supplies the want of any such suggestion or prayer.

Objection: That the information is abated by the death of Clark, one of the informers, before the trial or plea.

Solution: He agrees this case is not within 8 & 9 Will. III to prevent an abatement. He admits Buckley's Case is good law, for there could be no judgment because there was no man alive against whom to give judgment. But, where there are two plaintiffs and one survives, there is one for whom judgment may be entered.

This information is notice that such an offense has been committed. And here is a plaintiff and a defendant subsisting, which varies it from Buckley's Case. And there is no incongruity. Waller and Hanger, 2 Bulstrode 261. The death of the informer abated not the suit for the crown's duty of prisage nor for the crown where the Attorney General dies or is removed.

Note the difference between an informer that informs only for the king and that recovery must be for the king and when he himself is to recover. In the first case, it is plain that the death of the informer hinders not the Attorney General from proceeding in recovering all, because the informer has no interest, and, in the second case, where the informer has a part and dies, yet the Attorney General, at least for what appertains to the crown. But, here, the crown is no party, and so [it is] a more private suit.

[Other copies of this report: Georgetown Univ. Law Sch. MS. B88–9, f. 178.]

Lincoln's Inn MS. Misc. 533, ff. [117v], [119v]

27 April 1703.

Mr. Attorney General *Northey*, for the plaintiff Stringer: The defendants, in a [a motion] in arrest of judgment, made the objections.

First [objection]: The death of Clarke.

Solution: This is helped by the Statute 8 & 9 Will. III. The death is suggested on the roll. The words of the Statute are large, and it is a remedial law. He read the words of the law *prout*. This is not a *qui tam* action, though it is a penal law. Yet it is a personal action, and, with an exception, the statutes of jeofails would have extended to all penal law. The information is an action. A release of all actions releases writs of error. And it is an extensive term, and it includes all ways of remedy whatsoever. An action and a suit is the same; this is plain from 18 Eliz.; every informer shall exhibit his suit in proper person, which must be understood his information. The right of action in this case was in both the informers as a joint right, and then it must of necessity survive.

Second objection: The information is repugnant in laying the exportation out of Middlesex.

Solution: This is warranted by the practice and like to the common causes upon other informations laid in Middlesex though the facts were done elsewhere. Here, the words of the law are 'out of or through which'; so it goes to the carriage through as well as to the exportation out of the hundred. Besides, there is no impossibility in the thing, but the fact might be as laid. It stands upon the carrying through the hundred to be sufficient to maintain the information and verdict.

Mr. *Parker*, for the defendants: At common law, there is no doubt but there is an abatement by a death. And that is not opposed by Mr. Attorney [General]. And then he insists that it is not within the Statute 8 & 9 Will. III, and there is no distinction upon this law between *qui tam* [cases] and this information. In this Statute, there are distinct words of action, suit, bill, plaint, or information; so [there is a] difference between action and information. The preamble for protecting against unjust suits and, secondly, to recover just rights, neither of these extend to this case in question. This is not a penalty upon a hundred as offenders but to engage their search. And they are to recover treble against the offenders.

If the word 'action' should include informations, yet, here, there can be no survivorship nor help from 8 & 9 [Will. III]. And, before this Statute, [it is] sure [there was] no survivorship between informers, but, if one of them had died, the whole information was abated. The bringing of the action here is the sole cause of action for the plaintiff and the sole right of the plaintiff. He has none before. Therefore, there is no survivorship. This is all intended not to make a survivorship but in such cases only which, in their nature, the right survived. But that could not be before this law. There must be a right antecedent to the action which must survive, else nothing can survive. And, in this case, other persons might be concerned, as another informer who might plead a prior information by two, and yet, if one had died, that plea is lost.

So, here is no right to survive to the plaintiff alone, for both plaintiffs, by their information, pray both may have the forfeiture. *Vide* Raymond 463.

Second objection: [It was] against the venue from Ratcliff; as to the other information tried in Middlesex, that is where the law allows the laying in another county than that [is] well, but this law allows not laying but the trial of the information, which might and ought to be by alleging the fact in the proper county and then praying the trial to be by a jury of another county as the informers please, and this is yielded by Mr. Attorney General to be the best way. It is truly the only one.

The Attorney General [*Northey*] replies: An informer has a just right by exhibiting his information, and that vests the forfeiture in them. There is no need of a precedent right, but a joint right at the death of one does survive, and that is within the words of the Act. A third person is not to be considered. The second information gains nothing, for that was exhibited while both the informers in the first information were living, and, then, that second informer, at the time of his information, gained nothing, and so [it was] void, no interest or cause of action attaching in him by the exhibiting of his information. The penalty is turned into a right by the act of Parliament.

Ettrick, for the defendants: First, abatement by the death of one informer; second, the ill venue from Ratcliff [where] it ought to have been from Lincolnshire.

As to the first objection, Waller and Hanger, first case, 3 Bulstr., the solution [is] that replication was put in by Mr. Attorney [General]. No notice was taken of that abatement in that case as reported by Calthorpe, Moor, etc. But that it does abate, he cites these cases before 8 Will. III, 10 rep., Read and Alderman, 2 Cro. 19; Plo. 186; 2 Sidderfin 259; 1 Ventr. 235; 2 Levinz 82; 3d Mod. 248.

As to the Statute 7 & 8 Will. III, that Statute extends only to actions and not to informations. The preamble says 'to enable subjects to recover just rights'. Here, there is no cause of action in the informers but the bringing of the information is the informer's right or cause of action. He has no precedent right.

In Buckley's Case, the court was of opinion there is a distinction between an action and an information.

As to the fact charged by the information, it is not warranted by the Act in regard the exportation is laid to be from Ratcliff, which ought to be from Lincolnshire if the fact was true as laid in the information, yet it was no offense against the Act by the hundred, for, suppose the wool was carried through the hundred in Lincolnshire and then exported from Middlesex, that is no offense against that Act.

Objection: The Statute 21 Jac. allows such a venue as this to be laid as to wool at the pleasure of the informer.

Solution: It does so as against any that export, but it extends not to this case. The method should have been to have laid the offense in Lincolnshire and prayed a *venire* from Middlesex.

Browne, for the plaintiff: There is no authority in the law that says the death of one informer abates the information, but all authorities go to actions, which do abate. And, then, an information, being an action, is within the Statute of 8 & 9 Will. III. The trial here was proper. If the deceased informer had released, yet [it] proceeds by the other. (Query that.)

Ettrick replies: Every informer is a plaintiff. The judgment must be according to the information. Here, *tam quam* [makes a] difference. There are two several interests, and the informer's death hurts not.

The court will give an opinion in the next term.

In Michaelmas 1703, judgment was given for the defendant.

[Other copies of this report: Georgetown Univ. Law Sch. MS. B88–9, ff. 177, 182.]

Dodd 201

[On] 14 November [Michaelmas term 1703], judgment in Stringer and the Hundred of Candleshaw in Lincolnshire [was given] that an information brought by two against the hundred for loading and conveying wool within five miles of [the] sea shore and for exporting it contrary to 7 & 8 Will. III, ch. 28.[1] And a [writ of] *distringas* issued. And the hundred appeared and imparled. And, then, one of the informers died. And the other suggests it, and goes on and afterwards pleads. And the verdict [is] for the plaintiff.

[It was] resolved in arrest of judgment that the information was abated, and thus here. Upon argument, it was also adjudged a fault in the information, being tried at Ratcliffe etc. Thus the court held.

238

Stanton v. Child

(Ex. 1703)

A writ of extent can be awarded to an executor upon a bond to the decedent without an oath that the debt was originally due to him.

Lincoln's Inn MS. Misc. 533, f. [138]

24 November 1703. Stanton and Sir John Nicholas v. Leonard Child, in debt in aid.

The defendant, Mr. [Leonard] Child, being the queen's receiver general of the taxes in Surrey, obtained in his own name, first, a bond and, then, a judg-

[1] Stat. 7 & 8 Will. III, c. 28 (*SR*, VII, 118–120).

ment upon that bond for £70 debt from one Coldham, which was at first due to Child's father and to whom Child was executor. Child, upon [a writ of] extent against himself upon a bond he gave to the crown as receiver general procures this debt and judgment to be seized into the queen's hands and upon oath before me [Edward Ward] at the last Guildford Assizes that it was a just and true debt and not any trust nor put in suit and that Coldham was failed in his estate and absconded and the debt in danger to be lost, a [writ of] immediate extent was awarded, and Coldham's goods were seized, the plaintiffs to whom Coldham was tenant and owed rent and for which some distress had been taken, moved by *Ettrick* and *Phipps* to set aside the extent because it was not set forth in the oath that the debt was originally due to him for though he has observed the Rules of 1639 in all things except in the word 'originally', yet the omitting of that word, as was alleged, made the whole vicious, for all debts either to be assigned or found by an inquisition in aid must be such only as are originally due to the king's debtor, which, in fact, this was not, but came to Child as executor of his father. And, so, it was not a debt that could be seized in aid, nor could the defendant honestly swear that it was originally due to him. And these rules, being the stated measures for all debts in aid, must be strictly observed.

And of that opinion were the other three barons.

But I [Edward Ward] remembered the Case of Brediman and Coles, in Hobt. 253,[1] where the case was that the king's debtor by a bond of £600 married the administratrix of an intestate, to which intestate J.S. was bound in a statute of £2000. The king's debtor and his wife, the administratrix, assigned this statute to the king, which was payable after the assignment. And it was resolved in the Court of Wards that the assignment was good notwithstanding the Statute of 7 Jac. I, ca. 15,[2] which makes assignments of debts to the king void, other than such as did grow due originally and *bona fide* to the king's debtor for the purpose of the law was that no debtor of the king should procure another man's debt to be assigned, which was a common practice. But this here is the king's debtor's own debt, though not to his own use, which he may himself release and discharge, and, by the same reason, he may assign. And I wished that that case might be looked into and considered, for, if that case be law (and I never knew it denied), I could not see any reason why this extent should be set aside, for, if in judgment of law, this debt to Child is looked upon as an original debt to him, as it was in the other case, there can be no more reason to set aside this inquisition and proceedings than there was for the court to have set aside the assignment in the other case. And, surely, the words 'originally and *bona fide*' in the Act of Parliament are as forcible and operative as they can be in the Rules of 1639, which were made in imitation of that Statute and not otherwise so that, if, in the judgment and

[1] *Breadman v. Coales*, Hobart 253, 80 E.R. 399, *sub nom. Fawn's Case*, Croke Jac. 524, 79 E.R. 448.

[2] Stat. 7 Jac. I, c. 15 (*SR*, IV, 1171).

construction of law, this debt may be said to be originally due to Child, though it may be a scruple of conscience to swear it, it is hard to distinguish between the two cases and make the assignment good, which the Statute says shall be void. And when the truth of the case appears to the court and, if sworn, ought to be allowed without contest, it is hard to set it aside when it appears to be such a debt as by the true meaning of the rules was not intended to be restrained from being found. Besides, this seems to be something the stronger case in regard the first debt is now got into a judgment in Child's own name and in his own right. And many such debts as this have, without doubt all along, been seized and assigned without contradiction, not being within the mischief intended either by the Statute or the Rules to be prevented.

But though, at the first, two of the barons seemed willing to consider of it, yet, at length, they set aside the extent and proceedings upon it the same day without considering the case cited or the reason of it.

Ideo quaere, because it seems a hasty resolution.

[Other copies of this report: Georgetown Univ. Law Sch. MS. B88–9, f. 211v.]

Dodd 216

In the case of Child, receiver of Surrey, in the time of the present queen, where a debt was due to him as executor by a simple contract, and he took a bond for it and prayed [for a writ of] extent but he did not swear [that it was] originally due to him, the extent [was] granted by the Chief Baron [WARD].

And a [writ of] *supersedeas* [was granted] by the court against his opinion.

239

Robertson, qui tam v. Lowry

(Ex. 1704–1707)

The Court of Exchequer has jurisdiction to decide disputes arising from civil forfeitures granted by statutes even where the crown is not concerned.

Lincoln's Inn MS. Misc. 536, f. [8v]

There were two several informations of seizure in this court prosecuted this term, touching irregular trading to and from the East Indies, both founded upon the Act of Parliament made 9 & 10 Will. III, ca. 44, entitled an Act for Raising a Sum Not Exceeding Two Millions, upon a fund for payment of annuities after the rate of £8 per cent *per annum* and for settling the trade to the East Indies.[1]

In one of which, Robertson, *qui tam* for himself as the new East India Company, upon the seizure of the ship *Annandale* with her lading, guns, tackle, etc.

[1] Stat. 9 Will. III, c. 44 (*SR*, VI, 429–446).

was plaintiff, for that certain persons, to the informer unknown, being Her Majesty's subjects and such as might not lawfully go and trade to the East Indies by virtue of that Act, did between such time at London [. . .] put aboard divers goods and merchandises with the intent to trade, traffic, or adventure into or from the East Indies contrary to the true meaning of that Act, fo. 783, whereby the said ship and goods became forfeited, whereof he prays a fourth part to himself and the other three parts for the new East India Company, according to the form of the Statute. But he said nothing of the double value to be forfeited also as that Act provides nor of the charges of prosecution to be borne out of the Company's three parts.

And the other information was in the name of Gawen *qui tam* for himself as also for the new East India Company also upon a seizure of two ships and the cargoes from the East Indies belonging (since the time of the old and new East India companies to them) for that these two ships formerly belonged to the old Company did trade and arrive in England after the time limited by that Act, *viz.* at Ratcliff in Middlesex, whereby the said two ships and their cargoes became forfeited by the said Act and the forfeitures to be one-fourth to the seizer and three-fourths to the new Company. And he prayed by that information as and in the same manner with the other.

The ship *Annandale* was said to be a ship belonging to the subjects of Scotland and loaded there and here in England with a cargo intended for the East Indies and to trade there against the said Act and, therefore, seized by order of the new Company and the old united. And the other seizure said to be made by the direction and prosecution of one that had been a member of the old Company and was instrumental to the uniting the two companies and was in that respect to have £80,000 paid, which was not done and therefore the advantage of the strictness of law for the forfeiture was insisted upon.

But the new Company declined the advantage of the forfeitures in both cases. But the suits were carried on. And writs of delivery were prayed in both cases, in the first of which, *viz.* the *Annandale*, a writ of delivery was granted only for the ship and the *bona peritaca* in it because the prosecutor offered to go to trial this term at *nisi prius* in London, where the information and seizure were first laid, upon security.

But in the other, in regard the two ships and cargoes were estimated at £200,000, wherein the crown was concerned for a great sum for customs and duties and the seizers or prosecutors [were] not ready for trial so soon as by the rules of the court they might try it and those entitled to three parts of the forfeiture disclaiming and disowning it and consenting to the delivery, the court thought fit to grant a writ of delivery upon security with a writ of appraisement for the ships and goods to be first executed. And the informer against the ship *Annandale* having [been] mistaken in laying the fact and seizure to be in London, which ought to be in Middlesex and, therefore, could not be ready for trial as at first offered and the matter being of great moment and deserving of a trial at the bar which could not be laid in London, a motion was made to alter the information and lay it in Middlesex, which was granted by the court, but upon terms that the claimers of the ship *Annandale* and cargo might have a writ of delivery upon security for the ship and cargo, which was consented to and granted.

And, because the cargoes of the two ships inwards, which belonged to both the companies as now united would suffer much if not immediately put into the Company's own warehouse, which the informer and prosecutors insisted they ought not in regard the goods must be particularly appraised, which could not be ashipboard, but must be first put into other warehouses, which they had taken with the privity of the commissioners of the customs there first to be numbered, appraised, and security to be given before they could come into the Company's possession. It was upon a proposition in court agreed to on both sides to avoid that double trouble and charges that the goods should by degrees be removed out of the ships into the Company's warehouses upon security of £100,000 first given to the informer [. . .] the goods should be duly numbered and appraised with the privity and direction of the informer, who or [. . .] by his privity were to be present from time to time at the appraisement of the goods as taken out of the ships and brought into the warehouses and that when all that [. . .] the claimers should give the informer good and sufficient security as usual upon writs of delivery and that the informer should have one key to a lock upon each warehouse and the goods lodged there under and subject the seizure until security given to the informer as in cases of writs of delivery and the companies agreed to pay the charges of the warehouses which the informer had taken to put them in.

Note the jurisdiction of the Court of Exchequer upon such seizure for granting writs of delivery upon security and holding a plea in cases of forfeitures of goods where seizures are granted although no part of the forfeiture is granted to the crown. The like jurisdiction and practice in cases of exportation of wool and in several other cases of the like nature, no objection being made to the exercise of this jurisdiction nor any other court intermeddling therein.

[Other copies of this report: Georgetown Univ. Law Sch. MS. B88–9, f. 229.]

Lincoln's Inn MS. Misc. 538, p. 21, pl. 2

21 November 1707.

The court delivered their opinion in the case between Robertson, *qui tam* for the new East India Company v. Lowry upon the seizure of the ship *Annandale*. And all the court agreed that the judgment should be arrested.

But a writ of error was in the same term brought by the plaintiff and the East India Company conceived to be for the delay only, for it was never prosecuted, but discontinued, and the judgment of reversal stands.

[Other copies of this report: Georgetown Univ. Law Sch. MS. B88–9, f. 359, pl. 2.]

240

Jones v. Morgan

(Ex. 1704)

In the performance of a contract of sale, the buyer cannot have a remedy before tendering the purchase money.

Lincoln's Inn MS. Misc. 536, f. [10]

In the Office of Pleas in the Exchequer entered Michaelmas 13 Will. III [1701]. Carmarthen.

The plaintiff [Philip Jones] brought [an action of] debt upon a bond of £1000 entered into by the defendant [David Morgan] to the plaintiff the 23rd of October 12 Will. III [1700]. Upon *oyer* prayed, the condition was to this effect that:

> whereas it is this present day agreed upon by and between the above bounden Morgan and the above named Jones that, for and in consideration of the sum of £550 to be duly paid to the defendant [not saying by whom], he, the said [defendant] and Elizabeth, his wife, shall at or before the first of December next at the plaintiff's request to him and her in that behalf made by good and sufficient conveyances and assurances in the law such as counsel learned shall advise well and sufficiently convey and assure to the plaintiff or such as he [. . .] his heirs shall direct free from all encumbrances [divers lands and tenements therein particularly expressed] to hold to the plaintiff or such other persons as he shall direct to his and their heirs forever, now, if [the defendant] shall in all things well and truly fulfill, perform, and accomplish the said agreement on his and his said wife's part and behalf to be [. . .] by making such conveyances by fine or otherwise of the premises as aforesaid, then the bond to be void or else remain in force.

The defendant pleads *actio non*, for that, after the making of that bond and before said first of December, *scil. primo Novembris anno duodecimo supradicto*, the plaintiff gave notice at such a place to the defendant that the plaintiff, by the advice of his counsel learned (not naming anybody) had prepared conveyances [. . .] the premises in the condition mentioned by the defendant and his wife to be sealed and executed and that he, with his wife, for the execution thereof should come to such place and at such time as the [. . .] afterwards should give notice of to the defendant and him [. . .] that behalf should require, that, afterwards and before the [. . .] first of December, *viz.* 28 November *anno duodecimo supradicto* at such place the plaintiff gave notice to the defendant, and requested him and his said wife to come to Landovery, County of Carmarthen, the 30th of November to execute those conveyances, on such day, the defendant, with his wife, came to Landovery and then were present with the plaintiff to execute those conveyances and whereupon the plaintiff produced certain indentures of lease and release of the said premises to be by the defendant and his wife sealed and executed to one Nicholas Vanacker and his heirs at the plaintiff's nomination with covenants in the release contained for a fine after[wards] to be levied by the defendant and his wife and, then and there, requested the defendant and his wife to seal and execute the said indentures, whereupon the defendant and his wife were ready and offered to seal and execute the said indentures if the plaintiff would pay the defendant the said £550 in consideration thereof as aforesaid to be paid which the defendant then and there requested the plaintiff to pay which he utterly refused to do, by which the defendant refused to seal and execute the indentures unless the plaintiff would pay him the money *prout ei bene licuit secundum formam et effectum condictionis praedictis, et hoc paratus est verificare, et petit judicium si actio etc.*

The plaintiff replies that his counsel, the first of November, devised the indentures of lease and release whereof the plaintiff and his wife had notice that they were engrossed in parchment with wax affixed and tendered to the plaintiff and his wife to be executed the 30th of November, and they requested so to do according to the form and effect of the said condition which they then or at any time since have refused to do. *Et hoc paratus est verificare, unde petit judicium et debitum suum praedictum unacum damnis etc.*

The defendant demurs, and shows for cause that the plaintiff has not set forth the tenors of the said indentures of lease and release, nor does he deny nor anyways answers to the matter by the defendant pleaded in bar, but confesses the greatest part thereof by implication. The plaintiff joins in demurrer.

And the case was argued twice at the bar by *Henry Lloyd*, for the plaintiff, and by *Dodd* and *Turner*, for the defendant. And the principal point relied upon on both sides was whether, as this case [is], the defendant was obliged to execute the conveyances until he was paid the £550 or not.

On the part of the plaintiff, it was argued that here is a mutual agreement which affords to each party a mutual remedy, and, therefore, each having a remedy, there cannot be any construction made for the payment of the money to be a condition precedent or to oblige the payment of the money before the execution of the conveyances. And, for this, he mainly relied upon Pordage and Cole's Case, 1 Levinz 274 and 1 Sanders 319; he cited other cases as 1 Sidderfin 174; Ughtred's Case, 7 rep. 10, and others which seemed not material.[1]

The counsel for the defendant insisted here was no mutual agreement upon which the defendant could have any remedy against the plaintiff for the £550. All that appears of this mutual agreement is only in the reciting part of the condition of the bond, which is not obligatory upon the plaintiff, *non constat* that the defendant has any bond from the plaintiff or any security for the money. And the

---

[1] *Pordage v. Cole* (1669), 1 Levinz 274, 83 E.R. 403, 1 Williams Saunders 319, 85 E.R. 449, also T. Raymond 183, 83 E.R. 96, 2 Keble 542, 84 E.R. 339, 1 Siderfin 423, 82 E.R. 1194; *Ughtred v. Marquess of Winchester* (1591), 7 Coke Rep. 9, 77 E.R. 425, also Jenkins 260, 145 E.R. 186.

court can intend none. In the Case of Pordage and Cole, there it appeared that both parties sealed the agreement which created reciprocal remedies, but not so here, which is a substantial difference between that case and this. And, if this be not a precedent condition, which ought to be averred to be performed, for aught appears, the defendant has no remedy for his money. And, thus, it is hard to compel the defendant to part with his land and be remediless for his money, especially when the money is the consideration for which he parts with his land.

And of that opinion was the whole court, which was delivered by the Chief Baron [Edward Ward] the last day of Easter term. And judgment was given for the defendant.

Vide these cases following: 14 Hen. IV, 19; 5 rep. 21, Sir Arthur Mayne's Case; 2 Sanders 350; Peters and Opie, 1 Roll's Abr. 414 etc., 421; 1 Modern 57; 2 Lutwich 493 etc.; and 1 Lutwich 394 etc. and 245 etc.[1]

[Other copies of this report: Georgetown Univ. Law Sch. MS. B88–9, f. 230v.]

241

Pitt v. Hawkins

(Ex. 1704)

A disputed Parliamentary election can be settled in a court of law after the Parliament has been dissolved.

Lincoln's Inn MS. Misc. 536, f. [12]

Entered in the Office of the Clerk of the Pleas Trinity [term] 1 Queen Anne [1702].

The plaintiff [John Pitt] brings an action upon the case against the defendant, Mayor of the Borough of St. Ives in Cornwall, grounded upon the Statute

[1] *H. v. Glomer* (1413), YB Hil. 14 Hen. IV, f. 19, pl. 21; *Scott v. Main* (1596), 5 Coke Rep. 20, 77 E.R. 80, also Popham 109, 79 E.R. 1217, Croke Eliz. 449, 78 E.R. 689, 2 Anderson 18, 123 E.R. 523, Moore K.B. 452, 72 E.R. 689, Jenkins 256, 145 E.R. 182; *Peters v. Opie* (1671), 2 Williams Saunders 346, 85 E.R. 1141, also 2 Levinz 23, 83 E.R. 435, 1 Ventris 177, 214, 86 E.R. 120, 144, 2 Keble 811, 837, 3 Keble 45, 84 E.R. 512, 529, 586; 1 Rolle, Abr., *Condition*, pp. 414, 421; *Parker v. Welby* (1670), 1 Modern 33, 57, 86 E.R. 710, 728, also 2 Williams Saunders 150, 85 E.R. 887, 1 Siderfin 439, 82 E.R. 1204, 1 Ventris 55, 85, 86 E.R. 39, 59, 2 Keble 591, 626, 630, 657, 670, 84 E.R. 372, 394, 397, 413, 421; *Hilton v. Smith* (1690), 1 Lutwyche 493, 125 E.R. 259, also 2 Siderfin 35, 101, 82 E.R. 1242, 1279; *Brooke v. Jowett* (1693), 1 Lutwyche 347, 125 E.R. 182; *Thorpe v. Thorpe* (1696), 1 Lutwyche 245, 125 E.R. 128, also Holt K.B. 28, 96, 90 E.R. 913, 951, 1 Lord Raymond 235, 662, 91 E.R. 1054, 1341, 3 Lord Raymond 341, 92 E.R. 722, 1 Salkeld 171, 91 E.R. 157, 1 Comyns 98, 92 E.R. 980, 12 Modern 455, 88 E.R. 1448.

10 Will. III for a false return,[1] showing that he was duly chosen one of the burgesses to serve in Parliament for that borough, but the defendant refused to return him, but returned [. . .] Overton in his stead, who was not duly chosen and [. . .], contrary to the last determination in Parliament.

There was [. . .] special verdict in the case wherein the question was whether the burgesses at large of the ancient borough or the mayor and burgesses of the new corporation made by King James II had the right of election. The plaintiff claimed under the [. . .] of the burgesses before the new charter.

But no counsel appearing for the defendant, the cause indeed being compromised between them and the right or pretense under the new charter given up, the court upon hearing one counsel [. . .]ing the record and arguing for the plaintiff that the new charter made no alteration in the electing burgesses to serve in Parliament, that liberty or privilege not being touched by the [. . .] in the *quo warranto* or surrender, gave judgment for the [. . .] *nisi causa* the last day of this term. And no cause being shown, the judgment was [made] absolute.

Note, in this case, it was found that there was no determination in Parliament of the right of election, the Parliament being dissolved before that right was settled and that the plaintiff lost his place in Parliament and was put to great expense single damages £25, costs 40s.

[Other copies of this report: Georgetown Univ. Law Sch. MS. B88–9, f. 230v.]

242

Gee v. Perch

(Ex. 1704)

Tithes of hops must be set out when they are picked.

Tithes of milk are paid by the tenth meal.

Dodd 202, 1 Eagle & Younge 660

In a tithe bill, brought by the plaintiff as impropriator of Orpington in the County of Kent, [it was] resolved:

First, that tithe hops *de jure* must be set out when picked into the bin by measure and that the setting out either by hill or pole or by separating the tenth hill from the freehold or by laying them all in heaps before picked from the vine is not good. And [it was] so resolved between the same parties Thursday 17 November 1698 and then decreed by the court accordingly.[2] And it was now said

[1] Stat. 10 Will. III, c. 7 (*SR*, VII, 464).

[2] *Perch v. Gee* (Ex. 1699), see above, Case No. 183.

by the Chief Baron [WARD] that it was so decreed in Sir Thomas Vernon's case, in Farnham.[1]

Second, that tithe wood cannot to be set out in heaps on the falling but ought to be bound and made up in stackwood, faggots, bavins, etc., as the owner does his own; but, in this point, the court did not agree. Baron PRICE [held] that it was good setting out in heaps, and Baron SMITH doubting. But he and the others were satisfied in the proof that it was the custom of the parish and then thus they should be [set out] without any allowance for the charge, though, in this case, it was proved to be equal to the value of the wood.

Third, the Chief Baron [WARD] and BURY held [that] ash fallen above twenty years growth and used for the plough and cart shall pay tithe. But the other two [held] contrary, and so the point [was] waived, though the Chief Baron [WARD] and BURY said it must be used in building, which is not law.

Fourth, it was said in this case by the Chief Baron [WARD] that milk shall be paid not the tenth pint nor tenth quart nor the tenth day but the tenth meal for necessity and convenience.

1 Rayner 97, 1 Eagle & Younge 632, 658

[Upon a] bill by the impropriator of Orpington in the County of Kent, [it was] resolved:

First, as to the manner of tithing hops, see above;[2]

Second, that tithe wood is not to be set out in heaps on the falling, but ought to be bound up in stack wood, faggots, bavins, etc., as the owner does his own; but, in this, the court did not agree; Baron PRICE: it is good setting out in heaps; Baron SMITH doubted; but all agreed on the proof, that it was the custom of the parish that they should be so set out without any allowance for the charge, though that was proved to be equal to the value of wood;

Third, the Chief Baron [EDWARD WARD], and BURY held that ash fallen of above twenty years' growth and used for the plough and cart shall pay tithe, but the other two barons *contra*; and so the point was carried, the Chief Baron and BURY insisting that the wood must be used in building to exempt it; but query the law;

Fourth, the Chief Baron said that milk is to be paid every tenth meal, for necessity and convenience.

2 Gwillim 581

11 May 1704.

A bill [was brought] by the lessee of the rectory of Orpington in Kent, *inter alia*, for the tithe of wood, and stating that the defendant did not set out his tithe

---

[1] *Chitty v. Reeve* (Ex. 1687), Equity Cases Exch. 274.

[2] *Perch v. Gee* (Ex. 1699), see above, Case No. 183.

wood in such manner as he ought to have done, he leaving only some loose ranges or heaps of wood for his tithes without ingrain, binding, or making up the same, as by the law, custom, and manner of tithing used in the said parish he ought to have done, that the defendant did not in the said years set out his tithe hops as he ought to have done, but left, as he pretends, the tenth hill or pole without picking in lieu of tithes, and that the defendant ought to have picked his hops from the bines or poles before he set out the tithes thereof.

The defendant said that, for the years in the bill mentioned, he had held and occupied in the said parish about 100 acres of coppice wood and particularly Clay Wood, containing twenty acres, and the wood also adjoining to Crawton Heath, four acres, that, in 1698, he cut Crawton Heath Wood and, in 1701 and 1702, Clay Wood, but that, before he cut down and carried away any of the said wood, he applied to the plaintiffs to see the tithes of the said woods set out and separated from the nine parts as follows: *viz.* when his servants had cut down a small parcel, they piled it up in ten several heaps of equal size and goodness, and, to prevent disputes about the tithes, he had the said then heaps viewed by indifferent persons and caused the best of the said ten heaps to be left for the plaintiff's tithes, and then the defendant's workmen proceeded in the same method from place to place, until the tithes of both woods were duly and fully set forth. And he said that he believed that the like method of paying tithe wood is, and was, the only method used in the said parish, and that the said wood was not be size-bound or made up at the defendant's charge into a marketable ware, that the wood adjoining to Crawton Heath, when cut down, was not worth above 40s. an acre and Clay Wood £3 an acre to be sold and that, after the tithes set out, the said woods cost him more than the remaining nine parts of the same were worth, that, notwithstanding he set out the full tenth part of Crawton Heath Wood, wherein he had for his nine parts but 3670 bavins, that he had used 3423 of the same for necessary firing upon his farm, for which he need not to have paid any tithes, that, in 1702, he cut down and carried away one load and a half of ash trees of about 50s. value without setting out his tithes, he having occasion to use them to make and mend ploughs, harrows, and other utensils of husbandry about his farm, and sold no part thereof, for which reasons and because they were about twenty years growth, no tithes were due for the same.

The court were of opinion and declared that the way and method used by the defendant in setting out his tithe wood by loose heaps, in boughs, is no good way of setting out his tithe wood and that it appears by the proof taken in the cause that the usage and manner of tithing of wood in the parish was, and time out of mind had been, for the occupiers to bind up the wood before the tithes thereof are set out, and that no such manner of tithing by loose heaps or ranges was ever known in the parish.

It was, therefore, ordered and decreed that the defendant should pay to the plaintiff for all the tithes of the woods in the bill mentioned, to wit, for Clay Wood and the wood lying near Crawton Heath according to their respective values thereof when the wood is cut and bound, as usually had been done by the occupiers.

WARD, Chief Baron, said that, if wood has been used to be bound by the parishioners, the tithes of the said woods ought also to be bound up, that ash poles, not fit for timber, are to pay tithes.

BURY, Baron, said that the method set forth by the defendant for setting out the tithes of wood in heaps is not good, that ash poles are tithable though they are of twenty years growth.

PRICE, Baron, thought that ash poles used in husbandry were not tithable and, as to wood, that the defendant had rightly set it out, and that the plaintiff ought to have no account.

SMITH, Baron, said that, as to ash poles, he was of opinion that the defendant is not to account and that he ought to account for the tithe of wood, the plaintiff having proved the usage.

Note the plaintiff relinquished his claim as to the ash poles.

[Order of 11 May 1704: Public Record Office E.126/18, f. 424v.]

243

Ross v. Windsor

(Ex. 1704)

New mills pay tithes in the amount of the tenth toll dish.

Dodd 203, 1 Eagle & Younge 661

[It was] resolved: first, that tithes shall be paid of new mills; second, that it shall be the tenth toll dish.

Note: It was decreed by the Chief Baron [WARD] *vehementer* etc. Baron PRICE thought it ought to be a personal tithe but did not agree how [it was] to be paid.

Note that it was an ancient mill and it [was] pulled down and set up in another place; also the defendant insisted upon a *modus* in his answer but did not prove it; also there was a newly erected windmill. They were the mills of Hanley Castle in Shropshire.

Note: It seems to me [Samuel Dodd] that, if any tithe be due, it is only a personal tithe and then only payable where by custom personal tithes are payable. The objection was upon the Statute *Quod de molendino novo erecto non jacet prohibitio.*[1] See 1 Rolle Rep. 405; 2 Inst. 622; 1 Rolle 656; Degge 260; see below,

[1] Stat. 9 Edw. II, *Articuli Cleri*, stat. 1, s. 5 (*SR*, I, 172).

Newte and Chamberlain and others.[1]

[Order of 15 July 1704: Public Record Office E.126/18, f. 452.]

244

Ent v. Baynes

(Ex. 1704)

In this case, the court refused to allow a sheriff to amend his return to a writ of execution made after over a year before.

Lincoln's Inn MS. Misc. 536, f. [18], pl. 1

Michaelmas term 1704, 3 Queen Anne. The Sheriff of Essex's Case.

Bullock, sheriff of Essex, in Trinity term 1703, returned upon a *scire facias ad sectam Ent et uxoris versus Baynes* a *fieri feci* of £566 of the goods of Baynes, *quas paratus habet* to pay Ent, and that Baynes had no other goods.

The sheriff of Essex or rather the bailiff of the hundred that made the execution moved that the sheriff, against whom Ent and his wife had brought an action of debt upon that return for non-payment of the £566, might have leave to alter his return, that had been filed a year, and made it £300 and odd pounds instead of £566, making it out by affidavits that the execution being for the greatest part of corn standing and afterward carried into the barn and there appraised, the appraisers were mistaken in their appraisements, the corn not yielding so well as they expected, and, further, that what with the mistake in quantity and value and the charge of threshing etc., the whole did not exceed £360 and, further, by the same affidavits making it out that the plaintiffs' solicitor told the bailiff that his clients' debt was not above £300 and consented to omit wheat to the value of £120.

But the solicitor swore that, though, at first, he might say so and agree to leave out the wheat, yet, before the return of the execution, he told the sheriff and bailiff that he was mistaken and that his clients' debt was above £600 and wished him to levy all that could be.

The court thought it of dangerous consequence to give leave to a sheriff to alter and lessen his return filed a year ago and after an action brought upon that return and, though the appraisers might be mistaken in their calculations, yet the sheriff must [. . .] to his return and had caution for it before it was made.

And the motion was denied.

[Other copies of this report: Georgetown Univ. Law Sch. MS. B88–9, f. 237.]

---

1 *Jake's Case* (1616), 1 Rolle Rep. 405, 81 E.R. 568, also 3 Bulstrode 212, 81 E.R. 178; E. Coke, *Second Institute* (1642), f. 622; 1 Rolle, Abr., *Dismes*, pl. M, 3 and 4, p. 656; S. Degge, *Parson's Counsellor*; *Newte v. Chamberlaine* (1705), see below, Case No. 257.

245
Archbishop of York v. Duke of Newcastle

(Ex. 1704)

The question in this case was whether things of a tithable nature can be given as a modus in discharge of all tithes.

Dodd 204, 1 Eagle & Younge 661

[Upon an] English bill in the Exchequer chamber for tithes of the rectory of Kilburne against the farmers of part of the abbey of Byland, upon a case made upon three several *modus*es and [it was] debated before by counsel and standing now for the opinion of the court, the *modus*es were:

First, ten fleeces of wool and two and a half lambs or 18d. for the half lamb, payable at Midsummer in lieu of all tithes arising upon Bosomworth's Farm.

The Chief Baron [Ward] and Smith [held] that it is good, for it is not in discharge of wool and lamb only, but of all tithes, and anything, though of a titheable nature, may be given in discharge of tithes, as well as money, as an acre of land, etc., and the difference will be where it is in discharge of the species of tithe and where of the land. Litt. sect. 144; Noy 148; Dy. 349; Hob. 44, 45.[1]

[But it was held] by barons Price and Bury that it is not a good *modus*, for it is titheable matters for tithes, which is not good. Cro. Eliz. 446, 475; Mo. 554, 909; 1 Rolle [Abr.] 649, 651; Cro. Car. 276, 786; Dy. 149; Hard. 124; Rol. Rep. 120, Hob. 39.[2]

Second, *modus*, six fleeces of wool and three lambs in lieu of small tithes of Cawkerdale and Raper's farms. This as above.

Third, *modus* is eight fleeces of wool and 4s. in lieu of all tithes for Rowland's farm [was held] good by the Chief Baron [Ward], Baron Price, and Baron Smith, (Bury, *contra*).

---

[1] T. Littleton, *Tenures*, perhaps section 444 or 544; *Sharpe v. Sharpe*, Noy 148, 74 E.R. 1110; *Parson of Peykirke's Case* (1576), 3 Dyer 349b, 73 E.R. 784; *Cowper v. Andrews* (1615), Hobart 39, 80 E.R. 189, also Moore K.B. 863, 72 E.R. 957, Godbolt 237, 78 E.R. 138, *sub nom. Hooper v. Andrews*, 1 Rolle Rep. 120, 81 E.R. 372, 1 Gwillim 275, 1 Eagle & Younge 240.

[2] *Grysman v. Lewes* (1595), Croke Eliz. 446, 78 E.R. 686; *Sherington v. Fleetwood* (1596), Croke Eliz. 475, 78 E.R. 727; *Monday v. Lovice* (1596), Moore K.B. 454, 72 E.R. 690; *Bedingfield v. Feake* (1596), Moore K.B. 909, 72 E.R. 989, also Croke Eliz. 467 bis, 78 E.R. 719; 1 Rolle, Abr., *Dismes*, pl. D, 10, p. 651; perhaps *Green v. Piper* (1592), Croke Eliz. 276, 78 E.R. 531, also Moore K.B. 912, 72 E.R. 992; *Ingoldsby v. Johnson* (1600), Croke Eliz. 786, 78 E.R. 1016; perhaps *Parson of Peykirke's Case* (1576), 3 Dyer 349, 73 E.R. 784; perhaps *Wilson v. Redman* (1660), Hardres 174, 190, 145 E.R. 438, 445; *Hooper v. Andrews* (1615), *ut supra*.

[The court] directed [the parties] to try all, with other *modus*es, whether the fact be as alleged.

2 Salkeld 656, 91 E.R. 559

H. prescribed to pay ten fleeces of wool and two lambs in lieu of all tithes

And PRICE and BURY, barons, were of opinion this was an ill *modus*, because it is one species of tithe for another and there is great uncertainty, for one fleece may be twice as big and three times the value of another. See 2 Lutw. 1052; 3 Cro. 786, 276; Mo. 909; 1 Rolle, Abr., 649; Dy. 149; Hard. 174.[1]

WARD, Chief Baron, and SMITH, Baron, *contra*: First, a *modus* is nothing but a real composition, for or in lieu of tithes, or an annual profit certain and permanent; and they held that the payment of any one chattel for tithe, was or might be a good *modus* as well as money; for why might not the parson originally agree to take ten fleeces for his tithe, as well as a penny? They admitted that payment of tithe of one species, or payment of a *modus* for one species of tithe, could not be a discharge as to another species; but they held that this was not a payment of tithe, nor a payment for a species of tithe; because it was to be paid at all events, whether there be sheep or no. And they denied the case of 1 Rolle, Abr., 651,[2] and held it no more uncertain than to pay a *modus* of ten cheeses, which may differ vastly, both in nature, quantity, and value; and it tends to the disquiet of the country to break in upon customs and usages; and it ought not to be done but on plain and manifest reason.

2 Gwillim 583

9 November 1704.

A bill being filed by the lessee of the rectory of Kilburne in the County of York under the archbishop of York for tithes in kind of certain farms within the parish, the defendants, as to those farms, set up the following *modus*es, *viz.* as to two of the farms, a *modus* of ten fleeces of wool, and two and a half lambs, or 1s. 6d. in money in lieu of the half lamb, in full discharge of all tithes whatsoever, as to two other farms, a *modus* of six fleeces of wool and three lambs for all small tithes, and, as to a fifth farm, a *modus* of eight fleeces of wool and 4s. in money in discharge of all tithes whatsoever for this farm.

Upon these *modus*es, a case was settled for the opinion of the barons. And they, being attended by counsel, differed in opinion respecting them. We collect

[1] *Morton v. Briggs* (1696), 2 Lutwyche 1043, 125 E.R. 580; *Ingoldsby v. Johnson* (1600), Croke Eliz. 786, 78 E.R. 1016; *Scory v. Baber* (1592), Croke Eliz. 276, 78 E.R. 531; *Sherington v. Fleetwood* (1596), Moore K.B. 909, 72 E.R. 990, also Gouldsborough 147, 75 E.R. 1055, Croke Eliz. 475, 78 E.R. 727; *Market v. Knight* (1633), 1 Rolle, Abr., *Dismes*, pl. D, 7, p. 649; *Parson of Peykirke's Case* (1576), 3 Dyer 349, 73 E.R. 784; *Wilson v. Redman* (1660), Hardres 174, 190, 145 E.R. 438, 445.

[2] *Austin v. Lucas* (1598), 1 Rolle, Abr., *Dismes*, pl. D, 19, p. 651.

from Mr. Serjeant Salkeld's report and Lord Chief Baron Dodd's manuscripts that, as to the first *modus*, (and of course as to the second), PRICE and BURY, barons, were of opinion it was an ill *modus*, because it was one kind of tithe for another. Cro. Eliz. 446, 471; Moore 554; 1 Ro. Abr. 649, 659; Hardr. 174; Cro. Car. 276; 1 Ro. Rep. 120; Hob. 39. And there is great uncertainty, for one fleece may be twice as big and three times the value of another.

WARD, Chief Baron, and SMITH, Baron, *contra*, that it was a good *modus*, for it is not in discharge of wool and lamb only, and anything of a titheable nature may be given in discharge of tithes, as well as money, as an acre of land etc., and the difference is where it is in discharge of the species of tithe and where of the land, Litt. § 144; Noy 148; Dy. 349b; Hob. 44, that, to be sure, payment of tithe of one kind or payment of a *modus* for one kind of tithe could not be a discharge as to another kind. But this, they said, was not a payment of tithe, because it was to be paid in all events, whether there were sheep or not. And they denied the case of 1 Ro. Abr. 651. And they held the *modus* no more uncertain than to pay a *modus* of ten cheeses, which may differ vastly both in nature, quantity, and value, that it tended to the disquiet of the country to break in upon customs and usages, and it ought not to be done but upon plain and manifest reason.

As to the last *modus*, it was held good by the Chief Baron [WARD], PRICE, and SMITH, BURY *dissentiente*.

In consequence of this difference of opinion upon the bench, a trial at law was ordered upon the *modus*es. and, upon the trial of the issues, a verdict was found for the plaintiff, the lessee of the archbishop of York. But, on the motion of the defendants, a new trial was afterwards granted. However, it does not appear from the books of the court that any further proceedings were had in the case.

[Other reports of this case: Equity Cases Exch. 507.]

[The order of 9 November 1704, Public Record Office E.126/18, f. 465v, is printed at 1 Wood 446.]

246

Bishop v. Arundell

(Ex. 1704–1705)

Where an alleged modus decimandi is not void on its face, the parishioner must prove its existence and the rector has the burden of proving its unreasonableness.

Dodd 205, 1 Rayner 98, 1 Eagle & Younge 664

Between Bishop, rector of Tarant Kynston in Dorset, plaintiff, and Mr. Arundel and others, defendants, in a tithe bill, [the case was thus]. The defendant insisted upon a *modus* of £26 a year for the farm called Tarant Kynston Farm but set out no value of the farm, nor did the plaintiff prove any. And [the court] resolved:

First, that, if the plaintiff would avoid the *modus* as unreasonable in value, that he ought to have proved the value of the farm, and [it was] not [necessary for] the defendant to make it reasonable in respect of the value;

Second, that the *modus* was not on the face of it void in respect of its largeness and being for a farm only, nor would the court suffer the value to be inquired of but generally directed the *modus* to be tried, *quod mirum*, for I [Samuel Dodd] never knew a £26 *modus* before.

2 Gwillim 585, 1 Eagle & Younge 663

22 May 1705.

A bill [was filed] by the rector of Tarrant Keynston, in Dorsetshire, for tithes in kind.

The defendant Arundell, by his answer, said that the plaintiff was rector of the said parish and entitled as stated in the bill, that he, the defendant, was owner of Tarrant Keynston Farm and of several lands thereto belonging in the occupation of the other defendants, his tenants, that he had no part of the said farm in his occupation during the said time, except two coppices and wood grounds, called Ash Leys Coppice and Heath Coppice, that Ash Leys Coppice is reputed to be no part of the said farm, but that Heath Coppice is. And he set forth the particulars of the wood cut upon the said coppices in 1701 and 1702, part of which he said was used in fencing and the remainder sold, and that he had duly paid the plaintiff for the tithes thereof, that, in the year 1703, no wood was cut, that, time beyond the memory of man, no tithes in kind had been paid for the said farm and lands, but that the defendant and those, whose estate he had, paid to the rector a *modus* of £26 a year in full discharge of all tithes for the said farm, that the defendant had from time to time paid the plaintiff all the time he had been rector the said *modus* of £26 a year, which he had accepted, in discharge of the said tithes, except for one year only, ending at Michaelmas, which the defendant had tendered to him before the filing of his bill, and now offers the same by his answer.

The other defendants admitted the plaintiff to be rector, and set up the said *modus*, which they said they had tendered to pay their proportions of, and that no tithes in kind had ever been paid. And they set forth their titheable matters.

Two issues were directed to be tried,[1] first, whether there is, and, time whereof the memory of man is not to the contrary, has been a *modus* of £26 *per annum* payable to the rector of Tarrant Keynston for the time being by the own-

[1] It is to this part of the cause, no doubt, that the resolutions of the court, as given by Chief Baron Dodd, refer. He states that the court resolved, first, that, if the plaintiff would avoid the *modus* as unreasonable in value, it lay upon him to prove the value of the farm, and [it is] not necessary for the defendant to make it reasonable in respect of the value, second, that the *modus* was not on the face of it void in respect of its largeness and being for a farm only, nor would the court permit the value to be inquired into, but generally directed the *modus* to be tried. Dodd adds '*quod mirum*', for he never knew a £26

ers and occupiers of Tarrant Keynston Farm in satisfaction and discharge of all tithes arising upon the said farm and the lands and grounds thereunto belonging, secondly, whether the coppice and wood grounds in the said parish called Ash Leys Coppice is part of the said farm called Tarrant Keynston Farm.

A trial was accordingly had upon the said issues. And the jury found the same for the defendants. But, upon reading the said order and *postea*, a new trial was directed to be had upon the two following issues:

First, what was the annual value, one year with another, of Tarrant Keynston Farm now in question at the time of exhibiting the plaintiff's bill against the defendants and for the major part of sixty years before;

Secondly, whether there is and time whereof the memory of man is not to the contrary has been a *modus* of £26 *per annum* payable to the rector of Tarrant Keynston for the time being by the owners and occupiers of Tarrant Keynston Farm in satisfaction and discharge of all tithes arising upon the said farm and the lands and grounds thereunto belonging.

[It was] to be tried by a special jury, and the defendants [are] to have the costs of the last trial taxed and paid before they proceed to trial.

A trial was accordingly had upon the last-mentioned issues, and the jury found both the issues for the plaintiff, *viz.*:

As to the first issue, that the yearly value of Tarrant Keynston Farm for sixty years before the filing of the plaintiff's bill in this court was £400 a year, that, thirty years before filing such bill, the same was £350 and, at the time of filing, £300 *per annum*;

As to the second issue, the jury found that there was no such *modus* of £26 *per annum* payable in discharge of the tithes of Tarrant Keynston Farm, as by the defendants was pretended.

The defendants' counsel now alleging that the verdict was not to the satisfaction of the judge who tried the cause, Mr. Baron Smith was desired to speak to him.

Upon reading the order the 12th of November last and the return of the *postea*, whereby it appeared the verdicts were given as aforesaid, and upon hearing counsel on both sides, and it appearing to the court that the judge who tried the cause was not dissatisfied with the said verdict, it was ordered that the several defendants should account with, satisfy, and pay to the plaintiff for the tithes of the several titheable matters and things which they respectively had, renewing and arising on their respective tenements, lands, and grounds, and the heath coppice, which they respectively held and occupied within the said parish and rectory of Tarrant Keynston during the time in the bill charged.

[The order of 23 May 1703 is printed at 1 Wood 459.]

---

modus before. This note is referred to in [*Kennedy v. Goodwin* (Ex. 1731)] Bunbury 301. [Henry Gwillim's note]

247

Attorney General, ex rel. Lee v. Lane

(Ex. 1705)

Goods seized upon a writ of outlawry can be required to be produced in order to facilitate a trial for their forfeiture.

Upon a seizure of goods upon a writ of outlawry, the sheriff has the implied power to sell them without any further order.

Lincoln's Inn MS. Misc. 536, f. [50]

Trinity term 1705. Attorney General, *pro* Godfrey Lee v. Mr. Lane and the Sheriffs of London and Middlesex.

Sir John James, who married the countess dowager of Denbigh, was outlawed after a judgment at the suit of [Godfrey] Lee. And, upon a [writ of] *capias utlagatum* against Sir John James, the sheriffs of London by [a writ of] inquisition seized into the queen's hands divers household goods, in a schedule annexed to the inquisition at certain prices therein mentioned. The defendant Lane, brother to the countess, came before the sheriffs and made a claim to the goods in property, and left in the sheriffs' hands money to the value of the appraisement, and, thereupon, the sheriff delivered him the goods. But he returned the writ and inquisition whereby it appeared he had seized the goods themselves into the queen's hands without taking notice of selling the goods (indeed without selling them), they being necessaries for the countess's use, to whom her brother lent them for that purpose. The writ and inquisition were filed in the [Court of] Common Pleas, and the transcript of the outlawry was certified into the Exchequer, whereby the writ, inquisition, and return appeared to be as above.

And, to that transcript, the defendant Lane came in and, by a plea, claimed the property of the goods in the schedule, and traversed the title of Sir John James to the same at the time of the outlawry.

The Attorney General, by a replication, maintains the title of Sir John James, upon which, they were at issue. But the pleader, by his plea, does not pray delivery of the goods to him, nor does the Attorney General pray they may remain forfeited to the queen by the outlawry. But the record of the issue was made up wholly upon the property or not property of Sir John James, which was unusual.

And in order to this trial, Mr. Attorney General moved the Court of Exchequer that the prosecutor of the outlawry may have a view of the goods and that they may be produced at the trial so that evidence may be given concerning the identity of the goods, the goods themselves being necessary evidence in this case concerning the property to which the witnesses on either side may give evidence, and the more fit it is they should be produced in regard they in specie are forfeited if they prove to be the property of Sir John James.

First, it was moved in this case whether this court that had only the transcript before it (the sheriff's return being to the Common Pleas whence the [writ of] *capias utlagatum* issued and whence returnable) could order what [was] desired, which, if fit to be done, the court have thought it had the power to do in regard the defendant pleads here his title and property, which can be determined nowhere else and, the trial being to be in this court, no court else can judge of or intermeddle with the evidence. So, of necessity, this court by the transcript has power to try the title and determine it as in all other cases of outlawries transcribed [?], both touching lands and chattels.

The second question was whether the sheriff upon a [writ of] *capias utlagatum* only can sell the goods seized and valued in regard of the words in the writ '*ita quod nobis [. . .] de bonis praedictis vel vero valore eorundum*', which never are in the case of an extent. Besides, in an extent, there is a proviso that the sheriff sells not until further order and that is by [a writ of] *venditioni exponas*, which implies no sale without it.

In Hoe's Case, 5 Rep. 90b, if a sheriff sells goods on a *capias utlagatum* and the outlawry is reversed, the goods are to be restored and not the money, because the sheriff is not compelled to sell upon a *capias utlagatum* but may preserve them to the king's use. Dy. 263, 223; so is Dr. Drury's Case, 8 rep. 143, 1 Roll's Abr. 778; Eyre and Woodfine, Anderson and Cro. Eliz.[1] None of these blame, much less punish the sheriff for selling, so that a power to sell by a *capias utlagatum* is implied. Nor is there any great difficulty where the title of the goods is not contested.

But here it is. And the sheriff has not returned that he had sold the goods, as he ought if he had, and to have had the money ready. But he has returned that he had seized the goods into the queen's hands and, therefore, [it is] to be presumed that he still had them and, therefore, ought to produce them.

And, of that opinion, the court seemed to be.

The parties set up an agreement as to the sheriff, who proved what he did in delivering the goods was by the consent of the prosecutor, and so he was excused.

But the court made an order upon the pleader, who had the goods to show cause why the prosecutor should not have a view of the goods in order to give what evidence he could that they were the outlawed person's and not the pleader's, which was complied with.

And the cause was afterwards tried at law. And [there was a] verdict for the defendant that pleaded title to the goods that they were his and not the outlawed persons.

[Other copies of this report: Georgetown Univ. Law Sch. MS. B88–9, f. 243.]

---

[1] *Hoe v. Boulton* (Ex. 1600), 5 Coke Rep. 89, 77 E.R. 191, also Moore K.B. 468, 72 E.R. 701; *Lambert v. Proctor* (1563), 2 Dyer 222, 73 E.R. 493, also 1 Anderson 36, 123 E.R. 340, New Benloe 27, 73 E.R. 950; *Bray v. Drewry* (1610), 8 Coke Rep. 141, 77 E.R. 688, 1 Rolle, Abr., *Error*, pl. I, 1, 2, p. 778; *Eyre v. Woodfin* (1592), 1 Anderson 277, 123 E.R. 471, Croke Eliz. 278, 78 E.R. 533.

247a

Attorney General v. LeFevre

(Ex. 1705)

Salt imported from Guernsey pays the same duty as English salt.

Indiana Univ., Lilly Library
MS. Parker 'Cases in the Exchequer', vol. 4, p. 21

Trinity term 1705.

Upon an information for £222 for a certain quantity of bay salt imported from the Island of Guernsey at 3s. 4d. for every 56 pound weight, the defendant demurs. The question was upon a clause in the Statute 2 & 3 Anne, for regulating the duty on salt.[1] The clause is 'that, during the present war, it was lawful to import bay salt of the produce of Guernsey upon paying the same and no higher or other duty than shall be laid on salt made in England that there shall be but 4000 bushels imported in any one year.'

The question was what was the English duty on salt made in England.

Judgment was given for the plaintiff that the defendant was to pay the plaintiff according to weight not measure and that was most for the advantage of the crown, where the several acts relating to the salt duty were compared, that is to say 5 Will., c. [*blank*]; 7 Will., c. [*blank*]; 9 Will., c. [*blank*]; 1 Anne, c. [*blank*]; 2 & 3 Anne, c. [*blank*], in which last the proviso in question is.[2]

248

Lord Montgomery v. Anonymous

(Ex. 1705)

In this case, the court found no good reason or cause to allow a juror to impeach his own verdict.

Lincoln's Inn MS. Misc. 536, f. [53v]

In an [action of] ejectment brought by the plaintiff against the defendant for a mine of [*blank*] in a Welsh county, it came to trial by a special jury of quality last Lent Assizes at Shrewsbury. And a view was directed, which was had in July last, where the viewers were shown the place in question. And, it being then grousing time, divers persons and, amongst them, some friends and wellwishers, as it was

---

[1] Stat. 2 & 3 Ann., c. 16 (*SR*, VIII, 280–284).

[2] Stat. 5 Will. & Mar., c. 7 (*SR*, VI, 447–461); Stat. 7 & 8 Will. III, c. 31 (*SR*, VII, 130–148); Stat. 9 Will. III, c. 44 (*SR*, VII, 429–446); Stat. 1 Ann., c. 15 (*SR*, VIII, 60–66); Stat. 2 & 3 Ann., c. 16 (*SR*, VIII, 280–284).

thought, to both parties happened to be thereabouts and, by way of common discourse, vented their thoughts in the presence and hearing of some of the viewers, but no notice was taken of it by the jurors.

And, at the last Assizes before Baron Bury at Shrewsbury, the trial came on again, and the jury found for the defendant.

And now Mr. Solicitor General [*Harcourt*], upon affidavits that persons of kin to the defendant came to and were at the view and discoursed there with divers and uttered their opinions in favor of the defendant and that, after the trial was over, a baronet, who was the foreman of the jury, came to the judge and told him he was not satisfied with the verdict, moved for a new trial.

But, in regard nothing was made out that any came to the view at the desire nor so much as with the privity of the defendant and that any of the jurors [or] viewers took any notice of the opinions or discourses of any persons there and, if the foreman was not satisfied, why did he give the verdict and because, if what was done at the view was not right, yet it was known then to the plaintiff's agents and then why did they put in the record and try the cause, which was in their power to have avoided or why did not they challenge such of the viewers or others whom they thought not to be indifferent or to be influenced by anything done or said at the view and it being of dangerous consequence to give any regard to the juryman's declaration to the judge after the trial that, though he had given his verdict, yet he was not satisfied and this being in an [action of] ejectment when the plaintiff may try it again and as often as he pleases and Baron Bury, that tried the cause, not being dissatisfied with the verdict, the Chief Baron [Edward Ward] and Bury and Smith saw no cause for a new trial as this case is. And, therefore, the motion was not granted.

But Baron Price was, notwithstanding, for a new trial by reason of the presence of some of the defendant's friends at the view and the discourses there sworn, presuming, though nothing [was] made out, that the defendant's friends came at the defendant's desire, which seems strange, and, though the jury who were all of quality and four or five of them were at the view should be any ways influenced to give a verdict against or without evidence is not to be intended.

[Other copies of this report: Georgetown Univ. Law Sch. MS. B88–9, f. 246.]

249

Jeffs v. Mascall

(Ex. 1705)

In this case, the scire facias was properly and sufficiently pleaded by the plaintiff.

Lincoln's Inn MS. Misc. 536, f. [54]

Michaelmas [term] 4 Anne 1705. In the Office of the Pleas in the Exchequer, [entered] Hilary [term] 3 Anne.

Middlesex. *Praeceptum fuit vicecomitum Robertus Jeffs nuper in curia dominae reginae nunc coram baronum de Scaccario suo apud Westmonasterium per considerationem eiusdem curiae recuperasset versus Rodulfum Millet, armigerum, quoddam debitum de £802 13s. quam £9 9s. 9d. qui eidem Roberto in eadem curia adjudicata fuerunt pro damnis suis quae habuit actionem detentionis debiti illius unde convictus fuit prout per recordum inde in dicta curia reman' liquebat manifeste executo tamen judic' praedict' restabatur faciendum.* And then he sets forth that the defendant Mascall, the first of May *tertio reginae* [1704], before Baron Price, became bail for Millet (not saying where) to pay the debt if Millet did not do it nor yield his body to prison in case Millet should be condemned in that action and that Millet had not paid the defendant nor yielded his body to prison *prout ex informatione* of Jeffs *acceperat regin' et quia etc. quod per probas etc. scire feceret* to the defendant Mascall to be before the barons of the Exchequer *octabis Hilarii tunc proxime* to show cause why the plaintiff should not have execution against him for the debt and damages *juxta formam recuperationis praedictis si etc. et qualiter etc. vicecomes constare fac. baron' de Scaccario hic, scil. apud Westmonasterium praedict' ad praefatum terminum, ad quem diem*, the plaintiff came by his attorney, and the sheriff of Middlesex returned *nichil et non est inventus* against the defendant, and, thereupon, another [writ of] *scire facias* issues to the sheriff of Middlesex returnable *octabis Purificationis ostens' in forma praedicta et idem dies* to the plaintiff, who appeared by his attorney, and the sheriff returned another *nichil et non est inventus. Et super hoc*, the plaintiff prays execution against the defendant for his debt and damages *juxta formam recognitionis praedictis.*

The defendant Mascall comes in and pleads *executio non,* because he says that *ante impetrationem eiusdem brevis, scil. 25 Novembris tertio Annae* at the City of Durham in County Durham, he paid the plaintiff £812 2s. 9d. in full satisfaction of the said debt and damages *et hac paratus etc.*, and he prays judgment if the plaintiff ought to have execution against him for the said debt and damages.

To this plea, the plaintiff demurs generally. And the defendant joins.

Counsel were heard. And the plaintiff shows for cause of the demurrer that the defendant's plea of payment of the money, which is of a transitory nature, at Durham is not good to a *scire facias* awarded against him in Middlesex. But the payment, if true, ought to have been pleaded in Middlesex, where the *scire facias* was awarded.

The defendant did not contend that his plea was good, for the reason above. But he insisted that the *scire facias* was bad, insufficient, and uncertain for these reasons:

First, that the *placitum* here was of Hilary term and the first *scire facias* was returnable *octabis Hilarii*, which is the first day of term and so absurd to lay the *placitum* of Hilary term, which ought to have been of Michaelmas term before to warrant the first *scire facias*.

Sed non allocatur, for all the precedents are so, and it would have been naught; otherwise, the *placitum* must be of the term wherein the first process is returnable.

Second, *non constat* here when the judgment against the principal was had, which ought to have been, for, as this record is, it might be that the bail was given after the judgment and *non constat* in what action the bail was given.

Sed non allocatur, for it is not the course in such a *scire facias* to set forth the time of the judgment, neither in this court nor the Queen's Bench, though they do it in the Common Bench. Co. Entr. 624; Ra. Entr. 589; *Registrum Brevium* 228, 233, 234, 241–250.[1]

And, by the *scire facias*, it appears that the bail was given *in placito praedicto* and the judgment appears to be in an action of debt, which fully answers the objection that the bail was given to the action of debt and not after judgment. And it is well enough in a *scire facias*, which is only a short account of the matter and refers to the records of the court where the defendant upon *oyer* (had it prayed it) might have had the whole history at large.

Third, that it did not appear where Baron Price took the bail nor that he ever delivered it into court, and, if the bail was not taken in Middlesex and delivered into court, the *scire facias* could not be awarded to the sheriff of Middlesex.

Sed non allocatur, for *prima facie* it shall be intended to be taken in Middlesex and delivered by the baron in court according to the opinion of Hobart in Hall and Wingfield's Case and [*blank*] Case, Hobt. 195, at the latter end of the case, and Allen's rep., fo. 12.[2] And, if the defendant had prayed *oyer* of it, it would have appeared at large where taken and delivered into court.

The plaintiff had judgment *per totam curiam*.

[Other copies of this report: Georgetown Univ. Law Sch. MS. B88–9, f. 247.]

250

Murrey v. Johnson

(Ex. 1705)

In this case, the allegedly defamatory words were held not to be slanderous.

---

[1] *Eden v. Haward* (1573), E. Coke, *Book of Entries* (1614), '*Scire facias*', pl. 10, f. 624v; *Frowyke v. Sandys* (1571), E. Coke, *Book of Entries* (1614), '*Scire facias*', pl. 11, f. 624v.

[2] *Hall v. Wingfield* (1617), Hobart 195, 80 E.R. 342, also Moore K.B. 883, 72 E.R. 973, 1 Brownlow & Goldesborough 69, 123 E.R. 671; *Andrews v. Harborn* (1647), Alyen 12, 82 E.R. 888.

Lincoln's Inn MS. Misc. 536, f. [55]

Entered Easter term 4 Queen Anne [1705] in the Office of Pleas.

The plaintiff brings an action upon the case [for slander] against the defendant. And he alleges himself to be a good subject free from all faults and crimes of felony, deceit, or otherwise and that, for fourteen years, he had exercised the trade of a founder in London, and, for two years before, he had been employed in the Tower of London by the queen's Master Melter for melting gold and silver for the making of money and thereby gotten great gains for the support of himself and family and had demeaned himself faithfully in that employment without purloining or embezzling any of the queen's said metals or of any other or any fraud in his employment, yet the defendant, not ignorant of the premises and designing to injure him in his reputation and to bring him into the displeasure of the said Master Melter and other the queen's subjects and to bring him into shame and disgrace and to have him esteemed and reputed a purloiner and embezzler of the queen's silver from the Tower of London and to have him deprived from his said employment, spoke and published these false and scandalous words following in the presence and hearing of many of the queen's liege people, *viz.* I (the defendant *innuendo*) was at Murrey's Shop (meaning the plaintiff's[1] shop) and saw two pieces of shilling bars between three and four inches long (*innuendo argentum fusum in pecias monetae vocatus* shillings) *intendum ac insinuandum quod idem* the plaintiff *argentum illud de dicta domina regina praedicta Turre sua Londini clandestine, fraudulenter, illicite, et deceptive subduxisset, anglice* had purloined, *et imbezilasset, Anglice* embezzled. By reason of the publishing of which words, he was not only hurt in his good name and reputation but also afterwards (at such a day) was wholly amoved and deprived from his employment in the melting of gold and silver in the Tower for the coining of money and lost that employment and was much prejudiced in his other lawful business, *ad damnum* £500.

The defendant demurs generally to this declaration. And the plaintiff joins.

The words laid to be spoken are only that the defendant should say that he was at Murrey's shop (*innuendo* the plaintiff's) and saw two pieces of shilling bars between three and four inches long. What slander is this by these words? They import none in themselves. And the *innuendo* that follows is of a strange nature and cannot enlarge the sense of the words spoken nor make them actionable. He cites for that Danvers, Abr., 157, several cases there; to say a man has forsworn himself (*innuendo* at the Assizes) is not actionable; Cro. Eliz. 297; he burned my barn (*innuendo* barn with corn in it) is not actionable; Cro. Eliz. 609.[2]

---

[1] defendant's *MSS.*

[2] *Levermore v. Martin* (1593), Croke Eliz. 297, 78 E.R. 549; *Barham v. Nethersal* (1602), 4 Coke Rep. 20, 76 E.R. 908, also Yelverton 22, 80 E.R. 16, Noy 155, 74 E.R. 1116; *Anonymous* (1598), Croke Eliz. 609, 78 E.R. 852.

Special damages laid signifies nothing where the words are not actionable because they import not damage nor are any slander nor can an *innuendo* enlarge or alter the sense of the word.

On 27 November 1705, judgment [was given] for the defendant by the whole court.

[Other copies of this report: Georgetown Univ. Law Sch. MS. B88–9, f. 248.]

251

Garnett's Case

(Ex. 1705)

Money levied as a fine for a misdemeanor cannot be charged against a parish as for the non payment of a tax.

Lincoln's Inn MS. Misc. 536, f. [58v], pl. 1

Michaelmas [term] 1705.

In the receiver general's account for Middlesex for marriages, births, and burials declared (as the Act[1] directs) by the Chancellor of the Exchequer, there was a *super* set of £5 upon A., collector of that tax in Clerkenwell parish. And this being written in process against A., the sheriff, returned a *nichil* upon him, and, that Act directing that the parish shall answer for the insufficiency of the collector, the process went against the inhabitants. And it was levied upon the church wardens, who making it appear to the court that it was a fine set upon A. by the Commissioners for a misdemeanor and not for an arrear of any duty, the court ordered the Auditors of the Imprest to attend and the officers of the Pipe [Office].

And it appearing to be as above, the *super* was made right and set upon A. for a fine, and process [was ordered] to go against him first and the money levied to be restored to the inhabitants.

[Other copies of this report: Georgetown Univ. Law Sch. MS. B88–9, f. 252v, pl. 1.]

252

Veal v. Dix

(Ex. 1705)

Nul tiel record *is not a good defense to an action grounded upon a judgment in a court not of record.*

---

[1] Stat. 9 Will. III, c. 32 (*SR*, VII, 403–405).

Lincoln's Inn MS. Misc. 536, f. [58v], pl. 3

The plaintiff brings [an action of] debt for £4 19s. 9d. upon a judgment or recovery for damages in the county court of Norfolk. And he declares upon the recovery *prout patet per processum* of that court.

The defendant pleads *nul tiel record*. The plaintiff demurs.

And he had judgment, for the plea is idle, the county court not being a court of record, nor was anything of record mentioned by the plaintiff. And, though it may be a question whether *ley gager* lies upon a recovery, though it may for an amercement in a county court or a court baron, yet it never can be a question but that an action of debt lies for such recovery or amercement. Hobt. 206; Roll's, *Ley Gager*, 106, 9.[1]

[Other copies of this report: Georgetown Univ. Law Sch. MS. B88–9, f. 252, pl. 3.]

253

Walter v. Morgan

(Ex. 1705)

Where a defendant in an action upon a bond alleges that the bond was altered, he must allege the alteration with specificity in his own pleading.

Lincoln's Inn MS. Misc. 536, f. [59], pl. 1

Michaelmas [term] 1705.

[In an action of] debt upon a bond for the performance of covenants in an indenture of apprenticeship, the defendants plead *actio non* because they say that, after the making of the indenture and before this action, *quaedam verba materialia* (not saying what they were) were erased and obliterated by the plaintiff out of the indenture, *per quod* that indenture became void, *et hoc paratus sunt verificare etc.* The plaintiff demurs.

And he had judgment, for, first, the defendants must have shown what the words were which were erased that the court might judge whether they were material or no; secondly, if they had been set out and had been material, yet they should have concluded *et issint nient son fait*. Pigot's Case, 11 rep. 26.[2]

[Other copies of this report: Georgetown Univ. Law Sch. MS. B88–9, f. 253, pl. 1.]

---

1 *Speake v. Richards* (1617), Hobart 206, 80 E.R. 353, also Moore K.B. 886, 72 E.R. 974, 2 Shower K.B. 281, 89 E.R. 940, Hutton 11, 123 E.R. 1065, 1 Brownlow & Goldesborough 51, 123 E.R. 659, Noy 22, 74 E.R. 992; *Yewens v. Pound*, 2 Rolle, Abr., *Ley Gager*, pl. A, 9, p. 106.

2 *Winchcombe v. Pigot* (1614), 11 Coke Rep. 26, 77 E.R. 1177, also 1 Rolle Rep. 39, 81 E.R. 311, Moore K.B. 835, 72 E.R. 937, 2 Bulstrode 246, 80 E.R. 1096.

254

Attorney General v. St. John

(Ex. 1705–1706)

The crown can sue joint obligors severally.

Where a defendant pleads to the substance of an obligation, any defects in the writ are cured thereby.

Lincoln's Inn MS. Misc. 536, f. [59], pl. 2

The defendant St. John and two other persons entered into a recognizance to the late King William of £1000 penalty jointly and severally before the Chief Baron [Edward Ward]. And they were all written of London, and it was conditioned for the defendant St. John's performing such an order of this court as should be made in such a cause. A [writ of] *scire facias* upon that recognizance was awarded into London against two of them. And therein it is mentioned that the three had not paid the £1000, but that the same remains still due.

It was commanded that the sheriff *scire facias* to the defendants why the queen should not have execution against them for the said £1000.

The two defendants, upon a *scire feci* returned, came in and, after *oyer* of the condition, pleaded that there was not any order made in that cause.

The plaintiff replies, and sets forth the order, and assigns a good breach wherein the defendants had not performed that condition.

The defendants rejoin that they had not notice of the order, and conclude to the country, the Attorney General having in his replication alleged the defendants had notice of the order and required the money ordered to be paid, which they refused.

The Attorney General demurred, and had judgment, for the rejoinder was a plain departure from the plea, for, by the plea, they say no order was made and, when it is shown, notice or not notice is not material, for, indeed, being matter of record, they are bound at [their] peril to take notice of it. And it is a contradiction to say there was no order made and, when it is shown, to say they had no notice of it.

But *Dodd*, for the defendants, took an exception to the *scire facias* wherein it mentioned that the defendants *non solverunt vel solvi causaverunt* the £1000, and does not say *nec eorum alter seu aliquis non solvit*, for one or two might pay it, though all three did not pay.

Sed non allocatur, for, though in debt upon a bond where more than one is bound, it is usually said *nec eorum alter* or *aliquis non solvit* yet that is but an inducement to the purpose of the writ and just after it is said that the queen being willing to be satisfied that debt *nobis iam debitus* and, if any of them had paid that sum or the condition had been performed, the defendants would have had the advantage of it. Besides, the money was not otherwise due than that the condition was broken or observed, and, if observed, nothing was due so that that way of alleging that all had not been paid it is not material. Besides, it has always been the practice in the office to make a *scire facias* so.

The plaintiff had judgment.

And the like judgment was given in this court Easter [term] 1697 in Sir Edmund Wiseman's Case upon the like exception taken; L. M, 125, 126.[1]

[Other copies of this report: Georgetown Univ. Law Sch. MS. B88–9, f. 253, pl. 2.]

Lincoln's Inn MS. Misc. 536, f. [27]

Hilary [term] 1705[/06], [Entered] Easter [term] 4 Anne [1705].

A [writ of] *scire facias* goes out directed to the sheriffs of London reciting that the defendants St. John and Layfield of London, goldsmiths, and one Taylor of St. Clement's Danes, Middlesex, goldsmith, came before the Chief Baron [Edward Ward] at Westminster the 28th of May 10 Will. III [1698] and jointly and severally entered into a recognizance to the king of £1000 to be paid at a day past and that they had not paid nor caused the same to be paid to the queen and that the queen of the said £1000 *nobis iam debit' ei poternius [?] qua [. . .] satisfieri volentes ut est justum* commands the sheriffs (*sicut alios*) to make known to the two defendants to show cause why they *onerari non debent* with the said £1000 and pay the same to the queen. Whereupon a *nichil* was returned.

But those two defendants appear and pray *oyer* of the recognizance and condition. And, by the recognizance, it does not appear where it was entered into. And the condition recited that an order of court of the 21st of the same May in a cause depending between the Attorney General and the defendant St. John, whereby it was ordered by the consent of Joseph Bennet, the prosecutor in that cause, and the defendant St. John that Bennet should stand relator in that cause to answer costs and that Bennet, as well as St. John, should give security by a recognizance to abide such order as the court should make upon hearing of that cause as well touching the demand by the bill as touching the costs of the cause, if, therefore, St. John performs such order as the court shall make upon the said hearing as well touching the demand in the bill as touching the cost of the cause, then etc. or else etc.

The defendants plead that, after the recognizance and before the *scire facias*, no order was made by the court upon hearing the cause touching the demand in the bill or the costs in the cause, and pray judgment *si onerari debent etc.*

The Attorney General replies that *taliter processum fuit* in that cause that the 25th of November second [year of] this queen [1703] upon the hearing of that cause touching the demand in the bill and concerning the costs of that suit, it was ordered by the court, *inter alia*, that the defendant St. John should forthwith pay to the said Bennet, the relator, or his assigns £695 15s. 10d. to the use of the Regiment in the bill mentioned together with costs of suit to be taxed by

[1] *Attorney General v. Duke of Beaufort* (Ex. 1692–1697), see above Case No. 90.

the Deputy [Queen's] Remembrancer whereof St. John had notice and after was desired by Bennet to pay him the said sum for the use of the Regiment, which he refused and has not paid nor performed the order.

The defendants rejoin that, before the issuing of the *scire facias*, St. John had no notice of the order. And they concluded to the country.

The Attorney General demurred generally, and the defendants join.

It was agreed on all hands that the defendants' rejoinder that he had no notice of the order is a plain departure from his plea that no order was made.

But *Dodd*, on the defendants' behalf, took exceptions to the *scire facias* and also to the replication, as to the *scire facias*, first, that the recognizance is by three jointly and severally and the *scire facias* is only against two, which is neither jointly nor severally, for, if the conusors were to be charged jointly, they must all be sued so; if severally, then each one apart must be sued, but two of them, the three being living, cannot be sued together, for that is neither joint nor several. And, for that reason, the writ is insufficient, and ought to be quashed; as least, the defendants not [be] charged by it. And, for that purpose, were cited Hansard's *Entries* 237; *Officium Brevium* 350; 3 rep., Sir W. Herbert's Case, fo. [*blank*]; Lutwiche 1282; 4 Modern rep. 314 etc., for the third may have paid.[1]

First, this point, in the case of a subject, is certainly true. But it holds not against the queen's prerogative and the frequent practice in this court, and

Second, that the *scire facias* is only to bring the defendants in and, though the suggestion be that these two had not paid it, yet, as objected, the other might have done it, yet that is not material, for, if the other had paid it, these two might have pleaded it and had the advantage of it. L. M, 126, Sir Edmund Wiseman's Case.[2]

Third, if the writ had not been good, the defendants might have pleaded or demurred to it. But, having prayed *oyer* of the recognizance and condition and it appearing to be joint and several and having pleaded to the condition, that has cured all.

The second exception [was] that the writ is to show cause *quare onerari non debent*, which is not right, for it ought to have been there *quare* the queen *executio versus ipsos [?] habere non debent*, the recognizance being a judgment.

To that it was answered and affirmed by all the clerks that the writs of *scire facias* upon a recognizance are always so, *quare onerari non debet*. The judgment

[1] J. Hansard, *Book of Entries* (1685); *Officina Brevium* (1679); *Harbert's Case* (Ex. 1584), 3 Coke Rep. 11, 76 E.R. 647, also Popham 154, 79 E.R. 1252, Moore K.B. 169, 72 E.R. 510; *Redman v. Idle* (1698), 2 Lutwyche 1282, 125 E.R. 709; *Lampton v. Collingwood* (1694), 4 Modern 306, 314, 87 E.R. 411, 415, also Comberbach 325, 90 E.R. 506, 1 Lord Raymond 27, 91 E.R. 915, 3 Lord Raymond 327, 92 E.R. 714, 1 Salkeld 262, 91 E.R. 230, 3 Salkeld 145, 91 E.R. 742, Carthew 282, 90 E.R. 767, Holt K.B. 270, 90 E.R. 1048.

[2] *Attorney General v. Duke of Beaufort* (Ex. 1696–1697), see above, Case No. 90.

in Matthew Herbert's Case, 3 rep., fo. 11b and 18b, is so, and, though that judgment was found fault withal as to the charge against the heir to subject his own as well as his ancestor's lands, yet it was not objected against for any other purpose.

The third exception [was] that it is incongruous to charge defendant St. John by a decree to pay the demand in the bill to Bennet, who, though relator to answer costs, yet is not concerned in the demand.

To that, it was answered that is to object to the decree and order of the court, and, though he has not paid the costs, yet the condition is to pay as well the demand, which is settled to be £600 and odd pounds as the costs, and a failer in either is a breach of the condition.

And so judgment was given for the queen.

[Other copies of this report: Georgetown Univ. Law Sch. MS. B88–9, f. 257.]

255

Attorney General v. Venable

(Ex. 1705)

In this case, money was seized and forfeited for having been exported against the statute.

Lincoln's Inn MS. Misc. 536, f. [59v]

[There was an] information upon a seizure of £700 *de bonis personis ignotis* by Elrington, the Searcher of Chester, found aboard a ship *ibidem exitur in partes transmarinas ea intentione* to be carried into parts beyond the seas *contra formam statuti*. There was a verdict for the queen, no defense [being made].

It was moved in arrest of judgment that the offense is not laid as the Statute of 2 Hen. IV, ca. 5,[1] directs, for that the money must be found in the keeping of some[one] that is passing beyond the seas, which is not said here, as the precedent in Hardress is and upon the reason of Rooke's Case, Hardress, fo. [*blank*].[2]

Mr. Attorney General [*Northey*], for the plaintiff: It is said the goods of persons unknown and the word '*exitur*' may go as well to persons as the ship. Besides, the defendant claims property, and says the money was unjustly taken out of his possession and pleads that the money was not found by the searcher as the said ship or vessel *exitur extra portum praedictum in partes transmarinas modo et forma prout per informationem praedictam supponitur et de hoc ponit se super patriam*.

Judgment [will be given] for the plaintiff unless better cause [be shown] first day next term.

[Other copies of this report: Georgetown Univ. Law Sch. MS. B88–9, f. 254.]

---

1 Stat. 2 Hen. IV, c. 5 (*SR*, II, 122).

2 *Anonymous, qui tam v. Rook* (1655), Hardres 20, 145 E.R. 359.

256

Duckingfield v. Shaw

(Ex. 1705)

A plea of nil debet is a good response to an action of debt upon a bond.

Lincoln's Inn MS. Misc. 536, f. [60]

Michaelmas [term] 1705.

The plaintiff [Sir Robert Duckingfield, late sheriff of Lancashire] declares in [an action of] debt for £2000 upon articles between the plaintiff of one part and the defendants [William Shaw and Edmund Valentine] on the other part dated the 30 December 10 Will. III [1698] and sealed whereby the plaintiff being then the sheriff of Lancashire appointed the defendants *pro eis vel uno eorum* to be his undersheriff as long as he continued high sheriff and thereby authorized them *vel alter utrum eorum agere, recipere, et facere idem quod dicto officio spectabat* and then sets forth some part of the articles which related to fees and the division of them and *in consideratione inde*, the defendants, by those articles for themselves, their heirs, executors, and administrators, covenanted and agreed with the plaintiff that they or one of them should diligently and faithfully manage and discharge the duty of the said office of under sheriff and duly attend the assizes, sessions, and other occasions to the said office belonging *et omnia alia fideliter facerent idem concernendem et indemnificarent dictum vicecomitem in omnibus ab aliqua mala administratione vac' mismanagementa quae forent per alterutrum eorum vel eorum clericos tangente praemissa*. And, for the true performance of the several matters, covenants, and agreements *qualibet dictarum pertinent' per eosdem articulos obligasset seipsam et seipsas eius et eorum haeredes etc. alteri eorum eius et eorum executores et administratores in penali summa* £2000. Then he sets forth that the defendant Valentine, by virtue of that deputation, executed the said office of under sheriff during all the time the plaintiff was sheriff of that county then sets forth that, at the assizes at Lancaster in September 10 Will. III [1698], John Berisford, Esq., obtained a judgment against John Heap and Edward Whitehead for a £100 debt and costs and that Berisford sued out execution at the same assizes by [a writ of] *capias ad satisfaciendum* against the said Heap and Whitehead returnable at the then next assizes which was delivered to the plaintiff, then sheriff of Lancashire, to be executed, by virtue whereof the plaintiff arrested and took Whitehead in execution and had and detained him in execution *quousque* the defendant Valentine without the license and against the will of Berisford permitted him to escape and go at large, the said debt and costs not paid. And then he sets forth that Berisford brought [an action of] escape against the plaintiff, and declared against the plaintiff, as is usual in escapes, and he recovered against him by a verdict and judgment. And [he says] that the defendants or either of them *nullo modo conservaverunt indemnem* the plaintiff *ab implicatione illa aut de [. . .]*

convictione praedicta, but the plaintiff for his own discharge was forced to pay £60 *per quod actio accrevit* to the plaintiff to have and recover from the defendants the said £2000, which they or either of them have not paid, though often requested, *ad damnum* £20.

Upon *nil debent* pleaded, the plaintiff, upon a trial, had a verdict.

And Serjeant *Chesshire* and Mr. *Lutwyche* moved in arrest of judgment, first, that here was no good issue joined and so no judgment, but a repleader, for *nil debent* was no good plea to this action of debt upon the articles and for the penalty, but that is only to a matter *in pais* and not by a specialty, as this is, no more than payment can be pleaded to a single bill without an acquittance.

Note judgment was given for the plaintiff.

[Other copies of this report: Georgetown Univ. Law Sch. MS. B88–9, f. 254.]

257

Layton, qui tam v. Pierce

(Ex. 1705)

An amendment to an information charging an offense will not be allowed after the period of limitation has expired.

Dodd 207

An information [was] exhibited upon the Act of Navigation[1] but it mistook the clause, part of it being alleged only, which would not reach the case. Mr. Attorney [General] entered a *nolle prosequi* for the queen. The year passed, and then the informer moved to amend and added the whole clause so as to bring the information to his case.

And upon debate and consideration, it was denied because now the party is free, the year being gone, and to make him guilty by retrospect and amendment is not reasonable. Yet see above, Knowles against Merrick.[2]

258

Newte v. Chamberlaine

(Ex. 1705)

Tithes are payable for newly erected mills.

Tithes of mills are personal not praedial, and the measure of them is the net profit from the mill.

1 Stat. 12 Car. II, c. 18 (*SR*, V, 246–250).

2 *Knowles, qui tam v. Merrick* (Ex. 1693), see above, Case No. 109.

Dodd 208, 1 Eagle & Younge 679

A bill for tithe of malt ground at a horse mill in Tiverton in Devonshire erected within six years [was brought], and upon the hearing of this cause, the court took time, until 22d April, to deliver their opinion, and then all [held] for the complainant, and that the tenth toll dish should be paid, and decreed an account accordingly.

First, it is a predial [tithe] or in nature of a predial tithe;

Second, tithe of every newly erected mill shall be paid;

Third, *semble* that the Statute of *Articuli Cleri*[1] had allowed the canon and that all consultations or denials of prohibitions are resolutions in point. See Lindwood; 2 Rolle Rep. 84; 1 Brownl. 32; 3 Bulstr. 212; 1 Rolle 656; 1 Rolle 652; 2 Inst. 490, 1 Rolle 651, 1 Rolle 405; 2 Inst. 622; Cro. Ja. 523, 524.[2]

Note: All the Barons argued solemnly this day. See above 1694. See 1 Rolle 656.

Note: By the Chief Baron [EDWARD WARD], a mill built on lands that were abbey lands and discharged shall pay tithes (query by me); and afterwards [it was said] by *Ettrick*, [where there is] a *modus* for the land or land [is] discharged of tithes, a new mill erected thereon shall not pay [tithes]. 2 Inst. 490; 1 Rolle 652, 651.

In Hughes and my Lord Hereford's case, cited in Hall and Hart's case,[3] in the king's bench by Holt, in time of Hale, it was adjudged that [one] may prescribe in *non decimando* for old mills.

Note: In Hall and Hart's case, the court of king's bench [was] divided whether [it was a] predial or personal tithe.

Afterwards, in Hilary [term] 1706[/07], upon appeal to the House of Lords, this cause [was] heard, and the lords advised with the judges, who took time to consider; and afterwards all the judges of the king's bench and the common pleas gave their opinion for reversing the decree, and that it was only a personal title, and nothing [is] due but the tenth part of the clear profits, after charges [are] deducted; and the lords reversed the decree accordingly.[4]

---

[1] Stat. 9 Edw. II, stat. 1 (*SR*, I, 171–174).

[2] W. Lindwood, *Provinciale*; *Anonymous* (1619), 2 Rolle Rep. 84, 81 E.R. 674; *Anonymous*, 1 Brownlow & Goldesborough 32, 123 E.R. 647; *Jake's Case* (1616), 3 Bulstrode 212, 81 E.R. 178; 1 Rolle, Abr., *Dismes*, pl. M, 3, p. 656; *Goodwin v. Smith* (1637), 1 Rolle, Abr., *Dismes*, pl. F, 3, p. 652; E. Coke, *Second Institute* (1642), pp. 490, 662; *Jake's Case* (1616), 1 Rolle Rep. 405, 81 E.R. 568; *Johnson v. Dandridge* (1635), 1 Rolle, Abr., *Dismes*, pl. F, 1 and 2, p. 652; *Danderidge v. Johnson* (1619), Croke Jac. 523, 79 E.R. 448, also 2 Rolle Rep. 84, 81 E.R. 674.

[3] *Hart v. Hall* (1698), 12 Modern 243, 88 E.R. 1292, 1 Lord Raymond 441, 91 E.R. 1193, Holt K.B. 673, 90 E.R. 1272, 1 Eagle & Younge 632.

[4] *Lords' Journal*, vol. 18, p. 241.

I [*Samuel Dodd*] was of counsel in the Exchequer and afterwards the Lords for the decree.

Note: [It is] now a settled point, and well settled as I conceive, for I myself was all along of this opinion and in judgment against my client.

[Other reports of this case: 7 Brown 3, 3 E.R. 2, 1 Eq. Cas. Abr. 366, 21 E.R. 1107, 2 Eq. Cas. Abr. 731, 22 E.R. 617, 1 Rayner 101, 106, 3 Rayner 1087, 1090, 2 Gwillim 596, Equity Cases Exch. 552.]

[The order of 22 April 1706, Public Record Office E.126/18, f. 580v, is printed at 1 Wood 482.]

259

Haynes v. Parr

(Ex. 1706)

An administratrix of a deceased mariner can sue for his wages in the Court of Admiralty, even though the contract was made on land.

Lincoln's Inn MS. Misc. 536, f. [29]

The defendant, relict and executrix of Sampson Parr, sues the plaintiff in the Admiralty in a cause of substraction of mariners's wages. The plaintiff prays a [writ of] prohibition, suggesting the Statute of 15 Ric. II, ca. 3,[1] that all contracts made at land within the body of a county shall be tried and determined by the laws of the land and not in the Admiralty and that, contrary thereto, the defendant libelled in the Admiralty Court against the plaintiff as master of the ship called the *William Galley* for £16 for the wages of the testator, a mariner in that ship in a voyage, supposed to be due from the plaintiff upon a contract and agreement, whereas the said contract and agreement was by writing made at land, *viz.* at the parish of All Hallows, Barking, London, the 11th of August 1702 and not upon the high sea nor within the jurisdiction of the Admiralty and the ship was then and there also at land and not at sea nor within the jurisdiction of the Admiralty and, though he had alleged all this in the Admiralty Court, yet they refused to allow it, but proceed there against him in the said cause of substraction of mariner's wages. And, therefore, he prays a [writ of] prohibition, which was last term granted *nisi causa*.

The plaintiff produced the contract in writing made at land in England and dated as above signed by the testator and thirteen or fourteen more mariners whereby reciting that they had hired themselves to the plaintiff to go with him avoyage in that ship from London to Limerick in Ireland, there to load for Leghorn or some other port in the Straits and there to load back for England or Hol-

[1] Stat. 15 Ric. II, c. 3 (*SR*, II, 78–79).

land and each to receive a month's pay by way of advance and a month's pay at the unloading in Leghorn and to have a proportionable part of the net proceeds of all prizes taken during the voyage (if the commander takes a letter of marque). All the subscribing mariners, each one for himself, and not jointly, agree with the plaintiff to go and proceed on the said voyage and not to desert or leave the ship until the voyage be ended under forfeiture of all such wages as shall be due at such time of leaving the ship and do all unanimously agree to stay for the remainder of their wages until the ship be arrived in England or Holland. But there is no seal to it.

And, upon producing the libel, it appeared that it was styled Maria Parr, executrix of Sampson Parr, *et socii*, mariners of the ship in the schedule, and there were only she and one more that did not appear to sue, and the suit was generally for wages due for a voyage, and it was not against the ship at all; the two names and the sums due for wages were in the schedule.

And *King* now prays a [writ of] consultation because it has always been allowed for mariners to join in a suit for wages, though the contract was at land and that is in respect their service is performed at sea and that court allowing many to join, it is for the ease of poor seamen and not to compel each one to have a distinct suit, as it must be if sued at common law, that the courts at Westminster have thus far indulged suits in Admiralty for mariner's wages, though contracts at land. He cited these cases that follow, fo. 9, in the printed books and the agreement in the same, fo. 8, made by the judges 8 & 9 Car. I [1632 × 1634].

Dodd, for the prohibition, relied on the Statute 15 Ric. II and the special contract in this case that make further and other provision for the wages and the payment of them and for prizes to be taken than the law otherwise would allow the mariners.

Secondly, that the suit in the Admiralty is only by the defendant here and that, as executrix to her husband and a prohibition always went to a single mariner's suit for wages and to a master's suit also for his wages etc. and, though the mariners themselves have been indulged in such suits in the Admiralty, where many join in the suit for the saving of charges, yet that is not more than a favor of the courts at Westminster, not to prohibit such suits, being plainly and in express words against the Statute of 15 Ric. II and, but of late, allowed and took its rise from the agreement 8 or 9 Car. I, which nevertheless was not observed, *prout inde*.

Thirdly, the case of an executrix is not within the same reason of the indulgence, as the mariner himself is, who, while he lives, may be and is in a capacity to be useful and serviceable for sea service, which his executrix is not.

Reasons why the Admiralty court should not hold a plea for mariner's wages upon contracts or agreements for the same or their service or any other matter or thing made at land and within the body of a county in this kingdom, and not at sea, [are as follows].

First, the Admiralty is no court of record, but trial is by the civil law.

Second, it appears by the yearbook 48 Edw. III, 3, if a mariner makes a covenant (it is to be understood at law) to serve me in a ship at sea, if 'lowers' (that is the wages) is not paid, it shall be demanded in the court by common law, and not by the maritime law. 4 Inst. 141, and divers reasons and authorities in that book, at 134 to 147.[1]

Third, if any doubt could have been made of this, the statutes 13 Ric. II, ca. 5; 15 Ric. II, ca. 3; 2 Hen. IV, 11, have abundantly provided in that case that all contracts made and things arising at land within the body of a county shall be tried at common law, and not in the Admiralty, but that jurisdiction is excluded under a penalty.[2]

Fourth, that a contract and agreement between owners or masters of ships and mariners for going avoyage or sailing at sea, made at land, for wages or the like is plainly a contract and agreement at land within those statutes.

Fifth, Mr. Prynne, in his *Animadversions upon the Fourth Institute*, as to the chapter of the Admiralty, 22, fo. 75,[3] wholly agrees to this case of contracts etc. arising at land, and not upon the sea. And he says it is granted on all hands as an undoubted truth and settled by the statutes above and warranted by the yearbooks and precedents there cited.

But, as to contracts made and things arising in parts beyond the sea and on the sea, he wholly denies what Lord Coke says in his chapter of Admiralty. And he cites many records and reasons against that, though, as Lord Cooke says, that was yielded to by Dr. Dunn, judge of the Admiralty, and settled by King James I, 8 *regno sui*, and that *magna est veritas et praevaluit.*

But Mr. Prynne sets forth former agreements of the judges [in] 1575, which this case before us extends not to, but to things done upon or beyond the seas, which lasted until 7 Jac. I, when Coke came to be Chief Justice of the Common Bench. And, then, he and the other courts granted [writs of] prohibition in that case, as, fo. 100, he shows which lasted until about 8 or 9 Car. I, 1632. And, then, by order of the king in council and agreement of all the judges under their hands, it was settled that:

First, no [writs of] prohibition are to go upon contracts made or other things personally done upon or beyond the seas;

Second, suits in Admiralty for freight or mariner's wages or breach of charter parties for voyages beyond the seas, though charter parties made at land or money payable within the realm (so as a penalty [be] not demanded or a question

---

1 *Pole v. Tochess* (1374), YB Hil. 48 Edw. III, f. 2, pl. 6; E. Coke, *Fourth Institute* (1644), p. 141.

2 Stat. 13 Ric. II, stat. 1, c. 5 (*SR*, II, 62); Stat. 15 Ric. II, c. 3 (*SR*, II, 78–79); Stat. 2 Hen. IV, c. 11 (*SR*, II, 124).

3 W. Prynne, *Brief Animadversions . . . to the Fourth Part of Institutes . . . compiled by . . . Sir Edward Cooke* (1669).

whether a charter party be his deed or not or whether the plaintiff released or is discharged within the realm) not to be prohibited;

Third, as to building [or] repairing (saving necessary victualling) a ship where a suit is against the ship itself and not against any party by name but him that comes in *pro interesse*, no prohibition [goes], though done within the realm;

Fourth, no [writ of] prohibition [goes] to the Admiralty for enquiring and redressing nuisances and obstructions in navigable rivers beneath the first bridges that hinder navigation or passage to or from the sea or to try personal contracts and injuries done there which concern navigation upon the sea;

Fifth, in any imprisoned (upon *habeas corpus*) if any of these be returned to be the cause of the imprisonment, the parties are to be remanded.

These resolutions were printed in the first edition of Croke's reports of the time of King Charles I, but left out in the later edition.

And it seems they were not looked upon as Gospel, because, in Hilary term 16 Car. I [1641], seven or eight years after, three of the same judges that signed them and Berkeley, that came in after they were made, in the Case of Ball and Trelawny, Cro. Car. 603, where an action upon the Statute 2 Hen. IV[1] was brought against the defendant for suing in the Admiralty Court on a contract made at New England and there had judgment and execution against the plaintiff for £112, those four judges held that it was out of the Admiral's jurisdiction and that he had no authority to intermeddle therewith, but the suit in the Admiralty was *coram non judice*. And he was discharged upon [a writ of] *habeas corpus*.

This seems a sudden change of opinions, and the times [are] considerable.

Mr. Prynne has, indeed, in his *Animadversions*, set forth that the lords in Parliament 1645 ruled otherwise, fo. 124, that how that case came thither he thought original. The Rump Parliament, in 1648, 1649, 1650, made pretended acts thereby enabling suits for mariner's wages etc. generally to be sued in the Admiralty.[2] If they had supposed they might have been sued for there by the law before, there had been no need of that Act.

Now, after the restoration of King Charles II, 1660, [writs of] prohibition are granted for mariner's wages; 12 Car. II, Raymond's rep., fo. 31, Raymond and Bonithan, by Foster and Twisden against Mallet, who relied on the judges' resolution 8 Car. I, which the other two judges denied to be legal and contradicted by themselves *prout* Ball and Trelawny, *ut puto*, relying on the Statute 15 Ric. II as full against the suit, and he denied the opinion of Hobart, fo. 67, that prohibition is discretionary, for they say it is *ex merito justitiae*.[3]

---

[1] *Ball v. Trelawny* (1641), Croke Car. 603, 79 E.R. 1119; Stat. 2 Hen. IV, c. 11 (*SR*, II, 124).

[2] C. H. Firth and R. S. Rait, *Acts and Ordinances of the Interregnum 1642–1660*, vol. 1, p. 1121, vol. 2, p. 712.

[3] *Woodward v. Bonithan* (1661), T. Raymond 3, 83 E.R. 2; *Ball v. Trelawny* (1641), *ut supra*; Stat. 15 Ric. II, c. 3 (*SR*, II, 78–79); *Parish of Aston v. Castle Birmidge Chapel*,

[Writs of] prohibition for mariner's wages were denied in Hilary [term] 22 & 23 Car. II, Lord Hayne's Case, King's Bench, by Twisden, for the reason of many suing together. But the master was not sued there. Hilary [term] 31 Car. II, 1 Ventr. 343, for wages from port to port, being after a sentence, though the principal cause [was] allowed. 1681, Wilmot and Shaw, in the Exchequer; 1678, Potts and Green, in the Exchequer, L. H, 35; 1687, Inder and Brooke, L. L, 7, suits against the ship as well as the party; 2 W. & M., Allison and Marsh, 2 Ventris 181; 34 Car. II, 3 Levinz 60, Coke and Cretchet, for mariner's wages grow due by service at sea and the contract at land is only to ascertain them, and Chief Justice North cited it to be the opinion of Chief Justice Hale, which he enquired of him as Justice of the Court of Common Pleas.[1]

Note, if this is the reason, then why not a master or any single seaman sue in Admiralty, which is not allowed.

It may not be so unreasonable and unfit to allow suits for mariner's wages in the Admiralty when [there is] no contract in writing, as when there is one, for that, whether under seal or not, contains the contract from which none [is] to vary no more than if a man brings any action upon the case and there be a writing between the parties under hand, though not under seal, he can vary from it.

12 February 1705[/06].

Serjeant *Broderick*, against the prohibition, insists that Admiralty had jurisdiction of mariner's wages before the Statute of Ric. II and was not restrained or ousted by that Statute. (But he shows no authority for it, and the Statutes seem against it.) He further insists that, the service being done at sea, that and not the contract at land gives the cause of suit for wages, 3 Levins 60, that the ship is liable in Admiralty, but not at law. That is not the case here, the suit not being against the ship. He cites 2 Ventris 181, Allison and Marsh's Case, where a [writ of] prohibition was denied in the Common Bench, 2 W. & M., to stay a suit in Admiralty by some of the mariners against part-owners where there were more than those suing mariners and more than two part owners of the ship for mariner's wages. And it was held by the court that a purser, boatswain, or other officer may sue there for wages, they being mariners as well as the common seamen and that the Court of Admiralty may proceed in their own way, though different from our law, as to the joining of all the plaintiffs or defendants and, if the proceedings be not according to our law, the remedy lies there. It is then said the course of the Admiralty is not to charge some of the owners with the whole, but proportionably.

Hobart 66, 80 E.R. 215.

[1] *Anonymous* (1679), 1 Ventris 343, 86 E.R. 221; *Wilmot v. Shaw* (Ex. 1681), Georgetown Univ. Law Sch. MS. B88–7, p. 249; *Potts v. Green* (Ex. 1679), Exch. Cases *tempore* Car. II, p. 399; *Inder v. Brooke* (1689), Lincoln's Inn MS. Misc. 558, f. 7; *Alleson v. Marsh* (1690), 2 Ventris 181, 86 E.R. 380; *Coke v. Cretchet* (1682), 3 Levinz 60, 83 E.R. 576.

He also cited Wells and Osmand's Case, lately in the Queen's Bench,[1] where there was a ship in port, and not at sea, and, before the rigging, there was a contract with the mariners at land for wages. But, before the contract, a bill of sale was made of the ship, and yet the ship was made liable to the wages in the buyer's hands without notice of the contract, and [a writ of] prohibition was denied.

This cause in Admiralty proceeded to the examination of witnesses, and this contract in writing was never pleaded nor insisted upon, but went upon the merits of the cause and now comes in by suggestion for a prohibition when [it was] almost ready for a sentence, and, therefore, it is too late, nor does the contract alter the law. But the wages are to be recovered as the Admiralty law allows, without regard to the contract without being under seal alters not the case of wages.

Dr. *Lloyd*, on the same side, [argued] to the same purpose.

The plaintiff's counsel insisted as before.

The court will confer with the other courts that there may be a conformity in proceedings.

Query if the executrix of a mariner shall be under the same privilege of suing for wages as the mariner himself was if alive.

Note afterwards, Easter [term] 1706, the three barons reported that all the judges of the other two courts were of the opinion against the prohibition and so the rule for one was discharged, me dubitante.

[Other copies of this report: Georgetown Univ. Law Sch. MS. B88–9, f. 258v.]

260

Anderson, qui tam v. Allen

(Ex. 1706)

In this case, a criminal offense was not properly charged, and the conviction of the defendant by the jury was set aside.

Lincoln's Inn MS. Misc. 536, f. [32]

Scaccario, per Paschae recordum quarto Annae Reginae [1705].

The plaintiffs exhibit their information of seizure of a parcel of woolfells of the growth of England by them seized as forfeited because, at such a time and place, they were packed with an intent to be carried out of this realm into Scotland or parts beyond the seas contrary to the form of the Statute.[2]

The defendant comes in and claims the property, and pleads that the woolfells or any of them were not packed with an intent to be carried out of this realm

[1] *Wells v. Osmond* (1704), 6 Modern 238, 87 E.R. 987, 2 Lord Raymond 1044, 92 E.R. 193.

[2] Stat. 12 Car. II, c. 32 (*SR*, V, 293–296).

into Scotland or any the parts beyond the seas contrary to the form of the Statute in that case provided *modo et forma prout* by the information is alleged. And he concludes to the country.

And issue was thereupon joined. And [there was] a verdict at *nisi prius* in Middlesex, where the offense was alleged, for the informers and the queen.

In arrest of judgment, it was moved by *Browne* that there is no good cause of forfeiture by any law alleged in the information. The Statute upon which the information is grounded is that of the 12th of King Charles II, ca. 32, where, by § 1, it is enacted that none shall directly or indirectly carry or convey or cause or procure to be carried or conveyed out of England, Wales, Berwick, Jersey, Guernsey, Sark, Alderney, or Ireland into any parts or places out of them any sheep or wool of the breed or growth of those kingdoms or places or any woolfells etc., nor directly or indirectly pack or load or cause to be packed or loaded upon any horse, cart, or other carriage or load and lay on board or cause to be loaded or laid aboard any ship or other vessel in England, Ireland, Wales, or isles any such sheep, wool, woolfells, etc. to the intent or purpose to export or carry or cause the same to be exported or carried out of the said kingdoms, dominions, Town of Berwick, or isles or with the intent that any other should export or carry the same out of those places into Scotland or foreign places.

And, then, § 3 enacts that all the offenders and offenses aforesaid shall be liable to the penalties and forfeitures following, *viz.* the sheep, wool, woolfells, etc. so exported, carried, packed, or loaded contrary to the true intent of that Act to be forfeited and the offenders liable to 3s. 4d. for every pound weight of such wool, woolfells, etc. with penalties upon masters and owners of ships and mariners aiding therein.

And the sole question was whether, by this Act, the woolfells that were only packed, but not loaded or upon any horse, cart, or carriage nor put aboard any ship or vessel, with an intent to transport or carry into Scotland are forfeited or not.

Mr. Attorney General [*Northey*], for the queen and informer, urged that the fact of packing or loading only, though not on any horse, cart, or carriage are distinct offenses and are in the disjunctive and either of them with an intent to transport etc. is an offense that induces a penalty and forfeiture and that the succeeding words 'upon any horse, cart, or carriage' are relative only to the word 'loading', which is the next immediate term and proper upon that occasion and for such an act and not to the word 'packing', betwixt which and the word 'loading' there is the disjunctive 'or', which makes each an offense. And it is an impropriety to say 'pack upon any horse, cart, or carriage.'

On the other side, it was observed that it is no impropriety to say a man may pack upon a horse or carriage, which is the same with putting a pack upon a horse or carriage. Besides, the terms of packing or loading or causing to be packed or loading have a further description annexed to them before the words 'with an intent to transport' etc. can be applied to these acts and that is the words 'upon any horse, cart, or carriage', which words are not in this information. And it must be reasonably intended that the Parliament intended a further instance of the intention to transport etc. by packing or loading upon a horse or cart in order to transport and that there is as much reason to carry these words 'packing or loading or causing to be packed or loaded' to be upon a horse or carriage as to carry the words 'or load etc. lay aboard or cause to be loaded or laid aboard wool or woolfells on any ship or vessel', for all precede that within this case is the cause of forfeiture, *viz.* the intent to carry them beyond the seas or to Scotland and to construe the single fact of packing without loading upon a horse or carriage, is to vary the sense and make a forfeiture by construction, which is hard in the case of a penal law.

If the bare packing is to be the offense adding only an intent to it, which may be sworn by one witness only, then it may be, if a man has occasion to pack up any wool etc. in the middle of England having sold it to a chapman or to carry it to a market to be sold, such a construction to make a bare packing to be in danger of forfeiture may prove a great inconvenience.

By the 7th section in 12 Car. II, which gives the liberty of seizure, extends only to such wool and woolfells etc. as he or they shall happen to see, find, know, or discover to be laid aboard in any ship or vessel or to be brought, carried, or laid on shore at or near the sea or any navigable river to the intent to be exported etc. or to be packed or loaded upon any horse, cart, or carriage with the intent to be carried to Scotland and that last expression describes the packing to be on a horse etc.

By the 7th paragraph of 13 & 14 Car. II, ca. 18,[1] which made the exportation of wool, woolfells, etc. or the packing or loading on any horse etc. a felony, which is repealed as to the felony, makes a forfeiture of all woolfells etc. carried or laid at or near the sea coasts or shore or any navigable river with the intent to be transported etc., now the intent in such case is plain by the Act, for why should such things be brought to the sea shore or coasts but for transportation. But, here, *non constat*, that any act was done but barely packing and that and loading upon the horse or carriage is the same thing and cannot be severed by construction, but must both concur to make the forfeiture.

As to the verdict of the jury, that signifies nothing if the law be that the woolfells packed must be packed upon horses or carriages, which is wanting in the information and, if, [in] substance, the information is vicious and no judgment ought to be thereupon.

There seems to be no reason to make the word 'pack' to be a distinct offense by the disjunctive 'or' and to keep that from loading or causing to be packed or loaded upon any horse, cart, or carriage than to make the word 'loading' to be a distinct offense by the disjunctive 'or' in the next words 'or causing to be laid aboard any ship or vessel'; by such a construction, the words 'horse, cart, or car-

[1] Stat. 14 Car. II, c. 18 (*SR*, V, 410–412).

riage' and 'ships or vessels' must be laid aside, which are the ways and means of carrying the woolfells out of England into Scotland or beyond the seas. And, if packing only be a distinct offense without saying upon what, why may not loading only be so without saying upon what, for it is as proper to say and as usual to do, *viz.* pack upon a horse as load upon a boat.

And, afterwards, in Trinity term 1706, for the reasons above, the judgment was arrested by the Chief Baron [EDWARD WARD], BURY, and SMITH in the absence of Price *propter aegritudinem.*

[Other copies of this report: Georgetown Univ. Law Sch. MS. B88–9, f. 262v.]

Lincoln's Inn MS. Misc. 536, f. [91], pl. 1

12 June 1706.

Touching the loading of woolfells with the intent to carry to Scotland, judgment was arrested, because [it was] not said loaded on any horse, cart, or carriage.

[Other copies of this report: Georgetown Univ. Law Sch. MS. B88–9, f. 296v, pl. 1.]

261

Attorney General v. Walker

(Ex. 1706)

In this case, the administrators of a decedent's estate were not required to pay the debt in issue until the estate received a certain amount of assets in full.

Lincoln's Inn MS. Misc. 536, f. [34]

Hilary [term] 4 Annae Reginae in Scaccario [1706].

Upon a *scire facias* against the defendants [Walker and Mary, his wife, relict of Edward Sutton] to have execution against them upon a bond of £500 penalty entered into by the defendant Mary while unmarried seized into the queen's hands for and as a debt in aid for one Charles Berdoe, the defendants pray *oyer* of the bond and condition, which condition sets forth that:

> whereas the said Edward Sutton died intestate and left the said Mary his widow and at his death was indebted to Berdoe in £240 and administration of his goods was to be committed to [the defendant] Mary, if the said Mary, her heirs, executors, or administrators do pay or cause to be paid to Berdoe, his executors, [etc.], the said sum of £240 preferable before all other debts, if the assets of the decedent shall amount to so much and so soon as the said assets shall arise and be received and, if Berdoe save harmless the said Mary from all actions and demands due upon any bonds that hereafter may appear due from the decedent, the said Berdoe paying his due proportion or share of the said bonds, according to the quality and quantity of the said debt of £240, then the bond to be void.

The defendants plead *executio non quia omnia bona et catalla* which were the decedent's at his death to be administered and which the defendant Mary, while unmarried, at any time after the decedent's death did receive and also all the goods and chattels which were the decedent's at the time of his death and which they or either of them received after their intermarriage in the whole did not attain to the said sum of £240, *et hoc parati sunt verificare*, and they pray judgment whether the queen ought to have judgment against them for the said £500.

To this plea, the Attorney General put in a general demurrer, and the defendants joined therein.

The question upon this condition and plea is whether the defendants be bound to pay anything before assets to the full value of £240 of the decedent's estate come to their hands supposing that some assets, though not to the full, have come to their or one of their hands, which nevertheless appears not by the plea.

The very words of the condition being strictly and literally taken seem not to oblige the defendants to pay any part of the decedent's assets come to their hands until assets to the full value of £240 do come to their hands. But, if the defendants be bound to pay as assets come in, then the plea is bad, for they have not pleaded that nothing came to their hands, but that assets to the value of £240 did not come to their hands which may be true and yet some assets might come.

But Mr. Attorney General [*Northey*], on behalf of Berdoe, for whom this prosecution is, considers this case not under the strict and literal sense of the words of the condition, but according to the meaning and intent of the parties with respect to the subject matter and by a reasonable construction, which he takes to be this, that Berdoe shall have all his debt preferable to any other debts from the decedent, by bond, at least without controversy or competition out of the decedent's assets if and when and as soon as they amount to so much, but if [they do] not amount to so much, then the defendants are to pay the plaintiff so much of the said assets as the estate extends to when and so soon as they shall arise and be received, which he urges is but an equal and just way and rule, for there can be no doubt but it was the intent of the parties that Berdoe's debt should be first paid, and fully also, if the assets extended to it. And it is harsh to say that, if the assets fell short but a shilling or some other small matter, that he should lose all his debt. And the honesty and justice of the case is that there was a just debt of £240 due from the defendant's [first] husband, and, therefore, all securities, for it ought to be effectual. And the defendant Mary being to take administration to her husband, and willing to pay it out of her husband's estate that should come to her hands is but reasonable she should pay as far as his assets go, though they amount not to the full debt.

And, for authority in the point, he cited and relied on the Case of Ogle v. Quintin, 2d Jones 218, Easter [term] 34 Car. II, King's Bench,[1] where there was

[1] *Ogle v. Quintin* (1682), T. Jones 218, 84 E.R. 1226.

a bond for the performance of an agreement for paying £120 at a certain day, and, upon setting forth the agreement, which recited a controversy between the parties touching the probate of the nuncupative will of A.E. to whom the plaintiff was the next cousin and had entered a caveat about it now in consideration that the plaintiff had subducted the caveat so that the defendant might prove it. The defendant covenanted to pay to the plaintiff upon the 4th of January £120 out of such personal estate of A.E. as should come to the hands of the defendant in full satisfaction of all claims and demands out of it according to the intent of the bond. And, further, he pleads that, after the obligation huiusque no personal estate of A.E. came to the hands of the defendant to the value of £120 and that he had not, nor ever had of the said personal estate praeter bona to the value of £50. The court was there of the opinion that, if nothing had been received out of the personal estate before the 4th of January, that no payment should be made. But they held the defendant's plea bad in regard, he having confessed by it that he had £50 in his hands, he ought to have paid so much, for the meaning of the condition was that he should pay the £120 or so much of it as he should receive out of the personal estate before the said day, which not being paid or tendered at the day, judgment was given for the plaintiff.

On the defendant's behalf, it was urged (and I [Edward Ward] think very reasonably) that it appears in the case that the prosecutor has a bond from the intestate for his debt and the intestate's estate lies open to that payment of it and, here, it does not appear any consideration for this new bond from the defendant Mary (as there did in Ogle and Quintin's Case), but is only an additional security to the former bond without consideration, nor no certain time for the payment of the debt out of the assets (as there was in Ogle and Quintin's Case). The condition therefore of this bond is to be so understood as the intent of the parties that the defendant should not be bound to pay any part of the debt until she had received the whole out of the intestate's assets. And the words of the condition fully import so much, for here are two suppositions or rather conditions or qualifications for the payment, first, if the assets of the intestate shall amount to so much; secondly, so soon as the said assets, that is assets amounting to the debt, for so the word 'said' must be understood, shall be received.

So that I cannot from these words of the condition infer it to be the intent of the parties that anything should be paid unless assets to the full debt came to her hands and not sooner to be paid than until such assets come, which by the plea (which is issuable) are denied to have come and the plaintiff, by his demurrer, has confessed it. And the plaintiff is not without a remedy to charge the intestate's estate by his former bond, which differences this case and the construction of this condition from Ogle and Quintin's; so that I [Edward Ward] am of the opinion that judgment ought to be entered for the defendant.

12 February 1705[/06]; the opinion of the court.

Baron SMITH, for the defendant: Nothing shall be paid until [there be] sufficient to the debt, for the objection of Needler and Guest, Allen 12, the covenant went to quires and not sheets, and he brought [an action] for both; judgment [was] arrested, not being prorated. 2 Levinz 124; £3 per tun includes not a hogshead, not said *pro rata*; 21 Edw. IV, 52b; if I recover £20, the obligee [to] have a moiety, if but a condition, to be taken favorably for the obligor; Dy. 17; 3 Levinz 137, tied up to the word 'then' and not to any actions after.[1]

Note, for the plaintiff, 1 Rolls' Abridgment 114, Cross and Northey, there, the words 'after the rate of 8 per cent' ruled; Ogle and Quintin's Case, cited, differences that case.[2] There, [it was] out of assets to that value; here, when assets to that value come.

And, so, he concludes for the defendant.

Baron PRICE [held] for the plaintiff: He mentions as if this is a debt to the queen, where it is in aid. This rises upon a construction of the administration; [it is a] question upon granting administration. [This is] not so; she was to pay out of the assets. And he holds she should pay as far as assets came and when. This is not a precedent condition, but plead and tender as far as assets went. It is governed by Ogle and Quintin; [there are] parallels in the cases. These cases differ from the cases of tun and quire. There was a special agreement; here a previous agreement. Query.

Baron BURY [held] for the defendant: He complains of the [writ of] extent. He thinks the condition precedent and in favor of the obligor and nothing is to be paid until full assets come. A devise out of the rents and profits is as the rents and profits do arise; whereas a sum in gross would have been in fee, Brownlow 33;[3] to pay 100 marks during seven years is not to be construed annually.

Vide Chief Baron [EDWARD WARD's] argument above.

Judgment [was given] for the defendant.

[Other copies of this report: Georgetown Univ. Law Sch. MS. B88–9, f. 264v.]

---

[1] *Needler v. Guest* (1647–1650), Aleyn 9, 82 E.R. 886, Style 12, 254, 82 E.R. 492, 689; *Rea v. Barnes* (1675), 2 Levinz 117, 124, 83 E.R. 477, 480; YB Mich. 21 Edw. IV, f. 52, pl. 16 (1481); *Bold v. Molineux* (1536), 1 Dyer 14, 73 E.R. 31, also Benloe 13, 123 E.R. 10, 1 Anderson 1, 123 E.R. 321; *Stanley v. Fearne* (1683), 3 Levinz 137, 83 E.R. 617.

[2] *Cross v. Northey* (1632), 1 Rolle, Abr., *Covenant*, pl. C, 7, p. 518; *Ogle v. Quintin* (1682), *ut supra*.

[3] *Bird v. Kirton* (1615), 1 Brownlow & Goldesborough 33, 123 E.R. 645.

262

Jones, qui tam v. Oliver

(Ex. 1706–1709)

Where judgment is given for an informer upon a second information for a seizure, the bond to secure that seizure given upon the first information for the same matter is enforceable.

Lincoln's Inn MS. Misc. 536, f. [38]

Hilary [term] 1705[/06].

The plaintiff exhibits his information the 15th of May 4 Queen Anne. And he sets forth that he, between the 17th of January last and the day of exhibiting that information at Ratcliff in Middlesex, [was] seized to the use of the queen and himself 2390 ounces of wrought plate *pro eo* that it being molten silver of this kingdom and wrought within this kingdom *eskippatus et positus fuerunt* in and upon a certain ship to be transported into parts beyond the seas *absque aliqua certificatione a curia domini mayoris et aldermanorum Civitatis Londini de aliquo sacramento coram eis [. . .] per proprietorem inde [?] aut aliquos testes credibiles quod praedict' argent' conflatil'* (molten) *aut aliqua pars sive parcell' inde fuit argent' rude forinsec', Anglice* foreign bullion, *et quod nulla pars inde fuit (antequam constat fuisset) cun', Anglice* the coin, *huius regni Angliae aut tonsur', Anglice* the clippings, *inde nec argent' operat', Anglice* plate wrought, *infra hoc regnum prius habit' et obtent' contra formam statuti in huiusmode casus adit' et proviss'*, wherefore, as well for the queen as for himself, he prays the advice of the court, *ac praedicta bona praedicta ob causam praedictam reman' for'* and that he may have a moiety thereof according to the said Statute.

Upon a writ of appraisement returned whereby the value of the plate seized is returned to be £717, a proclamation is made for any to come in and inform why the said goods *dictae dominae reginae ob causas praedictas tanquam for' remanere non debeant etc.*

The defendant comes in [and] claims property of the goods and pleads that the said goods or any part thereof were not put aboard the said ship to be carried into parts beyond the seas *contra formam statuti praedicti modo et forma prout per informationem praedictam supponitur*, and he concludes to the country.

Upon a trial at *nisi prius* after the last term in Middlesex, there was a verdict *quod bona praedicta eskipat' et posit fuer' in et super navem infra mentionat' in parte transmarinas exportanda contra formam statuti infra mentionat' modo et forma prout per informationem praedictam interius supponitur.*

And this term [Hilary 1705], *Phipps* and *Turner*, for the defendants, move in arrest of judgment for three reasons or causes.

First, that this information is grounded only upon the Statute of 7 & 8 Will. III, ca. 19, fo. 460,[1] whereby it is enacted that, after the last of March 1696, no person shall ship or put aboard any ship or vessel any molten silver or bullion whatsoever unless a certificate be first had and obtained from the Court of the Lord Mayor and Aldermen of the City of London, oath having been made before the said court by the owners of such molten silver and likewise by two or more credible witnesses that the same molten silver and every part of it was and is foreign bullion and no part thereof was (before the same was molten) the coin of this realm or clippings thereof nor plate wrought within this kingdom, which oath the said Court of the Lord Mayor etc. are thereby authorized to administer and to examine strictly all such persons as shall make the said oath concerning the premises and to grant such a certificate thereof as aforesaid without a fee or reward, which certificate shall contain the names of owners of such molten silver and of the witnesses and of the weight thereof, which certificate shall be entered in the Lord Mayor's Court and shown to four or more of the Commissioners of the Customs before any cocket be granted for exportation and an entry thereof to be made in the books of the Commissioners of the Customs. And, if any person ship or put on board any ship any molten silver whatsoever as aforesaid without oath, certificate, and entry to be made and granted as aforesaid, in such case, it shall be lawful to the officers of the customs or other persons to seize the said molten silver so shipped as forfeited, one moiety to the king, the other to the seizer and the owner to forfeit double the value, a moiety to the king, the other to such as will sue or inform for the same to be recovered with costs, by [an action of] debt, bill, or information. Whereas, by a subsequent Act made 9 & 10 Will. III, ca. 28,[2] reciting the former Act and settling the fineness of silver manufactures at eleven ounces 10d. weight pound troy, it was enacted that, after 24 June 1698, it should be lawful to any person to export such wrought plate and silver manufactures made within this kingdom, being of the fineness above said according to the rules prescribed by the former Act as should be yearly allowed by three of the Commissioners of the Customs any former law to the contrary. And they allege that this Act ought to have been taken notice of in the information.

The second exception is that the information does not mention such a certificate, as the first act directs, the Act says the oath shall be that every part of it is foreign bullion. The information says *aut aliqua pars inde*, which ought to have been *quaelibet pars inde*.

Thirdly, that there is no time or place alleged where or when the wrought plate seized was put aboard the ship and, by consequence, no venue for the trial, and this is a penal law not within the statutes of jeofails, and, though there be a time and place for the seizure laid, yet that helps not for the cause of the forfeiture is the putting aboard and that must be tried, which, as this case is, cannot

[1] Stat. 7 & 8 Will. III, c. 19 (*SR*, VII, 94–97).

[2] Stat. 9 Will. III, c. 28 (*SR*, VII, 399–400).

be done without a venue and a proper trial for that forfeiture. And the verdict of the jury is that the silver was put aboard the ship to be carried to parts beyond the sea *contra formam statuti*, and yet there is no time or place where that [was] done, which is fatal.

As to the first of these exceptions, I [Edward Ward] think it not available, for, though the second Act indulges and allows the carrying out of silver of such a fineness and though this silver in bullion was of that fineness, yet that second Act directs it must be carried out according to the rules prescribed by the former Act and the allowance by three commissioners of the customs. And this Act is relative to the former, and imposes no penalty or forfeiture for the non-observance of it and, therefore, the penalties of the former Act remain and the means to recover them. And if the defendant would be excused from them, he must by pleading have shown that this was silver of that fineness and that it was put aboard according to the rules of the former Act and was allowed by three or more of the commissioners of the customs, all which are matters issuable. And, if any of them fail, it will be against the defendant in not observing those qualifications. And it is like to a proviso in an act that gives a man an ease in some particular from the body of the act which he must show himself entitled to. And it is not be taken notice of by the plaintiff, but averred and proved by the defendant. And this second Act has no penalty in it nor remedy appointed, which shows the first Act must enforce that and the second be pleaded in ease and excuse. Besides, in this case, the defendant was offered to have the matter found specially, which he declined, not having the least proof that three or more Commissioners of the Customs knew or allowed it nor pretended to any certificate, but it was proved that all the silver, except an old tankard, was of the fineness in the second Act, but that alone without the other requisites not being sufficient, and the defendant's counsel declining a special verdict, a general one passed for the queen.

[As to the] second exception, I [Edward Ward] think the defendant ought not to have put the silver aboard without a certificate or proof of the special matter to have enabled him according to law and that every exporter ought to perform everything that is necessarily previous to the exportation and the certificate, and must prove them.

But I cannot say that the want of a certificate as the information sets it forth is a transgression of the said Act *quoad* the certificate, for the Act directs the oath to be that every part of the silver was from bullion and the information sets forth that the oath was not made that the said silver or any part thereof was foreign bullion.

[As to the] third exception, that there is no venue laid in this case where the silver was loaded aboard for exportation nor any time when it was done, which I take to be fatal in this case, for that is the very cause assigned for the forfeiture and the only point to be found by the jury, for, if not found by the jury that it was laid aboard with an intent to transport beyond the seas, though there be no certificate nor other requisites by the acts founded, yet no forfeiture [was] incurred.

The time and place of the seizure helps not. That is only to entitle the seizer, in case there be a forfeiture proved and found, that he shall have his share according to the Act. I am surprised to hear from Mr. Attorney General that the proving of the seizure is enough in this case and all the rest of the matter to be intended where the seizure was made. And it is allowed by Mr. Attorney General that, in personal informations for forfeitures in like cases by way of *devenerunt*, it is necessary to allege the time and place for the offense. I must confess I never until this time heard of such a distinction between a seizure and a *devenerunt*, nor is there any reason for it, since the same cause of the forfeiture must appear in and be proved in one as well as the other.

That the verdict helps not in this case, being upon a penal statute and out of all statutes of jeofails, I think is plain by the reason of all our books that want of a venue is not supplied or helped by the verdict. The words '*contra formam statuti*' never did nor can help matters of substance, as want of a venue is in this case. Hardress 217, Pitcher and Jones.[1]

Besides, the Statute 31 Eliz.[2] having limited a time wherein an information upon penal laws must be brought, as well by the informer as the Attorney General, *viz.* one year for the first and three years for the last. It ought to appear that the supposed offense here was committed within the year to entitle the informer or within three years to entitle the queen, none of which appears nor, by law, can be intended. And, therefore, I am of the opinion that no judgment ought or can be given for the plaintiff or the queen, whereto the other three barons agreed, for the reasons above.

And, so, judgment [was given] for the defendant *per totam curiam*.

[Other copies of this report: Georgetown Univ. Law Sch. MS. B88–9, f. 267.]

Lincoln's Inn MS. Misc. 536, f. [88]

Trinity term 5 Anne 1706.

Upon a seizure of plate, there having been an information, trial, and verdict for the informer, but judgment was arrested for a fault in the information, no venue being laid for the shipping and the defendant's counsel praying now that the recognizance given by him upon the writ of delivery may be vacated, judgment being entered upon that information and proceedings for the defendant that the plaintiff should take nothing by that information, *et quod eat inde sine die salvo semper actione reginae si etc.*

The Attorney General [*Northey*] and others, for the queen and the informer, opposed that motion, there being another information for the same matter (only laying a venue for the shipping) exhibited in this court within the year after the offense committed, which they insisted the defendant ought to plead to, and that

[1] *Pitcher v. Jones* (1661), Hardres 217, 145 E.R. 461.

[2] Stat. 31 Eliz. I, c. 5 (*SR*, IV, 801–802).

the recognizance upon the writ of delivery ought not to be vacated, but to stand to the event and success of the trial that shall be upon this new information, the condition being to answer the value of the goods seized if, upon any information then lately exhibited *seu imposterum exhibendum*, the said goods shall be recovered so that, as the judgment arrested upon the first information whereon there was a verdict renders that information ineffectual, yet it is no bar to the informer or the queen's right to exhibit another information for the same matter no more than a nonsuit or judgment arrested in a subject's case is a bar to a new action, which none can pretend to. And the goods themselves not being *in esse*, but disposed by the defendant and so not liable to a second seizure, the recognizance being given as it is stands to answer the value of the goods upon a second information when not condemned upon the first, and, if it should be otherwise, it would be mischievous to grant writs of delivery. And the reason of putting those words '*imposterum exhibendum*' is for the purpose aforesaid and have been anciently, though not always, used.

The court did not think fit at present to vacate the recognizance, but left the informer to prosecute the new information, as he could by law, and the defendant to make such defense as by law he could, it not being proper for the court to determine the matter upon a motion.

To this second information, which was *in rem* and founded upon the first seizure, the defendant Oliver refused to enter any claim, whereupon the prosecutor's clerk in court proceeded in order to have a recovery of the silver and a condemnation thereof as forfeited for want of a claim. And, after that, intending a prosecution upon the recognizance given upon the writ of delivery as extending to this second information as well as to the first, for the reasons above, to prevent which recovery, there was a claim entered in the names of three dons in Portugal by the direction of the said Oliver, who offered to swear that they were the true promotors thereof at the time of the seizure, though he himself then claimed the property and had the goods delivered to him and he gave the recognizance upon that writ of security.

The court did not approve the entry of the said claim, none of the person being here but fictitious names, for aught appears, and, the goods being gone, no writ of delivery will be prayed and, by consequence, if the goods should be condemned, either without a claim or upon a verdict upon the dons' claim, the goods cannot be come at, so that, unless the first recognizance stands security upon a recovery or verdict and judgment upon this information, the whole proceeding upon this second information will be fruitless and vain.

Which claims of the dons being set aside and nobody else claiming, Oliver, who before claimed and had delivery upon security, now refusing to claim, though he still has as good a pretense of title to the goods as he had when he put in his claim, the goods were recovered and judgment thereupon was entered that they should be forfeited and the informer charged to pay to the queen one moiety of the value and to retain the other to himself.

And, thereupon, a [writ of] *scire facias* (upon a motion) was awarded upon Oliver's recognizance given upon his writ of delivery in the first information, whereto he may plead what he can why he should not be charged thereupon to the queen and the informer for the goods so recovered or the value thereof.

And, thereupon, the question will be brought into judgment whether, when goods are seized as forfeited and appraised and claimed and a writ of delivery granted upon security by a recognizance with a condition, as above, to answer the value if condemned upon any information then or after to be exhibited and upon that information then exhibited, then is judgment for the defendant *quod ipse ad praesens eat inde sine die*, though upon a second information there be a recovery for want of a claim whether the first recognizance shall stand to make good that recovery, as, without doubt, it would if the recovery had been upon the first information.

[Other copies of this report: Georgetown Univ. Law Sch. MS. B88–9, f. 292.]

Harvard Law Sch. MS. 537, pt. 2, p. 106, pl. 2

Hilary term 7 Anne.

The case was this. Jones presents an information as for goods seized for a quantity of wrought plate he had seized, having been shipped on board to be transported into foreign parts without having any certificate as provided by 6 & 7 Will. III, c. 17.[1] Oliver comes in and claims property, and has a writ of delivery upon giving a recognizance, if upon an information exhibited *sive exhibendum*, they should be condemned to answer for the value of them. And then he pleads the goods were not put on board with an intent to be transported beyond the sea.

And it was found for the plaintiff and the queen. But judgment was stayed because no venue was laid in the information where the goods were shipped.

Upon this, the plaintiff brings a second information, and he has judgment. And he brings a *scire facias* upon the recognizance to answer the value etc.

The defendant pleads to this the former information exhibited and the judgment thereupon, and, the two informations differing in time and place, he avers them to be the same etc.

And, upon a demurrer by the plaintiff, after arguments by *Turner, Phipps*, and Serjeant *Pratt*, for the defendant, and by *Northey, Dodd, Sir Peter King* for the plaintiffs, the court this term gave judgment for the plaintiffs.

N.B. I [Eden] was not at any of the arguments, the last of them being Trinity term last, as I was informed by Turner.

The court delivered themselves in substance as follows. They considered the occasion of granting writs of delivery, which was thus. The wisdom of the law in many cases having created forfeitures of goods in specie (and such forfeitures generally speaking are one-half to the queen and the other to the informer) and

[1] Stat. 6 & 7 Will. & Mar., c. 17 (*SR*, VI, 598–600).

because, in such a case, the right is not complete until the judgment and because, in many cases, it falls out that, before judgment, the goods may suffer prejudice and so may be of less value to the crown and inconvenient to the merchant if ended in his favor and because also no [action of] replevin lies in such a case, it has always been therefore thought fit to grant those writs of delivery upon great caution and taking sufficient security that the appraised value should be forthcoming if the goods be adjudged to be forfeited. This, therefore, being the occasion of such recognizances, the conditions of them were designed to put the queen in as good a condition as if the goods remained in court, for no reason the goods should be taken away. If the queen is to have any disadvantage and when the method prescribed the queen was not designed any, and, now, if the goods had been here, they might have well exhibited this second information, 11 Rep. 66; 1 Roll, Abr., 867; 5 Co., Robinson's Case; 1 Mod. 207,[1] for, in our case, the right and title is said for the queen and judgment [is] for the defendant only upon a slip.

They relied upon the words *in posterum exhibendum* and that, if it, the condition, had tied up the plaintiff more strictly, yet the first, being an insufficient information, is as none in law. 4 Co. 39b.[2]

And [it was said] by PRICE he needed not in this case to have assigned a breach. And he cited 1 Saund. 316; 1 Lev. 54; Yelv. 78.[3]

And [it was said] by him the time and place being not material in this case further than that a time and place must be alleged. 21 Hen. VII, fo. 39, pl. 52; Br., tit. *Averment*, 52; Perkins, pl. 147; a difference between them in that respect is made good by an averment that for the same etc.; Roll's Abr., 867, pl. 16.[4]

Objection: Here is a second information and a condemnation and no writ of appraisement so that the condition of the recognizance cannot be observed.

Answer: A writ of appraisement is not necessary upon all informations, as where the value appears to the court, as in a case of money etc. There, the information sets forth the value. Nor is it necessary to be at any particular time, as after the information etc., so as the time is material, for by BURY, if it appears there was any appraisement, though before the information, [it is] good. And, by

---

1 *Warren v. Smith* (1615), 11 Coke Rep. 66, 77 E.R. 1235, also 1 Rolle Rep. 151, 81 E.R. 394, 2 Bulstrode 146, 80 E.R. 1021, Croke Jac. 364, 79 E.R. 312; 1 Rolle, Abr., *Estoppell*, p. 867; *Robinson v. Robinson* (1603), 5 Coke Rep. 32, 77 E.R. 103, also Croke Jac. 15, 79 E.R. 13; *Kedgewin v. Lampen* (1675), 1 Modern 207, 86 E.R. 832, also *sub nom. Rozal v. Lampen*, 2 Modern 42, 294, 86 E.R. 930, 1081, 3 Keble 844, 84 E.R. 1045.

2 *Vaux v. Brook* (1586), 4 Coke Rep. 39, 76 E.R. 982.

3 *Hawkesworth v. Hillary* (1669), 1 Williams Saunders 313, 85 E.R. 433, also 1 Modern 2, 86 E.R. 682, 2 Keble 541, 592, 84 E.R. 339, 372; *Sayer v. Glean* (1662), 1 Levinz 54, 83 E.R. 293, also 1 Siderfin 27, 82 E.R. 949; *Jeffrey v. Guy* (1605), Yelverton 78, 80 E.R. 54, also 1 Brownlow & Goldesborough 89, 123 E.R. 684.

4 YB Mich. 21 Hen. VII, f. 39, pl. 52 (1505); J.Perkins, *A Profitable Book*; YB Hil. 6 Hen. IV, f. 4, pl. 25 (1405), 1 Rolle, Abr., *Estoppell*, pl. 16, p. 867.

PRICE, nor is the time material for it may be returned before the information be filed.

Objection: That [there are] no precedents of a second information upon a second seizure.

[It was said] by BURY that is caused perhaps by the frequent liberty given to amend.

[It was said] by WARD in his argument he thinks the recognizance ought to be contrived to answer the process as well as the value of the goods. And the court, by him, has granted writs of delivery without security where the party would not proceed within a reasonable time.

There was an objection of want of notice, but the second information, being a record, is notice sufficient, and no person is bound to give him notice. And it seems, being bound in a recognizance etc., he is bound at his peril.

Lincoln's Inn MS. Misc. 538, f. [98]

Upon an information grounded on the Statute [*blank*] Will. III,[1] for shipping plate for exportation without such a certificate as that Act requires, there had been a former verdict upon a seizure for the queen and informer and a writ of delivery upon security awarded. But judgment [was] arrested for a defect in the information. And, after that and within the year, a new information of seizure [was] exhibited for the same plate. And no claim being put in, there was a recovery of it and the security given upon the writ of delivery on the first seizure which respected a recovery upon that or any other information. And the crown obtained judgment upon the recognizance given for security upon the writ of delivery as extending to the second information upon which the recovery was had and that judgment [was] affirmed in [a writ of] error in the Exchequer Chamber and also in Parliament.

And this present informer was to recover the double value of the plate, which the same law lays upon the owner of it. But, throughout the whole information, no mention is made that the defendant was the owner of the plate, nor was it so laid, so that, though the plaintiff obtained a verdict on a trial, yet the defendant, by his counsel, moved in arrest of judgment by reason of that defect, which seemed to the court to be a fault and defect in substance.

And I [EDWARD WARD] remembered the like exception taken in the case of Dickenson against Stocker in this court, Pas. 24 Car. II, L. G, 139, upon the Statute of 18 Eliz., ca. 9, against transporting leather, tallow, etc. under forfeiture of the goods and treble the value of them by the owners and the ownership not being laid there, the verdict did not cure that defect, but the judgment was

[1] Stat. 9 Will. III, c. 28 (*SR*, VII, 399–400).

reversed in error Trinity 27 Car. II by the Lord Keeper and Lord Treasurer with the advice of Hale and North, chief justices.[1]

Some other things were in the principal case stirred also in arrest as if the offense was pardoned and that there was a defect in not properly alleging the oath according to the Act, but no stress was laid upon them. And the judgment in the principal case was stayed until further order. And nothing more was done in it.

[Other copies of this report: Georgetown Univ. Law Sch. MS. B88–10, p. 680.]

263

Presland v. Chambre

(Ex. 1706)

In this action based on an accounting, the defendant filed a rejoinder that was an improper departure from his plea.

Lincoln's Inn MS. Misc. 536, f. [68]

Entered in the Office of Pleas of the Exchequer, Michaelmas [term] 4 Queen Anne [1705].

The plaintiff [Richard Presland] brings [an action of] debt upon a bond of £1000 dated the 1st of October 11 Will. III [1699] entered into by the defendant [Charles Chambre] to the plaintiff conditioned that Arthur Chambre, the defendant's son, should from time to time observe, perform, and keep all the covenants, agreements, etc. on his part to be performed etc. specified in an indenture of apprenticeship of equal date, whereby the said Arthur became the plaintiff's apprentice, made between the plaintiff and his said apprentice, according to the true intent and meaning thereof, and should also during his apprenticeship truly and faithfully serve the plaintiff as his servant and apprentice and a just account and payment give and make to the plaintiff, his executors, etc. of all sums of money which he should or might receive and pay during the term when and as often as he should be thereunto required by the plaintiff, his executors, etc. And, if the apprentice did not at any time waste or embezzle the plaintiff's goods or wares or other of his master's things wherewith he should be entrusted but behave himself honestly and faithfully towards the plaintiff during the apprenticeship, then the bond to be void.

The defendant sets forth the indenture of apprenticeship, which is in common form with such like indentures and wherein there are both affirmative and negative covenants on the apprentice's part to be performed. And he pleads performance of the covenants affirmative in the affirmative and of the negative cov-

[1] *Dickenson, qui tam v. Stocker* (Ex. 1672), Exch. Repts. *tempore* Car. II, 250; Stat. 18 Eliz. I, c. 9 (*SR*, IV, 619–620).

enants in the negative, both as to what are in the conditions of the bond and in the indenture of apprenticeship from the time of the bond to the end of seven year's apprenticeship. And he pleads to the account according to the condition and that the plaintiff has not before the action brought sustained any damage or loss by the apprentice. And so he prays judgment if the plaintiff shall maintain his action against him.

The plaintiff replies that, after the making of the bond and before the 11th of October 1704, the apprentice received of one Robert Hulson and divers other people divers sums of money amounting to £3023 11s. 7d. to the use of the plaintiff and that, afterwards and before the exhibiting of the plaintiff's bill, *scil.* 15 October 1704, he was required by the plaintiff to give him an account of the moneys received and paid by the apprentice for the plaintiff's use according to the form and effect of the said condition, which he refused and still refuses to do, *et hoc paratus est verificare*, and he prays judgment and his debt.

The defendant rejoins that, the apprentice after the making of the bond and before the receipt of any money in the replication mentioned, *scil.* 2 October 11 Will. III [1699], the plaintiff ordered the apprentice to put all the money he should receive into a cupboard or iron chest of the plaintiff, having two keys to each, and constantly kept locked by the plaintiff and the keys kept by him and further that the apprentice after the bond and before the plaintiff turned him away, *scil.* 10 October 1704, constantly put all the money he received into that cupboard or chest for the use of the plaintiff and that the same 2d of October 11 Will. III, the plaintiff ordered the apprentice to enter into the plaintiff's books the receipts and payments of the money, which was done accordingly until [he was] turned away, and that, after the bond and before the request in the replication and before the exhibiting of the plaintiff's bill, *scil.* 11 October 1704, the plaintiff turned away his apprentice out of his service against his will and kept him out of his house and service and took the books out of his hands and custody and kept them ever since and that, since the turning away, the apprentice has neither received nor paid any of the plaintiff's money and that, at the time of such turning away, the apprentice, at the request of the plaintiff, gave him an account of all moneys by him received and paid to the plaintiff's use in this manner, *viz.* that he put all the money he had received for the plaintiff's use in the said cupboard or chest and the notes and memorandums thereof had entered in the plaintiff's books, which were taken and detained by the plaintiff out of the apprentice's power. *Et hoc paratus est verificare*, and he prays judgment and that the plaintiff may be precluded from his action.

To this rejoinder the plaintiff has demurred. And he shows for cause that it is repugnant and a departure from the plea in bar.

And the defendant has joined in demurrer.

Dodd, for the plaintiff, insists upon the departure [in the] rejoinder, [being] different from the plea. 1 Inst. 304; Dy. 371.[1] The bar is that the apprentice accounted for the whole time; the rejoinder says he accounted for part of the time.

Acherly, for the defendant: The matter of the rejoinder fortifies the bar, and there is no departure, for it is a special way of accounting and it is not different from the matter. 1 Inst.; 2 Levinz 57, Wood and Kirkham; Vere and Smith, 2 Levinz 5, is in point as affirmed.[2] [There was a] condition to account when requested; the plaintiff replies and shows the defendant's receipt of £26 whereof no account was given; the defendant rejoins and confesses the receipt and that he accounted for it to the plaintiff *modo et forma sequente, viz.* he put the money in the plaintiff's counting house and it was stolen out of by malefactors, and so he accounted for it, and it was held to be no departure. And so here.

Note in my report of the Case of Vere and Smith, L. 2, 146b,[3] which see, debt upon a bond to perform articles; one was to give a true account to the plaintiff of all sums the defendant should receive for him; the defendant pleads performance; the plaintiff asserts a breach that the defendant received for him £26 for which no account was given; the defendant, by rejoinder, says the money was locked in the plaintiff's counting house whereof the plaintiff had the key and that it was stolen out of by certain malefactors unknown with which the defendant acquainted the plaintiff, and thus he had made an account of it. Upon a demurrer, it was held, first, that the acquainting the plaintiff with the robbery should be a good account to excuse the defendants, for, though the robbery shall not be a plea to an action of account, yet it is a good discharge before auditors. 1 Inst. 89; Roll's, [Abr.,] *Account*, 124; 9 Edw. IV, 40b.[4] Second, for that reason, it is no departure but a fortifying of the bar by a special way of accounting. Third, that it had been bad if he had not concluded his plea, and thus he had accounted. No judgment [was given]. A demurrer was waived, and issue [was joined] upon the robbery.

On 4 June 1706, Mr. Attorney General [*Northey*], for the defendant, thinks the pretended dealings in the rejoinder are an account *prout* there set forth, and so there is no departure. And what other account could the apprentice give than by this thus set forth, though general, it being impossible to give any other. And the '*viz.*' and what comes after it is to be rejected.

---

[1] E. Coke, *First Institute* (1628), f. 304; *Rolt v. Neale* (1580), 3 Dyer 371, 73 E.R. 831.

[2] *Wood v. Kirkham* (1672), 2 Levinz 67, 83 E.R. 452; *Vere v. Smith* (1671), 2 Levinz 5, 83 E.R. 426, also 1 Ventris 121, 86 E.R. 83, 2 Keble 761, 779, 830, 84 E.R. 481, 492, 525.

[3] *Vere v. Smith* (1671), Lincoln's Inn MS. Misc. 500, f. 146v.

[4] E. Coke, *First Institute* (1628), f. 89; 1 Rolle, Abr., *Accompt*, part O, pp. 124–126; YB Mich. 9 Edw. IV, f. 40, pl. 22 or pl. 23 (1469).

But, upon consideration, judgment was given for the plaintiff *nisi melior causa*, [and], the last day of this Trinity term after, absolutely.

Afterward, [a writ of] error was brought, and the judgment was affirmed, 23 November 1708, both of the chief justices being of the opinion that the rejoinder is a departure.

[Other copies of this report: Georgetown Univ. Law Sch. MS. B88–9, f. 273.]

264

Herbert v. Ainsworth

(Ex. 1706)

Where a party has his own personal right and interest in the litigation, his prosecution of it is not champerty or maintenance.

Where damages are improperly pleaded, a verdict thereupon must be set aside.

Lincoln's Inn MS. 536, f. [69v]

Entered in the Office of Pleas, Hilary [term] 4 Queen Anne 1705[/06].

The plaintiff brings [an action of] covenant against the defendants [Ainsworth and Vicary], setting forth that, in December 3 Anne, 1704, he was possessed at London of a ship called the *Prince Frederick* of Christian's Land in Norway then sailing in the Downs upon the high sea and of the cargo of that ship, that, at the same time, one Shipman was the captain of a privateer called the *Neptune*, whereof the defendants and others were part owners, by virtue of letters of marque to him granted, took and seized in the said Downs the plaintiff's ship and his goods and merchandises therein as lawful prize to the use of the proprietors of the privateer, and that, 29th December aforesaid, a certain suit touching the capture or seizure of the plaintiff's ship and cargo was commenced and depending in the Court of Admiralty at London on the behalf of Shipman against the said ship and cargo and against one Prince[1] and the plaintiff and others *pro interesse* and against all others claiming title to the said ship and cargo with an intent to have them condemned as lawful prize. But Shipman and the defendants could not proceed to a condemnation for default of sufficient proof and witnesses in that behalf.

And, thereupon, the defendants, the 15th of January 1704[/05] at London etc. by a writing of agreement under their hands and seals between the defendants on one part and the plaintiff on the other, *in curia prolata*, reciting that Shipman, about the 2d of December then last, had seized the plaintiff's ship and lading of wine etc. and reciting that the defendants, two of the part owners of the privateer on the behalf of themselves and other the part owners had

[1] or Prens or Preus.

made some proceedings in the Admiralty towards a condemnation of the cargo of the plaintiff's ship as prize. They, the defendants, for themselves, their executors, etc., and other the part owners of the privateer did covenant and agree with the plaintiff that, in case he the plaintiff at the costs of the defendants *procuraret* the cargo of the plaintiff's ship to be condemned as prize for the use of the part owners of the privateer, then and in such case and not otherwise, the defendants within two months after the condemnation would pay or allow to the plaintiff the prime cost of the said goods with eighty guilders by the ton for freightage thereof and all that should appear to be insured upon policies of insurance when they should be produced.

And the plaintiff covenanted with the defendants that he would use his best power to procure the said cargo to be condemned as prize for the use of the part owners of the privateer.

The plaintiff avers that, according to his covenant, he, by the space of eleven days next after the said agreement, used his best power in the Admiralty Court in procuring the said cargo to be condemned. And, thereupon, in the said court, the 26th of January last past, the said cargo was condemned by the definitive sentence of Sir John Cooke, judge of the said court, *per operam, media, et procurationem* of the plaintiff *in ea parte usitata exhibit' et impens' debita juris forma* to the use of the part owners of the privateer and at their costs and whereof the defendants had notice.

And the plaintiff avers that the prime costs of the cargo did attain to £3000 whereof also the defendants had notice. And he avers also that the cargo of the said plaintiff's ship that was condemned did amount to 164 tons, whereof the freightage payable for the same at the rate aforesaid came to £1192 14s. 6½d., whereof the defendants had notice.

And he avers that the moneys paid for the insurance of that cargo upon the policies of insurance thereupon made and subscribed and by the plaintiff now produced amounted to the sum of £250, whereof the defendants had notice.

And the plaintiff, taking it by protestation that the defendants have not performed anything in the agreement mentioned on their parts to be performed, says the defendants, though often requested, at any time within two months next after the sentence, have not paid nor either of them have not paid or allowed to the plaintiff the prime costs of the cargo or any part thereof nor the said several sums above mentioned to be payable for freightage and insurance of the said goods and merchandises or any penny thereof. And so the defendants, though often requested, their covenants abovesaid with the plaintiff have broken and have and do refuse to hold the same, to the plaintiff's damage of £4000.

The defendants plead *actio non etc.*, taking by protestation the insufficiency of the declaration for that cause, amongst others, that it appears by the declaration that the contract was made upon champerty and unlawful maintenance of a suit or action and so invalid in law. But, for a plea, they say that they, at their own proper instance, suit, and prosecution, did procure the cargo of the plaintiff's ship to be condemned in the Admiralty as lawful prize for the use of themselves and other the part owners of the privateer. And they traverse *absque hoc* that the said cargo was condemned *per operam, media, et procurationem* of the plaintiff *modo et forma prout* he has above alleged and so pray judgment whether the plaintiff shall maintain his action against them.

The plaintiff replies *praecludi non etc.* for that he says *ut prius* that the said cargo was the 26th of January 1704[/05] condemned in the Admiralty as lawful prize *per operam, media, et procurationem* of the plaintiff for the use of the part owners of the said privateer *modo et forma prout* he has above declared against them. And he concludes to the country. And, thereupon, issue is joined.

And at *nisi prius* in London before the Chief Baron [Edward Ward], after a long and full evidence on both sides, there was a verdict for the plaintiff that the said cargo in the Court of Admiralty before Sir John Cooke, judge thereof, and by his definitive sentence *per operam, media, et procurationem* of the plaintiff was condemned as a lawful prize for the use of the part owners of the said privateer *modo et forma prout* the plaintiff *interius allegavit* and assess damages *occasione infrascripta* besides costs of suit to £1739 18s. 6d. and for costs 40s.

The defendants' counsel, Mr. Attorney General [*Northey*], Serjeant *Pratt*, and others, move in arrest of judgment as to what concerns the insurance of the cargo as set forth in the declaration, admitting the breaches good for cargo and freightage. And, for that, they take notice that the covenant is to 'pay or allow' to the plaintiff all that should 'appear to be insured upon policies' of insurance 'when' they should be produced. And the plaintiff's averment is that the 'moneys paid for the insurance of the cargo' upon the 'policies of insurance thereupon made and subscribed and by the plaintiff now produced did amount to the sum of £250,' whereof the defendants had notice. And then the plaintiff shows that the defendants, though often requested, had not paid or allowed the plaintiff the said several sums for freightage and insurance, but broke their covenant therein so that the covenant is for what should appear to be due upon the policies when produced. And the breach assigned is for non-payment of what was paid upon the policies, which are different things, and the damages being entire, the plaintiff ought not to have judgment, the jury having given damages for a thing not in issue. Besides, the action was brought too soon as to the insurance, for the policies ought to have been produced and shown to the defendant before the action that it might have appeared what was insured upon them, that being in the nature of a condition precedent to the action.

[Objection:] The breach assigned is good. Money insured must be understood.

[Solution:] The value of the goods includes both money paid and to be paid.

Second objection: The breach assigned is bad, for, until the policy be produced, no payment [is due] and the policies were not produced before the action, which [they] ought to have been, being in the nature of a condition precedent, and the defendants might have paid upon the producing.

Solution: Meaning all that appears when produced must be understood what money shall upon the policies appear to be insured, which must be understood to be paid by way of *premio*, the time of producing is not material because there was two months allowed to be paid and the breach is after the two months. But must not then the producing of the policies have been within the two months, which it is not, and so it is no breach before the action.

Ettrick, for the plaintiff: [As to the] first objection, the covenant goes to the money which is insured and the breach is what is insured upon it, which is different.

'*Pro*' is for or according to money paid according to the insurance, which is the *premio*. But note '*pro*' is not in the covenant, but in the plaintiff's averment. If wrong, [it is a] breach; yet, after a verdict, [it is] good, and the jury has not considered it. Hobt. 28; beating a servant *per quod servitium amisit*; Yelverton 35, Huish and Wright; Rolle rep. 79; Stile 111, 1 Rol. Abr. 577, Allen 67; 4 rep. 65b.[1]

[As to] the second exception, the action was brought before producing the policies, and not bound by the covenant. When produced shall appear that it shall appear at the trial. But note 'when' is an adverb of time and no action arises until it is produced, for the defendants, upon producing, might have paid. The case of proof is what shall appear at the trial and proved there. The time of proving is at the trial, and then [you] make all appear unless special proof [is] appointed, as Hobt. 217; 3 Cro. 205; Rolle, *Trial*, 594, 595; Hobt. 92, 2 Cro. 381.[2]

[As to the] third objection, champerty, inconsistency, and maintenance, the solution is [it is] not the definition here of thrusting himself into what he has nothing to do with, but, here, the plaintiff is concerned and willing to save what he can, which is lawful. The process is against Prince, but that [is] nothing. The plaintiff comes in *pro interesse*, and [it is] intended the possession carried the property. Moor 691; possession at London was laid for venue, and it excludes not title at sea.

Phipps, for the plaintiff, answers the champerty etc. *ut supra*.

Objection: The action was too soon.

Solution: [There was a] payment after the condemnation in two months, and that answered it. The intention to pay so much as was paid for insurance admits that this is no good breach; yet, as this case is, [it is] not intended the jury gave

---

[1] *Huys v. Wright* (1603), Yelverton 35, 80 E.R. 26; *Sell v. Fairee* (1614), 1 Rolle Rep. 79, 81 E.R. 341; *Pragnell v. Goff* (1648), Style 111, 82 E.R. 570, 1 Rolle, Abr., *Dammages*, pl. F, 5, p. 577, Aleyn 67, 82 E.R. 919; *Cartwright v. Roberts* (1591), 4 Coke Rep. 64, 76 E.R. 1031.

[2] *Crookhay v. Woodward* (1618), Hobart 217, 80 E.R. 363; *Scroggs v. Griffin* (1590), Croke Eliz. 205, 78 E.R. 462, also 2 Leonard 215, 74 E.R. 489; 2 Rolle, Abr., *Triall*, sect. G, 'Trial per Jury', pp. 594–595; *Gold v. Death* (1615), Hobart 92, 80 E.R. 242, Croke Jac. 381, 79 E.R. 325, also Moore K.B. 845, 888, 72 E.R. 943, 976, 3 Bulstrode 55, 81 E.R. 47, 1 Rolle Rep. 222, 261, 81 E.R. 447, 475, 2 Rolle, Abr., *Triall*, pl. G, 6, p. 595.

damages for this, for no issue [was] joined here upon the points objected; the only issue is whether the condemnation by the plaintiffs means [. . .].

1 Siderfin 38, Best and Jolly,[1] [there were] two considerations, one good, one bad, entire damages given for the good, the plaintiff [. . .] yet judgment was for the entire damages. Words spoken at the same time, some actionable, others not, Cro. Car. 327, the plaintiff [will] have judgment.[2] Supposing three breaches are assigned and some are not damageable, the like intendment. And, here, this is an idle and vain thing as to money to be paid for insurance. Crisp and Gamel, 2 Cro. 127,[3] two considerations, one good, one bad, the good proved suffices. [It is] in vain to allege the other, being idle and vain; he agrees; three *assumpsit*s, one bad, entire damages [was] bad, because all [was] in issue. But that is not so in this case after a verdict, though bad on a demurrer. [In the] case of an award, where the release ordered [was] larger than the matter submitted, [it was] bad in a bond, [it was] good in an action upon the award. 1 Roll's rep. 437.[4] And the like reason [is] here; a covenant and damages several.

Nothing in this cause is in issue but the condemnation.

Osborn's Case, 10 rep.;[5] '*fulcrum lecti*' with a too long *anglice*, though part bad and damages entire, yet the plaintiff had judgment. And the case there, 133, Gavin's Case,[6] there, insensible things carry no damages. A judge or jury is not intended to countenance insensible things. If all three are in issue, [it is] hard, but, here, [it is] only the condemnation.

Turner, for the plaintiff: There is no necessity to intend that money. 'Assurance' can signify insurance as well as insuring. The intent of the parties goes not further than what the parties paid.

[As to] breach, this is a breach out of the articles, and [it is an] answer *prout* Phipps.

The second objection: The action was too soon.

Solution: Producing policies [is] not for time, but when produced, to pay what appears. He relies upon the cases cited for proof and that at trial. 1 Siderfin 57, *plane manifestaret*; 2 Cro. 232; Cro. Eliz. 205, 2 Leon. 215.[7]

Pengelly, for the plaintiff: Where but one breach is to be assigned, if bad, it is against the plaintiff. But where more and some be bad and some good, the

---

1 *Best v. Jolly* (1661), 1 Siderfin 38, 82 E.R. 955.

2 *Penson v. Gooday* (1633), Croke Car. 327, 79 E.R. 886.

3 *Crisp v. Gamul* (1606), Croke Jac. 128, 79 E.R. 111.

4 *Vanlore v. Tribb* (1617), 1 Rolle Rep. 437, 81 E.R. 590.

5 *Osborn v. Middleton* (1613), 10 Coke Rep. 130, 77 E.R. 1123, also Jenkins 270, 145 E.R. 194.

6 *Gawyn v. Ludlow* (1594), 10 Coke Rep. 133b, 77 E.R. 1129.

7 *Traver v. Anonymous* (1661) 1 Siderfin 57, 82 E.R. 967; *Elve v. Sabe* (1610), Croke Jac. 232, 79 E.R. 201, also 2 Rolle, Abr., *Triall*, pl. G, 3, p. 594; *Scroggs v. Griffin* (1590), Croke Eliz. 205, 78 E.R. 462, 2 Leonard 215, 74 E.R. 489.

verdict cures the breaches assigned according to the intent and not strictly to the words.

Tracy and Poole, Stiles 143, '*scriptum suum*' is understood *scriptum obligatorum*. 4 Edw. IV, 29, a bond to one payable to another, if especially declared, is good.[1]

Proof: Bene and Bear, 3 Levinz 240; 1 Siderfin 214, 313; 2 Roll's, *Tryall*, 594, 2; 3 Cro. 333; Moor 351, the intent of articles is to be performed, and it answers maintenance etc. and fraud to the queen; 1 Roll's, *Cond.*, 433; 21 Edw. IV, a bad agreement binds not the queen, but [it does] parties.[2]

Mr. *Lloyd*, for the plaintiff: The goods came safe, and the insurance must be intended to be the *premio* and not the value of the goods.

Mr. Attorney General [*Northey*] for the defendants: Plaintiff's counsel agree [it is] bad, a breach, and not insensible. It is not intended that the *premio*, but the value of the goods, is within the words of the covenant. And no new covenant can be made. And, plainly, the words are that the defendants are to pay what shall appear to be insured, not when paid upon them, and their breach is upon the not payment of the money etc.

As to the case of 1 Roll's, *Condicion*, 433, 21 Edw. IV, he agrees it to be law, but [it is] not like this case.

Second, if the breach be good, yet the action is too soon, for the payment is to be *quando* the policies shall be produced.

Objection: *Quando*, though an adverb of time, yet it is not so here.

Solution: If that is true, yet the plaintiff here brought the action on the not producing the policies not within two months next after the condemnation. So, no.

Objection: It is not intended the jury gave any damages for this insurance.

Solution: He agrees [there are] no damages for insensible things or words not actionable. That hold right where all [are] spoken to at one time, but it is different if at several times. If there are three breaches and one is bad and judgment by default and entire damage [are given, it is] bad. Here is a pertinent and sensible breach assigned, though it is not within the covenant.

Objection: It is like the case of proof which is to be at trial.

Solution: Where no particular proof is directed, the trial is the time. But, here, there is no cause of action until the policies be produced. 9 rep. 25; suf-

---

1 *Tracy v. Poole* (1648), Style 143, 82 E.R. 596; YB Mich. 4 Edw. IV, f. 29, pl. 9 (1464).

2 *Beayne v. Beal* (1685), 3 Levinz 240, 83 E.R. 669; *Rex v. Rainer* (1664), 1 Siderfin 214, 82 E.R. 1064; *Butcher v. Vale* (1666), 1 Siderfin 313, 82 E.R. 1127, also 1 Levinz 191, 83 E.R. 363, 2 Keble 118, 84 E.R. 75; *Tedcastle v. Hallywell* (1590), 2 Rolle, Abr., *Triall*, pl. G, 2, p. 594, also Croke Eliz. 236, 78 E.R. 492, 1 Leonard 256, 74 E.R. 233; *Swayn v. Stephens* (1632–1633), Croke Car. 245, 333, 79 E.R. 815, 892, also W. Jones 252, 82 E.R. 132; 1 Rolle, Abr., *Condition*, p. 433.

ficient discharge of the annuity to be produced, he must set it forth that [. . .] no subjection to [*blank*]. 3 Cro. 85; [in a] promise to pay all sums expended, a special request and notice were necessary. 1 Sands, pl. 6; Cro. Car. 386; where a man is to do a thing, to entitle himself to an action, he must show that thing to be done before he can maintain an action to pay.[1] When policies produced implies not to pay until produced.

Objection: This of the insurance might have been left out.

Solution: If it had been so, it might have been well, but being not said when assurances were made nor for what.

Dodd, for the defendant: No breach was assigned according to the covenant. The money was insured upon goods and not the *premio* to be paid within the articles. Two policies are to be produced before an action [lies]. The producing is a precedent act to the action.

Objection: It is not intended that the jury gave damages for this.

Solution: It is a plain breach well assigned if true and against the covenant. And this was in issue.

Mr. *Lant*, for the defendant: 2 Bulstr. 145; notice is here necessary and [he can]not know what to pay until [it is] produced. And that is a matter of substance *prout*. Cro. Car. 139 *accord*. Entire damages, where [there were] three causes of action and one was not good, [see] Cro. El. 425; 10 rep. 135b; Dyer 370.[2]

Mr. *Mead*, for the defendant:

Objection: The intendment is that the jury gave no damages for this.

Solution: That is not to be supposed. Here, the matter not appearing to be insensible or impossible, but very possible, the value of the goods insured must be so, not the *premio*, the production of the policies is a cause precedent.

Proof must be at the trial of uncertain things. But this here is certain, and, therefore, must be precedently produced.

Objection: '*Pro*' is uncertain.

Solution: It is so, but that word is not in the covenant, but in the breach, and that makes the [. . .]. The insurance is, therefore, to be understood of the said goods and not the *premio*.

Harbin v. Green, Hobt. 187; it was ruled that it is not intended that laymen give a verdict according to law.[3]

---

[1] *Regina v. Vaughan* (1591), 9 Coke Rep. 24, 77 E.R. 765, also Moore K.B. 297, 72 E.R. 591; *Devenly v. Welbore* (1588), Croke Eliz. 85, 78 E.R. 344; *Palmer v. Knight* (1634), Croke Car. 385, 79 E.R. 936.

[2] *Child v. Horden* (1613), 2 Bulstrode 143, 145, 80 E.R. 1019, 1020; *Shutford v. Penow* (1628), Croke Car. 139, 79 E.R. 722, also W. Jones 194, 82 E.R. 103; *Germyn v. Rolls* (1595), Croke Eliz. 425, 78 E.R. 666; *Smith's Case* (1613), 10 Coke Rep. 135, 77 E.R. 1132.

[3] *Harbin v. Green* (1616), Hobart 189, 80 E.R. 336, also 1 Brownlow & Goldesborough 18, 123 E.R. 638, Moore K.B. 887, 72 E.R. 975.

Here, the plaintiff has made all the matters in the declaration material, and, first, joined all the damages together, Yelverton, in judgment; [. . .] mistaken reversed, antecedent things must be showed before the action. Cro. Car. 299, Sims and Smith.[1]

[It is] fraud to the *cestui que trust* and piracy.

The only question in this case is whether the court shall intend that the jury did not regard and so by consequence did not give damages for that part of the covenant which related to the insurance money.

First, it is plain there is no breach assigned upon that part, that which is said about it is by the averment that the money paid upon the policies came to such a sum, but that is no breach, being no part of the covenant.

Secondly, if there was no breach assigned, then may it be fairly intended (as the truth was, upon the evidence) that the jury took no notice of that part.

Thirdly, [there are] like intendments after a verdict.

If a man speaks words actionable and not actionable at the same time, [it is] not intended damages [were] given for the words not actionable, though it is very possible the jury might aggravate in respect of the words not actionable, as thief and cuckold or the like. Cro. Car. 327; 10 rep. 130b.[2] It supposes the court's direction. Cro. Jac. 127;[3] two considerations in *assumpsit*, one good, the other bad; if the good be proved, it suffices. And, though there is no proof of the other, [it is] not material because it was in vain to allege it and it is as if it had not been alleged.

Osborn's Case, 10 rep. 130; [an action of] trover, *inter alia, pro fulchro lecti, anglice* a field bedstead with a testerne and curtains of say, and entire damages [were given], yet the plaintiff had judgment, for the *anglice* was rejected as surplus, not being alleged *positive sed expositive* and, therefore, not directly put in issue, but obliquely inquired by the jurors.

Now, [in] our case, the direct issue is whether the plaintiff procured the ship to be condemned. And the damages are only the consequence of that.

'*Pro custodia haeredis et terrae*,' judgment was reversed, because there was no action for the custody of the body [and] entire damages; judgment was reversed. Moor and Bedell, 10 rep. 131;[4] submission to an award and the arbitrators award a release to be made of a thing not in issue or question. There were two breaches, one good, one bad; entire damages were agreed to be bad, for, when two points are put in issue and, for one, no action lies and there are entire damages, it is bad. But, when, in an action upon the case and nothing it is to be enquired of by the

---

1 *Symmes v. Smith* (1633), Croke Car. 175, 299, 79 E.R. 754, 861, also W. Jones 314, 82 E.R. 166, Godbolt 445, 78 E.R. 261, 1 Rolle, Abr., *Condition*, pl. A, 37, p. 466.

2 *Penson v. Gooday* (1633), *ut supra*; *Osborn v. Middleton* (1613), *ut supra*.

3 *Crisp v. Gamul* (1606), *ut supra*.

4 *Moor v. Bedell* (1587), 10 Coke Rep. 131, 77 E.R. 1125, also 1 Leonard 170, 74 E.R. 157, Gouldsborough 91, 7 E.R. 1016.

jury but damages, there [it was] supposed the court directed the jury. But, in that case, judgment was reversed.

But, in our case, it is not intended that the jury give damages for a thing wherein no breach is assigned. And the whole appearing upon the record that there is no breach, as to that part of the insurance, why [is it] not intended (as the truth was) that the jury should not nor did enquire of or give any damages upon that point of insurance.

But, [I EDWARD WARD] conclude for the defendant upon Moor and Bedell's Case, my private knowledge as judge of *nisi prius* vanishing, and my opinion must be as judge on the record.

[Other copies of this report: Georgetown Univ. Law Sch. MS. B88–9, f. 275.]

Lincoln's Inn MS. Misc. 536, f. [79v]

6 May 1706, last day of term. The judgment of the court.

Baron SMITH opens the record, and is of opinion for the defendant and judgment to be arrested.

First objection: [It was said] by Mead [it is] champerty and maintenance.

Solution: This is neither because the defendants here and the plaintiffs in the Admiralty are parties, and [there are] agreements, and [they are] not assignable as such. The defendant here had an interest in the whole cargo.

Second objections: The breach upon the covenant for insurance was ill assigned. [There are] considerable words of covenant and the breach and the difference of money paid for insurance is nothing; what is secured upon the policies [is] another, and the difference is plain.

And he held this breach ill assigned. The premium to be paid for by the letter of agreement is not to be contradicted by intendment [where the] words are full. The intent not appearing, it is not to be regarded, especially where it is doubtful and it may be otherwise and not impossible, as a case whereby a man binds himself to A. to pay to A.

Parties might agree to pay the loss though it appears that the goods be safe and condemned in the Admiralty.

He agreed as to the case of words actionable and not actionable at the same time.

Objection: [There was] no breach, nor was it well assigned nor necessary to be assigned.

Solution: If a thing assigned for breach is wholly foreign, it is not bad. But this having an affinity to the covenant, though not good, is a breach. And it is to be intended the jury gave damages for it. And a jury must give damages for all breaches. He concludes it was an ill breach and there were entire damages and judgment [is to be] arrested. He relies much on the case of Cro. Car. 286, Palmer and Knight, cited by the Attorney [General], a stronger case than this, to be intended that [*blank*].

Objection: The plaintiff has come too soon with his action before and during the policies.

Solution: [It is] not necessary to produce the policies before, but at trial, and [they] might and ought to have been produced. And he is of opinion with that point that is not necessary to produce before the trial, for the defendant is not bound by them if produced.

Baron Price, for the defendant: There are three parts of the covenant: for the first, prime [?] costs, second, freight, third money insured. And he averred breaches upon all. Two part are good.

The issue was upon the condemnation, but the damages are to be considered, first, whether, as to insurance, [it was a] good breach or action timely. There was not a proper breach assigned upon the insurance covenant. The covenant is one thing, and the breach is another; the premium in one value of the goods is another. And no intent is to be [found] against the words that are express, paying so much money as shall appear to be insured upon the policies and to pay money for the insurance are two things. And though he might have left out the insurance and declared without it, yet, having declared for all and one is bad [and there were] entire damages, it is bad for all. Beating a servant *per quod serviciam amisit, scil.* for six months, in Hobart. He relies upon the reason of Moor and Bedell's Case in Osborne's Case. He holds there is no action until the policies be produced. The plaintiff had them and [it was a] condition precedent. And it is not like the case of proofs to be made, which is distinguished between a general and special proof; if the last, it must be precedent; where general, there, the trial may do it. Hobt. 217 makes for the defendant, though cited by the plaintiff. Cro. El. 237 agrees the proof is to be precedent. Roll's, *Damages*, is otherwise. In this case, the plaintiff ought to have averred the producing of the policies and that so much appeared insured upon.

Baron Bury, for the defendant: There is a variance between the covenant and the breach; they are different things. Being insured and paid for insurance cannot be the same. He goes up on Smith's ground. And assurances may be understood to be for what is insured; it does not intend any policies for such money to be paid for insurance.

Objection: The issue was not upon the breach.

Solution: Moor and Bedell in Osborn's Case and in Sir Henry Constable's Case[1] answers all intendment; the case of the heirs, body, and lands.

Judgment was arrested, *me reluctante.*

[1] *Moor v. Bedell* (1587), *ut supra*; *Osborn v. Middleton* (1613), *ut supra*; *Constable's Case* (1601), 5 Coke Rep. 106, 77 E.R. 218, 1 Anderson 86, 123 E.R. 367, British Library MS. Lansdowne 1088, f. 69, S. A. Moore, *A History of the Foreshore* (1888), pp. 224–241 (Sir John Constable's Case and Sir Henry Constable's Case).

265

Gill, qui tam v. Fuller

(Ex. 1706)

Where, by law, anyone can make a seizure for the crown, there is no need for a warrant from a justice.

Lincoln's Inn MS. Misc. 536, f. [73]

For a £600 penalty, the case was this. An information was exhibited in the Exchequer against [John] Fuller upon the Statute 10 Will. III, ca. 13,[1] fo. 34, whereby it is enacted *inter alia* that, if an excise officer should suspect any to have concealed backs etc. and make an oath of it before a justice of the peace, it shall be lawful for the officer in the daytime and presence of a peace officer, by the warrant of such justice, to break and enter the suspected person's house and to seize such concealed backs etc. and, if they be not claimed in twenty days, then to be forfeited and sold, a moiety to the king, the other to the seizer, and, if claimed in that time, the claimer to forfeit and lose for every such concealed back etc. £200 and £200 more for the place where found. The informer shows that such an officer made such an affidavit and had a warrant from the justice to enter and search the defendant's house (but there was no power mentioned in the warrant to seize) and, upon the search, there were found two concealed backs etc., which the officer seized. And, within the twenty days, the defendant came in and claimed them. And the plaintiff prayed that the defendant might forfeit £600, *viz.* £200 for each of the two concealed backs and £200 for the place where they were concealed. And he prayed a moiety of the forfeiture, the Act, as to that forfeiture, giving a moiety to the king and the other to the informer.

The defendant pleaded not guilty. And, upon a trial, the fact was fully proved against the defendant, but a special verdict was found upon that point only that there was no power given by the justice's warrant to seize the concealed backs etc., after which, the defendant submitted to the commissioners of the excise, and they compounded with him for the forfeiture, generally intending thereby that the informer, who was their door keeper and for whom they took no care nor made provision for his part, should nor would make any claim in the premises. But he, insisting upon his moiety, was turned out of his place. And a *noli prosequi* was entered by Mr. Attorney General for the queen's moiety, it being insisted on that the informer's name was only used by the commissioners of the excise in trust and not with any intent that he should have any more than what the commissioners should think fit, all being transacted by them and he not cognizant nor concerned therein (only to the using of his name).

But the court would not nor could take any notice of that.

[1] Stat. 10 Will. III, c. 13 (*SR*, VII, 513–514).

And, after Mr. Attorney General [*Northey*] had entered his *noli prosequi*, he argued against the informer, insisting that no judgment ought to be given, the information being insufficient for want of the power in the justice's warrant to seize the concealed backs, there being no other power to seize but by such warrant, and, if there was no legal seizure, there could be no forfeiture and so no judgment for the informer.

But the whole court gave judgment for the informer to have his moiety in this case.

First, the officer, by law and upon the reason of that Act, had the power to seize without any power by the justice's warrant, the thing itself being by law forfeited, in which case, anybody might seize for the crown.

But secondly, the defendant coming and claiming the backs within the twenty days, they were never become absolutely forfeited, for, by that claim, the proceedings against the backs are discharged and then, in lieu of that forfeiture, there does emerge the forfeiture of the money, *viz.* £200 apiece for each back and £200 for the place where they were found, and that is the forfeiture for which this prosecution was and not for the forfeiture or interest of the concealed backs, which make it quite another thing.

Upon this judgment, Fuller brought a writ of error in the Exchequer Chamber, which being often argued before the two chief justices, the Attorney General [*Northey*] for Fuller, the judgment was affirmed the 23rd of April 1706, 5 *Annae Reginae*, by the Lord Keeper [Lord Cowper] and Lord Treasurer [Lord Godolphin].

And upon that affirmance, another writ of error in Parliament was in like manner brought in a like appeal by Fuller against Gill in order to reverse both judgments.

It seems hard that, after the crown had taken what belonged to it upon the forfeiture, which supposed a good suit, that it should not be as good for the informer etc.

But, afterwards, that writ of error in Parliament was surceased, and Fuller agreed with Gill, and gave him satisfaction. This proceeding in opposition to Gill was carried on by the commissioners of the excise or their agent, who prevailed with the Attorney General to appear all along against the information upon which the crown had recovered its moiety of the forfeiture, *quod nota et quaere*.

[Other copies of this report: Georgetown Univ. Law Sch. MS. B88–9, f. 281.]

266

Hardwick, qui tam v. Anonymous

(Ex. 1706)

Where perishable goods are seized as forfeited for non-payment of customs duties, they can be sold pendente lite, and the proceeds paid to the prevailing party.

A warehouse keeper must obey an order of the Court of Exchequer, regardless of any order by a commissioner of the customs.

The crown cannot have the customs duty and the forfeiture of the same goods also.

Lincoln's Inn MS. Misc. 536, f. [75]

27 April 1706.

Upon a seizure of a great quantity of wines as forfeited for non-payment of duties, after the seizure and a writ of appraisal awarded and a proclamation made in court *si quis plus dare volueret*, the appraised value being £1600, one Frampton bid £120 more, and, thereupon, was allowed by the court to be the best bidder and to have the wines for that sum, after which bidding and not before, there were three claims, each for the whole wines entered upon the back of the writ of appraisement, one claim in the name of one Aynsworth and another in the name of Guybon, who also bid for the owners, and the third in the name of one [*blank*].

And, upon affidavits made and the circumstances of the case that no claim was made until after the bidding and there being so great an under appraisement which induced a suspicion that there was some underhanded dealing in the valuation of the goods to the prejudice of the crown, it was upon motion in court some days since ordered that the claimers should each swear their property. And two of the claimers, *viz.* Aynsworth and Guybon, swore the same accordingly. But Guybon claiming under Aynsworth and there being a great opposition between their properties, as stated by their affidavits, the court ordered that both of them should join their claims. And, if either of them could defend the wines from being forfeited, there would be an end of the queen's and informers' pretenses, and, by consequence, the goods not forfeited would be discharged from all proceedings in this court, and each of the claimers might then contend their respective titles and properties between themselves, and the trial to proceed.

But it being fully made out by affidavits that the wines were in a perishing condition, having fallen in their nature and value many hundreds of pounds since the bidding and like to suffer more before a trial could be had, whereby the bidder could be a great loser if recovered and the claimers also if not recovered, it was proposed that, by consent, the wines should be forthwith sold and the money brought into court to attend the event of the trial and to be paid out accordingly, either to the queen and the bidder or to the claimers according to the event of the trial and this would answer everybody's interest, which, if the wines would perish, would be a great loss to the owner or the bidder, and, if not done, would be a discouragement to all bidders, if, after bidding and a charge upon record against the bidder for the sum bid, the wines should perish or be deteriorated under a pretense of subsequent sham claims preventing or delaying the trial or the recovery.

And this being the day for showing cause why such a sale should not be made and the money brought in (the claim of [*blank*] being set aside for want of swearing properly and none pretending to support it), Aynsworth, by his counsel, came in and consented to such a sale. But Guybon, by his counsel, would have opposed it (as so instructed overnight). But it appearing that this morning Guybon, by a writing under his hand, he directed [Thomas] Harris, one of the sworn clerks, or any other of the sworn clerks in the Queen's Remembrancer's Office to withdraw his claim and suffer the goods to be recovered.

Which claim being withdrawn, accordingly, the court, upon Aynsworth's consent, he being present in court and the bidder also consenting, ordered the wines to be sold and the money to be brought into court to attend the event of the trial and that the warehouse keeper should deliver the wines to the bidder, who brought the money into court. This was done for the good of everybody and that bidders that advance the crown revenue by exceeding the appraisement value, which bidding is the ancient and approved right and practice, may not be discouraged nor that the crown suffer.

Vide L. K, 84;[1] after bidding, a claim was entered and, upon the bidder's bringing the money into court, the goods were delivered to the bidder; *vide* this case and the reasons there, and [it was] without consent.

But, afterwards, *viz.* 30 April 1706, it appearing to the court by two affidavits that the bidder Frampton, having brought the £1726 into court, demanded of Dobson, the warehouse keeper, the wines to be delivered to him according to the order of the court, the warehouse keeper absolutely refused so to do, saying the commissioners of the customs had forbidden him to deliver them and that he would obey their order and, by the same affidavits, it appearing that the wines every day they lay in the warehouse wasted and were worse £20, the court, upon the motion of the bidder's counsel and hearing the counsel on the warehouse keeper's behalf, awarded an immediate attachment against the warehouse keeper for his contempt, it being a stratagem and contrivance below in the Custom House to render the wines of lesser value in order to discourage bidders, whereby the crown revenue will be much impaired and underhanded dealings in the Custom House as to appraisements encouraged, it being the ancient and proper business of this court to see the rights of the crown preserved and the insolence and disobedience of every officer in the Custom House, the commissioners themselves not excepted, to be punished.

---

1 *Chuseman v. Pierce* (Ex. 1685), see above, Case No. 5.

And the warehouse keeper or his agent, being in court and hearing the resolution of it, forthwith agreed with the bidder and paid him all his charges and went and delivered him the wines. And the [writ of] attachment was no further prosecuted.

Note, in this case, it appeared that Aynsworth was the importer of the wines, which were prize wines and liable to duties and were landed by the order of the commissioners of the customs and seized in order to secure the queen's duties, which were not nor are paid, and, in the order of the 27th of April, there is a clause that the money should be brought into court to secure the queen's duties. But the queen cannot have a duty and the forfeiture too. And this information and seizure is for a forfeiture for non-payment of the duty.

[Other copies of this report: Georgetown Univ. Law Sch. MS. B88–9, f. 282v.]

267

Regina v. Babb

(Ex. 1706)

A surety of a debtor to the crown can have relief by a court against co-sureties and executors of the debtor.

Wightwick 2, 145 E.R. 1152

6 May 1706.

John Babb was indebted to the queen by bond, against whom a [writ of] extent issued for the recovery of a debt of £2078 19s. 10d., and several goods were seized. A [writ of] *venditioni exponas* issued to sell them. And, after the return of that writ, stating the sum for which the goods had sold, John Babb died and left Sarah Babb and Thomas Babb, his executors. Thomas was also one of his sureties, together with Edward Hollister.

Mary Hollister, the widow of Edward, being desirous to exonerate the estate of her late husband, applied to the court that she might be at liberty to pay the remainder of the debt to the crown and have the aid of its process against Thomas Babb, the co-surety and executor of John Babb.

This the court ordered and also her costs and expenses, which she had already sustained or might hereafter sustain in prosecuting the prerogative process in her aid.

268

Fowler v. Anonymous

(Ex. 1706)

In this case of a seizure of wrecked goods, the seizer did not follow the proper procedures, and the goods were returned to the owner.

Lincoln's Inn MS. Misc. 536, f. [80]

9 May 1706.

Fowler, upon a seizure of brandy, at the setting down of causes after this term, a motion having been made for entry of a claim to a parcel of brandy which belonged to a Dutchman was wrecked in a vessel at sea and taken up on the shore and seized, as alleged by Fowler, and notice being given also of a motion for a writ of delivery, the case, upon examination in court appeared to be that, above a year ago, the vessel was wrecked, and the brandy was seized by Fowler, an excise officer, but, for what, *non constat*, and that no information was ever exhibited to this time and that, nevertheless, the goods had been proclaimed in court and a writ of appraisement awarded. And one of the sworn clerks had made a *debet* for paying the moiety of the appraised value into the Receipt [Office].

And, upon hearing the Attorney General [*Northey*], for the officer and the queen, and *Browne et al.*, for the claimer, the claim was admitted, and a writ of delivery was awarded. And a severe reproof was given for such illegal and unwarrantable proceeding without any information and keeping the goods by the excise officer so long and without any just cause, no duty being due for the brandy's being wrecked goods if exported.

[Other copies of this report: Georgetown Univ. Law Sch. MS. B88–9, f. 288v.]

269

Robertson, qui tam v. Anonymous

(Ex. 1706)

In this case, French wines that were unlawfully imported were seized, condemned, and sold for the benefit of the crown.

Lincoln's Inn MS. Misc. 536, f. [90]

Upon a seizure of a great quantity of French wines, the information sets forth the seizure to be between the first of June 1705 and the 10th of May 1706 for that they are forfeited, being French wines imported into this realm after the 25th of March 1705, not being goods taken as prizes and condemned as such in the High Court of Admiralty of England nor ordered by the said court before condemnation to be sold as perishable contrary to the form of the Statute.

The Statute is that of 3 & 4 *Annae Reginae*, ca. [*blank*],[1] for prohibiting all trade and commerce with France, which imposes a forfeiture of the goods, one moiety to Her Majesty, the other to the seizer or informer in any court of record.

After the seizure and information, a writ of appraisement issued, and the appraised value was returned to be £920. And, upon a proclamation in court *si quis plus dare voluerit veniat et audiretur*, one Hosier, who is the inspector and receiver of the moneys for the crown which accrue by forfeitures either for being prohibited or uncustomed goods, and one Frampton severally bid above the appraised value, each outbidding the other, but Frampton bidding the last sum, which made in all £460 above the appraised value, he was allowed by the court to be the best bidder and to have the wines for that sum above the appraised value, making in all £1380, which £460 was forthwith brought into court.

After this bidding and before any judgment or recovery was entered, divers noblemen and great officers and some private persons under pretenses [. . .] entered their several claims to some of the said wines, naming each what they claimed, but without any particular marks or distinctions so as to ascertain their claims or distinguish one hogshead or parcel from the other. And, upon enquiry, several of them disclaimed those claims and recoveries entered, and such as did not were directed by a day to ascertain their claims and join in a trial, all being an entire seizure in one ship and at one time and by the same officer and for the same cause of forfeiture, *viz.* being French wines, or else to be recovered.

It appearing by affidavit that, if the wines lie until next term, they would be much prejudiced and reduced to less than the value bid for them whereby the crown and the officer would be great losers, all those claimers, except three noblemen's which were allowed, appeared to the court to be set up and the whole business carried on for the purpose only to deter bidders and render bidding which is so advantageous to the crown and a great improvement of its revenue and a correction of the miscarriage in the low appraisement of goods in the Custom House, the solicitor and receiver of the forfeited goods appearing in opposition or prejudice to the bidders, useless, nevertheless, though the claims of several of the noblemen and others were not ascertained as to marks and distinctions, yet the court admitted them all to join in their claims wherein each of the claimers had liberty to defend for his own or the whole.

And, thereupon, a trial was had after the term, and several small quantities of each sort of the wines, there being Bordeaux, Champagne, Burgundy, and Hermitage, were produced upon oath at the trial and tasted by the witnesses and the jury, all the rest that were seized being either proved or agreed to be of the same sorts and kinds, and, upon proof of the seizure and testimony of divers witnesses well skilled in wines, no witnesses being produced by the defendants, though the seizure was made the 10th of May, above a month before the trial and

[1] Stat. 3 & 4 Ann., c. 12 (*SR*, VIII, 360).

it was a matter of opinion and judgment upon the last and hundreds might have been produced at a day's notice for that purpose, the counsel for the defendants contenting themselves with cross-examining the informer's witnesses.

The jury, after a long evidence and taste, as above, found and gave their verdict for the queen and the informer that the wines were French and they were recovered. And the bidder had them and sold some of them for £40, £38, and none of them under £30 a hogshead, as I [Edward Ward] was informed.

[Other copies of this report: Georgetown Univ. Law Sch. MS. B88–9, f. 295.]

270

Gratwick v. Earl of Denbigh

(Ex. 1706)

Where an executor sues a scire facias, the letters testamentary need not be set forth in the scire facias.

Lincoln's Inn MS. Misc. 536, f. [91], pl. 2

Officio Placitorum per Paschae recordum 4 Annae Reginae [1705].

In a *scire facias quare executio non* upon a judgment by the testator against the defendant, the *scire facias* was brought by the plaintiffs as executors. And they set themselves forth to be such but did not in the *scire facias proferre in curia* the letters testamentary.

And, therefore, the defendant demurred to the writ, and assigned that for cause.

But the plaintiffs had judgment, for, though the letters testamentary must be produced before the [writ of] *scire facias* issue, yet it is not the course nor of necessity to set forth in the *scire facias* a *profert in curia*.

Vide L. 1, fo. 298, Broyle and Noblett, Easter [term] 19 Car. II, the opinion of Lord Chief Baron Hale for that purpose.[1] And there is no precedent of such a profert set forth in the writ. But the constant practice is otherwise.

[Other copies of this report: Georgetown Univ. Law Sch. MS. B88–9, f. 296v, pl. 2.]

---

[1] *Broyle v. Noblett* (1667), Lincoln's Inn MS. Misc. 499, p. 298, pl. 5.

271

Parsons v. Earl of Peterborough

(Ex. 1706)

Where a defendant is abroad in the service of the crown, though his residence be close to the place of trial, he will be given additional time to appear and to plead.

Lincoln's Inn MS. Misc. 536, f. [91], pl. 3

[In an action of] debt upon a bond for the payment of £300 by £100 at every Midsummer day in three years, the defendant omitted the payment of the first £100 at the day but paid it after and had a receipt for it before the action was brought. But the plaintiff [Sir John Parsons], insisting that, in strictness, the bond was forfeited, put it in suit in order to recover the penalty. And the earl's agent having ordered an appearance, the plaintiff's attorney pressed for a trial this term upon six day's notice, insisting that the earl's house being within ten miles of London is bound to take such notice.

But the court, upon consideration of the strictness of the demand and it being made out to the court that the earl was at Barcelona in Spain and had been so for above a year in the service of the crown and, therefore, could have no personal notice of the trial and, upon a conference with some of the judges of the Common Pleas and the Queen's Bench that, in such a case as this, they do not tie up the defendant to take six day's notice and that it would be unreasonable in this case that the house should oblige the person, the court would not oblige him to take six day's notice.

[Other copies of this report: Georgetown Univ. Law Sch. MS. B88–9, f. 296v, pl. 3.]

272

Hanbury v. Lane

(Ex. 1706)

A trial will not be delayed because the cause of action sounding in tort accrued at a different place from the trial.

Lincoln's Inn MS. Misc. 536, f. [91v], pl. 1

A special *quo minus* in the nature of an original, containing the cause of action in it which was a battery, was directed to the sheriffs of Bristol. And he was taken thereupon and appeared and was pressed to take notice of a trial without an imparlance, that being the rule and course of the court in such a case to force to trial.

The defendant's counsel moved that the battery laid in the writ was at Bristol, but that, in his declaration and for which the plaintiff pressed, a trial was laid at Hereford; so, the declaration varying from the writ, the defendant ought not to be pressed to trial at those Assizes.

But the court held that variance not sufficient to put off the trial or hinder the defendant from pleading, the cause of action being the same and of a transitory nature and according to the practice of the court in like cases.

[Other copies of this report: Georgetown Univ. Law Sch. MS. B88–9, f. 297.]

273

Anonymous v. Wetherby

(Ex. 1706)

Special bail can be required only by the court or the Attorney General.

Lincoln's Inn MS. Misc. 536, f. [91v], pl. 4

22 June 1706.

Wetherby and Benson and others, merchants of Newcastle, were arrested upon *capias*es in debt upon several informations contracted by frauds. And the sheriff held them to special bail in exceeding great sums, and some of whom lay in prison for want of bail and others gave bail. And [there was] no order of court or warrant from the Attorney General for such bail, but [it was] marked by an attorney in court for such bail, which the court held unwarrantable. And, upon the return of the writ, the court, upon reading the affidavit, directed the sums for bail.

And, then, the writ was objected to as being one writ against divers for several distinct debts, which was said to be unwarrantable.

As to the matter of the writ, the queen's counsel held it was a common proceeding in the Queen's Bench and the Common Pleas to join several debtors to the same person in one writ. And this [writ of] *capias* is for the defendants to answer several informations of debt *seperaliter.* And there is no mischief to the defendants.

Curia: The *capias* is proper process, and it may be against five or six that are severally debtors to the crown, it being so in a subject's case in the other courts. But the making of writs by the clerk in court for special bail was ruled irregular and oppressive, and, for the future, is to be allowed only by a Baron or the Attorney General. And, in this case, as to those in prison, they are to be let out and those that appeared to give reasonable bail to be allowed as above.

And this was thus ordered because the nature of this case being a fraud and many others concerned at the same time, if the queen's witnesses should be discovered, they may be taken off.

[Other copies of this report: Georgetown Univ. Law Sch. MS. B88–9, f. 298v, pl. 1, and f. 297v.]

274

Hunt, qui tam v. Parry

(Ex. 1706)

Whether a church is impropriate or presentable is an issue for the common law courts, not for the ecclesiastical courts.

Lincoln's Inn MS. Misc. 536, f. [92]

Entered Trinity [term] 5 Queen Anne [1706] in the Queen's Remembrancer's Office in the Exchequer. Richard Hunt, Jr., qui tam v. Parry and Dr. Lloyd, official to the bishop of Worcester, in a prohibition.

The defendant [Dr. Lloyd], the official [to the bishop of Worcester], at the promotion of the defendant Parry libels and articles in the Consistory Court of the bishop of Worcester against the plaintiff, [Richard] Hunt, for that he, being church warden of the parish of Moreton Morrell in the County of Warwick and the Diocese of Worcester had taken an oath well and truly to execute that office, that the defendant Parry, the promoter, for eight months past, had been and still was the lawful and rightful rector of that parish, that the plaintiff Hunt, in neglect of his office and contempt of the laws of this realm and defiance of Parry, his lawful rector, did order the bells of the parish church to be rung or tolled for divine service and sermon as usual on such days being Sundays and festivals in December and January 1705 and, on some of them, did shut and lock the church doors and denied Parry, the rector, entrance to perform his duty in reading divine service and preaching to the parishioners met to serve God, as they ought, and, thereby, deprived both Parry and the parishioners of the benefit of divine service and sermon, and that Hunt kept the keys of the church from the parish clerk and hindered him from doing his duty in ringing and tolling the bells on those days and other days for divine service and sermon and that Hunt hindered Parry, his lawful rector, from administering the Sacrament at Christmas and from locking the chest in the church wherein Parry's vestments should be locked up, and that, on the days aforesaid or some of them, contrary to the duty of his office, procured or suffered one or more strange ministers without any authority from the ordinary of the diocese of Worcester to read divine service and preach in that church in opposition to and defiance of Parry, his lawful rector. And he did at the aforesaid times of hinderance of the said Parry take to his assistance his father, Richard Hunt, and Thomas Smith, the plaintiff's servant. And it was at the plaintiff's request and by his management that they assisted him in those pernicious and unwarrantable acts and in violation of his office of church warden.

The plaintiff Hunt here prays a [writ of] prohibition, suggesting that the master and confreres of the dissolved Hospital of St. John in the Town of Warwick, at the dissolution and suppression thereof in the reign of King Henry VIII and time out of mind were and had been seised in the right of the said hospital of and in the rectory and parish church of Moreton Morrell aforesaid and to the said hospital in due form of law appropriated. And that, after such dissolution, King Henry VIII by the laws and statutes of this realm became seised in fee in the right of his crown of England of and in the said rectory and church as of his lay fee and as his lay fee had and enjoyed and of right ought to enjoy the said rectory and church.

Then, he sets forth that King Henry VIII, by letters patent under the great seal of England, *in curia prolata*, dated 20 December in the 32d year of his reign [1540], granted to Anthony Stoughton *inter alia* the said rectory and church and the said hospital with all and all manner of lands, tenements, rents, services, rights, profits, commodities, and appurtenances to the said hospital belonging for the term of his life, whereby he was seised of the premises as of his lay fee for life and the reversion, continuing in the crown, came to Queen Elizabeth, who, by letters patent under the great seal of England dated 23rd June 5 *regni sui* [1563], reciting the grant to Stoughton, who was still living, granted the reversion of the said rectory, church, hospital, and premises and the said rectory, church, and tithes in Morton aforesaid to the said Anthony Stoughton as fully and in as large and ample manner as they came to the crown by virtue of any act or acts of Parliament or otherwise to hold to the said Anthony Stoughton and the heirs male of his body to be held of the crown *in capite* by the service of the fortieth part of a knight's fee for all rents, services, and demands.

Then there is a continuance of the estate tail in one Anthony Stoughton, and that King James I, by letters patent under the great seal of England dated 13 July 17 *regni sui* [1615], granted the reversion in fee expectant upon the aforesaid estate tail to John Buck, Walter Ligon, and William Wells, Gent., and their heirs, and that the said estate tail and the reversion in fee, by divers lawful conveyances, descents, ways, and means in the law, came to one Lawrence Fiennes, Esq., who now is and, for divers years last past, has had the lawful seisin of the said rectory and church with the appurtenances impropriate as of his lay fee and was and now is seised thereof as in his demesne as of fee and, long before the exhibiting of the said libel and articles, *scil.* 1 May 1705, did name and appoint one John Fancourt, clerk, to serve as his curate in the said church and to administer the Sacraments and celebrate divine service there during his pleasure and which curate, by virtue of the said nomination, ever since, has officiated and does officiate.

Then, he further suggests that pleas of advowsons of churches and presentations to vacant churches and whether presentable or not and all pleas and matters of and relating to lay fees and concerning the validity and exposition of royal charters and letters patent belong of right to the queen and her crown and not to courts Christian and by the laws of the land in the queen's courts of record and not in courts Christian or by ecclesiastical censures by any means to be determined, and that, by reason of the said appropriation of the said church to the hospital and the dissolution thereof, the said rectory and church ever after remained and was and still is a rectory and church impropriate and a lay fee and no way presentable nor has the ordinary of that place any ecclesiastical or other jurisdiction of inducting any clerk presented to him into the said church. Yet the said Parry knowing of the premises and being minded to oppress the plaintiff and draw the validity of the said letters patent by false allegations to be tried and determined in the court Christian and thereby to subject the said church to be ever after presentative and subject to the ordinaries' jurisdiction in a court Christian has prosecuted and sued the plaintiff in the court Christian, setting forth the libel and articles before set forth.

Ubi, revera et in facto, Parry never was nor is rector of the rectory and church aforesaid nor had or has any interest therein, but the said rectory and church were and are the lay fee of the said Mr. Fiennes, and impropriate and not presentable, nor subject to the bishop's jurisdiction. *Et ubi revera* all that was done by the plaintiff concerning the matters in the said articles mentioned or concerning the premises were done by him by the order and direction of the said Mr. Fiennes and of Mr. Fancourt, his curate, and for the preservation and asserting of their respective rights.

And then he suggests the refusal of his plea of the said matters by the official and his endeavors to condemn him in the premises by an ecclesiastical sentence to his great damage against the laws and customs of England. He prays a [writ of] prohibition.

And it was granted *nisi causa* the first day next term and to stay proceedings in the ecclesiastical court in the meantime, *ex motione Dodd*. And no cause being shown, the prohibition became absolute. And the defendants proceeded no further in the ecclesiastical court.

[Other copies of this report: Georgetown Univ. Law Sch. MS. B88–9, f. 298, pl. 2.]

275

Wyatt, qui tam v. Ferdinand

(Ex. 1706)

In this case of a forfeiture of French wines that were unlawfully imported, the court allowed the parties to settle the matter out of court with the consent of the Attorney General.

Lincoln's Inn MS. Misc. 536, f. [104]

Saturday 7 December 1706, setting down of causes after Michaelmas term. Frampton's Case, upon a bidding upon an information.

Upon a seizure of French wines as forfeited for unlawful importation, the case was this. A writ of appraisement was awarded, and the value of the wines was returned to be above £4000, the informer making it appear by several affidavits that the wines were much over-appraised, though the defendant entered a claim and the trial to be the day after the term and the first appraisement entered upon the roll, yet the court, upon those affidavits, awarded a new writ of appraisement *teste* 27 November and returnable the 28th and, upon the coming in of that new appraisement, which came to about £2900, and proclamation thereupon for any to give more, Frampton bid £50 more, which was accepted. And he [was] charged with the whole sum amounting to £2950. The trial not proceeding, the goods were recovered and the record made up (but the judgment was not signed) that the goods should remain forfeited that Frampton should be charged with one moiety of the £2950 to the queen and the other moiety to the informer and that, upon payment thereof, the goods should be delivered to him.

And now this day upon the producing of new affidavits whereby it appeared that this last appraisement was made by persons unskilled and in a private manner, that Frampton did apprehend that the second appraised value came but to £1900 and not to £2900, which encouraged him to bid the £50 more, and, in truth, it appeared to the court that the informer was prepared with affidavits of the over-appraisement of the goods this second time and intended to have moved for another appraisement or that the queen might take her moiety in specie, and this whole matter being communicated by the officers and persons concerned to the commissioners of the customs and they being sensible that the wines were not worth the money bid for them and that, if the wines lay until next term, they would be very much prejudiced and abate in their value and, therefore, thought it the best way that, by consent, the wines should be forthwith sold by inch of candle and the queen to have one moiety of the money and the informer the other and that Frampton should be discharged of his bidding if the court thought fit, and, thereupon, Mr. Attorney General, for the queen, and the informer, by his counsel, consented to all this.

But [it was] ordered that Frampton should pay £10 to the queen and £10 to the informer as part of the £50 because it was made out that he was told the second appraised value was £2900 before he bid the £50 more and, then, he to be discharged, and the wines sold and the money to be paid by moieties, as above.

Note the consent.

And the wines, upon the sale by inch of candle in December, were sold for £3474, which is £554 more than the second appraisement, *quod nota*.

[Other copies of this report: Georgetown Univ. Law Sch. MS. B88–9, f. 318.]

276

Greenway v. Earl of Kent

(Ex. 1706)

Tithes are due for all wood that has been cut and corded.

Bunbury 98, 145 E.R. 609, 1 Rayner 161

A bill was exhibited in 1704 by the vicar of Wasford in the County of Hereford setting forth that the defendant was possessed of a coppice called the Chace and other woodland within the said parish and to have the tithe of the wood cut down and bark. And he insisted that, if any of the wood was above twenty years growth, yet the same were but some few poles growing *sparsim* from the stubs or stocks of other trees and not fit for timber, but only for firewood or making laths and were accordingly sold to the iron masters, who used the same for fuel at their furnaces.

The defendant, in his answer, insisted that the woods etc. consisted of an innumerable quantity of timber trees of oak of thirty years growth and upwards and also of coppice and underwood under twenty years growth, that he caused the timber trees, which he hopes to prove were above thirty years growth, to be stripped and the bark to be perked by itself and so delivered to the buyers and the timber trees to be fallen and the sound and merchantable parts thereof to be sold by the country's use and the parts not employed in the defendant's own affairs for building and repairs, and the lops and offal he caused to be sized into billets and ranked and corded by itself apart from the coppice wood and he delivered the same to iron masters. And he insists that the timber trees were free from the payment of tithes.

But the court decreed that all the wood above twenty years growth, as well as underwood, cut and corded and the bark stripped from the same should pay tithes, but that no tithe was due from such wood above twenty years growth nor of the bark thereof which was not corded.

Note: This decree[1] was cited by the court, and it plainly makes timber trees above twenty years growth titheable if cut and corded for fuel, *per* Baron Bury, and Price and Smith, barons.

Ambler 134, 27 E.R. 86

There was a bill for tithes of wood and tops of pollards, all used for firing. It appeared in proof that all had been corded and used together.

And it was decreed that tithes should be paid of all trees of twenty years growth, as of underwood that was cut and corded.

The court was divided, and Chief Baron Ward differed with the other three barons, and delivered a very learned argument against the decree.

And I [Lord Hardwicke] think his the better opinion. I have informed myself of the ground on which the three barons went.

Baron Price said ancient statutes are to be construed according to the intent and meaning, that *gross bois* is not all sorts of wood above twenty years growth,

[1] *Buckle v. Vanacre* (Ex. 1693), see above, Case No. 103.

but timber, and used for building; so that the ground whether titheable or not is the being used for building.

But this is not agreeable to the Statute[1] and the determinations upon it. He [Price] cites Stat. 35 Hen. VIII.[2] But that Statute only gave protection to wood of such dimensions, and does not say that other timber shall not be privileged. And it might as well be said, although the law says a man shall be at age at twenty-one, yet it shall be determined by his sense or stature. As there was no precedent before that case, so there has been none since.

[Other reports of this case: Equity Cases Exch. 546.]

[The order of 31 January 1706, Public Record Office E.126/18, f. 567v, is printed at 1 Wood 479, 1 Eagle & Younge 677.]

277

Wyatt, ex rel. Robertson, qui tam v. Singleton

(Ex. 1707)

This case involved a release of court costs in a dispute over the priority of seizures of prohibited French wines.

This case, which was redolent of fraud, was settled out of court without any judgment by the court.

Lincoln's Inn MS. Misc. 538, p. 4

Robertson, having been a Custom House officer and not discharged but suspended only from the execution of his office by the Commissioners of the Customs, had an account and discovery made to him of a great quantity of French wines that would be imported into England against the law. And none but a Custom House officer being enabled by law to make a seizure, he was allowed, as he said, to make use of what officer he thought fit to make the seizure. And he made use of Wyat, who made the seizure. And an information thereof was exhibited in Wyat's name, who gave a bond to Robertson not to release or discharge the seizure or information or do any act to prejudice the same or the benefit thereby accruing (all which Robertson was allowed to have, he allowing such a sum to Wyat) without the privity and consent of Robertson or to that effect. And all was carried on at Robertson's charges, though in Wyat's name.

The commissioners or officers of the Customs did not well approve of this prosecution. And, therefore, as it afterwards appeared, the defendant Singleton was set up to make a seizure and to exhibit an information of seizure of the same wines in his own name. And then he came in and pleaded the same as a prior sei-

[1] Stat. 45 Edw. III, c. 3 (*SR*, I, 393).

[2] Stat. 35 Hen. VIII, c. 17 (*SR*, III, 977–980).

zure to that of Wyat's, which also he alleged to be exhibited by fraud, and so he claimed that moiety of the goods which was claimed by Wyat.

A replication was put in to this plea in the name of the Attorney General, whereby the time of Wyat's seizure was affirmed and the fraud and priority of Singleton's seizure were traversed. And there, upon an issue joined, [they were] ready for trial.

And, upon the same day the trial was to be and all things [were] ready and the jury [was] at the bar, Singleton came and withdrew his claim and plea. And so the goods were recovered upon the information in Wyat's name, there being no claim entered by or on the behalf of any proprietor, all being carried on at Robertson's charge, though in Wyat's name in trust for Robertson.

And thereupon, Robertson moved the court against Singleton for costs for not letting the cause proceed to trial, reckoning it to be a like case where informers pay costs upon seizures for not going to trial.

And, upon a day given to show cause, the Attorney General, for Singleton, produced Wyatt's release of all costs and demands against Singleton under hand and seal. And whether, against the release, the court should award costs against Singleton was the question, the commissioners of the customs taking part with Singleton.

It seems to me [Edward Ward], first, it is plain Wyatt was but a nominal trustee for Robertson, and why should his release bar costs more than the lessees in [an action of] ejectment.

Second, there is no statute that gives costs upon a seizure for not going to trial; that subsists by the authority and usage of the court only, and Singleton is an informer, though, in this case, he comes in as a defendant, yet so as, if he should prevail, he would be entitled to a moiety by his information.

Third, this trial was to have been between Wyatt and Singleton which of them had the priority of seizure, for none claimed property of the goods to avoid forfeiture and so [it was] a private cause between Wyatt and Singleton and wherein, if Singleton had prevailed, he would have a benefit, and then it being made out by affidavit that Wyatt was Robertson's trustee only, it brings it the nearer to the case of the lessee in ejectment, whose release of costs without consent of the lessor is every day set aside.

Fourth, the court took notice of the bond that Wyat gave to Singleton not to discharge or do anything to the prejudice of the right to the seizure or the recovery of the goods, Robertson bearing all the charges of the seizure, trial, and condemnation and to give Wyat so much.

And, it being made out by affidavit and producing the bond itself, that Singleton, the very day the trial should have been, had given a bond of £1500 to one Francia that, if he could and would at the trial prove that there was a collusion between Robertson and any other so as to make that a fraud and by consequence defeat any discovery on the information in Wyat's name, that then Singleton was to pay Francia £700 in a short time after. Upon which, it was resented by the court that such a bond should be given to procure and reward witnesses in a trial and some of the officers of the customs were witnesses to this bond and some of the commissioners were present in court on the behalf of Wyatt and Singleton. But this bond given by Singleton to Francia being produced, the court took time to consider what to do as to the costs.

And, in the meantime, the parties agreed. And (*prout audivi*) Singleton paid Robertson £100 for costs.

There was an odd recital in the bond to Francia that it would be an acceptable thing to have Wyatt's seizure and information proved to be a fraud and collusion, and that bond was delivered into court in order to have a prosecution upon it. But, after the agreement, it was heard no more of.

Note none appeared to prosecute the wines before Robertson did it in Wyatt's name, and, after that, Singleton was set up to baffle that prosecution. Query for what reason and upon what and whose account.

[Other copies of this report: Georgetown Univ. Law Sch. MS. B88–9, f. 346v.]

277a

Attorney General v. Pearce

(Ex. 1707)

No extent in aid can be superseded until the king's debt has been satisfied.

Indiana Univ., Lilly Library
MS. Parker, 'Cases in the Exchequer', vol. 4, p. 128

1 July 1707.

The Attorney General [sued] upon a [writ of] extent in aid of Mr. Sanson against Charles Pearce, whereby the sheriff of Devonshire seized a great quantity of timber. Mr. Sanson and Mr. Pierce, being agreed, I [PRICE] allowed of a [writ of] *supersedeas* to the extent.

And, it being moved that the [sheriff] should be allowed for his trouble, Chief Baron WARD said that no extent in aid could be superseded until it was known that the king's debt was satisfied, it being [come] to the king's hands by the extent and, though it be in aid, yet the king may detain it for his own debt and so in a judgment on a *quo minus*. The old books say that judgment is in aid for the crown and cannot be discharged before the king is satisfied.

And I [PRICE] [asked] him if that was the practice, which he could not say, but he was angry that he had not the profit, which was always a strong argument with him.

278

Attorney General v. Walker

(Ex. 1707)

In this case of a fidelity bond given by a deceased collector of duties due to the crown, the parties elected not to proceed to a trial.

Lincoln's Inn MS. Misc. 538, p. 15

Michaelmas 1707. Attorney General v. Walker *et ux.*, administratrix of one Bell, upon a *scire facias* upon a bond given by Bell to the late king for his well behavior in his office as collector of the salt duty at Newcastle, containing many particulars.

The defendants first pleaded *plene administravit* generally, which plea being demurred to, they waived it, and then pleaded performance of all things particularly as mentioned in the condition of the bond, which were in the affirmative and particular negatives to those that were in the negative. But there being mention made in the condition of a deputation to Bell and the words of the condition being that Bell should duly perform his duty and trust, which might as well respect what was in the deputation as well as in the condition, and there being no particular answer to that, the Attorney General again demurred. And a rule was given to join in demurrer or judgment [to be given] for the queen.

The defendants this term applied to the court, producing affidavits that neither of them ever saw or could find out or hear where the deputation was, but inclined to believe it was delivered up into the Excise Office, there being a clause in the condition of the bonds for the officers to deliver up their deputations to the commissioners when required. And, therefore, for want of that, they could not put in such a full plea as might be expected, but that, if the Attorney General would let them have either the deputation or a copy of any other usually given to such officers, they would amend their plea in that particular, though they steadfastly insisted that there was no more incumbent upon Bell by the deputation than was in the condition of the bond, the same particulars being in the one and the other.

The defendants' last plea came in time enough to have tried the cause at the Newcastle Assizes if Mr. Attorney General thought fit. And it appeared by an affidavit that the defendants' attorney, at the time when he delivered the last plea, told the attorney in the office for the queen and the solicitor for the excise who followed the suit that, if that plea was not as it ought, let it be known wherein defective, and it should be supplied so that a trial might be had at those Assizes. But these terms not being accepted and the demurrer coming in so late, no trial could be had, nor was had.

And, therefore, Mr. Attorney General [*Harcourt*] and Mr. Solicitor General [*Montagu*], *totis viribus*, insisted for judgment for want of a plea or to argue the demurrer this term.

The court thought either of those two things an extremity. And, therefore, though Mr. Attorney [General] and Mr. Solicitor [General] used very high and pressing arguments to have one or the other under pretense of the great delays used by the defendants, yet the court asserted their right to interpose as to forms of the court and matters of pleading so as not to hinder a trial where the defaults may be recompensed by costs and not have penalties run upon the subject. And, therefore, they thought it reasonable that the defendants should have a deputation given to them of the usual form that the matters alleged to be done or not done by way of breach should be alleged to be in Middlesex and that, by consent, that which would be good evidence at Newcastle should be allowed so in Middlesex and a trial to be in Middlesex next term and the defendants to pay all costs for both demurrers, otherwise, the last demurrer to be joined in and argued this term, to all which all parties agreed at last.

But no trial was ever proceeded to nor arguing of the demurrer nor further proceedings had in the cause, it being thought a needless prosecution, at least not upon reasonable or probable cause.

[Other copies of this report: Georgetown Univ. Law Sch. MS. B88–9, f. 348v, pl. 3.]

279

Ashton v. Firebrace

(Ex. 1707)

A sale upon an execution of a judgment will not be set aside because the purchaser at the sheriff's sale received a very good bargain unless the purchaser participated in a fraud.

Lincoln's Inn MS. Misc. 538, p. 16, pl. 1

Michaelmas [term] 1707. Ashton and Sir Basil Firebrass and Avery.

There having been a former complaint by [Sir Basil] Firebrace [1652–1724] of an extravagant execution for £300 due on a judgment to Ashton issued out of this court whereby it was said that goods to the value of above £500 were by combination between the sheriff of Middlesex's officer and Avery, who bought the goods sold for £300, and that Avery had them. And, *prima facie* upon the bill of sale, it looked very unreasonable.

Yet, after many affidavits on both sides and examining the matter, there could not be anything of fraud charged upon Avery, the former rules for attachments against him *nisi causa* were discharged. But Avery had no costs *propter violentam praesumtionem* and that he had a good bargain, nor can the court, in such a case, award any attachment against the buyer of the goods, as they may against the sheriff or his bailiffs in case they misbehave themselves in the execution unless it plainly appears that such buyer was *particeps criminis.*

[Other copies of this report: Georgetown Univ. Law Sch. MS. B88–9, f. 349v.]

280

Attorney General v. Butterworth

(Ex. 1707)

In this case, a claimant of land in execution upon a writ of extent was allowed to prove his right by producing a deed in court.

Lincoln's Inn MS. Misc. 538, p. 16, pl. 2

Michaelmas [term] 1707.

The defendants' [Alexander Butterworth's and one Holt's] lands were extended in Lancashire and, by an inquisition taken many years since, seized into the king's hands for a debt by bond to King Charles II and so remained extended to this day. The benefit of that extent was granted to Mr. Barnardiston. And he and Butterworth, by agreement between themselves, took the profits until about the year 1691. And, then, differences arising between them, contests at law touching the extended premises happened. And the grant of the extended premises proving defective by the mistake of the date of inquisition, the queen renewed the grant to the executors of Mr. Barnardiston with a grant of all the arrears of the extended premises, for which process of *levari facias* issued last term.

And one Holt, as terre tenant, comes in and pleads a conveyance of the extended premises to him before the inquisition, *viz.* 1663, and he traverses the seisin of Butterworth at or since the debt to the crown.

And, upon *oyer* of that conveyance, it appeared that it was not defeasible or redeemable upon certain provisos and conditions in an indenture tripartite contained. But what those conditions were *non constat.*

And, therefore, the Attorney General [*Harcourt*] moved the court that he might have *oyer* of the indenture tripartite or at least a copy of it, the plea being imperfect without it, for he may reply a performance of those conditions, then there will be either an estate or a trust for Butterworth, which, in the queen's case makes the lands liable and drives not the queen to her bill in equity, as in a subject's case it might. And if this was not done by Holt, that then he may not have a commission to take security in the country upon putting in his plea with and without security process issues to levy the arrears, besides, in the nature of the thing, the deed pleaded is not a substantive but a relative title and, without the tripartite indenture, there is not a complete title made to the lands in question to amove the queen's hands, whereto the court inclined.

But then Holt's counsel agreed to produce the tripartite indenture and let Mr. Attorney General have a copy of it and then the pleader to have a commission for taking the security touching mesne profits, which was agreed to be in £1000.

[Other copies of this report: Georgetown Univ. Law Sch. MS. B88–9, f. 350.]

[Related cases: Attorney General, *ex rel.* Barnardiston v. Butterworth (Ex. 1711), Equity Cases Exch. 666.]

281

Pemberton v. Beckwith

(Ex. 1707)

In this tithe case, the parson had received part of his tithe of wool and lambs and was allowed to sue for the remainder.

Dodd 210, 1 Rayner 110,
2 Gwillim 603, 1 Eagle & Younge 682

In a tithe bill, it appeared that the defendant had shorn his sheep and laid the wool up in a heap and set eight fleeces for the plaintiff and, when his tithe gatherer came, told him there was the tithe but would not let him break up the heap or tell the heap, and the man took them but said he took them in part, but that they were not his master's full due.

Also in the lambs, the defendant had a field in another parish and took out some lambs for that, and then the rest was tithed; but also in tithing, the defendant took out two and then bid the parson's man take out a third for his tenth lamb, but he insisted he ought to take a second, yet he took the third but said it was not right, and his master would sue.

And upon hearing, the court decreed for the complainant and [held] that the wool and lamb taken should go but in part and be allowed upon the account in part only, and not like the case where corn is tithed unequally and the tithe taken, there the parson shall be bound and cannot falsify and take only in part. Query the diversity. But [it was] asserted by the Chief Baron [Ward] *vehementer.*

Note: The Chief Baron [Ward] said that these eight fleeces should go for tithe as to the tale, and should not be examined as to the largeness of them but, if ten were due, then he should account for the rest.

282

Attorney General v. Tredinham

(Ex. 1707)

In this case, the proceedings to enforce the bond in issue were faulty, and the execution was denied.

Lincoln's Inn MS. Misc. 535, f. [216v]

The *scire facias* set forth that, the 24th of June 4 Will. & Mar. [1692], Brett and others became bound by bond of £200 penalty to Sir Robert Cotton and Mr. Frankland, who were then postmasters, though not so mentioned, and that the 10th of May 7 Will. III [1695], the obligees, by their deed enrolled in this court, assigned the said bond and certain articles dated 24th June 4 Will. & Mar. [1692] made between the said obligors and obligees and the whole benefit thereof and of all suits and judgments thereupon unto his said Majesty and that, by an inquisition of the 31st of May 7 Will. III [1695] taken in London upon a [writ of] extent against the said Brett, it was found that the defendant Tredinham and one Turner were bound in a bond of the penalty of £200 dated the 20th of February 1691[/92] unto the said Brett with a condition for payment of £114 with interest at a day past, which said writing obligatory and the debt thereupon due, the said sheriffs of London the day of the taking of the said inquisition *virtute brevis praedictis in manus nostras cepi et fieri fecerunt prout per brevem praedictam et return' eiusdem ac dict' inquir' eidem annexo in scrinium nostram certificat' etc. plene apparet.* Then the *scire facias*, to the sheriff of Middlesex directed, is for the defendant to show cause why the queen should not have execution against him for the said £200.

The defendant comes in and alleges that the writ of *scire facias* is not sufficient in law for the queen to have any execution for that £200 debt and that he is not bound in law to answer to it. And so, by way of demurrer, he prays judgment if the queen *ob insufficientiam eiusdem brevis* ought to have any execution against him upon the said *scire facias*.

The Attorney General, by way of joinder in demurrer, says the writ is sufficient to have execution upon it for the queen.

The fault assigned in the *scire facias* was that it sets forth that the defendant's bond was seized into the queen's hand by the sheriffs of London upon an extent and inquisition taken 7 Will. III, which is impossible and repugnant and the court have nothing before them in judgment but this writ which no doubt was a mistake as to the seizure and that it was into the late king's hands, yet this court must judge upon it and, therefore, cannot [upon] that mistake award execution. And, therefore, they must [and] did give judgment for the defendant and left Mr. Attorney [General] to take out a new *scire facias*, as by law he might.

[Other copies of this report: Georgetown Univ. Law Sch. MS. B88–9, f. 344.]

283

Hopkins v. The African Company

(Ex. 1707)

In this case, the defendants' insufficient plea in bar was held not to be a plea in abatement, and judgment was given for the plaintiff.

Lincoln's Inn MS. Misc. 535, f. [217]

[An action of] debt was brought upon several of the defendant's bonds entered into by the defendants under their common seal to the plaintiff for payment of divers great sums of money at [. . .] days past.

The defendants put in a rambling and utterly insufficient plea, upon which no issue could be taken, but pleaded it in bar to the action [. . .] plaintiff prayed his judgment alleging it to be a dilatory plea, within the late Act for Amendment of the Law,[1] and so not to be received.

But the court, after a conference with the judges of the other courts, held that [. . .] plea that is pleaded in bar is not to be understood a dilatory plea within that Act. And, therefore, they put the defendant to plead as they would abide by it by a [. . .], and they abiding by their plea, judgment upon a demurrer was given for the plaintiff.

And, thereupon, a writ of error was brought and security given [. . .] upon it for delay only.

[Other copies of this report: Georgetown Univ. Law Sch. MS. B88–9, f. 345.]

284

Winter v. Hodgson

(Ex. 1707)

A mistake in the record that was made by a clerk of the court can be cured by an amendment.

The void parts of an arbitral award will be disregarded, and the valid remainder of the award is good and enforceable.

An arbitral award of any matters not submitted by the parties to arbitration is ultra vires and, thus, unenforceable.

Lincoln's Inn MS. Misc. 535, f. [227]

Hilary [term] 5 Annae reginae 1706[/07]. John Winter, plaintiff; John Hodgson, Esq., defendant. In Officio Placitorum Scaccario.

---

[1] Stat. 4 & 5 Ann., c. 3 (*SR*, VIII, 458–461).

In [an action of] debt upon a bond of £500 entered into by the defendant to the plaintiff 24 August 3 Anne, 1704, conditioned for the defendant's performance of the award of three arbitrators there named, touching all matters in difference between the parties so as the said award of the arbitrators or any two of them for upon the premises be made under their hands and seals ready to be given up etc. on or before the 1st of December next.

The defendant pleads that the arbitrators took upon them the arbitration and made their award the said 1st of December *prout* and reciting thereby that they had examined the matters, pretensions, and demands between the parties and, *inter alia*, that the defendant demanded of the plaintiff £62 or thereabouts pursuant to an award then before made by Dr. Fenton in a cause wherein Bradly was the plaintiff and others and the now plaintiff the defendant and that these now arbitrators had taken into their consideration the said sum by the said other award given and that upon the stating and balancing of the whole accounts between the parties, the now arbitrators had made allowance to the now defendant for £31, his full provision of the said £62 so demanded by virtue of Dr. Fenton's award. The now arbitrators awarded *de et concernente* the premises in the manner following, *viz.*, first that the parties should each bear their own charges in any court of law or equity or otherwise before the 24th of August *tertio Annae Reginae* [1704]. Then, in reciting further that, upon a fair stating and balancing of all accounts and demands, the arbitrators found that the defendant was indebted to the plaintiff £54 8s. 10½d. [and] they awarded the defendant to pay that sum to the plaintiff in nine days after the date of the award or give the plaintiff good security for the payment of it within six months after the date of the award [and] that the parties, upon request, should seal and deliver mutual general releases of actions etc. and demands in law or equity for all things before the 24th of August.

The defendant avers that the plaintiff's bill was exhibited before the expiration of the six months for the security. And he prays judgment *si actio*.

The plaintiff replies *praecludi non*, confessing the award as set forth by the defendant and that, though he, the plaintiff, has performed all things on his part by the award to be performed, yet the defendant, within the nine days after the date of the award, did not pay him the £54 8s. 10½d. nor gave him security for the payment of it within six months after the date of the award *secundum ordinem et appunctuationem* of the award, *et hoc paratus*, and he prays judgment and his debt.

The defendant rejoins that the plaintiff has not performed all things on his part in the award to be performed as he has above alleged. *Et de hoc ponit se super patriam*.

To this rejoinder, the plaintiff demurs, and, for cause, shows, first, that the rejoinder is a departure from his plea, second, that the plea answers not the matter assigned for breach of the award if, to any things in the answer thereto, the defendant ought to be admitted. *Et non refert* whether the plaintiff had performed anything in the award unless the defendant had performed his part.

The defendant joins in demurrer.

Note, in this case, there was a great mistake for the defendant, praying *oyer* of the bond and condition, sets the condition forth to be if the plaintiff Winter, whereas it should have been if the defendant Hodgson performed the award, but this not being espied, it was thus entered of record and argued by counsel on both sides, and the mistake discovered by the court, which put the plaintiff to a nonplus, and having bail to his action was not willing to discontinue the action, which would loose his bail.

And, therefore, in Easter term 1707, Serjeant *Chesshyre* moved to have the mistake amended and a true *oyer* of the plaintiff's bond (the other set forth being the defendant's bond and he himself set it forth) to be had and alleged to be reasonable, because *oyer* is the act of the court and, therefore, the court may amend. 5 rep., Wymarke's [Case], if the fault of the clerk, [it is] amendable. He relies upon Cro. Car. 147, Forger and Sales; this was by consent, which the defendant refuses here. 1 Lutwych 508; Hetly 143, 148. But Cro. Car. was [. . .] wherein the material words that bound the heir were left out by the clerk's default, who owned it on examination; 1 Edw. IV, 2; 18 Edw. IV, 13; 22 Edw. IV, 22; L. 5 Edw. IV, 4b; Michaelmas 1694, Nurse and Frampton, words omitted [were] added; Cook and Hart [. . .] of bond mistaken amended.[1]

And, upon examination in court, it was amended, 16 May 1707.

[Other copies of this report: Georgetown Univ. Law Sch. MS. B88–9, f. 321.]

Lincoln's Inn MS. Misc. 535, f. [216]

The amendment being made as there appears, the defendant's counsel took exceptions to the award, first, that the award was void because it awarded the defendant to pay to the plaintiff £54 8s. 10½d. in nine days after the date of the award or give the plaintiff good security for the payment of it within six months after the date of the award and, that part of the award for giving security being void (as was admitted by the plaintiff's counsel), that vitiates the whole award, for arbitrators must make a certain final judgment, which they have not done here, but left that part of their judgment at the defendant's election, which, though it be void as to that part, yet it shows the uncertainty of their judgment.

To which was answered by the plaintiff's counsel and resolved by the whole court, according to the reason and authority of the cases 1 Leon., fo. 14 and 304,

[1] *Dun v. Law* (1593), 5 Coke Rep. 74, 77 E.R. 165; *Forger v. Sales* (1629), Croke Car. 147, 79 E.R. 730, also W. Jones 199, 82 E.R. 106; *Rooke v. Clealand* (1704), 1 Lutwyche 503, 508, 125 E.R. 264, 267; *Worthly v. Savill* (1629), Hetley 142, 143, 124 E.R. 408, 409, also Littleton 278, 124 E.R. 245; *Clotworthy v. Clotworthy* (1629), Hetley 137, 148, 124 E.R. 404, 413, also Hutton 82, 123 E.R. 1116, Croke Car. 436, 79 E.R. 979; YB Mich. 18 Edw. IV, f. 13, pl. 11 (1478); *Anonymous v. Hatley* (1482), YB Mich. 22 Edw. IV, f. 21, pl. 49 [1]; *Nurse v. Frampton* (1694), Comberbach 299, 90 E.R. 489, 1 Lord Raymond 28, 91 E.R. 519, 1 Salkeld 214, 91 E.R. 191.

and Owen 153, that, where two things are awarded and one of them is void and the other good, that a breach may be assigned for that which is good without taking notice of that which is void. So is the later resolution, *viz*. 2 Sanders 237.[1]

A second exception was taken that, here, the arbitrators had taken upon them to intermeddle and found their award upon matters between strangers, taking notice of Dr. Fenton's award, a cause wherein Bradly and others were plaintiffs and the now plaintiff, the defendant, and given an abatement and allowance of £31, part of the £62 therein mentioned, and it not appearing that that matter was submitted, but concerned a stranger, as Bradly was, the arbitrators had exceeded their authority and meddled with a matter relating to a stranger which vitiated their whole award. And for that, they relied upon the reason of the law and the authority of the case 2 Levins 235 and 1 Lutwich 541.[2]

And, of that opinion was Baron Price in the case in question.

The Chief Baron [Edward Ward] and the other two barons agreed the law to be that, where awards concerning stranger's matters not submitted, that, as to them, the awards are void. But they did not conceive this case to be so, for whatever was done here in relation to Fenton's award or Bradly was only an instruction to the arbitrators how matters stood between the plaintiff and the defendant by way of recital only and not in the awarding part, for the arbitrators *de et super praemissis*, which must be understood to be upon the premises submitted, first, that each party bear his own charges in law and equity, secondly, that, upon a fair stating and balancing of all accounts and demands, they found the defendant indebted to the plaintiff £54 8s. 10½d., which they awarded him to pay in nine days, for the non-payment of which, the breach was assigned, which is a substantive and final and certain award of itself and that, therefore, the plaintiff ought to have judgment, which was given accordingly.

[Other copies of this report: Georgetown Univ. Law Sch. MS. B88–9, f. 343.]

Indiana Univ., Lilly Library
MS. Parker 'Cases in the Exchequer', vol. 4, p. 131

[In an action of] debt on an award, the exception to the award was that the award was for the defendant, within six days after the award, to pay the plaintiff £54 or give security, and it does not say in what sum or whether by bond or in what manner. It is an uncertain and a void award for that, but [. . .] one part of the award to pay the money was certain, that is good. And, if the assignment had been only in that, it had been good, being void for the rest.

---

1 *Wilmer v. Oldfield* (1587), 1 Leonard 140, 304, 74 E.R. 130, 277, Owen 153, 74 E.R. 969; *Cooke v. Whorewood* (1671), 2 Williams Saunders 337, 85 E.R. 1135, also 2 Levinz 6, 83 E.R. 427, 2 Keble 767, 84 E.R. 485.

2 *Adams v. Statham* (1678), 2 Levinz 235, 83 E.R. 535, also *sub nom. Adams v. Staley*, 2 Shower K.B. 61, 89 E.R. 793; *Elliott v. Chevall* (1704), 1 Lutwyche 541, 125 E.R. 284.

5 Rep., Salmon's Case; Cro. Jac. 314, Thyn v. Right;[1] 1 Leon. 140, 304, Wilmar v. Oldfield; Hilary 5 Anne, Common Bench, rot. 28 [?], Alcock v. Gordon; 2 Sand. 337, Cole v. Sanders, [. . .] El. 4.

The second exception [was] that the award recited an award wherein [. . .] Bradley and Winter for £64 and that £32 thereof was allowed the defendant [on] that account which was awarding a [. . .] out of the submission contained after and that Winter might be sued by Bradley for the whole sum awarded, notwithstanding £32 was allowed Hodgson, nor does it appear that Hodgson was any way concerned in the submission.

Mr. Baron Price [held] that it was a void award as to that part and that, if Bradley sued Winter, this payment or allowance was no discharge. 2 Levinz 235. And though the allowance of £32 was but in the recital of the award, yet it was part of the award. 1 Lutw. 541, Elliot v. Chival; Yelv. 98.[2]

The Chief Baron [Ward], Bury and Smith were of the opinion that it was a good award, and judgment [was given] for the plaintiff.

Serjeant *Chesshyre, pro querente*; *Phipps*, for the defendant.

285

Marsh v. Williams

(Ex. 1707)

If a variance is to be cured by an amendment, the opposing party is entitled to a continuance.

Lincoln's Inn MS. Misc. 535, f. [231], pl. 1

The plaintiff sued the defendant on a bond of £2060, and took out a special [writ of] *quo minus* in debt which contains in itself the whole cause of action and declaration and to which writ the defendant is to plead forthwith without any imparlance. But, instead of £2060, £2000 only was mentioned in the writ, which varied from the bond.

The defendant was arrested upon this writ, and gave a warrant to appear and plead to it an issuable [plea] and no dilatory plea. But the defendant's attorney, espying the variance, offered a plea in abatement.

The plaintiff moved the court that he [the defendant] might plead forthwith in chief and the mistake be amended, which the court could not do in this case without an imparlance, which the defendant offered. But the plaintiff refused. And, so, nothing was done.

[Other copies of this report: Georgetown Univ. Law Sch. MS. B88–9, f. 329, pl. 1.]

---

[1] *Samon v. Pitt* (1594), 5 Coke Rep. 77, 77 E.R. 172, also Croke Eliz. 432, 78 E.R. 672, Moore K.B. 359, 72 E.R. 628; *Thinne v. Rigby* (1611), Croke Jac. 269, 79 E.R. 269.

[2] *Markham v. Jurex* (1607), Yelverton 97, 80 E.R. 66, also 1 Brownlow & Goldesborough 92, 123 E.R. 686, *sub nom. Gennings v. Markham*, Croke Jac. 149, 79 E.R. 130.

286

Johnson v. Boyse

(Ex. 1707)

Where salt is exported to a lawful destination, the specific destination is not material to the refunding of the export duties.

Lincoln's Inn MS. Misc. 535, f. [231v]

Thomas Johnson, Esq. vs. Boyse, in an action upon the case and a demurrer to the declaration, entered in the Office of Pleas in the Exchequer, Michaelmas [term] 5 Queen Anne. Lancaster.

The plaintiff declares and sets forth the Act of Parliament 5 Will. & Mar., ca. [*blank*],[1] for granting certain rates and duties upon salt etc. and that clause therein that, if any should export beyond the sea any such salt, the salt officer of that place where salt shall be made or imported and the duty paid or secured shall deliver *gratis* a certificate under his hand and seal that the duty was paid or secured. And, then, the officer of the place where the said salt shall be exported upon producing of that certificate and oath of the shipping and not re-landing of the salt in England or Wales shall give a debenture under his hand for the repayment of that duty, which being produced to the officers of the place where the duty was paid or secured, the security or money paid for the duty shall be re-paid and re-delivered without a fee or reward.

And he sets forth another Act of Parliament made 9 Will. III, ca. [*blank*],[2] that, if any should export beyond the sea foreign or home-made salt and pay or secure the duty, the officers of such place should give a certificate under their hands and seals that the duty for such salt was paid or secured upon producing whereof to the officer of the exporting port and oath made of the shipping and not re-landing thereof in England or Wales, the said officer said give a debenture under his hand for the repayment of that duty, which being produced to the officer of the place where the duty was paid or secured, the duty paid shall be re-paid or the security delivered up.

And he sets forth another Act made *primo Annae Reginae*, ca. 21, fo. 303[3] reciting that, by the acts for laying duties on salt to be transported, the persons exporting were entitled to drawbacks for the whole duty and that, by experience, it was found that the exporters, after they had obtained drawbacks or debentures re-landed the salt in England or Wales without paying duties upon such re-landing, to prevent which, it was enacted that, after 24 June 1702, no drawback should be allowed for or by reason of any exportation of any salt for the kingdom

---

[1] Stat. 5 Will. & Mar., c. 7 (*SR*, VI, 447–461).

[2] Stat. 9 Will. III, c. 6 (*SR*, VII, 302).

[3] Stat. 1 Ann., c. 15 (*SR*, VIII, 60–66).

of Ireland until the exporter should produce to the officer appointed to make such debenture a certificate under the hand of the collector of the customs of that port in Ireland where such salt shall be landed or the person executing that office of the particular quantity of the salt actually landed to be computed after the rates in that Act, *viz.* £56 a bushel English white salt, £65 a bushel for English rock salt, and £84 for foreign salt and that the same were weighed there, the certificate to be given *gratis* without delay and no drawback is to be allowed for more salt than shall be contained in such certificate to be actually landed in Ireland.

Then, the plaintiff shows that, after the 24th of June 1702 and before the 12th of January 1705[/06], *scil.* such a day, at Liverpool in Lancashire, as the true proprietor, he caused 5550 bushels of rock salt after the aforesaid rate of £65 to the bushel to be made and paid the duty of it to Carvile, the proper officer for the queen of Liverpool, and, the 4th of February 1705[/06], he entered the same in the Custom House of the port of Liverpool to be transported in the ship *Neptune* (Henry Smith, master) to Bergen in the king of Denmark's dominions. And, then and there, he caused that salt to be loaded aboard the said ship. And, after the 21st of May 1706, one Foster Cunliff, the plaintiff's agent, the plaintiff still being owner and exporter of the salt, at Liverpool, before such a one, collector of the customs there and the proper officer according to the Statute, made an oath that the salt was exported or shipped out in the said ship to be really therein and from thence exported to parts beyond the seas and not intended to be re-landed in England, Wales, or Berwick upon Tweed and that the duty for the same was actually paid without discount. And, afterwards, *viz.* 21 June 1706, the said Smith, the master of the said ship, with the said salt therein laden directly and voluntarily sailed from Liverpool to the port of Cork in Ireland, and there arrived. And, there, one Delahude unloaded the salt out of the said ship, and put it on land, and left it. [He said] that no part of the salt loaded aboard that ship was re-landed in England, Wales, or Berwick, that immediately after the landing of the salt at Cork, one Jamette, the collector of the customs there, caused the salt to be weighed. And it thereby appeared to him that there were of it 5530 bushels computed as aforesaid then and there landed, the residue before the landing begin wasted.

[He said] that, thereupon, Jamette, the same day, made a certificate in writing under his hand that the said quantity was landed there, which certificate the plaintiff, the 1st of August 1706 showed to the defendant then and before and after being the proper officer of the port of Liverpool and such a person to whom, according to the Act and duty of his place, it appertained to make such a debenture, and he offered to him the said certificate, and demanded a debenture from him according to the Act so that the plaintiff, by virtue thereof, might have a drawback, according to the Statute in that behalf.

But he, not weighing the Statute and fraudulently intending to damnify the plaintiff and deprive him of the benefit of the debenture and to hinder him from receiving to his own use a great sum of money against the form of the Statute and the duty of his office, utterly refused to make or give to the plaintiff any debenture concerning the premises, whereby the plaintiff is deprived of his proper or other remedy for his drawback, to the plaintiff's damage £1100 etc., *cum hoc* that the plaintiff avers that there is and time out of mind has been a custom in England among merchants and others *commercium habentes* and transporting merchandise beyond the seas, for the better security and profit of commerce that if any master or other such person intending to transport his goods out of England to any certain port or place purposed to himself not prohibited has used and accustomed to enter such his goods with the officers of the Custom House as if intended to be exported to any other lawful place out of England to carry at his pleasure and such entry and exportation has been allowed as good and lawful as if the real port of discharge had been named in the entry.

To this declaration, the defendant has demurred generally, and the plaintiff has joined.

The general question in this case is whether the merchant can maintain this action against the queen's officer for not granting him a debenture for the drawback of salt shipped and duty paid at Liverpool and entered for Bergen but willingly and directly carried to Cork in Ireland and there landed, measured, and certified as the Statute of 1 Anne directs in respect that Act, in express terms and for preventing deceits, provided that no debenture shall be made nor drawn back after 24 June 1702 be allowed for salt for or under the Act of exportation for Ireland until the exporter produces to the officer who is to make the debenture a certificate under the hand of the collector of the customs of the port in Ireland where the salt is landed of the particular quantity of salt there actually landed, computed, and weighed as aforesaid, and no drawback to be allowed for more salt than what appears by such certificate to be actually landed in Ireland.

First, this Act does not prohibit the exportation of salt to Ireland;

Second, but it regulates the way and manner of granting debentures for salt to be exported for Ireland, that none shall be granted until a certificate be returned from Ireland of the landing there and the quantity so landed;

Third, that the way of granting debentures for the exportation of salt to the other parts beyond the seas (not Ireland) is on oath made of duties paid and shipping for exportation and not re-landing, and, thereupon, to have the drawback, which is not touched on by the Statute 1 of the queen, but subsists by the precedent acts;

Fourth, whether there be any mischief follow upon the merchant's entering out for other parts beyond the seas than there would be in case the salt had been entered out for a port in Ireland, in regard no debenture is to be made out or drawback allowed until a certificate that all is punctually performed in Ireland as the Act directs.

But this action was not proceeded upon, for what reason, I [Edward Ward] know not, but that the parties agreed.

It seems to me [Edward Ward] a good cause of action, and [there is] no mischief to the queen or the revenue.

Note, afterwards, by a clause, fo. 288, in the 5th year of Her Majesty's reign, ca. [*blank*],[1] for the ease of Her Majesty's subjects in relation to salt etc., it is enacted that the merchant exporter, as this case was, shall be entitled to the drawback and all suits brought against any for such exportation to cease and determine, which clause was calculated for this very case.

[Other copies of this report: Georgetown Univ. Law Sch. MS. B88–9, f. 329v.]

287

Johnson, ex dem. Earl of Anglesey v. Earl of Derby

(Ex. 1707–1710)

In this case, the entail in issue was held to be a fraudulent contrivance and thus not within the Statute 34 Hen. VIII and thus the conveyance in issue was valid.

Where the parties consent, blanks in deeds may be filled up later after the execution of the deed.

N. Pigott, *Common Recoveries* (1739), p. 201

Trinity 6 Anne, in the Court of Exchequer, in [an action of] ejectment; Lancaster; John Johnson, on the demise of John, earl of Anglesey, and Henrietta Maria, his wife, and Lady Elizabeth Stanley, spinster, plaintiffs; James, earl of Derby, and others his tenants, defendants.

Of, *inter alia*, the Manor of Lathom and several thousand acres of land in Lathom and other places in the County of Lancaster, on not guilty pleaded on a trial at the Lancaster Assizes, the jury found several general verdicts as to parcels and *inter alia* as to Cross Hall in Lathom, and all the premises, except the residue of the Manor of Lathom, 2000 acres of land in Lathom, parcel of the same manor, the Manor of Newburgh, 250 acres of land in Newburgh in Lathom and New Park in Lathom, the earl is found not guilty, and, as to the particulars excepted, find a special verdict that William, earl of Derby, was seised thereof in fee, and being so seised, to the intent that Sir Thomas Leigh and others might convey the same to Queen Elizabeth, her heirs, and successors, and that the earl might accept from the queen a grant to the earl and heirs male of his body, and for default of such issue, to the heirs male of the body of Sir George Stanley, formerly lord Strange, and should leave the reversion in the crown, enfeoffed the said Sir Thomas Leigh, and others, and their heirs. And the said feoffees, being by virtue thereof seised in fee, did, in pursuance of the said intent, by deed enrolled, convey the same the eighth of December 43 Eliz. [1600] to the queen, her heirs, and

[1] Stat. 4 & 5 Ann., c. 23, s. 11 (*SR*, VIII, 509).

successors; that Queen Elizabeth, in further pursuance of the same intention, the seventh of January, by her letters patent, for divers good causes and considerations, the queen, specially moving and at the petition of the said earl, conveyed the same to the said William, earl of Derby, and the heirs male of his body and, for default of such issue, to the heirs male of the body of the said Sir George Stanley to be held of the queen, her heirs, and successors by the service of one knight's fee; that an Act of Parliament was made the eighteenth of November, 4 Jac. I [1606], whereby it was enacted, 'That the said William, earl of Derby, and the heirs male of his body, and in default of such issue, then the heirs male of the body of the said Sir George Stanley, should enjoy the last mentioned premises and that the king should hold such estate, right, title, interest, and reversion, as if the Act had not been made'; that the said reversion descended from the said queen to King James I and that the said reversion descended from him to King Charles I; that King Charles I, the eleventh of July in the eleventh year of his reign [1635], made an award under his privy seal that William, earl of Derby, and James, lord Strange, should grant a rent charge of £600 a year, out of an estate of sufficient value to Charles Stanley and the heirs male of his body, and for default of such issue, to James Stanley and the heirs male of his body; that King Charles I, afterwards, by letters patent the third of July, 13 Car. I [1637], reciting the letters patent of Queen Elizabeth, the Act of Parliament, and the award, and to enable the said James, lord Strange, to perform the award, granted the reversion to the said James, lord Strange, and his heirs, to be held by the same services; the king, by the same letters patent, willed and declared that the said James, lord Strange, within a year after the date thereof, should cause the reversion to be granted or limited that the lands etc. should revert to the king in the same manner as if the letters patent had not been made, chargeable nevertheless with a rent charge; the eleventh of August, 13 Car. I [1637], for performance of that award by indenture enrolled in Chancery, the said earl of Derby and James, lord Strange, covenanted to convey within two years the same premises by fine to the intent the rent charge might be paid according to the award, and that the premises in question should go chargeable therewith to the use of the said William, earl of Derby, and the heirs male of his body and, for default of such issue, to the heirs male of the body of Sir George Stanley, lord Strange, and, for default of such issue, to the use of James, lord Strange, his heirs, and assigns; twenty-first of August 15 Car. I [1639], a fine was levied of the Manor of Lathom to the uses in the covenant, and there were proclamation thereupon; that neither James, lord Strange, nor his heirs of assigns did within one year convey the reversion, so as the premises might revert; that Earl William was seised by virtue of the estate tail, which was descended to the said James, lord Strange, and afterwards to Charles, earl of Derby, and afterwards to William George Richard, earl of Derby; that William George Richard, being so seised in tail, made an indenture, bearing date the eighteenth of August 13 Will. III [1637] and sealed and delivered the thirtieth of the same August; the indenture is found *in haec verba*, and appears to be a bargain and sale for a year, from the earl of Derby to John Thornton and John Hayes of the Manor of Lathom, the capital messuage and demesne lands, park, wastes and rents of or in the said manor, and all lands and hereditaments in Lathom, in the actual tenure or occupation of the said earl, and divers lands and hereditaments in other places, in the possession of several tenants therein named; that the said William George Richard, earl of Derby, made another indenture, dated the nineteenth of August, but first sealed by him the thirtieth of August, the same year; this indenture is found *in haec verba*, and appears to be a release from the same earl of the same premises to Thornton and Hayes and their heirs in order to made them tenants to the *praecipe*; that, at the time of sealing the two indentures, there were blank spaces left immediately after the words 'John Harrock' in order to insert the names of other tenants of lands in the towns mentioned in those indentures; that a writ of entry was sued out of the Manor of Lathom etc.; the nineteenth of August 13 Will. III, returnable the first day of the next general session of the Assizes at Lancaster; that the first day of the next Assizes, to wit Wednesday the third day of September, 13 Will. III, the writ was returned; the second day the earl, who is vouched and summoned, appeared and vouched the common vouchee, and thereupon a recovery is suffered, and the demandants have judgment to recover seisin, and pray a writ of seisin, returnable on Monday next in the same session; that on Friday the fifth of September the spaces were filled up with the names of several other tenants of lands in the same manors and towns, which names were inserted by the said Thornton, party to the deeds; the jury further find that William George Richard, earl of Derby, being so seised as aforesaid of the said residue of the said Manor of Lathom and the said 2000 acres of land in Lathom, the said manor of Newburgh, 250 acres of land, parcel thereof Newburgh in Lathom, of New Park, and of the messuage and 60 acres in Lathom, called New Park, 2 August 29 Car. II [1677], in consideration of 5s., made a bargain and sale for a year to Heneage, lord Finch, and others of *inter alia* the said Manor of Newburgh and New Park in Lathom; that the third of August the same year, he made an indenture of release of the same premises to the same parties and their heirs; the release is found *in haec verba*, and is *inter alia* of the Manor of Newburgh and New Park, to hold the same to the trustees and their heirs, to the use of the trustees and their heirs, during the life of Dorothea Helena, then countess dowager of Derby, in trust to pay her a rent of £600 a year quarterly for her life and from and after her decease, then as to the Manor of Newburgh and New Park, to and for the uses of such persons for such estates and with such powers and with such remainders as in and by the said Act of Parliament of the fourth of King James I is limited and expressed and in such sort and manner as the same should have gone if this present settlement had not been made, and the said earl covenants to levy a fine to the uses in that deed; that a fine was levied accordingly the twentieth of August 30 Car. II [1678] with proclamations of *inter alia* the Manor of Newburgh and New Park in Lathom; that the Manor of Newburgh and 250 acres of land, part thereof, lie in Lathom; that New Park, at the time of the settlement, 29 Car. II, was parcel of the Manor of Lathom, and was ever since reputed parcel thereof; but both Newburgh and New Park, at the time of the settlement 29 Car. II and the recovery 15 Will. III, were in the possession of Dorothea Helena, countess dowager of Derby, and the said lord Finch and others the trustees, at the same times, were seised thereof for the life of the said countess dowager; they find that William, earl of Derby, had issue, James, who had issue Charles, who had issue William George Richard, who died without issue male 4 November 1702; that the defendant Earl James is heir male of the body of Charles and younger brother of the last earl, William George Richard, and great grandson and heir male of the body of the said Earl William; that the lessors, the countess of Anglesey and Lady Elizabeth Stanley, are daughters and coheirs of Earl William George Richard; that, on his death they entered and made the lease to the plaintiff *prout* etc., and whether the defendant the earl be guilty as to these, the jury submit to the judgment of the court.

Lord Chief Baron Ward was of opinion with the defendants, as to the Manor of Lathom etc. on the Stat. 34 Hen. VIII,[1] which restrains tenants in tail of the gift of the crown from aliening, against the opinion of the other three barons, who held the entail in this case was a fraudulent contrivance, not within the meaning of this Statute. The case on the Statute of Mortmain was cited, as it appears in Farmer's Case, 3 Co. 78b, and more largely in Magdalen's College Case, 11 Co. 73b, 74.[2]

As to the filling up the blanks after the first day of the Assizes, they all agreed, that, being by consent of the parties, though the words inserted might be void, it could not avoid the deeds as to what was contained therein at the time of sealing; and besides, the deeds had then done their office, and made a good tenant to the praecipe for the Manor of Lathom and what was comprised in the deeds the first day of the Assizes.

As to Newburgh and New Park, Baron Price cited the Case 1 Inst. 324b that, if a lease for life was made, the reversion remains parcel of the manor and passes with the manor, which was not denied by any of the barons, and seemed to be agreed by all. But they distinguished this case, as being by deed and fine, and held it therefore a discontinuance and a temporary severance during the life of Dorothea Helena, countess dowager of Derby; and, therefore, the recovery was void as to these for want of a good tenant to the praecipe.

And, pursuant to this judgment in ejectment, the whole Manor of Lathom (except Newburgh and New Park and except Cross Hall, which stood upon another title) was adjudged for the defendant, and therewith above £1000 *per an-*

---

[1] Stat. 34 & 35 Hen. VIII, c. 20 (*SR*, III, 919–920).

[2] Stat. 7 Edw. I (*SR*, I, 51); *Fermor v. Smith* (Ch. 1602), 3 Coke Rep. 77, 76 E.R. 800, also 2 Anderson 176, 123 E.R. 607, Jenkins 253, 145 E.R. 180; *Warren v. Smith* (1615), 11 Coke Rep. 66, 77 E.R. 1235, also 1 Rolle Rep. 151, 81 E.R. 394, 2 Bulstrode 146, 80 E.R. 1021, Croke Jac. 364, 79 E.R. 312.

num in leases for lives have been held and enjoyed under this recovery ever since, as parcel of the manor wherein the entail was barred by this recovery.

N.B. Upon the death of William George Richard, earl of Derby, Mr. Starkey of Preston was appointed by Earl James and Mr. Ward by the coheirs to inspect the writings and adjust their respective rights to the estates of the deceased earl. And this point, *viz.* that the reversions on leases for lives passed by this recovery as parcel of the manor, was agreed by them and, afterwards, upon a reference to the earls of Pembroke, Rochester, and Scarborough, the same point was admitted. And lastly, after the judgment given in the Exchequer upon a reference to Mr. Richard Webb and others, whereby at last all remaining disputes were settled between the heir male of Earl William and the right heirs of the late Earl William George Richard. All the Manor of Lathom in possession and reversion, except Cross Hall, Newburgh, and New Park, was awarded to the right heirs, and the same have since been sold and enjoyed accordingly.

And note the determination by the barons in the case of Newburgh and New Park that the fine in this case made the severance of these parcels from the manor, seems to imply that in other cases where there is no fine, there is no severance, but the reversion in fee remains parcel, and passes with the manor according to the former authorities.

Lincoln's Inn MS. Misc. 535, f. [234v]

Hilary [term] 1706[/07].

In an [action of] ejectment for lands in Lancashire upon the demise of the earl of Anglesey against the earl of Derby, defendant, et e contra, the earl of Anglesey complained of an order of the court for the [. . .] county palatine of Lancaster was ordered to produce the freeholders' book before the Master of the Office of Pleas in the Exchequer to strike an indifferent special jury, which was ordered unless cause [be shown to the contrary]. And to make out the justice and reasonableness of that order, two precedents were cited in the case between Sir George Warburton and Sir Roger Mostin against Mellot, Hilary [term] 1705[/06], where such an order was made to the county palatine of the [. . .] and a return made no obedience to it.

But note that, in those cases, Booth, the Prothonotary, was of [. . .] *viz.* these precedents and the pleadings and proceedings in this terms bundles.

But Serjeant *Parker*, for Sir Hervey [. . .], Prothonotary of Lancashire showed cause against that rule as invasive of his right [. . .].

In the principal case, the court upon advisement did not think themselves enabled to make any rule of this court to compel the bringing in of the freeholders' book in a county palatine where the whole proceedings after issue joined are to be carried on by the justices of assize for that county palatine constituted by a commission under the palatine seal by force and virtue of a commission under of the Exchequer seal to them directed for that purpose and by which the justices are required to command the sheriff to cause to come before the justices at the next sessions *duodecem liberas et legalis homines de vicineto de etc. as is usual in other venires ad faciendum juratores inter partes quia* the parties *posuere se in jurat' ill'* and to make other process against the jurors so to be empaneled as by the law and custom of the county palatine has used to be done in such cases until the said issue be fully tried and, when tried, then to make a return of all to the barons with that writ and to prefix the parties a day in the Exchequer *ad audiendum judicium suum*.

So that, by this, it appears that the awarding process for summoning the jury and all matters relating to the jurors and the trying of the issue are to be done by the justices of assize in virtue of the said commission out of the Exchequer and nothing is to be done by the Court of Exchequer after issue joined until the record of the trial be sent up by the justices, and then the judgment must be given by the Exchequer. But it seems lawful and is constantly practiced that the Exchequer grants new trials or sets the trials aside or awards by like commission a *venire facias de novo* where good cause shall be made out for that purpose.

Query, therefore, the precedents of the two rules for producing the freeholders' books to the Clerk of the Pleas for striking a jury, and the precedents of the rules of this court requiring the sheriff to attend the Prothonotary with the book for striking a special jury, upon what reason of law they stand.

And, therefore, the court set aside the rule for producing the freeholders' book to the Master of the Office of Pleas and for his striking the jury, and left the plaintiff to pursue his right and remedy in such case before the judge of assize in the County of Lancaster, who at Lancaster, after hearing the parties, directed the Prothonotary there to return a special jury. And the attorneys on both sides consented to a special jury. But there being no knight (but a baronet only, who not being a knight, was not sufficient) returned upon the panel (there being a peer of the realm concerned) the defendants challenged the array, which was allowed. And, thereupon, an entry was made that the panel be quashed immediately; whereupon, the plaintiff prayed a new [writ of] *venire facias*, which being carried to the seal keeper, who has his office under the defendant, the earl of Derby, then Chancellor of the County Palatine of Lancaster, where the lands lay, he refused to seal it as an unprecedented thing to have two *venire*s sealed in the same cause at the same assizes.

And so the cause was not tried, which caused a complaint to be made.

But, afterwards, upon a hearing before the queen in Council, it was declared that neither judge or officer or Lord Derby had done otherwise [than] well. And the complaint was dismissed, no warrant nor precedent or reason of law being made out for having a second *venire* to the same assize.

[Other copies of this report: Georgetown Univ. Law Sch. MS. B88–9, f. 332v.]

Harvard Law Sch. MS. 537, pt. 2, p. 163

Trinity term 9 Anne.

Lutwyche, for the plaintiff: This was an [action of] ejectment on the demise of my Lord Anglesey and his lady of several lands in the County of Lancaster and upon [a plea of] not guilty [and] a special verdict.

William, earl of Derby, was seised in fee of the manor of Latham, of Newberg, and New Park and the manor of Ormskirk and of the tithes of Dalton etc. And he, being so seised, did convey to Sir Thomas Leigh to that intent that he might convey to Her Majesty Queen Elizabeth and the queen to convey back to the earl to such and such uses as there mentioned. And accordingly, he enfeoffed to Sir Thomas Leigh, and he, by deed enrolled, conveyed [. . .]. And the queen afterwards conveyed the same to the earl of Derby and the heirs male of his body and, for default of such issue, to Sir George Stanley, lord Strange, in tail male.

And the reversion descended to King James I, and, then, an Act was made that William, earl of Derby, and lord Strange, and the crown should enjoy the lands as before. Then, the reversion descended to King Charles I. And, afterwards, several differences happening in the family, they were referred to the king. He, 11 July *anno* [. . .] of his reign, made his award that William, earl of Derby, and lord Strange should grant out of the premises a rent charge of £600 *per annum* to Charles Stanley in tail male with a remainder over. King Charles, reciting the letters patent of Queen Elizabeth etc., granted the reversion to James, lord Strange, within a year after, should reconvey to James, lord Strange, and to his heirs to the use of him and his heirs, in which letters patent, the king *voluit et declamavit* that the said lord Strange should within a year after reconvey to the king charged nevertheless with the rent charge of £600 *per annum* and that the king should be then in of his reversion as if no such conveyance had ever been made, and that a fine be levied accordingly and that the premises should go to the lord Derby and his heirs male and, for default, to Sir George Stanley and his heirs male.

And they find that the reversion was not reconveyed within the year, that the earl of Derby was seised by virtue of such estate tail, which descended to the earl of Derby, and that, in 13 Will. III [1701], there was an indenture which was a conveyance of the manor of Latham, New Park, and Newberg by way of lease and release to what uses. They find that, at the sealing of the indenture, there were great spaces left in order to insert other names of the tenants of the lands. They find a writ of entry sued out and returned and, thereupon, a recovery was suffered and judgment was given for the demandant to recover seisin.

N.B. The sealing of the indenture was 30 August, that the writ of entry was returned Wednesday the third of September, which was the first day of the assizes and then judgment was given; then the spaces were not filled until the fifth, which was the Friday following.

As to the manor of Ormskirk and the tithes of Dalton, [*blank*].

Lutwyche: As to the manor of Latham, New Park, and Newberg, which I shall look upon as part of the said manor, here is a distinct special verdict and upon which arises these three points:

First, whether the grant from Queen Elizabeth be such a one as is within the protection of 34 Hen. VIII;[1]

Second, admitting it within in, whether the grant of the reversion by King Charles to James, lord Strange, and his heirs and the fine levied many years afterwards, whether that has not destroyed the privilege;

Third, admitting that became a lien, whether or not the common recovery be sufficient to dock in entail of all those parcels.

As to the first, he takes it is not within the Statute, and he says the intent appears from the preamble because the body refers expressly to the preamble and the words in it are such as made for the recompense of services of such donees and that such lands may not only be a benefit to such grantees but likewise to such of their heirs as the estate is limited to. And he cites Wiseman's Case, 2 Co.[2]

By this verdict, it appears that this manor was an ancient estate in the family of the earls of Derby. Nothing appears to the contrary, and so it is mentioned to be in the grant to Queen Elizabeth. And, therefore, it does not appear that this family was in any way indebted to the crown for this land, for it is found that William, earl of Derby, by being seised in fee conveys to Sir Thomas Leigh and others to the end they might grant to the queen and the queen convey to the said earl to such and such uses and with the intent to leave the reversion in the crown and, accordingly, that they in 44 Eliz. [1602] conveyed to the queen and that the queen, so in possession, in 7 January grants, as was intended. Now, this law of 34 Hen. VIII, c. 20, being taken altogether, we take the intent of the Statute to be that such estates should originally flow from the crown.

He thinks that this grant of the queen, considering it under all of its circumstances, is no more than a new way of settling the earl of Derby's old estate so as his posterity should not alien. Here, the bounty does not flow from the queen to the earl, but quite otherwise, this conveyance leaves a reversion in the queen and her heirs. It is a plain design of bringing it within the Act of 34 Hen. VIII, which was never designed to reach so far. And he mentions Wiseman's Case. And this Statute is to be taken strictly, for it tends to a perpetuity. Indeed, it is otherwise where [it is] by provision of the crown, though no immediately from the crown, as Wiseman's Case.

Every grant is not within this Statute. A grant in consideration of money is not within it. Therefore, if a person purchase of the crown in consideration of money, that is not within it. Dyer 32, 5 Ch. I, the case between My Lord Nottingham and My Lord Mounson, the case mentioned in the margin in the new

[1] Stat. 34 & 35 Hen. VIII, c. 20 (*SR*, III, 919–920).

[2] *Wiseman v. Bernard* (1585) 2 Coke Rep. 10, 76 E.R. 410, also 1 Anderson 140, 123 E.R. 396, Moore K.B. 195, 72 E.R. 527.

[edition of] Dyer; and the case of the earl of Derby in Charles II's time.[1] It was so admitted and never denied. Then, if this is admitted, this great inconvenience would arise, a perpetuity might be made in any case whatever. The law has a long time labored against perpetuities. 6 Rept., Mildmay's Case.[2] And he mentioned John [. . .]'s Case, 1 Inst., but notwithstanding the Statute *de Donis*[3] had effectually introduced one until Edward IV's time.

Now, all the answer that he can find can be given to such things is that it cannot be presumed the queen would interpose in such a thing. There are some things the queen cannot do. And this is one of those things. And no one can say but, if such a power be allowed in this case, there will be such a one in all cases.

The law is against them upon the very finding the patent; in this case, [it was] not found in all the special verdict that it was for services. It is only *pro diversis causis et considerationibus* and which no more implies consideration of service than consideration of money, and, if money, then it is not certainly within the Act.

He cited [. . .] 261. The ejectment at that time was founded upon a patent in Richard III's time as 34 Hen. VIII that yet, if [there is a] conveyance over, the estate tail with the reversion is barable. 1 Inst. 372b.[4] And now, the words are full to pass the reversion to My Lord Strange.

Objection: That a clause in the same patent is to this effect, the king wills and declares that the lord Strange shall reconvey within a year in the same manner as if no such grant to him had been made, chargeable, however, with a rent charge of £600 and that this would amount to a condition, and, because it was not conveyed back to the king, it would revest to the crown.

First, that does not amount to a condition.

Second, that, if it did, it would not preserve the estate from being barred.

First, neither the words nor the intent of the patent import a condition. The king wills and declares that, within a year, he shall cause to be reconveyed. As yet the reversion may be in the crown in the same manner as if there were no conveyance. These words do no import a condition. He only expressed his will and pleasure. There are no words to make it appear that it was his intent it should be a condition. By virtue of these words, the party that accepts this patent may become liable to an action of covenant though there is no [. . .] in the case. And it was so resolved in 2 Cro. 399, 521.[5]

---

[1] *Earl of Nottingham v. Lord Mounson* (Ch. 1630); *Murray, ex dem. Earl of Derby v. Eaton* (Ex. 1679–1680), Exch. Cases *tempore* Car. II, p. 401.

[2] *Hethersall, ex dem. Mildmay v. Mildmay* (1605), 6 Coke Rep. 40, 77 E.R. 311, also Moore K.B. 632, 72 E.R. 805.

[3] Stat. 13 Edw. I, Westminster II, c. 1 (*SR*, I, 71).

[4] E. Coke, *First Institute* (1628), f. 372.

[5] *Brett v. Cumberland* (1616), Croke Jac. 399, 521, 79 E.R. 341, 446, also Popham 136, 79 E.R. 1238, 3 Bulstrode 163, 81 E.R. 138, 1 Rolle Rep. 259, 81 E.R. 533.

Second, if it had that effect, that the lord should reinstate the reversion in the crown and that this should preserve the estate tail and make it unalienable, as now, if this interposed a condition and that condition draw back the same estate tail again, then the rent charge would not be good, for it can never arise but only out of the estate out of the grantee.

And admitting it had been to reconvey again, yet it would not carry it further than if it were never reconveyed, for no such reconveyance would have been well barred. It would only have preserved the reversion, for he take it that in a case under 34 Hen. VIII, if the crown should convey with the intent to alien by a recovery etc. and so to reconvey that they may suffer a recovery anytime afterward and like the case where a lessee is restrained by a condition to assign, after one license and assignment, the assignee may assign *toties quoties*.

That quality is only annexed to the first estate tail, and there was a new estate on the fine. Ha. 405; Ra. 350; Gardner's Case; *vide* second 2 Jones, the last case, the same cited.[1]

As to the third point, it is found that, in the deed, there were spaces left for inserting tenants' names. And the objection was that the filling up the blanks had made this deed void; so the recovery was insufficient for want of tenants to the *praecipe*.

The [. . .] are it is found that the deed was sealed the 30th August, that the writ of entry was returnable Wednesday the 3d September, then the [*blank*] was given, yet the filling up was not until the Friday following, *viz*, the 5th September, by which it will appear, we hope, that these were good tenants to the *praecipe* as to that parcel of which one of the tenants is dead. That is not now in question at all.

When the judgment is given, the tenants to the *praecipe* are of no further use if a writ of entry be rightly brought against one that is a tenant to the *praecipe* at the time of the writ returned; though the tenant alien pending the writ, that will not make it insufficient; so, if a lease be surrendered upon a condition and the condition be broken after the recovery be suffered.

He takes it this filling up being not until 5th September, the recovery was well suffered though there was an erasure.

He thinks there is a difference when a bond is erased in any material part, which is only a chose in action, and when a deed is erased, without which an estate at law passes. 11 Rept., Pigott's Case.[2] If there is an erasure is in any material part, it avoids the bond. But it is otherwise in the case of a deed which conveys a freehold which is vested and remains in the alienee. How can an erasure revest that? 1 Cro. 197, 1 Jon. 354, 2 Roll, Abr., 29, pl. 6. And a deed was not necessary

[1] *Murray, ex dem. Earl of Derby v. Eaton* (Ex. 1679–1680), T. Raymond 338, 83 E.R. 176, T. Jones 237, 84 E.R. 1234, also Exch. Repts. *tempore* Car. II, 401.

[2] *Winchcombe v. Pigot* (1614), 11 Coke Rep. 26, 77 E.R. 1177, also 2 Bulstrode 246, 80 E.R. 1096, 1 Rolle Rep. 39, 81 E.R. 311.

in this case until 29 Car. II, the Statute of Frauds and Perjuries. Rolls' Abr., *supra*, Swanwic's Case, is in point; [. . .] 35, 36, pl. 16.[1]

But, admitting it void as to some of the tenants, yet it would not affect the rest. 2 Lutw. 35, Clare and [*blank*]. Admitting it no deed 5 September, yet it is a good one when the recovery was suffered.

As to New Park being a part of it, 24 Car. II finds it to be a conveyance to lord Finch and others. And the except[tion] is that this being an estate tail, the freehold being in another, the common recovery could not be well suffered without the tenant of the freehold. But he takes it sufficiently found to make it pass as the manor of Latham, for it was expressly said that it was part of the manor of Latham and it was found afterwards as [*blank*] part of it, and, after the suffering of the common recovery and being so reputed, it shall pass, as in Sir Moile Finch's Case.[2] There is no difference when it is by a common recovery and when by a bargain and sale. And there is no difference when it is a whole manor in reputation and when it is a part only. 1 Lev. 27, 1 Ven. 51, 1 Sid. 109. For admitting it part of the manor, 29 Car. II, and an estate for life granted out, [. . .] the reversion afterwards is parcel of the manor and is so in strictness and passes as such. 1 Inst. 324, 325; 2 R. [*blank*]; Br. Abr., pl. 3, tit. *Manner.*[3]

As to New Burgh, that is said to be in Latham *praedictum* [?] and is reputed parcel of the manor. It sufficiently passes, though not in strictness so.

As to the manor of Ormskirk and the tithes of Dalton, this arises upon finding a conveyance from the crown to the use of such persons with such matters as by an Act of 4 Jac. I is limited and expressed, and he found no limitation in the Act of Parliament concerning it at all. And since there are no uses, where it refers to, in such a case, the uses result to him that made the settlement and his heirs. It is found there were other manors wherein the Act limited to the earl of Derby and his heirs of his body, other to his heirs male, and so there is that insertion that no use can arise. Now, they say the name of the manor was not the manor of Ormskirk, but Ormskirk cum Halton, and they said expressly that there are not two manors. And then, if the manor does not pass, nothing at all passes. 1 Co. 46a, b.[4]

---

1 *Miller v. Manwaring* (1635), Croke Car. 397, 79 E.R. 947, W. Jones 354, 82 E.R. 186, 2 Rolle, Abr., *Interliner*, pl. U, 6, p. 29; Stat. 29 Car. II, c. 3 (*SR*, V, 839–842).

2 *Avery v. Crat* (1606), 6 Coke Rep. 63, 77 E.R. 348, 2 Leonard 134, 74 E.R. 420.

3 *Thinne v. Thinne* (1661), 1 Levinz 27, 83 E.R. 280, 1 Ventris 51, 86 E.R. 37, 1 Siderfin 190, 82 E.R. 1050, also 1 Keble 26, 591, 691, 716, 83 E.R. 790, 1129, 1188, 1203; E. Coke, *First Institute* (1628), ff. 324–325; YB 18 Edw. III, Lib. Ass., pl. 3, p. 55 (1344), 2 Brooke, Abr., *Manour*, pl. 3.

4 *Attorney General v. Bushopp* (1600), 1 Coke Rep. 26, 76 E.R. 64, also Jenkins 251, 145 E.R. 178, 2 Anderson 154, 123 E.R. 596, *sub nom. Welshe's Case*, Moore K.B. 413, 72 E.R. 664.

When My Lord Derby comes to settle by the name of Ormskirk cum Alton, in that case, it would have passed as he takes it. There is another case in Alton Woods [that] comes very near this, Hob. 123.[1] The intent in this case certainly was to pass the manor of Ormskirk.

Salkeld, e contra: [*blank*].

Viner, Abr., vol. 18, p. 234

William, earl of Derby, seised of the manors of Lathom etc. and Newburgh etc. conveyed the same to J.N. and J.S. with intent that they should convey the same to Queen Elizabeth and that she should re-grant the same to the said earl in tail male, with remainder to Sir George Stanley in tail male and the reversion to be made in the crown. J.S. and J.N. conveyed accordingly, and the queen, for divers good causes etc. and at the petition of the said W. re-granted to be held of the queen, her heirs, and successors, by the service of one knight's fee. An Act of Parliament made 4 Jac. I enacted that those to whom the limitations were made should enjoy and that the king should hold such estate, title, interest, and reversion, as if the Act had not been made. Afterwards, upon an award of a rent charge of £600 a year to Charles Stanley in tail male etc., King Charles I granted the reversion back to enable the grant of the rent charge and the reversion, within one year, to be again limited to the crown. After this, W. and his eldest son covenanted to levy a fine to make good the rent charge and that the lands chargeable therewith should be to the use of W. in tail male, remainder to Sir George Stanley in tail male, remainder to James, lord Strange, eldest son of W., his heirs, and assigns. The fine was levied. The reversion was not re-granted to the crown. The manors afterwards descended to William George Richard, earl of Derby, who, by lease and release, conveyed to Thornton and Hayes and their heirs to make a tenant to the praecipe to suffer a common recovery, in which William George Richard, earl of Derby, was vouched and he vouched the common vouchee. William George Richard died. In an ejectment brought by the daughters and coheiresses of William George Richard, earl of Derby, against the heir male of the body of Charles Stanley and younger brother of the said William George Richard, earl of Derby, deceased.

Lord Chief Baron Ward was of opinion with the younger brother, the heir male of Charles Stanley, as to the manor of Lathom etc. on the Statute 34 Hen. VIII, which restrains the tenant in tail of the gift of the crown from aliening.

But the other three barons held the entail in this case was a fraudulent contrivance, not within the meaning of this Statute.

[1] *Attorney General v. Bushopp* (1600), *ut supra*; *Pitts v. James* (1614), Hobart 121, 80 E.R. 271, also 1 Rolle Rep. 417, 81 E.R. 576, Moore K.B. 865, 72 E.R. 959, 1 Brownlow & Goldesborough 178, 123 E.R. 740.

288

Regina v. Newell

(Ex. 1707–1708)

In this case, an attachment was granted against a person who refused to be examined for the crown upon the execution of a writ of extent.

A witness is not required to answer any question that might subject him to any penalty or forfeiture.

Indiana Univ., Lilly Library
MS. Parker 'Cases in the Exchequer', vol. 4, p. 179

An immediate extent [issued] against [*blank*] Newell, and an inquisition found before the Secondary of the Compter, and Taylor was summoned in writing to attend to give evidence for the queen, who came and refused to be examined as to Newell's books, which were in his hands as assignee of the commission of bankrupt or to anything in the books being against himself and his own interest.

The Secondary certifies this contempt, and it was moved for an attachment against Taylor for his contempt in refusing to be sworn and examined.

It was said that he should have submitted to be examined and demurred in writing to any question that was not proper, which the Secondary might have certified to this court, and in case of contempt of this kind in a civil cause, an action upon the case lies and in a criminal [cause] to be indicted for the contempt but agreed in equity attachments are usually granted in this case.

It was ordered that an attachment should be granted.

[Other copies of this report: Dodd 353.]

Parker 269, 145 E.R. 777, Dodd 354

An immediate extent issued against the defendants directed to the sheriffs of London, in which there was the usual clause empowering them to call before them and to examine all persons proper to be examined in the premises. And an inquisition was taken before the sheriffs. And James Taylor was summoned in writing to attend and give evidence for the queen, who accordingly attended but refused to be examined as to Newell's books, which were in his hands, as assignee under a commission of bankruptcy, or to any thing in the books being against himself and his own interest.

The Secondary certified this matter, and it was moved for an attachment against Taylor for his contempt in refusing to be examined.

Though the power given to the sheriffs by the writ is only to propound fair and legal questions, yet the person summoned must answer all questions touching the matters to be enquired of, which he could not demur to if a bill in equity was filed against him, notwithstanding they may concern his own interest, provided they do not subject him to any penalty or forfeiture. And the court, thinking the questions which Taylor was required to answer were legal questions, granted an attachment against him.

Lincoln's Inn MS. Misc. 538, f. [24]

Hilary [term] 1707/8. John Taylor's Case.

A [writ of] immediate extent *teste* 3 December last returnable *Octabis Hilarii* was on oath awarded against the two Newells, goldsmiths, in Lombard Street for a great debt of above £20,000 due to the queen, they being sureties for one Dixon, receiver general of the taxes in Somersetshire, to whom he returned the same. But they failed to pay it. And this was directed to the Sheriffs of London. And, by virtue of the authority and command in the writ to call before them all such persons as they should think fit to be examined in and touching the articles in that writ which were to enquire of and seize into the queen's hands all the goods, chattels, debts, credits, lands, and tenements of the said two Newells.

The Secondary, who executed the writ, summoned by writing the said [John] Taylor to appear such a day and be examined in the premises he having possessed himself of the books of the Newells, wherein their debts and credits and other their estate were entered and to produce those books. And the examination, at Taylor's request, was put off to another day, when Taylor appeared. And he was required by the Secondary to take his oath or, being a Quaker, to make his affirmation in the premises, which he refused to do or produce the books pretending by himself and his counsel that he was not by law bound either to affirm or produce the books in regard, as he alleged, he and others were creditors and assignees of a commission of bankrupts sued out against the Newells, which, if any such were, none being made out to the court, they were long after the awarding of the extent, which bound their estates, real and personal, from the *teste* of the extent.

And the court, upon that certificate and hearing of divers counsel for Taylor, awarded a [writ of] attachment against him for his contempt in refusing to be examined, for he ought first to be sworn or affirmed and, then, if he had any just cause not to answer to the questions proposed, he might have demurred to the questions. But he ought not to have refused to swear or affirm, for, until then, he was under no obligation to speak the truth, and it would be of the utmost consequence to the crown revenue that persons that can discover the debtor's estate should refuse to be examined. And the court inclined that, having notice, he ought to produce the books which were part of the debtor's estate and bound by the extent and so were the debts and credits therein contained.

But, afterwards, in the same term, upon the application of the defendant Taylor and the assignees of the commissioners of bankrupts to the Attorney General, there was a consent that a new extent against the Newells should be taken of the same *teste* and return with the former and a new inquisition of the same day with the other should be taken and that Taylor should be examined as of the same day and fully give his evidence and make discovery as he ought to have done upon the former and that this new extent and inquisition by consent should be of and have the same force and effect as if taken the same days with the former and that the former should stand also and when all be done and the charges paid, Taylor to be discharged from his contempt, all which was done and complied withal.

[Other copies of this report: Georgetown Univ. Law Sch. MS. B88–9, f. 365.]

[Connected cases: Regina v. Arnold (Ex. 1709–1710), see below, Case No. 345.]

289

Bruse, qui tam v. Attorney General

(Ex. 1707–1709)

French wine bought in Holland by the queen with her own money and imported for the use of her family only is not forfeited by the Act of 3 Anne, c. 12.

Lincoln's Inn MS. Misc. 535, f. [231], pl. 2

Lowndes, upon a seizure of French wines, Hyems first claimed property *pro commodo reginae*. But that claim being waived, the Attorney General entered a claim in his own name as for the queen, whose wines they were said to be. And the appraisement was proclaimed. And [there was] a bidding £5 above by Frampton, which he waived if they were the queen's own wines imported for her own use, which they were affirmed to be.

Query, if the Attorney General claims in his own name, how can the informer try the cause with him and what is the consequence of such a claim and how the record [is] made up and who else can claim where the queen's own ships or goods are seized as forfeited.

See for this such an information, claim, special verdict, and judgment for the queen against the informer. A parcel of goods of several sorts were appraised and bid upon, the court awarded a writ of delivery for part, ordered the rest to be proclaimed again that they may be bid upon.

[Other copies of this report: Georgetown Univ. Law Sch. MS. B88–9, f. 329, pl. 2.]

Lincoln's Inn MS. Misc. 538, p. 17

Michaelmas [term] 1707. Parsons, qui tam upon a seizure of French wines and Bruse, qui tam on a seizure of the same wines and a claim by the queen.

The case appeared to be this.

11 October 1707, Parsons exhibited his information *tam quam*, and he lays the cause of the forfeiture to be because the wines, not being Rhenish, were imported from the Netherlands contrary to the Statute, which is a clause in the Act

against Frauds in the Customs,[1] whereby it is enacted that no sort of wines, other than Rhenish, should at any time be imported from the Netherlands or Germany into England upon any pretense whatsoever under forfeiture of ship and goods.

The writ of appraisement upon the first information was returnable 23 October and executed the 20th. And the wines were valued at £1690 and then proclaimed, and none claiming them nor bidding more, judgment was entered that the goods should remain forfeited and Parsons be charged with the moiety of the value to the queen and should retain the other moiety to his own use.

The queen's moiety was paid in, and a record of this [is] in the court.

After this, *viz.* the 10 November 1707, Bruse exhibits his information of seizure, and lays the cause of forfeiture because they were French wines and imported into England, not being taken prize nor condemned in the Admiralty as lawful prize nor sold by the Admiralty as perishable goods, contrary to the Statute (and that is the Act 3 & 4 Anne[2] for prohibited all trade and commerce with France).

A writ of appraisement *teste* 10 November and returnable 13 November was awarded, and the goods were appraised at £1608. The execution of which last appraisement being sometime delayed, upon a motion in court, it was ordered that the warehouse keeper should show the goods that they might be appraised and the appraisers directed to appraise and return, which was done, as above.

After which, Mr. Attorney General [*Harcourt*] moves the court that the wines in question were the queen's wines and imported for Her Majesty's own use. And he prayed the court would not proceed or let anything be done upon Bruse's information for that, as he alleged, the queen might import wines for her own use and the use of her family notwithstanding the statutes above and not be forfeited within either of them and that it sufficiently appeared by two affidavits he produced that these wines were imported for the queen's own use and of her family by order of the Board of the Green Cloth. And so he insisted that the two statutes above or either of them did not extend to the queen or her wines and though it has been of late practiced that the queen's wines have been colorably seised and condemned in this court, yet that was not of necessity but only to keep up a sort of regularity of management in the Custom House. And [he] did not inform upon the condemnation of those wines upon Parson's information but purely and only as the queen's own wines verified by affidavits as above.

All the counsel for Bruse upon his information, except Northey, late Attorney General, did not admit, but *Dodd* peremptorily denied that any wines, even for the queen's own table, could be imported against these two statutes, being so purely restraining as they are and the last reciting the importation of them to be a

[1] Stat. 14 Car. II, c. 11 (*SR*, V, 393–400).
[2] Stat. 3 & 4 Ann., c. 12 (*SR*, VIII, 360).

prejudice to the nation in general and that such laws bound the queen and forfeited the wines. And he relied on the reason of Magdalen College's Case, 11 rept.[1]

The court told Mr. Attorney [General Harcourt] and Mr. Solicitor [General Montagu] that whatever the law was whether the queen's wines were forfeited or no, that point not being before the court to determine, yet that being a matter of fact must, if insisted on, be tried by a jury and not by affidavits, which are not a sufficient foundation for the court to stop all proceedings upon Bruse's information, for that would be either *negare* or *deferre justiciam*[2] and the queen did never deny her subjects to contest their rights and titles at law with the queen in any cases whatsoever, and, if so as to land, liberties, and goods or the like, how came there to be a distinction between them and wines. And, therefore, they could not in justice put any stop to the proceedings upon Bruse's information. But, if a claim was not entered as usual, they must be proclaimed and recovered. And, there being a recovery upon Parsons's information, if that gave any property, it was fit to be tried between the informers or the queen according to the rules and methods of the law. And, then, if a property was made out in or for the queen, the point in law might be determined upon a special verdict or otherwise according to law.

And, therefore, the court could not deny that a proclamation should be made upon Bruce's information of a *si quis plus dare voluerit.*

But then, *Bridges*, of counsel for the queen, desired that the proclamation might be put off until the next day, which was done, not being opposed on the other side nor carrying with it any delay to the trial of the cause. The attorney sometime before saying he would enter no claim, and yet he prayed a writ of delivery, which he was told could not be granted until a claim was entered and, then, upon security only, if granted at all.

The next day being Saturday the 15th November, Mr. Attorney General having entered a claim for the queen in his name for her, after a proclamation and £100 above the appraised value being bid by one Robertson and accepted, he prayed a writ of delivery upon security, which was granted *nisi causa* Tuesday the 18th November, the wines being perishable in their nature and daily damnified.

The affidavits produced by Mr. Attorney General were of James Hayman, store keeper of the queen's wines under the Board of the Green Cloth, and of Luden Spiesmaker. The first swore that the wines in question were brought by him from Holland by the order of the Board of the Green Cloth for Her Majesty's and her family's use and for no other person whatsoever and that the queen's moiety was paid into the Receipt of the Exchequer the 6th of November instant out of an imprest of £1000 made to him by the order of the Board of the Green Cloth directed to the Cofferer of the Queen's Household to clear the charges of a

---

[1] *Warren v. Smith* (1615), 11 Coke Rep. 66, 77 E.R. 1235, also 1 Rolle Rep. 151, 81 E.R. 394, 2 Bulstrode 146, 80 E.R. 1021, Croke Jac. 364, 79 E.R. 312.

[2] Stat. 25 Edw. I, Magna Carta, c. 29 (*SR*, I, 117).

parcel of wines provided for Her Majesty's service and to be allowed to the Cofferer out of the buttery and cellar parcels for this Christmas quarter, which bill was dated the 30th of October 1707 and for which Hayman gave a receipt to the Cofferer.

Spiesmaker's affidavit was that he knew that Hayman was sent to Holland by the Green Cloth to buy wines for the use of the queen and her family and for which he paid the bills of exchange for the cost by the order of the Green Cloth. The wines in question were imported into the port of London, and seized by Parsons, who was employed by him to seize the same by the order of the Green Cloth.

And, upon Wednesday, the 19th of November, upon producing two affidavits that the wines were in a decaying perishable case and lay in a bad place and that, if not speedily removed, would be very much damnified in their nature and sink in value and that the queen had none for her own use, depending upon these, and, upon reading the affidavit of four persons for the informer that swore they believed the wines would not be damnified in three weeks if they remained where they are and on hearing counsel for Bruse, the informer (Robertson, the bidder, being in court), alleging that he is ready to try the cause this term or a day after and therefore opposing any writ of delivery and, upon hearing of Mr. Attorney General, Mr. Solicitor General, and others for the queen, showing that the information of Bruse came in but the 10th instant and, that, by the rules of the court, he could not be forced to trial this term nor until the next nor could sooner be ready and that he was willing and consented that the £100 brought into court should be delivered out to the bidder and the bidding discharged, which the bidder accepted of. And that since there was like to be a point in law whether the wines of the queen brought in for her own use would or could be forfeited and that, by reason thereof and of the greatness of the value, there might be either a trial at the bar or a special verdict, neither of which could be [had] this term and then by all the affidavits (even of the informer's part) these wines could not continue good above three weeks, it was but just and indeed necessary that there should be a writ of delivery, though Baron SMITH (at first seemed to doubt) yet now agreed there should be a writ of delivery upon security.

But then I [EDWARD WARD] proposed to whom the security should be given, whether to the queen, she being concerned in interest, or how else and how the cause should be carried on in regard the informer sues for the queen as well as himself and it would be improper that the suit for the queen should be carried on against the Attorney General, who claims for the queen. The informer's counsel electing to take a bond with sureties to the informer himself conditioned in all things as a security by recognizance upon writs of delivery usually are, and Mr. Attorney General agreeing to plead so as a trial may be had the next term, a writ of delivery upon such security was awarded by the court without opposition.

And that seems the more reasonable, because, though the queen claims all the wines in point of property, yet the informer, Bruse, by his information allows and entitles the queen to a moiety, which is without contest, and the queen's title to the whole in point of property is made out upon oath, which is more than is required from a subject that claims, though that oath was not required by the court for that purpose, but to show the fairness and reasonableness of entering the claim in the queen's name. And the opposition to a writ of delivery seemed more unreasonable because, on all hands, a moiety belonged to the queen and the other moiety only was in question. And it is hard for the queen not to have that on security.

Memorandum, first, that, if any person will seize the queen's ships or goods, which really belong to Her Majesty in property under pretense of forfeiture by any popular law, who should or could claim them but the Attorney General on her behalf, else she will be in a worse condition than any subject.

Secondly, if, by such a claim, the informer is put under any difficulty, who can help it? Must no claim be made at all? That must lose the goods absolutely, and, when nothing is done but what is necessary, if any unfortunateness, inconvenience, or disability happens to the informer or his pretense or remedy, he must submit to it. The law cannot be altered.

Thirdly, there is no more done in this case of the queen than in every private subject's case as to the writ of delivery. It is granted in the common case and upon security taken in such a manner as the informer chooses.

Fourth, in such a case of seizing the queen's goods upon a penal law for a supposed forfeiture whereof the informer is to have a part and the queen a part, the information must be *tam pro regina quam pro seipso*, being a seizure *in rem*, no person or name appearing until after the claim and when the Attorney General claims property of the whole as being the goods of the crown, query how the proceedings must be in order to trial. It seems in such a case the Attorney General must plead the goods were not imported or exported or otherwise forfeited for any cause in the information (as the case happens to be) and cannot insist upon the crown's property in bar, allowing the law makes a forfeiture for the offense in the information. And then, it seems that the informer must reply and carry on the trial as to the moiety claimed by him. And, if a verdict pass for the informer, judgment must be entered that the goods remain forfeited and that he have a moiety thereof to his own use and the other moiety to be for the queen's use. And the moieties are to be delivered in specie or, if delivered out before by a writ of delivery upon security (as it seems they may be), then, after the judgment is entered, *ut supra*, the informer will have the benefit of the security *quoad* his moiety.

[Other copies of this report: Georgetown Univ. Law Sch. MS. B88–9, f. 351.]

Lincoln's Inn MS. Misc. 535, f. [220]

Michaelmas term 1707.

First, where the crown claims the whole property of the goods which an informer seizes as forfeited, one moiety to the crown, the other to the informer, which, as to customable goods, goes as to one moiety of the rate thereof to the queen and the other moiety of the rate to the informer, there, the goods being in judgment of the law in the seizer's possession, the judgment upon the recovery in such case is that [. . .] seized and that the seizer shall be charged to the queen as to one moiety of the rate and that he shall retain the other moiety to himself and, in judgment of law, the goods [. . .] the seizer's possession though in the queen's warehouse of the port when the seizer has answered the [. . .] the queen's moiety which he bought by being so charged. The whole property of the goods is in the seizer, and he may justly retain them against all pretenders, the property being altered by the judgment of forfeiture [. . .] from the time when the forfeiture first commenced.

Second, where the seizer is entitled to one moiety and the crown to the other of the goods themselves and not to the rates or values [. . .] which generally is in case of goods prohibited to be imported or exported and fall not under the consideration of the customs acts, though the same judgment is given, as in the case of customable goods or a *devenerunt* for any sort of goods extending only to the values, as it must do in a *devenerunt*, where the value and not the goods themselves can be had or recovered. In such case, the queen may take her moiety in specie if she pleases, and bidding in such a case is vain because the property of the goods themselves, by the forfeiture, is vested in the queen and the informer after recovery. And the court can sell only the queen's part and not the informer's without his consent.

Third, from hence, it follows that nothing is sold but the queen's moiety only. And the difference between the forfeitures of customable and prohibited good, in that first case, it is at best but doubtful whether the queen may take a moiety in specie and, in the second case, that it is clear she may if she pleases, for this court is entrusted to sell and dispose the queen's moiety for her best avail, and, for that purpose, it is that the goods seized be appraised and, lest there should be a prejudice to the crown by the sworn appraisers and valuations, there is a public proclamation made for anybody to come in and bid more and, he that does so, the court generally sells the queen's part to him. But, in that case, there is a discretion in the court that guides the sale and not to take the bidder that will always give the most unless it be something considerable, for that, at that rate, the bidders may be vying one against the another by minute sums and, where the buyer is not known or is not taken to be sufficient, the court has of late obliged the party to bring in the *meus obtulit* [?] and not otherwise, for the entry on record contains no such matter.

This being the reason, extent, and limitation of the bidding and the discretionary power of the court in it, it is to be considered in what capacity and respect the bidder stands in the court and how chargeable and what interest he claims by his bidding and what influence it has in the cause between the informer and the crown or any that shall claim property in the goods and contest the forfeiture, wherein it is to be considered that this bidder is [. . .] his bidding charged upon record with the price of the goods which he bids for. But the fruit and effect of the bidding and charge is eventual and canting only, *viz.* that the goods prove forfeited and be recovered, then he is to have them. But, if not, his bidding and the charge upon him thereby is become ineffectual and to be discharged, for the goods remain where at first seized, and the trial and prosecution of the information is and must be carried on by the informer and in his own name as if no bidding had been. And, if there be a recovery, then the bidder being by his bidding charged on record, he is thereby become a third party to or outlier in the record and the goods as between the informer and the claimer; being recovered, the bidder must have them, paying the sum bidden. And he is thus brought in to be a party to or in the record in the nature of him that comes in by the way of receipt, aid prayer, or vouchee so as to bring a writ of error for his avail. But, if the claimer or the informer brings a writ of error upon the judgment, there is no need to make the bidder a party, because [he is] not concerned in the forfeiture further or otherwise than to advance the price of the goods if they be by law forfeit[ed].

Fifth, from hence, it follow that, where there is a claimer, the informer and the claimer, notwithstanding any bidding may by license of the court compound with the bidder not knowing the evidence which the informer or the crown has cannot nor ought in reason or justice to hinder such a composition, for that might be a prejudice to the crown and the informer to force them to a trial when it is possible there may not be sufficient evidence to make a forfeiture, though the claimer being conscious to himself may be willing to compound to save one and the law having provided that the informer shall not compound under a third of the appraised value and the crown has always as much and sometimes more, both which could be lost if the bidding should oblige the informer to a trial, though he has not sufficient evidence. This is and has been the practice. And it is justified by reason and precedents, and plainly shows that the bidder has nothing more to do in the cause than to have the goods, if recovered, for the price he bid for them.

Sixth, it comes now to be considered how far forth a bidder may and, by law or practice, can oppose a writ of delivery of the goods seized and by him bid for before a recovery of them by a trial and judgment. If he cannot hinder a composition, why should he hinder a delivery if and when the law allows it and the court sees reason and cause for it. *Quilibet potest renunciare juri pro se introducto.* The bidder is for the improvement of the queen's interest and profit under the seizure. And, if she desires it not, but [would have] her moiety in specie, what is the bidder concerned if his bidding in such a case be made ineffectual? He will not be bound by it, but his bidding is discharged. If any money was brought in, it ought to be delivered out as far as the queen is concerned in it. And, as to the informer, it is worse for him, for, in case of forfeiture, he is to have the goods themselves and, the cheaper they are, the better to him, for he will pay the queen less for them in case he has them. And, therefore, in the case in question, it looks suspiciously as if the informer and the bidder was all one. And, if the queen's Attorney General, who stands in the queen's stead *ad currandum et perdendum* for her, will either take her moiety in specie or will not have the wines bid upon to increase her part, why is the bidder concerned in a matter against the queen's mind and the informer's true and real interest?

Seventh, in this case, where the queen herself claims property and where it appears by affidavits that the wines were bought and brought in for the queen's own use and for none other, it must of necessity follow, and without dispute, that one-half of them must belong to Her Majesty, either in property or by forfeiture, and, as to them, there can be no prejudice to anybody. This court has no power to sell the queen's own wines in property but only by what accrues by forfeiture. So, it is fitting that both the informer and bidder should stand clear of the bidding, at least as to one moiety.

Eighth, therefore, as to the informer's moiety, the bidder and he may agree together as they please, for they seemed agreed and to be good friends to oppose a delivery, which must aim only as to the queen's moiety, which is otherwise disposed of, for, as to the informer, whose friend the bidder is, it is an injury to him, as before is said.

Ninth, it is proper to consider how the law stands as to writs of delivery. Before the Act against Frauds in the Customs, 14 Car. II, ca. 11, the court, at its discretion, granted writs of delivery. And it seems reasonable to think the restraint of granting such writs, unless where the goods were perishable or a delay used in not going to trial as the course of the court allows, was made for the benefit of the crown, as thinking the goods better than security, but, if the crown, which is entitled to the forfeiture of a moiety, claims property of the whole [and] desires a delivery, it seems to be a different case from all others.

And, therefore, for the reasons above and also besides:

First, an oath is made of the queen's property to the whole, and nothing is proved to the contrary;

Second, because here are two oaths made of the perishableness of these goods and damnification that will arise by their lying still for this winter season;

Third, because the information came in but the 6th of November this term and so no trial can be obliged or be had this term and must lie by until next term and, though the informer offers to try the cause this term or the day after, yet, in regard Mr. Attorney [General] says he cannot be ready with his witnesses to try it this term and no rule can compel him and if it would be hard to let the wines lie to perish in the meantime and deprive the queen of the use of them, at least of the moiety, which is incontestably true do belong to the queen;

Fourth, and there is like to arise a great point of law strongly stood upon on both sides whether the queen may have prohibited wines imported for her own use, notwithstanding the Act against Frauds and prohibiting all trade and commerce with France, and both seem to be confident of the law in the case, it may in all probability come to a special verdict, the case being of great consequence and also of value and fit for a trial at the bar, at the least if desired on either side, which, to be sure, cannot possibly be in this term and either a trial at the bar, which cannot be until next term, or, if tried at *nisi prius* this term and a special verdict, either upon the doubt of the judge or the prayer of either party and being, indeed, a point too weighty for any single judge at *nisi prius* to take upon himself to determine and;

Fifth, because there is no restraining clause in the last Act for prohibiting trade and commerce with France, upon which the information is grounded, from granting writs of delivery, as there was in the former Act for prohibiting trade with France, 29 & 30 Car. II,[1] which that Parliament thought necessary, and that, without such restraint, they might and would have been granted;

I am of opinion that a writ of delivery in this case, thus circumstanced and differed from all other cases (that I have met with) upon good security may well be granted. And, if the bidder be uneasy, by Mr. Attorney General's consent, he may be eased of his bidding, and that without any discouragement to bidders or any prejudice to the course of this court or the interest of the crown which is chiefly aimed at by the bidding. But this [is] under these cautions and limitations: first, that these wines be the queen's own and for her own use and not imported covinously under her name for the use of other of her subjects, for, if the importation be covinous, it will spoil all the defense; second, that Mr. Attorney [General] consents to try this cause the next term and that good security be given and the cause put into such a method for trial and, for having the security effectual, both for the informer and the crown, as shall be agreed upon before the goods be delivered.

In this case, first, query to whom to give the security because the queen is concerned in interest for the whole, second, query how this record shall be made up, for, here, the informer sues *qui tam* for himself as for the queen and, if the Attorney General claim the property, then, he is to be the defendant, and how can that be, both plaintiff and defendant?

In an ordinary information *tam quam*, the Attorney General may enter a *noli prosequi* for the queen's moiety, and the informer may go on for his moiety, there being a claimer to contest with. But, in this case, the informer must contest with the crown.

Query if [it be] not proper for the claim to be in another's name and not the Attorney General's, who, by consent, shall have leave to set up the queen's title and property and that to be insisted on and, if a property be proved in the queen, the case is to be considered and proceeded upon in all things as if the claim had been in the queen's name. And, if a verdict and judgment be for the informer, he is to have the fruit and benefit of the security for the recovery of his moiety.

Hyems and Lownd's case, last Hilary term, when [. . .] first claimed property of the French wines *pro commodo reginae*, which claim was waived and another was put in by the Attorney General. Query, what became of that case.

---

[1] Stat. 29 & 30 Car. II, c. 1 (*SR*, V, 852–864).

Who can claim property of the queen's goods but her Attorney [General]? What if a man of war imparts French wines and is seized, shall this be dispunishable or how shall the seizer proceed?

[Other copies of this report: Georgetown Univ. Law Sch. MS. B88–9, f. 351.]

Harvard Law Sch. MS. 537, pt. 2, p. 107

Hilary term 7 Anne, 1709.

Bruce brings an information *qui tam* of the seizure of wines imported against an Act 3d of the queen importing that all French wines, goods, etc. imported shall be forfeited, one-half to the queen and another to the informer.

Sir Simon Harcourt, the then Attorney General, claims them as belonging to the queen, upon which issue [is joined]. And [there is] a special verdict finding that the wines are of the growth of France, that they were not taken or condemned as prize nor ordered by the Court of Admiralty to be sold as such etc., but they find that they were bought in Holland [for] Her Majesty's use, and so it concludes, *si etc.*

Phipps, of counsel for the plaintiff, argued that they are within the general prohibition of the act.

Objection: That they are bought by the queen and paid for by her own money and that for her own use and that, as such, may be imported notwithstanding the Act.

But, by *Phipps*, there is no such saving in the Act, so that the question will be whether the queen can import notwithstanding this general prohibition.

He argued that they could not and that *ab inconvenienti*, for that, in this case, there were many tuns imported. But suppose the queen should buy 10,000 tuns, as she might if not bound, and so of other French goods and then suppose it more than she has occasion for; may she not sell this? There is no law to prohibit it. And, if so, the Act is utterly eluded and the monopoly of this French trade vested in the crown.

And, as for Her Majesty's dispensing with it, he cited 11 Rep. 68, where it was resolved the crown cannot dispense with any law *pro bono publico*.

And, if Her Majesty had had a mind to have had this liberty, she might easily have obtained it if she had thought fit.

He cited 3 Rep. 82,[1] where [it was] replied that all statutes made against fraud shall be liberally expounded to suppress that fraud, and the 5th Report, the same resolution.

In 4 Mod., it is laid down as a rule where any statute is made to suppress or prevent wrong, the king, though not mentioned, is bound by it because he can do no wrong. 5 Rep. 14. Acts that are made to suppress a wrong, to take away

[1] *Chamberlain v. Twyne* (1601–1602), 3 Coke Rep. 80, 76 E.R. 809, also Moore K.B. 638, 72 E.R. 809.

a fraud, or prevent the decay of religion shall bind the king though he be not named. And, for that reason, he shall be bound by Westminster II, c. 5, against wrongful usurpations, though not named. *Vide ibidem* and 2 Inst., upon this Act; so 32 Hen. VIII, c. 28, this binds the king, 2 Inst. 681; so 11 Co. 72, there the king cannot be exempted out of the general words to prevent wrong; *et ibid.* and Pl., Com., Berkley's Case, he is bound by the Statute *de Donis* and that he cannot alienate because this alienation is tortious; so, as to 27 Eliz., c. 4; *ibid.* 74, the king is bound by that Act for the same reason. And he cited the citation there out of Bracton.[1]

And [he said] that 32 Hen. VIII, 38, of fines, binds the crown. 7 Rep. 22, and Magdalen College Case, 75;[2] and he cited Magdalen College itself that hinders to convey to the crown to evade because of the impoverishing of the subjects. And he cited fo. 71b in that case and then compared the Act of 13 Eliz. with this French Act and the inconveniences. And he says the inconvenience is more in this case than that of 13 Eliz., this being to impoverish us and enable the French to carry on their war and the prince and subjects alike are bound by the war and ought to undergo the same fate and not the prince to live in amity while the subject in enmity. And the constant opinion since such Act has been that the crown was bound by this general prohibition and, for that reason, the crown always was at the charge of condemning the wines imported for their own use.

As for these that do not bind the king, as Westminster II, c. 16; 2 Inst. 391; Westminster III, c. 2; Plowd., Berkely's Case; Magna Ch., c. 11; 2 Inst. 23; and a great many others in Magdalen Coll. Case and in the same case, 2 Roll's Rep. But then he said that these were upon that rule, 11 Co. 74b, where the king has an estate, right, title, or interest, then, by general words, he shall not be bound by them, and that was the reason of those cases, but that is not our case. Here is no prerogative here. And so, he prayed judgment for the informer.

---

[1] *Attorney General v. Bishop of London* (1693), 4 Modern 200, 87 E.R. 347, also 3 Levinz 377, 83 E.R. 738, 1 Shower K.B. 441, 89 E.R. 688, Comberbach 205, 300, 90 E.R. 431, 490, Carthew 313, 90 E.R. 784, Holt K.B. 585, 90 E.R. 1223, 1 Lord Raymond 23, 91 E.R. 912, 2 Salkeld 559, 91 E.R. 472; *The Case of Ecclesiastical Persons* (1601), 5 Coke Rep. 14, 77 E.R. 69; Stat. 13 Edw. I, Westminster II, c. 5 (*SR*, I, 75–77); E. Coke, *Second Institute* (1642), pp. 353–365; Stat. 32 Hen. VIII, c. 28 (*SR*, III, 784–786); E. Coke, *Second Institute* (1642), p. 681; *Warren v. Smith* (1615), 11 Coke Rep. 66, 77 E.R. 1235, also 1 Rolle Rep. 151, 81 E.R. 394, 2 Bulstrode 146, 80 E.R. 1021, Croke Jac. 364, 79 E.R. 312; *Willion v. Berkley* (1562), 1 Plowden 223, 243, 74 E.R. 339, 371; Stat. 13 Edw. I, Westminster II, c. 1 (*SR*, I, 71); Stat. 27 Eliz. I, c. 4 (*SR*, IV, 709–711); *Bracton on the Laws and Customs of England.*

[2] Stat. 32 Hen. VIII, c. 28, c. 6 (*SR*, III, 785); *Anderson v. Sibthorpe* (1597), 7 Coke Rep. 21, 77 E.R. 443; *Warren v. Smith* (1615), *ut supra.*

Mr. Serjeant *Parker, e contra*: He observed in the first place that the tenor of the proclamations upon such informations as this in this court was always to show cause why the goods should not be forfeited to the queen.

He likewise observed that the forfeiture by the Act was one-half to the queen and the other to the informer.

And then, he cited a proviso in the Act, which was that nothing in the Act should hinder Her Majesty's subjects to import wines before the Act bought, by all which he argued it was meant the Act should only extend to Her Majesty's subjects.

And, as to the inconvenient objection, that the queen could not introduce them, and he said there were several cases where the queen is exempted yet could not be made a handle to evade the Act, as in the Case of the Statute of Mortmain; 17 Edw. III, 59; and that in 11 Co. 73b, shall not be an instrument of evading that Act. *Vide* the case, *ibidem*; so Magdalen College Case itself and none of the cases out of 11 Co., the Case of Monopolies, come to this.[1] And he thinks the question is whether the queen is within this Act or no.

He agreed with the rule of construing acts in restraining frauds more liberally. He agreed with the rule in Magdalen College Case that such a statute shall bind the king when the words are large enough. He agreed with those cases Phipps cited, as 27 Eliz., c. 4,[2] for wherever the subject is bound, the crown is bound. And there and in such cases, the subject is in the first place bound and who is to do the first act so that it proceeds from a disability of the subject and not of the crown. As to what is said of dispensing, he cited Hobt. 146; that Statute put things in form and to ease the sovereign [and] may be dispensed with. And he cited the case there cited.[3]

He says this Act comes in aid of the king's prerogative of levying war by a carrying on the war more effectually, so this act is an assistant to the prerogative. And where the queen has a special prerogative, a general act will not take it away. He cited 11 Co. 68b; the king is not within the Statute of *Nisi Prius* or the Statute of Limitations.[4]

[1] Stat. 7 Edw. I (*SR*, I, 51); Stat. 18 Edw. I, c. 3 (*SR*, I, 106); YB Mich. 17 Edw. III, f. 59, pl. 58, Rolls Ser. 31b, vol. 10, p. 262, pl. 58 (1343); *Warren v. Smith* (1615), *ut supra*; *Darcy v. Allen* (1602), 11 Coke Rep. 84, 77 E.R. 1260, also Moore K.B. 671, 72 E.R. 830, Noy 173, 74 E.R. 1131, British Library MS. Add. 25203, f. 678, J. I. Corré, 'The Argument, Decision, and Reports of *Darcy v. Allen*,' *Emory Law Journal*, vol. 45, p. 1261 (1996).

[2] Stat. 27 Eliz. I, c. 4 (*SR*, IV, 709–711).

[3] *Colt v. Bishop of Coventry* (1612), Hobart 140, 80 E.R. 290, also Moore K.B. 898, 72 E.R. 982, 1 Rolle Rep. 451, 81 E.R. 600, Jenkins 300, 145 E.R. 219; Stat. 25 Hen. VIII, c. 21 (*SR*, III, 464–471).

[4] *Warren v. Smith* (1615), *ut supra*; Stat. 27 Edw. I, Fines, c. 4 (*SR*, I, 130); Stat. 21 Jac I, c. 16 (*SR*, IV, 1222–1223).

But he also takes it from the import of the words of the Act that the queen is not within the intent of it. He observed the title of the Act and, as the fact is, found there is no color to [. . .] within it.

He said the Act, though styled such import etc. a nuisance, yet the Act does not make it criminal and nobody can be indicted for it as a nuisance. And he says it cannot properly extend but where the goods may be forfeited.

Then as to the queen's prerogative, she cannot undergo a penalty, and that also exempts her out of this Act. 1 Hen. VII, 4; 8 Rep. 61b.[1] The king cannot be amerced. He likewise takes it inflicting a penalty. It imports a superior power, and, none being her superior, none can inflict a penalty. And that the queen's goods cannot be forfeited is a consequence of the rule she cannot undergo a penalty.

He likewise argued the crown is not bound from the proving of imported wines [to have been] already bought, which only extended to the subject, so that [if] Her Majesty is within the Act, [she is] in a worse condition than her subjects.

He cited 9 Rep. 126b and the rule there, when the king and subjects concur [in interest], the king's shall be [preferred], and Hardr. 24.[2] And he made a comparison occasionally where a debtor made an executor, in which case, he said the debtor is not discharged as commonly supposed, but the debtor is discharged by supposing an immediate payment of it to himself so that he is still liable.

He observed the information to be *qui tam*, and he said the queen cannot be an informer against herself. It is true it is in this case a proceeding against the *rem*, but it affects the party by the *rem* being taken away.

And so he concluded for the Attorney General.

Harvard Law Sch. MS. 537, pt. 2, p. 142

Trinity term 8 Anne.

Dodd, for Bruce: First, the Attorney [General] has made the crown a plaintiff as to one-half of this information, for, having entered a *nolle prosequi* as to one-half, it seems to imply that he will proceed as to the other. But, instead of proceeding for the rem[edy], he claims property for the queen, which is quite contrary to the information before your Lordships so that we must, secondly, enquire whether he can claim property upon record, which he thought they could not do because it was directly contrary as to the first part of it, for claiming property must be an act of the defendant. But any other person might have been set up to have claimed the property, and the queen would have been in the same case as now they intended. The Attorney [General] then might have *nolle prosequi*ed

---

[1] YB Mich. 1 Hen. VII, f. 4, pl. 5 (1485); *Beecher v. Shirley* (Ex. 1608), 8 Coke Rep. 58, 77 E.R. 559, also Croke Jac. 211, 79 E.R. 183, Jenkins 283, 145 E.R. 204.

[2] *Floyer's Case* (1611), 9 Coke Rep. 125, 77 E.R. 913, also Croke Jac. 295, 79 E.R. 253; *Attorney General v. Andrew* (1655), Hardres 23, 145 E.R. 360.

as to one part and let the informer have gone on as to the other part against the defendant so set up.

If the Act extends to the queen, though not named but only generally, as to that, he said it was not only so prohibited by the Act upon which the information is grounded, *viz.* 3 Queen [Anne] but against several others, as, first, the Act of Navigation, which see, and he said that in fact it was a Dutch ship in which they were imported in; second, 14 Car. II, the Act to Prevent Frauds.[1] And he thinks those acts, for the reason of them binding to the crown. And he cited Magdalen College Case, and, though it is not laid upon these acts, yet if it appear upon the record that they ought not to have been imported, the court will take care of the crown and give judgment accordingly. And, thirdly, this is within the Act of 3 the queen [Anne]. And, for that purpose, he cited the preamble and the several reasons there given for making such an act. And he argued that, from those reasons, it should bind the crown, and the crown shall not be out of an act to prevent wrong. And, then, it is the office of judges, in construing acts to prevent wrongs, to suppress the mischief and advance the remedy and to suppress all evasions to continue that mischief. And that this was what the Act intended to remedy, he cited 11 Rep. 71; 3 Rep. 7; and Berkeley's Case, Commentaries,[2] and that all acts made *pro bono publico* will extend to the crown, though not named, 11 Rep. 88. And he thinks, in this case, the Parliament intended a general prohibition.

Objection: The queen cannot be a plaintiff against herself and, in this case, the information is for the queen, the proclamation and the other proceedings.

Answer: He thinks it is very odd after that they have said she is so much the plaintiff she should at last turn to be the defendant, for Sir Simon Harcourt, the then Attorney General, did not claim property for the crown until the proclamation after the appraisement was returned. And he thinks the Act intended to bind her in this case by reciting the causes so many and of such a nature in the preamble that she cannot be according to the rules of construing statutes, in such a case but be construed bound. And he thinks this way was the rather taken that she might be bound the more decently, and, if the Parliament had intended otherwise, it might have been an easy thing to have inserted a proviso to that purpose.

Objection: That the Act is to enable, the crown to carry on the war against France and in aid of the king's prerogative.

Answer: That it is otherwise for preventing the exhausting of the treasure of the kingdom, as appears by the preamble.

Objection: The title of the Act is to prevent all commerce with France.

---

[1] Stat. 12 Car. II, c. 18, s. 8 (*SR*, V, 248); Stat. 14 Car. II, c. 11 (*SR*, V, 393–400).

[2] *Chamberlain v. Twyne* (1601–1602), *ut supra*; *Warren v. Smith* (1615), *ut supra*; *Willion v. Berkley* (1562), *ut supra*.

Answer: The title of the Act of Tonnage and Poundage[1] seems to respect only merchants and yet, if anyone imports such goods for his own private use, yet he is as much within the Act, and this is the construction that has always been put upon it by Your Lordship and your predecessors. And that he always took it so.

Objection: It is not an offense for which one is indictable, by the punishment is the forfeiture of the goods.

Answer: He thinks an indictment may be, the Act having prohibited the importation as injur[ious], and an indictment or information may be for that misdemeanor.

Objection: That the penalty that the goods shall be forfeited and, if the crown had been particularly named and had imported notwithstanding, surely they would have been forfeited.

Objection: A penalty implies a superiority.

He thinks that an act giving the meanest subject a title to a forfeiture of the greatest nobleman that meanest subject would have a good title notwithstanding, for the law makes him superior as to that purpose (if he needs must be so) though he is much otherwise in person. And the greatest person is liable to the law. And, if the meanest, if entitled, may prosecute for the penalty.

Objection: Here is a forfeiture, and who shall have it?

Answer: The informer one-half and the crown the other, because nobody else is appointed to have it.

Objection: [There is] a proviso in the Act, which only seems to extend to the people.

Answer: This is only of [*blank*], and it may extend no further.

Objection: That the crown can dispense with this law.

Answer: He thinks there cannot be a dispensation in this case because it cannot be but under the great seal. It cannot be, as in this case, by parol.

Sir James Montagu, Attorney General, *e contra*: He argued much to the same effect with Sir Thomas Parker, who had argued against Phipps *quod vide antea*. He said, as to the objection that the queen cannot be both plaintiff and defendant. The queen cannot be plaintiff when it appears she ought to be defendant.

N.B. To me [Eden] this seems this is no objection if it appears upon the record that the queen had title, because, if in a case between subject and subject, the queen is, a stranger would have a judgment more strong where the queen irregularly; thus especially it is a special verdict in the case *nisi* perhaps objected that is not before us without two [. . .]. But the verdict, being a record that could be taken, seems in the case of the queen amounting to an office found. And the court would seize to the use of the crown *quousque* a right *melius ostensurus* by another party because of them.

---

[1] Stat. 12 Car. II, c. 4 (*SR*, V, 181–205).

And, as to what was said upon the Statute of Navigation and 14 Car. II, the conclusion of the special verdict ought to obviate that which concludes upon this Statute 8 of the queen and that, where the property vested in the crown, it was the rule that no general words in an act shall take it out of it. And he cited a construction [*blank*] Westminster II [*blank*] about wards.

Dodd: As to the objection that the proviso relating to bargains precedent to the Act extended to subjects, that might be because of their application to that end, whereas nobody put them in mind of the crown, as having none.

At another day, the court gave judgment.

Lovell was of opinion that a half ought to be given to the informer.

Objection: It was not brought in by way of merchandise; so it was not within the Act.

Answer: The law does not distinguish whether they are the queen's goods or a subject's. The penalty is in the remedy; the goods so imported shall be forfeited.

He takes this to be a popular action because it is a popular cause. If this construction might be allowed, any gentleman in England might do the same for their family, besides it is not defined what the word 'family' means. He takes it all the people of England are the queen's family, as *mater matriae*. It is made for the good of the people of England in general, a popular law, and not only made for the benefit of the queen.

And so he was of opinion for the informer.

Price: The plea is that it is not imported *contra formam statuti*. Now, it is to be observed that the general words take in the queen as well as the subject, and, therefore, if the queen is to be construed out of the Statute, it must be by her prerogative. He mentioned the preamble of the Act and agreed that, if the queen should constitute a monopoly or license any to import within that Act, it is to be looked upon as an evasion of it and the Act is to extend to it. The Act was there should be no commerce by way of merchandise with France. Now certainly, the queen could not be intended to be within the meaning of this law unless they would intend her to trade and merchandize. And, if the jury had that particular [intent], it would have had another consideration. It can never be intended the Parliament intended to deprive the queen, nor can it be thought that she designed it when she gave the royal assent. And this simple importation is not prejudicial to anybody. It can affect nobody.

He put the case of purveyance. 17 Stat. Hen. III; *de Tallagio non Concedendo*; 12 Rep., f. 19, which was law at that time, though altered now.[1] He agreed the grounds in Magdalen College Case and Berkley's Case to be good and legal. The

[1] Perhaps Stat. 3 Edw. I, Westminster I, c. 32 (*SR*, I, 34–35); Stat. 25 Edw. I, Tallage (*SR*, I, 125); *Case of Non Obstante* (1607), 12 Coke Rep. 18, 77 E.R. 1300.

Statute *de Donis* extends to the crown because it was to settle a common error; so the Statute of Eliz., of church leases; Hobt. 75, 2 Cro. 385.[1]

He thinks none of the reasons of those cases comes up to this. Though this Act prohibits trade, yet it does not prohibit the queen to trade for her own use.

He put the case upon the Statute of Mortmain,[2] that was to put a stop to the great mischief that hindered the defense of the kingdom etc., yet the king's prerogative could not be bound by that general law, for, where the crown has a precedent right or interest, a general act will not bind it, as the Statute of Marlbridge; the Statute of Magna Charta, c. 12; Westminster II, c. 3; Fitz., Abr., tit. *Receipt*, pl. 48.[3]

If the queen could dispense with this Act of Parliament, then she might certainly import for her own use. There is a great difference between a *non obstante*, which is *ius dare*, and a dispensation. (I [Eden] suppose in the crown's own case.) But he cannot reconcile it to his reason that a dispensing power should be in any but the legislature.

He mentions 12 Rep. 19; Com.; 2 Ric. II, f. 12. In that case, the king might dispense with that law, as it is there. So, if she had a dispensing power where such a prohibitory act relating to trades is, then she might certainly import, for it were absurd she could grant that to another which she cannot make use of herself.

The mischief of importing to her own use cannot by any, but the dispensing power may be of ill consequence.

He cited Thomas and Sorrell's Case, Vaughn, Levinz.[4] He takes it to be very good law.

He observed the penalty of importation is a forfeiture of the goods, which penalty is a trust committed to the queen for the good of the public. 7 Rep., Penal Law's Case.[5] And the queen cannot be possessed to the use of another. What is given to the informer is only an encouragement to him. The apportionment is by way of recompense to him. But the forfeiture is to the crown. It is very absurd the queen should thus proceed for her own wine, for, if it is forfeited, it is only forfeited to herself. It is like the case of pirate goods, 50 Edw. III; 35 Hen. VI,

---

[1] Stat. 13 Edw. I, Westminster II, c. 1 (*SR*, I, 71); Stat. 13 Eliz. I, c. 10, s. 2 (*SR*, IV, 544–545); *Rex v. Bishop of Norwich* (1615), Hobart 75, 80 E.R. 224, Croke Jac. 385, 79 E.R. 329, also 1 Rolle Rep. 235, 81 E.R. 456, 3 Bulstrode 88, 81 E.R. 75.

[2] Stat. 7 Edw. I (*SR*, I, 51); Stat. 18 Edw. I, c. 3 (*SR*, I, 106).

[3] Stat. 52 Hen. III (*SR*, I, 19–25); Stat. 25 Edw. I, Magna Carta, c. 12 (*SR*, I, 115–116); Stat. 13 Edw, I, Westminster II, c. 3 (*SR*, I, 73–74); YB Mich. 1 Hen. VI, f. 4, pl. 13, Fitzherbert, Abr., *Resceit*, pl. 48 (1422).

[4] *Thomas v. Sorrell* (1667), Vaughan 330, 124 E.R. 1098, 1 Levinz 217, 83 E.R. 376, also 1 Freeman 85, 137, 89 E.R. 63, 100, 2 Keble 245, 280, 322, 372, 416, 790, 84 E.R. 152, 174, 201, 233, 261, 500, 3 Keble 76, 119, 143, 155, 184, 223, 233, 264, 84 E.R. 603, 627, 642, 649, 665, 689, 694, 712.

[5] *Case of Penal Statutes* (1605), 7 Coke Rep. 36, 77 E.R. 465.

25, Br., [Abr., *Prerogative*], pl. 5, 120; Stamford, *Prerog.*, 72, fol. 74, 76, for, when a claim is made, it appears upon record they belong to the queen, and, being in the possession of the crown, they ought to apply by way of a petition and not by way of an information, which is an indignity upon the crown.[1]

Bury: He thinks this information is plainly restrained to be this Act by the concluding of the special verdict. But he is of opinion that it was not imported contrary to it. He took notice of the title of it, which is only of trade and commerce with France, and so the information suggests there is a great difference between the queen and a particular person only a private subject; these are within the Act because of the mischief that may be. By inflicting the penalty, it appears the Act does not design to extend to the queen. 11 Rep. 60.

There is an exception to that rule that, where a forfeiture is generally given, it shall go to the crown, *viz.* where any person, by the offense, is dispossessed of his property, it shall go to him though generally because of the prejudice it is to him, as, in the case of tithes, the treble value given by Edw. VI shall go to the party.[2] And, as to what is given to the informer, that is only an apportionment to him, the forfeiture being before. 2 Rich., fo. 12. Now, when the Act appoints a forfeiture to the queen, [there is] a great argument that it did not design the queen to be bound by it. The queen's goods cannot be forfeited to herself. If it had been intended that the queen's [goods] thus imported would have been of any ill use, they would have provided against that.

It was all that a man might be punished by way of an indictment upon this Act. Cro. Jac. 648.

He mentioned the provisos only extend to the subjects.

To the objection this may be a means of letting in great frauds, he thinks, when it happens so, it may alter the case.

He takes it the queen is not within the Act.

Ward: The Act of Navigation is not before us at this time. The Act about Rhenish Wines [is], so that this information wholly subsists upon this Act.

He took notice of the four parts of the Act and, as he termed it, anatomized it [*blank*] Statute Edw. IV [*blank*]. 3 Inst. 195. He can exhibit no information upon a penal law, but it must be *tam quam*.

He does not think there is any occasion for a petition, but that the Attorney General is properly the defendant; in this case, the nature of the case requires it should be so.

As to its being forfeited to the queen, it is already her own. And he remembered a case where it was attempted to seize the queen's own ship, but it was re-

---

[1] *Attorney General, ex. rel. Grimsby v. Eyre* (Ex. 1456), YB Mich. 35 Hen. VI, f. 25, pl. 33, also Exch. Repts. Middle Ages, 91, 2 Brooke, Abr., *Prerogative*, pl. 5; YB Mich. Hen. VI, f. 6, pl. 11 (1432), 2 Brooke, Abr., *Prerogative*, pl. 120; W. Staunford, *Exposition of the King's Prerogative* (1567), ff. 74, 76.

[2] Stat. 2 & 3 Edw. VI, c. 13 (*SR*, IV, 55–58).

jected. And he takes it the queen's goods are not liable to a forfeiture, nor capable of it. And so he was of opinion that judgment ought to be for the defendant.

Parker 274, 145 E.R. 778, Dodd 355

Information upon a seizure of French wine, as forfeited by the importation of it contrary to the Act 3d of the Queen, c. 13,[1] for prohibiting all trade and commerce with France; and which enacted, that no French wines, nor any other goods or commodities whatsoever of the growth, product or manufacture of any of the dominions or territories of the French king, should be imported into England, under the penalty of the forfeiture of all such goods and commodities, and of the ship or vessel in which they should be imported; one moiety to Her Majesty, and the other moiety to him who should seize, inform, or sue for the same.

A writ of appraisement was sued out; and by the indenture returned thereupon, the wine was valued at £1600. Mr. Attorney General entered a *nolle prosequi* as to one moiety; and as to the other, pleaded that the wine was not imported contrary to the form of the statute. A special verdict was found, that the wine was French wine, bought in Holland by the queen's order, with her money, and for the necessary use of her and her family: afterwards, by her order, imported into England, for the use aforesaid.

The question was, if this wine, being the queen's wine, and imported for the use aforesaid, was forfeited by the words or intent of the said act?

After several arguments, all the barons agreed, that the dispensing power was abolished by the Statute 1 Will. & Mar.,[2] but they differed in the construction of the Act 3d of Ann. And argued *seriatim*.

Baron Lovell was of opinion for the plaintiff, that the act was an absolute prohibition, without regard to person or quality, and extended to the queen as well as to her subjects: and as to the objection, that the queen could not forfeit to herself, he answered, that the forfeiture was formally to the queen, but substantially to the queen and informer, each a moiety.

Baron Price was of opinion for the defendant, that the statute was to restrain trade with France; but that this case was not within the mischief intended to be prevented, the wine being found to be for the necessary use of Her Majesty and her family. If the verdict had found that any person had traded for this wine under the queen's authority, it would have been forfeited; but here it was only imported for the use of the queen's own family; and not by way of trade or merchandize. This is a supposed forfeiture by act of parliament to the queen; but she could not forfeit to herself, and the moiety to the informer was only the method of distribution. He thought that this information could not be maintained but

---

1 Stat. 3 & 4 Ann., c. 12 (*SR*, VIII, 360).

2 Stat. 1 Will. & Mar., sess. 2, c. 2, s. 2 (*SR*, VI, 145).

that the plaintiff's remedy was by petition, if he had any right. Stamford's *Prerogative*, 72, 74, 76.

Baron BURY: This act related to trade; and the person importing is intended a merchant for his own benefit, and not for the use of the queen or her domestic family. All forfeitures by statute are to the queen, it not specially given. Dr. Foster's Case, 11 Co. 60.[1]

Lord Chief Baron WARD: A prohibition under a penalty is not an absolute prohibition, but *sub modo*; and the prohibition in this case extends not to the queen; the wine is found to be necessary for the use of Her Majesty and her family; and if had been imported in a British man of war, should the queen forfeit the man of war to herself?

The Barons argued more at large; and this is only a short account of their reasons. Judgment was given for the defendant.

[Notes of the evidence and argument of counsel: Lincoln's Inn MS. Misc. 536, f. [141].]

290

The Clerk of the Market's Case

(Ex. 1708)

Clerks of the market within the verge are required to send their estreats into the Exchequer.

Estreats of fines can be quashed for uncertainty.

Actions for levying the revenue of the crown should be begun or removed into the Court of Exchequer.

Lincoln's Inn MS. Misc. 538, f. [24v]

7 February 1707[/08]. Clerk of the Market within the verge of the queen's household.

The estreat was quashed for uncertainty; the fines returned were upon the constables of Greenwich for not making returns, not saying of what process, precept, or warrant and moreover the precepts were awarded to the high constables and not to the constables upon whom the fines and amercements were set and moreover no grant or deputation was enrolled in the court that the court could take notice of any such grant, for all which reasons, the court quashed and set aside the estreats returned into court.

But the court held that the estreats of the clerks of the market duly returned into court are a good charge to levy the sums unless discharged by a plea or other good cause and that they are part of the revenue of the crown, for which see the Statute 22 & 23 Car. II, ca. [*blank*], for the better recovery of fines etc. whereby the clerks of the market within the verge are required under penalties to return

[1] *Foster's Case* (1614), 11 Coke Rep. 56, 77 E.R. 1222.

their estreats into the Exchequer. *Vide* also the Statute of 32 Hen. VIII, ca. 20, § 6, and 17 Car. II, ca. 19, § 1.[1]

And though, in this and the last term, there were some proceedings in the Queen's Bench in the case of one [*blank*], who had brought an action there against [*blank*] for levying some fines upon estreats of the clerk of the market about the manor of Stepney, which were set over to him upon the sheriff's apposal, being within that liberty and were scheduled and the schedules under seal of the court delivered to him, but he had no order or process of the court for levying then, and, thereupon, the parties brought their action in the Queen's Bench, which, upon a motion in this court, were ordered to be laid in the Office of Pleas of this court, being as forward here as there, as is usual in cases of actions brought against officers for levying the crown revenues or duties, against which order, the Court of Queen's Bench took exceptions and ordered the party to show cause why a [writ of] prohibition should not go against him to stay his proceedings upon that order in the Exchequer and sometimes high and big words were uttered and some expressions in some rules used of prohibiting the Court of the Exchequer, which surely could not be done, the court being of equal antiquity and authority and the only court for determining the crown revenues. But, afterwards, the party that moved the Court of Exchequer for the order to remove the action perceiving that he had not pursued a proper way to have the fines levied as he had begun and attempted, nor was the court informed when they made that order of the true state of the case how it stood but only that an action was brought against an officer for levying the crown revenue by the process of the court, which, in truth, was not so, but had it been so, the court would have justified the order; he moved the Exchequer to discharge his own order, which was done.

But no doubt ever was or can be made but that, if an action be brought in the Queen's Bench, Common Pleas, or other court of law for levying the crown revenue by process or *virtute officii*, but such actions have been and ought to be removed into the Exchequer of Pleas and be as forward there as in the other court.

Mr. Earle's Case[2] was famous where, upon a seizure of wine and a condemnation for want of a claim, he brought an action in the Queen's Bench, which, being ordered to be removed, was refused and proceeded on, and, thereupon, the Exchequer awarded a [writ of] attachment against him, and the jurisdiction of the court in that case upon a view and producing of multitudes of precedents in all times vindicated, though, at first, big words were uttered about prohibiting the court, but nothing was done, nor could be. And after Mr. Earle's submission, the Exchequer discharged his contempt.

---

[1] Stat. 22 & 23 Car. II, c. 22 (*SR*, V, 739–741); Stat. 32 Hen. VIII, c. 20, s. 6 (*SR*, III, 771–772); Stat. 17 Car. II, c. 9 (*SR*, V, 580–583).

[2] *Earle v. Paine* (K.B. 1700), 2 Salkeld 550, 91 E.R. 466.

It seems to be the course of the Exchequer that, in the case of any Greenwax set over upon the apposal to any liberty or persons claiming a right thereto, that the schedules thereto sealed and writ of assistance granted for levying thereof is a good process for so doing to entitle such lord of a liberty or person, but why should not the sheriff, upon his first process, levy all and, at his apposal before the Foreign Apposer, and pay over what belongs to the liberty without further proceeding by estreats.

[Other copies of this report: Georgetown Univ. Law Sch. MS. B88–9, f. 366.]

291

Harris v. Richardson

(Ex. 1708)

The question in this case was whether court costs are payable where a plaintiff sues an action of debt on a judgment but fails to prove the judgment.

Lincoln's Inn MS. Misc. 538, f. [25]

Office of Pleas.

The plaintiff brings [an action of] debt upon a judgment in the [Court of] Great Sessions of Wales. The defendant pleads *nul tiel record.* A day is given to bring it in, but there is a failer, and judgment is entered *quod defendens eat inde sine die.*

Upon which, *Winnington*, for the defendant prays costs within the Statute of 4 Jac. I, ca. 3,[1] which gives costs to the defendant upon the nonsuit of the plaintiff or a verdict against him, supposing that this failer of the plaintiff's having the record at the day is either a nonsuit or at least to be considered as such within the meaning of that Statute, which enlarged the remedy for costs to other actions than the Statute of 23 Hen. VIII, ca. 15,[2] extended to. And both statutes were made to give recompense of costs against plaintiffs in vexatious actions, which that in question appears to be, as founding it upon a supposed judgment where none such is and so [it is] willfully vexatious, and remedial laws are beneficially expounded for the obtaining the remedy and preventing the mischief and is within the same reason and agreeable to like expositions of statutes. Cases cited were Moyle's *Entries*, 108; Cro. Car. 434, 449, 532; *et e contra*: Cro. Car. 545; 1 Siderfin 142; 2d Inst. 651; 2 Leon. 9, pl. 12; 2d book of Townesend's printed 1674, fo. 159, 161.[3]

---

[1] Stat. 4 Jac. I, c. 3 (*SR*, IV, 1141).

[2] Stat. 23 Hen. VIII, c. 15 (*SR*, III, 380).

[3] *James v. Tutney* (1639), Croke Car. 497, 532, 79 E.R. 1029, 1061, also W. Jones 421, 434, 82 E.R. 221, 228, March 28, 82 E.R. 396; *Lyster v. Home* (1639), Croke Car.

But *per curiam*: There is no rule for costs, there being no precedents for it, and this is not within the Statute, but a special case and [*casus*] *omissus* out of the Act.

[Other copies of this report: Georgetown Univ. Law Sch. MS. B88–9, f. 367v.]

292

Groobier v. Singleton

(Ex. 1708)

Customs house officers are liable in tort for wrongful seizures of goods that were lawfully imported.

Lincoln's Inn MS. Misc. 538, f. [33]

Tuesday, 27 April 1708. Office of Pleas in the Exchequer.

The plaintiff, being a merchant, brought an action of trespass against the defendants [Singleton and Hardwick], being Custom House officers, for taking and carrying away 65,000 weight of saltpeter of the value of £500 without any just or reasonable cause.

The defendants pleaded not guilty. And by the laws relating to customs, having liberty to plead the general issue and give the special matter in evidence, they did so.

And, upon a trial by a special jury in London last Hilary term in the Guildhall and after a long evidence on both sides, they found a verdict for the plaintiff, and gave £100 damages.

And, upon a motion for a new trial upon two grounds, first, that the defendants had a probable ground of seizure of the saltpeter as forfeited within the Act of Navigation, 12 Car. II, ca. 18,[1] for that it was in the opinion of divers knowing persons saltpeter of the growth of Asia, Africa, or America, *viz.* of the East Indies and was brought into England from Hamburg in Germany, not being of the growth or manufacture of Germany, contrary to that Act and, therefore, forfeited and liable to seizure, a moiety to the queen and the other moiety to the defendants, and that, therefore, it would be hard and discouraging to the officers to have actions brought against them where they had probable cause of seizure though they do not prevail at the trial of such seizures;

544, 79 E.R. 1069, also March 12, 82 E.R. 389; *Mayor of Southampton v. Richards* (1663), 1 Siderfin 142, 82 E.R. 1020, also 1 Keble 417, 467, 497, 504, 83 E.R. 1027, 1057, 1075, 1078; E. Coke, *Second Institute* (1642), p. 651; *Anonymous* (1576 × 1577), 2 Leonard 9, 74 E.R. 314; G. Townsend, *Second Book of Judgments* (1674).

[1] Stat. 12 Car. II, c. 18 (*SR*, V, 246–250).

Secondly, that in case an action should have been maintainable in this case against the defendants, yet that the damages of £100 are excessive and unreasonable.

There were no affidavits produced of any miscarriage or want of evidence.

I [*Edward Ward*] gave the court a full state of the case and evidence. The plaintiff imported the saltpeter, openly entered it as such at the Custom House, and paid the duty as imported from Germany and produced testimonials of it, and the defendants, after that, the same day, made the seizure. And, upon the plaintiff's agent's application to them to know the reason and to forego the seizure, they told him he must apply to the East India Company, they conceiving it to be East India saltpeter and not German. The defendants prosecuted the seizure in this court, and gave notice of trial. But the plaintiffs prayed a commission to examine witnesses in Germany, which was granted. And it was fully proved that it was of the growth of Germany and imported directly from thence, after which commission was returned, the defendants here did not proceed further upon their information so that the seizure being made in 1704 and the commission was returned in 1705, in 1706, the plaintiff had a writ of delivery, but he did not demand the goods by virtue of it full half a year after. And it was proved that, at the time of the seizure, the saltpeter was worth about £6 a hundred, but fell to about £3 a hundred at the time of the writ of delivery and of the delivery of it. There was no doubt but it was German saltpeter and duly imported. And it was proved that saltpeter had formerly been imported from Germany, though some of the custom officers knew it not, and that when saltpeter was dear in time of war and that it was distinguishable by its yellowness from Indian saltpeter, which is whiter. And it was proved that the defendants, pending the seizure, told the plaintiff's agent he must apply to the East India Company.

The defendants' counsel, at the trial and here, insisted that the plaintiff might have had a writ of delivery for the asking but did not. The jury was told that, where there is probable cause of seizure, no action should lie. But it seems the jury took this seizure to be made at the instance and on the behalf of the East India Company to deter the importation of any saltpeter from Germany, and, therefore, took it that it was a seizure at their peril. And they gave damages accordingly.

It seems hard, when merchants have imported and entered and paid duties, then to have seizures made at least without acquainting the commissioners or their officers of the customs with it, though no doubt they may but at their own peril, and, if a merchant be in the right, it is hard a bare suspicion should bereave him of goods and no law compels him to sue a writ of delivery. If the now defendants had offered the plaintiff to have had them upon security, it might in some measure have mitigated the damage, both in waste and value. And, as the complexion of this whole case was, it did seem the seizers referred the plaintiff all along to the East India Company. And, if they did not act at their desire or order, they might in order to a new trial at least have made an oath of it.

It appeared the plaintiff was put to very great charges about the seizure and that the goods were wasted and sunk in price above £100 and, in regard it was too hard to think that the plaintiff had not a cause of action when not in the least fault and that merchants should have their goods seized without just cause and it being as lawful to import saltpeter from Germany as the East Indies, a prosecution should not be carried in favor of one sort of trade against other lawful traders upon suspicion or pretense without very probable cause and merchants when trading lawfully ought to be encouraged. And, if the plaintiff had a cause of action, the jury are judges of the damages, and the damages do not exceed nor come up to what was proved the merchant lost and suffered.

The two barons, BURY and SMITH, to which I [EDWARD WARD] assented, *dissentiente* PRICE, were against a new trial.

[Other copies of this report: Georgetown Univ. Law Sch. MS. B88–10, f. 608.]

293

Blacket v. Thornton

(Ex. 1708)

Incorrect venue is cured by a failure to object before the trial and verdict.

Lincoln's Inn MS. Misc. 538, f. [36v]

Yorkshire.

The plaintiff [Blacket, executor of John Blacket] brings an action of covenant against the defendant [Roger Thornton] upon an assignment of a lease to the defendant wherein the defendant covenanted to pay the rent upon the original lease to the original lessor. And, for non-payment, this action is brought.

The defendant pleads that the premises leased and assigned to him was a copyhold estate lying in Durham and he held of the bishop there and that, before the assignment to him, the bishop entered for a forfeiture. The plaintiff, who had laid his action of covenant in Yorkshire, where the assignment was made, replied and, by protestation that the premises were not copyhold, traverses the bishop's entry. And thereupon, issue was joined. And there was a trial in Yorkshire and a verdict for the plaintiff, and damages were given.

And now, *Bridges* moves in arrest of judgment that here was a mistrial, for the issue being entry or not an entry by the bishop, the trial ought to have been in Durham, where the lands lay and where only the entry could be.

Serjeant *Chesshyre*, for plaintiff, admitted it to be a good exception if not helped by the Statute 16 & 17 Car. II, ca. 8,[1] which after a verdict helps all trials where there is no right venue so as the cause was tried by a jury of the proper

[1] Stat. 16 & 17 Car. II, c. 8 (*SR*, V, 556–557).

county or place where the action is laid, and, here, the action was laid in the County of York, and [there was] a verdict by a jury of that county. And so it is within the words of that Statute.

And he cited these cases to be resolved in point, viz. 1 Sanders 246, L. 2, 30, Craft and Boit,[1] where an action of slander was brought by the plaintiff for the defendant's saying the plaintiff had stolen plate out of Wadham College in Oxford. The defendant, by a plea, justified the saying of those words for that the plaintiff did steal the plate out of Wadham College, and the trial was in London, and the verdict was for the plaintiff. And it was moved in arrest of judgment for a mistrial ut supra and that Statute ought not to be construed to help a trial in a wrong county, but only a wrong venue in the right county. But, by Keeling, Rainsford, and Morton, dissentiente Twisden, fortiter, the Statute has helped, it being within the very words, and the plaintiff had judgment. And this has been followed by several resolutions. 3 Levins 394, 6 W. & M., Common Bench, Hunt's Case, upon a writ of error on a like judgment, where an entry and expulsion in Essex was laid and tried in London, affirmed by four against three. But he said it was per majoritatem numero non pondere. 3 Keble 371, 654; and Michaelmas [term] 9 Will. III [blank], Lady Calverly against Sir Richard Levins, upon a covenant to repair a house in Chester, the action was laid in Derbyshire, and the question was about the repairs, whether they were made or not; and the trial was ruled good, for the reason above of the Statute.[2]

And the plaintiff had judgment here by reason of the Statute and those resolutions upon it, which if *res integra* at this day seem not to be so reasonable, though not now to be unsettled.

[Other copies of this report: Georgetown Univ. Law Sch. MS. B88–10, p. 615.]

294

Leigh v. Booth

(Ex. 1708)

In this case, the defendant's pleading did not sufficiently respond to the plaintiff's allegation of tort.

---

[1] *Craft v. Boite* (1669), 1 Williams Saunders 241, 85 E.R. 276, *sub nom. Craft v. Winter*, Lincoln's Inn MS. Misc. 500, p. 31, also T. Raymond 181, 83 E.R. 95, 1 Ventris 22, 86 E.R. 16, 2 Keble 496, 84 E.R. 311.

[2] *Hunt's Case* (1694) 3 Levinz 394, 83 E.R. 747; *Jennings v. Hunkin* (1674), 3 Keble 350, 371, 509, 84 E.R. 760, 772, 849; *Aynsworth v. Chamberlain* (1676), 3 Keble 654, 675, 691, 84 E.R. 934, 946, 956, also T. Jones 82, 84 E.R. 1157; *Leving v. Lady Calverly* (1698), 1 Lord Raymond 330, 91 E.R. 1116, Carthew 448, 90 E.R. 859, Comberbach 472, 90 E.R. 598, 5 Modern 405, 87 E.R. 733, Holt K.B. 710, 90 E.R. 1292; Stat. 16 & 17 Car. II, c. 8 (*SR*, V, 556–557).

Lincoln's Inn MS. Misc. 538, f. [37]

The plaintiff declared in an action of trespass assault and battery against the defendant for that he did at such a time and place beat, wound, and evil entreat him and a certain hat of the plaintiff valued at £5 *ad tunc et ibidem cepit, laceravit, et in ignem projecit, combussit, et spoliavit et alia enormia etc. ad damnum* £500.

The defendant after imparled. And, as to force and arms and everything against the peace and, as to the wounding, he pleads not guilty. And, thereupon, [there is an] issue. *Et quod residuum transgressionem praedictum*, he pleads *actio non* for that the plaintiff *tempore quo etc.* at the place aforesaid made an assault upon him and would have beaten and evilly entreated him, *per quod*, the defendant then and there his hands upon the plaintiff (his hat upon his head being) did *molliter imponere* to defend himself and restrain the plaintiff *ne damnum ipso* the defendant *ulterius inferret prout ei bene licuit, et si quod damnum* to the plaintiff or his hat *inde evenit*, it was *ex insultu* the plaintiff and in the proper defense of the defendant, *et hoc paratus est verificare*, and he prays judgment *si* the plaintiff *actionem suum manutenere debeat.*

To this plea, the plaintiff demurred specially, and assigned for cause that the defendant, by his plea, has not shown any sufficient cause why he tore, cast in the fire, burned, and spoiled the plaintiff's hat, which is part of the trespass in the declaration mentioned and is not defended nor justified by the defendant's plea. And because the defendant has not shown any special necessity why he spoiled the hat or that he without such spoiling could not have defended himself against the plaintiff's assault. The defendant joined in demurrer.

And, after two several arguments by *Chesshyre* and *Lutwyche*, for the plaintiff, and by Serjeant *Parker* and *Sir Edward Northey*, for the defendant, the court unanimously gave judgment for the plaintiff that the defendant's plea as to the matter charged about the hat did not answer and, principally, for the reasons and causes assigned by the plaintiff's demurrer. Hobt. 134; [*blank*] Levins [*blank*], Gibson and Pepper; 1 Sanders 84; 12 Hen. VII, 14; 21 Hen. VII, 39; 8 Edw. IV, 8; 2 Roll's Abr. 448, pl. 8; 1 Mod. rep. 36; Moor 864.[1] And *molliter manus imposuit* cannot extend to violent and willful actions, as tearing and burning the hat, and *in son assault demesne* the tearing of clothes without cause shown and how and inevitable cannot be justified.

[Other copies of this report: Georgetown Univ. Law Sch. MS. B88–10, p. 617.]

---

[1] *Weaver v. Ward* (1616), Hobart 134, 80 E.R. 284, Moore K.B. 864, 72 E.R. 958; *Wright v. Ramscot* (1667), 1 Williams Saunders 82, 85 E.R. 92, also 1 Siderfin 336, 82 E.R. 1141, 1 Levinz 216, 83 E.R. 376, 2 Keble 237, 84 E.R. 147; YB Hil. 12 Hen. VII, f. 14, pl. 1 (1497); YB Mich. 21 Hen. VII, f. 39, pl. 51 (1505); *Cole v. Maunder* (1635), 2 Rolle, Abr., *Trespas*, pl. G, 8, p. 548; *Jones v. Tresillian* (1670), 1 Modern 36, 86 E.R. 713, also 1 Siderfin 441, 82 E.R. 1205, 1 Levinz 282, 83 E.R. 408, 2 Keble 597, 84 E.R. 375.

295

Henery, qui tam v. Richardson

(Ex. 1708)

In an action for importing prohibited French wines, the defendant cannot plead that the wines were taken as prize and that the Court of Admiralty is the proper court to decide the case, but the defendant must plead to the merits of the case.

Lincoln's Inn MS. Misc. 538, f. [38]

Michaelmas [term] 6 Anne, Queen's Remembrancer's [Office], Exchequer.

The plaintiff exhibits a Latin information by way of *devenerunt* grounded upon the Statute 3 & 4 Anne,[1] for prohibiting all trade and commerce with France, and he sets forth that certain merchants unknown between such days imported from parts beyond the seas to Ratcliff in Middlesex in the ship the *St. Peter* seventy tuns of French wines of the value of £7000 of the growth or product of France or of some of the French king's dominions before the importation thereof not being taken as prize contrary to the form of the Statute, whereby they became forfeited, and, so being forfeited, came to the hands of the defendants [Richardson and Devereux] within the said time. And he prays the said goods may remain forfeited for that cause and that he may have a moiety of the forfeiture and that the defendants may answer for the goods or for £7000, the value thereof.

The defendants, after *oyer* of the information, plead to the jurisdiction of the court, and they say *quod cognitio placitorum predarum anglice* prizes taken upon the high seas belong and time out of mind have belonged to the Court of Admiralty of the queen of Great Britain and not to any other court and that such pleas in the said Court of Admiralty, according to the maritime law, and not otherwise, ought and have used to be tried and determined. And then [they] say that, before the supposed importation of those wines in the information to Ratcliff, they were taken as prize upon the high seas by Nathan Pygram and others, subjects of the queen, *viz.* at Ratcliff aforesaid, and after they were so taken as prize, they came to the hands of the defendants by the delivery of Pygram, which said taking of the said wines as prize and coming to the defendants' hands is the same coming to the defendants' hands of the said wines whereof the plaintiff in the said information complains. *Et hoc paratus est verificare unde ex quo* the conusance of the pleas of the taking of prizes appertains to the Admiralty Court. The defendants pray judgment whether this court will or ought *placitum praedictum in et super eandem informationem versus* the defendant *cognoscere.*

[1] Stat. 3 & 4 Ann., c. 12 (*SR*, VIII, 360).

To this plea, *Montagu*, the Queen's Solicitor [General], in the vacancy of an Attorney General, demurs in common law, and, for the insufficiency of the plea, *petit judicium* without more.

The defendants join, and pray judgment whether the court here will or ought further to *cognoscere* this plea in and upon that information.

The defendants' counsel, *Ettrick, Dodd*, and *Whitaker* did not insist against the jurisdiction of the court in proceeding upon informations rightly founded upon the Act 3 & 4 Anne, where prize or not prize was not in question. But they cited many authorities to show that the Admiralty Court had the jurisdiction of prizes taken at open sea, which was not contested, where that was the only original question and did not come incidently into the cause.

But the whole court held they had a proper jurisdiction here, for the Act having made the importation of French wines not taken as prize a cause of forfeiture and recoverable by information in this court, and it being set forth in the information that these wines were imported, not being taken prize, it seems absurd to plead to the jurisdiction where the principal and original matter is the importation, which cannot be tried in the Admiralty any more than taken or not taken prize at the open sea can originally be tried in this court, and, then, upon this information, this court must proceed to try the importation and then the matter of taken or not taken prize, coming in incidentally, must be determined in this court, as the cases of Parliamentary privileges, marriages, or other ecclesiastical matters coming in incidentally must be tried and determined by the court where the original cause is triable.

And, upon the trial of this information, the defendants will have the benefit upon evidence of proving that the wines were taken and condemned as prize before importation or have pleaded that to the information, if thought fit.

But, then, the defendants' counsel insisted that the plaintiff's replication by way of demurrer did not conclude right, for he does only *petere judicium* without praying that the court's jurisdiction should be allowed, as Rastall, *Entries*, 419 and 636.

But the court held the general prayer of judgment good, for thereby, he prays the court's judgment in the matter, which is supposed will be such as the law ought to be.

Something was said that this was a new and introductive law and then giving the Admiralty a jurisdiction to enquire and proceed in collusive captures, it was an exclusion of all other ways of enquiry, for which was cited Plowden 113a and 11 rep. 64.[1]

But, to that, it was answered that, by the scope of this Act, this cause was within the jurisdiction of the court. And collusion or not collusion is an incident

---

[1] *Thynne v. Earl of Pembroke* (1554), 1 Plowden 111, 75 E.R. 173; *Shoyle v. Foster* (1614), 11 Coke Rep. 56, 77 E.R. 1222, also 1 Rolle Rep. 88, 81 E.R. 349, 2 Bulstrode 324, 80 E.R. 1158.

only and enquirable in this court upon an information for unlawful importation and, though the Admiralty may according to the power and in the case and manner directed by the Act proceed to examine and try the matter of collusion, yet there is no exclusion of this court to try any fraud or collusion in a matter triable in this court, there being no negative words in the Act.

And so, upon the whole matter, the court gave judgment for a *respondeat ouster.*

And the defendants' counsel submitted, and prayed time to plead in chief an issuable plea, and would take notice of a trial next term.

[Other copies of this report: Georgetown Univ. Law Sch. MS. B88–10, p. 619, p. 2.]

296

Eyres v. Andrews

(Ex. 1708)

Officers of the Exchequer have a privilege to be discharged of all tolls for their goods carried over Windsor Bridge.

Lincoln's Inn MS. Misc. 538, f. [40]

Trinity [term] 1708.

The plaintiff, being an attorney of the Queen's Remembrancer's Office, brings a writ of privilege to be discharged of all tolls for his goods carried over Windsor Bridge. And he produces the writ and an order or record in the Queen's Remembrancer's Office *per* Hilary record 14 Car. I, ro. 143.

The writ of privilege was now brought and *teste* the 12th of February last, reciting that *tam ex dignitate nostra regia quam ex consuetudine antiqua secundum eandem a tempore quo non existat memoria hominum usitat' huiusque [?] fuer' obtent'*, the barons of the Exchequer, resident clerks, and all other ministers *sive de clero sive de regia cur' qui assident' ex mandat'* to any other causes out of the Exchequer under any other judges *sub qualis mota fuerit*, whether ecclesiastical or secular, ought not to be called and, if called, *ratione regiae potestatis publica auctoritate excusantur* and then sets forth their being free from all common assises, suits, counties, hundreds, and courts whatsoever *tam de et pro [. . .] suis quam de et pro feod' suis ac etiam de murdris, scutagiis, vigiliis, et dangeldis necnon de quibuscunque provisionibus seu provisoribus et al. soluc' nomine consuetud' pro quibuscunque victualibus [. . .] suarum in quibuscunque urbibus, castellis, et locis maritimis empt' ac de quisbuscunque assertis dominorum suorum necnon de sollitione alicuius theolon' sive tolnet' liberi et quieti esse debentur*, and that they ought not to be impleaded *alibi* than in the said Exchequer so long as the Exchequer shall be open *prout per inspectionem Rubei Libri de Scaccario nostro praedicto sub titulo, viz. quae sunt jura et dignitates residentium ad scrinum destinavit Rex Henricus primus ita breve suum ad [. . .] ut assidentes illic' ab hiis liberi erunt jure perpetuo.*

Then, this writ commands all to whom it shall come that Thomas Eyre, Esq., one of the sworn clerks of Henry Ayloffe, Esq., the Queen's Remembrancer of her Exchequer *cujus continua residentia ibidem requiritur contra tenorem libertatum praedictum* not to molest nor as much as in them is permit to be molested *sed firmam pacem ei inde habere faciatis sub [. . .] incumbent'*. And, if they have any distress from him taken for these occasions or any of them that they do redeliver the same to him, and, if they have arrested him, *tunc ipsum ad largum ire permittatis indilate sub poena que incumbit in cuius rei testimonium has litteras nostras fieri fecimus [. . .] patentes teste* the Chief Baron, *per Rubeum Librum praedictum et per Barones*. And, upon an affidavit made that the defendant, being served with this writ of privilege left with the party to consider, did nevertheless insist upon to have and, accordingly, did receive from Mr. Eyres's servant at several times several sums for money for toll for his goods arising from his estate and other goods of his being carried over the bridge at Windsor as belonging to the Corporation of Windsor. And, therefore, Mr. *Ettrick*, of his counsel, prayed a [writ of] attachment.

And the court ordered the defendant to show cause why not a [writ of] attachment [should not go] upon the reading of a record Hilary [term] 14 Jac. I, rot. 143, ex parte Rememeratoris Regis in Scaccario where the case was that, upon an affidavit made that the tenants of John Wingfield, Esq., one of the attorneys in the Treasurer's Remembrancer's Office coming through Gunworth, Northamptonshire, with a carriage laden with goods for the furniture and provision of Wingfield's house, a farmer of the tolls of Gunworth ferry with others demanded a toll for the said carriages for Sir William Fitzwilliam, and that they, being acquainted with the privilege of Wingfield to be free from the tolls, refused to allow it, though they were offered a knowledge penny, but insisted on the toll and endeavored in a violent manner to seize a horse, which the servant of Wingfield endeavored to hinder, and were assaulted and beaten by a woman and Sir William Fitzwilliam insisted on the toll and bade Wingfield try his charter. And, thereupon, an attachment issued against them that seized the horse and committed the assault and were bound by a recognizance to appear de die in diem etc. And they were after[wards] committed to the Fleet [Prison] and presently brought to the bar, and submitted to the court. And Wingfield being satisfied for his goods taken etc. and the trespass and for his charges and they being poor, ex gratia curiae, they were discharged, and the recognizance vacated.

Note, in the principal case of Mr. Eyres, the writ of privilege was obeyed, and his goods then and ever after suffered to pass toll free, as Eyres himself informed me [Edward Ward].

[Other copies of this report: Georgetown Univ. Law Sch. MS. B88–10, p. 624.]

297

Stiles, qui tam v. Dickinson

(Ex. 1708)

An out of court settlement is a valid and enforceable contract regardless of later unforeseen developments in the law.

Lincoln's Inn MS. Misc. 538, f. [41]

Trinity [term] 1708.

Upon an information of seizure of turmeric for not being garbled according to the Statute 1 Jac. I, ca. [*blank*],[1] exhibited Michaelmas term last. And there was a trial upon it. And, by consent, a juror was withdrawn upon the defendant's payment of the duty and such costs as the prosecutor shall make oath of [and] the goods shall be delivered to the defendant. And that order being made an order of the court 28th November 1707 and entered by consent of the Attorney [General and the] defendant that a juror be withdrawn *quodque* upon payment of the duty and such costs as William Stewart, the prosecutor should swear to be expended in the prosecuting of that suit, the goods seized should be delivered to the defendant. And it was further ordered by like consent that the rule should be made a rule of court, which was done accordingly.

And the prosecutor having sworn the costs to be [*blank*] and the defendant being served with the order to pay them and having refused, a [writ of] attachment was prayed for non-payment, the goods having been long since delivered to the defendant, the costs not then sworn to, but now insisted upon.

After that trial, there was an Act of Parliament[2] passed for taking away the garbling of spices and giving Stewart a recompense for his office of Garbler and repealing the Statute of 1 Jac. I, for garbling of spices, from henceforth and whereby all suits and informations in the Exchequer now depending or hereafter to be prosecuted for any seizure or for seizure upon the said repealed Act or for any offense against it should be and were thereby declared to be discontinued, discharged, and determined and no proceedings to be had thereupon and all seizures upon that Act made or to be made are discharged, released, and declared nul and void and that from and after the full payment of £967 10s. to Stewart for a compensation for his interest in the office, all the moneys arising by the admissions of brokers shall go to City of London and Stewart's lease from the end of that session of Parliament to be void.

The defendant insists, first, that this Act referring to the first day of Parliament which began 23 November 1707, which was before the trial, and so making that suit and all the proceedings void has discharged not only the trial but the

[1] Stat. 1 Jac. I, c. 19 (*SR*, IV, 1036–1037).

[2] Stat. 6 Ann., c. 68 (*SR*, VIII, 816–817).

rule and order of the court for costs and so [he is] not liable for the costs. Second, the rule and order are not to be interpreted as the defendant's consent absolutely to pay the costs so as to be binding to him to pay the costs in all events for that payment of costs depends upon the delivery of the goods, it being said upon the delivery of the goods, the costs are to be paid so that the costs do not depend or subsist upon the defendant's consent, but only upon the delivery of the goods and the defendant need not have delivered the goods until he had received the costs.

Per me [Edward Ward]: The order of the court is not touched by the Act of repeal, by the consent of the parties, the cause was determined before; the repealing of that Act was so much as [. . .] though, by relation, it precedes the trial and order, yet such relation shall not work an injury nor discharge the defendant's consent, which is a collateral thing to the Act and the intent of it. And though the prosecutor need not have delivered the goods before he had his costs, yet it being the intent and, by consequence, the agreement of all the parties that the defendant should have his goods and pay the costs, and having taken his goods, he ought to pay the costs, his consent going to that payment of them. If he had his costs and his goods, in all probability, would have been forfeited if such consent had not been.

And after[wards], the costs were paid; else [a writ of] attachment [would have been issued].

[Other copies of this report: Georgetown Univ. Law Sch. MS. B88–10, p. 627.]

298

Harris and Townsend's Case

(Ex. 1708)

The Court of Exchequer can discharge or reduce the penalty of a bond to keep the peace.

Lincoln's Inn MS. Misc. 538, f. [42]

[Walter] Ducain being indicted for seditious words at the Oxford Assizes, two trials were had against him, upon which there were two special verdicts, and two recognizances entered into by Ducain and by Harris and Townsend, his two sureties, of £20 apiece which being forfeited and estreated into the Exchequer on the petition of the sureties to the Lord Treasurer and certificate of the Recorder of Oxford that Ducain was expelled [from] the university and gone from Oxford and thereby the university and town and the prosecutors were satisfied and desirous that the recognizances of the sureties might be discharged or compounded, they being very poor, upon a letter from the Lord Treasurer to the Chief Baron where His Lordship, signifying his being well informed of the sureties' great poverty, desired the Chief Baron and the rest of the barons to admit them, the said sureties, to compound their said recognizances in the most easy manner that might be, whereupon, on their counsel's motion in open court, their recognizances were compounded by the court for a 13s. 4d. fine, the composition fees amounting to about £6.

Note the court, by a [writ of] privy seal, might discharge as well as compound. But the desire here was only to be compounded.

[Other copies of this report: Georgetown Univ. Law Sch. MS. B88–10, p. 633.]

299

Mansell v. Mansell

(Ex. 1708)

No court costs are given for the failure to execute a writ of enquiry of damages.

Lincoln's Inn MS. Misc. 538, f. [43]

Trinity [term] 7 Queen Anne.

Mr. *Lloyd* had formerly and now moved again for costs to be paid by the plaintiff for not executing a writ of inquiry of damages having given notice thereof. And the defendant attending, the court formerly enquired of the judges of the Queen's Bench, and the Chief Justice said they awarded costs. But the other judges said to the contrary. And the judges of the Common Pleas [were] said never [to] give costs in such a case.

And *Marriot*, Clerk of the Pleas, said [they were] never given in this court, and upon his enquiry amongst the officers of the other courts, and they told him no costs [. . .] unless for some special reason or cause, but, in ordinary cases, never. And 1st Ventris 305[1] there is a note that the King's Bench never gives costs for not executing a writ of enquiry of damages though notice be given.

So, the motion here was denied.

Query the reason of the case, but the practice prevails.

[Other copies of this report: Georgetown Univ. Law Sch. MS. B88–10, p. 634.]

300

Child's Case

(Ex. 1709)

Debtors to the crown cannot use writs of extent to procure assignments of other person's debts.

---

[1] Note (1677), 1 Ventris 305, 86 E.R. 197.

Lincoln's Inn MS. Misc. 538, f. [55]

Hilary term 1708/9, 7 Queen Anne.

Note upon a motion in court, [a writ of] immediate extent was awarded in aid of a receiver general of the taxes against an obligor in a bond entered into by him to a woman, who, afterwards, married the receiver general, upon an affidavit that it was for a debt originally and *bona fide* due to the receiver general and that the obligor was decayed in his estate and the debt in danger to be lost etc., as is usual in such cases of extents in aid. And this was after a consideration of the Statute 7 Jac. I, ca. [*blank*],[1] and the Rules of this court 1639, touching assigning or finding debts in aid and, in both which, they carry it no further than for debts originally and *bona fide* due to the receiver, which, according to the letter, is not a debt originally due to the receiver, but to a woman whom he afterwards married. And this was done upon the authority and reason of the case of Breadman and Coles, Hobt. 253, and 2 Cro. 524, by the name of Fawne's Case,[2] wherein the words of that statement (upon which the Rules in 1639 were made), *viz.* 'originally' due to the receiver were considered and where the case in effect is the same with this, that a woman administratrix to the conusee of a statute married the king's debtor, who both, by a deed enrolled, assigned the statute of £2000 to the king, which was for payment of [. . .] debt to the king from the husband and the king's debtor. And it was resolved by the court to be a good assignment and not restrained by the Statute though not strictly originally due to the king's debtor but esteemed his own debt, though not to his own use but such as he might release or discharge and by the same reason assign. And the meaning of the Statute was to restrain the king's debtors from buying in or procuring another man's debt to be assigned, which then was a common practice.

And, in this case, it was owned to be a mistake in the case of one Child, receiver general of Surrey, who had an immediate extent set aside because it was not originally due to him in regard he, being executor to his father, took a bond in his own name for it from the debtor, which, when done, the debt by bond was thereby become an original debt to him, but Child was [. . .] as to his oath for the original because of the debt, in truth, at first, because due to his father, but now agreed to such a debt for which he ought to have had an immediate extent.

[Other copies of this report: Georgetown Univ. Law Sch. MS. B88–10, p. 644.]

---

1 Stat. 7 Jac. I, c. 15 (*SR*, IV, 1171).

2 *Breadman v. Coales*, Hobart 253, 80 E.R. 399, *sub nom. Fawn's Case*, Croke Jac. 524, 79 E.R. 448.

301

Note

(Ex. 1708)

Damages for goods wrongfully detained upon a distress are not recoverable where the owner could have recovered the goods immediately.

Lincoln's Inn MS. Misc. 538, f. [33v]

If a landlord distrains wrongfully for rent not due and detains the goods distrained or sells them, shall not the tenant recover his damages for the detainer of the goods for a long time because the tenant might have replevied them the next day if he pleased.

[Other copies of this report: Georgetown Univ. Law Sch. MS. B88–10, f. 612.]

302

Scott, qui tam v. Pigram

(Ex. 1708)

A verdict can be amended.

Dodd 214

In a [action of] *devenerunt* tried in Winchester [?] before the Chief Baron [Ward] and [upon a] verdict for the plaintiff, it was moved in arrest of judgment that the *venire* upon this roll awarded was 23 of October but the *teste* was the 31st of October.

And upon debate, the court amended it and said that [verdicts are] amendable at common law or, at least by two of them, by the Statute of Hen. VIII.[1] And upon this, a bill of exceptions [was] prayed and, this term [Trinity, 7 Anne, 1708], tendered. And whether it lies in such a case was the question. And that it does, these books were cited: Fitz., *Inquest*, 22; Br., *View*, 103; 9 Hen. V, 5; 11 Hen. VI, 30; *Old Entries* 96 B; Fitz., *Quare non admisit*, 3; 1 Ventr. 366; D. 179; 10 Hen. VII, 8; Br., [Abr.], *Error*, 50; 27 Hen. VI, 3; Regist. 122; 9 Ass. 8; 8 Hen. IV, 15, 20; 11 Hen. IV, 92; 17 Edw. III, 22; 24 Edw. III, 11; 21 Edw. IV, 20, 63; N.B. 21, 22; 27 Hen. VIII, 24, 25;[2] *Old Entries* 136; Rastall 96, 346; Brownlow, *[Latine] Redivivus*, and Wright.

---

[1] Perhaps the Statute of Jeofails, Stat. 32 Hen. VIII, c. 30 (*SR*, III, 786–787).

[2] YB Pas. 4 Edw. IV, f. 1, pl. 1 (1464), Fitzherbert, Abr., *Enquest*, pl. 22; YB Mich. 10 Hen. VII, f. 8, pl. 18 (1494), Brooke, Abr., *View*, pl. 103; YB Pas. 9 Hen. V, f. 5, pl. 16 (1421); YB Pas. 11 Hen. VI, f. 30, pl. 16 (1433); YB Pas. 16 Edw. III, pl. 5, Rolls Ser. 31b, vol. 7, p. 162 (1342), Fitzherbert, Abr., *Quare non admsit*, pl. 3; *Denison v. Ralphson*

See the opinion of the court in my notes tied to this bill and the lord Wharton's bill of exceptions.[1] As to the bill (in the amendments) of Scott, *qui tam*, the court was of the opinion that it did not lie. And in the lord Wharton's [case] that, not being taken in time, *viz.* when the evidence is given and notes in writing then made (as in the case of a special verdict) to ascertain the fact, that it ought not to be received.

Note in that case, no bill was prayed until after a private verdict was given (which was on a Saturday), and the jury, at the bar on Monday, declared they did abide by it and then a bill was offered containing many disputed facts.

303
Regina v. Wood
(Ex. 1708)

In this case, witnesses not attending the execution of an extent, a new one was ordered, and costs were reserved.

Parker 271, 145 E.R. 777

On complaint that persons had not attended the execution of a [writ of] extent, a new extent was ordered to be taken out, and the persons complained of were ordered to attend the execution of it; and after, the court would consider of their behavior and costs: and they to show cause why the prosecutor of the extent should not have costs.

304
Delove v. Bellamey
(Ex. 1708)

A bill of discovery does not lie against a public officer to set forth public records that are in his keeping.

(1682), 1 Ventris 365, 86 E.R. 235; *Herbert v. Vernon* (1560), 2 Dyer 179, 73 E.R. 394; YB 11 Hen. IV, ff. 52, 65, 92 (1410), Brooke, Abr., *Error*, pl. 50; *Torel v. Bourchier* (1448), YB Mich. 27 Hen. VI, f. 3, pl. 25; *Registrum Brevium*; YB 9 Edw. III, Lib. Ass., p. 21, pl. 8 (1335); YB Mich. & Hil. 8 Hen. IV, ff. 14, 20 (1407–1408); YB Trin. 11 Hen. IV, f. 92, pl. 49 (1410); *Raly v. Grenevil* (1343), YB Pas. 17 Edw. III, f. 21, pl. 4; YB Pas. & Mich. 21 Edw. IV, ff. 31, 63 (1481); *Natura Brevium*; YB Mich. 27 Hen. VIII, f. 24, pl. 3 (1535).

[1] *Attorney General, ex rel. Marriot v. Lord Wharton* (Ex. 1706–1708), Equity Cases Exch. 536, T. Gates, ed., *'The Great Trial' A Swaledale Lead Mining Dispute in the Court of Exchequer, 1705–1708* (2012).

2 Eq. Cas. Abr. 66, 22 E.R. 58

Easter 7 Ann. [1708].

The bill was brought against an Auditor of the Duchy, who answers that he does not know anything that is prayed in the bill, but as an officer.

[It was] resolved by all the Barons that he is not obliged to answer the bill, because every subject may have knowledge of it, paying the usual fees, and it is not charged in the bill that the defendant had any interest in the thing which is demanded, neither is it alleged that he hindered any person from searching.

305

Poole v. Wilshaw

(Ex. 1708)

A devise of an annuity is in support of, and not in addition to, an inter vivos gift of the same annual sum to the same person.

Lincoln's Inn MS. Misc. 9, p. 80

9 December 1708.

Francis Wilshaw, having two sons by his first wife and one son by his second wife, makes his will and devises his personal estate between his two sons by his first wife, who were named Francis and Benoni. And he made Thomas Wilshaw, his brother, executor.

Francis, the son, after the death of his father, died, having received his share of his father's personal estate. And Thomas, the executor, took administration during the minority of the other sons. And, thereupon, the plaintiff, who was the mother of the testator's first wife and grandmother of Francis, the son, prefers her bill for a share of Francis's, the son's, personal estate with Benoni, the brother of the whole blood, and Richard Wilshaw, the defendant, brother of the half blood.

The cause was first heard upon the 9th July 1708. And it was then strenuously argued by the civilians that she was entitled to a share and stood in equal degree with the two brothers.

But the court was of another opinion and decreed she should have no share.

Afterwards, *viz.* 9 December 1708, this cause came on again upon another point, which was this. Francis, the testator, having in his lifetime a kindness for the plaintiff, his mother-in-law, and knowing her to be in mean circumstances, voluntarily gave her a bond to pay her £25 a year for her life. Afterwards, he went into the East Indies and died, having there made his will and devised an annuity of £25 a year to the plaintiff for life and charged it upon some fee farms rents in Poplar in Middlesex. But he takes no notice in his will of the bond nor the annuity payable thereby.

And now the question was whether she should have two annuities or but one.

And the opinion of the court was that she should have but one and that the bond and the will were for one and the same annuity.

See the Case of Nelthorp, *ante* 30.[1]

[Other reports of this case: Equity Cases Exch. 582.]

306

Poole v. Attorney General

(Ex. 1709)

Legacies charged on land will be paid even though the land has been extended into the crown's hands.

Dodd 217, Parker 272, 145 E.R. 777

Poole devised his estate to A. paying £200 apiece to his grandchildren and [there was] a power to enter for nonpayment, and he died. A. sold to B., who had notice of the charge. B. being in debt to the queen, the estate was seized and extended. And his grandchildren brought a bill in the Exchequer against Mr. Attorney [General] and B. to have the legacies and to charge the estate therewith. And [it was] decreed accordingly.

307

Regina v. Lucy

(Ex. 1709)

The court can grant a new trial on its own motion.

Harvard Law Sch. MS. 537, pt. 2, p. 98, pl. 1

Hilary [term] 7 Anne.

A new trial was granted in this case upon the dissatisfaction of My Lord Chief Baron [Ward], who tried it, without the queen's counsel's pretending any misbehavior in the jury and though the evidence was only circumstantial to prove the fraud, which the jury were judges of and likewise of the credit of the witnesses.

N.B. The trial was to prove the defendant guilty of fraudulent drawbacks.

---

[1] *Anonymous v. Nelthorp* (Ch. 1702), Chancery Repts. *tempore* Anne, 13.

308

Regina v. Thornton

(Ex. 1709)

A debt to a man jure uxoris is considered as a debt originally due to him within the meaning of the Statute 7 Jac. I, c. 15.

Harvard Law Sch. MS. 537, pt. 2, p. 98, pl. 2

Hilary term 7 Anne.

A. was indebted by bond to B.; B. marries one Thornton, a debtor to the king. A [writ of] immediate extent was now prayed against A. in aid of Thornton. The question was whether, such debt being in the right of his wife and not his own original debt, it might be so extended.

It was moved the first day of the term, but, the court no then agreeing, they ordered it to be moved again.

Accordingly, Mr. *Dodd*, who at first moved it, on the second day after, moved it again.

And Bury and Price were of the opinion it might.

Price cited Roll's *Abridgment*, tit. *Prerogat.*, 159,[1] where it was adjudged, if a conusee of a statute die intestate and administration be committed to his wife who marries J.S., a debtor to the king, the chattels J.S. had in the hands of his wife as administratrix should not be extended for the king's debts as to pay debts etc., which he thought, seemed for him. But what he principally relied upon was Roll's *ibidem* 157,[2] where it was adjudged, if a husband and wife purchase lands to them for years, this shall be put in execution against the wife because the husband had power to dispose of the term. He went upon the power of disposition he is said to have in this case, though he agreed with My Lord Chief Baron [Ward] and the rest of the court that, as to the point itself as to the levying of the debt upon the wife was not law.

And [it was said] by *Dodd* that is contradicted by Fleetwood's Case, 8 Co.[3]

And Bury and he made a difference when he had a debt as executor and when as husband. In the latter case, he had it for his own advantage; in the first case, as a trust only. And, then, Bury went too upon the power of disposition he had.

Ward: He differed in opinion. He went upon its not being originally due to the husband. He insisted upon the rule of court for that purpose, second, for

[1] *Buckler v. Rogers* (Ex. 1622), 2 Rolle, Abr., *Prerogative le Roy*, pl. I, 7, p. 159.

[2] YB 50 Edw. III, Lib. Ass., p. 324, pl. 5, 2 Rolle Abr., *Prerogative le Roy*, pl. E, 5, p. 157 (1376).

[3] *Fleetwood's Case* (1610), 8 Coke Rep. 171, 77 E.R. 731, also 2 Rolle, Abr., *Prerogative le Roy*, p. 157.

extents of debts in aid which was only of debts originally due to the king's debtor and seemed as if the rule made with resemblance to the Statute 7 Jac. I, c. 15, which prohibits assignments of debts to the king other than such as grew due originally to the king's debtor. And he cited Hobt. 258;[1] B., conusee, dies intestate; administration is committed to his wife, who marries the king's debtor; her husband assigns this debt to the king, and it was adjudged not assignable within that Statute. He thought this no more originally due than that. He likewise cited one Child's Case,[2] lately in this court, which case was Child was a debtor to the king and was executor to this father. And, as executor, he had a debt due by simple contract, for which he, afterwards, took a bond of the party indebted. And the question then was if that might be then extended. And the court then was of opinion it could not because Child would not swear it was originally due to himself, though the simple contract was determined by the bond. He likewise cited one Nichol's Case,[3] lately too in this court, in which Mr. Ettrick was of counsel. That case was A. was a covenantee in trust for Nichol, the king's debtor, and the question was if that could be extended. But he said it was not then resolved, but it went off. But he expressed himself now as if he was of opinion it was not extendible.

But upon PRICE and BURY's opinion, I [*Eden*] took it he [WARD] ordered the [writ of] extent might go.

Dodd 216, Parker 271, 145 E.R. 777

Wednesday, 26 January 1708[/09].

Thornton was receiver of Lancaster. A. was indebted to him in £20 and also to B. a single woman, by bond in £50. Thornton married B. and afterwards took out a [writ of] extent in aid against himself; and these two debts were found and seized into the queen's hands. And Thornton made an affidavit for an extent against A. and set out these matters in his affidavit. But whether an extent should issue, because the debt of £50 was in the right of his wife, and not originally due to him (as the words of the Act of 7 Jac., c. 15,[4] and the rules are) was the question. And upon debate, the extent did go, for it is now the husband's, and is not a trust, as the word was originally intended to meet with, and [it was] so held in Hob. 253, Cro. Jac. 524.[5]

The Case of Child, receiver of Surrey, was cited to the contrary, in the time of the present queen, where a debt was due to him as executor by a simple con-

---

[1] Stat. 7 Jac. I, c. 15 (*SR*, IV, 1171); *Duncombe v. Wingfield* (1617), Hobart 254, 258, 80 E.R. 400, 404, also 2 Rolle Rep. 447, 91 E.R. 908.

[2] *Child's Case* (Ex. 1709), see above, Case No. 300.

[3] *Stanton v. Child* (Ex. 1703), see above, Case No. 238.

[4] Stat. 7 Jac., c. 15 (*SR*, IV, 1171).

[5] *Breadman v. Coales*, Hobart 253, 80 E.R. 399, *sub nom. Fawn's Case*, Croke Jac. 524, 79 E.R. 448.

tract, and he took a bond for it, and prayed [for a writ of] extent, but he did not swear [that it was] originally due to him, and the extent [was] granted by the Chief Baron [Ward], and a [writ of] *supersedeas* [was granted] by the court against his opinion. And the court now seemed not to relish that precedent.

309

Note

(Ex. 1709)

A party cannot sue at common law and in equity for the same matter against the same defendant at the same time.

Harvard Law Sch. MS. 537, pt. 2, p. 99, pl. 1

Dodd having moved, the plaintiff having sued both in the equity side and the plea side of the Exchequer for the same cause, that the plaintiff should make his election and it being granted and the plaintiff's electing to go on in the plea side, he now moved that the bill might be dismissed with costs.

And it was granted. This is a common motion.

310

Note

(Ex. 1709)

A case must be moved by a barrister, and cannot be moved by a clerk in court.

Harvard Law Sch. MS. 537, pt. 2, p. 99, pl. 2

The Warden of the Fleet having brought up one to the court to show why he should not be in execution at such a one's suit, one of the clerks called him to bring him to the bar.

But [it was said] by Price it ought to have been moved by one of the counsel at the bar to have him called etc., and, if at the plaintiff's suit, by the Attorney General.

311

Crow v. Hughes

(Ex. 1709)

A defendant can tender into court what he thinks that he owes upon the plaintiff's claim and, if the plaintiff proceeds and does not recover more, the defendant is not liable for court costs that accrued after the tender.

Harvard Law Sch. MS. 537, pt. 2, p. 99, pl. 3

Hilary [term] 7 Anne.

The case was the plaintiff brings [an action of] debt for so much rent upon a parol lease. The defendant, admitting part due but not so much, moved upon the late Statute for the Amendment of the Law[1] that he might bring into court so much and the plaintiff to proceed at his peril.

Upon the first motion, the court doubted of it, whether [it was] within the equity of the Statute, and, therefore, they ordered the Master to enquire of the practice of the courts below.

And now, at a day after, the Master informed the court he had enquired of the Secondary of the Queen's Bench that they told him they had had such motions and the court always referred it to the Master to enquire how much was due and the defendant was to bring so much into court and the plaintiff to proceed at his peril and that, for the practice of the Common Pleas, he had enquired of Prothonotary Borret and Cook, who told him that the practice was likewise after the same manner.

WARD seemed dissatisfied with that practice of referring it to the Master etc. because it made the officers too much judges. The rest of the court said nothing to that. But, however, the motion was granted, and a rule was made, as I [Eden] suppose, that the defendant might bring in what he desired and the plaintiff to proceed at his peril.

I [Eden] did not perceive the court directed there should be any reference to the Master, and the rest of the judges said they had enquired of the judges of both courts and that they said it was their constant practice in this case of a rent and that they went so far as to do it in a *quantum meruit* with the object in its nature uncertain yet answered by this means reduced to a certainty.

N.B. This was *ex motione* Master Floyd.

312

Attorney General v. Rouse

(Ex. 1709)

The question in this case was whether, in an information upon a seizure, the prosecutor must plead the particulars of the alleged offense.

Harvard Law Sch. MS. 537, pt. 2, p. 100, pl. 1

Hilary term 7 Anne.

In an information against the defendant as for goods seized for that he found several parcels of wrought silk and brocade in the defendant's shop etc., upon [a

[1] Perhaps Stat. 4 & 5 Ann., c. 3, s. 10 (*SR*, VIII, 459).

plea of] not guilty, the defendant being a retailer of such goods and bringing into his shops great quantities weekly and having always a great quantity in his shop, now, by *Northey* and *Ettrick*, [it was] moved the court would rule the Attorney General to tell the time when, or at least to confine him more, as what six months it was, in that the defendant might be enabled to make a defense and as to what sorts.

But, as to the latter, [it was] immediately denied, as it was also as to the suit, by WARD and BURY, who said that was to both alter the law and make a man tell his evidence beforehand. And they could not do it in the crown's case without the Attorney General, who would not comply.

But PRICE and LOVELL *e contra*, and they said a man must bring a riot of evidence to prepare himself against such a charge. And Price said he believed he had known it done but would not be positive.

But WARD said he was sure he never knew it.

And *Northey* [said] he meant the Newcastle Case, where he said the court ordered they should discover both the ships in which and the time when.

And *Ettrick* cited a case, which was against the Sussex Carrier, who brought always great quantities of goods often, and, there, [one was] obliged to discover the time (as I suppose).

Query how far they will go in a common case and if [there is] any difference, *per que dict. semble [. . .] est mes.*

Vide 9 & 10 Will. III, c. 48,[1] similar. It has been an information upon that Act. N.B. its name was *ut supra* as I understand or else the motion precedent to it. *Vide* the rules for it of this term.

313

Regina v. Cambridge

(Ex. 1709)

Where a receiver of the crown lends his own private money, his debtor is not a debtor of the crown.

Harvard Law Sch. MS. 537, pt. 2, p. 100, pl. 2

Hilary term 7 Anne. Regina or Caswell v. Cambridge.

[It was said] by the Chief Baron [WARD], if I borrow money of the queen's receiver, but not as the queen's money, I shall not be answerable as the queen's immediate debtor. But, if as the queen's money, I shall. And that being the question in this case, a trial was directed upon it. And he said it had been settled upon that difference.

---

[1] Stat. 9 Will. III, c. 44 (*SR*, VII, 429–446).

314

Attorney General v. Bradshaw

(Ex. 1709–1712)

In this case, the question was whether the land of an accountant to the crown is bound in an execution before the account of the accountant was stated and settled or is not bound.

Harvard Law Sch. MS. 537, pt. 2, p. 101, pl. 2

This case was this. Sir Cornwall Bradshaw, 9 December 30 Car. II [1678], was made a collector of the hearth money,[1] and, of that year, he entered upon the execution of that place by receiving several sums of money amounting in all to £60,000. In 1692, 3 Will. & Mar., upon the marriage of Caesar Bradshaw, his eldest son, with the daughter [in law] and in consideration of £2600 marriage portion, he settles the lands in question and which he was then seized of in fee to the use of himself for life, remainder to this son for life, remainder to the daughter [in law] while she continued the son's widow.

[In] 9 Will. [1697], [a writ of] process of distress *ad computandum* issued against Sir Cornwall to account and issues returned upon his defaults at several times in all £450. The son dies. Sir Cornwall afterwards dies, having not yet accounted. And, now, a [writ of] *scire facias* went to levy those issues. And, by an inquisition upon it, it was said, *inter alia*, that Sir Cornwall Bradshaw was receiver etc. and seised of those lands etc. But it did not find he had not accounted, upon which they were seized into the queen's hands.

The daughter comes in and pleads the settlement by which she was seised *durante viduitate*, but she had not averred herself a widow of Caesar Bradshaw and so continuing, though it was otherwise apparent upon the pleading, nor had she concluded with the prayer of an amotion of the queen's hands *durante viduitate*, but for life generally.

The Attorney General replied he was a collector *ut supra* and being so a collector was seised of these lands and had received so much for which he had accounted and then much the same with the *scire facias*.

The rejoinder was to the same effect with the plea, upon which the Attorney General demurred.

It was argued Michaelmas term by *Northey*, for the queen, and by Serjeant *Chesshyre*, for the defendant.

[It was said] by *Northey* that both at common law and by 13 Eliz., c. 4, the lands the accountant had at any time he was accountant were liable to the arrears of the account and he cited 10 Co. 55b, Sir Christopher Hatton's Case, and that process *ad computandum* against the terre tenant, Dy. 225; 2 Roll, Abr., 162; N.B.

---

[1] Stat. 14 Car. II, c. 10 (*SR*, V, 390–393); Stat. 15 Car. II, c. 13 (*SR*, V, 493–495).

288, pl. 321; Sir W. Candish's Case, 11 Co. 90.[1] And all subsequent conveyances [are] void as to the crown and like where a man entered by judgment and makes afterwards a fraudulent conveyance, the judgment [*blank*] may plead *non concessit.* He cited 2 M. 247; f. 3, Br., *Prec.*, 59, 65; Co., Jurisdiction, 209; 7 Hen. IV, 33.[2] And he argued to the same effect with the Chief Baron.

Chesshyre: The entry of the issues is because *in defaltum*, and it is for that reason they are forfeited to the crown and affect the land from the judgment of that default. In the case of a fine upon an information for not executing his office aright, that fine will not lie upon the land in the hands of a precedent purchaser. Suppose in a case of a common person, one is adjudged to account, the judgment is *quod computet et in misericordia*, because he did not account sooner. He takes this amercement to be the same as issues in cases of the crown. And yet these issues would not bind the land if they had have the king's. 8 Co., Griesly's Case.[3] They bind only from the judgment *in misericordia* and not from the time he first became accountant. He cited Cro. Jac. 449 and Hoe's Case, and he compared this to that in Cro. Jac. And that he took the better opinion of that case to be that the land is bound only from the time of the judgment.[4]

And now this term, judgment was given by the court *seriatim.* And all but the Chief Baron [Ward were] for the defendant.

PRICE: He was of the opinion *quod manus dominae reginae amoveantur.* He argued that the defendant account from the time of the grant and that the course of the Exchequer to proceed by [a writ of] *distringas ad computandum* and the sheriff to return issues upon default, which issues [are] a charge upon the accountant's estate from the time they were returned and recorded. He likewise agreed, since the death of the accountant, process might go out against the heir and for that of such against the terre tenants and for their, defendant, issues returned against them. And this is the known course and law of this court. 11 Co., Dev's Case; 2 Roll, [Abr.], tit. *Prerogative*; Dy. 224; Comm. 321.[5]

---

[1] Stat. 13 Eliz. I, c. 4 (*SR*, IV, 535–537); *Hatton's Case*, 10 Coke Rep. 55, 77 E.R. 1009, also *sub nom. Coke's Case*, 2 Rolle Rep. 294, 81 E.R. 809, Godbolt 289, 78 E.R. 169; *Seyntloo's Case* (Ex. 1563), 2 Dyer 224, 73 E.R. 479; *Anonymous*, 2 Rolle, Abr., *Prerogative le Roy*, pl. Q, 1, p. 162; *Natura Brevium*; *Cavendish's Case*, 11 Coke Rep. 93, 77 E.R. 1271, 1 Plowden 321, 75 E.R. 487, Godbolt 292, 78 E.R. 171, 2 Dyer 224, 73 E.R. 497, Benloe 118, 73 E.R. 983.

[2] Perhaps *Attorney General v. Alston* (1677), 2 Modern 247, 86 E.R. 1053; YB Trin. 3 Hen. VII, f. 2, pl. 10 (1488), 2 Brooke, Abr., *Prerogative le roy*, pl. 59; YB Pas. 7 Edw. IV, ff. 5, 6, pl. 16 (1467), 2 Brooke, Abr., *Prerogative le roy*, pl. 65; *Earl of Kent's Case* (Ch. 1405), YB Mich. 7 Hen. IV, f. 32, pl. 19, Chan. Repts. Middle Ages 76.

[3] *Griesley's Case* (1588), 8 Coke Rep. 38, 77 E.R. 530, also Savile 93, 123 E.R. 1031.

[4] *Baskerville v. Brocket* (1617), Croke Jac. 449, 79 E.R. 384; *Hoe v. Belton* (Ex. 1600), 5 Coke Rep. 89, 77 E.R. 191, Moore K.B. 468, 72 E.R. 701.

[5] *Earl of Devonshire's Case* (1607), 11 Coke Rep. 89, 77 E.R. 1266, 2 Rolle, Abr., *Prerogative*, pl. O, 1, pl. P, 1–4; *Seyntloo's Case* (Ex. 1563), 2 Dyer 224, 73 E.R. 479; *Re-*

But the issues he thinks [are] no part of the king's debt nor can they go in discharge of it, for, if the accountant appear after such issues and the issues appear levied to the value of the debt, this is no satisfaction of it for that they are different things and of a different nature, nor, if he appear, can he have the issues restored to him. And he cited the Book of Assizes, *anno* 22, pl. 33, Bro., tit. *Amerciament*, 37, 5c, and Brook's opinion there, and that is a great diversity between this case and that. 12 Hen. VII, p. 4 [. . .].[1] He cited 2 Cro. 449 and that a bail recognizance does not bind the land from the time it was given, but from the time judgment [was had] against the principal. The reason is because the condition of the recognizance is *si judicium reddit*, then it shall affect the bail from the time of the judgment against the principal (which N.B. for though in the book [it is] not adjudged, yet, by this argument, his opinion seemed to be that it bound only from the time of the judgment) which agreed with Chesshyre's *antea*. He cited 8 Co., Grisley's Case, and he said all the cases there run are quite different from the debt itself and upon a different foundation.

And [it was said] by him, in the case of an outlawry, the issues and forfeitures [are] answerable only to the crown; nothing goes to the party in satisfaction of his debt and that the judgment given by the coroners does not bind until removed above and recorded, nor can the outlawry be pleaded in disability or in bar until that done nor does it relate to the first judgment. But it is the judgment above which affects the lands which it is given [. . .] when recorded. So he thinks the issues only bind the land from the time of their being forfeited and recorded.

Second, whether the replication be a departure, the *scire facias* is of issues forfeited and after the plea of the settlement etc. the replication that Cornwall Bradshaw [was] collector of the hearth money and had received great sums, amounting to £60,000, and never had accounted. But then, as I apprehend, [. . .] and much to the same effect as the *scire facias* (*mes et vide le record*).

As to that, he thinks the replication sets forth the same thing with the declaration, no way different, but only in fortification of it, and that it does not set forth any new matter. It only shows the issues came to be forfeited. He agreed it would be so if, in the replication, there had been a debt set forth, for that, by 13 Eliz., would have bound the land from the time he became collector.

Third, whether the plea [was] a good bar in substance, and he was of the opinion it was. He cited 2 Mod. 247,[2] and he takes that case [to hold] for the crown, though it was not adjudged, as there reported.

Fourth, admitting it good in substance, if ill in form, as to the objection that, the defendant having but an estate during widowhood, she does not aver herself

---

gina v. Earl of Northumberland (Ex. 1568), 1 Plowden 310, 321, 75 E.R. 472, 487.

[1] YB 22 Edw. III, Lib. Ass., pl. 33, p. 92 (1348), 1 Brooke, Abr., *Amercement*, pl. 37; perhaps YB Mich. 12 Hen. VII, f. 4, pl. 2 (1496).

[2] *Attorney General v. Alston* (1677), 2 Modern 247, 86 E.R. 1053, Exch. Repts. *tempore* Car. II, 341.

Caesar Bradshaw's widow and so continuing, it is true affirmative pleas must be with an averment of the particular estate, but he says it may be averred sufficiently by appearing upon the precedent part of the plea where, laying that precedent part of the plea and the conclusion together, it must be intended so. He said indeed Dyer 142 was strongly against the defendant if [good] law, but, in opposition to it, he cited Pl. 342, 326; Dyer 304; Cro. Jac. 622.[1] There, the life being necessarily implied, it was not necessary to be averred. So, if the party whose life [is] to be averred be a party to the suit. But all the pleadings being as a widow and the replication taking notice likewise of it by saying *praedicta vidua* and the demurrer admitting all matters of fact well pleaded and the plea being by Joanna Bradshaw, *vidua* and married to Caesar Bradshaw and so appearing upon the settlement pleaded, it sufficiently appears she is Joanna Bradshaw, widow, and so continues. And a plea in bar being likewise [is] sufficient if to a common intent.

Fifth, as for the objection to the conclusion which prays restitution to her for life generally, that is to be understood according to the estate which she is entitled to. And she does say for life. It is not improperly so, for an estate *durante viduitate* is an estate for life, and it would be incumbent on the other part to show her [re-]marriage.

But, if it all does not amount to an averment, yet this being an estate for life *durante viduitate*, it is a condition subsequent, as 7 Co., Ughtred's Case; Pl. Com. 26.[2] And, if this be a condition subsequent, this being a plea and defense, the defendant is not bound to show anything to defeat her own estate.

And, if [there is] any difference in the case of the crown and in the case of the subject, it is more than he can find any precedent or reason for. And, if she was not a widow, the Attorney General might have shown it in his replication.

And so he concluded for a [writ of] *amoveas manus*.

Bury was of the same opinion. He agreed the land he was seised of in fee anytime after an account was liable to the account. But he was of the opinion that this forfeiture for not appearing upon the *distringas* is distinct from the account and of a different nature with it, and, when it is levied, it shall not go in discharge of the account. And [as to] lands sold before issues and after, an accountant is not liable to the issues. They are only a penalty and not otherwise belonging to the king than issues forfeited for not appearing upon other process against other persons, and not upon the king's account and are only to be levied upon such land as he then had.

---

1 *Putbury v. Trevelian* (1557), 2 Dyer 142, 73 E.R. 310; *Brett v. Rigden* (1568), 1 Plowden 340, 75 E.R. 516, also 1 Eq. Cas. Abr. 172, 21 E.R. 966; *Regina v. Earl of Northumberland* (1568), 1 Plowden 310, 75 E.R. 472; *Anonymous* (1571), 3 Dyer 304, 73 E.R. 684; *Boston v. Tatam* (1621), Croke Jac. 623, 79 E.R. 535.

2 *Ughtred v. Marquess of Winchester* (1591), 7 Coke Rep. 9, 77 E.R. 425, also Jenkins 260, 145 E.R. 186; *Colthirst v. Bejushin* (1550), 1 Plowden 20, 26, 75 E.R. 33, 41.

[As to the] objection [they are] the issues of an accountant and they ought to relate to the first time he became an accountant, he thinks they cannot be properly called the issues of an accountant [. . .] of others. The issues are only for not appearing upon the *distringas*. And, if the queen had gone any other way, there had been none such, as she might, as in Sir W. Candish's Case, Pl. Com. 321.[1]

Then, he said that, in 2 Mod. 248, it is there said that, by the common law, the land is bound only from the time the accountant became indebted and not from the time he first became an officer. And so Moor 127 seems to be. Now, if by the common law, it was so, surely the *distringas* cannot make the land further liable than the account itself. And the Statute of Elizabeth does not make them relate. And he argued as if inclined the lands [are] only so liable at common law, as in 2 Mod. and Moor, *supra*.[2]

Objection: If the queen seized, although wrongfully, yet, if a title appears, her hands shall not be amoved. And 2 Mod. 247 was cited.

Answer: That case is not like ours, for the replication there was for maintaining the extent sued forth and for the same debt, but, in our case, the land was seized for one debt, and the Attorney General, by his replication, would maintain it for another and upon another account and which is of a different nature. He cited Br., *Prerog.*, 56, 65; Va. 62, where the king's title appears by record.[3] There, the defendant must make a good one against it. And it is true where it appears by matter of record, as if by a confession or that the king has a right, he shall have the benefit of it, as in an [action of] *quare impedit*, if a title appears for him, he shall have a writ to the bishop, but here it is not confessed by the party nor does it otherwise appear by matter of record, for the inquisition has only found him a receiver, not that he has not accounted. It only appears by the Attorney General, alleged in his replication; [it is] not sufficient.

As to the exception to the plea for want of an averment, he argued after the same manner as Price. And he cited 1 Inst. 42 and 302,[4] and so after the same manner as to the exception to the conclusion of the plea.

As to the objection to the rejoinder, that it is no more than what she said before in her plea and does not traverse the Attorney General's replication; he takes it the replication is impertinent and she is not bound to answer it.

And so he concludes for the defendant.

N.B. Mr. Baron Lovell, having not been here at all of the arguments, delivered at first no opinion. But Baron Bury, saying he was at one, seemed to in-

---

[1] *Cavendish's Case, ut supra.*

[2] *Attorney General v. Alston* (1677), *ut supra*; *Anonymous* (Ex. 1583), Moore K.B. 126, 72 E.R. 484.

[3] *Rex v. Bishop of Worcester* (1669), Vaughan 53, 124 E.R. 967, also 1 Modern 276, 86 E.R. 878, T. Jones 8, 84 E.R. 1120, 1 Freeman 7, 89 E.R. 7.

[4] E. Coke, *First Institute* (1628), ff. 42, 302.

sist he should give his opinion, which he did to the same effect as Bury and Price had.

But Ward, he differed in opinion. And he said that, at common law, the accountant's lands he had at any time are liable. And he cited Sir Christopher Hatton's Case, 10 Rept. 55, and the same case in 2 Roll's Repts. and Godbolt. He cited 2 Mod., Alston's Case, and that case was adjudged for the crown and there was no departure.

He agreed that issues only bind from the time of the return, but he insisted that no *amoveas manus* should be [granted] while the lands appeared liable. (So that he took it that it appeared sufficient.)

He is not satisfied that it is not necessary to aver her a widow, for, wherever one pleads against the crown and comes to take lands out of the crown, he must make a complete title to the lands.

He likewise said the cases of conditions subsequent and those of averments of lives would not come up to this and that, if an estate so qualified as this, it is necessary to show that it is not taken off by such qualifications and that she should have done [so] in her pleading and must not put the showing of it upon the king. And, as for being named a widow in the pleadings, she might be the widow of another.

And then that those issues affect the land as much as the issues of jurors. They are *exitus terrae* as well in the one case as the other. And he cited 47 Edw. III, the same case abridged, Br., tit. *Issue*, 15; and Br., *ibid.*, 23.[1] And, if so, then they charge the remainderman as well as those. And so he [held] that the king's hands are not to be amoved.

So judgment [was given] *quod manus dominae reginae amoveantur.*

Lincoln's Inn MS. Misc. 539, f. [10]

21 June 1712.

Upon a [writ of] *diem clausit extremum*, prayed to be superseded, wherein the court happened to be divided, and that writ having issued by order of the court and an inquisition seizing of lands into the queen's hands being returned and filed on record and a [writ of] *levari facias* having issued thereupon and money returned to be levied for the crown, no [writ of] *supersedeas* to the writ nor stay of process was granted by the court. But Mrs. Bradshaw, who is not in court as terre tenant or otherwise nor any title appearing for her, may, if she please, come in as terre tenant or otherwise and put in her claim by a plea, for which purpose, she is to have a month's time, which was allowed her in regard, as her counsel alleged, she must have an *oyer* of the indenture of contract thereby to show, if she can, that Sir Cornwall Bradshaw, one of the collectors of the hearth money and

---

[1] YB Mich. 47 Edw. III, ff. 7, 8, pl. 4 (1373), 2 Brooke, Abr., *Issues retornes sur terres*, pl. 15 and pl. 23.

whose estate she occupies and for whose debt the writ issued was not a debtor, but an accountant only, to the crown.

Vide the whole case stated both upon the indenture and writ and my argument in a paper by itself. And my argument in the case between the Queen and the same Mrs. Bradshaw 12 February 1708[/09], when judgment was given by the three barons against the Chief Baron [WARD], for the reversal, to which, Mr. Attorney [General *Northey*], this day, declared he had ordered a writ of error.

[Other copies of this report: Georgetown Univ. Law Sch. MS. B88–10, p. 935.]

315

Anonymous

(Ex. 1709)

The question in this case was whether a discharge of a judicial seizure can be asserted by a mere motion or must be by a formal pleading.

Harvard Law Sch. MS. 537, pt. 2, p. 119, pl. 1

A motion was made to discharge a seizure (of a Roman Catholic's estate, as I [Eden] took it) upon a certificate that he had complied so as to save it. But the court would not discharge a seizure upon a motion, but they must plead to it. But, at last, I [Eden] think the court put it upon the other side to show cause the first day of next term.

316

Anonymous

(Ex. 1709)

A deposition cannot be admitted as evidence to explain or to vary the meaning of a writing that is clear on its face.

Harvard Law Sch. MS. 537, pt. 2, p. 119, pl. 2

Before the rule of refusing depositions almost [. . .], as I [Eden] am informed by Dormer, one of my Society, and, as to the course, it was to be allowed to them [. . .] in this case, but where the intent is full and plain. And N.B. Baron PRICE, in Long's Case,[1] said that there was no occasion, for the intent appeared sufficient without them, which *nota bene*, for by it and others putting off the case, it seems they took the law for the plaintiff.

[1] *Long v. Beaumont* (Ex. 1709), see below, Case No. 340.

317

Eyle's Case

(Ex. 1709)

Where a court does not have subject matter jurisdiction, the parties cannot confer jurisdiction by consent or otherwise.

Lincoln's Inn MS. Misc. 538, f. [55v]

Saturday, 29 January.

Eyles, of the Devises, was cited to the bishop of Salisbury's consistory court for making a disturbance in the church, to which citation, he appeared and pleaded in chief. And the cause was proceeding. But, before any sentences, Eyles prayed a [writ of] prohibition upon the Statute of 23 Hen. VIII, for citing out of the diocese etc.,[1] the truth being that both the offense and the person were within a peculiar and exempt jurisdiction, though within the diocese of Salisbury and no remission of the court.

And, upon debate, the rule for the prohibition was made absolute, for, though Eyles had so far submitted to the bishop's court, yet that had not given it a jurisdiction against the Act of Parliament, it being before the sentence, nor, in truth does a sentence in such a case give a jurisdiction but that the temporal court will not in discretion grant a prohibition after the matter had passed *in rem judicatam* by the sentence and he had so far affirmed the jurisdiction. Roll's, *Prohibition*, 318, Lre. L, fig. 40.[2]

But, in my [Edward Ward's] apprehension, that discretionary way of denying a prohibition after a sentence [be]cause the party has submitted to the jurisdiction does not seem well grounded, for, if the court has not jurisdiction of the cause, the proceedings are *coram non judice*, and no submission can give a jurisdiction where the law does not.

[Other copies of this report: Georgetown Univ. Law Sch. MS. B88–10, p. 645.]

318

Leigh v. Maddox

(Ex. 1709)

The question in this case was the sufficiency of the pleadings.

---

[1] Stat. 23 Hen. VIII, c. 9 (*SR*, III, 377–378).

[2] *Pudsey v. Richardson* (1617), 2 Rolle, Abr., *Prohibition*, pl. L, 1, p. 318.

Indiana Univ., Lilly Library
MS. Parker 'Cases in the Exchequer', vol. 5, p. 184

Hilary [term] 1708[/09]; John Leigh v. Mordecai Maddox.

[There was an action of] debt on a bond with a special condition that he, the defendant, would pay the plaintiff £48 *per annum* at certain days for so long a time as Claridge had a lease from Broom.

The defendant demurs to the replication, which assigns that £24 was not paid, due at such a time, and that the term was still in being.

Dodd, for the defendant, objected [that it] ought to set forth the term and how many years; 2 Cro. 359, pay when he came of age ought to set forth the time; Styles 473.[1]

Second, it was to pay the plaintiff or his assignee [and it does] not mention who was the assignee.

Serjeant *Chesshyre*, for the plaintiff: The plaintiff was not privy to the term made by Broome to Claridge. The defendant is estopped to say [there was] no term, it being mentioned in the condition. 1 Roll. 872; Moor 420; Dyer 196; 3 Cro. 756, 362. The defendant shows the term and ought to show the surrender of it.[2]

Second, the condition is in the disjunctive to pay the rent or term. and so [is] the case, 2 Cro. 359; plead payment or age, either; Lutw. 421; pay all charges and taxes, in a plea that he paid, he ought to show what was taxed.[3]

Third, the defendant ought to show how long the term continued that was to pay the rent in his rejoinder, and it is no departure from the plea.

Fourth, to pay him or assigns need not show or have any assigns.

Dodd replies for the defendant that the plea is good, being general, but the replication is bad. Cro. El. [*blank*], to deliver all such tallow, he ought to show what he had.[4]

Judgment [was given] for the plaintiff.

---

1 *Halsey v. Carpenter* (1614), Croke Jac. 359, 79 E.R. 308; *Arnold v. Floyd* (1655), Style 473, 476, 82 E.R. 873, 875.

2 1 Rolle, Abr., *Estoppell*, p. 872; *Paramour v. During* (1595), Moore K.B. 420, 72 E.R. 668; *Rainsford v. Smith* (1560), 2 Dyer 196, 73 E.R. 432; *Willoughby v. Brook* (1600), Croke Eliz. 756, 78 E.R. 988; *Strowd v. Willis* (1594), Croke Eliz. 362, 78 E.R. 610, also Owen 110, 74 E.R. 937, Popham 114, 79 E.R. 1221, Moore K.B. 405, 72 E.R. 658.

3 *Parkes v. Middleton* (1704), 1 Lutwyche 419, 125 E.R. 220.

4 *Mints v. Hethil* (1600), Croke Eliz. 749, 78 E.R. 981.

319

Mees v. Snige

(Ex. 1709)

The question in this case was whether a dispute over a rectory where a resignation had been made and then revoked should be tried in a temporal or an ecclesiastical court.

Lincoln's Inn MS. Misc. 538, f. [81]

Easter term 8 Anne 1709.

In [a writ of] prohibition to the Court of Arches, in order to obtain which, the suggestion was that the defendant Snige, being vicar of Stratford upon Avon in the County of Warwick, did for divers good causes duly make and execute to a notary public an instrument of resignation of that vicarage and of all his right and title to it with authority to exhibit it to the ordinary of the bishop of Worcester in form of law, therein renouncing his right and title to the vicarage to the intent the same may become void and the patron to present. And this was dated the 25th of March 1708, the first day of that year. And, on the 8th of March 1708[/09], near a year after the date of the resignation, the notary public exhibited that resignation in due form to the bishop, who accepted the same and declared the vicarage vacant and ordered a notice to the patron and awarded a sequestration of the profits during the vacancy. After this, *viz.* 30th April 1709, the earl of Dorset, the patron, having had notice from the bishop, presented the plaintiff Mees to that vicarage, who, the 4th of April 1709, was instituted and inducted into the same. And he thereupon became the lawful vicar of the said vicarage, and he ought to hold and enjoy the same by the laws of this realm.

But the defendant had against the law sued and prosecuted the plaintiff in the Court of the Arches in order to avoid the plaintiff's title to the said vicarage under color of an appeal to the Arches for a pretended revocation of the said instrument of resignation, which the plaintiff suggests to be (if any was) after the bishop's acceptance of the said resignation and notice to the patron and after the plaintiff's presentation, institution, and induction when the said church was full. And, therefore, he prayed a [writ of] prohibition to the proceedings in the Arches, it being (as was insisted) in this case and as appears in this suggestion a matter properly determinable at law, the church being full by the induction, which is not to be drawn into question in the spiritual court, and it is plain by all laws that the resignation and acceptance of it by the bishop makes a vacancy, and then, when a presentation, institution, and induction follows such resignation and acceptance, though, in a proper time, they might be appealed from as an ecclesiastical act, being no more of ecclesiastical conusance than an institution, they must be of no great force nor give more jurisdiction to the spiritual court to examine than after induction than an institution, which is of ecclesiastical jurisdiction, can be called in question by that law after an induction which surely cannot be, as, by multitudes of authorities in our books, appears. Dyer, 228, 233; Roll's, *Tryall*, 582, etc.; Hitchin and Glover's Case, Roll's, *Prohibition*, 282, 2 Cro. 463, 1 Roll's rep., 191, 229, 293.[1]

And it was insisted that the rule of law is that ecclesiastical jurisdiction must consist of the whole cause spiritual, for, if any part be temporal or a temporal ingredient, the cause appertains to the common law. 7 rep. 44, Ken's Case.[2] Whether a church be void by resignation or not is triable *per pais*, but whether full or not full is triable by the bishop. And the reason of that is because the church is full by institution against all but the crown and the bishop is the judge of the institution. But void or not void is triable *per pais, prout supra*. Roll's, *Triall*, 282 etc.

All must agree induction is triable *per pais*. And so, if issue be joined upon institution and induction, trial is *per pais, ubi supra*.

And it was further insisted that, though it is said in Manknoll's Case, Roll's, *Prohibition*, 293,[3] that if, upon a resignation, another be instituted and then the resigner denies the resignation and makes a lease, wherein issue is joined whether parson at the time of the lease or not, no prohibition is to be granted because the question only touches the resignation, which properly appertains to the ecclesiastical court.

That case receives two answers, first, it does not appear that there was in that case any more than an institution of which the bishop is judge, secondly, it does not appear that the resignation was accepted by the bishop so as to make a vacancy. At least, there was no induction or temporal act here to entitle a temporal court to a jurisdiction, so that, as this case appeared upon the suggestion, it is no more but that the living was vacant by the resignation and acceptance and then after notice to the patron and his presentation and the institution and induction of his clerk, the spiritual court can hold a plea of a thing to enervate the incumbent's title who has performed all things requisite to make him a complete incumbent by the laws of the realm, which surely cannot be done.

And so, upon that ground, the prohibition issued, but to be declared upon at the defendant's request.

Now, in truth, upon the perusal in the court of the proceedings in the [Court of] Arches, they stood thus:

First, the resignation was the 25th of March 1708;

---

[1] *Sidney v. Bishop of Gloucester* (1564), 2 Dyer 228, 73 E.R. 505; *Parkchusts's Case* (1552), 2 Dyer 233, 73 E.R. 515; 2 Rolle, Abr., *Triall*, p. 582; *Hitchins v. Glover* (1618), 2 Rolle, Abr., *Prohibition*, pl. F, 3, 5, p. 282, Croke Jac. 463, 79 E.R. 396, 1 Rolle Rep. 191, 227, 81 E.R. 423, 451.

[2] *Robertson v. Lady Stallenge (Kenn's Case)* (1606), 7 Coke Rep. 42, 77 E.R. 474, also Croke Jac. 186, 79 E.R. 162, Jenkins 289, 145 E.R. 209.

[3] *Manknoll's Case* (1612), 2 Rolle, Abr., *Prohibition*, pl. M, 11, p. 293.

Second, the bishop's acceptance of it and declaration that the church was void and notice decreed to the patron and a sequestration of the profits during the vacancy were all on the 8th of March 1708[/09];

After which, *viz.* 17 March 1708[/09], the defendant revokes the resignation, but the bishop refuses that revocation;

24 March 1708[/09], the defendant appeals from that refusal to the [Court of] Arches;

31 March 1709, the plaintiff is presented by the patron;

31 March 1709, the defendant appealed against the sequestration;

4 April 1709, the plaintiff was instituted and inducted;

14 April 1709, a [writ of] inhibition is granted by the Arches.

Now, what the defendant's counsel labored for against this prohibition was to make it out by law that, though the bishop had accepted the resignation and declared the living void and notice to the patron and sequestration awarded before the defendant revoked his resignation, yet that such revocation, coming at any time before the presentation, institution, and induction, ought to have been received by the bishop and that all that was done after the revocation tendered was void and that, therefore, the resignation and acceptance thereby became nul, at least a *gravamen*, to the defendant and that, by the spiritual law, the resignation and acceptance of it and the revocation and the bishop's refusal of it are all of spiritual conusance and not temporal and that, therefore, the institution and induction of the plaintiff pending that appeal or *gravamen* did not nor could deprive the defendant of having the validity of that revocation tried in the spiritual court where, as they allege, they are properly conusable and determinable.

And they compared this case to that of a deprivation by the ordinary from which, if the party appeals, it extinguishes the sentence and if it be reversed, there needs no new institution or induction. No more will the defendant want it here in case his revocation be by the spiritual law allowed to be good, for, then, he is in of his first title before the resignation and the institution and induction built upon that resignation must fall, the church being always full of the defendant. And nothing ought to be binding until the validity of that revocation and refusal of it be determined in the Arches.

But the suggestion laying this pretense of revocation not to be until after the institution and induction, the court granted the prohibition upon the matter as alleged in the suggestion, and ordered the plaintiff to declare upon it at the defendant's desire, which is done.

[Other copies of this report: Georgetown Univ. Law Sch. MS. B88–10, p. 648.]

Lincoln's Inn MS. Misc. 538, f. [84v]

The plaintiff declared upon the prohibition to the effect of the suggestion. But the defendant, by his plea, pretended that his revocation of the instrument of resignation was the 27th of February 1708[/09] and so before the presentation of the resignation was delivered to the bishop or he [had] done anything upon it and, if anything was done, that it was void, the resignation being become void by the revocation, and so, that matter being wholly of ecclesiastical conusance and varied from the times laid in the suggestion in other things but the plaintiff having oyer of them and set them forth in his replication and so insisted, he prayed the prohibition to stand.

And, thereupon, a demurrer being joined, the arguing of it was put off by counsel's consent several days.

But it never was argued. But upon what appeared by the counsel on both sides, it seemed as it were by consent that the prohibition should stand. And, accordingly, it stood without opposition.

Upon the debate of the case before the prohibition was granted, these books were cited for the plaintiff, Moor 61; 12 rep. 67; Sidderfin 290; 2 Cro. 63, 194; Noy 147; for the defendant, some of the same cases, Roll's, *Tryall*, 583; Lutwyche 115, 116; 2 Cro. 197, 198; Roll's, *Prohibition*, 293, 294; 2 Levins 125; Fitzh., *Quare Impedit*, 143; 6 rep. 18, Packman's Case.[1]

[Other copies of this report: Georgetown Univ. Law Sch. MS. B88–10, p. 660.]

320

Parran v. Hart

(Ex. 1709)

A proceeding upon a writ of extent to seize a bond will be discharged if the bond is not produced.

Harvard Law Sch. MS. 537, pt. 2, p. 121, pl. 3

Easter term 8 Anne; Attorney General v. Hart.

A [writ of] immediate extent was now prayed and, as the counsel said, at the suit of the crown against one Hart as defendant, debtor to one Paron, against whom a [writ of] extent was gone out upon a Custom House bond and an inquisition upon which was found this debt. And, upon Paron's affidavit of his own

[1] *Anonymous* (1564), Moore K.B. 61, 72 E.R. 441; *Roberts's Case* (1610), 12 Coke Rep. 65, 77 E.R. 1344, also Croke Jac. 269, 79 E.R. 231; *Fairchild v. Gayre* (1605), Croke Jac. 63, 79 E.R. 53, also Yelverton 60, 80 E.R. 42, 1 Brownlow & Goldesborough 201, 123 E.R. 754, Moore K.B. 765, 72 E.R. 892; *Staineroid v. Locock* (1607), Croke Jac. 194, 79 E.R. 169; *Smith v. Foaves*, Noy 147, 74 E.R. 1109; 2 Rolle, Abr., *Triall*, sect. O, pp. 583–584; *Reynolds v. Hewett* (1700), 1 Lutwyche 115, 125 E.R. 60; *Fane's Case* (1607), Croke Jac. 197, 79 E.R. 172; *Manknoll's Case* (1612), *ut supra; Rex v. Abbot of Gloucester* (1378), YB Mich. 2 Ric. II, Ames Found., vol. 1, p. 80, pl. 10, Fitzherbert, Abr., *Quare impedit*, pl. 143, Bellewe 280, 72 E.R. 122; *Wilson v. Packmam* (1595), 6 Coke Rep. 18, 77 E.R. 281, also Croke Eliz. 459, 78 E.R. 698, Moore K.B. 396, 72 E.R. 651.

inability etc. and of Hart's absconding etc., to prevent the crown's debt being lost, which, upon that affidavit, seemed in danger, was now this [writ of] immediate extent prayed by Mr. *Dodd* and Mr. *Ward.*

[It was said] by the Chief Baron [WARD] we shall not help the crown's debtors to fetch in their debts when they themselves are sufficient to pay them. And Paron's insufficiency only appears by his own affidavit so that the question is whether a *scire facias* (as it may be the debt being said [?] in the inquisition) or any immediate extent must go; indeed, if the queen's debt was in danger, an immediate extent should go. But he was not satisfied of that appearing only upon Paron's affidavit. And he seemed to make this difference between levying this debt by a *scire facias* and by an immediate extent. In the first case, part cannot only, but the whole must be levied. But an immediate extent being of the court's granting, it may be governed as the court shall think fit.

He [WARD] told us he remembered these immediate extents to occasion a great deal of clamor once, for, in King James II's time, Sir Basil Firebrace [1652–1724] and several others,[1] upon importing their wines, gave a bond for the customs [duties] and then sold them to the vintners and, oftentimes, upon the vintner's seeming to fail etc., by these immediate extents, came and swept all away. And he seemed to speak as if that had occasional a less readiness to favor those Custom House bondsmen than receivers and such like, though he said the customs bonds as they related to the crown were as much to be taken care of. He said, likewise, an immediate extent might go to the third degree.

And he cited a case in King Charles II's time, the case of one Jolly and Ewen,[2] and it was this. Ewen was indebted to Jolly, who was a receiver to the crown and by a simple contract only, and one Lindsey and Goldsmith were indebted likewise and by a simple contract only to Ewen. And Lindsey, he said, was then fetched in in aid of Jolly. But we will never go further.

[It was said] by PRICE this is contrary to the rules in King Charles I's time.

But because they were acquainted by Mr. *Armiger*, on the behalf of Hart, that it was a contrivance of Paron only, it was put off as to giving any rule until the day following. As to the difference between a *scire facias* and an immediate extent, query, as to the first part, because I am not so sure of it as the latter.

Lincoln's Inn MS. Misc. 538, f. [82v], pl. 1

Parran was indebted by bond at the Custom House to the queen of a great penalty, but £200 was sworn due thereupon. And, upon Parran's affidavit that he was unable to pay that debt to the queen unless a debt of £500 due from Hart to Parran on a bond of £1000 be seized into the queen's hand and a [writ of] immediate extent awarded thereupon, the defendant Hart absenting himself from his

[1] *Attorney General v. Hart* (Ex. 1686), see above, Case No. 18.

[2] *Ewin v. Lindsey* (Ex. 1678), Exch. Cases *tempore* Car. II, p. 389.

house and absconding for debt, Hart's bond to Parran, upon a [writ of] extent to find debts founded on the queen's bond, was seized into the queen's hands by an inquisition. And, upon a motion in court for an immediate extent against Hart upon Parran's and another man's affidavit of Hart's absconding and Parran's inability to pay the queen's debt otherwise than out of the debt due from Hart to Parran, it was granted accordingly unless cause [be shown], the court holding in this case that there being a just debt due to the queen by bond and that it was like to be lost unless by this way of immediate extent and that the queen in an adversary manner might subject her debtor's debtor's estate to the payment of her debt and that the immediate extent was only to secure that debt which was like to be lost was fitting in this case.

But, on the day to show cause, Hart's counsel demanded a sight of the bond from Hart to Parran, denying there was any such, though found and seized by the inquisition, whereupon the court stayed the immediate extent until the bond be produced, in regard no process ought to issue until the bond seized be in court and disapproved of finding and seizing a bond not produced.

And no such bond being produced (nor, as appeared after, was produced at the time of the taking of the inquest), the court stopped the immediate extent, and set aside the inquisition and proceedings.

Vide Michaelmas term 1710, Abbot and the African Company.[1]

[Other copies of this report: Georgetown Univ. Law Sch. MS. B88–10, p. 653.]

321

Egerton v. Wheeler

(Ex. 1709)

The Court of Admiralty does not have jurisdiction to hear a dispute as to repairs made to a ship at land.

Lincoln's Inn MS. Misc. 538, f. [82v], pl. 2

A prohibition was prayed to the Admiralty to stay a suit there against a ship and the owners for carpenter's work and service said to be done in that ship by the defendants upon a suggestion and affidavit that, if any contract was made or work done in or about that ship, it was at land in Middlesex and nothing was done at sea.

And it was granted *nisi etc.* and after[wards] absolutely.

[Other copies of this report: Georgetown Univ. Law Sch. MS. B88–10, p. 654.]

[1] *Albert v. The African Company* (Ex. 1710), see below, Case No. 381.

322

Anonymous

(Ex. 1709)

After a hearing on a bill to recover tithes, the defendant cannot be examined as to the amounts due, but the plaintiff must prove that by other evidence.

Lincoln's Inn MS. Misc. 538, f. [83], pl. 1

28 May 1709.

A motion to have the defendant to a tithe bill, after hearing, to be examined upon interrogatories as to quantities and values, was denied, no exceptions being taken nor order for it at the hearing. And it was the plaintiff's fault to proceed to hearing against the defendant without having such a discovery by answer or proof. And it seems to be the reason of the course of the court to compel defendants to answer to quantities and values, though they have legal discharges from the payment of tithes because the court has not used to enforce the defendants to be examined upon interrogatories after a hearing to quantities and values.

But they left the plaintiff to make his proofs by commission or otherwise, the defendant's counsel opposing the motion.

[Other copies of this report: Georgetown Univ. Law Sch. MS. B88–10, p. 655, pl. 1.]

323

Bert v. Anonymous

(Ex. 1709)

Only a credit-worthy person of quality should be made commissioners of a high court.

Harvard Law Sch. MS. 537, pt. 2, p. 123, pl. 1

Easter term, 8 Anne.

A bailiff and a bailiff's follower were inserted in a commission of sequestration as commissioners. And the court were very angry such men should be put into such commissions and that it was an indignity put upon the court.

324

Anonymous

(Ex. 1709)

In a case of the crown, the court or the Attorney General can set the amount of bail that is appropriate.

Harvard Law Sch. MS. 537, pt. 2, p. 123, pl. 2

N.B. Upon a bond put in suit with a £10,000 penalty for the performance of covenants, upon an affidavit of such damnification etc., before one of the barons for non-performance (as, in this case, it was by PRICE), the baron may order the writ to be marked as he thinks reasonable as in this case for bail as for £1500 and though it be in a crown case, as this was.

And so it was said by WARD and urged by the counsel to have been done in some of the Newcastle men's cases which they proceeded against because of the drawback business, where WARD himself upon affidavits etc. marked the writs for bail.[1] And the court upon any writs marked so by one of them will hardly be brought to discharge it and suffer a common appearance.

And [it was said] by WARD nothing is more common upon such cases between party and party upon affidavits of so much etc. to mark for bail.

N.B. In this case, Baron PRICE, upon examination, as before, sent them to the Attorney General and that he might mark it [as] he thought for about so much. However, he sent his thoughts along with it, upon which it was marked for so much as before.

Upon that, [it was] said by *Northey* the Attorney General may mark the writ for bail in the crown case himself upon affidavits and examinations before him.

325

Note

(Ex. 1709)

When lands are seized upon an outlawry, the court will lease them to the plaintiff.

Harvard Law Sch. MS. 537, pt. 2, p. 123, pl. 4

It seems the court always grants the lands of the persons outlawed by way of a lease to the parties at whose [writ] the outlawry [was], but under such directions as the court thinks fit [. . .] concerning it.

326

In re Petition of Dyer

(Ex. 1709)

Trustees of infants may convey mortgaged lands and give good title.

In such cases, the court will proceed upon a petition, and the infant must be represented by a guardian ad litem.

---

[1] *Anonymous v. Wetherby* (Ex. 1706), see above, Case No. 273.

Harvard Law Sch. MS. 537, pt. 2, p. 123, pl. 5

Doyly Dyer petitioned this court in pursuance of an Act[1] this last session that the informant trustee might convey as provided by that Act.

Upon reading the petition, the court was of opinion the petition ought to name the party to whom the money is payable and when all the parties concerned. And the petitioner not doing it, it was ordered to be amended.

And now, the court being moved again, they were of the opinion, as they had expressed themselves and the day before, that the infant must not, it is not expressed so in the Act by his guardian. And, if he has not one with him, the court must assign him one.

And, now, the question was whether the parties concerned should put in their examination in writing or say what they had to say in writing.

They agreed it should be by way of a petition and not by a bill, as had been formerly the opinion of some of them.

And My Lord Chief Baron [Ward] and Bury were of opinion the parties concerned ought only to be examined verbally and everything done was in as summary a way as could be. And My Lord Chief Baron [Ward] said he had spoken to My Lord Chancellor [Cowper] about it and he was of the same opinion. But Price and Lovell were of the opinion that it ought to be in writing, second, that they ought to put in their assents in writing, not in any form, but in some summary way. And so Lovell said My Lord Chief Justice Holt and Mr. Justice Powell had told him their opinion were.

Et sic curia divisa, adjornatur.

327

Williamson v. Hewet

(Ex. 1709)

An omission of a formal recital in an arbitral award can be cured by a court.

Harvard Law Sch. MS. 537, pt. 2, p. 124, pl. 1

Easter term, 8 Anne.

It was objected by *Phipps* to an award upon a submission by a rule of the court after the day *nisi* past that the submission was of a particular suit and the wardsmen had awarded a general release until the date of the releases of all matters in controversy, all demands, etc. and did not conclude *de et super praemissis*. And he cited 2 Roll Repts. 1, Maw and Samuel, and Popham 134, the same case.[2] He said there were several cases where such would be aided by the intend-

[1] Stat. 7 Ann., c. 19 (*SR*, IX, 89).

[2] *Mawe v. Samuel* (1618), 2 Rolle Rep. 1, 81 E.R. 619, Popham 134, 79 E.R. 1236.

ment when it was *de et super praemissis*, but the two cases above were authority for him; it was otherwise where they were wanting.

Curia: We will intend it was *de et super praemissis*.

Query as to this case. It was little argued, being only a motion and the court a little in haste with it. And, as I remember, it was adjourned.

In this case, [it was] said by Chief Baron WARD and BURY that they may take [a writ of] execution to the award, though an order of court in confirmation of it if it is void. And so he said Chief Justice Hale said in one [*blank*] Tresilian's Case.[1]

But PRICE doubted they could not.

And query if they can after the day *nisi*. And [query] if their only relief then be not by a bill and if that will free them from the award as void or only rectify it. Query of this.

328

Goring v. The African Company

(Ex. 1709)

The question in this case was how to levy a distress against a corporation.

Harvard Law Sch. MS. 537, pt. 2, p. 124, pl. 2

A [writ of] *distringas* went out against the [African] Company, and the sheriff distrained them by their transfer book, and, afterwards, he returned it. And so he returned to the court issues, which was £4.

And, upon a motion by Mr. *Dodd* against the sheriff [and], second, against the Secondary of the Compter, who is in the nature of a sheriff (but for what I did not hear).

But a question thereupon happened whether the Company could be distrained by their transfer book.

Phipps insisted they could not, because it was not the Company's, but it belonged to those who had the stock and, though, perhaps, several might for that reason have an interest in it, yet it was in their private capacity and not as members and that, therefore, he did well in returning it, because he had no right to meddle with it.

But the court rather inclined they might, as having what would compel them to appear the soonest and that they were at the expense of the book [and] had the custody of it.

Then, on the other side, it was objected that he ought not to have returned the book and so returned issues.

---

[1] *Tremenheere v. Tresilian* (1670–1672), 1 Siderfin 452, 82 E.R. 1213, 2 Keble 664, 84 E.R. 418, 3 Keble 91, 84 E.R. 612.

And to this opinion, LOVELL inclined.

But WARD [said] he never knew them do otherwise; the constant practice was so. And so the rest seemed to think. And so it was affirmed by those at the bar.

Then, it was objected the issues were not large enough.

WARD: The sheriff is to return and charge himself with no more issues than he can sell the goods for. And, if the other side think the issues be too low, then they come and have their writ of averment, according to the Statute Westminster II.[1]

WARD, in speaking as to the first point, remembered the Corporation of Saltash's Case, in Hale's time, which was a [writ of] *distringas* issued against the Corporation and the officers seized the mayor's mace and went in triumph with it, and, the matter coming before the court, Chief Baron Hale said that, truly, they ought not to distrain the regalia if they could get anything else.

Dodd mentioned the Company of Grocers' Case,[2] in Chief Justice North's time, where, upon a *distringas* against them, they not appearing and standing out a little contempt, they ordered a day or two before they were to have a feast, upon the feast day, they should seize most of their plate, which was done accordingly.

[It was] put off to another day.

And [it was said] by PRICE it seems they cannot distrain the regalia if they can get sufficient [goods] besides.

And [it was said] by BURY that seems to be the law of distresses sp[. . .] as to Saltash's Case.

But then, [it was said] by *Dodd*, you must come on the other side and make affidavits they might have had sufficient [goods] besides.

329

Attorney General v. Bartlett
Attorney General v. Bowdage

(Ex. 1709–1710)

A bond given as security for a collector of the customs does not extend to a subsequent duty upon coals where the collector had a new deputation.

[1] Stat. 13 Edw. I, Westminster II, c. 39 (*SR*, I, 90–91).

[2] *Hussey v. Grocers Company* (1672–1673).

Dodd 218, Parker 277, 145 E.R. 779

Clarke in 1691 was made collector of the customs in the port of Boston. Bartlett and others were security for him. In 1698, 10 Will. III, the duties were granted upon coal etc., which by the Act[1] were to be managed by commissioners of the customs, and several clauses for that purpose [were put] in the Act. The commissioners gave Clarke a deputation for that purpose and took security. Afterwards Clarke died, the customs were paid, but on this new coal they were unpaid [in the sum of] £2000. Upon this, the bond is sued against Bartlett (*viz.* the widow and executrix of Bartlett), who brought her bill. And whether the bond where Bartlett was security extended to this future duty of coal was the question.

And the Chief Baron [Ward] inclined that it did, but he ordered the cause to be adjourned to consider of it.

In the case of Bowdage, the point was the same except that no security was given on the second deputation.

Afterwards, it was resolved that it did not extend to this, and the plaintiff [was] relieved, and a perpetual stay of process [was] awarded.

[Other reports of this case: Equity Cases Exch. 561.]

[Orders of 26 February 1707: Public Record Office E.127/26, f. 70; 10 December 1707: Public Record Office E.127/27, f. 33; 10 December 1709 and 5 May 1710: Public Record Office E.126/19, ff. 166, 192v.]

Harvard Law Sch. MS. 537, pt. 2, p. 156, pl. 2

Attorney General v. Bowdage, 1710.

The case was one Savil, in 1695, was made collector of the customs at Poole. And this Bowdage was his security in a bond of £1000. In 1697, [*blank*] Will. III, an Act was made laying a duty upon coals and culm. And it proves that officers were appointed for the receipt of it as collectors etc., for which see the Act. And, in pursuance thereof, this Savil was made a collector of it. Also, after some time, upon account, this Savil was found in arrear for customs in £300 and by the duty of coals and culm because the duty was subsequent to the bond and the bond, as I suppose, was to answer all collections etc. (or, as the common form is *quae quaere*).

And for this reason and upon one Bartley's Case, which is said to be the very same by the court, which was adjudged within a year before, they decree with[out] any hesitation thereby for the plaintiff.

N.B. They took notice that Baron Bury differed in opinion from the others in Bartley's Case.

[1] Stat. 11 Will. III, c. 13, s. 8 (*SR*, VII, 602); see also Stat. 6 & 7 Will. & Mar., c. 18, ss. 12–16 (*SR*, VI, 603–604).

N.B. In this case, they would not allow Mr. Holt, the Comptroller of the Customs, account, though, as the Chief Justice said, he is sworn to his account and though sworn to be Mr. Holt's hand etc. and a true account, but they sent it to the Master to take it because it was not sufficient for them to found their decree upon. Query, for it seems the Deputy [Remembrancer] has his power from them and only in their ease. And this would be sufficient to guide the Deputy and not them.

N.B. Likewise upon hearing an affidavit, [it was] refused to be heard because he should have been examined that the others might have had an opportunity to cross-examine [. . .] the method is upon a motion to allow of proving exhibits at the hearing *viva voce* upon a notice sometime precedent to the hearing to the other party what the exhibits are.

330

Lloyd v. Green

(Ex. 1709)

In this case, the court decreed the defendants to account for past due tithes but for only a part of the time they were proved to be due.

Dodd 218, 1 Rayner 114, 1 Eagle & Younge 684

In the Exchequer Chamber, by English bill, in a tithe bill, as executor for part of the time, against Green, as administrator for part of the time (twenty years) but in his own right for eight or nine years, against the [other] defendants in their own right for that time for the tithes of Nonsuch Park,[1] the plaintiff's title [was] established upon two trials at law, yet the court would not decree an account for the whole time. And then the plaintiff's counsel waived the time which was sued for as executor against the defendant as administrator and prayed a decree for their own time, and the Chief Baron [Ward] would not do it but only for four years.

Query by me [Samuel Dodd], for it seems very strange when it was agreed that the five and six years etc. were as plain for the plaintiff as the four years before the bill, but he would not be contradicted, and the rest of the court said little or nothing.

Note: No tithes had been before paid, but it had been disparked about twenty or twenty-five years; and the Chief Baron [Ward] said, if we stood still and would let it run so long, we should only have an account for four years.

Query by what law or statute of limitation; and why four years; why not three years or five years? I never observed such a decree before etc.; therefore, query.

[1] In the rectory of Cuddington, Surrey.

[The order of 6 November 1707, Public Record Office E.126/18, f. 687, is printed at 1 Wood 501.]

331

Scory, qui tam v. The Lord Admiral

(Ex. 1709)

In this case, a ship was seized by the Admiral's officers and, afterwards, seized by a custom house officer as forfeited, and the case was removed out of the Court of Admiralty.

Dodd 219, Parker 273, 145 E.R. 777

Score, *qui tam* v. The Lord Admiral.

In a prohibition, a ship with French goods came into the port of Penzance, and [was] there seized by the admiral's officers as a perquisite of the admiralty. A custom house officer, afterwards, seized [the ship], as forfeited on the French Prohibition Act,[1] and exhibited an information and moved for a [writ of] prohibition.

And, upon debate, it was granted, for [the ship was] presently forfeited by the Act of Parliament upon coming into port, and the seizure afterwards of the admiral did not prevent this forfeiture. Also, it was a seizure at land.

Note: Lord Chief Baron [Edward Ward] cited a case in the time of Hale, where goods were put on board, duties not [being] paid, and carried to sea, and became flotsam; and a suit [was] commenced in the Admiralty, who have jurisdiction of flotsam; and, upon an information in the Exchequer for the forfeiture, in regard they were shipped before duties paid, a prohibition was granted, for the crown had a title by the forfeiture and [the goods] becoming flotsam after did not purge the forfeiture.[2]

332

Scory, qui tam v. The Ship Adventure

(Ex. 1709)

In this case, a ship was seized by the Admiral's officers and, afterwards, seized by a custom house officer as forfeited, and the case was removed out of the Court of Admiralty.

---

[1] Stat. 3 & 4 Ann., c. 12 (*SR*, VIII, 360).

[2] *Anonymous* (Ex. 1664), Exch. Repts. *tempore* Car. II, 25.

Lincoln's Inn MS. Misc. 538, f. [83v]

Scory, *qui tam* against the ship *Adventure* of Dublin and French goods imported in it upon a [writ of] prohibition to the Admiralty, the case was thus. The ship with the goods in it were all French and French property belonging to enemies and were imported and came into the port of Falmouth 17 of April 1709. And, there, an officer of the Admiralty seized them as enemies' goods and a prize and so a perquisite of Admiralty and, as such, condemned in the Admiralty Court the 17th of May 1709. But before the condemnation, *viz.* 30th of April 1709, the informer having before that time, but after the seizure by the Admiralty, seized the said ship and goods [and] exhibited an information thereof grounded upon the Act 3 & 4 Anne,[1] which makes a forfeiture of all French goods imported into England etc. and of the ship also wherein such goods shall be imported with the privity of the master, one moiety to the queen, the other to the informer. And, in regard the Admiralty pretended to have the jurisdiction and determination of this cause, the informer suggesting the two statutes of Ric. II and that of 3 & 4 Anne and that, in this case, the sentence and proceeding in the Admiralty were void, the Attorney General and others prayed a [writ of] prohibition, which was granted *nisi causa*.

And, upon hearing counsel, as well for the queen and informer as for the Admiralty, the prohibition was absolutely granted, for, though the seizure and proceedings in the Admiralty before sentence were precedent to the informer's seizure and information, yet the cause of forfeiture of the ship and goods accruing by force of the Act of Parliament was in the nature of the thing and by due construction of law precedent to all Admiralty pretenses of prize or a perquisite of the Admiralty, which carries no pretense of title until sentence. But, by the very coming in of the ship into port, nothing of force appearing in the case, the forfeiture by the Act of Parliament, the construction of and proceeding upon it belonging to this court, and not to the Admiralty, immediately incurs and the subsequent seizure and information and proceedings in this court respect and relate to the very first cause of forfeiture, which was coming into port, and that carries a priority to the queen and informer, for, where the crown and the Admiral may each pretend to jurisdiction, the crown shall be preferred. Nay, though the Admiralty be in the crown, the law makes it so by construction, for all Admiralty jurisdiction being under and derived from the crown, it must therefore be inferior to it. And the forfeiture here incurring by Act of Parliament by coming into port and nothing done at high sea, though it should be admitted, as the civilians argued, that, by an order in Council in 1665, enemies' ships taken in port should be a perquisite of the Admiralty, yet that would not alter the case where an Act of Parliament creates a forfeiture for coming into port. And, though, in this case, there be a sentence in the Admiralty, that will not toll the jurisdiction of this

[1] Stat. 3 & 4 Ann., c. 12 (*SR*, VIII, 360).

court over the cause of forfeiture which was precedent to all that the Admiralty could pretend to. And there was not in this case any concurrence of jurisdiction upon the Act of Parliament.

In this case, I [Edward Ward] remembered a case in this court (whereof I have a note, L. J, 115) Michaelmas term 16 Car. II,[1] where upon great argument and hearing the civilians and common law counsel for the duke of York, then Lord Admiral, a prohibition was granted to the Admiralty after a sentence there for flotsam goods which were first put on board a ship in England that was broken at high sea and the goods taken up as flotsam and condemned in the Admiralty as such because those very goods were put aboard the ship without payment of duties and thereby became immediately forfeited and so carried their forfeitable quality along with them and were never purged of it, and that being a precedent forfeiture, though the information, nay, even the seizure itself, by an informer *tam quam* were after the sentence and that the Admiralty doubtless has a proper jurisdiction in the case of flotsams, yet the law respecting the original cause of forfeiture which, in that case, appeared to be by an Act of Parliament, the proceedings in the Admiralty were held insufficient, and the [writ of] prohibition was granted.

And, in the principal case, it was insisted that, in all cases, the title for the crown must be preferred to that of the Admiralty and that the Admiralty has no jurisdiction of enemies' goods in port not taken at sea and that all subjects may seize enemies' goods (*qua* such) at land. And the sentence here is grounded upon the foot of prize, which must be by a capture at sea, which this was not.

[Other copies of this report: Georgetown Univ. Law Sch. MS. B88–10, p. 657.]

333

Oldfield, qui tam v. Blagden

(1709)

Where an informer sues for a forfeiture but is not entitled to any part of it, the verdict will nevertheless stand and the crown will have the full forfeiture.

Lincoln's Inn MS. Misc. 538, f. [85v]

Oldfield, *qui tam* v. Bladwyn.

Upon a seizure of wool, the said Oldfield exhibits an information as well for the queen as for himself grounded upon the Statute 1 Will. & Mar., ca. 32,[2] setting forth that, between such times, he had seized to the use of the queen and himself as forfeited a parcel of English wool at Boston in Lincolnshire because

[1] *Anonymous* (Ex. 1664), Exch. Repts. *tempore* Car. II, 25.

[2] Stat. 1 Will. & Mar., c. 32 (*SR*, VI, 96–98).

it was loaded and carried by wagon or cart drawn with horses to a certain place upon the coasts of the sea, *viz.* to Boston aforesaid, with an intent to be conveyed from Boston to another place upon the coast of the seas within England to the informer unknown from whence the wool might be conveyed into ports beyond the seas and that the said wool at Boston within the times in the information was carrying in the said carriages towards the seas within five miles of that place on the coasts of the seas from whence the wool was to be conveyed before any due entry thereof was made at the port from whence it was intended to be conveyed of the weight, marks, and numbers of the wool *contra formam statuti etc.* And he prays that he may have a moiety of the forfeiture according to the Statute.

The defendant comes in and claims property of the wool, and pleads it was not carried *contra formam statuti modo et forma* as by the information is alleged.

And, upon a trial in the County of Lincoln, there is a verdict for the queen.

And, now several exceptions were moved in arrest of judgment, the principal of which was that the Statute upon which this information is grounded gives no part of the forfeiture for the supposed offense in the information to an informer but generally makes the wool in that case to be forfeited. (And, upon looking into the Act, it is so.) And therefore, it was urged that this was an insufficient information, and, though there has been a trial and verdict upon it, yet no judgment ought to be entered upon it, for, then it must be that the informer must have a moiety which the Act does not warrant.

But, to that, it was insisted upon by the Attorney General [*Montagu*] and others that it is a good information for the queen for the whole.

And so was the opinion of the court according to the authorities after mentioned, *viz.* Moor 28 and 556; 2 Cro. 366, 530; Hardress 185; Cro. Car. 581, 582; 11 rep., Foster's Case,[1] which, as also the reason of the law, make it out that an information by an informer *tam quam*, though it is not to have any part of the forfeiture or the information be out of time for the informer, yet, in both cases, it is good for the crown for the whole and the court can give judgment accordingly, for the law having imposed the penalty for the offense and the distribution of it being only so much to the informer, which is a reward only if he prosecutes, and so much to the crown if nothing be given to the informer or where the informer is out of time or where the Attorney General for the crown exhibits an information within the year before any information is exhibited by the informer, that, in all such cases, the crown shall have the whole forfeiture, for, where the informer has nothing given him or he comes after the year wherein, by law, he is to pros-

[1] *Anonymous* (1564), Moore K.B. 58, 72 E.R. 439; *Syvedale, qui tam v. Lenthall* (Ex. 1615), Croke Jac. 365, 79 E.R. 313, Exch. Repts. 1604–1648, p. 145; *Parker v. Curson* (1619), Croke Jac. 529, 79 E.R. 453; *Cross, qui tam v. Roe* (1661), Hardres 185, 145 E.R. 443; *Plowden v. Oldfield* (1640), Croke Car. 581, 79 E.R. 1099, also W. Jones 454, 82 E.R. 238; *Shoyle v. Foster* (1614), 11 Coke Rep. 56, 77 E.R. 1222, also 1 Rolle Rep. 88, 81 E.R. 349, 2 Bulstrode 324, 80 E.R. 1158.

ecute, though he pray a moiety, yet the court cannot give judgment for him, but must take notice of the law, and give the whole penalty of the law to the crown, the information in such a case being a record of the court. And such a title to the crown appearing to the court, it seems to be a far stronger case than for a court in the case of a *quare impedit* depending between two subjects; yet, if a title appear for the crown, judgment is to be given for the crown. Cro. Car. 590, 591.[1]

There were other exceptions taken that the Act upon which the information is grounded appoints commissioners to see the laws against transporting put in execution. But that saves all other ways of prosecution. And if it did not, yet being an affirmative law only, this court's jurisdiction is not touched.

It was further objected that the Statute 1 Will. & Mar. was a temporary law only and the last continuance of it and making it perpetual was by the Statute 9 & 10 Will. & Mar., which continued 7 & 8 and, as part of that is only made perpetual and, in that of 7 & 8, there is a clause that all actions and suits prosecuted by virtue of that Statute shall be tried by a jury summoned out of another county so that, in virtue of that clause, the cause in question is mistried, and so no judgment ought to be given.[2]

But, upon looking into those laws, it plainly appears that 1 Will. & Mar. is made perpetual as a distinct and substantive law of itself without any dependence upon any other law and that clause for trials respects not proceedings upon 1 Will. & Mar. nor the offenses thereby created, but only such offenses as are created by 7 & 8, which this in question is not.

There were also some other exceptions taken about variances between the Act and the information and uncertainties therein, which, being looking into and considered, proved mistakes.

And so, by the opinion of the whole court, judgment was entered for the queen for the whole parcel of wool.

[Other copies of this report: Georgetown Univ. Law Sch. MS. B88–10, p. 663.]

Harvard Law Sch. MS. 537, pt. 2, p. 131

Easter Term 8 Anne. Opkield, *qui tam* v. Bladwell.

This was an information upon 1 W. & M., sess. 1, c. 32, upon a seizure of wool. And, upon [a plea of] not guilty and a verdict against the defendant, it was now moved in arrest of judgment by Mr. *Ettrick* and Mr. *Blencowe*:

First, that this information is brought by the informer as well for himself as the queen and he concluded praying a half according to the Statute, *supra*, which

[1] *Rex v. Dryden* (1640), Croke Car. 511, 574, 583, 585, 589, 79 E.R. 1040, 1093, 1100, 1103, 1106.

[2] Stat. 7 & 8 Will. III, c. 28 (*SR*, VII, 118–120); Stat. 9 Will. III, c. 40 (*SR*, VII, 421–423); Stat. 10 Will. III, c. 16 (*SR*, VII, 524–528).

has given him no part of the forfeiture and that this is fatal; they cite Pie and Westley's Case, Hobt. 246;[1]

Second, that they had not pursued the directions of the Statute and entitled themselves to inform, for it only allows that such and such may, and when any act prescribes a particular way of punishing an offense, then no other way can be taken; for that they cited 2 Cr., Castle's Case;[2]

Third, that this Statute was only a temporary law, for three years; it is true it was continued, but only as merged and incorporated with 7 [Will. III], c. 28;

Fourth, it appears that the trial was where the fact was committed, and it is expressly proved to the contrary by 7 [Will. III];

Fifth, that the information does not name the owner or his agents, and suppose a stranger's goods had been taken and carried, so nobody will say they had been forfeited in that case.

Mr. Attorney General [*Montagu*], Mr. *Dodd*, and Mr. *Bridges, e contra*: As to the first, that it is grounded upon a mistake, for the Act has relation to an Act 12 Car. II, 32,[3] and that Act gives one-half to the informer and that this has a relation appears by the words 'and the persons [. . .] etc. shall forfeit and suffer as by the laws and statute now in force against the exportation of wool'.

But, however, if this were not sufficient, there is no question but it would be a good information in this case, for the information does not entitle the informer to anything, yet, so long as it appears upon record that it is an information for the benefit of the crown, the court will take notice of it for the benefit of the crown. And this is every day's practice almost, and so in Hardr. 185. And, in a *quare impedit*, if a title appear for the crown, it is common to give judgment for the king as appearing. Cro. Car. 589, 592.

As to the second, that rule does not hold where an offense [was] before that Act, as it was in our case by that act in Charles II's time. And the power given to the lessors [?] there named was so far from being excluded that there was an express proviso to that purpose afterwards.

And, as to any objection that it does not appear that we are lawfully authorized, we have a verdict in this case, and such an objection ought to have been made at the trial.

As to the third, it is continued by 7 & 8 W. and by 9 [Will. III] and to be made perpetual, and it is still a subsisting law.

As to the fourth, this is proved by 7 & 8 [Will. III]; it is only intended when the hundred is to be sued, as they are made liable by that Act, and not when the thing itself is seized. And we take it that then it was only giving the informer liberty. And, besides, though it be tried in any other court, yet, notwithstanding, the fact must be tried in the [. . .] *et non constat* but only upon the record that it

[1] *Pie v. Westly* (1618), Hobart 245, 80 E.R. 390.

[2] *Castle's Case* (1622), Croke Jac. 644, 79 E.R. 555.

[3] Stat. 12 Car. II, c. 32 (*SR*, V, 293–296).

was committed in Stone. If Lincoln was a strange county and they had a mind to try it there and [it is] no more than the common case of customs every day which they lay at Ratcliff, though not committed there, in order to try it in Middlesex. And, if they would have made anything of this point, it ought to have been found specially, *et non constat* but it was a commission in another county, for he cannot lay it in one county and try it in another.

As to the fifth, that cannot be an objection to this inference, for the officers seized the wool as forfeited and the person was unknown from whom and the court will intend them the owners who have it in their custody and possession. And they are said to be the goods of persons unknown, which is the common allegation in informations of this nature. And, besides, what now ascertains the owner is the defendant's coming in an claiming the property, and he is by that the owner upon record.

N.B. As to the third, it was further answered that it appeared plainly upon 7 [Will. III] that that manner of trial was tied up to offenses against 7 [Will. III] only and this upon 1 [Will. & Mar.]. And there are several new offenses created in 7 [Will. III].

They replied, as to the relation to 12 Car. II, there are several sorts of forfeitures by that Act. And this refers only to that as to what shall be forfeited and not to what shall afterwards become of it. It relates only so far as that the thing shall be forfeited and vested in the crown and not as to anything of distribution.

And that prerogative is not to be given away by acts of Parliaments, no more than in grants, but by express words. And, as to the case in Hardr., it does not appear that, in that case, it was afterwards moved in arrest of judgment. And as for the rem[edy] of the *quare impedit*, that was only for the ease of as much; so that was found upon a particular reason. If it appear upon the pleading in any other real action the king has a right, the court will not give judgment for the king upon that record. Now, in the case of an indictment, if he restore himself to a particular statute which does not support his demand, the court will not give judgment in such a case because he has tied himself down to that particular one.

As to the second, suppose there had been exclusive words that J.S. had brought an information and a trial, certainly, we might notwithstanding, have taken the execution. It is said, indeed, they had had an authority or that it did not appear to the contrary; they had there, indeed, after a verdict been right enough. And, besides that, all acts of parliaments which introduce a new law in the affirmation implies a negative.

And fourth [*blank*].

As to the third, the Act [*blank*], it shall not be in that county, and it cannot now be said to have been done in any place else than where laid in the information. [It was] objected the offense was not against 7 [Will. III] and 9 & 10 [Will. III], we do not take in 1 [Will. III] but only 7 [Will. III] and the words so incorporated in 7 [Will. III] and one part of it and the occasion of this proved was because they were looked upon to be as accessories in the same fact.

As to the fifth, it does not appear that the defendant was the person who carried the wool. And they must pursue the Act. They might have named the person who seized, [for] there would not perhaps have been a necessity to prove it, for the judge would intend it.

Edward Ward: He thinks it does not relate to 12 Car. II, but the true answer is, though he does not derive a half to himself when not entitled to it, that, notwithstanding, the crown shall have judgment, and anybody may inform and seize for the crown. He cited for this Agar and Candish's Case; Moor 28; 2 Cro. 366, 530; and Hard. 185; and Cro. Car. 581.[1] And he spoke as if one of them reported in Anderson wherein Anderson would make a difference of taking advantage before eight and after. But he had known when the difference was denied since. And he mentioned one Standen's Case, in this court, as the case wherein it was denied, which was judgment was given in this court in that case for the king with costs. And, likewise, there was costs added *de incremento*, whereas the king could have no costs, and that judgment was reversed in the [Court of] Exchequer Chamber for that reason and a new judgment was there given, which new judgment afterwards was affirmed in the House of Lords. He remembered that the now Chief Justice and himself argued it in the House of Lords. He said, as to Pie's Case, there was no such act as the information was brought upon.

As to the second, the power of the commissioners is not exclusive, but, however, there is likewise an express proviso to enable anybody else.

Third, as to 1 W. & M. being a temporary law, it is true it was so, but it was continued by 7 [Will. III] and made perpetual by 9 & 10 [Will. III]. He said it is certainly a subsisting law. It is continued only, not merged. Besides, if any statute supports the information, it is well enough upon this information, because the conclusion is general, *contra formam statuti*, and, therefore, any will support it.

Fourth, as to the fourth, that the trial was well enough, it being a subsisting law, and 21 Jac., 4, gives the informer, in this case, liberty to bring it in any county.

As to the last and as to its being alleged that the defendant's having claimed property etc. if it be necessary to show the owner that they shall now be presumed the defendant's goods, he cited one Dickinson and Stockdon's Case, in Charles II's time.[2] It was an information upon 18 Eliz.,[3] where [there was] a penalty (a person and a corporate one, as I apprehended) laid upon the owner and it was not said in the information that the defendant was the owner and [there was

[1] *Agar v. Cavendish* (1594), Moore K.B. 564, 72 E.R. 761, Croke Eliz. 327, 78 E.R. 576, also Savile 134, 123 E.R. 1055; *Anonymous* (1564), Moore K.B. 58, 72 E.R. 439; *Ward v. Ayre* (1615), Croke Jac. 366, 79 E.R. 314; *Parker v. Curson* (1619), Croke Jac. 529, 79 E.R. 453; *Cross, qui tam Roe v. Roe* (1661), Hardres 185, 145 E.R. 443; *Plowden v. Oldfield* (1640), *ut supra*.

[2] *Dickenson, qui tam v. Stocker* (Ex. 1672), Exch. Cases *tempore* Car. II, 250.

[3] Stat. 18 Eliz. I, c. 9 (*SR*, IV, 619–620).

a] verdict and judgment and, upon a writ of error in the Exchequer Chamber before Hale, it was said by Hale we will not presume a man to be a forfeiture etc. though he claims and defends etc., but, in a case of goods, it may be otherwise, but, if you do not know who, it is sufficient to assign it that they belonged to *personis ignotis et sic*, he was of opinion that judgment should be given for the queen.

And so the rest declared themselves without giving their reasons.

Dodd 220

In an information upon [the Statute] 1 W. & M. about wool and a verdict given, [it was] moved in arrest of judgment that the informer [was] entitled to no part, and, therefore, the information [was] bad etc.

But [it was] adjudged upon debate that the queen will have all and the information [was] good for the queen. And judgment [was given] accordingly. Moo. 564; Hard. 185; Cr. Car. 381, etc.; Hob., Pye and Westley, 245.

Parker 111, 145 E.R. 729

Entered Michaelmas term 7 Anne, roll 51.

An information [was exhibited] upon the Statute 1 W. & M., c. 32, continued by 4 & 5 W., c. 24,[1] for carrying 386 fleeces of wool, containing 66 tods and 14 pounds weight within five miles of the seacoast in order to exportation without due entry made of it, and the plaintiff demands a moiety.

After a verdict for the plaintiff, the defendant, in Easter term, 8th of Anne 1709, moved in arrest of judgment. And the exception taken to the information was that the whole forfeiture was given to the queen and yet the plaintiff demands a moiety of it.

And, on great debate by eminent counsel on both sides, judgment was given in Trinity term following for the queen for the whole forfeiture.

334

Lord Raby v. Lord Pelham

(Ex. 1709)

In this case, the court held that the plaintiff was entitled to have certain moneys that were in issue that were due to the crown before his grant of them began.

Harvard Law Sch. MS. 537, pt. 2, p. 133

Easter term 8 Anne.

The case was the crown had granted at one time all the post fines of lands in the liberty of A. to My Lord Pelham and, at another time, all those of lands

[1] Stat. 4 Will. & Mar., c. 24, s. 9 (*SR*, VI, 417).

in the liberty of B. to him. And a fine being of lands in both liberties, the question was whether My Lord Raby as general grantee of the crown of the post fines should have it or My Lord Pelham.

It was said that, though the liberties had been in distinct hands and a fine levied of lands in both, that the crown must have the post fine because there could be no apportionment, but, being both in one, the reason failed.

And so, as I [Eden] apprehend, the court inclined. But it was put off.

Per curiam: If lands are asserted [to be] out of the liberty, we will examine whether it was with an intent to defraud the patentee or no. It lies upon the patentee to make it appear to be within the liberty.

Lincoln's Inn MS. Misc. 538, f. [85]

The Lord Raby had a grant under the great seal dated the 18th of January 1696 of the benefit of all post fines for the term of forty-eight years from Michaelmas 1708, when a former grant of the post fines for a like term made by King Charles II in April 1661 to the earl of Berkshire and Sir Robert Howard determined.

A question arose whether the Lord Raby's grant carried the post fines that grew due to the year ended at Michaelmas 1708 in regard that, by a proviso in the earl of Berkshire's grant, the earl and Sir Robert were restrained from receiving that year's post fines but that they should remain to King Charles II and his successors and the like restriction was in the Lord Raby's grant as to the post fines that should grow due in the last year of his term so that whether the post fines that grew due in the year ended at Michaelmas 1708 belonged to the queen or the Lord Raby was the question.

And it appearing upon the inspection into both grants and the certificates of the deputy to the Lord Treasurer's Remembrancer and the Clerk of the Pipe that the first grant passed the arrears for the year preceding the commencement of it so that, there, the grantees received forty-eight years post fines for their annual rent of £2276 payable to the crown without the last year's post fines. And the Lord Raby's grant carried the arrears of post fines due at the commencement of it and that he was to pay the like yearly rent of £2276 during his term. And he stands excluded in like manner from receiving the post fines that shall grow due in the last year of his term (the post fines in each last year not being accounted for within that year), it seemed just and was so ordered by the court that the Lord Raby should have the post fines grown due within the last year of the earl of Berkshire's grant, else he would be obliged to pay forty-eight years' rent and have but forty-seven years' profits, which could not be the intention of the parties. And, moreover, the Lord Raby having a grant of the arrears at the commencement of his grant well warrants the passing the post fines to him that grew due in the year preceding his grant which the earl of Berkshire's grant did not carry to him for the reasons aforesaid.

[Other copies of this report: Georgetown Univ. Law Sch. MS. B88–10, p. 661.]

334a

Lord Pelham's Case

(Ex. 1709)

Where post fines are partly out of a manor, they are payable to the crown.

Indiana Univ., Lilly Library
MS. Parker 'Cases in the Exchequer', vol. 5, p. 170

He claimed the post fines of the rape of Hastings and the rape of Pevensey in Sussex upon a fine levied by the earl of Sussex. King Charles II, 4 July, 36th of his reign [1684], under the seal of the duchy of Lancaster, did grant to Benjamin Ayloff in trust for lord Hollis all fines and amercements within the fees and liberties of the duchy of Lancaster in Surrey and Sussex for thirty-one years. The duke of Newcastle assigned to lord Pelham 30 June 1707 his interest in the said post fines. And so he claims the said post fine as in the rape of Pevensey under the seal of the duchy of Lancaster. The lord Pelham and his ancestors have the post fines in the rape of Hastings in Sussex, which is contiguous to the rape of Pevensey.

The objection against setting over the post fines to the Lord Pelham is because there are lands in this fine that are not in either of the said liberties, as appears by the *Nomina Villarum*, before the Foreign Apposer, and so, by the usage of the Exchequer, the post fine ought not to be totted, as the agent of the farmer of the post finds insists.

By the like usage of this court, if post fines arise out of two distinct liberties, by which it is uncertain to which it belongs, such post fines ought not to be totted and go to the crown. If part be out of a liberty, it is gildable, and ought to go to the crown, and not be set over.

Chief Baron [Ward]: Where liberties are granted, the officer cannot set over without a judgment of the court or a confession of the Attorney General. Where two cannot divide, it must go to the crown.

It was referred to the Lord Treasurer's Remembrancer that all the land was in one or both of the liberties.

We, on 13 July 8 Anne, *reginae*, 1709, ordered the post fine to be set over to lord Pelham by the Foreign Apposer upon his yearly claim.

Lord Raby is now the farmer of the post fines.

335

Cartwright v. Anonymous

(Ex. 1709)

An arbitral award must decide and end all of the disputes that were submitted to the arbitrators.

Harvard Law Sch. MS. 537, pt. 2, p. 139, pl. 2

The case was there had been a suit by the plaintiff against the defendant. And they enter into arbitration bonds submitting all debts, quarrels, suits, strifes, etc. It went on in such general words. And an award is made that the defendant shall pay the plaintiff £10 and £8, and it likewise awarded that the plaintiff should accept the said £18 in full satisfaction of all debts and sums of money.

To this, *Lutwyche* objected that it did not make an end of all matters in controversy, as the plaintiff might have a title to an action of trespass against the defendant and this is within the submission but yet not within the award. And this objection is the stronger because the submission concludes *ita quod fiat de praemissis.*

Chesshyre: It lies upon them to show that there was anything else not by this determined, and, then, it well might have denied it, and, if it had found with the denial, then, it would have been a good award still.

Curia: The premises must be made an end of, expressly or impliedly, and it awarded an acceptance in full, the same whether an award or a release, and make it as much an award of both sides. But there is a difference where there is a general submission of things and where there is a submission only of particular controversies etc. In the first case, though it be *ita quod*, it is good until it is shown on the other side there was something else not determined and which was notified to the arbitrators. And this though the award was not equally extensive with the submission, but, in the latter, it is otherwise.

And, so, judgment [was given]. It was, indeed, *nisi*, not but that the court was clear of the award being good.

336

Anonymous

(Ex. 1709)

Where a master of the court makes a finding upon a reference and the defendant absconds, the order will be discharged.

Harvard Law Sch. MS. 537, pt. 2, p. 139, pl. 2a

N.B. [There was] a rule of reference to the Master and that the defendant should pay so much as the Master, upon examination, [should find]. The Master finds so much. The defendant runs away, and does not pay it.

And the court ordered the rule to be discharged *nisi*, though they had made no demand or given him notice of it.

But it seemed by those speaking in it that, in case he could have been demanded, they must have demanded it of him first.

Ex motione Lutwyche.

N.B. It seemed to be in an action upon a bond, for it was said the rule was an equitable one by the interpretation of the court.

337

Peacock v. Stollard

(Ex. 1709)

The Court of Admiralty does not have jurisdiction to settle disputes that arose on land in a foreign nation.

Lincoln's Inn MS. Misc. 538, f. [95]

28 October 1709. Entered Trinity 8 [Anne] in the Office of Pleas. Peacock *et alii versus* Stollard *et alios* and the ship called the *Phoenix Foy* upon a motion for a [writ of] prohibition to the Court of Admiralty wherein the case was thus.

Stollard, a merchant of Amsterdam, libels in the Admiralty Court here *querelando* showing that, in March and April 1708, that ship, whereof Perry was master, lay in the port of Rotterdam in Holland beyond the sea *infra fluxum et refluxum maris* bound for Fareham or some other port in England and that, while the ship lay there, she wanted several necessaries without which she could not proceed on her intended voyage. And, thereupon, Perry, the master, borrowed so much money of Green, Stollard's agent, on the bottom of that ship in order to refit her and provide her with necessaries for her voyage to be repaid within eight days after the ship's arrival at Fareham with 5 percent, Stollard running the risk and perils of the sea. Perry, at the borrowing of the money declaring and protesting that the ship wanted necessaries and could not perform her intended voyage without the said money and then and there, by a writing duly executed, did stake and hypothecate the said ship for the repayment of that money with £5 percent interest as aforesaid and that the money was laid out for refitting the ship and finding necessaries and, after that, sailed for Fareham. And there she arrived May following with her goods and cargo. And the money borrowed has been demanded, and eight days and more passed. And, thereupon, he caused the said ship to be arrested for the same.

Note it is not laid in the libel that the ship lay *infra jurisdictionem Admiralitatis.*

The defendants Peacock and others, owners of the ship, who come in *pro interesse*, pray a [writ of] prohibition, suggesting the statutes of Richard II[1] and that the contracts and matters in the libel were all made and done at land beyond the seas, *viz.* at Rotterdam and not upon the high sea and so not to be sued for in the Admiralty, but at common law. And a rule for a prohibition was granted *nisi causa* this day [28 October 1709].

[1] Stat. 13 Ric. II, stat. 1, c. 5 (*SR*, II, 62); Stat. 15 Ric. II, c. 3 (*SR*, II, 78–79).

And *Ettrick* and *Pengelly* showed for cause that the master of a ship, by the civil law, has power in such a case as this, either at sea or at land, to hypothecate a ship for necessaries without the consent of the owners (though not to sell it) and that it is most reasonable it should be so, else the ship and voyage be lost, and, therefore, our law allows it also, though it is suggested here that the hypothecating was at land beyond the sea, yet it was done for necessaries, which is proper to be determined in the Admiralty. It is as valid as if at sea, notwithstanding Lord Hobart's opinion in Bridgman's Case, Hobt., fo. 11, which is also in Roll's, title *Admiralty*, 530.[1] And all agree with the master's power to pawn the ship at sea for necessaries. And, by parity of reason, where the ship receives damage at sea and in voyage, the supplies may not be had at sea, but must be had in port. And, where they are had or furnished, there, the necessity rises and, therefore, must be supplied. Latch 252, Noy 95.[2]

Nevertheless, here, the pawning was at sea and not avoyage. But that did not so appear, but that the pawning was in port at land and the ship was in port also.

The only question in this case is whether the master of a ship can pawn his ship for necessaries in port beyond the seas when it does not appear that she had been in any voyage or ever at sea or sustained any damage or became in want of any necessaries by any voyage.

By these cases in Latch and Noy *supra*, it appears the pawning was at sea and the ship was in a voyage and [it was] good in such a case if done beyond the sea. Watson's Case is that the factor pawning at Bayonne, beyond the seas is good.[3] It seems to intend in voyage. The only question in that case was whether the pawner was such a person as was in power to pawn, which the court left to be tried if they would in any action.

The anonymous case, 3 Modern 244, was a libel against a ship that wanted necessaries at open sea and was pawned by the master for those necessaries on the coasts, and that was allowed to be good.[4] But this case differs. Statute 28 Hen. VIII, ca. 15, does not allow a power of pawning the ship for necessaries upon the seas, but they are to pay ready money or demand a bill obligatory for payments at a day.[5]

The reason of the power of pawning is for necessity, that the voyage be not lost. And, in that case, it is said the pawning must be at sea, which I [EDWARD WARD] would interpret to be in the voyage, and for a necessity arising in the voyage, for no necessity can arise but from some accident or want arising from the

---

[1] *Barnard v. Bridgeman* (1614), Hobart 11, 80 E.R. 162, 1 Rolle, Abr., *Court of Admiralty*, pl. C, 2, p. 530, also Moore K.B. 918, 72 E.R. 996.

[2] *Scarborough v. Lyrus*, Latch 252, 82 E.R. 371, Noy 95, 74 E.R. 1061.

[3] *Watson v. Jackson* (K.B. 1596 × 1597), Latch 252, 82 E.R. 371.

[4] *Cossart v. Lawdley* (1688), 3 Modern 244, 87 E.R. 159, also Comberbach 135, 90 E.R. 389, Holt K.B. 48, 90 E.R. 924.

[5] Stat. 28 Hen. VIII, c. 15, s. 4 (*SR*, III, 671).

voyage. And it is there said that this power of pawning arises from some extraordinary and invincible necessity at sea, but not at land.

And, when that necessity arises at sea, that gives the Admiral jurisdiction, for, in such a case, the ship was once under the Admiral's jurisdiction, *viz.* at sea, but not so here.

It is objected that, in Costard and Lusely's Case, Trinity 1 Will. & Mar., King's Bench,[1] where it was adjudged the pawning was good at land, it does not appear that the ship had been at sea or received any distress there.

Solution: That point might never come in question there nor be the same case with this and so conclude nothing, but the former cases favor it as appearing to be in the voyage, and to say it does not appear the ship had been at sea is not an answer, for it is more reasonable to think it had been at sea than not and so touches not this case, since the reason of the thing leads to a voyage had and necessity arising therein. And, since there can no necessity arise at land before any voyage begins since it is not safe to trust a master of a ship that never went avoyage to buy provisions or order the ship as he pleases at land where he may acquaint and have consent of the owners (for, in this case, *non constat* that the owners were English), I [Edward Ward] think it is not fit to make a precedent in this case or to enlarge the power of the master to pawn the ship to provide necessaries for a ship for a voyage when there is no such thing ever yet allowed, nor does the reason of the thing allow it.

Now besides the authorities already cited, that the pawning must be to supply defects and necessities arising at sea in a voyage, these and the reason of them that follow [are] to be considered: Molloy, *Jure Maritimo*, fo. 197, a master's fault in port [is] punishable at law; if, at high sea, in the Admiralty, Dowdale's Case, 6 rep.;[2] fo. 202, if a ship at sea leaks or wants necessaries, [he] may impawn to relieve such necessities; he cannot pawn without the consent of the mariners, and the obligation on the vessel must be in foreign parts where the necessity came upon the vessel; fo. 203, merchants freighting a ship and setting her to sea and is there waterbound, the vessel he may pawn for necessaries rather than lose the vessel. [Laws of] Oleron, ca. 22.

It has formerly been much stood upon that, as to ships built in port, the shipwright or builders may sue the ship for wages. And [he] cited the case of Tasker and Gale, Roll's, *Admiralty*, 533, 19, Pas. 9 Car. I, and so for a charter party etc.[3]

I agree the book is so, but I give it this answer that this was after the judges' agreement 8 Car. I[4] and before they were exploded. There are other cases there which are otherwise resolved since. Now, as to that agreement, it certainly is

---

1 *Cossart v. Lawdley* (1688), *ut supra.*

2 *Richardson v. Dowdale* (1605), 6 Coke Rep. 46, 77 E.R. 323, also Croke Jac. 55, 79 E.R. 47.

3 *Tasker v. Gale* (1633), 1 Rolle, Abr., *Court of Admiralty*, pl. E, 19, 20, p. 533.

4 18 February 1632[/33], W. Prynne, *Brief Animadversions* (1669), p. 100.

not law, nor binds, nor now practiced. Some of the very judges that subscribed changed their opinion, as appears, first, by the uniform opinion of the court of King's Bench in the Case of Ball and Trelawny, last case in the same book, where they discharged one from imprisonment in the Admiralty on a judgment obtained against him upon a contract for goods in New England beyond the seas, which was the very first case in that agreement to be made; second, by the opinion of Foster and Twisden, 12 Car. II, Raymond 3, where a prohibition was granted against that agreement, it being by them said that they had known several judges deny them and that they had been renounced by several of those that subscribed them; third, the constant current of our books are, at this day, the Admiralty has nothing to do with contracts or matters done on land beyond the seas. More full restraint cannot be put by words to the Admiralty jurisdiction than what [is] contained in the Statute of Richard II and Henry IV, and here to make an exposition against them is too hard.[1]

The cases cited [were] Hobart, Bingly's Case, Pope's Case, etc. [It is the] constant practice since Jurado and Gregory, 1 Ventr. 32; 12 rep. 103, 104; 79; Justice and Browne, 20 Car. II, L. 1, 391, in the Exchequer.[2] Nay, the counsel themselves that are against the prohibition do allow the law to be that, generally speaking, the Admiralty cannot hold a plea of anything done at land beyond the seas. But they only insist upon the master's power of hypothecating the ship for necessaries. Then, while that extends to necessaries to fit out a ship in port for a voyage or only to supply the ship with necessaries which has been damnified in a voyage is the now question. And I hold the last only. Suppose the master or any of the owners had sold or mortgaged the ship by a writing at land, the Admiralty [may] not try that. And this is the same thing.

[Other copies of this report: Georgetown Univ. Law Sch. MS. B88–10, p. 669.]

---

1 *Ball v. Trelawny* (1641), Croke Car. 603, 79 E.R. 1119; *Woodward v. Bonithan* (1661), T. Raymond 3, 83 E.R. 2; Stat. 13 Ric. II, stat. 1, c. 5 (*SR*, II, 62); Stat. 15 Ric. II, c. 3 (*SR*, II, 78–79); Stat. 2 Hen. IV, c. 11 (*SR*, II, 124).

2 *Don Diego v. Bingley*, Hobart 78, 113, 80 E.R. 228, 263; *Palmer v. Pope* (1611), Hobart 79, 212, 80 E.R. 229, 359; *Jurado v. Gregory* (1669), 1 Ventris 32, 86 E.R. 23, also 2 Keble 511, 610, 84 E.R. 320, 384, 1 Siderfin 418, 82 E.R. 1191, 1 Levinz 267, 83 E.R. 400; *Thomlinson's Case* (1605), 12 Coke Rep. 104, 77 E.R. 1379; *Justice v. Brown* (Ex. 1668), Exch. Repts. *tempore* Car. II, 128.

338

Poulson, qui tam v. Anonymous

(Ex. 1709)

Where there are two informations of seizures of the same alleged illegally imported goods, the second seizer must prove his priority and then the common defendant pleads auter action pendant and then the Attorney General elects which information to prosecute.

Lincoln's Inn MS. Misc. 538, f. [96v]

Trinity term 8 Anne.

Gilbert Poulson exhibits two informations of seizures the 22nd of June 8 Anne [1709], by one of which he shows that, between the first of July then last and the day of exhibiting that information, at Ratcliff in Middlesex, he seized to the use of himself and the queen the ship called the *King David* of Rotterdam with the apparel and furniture thereof, for that several parcels of French wines, French prunes, and French cork, being of the growth of France etc., were within that time imported in that ship from parts beyond the seas to Ratcliff aforesaid with the knowledge, privity, and consent of [*blank*], then master of that ship, the said goods before the importation thereof not being taken as prize *contra formam statuti*. And so he prays the ship may be forfeited and the queen may have one moiety and the informer the other.

The other information is in the same time and for the same goods mentioned in the first information and for the same cause, *viz.* for being imported French goods and not being first taken as prize nor condemned in the Admiralty nor ordered to be sold as perishable goods.

The property of the ship is claimed by [*blank*], and Binks comes in and claims the property of one. And the property of the goods is claimed by [*blank*]. And Binkes claims the property of one moiety.

The same Trinity term, *viz.* 5 July, Samuel Binkes exhibits his information into the court, and lays his seizure of the same ship and all the goods in Poulson's informations mentioned to be between the first of August then last and the day of the exhibiting of that information for the same reasons and causes in Poulson's two informations mentioned. And he makes a like prayer. But this information mentions nothing of condemnation or sale of goods as perishable. The property of the ship and goods is claimed by the same claimers to Poulson's informations.

The claimers and proprietors of the ship and goods, but not the said Binks, move the court that, inasmuch as here are two several informers and three several informations depending for the same thing, that they may not be compelled to plead so as to go to any trial before the two informers have between themselves settled the right and title of their respective seizures, for, otherwise, the claimers must be put to attend two trials, which will be chargeable and is not reasonable, for, if the claimers make good their case against one, it will be hard to fight a second battle with the others, for, as to the queen, she can have but one moiety if forfeited, and therefore, the question for the other moiety must be between the two informers, for the ship and goods cannot be double forfeited nor ought the claimers, who are willing to try it upon either of the informations, be doubly vexed for the same thing.

And I [Edward Ward] observed that, in this case, here is a difference of time between the exhibiting of the informations and the times of seizure alleged, and, in such a case, regularly, the junior informer ought to come in and claim the property as to one moiety of the ship and goods claimed by the first informer and say that he was the first seizer and, thereby, became the first entitled to the moiety and show the time and manner of such seizure and, if he prevails therein or if he pleads his seizure and that the first seizure and information exhibited and made by the other informer were had and made by fraud and to deceive the queen and him of the forfeiture of the ship and goods and prevails therein, then the defendants will be rid of the first informer and his informations or else the claimers may to the second information plead in abatement the pendency of the first informations for the same thing, and pray judgment which they shall answer to that pending the other one determined, and then the Attorney General and informers must agree or be determined by the court upon that plea or examination of the matter which to proceed upon and, if the Attorney General should elect which to proceed upon, yet, inasmuch as there may be a question of right between the informers, who, by their seizures and informations, have a right attached in them, Mr. Attorney General, by anything he can do, cannot divest them from trying their rights. But then they must agree to it, else the court will determine it.

Singleton and Wyat were two seizers of the same goods and the court 19 November 5 Queen [Anne] 1706, whereby the court ordered the two informers to try and [. . .] the cause between the two informers, which [was the] first or lawful seizer, and that the trial should be the day before the claimer's trial should be, which was to be the next day, in which Case of Wyat and Singleton, Michaelmas 5 Anne,[1] Singleton claimed the property of a moiety of the ship and goods, being seized for the same cause with this of Poulson and Binks and pleads that Wyat's information and seizure were by fraud and covin between Wyat and the importers and others to avoid the Act of Parliament which gives the forfeiture and the real forfeiture of the ship and goods and to deceive him, the said Singleton, of his moiety, for which cause Wyat's seizure was and is void. And then he shows that the said Singleton, being an officer of the customs, the 30th of July 5 Anne, Wyat's information being on the French Act[2] and entered the 27 of July 5 [Anne], exhibited his information of seizure on the French Act for the same cause of forfeiture of the ship and wines and, at the same, also exhibited another

[1] *Wyatt, ex rel. Robertson, qui tam v. Singleton* (Ex. 1707), see above, Case No. 277.

[2] Stat. 3 & 4 Ann., c. 12 (*SR*, VIII, 360).

information of seizure of the same ship and goods for that the wines, not being Rhenish, were imported from the Netherlands or Germany against the form of the Statute against Fraud in Customs, 14 Car. II, ca. 11, which gives a forfeiture of the ship and goods.[1] And he avers his informations to be depending undetermined *prout per recordam*, and he avers the ships and goods in all the three informations to be the same, and prays judgment and that the moiety of the ship and goods may be delivered to him, and he, *quoad praemissa, ab hac curia, dimittatur.* Wyat replies and avers his seizure and information and cause of forfeiture to be good, and he traverses the fraud and covin alleged by Singleton, and prays judgment and that he may have his moiety. Singleton rejoins and maintains the fraud and covin, and concludes to the country. And, thereupon, issue is joined. And, at the day of *nisi prius* and before trial, Singleton withdraws his claim *et relicta verificationem* released the goods and his claim.

And so, at length, did Binkes here by the direction of the Attorney General. And the cause on Poulson's information was to proceed.

And it was tried the same term, and [there was] a verdict for the defendant against the opinion of the Chief Baron who tried it.

[Other copies of this report: Georgetown Univ. Law Sch. MS. B88–10, p. 675.]

339

Smith v. Johnson

(Ex. 1709–1713)

A custom of not paying tithes of herbage in a hundred can be valid where the rector has sufficient other income from the hundred.

Agistment tithes are due for unprofitable cattle.

Dodd 221, 1 Eagle & Younge 692

In a tithe bill as rector of Bishop's Wearmouth, a custom was alleged that tithe herbage is not payable within the hundred or ward of Easington in Durham and that there was a sufficient maintenance, *viz.* above £300 *per annum*, besides herbage, to the plaintiff.

And upon debate, [it was] resolved: first, that [it was] not a good *modus* and [they] grounded their opinion on Hicks and Woodhouse case, 4 Mod.[2]; second, that the defendant proved no tithe [was] paid in the hundred, yet as to the maintenance, he examined only to this parish, and not to all the rest, which the court held naught, for the whole hundred must be discharged, because in this parish

[1] Stat. 14 Car. II, c. 11 (*SR*, V, 393–400).

[2] *Hicks v. Woodhouse* (1697), 4 Modern 324, 336, 87 E.R. 422, 429.

there is a sufficient maintenance, but *non constat* if so in the other parishes. Baron LOVELL [was] against the other three barons.

2 Gwillim 606

Trinity term 8 Anne, 1708.

To a bill by the rector of Bishop Wearmouth, in the County of Durham, for an account of all tithes, both great and small, within the parish, the defendants, as to agistment tithe, pleaded that the said parish is parcel of the hundred or ward of Easington in the said County of Durham and that, by ancient custom within the said hundred, the owners, tenants, and farmers of any lands and tenements within the said hundred have been, and ought to be, discharged from the payment of tithes for all barren and unprofitable cattle bred, fed, or depastured, or for or in respect of the agistment or depasturing thereof, or of any other cattle in or upon the said lands or ground, or any part thereof and that, accordingly, no tithes had at any time been paid for any such barren cattle or the agistment or depasturing of the same or of any other cattle within the said hundred for that the rector of the said church had enjoyed glebe lands and other tithes and profits yielding a competent reasonable maintenance and subsistence for him and them without the tithes for barren and unprofitable cattle or agisting or depasturing the same or any other cattle, amounting to £300 *per annum*, and then to £400. And they insisted that they were exempt from the payment of the said tithes.

The court declared that the said custom, if any such there were, was void in law, and, therefore, overruled the same.

And as to tithes demanded for sheep bought in after shearing and wintered and sold or killed unshorn, they ordered the defendants to account for the same.

Bunbury 1, 145 E.R. 574, 1 Eagle & Younge 705

If a man depastures unprofitable cattle in his ground, he shall pay tithes in proportion to the number of the cattle and the value of the land, generally at the rate of 2s. in the pound. And the same proportion is to be observed if they are travelling cattle that come and go successively. Cattle fed upon meadow ground, after it is mowed, shall not pay tithes, unless by custom.

[Other reports of this case: Equity Cases Exch. 606, 1 Rayner 121.]

[The decree of 14 July 1709, Public Record Office E.126/19, f. 144, is printed in 1 Wood 514; see also order of 19 May 1709: Public Record Office E.126/19, f. 118v.]

340

Long v. Beaumont

(Ex. 1709)

A devise to the heir of a living person is valid.

Since a will must be in writing, a deposition to explain the will cannot be considered.

Indiana Univ., Lilly Library
MS. Parker, 'Cases in the Exchequer', vol. 5, p. 131

Lay v. Beamont.

This was a bill on the will of Colonel Sprot, who devised his real estate to trustees for twenty-one years to pay his debts and legacies and then to his cousin John Sparks for ninety-nine years if he so long lived, remainder to [his] first son in tail male etc., remainder to Jonathan for ninety-nine years if he lived, then to [his] first son in tail male, and [the] remainder to the heirs male of Richard and Elizabeth Lay in tail male.

John and Jonathan Sparkes died without issue male; the plaintiff Elizabeth [Long] was aunt to Colonel Sprot and had issue then living, the plaintiff Thomas and others.

[The issue was] whether this was a good limitation to the son of the plaintiff Elizabeth, the mother then living, for which was quoted Noy 43; 4 Modern, Goodright v. Cornish; 1 Modern, Pybus v. Mitford, 2 Levinz 78, *idem*; 2 Rep., Cholmley's Case; 4 Modern, Tipping v. Cosins; 2 Levinz 230, James v. Richardson; Syderfin 153, where [to] one *en ventre sa mere* [is] a good devise; Moor 593, Clark v. Day.[1]

The court decreed the plaintiff [to be] at liberty to affirm his title at [common] law[2] [and decreed] the lease and all obstacles to be removed.

Secondly, it was objected against [the] reading [of] the deposition for explaining the will and that the Lords in the Lord Falkland and Mr. Lytton's Case,[3] on Sir William Lytton's will, they blamed the reading of it in Chancery, and yet, in the case of Nicolas v. Nicholas before lord Somers, it was allowed, where [there was] a devise of land to a wife and [there was] proof that it was in-

---

1 *Payne v. Ferrall*, Noy 43, 74 E.R. 1012; *Goodright v. Cornish* (1694), 4 Modern 255, 87 E.R. 380, also 1 Salkeld 226, 91 E.R. 200, Holt K.B. 227, 90 E.R. 1024, Comberbach 254, 90 E.R. 461, Skinner 408, 90 E.R. 181, 12 Modern 52, 88 E.R. 1159, 1 Lord Raymond 3, 91 E.R. 898, 1 Eq. Cas. Abr. 189, 21 E.R. 980, 2 Eq. Cas. Abr. 337, 22 E.R. 287; *Pybus v. Mitford* (1673), 1 Modern 98, 121, 159, 86 E.R. 761, 780, 800, 2 Levinz 75, 83 E.R. 456, also 1 Ventris 372, 86 E.R. 239, 3 Keble 129, 239, 316, 338, 84 E.R. 634, 697, 741, 754, T. Raymond 228, 83 E.R. 119, 1 Freeman 351, 369, 89 E.R. 262, 275, 3 Salkeld 337, 91 E.R. 859; *Cholmley v. Hanmer* (1597), 2 Coke Rep. 50, 76 E.R. 527, also Moore K.B. 342, 72 E.R. 617; *Tippin v. Coson* (1694), 4 Modern 380, 87 E.R. 455, also Comberbach 312, 90 E.R. 498, Carthew 272, 90 E.R. 761, Holt K.B. 731, 90 E.R. 1303, 1 Lord Raymond 33, 91 E.R. 918; *James v. Richardson* (1678), 2 Levinz 232, 83 E.R. 533, also T. Jones 99, 84 E.R. 1166, Pollexfen 457, 86 E.R. 610, 3 Keble 832, 84 E.R. 1039, T. Raymond 330, 83 E.R. 172, 1 Ventris 334, 86 E.R. 216, 1 Eq. Cas. Abr. 214, 21 E.R. 998, 1 Freeman 458, 472, 89 E.R. 343, 353, Dodd 60; *Snow v. Tucker* (1663), 1 Siderfin 153, 82 E.R. 1027; *Clerke v. Day* (1593), Moore K.B. 593, 72 E.R. 779, also Croke Eliz. 312, 78 E.R. 564, *sub nom. Lilly v. Taylor*, Owen 148, 74 E.R. 965.

2 See *Darbison, ex dem. Long v. Beaumont* (1713), below, Case No. 436.

3 *Viscountess Falkland v. Lytton* (1709), 3 Brown 24, 1 E.R. 1152.

tended in bar of dower, though [it was] read, yet [it was] not admitted against a will. The Statute of Wills and Frauds and Perjuries[1] says that wills must be in writing, so it was passed over.

Harvard Law Sch. MS. 537, pt. 2, p. 115

Hilary term 7 Anne.

The case was A., by his will, devised lands to trustees for twenty-one years for the payment of debts, remainder to J.L. for ninety-nine years if he so long lived, remainder to his first and every other son in tail male, remainder to the heirs male of the body of his Aunt Long, and, for default of such issue, remainder to his right heirs. He devises likewise in the same will several legacies to his Aunt Long, whereby he took notice of her being then living. J.L. dies without issue male. The plaintiff Thomas Long, upon that, being at the time of the devise heir male apparent to the Aunt Long, preferred a bill against Beaumond, the right heir and the trustees of the term to account etc.

And the question was whether the plaintiff was well entitled to the estate after J.L.'s dying without issue male by virtue of this will.

It was argued by the Solicitor General [*Robert Eyre*], *Sir Thomas Parker, Sir Peter King*, Mr. *Dodd*, and Mr. *Ward* that he was well entitled.

Solicitor General [*Eyre*] argued that there was a good estate devised to him notwithstanding there was no particular estates of freehold and that it was a contingent remainder, for, by him, it is in this case devised to a stranger and not to the heir at law and there is a freehold that descends to the heir at law during the Aunt Long's life. If the estate had been given for years, remainder to the heir at law during the Aunt Long's life, remainder to the heirs male of his Aunt Long, here the remainder would have been good because not a contingent remainder upon a lease for years, but there is a freehold likewise to support it. And [it was said] by him [there is] no difference when the party and when the law gives it. And, in this case, here being a lease for years and a contingent remainder and a sort of a gap left open, it will descend in the meantime to the heir at law. He cited Noy 43, Cro. Eliz. 878, the same case.

Supposing it had been by way of a use, it would have been good. 1 Mod. 98, Pybus and Mitford's Case. He cited 4 Mod., Goodright and Cornish's Case, 255. And though it is true the remainder was not held good in that case, yet the said the reason in that case was, if it had been construed in that case as an executory devise, then it would have merged the term for years and so have destroyed an express limitation, because, there, the term was devised to him who was the devisor's heir. But, where there is no danger of that, as where the term is to a stranger,

[1] Stat. 29 Car. II, c. 3 (*SR*, V, 839–842).

there it may be held otherwise and good by way of executory devise. He cited Tippin and Cousin's Case, in the same book, 100.[1]

(But it seems that does not seem much to the purpose that when there shall be an implied estate joined with a limitation to the heirs male of the feoffor etc.)

And the law takes notice of [*blank*] between the lease for years and the remainder and, for that reason, it is why a term for years does not execute with a remainder limited to the right heirs of the same person, as an estate for life is, because possibly it may determine before the party to whom's death.

Second, [he said] that if it is not good by way of an executory devise, yet it is good by way of a present remainder. He cited James and Richardson's Case, 2 Lev. 232, that, though our case have not the words 'now living', yet he has sufficiently taken notice that the Aunt Long, was then living by leaving her a legacy and that a will is to be construed accordingly as acts of Parliament. And, in both, the intent is to be pursued. And he cited Lord Cobham's Case, 2 Lev. 78, where he settled lands to the heirs male of his body, and he is attainted of treason, afterwards, [it was] enacted by Parliament that the heirs male of his body will enjoy the land though, by the law, he could not have any heir male; he was attainted, yet it was adjudged his son will enjoy it according to the intent of the Act. And he cited Siderfin 153. A devise to one *in ventre sa mere* was adjudged a good devise. But *vide* 1 Lev. 135; it seems it is a future devise, because, there, it was held by them that [. . .] it a good devise, as a devise to the infant *in ventre sa mere* and, as to the land, it is not the same because [. . .] it is a sort of executory devise. Query this, but it seems this case is more applicable to the first point than the second.

And so he concluded for the plaintiff.

Sir Thomas Parker, to the same intent: He takes it a good *designatio personae* and an estate tail in him. [It was said] by him 'issue male' and 'heirs male' are synonyms in wills, and the one gives an estate tail as well as the other. And, if, in our case, it had been 'issue male', he would have had a present remainder. And, if 'issue male' is the same with 'heirs male' in wills, why not is 'heirs male' the same with 'issue male'?

But N.B. If the devise had been to the issue male of J.B., query if they will take jointly, it is several or successively. And *vide* for this 6 Co. 17b; 2 Lev. 61. It appears he takes notice of her being alive, that the law itself often takes notice of the heir in the ancestor's lifetime, as in the Register, *Hered.*, [. . .]; 31 Ass., fol. 47, Bro., Abr., tit. *Devise*, 17, the same case; and 15 Edw. III, 25. It is likewise a vulgar expression to call an heir apparent heir. And the law will construe in this case according to the intent of the party.

Sir Peter King: The questions are, first, whether it may not be taken as an executory devise and so no freehold is requisite to support it or, second, as a re-

[1] *Tippin v. Coson* (1694), 4 Modern 380, 87 E.R. 455, also Comberbach 312, 90 E.R. 498, Carthew 272, 90 E.R. 761, Holt K.B. 731, 90 E.R. 1303, 1 Lord Raymond 33, 91 E.R. 918.

mainder vested. He rather takes it that it is a remainder vested, that the intent of the testator may be complied with. He thinks it is such if a person then in being as described and that we may be admitted to our proofs to prove that it was his intent to give it to him. The restriction, *vide* in Cheney's Case, is generally true. And he put the two cases of 2 [*blank*] and where two places of the same name and that, in such cases, he likewise said it is to be allowed where [there is] a doubtful description of the person who he meant [so] that that doubt may be cleared and it may appear who it was. It is plain he designed to give something and who must have it; certainly, who is described. And this, in common parlance, is a description of him. And, when a man makes a will, he is not to be considered as a lawyer, but as one that does not understand it. And this is a description, a common description, of the plaintiff; it is a *designatio personae*. And, if it be a doubtful one, we must read our depositions.

Dodd: The law in wills takes notice of common parlance,[1] and, for that reason, if I give my lands to A. forever or all my estate to him, this is an estate in fee, and for no other reason but it is understood generally by those ignorant of the law. And it is so. This is as strong as Richardson's Case, though we [. . .] the words 'now living', yet he sufficiently takes notice of her being alive, which is as much. And it is the eldest son-in-law which is intended by the word 'heirs male'. And, if I devise lands to such a family or to the head of such a family, the eldest son takes it.

Ward, [argues] to the same intent. And he cited Moor 593, Clarke v. [*blank*].

After they had done, they moved to read their depositions to explain the testator's intent that he always designed that the land should go to Thomas Long, then plaintiff, as being then heir male apparent of the Aunt Long.

Upon that, *Sir Joseph Jekyll*, on the other side, took exception to it. And he insisted that they should not be read, that it had been no longer since than the other day resolved in the House of Lords in Litton and Frankland's Case that depositions could not be read to explain a will as being against the Statute Hen. VIII and 29 Car. II and of the great inconveniences that that way might be let in and accordingly in that case, the reading was denied and notwithstanding they had been admitted to be read in the same case in Chancery. But *Sir Joseph* [*Jekyll*] said (and it was so) it was true My Lord Chancellor did allow them to be read and the judges present assented to it. But My Lord Chancellor told them at the same time that it was upon the counsel's great importunity he allowed it, not that they should be of any great weight with him, and the court could entrust themselves with them, but they should not be read to a jury, for, though the court could entrust themselves, yet they would not entrust a jury.

And [it was said] by *Jekyll* it is true it was allowed at the same time in the House [of Lords] they might be read, where lands be devised to John [*blank*]

[1] pl. *MS*.

and to two of that name, where the [. . .] of [*blank*] and two of that name, but that, in that case, it was because of the necessity of the thing, but they could not be allowed in any other court, where there was no such necessity.

And LOVELL, who was in the House of Lords when Litton and Frankland's Case was affirmed, with Ward, Gould, and Dormer, confirmed what Sir Joseph Jekyll had said.

The court, at first, seemed they might entrust them with the reading of them, though a jury should not.

And PRICE cited Nicolls and Nicholls' Case, lately in Chancery, where one had devised an estate for life to his wife, remainder over etc. And the case coming into Chancery, it was moved to read the depositions that it was designed to her as her jointure. And he said there was a learned judge then upon the bench, who said they might read them if they would, but that they should not be of any effect, and, accordingly, though they were read, it was decreed she should have her estate for life devised to her and be at liberty to proceed as to her dower.

The, [it was said] by *Ward*, they must be read because the court, before then could not know what they were about. And it should not be a hindrance to read depositions because it was barely alleged they were concerning the exposition of a will.

But it was answered by Serjeant *Pratt* that the other side did not pretend they related to anything else. And, if so, the court might beforehand know what use they would be of and so it was to no purpose to read them. And [it was said] by him that, if they were read and should have any effect upon a court, why then the estate passed by the depositions by a parol will and not by a will in writing.

Upon that, the court said they would make no rule, but would consider of it.

But the cause went off [. . .] dismissed to law upon the objection that this was an ejectment bill that the plaintiff's title was a mere title at law and only triable there, the question being whether he had a good title by that will to the estate after the term for twenty-one years expired, that after the court had removed everything out of the way that might hinder the plaintiff to proceed at law, as in this case that the term might be put out of the case, for, as long as it was in being, the plaintiff could not be entitled to bring [an action of] ejectment, that these they must be dismissed to law. The court inclined accordingly and, where a point was of any difficulty and of any real consequence and only a point in law, that then they must be sent to law, only they should have the aid of this court to enable them, as they had in this case.

And [it was said] by WARD, Holt used to say, while he was of the equity side, he could not determine anything as a lawyer, but, as a chancellor, and so *e converso* of the other side.

And it was accordingly dismissed. But query.

Sir Joseph Jekyll, Serjeant *Hooper*, Serjeant *Pratt*, Mr. *Ettrick, Dodd*, were for the defendant.

[It was said] by *Jekyll, arguendo*, in Bertie and Frankland's Case, *q.v.* reported 3 Chanc. Cases, letters were desired to be read in explanation of the will in that case, but it was denied there, and so in the House of Lords, which he said was the same with depositions.

But *Dodd*, who was in the case when it was in the House of Lords, said that two of them were read.

N.B. One Long and Long's Case[1] was cited in which the [*blank*] had formerly been used.

[Connected cases: Darbison, ex dem. Long v. Beaumont (Ex. 1713), see below, Case No. 436.]

[Order of 24 February 1709: Public Record Office E.126/19, f. 93.]

341

Jones v. Owens

(Ex. 1709–1711)

It is not defamation to accuse a person of doing something that was not ever done according to the accusation itself.

Lincoln's Inn MS. Misc. 538, f. [99]

16 November 1709.

The plaintiff alleges himself to be a wet glover, and brings [an action of] slander against the defendant for the speaking of divers Welsh words mentioned in the declaration. And he says that '*quae quidem Wallica verba sic interpretantur* you (*innuendo* the plaintiff) have perjured yourself at Harlech for Rowland Jones' maid's money,' *ubi revera* that the plaintiff at any time did not make any oath in the cause aforesaid or concerning any of the money of the said Rowland Jones' maid's money, by reason of which he is not only greatly damnified in his reputation, but he has sustained in the loss of his trade to his damage of £500.

The defendant pleads not guilty. And [there is a] verdict for the plaintiff and £20 damages.

The defendant's counsel, *Dodd* and *Ward*, move in arrest of judgment.

First, the Welsh word '*anydon*' does not signify perjured, but, there being no such word but the word '*anudon*', it only signifies false swearing but not perjury.

[1] *Long v. Long* (H.L. 1694), Dodd 142, 1 Freeman 505, 89 E.R. 381, *sub nom. Reeve v. Long*, Comberbach 252, 90 E.R. 460, Carthew 309, 90 E.R. 782, Skinner 430, 90 E.R. 191, Holt K.B. 228, 286, 90 E.R. 1025, 1057, 3 Levinz 408, 83 E.R. 754, 4 Modern 282, 87 E.R. 395, 12 Modern 53, 88 E.R. 1160, 1 Salkeld 227, 91 E.R. 202, 1 Eq. Cas. Abr. 173, 21 E.R. 967, 2 Eq. Cas. Abr. 336, 22 E.R. 286.

And, for saying a man is forsworn, unless it be in a court or course of justice, no action lies.

Second, the plaintiff has, by his averment in his declaration that he never took any oath in the cause in the declaration, destroyed his cause of action, which subsists only by the word 'perjured', and no perjury can be where no oath was taken. Yelverton 72, 117; Hutton 34; 2 Cro. 436; 4 rep. 16, Snag's Case; Hobt. 191; Roll's, *Action sur le*, 74, Pett's Case, 'you have murdered A.' is actionable, but, if [it was] said she is living, [it is] otherwise.[1]

Phipps, for the plaintiff: The signification of the Welsh words are rightly interpreted and ascertained by the verdict. And that objection is too late. The colloquium [was] laid concerning a suit and cause of proceeding at law though it does not say where or what the cause or suit was nor in what court, yet, being in a legal course, that it must be intended perjury. And the subsequent averment by the plaintiff himself that no such oath was made does not excuse the slander that arose when the words were spoken, but are evidence of the defendant's great malice to slander the party because no oath was taken at all.

Turner, on the same side: As to the interpretation of the words *ut supra*, the word 'perjured' is actionable, and [there was] no qualification upon them by the plaintiff's subsequent averment that no oath was made. The slander is the greater when no oath was taken; by slanders, [one] must understand that it was an imputation of a crime. And, whether an oath was taken or not, a cause depending [is] all one. Cro. Car. 337, 509; Cro. Jac. 158.[2] The difference between saying 'murdered' A. or 'poisoned' [is it is] not necessary to show [he was] dead in the first, as it is in the last; 1 Sid. 52, 53; 3 Keble 624, because a man may be poisoned and yet not die, but he cannot be murdered unless he die.[3]

---

1 *Stile v. Heape* (1605), Yelverton 72, 80 E.R. 50, also Croke Jac. 80, 120, 79 E.R. 68, 103; *Arundell v. Tregono* (1607), Yelverton 116, 80 E.R. 79; *Adams v. Flemming* (1617), Hutton 34, 123 E.R. 1081, also Hobart 283, 80 E.R. 428, 1 Brownlow & Goldesborough 13, 123 E.R. 634; *Bradshaw v. Walker* (1619), Hutton 34, 123 E.R. 1081, also Hobart 249, 80 E.R. 395, Palmer 29, 81 E.R. 962, 1 Brownlow & Goldesborough 13, 123 E.R. 634; *Page v. Keble* (1617), Croke Jac. 436, 79 E.R. 372; *Snag v. Gee* (1597), 4 Coke Rep. 16, 76 E.R. 896; *Gibbs v. Jenkins* (1617), Hobart 191, 80 E.R. 338, also Noy 19, 74 E.R. 990, Hetley 175, 124 E.R. 433, Hutton 8, 123 E.R. 1062; *Pett's Case* (1614), 1 Rolle, Abr., *Action sur Case*, pl. B, 2, p. 74.

2 *Anonymous* (1633), Croke Car. 337, 79 E.R. 895; *Ceely v. Hoskins* (1638), Croke Car. 509, 79 E.R. 1039; *Harris v. Dixon* (1607), Croke Jac. 158, 79 E.R. 139, also Yelverton 72, 80 E.R. 50.

3 *Dacy v. Clinch* (1661), 1 Siderfin 52, 82 E.R. 964, also T. Raymond 35, 83 E.R. 20, 1 Keble 140, 181, 184, 83 E.R. 862, 887, 889; *Grene v. Warner* (1676), 3 Keble 624, 84 E.R. 916.

22 May 1710.

Mr. *Thomas Price*, for the plaintiff: Cro. Car. 10 and 11, Smith and Crashaw, conspiracy [was sued] for indicting for treason maliciously, and it was good. And, here, this action is laid that the defendant spoke these words *falso et maliciose* and laid special damage. Averments by *revera* generally [?] and of a thing not to be proved, Winch, *Entries*, 74, 75, 96, 97; Brownlow, *Latine Redevivus*, 20, 21; 1 Sanders 241, Croft and Bois, '*Ubi revera*, he was not guilty of any perjury' [is] good; Cro. Eliz. 569, 30 Eliz., Webb and Cole, 'I will call him in question for [he] poisoned my aunt' [is] no averment.[1] To say a man is perjured in this court is actionable though he was never sworn, for it is a slander. Cro. Eliz. 620, Poe and Munford, 40 Eliz., poisoned, *ubi revera* he never administered physic.[2]

This is in point with this in question as to the '*revera*' which is the averment that the plaintiff never took any oath. Cro. Car. 255; 'you have given J.S. £9 for forswearing himself in Chancery and have hired him to forge a bond'; though it was not shown that he swore at all, yet [it was] actionable being scandalous, his reputation being impeached.[3] Snag's Case is 'you have murdered my wife'. 4 rep., 39 El., [it was] manifest that the wife was living; so it was not true nor damage. 1 Sid. 52, 53; an action lies without an averment.[4] It is all one in this case which forsworn or not, for the bystanders who know nothing of the matter, for they must need understand it to be slanderous. Snig's Case and Webb and Cole's Case seem to contradict. The first is contradictory to itself, the wife living; the other is good. Cro. Eliz. 250; as to the Welsh, Coles and Haviland, 'Coles strained a mare, *innuendo carnaliter cognovit*', the court takes notice of the words as to the place of perjury; Cro. Car. 366, 275, intend in a court of record; Cro. Eliz. 583, 709, forsworn in the leet, 492.[5]

Dodd, for the defendant, relies on Snag's Case; the plaintiff kicked down his cause of action by making a contrary averment.

Curia advisare vult.

---

[1] *Farrington, qui tam v. Prince* (1625), Croke Car. 10, 79 E.R. 614; *Rex v. Shale* (1614), Winch, *Entries*, p. 74; *Horwood v. Corderoy* (1613), Winch, *Entries*, p. 96; *Anonymous* (1591), R. Brownlow, *Book of Entries* (1693), p. 20; *Craft v. Boite* (1669), 1 Williams Saunders 241, 85 E.R. 276; *Webb v. Poor* (1597), Croke Eliz. 569, 78 E.R. 813, 1 Rolle, Abr., *Action sur Case*, Pl. E, 7, p. 77, also Noy 63, 74 E.R. 1031.

[2] *Poe v. Mondford* (1598), Croke Eliz. 620, 78 E.R. 861.

[3] *Anonymous* (1633), Croke Car. 337, 79 E.R. 895.

[4] *Dacy v. Clinch* (1661), *ut supra.*

[5] *Coles v. Haveland* (1591), Croke Eliz. 250, 78 E.R. 505; *Seagood v. Hone* (1634), Croke Car. 366, 79 E.R. 920, also W. Jones 342, 82 E.R. 180; *Gryffyth v. Biddle* (1632), Croke Car. 275, 79 E.R. 840, also W. Jones 300, 82 E.R. 158; *Harrison's Case* (1597), Croke Eliz. 583, 78 E.R. 826; *Spencer v. Shory* (1599), Croke Eliz. 709, 78 E.R. 944; *Wyld v. Cookman* (1596), Croke Eliz. 492, 78 E.R. 743, also Moore K.B. 404, 537, 72 E.R. 657, 742, Noy 34, 74 E.R. 1004.

The only question is whether the plaintiff has by his averment in his declaration destroyed his cause of action, this appearing in the declaration, which contains his cause of action, to be repaired in damages for the slander of being perjured when the plaintiff himself says he never took any oath in the case and, if so, he could not be perjured and so [there is] no cause to recover damages.

Snag's Case, 4 rep. 16; to say the defendant has murdered his wife when it appears by the declaration the wife is living [is] no slander and so no damage; the words [are] vain. But had the wife been dead or [it was] said *nuper* his wife, the action would have lain. Cro. Car. 489; Pett's Case, 11 Jac., 1 Roll's, Abr., f. 74, 'you have murdered J.S.'; no action lies if it is averred that J.S. is yet alive; Kemer and Hallet's Case, 2 Car., 1 Roll's 75, an action for saying the plaintiff was incontinent with A. and had several children by her which he murdered and, [it was] averred he was never incontinent with A., but the averment was not that he had no child by her, and, therefore, the plaintiff recovered because the averment was general. And, there, it is said, if a man says to another that he had killed J.S. and avers there never was such a person as J.S., no action lies.[1] Bettridge's Case, 4 rep. [*blank*] 'you are perjured and that is to be proved by a stake between the lands of A. and B.'[2]

I [Edward Ward] think this is the difference, when an action is brought by a plaintiff as for saying such a one gave money to A. for forswear[ing] himself in such a court or for saying he was perjured, the court will intend them slanderers without showing that the party took any oath or was forsworn at all, because, as laid in the declaration, they are actionable. And that answers the cases Cro. Car. 337, where a man said A. had given B. £9 for forswearing himself in Chancery without showing any suit or examination there, for, if he never was sworn, it is scandalous. And so is the Case of Webb and Poor, Cro. Eliz. 569, 1 Abr., Rolle 77, 'poisoned my wife'; Hobt. 6.[3] But, when the same person that sues for damages for slander does in that action aver that he never did or said the thing which he supposes scandalous and for which he would have damages, there is no reason that he should recover for a thing that is impossible of his own showing, according to the reasons and authorities of Snagg's and Pett's and Kemer's cases, before cited. And so I concluded to arrest judgment.

By all of the court, judgment was arrested upon the reason of Betteridge's Case and Snagg's Case, 4 rep., 9 February 1710[/11].

[Other copies of this report: Georgetown Univ. Law Sch. MS. B88–10, p. 682.]

---

1 *Kemer v. Hallet* (1626), 1 Rolle, Abr., *Action sur Case*, pl. B, 4, p. 75.

2 *Brittridge v. Atkins* (1602), 4 Coke Rep. 18, 76 E.R. 905, also Moore K.B. 666, 72 E.R. 827, Yelverton 10, 80 E.R. 8.

3 *Webb v. Poor* (1597), *ut supra*; *Miles v. Jacob*, Hobart 6, 80 E.R. 156.

342

Child v. Lord Howard of Effingham

(Ex. 1709)

The question in this case was whether 'baron' and 'lord' are the same title of nobility.

Lincoln's Inn MS. Misc. 538, f. [100], pl. 1

The plaintiff sues the defendant in an [action of] *indebitatus assumpsit* for goods and wares sold and delivered to the value of £24 10s. by the name of *praenobilem Thomam Dominum Howard de Effingham.*

The defendant puts in a plea of abatement in these words, *et praedictus Thomas modo defendens versus quem idem Johannes Child exhibuit billam suam praedictam per nomen Thomae, Domini Howard de Effingham, in propria persona sua venit et defendit vim et injuriam et dicit quod ipse modo est et tempore exhibitionis billae praedictae et per nullas annos tunc utlimos elapsos fuit Thomas, Baro Howard de Effingham, absque hoc quod ipse idem modo defendens fuit Thomas, Dominus Howard de Effingham, prout per billam praedictam superius supponitur, et hac paratus est verificare prout curia etc., unde petit judicium de billa praedicta et quod billa illa cassetur.*

The plaintiff's counsel obtained a rule for the defendant to show cause why his plea should not be set aside and plead in chief.

The defendant's counsel produced in court the original creation of honor to that noble family under the great seal whereby the noble lord was created by the name and title of Baron Howard of Effingham. And this was to satisfy the court that there was a reason for his plea in abatement according to the clause in the late Act for Amendment of the Law.[1]

Vide Davis 60, which cites 8 Hen. VI, 10a, Lord Lovell's Case, that the name or title of baron is not a name of dignity or addition; 32 Hen. VI, 30; Thelw., *Digest of Writs*, 67; Bro., *Amercement*, 52.[2]

This cause was no further proceeded in; query for what reason. Shower's reports in the King's Bench, fo. 392.[3]

[Other copies of this report: Georgetown Univ. Law Sch. MS. B88–10, p. 687.]

[1] Stat. 4 & 5 Ann., c. 3 (*SR*, VIII, 458–461).

[2] *Case of the County Palatine of Wexford* (1611), Davis 58, 80 E.R. 544; YB Mich. 8 Hen. VI, f. 9, pl. 22 (1429); *Talbot v. J.L.* (1454), YB Hil. 32 Hen. VI, f. 28, pl. 23, Brooke, Abr., *Amercement*, pl. 52; S. Theloall, *Digest.*

[3] *Rex v. Lord Dover* (1692), 1 Shower K.B. 392, 89 E.R. 660, also Comberbach 189, 90 E.R. 421.

343

Franklin v. Lee

(Ex. 1709)

In order to receive the double costs provided by the Statute against Frauds on the Customs, the plaintiff must specifically request them in his pleading.

Lincoln's Inn MS. Misc. 538, f. [100], pl. 2

The plaintiff brought [an action of] trover and conversion of linen cloth against the defendant, and obtained a verdict with single costs.

But Justice Powell, who tried the cause at the Winchester Assizes, certified on the [writ of] *distringas* that it appeared upon the evidence that the cause of action was that the defendant, being a Customs House officer, illegally took and detained the goods in the declaration.

And, thereupon, *Ettrick* and *Ward* prayed that the Master of the Office might tax double costs according to the 34th paragraph of the Act against Frauds, 14 Car. II, ca. 11, which provides for double costs in such a case. And they cited the Case of Willet and Tidy, Shower's rep., fo. 214, 215.[1]

But the court did not think the case cited to be like this nor fit to give any direction for double costs in this case, for that the judge's certificate does not warrant any such thing, for that paragraph is a private clause and the plaintiff must have declared specially upon it, as the constant practice has been in Pecket and Shaw's Case[2] and all other actions founded on that clause. And the judge has no power to make such a certificate by any law. And, therefore, the court can take no notice of the judge's certificate, and the declaration warrants no such action, but it is a mere [action of] trover and conversion between two persons, and the defendant does not appear in the record to be any Custom House officer or that the cause is concerning any matters relating to the customs.

But the court gave leave to the plaintiff to move it again if the plaintiff pleased. But all inclined against it with great clearness. And nothing more was done in it.

[Other copies of this report: Georgetown Univ. Law Sch. MS. B88–10, p. 688, pl. 1.]

---

[1] Stat. 14 Car. II, c. 11, s. 32 (*SR*, V, 400); *Willet v. Tidey* (1691), 1 Shower K.B. 214, 89 E.R. 544, also 12 Modern 6, 88 E.R. 1128, Carthew 188, 90 E.R. 714.

[2] *Peckett v. Shaw* (Ex. 1671), Exch. Repts. *tempore* Car. II, 233.

344

Attorney General v. White
Attorney General v. Norris

(Ex. 1709)

Carrying salt without a license is a separate offense from not paying customs duties on salt.

Lincoln's Inn MS. Misc. 538, f. [101], pl. 1

25 November 1709.

In two distinct informations against carriers of salt without a permit whereby [there was] a forfeiture of £20 on each, by the opinion of the whole court after argument, the offenses are pardoned, they being offenses merely collateral to the duty and *non constat* that the queen was at all defrauded of her duty, which is the crime excepted, and the defendants are only carriers and no ways liable to the payment of the duties nor examinable in these causes whether duties are paid or not.

[Other copies of this report: Georgetown Univ. Law Sch. MS. B88–10, p. 690, pl. 1.]

[Other reports of this case: Indiana Univ., Lilly Library, MS. Parker 'Cases in the Exchequer', vol. 5, p. 185.]

345

Regina v. Arnold

(Ex. 1709–1710)

The first issue in this case was whether the facts of bankruptcy must be specially pleaded in detail where the crown is a party.

The crown is not bound by the Statute of Frauds.

In the case of the crown, a chose in action is assignable and subject to execution.

Upon proceedings on a writ of extent, the lien of the crown attaches as of the date of the writ.

Lincoln's Inn MS. Misc. 501, p. 189

On a *scire facias* on an extent, the case was this. Dixon, a receiver general, as principal [debtor], and George Newell and Joseph Newell, as his sureties, became bound to the queen in £23,000. Upon this bond, an extent issues against the body, lands, and goods of George Newell and Joseph Newell dated 3d December, and, upon the 8th of December, an inquisition was taken upon the said extent, whereby it was found that the defendant Arnold was indebted to George Newell in £109 12s. Upon the return of this inquisition, a *scire facias* is sued out against

Arnold, and he comes in and pleads that upon the second of the same December, George Newell became a bankrupt and that thereupon issued a commission of bankruptcy and that proceedings were had thereupon according to the several statutes made concerning bankrupts[1] and that [on] 6th December, George Newell was found a bankrupt and that, thereupon, the commissioners assigned over his estate and effects to one Taylor so that he, the defendant, was not indebted to the said George Newell but to the assignees of the commissioners of bankruptcy.

Upon this plea, the Attorney General demurs and shows for cause two things:

First, that it was not set forth what act of bankruptcy the said George Newell had committed, and

Secondly, that he had not set forth the commission and that the commissioners had adjudged and declared George Newell to be a bankrupt and that the plea amounted to the general issue.

The barons delivered their opinions *seriatim*.

And Baron Lovell said that the plea in this case was nought:

First, because the defendant had not set out what act of bankruptcy George Newell had committed, for this being in the case of the crown, it is not sufficient to say only that [on] such a day George Newell manifestly became a bankrupt, though this sort of pleading to bar a subject may be good enough, a plea to a common intent being good, but in [the] case of the crown, it must be certain, and

Secondly, because the commissioners had not set forth that the commissioners had found him a bankrupt, for the commissioners are to proceed upon the statutes and they ought to bring the party within the extent of the acts.

And of this opinion was Chief Baron Ward.

But Baron Lovell observed that there was another fault in the plea, because, in setting out the assignment, it was not pleaded with a profert *in curiam*.

Baron Price held that the pleading was sufficient. As to the first cause assigned, he said that the old precedents in the case of bankrupts did set forth all the proceedings, as the petition, the granting of the commission, etc., and what was done thereupon, but the precedents of late were otherwise, and they do not set forth any particulars but only in general that, [on] such a day, he became a bankrupt.

Lut. 104, in an assumpsit by assignees of commissioners of bankrupts, the short way is now only used when a person is declared a bankrupt by commissioners. It is not any way material, for on an issue whether a man be a bankrupt or not, though a particular act of bankruptcy is assigned in the plea, yet any other act of bankruptcy may be given in evidence. The judgment or declaration of the commissioners is not evidence in a trial and consequently it cannot be material. But now as to the matter whether this matter ought to be more particularly set

---

[1] Generally Stat. 1 Jac. I, c. 15 (*SR*, IV, 1031–1034).

out in the case of the crown, he did not think it necessary, for by the same reason that one act of bankruptcy is set forth, all the acts of bankruptcy ought to be set forth and the act of bankruptcy or the declaration of the commissioners is not anywise material, neither is it any evidence.

As to the second exception, that this sort of proceeding amounted to the general issue and that though this sort of pleading might be good in the declaration yet it is not good in a plea, he said that a declaration required more certainty than a plea. Coke Litt. 303.[1] In a declaration, everything must be affirmed particularly. Now, as to the saying that he was indebted to Taylor and not to the crown, whether or not this amounted to the general issue, he said that to make a general issue, they should have gone into a particularity, but here this is done not full enough. By 21 Jac., ca. 14,[2] it is enacted that:

> whensoever the king . . . and such from and under whom the king claims or has been or shall be out of possession for twenty years and shall not etc. have taken the profits of any lands etc. within twenty years before the information of intrusion to be brought to recover the same . . . the defendant etc. may plead the general issue, if he etc. think fit and shall not be pressed to plead specially . . . . And where any information of intrusion may fitly and aptly be brought on the king's behalf, no *scire facias* shall be brought whereunto the subject shall be forced to a special pleading.

But the party was before obliged to set forth his title where a man would take advantage of a matter pleaded that amounts to the general issue; upon a demurrer, he must assign it for cause. 1 Cro. 146, Ward v. Blunt.[3]

Baron Bury was of the same opinion that the pleading was good.

The question of law in this case was what operation this extent had and whether or not the goods and chattels of George Newell were not bound from the *teste* of the writ of extent. As to this point, it was resolved by the whole court that judgment should be given for the queen.

Baron Price's argument: It is agreed of all hands that in [the] case of an execution for a subject, whether it be on *elegit* or *fieri facias* or an extent, the goods and chattels of the party were bound from the *teste* of the writ before the Statute of Frauds and Perjuries, 29 Car. II, ca. 3, § 16,[4] by virtue of which Statute, the property of the goods of the party against whom a writ of execution is sued out is not bound but from the time that such writ is delivered to the sheriff etc. to be executed. But this Statute does not extend to the case of the crown. On an extent

[1] E. Coke, *First Institute* (1628), f. 303.

[2] Stat. 21 Jac. I, c. 14 (*SR*, IV, 1221).

[3] *Ward v. Blunt* (1589), Croke Eliz. 146, 78 E.R. 404, also 1 Leonard 141, 178, 74 E.R. 131, 164.

[4] Stat. 29 Car. II, c. 3, s. 15 (*SR*, V, 841).

on a statute acknowledged according to 23 Hen. VIII,[1] when a [writ of] *liberate* is sued out and the goods are delivered by the sheriff according to the appraisement in the extent, the goods of the party are so bound hereby that he cannot either give, sell, or dispose of them neither can he forfeit them nor can they be distrained for rent. The *liberate* here has relation to the *teste* of the extent though the extendee had no right in the goods until the *liberate*. 1 Cro. 148, Jones 202, Awdley v. Halsey.[2]

The writ to seize does not give a property, but it is only a protection from the crown to have the goods delivered over to the party. The *liberate* is but a finishing of the execution. There is such a lien upon the goods from the *teste* of the execution that if the party die or assign away his goods, the sheriff may execute the writ against the executor or against the assignee. J.R. at 896. The interest of the goods is bound, though the property be not transferred. See Keb. 930, 932, Baily v. Bunning, Syd. 271, 1 Lev. 173.[3]

Now it will be hard to vary this in the case of the crown or to make a construction to lessen the prerogative of the crown.

Of extents, there be several sorts, for some are general to seize body, land, and goods, some have a commission in them to find debts by inquisition or otherwise, some are to seize into the queen's hands until the debts are satisfied, and some of these extents are to sell the goods of the party, and others are that the goods should not be sold but by order from the court, but this is only as a check upon the officer, but not that the crown has the property.

In [the] case of a statute staple, according to 27 Edw. III, ca. 8,[4] the goods of the party are to be seized and delivered to the party; now this gives an immediate property. But in [the] case of a statute merchant, this is not so, for there goes first process against the body and then, upon a return of a *non est inventus* or a *mortuus*, there goes an extent against the lands and goods. This must be much stronger in the case of the crown.

Executions for the crown have relation to the time of the execution awarded. And the goods and chattels of the party are bound from that time into whose hands soever they come. 2 R. Ab. 157, Co. 8, 171, Sir George Fleetwood's Case.[5]

In Dyer 67, Stringfellow's Case,[6] Stringfellow sued a writ of *extendi facias* out of the chancery to have execution of a statute staple against one Brownesope

---

[1] Stat. 23 Hen. VIII, c. 6 (*SR*, III, 372–373).

[2] *Audley v. Halsey* (1629), Croke Car. 148, 79 E.R. 731, W. Jones 202, 82 E.R. 107.

[3] *Bayly v. Bunning* (1665), 1 Keble 637, 930, 932, 83 E.R. 1157, 1326, 1327, 1 Siderfin 271, 82 E.R. 1100, 1 Levinz 173, 83 E.R. 355, also 2 Keble 32, 84 E.R. 21.

[4] Stat. 27 Edw. III, stat. 2, c. 8 (*SR*, I, 336).

[5] *Fleetwood's Case* (1610), 2 Rolle, Abr., *Prerogative le Roy*, p. 157, 8 Coke Rep. 171, 77 E.R. 731.

[6] *Stringfellow v. Brownsoppe* (1549), 1 Dyer 67, 73 E.R. 142, also 2 Rolle, Abr., *Prerogative le Roy*, pl. G, 2, p. 158.

and takes the goods accordingly and seized them into the king's hands, but there is no *liberate*, then there comes a prerogative writ out of the Exchequer rehearsing the king's prerogative that he ought to be satisfied his debts and commanding the sheriff to levy upon Brownesope a debt of £500 which he owed the king and if he had not sufficient [personal goods] to extend his land, and this writ was delivered to the sheriff after the day of the return of the first writ, but the first was not returned at the day, and the sheriff hereupon returned the special matter. And it was held in the Exchequer that the sheriff should be amerced if he would not amend his return, *i.e.* return that he had saved the king's debt, for the property of the goods was not in Stringfellow before that the goods were delivered to him by virtue of the *liberate*.

There is a very ancient statute, 25 Edw. III, c. 19,[1] reciting that:

> forasmuch as . . . the king had made . . . protections to divers persons which were bound to him in some manner of debt, that they should not be impleaded of the debts which they owed to others till they had made gree to the king of that which was due to him by reason of his prerogative and so, during such [time], no man has used or durst implead such debtors, [whereby] it is assented and accorded that notwithstanding such protections, the parties which have actions against their debtors shall be answered in the king's [bench] by their debtors and, if judgment be thereupon given for the plaintiffs, the execution of the same judgment shall be put in suspense till gree shall be made to the king of his debt, and, if the creditors will undertake for the king's debt, they shall be thereto received and shall have execution of the debtors of the debt due to them and also shall recover against them as much as they shall pay to the king for them.

As to the objection that this case differs from the common case of extents for the crown, for that here is a debt found which is in a three-penny person's hands, the extent has bound the money, goods, and chattels of the party himself but not the debt in the hands of Arnold.

Now this debt in Arnold's hands is a chattel though it be but a chose in action, which, in the case of a subject, is not assignable nor liable to any execution. But in the case of the crown, it is assignable and liable to execution. But it is said that this is not the chattel of George Newell, see Stam., Pr., 45; 17 Edw. II, ca. 16,[2] under the word '*catalla*' are only comprehended leases for years, the issues and profits of the lands of those that fly for felony until such time as they be attainted and acquitted, and of clerks convict until he has made his purgation, emblements growing upon the ground at the time the forfeiture of the goods first began to take place, a right of action to goods, as where goods are taken away

[1] Stat. 25 Edw. III, c. 19 (*SR*, I, 323).

[2] W. Staunford, *Exposition of the King's Prerogative* (1567), f. 45; Statute of the Chattels of Felons (*SR*, I, 230).

wrongfully from a felon or where one is indebted to a felon by obligation or is accountable to the felon for any receipts or otherwise. This Statute of Edw. II does not give anything but only shows what shall be forfeited under the word; '*catalla* are sometimes taken goods wherein the felon has no property, as if a man deliver money out of a bag or corn out of a sack to one to keep, who is afterward attainted of felony, the money or corn, in such case, is forfeited'. Stamf., *Prerog.* 45b; 6 Hen. VII, 9a; 19 Hen. VII, 47.[1]

It was objected that it was not the extent but the inquisition that bound the goods. But it was answered that the inquisition was only an act in pursuance of the extent and implied within the extent itself. It is an inquisition of information and instruction only and not of entitling. It has such a relation to the extent that the whole together makes but one execution. Suppose that there should be an extent and no inquisition at all should be taken upon it but the sheriff should return that he had seized the debt; this would have been good, though the debt were in the hands of a third person. Now, if this be sufficient grounds for you to bring an action for the crown, the inquisition is not material. It is but an inquiry to find the debt. But when there is an inquisition, it is fuller and more entire. And there is a mistake in the conclusion of the plea *absque hoc* that the defendant was indebted to the queen *tempore inquisitionis*, for it should be that he was not indebted to the queen at the time of the *teste* of the extent.

If there be a difficulty in making this relation, the inquisition finds everything that was before the extent but not anything since the extent. But, in pursuance of the power of the extent, it is but a bare information and it does relate to the extent. An inquisition upon an elegit relates to the elegit. So a bargain and sale enrolled relates to the date of the bargain and sale. So, if a feoffment be made with a letter of attorney to deliver seisin and after[wards] an assignment is made by commissioners of bankruptcy and then livery is made, this shall relate to the feoffment, for all is but one conveyance. If goods are bailed or sold upon condition and the bailee or vendee becomes bankrupt and the commissioners assign his estate and effects and then the condition is performed, this overreaches the bankruptcy.

It was further objected that it would be of dangerous consequences that extents should overreach the debts which are to be distributed among the creditors. But it was answered that an extent was a matter of record whereof every person ought to take notice. When an inquisition is taken, though it be one hundred miles off, it is no more than the extent itself. But it was said that without this proceeding, it might be of great damage to the crown, for tradesman may commit an act of bankruptcy in a covinous manner and so as it cannot be known, as it was done in this case, for here the creditors were very quick and a commission of bankruptcy was taken out before the inquisition was taken and it was their

[1] W. Staunford, *Exposition of the King's Prerogative* (1567), f. 45b; *Broker's Case* (1490), YB Mich. 6 Hen. VII, ff. 7, 9, pl. 4; YB Mich. 19 Hen. VI, f. 47, pl. 100 (1440).

interest to defeat the extent so that the danger attends the crown more than the subject. The person indebted is not [in] any way prejudiced, for it is the same thing to him whether he pays the money to the one or to the other.

The act of bankruptcy itself does not bind the property, but that continues in the bankrupt until the assignment is made. 3 Keble 616. 'In debt on an obligation, the defendant pleaded that before the action [was] brought, the plaintiff became bankrupt, to which the plaintiff demurred and [it was held] by the court [that] the plea is ill and, until an assignment, the debtor is defenseless. . . . Payment of a debt to a bankrupt before commission sued out is good enough and so it is before his debt be assigned.' Andrews v. Spicer; 1 Jac., ca. 15, § 14.[1] 'No debtor of the bankrupt shall be endangered for the payment of his or their debts truly and *bona fide* to any such bankrupt before such time as he shall understand and know that he is become a bankrupt.'

Now, in this case, Arnold could not be damaged for he did not know that Newell had committed an act of bankruptcy, but, after he had notice of the bankruptcy, it was equal to him whether he paid it to the queen or to the assignees of the commissioners.

Besides, the crown is taken notice of in 21 Jac., ca. 19, § 10.[2]

It is thereby enacted that if it shall happen any the lands, tenements, goods, chattels, debts, or other estate of any bankrupt to be extended after such time as he or she is become bankrupt by any person or persons under color or pretense of his or their becoming an accountant or any way indebted to the king, his heirs, or successors, it shall be lawful to and for the commissioners to examine upon oath whether the said debt were due to such debtor or accountant upon any bargain or contract originally made between such accountant and the said bankrupt, the said debtor and accountant, and his or their servants, and if such bargain or contract was originally made to and with any other person or persons, then the said debtor or accountant and for the use and trust of any other person or persons, the commissioners or the greater part of them may order and dispose of all such lands, etc., goods, chattels, and debts so extended as aforesaid to and for the use of the creditors etc.

And this is now as if it had said that where a man shall be a bankrupt before such time as that there is an extent sued out for a just and true debt, the commissioners should not intermeddle with nor sell the goods, there being such a lien upon them by the extent, so that upon the whole, the mischief and inconvenience will be on the part of the crown.

Judgment for the queen [was given] by the court.

[Other copies of this report: Viner, Abridgment, vol. 7, p. 104, Dodd 356.]

---

[1] *Andrews v. Spicer* (1676), 3 Keble 616, 84 E.R. 911; Stat. 1 Jac. I, c. 15, s. 9 (*SR*, IV, 1033).

[2] Stat. 21 Jac. I, c. 19, s. 9 (*SR*, IV, 1228).

5 Price 631, 146 E.R. 716

The defendant pleaded that George Newell, to whom he had been found to be indebted, between the *teste* of the [writ of] extent and the caption of the inquisition, became bankrupt and that, thereupon, a commission of bankruptcy issued and that proceedings were had thereupon, according to the several statutes made concerning bankrupts, and that he was found a bankrupt. And, thereupon, the commissioners assigned over his estate and effects to one Taylor, so that he, the defendant, was not indebted to the said George Newell, but to the assignees of the commission of bankruptcy.

To that plea, the Attorney General demurred and showed for cause, first, that it was not set forth what act of bankruptcy the said George Newell had committed, and secondly, that he had not set forth the commission and that the commissioners had adjudged and declared George Newell to be a bankrupt and that the plea amounted to the general issue.

Ward, Chief Baron, and Lovell, Baron, were of opinion that the plea was bad, first, because the defendant had not set out what act of bankruptcy George Newell had committed, for being the case of the crown, it was not sufficient to say only that, such a day, George Newell manifestly became a bankrupt, although that sort of pleading might be good to bar a subject, a plea to a common intent being good, but, in a case of the crown, it must be certain, and secondly, because he had not set forth that the commissioners had found him a bankrupt, for the commissioners should proceed upon the statutes and they ought to bring the party within the extent of the acts.

Barons Price and Bury held the plea good.

Thus, on the one hand, it appears, that two of the barons in that case took a distinction between pleas pleaded in bar of the crown, holding that a greater degree of certainty and particularity were necessary in such cases than in pleas between subject and subject. On the other, it is observable that the Attorney General demurred specially for the want of sufficient particularity in the plea.

Indiana Univ., Lilly Library
MS. Parker 'Cases in the Exchequer', vol. 5, p. 173

25 November 1709.

[There was a] *scire facias* which sets forth a bond of £24,000 entered into by George Newell, Joseph Newell, and George Dixon, Sr., and George Dixon, Jr., to the queen 17 May 6 Anne [1707] and a [writ of] extent thereon and an inquisition taken 13 December 6 Anne [1707], which found Tannar Arnold indebted to George Newell £109 12s. 0d. for goods sold, and that was seized into the queen's hands.

The defendant pleads, *protestando*, that he did owe George Newell £109 12s. 0d., that, 1 December 6 Anne [1707], George Newell was indebted to Taylor £200, the 2d December, George Newell became a bankrupt, the 8th December,

Taylor petitioned for a commission of bankruptcy the same day granted, the 9th, the debts and effects were assigned to Taylor toward his debt. And he traverses that he was indebted to George Newell after the 8th December 6 Anne.

The Attorney General demurs and for cause that the defendant does not show any act of the bankruptcy nor that the commissioners declared him a bankrupt.

Mr. *Eyre*, Solicitor General: If the commissioners exceed their jurisdiction, it is *coram non judice*, and the officers are liable. Hard. 480, Terry v. Huntington; Styles 301, Watson v. Horbury; 1 Lutw. 274, Lawson v. Lamb; 451, Slaughter v. Perpoint; 2 Vent. 63, Bliss v. Frost; Ashton 227; Brownl. 83; 1 Brown 103.[1]

If you take advantage of the acts against bankruptcy, you ought to show they are within the acts. The bar is not good, and not well pleaded. 1 Inst. 303; 3 Cro. 698; Moor 573; 3 Cro. 748; 3 Modern 137, Matthew v. Cary; Litt. 356; 3 Keb. 134, 616, Haislop v. Hales; Andrews v. Spicer.[2]

Second, if the £109 is to be paid the queen or the assignee of the bankrupt, if the goods are bound from the *teste* of the extent, which is so in the case of a subject, then it is for the queen, before the Statute of Frauds and Perjuries, the same; the same in *elegit* and *fieri facias*. Moor 21; 1 Ro. Lib. 393; 2 Ro. 157; Moor 873, Canning v. Bradley; Sir George Fleetwood's Case, 8 Rep.; Stamf. 84.[3]

There is no difference between money or debt and goods save execution. The inquisition relates to the fact. Execution [is] to the awarding which binds the goods.

Mr. *Ettrick*, for the defendant: First, it appears by the plea that he was a bankrupt; second, if bound from the *teste* of the extent or inquisition; third, if it amounts to a [plea of the] general issue. The printed precedents are '*manifeste devenit decoctor*'. The traverse is bankrupt, not act of bankruptcy. The crown loses nothing by this pleading. Fourth, if it is the general issue. 1 Inst. 303, as before; 3

---

[1] *Terry v. Huntington* (Ex. 1667–1669), Hardres 480, 145 E.R. 557, Exch. Repts. *tempore* Car. II, 122; *Lawson v. Lamb* (1704), 1 Lutwyche 274, 125 E.R. 144; *Slaughter v. Pierpoint* (1704), 1 Lutwyche 451, 125 E.R. 237; *Blisse v. Frost* (1689), 2 Ventris 63, 86 E.R. 310; *Weaver v. Clifford* (1613), 1 Brownlow & Goldesborough 83, 118, 123 E.R. 681, 702, also 2 Bulstrode 62, 80 E.R. 960, Croke Jac. 3, 79 E.R. 2, Yelverton 42, 80 E.R. 30.

[2] E. Coke, *First Institute* (1628), f. 303; *Scrogs v. Stevenson* (1599), Croke Eliz. 698, 78 E.R. 933, Moore K.B. 573, 72 E.R. 767; *Rowleston v. Alman* (1600), Croke Eliz. 748, 78 E.R. 979; *Matthews v. Cary* (1689), 3 Modern 137, 87 E.R. 88, also 1 Salkeld 107, 91 E.R. 98, 1 Shower K.B. 61, 89 E.R. 449, 3 Salkeld 52, 91 E.R. 686, Comberbach 76, 90 E.R. 353, Carthew 73, 90 E.R. 646, Holt K.B. 408, 90 E.R. 1125; T. Littleton, *Tenures*, sect. 356; *Hanslop v. Hales* (1673), 3 Keble 134, 84 E.R. 637; *Andrews v. Spicer* (1676), 3 Keble 616, 84 E.R. 911.

[3] *Anonymous*, Moore K.B. 21, 72 E.R. 413; *Comyn v. Brandlyn* (1614), Moore K.B. 873, 72 E.R. 965, also 1 Rolle, Abr., *Execution*, pl. A, 3, p. 893; *Fleetwood's Case* (1610), *ut supra*; W. Staunford, *Exposition of the King's Prerogative* (1567), f. 84.

Cro. 871, Pain v. Rochester; 900; Moor 600, Chambers' Case, *idem.*[1] [Fifth], if a debt found to the king's debtor is a debt to the king before the inquisition. *Cursus Scaccarii est lex Scaccarii.* There are no precedents of this kind. The extent against Newell does not give his debtors notice.

King v. Burnett. Since receipt of the king's money *in pais* has preference to a debt of the subject, and, if in a case of the crown, the same in aid.

This overreaches all bankrupts and acts of bankruptcy, extent and find debts. The *scire facias* is *tempore inquisitionis captus.* In the case of goods, it is agreed to bind from the *teste.* They are the persons', and in his hands.

But a debt in a third person's hands and not a debt [to the crown], it is not a debt until the inquisition. This is a novelty and no practice.

Judgment [should be] given for the queen and that the extent against Newell bound the debt due from Tannar Arnold from the *teste* of the extent as much as if it had been goods or chattels.

Attorney General *Sir James Montagu, pro querente*: First, he does not show in the plea any act of bankruptcy. Second, it does not appear that the commissioners found him and he declared him in a bankruptcy. Second, it does not appear that the commissioners found him and declared him a bankrupt. A general intent is good in a declaration, but not in a plea. Co. Litt. 303; 701, Lutw. 74, 452, before, are general in declarations.[2] But the plea is *manifeste devenit decoctor*; [this is] not resolved.

The execution from the *teste* binds property, chattels real and personal, the Statute of Frauds and Perjuries, from being marked by a sheriff. A chose in action is liable to execution as a chose in possession in a case of the crown. If there was no assignment, the money was liable to the execution for the crown. The doing an act of bankruptcy does not change the property. Easter 1 Will & Mar., Crisp v. Cary,[3] in *indebitatus* [*assumpsit*], he pleads that he was a bankrupt, [this] does not alter the property. 3 Keble 616, Andrew v. Spice. The inquisition finds the facts before, but the seizure has a relation to the extent. 1 Syd. 271, Baily v. Bunning; Statute 21 Jac. I, c. 19.

Mr. *Phipps*, for the defendant: In [an action on a] bond or covenant, a general performance [can be pleaded] in a case of a subject, but, in a case of the crown, it must be special, because the title of the crown must appear on the record, and the subject must plead specially that his title may appear on the record. There is no need to plead a particular act of bankruptcy. Formerly, pleading was longer, as in bills of the Exchequer *devenit onerabilis* or judgment *taliter processus fuit etc.*

---

1 *Pain v. Rochester* (1602), Croke Eliz. 871, 78 E.R. 1096; *Chambers v. Taylor* (1602), Croke Eliz. 900, 78 E.R. 1123; *Varrell v. Wilson* (1594), Moore K.B. 600, 72 E.R. 785.

2 *Hepworth v. Haigh* (1704), 1 Lutwyche 701, 125 E.R. 367; *Lawson v. Lamb* (1704), 1 Lutwyche 274, 125 E.R. 144; *Slaughter v. Pierpoint* (1704), 1 Lutwyche 451, 125 E.R. 237.

3 *Cary v. Crisp* (1689), 1 Salkeld 108, 91 E.R. 99.

Attorney General v. Oliver, in this court; all proceedings to the judgment were left out. Lutw. 274, 701; 3 Keb. 134, Hansell v. Hall, before; 3 Keb. 616; 1 Will., Crispe v. Cary [is a] precedent not much to be relied on.[1]

Whether commissioners declared him a bankrupt is not traversable. The assignment implies a bankruptcy and that there was a commission.

Second, if the assignment by the commissioners bars the crown before the Statute of Frauds and Perjuries, the king is not bound by the Statute of Frauds and Perjuries. Moor 21, 873, before. To sell goods or wine to anyone is good. The title of the crown to the money is from the inquisition, which is an entitling office, not [an office] for instruction. The inquisition is a seizure in the law, but it cannot take upon it an inquisition of idiocy. 8 Rep., Fleetwood Case. Payment before the *teste* is good.

An inquisition for the crown is the same as [a writ of] *fieri facias*. An act of bankruptcy and assignment between the extent and the inquisition is good. The [writ of] extent is a commission to enquire and seize, and it relates to the inquisition. It is a great mischief if I pay in the vacation and the extent and inquisition is in the term before.

In reply, a chose in action in the case of the crown is bound. The case of idiocy by the Statute *Praerogativa Regis*; that is from the inquisition.

Baron Bury: An extent binds goods and money from the *teste* of the extent. 2 Inst. 8, on the Statute Magna Carta; 33 Edw. III, c. 39; Statute 25 Edw. III, c. [*blank*], an act of grace could not proceed to judgment; 4 Inst. 111 cites Briton, that the Exchequer may take notice of the debts of the king's debtor.[2]

Objection: A debtor may be prejudiced by paying a bankrupt after the *teste* of the extent and without notice.

The Statute 1 Jac., c. 5; no debtor is prejudiced who pays without notice, and, by the Statute 33 Hen. VIII, c. 39, it is a good plea in equity on the Statute.

I [Bury] agree the inquisition is an office of entitling and no more notice of the inquisition than of an extent, and all agree to bind from the inquisition. [There is] the same mischief if goods are sold after the *teste* of the extent, and yet [it is] bound by the *teste* of the extent. 20 Edw. III, Fitz., Abr., *Ley*, 52.[3]

No wager of law is allowed in a case of the crown where there is an extent. And, if not answered, a commission goes to enquire after the debt to the crown.

---

[1] *Lawson v. Lamb* (1704), 1 Lutwyche 274, 125 E.R. 144; *Hepworth v. Haigh* (1704), 1 Lutwyche 701, 125 E.R. 367; *Hanslop v. Hales* (1673), *ut supra*; *Andrews v. Spicer* (1676), *ut supra*; *Cary v. Crisp* (1689), *ut supra*.

[2] E. Coke, *Second Institute* (1642), p. 8; Stat. 25 Edw. I, Magna Carta (*SR*, I, 114–119); Stat. 33 Hen. VIII, c. 39, s. 36 (*SR*, III, 886); Stat. 25 Edw. III, stat. 5, c. 19 (*SR*, I, 323); E. Coke, *Fourth Institute* (1644), p. 111; F. M. Nichols, ed., *Britton* (1983), vol. 1, p. 5, sect. 9.

[3] *Anonymous* (Ex. 1346), Fitzherbert, Abr., *Ley*, pl. 52, also Exch. Repts. Middle Ages 11.

The king distrains a rent seck, which a subject cannot do. [Where there is a] judgment for the king, he has the whole; the subject has a moiety; Fitz., Abr., *Execution*, 166; 2 Cro. 513; public debts are strictly looked over in all [. . .], even though the pleading says *a captione inquisitionis*, yet that is no precedent to alter the law.[1]

The extent is to inquire what goods and debts he *modo habet*, that is at the time of the extent, not the time of the inquisition. Cro. Jac. 451; Jones, *idem*; Dyer 67, Stringfellow's Case, 2 Rolle [Abr.] 158. This inquisition is instructive and entitling.[2]

Objection: The inquisition is entitling as to the goods, and, as to the debts due to the queen's debtor, it is an office of instruction or information. Cro. Car. 451; Jones rep., *idem*.

Inquisition of entitling are of land and vest in the king a possession where he had but a right before. 5 Rep., Page's Case. If it were entitling, the queen has a right and possession to the money from the extent. The assignee of a commission of bankrupt takes as the right was, being bound by the extent. Com. 23b.[3] The queen is not bound by a statute which gives penalties, as the Act against Bankrupts.

The traverse in the plea *a die inquisitionis* is bad, but *a die* the extent is good.

[There is] no need of any act of bankruptcy to be averred, for it is not traversable, but he may give any other act of bankruptcy in evidence. In a case of the crown, it is a matter of law and so not a general issue, which is not to be left to a jury.

And he gave judgment for the queen.

Lord Chief Baron Ward: The defendant, in his plea, did proffer *in curia* their title. The traverse in the plea *tempore inquisitionis* is not a good traverse and does not deny, but rather admits he was indebted *tempore* of the extent. The Statute of Bankrupts extends not to the case of the crown. The crown overreaches the Statute of Bankrupts on the extent. The *teste* of the extent binds the goods and the property of them; an so it does money and debts.

They confess in the plea that the defendant was indebted *tempore* the extent. 8 Rep., Sir George Fleetwood's Case; Dyer 67, Stringfellow's Case extends to *bona et catalla* and extends to the *teste* of the extent. Dyer 179; an extent before [the writ of] *capias ad satisfaciendum*. A [writ of] *fieri facias* before the Statute 29 Car. II, c. [*blank*], of Frauds, binds goods from the *teste* and can be executed on executors. Moor 21; Cro. El. 174, 440; 1 Lev. 145; Cro. Car. 459. Goods sold

---

1 *Rex v. Death* (Ex. 1618), Croke Jac. 513, 79 E.R. 438, also Exch. Repts. 1604 to 1648, p. 201.

2 *Baskerville v. Brocket* (1617), Croke Jac. 449, 79 E.R. 384; *Stringfellow v. Brownsoppe* (1549), *ut supra*.

3 *Attorney General v. Page* (Ex. 1587), 5 Coke Rep. 52, 77 E.R. 133; *Willion v. Berkley* (1562), 1 Plowden 223, 75 E.R. 339.

bona fide, yet the lien holds good. Syd. 271, Bayly v. Bunning; *scire facias* made after bankruptcy, but made *teste* before did bind the property. Stat. 21 Jac. I, c. 19. Clause where execution executed and that before the *teste*, as before; 3 Lev. 191, Philips v. Tomson.[1]

There is no difference between *bona et catalla* and the debt found; personal things and choses in action differ only on the way of the recovery, but they are the same in nature.

Things come to the crown by the act of the party or an act in law or by forfeiture or grant. 39 Hen. VI, 35; [upon] a grant of *bona et catalla*, a rent reserved on a lease passes.[2]Magna Carta, c. 48; the king cannot seize the body [of a debtor] if he has goods or chattels. *Diem clausit extremum* is founded on this Statute if not at common law and which takes in upon the inquisition the debts due to the debtor of the crown. 2 Ro. Abr. 150, 151. A *depositum* or occupier of *bona et catalla* are chargeable. Statute 33 Hen. VIII, c. 39; the king has an equal liberty against lands or goods, though Magna Carta restrains him to goods. Stanford's, *Prerogative Regis*, 45.[3]

Felons' goods are forfeited by condition in law, and are *bona et catalla*. 2 Leon. 56; Dyer 262. Debts and credits pass by the name of *bona et catalla*. 12 Rep. 1, Ford v. Sheldon. Statute 4 Jac., c. [*blank*]; 29 El., c. 6. A chose in action is the same as goods because the crown takes it in specie. Debts and goods are the same in respect to the crown. 21 Hen. VII, 19; if an oblige assign a bond to the crown without an enrollment, being a chattel interest, it passes. Moor 352; upon a devise of *omnia bona*, a lease for years passes.[4]

[A writ of] extent says *quae bona et catalla modo habet*. An inquisition is not an office entitling for goods or debts. 6 Rep. 171, Tourson's Case, where a *nomine districtionis* or in case of outlawry, there must be an office of entitling; [there is] no need of an office if they king's title is precedent to the inquisition. 3 Jac. I, 2

---

[1] *Anonymous*, Moore K.B. 21, 72 E.R. 413; *Anonymous* (1590), Croke Eliz. 174, 78 E.R. 431; *Boucher v. Wiseman* (1595), Croke Eliz. 440, 78 E.R. 680; *Finch's Case* (1591), 2 Leonard 134, 145, 74 E.R. 420, 429; *Cleve v. Veer* (1637), Croke Car. 450, 457, 79 E.R. 992, 996; *Bayly v. Bunning* (1665), *ut supra*; Stat. 21 Jac. I, c. 19, s. 9 (*SR*, IV, 1228); *Philips v. Thompson* (1682–1684), 3 Levinz 69, 191, 83 E.R. 581, 645.

[2] YB Mich. 39 Hen. VI, f. 35, pl. 48 (1460).

[3] Stat. 33 Hen. VIII, c. 39, s. 36 (*SR*, III, 886); W. Staunford, *Exposition of the King's Prerogative* (1567), f. 45.

[4] *Lord of Northampton v. Lord St. John* (1587), 2 Leonard 56, 74 E.R. 354; *Anonymous* (1567), 3 Dyer 262, 73 E.R. 582; *Attorney General v. Ford and Sheldon* (Ex. 1606), 12 Coke Rep. 1, 77 E.R. 1283, 117 Selden Soc. 345, Exch. Repts. 1604 to 1648, p. 19; Stat. 29 Eliz. I, c. 6 (*SR*, IV, 771–772); YB Hil. 21 Hen. VII, f. 18, pl. 30 (1506); *Portman v. Willis* (1594), Moore K.B. 352, 72 E.R. 623, also Gouldsborough 129, 75 E.R. 1042, Croke Eliz. 386, 78 E.R. 632.

Cro. 82; Savill 130. All inquisitions are offices of instruction, not of entitling, and extend to goods or debts.[1]

The mischief [is where] a debtor pays before notice. The defendant admits that it is not paid. And the mischief is equal if goods are sold after the *teste* of the extent, which binds the property.

The plea is bad; he has no defense or title; being a debtor, he might plead *non indebitatus*. If he pleads as assignee of a commission of bankruptcy, he might plead this plea and pray for a [writ of] *amoveas manus*.

5 Rep., Knight's Case;[2] where a debt be assigned, one cannot wage his law. A rent seck is a rent charge. And there are many cases where the king has the preference.

1 Jac. I, c. 15. The crown is not within the Statute of Bankrupts. Magdalen College Case. The king's title is not taken away by general words. Statute 25 Edw. III, c. 19; 3 Rep., Herbert's Case; Statute 33 Hen. VIII, c. 39, the Statute of Equity, may award process for the queen's debt; 21 Jac. I, c. 19.[3]

Easter 20 Car. II, 20, 80, in the Exchequer, King v. Crump and Hanbury;[4] one was indebted to the crown and became a bankrupt, and a commission and assignment was made of his estate; an extent issued from the crown tested the day of the date of the assignment, and yet the extent of the crown was preferred, and this was adjudged by Chief Baron Hale.

The pleading is not goods in cases of the crown. It must be special, and the defendant must make [out a] title, which the queen may traverse.

21 Jac., c. [*blank*]; to an information of intrusion, if there were twenty years of possession against the crown, one may plead the general issue, but one must give up the possession to the crown if not twenty years' possession [and one] must plead specially in intrusion. Statute 21 Jac. [*blank*], the Statute of Limitations, does not bind the king unless sixty years out of possession before the Statute, not since the Statute. 24 Car. II, Exchequer, King v. Morgan; if one sue on a bond for the crown, one must plead to every item of the bond, though affirmative, and a general plea is not good.[5]

---

[1] *Tourson's Case* (1610), 8 Coke Rep. 170, 77 E.R. 730; *Rex v. Wendman* (1605), Croke Jac. 82, 79 E.R. 69; *Hitchcock v. Skynner* (1594), Savile 130, 123 E.R. 1052.

[2] *Knight v. Breech* (1588), 5 Coke Rep. 54, 77 E.R. 137, also Anderson 173, 123 E.R. 414, Gouldsborough 15, 75 E.R. 965.

[3] Stat. 1 Jac. I, c. 15, s. 9 (*SR*, IV, 1033); *Warren v. Smith* (1615), 11 Coke Rep. 66, 77 E.R. 1235, also 1 Rolle Rep. 151, 81 E.R. 394, 2 Bulstrode 146, 80 E.R. 1021, Croke Jac. 364, 79 E.R. 312; Stat. 25 Edw. III, c. 19 (*SR*, I, 323); *Harbert's Case* (Ex. 1584), 3 Coke Rep. 11, 76 E.R. 647, also Popham 154, 79 E.R. 1252, Moore K.B. 169, 72 E.R. 510; Stat. 33 Hen. VIII, c. 39, s. 36 (*SR*, III, 886); Stat. 21 Jac. I, c. 19, s. 9 (*SR*, IV, 1228).

[4] *Rex v. Crump and Hanbury* (Ex. 1668–1670), Exch. Repts. *tempore* Car. II, 134.

[5] *Attorney General v. Morgan* (Ex. 1672), Exch. Repts. *tempore* Car. II, 239.

Here, the defendant that is the debtor may plead *non indebitatus* to Newell, but he cannot traverse the queen's office, nor remove the queen's hand. But the assignee, who has a title under the bankruptcy may plead the same to the *scire facias* or the extent and inquisition. But, if the assignee brought an action against Tannar Arnold, the debtor, he may plead the extent *prout patet per recordam*, and so avoid the debt. The defendant should have come as an interpleader until the suit ended. Stamf., *Prerog.*, 64; Bro., *Prerog.*, 55; Com. 243.[1]

Baron PRICE's argument is with the copy of the record. And judgment by all was for the queen that the debt due from the defendant to Newell for goods sold, who being the queen's debtor, was bound from the *teste* of the extent.

The Chief Baron [EDWARD WARD] was of opinion the plea was not good, contrary to BURY and PRICE. But all four agreed in the main point.

Harvard Law Sch. MS. 537, pt. 2, p. 147

Hilary 8 Anne, 1710.

The case was Newins was indebted to the crown by a bond the 3d December 6th of the queen [1707]. A [writ of] extent was issued out upon it. And, the 13th, there was an inquisition which found that A. was indebted to Newins £109 12s. And, upon that, a [writ of] *scire facias* [issued] against A.

A. comes in and pleads *quod bene et veram est* the 3d of December *supra* he was so indebted to Newins £109 12s. but that, 3rd December *superdictus et diu antea* in Cheapside, Newins was a goldsmith and got his living by buying and selling and was indebted to Taylor and others in £1000 *et quod secundo Decembris manifeste devenit decoctor*, setting out no act of bankruptcy, and that, upon their *petitionem 8 ejusdem mensis*, a commission of bankruptcy was awarded against them and that the 9th the debt was assigned to Taylor and then he traverses that he was indebted to Newins *tempore inquisitionis praedictis*.

Upon which a demurrer [was filed and it was shown] for cause (1) that no act of bankruptcy was set forth [and] (2) that [it was] not shown that the commissioner declared him to be a bankrupt. And, Hilary [term] 7 [1709], it was argued by Dodd, for the queen, and by Northey, for the defendant.

Dodd: First, no particular act of bankruptcy is set forth. Second, if the plea was good, it amounted to no more than the general issue *non assumpsit* then that he was not indebted to Newins at the time of the inquisition. Third, that it was not a sufficient answer to the *scire facias*, for it only traverses *quae indebitatus* at the time of the inquisition and does not traverse *quae indebitatus* at the time of the *teste* of the [writ of] extent.

[1] YB Pas. 1 Hen. VII, ff. 17, 19, pl. 3 (1486) and YB Hil. 4 Hen. VII, f. 1, pl. 1 (1489), 2 Brooke, Abr., *Prerogative le roy*, pl. 55; *Willion v. Berkley* (1562), 1 Plowden 223, 75 E.R. 339.

For the first, he cited Thompson 106; Brownlow, *Redivivus*, 83, 185; Brown's *Entries*, 1st part, 104; Ashton 228; Levinz, Entries, 15; 3 Levinz Rept. 191; and Lutw. 15; 2 Ve. 63; Lutw. 451; Ashton [Entries] 195, 196.

For the second, if the assignment of the commissioner did prevent the extent, then the general issue [is] *non assumpsit*. 1 Inst. 303b.

As to the third, the question is whether the debts of the king's debtor are not bound by the extent, *viz*. by the *teste* of it.

He observed this was the queen's immediate debt and not a [writ of] process in aid, that the crown is not within the Statute of Bankrupts, that this extent is a [writ of] execution and is the crown's execution, and, if an execution, it is not at all doubted but that it bound from the *teste* until 29 Car. II, and that restrains between party and party only. And one Ben Higden's Case, in this court, was cited. The case was there went an extent after an act of bankruptcy, and though after that act, the bankrupt's power of disposal is gone, yet the court did not doubt but an extent might well go, notwithstanding an act of bankruptcy. And the King and Thomas's Case in Charles II's time, in this court.[1] The case was an act of bankruptcy was committed and a commission was taken out, but no assignment. And it was there resolved the extent did well issue notwithstanding the act of bankruptcy and the commission taken out.

He cited the King and Lechmere's Case in King James II's time, in one of the Moderns.[2] There, they made no doubt of it, notwithstanding the commission had gone out, that the extent well issued. And, if so, the subsequent assignment cannot defeat the extent.

Sir Edward Northey, for the defendant: As to the first, he confesses there are many precedents, so, but the practice of late has been quite otherwise. As to the second, it should have been shown for cause. As to the third, they do not pretend the crown is bound by the Statute of Bankrupts, nor that the Statute of Frauds extends to the Crown, but that, when a stranger's debts come to be asserted by the process of the crown, that the constant opinion has been that they are bound only from the inquisition. Coke's prerogative of the crown in Auditor Povey's Case, 4 Inst. 115; Stamford's, *Prerogative*, fo. 84; Roll's (I believe) 440; 2 Inst. 145; 2 Leon. 145;[3] Popham 45, 25; 1 Leon. 50; Savil 41; 8 Co. 178.

And [it was said] by *Northey* the crown cannot take advantage of double pleading without showing it for cause. And that was admitted by the two chief justices in a case which he mentioned had been lately in the Exchequer Chamber.

---

1 *Attorney General v. Thomas* (Ex. 1684), Exch. Repts. *tempore* Car. II, 588.

2 *Letchmere v. Thorowgood* (1688), 3 Modern 236, 87 E.R. 153, also Comberbach 123, 90 E.R. 381, 1 Shower K.B. 12, 146, 89 E.R. 416, 502, 2 Ventris 156, 86 E.R. 365.

3 *Povie's Case* (1615), E. Coke, *Fourth Institute* (1644), p. 115; W. Staunford, *Exposition of the King's Prerogative* (1567); *Finch's Case* (1591), 2 Leonard 134, 145, 74 E.R. 420, 429.

PRICE cited for the first, that a general plea is sufficient. Lutw. 274, 451, 701.[1]

It was argued at another [day] in Trinity 8 [1709] by *Sir James Montagu*, Attorney General, for the crown, and Mr. *Ettrick*, for the defendant.

Sir James Montagu: In all the old precedents, the act is particularly set forth, and Lutw. 274 only is against them. And he mentions the precedents *supra* in Dodd's argument. If a man will bring an action upon a law, he must make his case come within it. Though a man may perhaps declare so, yet he may not plead so, because, in a declaration, it is oftentimes helped by the verdict. Cro. Eliz. 698; Moor 573. He mentioned the difference in Matthews and Cary's Case, in Sir B. Shower and 3 Mod. 137, 138.[2] No case nor precedent was cited to maintain the plea. He cited Littleton 356; 3 Keb. 134.[3]

As to the third point, he cited Moor 21; Roll's, Abr., 893, pl. 30; Moor 873; Sir George Fleetwood's Case.[4] It is awarding the execution which binds, which appears by the *teste*.

Ettrick: As to the first point, he cites Cro. Eliz. 871, 900; Moor 600. And [it was said] by him the act of bankruptcy is not traversable, but whether he committed an act of bankruptcy or no is traversable.

N.B. query as to that distinction, for I [Eden] cannot be positive he made it.

And he argued to the same effect with Northey, which I did not take or, if I did, lost it. But I believe it was the first. And this term, the court unanimously gave their opinion for the crown. I did not hear much of Lovell's argument.

LOVELL was of opinion that whatever was extendable was attached even from the *teste* of the extent. He cited Stringfellow's Case, Dyer 67, and Cro. Car., Audley's Case. And he was of opinion that the plea was not good because of the generality of it.

PRICE: As to the first point, most precedents are indeed that it ought to be particularly set forth. But, of late, the method of pleading in that respect has been otherwise. Lutw., Shaley's Case, 455; *et id.*, Lawson and Lane's Case. And though it be in the case of the crown, yet it will not require anything that is unnecessary. Kepworth and Hayes, in Lutwich.

---

[1] *Lawson v. Lamb* (1704), 1 Lutwyche 274, 125 E.R. 144; *Slaughter v. Pierpoint* (1704), 1 Lutwyche 451, 125 E.R. 237; *Hepworth v. Haigh* (1704), 1 Lutwyche 701, 125 E.R. 367.

[2] *Steverton v. Scrogs* (1599), Croke Eliz. 698, 78 E.R. 933, Moore K.B. 573, 72 E.R. 767; *Matthews v. Cary* (1689), 1 Shower K.B. 61, 89 E.R. 449, 3 Modern 137, 87 E.R. 88, also 1 Salkeld 107, 91 E.R. 98, 3 Salkeld 52, 91 E.R. 686, Comberbach 76, 90 E.R. 353, Carthew 73, 90 E.R. 646, Holt K.B. 408, 90 E.R. 1125.

[3] *Anonymous* (1631), Littleton 356, 124 E.R. 282; *Legar v. Randall* (1673), 3 Keble 134, 84 E.R. 637.

[4] *Anonymous*, Moore K.B. 21, 72 E.R. 413; *Comyn v. Brandlyn* (1614), 1 Rolle, Abr., *Execution*, pl. A, 3, p. 893, Moore K.B. 873, 72 E.R. 965; *Fleetwood's Case* (1610), *ut supra*.

As to the objection that it may be good in a declaration and yet not in a plea, he cannot allow the difference, for that a declaration requires more certainty than a plea. 1 Inst. 304.[1]

As to the second point, its amounting to the general issue, Cro. Eliz. 146, Ward and Blood's Case, there, it is laid down as a rule that you must assign such a thing specially for cause upon your demurrer and not to take advantage of it upon a general demurer.[2]

Objection: Littleton's Reports 356. He cannot make any such difference.

As to the third point, 29 Car. II extends not to the crown, that the conusee has no perfect title until the [writ of] *liberate*, yet the conusor cannot dispose of it in the meantime. And the *liberate* relates to the writ of extent, and it makes all but one execution. Audley's Case, which is likewise in Jones 282 and, where better reported; 1 Roll's [Abr.] 896; 1 Sid., Baily and Buning's Case; 2 Roll's Abr. 157; 25 Edw. III, 13, which is a very strong Statute for the crown. And this debt is a chattel of George Newins; it is forfeitable, assignable to the crown, and liable to its execution. Stamford, 45.[3]

Objection: That it is not the extent but the inquisition that binds the property. The inquisition is only in pursuance to the extent. It is an inquisition of the instruction only, not an entitling one. And this has such a relation to the extent as it is all but one execution.

As to the mischief objected for want of notice, etc., the proceedings are matter of record and thence notice may be had. And suppose an inquisition be taken 200 miles off; will anybody [think] that there may not be better notice had of a record in Westminster Hall? If that position should prevail, it would be of great mischief to the crown, for they might manage so by a quick dispatch as to prevent the crown, as it seems they did design in this case. Pearson and Hall Spier, etc., in Keble, cited, 21 Jac. 19. The crown is taken care of.[4]

And [it was] said by him, suppose in a case of a bargain and sale, there be an assignment or an act of bankruptcy committed before enrollment, yet, after enrollment, it shall relate so as to make all one conveyance. *Et sic conclusit pro corona.*

Bury: He looks upon it as no good plea because it has not answered the *teste*. Magna Charta, [*blank*]; 25 Edw. III, c. 19; both, by Cook, are acts of grace, through these have restrained the king's execution. He cited Britton for the extent and execution of the king, *viz.* that he [. . .].

Objection: A difference between debts and chattels, as to debts, they are not entitled until an inquisition, but the goods they allow are bound from the *teste* of

[1] E. Coke, *First Institute* (1628), f. 304.

[2] *Ward v. Blunt* (1589), *ut supra.*

[3] *Audley v. Halsey* (1629), *ut supra; Baily v. Bunning* (1665), *ut supra; Fleetwood's Case* (1610), *ut supra*; Stat. 25 Edw. III, c. 19 (*SR*, I, 323); W. Staunford, *Exposition of the King's Prerogative* (1567), f. 45.

[4] *Andrews v. Spicer* (1676), *ut supra.*

the extent, they say it may be inconvenient to a third person, but have instanced in nothing but one as perhaps a good plea upon 33 Hen. VIII. And yet it must be, according to their objection, still be inconvenient as to the goods. 20 Edw. III, B. Abr. 99, 52, because the king is party in a manner; the king may distrain a rent seck. Fitz., tit. *Execution*, 166; 2 Cro. 513. The debtor's debtor's debtor may be affected.[1]

They rely upon the forms of the inquisition, which they say are always that he was *ind[ebitatus] tempore inquisitionis*. But he says none [are] cited, and he believes the precedents generally [are] otherwise. And the writ of extent says *quae bona* at the award, which is the *teste* of the extent.

As to its being an office entitling as to debts but an office of instruction as to goods, it is no more an office of entitling in this case than upon a statute staple. Cro. Car. 450; Stringfellow's Case, Dyer, Roll's, Abr., 158; Page, 5 Rept.; Pl. Comm. 23b.[2]

As to the first point, *quod guarniseste devenit decoctor*, he answered, if he sets forth the act of bankruptcy, he must be bound by it, and cannot give another in evidence, nor is it traversable.

As to its being a general issue, it is a matter of law, *ergo pro corona*.

Ward: First, he observed the crown had in its execution only a preference, but a more extensive power; second, that the act of bankruptcy does not affect their remedy; third, that the *teste* of the extent of the crown did equally bind the goods and chattels and personal estate [. . .] since 29 Car. II as before.

For the first, he cited Dyer 179; Cro. Eliz. 174, 181, 440; 3 Leon. 145; Baily and Bunning's Case, 1 Sid. 21 [. . .], c. 9. Indeed, Philips and Thompson's Case, 3 Lev. 17. And [. . .] doubted Baily and Bunning's Case, and the judgment seems to be against it.

As to the objection this execution only extends to *bona et catalla* and that is not debts, he answered *bona et catalla* extends to and includes the whole personal estate. That difference, however, makes nothing in the case of the crown, though it might be pretended to be in the case of the subject. 39 Hen. VI, f. 35; Magna Charta, c. 8 and 18, that it is upon this Statute that the writ *diem clausit extremum* was founded. That *bona et catalla* extends to debts, [see] Roll's Abr., *Prerogative*, 158a and 159; Magna Charta, c. 8, put a restraint upon the crown, which the subject has not. 17 Edw. II, [*blank*].[3]

---

[1] *Anonymous* (Ex. 1346), Fitzherbert, Abr., *Ley*, pl. 52, also Exch. Repts. Middle Ages 11; *Rex v. Death* (Ex. 1618), *ut supra*.

[2] *Cleve v. Vere* (1636), Croke Car. 450, 457, 79 E.R. 992, 996, also W. Jones 385, 82 E.R. 201; *Stringfellow v. Brownsoppe* (1549), *ut supra*; *Attorney General v. Page* (Ex. 1587), 5 Coke Rep. 52, 77 E.R. 133; *Willion v. Berkley* (1562), 1 Plowden 223, 75 E.R. 339.

[3] YB Mich. 39 Hen. VI, f. 35, pl. 48 (1460); Stat. 25 Edw. I, Magna Carta, cc. 8, 18 (*SR*, I, 115, 116); 2 Rolle, Abr., *Prerogative le Roy*, pl. H, 5, p. 158; Statute of the Chattels of Felons (*SR*, I, 230).

But [it was] objected Dyer 368, that, in the case of a grant of *omnia bona et catalla felonum*, debts do not pass.[1]

He answered that, by way of grant, they shall not pass because *de praerogativa de coronae* that, by the grant of a liberty *de omnibus bonis et catallis felonum*, they shall pass. And [it was] so adjudged in a case in the King's Bench in Keeling's time. He cited 12 Co., Ford and Sheldon's Case; 21 Hen. VII, 14b.[2]

That it is no more an office entitling for debts than for goods, [see] 8 Co., Curson's Case, 3 Jac. I; 2 Cro. 62.[3]

As to the pleading, he never knew such a one as this, one comes to pray an *amoveas manus*, who is a third person.

He cited a case between King [v.] Compton and Andrews in Charles II's time, Easter 22d [1670], it was an extent went out tested the same day an assignment of a bankrupt's goods was made, and [it was] adjudged the extent took place.

But he cannot be of opinion the pleading [is] good. He thought the way was to express what trade that he might appear liable to be a bankrupt, then to show the act that made him one, and the precedents have been generally so until of late. But, admitting it good in the subject, yet it cannot be so in the case of the crown. So judgment [goes] for the queen.

[Connected cases: Regina v. Newell (Ex. 1707–1708), see above, Case No. 288.]

346

Burton v. Davis

(Ex. 1709)

The limitation on receiving court costs for small verdicts applies only to torts and not to actions for disturbing a right of common.

Lincoln's Inn MS. Misc. 538, f. [101v], pl. 1

The plaintiff brought an action on the case against the defendant for disturbing him in his right of common at such a time and place, and he had a verdict and 2d. damages only. And the defendant insisted that the damages being 2d. only, the plaintiff ought to have no more costs than damages.

But, *per curiam*, that Act[4] goes only to trespasses and not to actions on the case, nor where the title is in question. This is the common experience. 3 Keble

[1] *Anonymous* (1567), 3 Dyer 262, 73 E.R. 582.

[2] *Attorney General v. Ford and Sheldon* (Ex. 1606), *ut supra*; YB Hil. 21 Hen. VII, f. 14, pl. 21 (1506).

[3] *Tourson's Case* (1610), 8 Coke Rep. 170, 77 E.R. 730; *Rex v. Wendman* (1605), Croke Jac. 82, 79 E.R. 69.

[4] Stat. 22 & 23 Car. II, c. 9, s. 9 (*SR*, V, 719).

[*blank*].[1] Besides, an action upon the case, as this is, implies a title. And so the plaintiff had his costs.

[Other copies of this report: Georgetown Univ. Law Sch. MS. B88–10, p. 691.]

347

Anonymous

(Ex. 1709)

The Attorney General, but not the Lord Treasurer, can acknowledge the satisfaction of a fine and discharge the debtor from imprisonment.

Lincoln's Inn MS. Misc. 538, f. [102]

It was signified by the Lord Treasurer in writing that Her Majesty was pleased that A., who was in execution for a fine, should be discharged from the fine and imprisonment.

But the court could not do it until the fine was discharged, which could not be but by the Attorney General's acknowledging satisfaction of it on record, and when that appears to be done, the court here will stay all upon the estreat made into this court, which is all that is before the court. The record itself is below. And this method has been heretofore observed in all cases of estreats of like nature. But, when the party that lies in execution pays the fine, which is to be by tally, into the Receipt, then, upon producing that tally, the court awards a writ of *liberate* to the sheriff or officer in whose custody he is for setting the party at liberty *si ea de causa tantum* he is detained.

[Other copies of this report: Georgetown Univ. Law Sch. MS. B88–10, p. 693.]

348

Rice's Case

(Ex. 1709)

Where a person is charged by an act of Parliament with a debt to the crown, the procedure for collecting it is an action at law upon a writ of account.

[1] *Earl of Pembroke v. Westall* (1673), 3 Keble 121, 84 E.R. 629; *Claxton v. Laws* (1673), 3 Keble 247, 84 E.R. 702.

Lincoln's Inn MS. Misc. 538, f. [102v]

By an Act of Parliament made 5 Anne, ca. [*blank*], fo. 313,[1] [Colonel John] Rice is thereby charged and made chargeable in the Exchequer with £11,420 17s. 06d. and liable to render an account thereof according to the course and method of the court as if immediately impressed to him on account of the services of the Army. And the Earl Ranelagh[2] is thereby directed to transmit a certificate into the court of the said sum so issued and of the days when paid to Rice to be filed of record there and such charge to be taken as a debt by obligation or statute staple according to the Statute 33 Hen. VIII, ca. 39,[3] to oblige Rice to answer and account for it.

Upon consideration and hearing of the Queen's Counsel what process should issue against Rice upon the Lord Ranelagh's certificate and the Act, because the words of the Act seemed sometimes to fix the sum as a debt stated and determined, which, if so, then an immediate process of extent was to issue against body, lands, and goods. But other words in the Act looked as if an account was to be made and that sum to be taken only as a stated sum for which he ought to account and to be allowed what he could prove paid and duly disposed.

It was resolved by the court that the process should be to fetch him into account. But, because the ordinary process of *distringas* was in all probability too weak and ineffectual to fetch him in and, having no lands in England, would be wholly avoided by going into Ireland, of which country he was, and oath being made of his secreting and concealing himself in England, upon the motion of the Attorney General, the court awarded a *capias ad respondendum et computandum* against him for the £11,420 17s. 06d., which are the words of the Act of Parliament, to answer and account for the same, and a *capias* as well as a *distringas ad computandum* lies in the crown, the law allowing it law against a lord's or person's bailiff according to the Statute of Marlebridge.[4]

And, after some time, Rice was taken upon the *capias*, and carried to Newgate [Prison]. And the 28th of October 1709, he removed himself to this court with the cause of his imprisonment.

And his counsel prayed he might be committed to the Fleet [Prison] there to account. And one of his counsel objected to the form of the writ as containing more than the Statute of Marlbridge warranted, but he was not willing to demur to it, this being a case subsisting by the words of the Act that charge him and not within the Statute of Marlbridge, nor is the case of the crown confined to it. The court committed him to the Fleet [Prison] to account in custody, and, in open

---

1 Stat. 6 Ann., c. 33 (*SR*, VIII, 631–632).

2 C. I. McGrath, 'Jones, Richard, earl of Ranelagh (1641–1712)', *Oxford Dictionary of National Biography*, vol. 30, pp. 616–618.

3 Stat. 33 Hen. VIII, c. 39, s. 36 (*SR*, III, 886).

4 Stat. 52 Hen. III (*SR*, I, 19–25).

court, assigned Auditor Manwaring, one of the Auditors of the Imprests, to take the account. And Rice was to have liberty at all proper times to attend the Auditor upon his first giving good security in this court for his rendering him to the Fleet or payment of the money as the court shall from time to time direct. *Vide* Rives's printed case.

Upon perusal of the ancient records in the King's Remembrancer's Office in the Exchequer, the method of charging accountants and assigning to them auditors and their discharge upon a *plene computavit* appears to be this. If it be an imprest accountant, the entry is to this effect: *memorandum* that such a day and year such amount the Lord Treasurer, by the hands of such a one, his clerk (supposed to be the Clerk of the Pells or Auditor of the Revenue), delivered into court an imprest roll (describing it) for examination thereupon to be made, and then it mentions the particular sums that are imprested and the persons to whom and for what uses or occasions, as for example, prested to A.B., Clerk of the Wardrobe, for such uses, naming them, and received of such a teller by name such a sum, and so the rest. But, if it be another sort of account, then it is first mentioned that such a one, showing how and for what he is an accountant, ought to account for such a sum and how it arises and by what record or other way charged.

And, in both cases, it thus follows, *super quo concordatur* that the accountant (or his heirs, executors, administrators, terre tenants, or occupiers of his lands and tenements at the time of his death as the case shall happen to be) be distrained etc. to render an account of that money, naming it, returnable at such a time. At which time, the accountant appeared by his attorney and made oath truly to account in the premises. And then an Auditor is assigned by the court to audit the account, which, when fully and truly done, the entry of the court's award or judgment is *quod plene computavit et ideo non fiat ulterior executio*. And, if all is not paid or cleared, it is so to be before he is discharged.

Vide Hilary [term] 1 Jac. I, rot. 151, ex parte Rememeratoris Regis.

[Other copies of this report: Georgetown Univ. Law Sch. MS. B88–10, p. 694.]

349

Symes, qui tam v. Anonymous

(Ex. 1710)

The Statute of 6 Anne extends only to French goods, and it does not make foreign brandy and rum liable to an import duty.

Indiana University, Lilly Library
MS. Parker 'Cases in the Exchequer', vol. 5, p. 182

Hilary [term] 1709[/10].

[This was] the case of foreign brandy and rum from the English plantations in America taken as prize or seized and condemned for unlawful importation or brought in by collusion. Robert Symes, officer of the Customs at Bristol, seized several parcels of rum and brandy from English plantations in America as forfeited, being imported in small casks under sixty gallons, being appraised and condemned in the Exchequer for want of a claim, the moiety forfeited paid into the Exchequer as by a tally, and there was a writ of delivery. But Jacob Reynardson, Collector of the Excise, refused to deliver it to Symes, demanding a duty of excise by the Act of 6 Anne,[1] being an act for continuing half subsidies etc. and for charging prize goods and seizures.

He declares that over and above the duty of £25 per ton for prize wines by the Act all ships, vessels, wines, and other goods and merchandises seized and condemned for unlawful importation brought in by collusion or taken from the enemy and condemned as lawful prize during the war shall be subject to the like customs and duties, which ships, goods, and merchandises taken and condemned as prize were subject to by the queen's declaration 1 June 1702 for the encouragement of Her Majesty's men of war.

[On] 1 June 1702, [there was a] declaration, if any ship, vessel, or goods belonging to the enemy or otherwise liable to confiscation shall be seized and taken at sea by a man of war or merchant's ship employed in the queen's service and condemned and adjudged a lawful prize, the same shall be appraised and sold and, after satisfying all duties and customs payable by law (other than the £25 percent by the Statute 7 Will.[2] on French wines) one half of the real produce of such prize to the flag officers etc.

Attorney General, *Sir James Montagu*: No duty is payable for prize goods or goods unlawfully imported, being all forfeited. The queen by a declaration gives a moiety, paying to duty. If a clause is not substantive, then it relates to no French goods but wine and brandy. As aforesaid, it relates not to the goods but the manner of information. The title of the Act charges prize goods and seizures.

Solicitor General *Eyre*: Prize goods are not liable, but, by this Act and declaration. Prize [and] wine are set together during the war in the Act [and] is the time the duty is to continue. All other duties extend to the excise as well as the customs. This Act makes the declaration law.

Mr. *Dodd*, for the defendant: The Statute of 6 Anne extends only to the French goods over and above those duties, and it is confined to the French by collusion; it is tied to French wine, as aforesaid, [and] is relative during the war. It shows an invention not the.[3] It extends only to such goods which were less subject to be prize [that] should by an unlawful importation or collusion be liable.

---

[1] Stat. 6 Ann., c. 27, s. 4 (*SR*, VIII, 614).

[2] Stat. 6 & 7 Will. & Mar., c. 1 (*SR*, VI, 508–509).

[3] Sic in MS.

The queen's two declaration in May 1703 extend to goods of France and Spain.

The Statute 12 Car. II gives 4d. each gallon on brandy on entry and before landing. [The Statute] 15 Car. II; additional of excise shall make entry with the collector of excise. [Statutes] 5 Will. [and] 4 Will. & Mar., Act of Additional Imposition, forbids any importation of brandy under sixty gallons. [Statute] 12 Will. grants a duty on low wine; no brandy imported under fifteen gallons is forfeited. The Statute 8 Will. does not extend to prize wine. Such and the like duty is not the same. This duty will injure, if not ruin, our plantations.[1]

The court gave opinion that this foreign brandy and rum was not liable to the duty by the Statute 6 Anne and that that Act extended only to French goods.

350

Sturt's Case

(Ex. 1710)

A Cashier for the Victualling of the Navy is not an accountant to the crown, but the accountant is the Treasurer of the Navy.

Lincoln's Inn MS. Misc. 538, f. [103v]

7 February 1709[/10].

Process of *distringas ad computandum* having issued by warrant from the Lord Treasurer to the Queen's Remembrancer directed against Mr. [Anthony] Sturt by the name of Anthony Sturt, Esq., late Cashier for the Victualing of the Navy to render an account to the queen for money by him received and unpaid for the victualing of the Navy from such a time to such a time (naming them) returnable etc., *Phipps*, of counsel with Sturt, moved that the process should be discharged and none other for the future might issue in regard he is no accountant to the crown in this court or otherwise, there being no such officer or office created or granted by the crown, nor has any *super* or arrear been set or charged upon him in any account or by any charge or record in this court nor any of the crown's money impressed to him or any bond or security given by him, by or upon which or in any other manner he is or may be charged or accountable or any foundation or ground to warrant the *distringas*, only the Lord Treasurer's warrant which contained no certain charge or sum or other just cause or reason wherefor or for which he is or ought to be liable to account to the crown.

---

[1] Perhaps Stat. 12 Car. II, c. 18 (*SR*, V, 246–250); Stat. 15 Car. II, c. 11 (*SR*, V, 488–492); Stat. 4 Will. & Mar., c. 3 (*SR*, VI, 373); Stat. 5 Will. & Mar., c. 7 (*SR*, VI, 452); Stat. 8 & 9 Will. III, c. 3 (*SR*, VII, 164–165); Stat. 12 & 13 Will. III, c. 11, ss. 5, 16 (*SR*, VII, 717, 719).

Whereupon, the court thought fit to refer it to the two Auditors of the Imprest and the Deputy of the Queen's Remembrancer to state and certify to the court the whole matter appearing in their respective offices touching the Cashier for the Victualling of the Navy.

Upon the return whereof, it was certified by Auditor Harley of the Imprests that, between Midsummer 1681 and 1689, all money impressed for the service of the Navy or the victualling was only to the Treasurer of the Navy and not to the Cashier for the Victualling, that, by two general certificates of accounts made by the Auditors of the Imprests to the Commissioners of the Treasury 1691 and 1692 and to the Court of Exchequer, no other person was certified as accountant for the Navy or victualling but the Treasurer of the Navy only, after which times, the Commissioners for the victualling and Sturt's late father as Cashier of the Victualling in several certificates were certified as accountants for the victualling, but have been omitted in others, that, in Lord Falkland and the earl of Orford's treasurerships, no notice is taken of the Cashier of the Victualling, but all the charge for the Navy and victualling was placed to and accounted for by the Treasurers of the Navy, no commission from or security was given to the crown appearing.

And, by the Deputy Remembrancer, it was certified that no money appeared in the imprest rolls to be impressed to the Cashier of Victualling, but all to the Treasurer of the Navy, who accounts for it and that the first warrant for issuing a *distringas* against the Cashier for the Victualling was in February 1 Queen Anne [1703].

And there is no other ground or foundation for the *distringas* but the Lord Treasurer's warrant, nothing of charge appearing by the imprest roll or any record to make the Cashier for the Victualling any ways liable to account with the crown.

Upon consideration of all which, it did not seem to the court that the Cashier for the Victualling of the Navy is a person accountable to the crown, but to the Treasurer of the Navy only, who is charged with and, in his account, answers for all that is paid or impressed for the service of the Navy or victualling by or from the crown. And, if any further process by any warrant from the Treasury should issue, Mr. Sturt, if he thinks so fit, may plead to the *distringas* that he is not an accountant to the crown nor any ways liable or chargeable to render any account to the crown nor that there is any record in the court by which he is or may be liable or chargeable to render any account to the crown for any of the money or touching any of the matters in the writ mentioned or what else he shall be advised to.

But note that, in some part of the earl of the Oxford's treasurership, Philip Papillon, Esq., was by a warrant under hand and seal made Cashier for the Victualling and to issue and pay such money as he should receive to such uses and in such manner as the Commissioners of the Victualling should order and direct and he never received any but upon the account and in the name of the earl and, for all which, the earl was charged with and accounted for to the crown. And yet (by what advice or direction does not appear) for several years, he passed accounts in this court as Cashier of the Victualling. But query what effect such account was of, for the charge not arising from any money paid or imprested to him from the crown nor the discharge to him as against the crown so that no *super* could be set thereupon to enable any process for the recovery of it, it seemed to be only for the earl's private satisfaction, he well knowing that he was charged and accountable for the whole without any regard to the Cashier.

The more accountants, the more fees to the officers.

[Other copies of this report: Georgetown Univ. Law Sch. MS. B88–10, p. 698.]

351

Wright v. Elderton

(Ex. 1710)

In this case, a vicar was held not to be entitled to tithes of turnips.

Dodd 224, 1 Rayner 119, 1 Eagle & Younge 694

[Upon a] bill for small tithes by the plaintiff, vicar of Stepney, [Middlesex], [it was] resolved that he having generally taken the tithe of turnips sown but not having had tithes of turnips sown after the corn reaped nor those paid to any person, that the plaintiff should not have them, for he appears not to have any endowment or possession of them, and cited Barry and Bridges' case, impropriator of Fulham,[1] decreed accordingly.

Note: Baron Price [held] *contra*, and [that it] shall be intended to be endowed of the whole, and not partial.

[Other reports of this case: Equity Cases Exch. 659.]

[The order of 23 July 1709, Public Record Office E.126/19, f. 149, is printed at 1 Wood 518, 1 Eagle & Younge 694; see also order of 8 December 1710: Public Record Office E.126/19, f. 250.]

352

Mead v. James

(Ex. 1710)

The question in this case was the date to which a plea of tender refers.

[1] *Barry v. Bridges* (1706), Public Record Office E.126/18, f. 566v.

Harvard Law Sch. MS. 537, pt. 2, p. 156, pl. 1

The point was an [action of] *indebitatus assumpsit* was brought against James. And he comes and imparls. And then he pleads a tender such a day with a *semper paratus* from that time.

And, upon a demurrer for this, *Lutwyche* argued that the *semper paratus* should be from the time of the promise. And, for this, he cited two cases in the [Court of] King's Bench, one Easter term 9, Giles v. Hart;[1] the other, 10 Easter term, Holden v. Bridges, where it was ruled accordingly in both cases.

[It was said] by LOVELL it is laid *cum inde requisitus esset* and since no *requisitus* is laid but the action or that appears to be before the tender, therefore, he thought it might be good.

[It was said] by *Lutwyche* an *indebitatus cum inde requisitus* is payable immediately and, therefore, the *paratus* must be from that time. And he believes *non requisitus* in such a case is no plea.

(But N.B. that may be because the action is a request.)

Such declarations have a general *licet saepius requisitus*, which shall be intended a precedent partic[. . .] unless shown the contrary. The case seems to be this: I promise to pay upon demand; if [it is] never demanded, am I obliged to pay it?

Lutwyche: The pleading of a tender alone is no good plea, but he must plead *semper paratus*. And, now, the question is from what time and why from the time of the tender more than any other time. If he will plead from anytime, he must plead from the time that it was always due.

BURY: The plea may be true, and yet he may have denied from the tender.

LOVELL agrees it is ill if a demand had appeared before the tender.

PRICE: If it is due immediately, it ought to be prayed immediately, and the pleading *semper paratus* from the tender is only from the time he was pleased to pay it.

LOVELL, *ut prius*: If laid *cum inde requisitus*, it makes a request necessary.

Lutwyche: But, however, here is an imparlance in this case.

And, so, the demurrer stood.

---

[1] *Giles v. Hart* (1697), 12 Modern 152, 88 E.R. 1229, 2 Salkeld 622, 91 E.R. 526, Comberbach 443, 90 E.R. 580, Carthew 413, 90 E.R. 839, 3 Salkeld 343, 91 E.R. 863, Holt K.B. 556, 90 E.R. 1207, 1 Lord Raymond 254, 91 E.R. 1066.

353

Anonymous

(Ex. 1710)

The question in this case was whether the Court of Exchequer can discharge an estreat of a fine imposed in another court.

Indiana Univ., Lilly Library
MS. Parker 'Cases in the Exchequer', vol. 5, p. 181

Easter [term] 1710.

A. was fined at the Old Bailey for a battery, and there was an estreat into the Exchequer.

The Attorney General, *Sir James Montagu*, moved that the court, by virtue of a privy seal, would discharge the fine by reason of poverty.

The Chief Baron [EDWARD WARD] held that the Attorney General should acknowledge satisfaction on the record where the record lies and that it was only an estreat here, upon which the court could discharge the estreat roll.

Then, it was moved to compound the fine, it being after execution, and, where fines were imposed in judicial matters, the court seldom compounded them, though the privy seal is in general words.

Curia advisari vult.

354

Poulson, qui tam v. Mendes

(Ex. 1710)

A new trial can be granted in a penal forfeiture where there was a verdict that was given against the instructions of the judge.

Lincoln's Inn MS. Misc. 538, f. [119]

Tuesday 2 May.

In an information of seizure of French wines, this cause was tried at *nisi prius* the second of December last, and [there was] a verdict for the defendant against the direction and expectation of the court. And, in Hilary term last, [there was] a motion for a new trial. And, at the defendant's request, it was put off from time to time to this term in order to accommodate the matter, which not being effected, the Attorney General [*Montagu*] and others moved for a new trial.

And, on hearing the counsel of Mr. Francia, who, in the right of Mendes or rather his own right, defended the cause and the Chief Baron [WARD], who tried the cause, giving a full account to the court of the evidence on both sides, the court granted a new trial on the payment of costs, notwithstanding it was upon a penal law and £4000 value, the precedents of the court warranting such trials, L. M, 97,[1] for here, the wines were before the trial delivered upon a writ of delivery and security as to Mendes, who was then alive, and were pretended to be carried from Bordeaux to Rotterdam. But Francia brought the wines to London, and exposed them to sale, and no duties were paid so that the wines are or are like to be spent in England, against the Act of Parliament,[2] and the crown not to have either the duty or the forfeiture.

The cause was afterwards agreed [out of court] without a trial.

[Other copies of this report: Georgetown Univ. Law Sch. MS. B88–10, p. 729.]

355

Attorney General v. Rowe's Executors

(Ex. 1710)

A writ of diem clausit extremum cannot be issued where a debtor of the crown had no debt stated against him in his lifetime.

Lincoln's Inn MS. Misc. 538, f. [120]

6 May 1710.

The Attorney General [*Montagu*] moved for a [writ of] *diem clausit extremum* against the estate, real and personal, of Anthony Rowe, Esq., deceased, it being found by inquisition of the second instant taken in pursuance of a commission awarded by the Lord Treasurer's warrant directed to the Queen's Remembrancer, where the case was thus.

The queen, by a privy seal of the 23 December 1709, directed to the Lord Treasurer, Chancellor, Barons, etc., reciting that the Commissioners of the Customs had represented to the Lord Treasurer that there are standing out in the general account of the customs several sums amounting to £8930 14s. 7d. qa. due from several late collectors of the Customs, naming them and the sums due from each of them respectively and the years wherein they became due, and that they died insolvent and, process having issued ineffectually and that carrying them on in the accounts from year to year with interest at 12 percent pursuant to the Statute 20 Car. II[3] is a matter of trouble and delay to the accounts, and these being precedent to any Parliamentary appropriations, the Commissioners proposed they might be left out of the accounts. And, further reciting that, at the time of the Revolution of 1688, several sums of money, amounting to £2883 11s. 9d., were taken up by Anthony Rowe and other persons therein named from

[1] *Pritchard, qui tam v. Boyle* (1696), Lincoln's Inn MS. Misc. 559, f. 97, pl. 3.
[2] Stat. 3 & 4 Ann., c. 12 (*SR*, VIII, 360).
[3] Stat. 19 & 20 Car. II, c. 7 (*SR*, V, 636).

several collectors of the customs at Exeter and other of the western ports (naming the collectors and ports) the same alleged to be taken up by Mr. Rowe being £1767 11s. 6d., and that the commissioners of the customs have desired the same might also be discharged out of the accounts of the customs, the queen, by that privy seal, directs that an allowance be given in the next general account of the customs for the same with the interest but so as not to discharge the collectors or other persons or their sureties or representatives from those debts, but process to issue by her Remembrancer to recover what can be, and requires all to whom the privy seal is directed to give all necessary orders and directions that all of the aforesaid sums may be allowed in the next general account of the customs without being carried over to the subsequent account, but so as the collectors and other persons or their representatives be not discharged, and directs process to issue against them all for the recovery of what can be had.

24 March 1709, the Lord Treasurer, by his warrant to the Queen's Remembrancer, reciting the privy seal as to so much as related to Row and others that received the money from the collectors of the customs, directs a commission to issue to seize the sums (there called debts) into Her Majesty's hands and to enquire what estate Row died seised or possessed of at his death and to make out such further process as he shall find to be requisite for that purpose.

24 May 1709, a commission issues, reciting that *datum est nobis intelligi* that Anthony Row, Esq., received in his lifetime, *scil.*, in the year 1688, did receive to the use of the late King James of the collectors of the customs in several ports (naming them) several sums of money arising out of the customs and subsidies for merchandises imported and exported into and out of those ports due and payable to the said late king, which Rowe had not paid to the said late king or to King William or Queen Mary or to her present Majesty, and, therefore, authority is given to the commissioners to enquire of the truth of the premises and whether Rowe had received any and what such money and whether, at the time of his death, he was indebted and in what sums to the queen and at what time he died.

2 May 1710, an inquisition is taken whereby it is found by a jury that Row, in his lifetime, *scil.* in the year 1688, had and received to the use of the said late king from such and such collectors of the customs in such ports such and such sums, naming all of them in certain, amounting to the sum of £1767 11s. 6d., arising out of the customs and subsidies for goods and merchandises imported and exported into and out of the said ports and that he died the 15th of October 1705 indebted to the queen in that sum and that the same is still due and unpaid.

I [Edward Ward] am of the opinion that no *diem clausit extremum* ought to issue in this case, for here was no debt stated in the life[time] of Row, the money received being only to be accounted for and is a mere matter of account in the nature, at best, of an imprest, it was received for the supply of the Prince of Orange and his troops at the time of the Revolution and what Row paid away upon that account ought to be allowed him, which cannot be in case this be a stated and determined debt against him. There was no specialty nor record of any debt or charge against Row in his life[time], and [it is] too hard by taking an inquisition after his death to make him a debtor for money received *in pais* above twenty years since and never called for in all that time. If the collectors from whom he received the sums had upon their accounts passed, *scil.* any *super*s on Rowe for those sums, yet, even in such a case, *distringas*es *ad computandum* only could have issued against him during his life[time] and against his heirs, executors, terre tenants, and occupiers of his goods after his death. And I [Edward Ward] conceive that the process that ought to go upon this inquisition is but a [writ of] *scire facias* whereto the parties may plead, and not to have a [writ of] immediate extent, which a *diem clausit extremum* is, to issue, which carries execution against all Rowe's estate at the time of the death.

Vide Statute 1 Will. & Mar., ca. 14, § 5; the word 'answerable' there imports only account.[1]

The court ordered it to be moved again, but it was not. Query why. It seems they were satisfied it was not a debt stated against Rowe, neither in his life[time] nor at his death.

Vide Bradshaw's Case, Trinity 1712.[2]

[Other copies of this report: Georgetown Univ. Law Sch. MS. B88–10, p. 730.]

356

Maddy v. James

(Ex. 1710)

A plea of tender must be made before a motion for an imparlance.

Lincoln's Inn MS. Misc. 538, f. [121v], pl. 1

In Officio Placitorum Scaccarii.

The plaintiff brought an action on the case by *indebitatus assumpsit* and *quantum meruit* for three causes, and laid several damages.

The defendant, as to all of the three sums laid in the three promises (except as to 8s. in the first promise), pleads (after an imparlance) *non assumpsit.* And, thereupon, issue is joined. And, as to the 8s., he pleads that the plaintiff ought not to recover any damages for the non-payment of that, because that, after the time of the supposed making of the first promise and before the exhibiting of the plaintiff's bill, *scil.* at such a time and place, he was ready and tendered to pay to the plaintiff the said 8s., which the plaintiff refused to accept and that he, the defendant, ever after, was and yet is ready to pay them to the plaintiff, *et illa modo*

[1] Stat. 1 Will. & Mar., c. 14, s. 2 (*SR*, VI, 71).

[2] *Attorney General v. Bradshaw* (Ex. 1709–1712), see above, Case No. 314.

hic in curia profert paratus ei solvendum et hoc paratus est verificare. And he prays judgment if the plaintiff ought to receive any damages for non-payment thereof against him.

There were several impertinent pleadings over, even to a sur-rejoinder. And a demurrer was joined in. But the only question was whether this tender was well pleaded or not so as to bar the plaintiff.

And, by the opinion of the court upon hearing Mr. *Lutwyche*, for the plaintiff (none attending for the defendant), it is not well pleaded.

First, it is a plea of a tender after an imparlance, which comes too late.

Secondly, the action being laid that the *assumpsit* for paying the money was *cum inde requisitus esset*, which, in judgment of law, is presently without any formal request or staying until the action be brought, the defendant's plea of a tender after the time of the first promise though before the action was brought comes too late, for it ought to have been that at and from the time and not after the time of the first promise he tendered and was then and at all times after and still is ready to pay. And the imparlance contradicts that.

Judgment [was given] for the plaintiff *nisi causa* and, afterwards, absolutely.

[Other copies of this report: Georgetown Univ. Law Sch. MS. B88–10, p. 736.]

357

Povey v. Puleston

(Ex. 1710)

A covenant not to sue a debtor does not release any joint obligees.

Lincoln's Inn MS. Misc. 538, f. [121v], pl. 2

The plaintiff brings [an action of] debt upon a bond for the payment of money at a day past.

The defendant prays *oyer* of the bond and condition that one Hoply was bound with the plaintiff jointly and severally in the bond to the plaintiff and that, afterwards, the plaintiff with others of the creditors of Hopley by a writing under their hands and seals of such a date, reciting that Hoply stood bound to the plaintiff and others, the creditors, in several sums by several obligations, the plaintiff and others, the said creditors, by that writing did give leave and liberty to Hopley freely to attend and manage his own affairs and business from the date thereof for three years without any obstacle, impediment, or interruption to be given to Hoply, his goods, or chattels by any of them or their executors or administrators within that time. And he further pleads that the plaintiff and others, the said creditors, severally covenanted and agreed with Hoply that, if he, the said Hoply, during the three years, should be troubled or molested in his body, goods, or chattels by the plaintiff or any of his creditors against the true intent and meaning of that writing that, then and from thenceforth, Hopley, his executors, and administrators should be and remain *libere exonerato* from the debt or debts due to such of them who should molest or sue Hoply in his person, goods, or chattels. And, then, he shows that, after the making of that letter of license, at such a time, which was within the three years, a writ of subpoena issued out of this court at the suit of the plaintiff directed to the defendant and Hoply commanding them to appear in this court at such a time to answer the queen to certain articles on the part of the queen then to be objected against them under pain of £100, by virtue of which writ, the plaintiff before the return of it, caused the said defendant and Hopley to be summoned to appear in this court at the return of it, at which return, they did appear at the suit of the plaintiff *prout* by the record of that appearance still remaining may appear and that, after such appearance, the party, by his bill, declared against the defendant upon the bond entered into by the defendant and Hoply. *Et hoc paratus est verificare.* And he prays judgment if the plaintiff ought to maintain his action against him.

To this plea, the plaintiff has put in a general demurrer, and the defendant has joined.

And *Agar*, for the defendant, to make good the plea, insisted:

First, that a release by the obligee to one of the obligors where [they are] jointly and severally bound is a release to both, which was not contested;

Second, that the suing out and serving of this subpoena on the defendant and Hoply and the plaintiff's declaring against the defendant upon that bond is a breach of the plaintiff's covenant in the letter of license not to sue or molest Hoply under the loss and forfeiture of his bond and debt, for Hoply being released thereby, the defendant is thereby released also and so the bond to the plaintiff is discharged and ought not to be put in suit. And, though the cause of action does not appear in the subpoena so that it does not appear that it was upon the bond in question (which nevertheless may fairly be intended and presumed), yet the agreement not to molest Hodder being general and not under any particularity, any suit or molestation is a breach of that covenant and, consequently, a forfeiture of the bond wherein Hoply with the defendant is bound to the plaintiff.

But *Ettrick*, for the plaintiff, insisted (and with whom the court agreed) that, thought [the] subpoena and serving it by the plaintiff or [his] order on Hoply and the defendant might be a molestation, yet it does not appear that it was in order to sue Hoply upon this bond and that, unless that appeared, there can be no pretense of a release, for it does not appear that this bond was under that agreement, but that the agreement respected some other bond that Hoply stood bound in to the plaintiff, the bond in question not being recited in the agreement. And it will be hard to carry this to be a release of the debt due upon the bond where both the defendant and Hoply were bound.

Judgment [was given] for the plaintiff *nisi* and, afterwards, absolutely.

[Other copies of this report: Georgetown Univ. Law Sch. MS. B88–10, p. 737.]

358

Knapp and Garway v. The African Company

(Ex. 1710)

In this case, the assets of the defendant stock company were distrained in order to satisfy a judgment against it.

Lincoln's Inn MS. Misc. 538, f. [123], pl. 2

The plaintiffs, creditors of the [African] Company, sued them upon bonds for debts and for non-appearance, and a motion to compound issued [. . .] £892 returned estreated against the defendants and levied, and by a privy seal, granted to the plaintiffs, whose debts are thus, *viz.* £1350 to Knap, for which £672 issues, and £280 to Garway, for which £200 issues. And the order of the court 22 May instant [was] read; all these issues were returned in Easter and Trinity [terms] 1709.

And by a rule of court 12 July 1709, it was ordered not to be compounded until the plaintiff's costs be paid and the court otherwise order.

17 May 1710, the queen, by a privy seal, grants all these issues to the plaintiffs to their own use, but subject to such compositions as the Barons of the Exchequer or two of them shall think fit to make.

Northey, *Ettrick*, and *Phipps* move for a composition upon the payment of costs, the defendants having now appeared. They urged that it was unprecedented that issues should go to the payment of the debt or beyond the costs and charges.

Hawles, *Harcourt*, and *Dodd* insist against any composition for the great delay had and great charges the plaintiffs were put to and the company aliened an estate so that after *distringas*es were returned *nichil*s and, in the case of delay upon bail bonds where past assizes where a trial might have been, the court [would] not relieve the plaintiffs' debts from the company with [. . .] interests.

[It was] agreed to be thus: first, Knap's principal £675 and £75 interest; second, Garway's principal £140 [and] £15 interest; £795 [and] £90, which do amount to the issues returned. The case of Sir John Briscoe *versus* Earl Banbury was cited, where issues granted much exceeding the debt,[1] and Lady Wood against Anthony Rowe, where the issues granted exceeding the charges, costs, and interest of the debt and [. . .].

Per curiam: Let the Treasurer's Deputy Remembrancer state the principal, interest, and all of the costs and charges the plaintiffs have been at and report it

---

[1] *Brisco v. Lady Banbury* (1675–1680), 1 Freeman 309, 22 E.R. 1231, 89 E.R. 227, 2 Freeman 8, 22 E.R. 1021, 1 Chancery Cases 287, 22 E.R. 804, 2 Chancery Cases 42, 22 E.R. 837, 73 Selden Soc. 224, 308, 385, 437, 79 Selden Soc. 462, Repts. *tempore* Finch 237, 23 E.R. 130.

to the court and the plaintiffs immediately to be paid the costs and charges and the court then consider how far they will apply anything to [pay] principal, the money to be brought into court and the plaintiffs at liberty to deliver their declarations without prejudice to what past, [?] the sheriffs to have poundage for what [they] levied.

In Michaelmas term 1710, after the Treasurer's Deputy Remembrancer had made his report and stated the whole matter and the money levied brought into court and the plaintiffs received their full costs and the sheriffs paid their fees, the parties came to an agreement whereby the whole residue of the money was agreed to be paid out of court to the plaintiffs for and upon the account of their respective debts due upon their bonds from the Company, which was ordered by the court by consent accordingly. And so that matter was ended.

Note that, in or about Easter term 1709, the plaintiffs sued out process of *distringas* against the Company to the sheriffs of London, who thereupon distrained the defendants by their Company's book wherein they make the entries and keep accounts of their business, which, for some time, the Secondary kept in his hands and was desired by the plaintiffs so to do as the most proper means to compel them to appear, no other goods being to be found. But the book being so necessary for the Company, the Secondary returned it to them, and returned for issues £4, for which contempt, the plaintiffs' counsel prayed a [writ of] attachment, for, in such case, the goods distrained ought, as they said, to be brought into court there to remain until appearance, for the [writ of] *distringas* is to distrain them *per omnia bona et catalla, terras et tenamenta ita quod de exitibus terrarum nobis rendeas* and that the defendants may not put their hands upon any of the goods until the court make other order therein so that 'issues' answers to lands but the goods remain in specie.

But, *per curiam*, the proper return upon a *distringas* is issues, and goods on lands by the Statute of [*blank*] are defined to be issues. And, what if the goods destrained be cumbersome or of a perishable nature, what must the sheriff do with them? Therefore, no attachment [was ordered].

Afterwards, upon another distringas, the plaintiffs got intelligence of many of the Company's goods at the Custom House ready to be shipped off as merchandize for transportation and showed those goods to the officer that had the distringas, and required him to seize them, promising security and indemnity for so doing. And yet the Secondary refused to return any considerable issues, whereupon the court required the Secondary to return goods [and] issues according to the value of the debts and with regard to the worth of the goods shown to the officer, whereupon the Secondary, in court, returned considerable issues, which were those before mentioned. And, by this way and the means aforesaid, the plaintiffs got their debts, which else were in danger.

[Other copies of this report: Georgetown Univ. Law Sch. MS. B88–10, p. 742.]

Lincoln's Inn MS. Misc. 538, f. [145], pl. 2

Actions of debt are brought against the [African] Company by Knap and Garoway, and laid in London. And the plaintiffs' counsel moved for a special jury and that the Secondary of the Counter may attend the Master of the Office of Pleas with the Book of Citizens to take out the names of forty-eight and each side to strike twelve, as usual in like cases in the counties for freeholders.

And it was by me [Edward Ward] doubted whether the secondaries in London have been used or ought so to attend out of the City. But it was asserted by the clerks that there are many instances of such orders and attendances. And the order for that purpose in this cause was made absolute that if the former order were not made where the Secondaries or Sheriffs [were] concerned in interest or contempt.

And now, in these actions, the defendants, by consent, gave [confessed] judgments and the issues estreated and granted, prout notes in Easter [term] 1710, and the money brought into court was paid out by the consent of the same.

Vide such a motion denied in the County Palatine, Hilary 5 [Anne], fo. 18, Earl of Anglesey and Earl of Derby's Case.[1]

[Other copies of this report: Georgetown Univ. Law Sch. MS. B88–10, p. 798.]

359

Bell v. Price

(Ex. 1710)

A pleading for the tortious interference with a right of way need not allege the plaintiff's right to the land at the end of the easement.

Lincoln's Inn MS. Misc. 538, f. [129], pl. 1

The plaintiff brings his action upon the case for stopping up a way which the plaintiff ought to have the use of, leading from his house over certain closes, naming them, *usque* Blackacre. It was averred for the defendant, and moved in arrest of judgment that the plaintiff had made no title to Blackacre, which was the *terminus ad quem*, which he ought at least to have laid.

For the plaintiff was cited Palmer 420, Latch 110, 3 Bulstr. 344; 1 Sidderfin 167, Palmer and Plashee, Winch's, *Entries*, 1125; Rastall 616.[2]

---

[1] *Johnson, ex dem. Earl of Anglesey v. Earl of Derby* (Ex. 1707–1710), see above, Case No. 287.

[2] *Harrison v. Rooke* (1625), Palmer 420, 81 E.R 1151, Latch 110, 82 E.R. 299, 3 Bulstrode 334, 81 E.R. 277, also Benloe 160, 73 E.R. 1025; *Palmer v. Fleshees* (1663), 1 Siderfin 167, 227, 82 E.R. 1035, 1073, H. Winch, *Entries* (1680), 1125, also 1 Levinz

For the defendant was cited 2 Modern rep. 318,[1] and, if the plaintiff has no property or possession, there is no damage to him by the stopping.

But the court, upon consideration of the case and of the authority of 2 Levins 148, 266, held it not necessary in an action upon the case that the plaintiff should show any title to the *locus ad quem etc.*[2] And so the plaintiff had judgment.

[Other copies of this report: Georgetown Univ. Law Sch. MS. B88–10, p. 747, pl. 2.]

360

Dawson v. Nicholson

(Ex. 1710)

Where a sentence in an ecclesiastical court has been affirmed by the Court of Delegates, the parties cannot thereafter attack the jurisdiction of the ecclesiastical court, having submitted to it.

Lincoln's Inn MS. Misc. 538, f. [129], pl. 2

The steeple of Woodford Church in Essex was greatly decayed, and a rate was made for the repair thereof under the title of repair of the church. But the decay of the steeple was so great that it could not be repaired without wholly taking it down, which was done accordingly. And [it was] newly built. But the new built one was made larger and something beyond the foundation of the old steeple.

And the plaintiff here being sued in the ecclesiastical court for not paying his rate, it was so far proceeded therein that there was a sentence against the plaintiff and [it was] affirmed by the Delegates. And now, he prayed a [writ of] prohibition, suggesting the rate was not made by the major part of the parishioners as it ought to be. 1 Ventr. 267; Poph. 197; Roll's, *Proh.*, 291; 2 Mod. 222; Hetley [*blank*] Robert's Case.[3]

But, more especially, it was insisted upon that the enlargement of the steeple was not within the power or jurisdiction of the ordinary to compel what is, for the necessary repairs of the church and steeple is within their jurisdiction, but to enlarge a church or steeple beyond the old foundation is not.

122, 83 E.R. 329, T. Raymond 87, 83 E.R. 48, 1 Keble 553, 625, 794, 836, 83 E.R. 1108, 1149, 1247, 1272; W. Rastell, *Entries.*

[1] *Scoble v. Skelton* (1682), 2 Modern 318, 86 E.R. 1097, also Skinner 36, 90 E.R. 18, 2 Shower K.B. 195, 89 E.R. 886.

[2] *St. John v. Moody* (1675), 2 Levinz 148, 83 E.R. 492, also 1 Ventris 274, 86 E.R. 184, 3 Keble 528, 531, 84 E.R. 860, 862.

[3] *Anonymous* (1675), 1 Ventris 267, 86 E.R. 179; *Anonymous* (1626), Popham 197, 79 E.R. 1288; 2 Rolle, Abr., *Prohibition*, section K, p. 291; *Rogers v. Davenant* (1677), 2 Modern 222, 86 E.R. 1038, also 1 Modern 194, 236, 86 E.R. 823, 852, T. Jones 89, 84 E.R. 1161; *Roberts' Case*, Hetley 61, 124 E.R. 343.

Northey, for the defendant, did not take upon him[self] to justify the ecclesiastical court's power to enlarge the steeple, but insisted upon it, first, that that was not alleged or contested below nor within the pleadings, secondly, that the prohibition is prayed too late, being after a sentence and confirmed upon an appeal, and the plaintiff had submitted to the jurisdiction. And he laid this down for a rule that, where it does not appear in the face of the libel that the court has no jurisdiction of the cause, then, after sentence, no prohibition is to go.

The court denied the prohibition because [it was] after a sentence affirmed by the Delegates, as the Queen's Bench had done.

But it seems the rule laid down that the defect of jurisdiction must appear in the libel, else no prohibition after sentence is not [. . .] for the libel may contain a cause within the jurisdiction. But, if a *modus* [*decimandi*] be alleged and not allowed, a prohibition lies after sentence, and so upon any other ground where, upon the pleadings, it shall appear the ecclesiastical court has not a proper jurisdiction or shall refuse a proper plea, it may be true that, where the defendant admits the jurisdiction by pleading and submitting to it, no prohibition goes after sentence unless, by the libel, [it] appears there is no jurisdiction of the court, like in Admiralty. 2 Brownl., Jennings and Awdley; Baxter and Hope, etc.[1]

[Other copies of this report: Georgetown Univ. Law Sch. MS. B88–10, p. 748.]

361

Worthy, qui tam v. Levy

(Ex. 1710)

In this case for import duties for silk, the cause of action was properly pleaded against the defendant.

Lincoln's Inn MS. Misc. 538, f. [130v]

Trinity term 1710. *Ex parte* Queen's Remembrancer.

The plaintiff, in Easter term 8 Anne, exhibited an information grounded upon the Act 11 & 12 Will. III, ca. 10,[2] showing that, between the first of June last and the time of the exhibiting of that information, 51 *pec[ia] stuffur operata cum serico vocata* sufas *de manufactur' Indiarum oriental' in partibus transmarinis et in Indiis oriental' praedict' operat'* were imported into England, *viz.* to Ratcliff in the port of London, that the defendant well knowing the said goods between the times aforesaid had and retained and in his custody had, the said goods were

[1] *Jennings v. Audley* (1611), 2 Brownlow & Goldesborough 30, 123 E.R. 797; *Baxter v. Hopes* (1611), 2 Brownlow & Goldesborough 30, 123 E.R. 797.

[2] Stat. 11 Will. III, c. 3 (*SR*, VII, 582–586); Stat. 11 Will. III, c. 10 (*SR*, VII, 598–599).

found at Ratcliff out of any warehouse approved by the Commissioners of the Customs for keeping the said goods according to the form of the Statute, these goods not being *operatus, anglice* made up and used in any garment or furniture before the 29th of September 1701 *contra formam statuti* in that case made and provided with an averment that the Commissioners of the Customs before the said 29th of September had appointed warehouses for the receipt of all goods of the manufacture of Persia, China, or the East Indies that then were or should be imported into England according to the form of that Statute, and so prays the judgment of the court and that the defendant, for his said offense might forfeit £200 and that he might have two third parts thereof according to the form of the Statute etc.

The defendant pleads not guilty of anything charged against him by the information *contra formam statuti*. And, upon a trial, there was a verdict for the queen and the informer last term.

And it was this term [Trinity 1710] moved in arrest of judgment by *Phipps et al.* that the offense charged by this information is not the same with that created by the Act of Parliament which respects and provides only against all wrought silks, Bengals, and stuffs mixed with silk or herba of the manufacture of Persia, China, or East India, to which the words of the information do not extend, for, by the Act, they must be wrought stuffs mixed with herba and of the manufacture of Persia, China, or the Indies and the information describes these to be stuffs *operata cum serico vocata* sufas of the manufacture of the East Indies without any *anglice* to the word '*operata*', which is by no means to be construed mixed but only wrought, which answers the first part of the description, which is wrought stuffs, for so they must and are described to be. And, though, afterwards, they are laid in the information to be wrought in the East Indies, that will not supply the former defect of laying them to be wrought stuffs because the Act provides they must be of the manufacture of the East Indies etc. and so the Act prescribes a double qualification, *viz.* they must be wrought silks and also of the manufacture of the East Indies etc. And, if so, then both the words '*operata*' in the information are properly applied to these two qualifications in the Act. And, then, there wants a word in the information to express them to be mixed with herba, for *operata* can never (at least without an *anglice*) be construed mixed, for there is a proper word for mixed, *viz. misto* or *mixto*. And, then, a term for which there is a proper Latin word neither can nor ought to be construed to signify another term for which also there is a proper significant word. And, therefore, if, for the reasons before, the word 'mixed' in the Act is not comprised in the information, then the information is not pursuant to nor warranted by the Act. And, therefore, no judgment can be given for the penalty of £200 to be incurred by the defendant.

It was much stood upon by the Attorney General [*Montagu*] and others that the words '*operata cum serico vocata* sufas' must be understood in the nature of the thing to import to be mixed with silk because, if the stuff was wrought with silk, it must of necessity be mixed with silk. And, then, it is all one as if the word 'mixed' had been in the information, which is tantamount and specially being after verdict when the jury have given a verdict upon the information which concludes *contra formam statuti* and so all that can be intended to make it an offense against the Statute is found. The word '*murdravite*' implies malice, and the word *furate* implies *felonice cepit*; Dyer 68, 69. And, where the conclusion is *contra formam statuti*, it supplies many defects; Dy. 312.[1]

And to this opinion, PRICE and LOVELL inclined, and were of opinion that the plaintiff should have judgment.

But BURY and myself [EDWARD WARD] were of opinion for the defendants for the reasons before mentioned and upon consideration of these cases, Dy. 183, pl. 59; 1 Anderson, fo. 49; and 11 rep. 58, where, in an information for usury, though it plainly appeared by it that the defendant took above 10 percent and the information concluded *contra formam statuti*, yet judgment [was] reversed and that [was] affirmed in error because it was not laid to be by a corrupt contract, as the words of the Act[2] are, and they must be expressly alleged, and not by implication, for, though the taking more for usury contrary to the Statute must imply corrupt means, else [it is] not contrary to the Statute, yet it must be laid in the words. 10 Hen. VII, fo. 10; and Pitcher and Jones' Case, Hardres, fo. 217, where that information laid that spices of the growth of Asia, Africa, or America were brought from Holland, not being the place where the goods are usually shipped for transportation *contra formam statuti* and a verdict for the plaintiff [was given], yet judgment was arrested because [it was] not alleged not to be of the growth of Holland, though that might be fairly implied, it being before said they were of the growth of Asia etc., but no implication will serve their turn.[3]

The like [case is] Cro. Car. 464,[4] an indictment for beating, wounding, and evil entreating a man in the churchyard *contra formam statuti* [was] not good because [he was] not said to be armed with a weapon or weapon drawn, which are the words of the Act. *Vide* Dy. 363, 25; *contra formam statuti* supplies not substance.[5] And, here, no stuffs are prohibited but wrought stuffs mixed etc.

At the first motion in arrest of judgment in the principal case, the defendant's counsel not having fully stated the case to the court, there was a rule for

---

[1] *Rex v. Buckler* (1551), 1 Dyer 68, 73 E.R. 145; *Dawson v. Alford* (1572), 3 Dyer 312, 73 E.R. 706.

[2] Stat. 12 Car. II, c. 13 (*SR*, V, 236–237).

[3] *Anonymous* (1560), 2 Dyer 183, 73 E.R. 404, also Jenkins 221, 145 E.R. 152, 11 Coke Rep. 37, 77 E.R. 1193; *Emmot, qui tam v. Fulwood* (1575), 1 Anderson 49, 123 E.R. 347; *Shoyle v. Foster* (1614), 11 Coke Rep. 56, 77 E.R. 1222, 1 Rolle Rep. 88, 81 E.R. 349, 2 Bulstrode 324, 80 E.R. 1158; YB Mich. 10 Hen. VII, f. 10, pl. 25 (1494); *Pitcher v. Jones* (1661), Hardres 217, 145 E.R. 461.

[4] *Rex v. Cholmley* (1636), Croke Car. 464, 79 E.R. 1002.

[5] *Anonymous* (1579), 3 Dyer 363a, 73 E.R. 815, also Jenkins 243, 145 E.R. 171.

judgment for the plaintiff *nisi*, at which day, upon further argument, the court was divided *ut supra*, so no rule could be given then for entering or arresting judgment nor for discharging the former rule for judgment *nisi*. The court could now make no rule in it, but left the plaintiff to do as he could by law and to enter judgment if, by the rules of law and the court, he could do so without other direction from the court.

This £200 is a penalty besides the forfeiture of the goods.

[Other copies of this report: Georgetown Univ. Law Sch. MS. B88–10, p. 752.]

Harvard Law Sch. MS. 537, pt. 2, p. 159, pl. 2

This was an information upon 11 & 12 Will. III,[1] which enacts that all wrought silks and bengals and stuffs made in Persia, China, or the East Indies or silk or helba or mixed therewith etc. should pay a duty of 15 percent. And there was a verdict for the queen.

It was moved in arrest of judgment by *Phipps*. The information was for importing several pieces etc. *operatus cum serico etc.* and, being brought, was found in the custody of the defendant.

Objection: The words of the act are not pursued, and penal laws are to be taken strictly, and the words are to be pursued. In Dyer 183, pl. 59, *tantament coordarum* was not sufficient upon 4 & 5 P. & M.; so Peacher and Jones' Case, in Hardr., upon the Act of Navigation,[2] where the information was for importing thirty-two bags of spices and being of the growth of Asia, Africa, or America from Holland *contra formam statuti* after a verdict and motion for arrest of judgment because they were not all of the growth of Holland, though implied [is] sufficient, there is an *anglice*. Indeed, in another part of it which says '*anglice* mixed with silk', but an *anglice* shall not carry the words to another signification, especially when that signification might have been expressed in proper words, and '*operatus*' does not signify mixed. And there is a proper word for it. And then, in another place [it is] right *minime operatus, anglice* not made up.

Another distinct part of the Act says that, if [it is] imported and not entered, then [it is] forfeited. And, now, it appears no entry was made of them, and so they were forfeited under the other part.

Attorney General [*Montagu*] and Mr. *Turner e contra*: '*Operatus cum serico*' is more agreeable to the intent of the Act than 'mixed', for it might be only mixed as there being two or three parcels amongst others, and the meaning of the Act is mixed in the working. He agrees, if a man will, an information [lies] upon an

---

1 Stat. 11 Will. III, c. 3 (*SR*, VII, 582–586); Stat. 11 Will. III, c. 10 (*SR*, VII, 598–599).

2 *Anonymous* (1560), *ut supra*; Stat. 4 & 5 Phil. & Mar., c. 4 (*SR*, IV, 322); *Pitcher v. Jones* (1661), *ut supra*; Stat. 12 Car. II, c. 18, s. 8 (*SR*, V, 248).

Act of Parliament. He must make his case within it, and he thinks '*operatus cum serico*' is a sufficient expression of the sense of the Act.

As to that objection of the venues nowhere laid as to the app[. . .] of the [. . .], he thinks that is not necessary since 4 Anne, for the Amendment of the Law.[1]

Turner: It is true, where a matter of fact is not alleged in the information, it shall not be supplied, as in the [. . .], the court shall not take notice whether Holland is not in Asia or no without being alleged, but that is not the question here. Here it is sufficiently alleged, for, if the fact has been sufficiently well alleged, it has always been held so, so, in courts it is adjudged that the breach not be all in the precise words of the covenant, Cro. Car. [. . .], but, where we make use of it to another purpose, it has.

As to the objection that we have not said the goods were entered and that they are two several clauses and no ways relate, it is after a verdict, and a great many things are intended after a verdict [. . .] in an information. Cro. Jac. 609.[2]

[It was said] by *Phipps* malice was implied in the case in Dyer and men shall not be subject to punishment by construction or intendment and that the reason here there should have been an entry laid, and 4 & 5 [Anne], Amendment of the Law, does not say there shall be no venue laid.

BURY: They lay the venue now generally within the county.

WARD: The law is not so nice in a case of forfeitures as in a case of cr[. . .].

Et adjornatur.

Harvard Law Sch. MS. 537, pt. 2, p. 172

I [Eden] did not hear LOVELL, but he gave his opinion for the plaintiff, and so PRICE. I was present at the end of his argument. And he said '*operatus*', it seems has a double meaning, made up and wrought in the piece and made up as sewed together and made into anything. In the latter case, there is an *anglice* 'made up'. Therefore, he thinks that there being no *anglice* in the first place, it must be intended to have the other meaning, *viz.* wrought up. And this is after a verdict. And, if it had not upon the trial appeared to be mixed with silk, *viz.* wrought up, it must have gone against the crown. And, likewise, since it has a double meaning, after a verdict, it must be intended as the Act of Parliament requires it, especially since the information concludes *contra formam statuti*.

BURY: *Operatus cum serico* having no *anglice*, he cannot see it necessarily implies mixed with silk in the manufacture. He rather thinks it implies otherwise, having no *anglice*. And, if it signify made up in the garments, he thinks it should have had an *anglice* in the first place.

---

[1] Stat. 4 & 5 Ann., c. 3, s. 13 (*SR*, VIII, 459).

[2] *Gerrard v. Wright* (1621), Croke Jac. 607, 609, 79 E.R. 518, 520, also W. Jones 2, 82 E.R. 2, Hobart 306, 80 E.R. 449.

WARD: He never knew that *contra formam statuti* signified anything, nor that it concluded anything at all if the Statute, as laid in the information, did not come up to what was to make an offense within the Statute, though after a verdict. *Operatus* is properly for the word 'wrought'. Now '*operatus*' must be amiss in one place. Here is but the word *operatus* in both places. And he cannot make it serve both. And, in all cases, if the Latin word has a doubtful signification, it must have an *anglice*. But, if there is a more proper Latin word, it must be taken. He takes the case of Pitcher and Jones, in [. . .] to be stronger than this, and, there, he held *contra formam statuti* helped nothing, because it is the statute, and not the verdict of the jury, that makes the offense. Cro. Car. 464; there judgment was arrested after a verdict though *contra formam statuti* was there; so 1 Anderson, fo. 49, and 5 Rept. 58; so Dyer 68, 69.[1] And, here, there is no word to signify mixed, and that must be in. And he does not think it is helped by *contra formam statuti*.

PRICE said he took Pitcher and Jones' Case to be somewhat extraordinary.

WARD: It was because the words of the Act were not pursued. And it is not fit we should take upon ourselves to vary from the words as we plead.

It was then debated what should be done, seeing the court was divided. But [judgment was] given for the crown. But query if this may not be prevented by having rules to show cause why judgment should not be arrested etc.

362

Attorney General v. Kempston

(Ex. 1710)

A surety of a fidelity bond has the burden to show that his principal has faithfully discharged his office.

Lincoln's Inn MS. Misc. 538, f. [141v]

John Parker and the defendant [William Kempston] with one Molineux, 3 Anne, became bound to the queen jointly and severally in £1000 conditioned that, whereas the Commissioners for Prizes had appointed Parker one of the agents in the port of Falmouth, if the said Parker did not commit any waste or embezzlement upon or of any ship, vessel, or goods brought as prize into that port and did not nor should do in any other acts (in the negative) and there were affirmative clauses and things to be observed and done by Parker.

The defendant, who is but a surety and not privy to Parker's actings, pleads that Parker, at any time after the making of that bond and before the day of exhibiting that information, did not commit any waste nor did any of the things

[1] *Rex v. Cholmley* (1637), Croke Car. 464, 79 E.R. 1002; *Emmot, qui tam v. Fulwood* (1575), 1 Anderson 49, 123 E.R. 347; *Rex v. Buckler* (1551), 1 Dyer 68, 73 E.R. 145.

(showing the particulars *prout* the condition) that are in the negative and that he had performed all the things in the affirmative *prout* the condition, showing the particulars how. And he prays judgment.

The Attorney General [*Northey*] demurs for two causes:

First, because the defendant has not showed in his plea how long Parker continued in that office so that the court might judge whether Parker had performed all things in the condition during his continuance in the office;

Secondly, because the defendant did not show in his plea what were the directions and instructions which Parker had and received from the Commissioners of the Prizes so that the court might judge whether Parker had performed his office in the matters and things therein contained according to such directions and instructions.

The defendant having pleaded as to that part that Parker had duly executed that office in all matters and things thereto belonging according to such directions and instructions as he from time to time received from the Commissioners of the Prizes, and [it is] not shown the instructions, as in strictness he ought, judgment for the queen [was given] *nisi causa* last Wednesday in term, no counsel appearing for the defendant.

And it seems a hard case upon sureties, yet, though this be the case of a surety, who is not supposed [to be] privy to the constitution or instructions to the officer, yet, since he undertook for the officer, he must enable himself at his peril to make it out that the officer has truly observed and done all that is expressed in the condition of the bond.

But, afterwards, within the term, the Commissioners of the Treasurer directed the Attorney [General] to stay all proceedings until further order. And so no judgment was entered this term, it not be[ing] shown that Parker was dead or insolvent.

[Other copies of this report: Georgetown Univ. Law Sch. MS. B88–10, p. 813.]

363

Anonymous

(Ex. 1710)

A court cannot increase court costs beyond what is taxed even though more was actually spent by the successful party.

Lincoln's Inn MS. Misc. 538, f. [142v]

Upon the Lottery Act, an informer brings an action of debt *qui tam* in the Office of Pleas against the defendant for the recovery of £500 for keeping a lottery contrary to the Statute of 10 & 11 Will. III, ca. 17, which directs the penalty to be divided into three parts, *viz.* one to the king, one to the poor of the parish, and a third to the informer and he to recover double costs.[1]

There was here judgment entered for want of a plea, the defendant, being a poor French refugee, refusing to plead. And costs were taxed at £5. Execution by [a writ of] *fieri facias* issued, and there was levied £24, which was brought into court.

And, upon hearing the Attorney General [*Northey*] and the defendant's counsel, the court ordered that the informer should have his £5 costs and the poundage of the sheriff first paid him and, then, the residue to be paid in thirds, as the Act directs, for, though the informer might spend more money in the prosecution than £5, yet that being the sum taxed, the court could not enlarge them.

[Other copies of this report: Georgetown Univ. Law Sch. MS. B88–10, p. 819, pl. 1.]

364

Roberts v. Hughes

(Ex. 1710)

A plaintiff who had a verdict as to the principal sum due but not as to the interest thereupon can be nonsuited and have a new trial, but he cannot accept the verdict, and have a new trial as to interest only.

Lincoln's Inn MS. Misc. 538, f. [144]

The plaintiff, as an executor, brought an [action of] *indebitatus assumpsit* against the defendant as an executrix. And, upon a trial before Justice Dormer, [the plaintiff] had a verdict. But the jury, contrary to the direction of the judge, did not think fit to give any interest for the non-payment of the money due upon a note under hand only. And they were sent out again by the judge, but they would not find anything for that. So the plaintiff took the verdict, and, now, moved for a new trial upon the certificate of the judge signified to one of the barons of the court that he thought it was fit for a new trial upon the ground that the jury did give their verdict against the direction of the court in the point of interest.

And, now, *Lechmere*, one of the Queen's Counsel, for the defendant, opposed the granting of a new trial at the plaintiff's prayer, who had a verdict for him. And, if he thought he had not damages sufficient (of which the jury are the sole judges), he might (by leave of court at least) have been nonsuited. But it is without precedent that a plaintiff who has a verdict in an action for damages only shall pray and have a new trial because the jury (as he conceives) give him too little damages which he might have prevented by being nonsuited, which wholly dif-

[1] Stat. 10 Will. III, c. 23 (*SR*, VII, 532–533).

fers from the case of a defendant's having a verdict against him, which he could not prevent.

The court in this case gave all the respect imaginable to the judge's report, and took it to be his opinion that the plaintiff had not what he ought to have by the verdict, but did not conceive that the plaintiff, who perceived the opinion of the jury to be against him as to interest and would not be nonsuited but took the verdict, was entitled to a new trial in this case, where the question was only as to the interest, which is damages only and the jury is the judge of them, and the case is between executors on both sides.

And *Northey*, Attorney General, as *amicus curiae*, informed the court that the Court of the King's Bench was wholly of the opinion in such a case as this between Stephens and Ettrick[1] that the plaintiff ought not to have a new trial.

And I [Edward Ward] put this case to Parker, Chief Justice of the Queen's Bench, and Powys, Justice of the same court, and they were both of the opinion no new trial ought to be had in this case.

Neverthe[less], the court gave a day to the plaintiff to produce precedents, if he could, of any new trials granted in the like case. But none being produced, the new trial was denied. The Case of Stevens and Ettrick is reported in Shower's Reports, fo. 63.

There are cases where a plaintiff that has a verdict may pray that it may be quashed, but that is when it is wholly uncertain and defective or that the judgment upon it must be erroneous. 18 Edw. III, 55; Cheney's Case, 10 rep. 119; Benthem's Case, 11 rep. [*blank*]; 2 Roll's, Abr., 721; Roll's, *Continuance*, 487.[2] But these cases carry their reasons with them, which none of them hold in this case, where there is no defect, but [it is] a complete verdict. *Vide* Hardress, fo. 219, leave was given to a defendant to enter up the plaintiff's judgment where the plaintiff would not [for] small damages.[3]

28 November, [it was] moved that the defendant may have, first, the surplus money above what [was] recovered that was brought into court may be had out; secondly, the defendant may have his costs; thirdly, the defendant may have liberty to enter up the judgment if the plaintiff will not. Hardress 219, accord.

Objection: The plaintiff is an executor, and so ought to pay costs, being not the possession or property of the plaintiff but purely testamentable.

---

[1] *Stephens v. Etterick* (1689), 1 Shower K.B. 63, 89 E.R. 450, also Carthew 86, 90 E.R. 654, Comberbach 170, 90 E.R. 411, Holt K.B. 155, 90 E.R. 983.

[2] YB Mich. 18 Edw. III, f. 55, pl. 73 (1344); *Cheyney's Case* (1612), 10 Coke Rep. 118, 77 E.R. 1106; *Marsh v. Bentham* (1614), 11 Coke Rep. 56, 77 E.R. 1222, also 2 Bulstrode 279, 80 E.R. 1122, 1 Rolle Rep. 88, 81 E.R. 348, Jenkins 286, 145 E.R. 207; 2 Rolle, Abr., *Triall*, '*Venire facias de novo*', p. 721; *Thorpe v. Davenant* (1641–1642), 1 Rolle, Abr., *Continuance*, Pl. D, 1, p. 487.

[3] *Andrews v. Anonymous* (Ex. 1661), Hardres 219, 145 E.R. 462.

By *Grove*: 2 Cro. 29, ravishment *tempore* testator, seizure after, no costs; Hutton 78; 1 Jones 341; Eckinham and Glasier, in [an action of] trespass this term; *post mortem* intestate that were the goods of the intestate, no costs.[1]

Allows the [costs]: Thorpe and Davenant, Roll's, *Continuance*, 487, the defendant to enter judgment, leave to enter it by the court, no authority, no experience by Marriot as to the rule for bringing money into court and defendants. The court will consider touching money out of court and a defendant's entry of judgment.

[Other copies of this report: Georgetown Univ. Law Sch. MS. B88–10, p. 825.]

365

Dowall v. Brewster

(Ex. 1710)

A suit to perpetuate evidence will not be dismissed until after the death of the witness who was examined.

Lincoln's Inn MS. Misc. 538, f. [144v]

The plaintiff [Sir Thomas Dowall], being an inhabitant and owner of divers houses in Aldgate parish whereof the defendant is the impropriator lying part in London where tithes are by 37 Hen. VIII[2] to be 2s. 9d. in the pound and part in Middlesex where tithes are laid to be due by custom, and the plaintiff apprehending or being threatened to be sued by the defendant for tithes of those houses, exhibited his bill in this court to examine his witnesses *in perpetuam rei memoriam* to make out his discharge from the payment of tithes by some *modus*es or otherwise. And he prayed not any relief, but only the examination of his witnesses to preserve their testimonies.

The defendant answered, and the plaintiff replied, and witnesses were examined. And, because the plaintiff did not proceed to publication or bring his cause to a hearing, the defendant moved the court to dismiss the plaintiff's bill for want of prosecution or, at least, that the defendant may have his costs he has sustained in that cause. And whether there should be any such dismission or costs was the question.

And it was afterwards enquired into how it was practiced in Chancery. And nothing was found that such a bill to perpetuate testimonies was ever dismissed or publication passed until after the death of the witnesses [who were] examined.

---

1 *Mackworth v. Shipward* (1604), Croke Jac. 27, 79 E.R. 21; *Townley v. Steele* (1626), Hutton 78, 123 E.R. 1113; *Todderidge v. Mackalley* (1634), W. Jones 341, 82 E.R. 180, also Croke Car. 337, 353, 361, 79 E.R. 895, 910, 915.

2 Stat. 37 Hen. VIII, c. 12 (*SR*, III, 998–1000).

But this seems to make the witnesses' perjury dispunishable.

[Other copies of this report: Georgetown Univ. Law Sch. MS. B88–10, p. 827.]

366

Jones, qui tam v. Locker

(Ex. 1710)

Carrying letters at no charge is not a violation of the Post Office Act.

Lincoln's Inn MS. Misc. 538, f. [145], pl. 1

Easter 9 [Anne]. *Ex parte* Queen's Remembrancer.

This information, intended to be grounded upon the Act 12 Car. II, ca. 35, for erecting a post office,[1] sets forth that, at such a time and place and for forty days after, the defendant [Elizabeth Locker] at such a place (naming them) without any authority from the queen or the Postmaster General or his deputy and without any authority whatsoever sounded a bell and, by reason thereof and by a great vociferation obtained and had from divers of the queen's subjects ten letters upon each of the four days there mentioned, amounting in all to forty letters *ad carriandum* to the general post office in London at such a parish there *contra formam statuti*.

But the statute extending only to such as carry letters for hire and those words not being in the information, the court arrested the judgment, for to carry for hire being the essence of the offense, the finding of the jury or the words '*contra formam statuti*' in the information helps not the want of substance.

[Other copies of this report: Georgetown Univ. Law Sch. MS. B88–10, p. 797.]

367

Bower v. Forte

(Ex. 1710)

A landowner cannot be compelled to contribute to the construction of a gallery within the parish church.

A majority cannot lay a tax upon other persons unless it be for things of a public and not of a private concern.

[1] Stat. 12 Car. II, c. 35 (*SR*, V, 297–301).

Lincoln's Inn MS. Misc. 538, f. [145v], pl. 1

[There was a] libel in the ecclesiastical court of Exeter by the defendant as churchwarden of the parish of Burlescomb [Devonshire] against the plaintiff to compel him to pay a rate upon land for the erecting of a gallery in the church by license from the ordinary.

And *Ward* and *Dodd* pray a [writ of] prohibition upon a suggestion, first, that to erect a gallery, though by the ordinary's license, is not of ecclesiastical conusance nor power, second, that, if it was, yet the rate demanded is an old rate in the parish and not a rate newly made for this purpose nor is it by the consent of the major part.

Ward: The ordinary's [jurisdiction] extends not to new erections but to disposing of seats. [It is a] mixed jurisdiction. Roll's, [Abr.], *Reperation*. All parishioners must be equally rated. 1 Mod. 236; a tax for repairing a church and chancel is bad because one is not a charge on the parishioners. This matter is not a reparation, but a new charge for a new erection [and] out of the ordinary's power. Noy [*blank*], against the rate [. . .]; [it] must be *ex re nata*.[1]

Dodd: [As to a] license to erect a gallery at the charge of the parishioners, this is neither a repair or an ornament. No necessity [is] surmised, only convenience. 3 & 4 Will. & Mar.; united churches, [and] the inhabitants were obliged to repairs and ornaments.[2] And this is neither. Prohibition [lies] for rates about communion tables. The rate here is not just. It ought to be a new, and not an old, rate [for those] who wanted convenient seats to sit and kneel in.

[Other copies of this report: Georgetown Univ. Law Sch. MS. B88–10, p. 799.]

Lincoln's Inn MS. Misc. 538, f. [147v]

Upon several libels, the plaintiffs pray prohibitions in all. The defendant [churchwarden of Burlescomb, County Devon] libels in the ecclesiastical court of Exeter against the plaintiff Bower to compel him to pay 6d. a rate for six rates for his estates in that parish held by him [in] 1705 and 1706 agreed to be raised by the common consent of the parishioners or the major part of them towards building and erecting a loft or gallery in the church, twenty feet long, fifteen feet broad, for the more convenient placing the parishioners there, who wanted convenient seats to sit in and kneel in time of divine service at the public costs and charges of the parishioners. It was agreed by the major and better part of the parishioners that this gallery should be so erected at the public charge of the parish in general and that it should be raised according to the ancient rate and proportion of the parish where, for several years past, there was a standing rate used to be gathered

[1] 2 Rolle, Abr., *Prohibition*, section K, p. 291; *Rogers v. Davenant* (1677), 1 Modern 194, 236, 86 E.R. 823, 852, also 2 Modern 222, 86 E.R. 1038, T. Jones 89, 84 E.R. 1161; *Carleton v. Hutton*, Noy 78, 74 E.R. 1045.

[2] Stat. 4 Will. & Mar., c. 12 (*SR*, VI, 393).

by in all times as the necessity of the church should require. And the parishioners always paid the sums rated therein upon their respective estates. Six pence was a single rate for the plaintiff's estates held by him there. And the six rates making 3s. are still due, the gallery being erected, which all or most of the parishioners well approve and have paid their rates. [There are] the like libels against several other parishioners.

The plaintiff, for a prohibition, suggests that, by the laws of the land, no levy or demand of money upon the parishioners of any parish in England by any churchwarden without notice first to be given to the parishioners under pretense of a parish rate or assessment with the consent of the parishioners or the major part of them first made and allowed to authorize the levying or demand thereof ought to be made. No parishioner ought to be charged by levies to erect galleries in their parish churches without his own consent. By law, every rate ought to be by the consent of the major part of the parishioners present for the occasion, and none ought to be collected by an ancient standing rate. This had been moved in the Queen's Bench this term, and a prohibition was denied.

Yet, by Chief Baron [EDWARD WARD], BURY, and LOVELL (*dissentiente* PRICE), the defendant [was] to show cause the first day next term why a prohibition ought not to be granted and, in the meantime, all proceedings in the ecclesiastical court are stayed against the plaintiff Bowyer and the other parishioners against whom the like libels are exhibited and who have put in the like suggestions.

These things are plain:

First, the soil of the church and the yard are the freehold of the parson, and the ordinary [can]not license to bury;

Second, the use and repairs of the church are common to all of the parishioners;

Third, the disposal and placing of parishioners in seats belongs to the ordinary (where [there is] no right by prescription in others) to avoid confusion;

Fourth, churchwardens, by custom, may place and displace;

Fifth, seats append to a house, 1 Inst. 121, 122; Noy 78;[1]

Sixth, priority of sitting [is] by prescription. Godolphin, 140, 146.[2]

The case, in short, is this. The major part of the parishioners of a parish apply to the bishop of the diocese for leave to erect a gallery in their church for placing some of the parishioners who, as it is alleged, wanted convenient seats to sit and kneel in time of divine service. And they agreed that the gallery should be erected at the public charge of the parish in general and to be raised according to the ancient rate and proportion of the parish where, for several [years] past, there was a standing rate used to be gathered by in all times as the necessity of the church

[1] E. Coke, *First Institute* (1628), ff. 121, 122; *Carleton v. Hutton*, Noy 78, 74 E.R. 1045.

[2] J. Godolphin, *Repertorium Canonicum*.

should require and the parishioners always paid after those rates. And the gallery is built. And the major part of the parishioners have paid their rates, except the plaintiffs in the prohibition, who refuse, showing what rates theirs are. And to compel the payment of them, the churchwardens libel in the ecclesiastical court. And a prohibition is prayed upon suggestions that, by the law of England, no rate or levy ought to be made nor demanded of money upon any parishioners by any churchwarden without notice first given to the parishioners under the pretense of a parish rate or assessment with the consent of the major part of them to authorize the levying or demand thereof.

Secondly, no parishioner ought to be charged by levies to erect galleries in their parish churches without his own consent.

Thirdly, by law, every rate ought to be by the consent of the major part of the parishioners present for the occasion, and none ought to be collected by an ancient standing rate.

First, it does not appear in this case there was any occasion for the erecting of this gallery for want of seats for any parishioners in the body of the church. The occasion alleged for erecting it is only for the more convenient placing of the parishioners there who wanted convenient seats to sit and kneel in, so that all is tied up to convenience. And it does not appear that the bishop has made any enquiry whether any seats are wanted or made any judgment of the convenience; that seems only to be done by the parishioners. And no complaint was made by any particular parishioner for want of a seat or a convenient one.

Second, doubtless, the bishop has the power to compel the churchwardens to repair the church and support the fabric of it and to provide ornaments and to order and dispose the placing of parishioners in seats in their church (not meddling with such as have seats by prescription which they are bound to repair or to displace any who or whose ancestors or predecessors in respect of any house have used to sit uppermost or in any other certain place in a seat), but it must be considered that the bishop has not any power to compel churchwardens, at the parish charge, to erect new seats for any parishioners that want, but such as do want may have a faculty (as the general usage is) from the bishop at their own charge to erect seats in the body of the church and to sit in them exclusive to any others, but not in fee, what reason have the other inhabitants who have seats of their own to contribute to the new erecting of others that want; they cannot be reimbursed by any payment to be made by the sitters. As to the fabric of the church and ornaments, they are of public concern and touch every parishioner, the first as to a rate upon lands, the ornaments touch only the inhabitants in respect of their personalities and residences in the parish.

Foreigners, owners of land, are not liable to repairs of seats in the church nor for ornaments. Godolphin 150; 2 Brownl. [*blank*]; Moor [*blank*], prohibition granted after a sentence and appeal for a tax for re-edifying seats pulled down, to which [it was] never assented; Hetly 61.[1]

Thirdly, it is without precedent that ever a tax was laid by the majority of the parishioners to erect a gallery or seats for such of the inhabitants as either have no seats or what are not thought convenient seats at a public charge nor can there be any reason at law for it. It is to raise a tax by a subject upon a subject for a private use; to allow such a tax may be greatly inconvenient without consent and upon due notice as tending to the oppression of many parishioners when they happen to be the minority. A great man and his tenants, being the majority, may think his seat not convenient or not in a convenient place and may compliment him[self] with a fine gallery at the charge of others *et sic vice versa*.

By law, no majority of subjects can lay a tax upon other subjects unless it be for things of a public and not of a private concern, as this is.

All the cases go to the repairs of the fabric [or] ornaments as to the ordinary's jurisdiction.

Fourthly, this tax new laid is irregular, for it is laid by an old rate made for church affairs many years ago. And, then, it might be an equal rate according to the values of the lands, but it can hardly be so now because of the changes which must necessarily happen in the course of so many years. And every rate must be proportionable upon the view and consideration of the present occasion. A rate made *in perpetuis temporibus duratura* is not good.

The prohibition went and stood in this case.

[Other copies of this report: Georgetown Univ. Law Sch. MS. B88–10, p. 808.]

Harvard Law Sch. MS. 537, pt. 2, p. 177

The case of the parish of Burscombe in Devonshire, it was this. The parishioners, finding it necessary to have a gallery in their church, by a majority of them, assess a rate towards the building of it. One of them refuses to pay this rate, upon which there was a libel in the spiritual court. And to that, [a writ of] prohibition was prayed. And the question was whether the spiritual court had a jurisdiction in this matter.

N.B. They had first of all a license for that purpose of building from the ordinary.

Dodd [and] *Ward* [said] that a [writ of] prohibition should go. They cited Roll, tit. *Prohibition*, 288; 1 Modern 236; Noy 41.[2]

Chief Baron WARD [held] that it should go, that the ordinary had only *jus disponendi*, not *erigendi*. And, though he had jurisdiction as to the repairs of the church, yet building could not be called repairs. And he did not look upon a gal-

[1] J. Godolphin, *Repertorium Canonicum*; *Roberts' Case*, Hetley 61, 124 E.R. 343.

[2] 2 Rolle Abr., *Prohibition*, pl. G, 'Pur Seats in l'Esglise', p. 288; *Rogers v. Davenant* (1677), *ut supra*; *Denford Churchwardens' Case* (1562), Noy 41, 74 E.R. 1011.

lery or rails as things of necessity, nor was it said so expressly in the libel, that it was charging a man's freehold and inheritance, which the ordinary could not do etc., and that the consent of each parishioner would be requisite in such a case.

BURY [held] that a prohibition should not go. He took seats to be of necessity. And he took seats in a gallery to be as much of necessity as any other. Jeoffr., c. 5, Co.[1] The court has jurisdiction for ornaments as well as repairs. So is the Statute *de Circumspecte Agatis*.[2] Rates of ornaments are to be levied in respect of the person, not in respect of the real [estate], as in the case of repairs. And the ordinary cannot compel such a rate as this and for such purpose. But when the persons have assessed themselves, the ordinary may compel a contribution in his court. And he thinks they may be compellable here as to an ornament.

PRICE was of the same opinion. The inhabitants, in a case of ornaments, are taxed with respect to their personal estate; in a case of repairs, 1 Bulstr., fo. 20; 2 Bulstr. 250; and, as to Roll's [Abr.] 288, fo. 290, a later case,[3] it is directly otherwise. He take it all parishioners may agree to make seats or galleries, and the ordinary can dispose of them. He takes it the ordinary has jurisdiction in a case of repairs, things of necessity, or ornaments. Indeed, bells have been adjudged ornaments. But a pulpit, he takes [to be] of necessity, so that he was against a prohibition. And it was agreed this had been moved in the Queen's Bench the same term, and they had been of the same opinion.

LOVELL [held] accordingly. He took it a majority was sufficient to assess the rate and that it appeared sufficient that the gallery is necessary.

N.B. *Vide* 1 Mod. 236, 237, as to repairs.[4] N.B. As to the Case of Hall and Filty, *antea*.[5]

Turner told me that the counsel had waived that of their paying as unprofitable cattle and given it up and only cont[inued] in the paper as the points of costs.

Harvard Law Sch. MS. 537, pt. 2, p. 180

Hilary term 9 Anne.

And it was now argued by *Ettrick* and *Turner* that the [writ of] prohibition which was ruled *nisi* should be discharged.

Ettrick cited 2 Roll's Abr., 290, pl. 10;[6] there, if a summons upon a libel to repair, that other persons have lands within the parish which ought to be charged as well as them, if that be true, it is a good plea in a spiritual court, and, if they do not allow it, they may appeal and a [writ of] prohibition [will be] denied, by which he argues that there is no question there whether they may levy such a rate. But so much if, by non-equality, prohibition lies and that the matter suggested

1 *Jeffrey v. Kenshley* (1589), 5 Coke Rep. 64, 77 E.R. 153.
2 Stat. 13 Edw. I, *Circumspecte Agatis* (*SR*, I, 101–102).
3 *Anonymous* (1610), 1 Bulstrode 20, 80 E.R. 725.
4 *Rogers v. Davenant* (1677), *ut supra*.
5 *Hall v. Filts* (Ex. 1708), Equity Cases Exch., p. 589.
6 *Anonymous* (1633), 2 Rolle Abr., *Prohibition*, pl. H, 10, p. 290.

is pleaded there and, if not allowed, they may, as in that case, appeal. And he cited 2 Mod. 237, where it is said, if a church be down[1] and the parish increased so that, of necessity, they must have a larger church, the major part of the parish may raise a tax for the enlarging of it as well as repairing it. And the same case is 2 Mod. 222.[2]

Turner: The libel suggested that the gallery was necessary for their want of seats for the parish, and, for this reason, by the majority of the parish, this rate, by which the libel, was assessed according to an ancient rate for the repairing of the church.

If the rate be necessary, the suggestion admits it was well assessed, and it, as before, is allowable in the libel. If a custom has been suggested, then [a writ of] prohibition [lies] because it is not triable in a spiritual court, as 2 Lev. 186,[3] but, if no custom be allowed nor anything but which is properly triable in the spiritual court, and [see] Latch 252, there, for the rule that none ought to be suggested which is properly triable is a spiritual court; so, 5 Rep. 67.

And, as to the assessment of that rate, it is admitted. 2 Rolls, tit. 1291, no. 4, there, admitting that the rate was assessed by the majority is sufficient. 2 Inst. 489.[4]

And, though this appointment of the rate for the repairs was properly made, yet, if this gallery is necessary and convenient, yet there it is properly for their rate. 5 Co., Jeffries' Case.

And as the objection that it is hard for them who had seat *infra* for them to contribute to building seats for others, the answer is this is for their ease to congregate generally, for though it is not necessary for them who had not, yet it gave ease to the others, for it thins the crowd *infra*, and it is of ease for them.

And, as to the other objection that, in this, there ought to be the consent of every individual, the majority binds the rest. This is so adjudged in Popham 197; 2 R. Abr. 291; and a rate may be made for the enlargement of a church, though 1 Mod. 236, so for rebuilding, 2 Mod. 222; 2 Lutw. 1022, a prohibition was denied where a rate was for more chimes, for not so [as] ornamental, but useful and of delight and convenience.[5]

---

[1] Sic in MS.

[2] *Case of the Church of St. Mary Magdalen* (1677), 2 Modern 222, 86 E.R. 1038.

[3] *Wise v. Creek* (1677), 2 Levinz 186, 83 E.R. 510, also 3 Keble 727, 791, 809, 84 E.R. 976, 1014, 1025.

[4] E. Coke, *Second Institute* (1642), p. 489.

[5] *Anonymous* (1626), Popham 197, 79 E.R. 1288; *Bromsgrove Parishioners' Case* (1626), 2 Rolle Abr., *Prohibition*, pl. K, 4, p. 291; *Rogers v. Davenant* (1677), *ut supra*; *Case of the Church of St. Mary Magdalen* (1677), *ut supra*; *Watkins v. Seaman* (1704), 2 Lutwyche 1022, 125 E.R. 567.

As to notice, it was sufficient, for it is not to be given from house to house, but if, at the church, it is sufficient enough. 1 In. 286, 194; 1 Ve. 367.[1]

As to the making of the rate, which is not a new rate, but an old rate, which was assessed for repairs, that it ought to be the rate and rates of repairs affect a house discrete from one for things, so ornamental. This is a new rate only made with reference to the old rate. The words of the libel are that the rate shall be with relation to the ancient rate.

But, if the rate was not well assessed, it is properly conusable there, if it is well or not conusable there so if it is necessary or does not appear to them. And in this case, a prohibition was denied in the King's Bench. And, so, we apprehend it ought to be there.

Mr. *Belfield* [argued] of the same effect.

368

Harper v. Keat

(Ex. 1710)

A general pardon includes ecclesiastical offenses.

Lincoln's Inn MS. Misc. 538, f. [145v], pl. 2

The defendants, churchwardens of Church Hanny, Berkshire, exhibit articles *ex officio* in the Archdeacon's Court in Berkshire against [Jane] Harper for incontinency with one Ayscomb for the space of five, four, three, two, or one year past.

Harper insists upon and pleads the queen's pardon[2] to all offenses before the 19th of April 1709, the last pardon extending to the time and that offense is not excepted.

A [writ of] prohibition was granted to the suit *quoad* all offenses before the Pardon *nisi causa* such a day [and a] stay in the meantime *quoad etc.*

[There was a] like prohibition for Ayscomb, the knight.

[Other copies of this report: Georgetown Univ. Law Sch. MS. B88–10, p. 800.]

---

[1] *Thursfield v. Jones* (1683), 1 Ventris 367, 86 E.R. 236, also T. Jones 187, 84 E.R. 1209.

[2] Stat. 7 Ann., c. 22 (*SR*, IX, 95–101).

369

Poole's Case

(Ex. 1710)

The question in this case was whether a default judgment can be set aside for the lack of notice to the party.

Lincoln's Inn MS. Misc. 538, f. [146]

Upon two *nichil*s, [writs of] extent and *levari* [*facias*] issued. And an English bill [was filed] to be relieved, having no notice, living in another county, and to have leave to plead. [It was] referred to the Attorney [General].

In Sir William Herbert's Case, 3 rep. 11b, etc., judgment against an heir upon a *scire facias* [was] returned and, after[wards], the heir was relieved by an English bill for a matter in equity, as not being summoned and having good matter to have pleaded; 7 rep. 20a; there [it was] said to be by the advice of the two chief justices upon conference with the barons.[1]

Note an *audita querela* may be [filed] after two *nichil*s, but not a summons returned.

Query the reason of the difference. The like clause in the Statute 33 Hen. VIII, ca. 39.[2]

[Other copies of this report: Georgetown Univ. Law Sch. MS. B88–10, p. 801.]

370

Egerton v. George

(Ex. 1710)

The question in this case whether a verdict should be set aside because some of the jurors were shown a map upon a view of the premises in issue.

Lincoln's Inn MS. Misc. 538, f. [147], pl. 1

In [an action of] ejectment, a view before the trial was agreed to. And [it was] mentioned in the [writ of] *distringas prout* that such, which the Act for Amending of the Law[3] directs to be the first six, were agreed to and named. And upon the view, a map was produced and showed to the jury by the plaintiff's shower in the absence of the defendant's viewer, it being affirmed and proved that the plaintiff's attorney said it was the course not to have both of the viewers present

---

[1] *Harbert's Case* (Ex. 1584), 3 Coke Rep. 11, 76 E.R. 647, 7 Coke Rep. 20, 77 E.R. 442, also Moore K.B. 169, 72 E.R. 510.

[2] Stat. 33 Hen. VIII, c. 39, s. 55 (*SR*, III, 891–892).

[3] Stat. 4 & 5 Ann., c. 3, s. 8 (*SR*, VIII, 459).

at the same time and that the plaintiff's shower made remarks to the jury upon the map. And this appeared by affidavits of one of the jury and of two other witnesses.

And, for that reason, the plaintiff [Sir John Egerton] having obtained a verdict, the defendant prayed a new trial. And whether that be a cause for it is the question.

The defendant's counsel insist upon it as against reason and the Act for Amendment of the Law, which points at showing only but not evidence, as surely the map was, the Act and record mentioning only to view that place and that the view by the six first of the jury *prout* the Act, but the word '*primos*' is erased out and [it was] said to be by consent before the trial. And it appeared by affidavit that, after the plaintiff's attorney had showed the place and observed upon the map to the jury, the jury refused the defendant's viewer to go with him, and said it was late and [they could] not get home in time.

For the plaintiff: [First,] this map was no evidence;

Second, [it was] showed by agreement of the viewers to be distinct;

Third, if it not be good, yet it is a cause of challenge which ought to have been at trial, and the defendant had notice of this after and makes a full defense and so makes an allowance of the view. This is a vast district of land not discoverable but by some help by a map. The defendant had a map, though it was not shown. The map was shown at the desire of the jury that viewed to inform the situation, and it did not influence the verdict, nor was it shown at the trial. But the verdict was given upon the merits of the cause and the evidence at trial. And all this appears by the affidavits of eight jurymen. And it was viewed distantly [?] by agreement.

By consent, the plaintiff was to have time to answer the matter of an affidavit of one Hughes filed last Friday, according to the rule of the court, which swears the jury refused to go with the defendant's shower, saying they had seen all and it would be too late (and their horses were tired) to go home.

26 January 1710[/11], it was moved again, and the affidavits of the jury were against Hughes' affidavit.

[Other copies of this report: Georgetown Univ. Law Sch. MS. B88–10, p. 866.]

371

Weddell, qui tam v. Thurlow

(Ex. 1710–1711)

The crown's share of forfeitures can be pardoned by a statute, but not an informer's share.

Harvard Law Sch. MS. 537, pt. 2, p. 159, pl. 1

Trinity term 9 Anne.

The case was an information was exhibited against the defendant upon 4 & 5 W. & M., relating to distilling.[1] And, pending the information and before the trial, this general Act of Grace[2] came, which, however, excepts such offenses whereby the queen is defrauded of her duty. Now, the information being before the Act, as the fact charged there the offense was pardoned.

But, as affirmed by the Attorney General [*Montagu*] and the Solicitor General [*Raymond*], the fact was so as the queen was defrauded and so [it was] excepted.

And the verdict being for the queen, it was moved in arrest [of judgment] by *Ettrick* and *Dodd* that it was produced, and so judgment should be stayed.

And, now, it was argued by the Attorney [General *Montagu*] and the Solicitor [General *Raymond*] that the defendant might enter a suggestion of the pardon and that he was not within the exception that they might have an opportunity of replying and having the fact tried on which would depend his being or not being within the Act. And they cited Rastall's *Entries*, 107; 2 Leon. 40, Green and Edward's Case; 1 Brown's *Entries* 360; and one Merriell and Edwards's [Case] in the Queen's Bench lately, which was upon the Statute of Will. III, of Arbitrations.[3]

And My Lord Chief Justice Holt said, if they had any ill practices to charge it with, they must suggest them upon the roll that the others may reply etc. Cr. Eliz. 380; Townsend, 2 Book of Judgments, 176; Rastall, *Entries*, 260, 86, 51.

In this case, the Attorney General [*Montagu*] said, if they had been aware of that Act, they could have said *per quod* the queen was defrauded, though it was useful to no other purpose.

But [it was said] by Ward and Bury, it would have been ill.

Then query the reason.

Adjornatur.

Vide Hardr. 191, Vandebergh v. Blake,[4] where the defendant, as it seemed, might have suggested the pardon, but only [if] it was after a special verdict and he did not come upon the first continuance.

Harvard Law Sch. MS. 537, pt. 2, p. 160

This was an information upon a *devenerunt* for importing brandy in undersize casks *contra* 4 & 5 W. & M., in the Book of Rates, 389, whereby the queen, as [by] the act, is defrauded. And the case was, after the information was exhibited and before the verdict, comes the Act of Grace, which pardons everything the queen can pardon, excepting *inter cetera* such offenses whereby the queen was

[1] Stat. 3 Will. & Mar., c. 15 (*SR*, VI, 321–322).

[2] Stat. 7 Ann., c. 22 (*SR*, IX, 95–101).

[3] *Green v. Everard* (1588), 2 Leonard 40, 74 E.R. 340; Stat. 9 Will. III, c. 15 (*SR*, VII, 369–370).

[4] *Vandebergh v. Blake* (Ex. 1661), Hardres 191, 194, 145 E.R. 446, 447.

defrauded. And a verdict being for the queen, it was moved in arrest of judgment by *Ettrick* and *Dodd.*

But it was insisted upon by the Attorney [General *Montagu*] and the Solicitor [General *Raymond*] that the Act should be pleaded by way of a suggestion upon the roll that they might have an opportunity of showing the fraud *ut antea* 133.

And, now, it was argued in opposition to that by *Ettrick* and *Dodd, e contra*, and at the same time there being another case of the same nature, but the fact found in the special verdict was that the queen was deceived.

It was argued by *Ettrick* that the finding by the verdict that the queen is deceived of her duty when no duty was due that is inconsistent, for they cannot proceed for the forfeiture of the goods and the duty both, and, having made their election for the goods themselves, the information being for them, and the finding that by the jury is inconsistent with what they had already and before that found.

Another question was whether the informer's part was pardoned. The Act, indeed, pardoned all things whereby Her Majesty, by any ways and means, can be pardoned. But he then took notice of an exception[1] afterwards, which was that the exceptions of all informations wherein a verdict was obtained, which implies no verdict, no execution, and so it is pardoned. He mentions the acts of pardon as different from this, 2 W. & M. and 6 & 7 W.,[2] and such a solemn pardon as this by the legislature seems to design more than Her Majesty alone could. There is likewise another exception[3] of informations depending, which implies all others are not. He cites Burton's Case, in Dyer and Co.; [if] an offense is pardoned, all consequences are so too.[4]

Attorney General [*Montagu*] *e contra*: The Act takes notice of Her Majesty's being defrauded of her duty by such means. And this is an answer to the inconsistency that was objected. And the Act excepts all offenses whereby Her Majesty has been defrauded; so this offense is plainly within the exception.

Then, as to the informer's part being pardoned, nothing is pardoned by the Act but as against the queen. It is said expr[essly] as by Her Majesty may be pardoned; this cert[ainly] means to extend only to where Her Majesty alone, by a charter, might pardon.

This [action of] *devenerunt* is in the nature of an [action of] trover. And, as to the objection that the means being pardoned, all the consequences are so too, and Burton's Case is in maintenance of that, he does not think that holds, for, by this suit, a property is fixed that is not altered by the pardon. He admits the

1 execution *MS.*

2 Stat. 2 Will. & Mar., c. 10 (*SR*, VI, 174–179); Stat. 6 & 7 Will. & Mar., c. 20 (*SR*, VI, 607–619).

3 execution *MS.*

4 *Burton's Case*, 6 Coke Rep. 13, 77 E.R. 272.

case of an attainder being reversed that the party's heirs are entitled to all again. But, if a pardon does not alter the property that is fixed, as if a lord of a manor be entitled to a forfeiture by a felony etc. and that is pardoned, the party shall not be again restored.

As to the point of the suggestion, they have given no answer to the precedents that have been cited as to the suggestion, practices used by arbitrators, etc., that, indeed, [there was] never a suggestion, but, when [it was] heartily contested, then a suggestion must be put in to by it. That precedent of the case of the outlawry he takes to be the very same case. 1 Brown's *Entries* 360, Walter Vaughn's Case.

Solicitor General [*Raymond*]: The information, being before the Act of Grace, states the Act so only as it appears within the Act, though the fact is so as not intended to be pardoned. Now, since the fact is so and that found by the jury so that, upon the whole record, it appears expressly excepted.

Second, that the informer's part can never be pardoned, it is admitted that, in the case of actions *qui tam*, the king cannot pardon the informer's part, M. 1 Hen. VII, pl. 2, fo. 3, and an abundance of other cases there are that are founded upon that, as 3 Inst. 238; Cro. Eliz. 138; 11 Co. 65, etc. And this goes further than the queen's pardon as appears by the qualifications. And [it was said] by him [it was] never known made a general pardon by a charter and that the reason of making those general ones [was] after a solemn manner and no other. Cro. Car., Brigenden's Case; 5 Co., Biggen's Case; Hall's, *ibidem*.[1]

Now the contempts for which [there is] any execution are always looked upon to be pardoned, but yet the costs are not, though the pains be this to be understood only where the execution is only for contempts and where there is no interest in the party. But where the suit is grounded upon the interest of the party and where the party has costs, in such a case, they have [not] been pardoned.

There is a case now depending in the Queen's Bench which is of a conviction for deer stealing removed by a [writ of] *certiorari*, and the question is whether the penalty given to the party be pardoned. The court inclined as to the party. They said it could not be pardoned though it be pardoned so far as concerns the crown. But it still hangs upon the other point, whether the corporal punishment be pardoned or no as [. . .] pillory, etc. But, as to the information part of the pen[alty], they seemed pretty clear it was not.

Dodd: It is not only an offense against a prohibitory law, but there was likewise a duty due upon it if imported in unsizeable casks. And the queen may sue for the penalty and likewise for the duty too. Why then, if those goods that pay

[1] YB Mich. 1 Hen. VII, f. 2, pl. 2 (1485); E. Coke, *Third Institute* (1644), p. 238; *Stretton v. Tayler* (1589), Croke Eliz. 138, 78 E.R. 395; *Foster's Case* (1614), 11 Coke Rep. 56, 65, 77 E.R. 1222, 1234; *Brikenden's Case* (1625), Croke Car. 9, 79 E.R. 613; *Shugborough v. Biggins* (1599), 5 Coke Rep. 50, 77 E.R. 130; *Cooke v. Hall* (1604), 5 Coke Rep. 51, 77 E.R. 132.

a duty to the crown and this method of importing such a method that defrauds the crown, then it cannot be excepted.

At the trial, it being objected that it was pardoned and that, then controverted, was it not then proper to be found and now that it is so, he cannot imagine why this is not a proper special verdict. And he does not take it to be an idle finding. In case of the death of the party before the day in bank, sometimes they take notice of it by a suggestion and sometimes by an affidavit; that is in the discretion of the court and as they please. But, if these are looked upon as sufficient to apprise the court, surely this verdict is so too.

Objection: This is to put the party to plead in all cases whatever.

He thinks it proper they should plead in all cases where it is questioned whether it be pardoned or no. And, wherever a man pleads a pardon, he never pleads it generally, but always that he is not excepted.

He cited 2 Mod. 52 as to what was said concerning pardons which pardon the offense that it pardoned likewise all the consequences. He said it was there made a difference between natural and legal consequences. He cited 11 Co., the end of Foster's Case; Dyer 288; Lord Chandois' Case.[1]

Phipps, e contra: He spoke only as to the suggestion. The offense, as it is in the information, is pardoned. Now, the question is if the Attorney General is at liberty to plead anything so as it may come to a new trial. If so, in all cases the Attorney [General] might come and suggest a fact that it might appear within the exception and so carry the matter to a new trial. And he said the precedents that have been cited did not come up to this case and that it was never yet heard of.

Attorney General [*Montagu*]: In the Regicide's Case, when attainted by an Act of Parliament, they then suggested that they were not the persons, and that was tried.[2] And he said it was My Lord Chief Justice Holt's opinion that it should have been tried in the Duke of Monmouth's Case, and he should not have been hurried to execution as he was, and that gave the occasion to say that he was afterwards alive.

Ettrick: If the Act had stopped at the first qualification, then that would have been a good answer. And, where the thing is gone so far as a judgment, it may be as they say. But, where there is only an information, as this, it is perhaps all[owed].

As to the cases of costs mentioned, though they are that the costs may not be pardoned, yet the pardon has that effect. He shall never come to have his costs taxed. And [it was said] by him there was in King James's time a general charter offered [. . .] now [. . .] they designed something more when the legislature [is] concerned in it, and then they have proceeded in this case for the forfeiture.

---

1 *Foster's Case* (1614), *ut supra*; *Bishop of Durham's Case* (1570), 3 Dyer 288, 73 E.R. 648; *Duke of Chandois's Case* (1606), 6 Coke Rep. 55, 77 E.R. 336.

2 *Regicides' Case* (1660), J. Kelying 7, 84 E.R. 1056; Stat. 12 Car. II, c. 30 (*SR*, V, 288–290).

They could not at the same time have the forfeiture and the duty; that would be double. And the information for the forfeiture is an election; he would have the goods.

Price: If this finds the crown deceived out of the issue, it is surplusage. Indeed, the Attorney [General] may proceed for the forfeiture or the duty at his election.

As to the suggestion, if it is so now, it may be so in all cases. It seems the informer's part was indeed not pardoned.

Adjornatur.

That case, in which the suggestion was, was the Queen and Hinton.[1]

Lincoln's Inn MS. Misc. 538, f. [163], pl. 1

The question was whether the queen's late Act of Grace[2] pardoned the informer's moiety of the value of goods upon a *devenerunt*, the information being depending before the Act took place.

And, by the opinion of all of the judges of England, it is not pardoned.

And with that, a case in the Queen's Bench about deer stealers was mentioned, and, afterwards, [it was] ruled that the informer's and poor's shares of the penalty were not pardoned where the conviction was before the pardon, but [it was] held that the offender's imprisonment for want of payment and of goods to be distrained is pardoned, that being a distinct punishment of itself and not limited or confined to be until payment of the penalty, in which case, had it been so, it had not been pardoned, for it had been a further remedy for the forfeiture.

[Other copies of this report: Georgetown Univ. Law Sch. MS. B88–10, p. 844, pl. 1.]

Dodd 226, Parker 280, 145 E.R. 780

Upon a motion in arrest of judgment, it was resolved by the court (upon consultation with all the justices) that the queen's part was pardoned, but the informer's part [was] not, because the words of the late Act of General Pardon,[3] are, 'all that the crown could pardon'. But by the information filed (which was before the pardon), the informer's part was fixed and vested etc.

This matter was depending several terms in the Exchequer.

And on Tuesday, 19th of June 1711, [the court was of opinion that the informer's moiety was not pardoned but gave judgment for the defendants as to the queen's moiety. 1 Hen. VII, pl. 2; Cro. Eliz. 138; Jenk. Cent. 164; 2 Strange 1272].[4]

---

[1] Note *Attorney General v. Thomas* (Ex. 1684), Exch. Repts. *tempore* Car. II, 588.

[2] Stat. 7 Ann., c. 22 (*SR*, IX, 95–101).

[3] Stat. 7 Ann., c. 22 (*SR*, IX, 95–101).

[4] YB Mich. 1 Hen. VII, f. 2, pl. 2 (1485); *Stretton v. Tayler* (1589), Croke Eliz. 138, 78 E.R. 395; *Anonymous*, Jenkins 164, 145 E.R. 106; *Howel, qui tam v. James* (1747), 2

372

Attorney General v. Crosley

(Ex. 1710)

In this case, the defendant did not have the right to have oyer of the bond that was in execution.

A verdict must be set aside where the defendant did not receive due and fair notice of the trial date and did not appear at the trial.

Lincoln's Inn MS. Misc. 538, f. [142]

4 November.

A [writ of] extent *quoad bona et catalla debita et credita et specialitates* having issued against Jacob Reynardson, receiver of the customs at Bristol, on a bond of a great penalty to the queen for the due performance of his office and paying the money received to the Cashier of the Customs at London for Her Majesty's use, there was an inquisition taken at London, whereby it was found that one Hickman of Bristol was then indebted to Reynardson £492 12s. 11d. (showing how), being the queen's money, which debt was seized into the queen's hands the 13th of February 9 Anne [1711][1] and returned into the court and, on an oath made of the inability of Hickman and that the debt was in danger of being lost, a [writ of] immediate extent issued *teste* the same 13th of February directed to the sheriffs of Bristol to take the body and seize the lands and tenements, goods and chattels etc. of Hickman into the queen's hands that the queen may have them until the debt of £492 12s. 11d. be fully paid with a proviso not to sell the goods etc. until a further command.

13 March following, an inquisition was taken upon this last extent whereby it was found that Hickman, the day of the *teste* of the extent, *scil.* the 13th of February, and also on the day of the taking of the said inquisition, was possessed of the several goods and chattels in a schedule to the inquisition annexed as of his own proper goods of the value (in the whole) of £1500, which were then seized into the queen's hand, according to the writ which was returnable *quindena Paschae* next.

The defendants, claiming property of the goods by assignment from the commissioners of bankrupts against Hickman made and dated the same day with the *teste* of the last extent at the day of the return of the writ upon a rule given for that purpose, pray an imparlance, which is entered to be granted until [*blank*]. And, then, they pray *oyer* of the bond given by Reynardson to the queen and of the condition of that bond, which, without any order of court or consent of the Attorney General, is entered to be granted to them. And, then, they plead

Strange 1272, 93 E.R. 1175.

[1] Sic in MS.

the Statute of Equity, 33 Hen. VIII,[1] showing for equity that, before the issuing of the last extent, Hickman became a bankrupt and that a commission of bankruptcy before that extent issued against him and that, on the 13th of February, being the day of the *teste* of the last extent, the commissioners of bankrupts made an assignment of the same goods to the defendants for the benefit of Hickman's creditors and that the defendants, the 12th of March, before the last inquisition, paid Hickman's debt to Reynardson unto Ferne, the Cashier of the Queen's Customs, according to the bond.

Upon a motion by the Attorney General and others, this *oyer* was held by the court to be irregular, and set aside, it not being the defendant's right in this case to have *oyer* of the bond and condition, at least without the leave of the court.

Upon Friday the 16th of June last term, the court ordered the *oyer* to be set aside unless cause to the contrary [be shown] the next day and the Attorney General to be that day in the same condition as on the 16th as to his proceedings upon the extent.

The next day, *viz.* the 17th, on hearing counsel on both sides, the court ordered that the *oyer* should be struck out and that the defendants do plead by Monday next as of the 16th and pay 40s. costs, which they did, an issuable plea alleging a title to themselves and traversing the queen's inquisition.

After this, the plaintiff's attorney, on the 22nd of June, gave notice of trial, which was had the 28th, and the defendants made no defense. So the verdict was for the plaintiff.

And the defendant moved for a new trial, because the notice for the trial was not right nor timely, according to the rules of the court, which were agreed to be ten days in Hilary and Trinity terms where the defendant lives above forty miles off (as, in this case, they did) and fourteen days in the other two terms, and here is but six days notice.

And the court held the notice not sufficient, and, therefore, set aside the trial, for neither of the orders extended to oblige the defendants to take any notice of the trial. And, therefore, such notice should be given as is according to the rules, which must be ten days, which is not here.

But, afterwards, the cause was tried at *nisi prius* this term. And a verdict [was given] for the queen.

[Other copies of this report: Georgetown Univ. Law Sch. MS. B88–10, p. 815.]

[1] Stat. 33 Hen. VIII, c. 39, s. 55 (*SR*, III, 891–892).

373

Gibbons, qui tam v. Seddon

(Ex. 1710)

A judgment based on a defective pleading is not res judicata.
Res judicata *must be pleaded in bar and not in abatement.*

Lincoln's Inn MS. Misc. 538, f. [150], pl. 2

The information was exhibited the 17th of May last. And, therein, [it was] laid that, between the first of July last and the time of exhibiting that information, the ship *Anne* arrived at the port of London in a voyage from Rotterdam laden with several parcels of silks wrought and other goods, of which ship, the defendant was the master for that voyage and that he or the purser of the ship, at the time of the arrival of that ship in the port of London, being the port of her discharge or before, did not make a just and true entry upon his oath of the burden, contents, and lading of the said ship with the particular marks, numbers, etc., as are mentioned in the Act against Frauds in the Customs, 14 Car. II, ca. 11, § 2,[1] to the best of his knowledge, whereby he forfeited £100, a moiety to the queen and the other to the informer.

The defendant pleads in abatement a former information and a trial and verdict for the defendant for the same offense, with a proper averment. And so he prays judgment of the now information.

The Attorney General [*Northey*] prays *oyer* of the former information, and he has it *in haec verba*. And then he says that the defendant was acquitted by the jury of that former information for several defects in it and because in that the defendant was not accused with any offense in not making a true entry upon his oath as the Act directs and because the offense laid in the first information is not the same that, by this information, is charged against the defendant, *et hoc paratus etc.*, and he prays judgment etc.

The defendant rejoins, and says the offenses in both of the informations are the same and not diverse.

To which the Attorney General demurs, and shows for cause that the defendant was acquitted of the first information for divers defects in it and because it was not alleged in that as it is in this that the defendant had not made an entry upon his oath etc. and, further, because the matter of the defendant's rejoinder is not issuable, but a departure from his first plea. And he prays judgment. The defendant joins in demurrer, and prays the information may be quashed.

And, upon the opening of the matter by the Attorney [General *Northey*] and the Solicitor General [*Raymond*] and comparing the two informations, it evidently appeared that the defendant, by the first information, was not charged

---

1 Stat. 14 Car. II, c. 11, s. 2 (*SR*, V, 393–394).

with his not making his entry upon oath, the omitting of which was the only reason why he was acquitted. And, then, his acquittal upon a defective information and wherein he was charged with no offense can be no bar to this information where he is charged with an offense against the Statute fully and plainly and which was not in issue in the former trial.

Besides, an acquittal upon a trial cannot be pleaded in abatement, but [must be pleaded] in bar.

And, therefore, the plaintiff had judgment by the uniform opinion of the court. But he chose to have it a *respondeat ouster*, which was granted.

But *Phipps*, for the defendant, offered to take an exception to the present information.

But that was not allowed him as this case stood in court.

[Other copies of this report: Georgetown Univ. Law Sch. MS. B88–10, p. 771, pl. 2.]

374

Attorney General v. Tym

(Ex. 1710)

A maltster must allow an officer of the revenue to measure the amount of malt in his place of business for the purpose of determining the amount of the taxes that are due to the crown.

Lincoln's Inn MS. Misc. 538, f. [149]

28 November 1710.

The case upon the pleadings was this. The Attorney General exhibits a Latin information against the defendant founded upon the Act 1 Anne, ca. 3,[1] for granting a supply to Her Majesty by several duties imposed upon malt, mum, cider, and pesey continued down all along from that time to the time of the information by several acts of Parliament setting forth that the defendant was a common maltster for the making of malt for sale for six months before the 5th of February 7 Anne and exercised the occupation of a common maltster and had kept a malting house, *viz.* at Westminster. And he charged the defendant with five several times refusing one Ward, the queen's officer, to measure and take an account of the quantity of the defendant's barley, which was then wetting and steeping or had been wetted or steeped in the defendant's malt house there then being and within the time in the information, had been divers great quantities of barley wetted and steeped to be made into malt for sale, and lay fifteen offenses, £20 for each offense *contra formam statuti*. The defendant pleads *non culpabilis*.

---

[1] Stat. 1 Ann., stat. 2, c. 3 (*SR*, VIII, 155–161).

A special verdict was found that the defendant was a common maker of malt for sale and was a maltster and exercised the occupation of a common maltster, that Ward was the queen's officer duly authorized for measuring, gauging, and, taking an account of malt and corn for malt within the times in the information, twice within those times, came to the defendant's malt house in the daytime to measure and take account of the barley and other grain there found wetting and steeping and which had been there wetted and steeped, at which times, he there found great quantities of the defendant's barley and other grain then wetted and steeped to be made into malt for sale, which he endeavored to measure and take account of, but the defendant had so depressed the barley in his cisterns and couch that the officer could not take an account thereof by his gauging rod or other instrument for gauging and, thereupon, he requested the defendant to permit him to measure the same by the Winchester bushel, which the defendant refused and wholly hindered and obstructed him to measure and, by reason of that, all the said barley escaped measuring. And the jury concluded, if the defendant be guilty of those two offenses in the information, they find him so, if not guilty, they find him so.

Serjeant *Grove* and Mr. *Ettrick*, for the defendant, insisted that the defendant is not guilty within this special verdict of any offense within the Act of Parliament in regard the penalty of £20 is annexed only by the Act for refusing the officer to gauge, and not for refusing him to measure, the design and meaning of the Act being that the officer was to gauge the barley in the cistern and couch and not measure it there, which would certainly spoil the corn from ever being made into malt, for the malt only is to measured when made and, before it is made, the account to be taken is only by the gauge, which, in the nature and reason of the thing must be so, since measuring in the cistern or couch would manifestly spoil the making of the barley wetted in the cistern or put into the couch into malt.

On the other side, it was insisted, and so held by the whole court, that the Act expressly provides that the queen should have a certain duty of 6d. a bushel for the malt, that, in order to ascertain that duty and prevent frauds and to have an account of the barley wetted for making malt previous to the making it into malt, the acts had provided that, to ascertain the charging and levying of that duty, the gaugers and officers to be appointed should have the power, in the daytime:

First, to gauge cisterns and other vessels for the steeping of corn for the making of malt;

Second, to gauge, measure, and take an account of the just quantity of the barley etc. which should be found wetting or steeping or which should have been wetted or steeped in any cistern etc. for making malt and make a report thereof to the Commissioners of the Excise, leaving a copy with the maltster, which should be a charge upon him;

Third, and, if any maltster or person making malt for sale or private use shall refuse any gauger or officer to enter his malt house or to measure, compute, or take an account of all his malt and to gauge all and every of the cisterns etc. and to gauge and take an account of his barley in such cistern etc. or which have been steeped or wetted and shall be upon any floor or other place, shall, for every such offense, forfeit £20.

Which last clause plainly extends to the case in question, for, when the defendant has so pressed the barley both in the cistern and the couch as to disable an account to be taken thereof by the gauge there then remaining no other way to have an account but by measuring (which also is one of the ways prescribed for taking the account of the barley in the cistern or on the floor) and the defendant refusing to permit the measuring, he is an offender within the Act and liable to the penalty of £20 for each of the two offenses, *qui derimit [?] medium [?] adimit [?] fine[. . .]*. And, when the defendant, by his own willful act, disables the officer from taking an account by gauging, he ought to have let him to have measured, which, though it might be inconvenient or prejudicial to him in making the malt, it must not deprive the crown's having a true account of the corn, which could not otherwise be than by measuring, and refusing that is a refusal to take an account and so within not only the meaning but the very words of the Act that gives the forfeiture.

And, therefore, judgment was for the queen.

And, in this case, by mistake, the word '*que*' which was added to the word '*quod*' and made the verdict uncertain was amended in the verdict by the notes of the special verdict after an argument but before judgment. And the defendant's counsel were heard thereto.

Note the matters and jurisdiction of this case was altered by a subsequent Act[1] laying a duty on malt.

[Other copies of this report: Georgetown Univ. Law Sch. MS. B88–10, p. 766.]

375

Natt, qui tam v. Bartlet
Natt, qui tam v. Barker

(Ex. 1710)

An information on a devenerunt for a parcel of wine that expresses the value but not the quantity or kind is bad. It is otherwise upon a seizure.

A judgment can be arrested after a verdict where the complaint is uncertain.

1 Stat. 12 Ann., c. 2 (*SR*, IX, 753–762).

Lincoln's Inn MS. 538, f. [118]

The information [of *devenerunt*] sets forth that, between such times, *separalae parcellae vini valor'* £100 (without showing any certain quantities nor in what vessels or casks nor of what sort or kind the wines were) were imported by merchants unknown from beyond the sea into England, *viz.* to Ratcliff in Middlesex, and there unshipped to be laid on land, the duties due and payable for the same not being paid or secured etc., whereby they became forfeited, and, so being forfeited *ad manus et possessionem* of the defendant *devenerunt*, and so prays that the defendant may answer for the wines or for £100, the value thereof, as is usual in an information of *devenerunt*.

Upon the trial last term, the plaintiff [. . .] evidence that they were French and Madeira wines, *viz.* two hogsheads of French and two tuns of Madeira and that they were privately unshipped and came to the defendant's hands and no duties were paid and they were of the value of £100.

And the jury found a verdict accordingly, which was a general verdict, and nothing was specially found nor insisted on.

And now, *Northey* and *Ward* move in arrest of judgment that this information is too general and uncertain, it not containing any certain quantity of wine nor what sort or kind of wine, which, though it might be good in a seizure because, there, the quantities and sorts of wines are ascertained by the return of the ind[enture] of appraisement which supplies the uncertainty in the information, yet, here, this information is personal and not *in rem*, and it is in the nature of an [action of] trover and conversion, which, in all cases, as well in the case of the crown as the subject, must have an express certainty; otherwise, a verdict or an acquittal cannot be pleaded to another information for the same thing and that such uncertainty is as bad in the case of a subject, even after a verdict.

These cases were cited, 2 Levinz 195; Cro. Eliz. 865; Playter's Case, 5 rep. [*blank*]; Stiles 360; 1 Ventr. 272; 2 Ventr. 262 and 73.[1] And, if there be any precedents in this court of a like information with this, they passed *sub silentio*.

The Attorney General insisted this is as great a certainty as *indebitatus assumpsit pro diversis bonis etc.* and as *pro opere et labore*, where all rises upon the evidence, and then the certainty will appear. He relies upon several precedents produced of such informations of *devenerunt* by the names of *parcella vini* and the like. And they are the more reasonable because it may often fall out that the quantity, quality, or value of the goods cannot or may not be certainly known at the time of exhibiting the information.

---

1 *Wade v. Hatcher* (1677), 2 Levinz 195, 83 E.R. 515; *Gramvel v. Rhobotham* (1601), Croke Eliz. 865, 78 E.R. 1092; *Playter's Case* (1583), 5 Coke Rep. 34, 77 E.R. 105; *Webb v. Washborn* (1652), Style 360, 82 E.R. 777; *Anonymous* (1675), 1 Ventris 272, 86 E.R. 182; *Tregonwell v. Sherwin* (1691), 2 Ventris 262, 86 E.R. 429; *Blake v. Clattie* (1689), 2 Ventris 73, 86 E.R. 316.

But surely an *indebitatus* always implies a contract between certain persons, and it gives notice of it accordingly, but this mentions not whose the wines are nor the least certainty for defense. And, as to the precedents, they are not of the moment and are answered after.

The answer insisted upon by the defendant's counsel and which move me are:

First, that the word '*parcella*' is wholly uncertain as to quantity;

Second, that the word '*vinum*' is as uncertain as to the kind;

Third, that both are uncertain as to the value to be recovered as there being divers sorts of wines which are of different values;

Fourth, a defendant is wholly unprovided to defend such a charge;

Fifth, what verdict or judgment can be given or entered upon such an information;

Sixth, what if the word '*parcella*' should include several vessels or distinct quantities arising upon the evidence and some are proved to come to the defendant's hand, others not proved, how that there be a distinction made either by the verdict or judgment, for as there must be a verdict and judgment for the informer as to these come to the defendant's hands, so there must be a judgment of acquittal for the rest that may be pleadable to any other information for the same which, in such a case as this, cannot be, and so, for ought appears upon the record, he may be liable over and over again for the same goods. And this happens to be the case almost in every *devenerunt*.

2 Levinz 195; a parcel of woollen yarn, in [an action of] trespass, judgment was arrested. 1 Ventr. 272; in [an action of] trespass *pisces cepit*, arrest [of judgment], and, there, considerations had by Hale of the *indebitatus* for goods and *pro opere et labore* and yet judgment was arrested for uncertainty there put. Trover for a ship *cum velis* [was] good because [there was] but one body, but *pro velis* only [is] bad. Style 352, 361; 2 Ventris 262; *diversas per maerem*' is bad in [an action of] trespass. [*blank*] 73; the like *diversa onera equin*' of gravel [was] arrested; Cro. Eliz. 865; *parcella piscium* the like; 5 rep. 34, Playter's Case; *pisces suos cepit* without number or nature, [on] settled authority, is bad after a verdict.

As to the precedents, [they are] too modern; none are earlier than [the] information 27 Car. II, no judgment, until 11 Will. III and but seven judgments. [There are] none upon debate nor question, *sub silentio* among the clerks, and misled by a precedent of seizure, but that uncertainty [was] helped by indentures of appraisement parcel of the record.

I have no memory of such precedents. What I have seen or observed have been particulars.

If this be good, why may not an information in debt be good without showing how grown due, for that may come in evidence.

In Agar and Candishe's Case, Moor [*blank*],[1] sixty precedents were laid aside. Shall the judgments *sub silentio* prevail when 700 mention a quantity and quality?

In all cases for exporting wool, a certain quantity is charged for masters making a short report the goods omitted mentioned in the information to be aboard.

Nothing of quantity or quality of the wines appears within the whole record. The verdict only finds that the goods in the information were of the value of £100 and came to the defendant's hands, and were brought in and imported by strangers unknown and not by the defendant. The judgment is that he be charged with one moiety of the value to the queen, the other to the informer.

Will an information in the nature of an action of debt lie for the duties of one or several parcels of wine, not saying what the parcel is nor of what sort or kind or that J.S. is indebted to the crown in such a sum, not saying for what nor upon what account?

And yet, in both cases, it may be said that they may be given in evidence and the certainty and particulars appear. What defense can the defendant make in proving the duties paid when he does not know the goods? He is not charged to have imported them, but that they were imported by merchants unknown.

28 November 1710.

The court gave judgment in this case. And, by the opinion of the Chief Baron [Ward] and Bury and Lovell, barons, against the opinion of Price, judgment was arrested for the very reason and causes before in my argument.

Price did not go about to make the words '*parcella vini*' to import in themselves any certainty, but only thought that, in the case of the crown, it might be well in respect only of the precedents produced of several informations in the court of that sort between the [year] 27 Car. II and this term, which were only filed in the court and no pleas or proceedings had upon them and were in number thirteen and eleven informations of the like sort exhibited in and between the tenth and twelfth years of King William III, upon which, verdicts and judgments were had. But all passed *sub silentio*, and not upon any debate or opinion of the court or any notice taken of them.

And what are those to the ancient and uniform practice of the court in all times wherein some certainty, both as to quantity and quality, were always mentioned and exceed hundreds of times the others? And the modern practice for the bulk exceed them, the others taking rise only from the ignorance of under clerks, being in all probability led into that mistake of *parcella vini* commonly used in informations of seizure of goods, which, nevertheless, in that case, are particularly ascertained both as to quantity, value, and quality by the indentures of appraise-

[1] *Agar v. Cavendish* (1594), Moore K.B. 564, 72 E.R. 761, also Croke Eliz. 327, 78 E.R. 576, Savile 134, 123 E.R. 1055, 2 Anderson 127, 123 E.R. 581.

ment, which is always parcel of the record and returned before the defendant is bound to plead.

The crown has privileges and prerogatives in pleadings, but none for uncertainties of its duty or demand, as appears before in my argument and the instance there. And an [action of] *devenerunt* is the crown's [action of] trover and conversion. And, therefore, it must demand a certainty, else no defendant can make a defense.

Precedents in no case can make a good thing void nor a void thing good. In doubtful and questionable things, they are of use. And, in Agar and Candish's Case, Moor [*blank*], there were sixty precedents, a far larger number than now for the plaintiff, were set aside and not regarded as not warranted in the reason of the thing and not being upon debate, but passing *sub silentio*, as, in this very case, it was.

Judgment was arrested.

Note where the landing or omitting any goods out of the master of the ship's report or the like lead to a collateral penalty or forfeiture, and not of the goods themselves, it may not be so necessary to lay a precise or particular certainty of the quantity of the goods supposed to be so landed or omitted because, if any quantity was so landed or omitted, the collateral penalty or forfeiture is incurred. But that stands upon a different reason from this, where the goods themselves or the value is to be recovered; in such, a certainty ought to be in the quality of the goods; in that case, [it] is always set forth.

[Other copies of this report: Georgetown Univ. Law Sch. MS. B88–10, p. 722.]

Dodd 221

[In] an [information of] *devenerunt* and the information alleges *quod parcella vini* without any particulars of quantities or kinds. [There was] a verdict for the king. And [it was] moved in arrest of judgment that [it was] bad and not like *parcella* in an information of seizure, for there the seizure and writ of appraisement make it certain, but here it is in a personal information and [is] altogether uncertain, as trover, trespass, etc. [is] bad. 2 Levinz 195; Cr. Eliz. 865; Plater's Case; Style 360; 1 Ventr. 272; 2 Ventr. 262; C. J. Jones 109.[1]

[It was argued] to the contrary, that [it is] good and warranted by a multitude of precedents and [is] like a general *indebitatus assumpsit pro opere et labore, pro bonis et merchandis sic concessit solvere.*

Curia advisare vult.

---

[1] *Wade v. Hatcher* (1677), 2 Levinz 195, 83 E.R. 515; *Gramvel v. Rhobotham* (1601), Croke Eliz. 865, 78 E.R. 1092; *Playter's Case* (1583), 5 Coke Rep. 34, 77 E.R. 105; *Webb v. Washborn* (1652), Style 360, 82 E.R. 777; *Anonymous* (1675), 1 Ventris 272, 86 E.R. 182; *Tregonwell v. Sherwin* (1691), 2 Ventris 262, 86 E.R. 429; *Hevel v. Reynolds* (1678), T. Jones 109, 84 E.R. 1171, also 1 Ventris 329, 86 E.R. 212.

Note: Precedents are some general and some particular. Query, for [it was] never stirred before in all my time. See the information.

There was another [information] of the same nature between Nat, *qui tam* and Barker.

Harvard Law Sch. MS. 537, pt. 2, p. 152, pl. 1

Easter term 9 Anne. Nat, *qui tam* v. Bartlett.

It was moved in arrest of judgment upon an information of *devenerunt* after a verdict that it was too uncertain because it was *pro separale parcella vini* without saying what sort or what quantity. And [it was] compared to [an action of] trover. And thereby were cited 2 Lev. 195, where [an action of] trespass was brought for entering into the house and taking, *inter alia, unam parcellam pensarum laniarum, Anglice* a quantity of woolen yarn, and, being entire damages, judgment was stayed. Cro. Eliz. 865, an [action of] trover, *inter cetera, de una parcella piscium, Anglice* lings, and not being alleged what parcel, and [it was] reversed, though [there was a] verdict, in the case, and 5 Rep. Plaister's Case.

And a difference by Ward was taken between such an information as this and an information of seizure, because, in the latter case, the parcels and quantities are specified in the writ of appraisement. And he cited Style 360, where a declaration in trover for four pair of hangings was uncertain, and 1 Ve. 272, an [action of] trespass for fishing in his several piscaries and *pisces* taken, and it was ill after a verdict, and 2 Ve. 262 and 73. And he said informations always specified the tuns or hogsheads *ad valorem* of so much.

Chief Baron [Ward]: We are in the case of the crown. And it is not a criminal prosecution.

But [it was said] by *Northey* upon a penal law, and there can be no knowing how to make any defense upon such an information.

Chief Baron [Ward]: We always in such a case confine them to such a time and such vessels and, by the Attorney General, the court directs them to assign the particular time etc. in such a case.

But [it was said] by *Northey* and Ward, they sometimes deny it.

Adjornatur.

Dodd 223, Parker 278, 145 E.R. 779

In an information of *devenerunt*, the charge was *parcella vini valoris* £100. And after a verdict for the queen, [the defendant] moved in arrest of judgment for the uncertainty, because neither the quantity, as hogsheads etc., nor the sorts, as French, Spanish, etc. [were mentioned]. And upon debate and consideration, judgment was for this omission arrested, notwithstanding many precedents produced within twelve or fourteen years [last] (but no ancient ones appeared). And a difference [was] relied on in this information, which is in the nature of a trover or trespass and informations of seizure, which are made certain by the writ of appraisement. And as to the objection of a general indebitatus assumpsit, it was said that that is upon a contract and so I may know what the matter is or what I contracted for; but this a tort. And, by the Chief Baron [Ward], [it was said], for the queen, it does not lie for the duty *parcella vini*, because [it is] uncertain. 2 Lev. 195; 1 Ventr. 272; Style 360; 2 Ventr. [262; 2 Jones 109; Cro. Eliz. 865].[1]

Note: Baron Price [was of the] contrary [opinion and thought the information] good; but judgment [was] arrested by the other barons on the 28th of November 1710.

Harvard Law Sch. MS. 537, pt. 2, p. 178

The court now give their opinion.

Lovell: As I [Eden] apprehended him, [he was] of opinion that it is sufficiently certain, that the information was *quandam parcellam vini*. It is certain enough in a *devenerunt*. And he thinks it good if the precedents be so.

But N.B. Ward told me Eyre took it down as for arrest of the judgment. *Ideo query*.

Price: He thinks it [was a] certain enough judgment. It has been compared to trover and detinue etc. and, in these, there must be certainty. He takes this to the stand upon its own bottom upon the precedents of this court. And he finds the method has run so, and there are above one hundred of these informations that have been so. Therefore, upon the account of the inconvenience of rev[iewing] all those in case it now be adjudged uncertain, he takes it to be good.

This differs from trover etc., being a crown case. In trover etc. the party knows what he brings it for, which it is imp[ortant] to him he should do in a case of this nature. And [writs of] *indebitatus assumpsit* are even as general [as] this. And he does not know any reason there is to distinguish them.

And he believes it is admitted, if the proceeding had been *in rem* by way of a seizure, there had been no occasion for such express certainty and that is because of the writ of appraisement, which they say ascertains it in finding the value. Now, this case is after a verdict, whereby it equally ascertained.

And suppose I see a man carry off a bundle of goods upon his back; I may perceive it wines and not be able to discover the quantity or quality. He thinks the practice has gone certainly so and that, if it had been error, it would not have passed so long.

Bury: All those precedents have passed *sub silentio* and very lately, the oldest only about 27 or 26 Car. II [1674 × 1676]. He can find no reason why they must encourage informations of *devenerunt*. He thinks they should be the certaintest

[1] *Wade v. Hatcher* (1677), 2 Levinz 195, 83 E.R. 515; *Anonymous* (1675), 1 Ventris 272, 86 E.R. 182; *Webb v. Washborn* (1652), Style 360, 82 E.R. 777; *Tregonwell v. Sherwin* (1691), 2 Ventris 262, 86 E.R. 429; *Hevel v. Reynolds* (1678), T. Jones 109, 84 E.R. 1171, also 1 Ventris 329, 86 E.R. 212; *Gramvel v. Rhobotham* (1601), Croke Eliz. 865, 78 E.R. 1092.

of any proceeding. And yet [a writ of] trover must always be certain. 2 Lev. 106, 85.[1] And so are several other cases. And so he was for arresting the judgment.

WARD was of the same opinion with BURY. Of the precedents mentioned, but four [are] with verdicts upon them; the rest were only filed. He cannot think a thing uncertain in itself can be made good by any law and that they must never attempt to make good the mistakes of the clerks. And such informations as had been mentioned cannot be called precedents.

He thinks to call anybody in question for a duty for *parcella vini* such an uncertainty as nobody can know how to make an answer to.

[As to writs of] *indebitatus assumpsit*, those are upon contracts and deliveries between the parties themselves. And yet these [. . .] in former times.

In Cavendish's Case,[2] sixty precedents were laid aside. The information is for *parcella vini per se importata* without asserting quantity or quality, which he thinks they ought to do in both.

If it be upon a man's back in a bundle, it may as well be a pig as a parcel of wine.

Suppose the Attorney [General] says J.S. [. . .] 500 [. . .] crown without saying how this must be proved upon the trial and, if it is, yet it is ill because of the impossibility of making his defense. The wisdom of the law requires certainty in all declarations. This word 'parcel' is always adjudged uncertain. 2 Lev. 272; Style 361, 392; 2 Ve. 362; Cro. Eliz., *parcella piscium* was ill; 5 Co., Playster's Case.

And so the judgment was arrested.

Lincoln's Inn MS. Misc. 538, f. [150], pl. 1

[A writ of] *devenerunt pro parcella vini*, after a verdict, was adjudged not good by reason of the uncertainty, both in the quantity by the word '*parcella*' and in the quality by the word '*vini*', which is uncertain what sort or species of wine is meant by it.

Judgment was arrested the last day of this term.

[Other copies of this report: Georgetown Univ. Law Sch. MS. B88–10, p. 771.]

---

1 *Blackborne v. Greaves* (1674), 2 Levinz 107, 83 E.R. 472; *Miller v. Green* (1673), 2 Levinz 85, 83 E.R. 451.

2 *Agar v. Cavendish* (1594), *ut supra*.

376

Hancock v. Hogg

(Ex. 1710)

Customs officers, when sued for performing their official duties, can plead generally, and then produce at the trial evidence of judicial orders of forfeitures.

Lincoln's Inn MS. Misc. 538, f. [150v]

30 November.

The plaintiff brought [an action of] trespass against the defendant [Hogg *alias* Webb], a Custom House officer, for taking thirty gallons of English spirits drawn from molasses, valued £30. The defendant pleaded not guilty, and, upon the trial, the defendant confessed the taking. But he gave in evidence that he seized the goods because they were carried coastwise from the port of London at open sea into the port of Sandwich without any cocket or certificate, as the Act 14 Car. II, ca. 11,[1] directs, whereby they became forfeited. And he proved a copy of the record of this court, whereby it appeared that an information was exhibited and a recovery of the same by a judgment of the court had that they should remain forfeited.

Dodd, for the plaintiff, insisted that the action was brought before the information was exhibited and that this being [an action of] trespass, and not trover, the defendant should have pleaded the recovery and, then, it might have been tried whether they were the same goods which nevertheless the defendant here proved.

And *Ettrick*, for him, insisted upon a clause in the same Act that gives leave to the officers of the customs to plead the general issue and give the special matter in evidence and directs that the judges admit the same and acquit the officers from all suits etc. for anything done by them in the due and necessary performance and execution of their offices or employments. And it fully appeared in this case that the defendant had done what was his duty according to law. And, therefore, he was to have the benefit of that law in giving this condemnation in evidence. And, though this action was brought before the information was exhibited, yet the seizure of the goods gives the right of recovery and that relates to the time of the seizure which gave the pretense to the plaintiff's action. And it would be a great grievance to the officers, after they have recovered goods upon due proceedings in law and wherein the plaintiff might have made his claim and defended his property to have the same thing tried over again in an action of trespass.

[1] Stat. 14 Car. II, c. 11 (*SR*, V, 393–400).

Which being observed to the jury, being a substantial jury in London, and they ready to give a verdict for the defendant, the plaintiff became nonsuited, for it fully appeared that the officers had done all things according to law.

Note that a seeming objection may be made upon that clause that gives liberty to plead the general issue etc. as if it respected only to suits upon the Act for Navigation[1] there mentioned, but, being well considered, it extends to all suits etc. brought against any appointed by the king for managing the customs or officers of the customs or persons authorized to put in execution the Act for Navigation, their deputies, or servants or others acting in aid of them, which are all in the disjunctive and must be considered so and authorizes them all to give that Act against Frauds or the aforesaid acts of Parliament relating to the customs and navigation in evidence (several acts relating to customs being before mentioned). And the opinions and practice have been so constantly.

[Other copies of this report: Georgetown Univ. Law Sch. MS. B88–10, p. 773.]

377

Attorney General v. Cresner

(Ex. 1710)

A party cannot be required to make discovery of anything that might result in a penalty. A demurrer lies to a bill or information that would subject the defendant to a penalty.

Dodd 223, Parker 279, 145 E.R. 779

An English information [was] brought to discover what stock in hand of pepper the defendant had on 8 February last and to recover the duty of 1s. 6d. in the pound laid upon it by Act[2] the last session, which enacted that the person shall enter the same at the Custom House before 15 May or, in case of neglect, he forfeit the pepper or [the] value thereof. To this bill, the defendant demurred because [it] subjects him to a penalty and, the year not being past, he [is] liable to the common informer and Mr. Attorney [General's] waiver will not prevent the common informer nor is this bill pleadable to a *qui tam* information nor can an injunction be granted to the common informer's suit. And the demurrer [was] allowed by all [the barons], 8 December 1710, at Serjeants' Inn.

See the precedents: Michaelmas [term] 1705, Attorney General v. Smyth, for duties of wines; Michaelmas [term] 6 Anne [1707], Attorney General and Pocock v. Maulsters; Michaelmas [term] 1707, Attorney General v. Bevis and others [for] duties of coals.

---

[1] Stat. 12 Car. II, c. 18 (*SR*, V, 246–250).

[2] Stat. 8 Ann., c. 12, s. 7 (*SR*, IX, 219).

Note: If the year be past so that the common informer cannot sue, then an English information lies for the attorney general to discover, he waiving penalties and forfeitures, otherwise not.

Note: The Chief Baron [Ward] said, if Mr. Attorney [General] within the year first prefer an information whereby the common informer is barred and then bring a bill to discover, it will be good. Query.

Lincoln's Inn MS. Misc. 538, f. [152v]

9 December.

The Act of Parliament 8 Anne, ca. 7, fo. 118, etc. charges all wholesale traders and dealers in pepper for all pepper they have or may have in stock on the 8th of February 1709[/10] with a duty of 18d. a pound to the crown and directs an entry to be made thereof in the Custom House nearest the place where the pepper is before the 8th of April 1710 and the proper officers to make a search and take an account thereof where it may be found before the 15th of May 1710, and, if the trader or dealer neglect to make such an entry or refuse the officer to enter or take an account, as aforesaid, or shall hide, remove, or convey away the stock of pepper to defraud the queen or shall not pay the duty according to that Act, then, for every such offense, the offender shall forfeit and lose his stock of pepper or the value, one moiety to the queen, the other to the informer.

The Attorney General's bill was to compel the defendant, being a wholesale trader and dealer in pepper to discover what stock of pepper he had the 8th of February 1709[/10], alleging that he had then great quantities which he had not entered by the 8th of April 1710 nor had paid the duty of 18d per pound for the same. And he waived all penalties for any of the offenses the defendant might be subjected to by a discovery.

To this bill, the defendant demurred as to any discovery, alleging that the matters charged against him, if true, would subject him to the penalties in the Act, being for matters done within a year.

And, upon debate, the court allowed the demurrer upon this ground only, that the discovery prayed referred to matters wholly within a year next before the bill as to all offenses within that year an informer had liberty at any time within the years to prefer an information to be entitled to a moiety of all the forfeitures that had or might incur for any offense within that year and the waiver of all forfeitures by the bill extended only to the queen's moiety and not to any information that should be exhibited by an informer within the year so as to have his moiety.

But, if the bill had been exhibited after the year so as no informer could come in, the demurrer must have been overruled, as such a one was in the Case of the Attorney General and Pocock *et al.* for the duty on malt after the year, which see 8 November 1707 and the case at large with the reasons and authorities and precedents, Hilary 5 Anne, in my notes.

Query if the Attorney General within the year and before any informer exhibits any information does exhibit a Latin information for the penalty, which, by law, he may do, and so appropriate the whole forfeiture to the crown if, pending such a Latin information which is pleadable against any Latin information by an informer, the Attorney General may not exhibit an English information and, waiving all forfeitures, may not have a discovery and relief for the duty the party then being free from all penalties, the pendency of the Latin information for the penalties being a bar to any informer and the English bill being for the duty only cannot be pleaded in abatement, not being for the same thing.

[Other copies of this report: Georgetown Univ. Law Sch. MS. B88–10, p. 780.]

378

Smith, qui tam v. Haynes

(Ex. 1710)

A wrecked foreign-built ship becomes English-built when re-built with a new keel in England.

Lincoln's Inn MS. Misc. 538, f. [151]

At a trial at *nisi prius* before me [Edward Ward] after the term upon the Act 7 & 8 Will. III, ca. [*blank*], touching the plantation trade,[1] it is provided that no ships shall be permitted to carry out of any of the English plantation in Asia, Africa, or America any of the goods of their growth or production but in English built ships and navigated and owned as that Act directs under forfeiture of ship and goods.

And the question was whether the ship *Leviathan*, whereof the defendant is the owner and wherein great quantities of tobacco and pipestaves were imported from Virginia, a plantation in America, was to be esteemed an English built ship within that Act in regard she was originally Flemish built and so foreign and, about nine years ago was wrecked at Guernsey and bought by one there for £80, who put a new entire keel to her at Jersey and newly planked her with other new work, which cost £210 in all, and some years after, the ship [was] navigated to Newcastle. And, there, she had other new materials put upon her, which cost above £300, and, afterwards, in 1707, she was repaired and doubled at one Burchetts, a builder in the river of Thames, and new tops and decks were made and another lower keel under the main keel was put to her, for which the defendant paid him £493, so that, besides the first cost, there has been laid out in new keeling and other work near £1000. But the shape and form of Dutch-built was continued by these new fabrics and little or nothing of the first Flemish materi-

[1] Stat. 7 & 8 Will. III, c. 22 (*SR*, VII, 103–107).

als were left, nothing of the keel bottom, ribs, or decks were now foreign, but all English.

And, by the opinion of judicious persons, the new building and fabric of such a ship all of English materials would not cost above £1000. And it was the opinion of the jury and, indeed, of the Attorney General under his hand that this ship was in judgment of law an English, and not a foreign, built ship. And the jury found for the defendant.

The Attorney General [*Northey*] started a question that, since the new keel and bottom, which were the principal things to make it a new ship and without which it could not be so were done and made in Jersey, which is no part of England, though all the other reparations were in England and by Englishmen, whether this ship could be esteemed an English built ship within that Act, Jersey or Guernsey not being named in it. If that had been stood upon, it should have been specially found (though I [EDWARD WARD] had no doubt of it). But, looking into the Act further, there is a clause which takes notice of Jersey and Guernsey as if within that Act. And then the Attorney General gave it up.

And the verdict passed for the defendant *ut supra*.

[Other copies of this report: Georgetown Univ. Law Sch. MS. B88–10, p. 776.]

379

Bligh, qui tam v. Santlebury

(Ex. 1710)

A person who has an interest in the outcome of a lawsuit is not competent to be a witness in that suit.

Lincoln's Inn MS. Misc. 538, f. [151v]

At a trial at *nisi prius* after term upon the French Prohibition Act, 3 & 4 Anne,[1] an information of seizure, both of ship and wine, was brought. And the defendant, claiming the property of both, produced the master of the ship to be a witness for him in the cause in defense, both of ship and goods. And, because the forfeiture of the ship depended wholly upon the importation with the privity of the master of the ship, the Attorney General [*Northey*] and the Solicitor General [*Raymond*] objected against the master's being a witness in regard he is a party concerned to prove there is no forfeiture and so he would swear himself out of an action that might be brought against him by the owners for his forfeiting the ship or goods without and against the will of the owners.

But, in regard the ship and goods in question were all claimed by the defendant and nothing of the property appeared in the matter, but that he was a

[1] Stat. 3 & 4 Ann., c. 12 (*SR*, VIII, 360).

servant only to the owners and that it would seem hard to the owners to lose the testimony of an uninterested master of a ship for the sake of a presumptive action at law that the owners may have against the master and wherein the master probably may prevail by proving their direction for the voyage etc., for which reason, I [EDWARD WARD] was inclined to have allowed the master [to be] a witness, as, indeed, he generally is to prove the whole voyage and direction of it.

But, then, the Attorney General [*Northey*] called witnesses to prove that the master at the time of the seizure claimed the ship and goods as his own and affirmed them so to be, for which reason, he was disallowed [to testify] without contest.

[Other copies of this report: Georgetown Univ. Law Sch. MS. B88–10, p. 778.]

380

Attorney General v. Watson

(Ex. 1710)

In pleading a scire facias, it is only necessary to state the matter briefly and then refer to the record where the particulars can be found.

Lincoln's Inn MS. Misc. 538, f. [152]

In a *scire facias* upon a [writ of] extent for a debt to the queen issued against one Rutherford and by an inquisition thereupon, he was found to be possessed of several parcels of corn and grain, naming the species but not the quantities by bushels or other certain measure of the value in the whole of £54 without mentioning the values of each particular.

The defendant comes in, and claims the property of all the corn and grain in the inquisition. And, upon putting in his plea, [he] laid the property in himself and traversed the property of Rutherford, and, thereupon, he had the corn and grain delivered to him. And, upon the trial, the verdict passed for the queen against the defendant Watson.

And a *scire facias* was awarded against the defendant to show cause why he should not answer the queen the £54.

And *Dodd*, for the defendant, took exception to the writ for the uncertainty in regard no certain quantities of the corn and grain were set forth nor the particular value, but only a gross sum of £54 and also because it does not appear that the goods were ever seized in execution or how made liable to the queen's debt.

But these objections were all overruled as insufficient, for these proceeding being upon a *scire facias*, the substance only in short was set forth, but the whole referred to records depending in court. And it does not lie in the defendant's mouth to object any of those things in regard he had the corn and only coming into court and making himself party to the whole proceedings by pleading with the queen he is privy to all. And it is not usual to set forth the whole records in the *scire facias* but the matter shortly and say *prout patet per recordum*.

And the queen had judgment.

[Other copies of this report: Georgetown Univ. Law Sch. MS. B88–10, p. 779.]

381

Albert v. The African Company

(Ex. 1710)

Writs of immediate extents are only granted where the crown's debt is otherwise in danger to be lost.

If bonds are to be seized into the hands of the crown, they must be actually brought into court before any writ of extent or process can be made upon them.

Lincoln's Inn MS. Misc. 538, f. [154v]

Albert was receiver general of the land tax and other taxes in Worcestershire in 1707 and 1708, for which or some of them, he had not passed any accounts, but great sums remained unaccounted for, and, therefore, he was not appointed receiver general for the taxes for [1709]. And, being called upon to clear his accounts, he then pretended that he had remitted to his brother, Fletcher Albert, in London £10,000 or £11,000 of those taxes in order to be paid into the Exchequer, who had failed to pay the same. And, therefore, in December 1710, he applied to me [Edward Ward] for a [writ of] immediate extent against his brother, whom he swore to be decayed and failed in his estate and that the money was really the queen's money and that, unless some more speedier course than ordinary was taken, the debt from him was in danger to be lost; whereupon, a [writ of] immediate extent *quoad bona et catalla, debita, credita, et specialitates*, which was all he desired, was awarded. And, by an inquisition thereupon, it was found that the African Company, by a great number of bonds under their common seal, became indebted to Fletcher Albert in several great sums payable to him at certain days and times past with interest for the same. But many of the bonds were not produced at the time of taking the inquisition, nor were they thereby seized into the queen's hands as they ought to have been. Upon the returning of which extent and inquisition into the office and affidavits of Fletcher Albert that the money due on those bonds was the money which the receiver returned to him and that the African Company was decayed in their estate and were not able to pay their debts but had refused so to do so that, unless some speedier course than ordinary was taken, the said debts were in danger to be lost, application was made to me [Edward Ward] to award a [writ of] immediate extent against the African Company, which I refused to do, for that this would be a pure aid for the queen's debtor's debtor who, for his private benefit and in breach of trust and to the queen's apparent damage had lent out the money to strangers (admitting it to be the queen's money, which nevertheless did not fully appear, nor did it appear that the Company knew it to be so).

And, it being plain that the receiver and his security were abundantly sufficient so that the queen's debt from the receiver was in no danger, it had not in such a case (which was an odious one and a fraud to the crown) been so far carried to award an immediate extent against the debtor's debtor, who is made so to the crown only by an act of law, and such immediate extents are not granted unless where the crown's debt is otherwise in danger to be lost, for, in such a case, by that prosecution of the crown for its debt and not in aid of the party, immediate extents have and may be granted. And, even in this case, proceedings may be had against the Company by *scire facias* [whereto] they may plead as they shall be advised. And, in such a case, it has been held to be a hard case that the queen's debtor's debtor who possibly may be a trader (as in this case happened) and may owe money debts to subjects by bonds, judgments, or otherwise, whose debts will be postponed in such a case and a preference given to one who stood in equal (it may be inferior) degree to the other. But, in regard these bonds for the most part of them were not in court nor seized by the inquisition, I refused, as above.

But after[wards], application being made to Mr. [Robert] Harley, the Chancellor and Under-Treasurer of the Exchequer, without acquainting him that I refused it, he granted a *fiat* for an immediate extent, which was forthwith executed and the Company's books and papers were seized and their house was locked up. Whereupon, they applied to the Lords Commissioners of the Treasury, whereof Mr. Harley was one for a [writ of] *supersedeas* to the extent, who referred the case to the Attorney General Northey, who, upon an enquiry into the matter and hearing counsel and perusing the rules of the court of 1639 touching debts in aid and the practice of the court and the defects touching the want of the bonds being in court or so much as was seized into the queen's hands, made his report to the Treasury, and, after that, the Chancellor of the Exchequer superseded the immediate extent before the return of it.

And note that the first extent, though made in the vacation, was not returnable until the first return [day] the next term, until which the court is not possessed of that or the inquisition thereupon. And though, for the recovery of a debt from the crown's debtor's debtor where the crown's original debt will be otherwise lost, the court has allowed a second extent returned into court before the return of the first. Yet, in the case of a debt in aid purely of the crown's debtor's debtor, no such course is allowed.

And, if bonds shall be really seized into the hands of the crown, yet, in such a case, they must be actually brought into court before any extent or process can be made upon them for, upon them, the process is grounded and, without them, [there is] no warrant to issue any process. And the court, in like cases, have set aside extents and inquisitions. *Vide* Parran's Case, Easter term 1709.[1]

[Other copies of this report: Georgetown Univ. Law Sch. MS. B88–10, p. 788.]

382

Floyd v. Abel

(Ex. 1710)

In this case, the contract in issue for repairs to land was not within the Statute of Frauds.

Harvard Law Sch. MS. 537, pt. 2, p. 173, pl. 1

Exchequer sittings.

[It was said] by *Dodd* in this case *arguendo* Lester and Foxcroft's Case[2] was decreed by this court and affirmed in the House of the Lords. The case was the landlord and tenant had agreed that the tenant should have such lands for twenty-one years. They wanted repairs much; the landlord was not willing to repair them, whereupon the tenant did. And [. . .] the agreement [. . .] in part notwithstanding it was only a parol agreement. Yet it was adjudged not to be within 29 Car. II.[3] So he cited another case of Hatley and Bowayl in 1696 [which was] decreed so upon the like reason.

Bridges cited, as to the principal case, 2 Ch. C. 143 and p. 8.[4]

N.B. [It was] said by *Bridges* and *Ward* that, where a witness deposes against an answer, in that case, it generally goes to a trial at law.

Phipps cited one Webb and Rogers' Case. The case was there was a memorandum of a demise of Woodland Farm and, the land having some meadow ground too, the tenant possessed himself of all, and, it was not within 29 Car. II, because the words did not extend to the meadow.

Query the case [*blank*] in this court and lately.

383

Regina v. Watson

(Ex. 1710)

An objection to the certainty of a scire facias must be made by craving oyer and not by a motion in arrest of judgment.

---

[1] *Parran v. Hart* (Ex. 1709), see above, Case No. 320.

[2] *Lester v. Foxcroft* (1700), Colles 108, 1 E.R. 205.

[3] Stat. 29 Car. II, c. 3, s. 3 (*SR*, V, 840).

[4] *Foot v. Salway* (1683), 2 Chancery Cases 142, 143, 22 E.R. 885, Chan. Repts. *tempore* North 147.

The finding by inquisition is by itself a seizure in a case of the crown without an actual, physical seizure.

Harvard Law Sch. MS. 537, pt. 2, p. 176

[There was an] inquisition upon an extent finding that Rutherford, a collector to the queen, was possessed of certain quantities of corn, *viz.* wheat, rye, etc., which now came to the hands of Watson. And, upon that, a *scire facias* [was issued] against Watson. And, upon a traverse of property and a verdict against him, it was moved by *Dodd* in arrest of judgment that the *scire facias* was uncertain, which was against Watson and only with reference to the inquisition and that Watson could not, for that reason, make a good defense that the goods were only found by the inquisition, but were never seized.

Curia: The *scire facias* is as they always are. It has reference to the inquisition, which, if you had any objection to, for certain, you should have craved oyer and demanded [profert], and not now after the issue was taken upon another point whereby the quantity in the inquisition and the value is confessed and admitted (for it was laid *ad valorem* £34) and a verdict went against you, finding the property and the good *ad valorem* £24.

And, as to the seizure, in the crown's case, there is a seizure in fact and in law. The finding by inquisition is a sufficient seizure in the crown's case without an actual one, and so it always has been, and so in the Queen and Arnold's Case, lately here, *antea.*[1]

But, in the case of the subject in execution upon a [writ of] *scire facias*. So, in a case of an inquisition upon [a writ of] *elegit*, there must be an actual seizure.

Attorney General [*Montagu*], *pro regina.*

384

Spateman v. Know

(Ex. 1711)

Woodlands that are within the Weald of Kent do not pay tithes of wood.

1 Wood 525, 1 Eagle & Younge 697

19 February 1711.

The rector of Leybourne in the County of Kent claimed tithes of wood.

The defendant confessed that, ten years ago, he purchased from Mr. Clarke forty-nine acres of woodland situated in Little Leybourne, otherwise Little Comp, in the Weald of Kent, distant three miles from Leybourne and a distinct parish and that he cut about twenty-five acres of the same and made thereof core

[1] *Regina v. Arnold* (Ex. 1709–1710), see above, Case No. 345.

wood, brush wood, or spray, broom staves, hop poles, and bark. But he said that, as the woods lie in the Weald of Kent, they are exempt from tithes.

An issue was directed to try whether the said woodlands are within the Weald of Kent or without the said Weald. And, upon a full evidence given on both sides, a verdict passed for the defendant.

The court, therefore, dismissed the bill.

385

Attorney General v. Child

(Ex. 1711)

In this case, the question was whether the crown's title by an outlawry after a judgment relates to the judgment or to the inquisition only.

Harvard Law Sch. MS. 537, pt. 2, p. 184

Easter term 10 Anne; Sir Laicon William Child's case.

The question was if the queen's title by an outlawry after a judgment relates to the judgment or to the inquisition only.

Serjeant *Floyd*: He distinguished between an outlawry before and after judgment. In the latter case, the queen's title was from the time of the judgment. He cited Statute 5 Edw. III, c. 12; Dyer, f. 172; 13 Hen. IV, Fitz. 28; F.N.B. 247 B; Reg. 288; Noy, f. 143. He cited a case between Cotton and Gristill, 36 El., Common Bench, out of a manuscript report he had, that when a man is outlawed after judgment, the queen has a title to the lands and goods and the party has no means to get his execution; the queen's title stands in his way. 8 Rep. 117; Sty., *Prerog.*, 84; 28 Ass., pl. 18; Fitz., *Entry Congeable*, 39; 41 Edw. III, f. 21; Keilw. 142; Br., *Select*, c. 33, 205, 414; 8 Edw. IV, 4; Br., *Ass.*, pl. 36; Keilw. 52, pl. 6, 63, 12.[1]

Dodd, e contra: This outlawry is for the contempt only. The court is only entitled from the time of the inquisition, that anything done between the outlawry and the inquisition binds the crown. [There is] no manner of differences between

[1] Stat. 5 Edw. III, c. 12 (*SR*, I, 268); *Ratcliffe's Case* (1559), 2 Dyer 172, 73 E.R. 377; A. Fitzherbert, *Natura Brevium*; *Registrum Brevium*; *Anonymous*, Noy 143, 74 E.R. 1105; perhaps *Bonham v. Atkins* (1610), 8 Coke Rep. 107, 77 E.R. 638, also 2 Brownlow & Goldesborough 255, 123 E.R. 928; YB 28 Edw. III, Lib. Ass., pl. 18, p. 148 (1354); YB Hil. 19 Edw. III, Rolls Ser. 31b, vol. 12, p. 492, pl. 30 (1345), Fitzherbert, Abr., *Entre congeable*, pl. 39; YB Mich. 41 Edw. III, f. 21, pl. 7 (1367); *Rex v. Abbot of Peterborough* (temp. Edw. III), Keilwey 141, 72 E.R. 313; *Anonymous* (Ch. 1468), YB Pas. 8 Edw. IV, f. 4, pl. 11, also Chan. Repts. Middle Ages 165; YB Trin. 48 Edw. III, ff, 15, 16, pl. 10 (1374), 1 Brooke, Abr., *Assise*, pl. 36; *Anonymous* (1504), Keilwey 52, 72 E.R. 210, also 116 Selden Soc. 424; *Anonymous* (1505), Keilwey 63, 72 E.R. 221.

an outlawry before and after judgment, nor can either have any relation but to the time of the inquisition. It has indeed been held that a feoffment after an inquisition defeats the king's interest, but it is otherwise held now.

In the case of two outlawries, the precedent inquisition and not the precedent outlawry takes place. Brudenell's Case. An inquisition at the suit of another takes place of any judgment, for the judgment not being [. . .] (or the interest in the land fixed but by [a writ of] *elegit*), I may take place in that case. So is Baden's Case [. . .].[1]

If [there are] two outlawries, the first inquisition shall take place. If there are two outlawries on one day, that outlawry upon which the first inquisition is will take place. If there are two inquisitions the same day, here, the first outlawry shall take place. If there are two outlawries and two inquisitions upon the same days, the first lease shall have the preference. If there are two leases the same day, as he thought, the first [. . .].

It is the inquisition that makes the crown's title. And it is occasioned only by the taking; the inquisition supposes a debt upon a judgment and is a judgment upon that. That judgment can never relate further than the judgment upon which he grounded his action.

Ward: The contempt is equally so before and after judgment. And he mentioned the Case of Edwards and Sir Robert Viner before Chief Justice Herbert, in the King's Bench, where the question was if a [writ of] *elegit* could be executed upon the estate of a person outlawed and after inquisition, and it was then held it might.

An outlawry before and after judgment are equal before and after judgment as to forfeiture of lands. The queen's title is upon the contempt.

He has known a plaintiff nonsuited for deliv[ering] a declaration in ejectment upon the land of a person outlawed. (And I by an inquisition upon it.)

The conusee of a judgment may extend notwithstanding the outlawry, because the execution gains an interest, not the profits.

He held that a [writ of] *levari facias* upon an outlawry will affect cattle levant and couchant or not levant and couchant upon the land if the land *exitus* [. . .][2] and subject to a *levari* [*facias*] upon the outlawry.

Per Ward: The goods are forfeited by the outlawry; the lands [and] the issues are forfeited by the inquisition. But how the inquisition affected real chattels, he thought was a question. The lands in the case of outlawry are as much seized by the inquisition as in the case of [writ of] extent; only they differ in consequence. 21 Hen. VII [*blank*]; Hen. VI [. . .] guides most in Westminster Hall.

---

1 *Brudenell v. Norwood* (Ex. 1681–1682), Exch. Repts. *tempore* Car. II, 489; *Rex v. Baden* (Ex. 1693–1694), see above, Case No. 101.

2 lane *MS.*

Paine and Lewis' Case, 20 Car. II, in Hale's time,[1] the second outlawry takes place if the first inquisition was upon it.

The lease upon the outlawry is *tam diu. Vide* Hardr. 101, 422.[2]

Dodd: I have often pleaded a lease made before the inquisition to the inquisition and always prevailed.

[It was] adjourned to be argued next term.

Lincoln's Inn MS. Misc. 538, f. [231], pl. 2

27 November. Attorney General v. Sir Laicon Child upon the outlawry of Sir Rowland Gwyn.

The case upon the pleading stood thus. [In] Michaelmas term 2 Jac. II, Sir Rowland Gwyn was outlawed after a judgment in debt at the suit of one Hawes.

23 January 8 Anne, a [writ of] *capias utlagatum* issues thereupon to enquire and seize the goods and chattels, lands and tenements of Sir Rowland which he had at the time of the outlawry or at any time after.

8 February 8 Anne, an inquisition was taken thereupon, which finds that, on the 25th of March 1698, Sir Rowland was seised in the right of his wife then (and still) living of divers manors and lands, mentioning them, in the County of Glamorgan of such yearly values respectively and them seized into the queen's hand *prout* the writ requires.

April 9 Anne, the transcript of the outlawry, containing the writ and inquisition, is sent into the Exchequer.

And process of levari [facias] going thereupon Trinity [term] 9 Anne, the defendant, as terre tenant of the premises seized comes in and pleads in discharge of that seizure upon the outlawry that, long before the seizure, viz. [blank] Trinity [term] 4 Jac. II, he obtained a judgment for £1000 debt in the Court of Common Pleas against Sir Rowland and that, in Michaelmas term 2 Anne, he sued a scire facias and, in Hilary term 2 Anne, he sued out a [writ of] elegit upon his judgment returnable next term, before which, viz. 29 April 3 Anne, an inquisition was taken thereupon that found Sir Rowland's seisin in the right of his wife for her life and ambarum vitarum suarum adjungendum in dominico suo ut de feodo of the same lands which were contained in the inquisition upon the outlawry at certain yearly values and delivered the lands in question to the defendant as one moiety of the lands as his freehold quousque his debt and damages should be levied. And he made all proper averments that his judgment is in force and his debt and damages were not satisfied. And he prayed the queen's hands may be amoved from the possession of the premises delivered to him for and as his moiety and the defendant to be restored to his possession of them.

[1] *Payne v. Dewy* (Ex. 1669), Exch. Repts. *tempore* Car. II, 157.

[2] *Attorney General v. Freeman* (1657), Hardres 101, 145 E.R. 402; *Attorney General v. Fox* (1665), Hardres 422, 145 E.R. 528.

To this plea, the Attorney General demurred. And he showed for cause that the defendant, by his plea, does not deny the seisin of Sir Rowland at the time of the outlawry nor at the time of the judgment nor at the time of the inquisition upon the outlawry so that it plainly appears that the defendant's judgment and execution upon it were long after the judgment upon which the outlawry was had and so it was lawful to seize the lands upon the outlawry into the queen's hands. The defendant joins in demurrer.

And, upon the argument of this case formerly by Serjeant *Lloyd*, for the plaintiff, and *Dodd*, for the defendant, and now again this day *Lutwyche*, for the plaintiff, and *Dodd*, for the defendant, the whole court held that the plea was good and sufficient to amove the queen's hand and that the queen's hands should be amoved, for, though the judgment of Hawes and the outlawry thereupon were the first, yet, inasmuch as the defendant's extent upon his judgment and the inquisition and delivery of the moiety upon the *elegit* were long before the inquisition upon the outlawry, the defendant had a good title against the outlawry which only, in this case, gave a title to the pernancy of the profits of lands which does not affect the lands themselves, only the profits, and not them neither until an inquisition and seizure thereupon be made. And the difference lies thus. The *capias utlagarum* and the inquisition thereupon gives title of forfeiture to the goods and chattels at the time of the outlawry, but not to the profits of any lands until the lands be seized upon the inquisition, for any alienation of lands before such inquisition avoids the outlawry as to them and their profits. And that is the constant learning and practice of this court. And it is agreeable to the reason of Tourson's Case, 8 rep. 170,[1] and Standford, 'Issue de mesne', 84. There, where the crown claims *nomine districtionis* etc., it has no right to any mesne rates but from the time of the inquisition and if aliened before to nothing at all. It is possible the outlawed person may alien the estate in the land even after an inquisition upon an outlawry. But the crown, by the seizure upon the outlawry, being entitled to the profits, shall not be deprived of them by any such alienation of the lands so long as the outlawry remains in force.

There have been some later opinions that favor the conusees of judgments, extending them after an inquisition upon an outlawry, which formerly was not allowed. But none say that that touches the profits of the lands. *Vide* Baden's Case, Shower's rep., fo. 70, [which] was cited and relied upon and is the very case in question, adjudged and settled in Parliament.

Some exceptions to the pleadings [were]: first, because, in the pleader's inquisition upon his *elegit*, no certain estate was set forth, for, first, it is mentioned that Sir Rowland was seised in his wife's life and for both their lives and in fee, but there is plainly found a seisin for the wife's life and what follows is senseless, at most, a redundancy; secondly, it was said that, by comparing the lands and the

1 *Tourson's Case* (1610), 8 Coke Rep. 170, 77 E.R. 730.

values in the inquisition, it appears that the moiety delivered to the conusee was not of equal value with the other moiety and then the whole proceeding upon the *elegit* is void and, by consequence, no good title was pleaded to avoid the inquisition upon the outlawry.

But it was answered that, though the values are found upon the inquisition, yet the lands delivered as a moiety have not any value put to them, and they may be, for aught appears, a full and just moiety of the lands though it may be not of the values. But, if that was an objection, it must be helped upon a writ of error in the award of execution, and [it is] not a thing void, but, at best, if at all, voidable. And this court has only the transcript before it. The record lies below in the Common Pleas.

So, judgment was given that the queen's hands should be amoved.

[Other copies of this report: Georgetown Univ. Law Sch. MS. B88–10, p. 889.]

386

Bully and Osborne, qui tam v. Lynch

(Ex. 1711)

Where a ship is forced into a port by foul weather, this is not an importation.

A witness who has an interest in the outcome of the litigation is not competent to testify as a witness.

Lincoln's Inn MS. Misc. 538, f. [161]

Saturday 2 June 1711.

There was a trial before me [Edward Ward] at *nisi prius* after last term upon a seizure of a ship and French goods in it imported to Fowey. And the questions were three: the first was whether the goods were French, which the defendant [Francis Lynch] insisted they were not; and, secondly, whether the ship came by stress of weather or voluntarily into port; and a third question arose whether the importation was with the privity and knowledge of the master of the ship, for that only could forfeit the ship within the French Act, 3 & 4 Anne, ca. [*blank*].[1]

As to the first, there was sufficient proof by persons skilled in French goods that the silks, glass, and several others (but not all) the goods aboard were French, though [it was] pretended to be taken aboard at Rotterdam (of which there were no bills of lading or invoice produced or pretended to) to be carried to Ireland (where they were as much prohibited by that law to be imported as into England).

After which proof, the defendant's counsel then insisted upon the second point that the ship was forced into Fowey by stress of weather and came not

[1] Stat. 3 & 4 Ann., c. 12 (*SR*, VIII, 360).

in voluntarily and so [there was] no importation within that Statute to make a forfeiture. Three witnesses for the plaintiffs were examined, and they swore the weather was fair when the ship came in and might have pursued her voyage for Ireland if they pleased. But, when they came into port, they did not pretend any stress of weather. But the Custom House officers, according to duty, coming aboard, enquired what their cargo was and whether they had not French goods aboard, who denied having any such, saying they had only such and such which were not prohibited, and the master said, if they found any French [goods], it was a good seizure. And, upon the search, they found several boxes of French alamodes and lustrings and several quantities of French glass and linens, pichures, beads, iron pots, etc. covered and concealed under deal boards and the bread room under the master's cabin in the scuttle, some of which were proved to be owned by the master. After which, the defendants produced one witness, who was a seaman belonging to the ship, and, upon a *voir dire*, denied his being any way concerned in gain or loss, and he and another that was the master of another vessel that lay out at sea both swore that the ship was forced in by stress of weather and was necessitated to come in for safety. And, then, the defendants offered to produce another of the seamen to prove the like.

But the Attorney [General *Northey*] and Solicitor [General *Raymond*] objected against him as one interested in some of the French silks under seizure, but would not have him examined on a *voir dire*, but would prove it upon him, which they did by one or two witnesses, who swore that the witness produced did own and acknowledge to them such and such pieces or remnants of silk and linen seized were his own and they had either his name or mark upon them. Which owning the defendant's counsel insisted was not sufficient to bar his testimony, but only went to his credit, for that he being a witness for others, they ought not to lose the benefit of it by this tittle-tattle. And that seemed to have been ruled so in cases where the witness was not concerned in interest.

And, after long debate upon that point (which was not ruled one way or the other), the defendant's counsel then called the master of the other ship and another, who swore the stress of weather, as aforesaid. And, by the evidence, it fully appeared that the importation or coming into the port of Fowey with the French goods was with the privity, consent, and knowledge of the master.

After all which evidence was given and fully summed up to the jury on both sides with directions that, if they found the goods sworn to be French to be so and that the ship came voluntarily and not by stress of weather into Fowey with the master's privity, then the law was for the queen and informer as to the ship and French goods, but not for the goods not French, but, if the ship was forced into port by stress of weather and came not in by good will or [. . .] own accord, though it might be designed for Ireland, where they are as much prohibited as in England, yet then the law was for the defendant. And the credit of the witnesses that proved the defendant's witness's owning that part of the goods seized were his own was left to the jury, who, after some time, brought in a verdict for the queen and informer as to the ship and French goods, but, as to the other, for the defendants.

And now this day, *Ettrick*, *Dodd*, and *Ward* move for a new trial, principally upon the point that the witness for the defendant who was proved by one or two witnesses to have owned himself interested in part of the French goods seized was not admitted to give his evidence, his so owning not being an absolute proof of interest or, if it was, yet not to debar the master or other of the parties concerned in the cargo of the benefit of his testimony. And, for further reason for a new trial, an affidavit was made that the defendant had many other witnesses at Fowey that can prove the stress of weather, which, by reason of the badness of the waves [?] (and little thinking of the objection to their witness's being interested), they could not then, but now shall be able to, bring up.

But the three other barons, to whom I [Edward Ward] gave a full account of the whole trial, would not grant a new trial, declaring that they held the law to be that a seaman that has any French goods aboard a ship prohibited to be imported under forfeiture and they are seized cannot be a witness nor ought to be sworn to evidence or upon a *voir dire* and that proof of his owning himself to be so interested by a witness is a bar to his testimony, and it goes not to his credit only, and that the having new witnesses not at the former trial is no reason for a new trial, for they ought to have had them there or the cause put off, it being of dangerous consequence to admit of new trials after all the evidence for the queen is discovered.

[Other copies of this report: Georgetown Univ. Law Sch. MS. B88–10, p. 837.]

387

Fizackerly v. Browne

(Ex. 1711)

A municipality can make by-laws regulating carts and carters.

Lincoln's Inn MS. Misc. 538, f. [162], pl. 2

9 June 1711.

Upon a [writ of] *habeas corpus* directed to the Mayor, Aldermen, and Sheriffs of London to remove an action of debt brought in one of the Sheriff's Court by the plaintiff [Sir William Fizackerly, Chamberlain of London] against the defendant [Elizabeth Browne, widow,] for £2 13s. 4d. become due for transgressing a by-law made by the City the 15th of October 1681 for the regulating, ordering, and disposing of cars, carts, caroons, carters, and carmen and all other persons that thereafter should work any cars or carts within the City of London or the liberties thereof for hire, the court upon hearing Mr. Attorney [General *Northey*] and Mr. Solicitor [General *Raymond*] and Mr. *Turner*, for the defendant, and *Sir Peter King*, Recorder of London, Mr. *Ettrick*, and Mr. *Dodd*, for the City, and upon a view of two rules of court, one in the Common Pleas, 13 November 4 Jac. II, in the Case of one Langley, and of a like rule made in the Office of Pleas of this court in the Case of one Greenaway, 21 June 5 Will. & Mar., by the opinion of both which courts (being after the Case of Player and Vere, reported by Justice Raymond,[1] the fine and rent being the objection in that case and by this by-law left out), the by-law was held good. This court, being now of the same opinion, declared the same to be a good by-law, and, *per totam curiam*, awarded a [writ of] *procedendo*.

[Other copies of this report: Georgetown Univ. Law Sch. MS. B88–10, p. 842.]

388

Attorney General v. Munden

(Ex. 1711)

The improper receiving of rents and profits of royal manors was not pardoned by the general pardon in issue.

Lincoln's Inn MS. Misc. 538, f. [163], pl. 2

In an information of intrusion for setting up posts in Kew Green in Richmond in Surrey and receiving the rents and profits of the manor, the intrusion was laid 24 May 1708 and the receipt of the rents from that time to the time of the information Easter [term] 1709, 3 June.

The intrusion was pardoned by the Pardon to 9th of April 1709,[2] but there is a particular exception in the Pardon, fo. 298, of persons that have converted to their own use any rents or profits of the crown lands, which was insisted upon by Mr. Attorney [General *Northey*] that the defendant Munden do now, though the time of the first intrusion is before the Pardon, yet part is after the Pardon. And, as to the profits, they are not pardoned, and so the party is not wholly pardoned. Therefore, the court awarded an injunction for possession.

But the defendant being poor and had long use of the posts for boats upon the Thames, the Attorney General will be attended, and [he will] deal mercifully.

[Other copies of this report: Georgetown Univ. Law Sch. MS. B88–10, p. 844, pl. 2.]

---

[1] *Player v. Vere* (Ex. 1678–1680), T. Raymond 288, 324, 83 E.R. 149, 168, also Exch. Repts. *tempore* Car. II, 358.

[2] Stat. 7 Ann., c. 22 (*SR*, IX, 95–101).

389

Leigh v. Mottershead

(Ex. 1711)

The land owner must set out tithes; the rector's agent cannot sever and take the tithes himself.

Lincoln's Inn MS. Misc. 538, f. [163v], pl. 1

The plaintiff brings a common action of trespass for breaking and entering his close and taking away two pigs, damages £5.

The defendant pleads not guilty as to the force and arms, and, as to the residue of the trespass, *actio non* for that, at the time of the supposed trespass and for a year before, one Joshua Wakefield was rector of the rectory of Wilmeslow in that county and had the right to the tithes of all pigs within that parish and that the plaintiff was an inhabitant and parishioner there and, within the said year, kept within that parish twenty sows and above, from which, within that time, he had twenty pigs and more, out of which the plaintiff disposed of four and was possessed of the residue and that the defendant, as servant to the rector and by his command after he had demanded the tithes of the said twenty pigs, entered into the close where the said residue of the pigs were to take the tithes. And, there, he did take the said two pigs by the showing and direction of Joseph Clarke, the plaintiff's servant, for the said tithes due and payable as aforesaid. And, in doing so, he trod down a little grass, doing as little damage as he could, by reason thereof, which is the residue of the said trespass. And he prays judgment whether the plaintiff shall maintain his action.

Upon a demurrer to this declaration and [being] shown for cause that it does not appear by this declaration that the said tithes of the said pigs were set out, the court was of opinion, upon hearing of *Lutwyche*, one of the Queen's Counsel, for the defendant, and *Turner*, for the plaintiff, that the defendant's justification or excuse was not good because that it is not shown that the plaintiff's servant had any direction or authority from the plaintiff to show or direct the defendant to take the two pigs, which, if he had any, ought to have been set forth, and, if he had not any, the defendant ought not to have taken them, for no man's servant has a power to do such a thing without his master's order, which must be shown. And it is not to be presumed. The owner must set them out, and make the severance before any certain thing can be taken for and as tithes.

And judgment was given for the plaintiff *nisi*, and, afterwards, absolutely.

[Other copies of this report: Georgetown Univ. Law Sch. MS. B88–10, p. 846.]

390

Pryor's Case

(Ex. 1711)

Where a sheriff or his deputy executes a lawful order that is later discharged, he is entitled to have and keep his fees for executing the order.

Lincoln's Inn MS. Misc. 538, f. [163v], pl. 2

Pryor, Under Sheriff of Northamptonshire, [sued] his case about sheriff's fees for executing a [writ of] *levari* [*facias*] upon an outlawry and, then, a plea was put in and [there was an] order upon security to restore the money.

But the court would not compel the under sheriff to do it without deducting his fees or some satisfaction for them.

Vide Michaelmas notes 13 November 1711, the Case of the Sheriff of Montgomeryshire and Mason.[1]

[Other copies of this report: Georgetown Univ. Law Sch. MS. B88–10, p. 847.]

391

Nicholas v. Elliott

(Ex. 1711)

Fish in a pond that are caught and sold are not tithable without a custom.

Beans and peas in a garden are small tithes payable to the vicar regardless of the method of cultivation.

Dodd 227, 4 Gwillim 1581, 1 Eagle & Younge 698

20 June 1711.

Upon a case stated and argued, the court resolved:

First, that fish in a pond, caught and sold, are not tithable without a custom, as deer in a park, rabbits in an inclosed warren, etc., for they are wild in their nature and are *quasi* in the realty, for they go to the heir, etc.;

Second, that beans and peas set by the spade, or the plough and spade, and hoed and managed in a garden [in] like manner belong to the vicar, so here, though inventing a plough which does the work of a plough and spade, and managed with the hoe, for it is not the nature of the grounds or the varying the manner of preparing from the spade, or the spade and plough, to the plough only [that] will alter the right of the tithe, the peas and beans being still set or sown in rows and banks and commonly with carrots sown between and managed with the hand or hoe in a garden fashion.

---

[1] *Montgomery Sheriff v. Mason* (Ex. 1711), see below, Case No. 396.

Stephens v. Martin was cited and Greaves and Tongue, Tr. 32 Car. II. Fish in water nets and lobsters in nets.[1]

1 Rayner 119

Matthew Nicholas, clerk, vicar of Shalford, preferred his bill in this court against the defendant Elliot, the farmer of the impropriate rectory, among other things, for tithes of pease and beans. And he also preferred his bill in the same court afterwards against Austen, the defendant in the other cause,[2] the impropriator. And he had a decree for the same though it was insisted by the defendants that the vicar was only entitled to the tithes of peas and beans set and planted in rows and ranks that have been hoed and weeded with the hand where the ground had been turned with the spade, as well in the open fields as in gardens, but not where they have been set in rows and ranks and hoed and weeded with the hand where the ground had been turned only with the plough.

[The order of 1 February 1711, Public Record Office E.126/19, f. 268v, is printed at 1 Wood 523.]

[Affirmed on appeal: Bunbury 19, 145 E.R. 580, 7 Brown P.C. 9, 3 E.R. 7.]

392

Cole's Case
(Ex. 1711)

It is the priority of seizure and not of the time of exhibiting the information that gives the title to the recovery.

Such a priority can take place within the same day.

Lincoln's Inn MS. Misc. 538, f. [221v], pl. 2

Note one Coles, a Custom House officer, having by diligence, charge, and trouble discovered divers silks imported without payment of duty and against the law, exhibited a personal information for the treble value thereof before me [EDWARD WARD] the 22nd of October, which was actually engrossed and signed by me in the evening of that very day. And, suspecting that the offenders themselves might set up some of their friends to exhibit some informations against the offenders for the same offenses, he and his clerk in court entered a *caveat* with me

---

[1] *Stevens v. Martin* (1696), Equity Cases Exch. 362; *Gwavas v. Teague* (1680), Equity Cases Exch. 111, *sub nom. Gwavas v. Kelynack*, 1 Rayner 61.

[2] *Nicholas v. Austen* (1715–1718), Exch. Repts. *tempore* Geo. I, vol. 1, p. 2, 2 Eq. Cases Abr. 734, 22 E.R. 622.

and the rest of the barons to be heard before any other informations for the same goods and offense should be signed.

The next day, *viz.* the 23rd of October in the afternoon, Mr. Penrose, an underclerk in the office, brought four or five informations for the same offense to be signed by me as of the 22nd of October, for which and by reason of the *caveat,* I refused then to sign them, offering to sign them as of the 23d, being the very day they were brought to me, but that would not be accepted, it being affirmed that instructions for those informations were actually entered in the office book the 22nd but could not be engrossed until the 23d, in which cases, the informations bear the same date with the entry in the book and that this entry in the book was made before any instructions were given by Cole, upon which these considerations offer themselves by the Statute 18 Eliz., ca. 5, to redress disorders in common informers upon penal laws and for the better execution of penal laws,[1] it is enacted:

First, that every informer upon any penal statute shall exhibit his suit in proper person and pursue it by himself or attorney;

Second, that, upon every information to be exhibited, a special note be made of the very day, month, and year of the exhibiting thereof into any office or to any officer which lawfully may receive the same without any antedate and the information to be accounted and taken to be of record from that time forward and not before;

Third, no process is to issue until the information be exhibited as aforesaid and the prosecutor's name and the statute upon which the information is grounded be endorsed upon the process under a penalty;

Fourth, no composition is to be made by any informer but after an answer to be made in court to the information and by license of the court and the informer is to pay costs in case of delay, discontinuance, nonsuit, or verdict against him.

It seems probably that this Statute extends to all informers and informations upon penal and popular laws, as well touching revenues as otherwise, where a penalty is to be recovered upon a personal information, but not to the time of exhibiting an information of seizure, because the priority of seizure and not of the time of exhibiting the information gives the title to the recovery.

But, in the Exchequer, there never was any usage of endorsing the prosecutor's name or the statute upon any personal information.

The difficulties occurring in the case in question are these two:

First, that, if the first entry in the book, which is the first step that an informer can take, should not answer the words or intention in the act of being a special note of the very day of exhibiting the information, it may so fall out that it may be impractical to get an information drawn at large in form and then an-

[1] Stat. 18 Eliz. I, c. 5 (*SR*, IV, 615–616).

other that made no such entry in the book may get an information in form to be first signed and the first and true discoverer of the crime be disappointed;

Second, that, where a contest happens between two informers who exhibit two informations on the same day for the same offense, the offender may take advantage thereof by a plea, and so no judgment is to be given for either, there being no priority of suit to attach in either, according to Pye and Coke's Case, Hobt. 128.[1]

Now, in questions arising upon priority in seizures, it has often happened that a priority in the same day has been insisted upon and allowed. And why should it not be the like in apersonal information upon specially showing the time of the day when the entry or information was first made or exhibited, the law allowing a priority in an instant in some cases? 6 rep. Fitzwilliam's Case, fo. 33a, b.[2] And I take that to be the meaning of pleading that matter in Pye and Coke's Case.

But, in the case in question, the court was of opinion that Cole's information, being exhibited in proper person and actually signed the 22nd day, should so stand and the other informations tendered the 23rd not to be signed or bear date until the 23d, which, afterwards, were done accordingly.

But it seemed to the court that personal informations may be signed as on the day of entry in the book when instructions come in the vacation and no baron is in town to sign or for some allowable cause and that no other information was before actually exhibited and signed, there being in such cases no mischief or prejudice to anybody within the meaning of the Statute. Exchequer Rules 1687, 48th Rule.

[Other copies of this report: Georgetown Univ. Law Sch. MS. B88–10, p. 851.]

393

White v. Keate

(Ex. 1711)

In this case, a copy of a record in an ecclesiastical court was refused to be admitted in evidence.

Dodd 228, 1 Eagle & Younge 699

The plaintiff was vicar [of a parish] in Berkshire. The defendant produced a copy of a terrier out of the ecclesiastical court at Salisbury in 1637 to prove that the lands and tithes in question are not in that terrier, although the parson had got

[1] *Pie v. Coke* (1616), Hobart 128, 80 E.R. 277, also Moore K.B. 864, 72 E.R. 958.

[2] *Fitz-William v. Fitz-William* (1604), 6 Coke Rep. 32, 77 E.R. 300, also Moore K.B. 681, 72 E.R. 836.

them in a subsequent terrier. And the court refused to allow a copy to be proved out of the ecclesiastical court.

Query, for [it] has been done several times.

[Order of 5 December 1711: Public Record Office E.126/19, f. 331v.]

394

Attorney General, ex rel. Dawkes v. Finlosin

(Ex. 1711)

Where prosecutors for the non-payment of import duties cannot prove their accusations, court costs will be awarded to the defendants.

Lincoln's Inn MS. Misc. 538, f. [222v]

7 November 1711, Attorney General, by the procuration and prosecution of Dawkes and Lane, two Custom House offices v. Finlosin, upon a contempt.

The two Custom House officers, in a former term, made an oath that, being upon their duty on Wednesday the 19th of July 1710 about 9 or 10 o'clock at night, they saw two men go from the Thames into the defendant's house with a sack full of goods, which they believed and suspected to be prohibited or uncustomed goods and, therefore, would have seized them, being assisted by a constable. But they were opposed and hindered from so doing by the defendant, into the cellar of whose house, one of the officers swore the sack was put, by reason of which the goods were conveyed away so that no seizure could be made.

And upon the Attorney General's motion, a day was given for the defendant to show cause why a [writ of] attachment should not be granted against him for this misdemeanor in resisting and hindering the officers to see and search for the goods brought ashore in so suspicious a time and manner.

The defendant appeared, and, by his own and several other persons' affidavits, denied the charge of his resisting and refusing the officers to search or that any goods were brought into his house but that, on the 20th day, the officers came to his house with a constable and that they had full and free leave to search and they did search his house and found nothing. And this was verified also by the constable's affidavit, who was sent for by the officers.

The court inclined that no attachment should issue.

But Mr. Attorney General *Northey* and others insisted vehemently that it was plain by the officer's affidavits that the defendant, though he has denied the contempt by affidavit, yet, by the course and rule of the court, there being two affidavits against him, he ought to be examined upon interrogatories, laying great stress upon it that, if the officers of the customs should be so resisted and hindered, that it would tend to the discouragement of officers and diminution of the revenues of customs.

And, thereupon, the defendant was ordered to appear upon an attachment and be examined, which, accordingly, he was. And, thereby, he fully and absolutely denied the contempt and matters charged upon him by the officers' affidavits, which the Attorney General admitted he had done sufficiently. Yet, in regard the officers, by their affidavits, swore they had witnesses to prove the matters charged upon the defendant, he pressed for a commission for the examination of witnesses to prove the said matters upon the defendant which is usually granted in courts of equity and cases of revenue in this court where the party has upon examination denied the contempt (though, in the other courts of law, no such commissions are granted).

And, thereupon, a commission was awarded, and the same officers were examined as witnesses (which I [EDWARD WARD] take to be irregular and against practice). But, in their examinations, it came not up so far to prove the contempt as they has done in their affidavits and not having produced any other witnesses save two Custom House officers to prove that the prosecutors were entered in a book that they were watchmen the 19th and two others the 20th (which made nothing in the case, there being but one offense charged) and the defendant having examined several material witnesses (among whom the constable who was sent for by the prosecutors was one) all proving that the defendant never refused or opposed the prosecutors from searching his house, but, on the contrary, willingly suffered and showed them every room and place in his house which they desired and that Dawkes had owned the same, the court *seriatim* delivered their opinions that the defendant was not proved to be guilty of the contempts charged upon him, and, therefore, ought to be discharged.

And he was accordingly discharged. And his counsel, Mr. *Dodd*, praying that the prosecutors might be ordered to pay the defendant his costs sustained by and since the awarding of the commission, the court on the hearing of Mr. Attorney General [*Northey*] ordered it accordingly, this being a vexatious and groundless prosecution, and ordered the defendant's costs to be taxed and that the prosecutors shall pay the same, for, though, where the case is probable, costs may not be paid, yet here, there appeared not the least ground of proof against the defendant upon the examination but what was contradicted by the defendant's witnesses.

Vide Exchequer orders and rules 1687, Rules 38 [and] 39.

[Other copies of this report: Georgetown Univ. Law Sch. MS. B88–10, p. 855.]

395

Tax Commissioners v. Briddis

(Ex. 1711)

An action of replevin does not lie against a commissioner of the revenue of the crown for actions taken to collect the crown revenue.

Lincoln's Inn MS. Misc. 538, f. [226]

7 November 1711. The commissioners for the 4s. tax for this year for the County of Surrey, plaintiffs; Briddis and Roake, assessors of that tax in the Town of Chertsey in that county and the clerks and officers of the Court of Record within the Town of Windsor in the County of Berkshire, defendants.

Upon a motion made to the court the first day of this term by Mr. Attorney General [*Northey*], *Ettrick*, and *Dodd*, on the behalf both of the queen and of the said commissioners against the defendants for suing out and granting a [writ of] replevin in that court for a mare of one of the assessors seized by virtue of a warrant from three of the commissioners for a fine of £5 set upon the assessors by the said commissioners for not making a re-assessment of 1d. in the pound upon the inhabitants and landholders in Chertsey to supply the deficiency of a former assessment made by the assessors, the case appeared to be thus that one Mr. Perkins, one of the commissioners and an inhabitant and landowner in Chertsey, upon his appeal, was relieved by the commissioners and his tax in the former assessment lowered and abated so much as required a re-assessment upon the parish of so much as 1d. in the pound came to to make good the proportion of that whole tax upon the parish.

The court, upon affidavits of the whole matter awarded a [writ of] attachment unless cause this day.

And now *Sir Peter King*, Recorder of London and one of the commissioners for the tax in Surrey, and others of counsel for the defendants, insisted that the commissioners, upon the appeal, had abated Perkins's tax without any good reason or ground, alleging that his estate there ought to be taxed as it was before the appeal. Therefore, the commissioners could [not] nor ought to have ordered any reassessment nor the commissioners have fined the assessors for not making it and that, therefore, the replevin well lay.

But the Attorney General [*Northey*] and counsel for the queen's commissioners insisted that, by the Act,[1] the appeal is to be final and that, when an abatement arises thereby, it must be supplied by a re-assessment upon the whole parish when it cannot be laid upon any particular estates, as, in this case, it could not. And the Act enables the re-assessment in such a case, and the assessors ought not to have refused the making of it, but are subject to the commissioners' power

[1] Stat. 10 Ann., c. 1 (*SR*, IX, 509–538).

in such a case, who are enabled by the Act to fine any assessors etc. refusing or neglecting to do their duty in any sum not exceeding £40 to be either by their warrant levied by distress and sale of their goods or may be returned into this court by the Receiver General, and, therefore, it was an offense in the assessors and to the revenue to have it delayed by any pretense of replevin, which ought not to have been granted in this case, being the case and revenue of the crown for the great mischief that would ensue thereby then when the remedy is given by distress and sale in so many days a replevin would delay the bringing in the tax contrary to the intent of the Act and great prejudice of the crown, there being no instance that any replevin was allowed against the crown. But the contrary [was] adjudged often in this court and, though a distress for a seizure may differ from an execution where replevins never lie, yet, where there is a time limited for the sale in the case of non-payment, no replevins ought or can prevent such a sale, but, if anything be illegal or unwarrantable, the party must resort to his action.

The Statute [*blank*] *de Districtione Scaccarii*[1] enables a sale after fifteen days, and a replevin was never heard of in such a case. The party must submit to the sale that the crown may not be delayed in its duty, and, after[wards], if he think himself aggrieved, pursue his action. *Vide* the Act, fo. 135–136, etc. [It is a] mischief for replevins to lie to the whole as being leviable if refused by distress.

And it was touched in this case that the Court of Windsor Town, though of record and extending its jurisdiction into Surrey, yet it was but an inferior court and not of jurisdiction to grant replevins, that being properly the sheriff's power, as appears [in] F.N.B [*blank*], title *replevin*, and Fitzherbert's and Brooke's abridgments, titles *replevin, avowry*, etc. and that usage, though time of which etc., will not enable a jurisdiction in such courts. Dalton, *Sheriffs*, 430, etc.

And the court, upon hearing counsel on both sides, was unanimously of opinion that the commissioners had acted according to law and that the replevin was not proper in this case and ought not to have been prosecuted by the assessors nor granted by the steward or officers of Windsor Court (in case that court had a jurisdiction to grant replevins). But it being made out to the court by affidavits that the clerks of the court who made out the replevin did not know the cause or that the crown was concerned, the court did not think fit to punish them, though it was alleged that the steward of the court did advise the replevins, which was denied by him.

But the court directed a [writ of] attachment against the assessors for their contempt in suing the replevin and taking the mare out of the officer's hands, who had distrained her in order to be sold for the fine before that fine was paid.

But a proposition being made to spare the execution of the attachment if the assessors would pay the fine set and the commissioners' costs and forbear actions, the defendant Briddis took time to consider of the proposition. And,

[1] Statutes of the Exchequer (*SR*, I, 197).

afterwards, he agreed to it, and observed it. But, as to the defendant Roake, he sued no replevin, but brought his action, and Briddis being after taken upon the attachment because Roake had not released his action though he never agreed to procure Roake so to do, it being unjust without such an agreement to imprison Briddis because Roake had not withdrawn his action, the court superseded the attachment, the fine and costs (when taxed) being undertaken to be paid.

[Other copies of this report: Georgetown Univ. Law Sch. MS. B88–10, p. 865.]

396

Montgomery Sheriff v. Mason

(Ex. 1711)

Sheriffs can charge fees for monies levied on lands seized upon outlawries and for debts to the crown.

Lincoln's Inn MS. Misc. 538, f. [227]

13 November 1711.

Upon a motion made formerly this term to the court by *Ettrick* and *Dodd*, for the under sheriff of Montgomeryshire, that the defendant Mason may pay him the poundage fee of 12d. or 18d. in the pound for executing a [writ of] *levari [facias]* £200 or £300, the issues and profits of the defendant's land which the defendant's agent promised to pay if the under sheriff would forbear the execution of it for some time and in respect the under sheriff had taken some pains and been at some charges preparatory to it, but was prevented in the execution of it by a [writ of] *supersedeas* procured by the defendant to the *levari* and so the under sheriff [was] deprived of his poundage, which he would have had if he had executed the *levari*, alleging it would be a discouragement to sheriffs to levy if they lose the fees.

And the court (*reluctante* Price) denied to interpose in this matter, as having nothing before them or indeed any authority in this case, for the defendant, being a surety for a Custom House officer and having his land seized upon a [writ of] extent as soon as he was acquainted with the seizure and that a *levari* had issued, paid to the crown the full debt and, thereupon, had a *supersedeas* to the *levari* which imported a stay of the execution and, if anything [had been] levied, to restore it, and nothing being levied when the *supersedeas* was delivered, the sheriff was not entitled to any poundage, for that subsists only by an ancient order made in this court in the time of King Charles II when the earl of Southampton was Lord Treasurer and Hale Chief Baron, which has ever since been observed, whereby to encourage the diligence of sheriffs in levying the crown debts; there is an allowance made to them to them of 12d. in some and 18d. in the pound in other cases for all monies which they should levy and pay to the crown's use. So there is no title to poundage but for what is levied and paid and, without that order, the sheriffs can claim nothing, being, by virtue of their office, obliged to execute the crown's process without a fee.

And it seemed too hard in this case to force the defendant to pay fees for executing process after he had paid the debt and had a *supersedeas* if it had been in the power of the court so to do, which it was not. Besides, if fees were due by that order, they must be paid and deducted out of the queen's money levied, and not by the defendant, for that would be to make him pay more than the debt. And here is no penalty to enforce or allow the levying of more than that certain sum for the issues and, in all executions, the plaintiffs, not the defendants, pay the poundage. And it was never known that, before the levy, the court interposed, but, when the sheriff has executed the writ and levied the money and, after that, a *supersedeas* comes, the court has not in some cases and under some circumstances compelled the sheriff to repay the money levied without an allowance of the poundage, as it was done last term or setting down of causes in the Case of Pryor, Under Sheriff of Northamptonshire,[1] who had levied goods upon an outlawry and another came in as terre tenant and pleaded to the seizure and, thereupon, it was moved to have the sheriff return the money levied without a deduction of poundage, but the court thought it not reasonable the sheriff, who had done his duty in levying, which was the laborious and chargeable part, that he should be deprived of the allowance because it was not actually paid into the Exchequer, which was as easy for him to have done as to pay it to the pleader. And that was in the case of an outlawry whereupon lands might be wrongfully seized, yet the sheriff taking an inquisition is justified though the lands were not the outlawed person's, but, upon a *fieri facias*, he must take the right person's goods at his peril. And, though it may seem hard that a man must pay fees for having his lands unjustly seized, yet the case of the sheriff and his merit being equal in the case of an outlawry as of an extent for debt, the reason of the fees is the same in both cases, being for the encouragement of sheriffs to execute the process which otherwise would be but poorly if at all done.

And, in this last instance, it was affirmed by all of the sworn clerks that poundage has been allowed constantly for monies levied on lands seized on outlawries as well as for debts to the crown.

And, as to the defendant's agent's promise in the principal case, the court left the under sheriff to take his remedy at law against him, and he was less to be considered in this case because it appeared by affidavit that, though the *levari* had been for some time in his hands, yet he had not made any steps to the execution of it, but that, being in Shropshire, he was informed that a *supersedeas* was sent thither to the like process for lands in Shropshire and thereupon he said he must

1 *Pryor's Case* (Ex. 1711), see above, Case No. 390.

make haste or else he should have the same to him. And he was served with it before any actual levy was made.

But the clerk in court for the queen said he would take care that he should be paid what he was really out of purse as a voluntary thing. But the court could compel nothing, but discharged the former order.

The like with this was denied 1st June 1712, in the Case of the Sheriff of Surrey, who seized and was at the charge in detaining a ship until delivered by an order, though the party promised to make allowance, the court having no power to interpose upon a promise.

[Other copies of this report: Georgetown Univ. Law Sch. MS. B88–10, p. 869.]

397

Attorney General v. North

(Ex. 1711)

Manorial records kept by the lords of the manor are not admissible into evidence.

Land lying below the low water mark of the sea cannot be part of a manor, because it belongs to the crown by prerogative.

If the sea washes away part of a manor, and then leaves that part again as dry land, it is a part of the manor.

Lincoln's Inn MS. Misc. 538, f. [228]

Friday 16 November 1711.

Mr. Attorney General exhibited an English bill or information as well for and on the behalf of Her Majesty as also on the behalf of His Grace Charles, duke of Grafton, vice-admiral of Suffolk, claiming also under the right of the Lord High Admiral of England for discovery and relief against the defendant [Anne North, widow,] for a great wreck of wines, brandy, and other goods cast on shore on the coasts of Suffolk of very great value, near £4000, which the defendant took and claimed as her own by right of prescription to all wrecked goods cast on shore within her manor of Benacre in Suffolk.

And the court, upon hearing of the cause, before any decree or dismission could be made whether the wreck belonged to the crown or the Lord Admiral or unto the defendant, directed these two issues to be tried at law:

First, whether the defendant has a right by prescription to all wreck goods cast on shore within her manor of Benacre in the Country of Suffolk and the limits thereof or not;

Second, whether the place whereon the goods in question or any or what part thereof were cast on shore [were] within the said manor of Benacre or the limits thereof or not.

Five of the jury had a view of the place in the second issue. The cause lasted until nine at night. And the defendant gave evidence by a record *tempore* Edw. I upon a commission of enquiry and also upon a *quo warranto* that the lord of the manor claimed wreck by prescription from the Conquest [1066] and, thereupon, no further proceedings were had. And then [it was] showed that wreck of sea was mentioned in ancient conveyances of that manor in the 19th [year] of Queen Elizabeth [1576 × 1577] and so downwards to the Norths, under which the defendant claimed and the taking of divers wrecks for above fifty years without interruption or claim of any other. And she would have given in evidence an ancient manuscript book made by some of the lords of that manor wherein entries were made of wrecks taken, but being only the lord's own entries without respect to any surveys or inquisitions or verdicts of juries, that book was not allowed to be given in evidence. But what else was offered was allowed to be very probable evidence to maintain the defendant's right by prescription as to the first issue. And the jury found it accordingly.

But, as to the second issue concerning the place, whether that was within the plaintiff's manor or the limits of it, admitted of great debate and consideration, the defendant endeavoring to prove the place in her manor by witnesses, who proved the taking of wrecks in the very place and nearer to the sea, and endeavored to make that to be parcel of her manor as being land lying between high water and low water mark, which, by Constable's Case, 5 rep.,[1] is allowed, may be part of a manor if there has been usage of taking wrecks there or other proper evidence to prove it so.

But the plaintiff produced many witnesses, some being fishermen and others seafaring men and others near inhabitants to the place, who swore that, sixty years ago and for divers after, the low water mark was much nearer to the land than now it is and, by consequence, the place where the goods were cast on shore was within times of memory much below the low water mark, and so, by law, could not be time out of mind parcel of the defendant's manor, to which prescription for wreck could appertain, and so the defendant's prescription could not hold in that case, for, if that land was not time out of mind parcel of the manor, as it could not be if, anciently, it lay below the low water mark, for, then, it was the soil of the crown and, though, in time of memory, the sea left it, yet it then must be the soil of the crown and not parcel of the manor.

And the law was taken to be so by the whole court, for, though Constable's Case and other books seemed to allow that land lying between high water and low water mark of the sea may be parcel of a manor, yet it may be otherwise. And there is no book, case, or authority that says that land lying below the low water mark of the sea can be parcel of a manor, for that is the crown's by prerogative.

---

[1] *Constable's Case* (1601), 5 Coke Rep. 106, 77 E.R. 218, also 1 Anderson 86, 123 E.R. 367, British Library MS. Lansdowne 1088, f. 69, S. A. Moore, *A History of the Foreshore* (1888), pp. 224–241 (Sir John Constable's Case and Sir Henry Constable's Case).

And the defendant's counsel, being pressed with that, endeavored to show that this land in question was formerly parcel of the defendant's manor and taken away and covered by the sea and the sea now having left it, it became and remains parcel of the manor as before. And, if it was so, it was agreed by all that, if the sea takes away and covers part of a manor yet if and when it leaves it again, it shall be taken as part of the manor, because the lord has only his own again. 2 Roll's, *Prerog.*, 168.[1] And, indeed, it is but natural justice.

And, to prove this, the defendant called some witnesses. But none of them spoke anything to that but only Sir John Playters, whose observation took its rise from riding or hunting that way about fifty years since, when he observed and believed that this place in question then lay between high water and low water mark. But no other of the defendant's witness could come up to that. But they said it was below the low water mark. And they and four or five of the plaintiff's witnesses all proved that that place was in their times and, other than Sir John, spoke to the high sea and they fished upon it for herrings and ships navigated there and it was between the low water mark some thirty, some fifty, others near one hundred yards. And upon that evidence, it was left to the jury whether that place had been formerly part of the manor and now left by the sea again or not.

And the jury thought fit to find for the defendant, one of the barons observing to the jury whether they would not rather respect the evidence of one single gentleman of good quality than of five or six tars etc.

The cases and authorities of the Abbot of Peterborough and the Abbot of Ramsey, Roll's, title *Prerog.*, 168, 169, and Dyer 326,[2] were cited and observed upon by the defendant's [counsel], and he thought they made for him that derelict land adjoining to the manor might by like reason belong to the lord of the manor.

But, to that, it was answered that those cases were ancient and nothing of late justifies them. And, there, the *consuetudo patriae* was an ingredient. And, though, in those cases, derelict land might be allowed to belong to the lord of the manor by such a right and *ratione scutagii*, yet that did not make such derelict land parcel of the manor if it had not been so before, and so it could not help the defendant in his prescription and that such a right *ratione scutagii* might belong to the owner of the land next to the sea which was not a manor.

I [Edward Ward] cited the Case of Winter and Jones, upon a trial at the bar in this court, Michaelmas [term] 1685, q.v. L. L, 36.[3]

---

[1] *Abbot of Peterborough's Case* (1349), 2 Rolle, Abr., *Prerogative le Roy*, pl. B, 3, p. 168, *Abbot of Peterborough's Case* (1367), S. A. Moore, *A History of the Foreshore* (1888), pp. 157–158.

[2] *Abbot of Peterborough's Case* (1349), *ut supra*; *Abbot of Ramsey's Case* (1369–1371), 2 Rolle, Abr., *Prerogative le Roy*, pl. B, 9, p. 169, S. A. Moore, *A History of the Foreshore* (1888), pp. 158–159; *Anonymous* (1573), 3 Dyer 326, 73 E.R. 737.

[3] *Winter v. Jones* (1685), Georgetown Univ. Law Sch. MS. B88–7, p. 613.

Note [it was] agreed by all that a prescription for wreck may be notwithstanding the Statute *Prerogativa Regis*, 17 Edw. II, ca. 11; and Stamford's *Prerogativa Regis*, title *Wreck*, fo. 37b.[1]

[Other copies of this report: Georgetown Univ. Law Sch. MS. B88–10, p. 874.]

398

Pritchard v. Harris

(Ex. 1711)

A special plea that amounts to no more than a plea of the general issue is bad pleading.

Lincoln's Inn MS. Misc. 538, f. [230], pl. 2

21 November 1711.

[In an action] in trover for a gold ring, the defendants pleaded *actio non,* because, though the ring was found by the defendants, yet, at the time of the finding, the defendants were ignorant that the ring belonged in property to the plaintiff and that, as soon as the defendants had notice that it belonged to the plaintiff and before the exhibiting of the plaintiff's bill, *scil.* such a day, they were ready and offered to deliver it to the plaintiff, which he refused to receive. And they produced the ring in court to be delivered to the plaintiff if he will receive it.

The plaintiff demurs specially to this plea, first, because the plea goes in bar of the action, whereas it ought to have been to the damages only and, secondly, because the plea amounts to the general issue only and is double and not issuable.

And, by the opinion of the whole court, the plea is not good for want of a traverse that they had converted the ring to the defendants' use, which ought to have been, for the conversion is the main thing, which, here, is neither confessed nor traversed, for, if a man loses a ring or horse and delivers them before the action, yet in regard the party might have converted them before, yet an action lies for it and, here, the plea amounts to no more than the general issue.

Authorities cited for the plaintiff were Goldesborow 155; Style 261; second point, 1 Keble 305; Hobt. 186; 2 Cro. 165; Cro. El. 435; 1 Leon. 221; 10 rep. 56, 57.[2]

[Other copies of this report: Georgetown Univ. Law Sch. MS. B88–10, p. 884.]

---

[1] *Prerogativa Regis* (*SR*, I, 226); W. Staunford, *Exposition of the King's Prerogative.*

[2] *Anonymous* (1601), Gouldsborough 155, 75 E.R. 1061; *Gowr v. Anonymous* (1651), Style 261, 82 E.R. 695; *Devoe v. Coridon* (1662), 1 Keble 305, 83 E.R. 961; *Johnes v. Williams* (1607), Croke Jac. 165, 79 E.R. 145; *Dee v. Bacon* (1595), Croke Eliz. 435, 78 E.R. 676; *Vandrink v. Archer* (1590), 1 Leonard 221, 74 E.R. 203; *Chancellor of Oxford v. Bishop of Coventry* (1613), 10 Coke Rep. 53, 56, 77 E.R. 1006, 1010.

399

Watson v. Pugh

(Ex. 1711)

Where a defendant sets a case for trial but does not proceed, the plaintiff is entitled to receive court costs.

Lincoln's Inn MS. Misc. 538, f. [231], pl. 1

27 November. *In Officio Placitorum.*

The plaintiff at law having failed to carry down the cause at the assizes, the defendant carried it down the next assizes by proviso. And he gave notice of the trial, but he did not proceed to put in the record, for which reason, the plaintiff prayed costs might be taxed.

And, upon enquiry of the practice in the Queen's Bench and the Common Pleas, it was reported that, in such a case, the defendant has been ordered to pay costs as well as where a plaintiff carries down the cause and does not proceed to trial after notice of it given, though, here, if the defendant had entered the cause, the plaintiff, if he had not opened the declaration, must have been nonsuited and paid costs.

[Other copies of this report: Georgetown Univ. Law Sch. MS. B88–10, p. 888.]

400

Wood v. Cleater

(Ex. 1711)

The contract made in this case was not within the Statute of Usury.

Lincoln's Inn MS. Misc. 538, f. [232], pl. 1

27 November.

The plaintiff brings his action upon a promissory note, and he lays also a *mutuatus* and an *insement computasset* for the like sums, being £12.

The defendant pleads *action non* for that, at the time of making the note and of tendering the money and making the promise, *scil.* such a day and place, the plaintiff, corruptly and against the form of the statute in that case made and provided, received from the defendant 24s. for giving a day and forbearing of the £12 for a year next following, being above the rate of £6 percent for a year.

And the plaintiff had judgment, the plea being nugatory and the Statute of Usury[1] nothing in this case, for here is not any corrupt agreement for lending, which must be to make the contract void. No defense was made.

---

[1] Stat. 12 Car. II, c. 13 (*SR*, V, 236–237).

[Other copies of this report: Georgetown Univ. Law Sch. MS. B88–10, p. 893.]

401

Bayly v. Brown

(Ex. 1711)

Discharge in bankruptcy can be pleaded puis darrein continuance.

Lincoln's Inn MS. Misc. 538, f. [232v]

28 November 1711.

The plaintiff brings [an action of] debt upon two bonds of £100 penalty each against the defendant who, at first, pleads *non est factum* to each, but, after *relicta verificationem*, he pleads himself to be a bankrupt with all the circumstances conducing thereto pursuant to the Statute of 4 & 5 Anne[1] and a commission issued and the commissioners' declaring him so and his being summoned and appearing before and being examined by the commissioners and his discovering his estate and performing the requisites by that Act of 5 [Anne] and that, pending the plaintiff's bill, the commissioners made a certificate to the Lord Chancellor that the defendant had performed all things required by the Act and that four parts in five of his creditors in number and value certified their consent thereto and that, after the last continuance of that plea, that certificate was allowed and confirmed by the Lord Chancellor, by reason of which and of the Statute 4 Anne, ca. [*blank*], he became discharged of the debts. And he prays judgment if the plaintiff can maintain her action against him.

The plaintiff demurs to this plea for that this plea, being *puis darrein continuance*, was not to be allowed, for the discharge respecting the original cause could not be pleaded *puis darrein continuance*. 2 Cro. 82; Yelv. 141; Lutw. 1141.[2]

But the court held that the confirmation of the certificate not being had while the plea depended, but after, it could not be pleaded sooner and the Act 4 Anne, ca. 17,[3] directing that bankrupts' surrendering themselves to the commissioners and conforming in all things as the Act directs shall be discharged from all their debts owing at the time they became bankrupts and, if arrested or impleaded for any debt before, shall be discharged on common bail and plead in general that the cause of such action accrued before such bankruptcy and give the Act and special matter in evidence and, if [there be] a verdict for the defen-

---

[1] Stat. 4 & 5 Ann., c. 4 (*SR*, VIII, 461–465).

[2] *Baker v. Gough* (1605), Croke Jac. 82, 79 E.R. 70, also *sub nom. Lord Abergavenny v. Edwards*, Moore K.B. 775, 72 E.R. 898; *Ewer v. Moile* (1608), Yelverton 140, 141, 80 E.R. 94, 95; *Campion v. Baker* (1704), 2 Lutwyche 1139, 125 E.R. 633.

[3] Stat. 4 & 5 Ann., c. 4 (*SR*, VIII, 461–465).

dant or the plaintiff [be] nonsuited or judgment [be] against him, the defendant [is] to have his costs.

And the defendant here had no day during the continuance of the plea to show the Lord Chancellor's confirmation of the certificate, and, therefore, of necessity, he must do it after to show the defendant had performed all that the Act requires and he having generally pleaded and shown that he had done and performed all the requisites by the Act and that he had surrendered himself within the thirty days after notice in the *Gazette*, though he did not show when the precise day of the notice in the *Gazette* was, it was held sufficient upon the general allegation, for it was not intended to be so precise in the showing of all of the particulars, it being now held sufficient to show that he was a bankrupt within that Act and had done all things required thereby generally and, if he had not, the plaintiff might have taken issue and not demurred, the Act intending a general showing of the performance.

And the defendant had judgment delivered by Chief Baron [Edward Ward] at the desire of all of the other barons concurring therein.

[Other copies of this report: Georgetown Univ. Law Sch. MS. B88–10, p. 894, pl. 2.]

402

Attorney General v. Johnson

(Ex. 1711)

In an action for a debt to the crown, the Attorney General can end the prosecution of the case during the trial and have a new trial.

Lincoln's Inn MS. Misc. 538, f. [213v]

29 November 1711.

The information was in the nature of an action of debt for £91 18s. 4d. for so much of the queen's money received by the defendant [Thomas Johnson of Liverpool] to the queen's use. And the case was this.

The defendant shipped out from Liverpool for Belfast in Ireland in the ship *Anne* of Milford (Edward Mark Donnest, master) 551 bushels and four gallons of salt 22 August 1707. And he gave a bond for the payment of the duties or for returning a certificate from the officer at Belfast of the landing of the salt there. And, upon the producing of that to the officers at Liverpool, he obtained a debenture from them for the payment of £91 18s. 4d. to him for the duties of the salt so entered by the defendant outwards and then, upon such certificate, he was to have a debenture and his bond was to be delivered up. But, to deceive the queen of that duty, it was given in evidence that the salt was carried to Goodwick in Wales and there he landed it. The ship went empty to Dublin, and there took in the like quantity and carried it to Belfast and there obtained a certificate as if it came from Liverpool. And, thereupon, the defendant had a debenture for the £91 18s. 4d. And the defendant's endorsement on the debenture under his hand was produced in these words 'received of the Commissioners of Excise for the duty of salt an allowance of the sum of £91 18s. 4d. in full of this debenture in discharge of my bond entered into the 22nd of August 1707 whereby the duties on the salt herein mentioned are secured.'

The matter of fact of the landing of the Liverpool salt at Goodwick was sworn by two or three witnesses and, by one, of the ship's going empty to Dublin and there taking in salt and landing it at Belfast and bringing the certificate from thence to Liverpool and having the debenture which seemed all that was unlawful to be done by the family of the Rogers living at Goodwick without the defendant's privity.

But it could not be proved that the defendant's bond was delivered up or vacated, but that it stood out against him. And, thereupon, the defendant's counsel insisted that this evidence did not maintain the information that the money was received by the defendant at all, it being only a receipt by allowance in full of the debenture in discharge of the bond, which still, in truth for aught appears to the contrary, stands out against him not delivered up or vacated, and so, at law, he may be liable upon it, though probably, in equity, he might be relieved against it if he had truly performed the condition. And so he cannot be charged for money actually received for which no evidence was given. And, therefore, he is not chargeable upon this information.

And, thereupon, the Attorney General [*Northey*], without any consent (as he might) withdrew a juror in order to [have] another suit.

403

Marquess of Carmarthen v. Morton

(Ex. 1712)

Special bail cannot be required in actions of scandalum magnatum.

Lincoln's Inn MS. Misc. 539, p. 1

The first Thursday of this term [Easter term 1712] in the Exchequer Chamber, Mr. *Dodd* moved the court for a special *quo minus* to be awarded for the marquess [of Carmarthen], who is a peer of this realm, *viz*. Lord Osborne,[1] against the defendant, Mary Hill Morton, to be marked for special bail to the value of £5000 at least whereupon the marquess will upon an appearance declare against her in a *scandalum magnatum* for words by her spoken against the marquess tending to

[1] M. Knights, 'Osborne, Thomas, first duke of Leeds (1632–1712)', *Oxford Dictionary of National Biography*, vol. 42, pp. 24–36.

charge him and his father, the duke of Leeds, with the murder of one Monsieur Robart and that to bring him into the ill opinion of his father.

The defendant claimed to be his wife under the title of the marchioness of Carmarthen. And he produced the affidavits of four persons who heard her speak the words that he and his father murdered Robart several times and in the presence of several persons and, after[wards] produced the affidavits of two other persons whom the marquess employed to obtain his father's reconciliation to him, being under his displeasure, who both swore that they often endeavored it and that, as far as they apprehended by the duke's expressions, do in their consciences believe that the defendant's pretending to be and publicly going by the name of the marchioness of Carmarthen unjustly has been the chief cause of hindering the reconciliation of his father to the plaintiff, on which account, they believe the plaintiff has been a sufferer to the value of £5000 or more and may yet be a greater sufferer on the same account if not prevented by a speedy course of law.

The court enquired whether they had any precedents of special bail in actions of *scandalum magnatum*.

The counsel said they had not, but took it to be a matter of course upon such affidavits.

Which the court, doubting, wished it might be moved another day, which was so done two days after. And, then, they cited only the Duke of Richmond's Case, wherein they said there was special bail ordered by the Court of King's Bench for £1500 in a *scandalum magnatum*.[1] But that was a mistake, for it was only bail at a judge's chamber submitted or agreed to and never came before the court. And, by Raymond's reports, fo. 74, there was a rule for special bail *nisi*; that by 1 Keble, fo. 173, in a commoner's cause, there was special bail ordered for calling a woman a whore whereby she lost her marriage, but the authority of that book and case was suspected. There were also cited 1 Mod., fo. 2; 1 Siderfin 207; 1 Ventris 60. But those cases seemed not to concern bail.[2]

But the court denied special bail in the case in question, as well upon the reason of the law that there is no rule to go by as to damages in case of words which is altogether uncertain and differs from a special writ for bail in the case of a battery or mayhem, where the thing itself necessarily imports damage apparent, which, in case of words, is only imaginary. And to give leave to have a *quo minus* to hold the defendant to special bail at all, especially to so great a value, is indeed to condemn the defendant to a perpetual imprisonment for want of it and, in effect, never to try the cause, for it can never come to trial without such bail, which the defendant may not be able to give. And, by 2 Modern reports, fo.

---

[1] *Duke of Richmond v. Costelow* (1709), 11 Modern 234, 88 E.R. 1010.

[2] *Earl of Stamford v. Gordal* (1663), T. Raymond 74, 83 E.R. 41; *Anonymous* (1661), 1 Keble 173, 83 E.R. 882; *Anonymous* (1669), 1 Modern 2, 86 E.R. 682; *Rex v. Crosse* (1664), 1 Siderfin, 204, 207, 82 E.R. 1058, 1059; *Earl of Peterborough v. Mordant* (1670), 1 Ventris 59, 60, 86 E.R. 42.

215, in the Marquess of Dorchester's Case, Easter term 29 Car. II, it was denied as it was in 3 Mod. 41, in the Earl of Macclesfield's Case, and though that book says the court said it was discretionary and [it was] there said to be denied in the Duke of Norfolk's Case unless oath be made of the words.[1]

Yet, upon conference in the case in question with the judges of both the courts of Queen's Bench and Common Pleas, who agree that, of late, they never hold to special bail in the case of *scandalum magnatum* for the reasons above and the ill consequence that may attend it by a perpetual imprisonment for want of it and that this action, which is founded upon a Statute and is *tam quam*, in which cases of *tam quam*, no error lies in the [Court of] Exchequer Chamber, as Cro. Car. 142, nor special bail in [an action of] debt for tithes, L. 2, 51, nor a change of venue, it differs from other cases, the court delivered their opinion *seriatim* that no *quo minus* ought to issue marked for special bail in this case though the words were, as sworn, very scandalous for the reasons and authorities before mentioned.[2]

Note, afterwards, in the Common Pleas in the same term, the marquess brought an [action of] *indebitatus assumpsit* against the defendant and upon oath made thereof had special bail ordered where she could not procure so lay by it. And though the plaintiff brought down his trial twice, he did not proceed. And the court made a rule that, unless the plaintiff tried the cause the sitting after term, she should be discharged on common bail, two judges being of opinion that she ought to have been so after twice notice of trial and not going on. The cause was not tried after term.

But the duke of Leeds tried his [action of] *scandalum magnatum* against the defendant wherein there was no special bail and had a verdict for 1000 marks. The words were that the duke murdered Mr. Robart.

[Other copies of this report: Georgetown Univ. Law Sch. MS. B88–10, p. 914.]

404

Attorney General v. Campbell

(Ex. 1712)

A proposed amendment to correct a mistake in a record that goes to the foundation of an execution will not be allowed.

---

[1] *Marquess of Dorchester's Case* (1677), 2 Modern 215, 86 E.R. 1033; *Earl of Macclesfield, qui tam v. Starkey* (Ex. 1685), see above, Case No. 11; note *Duke of Norfolk v. Alderton* (1697), Carthew 400, 90 E.R. 832, 2 Salkeld 668, 91 E.R. 568, 12 Modern 121, 88 E.R. 1207.

[2] *Viscount Say and Sele v. Stephens* (1628), Croke Car. 135, 142, 79 E.R. 719, 725, also W. Jones 194, 82 E.R. 103; *Wheeler v. Potter* (1669), Lincoln's Inn MS. Misc. 500, f. 51.

Lincoln's Inn MS. Misc. 539, p. 3

A motion was made for an amendment to be made where the case appeared to be thus. An information was exhibited Michaelmas term 6 Anne [1707] by Hendry, *qui tam*, against Richardson in an [action of] *devenerunt* for a great quantity of French wines imported and forfeited and came to his hands forfeited. And a verdict and judgment were for the queen and informer for £3990, the value thereof. And the judgment was entered for £1995, for Her Majesty's moiety and the like sum for the informer's moiety. After which a writ of extent grounded upon the said judgment was awarded against the said Richardson to recover Her Majesty's moiety and, in order thereunto, to enquire and seize into Her Majesty's hands the lands, tenements, goods, chattels, debts, credits, and specialties of the said Richardson therein reciting that the queen had recovered a judgment against Richardson for £3990 for Her Majesty's moiety which, in truth, was a mistake, for the queen's judgment was only for £1995, a moiety thereof.

And, by virtue of that writ of extent so falsely reciting the judgment, there was an inquisition found that the defendant Campbell and divers others persons therein named at the time of the *teste* of the extent and on the day of the taking of the inquisition were indebted to Richardson in divers sum of money, showing what and for what causes, which were seized into the queen's hands so that she might have them until she should be satisfied the debt aforesaid, no other debt therein being mentioned but £3990.

And, upon an information in debt so made upon the said extent and inquisition against the said Campbell for his said debt, which was found to be £3409 13s. 4d., Campbell appeared and put in bail to it and prayed *oyer* of the original judgment, extent, and inquisition. And he pleaded *non indebitatus etc.* But the prosecutors for the queen, perceiving the mistake of the sum of £3990 in the recital of the extent against the defendant instead of the true sum of £1995, moved the court by *Dodd* to have that mistake between those two sums to be amended.

The court ordered the first day of this term that the defendant should show cause why it should not be amended accordingly, it being only a mistake of a sum in the recital of the extent, the judgment upon the record of the court showing it to be so.

But upon hearing *Sir James Montagu, Ettrick, Turner*, and *Ward*, for the defendant, the court declared unanimously that it was not amendable, for the extent reciting the judgment to be for £3990 and to enquire and seize Richardson's estate, debts, credits, and specialties until the queen should be satisfied that mistaken debt and the inquisition being founded upon that extent and debt mistaken and the seizure itself of the defendant's [. . .] being that the queen should have them *donec* and *quousque* [it] should be satisfied that mistaken debt, the amending the £3990 to £1995 quite alters the jury's finding by the inquisition and the seizure by it which is the foundation of the queen's title and makes quite another case and differs from other amendments where there is no inquisition.

And, afterwards, in this term, by a motion on behalf of the crown, the information was quashed, and the extent also. And the crown was left to proceed upon the judgment as Mr. Attorney General shall think proper.

[Other copies of this report: Georgetown Univ. Law Sch. MS. B88–10, p. 918.]

405

Jenkins, qui tam v. Horne

(Ex. 1712)

If a ship be seized and set at large upon security, the security shall not be discharged on account of the neglect of the prosecutor of an information in support of the seizure to try it according to notice if he declare he intends to try it the term after the application for the discharge.

2 Lord Raymond 1311, 92 E.R. 358

In an information upon a seizure of currants imported in the *William and Ann* of Plymouth into the port of London contrary to the Act of Navigation, 12 Car. II, c. 18, s. 14,[1] from Algiers in Africa, the currants not being of the growth, product, or manufacture of that place or of the region where they were shipped etc., the defendant claimed property, and, on issue joined, notice was given for trial in Trinity term last and for the sitting after Trinity term last. And on motion on behalf of Charles Moone, a security for Horne on the writ of delivery, the following order was made, *viz.*:

> Middlesex. Whereas a writ of delivery for the said ship with her apparel and furniture has been awarded under the seal of this court upon a recognizance entered into to Her Majesty by Edward Grose of East Smithfield, baker, and Charles Moone of Mowell in the County of Cornwall, cooper, dated the 11th day of February last in the sum of £252, now, upon the motion of Mr. Dodd, of counsel with the said Charles Moone, informing the court that the plaintiff gave notice of trial to be had in this cause, the sitting of the lord chief baron within the last Trinity term in Middlesex; in pursuance of which notice the said Charles Moone attended with his counsel and witnesses on the day appointed for the said trial, as also on the day of sitting after the said term in Middlesex, not having received any countermand from the said plaintiff, whereby the said Charles Moone, who is at the whole charge of the defense made in this cause, was put to great expense, it was, therefore, now prayed that the said recognizance might be discharged and that the said Charles Moone might have his costs, it is this day ordered by the court that the said recognizance entered into by the said Edward Grose and Charles Moone shall be vacated and discharged and that it be

[1] Stat. 12 Car. II, c. 18, s. 14 (*SR*, V, 249).

> referred to John Morgan, Esq., deputy to Her Majesty's Remembrancer of this court, to tax the said Charles Moone his costs against the plaintiff in this cause, unless cause be showed to the contrary on the last day of Michaelmas term next.

Upon the motion of Mr. Attorney General [*Northey*], the Solicitor General [*Raymond*], and Mr. *Ward* at the setting down of causes after this term, to which time the order was enlarged, it was discharged: first, as to the discharging the recognizance upon declaring the plaintiff intended next term to try the cause; secondly, as to the payment of costs for not going on to trial, because such order can be made only in behalf of and upon the motion of the defendant and his counsel, and not in behalf of the security. Lord Chief Baron [Ward], Bury and Lovell, barons, [were] present in court.

Note: The Lord Chief Baron [Ward] exclaimed against the order, as being obtained perfectly irregularly without an affidavit and by surprise.

406

The Case of The *Batchelor*

(Ex. 1712)

A court cannot prohibit purchasers of goods that were forfeited as prizes from disposing of them as they please.

Lincoln's Inn MS. Misc. 539, f. [10v]

The case of the Acupulto ship called The *Batchelor* and the cargo of thrown silk in it.

Some merchants of Bristol who sent the ship *Duke and Duchess of Bristol* on a trading voyage to the South Seas, which returned from thence by the East Indies and took the Acupulto ship with a rich cargo by goods in her as prize, amongst which there were divers balls of thrown silk, which, by the acts 1 & 2 W. & M. and 1 Anne,[1] might not be imported into England as merchandise, which ship and goods were lawfully condemned as prize in the Admiralty and, being ready to be exposed to sale and the Silk Throwers Company conceiving that, if this great quantity, being above twenty bales and valued at above £6000 should be used in England, it would be great prejudice to their trade, caused a forfeiture thereof to be made by Groves, the Master of the Company, as forfeited, being prohibited goods.

Mr. Attorney General [*Northey*], for the proprietors of the ship and silk, prayed that the seizers might appear and show the cause of seizure and that, in

[1] Stat. 2 Will. & Mar., c. 9 (*SR*, VI, 173); Stat. 1 Ann., cc. 21, 22 (*SR*, VIII, 73–74).

the meantime, the proprietors might have leave to view and show the title in order to [have a] sale, which was ordered accordingly the 31st of May 1712.

The 3rd of June afterwards, the proprietors of the silk by *Ettrick*, their counsel, prayed a writ of delivery, the seizure being made to prevent the sale upon the condemnation in the Admiralty, which, upon hearing counsel on both sides by consent, was granted on security to be given for the appraised value, which was £6000. And, upon the return of the writ of appraisement, security was given accordingly.

And now, Mr. Attorney General [*Northey*] prays that the proprietors may not be admitted to sell or use the silk in England, which would be so prejudicial to the silk throwsters and almost starve them for want of work.

But the court denied the motion as being out of their power to hinder the proprietors to sell the silk or to compel them to export it, for, being condemned as prize, it could not otherwise be liable to seizure as prohibited goods by way of merchandise, for the Statute of 3 Edw. IV,[1] which restrains the importation of foreign manufactures under forfeiture *toties quoties* they shall be found to be sold, yet, when once condemned, they may and always are vended and used here. And no law less than an act of Parliament can restrain the use or compel the exportation, as is provided by some acts about East India goods for that purpose and after such proceedings by consent and, as the law stands, the court has no power to stay the sale or enjoin the exportation. L. H, 54.[2]

The case was afterwards, in Michaelmas term 1712, tried at *nisi prius* and a special verdict was found.

[Other copies of this report: Georgetown Univ. Law Sch. MS. B88–10, p. 936.]

407

Meadow v. Gardner

(Ex. 1712)

In this case, an estreat of improper fines was found by the court to be irregular, and then they were voluntarily withdrawn.

Lincoln's Inn MS. Misc. 539, f. [11]

28 June 1712. The case between Meadow and others, inhabitants of Sawbridgeworth in the County of Hertford, and Mr. Gardner and others, commissioners for the present 4s. tax in that county.

The commissioners having sent up an estreat under their hands and seals of certain fines by them set upon Meadow and two others, which was received by an

[1] Stat. 3 Edw. IV, c. 3 (*SR*, II, 395–396).

[2] *Slater, qui tam v. Pidgeon* (Ex. 1679), Exch. Repts. *tempore* Car. II, 441.

under clerk in the Queen's Remembrancer's Office of his own head without any oath or delivery before a baron, purporting a fine of £20 to be set by the commissioners upon the said Meadow, who appeared to have been returned by the assessors of that parish to be a collector of that tax and was authorized also by the commissioners by a warrant and duplicate to be a collector for the whole year's tax and had collected and paid the first payment, because they, having been informed of his inability, superseded his collectorship and demanded of him to deliver up the duplicate of the tax delivered to him that they might rectify some mistakes and abuses in the assessment and, for his refusal so to do, the commissioners set the said fine of £20 upon him.

There was also a charge of £10 set upon one Gwyn, a constable, for so much money which he had in his hands for the queen's use levied by virtue of a warrant from the commissioners, which was in truth part of Meadow's fine.

There was also a fine of £40 set upon one Ferguson, a high constable of the hundred, for not executing two warrants from the commissioners for levying the said two sums of £20 and £10.

The court was moved to discharge this estreat, supposing it to be irregular. And, upon the reading of many affidavits touching the matter, the court ordered that process should stay and, if Mr. Gardner, who was sworn to have a great hand in the matter, or any other of the commissioners thought fit to say anything about the matter, they might be heard, having notice thereof.

And this day, Mr. Solicitor General [*Raymond*], *Ettrick*, and *Ward* insisted that the commissioners had acted legally and yet been reflected upon in the affidavits. And they also produced affidavits for their own vindication.

But, upon the hearing, Serjeant *Comyns* and *Dodd*, for the officers, the whole court was of opinion, and so declared:

First, the estreat was not regular nor justified by the Act, for, by the express provision of it, they are to be levied by warrants from the commissioners and paid to the receiver general and duplicates to be sent to him and into the Exchequer, but this when the receiver general passes his account;

Nor did it come regularly into court, the under clerk in the office having no power to receive it, that Meadow having been duly returned collector by the assessors and having his warrant's and duplicates from the commissioners and having collected and paid the first payment and, as appeared, had advanced £30 for some inhabitants upon credit and being superseded, he did offer to deliver up the duplicate and warrant to the commissioners under a promise to have it again, which he not obtaining, he did refuse to deliver it, which not being any contempt in relation to his office and being his justification for what he had done and the means to obtain his £30 and, if there was a fault in the assessment, it was none of his, but the assessors and the fault might have been rectified by the duplicate the commissioners had, it was thought no such contempt for which he could be fined, it being plain by the Act that, though it may be that collectors, once lawfully authorized, may for just reasons be discharged, yet no new one can be appointed by the commissioners without a return from the parish, because the parish is answerable for them and no new one appointed in his place was not so returned, and no contempt within the Act or the commissioners' power for which a fine could be imposed;

Third, as to the charge upon him, it is no fine but a *super* signifying he has so much of the queen's money in his hands and that really was that £10, part of the £20 fine set upon Meadow, had been levied by him by warrant of the commissioners and not paid, which seemed not to be any fine, but a *super*, and not within the commissioners' power;

Fourth, as to the £40 on Ferguson, if the commissioners could compel a chief constable to execute their warrant for levying the fines, not showing any default in the constables of the parish, yet he acquainting the commissioners that he was advised by counsel that he could not lawfully execute the warrants, and, in truth, the warrants not being justifiable to levy both the £10 and £40, for, as to the £10, it was not in the commissioners' power to levy it, it was thought the setting of that fine might have been spared and ought not to be levied.

So, upon the whole matter, the court thought fit to stay all proceedings upon the estreat, but, at present, not to discharge it without hearing Mr. Attorney General, it appearing that the levying and answering of the tax so far had been duly observed and the whole tax laid upon the parish raised and the question only who should be collector, it appearing that the major part of the town appeared for Meadow, and the new collector was not nominated by the parish, who is to answer for him, but by the commissioners only, which is not warranted by the Act.

But, after the commissioners and other the officers had heard the inclination of the court, they fell into an agreement that the £10 levied on Meadow should be restored and he and other officers that had brought actions against the commissioners should withdraw them and that the estreat that was, in truth, not a regular nor formal estreat nor could warrant any process nor came regularly into court [and] should be withdrawn by the commissioners, which was agreed accordingly. Mr. Solicitor [General *Raymond*], for the commissioners, agreeing to it and so the matter ended.

I [EDWARD WARD] observed that the Act of Parliament is the measure and direction of the duty and power, both of the commissioners and subordinate officers, and, therefore, all proceedings must be governed by it. The collector meddles not with fines set, levied, and answered pursuant to the Act, for they must be as the acts direct. But they can be set only for offenses relative to their duties to be performed as the Act directs and not otherwise. And so [*blank*].

[Other copies of this report: Georgetown Univ. Law Sch. MS. B88–10, p. 938.]

408

James v. Philips

(Ex. 1712)

A plaintiff must allege a specific sum as damages in a tort case.

Lincoln's Inn MS. Misc. 539, f. [12], pl. 1

2 July 1712. *In Officio Placitorum.*

An action of assault and battery was brought by the plaintiffs [James and his wife] for a battery upon his wife. And [there was] a verdict for the plaintiffs, and damages were assessed by the jury to the sum of [*blank*]. Exceptions in arrest of judgment were taken to the declaration because it laid the battery to be done on the wife *ad damnum* of the wife (not saying what sum) but, then, it goes on, *unde* the plaintiffs *dicunt quod deteriorati sunt et damnum habent ad valentem* £20. And the exception was to the first laying to the damage of the wife, which, by law, could not be allowed to lay any damage to the wife only and, for that purpose, the cases in Palmer's reports 338; 2 Cro. 664; and 1 Siderfin 387, were cited.[1]

But the court was of opinion that the saying to the damage of the wife in the first place was but surplusage and void, there being no sum mentioned, and some sum must be laid for damages. And, therefore, what comes under the *unde dicunt* that they are deteriorated *ad damnum habent ad valentem* £20 is the true and right declaration for damages and well enough to be laid to the damage of both, being a battery upon the wife, wherein she may have the benefit if she survives.

And the plaintiff had judgment after hearing counsel twice, the rule formerly given being for judgment *nisi* better cause this day and no better cause [was] shown.

[Other copies of this report: Georgetown Univ. Law Sch. MS. B88–10, p. 943.]

409

Thorpe, qui tam v. Hannoway

(Ex. 1712)

The question in this case was whether a defendant in a qui tam prosecution can be allowed to set the case for trial.

---

[1] *Buckley v. Haley* (1623), Palmer 338, 81 E.R. 1112, also Croke Jac. 655, 79 E.R. 565; *Thomlins v. Hoe* (1623), Croke Jac. 664, 79 E.R. 574; *Horton v. Byles* (1668), 1 Siderfin 387, 82 E.R. 1173.

Lincoln's Inn MS. Misc. 539, f. [12], pl. 2

An information *tam quam* was brought against the defendant upon a penal law for a great penalty. And the issue [was] made up and joined by the Attorney General, as usual, and notice [was] twice given for trial. But he did not proceed. And, now, a motion was made that the defendant might carry down the trial by provisoes, it being a great demand hanging over the defendant's head and he at a great charge in keeping many witnesses and the hazard of their deaths, being seafaring men.

The Attorney General [*Northey*] not opposing the motion, but I [EDWARD WARD] doubted whether any defendant in a *tam quam* [action] was ever allowed to carry down the record by proviso in any case, and, if he could, yet whether it could be done as this issue is joined by the Attorney General and, if the Attorney General should enter a *noli prosequi*, yet whether, in that case, there must not be a new issue joined between the informer and the defendant before such carrying down by proviso. It being so practiced in the Case of Robinson as to the issue joining after a *noli prosequi*, though, in that case, there was not anything relating to a proviso. *Vide* L. M, 14, trial after *non prosequi*; 1 Ventr. 315, no proviso in the indictment; L. 2, 142b, upon the general issue, the informer draws up the record without the Attorney General.[1]

[Other copies of this report: Georgetown Univ. Law Sch. MS. B88–10, p. 944.]

410

Miles v. Metcalfe

(Ex. 1712)

In the case of a forfeiture for non-payment of customs etc., the expenses of the seizure are paid by the seizer until the bidding and, from then, they are jointly paid by the seizer and the bidder.

Lincoln's Inn MS. Misc. 539, f. [12v]

2 July 1712.

[In a case] between Miles, a bidder, and Metcalfe, a seizer of wines and other goods, the court was of opinion that the officer that seizes and exhibits the information in a case of a condemnation for want of a claim and a sale of the goods to a bidder is to bear all the charges to the time of the bidding and, from thence, the seizer and the bidder to bear the subsequent charges between them.

[Other copies of this report: Georgetown Univ. Law Sch. MS. B88–10, p. 945.]

---

[1] *Allen, qui tam v. Brittiss* (Ex. 1695), see above, Case No. 131; *Anonymous* (1677), 1 Ventris 315, 86 E.R. 203; *Anonymous* (1671), Lincoln's Inn MS. Misc. 500, f. 142v, pl. 4.

411

James, qui tam v. Rogers

(Ex. 1712)

All salt imported for the curing of fish is excepted out of the Salt Act of 2 & 3 Anne, not just salt for fish caught in the particular voyage.

Lincoln's Inn MS. Misc. 539, f. [14v]

Upon a seizure of a ship called the *Elizabeth* of Dublin and 246 bushels of salt in it, upon a trial on the information and a special verdict thereupon, the case appeared to be thus. The information was grounded on the Act 2 *Annae Reginae*, entitled an Act for the Better Securing and Regulating the Duties upon Salt,[1] whereby it was enacted that no salt coming from Ireland, Scotland, or the Isle of Man should, after the first of June 1704, be imported or brought into any port or place in England, Wales, or Berwick nor taken out of any ship nor put on shore in any of those ports or places on pain of forfeiture of the ship and the salt in it. But, after, in the same Act, there is a proviso that, in case any ship or vessel should come into any port of England, Wales, or Berwick from Ireland or other foreign part having on board any quantity of salt which was taken in only for the necessary provisions of the ship for such voyage or for the curing of fish, then the master of the ship might land such salt, so as entry be made thereof within ten days next after his first coming into such port and duties paid or security for the same before landed or taken out of the ship in the same manner as duties of foreign salt imported are to be paid or secured, anything in that Act or any other statute to the contrary notwithstanding. And the information set forth the seizure of the ship and salt between such times for that the salt was imported in that time from Dublin in Ireland to Ratcliff in Middlesex within the port of London, not being for the necessary use of the ship for that voyage nor for the curing of fish *contra formam statuti*, and so prays a moiety for the informer and the other for the queen.

And though, upon perusal of the Act and hearing the evidence at the trial, I [Edward Ward] was not under any doubt but that foreign salt taken in in Ireland for the curing of fish might be brought into England or Wales under and subject to the entering and paying or securing the duties according to the directions in the proviso, yet, upon the pressing instance of the Attorney [General *Northey*] and the Solicitor General [*Raymond*] that such importation was not allowable by the Act, but would be a great deceit to the crown and prejudice to the salt makers in England, who pay great duties, I [Edward Ward] allowed a special verdict to be found, which was to this effect, that the salt was Portugal salt brought in the ship within the times in the information from Dublin to Fishgard

[1] Stat. 2 & 3 Ann., c. 16 (*SR*, VIII, 280–284).

in the port of London and there to be landed with the intention that one third part of it should be used and spent there for the curing of fish and that the other two-thirds should be carried from Fishgard to any other place where fish could be taken for the curing of such fish, that, upon arrival in the port and within the times in the proviso, entry of the salt was made and the duties secured as directed, that the cocket that was taken at Dublin for the said ship and salt was made and taken generally from thence *usque ad* Glasgow in Scotland, that the informer [Arthur James] was an officer of the salt and seized within time. And the doubt that the jury made was whether the salt was brought in that ship from Dublin in Ireland into the port of London contrary to the said Act or not. If it was, then they find for the queen and the informer; if it was not, then for the defendant.

The case was argued the first of July by *Raymond*, Solicitor General, for the plaintiff, and by *Ettrick*, for the defendant, and again, at the defendant's earnest request, his salt wasting and his way of trading in fetching foreign salt from Ireland for curing fish in England being under question, Mr. Attorney General consenting to argue it the last day of this term and submit it to the court, he argued it accordingly, and *Ettrick* again for the defendant to the same effect as before.

And the court gave their opinion and judgment the same day, being thought a plain case and Mr. Attorney General not opposing it.

The matters insisted upon by the Attorney [General] and the Solicitor General were that they thought that the proviso did not enable any to bring salt from Ireland even for any purpose because of the restraint put upon it by the body of the Act, which was to remedy a mischief recited in the preamble [. . .] of the Act of the crown's being defrauded in drawbacks and the mentioning of salt for the curing of fish ought to be extended no further than for the curing of fish caught at sea in that voyage or at sea in Ireland and that, as the verdict has found it, there is no certain place appointed where the fish were to be cured specially for two-thirds of the salt.

But I [Edward Ward] offered my reasons why judgment must be for the defendant, for the mischief in the preamble arose by importing salt from England into Ireland and obtaining a drawback and then bringing to back by stealth, to prevent which, the Act did at first totally prohibit the importation of salt from Ireland, but the proviso sets at large if imported for the curing of fish, which the Parliament had always an intent to encourage, it tending to so great an advantage to the kingdom. And, since the laws allow the importation of foreign salt under the payment of duties, the only restraint of importing it from Ireland was that what was to be so imported should be tied up to be for the curing of fish, the words are rendered plain, and there is no mischief in the case, for it advances the revenue and furthers the trade of curing fish and being to be employed for that use. So it stands upon the same reason of law to have foreign salt imported from it as from any other place, bay, and seas.

And the jury have found that this salt was imported for the curing of fish, one-third at Fishguard and the other two-thirds where fish could be caught. And it was all prevented from being so employed by being seized after entry and securing the duties. And the proviso does not restrain the curing of fish with it to any certain place, nor indeed was it reasonable to do it. The cause of forfeiture laid in the information is for that the salt imported was not for the curing of fish, and that is expressly found by the jury otherwise, and so [there is] no cause of forfeiture.

And, the other three barons clearly concurring, judgment was given for the defendant.

[Other copies of this report: Georgetown Univ. Law Sch. MS. B88–10, p. 952.]

412

Attorney General v. Barret

(Ex. 1712)

In this case, a common brewer was allowed the statutory allowances for beer that was sold to the customers of a near-by inn.

Lincoln's Inn MS. Misc. 539, f. [15]

An information in debt was brought for £54 11s. 3d. against the defendant for the duty of excise for 185 barrels of beer above 6s. a barrel and for 88 barrels of beer under 6s. a barrel brewed and tapped out for sale within the times in the information. And, upon the trial, it appeared that the defendant was both a common brewer of beer and kept an inn and a tavern in Windsor and that, before any of the excise grew due, he, by a lease in writing demised to one Dixon the outhouses and summer cellar and rooms over them within the yard of the defendant's inn, not far from his dwelling house and wherein Dixon lived and furnished out beer which he bought of the defendant at a certain price to any persons that sent to him for it, from year to year at £30 rent *per annum*. And, when and often as any guest came to the defendant's house and wanted beer, Dixon was sent to for it, and furnished it and for which he made a distinct bill for such a guest and was paid distinctly from their other reckonings. And the point depended wholly upon this, whether Dixon taps out this drink upon his own proper account or as servant or agent for the defendant, for it was agreed that the defendant was a common brewer of beer and furnished almost [all of] the town with beer in barrels and other vessels.

But, by the Statute of 1 W. & M., ca. 24,[1] no common brewer that taps out any beer by retail for sale shall have the allowance of two barrels and half out of twenty-three without the bills of mortality so that, though the defendant should be a common [brewer], yet, if he sold and tapped out any beer by retail, he was

[1] Stat. 1 Will. & Mar., c. 24 (*SR*, VI, 88–91).

to have no allowance, which he insisted to have and had tendered all the excise due besides the allowance.

And after a long and considerable evidence on the defendant's part that his lease was *bona fide* and thereby the things leased several from the inn during such lease and that Dixon always furnished the beer to the guests on his own account and his money for it by and upon his distinct bill and that he ran all the risks of loss of the beer after furnished to him (except proving bad, in which case only, the defendant was to change it), the jury found for the queen as to all the excise except for the allowances, which they found for the defendant.

[Other copies of this report: Georgetown Univ. Law Sch. MS. B88–10, p. 957.]

413

Moreton's Case

(Ex. 1712)

The date of a later writ of execution does not relate back to the date of the first such writ unless there was fraud or hinderance against the first writ.

Lincoln's Inn MS. 539, f. [75], pl. 3

In the Case of Moreton, Elliot, and Farington, the court declared, and it has been so practiced, that, where the crown's [writ of] extent has been unlawfully hindered from being extended fully before the return, that another or more extents of the *teste* of the first extent may issue in order to have such a complete execution made, as would have been had in case there had been no such unlawful hindrance at first.

And the court held to that rule and distinction whenever made for an extent of an older *teste* than the time it really issued, unless where [. . .] defeated of full execution by fraud and contrivance, it being of a dangerous and mischievous consequence to award extents of a former *teste* with precedent extents [. . .] not to be fully executed against all the goods of the debtor unless the complete execution of the former extent as to goods after discovered was avoided or rendered ineffectual by fraud and contrivance, for, according to Sir Gerrard Fleetwood's Case, 8 rep.,[1] the goods and chattels of the king's debtor are not bound but by and from the *teste* of the execution. If such new or other extents with precedent *testes* should be allowed, it might avoid executions and sales *bona fide* after the first extents returned and before the times of the real issuing of the second extents, which would be unjust where there was no fraud or collusion used to defeat or render ineffectual the king's first extent.

[1] *Fleetwood's Case* (1610), 8 Coke Rep. 171, 77 E.R. 731.

And a motion by Mr. Attorney General [*Northey*], Mr. Solicitor General [*Raymond*], and *Ward* in Michaelmas term 1712 for such a new extent with a precedent *teste* was denied, there not appearing any fraud or collusion whereby the first extent was rendered ineffectual.

414

Pye v. Eastwick

(Ex. 1712)

Upon a seizure for non-payment of import duties etc., the bond given as security must be in the sum of the double value of the goods and the ship seized.

Lincoln's Inn MS. Misc. 539, f. [78v], pl. 2

A seizure was made last vacation at Falmouth of a ship laden with French salt and other goods imported, as forfeited upon the French Act.[1] The defendant claimed property, and prayed a writ of delivery upon security, the which was granted. The appraisement was £800 and odd pounds (*debitis dominae reginae exclusis*). The defendant was willing to give security in double the £800, which was opposed by Mr. Attorney General [*Northey*] and *Dodd*, insisting that security ought to be given in double the value of the ship and goods, for the queen and the informer, if they recover, must be answered the ship and goods in specie without regard to duties and, when the defendant has them by [a writ of] delivery, the security must be such as may answer the full value. Also, in the case of a recovery, the queen and the informer, upon the new appraisement, will lose above £1400, the ship and goods being said to be worth £2300 single value and the security ought to be double, lost duties in this case not being to be taken notice of or considered, for, in case of a forfeiture, the queen cannot have duties also unless so provided for by statute (as, in some cases, it is, but not in this). And the way of appraising goods besides or excluding the queen's duties is no certain way, but the appraisement must be of their full value, else the court has no certain account of the value, for how can they know or consider what the duties come to, and directions have been often given to return the full value upon appraisements, so that, in case of a forfeiture, the goods in specie or their full value by the appraisement must be answered to the queen and the informer. Indeed, if the defendants submit to a license and composition, in that case, the queen's duties will be considered and, in the first place, taken out of the appraised value and the composition go upon the rest, And, then, everyone has their due. But, here, if goods of the value of £2300 should be let go upon £800 security and, at the trial, they shall be found forfeited, what remedy is there for the queen or the informer to come at the overvalue?

---

[1] Stat. 3 & 4 Ann., c. 12 (*SR*, VIII, 360).

Ettrick and *Ward, pro defendentibus.*

[Other copies of this report: Georgetown Univ. Law Sch. MS. B88–10, p. 969.]

415

Morset v. Barnardiston

(Ex. 1712)

A prosecution for a clandestine marriage is to had in the ecclesiastical court of the diocese where the defendants live.

Lincoln's Inn MS. Misc. 539, f. [79v], pl. 2

Adam Morset and Mary, his wife, plaintiffs; George Barnardiston, archdeacon of Huntington.

In a prohibition prayed by the plaintiffs, who live at Huntington in the diocese of Lincoln and are there sued for a clandestine marriage without banns or license, against the ecclesiastical laws, suggesting that they were married at Cambridge in the diocese of Ely lawfully and by license, and so ought not to be sued in the defendant's court and that they had offered this by way of plea, which the court refused. And so they pray [a writ of] prohibition.

But the court denied it, for, though the marriage was at Cambridge, yet, since the offenders live in the defendant's jurisdiction, they must be sued where they live, and cannot be sued in Ely diocese, for that would be against the Statute 23 Hen. VIII, for citing out of the diocese, and, if they cannot be sued where they live, the supposed offense would be dispunishable. Hardress 421, Dr. Blackmore's Case.[1]

And the Recorder of London [Sir Peter King] cited a case in the Queen's Bench, Trinity [term] 5 Anne, Wilmot and Lloyd, where as incestuous marriage was celebrated in Worcestershire and the parties removed and inhabited in Yorkshire, but the man coming occasionally only into Worcestershire to vote at an election, he was cited and prosecuted there, and he prayed a [writ of] prohibition because of his habitation in Yorkshire for being sued and cited out of his diocese, and [it was] granted, it not being flagrante crimine.

And, in the principal case, the plaintiffs may be assisted by the proofs from Cambridge of the legality of the marriage. And it being a pure matrimonial case, the jurisdiction appertains of right to the ecclesiastical court. And [if they be] aggrieved, [they] must be remedied by an appeal and not by a prohibition.

[1] Stat. 23 Hen. VIII, c. 9 (*SR*, III, 377–378); *Blackmore's Case* (1665), Hardres 421, 145 E.R. 528.

Vide 1 Jones 257, Mattingley and Martin; L. G, 50, Bengoe and Bishop of St. David's.[1]

[Other copies of this report: Georgetown Univ. Law Sch. MS. B88–10, p. 971.]

416

Doddington's Case

(Ex. 1712)

The Court of Exchequer can correct accounts and charges of those who contracted with the crown for goods delivered.

Lincoln's Inn MS. Misc. 539, f. [80], pl. 1

14 November 1712.

He [Doddington] and others were appointed clothiers for the Army in Ireland in the reign of King William and Queen Mary to furnish clothes to the army at a certain rate and price agreed upon. And the treasurer and paymaster of the army there had money imprested to them to pay for these clothes when certificates should be brought to them by the clothiers from the proper officers that the clothes were delivered according to the contract, which the clothiers did.

But Mr. Done, Auditor of the Imprest, in making up the account of the treasurer and paymaster, instead of giving them an allowance at the payment in that account, which he ought to have done, sets a *super* of £27,817 4s. upon the clothiers as so much money imprested to them by the treasurer and paymaster. And, thereupon, a process of *distringas* issued against them to render an account for that sum.

But, upon a motion to the court and reading the king and queen's warrants for the imprest to the treasurer and paymaster, upon hearing Mr. Attorney [General *Northey*], it was referred to Auditor Harley, one of the Auditors of the Imprest, to examine and state the whole matter, which he did by his certificate of the 8th of July 1712. And, thereby, he did certify the court of the mistake of setting the *super* on the clothiers as money imprested to them, it being an absolute payment for the clothes furnished at a certain price and that they had no more than what was due to them according to the price and contract.

The court in the presence of the Attorney General [*Northey*], who thought it just and reasonable, by order of this day [14 November 1712], discharged the *super* and process and all issues, and ordered that no further process should issue.

[Other copies of this report: Georgetown Univ. Law Sch. MS. B88–10, p. 974.]

---

[1] *Matingley v. Martyn* (1632), W. Jones 257, 82 E.R. 134; *Bengoe v. Bishop of St. David's* (Ex. 1682), Exch. Repts. *tempore* Car. II, 499.

417

Short, qui tam v. Tyler

(Ex. 1712)

A new trial will not be granted upon evidence that the prosecutor entrapped the defendant into committing an offense and the jury so found.

Lincoln's Inn MS. Misc. 539, f. [81]

An information was exhibited against the defendant as being a common carrier for carrying letters for hire against the late Act of Parliament and a former Act for Settling the Post Office.[1] Upon not guilty pleaded, the cause came to be tried before Justice Dormer at the last Assizes at Oxford. And a verdict was given for the defendant. And the Attorney General [*Northey*] and *Jeffreys*, one of the Queen's Counsel, moved for a new trial, alleging the verdict to be against the evidence, producing the affidavit of one Waters, one of the messengers of the Post Office, swearing the evidence that he gave on the trial that the defendant carried four letters for hire for the witness and that he proved the issue.

The court, by order of the 4th instant, gave the defendant a day to show cause why not a new trial should be granted, and ordered that, if the defendant should produce any affidavits, that they should be filed three or four days before the day of showing cause, which was appointed to be this day, and, in the meantime, one of the court should speak with the judge that tried the cause whether he thought it proper or fit for a new trial. And the defendant had filed his affidavits accordingly.

But the Attorney General, having been acquainted therewith, opposed the reading of them, depending upon the judge's certificate, who reported that evidence was given on both sides and that, upon the trial, it appeared that Waters, by contrivance and in order to entrap the defendant, applied himself to the defendant to carry those letters, which the defendant refused to do, saying it was against the Act of Parliament and a forfeiture upon him if he did it. But he said, if they were tied up and put into a packet and tied around with parchment, he could carry them as a parcel, which being so done, he carried them, and received 6d. for it. And he believed the parcel was delivered accordingly, *viz.* the four letters, one whereof was directed to Waters himself. And the defendant's porter, at the trial, owned the receipt of the four letters and the delivering of them and his receiving of 2d. apiece at the delivery.

And the judge certified that it appeared at the trial that Waters did all this to draw in the defendant and to subject him to the breach of the law and so to incur the penalty and that his direction to the jury was indifferently delivered to them

[1] Stat. 9 Ann., c. 11 (*SR*, IX, 393–404).

and left upon the credit of the evidence and, being a substantial jury, they found for the defendant. And he did not think that it was a verdict against evidence.

And thereupon, the court did not think fit to grant a new trial. And so the defendant's affidavits were not read, whereby, as it was alleged, a notorious trap and cheat upon the defendant would have appeared.

[Other copies of this report: Georgetown Univ. Law Sch. MS. B88–10, p. 979.]

418

Stuart v. LeNeve

(Ex. 1712–1713)

When a Chamberlain of the Exchequer's office ends, his deputies' offices end also.

Lincoln's Inn MS. Misc. 539, f. [81v]

The case between Sir Simeon Stuart, baronet, one of the Chamberlains of the Exchequer, plaintiff, and Peter LeNeve and Henry Ballew, claiming to be under chamberlains or deputy chamberlains of the said Exchequer, defendants.

Sir Simeon Stuart, by letters patent under the great seal dated 8 July last was made one of the Chamberlains of the Exchequer or of the Receipt of the Exchequer, and he had that whole office granted to him for his life to be held and occupied together with the constitution and ordination of all officers and ministers to that office belonging by himself or his sufficient deputy or deputies with all fees, profits, etc. to the said office belonging and of ancient time due and accustomed, which office became void by the death of Charles Cole and was formerly granted by King Charles II to Philip Hildyard, Esq., for his life, and, by the same grant, to the said Cole for his life in reversion after the death of Hildeyard in like manner and by the same words, *mutatis mutandis* as in Sir Simeon's grant, Cole surviving Hildeyard.

And the said Sir Simeon, being sworn and admitted into the said office in open court the same day his grant bears date, came personally the 24th of October this term into court, and brought with him into court two instruments under his hand whereby he constituted Dudley Downs to be his deputy in the Lower Exchequer and George Lesley to be his deputy in the Upper Exchequer during pleasure.

He, by Mr. Attorney General [*Northey*] and Mr. *Ettrick*, his counsel, prayed the two deputations then acknowledged in court might be enrolled in court and those two persons then present in court to be admitted and sworn. Sir Simeon's grant and those two instruments were read.

But *Dodd*, *Turner*, and *Ward*, of counsel with LeNeve and Ballew, opposed the swearing and admitting of Downs and Lesley, insisting that the said LeNeve and Ballew having had deputations from Hildeyard in his life and which Cole, by writings under his hand and seal, acknowledged and confirmed to them, they were lawful deputies and under chamberlains, having all along hitherto been in possession and executed their said offices and ought not to be molested in nor turned out of the same, claiming the same as their freehold, their grants being for their respective lives, at least during their good behaviors therein, having been duly sworn and admitted to the same, their deputations from Hildyard being a constitution of them respectively to be his true and lawful clerks or deputies in the upper and lower Exchequer and to give to them respectively the offices of his clerks and deputies in the upper and lower Exchequer to hold and enjoy the said offices during their natural lives respectively if he the said Hildyard should so long live and to take, receive, and enjoy yearly all fees, wages, profits, advantages, rewards, and emolument whatsoever to the said office pertaining, due, or accustomed without account in as ample manner and form as any other before them had held, received, or enjoyed the said office. And the defendants' counsel insisted upon many precedents produced and read, which they offered to make out their rights and usages and that it was never known that any such deputy put in by a predecessor had been turned out by a successor and how inconvenient and mischievous it would be for to turn out ancient and experienced officers and to take in new ones without some just cause assigned, which has always been disallowed in courts of justice.

Whereupon, the court forbore to admit and swear the new deputies and the plaintiff's counsel praying time to answer these things, the court allowed it.

[Other copies of this report: Georgetown Univ. Law Sch. MS. B88–10, p. 982.]

Lincoln's Inn MS. Misc. 539, f. [83], pl. 1

9 December 1712.

Sir Simeon Stuart's counsel produced a large volume of cases and precedents endeavoring to make it out as well by them as by reason of law that chamberlains for life only or at pleasure by a grant from the crown cannot make nor have made under chamberlains or deputy chamberlains to continue longer than the life of the grantors and that it so appears by the cases and precedents produced on his behalf.

And the counsel for LeNeve and Ballow insisting upon their right and title to their places as their freehold, from which they ought not to be amoved until evicted by law, having produced many precedents and urged several arguments for that purpose, the court thought fit that there should be a trial at the bar the next term in an action upon the case wherein the question to be whether the defendants, the two deputy chamberlains, have a right to continue in their former places without new deputations from Sir Simeon or not, Sir Simeon to be plaintiff and they defendants, and all things to be admitted which may bring the right in question in both sides and, for preventing any disputes or disturbances in the execution of the under chamberlains' places in the meantime and that the duties thereof may be performed, the two present under chamberlains are to continue in the execution of those places until after the trial without prejudice to the right on either side and be accountable for the fees and profits thereof as the court shall direct which they agree to be and, if the verdict goes against them, to quit their places and be accountable for the profits, having a reasonable allowance for the execution of their places as the court thinks fit.

[Other copies of this report: Georgetown Univ. Law Sch. MS. B88–10, p. 985.]

Lincoln's Inn MS. Misc. 539, f. [87]

The cause between Sir Simeon Stuart, one of the Chamberlains of this court, and LeNeve and Ballow, the two under or deputy chamberlains, *prout ante*, fo. 15 and 25, was tried at the bar by a special jury of Middlesex, Saturday, the 7th of February [1713], *prout* the paper of that trial, upon the issue directed, which was whether the defendants or either of them have a right to continue in their respective offices of under or deputy chamberlains wherein they were placed by Mr. Philip Hildyard, deceased, when he was Chamberlain notwithstanding the grant of the office of Chamberlain to Sir Simeon for his life and his deputations made to Dudley Downe and George Lesley. And, after a trial, which lasted ten hours and above, there was a verdict for Sir Simeon against the two defendants.

And, on Monday following, the defendants delivered up to Sir Simeon the keys of their offices, and Downes and Lesley were sworn and admitted his deputies.

[Other copies of this report: Georgetown Univ. Law Sch. MS. B88–10, p. 993.]

419

Morgan v. Bowen

(Ex. 1712)

Customs and prescriptions as to tithes are within the jurisdiction of the temporal courts and not the ecclesiastical courts.

Lincoln's Inn MS. Misc. 539, f. [82]

22 November 1712, *In Officio Placitorum*.

The defendant as Clerk or Sexton of the parish and parish church of Kinnersley in the County of Salop in the Diocese of St. Asaph libels against the plaintiffs here, as they are severally farmers of the tithes within several vills within the parish of Kinnersley, before Dr. Wyn, vicar general and official of the bishop of St. Asaph, setting forth that, by custom or prescription, time out of mind, the farmers or sub-farmers of all tithes of corn and grain belonging to the rectory or impropriation of Kinnersly in each of those vills have time out of mind paid or compounded to and with the parish clerk or sexton of Kinnersly for the time being for his proper tithable place one sheaf of winter corn, wheat, and rye and one sheaf of barley and another of oats by the name of a bell sheaf for every landholder, parishioner, and inhabitant in each of the said vills (naming them) who sowed any strike or measure of wheat, rye, barley, or oats in the parish or vills aforesaid as his fee, wages, or salary yearly due from the rector or impropriator or their tenants or subtenants of the tithes aforesaid to the clerk or sexton of the said parish for the execution of the said office.

The plaintiffs here pray a [writ of] prohibition to the said suit upon a suggestion that the conusance and jurisdiction of all customs and prescriptions, time out of mind, belong to the temporal and not to the spiritual courts within this realm.

And the [writ of] prohibition was granted *nisi causa* first day next term as a plain case that all trials and determinations of customs and prescriptions, time out of mind, must be at common law.

And, afterwards, no cause being shown, the prohibition went absolutely.

[Other copies of this report: Georgetown Univ. Law Sch. MS. B88–10, p. 986.]

420

Attorney General, ex rel. Harris v. Jones

(Ex. 1713)

Where a court finds that a relator prosecuted a claim in bad faith, the relator will be ordered to pay court costs to the prevailing party.

Lincoln's Inn MS. Misc. 539, f. [89]

Attorney General *pro* Harris v. Rice Jones, William Jones, and John Evans.

Mr. Attorney General [Northey] having obtained an order of the 18th of February last [1713] upon the affidavit of Harris, an officer of the Excise, for the defendants to show cause this term [Easter term 12 Anne 1713] why [writs of] attachment should not issue against them, *viz.* against Rice Jones for suing an [action of] replevin and William Jones for granting it and against Evans for executing it whereby a horse of Rice Jones that was seized by a warrant of two justices of the peace for a fine of 50s. set upon him for an offense against the laws of excise.

And, upon a hearing, *Ettrick, Dodd,* and *Ward,* for the defendants, the court discharged the order, and ordered Harris, who prosecuted the defendants in this court, to pay costs, for it appeared by affidavits that Rice Jones was cleared of the offense for which he was summoned before three justices in the forenoon, but, in the afternoon, another justice, who heard nothing of the matter joining with one who was there in the forenoon, pretended to set the fine for the offense for which he was cleared in the forenoon. And this was at Ruthin in Denbighshire on the ninth of October last. And, thereupon, the said two justices made a warrant directed to all high and petty constables and, more especially, to Her Majesty's officers of Excise and their assistants, reciting that:

> the several persons in a schedule annexed [whereof Rice Jones was one] being maltsters, seller and dealers in malt, having neglected or refused to make their due and true and particular entries and have committed several fraudulent practices contrary to law [not setting forth any conviction or oath in the case], those officers were thereby required forthwith to repair to the dwelling houses of the offenders or to any other places where any of the offenders had any goods or chattels or utensils for making malt of their own or of any other by them used or of what title soever the same may be claimed, and, there, to enter, distrain, and carry away as much of the same as may be sufficient to satisfy the respective sums at their respective names appearing with reasonable costs and charges to the said officers for the prosecution thereof and to keep the distresses for fourteen days and, if not redeemed, to sell the same, rendering the overplus to the owners or, in case of opposition or want of sufficient distress, then to apprehend the bodies of such opposers or insufficient persons and to bring them before us or either of us to be proceeded against as the Acts of Parliament in such case directs. /s/ *John Roberts; Ellis Meredith.*

It appeared that this warrant was kept private by Harris from the date until the ninth of December following, two months, and that Rice Jones being going ajourney for his usual business and his horse being brought out for that purpose, the said warrant was delivered by Harris, who appeared to have a grudge against Rice Jones, unto Henry Roberts, constable of Ruthin, and they then acquainted Jones with it, who never heard of it before, and he to prevent the distraining of his horse, which Harris required the constable to do, deposited into the constable's hands three guineas as a pledge for the fine until relieved upon his intended appeal at the next Sessions, notwithstanding which Harris commanded the constable to distrain the horse, which was done. And, to prevent the losing of his journey, he did sue out the replevin.

And, upon consideration of this whole matter, the warrant not mentioning any conviction or oath of the concealing the warrant and causing the horse to be seized after depositing the three guineas and the necessity Jones had for his horse, the court thought it was a hard thing to punish the party or grantor of the replevin and that it was no such contempt to this court that it could take notice of nor indeed any contempt in the nature of it and that it would be too hard for this court to be subservient to the justices in their proceedings, especially upon a warrant that was so insufficient, and so allowed the cause. And they ordered Harris for his malicious prosecution here, to pay the defendant's costs.

The order granted by this court was thought hard and not to be followed and a surprise on the court.

[Other copies of this report: Georgetown Univ. Law Sch. MS. B88–10, p. 997.]

421

Anonymous

(Ex. 1713)

An action for assaulting a customs officer cannot be joined with an action for not paying customs duties.

Lincoln's Inn MS. Misc. 539, f. [90v], pl. 1

1 May 1713.

Upon the occasion of a [writ of] attachment moved for and cause to be shown against it for affronting Custom House officers aboard a ship, whereby it was said customable goods were taken away without paying the queen's duty, it was the opinion of the court that, as to the beating and resisting of the officers in the execution of their office, this court, notwithstanding the Statute 14 Car. II, ca. 11,[1] in such case, may attach offenders in that kind, but not in any case to call the offenders in question for anything that may subject them to any forfeiture or penalty which they may be liable to by any law, but merely for the point of beating or resisting, the Statute of 14 Car. II being only an affirmative law and introductive of a new and further way of punishment. But it takes not away the jurisdiction of this court to punish offenders for personal violences only touching the revenues in this court, but not to enquire into what, if any, customable goods were taken away by the offenders, that being an offense tending to a forfeiture and examinable by an information.

[Other copies of this report: Georgetown Univ. Law Sch. MS. B88–10, p. 1003.]

422

Anonymous

(Ex. 1713)

A married woman's debts are not enforceable.

Lincoln's Inn MS. Misc. 539, f. [90v], pl. 2

1 May.

A married woman is arrested and held to bail by the sheriff, it not appearing otherwise than that she was an unmarried woman at the return of the writ, she

[1] Stat. 14 Car. II, c. 11, s. 6 (*SR*, V, 395).

being gone to her husband beyond the sea and the debt contracted in England during the marriage, her husband beyond [the sea].

The bail moved to have the woman discharged upon a common appearance, it being made to appear that she was married when the debt of £75 was contracted.

The court ordered a common appearance, for, though it may be a prejudice in some sort to trade, yet no man is bound to sell his goods upon credit. If he will, it is at his peril. And, in this case, *caveat venditor.*

[Other copies of this report: Georgetown Univ. Law Sch. MS. B88–10, p. 1004.]

423

Style's Case

(Ex. 1713)

Fines estreated by sheriffs into the Exchequer can be discharged by the Court of Exchequer where they are unreasonable or unjust.

Lincoln's Inn MS. Misc. 539, f. [90v], pl. 3

12 May. The sheriff of Kent's case of a fine.

Humphrey Style, Esq., was the sheriff [of Kent], and Polhill [was the] undersheriff. And a Quarter Sessions was held at Maidstone three days and adjourned to Canterbury, and, there, held two days, at all which, the undersheriff attended, and paid the justices for their wages at each Sessions 48s. though all the fines of both Sessions came but to £29 8d. And, at the last Sessions, the justices discharged all the juries, but thought fit to make two successive adjournments to other places only in order to swear two new justices, at both of which last adjournments, there were deputies appointed under the sheriff's seal to attend the justices. But not paying the justices' wages at those two adjournments though more had before been paid than all the fines came to and wages arise only out of fines, the justices fined the sheriff for the first adjourned Sessions [to do his duty] £10 and, for the second, £20. And they estreated them into this court, and returned the cause to be for that neither the sheriff by himself or the deputy did attend those adjourned sessions to do his duty.

All which appearing by affidavits, the court, upon motion, discharged the fines as set unreasonably and without any just cause.

[Other copies of this report: Georgetown Univ. Law Sch. MS. B88–10, p. 1005.]

424

Owen v. Purcell

(Ex. 1713)

A false accusation of stealing sheep is actionable defamation.

Lincoln's Inn MS. Misc. 539, f. [91], pl. 1

An action [in slander] was brought for these words spoken by the defendant of the plaintiff 'Owen is a thief and has stolen several of his neighbors' sheep and has altered the marks of other persons' sheep and feloniously converted the same to his own use.'

Upon a trial before [Baron] Price at Shrewsbury, the defendant was found guilty of speaking all the words except the last of 'feloniously converting the same to his own use', and damages were found for the plaintiff.

And *Jeffreys*, queen's counsel, moved in arrest of judgment that, the plaintiff having failed in proving all the words laid in his declaration, that he had failed in his action. And he prayed the *postea* might stay until moved by the other side.

Ward, for the plaintiff, prayed for judgment in respect to other words of calling the plaintiff a thief and that he had stolen several of his neighbors' sheep substantially were of themselves actionable without any regard to the rest and, for which, it must be intended and the jury was directed, if they found they were spoken, to give damages and that adding the other words of altering the marks of other persons' sheep and those other words not found not being relative to or depending upon nor any way qualifying the actionable words did not hurt the plaintiff's remedy for what is actionable, for which he cited Dyer 75. One said Sir John Bruges is a strong thief, and the jury found all the words except the word 'strong', and the plaintiff had judgment, the word 'thief' being actionable of itself without the word 'strong'. 4 rep., 19, 20, the diversity in Britteridge's Case; Allen 31.[1]

And judgment was given *pro querente nisi*, and, afterwards, absolutely.

[Other copies of this report: Georgetown Univ. Law Sch. MS. B88–10, p. 1006.]

[1] *Brugis v. Warenford* (1552), 1 Dyer 75, 73 E.R. 160; *Britteridge v. Atkyns* (1602), 4 Coke Rep. 18, 76 E.R. 905, also Yelverton 10, 80 E.R. 8, Moore K.B. 666, 72 E.R. 827; *Yearworth v. Pierce* (1647), Aleyn 31, 82 E.R. 900.

425

Miles, qui tam v. Clarke

(Ex. 1713)

When goods, including tin, are once legally condemned and the crown's part paid, that purges all precedent duties for the same and vests the property in the buyer, discharged of future demands, as for coinage.

Lincoln's Inn MS. Misc. 539, f. [91v]

18 May.

Upon a seizure of tin at Plymouth as forfeited for being shipped for exportation, duties not paid, an information was exhibited, and, no claim being put in, the tin was recovered and appraised. And, thereupon, Miles came into court and bid and advanced upon the appraised and was allowed the buyer and paid the queen's moiety and, thereupon, had a writ of delivery directed to the officers at Plymouth that made the seizure that, upon Miles's paying him the other moiety, they and all others that had the tin should deliver to Miles, which should be their discharge. The officers delivered the tin accordingly. But, immediately thereupon, Clark seized the same tin as forfeited for being carried from the melting house to Plymouth before it was stamped for coinage or paid the queen's duty of coinage. And it appeared that Clark, the agent for the coinage was privy to the seizure for being shipped for exportation, duties not paid, and, then, no pretense was made that the coinage duty was not paid nor until after the recovery in the Exchequer and the queen's moiety paid. And the said Clark detained the tin, and refused to let it go unless Miles would pay the coinage, who, thereupon moved the court upon affidavits of the matter for a [writ of] attachment, which, upon the hearing of counsel for both sides was granted against Clark unless he delivered the tin to Miles, for, though the court would be tender to injure the queen's duty of coinage or any legal remedies for the recovery thereof, yet, in this case, instead of the coinage duty, she has much more by her moiety of the forfeiture. And it seemed a trick amongst the officers to oppress Miles. And the court was of opinion that, when goods are once legally condemned and the crown's part paid, that that purges all precedent duties for the same and vests the property in the buyer discharged of future demands for coinage. And, though the pretense of right to seize as forfeited tin for non-payment of coinage, yet the court entered not into that but was clear upon the former part and, therefore, awarded the attachment.

But the defendant's counsel to avoid that agreed to deliver the tin to Miles upon oath and in the same plight and at the same place where it was seized and to pay Miles his charges. And so it ended.

[Other copies of this report: Georgetown Univ. Law Sch. MS. B88–10, p. 1009.]

426

Miles's Case

(Ex. 1713)

Where goods have been seized for non-payment of duties and the bidder has paid his money, the court cannot set the bid aside.

Lincoln's Inn MS. Misc. 539, f. [94v]

Trinity term 12 Anne 1713; upon a bidding.

There was an information *tam quam* exhibited into the court last term upon a seizure of French brandies for non-payment of duties. And, for want of a claim, they were condemned and recovered. And, upon a writ of appraisement into one of the out ports, they were appraised at 3s. per gallon *debitis dominae reginae exclusis*. And, upon a proclamation in court *si quis plus dare voluerit*, Miles came in and bid more money upon the appraisement. And he was admitted the buyer. And, upon a *debet* made out by Armiger, the clerk in court for the queen and the informer, Miles paid the queen's part into the Exchequer and had a tally for the same. And he was ready to pay the informer his part, which is usually done upon the bidder's having a writ of delivery directed to the officers of the port and the informer testifying the tally and payment of the queen's part and, upon payment of the informer's part and payment of the queen's duties to deliver him the goods. Now, the usual duties for brandies lawfully imported were 4s. per gallon over and above the appraised value where such an appraisement is returned *debitis exclusis* as which sort of return has been all along condemned by the court and directions given that the appraisement should always be made of the goods according to the full and true value of them without regard to any duties, that being the best and surest way for the crown and informer. But the officers willfully neglect to observe it in many cases.

And, now, it appearing in this case in question under the Attorney General's hand (and the law is clear) that no duties are due for these brandies, being French and prohibited, Miles refused to pay any duties. And, therefore, the Attorney General moved that he might either pay the 4s. a gallon or take back the money he had paid in or that the proceeding in the whole bidding might be set aside and no writ of delivery be awarded, this being, upon the face of the matter, a fraud and wrong to the queen, for, though, in strictness of law, there be no duties due, yet it is plain the appraised value of 3s. per gallon was set with respect to the queen's duties of 4s. per gallon. And, if the queen cannot have the 4s. as a duty, she and the informer ought to have had in the appraisement of the goods as to their true value.

The court, considering that the bidder had paid his money, could not set aside what had been done upon record last term. And, upon a proposition made and accepted by the Attorney General, the bidder advanced the queen's moiety of the 4s. a gallon, all things stood as they were, and the bidder saved the informer's moiety of the 4s. a gallon had the brandies been appraised at the full value in the indenture of appraisement.

[Other copies of this report: Georgetown Univ. Law Sch. MS. B88–10, p. 1015.]

427

Whitfield v. Petre

(Ex. 1713)

Writs of immediate extent should be issued in open court, but, in cases of emergency, they can be issued in vacation by a warrant.

Lincoln's Inn MS. Misc. 539, f. [108]

9 June 1713.

A [writ of] *diem clausit extremum* having issued against Whitfield, deceased, a debtor to the queen as an officer and accountant to the queen for a considerable debt due to her Majesty from him, it was thereupon found that Petre was indebted to the said Whitfield in great sums of money by two bonds, which were seized into the queen's hands. And, upon an affidavit made that the said debts were real and just debts originally and *bona fide* due from the said Petre to the said Whitfield and that the same were still due and owing and had not been put in suit in any court and that Petre was become decayed in his estate and insolvent, a [writ of] immediate extent was upon *Dodd*'s motion granted against the said Petre and his estate, being in aid of Whitfield's estate and representatives in order the better to secure the queen's debt from Whitfield. But the same being an aid only and not for the queen's immediate debt or money due originally to her, I [Ward] refused to give a warrant for a [writ of] immediate extent, but directed it to be moved in open court according to the Rules of 1639 and the usual practice of the court, though it has sometimes been done by a warrant in the vacation and sometimes in the term time. But it is the safest and best way to have immediate extents in cases of debts in aid for a subject debtor or accountant to be by a motion in open court in term time, but, in cases of exigency, they may be by a warrant in the vacation.

[Other copies of this report: Georgetown Univ. Law Sch. MS. B88–10, p. 1034.]

428

Mason's Case

(Ex. 1713)

Courts cannot appoint receivers to execute writs of extent however convenient it might be.

Lincoln's Inn MS. Misc. 539, f. [108v], pl. 1

17 June.

In the case of Mr. Mason, [writs of] extent issued against Mason, and his lands in three counties, *viz.* Salop, Montgomery, and Radnor, were seized into the queen's hands. And [writs of] *levari facias* issued, and the profits answered. But, because there were many tenants of the lands and great trouble and charge in getting in the extended values, Mr. Attorney General [*Northey*] prayed that, for the ease of all, *viz.* the crown, the tenants, and Mr. Mason, the debtor, that the court would appoint a receiver who should collect the rents and profits of the extended premises and answer for the extended values to the crown and the overplus to be accounted for to the tenants and Mr. Mason upon good security to be given, which would be easy and safe for everybody.

But the court told him they had nothing before them but the [writs of] extent and the extended values, which could be levied no other way but by [a writ of] *levari facias* unless the queen would lease the extended premises to anybody under the extended values, and, if anybody disturbed such lessee, the court would grant an injunction until such disturber had pleaded a prior title to the crown's extent and evicted it. But as to appointing a receiver as things stand, it was *res inaudita* and not warranted by any rule or course of the court or by any precedent or authority in law.

[Other copies of this report: Georgetown Univ. Law Sch. MS. B88–10, p. 1036, pl. 2.]

429

Bean v. Lee

(Ex. 1713)

A modus decimandi that is unliquidated is void.

2 Gwillim 609

2 July 1713.

The plaintiff, a vicar of Lidd, by his bill, demands the tithes in kind of hay, lambs, pigs, turkeys, hens, geese, calves, milk, honey, wax, and agistments, etc. The defendants, by their answers, admit the plaintiff is vicar of the said parish, and is thereby entitled to all the tithes arising in the said parish, except the tithes of corn and grain, or to some rate, *modus*, or customary payment, in lieu thereof. And they say they believe, and doubt not but to prove, that no tithes of hay, lambs, wool, calves, pigs, eggs, agistment, or any other small or vicarial tithes were ever paid, or ought to be paid, in kind to the vicar of the said parish for the time being, but that there is, and time out of mind has been, a custom, usage, or *modus decimandi* in the said parish that all the occupiers of marsh, meadow, and pasture land in the said parish have used to pay yearly for all the said marsh, meadow, and pasture lands by them respectively used and occupied in the said parish to the vicar of the said parish for the time being in lieu and satisfaction of the tithes of hay, lambs, wool, calves, colts, pigs, eggs, honey, wax, fruit, agistment, and all other small and vicarial tithes arising upon the said lands the yearly rate or sum of 1s. in the pound and so proportionally for every greater or less sum than £1 according to the yearly rent of such of the said lands as are rented or let at a full or rack rent without fine and according to the yearly value of such lands as are not let or not let at a full rent without fine as aforesaid. The question was whether this *modus*, as laid, were a good *modus* in law or not.

Upon hearing counsel on both sides and on full debate of the matter, the court was unanimously of opinion that the *modus* in question, as laid and insisted on by the defendants in their answer and stated by the case, was a void *modus* in law.

Dodd 231, 1 Rayner 120, 1 Eagle & Younge 703

The plaintiff, [vicar of Lydd in Kent], brought his bill for small tithes. The defendant insisted upon a *modus*, that the occupiers of any marsh, meadow, or pasture lands have used to pay and ought to pay yearly for all their marsh, meadow, and pasture lands by them occupied to the vicar in lieu and satisfaction of the tithes of hay, lambs, wool, calves, colts, pigs, eggs, honey, wax, fruit, agistment, and all other small tithes arising upon said lands the yearly rate or sum of 1s. in the pound and so in proportion for every greater or smaller sum than a pound, according to the yearly value of such lands as are let or rented at a full or rack rent without fines and according to the yearly value of such lands as are not let at a full rent without fine as aforesaid. And [it was] resolved upon a case stated and debated that the first [was] a void *modus* for the uncertainty and impossibility of the parson's knowing the value without annual and constant suits.

See Dodderidge and Startup.[1]

These cases were cited: 11 Rep. 16; Hob. 11; 3 Mod. 73; Cro. Jac. 621, 671; 2 Leon. 117; 2 Keb. 280, 318; Latch 210; Sid. 49; 3 Mod. 132; Calthorp, tithe of houses in London and by custom; Godolphin 425; 1 Keb. 602; 1 Leo. pl. 127.[2]

---

[1] *Doddridge v. Startop* (1690), Eq. Cases Exch. 324.

[2] *Dr. Graunt's Case* (1613), 11 Coke Rep. 15, 77 E.R. 1165; *Leifield v. Tysdale*, Hobart 10, 80 E.R. 161; *Mason v. Beldham* (1685), 3 Modern 73, 87 E.R. 47; *Page's Case* (1623), Croke Jac. 671, 79 E.R. 581; *Carpenter's Case* (1667), 2 Keble 280, 84 E.R. 174;

British Library MS. Hargrave 81, p. 57, pl. 2

30 July.

The barons this day gave judgment in this cause. The suit was for tithes in the parish of Lydd in Romney Marsh. The defendant insisted on a *modus* of 2s. per pound according to the yearly rent of the land more or less according as the rent happened to be. And the question was whether this was a good *modus.*

And the barons were unanimous that it was not good because it was variable and uncertain and, as the tithe in kind is due in common right and is certain in its nature, so whatever is by custom substituted in the place of those tithes must be very clear and certain and of constant continuance.

And Baron Price cited for that Godophin's, *Repertorium Canonicum*, 407; 1 Keble 602.[1] And though Doctor Grant's Case[2] was cited on the other side, no regard was had to that judgment.

[Other copies of this report: British Library MS. Hargrave 82, f. 55, pl. 1, British Library MS. Hargrave 77, f. 15v, pl. 2, British Library MS. Hargrave 303, f. 29v, pl. 2.]

[The order of 2 July 1713, Public Record Office E.126/20, f. 71, is printed at 1 Wood 537.]

430

Regina v. Quash

(Ex. 1713)

Immediate extents have priority according to the dates of the teste and before extents in aid.

Lincoln's Inn MS. Misc. 539, f. [108v], pl. 2

[In the] case of many [writs of] extent issued against one Quash, a late receiver of the queen's revenues, as land tax, house, post office duties, etc. in the County of Devon etc., for debts due from him immediately to the crown and for debts in aid, *viz.* of Mannaton *et alii*, to whom Quash was indebted and in great sums which were the crown's money paid by them to Quash in order to pay into the Exchequer for the use of the crown, wherein two points are in question:

Clark v. Prowse, Latch 210, 82 E.R. 350; *Cole v. Banbery* (1661), 1 Siderfin 49, 82 E.R. 962; *Perkins v. Titus* (1687), 3 Modern 132, 87 E.R. 85, also 2 Shower K.B. 507, 89 E.R. 1069, 3 Levinz 255, 83 E.R. 677, Comberbach 43, 90 E.R. 333, Carthew 12, 90 E.R. 612, Skinner 247, 90 E.R. 113; *Case Concerning Payment of Tithes in London* (1617), Calthrop, 80 E.R. 672; J. Godolphin, *Repertorium Canonicum*; *Baudink v. Bushel* (1663), 1 Keble 602, 83 E.R. 1136; *Stebbs v. Goodlack* (1588), 1 Leonard 99, 74 E.R. 92, also Moore K.B. 913, 72 E.R. 992.

[1] *Baudink v. Bushel* (1663), 1 Keble 602, 83 E.R. 1136.

[2] *Dr. Graunt's Case* (1613), 11 Coke Rep. 15, 77 E.R. 1165.

First whether, when money is levied for the queen's original debts and also in aid of any other in the queen's name, the queen shall be satisfied all her original debts before anything shall be delivered out for the debts in aid, though some of the debts in aid were levied by process in the queen's name even before the levies or process for the queen's original debts issued or were made.

And it was held that, where goods and debts are seized into the queen's hands in aid, the party cannot have them until the queen's original debts are paid.

Secondly, where a third person is indebted to the queen's debtor and a [writ of] extent in aid is granted to such debtor to the queen to find debts due to him and which are found by inquisition and seized into the queen's hands and the debts to the queen's debtor being proved by affidavit to be part of the queen's revenue which her debtor trusted his debtor to pay to the queen's use, but did not, therefore, in such case upon an affidavit made that such debtor to the queen's debtor is decayed in his estate and the debt in danger and, thereupon, a warrant for an immediate extent is issued against him whether the *teste* of that immediate extent ought not to be upon the same day that the warrant bears date though in a vacation which in such case may be and is warranted by practice or whether that extent may be tested the last day of the precedent term when there was no judgment to bind lands, debts, or goods or whether they can be bound sooner or otherwise than by and after the date of the warrant, which, in such a case, is in the nature of a judgment by the prerogative, for, in the case of the crown, goods or debts are not bound but from the *teste* and awarding the execution according to Sir Gerard Fleetwood's Case, 8 rep.,[1] and, this warrant being for that purpose in the nature of a judgment (which a bare bond is not), it is not reasonable nor agreeable to any rule of law or practice of the court that any such immediate extent should bear *teste* before the warrant but, where there was a judgment in the court for the crown in term, there, the extent may be tested the last day of the term, for the crown is not within the Statute of Frauds and Perjuries[2] in point of delivery of executions.

And the court was of opinion that the *teste* of the immediate extent, whether the debt be for the crown or in aid, where there is no precedent judgment, ought to be *teste* with the warrant for the immediate extent and to bind no further or sooner as to goods or debts. But, as to lands, they are bound from the time of the bonds to the crown and from the *teste* of the immediate extent in cases of debts in aid. And this resolution was held to be good against the sudden opinion of Northey, the Attorney General, who directed some immediate extents, which were awarded by a warrant in a vacation and for which there were no judgments precedent, but bonds only, to bear *teste* the last day of the precedent term with-

---

1 *Fleetwood's Case* (1610), 8 Coke Rep. 171, 77 E.R. 731, also 2 Rolle, Abr., *Prerogative le Roy*, p. 157.

2 Stat. 29 Car. II, c. 3 (*SR*, V, 839–842).

out any order or direction from the court or any of the barons. But he, being acquainted with that mistake, took out other extents *teste* the day of the warrants.

[Other copies of this report: Georgetown Univ. Law Sch. MS. B88–10, p. 1037.]

Parker 281, 145 E.R. 780, Dodd 365

It was adjudged, that the immediate extents for the crown, finding the same goods found upon a former extent in aid, shall be preferred and paid before it; and among immediate extents, they shall take place according to the *teste*.

The court gave their opinion, that the extents for debts immediately due to the crown shall be first satisfied and paid; and that the extents in aid shall be postponed until such debts be paid and satisfied; and ordered that all further proceedings upon the several extents against the defendant for the several debts seized in aid of A., B., and C. shall be and hereby stayed, until Her Majesty's debts, due from the said defendant upon the post office account, the old duty on houses, the land tax, and new duty on houses, shall be satisfied and paid, with costs and charges; and the debt due upon the post office account, together with costs and charges, to be first paid.

431

Livermore, qui tam v. Leving

(Ex. 1713)

A bid for forfeited goods cannot be set aside on the ground that it is less than the appraiser's valuation.

An offense, such as smuggling, that took place on the high sea is not within the jurisdiction of the Admiralty Court of the Cinque Ports.

Lincoln's Inn MS. Misc. 539, f. [112]

On a seizure of the ship with wines, brandies, and other goods for unlawful importation, a writ of appraisement issued and the ship and goods *debitis reginae exclusis* (according to that irregular way practiced by the appraisers against the court's orders) were appraised at £800. And, upon that appraisement and proclamation, Frampton bid £40 more, but the court, upon motion, ordered a new appraisement to the full value without respect to the queen's duties *de bene esse* without prejudice to the bidder. And, upon the second appraisement, the goods were appraised at above £3000. Frampton, in court, bid the same £40, which lay in court from the first bidding above that second appraised value.

And, upon hearing the Attorney General [*Northey*] and *Stevens*, Solicitor of the Customs, for the queen and the officers, the court ordered that the £40 in court should be transferred to the second appraisement and Frampton to be admitted the bidder and to have the goods, which was entered upon the record on the back of the writ of appraisement, as usual. And, though it was admitted by the Attorney General that Frampton for that £40 should be the bidder after that order and admission of being the bidder under the pretense that the goods were worth more, Mr. Attorney [General] was prevailed with by some third persons, Huggins, Deputy Bailiff of Westminster, and one Whitehall, named a commissioner in the last appraisements, so moved to set aside Frampton's last bidding.

But the court could not in justice do it, none having come in to bid more. And, if the second appraisement was not of the full value, it was a trick to deceive the queen and the bidder, as is too much practiced between the officers and the appraisers and no notice taken of such under-appraisement unless bidders come in, who are much discouraged by the officers below. But the court finds them to be of good service for the crown by advancing under-appraisements, and, therefore, will and do encourage and assist them.

But note that, afterwards, the cause itself was tried upon the merits, and found to be no forfeiture or cause of seizure. And, so, the bidding was out of doors, and the bidder had his money again.

[Other copies of this report: Georgetown Univ. Law Sch. MS. B88–10, p. 1041.]

Lincoln's Inn MS. Misc. 539, f. [123]

In Trinity term last [1713], there was a trial had before me [Edward Ward] at *nisi prius* upon a seizure of the ship *St. Peter* of Bremen and a cargo of French wines, as being supposed to be forfeited for coming into a port in England and not manned, owned, or navigated as the Act for Navigation 12 Car. II[1] required. And the great question was whether the ship came into any port of England. And, in order to make out the forfeiture, the plaintiff gave evidence of divers quantities of wines which were sold out of the ship to and were fetched by people that lived at Rye and elsewhere. But the verdict was for the defendant, and no fault found with it. And the defendant, after judgment was entered, had a writ of delivery for the ship and goods. But, before she could get clear to proceed in her voyage, which was always intended for Bremen, the ship and the lading were seized upon at Dover as forfeited to the duke of Ormond as Lord Admiral of the Cinque Ports for transgressing the laws and statutes of this realm. And a suit was instituted, and a libel and articles thereupon were exhibited in the Admiralty Court of Dover, endeavoring a condemnation therein of the ship and the cargo.

And, thereupon, a [writ of] prohibition was prayed wherein John Ration, master of that ship, was the plaintiff against Isaac Lamb, the duke's proctor on the duke's behalf, and William Richess, the Serjeant of the Admiralty, who seized the ship, defendants, the suggestion being that all pleas and business touching the validity, construction, and exposition of statutes and the conusance of all pleas touching the same belong to the queen and her crown and not to the

---

[1] Stat. 12 Car. II, c. 18 (*SR*, V, 246–250).

Court of Admiralty, nor ought to be tried or determined there or otherwise save in the queen's courts of record before the queen or her justices, yet nevertheless, the defendant as proctor for the duke as Admiral of the Cinque Ports, to oppress and aggrieve the plaintiff against the law before the judge and in the Court of the Admiralty of the Cinque Ports, the 29th of August last [1713], has exhibited a libel setting forth the aforesaid Act of Navigation, 12 Car. II, whereby it is enacted that, if any goods or merchandise shall be unloaded out of any ship with an intent to defraud the crown of its duties without a sufferance and entry as that Act directs, the said ship with its lading shall be forfeited. And it sets forth another Act of Parliament made the 9th Anne,[1] repealing the Act for prohibiting all trade and commerce with France, whereby foreigners in amity during the war might import from France into Great Britain in foreign ships French wines taking in their outward bound lading of British manufactures in some port of Great Britain before they proceed in their voyage to France, and, then, shows that the plaintiff, being a foreigner, *viz.* a Bremener, in his said ship of the build of Bremen did in March last [1713] take in a cargo of French wines and brandy in France and came to an anchor at Dungeness upon the high seas and within the jurisdiction of that court of Admiralty and that the plaintiff and his company broke bulk of the said ship there and sold and delivered out two tierces of brandy and four tierces of French wines, which were privately put ashore at Hythe etc. within the jurisdiction of that court and on purpose to defraud the queen of her duties and were seized at or near Hythe, by reason of which breaking bulk and taking the wines and brandies out of the said ship without any lawful authority from the custom officers, the said ship and her whole lading became forfeited for breaking bulk contrary to the said acts of Parliament and laws of England and that the Act of 9th Anne was not observed by the plaintiff by taking in her outward bound lading of British manufactures for France, but the ship came to Dungeness and bulk was there broken, as aforesaid, and the wines and brandies so unladen, by reason of which, the said ship and her cargo, by the acts of Parliament and laws of England became forfeited. And, thereupon, the said ship and cargo were seized as forfeited upon the high seas within the jurisdiction of that court by William Richess, Serjeant of the Admiralty of the Cinque Ports, for the use of the Admiral of the Cinque Ports, being a right and perquisite to him, being found, seized, and taken within the jurisdiction of the court and that the defendant, the fourth of September, articled in that court against the plaintiff ship and lading to the like purpose and for the like causes in the libel, laying the reason and cause of seizure and forfeiture to be for breaking bulk contrary to the said acts and the laws of the realm interspesing therein the Admiral's right to all forfeitures within his jurisdiction and praying that this ship and lading may be adjudged forfeited for the causes aforesaid to the duke as a perquisite of his Ad-

[1] Stat. 9 Ann., c. 8 (*SR*, IX, 388–389).

miralty jurisdiction subject to such distributions as are usual in such cases. And the suggestion further sets forth that, though the offenses, if any there were, were committed *infra corpus comitatus* and not at high sea nor belong to the jurisdiction of the Admiralty, and, though the plaintiff here has been acquitted in this court of record of the said offenses upon a trial at law upon an information, as by the record of this court appears and whereof the judge of the Admiralty had notice, yet the duke, by his said proctor, proceeds in the said Admiralty in order to the condemning of the ship and lading contrary to the laws of this realm and to the prejudice of the plaintiff. And so he prays a [writ of] prohibition to the judge of the Admiralty from further proceeding.

And a rule was made for a prohibition and also for a [writ of] attachment for not obeying the writ of delivery *nisi causa* such a day and proceeding in the Admiralty to stay in the meantime, upon the motion of *Ettrick* and others, which time being enlarged at the defendant's desire, *Raymond*, the queen's Solicitor General, on the defendant's behalf, endeavored to show cause both against the prohibition and the attachment, alleging that the Admiralty, in a case of breaking bulk in such cases at high sea, claimed and had a jurisdiction. (But he showed no authority for it.) And, though, by the libel and articles, there are expressions as if the proceeding there and the forfeiture thereby sought were in virtue of the acts of Parliament therein mentioned, if so, he agreed, as to them, the prohibition ought to go for the reasons in the suggestions as to the exposition etc. of acts of Parliament as to what arose at land and as to what related to the matter of the trial at law, verdict, and acquittal. But he seemed to insist upon crimes committed at open sea, which were breaking the bulk and selling wines, which he said were crimes that induced the forfeiture of the ship and lading by the admiralty law. But he showed nothing to make that out. And, in truth, there is nothing in the libel or articles which entitle to any forfeiture, but in virtue of the act of Parliament, which with or for any forfeiture arising thereby, the Admiralty has no jurisdiction.

And the prohibition was awarded absolutely. But, at first, he desired that the plaintiff might declare upon it. But, afterwards, he said he would consider whether to insist upon it or not. And the attachment was awarded against Richess, who arrested and detained the ship against the writ of delivery. No desire afterwards [was] made that the plaintiff in the prohibition should declare thereupon, and so the prohibition went absolutely.

[Other copies of this report: Georgetown Univ. Law Sch. MS. B88–10, p. 1077.]

432

Bishop of Norwich v. Bucklea

(Ex. 1713)

The bishop and a sequestrator of a rectory can join as co-plaintiffs in a suit for tithes.

A bishop has the right to recover the tithes during the vacancy of a parish.

The Court of Exchequer, as a court of revenue, can determine disputes involving tithes.

Lincoln's Inn MS. Misc. 539, f. [113]

The Bishop of Norwich and Thomas Echard, clerk, plaintiffs, against George Backler, defendant, in a bill for tithes. Michaelmas term 11 Anne.

The bill sets forth that the bishop has been so for four years past and that the rectory of Boulge in Suffolk lies in his diocese and jurisdiction and that it became vacant in 1709 by the death of the last incumbent that, no clerk being presented to it, the bishop sequestered the profits of it and, under his episcopal seal, appointed Echard sequestrator to collect, levy, and receive all the tithes and ecclesiastical profits of that rectory and to serve and provide for the cure of the said parish and appointed him the curate thereof, as by that appointment made under seal ready to be produced might appear, that Echard has ever since served the cure there, and that the plaintiffs or one of them became entitled to all the profits arising from that rectory. And, then, he shows that the defendant did in 1709, 1710, 1711, and 1712 occupy and possess divers lands and grounds in that parish and had divers quantities of corn, grain, and hay there growing, which he cut and inned and had divers other tithable matter, great and small, there, the tithes whereof or some rate for the same were due and ought to have been paid to the plaintiffs or one of them, but were not. And, therefore, the bill prays discovery and relief for the same.

The defendant demurs to the whole bill and the matters and things therein as uncertain and insufficient in law and shows for cause, first, that the plaintiffs or one of them entitle him or themselves to the tithes in the bill by a sequestration from the bishop, one of the plaintiffs, under his episcopal seal and constituting the other plaintiff sequestrator of the profits of the rectory and for providing for the cure there. And, by constituting the plaintiff Echard curate of that rectory to perform divine service there and by his the said Echard's performing the same. But the bill does not set forth when the profits of the rectory were sequestered nor when Echard was appointed sequestrator or curate of that rectory or how long he served the cure there, the words 'ever since' in the bill being uncertain to what time they refer, and so no certainty for the plaintiffs' title to the tithes to or for what time they are entitled.

Secondly, the charge in the bill is that the plaintiffs or one of them is or are entitled to the tithes, whereas it ought to have been that both of them had right.

Thirdly, it appears not by the bill that the plaintiff Echard is in any way entitled to any of the profits of the rectory, because he is set forth [to be] but a sequestrator thereof and a curate of the parish, which is no more than a servant to the other plaintiff, the bishop, and, as such, accountable to him for the profits and he is to pay Echard thereout for serving the cure and to pay the surplus to the next incumbent. And no time appears when or how long Echard was the sequestrator or curate or that he served the cure so much as a fortnight.

The point principally to be considered by the court in this case is whether the bishop, as such, having in or during the vacancy of a living granted a sequestration of that living and the profits thereof and appointed the other plaintiff, a clergyman, to be the sequestrator to collect and receive the profits and to be the curate and serve the cure there, can together with the said sequestrator and curate jointly or either of them separately maintain a suit for the tithes arising during such a vacancy against a parishioner that withholds the same and neither pays nor sets them forth, though tithes in kind be due and no pretense of a *modus* or discharge or, if there were any *modus*es, whether such *modus*es should not ensue and be payable to such as have a right to the tithes, which any such *modus* does not cover, or whether any and what remedy can be taken in such case against the parishioner.

As to the determination of this case, I [Edward Ward] think these things must necessarily fall under consideration:

First, that tithes not impropriate but belonging to an ecclesiastical person in a parochial right serving the cure are in judgment of law a maintenance for the clergy and are *beneficia propter officiae* and ordinarily are of special conusance, though the remedies for the recovery thereof may in some cases by act of Parliament and the jurisdiction of the Court of Exchequer, *temps dont*, as a court of revenue where the clergy rights and dues from others to them and from them to the crown and others have been determined, no act of Parliament before 2 & 3 Edw. VI[1] having given any temporal court any jurisdiction therein, but the Court of Exchequer in the capacity of a court of revenue was always invested with that jurisdiction, but no other court. And, therefore, it is strange that the Chancery, as a court of equity, should intermeddle therein, many worthy Chancellors and Lord Keepers having declined intermeddling therewith, though others, by the pretense of precedents only, suggested by practicers and clerks of the courts for their own advantage and to enlarge jurisdictions, have sometimes intermeddled therein, though generally, if not always, under pretense of preserving the testimony of witnesses to prove *modus*es or customs, bounds of parishes, and prescriptions, and not upon the mere right of tithes between the incumbent and parishioners without such ingredients;

[1] Stat. 2 & 3 Edw. VI, c. 13 (*SR*, IV, 55–58).

Second, that, notwithstanding the right of tithes does or may belong to the incumbent of every parish serving the cure and the patron has not any right to the tithes, but only to present a fit person to the bishop of the diocese to be instituted and inducted into the rectory or vicarage, which, when done, the person so instituted and inducted becomes entitled to the tithes, yet, in judgment of the law, every bishop has the cure of souls of all the inhabitants within his diocese and jurisdiction, if not actually, yet habitually and, at least, until he discharges himself (if indeed it be a discharge) by conferring upon the person instituted and inducted the bishop's cure by the words *accipe curam tuam et meam*;

Thirdly, that it was, I [Edward Ward] conceive, upon the grounds and reasons aforesaid that, until the Statute of 28 Hen. VIII, ca. 11,[1] that the bishops were supposed to be entitled to all the tithes and duties that arose and grew due during the vacancy of any rectory or vicarage within his diocese and, in fact, received the same, but the year for the commencement of the payments of first fruits by the Statute 26 Hen. VIII, ca. 3,[2] being to be computed from the death of the last incumbent and in regard it is not declared by that Statute who should have the tithes and profits during the vacancies of the livings, divers of the archbishops and bishops, taking and receiving the tithes, great and small, at Easter, have deferred the collation of their own clerks and the institution and inductions of the patron's clerks to the intent they might receive what grew due in the vacation, which was a mischief and prejudice to the incumbents and patrons, the right of tithes arising in the vacation was declared to be to the next incumbent. It is enacted by 28 Hen. VIII, ca. 11, that, if any of the archbishops or bishops, after that time, shall by themselves or others for their use receive any of the fruits or profits of any parsonage, vicarage, etc. during the vacancy thereof and the same upon request, do not restore to the next incumbent, he shall forfeit the value thereof, a moiety to the king and the other to the incumbent. But there is a proviso that the archbishops, bishops, etc., their officers, and ministers may retain so much of the said tithes and profits as shall amount to pay such persons as have served the cure during the vacancy their reasonable stipend or salary and for the collecting and levying of such tithes and fruits rising during the vacation anything in that Act to the contrary notwithstanding;

Fourthly, so that, by this last Act, it seems plain that a bishop's right or pretense of title, as in his own episcopal right, to the tithes arising during the vacancy is determined and destroyed and the next incumbent entitled thereto after the charge of serving the cure and the collecting and levying of those tithes, but it respects only the matter between the bishop and the next incumbent, but meddles not with the parishioners liable to the payment of those tithes in case they should refuse to pay the same nor is any remedy thereby provided how the tithes during the vacation shall be recovered;

[1] Stat. 28 Hen. VIII, c. 11 (*SR*, III, 666–667).

[2] Stat. 26 Hen. VIII, c. 3 (*SR*, III, 493–499).

Fifth, now, ever since the making of that Act, the practice has been that the bishop or ordinary, during the vacancy of a living, has usually awarded a sequestration under seal sometimes to the churchwardens or others and sometimes to some ecclesiastical person, who is by the bishop appointed to serve the cure there to sequester the tithes and profits of such vacant living and to make them *custodes* of that sequestration and to demand of all persons liable to pay those tithes to pay the same to the sequestrators and they to account for the same to the bishop or his commissary so that thereout the service of the cure and charges of collecting and levying the tithes being deducted and the residue may be restored (if any be) to the next incumbent. But here is no compulsory power against the parishioners to pay the same unless there may not result a contempt against them for not giving obedience to the sequestration which was duly published in the church and whereof the parishioners had full notice to set out, compound, or agree for the same with the sequestrators, as, doubtless, it would be a contempt in the sequestrators to refuse to act thereby in all lawful things;

Sixth, so that though there is no person during the vacation in whom the mere right or title in law of the tithes arising during the vacation is invested further or other than as the bishop as ordinary and as one bound to see the cure served, which must and ought to be out of the profits of the living, there being no incumbent and the patron having no pretense nor obliged to present, what remedy can be taken against refractory inhabitants refusing to set out or pay their tithes and dues if a bill of this nature is not proper? The defendant in such a case as this cannot deny but his tithes are due and payable and that he has no right to detain them but under pretense that the plaintiffs have no strict legal right to recover them and that he may be questioned for them by the next incumbent. Now, in answer to this, the defendant may set out his praedial tithes of corn, grain, hay, wool, lamb, and other mixed tithes which are severable in their natures and he must be free, there being no incumbent, to demand the same or to whom he can give notice thereof, and he is not bound by any but to keep them. But, having thus set them out, whoever takes them, he is not answerable for them. The Statute has declared a right to the next incumbent for vacation tithes but made no provision against the bishop and his officers but for what they have received and to have an account thereof and relief for the surplus above cure and charges;

Seventh, so that, in such a case as this is and thus circumstanced, this court, to enable the payment of first fruits and tenths and other ecclesiastical duties chargeable upon the living and to prevent the loss of the rights of the church, which a wrongdoer endeavors to turn to his own account, may in the nature of a provision and in aid of the true intent of the Statute of 28 Hen. VIII that the cure should be served and the tithes gotten in and the surplus, if any, answered to the next incumbent, which, in the case of poor livings, it may be doubted whether ever there will be a legal incumbent to take it or not, there being multitudes of such instances where the cure is served under the bishop's sequestration only, which may be hoped to be remedied by the proceedings of the Trustees for the

Queen's Bounty to the Poor Clergy. And this court, upon any contest about the rights or quantities or qualities of tithes may settle the same during the vacation and upon any bill or suit by the next incumbent against any of the parishioners having paid their tithes pursuant to a decree or order of this court will establish the same and leave the incumbent to take his course against the bishop and sequestrators touching the cure, charges, and surplus, as he shall be advised. And, if some such course be not admitted (as of necessity it must), the parishioners of poor livings have a way chalked out not to pay any of their tithes or duties arising during the vacancy and so, by necessary consequence, no service of the cure nor divine service nor administration of the Sacraments in that parish for which the tithes are due and for which they ought to be applied will be performed to the prejudice of religion.

And I [Edward Ward] am not aware of any other authority or jurisdiction that can give aid or a remedy in such a case as this, but this court only, and that this court which has an original jurisdiction and privilege in a case of tithes and for the benefit and advantage of the crown's debtors and accountants, which the plaintiffs here are, may give relief and, since this court has such a jurisdiction, I see no reasonable objection can be made why the parishioners should not be as liable to discovery and account for his tithes to the bishop and the sequestrator or one of them as to any incumbent, so as he be indemnified against the next succeeding incumbent, no such being during the vacancy when the tithes grow due nor certain that there ever will be in poor livings, where the tithes and profits will not extend to discharge the service of the cure, which rests in the bishop's discretion and must be reasonable.

The bishop or nobody must be allowed to have a right of a remedy to recover the tithes during the vacancy, else the cure ceases, for none can compel a patron or any other to present.

The great objections made are two:

First, that the title to sue for tithes only by virtue of the bishop's right or sequestration is too feeble a title to recover them by during the vacation and that none but he who has a legal title by institution or induction or by lease or title under such can maintain such a suit;

Second, that there are many precedents in this court whereby it appears that such sequestrator's bills, even when brought to a hearing and the title not contested by the defendants, have been dismissed for a defect or incompetency of right or title to maintain such suits.

As to the first, I [Edward Ward] have before offered my reasons and shall not repeat them. And, secondly, and as to the second, which is the case of the precedents, I acknowledge there have been some against relief upon a bill founded by a sequestrator alone and merely and only as his own right and title by virtue of his sequestration. But none of those cases that I remember or have heard of were ever where the bishop, either alone or with the curate, his sequestrator, did ever bring such a bill which was refused, and, therefore, this being in that respect a different case and wherein for the reasons and causes before mentioned, I conceive much stronger than the other, and, there being no precedent in this case against the now bill and case, it must subsist upon those grounds and reasons I have before mentioned and which, in my opinion, are sufficient to maintain this bill, notwithstanding the joint and disjunctive title laid that the bishop and curate or one of them ought to receive the tithes, for the court, if they see cause, may make the decree for both or one, the demurrer saying it ought to have been that both of them have the right.

And, therefore, as to the cause of demurrer to that part of the bill, I think it not good. But, as to the other causes of demurrer, that there is no time set forth when the sequestration issued nor how long he continued sequestrator or served the cure, the bill is not so full as it might be, but that, being a slip only, may be amended upon payment of costs if the court pleases, at least, it is plain the vacancy of the living happened in 1709 and the defendant inhabitant had tithable matter during the four years of the vacancy and the sequestrator is truly but the bishop's collector and the right of recovering the tithes must reside in the bishop and the sequestrator, an accountant to the bishop, for what he receives, and the bishop to allow cure out of the parish tithes.

Now, as to the precedents, that of Berwick and Swantons, in this court, Trinity term, 22 June, 4 Will. & Mar.,[1] was by the sequestrators only for the small tithes of Stanford in Norfolk, for two years, which defendant said might be due to the plaintiff as sequestrator for one year of which he paid the plaintiff and, having overpaid him for other things, the plaintiff refused to allow such overpayment in part of the second and the defendant, insisting that an account was stated and a certain sum there mentioned, tendered, and [it was] refused, and the bill was dismissed, as it might justly be for that cause. But it is put into the decree (though I think not necessarily) that the three barons, Lechmere, Turton, and Powell, were all of the opinion that the plaintiff, being a sequestrator only, was not properly relievable touching the tithes arising in that parish, but this dismission was without costs unless better cause be shown at a day to come. I find Sir Robert Sawyer and I [Edward Ward] were counsel for the defendant, and Mr. Browne and Mr. Dodd were for the plaintiff.

L. K, 140; in the Case of Bankes and Rye, which was the 30th of November 1686, the plaintiff was a sequestrator by one instrument of the tithes of the vicarage in Suffolk which had been vacant from 1677 and for three years after and, by another instrument under the seal of the bishop, was made appointed to serve the cure there and had the power to collect the tithes for that time *ita quod* he gave a true account thereof to the bishop and, by a bill in his own name as collector and sequestrator of the tithes, sued the inhabitants for their small tithes for three years. And, upon the hearing, the bill was dismissed by reason he had only a bare

---

[1] *Berwick v. Swanton* (Ex. 1692), see above, Case No. 95.

authority to collect the tithes and to account for them to the bishop, wherein I [Edward Ward] was for the defendants. And a note was then taken that divers such bills had been formerly dismissed.[1]

L. J, 79; on 18 November 1682, upon hearing the cause between Husbands, the impropriator of Horsely in Essex, and Brand and others, the inhabitants there where the plaintiffs sued the defendants for their tithes of all sorts, there being no vicarage endowed, but the impropriators had for fifty years provided one to serve the cure there at his own charges, though nothing of obligation upon him appeared until within three years that he provided none and the bishop of London, upon a complaint, admonished the plaintiff to provide one to serve it, which he refusing, the bishop sequestered the tithes of the parishioners towards serving the cure, which they procured to be served, and showed this for their defense against the plaintiffs' demands of their tithes not exceeding the charge of the cure amounting only to £25 *per annum*. But the court decreed the defendants to pay the plaintiff their tithes, the bishop's sequestration not being of any force against an impropriator who claims a lay fee. But the court moderated the costs of the defendants to £5. Here, the bishop was no party, but acted only provisionally and sequestered a lay fee, which was not in his power. The parishioners paying their tithes to him that served the cure not having any notice or warning to the contrary for the defect of title not to pay again service of the cure by a clergyman without a contest of title [is] constantly allowed for a title to tithes against a parishioner.[2]

A curate is not to maintain a title by prescription to tithes against him that put him in and may turn him out. Noy's rep.[3]

9 July 1713, Bishop of Norwich and Backler, by the opinion of the whole court, that the demurrer be overruled, but, being an original matter, no costs [were given].

[Other copies of this report: Georgetown Univ. Law Sch. MS. B88–10, p. 1043.]

Dodd 231, 2 Gwillim 610, 1 Eagle & Younge 705

Upon a demurrer in the Exchequer to a tithe bill brought by the bishop [of Norwich] and Eachard, as sequestrator of the rectory of Boulge in Suffolk, the bill charges that the bishop was bishop of the diocese and that the rectory is within it and has been vacant so long, that the bishop sequestered and granted it to the other plaintiff.

And [it was] resolved: first, that a sequestrator cannot maintain a bill; second, that the bishop and sequestrator joining may maintain a bill. And, accordingly, the demurrer was overruled.

See above, the Case of Berwick and Swanton.

---

1 *Bankes v. Rye* (Ex. 1686), Eq. Cases Exch. 247, 1 Rayner 65.

2 *Husbands v. Brand* (Ex. 1682), Eq. Cases. Exch. 163.

3 *Bott v. Brabalon*, Noy 15, 74 E.R. 986.

433

Philips v. Evans

(Ex. 1713–1714)

The question in this case was whether the words spoken were defamatory or not.

Lincoln's Inn MS. Misc. 539, f. [121v]

Michaelmas 12 Anne, 1713, 28 October.

The plaintiff [Richard Phillips] brought an action on the case for slander against the defendant [Evan Evans] for speaking these words *de querente*, setting forth the Welsh words particularly and averring that they, in the English tongue, are thus interpreted and bear this sense, *viz*. he (*innuendo* the plaintiff) is a thief of my brother's goods (*bona cuiusdam fratris sui innuendo*) and that he (*innuendo* the plaintiff) is worse in his actions than a highwayman that keeps the highway.

And *Ward*, for the defendant, took these exceptions in arrest of judgment, there being a verdict and £5 damages for the plaintiff:

First, that, in the Welsh words, there is no *innuendo* nor can there be any supply to make a certainty of the person in English and that *de querente* is not certain enough. Rolle, *Action sur le case*, 84, 85, Burrows and Usher,[1] and the word 'highwayman' is not a Welsh word, as it is laid to be;

Second, that, though to call a man a thief generally may bear an action, yet, when there are words following which point at or describe wherein that theft does consist and that is not to be understood in the law to be a theft (words being always to be taken *in mitiori sensu*), those subsequent words take off the force and qualify the sense of the word 'thief', as 'you are a thief and stole my trees', Hobt. 77; and 'you have picked my pockets, and took away my money; you are a pick-pocket', 2 Levins 51; 1 Ventris 233.[2]

Thirdly, it ought to have been laid whose goods they were in certain and what the goods were, which is not so here, but it is only said *bona cuiusdam fratris sui*, not naming him nor saying what. Rolls, *Action sur le case*, fo. 78.

Fourthly, as to the last words that the plaintiff is worse in his actions than a highwayman that keeps the highway, they are no slander, not being said that he did rob or do any unlawful thing in the highway, the words 'worse in his actions than a highwayman that keeps the highway', importing no slander, stronger words than these, *viz*. 'he has stolen by the highway' being held not actionable. Rolls, *supra*, 73.[3]

Per curiam: Stay until moved by the plaintiff.

---

1 *Burrowes v. Usher* (1653), 1 Rolle, Abr., *Action sur Case*, pl. K, 9, p. 85.

2 *Coote v. Gilbert* (1613), Hobart 77, 80 E.R. 227; *Watts v. Grymes* (1672), 2 Levinz 51, 83 E.R. 445, also 3 Keble 34, 84 E.R. 579, 1 Ventris 213, 86 E.R. 143.

3 *Denyson v. Burke* (1596), 1 Rolle, Abr., *Action sur Case*, pl. Z, 12, p. 73.

[Other copies of this report: Georgetown Univ. Law Sch. MS. B88–10, p. 1072.]

Lincoln's Inn MS. Misc. 539, f. [211]

Easter [term] 13 Anne, 1714.

'He is a thief of my brother's goods; he is worse in his actions than a highwayman that keeps the highway.'

Serjeant *Lloyd*, [upon a motion] in arrest [of judgment], begins with the last set of words, and [he says] they are not actionable. 3 Cro. 746, maintainer of thieves etc.; Yelverton 64; 2 Cro. 54; 3 Cro. 459, 31; 470. And, if they are not actionable and [there are] entire damages, 3 Cro. 282.[1]

First, the words are not actionable, for, *non constat* that the plaintiff had a brother and, if he had no brothers or he had no goods, no action [lies]. Noy 116, Williams's Case; if any man was ever perjured, Williams was; no averment that any perjured [for] want of an averment for a relative. 2 Cro. 331, 'murderer', words and things fatal, as 'arrant a thief as any in Gloucester jail' without an averment is not actionable. 2 Cro. 243; Cro. Car. 92, 420. 'I will take my oath your son stole my horse'; [there was] no averment of a son. Marsh 62; Noy 65, in point. Saying a man is a thief generally is actionable, but, where relative to any thing or person, there must be a certainty, and where not. Rolls, *Action*, 80; Plowden 132. *Non constat* that the plaintiff had a brother, which ought to appear. This charge is entire, and part is not actionable; [it is] bad. 1 Cro. 155, 156; 3 rep. 88, 31; 8 rep. 75. These books exclude intendment.[2]

If it intended a brother, it did not intend goods. 2 Cro. 331; 'You are as bad as your wife when she stole my cushion'; 'you are a murderer, for you are the fellow that killed Sidenham's man.'[3]

Mr. *Winnington Jeffreys, pro querente*: These [words are] an entire sentence, and must be so intended, and not divided, but follows [. . .]. 'He keeps thieves and is a maintainer, He keeps company with none but thieves; you have stolen by the wayside.' The first part of the words are actionable. Noy 55. The want of an averment may be bad, but no averment is necessary here. Where [there is] uncer-

---

1 *Ball v. Bridges* (1600), Croke Eliz. 746, 78 E.R. 978; *Hollis v. Briscoe* (1605), Yelverton 64, 80 E.R. 45, also Croke Jac. 58, 79 E.R. 49; *Harper v. Beamond* (1605), Croke Jac. 56, 79 E.R. 47, also Yelverton 57, 80 E.R. 41; *Webb v. Nicholls* (1637), Croke Car. 459, 79 E.R. 998; *Crumpe v. Barne* (1626), Croke Car. 31, 79 E.R. 630; *George v. Harvy* (1632), Croke Car. 282, 324, 79 E.R. 847, 883, also W. Jones 325, 82 E.R. 171; *Collis v. Malin* (1632), Croke Car. 282, 79 E.R. 847, also W. Jones 304, 82 E.R. 161.

2 *Wittam's Case*, Noy 116, 74 E.R. 1081; *Barrons v. Ball* (1613), Croke Jac. 331, 79 E.R. 282; *Phelps v. Lane* (1627), Croke Car. 92, 79 E.R. 681; *Spencer v. Medburne* (1635), Croke Car. 420, 79 E.R. 965; *Johnson v. Dyer* (1639), March 62, 82 E.R. 412; *Wicks v. Shepherd* (1629), Croke Car. 155, 79 E.R. 735.

3 *Barrons v. Ball* (1613), *ut supra*; *Ratcliffe v. Michell* (1612), 1 Rolle, Abr., *Action sur Case*, pl. F, 1, p. 78.

tainty as to person, [it] needs an averment, but that is not here. Hobt. 77; a thief stole a tree agrees not. The plaintiff's person is certain. 1 Rolle's [Abr.] 73; stole by the highway side. He relies upon Noy. And the judgment [was given] there, though 'son' is uncertain; these words are not divided.[1]

Objection: No *colloquium* is necessary about 'brother.'

Solution: Thief of goods *cujusdam ignoti* so [. . .] he is a thief. 1 Rolle's 42, ltr. G, fig. 1. 'You are a thief and have stolen my dung' is actionable, 1 Rolle's 52; so [is] 'thief [who] stole my turnips and grass and corn.'[2] Thief of goods necessary [is a] felony, and the latter words aggravate [damages].

Lloyd replies 'thief' alone is actionable, but here they are coupled. 2 Cro. 423, Poph. 128; 2 Bulstr. 141.[3]

Curia advisari vult.

[Other copies of this report: Georgetown Univ. Law Sch. MS. B88–10, p. 1147.]

434

Tomblin v. Hall

(Ex. 1713)

In this case, the plaintiff failed to prove the alleged trespass to land.

Lincoln's Inn MS. Misc. 539, f. [122]

The plaintiff [Margaret Tomblin] declares in [an action of] trespass for that, at such a time and place, the defendant [George Hall] broke and entered her close called The Yard, and walked over it and disturbed her in the quiet possession thereof and cut down and carried away six posts in her fences to her damage of £20.

The defendant, as to the six posts, cutting, and carrying away, pleads not guilty. And, thereupon, issue is joined. And, as to the rest of the trespass, he pleads specially that one Geoffrey Tomblins was seised in fee of the said close called The Yard and of a messuage and piece of ground adjoining, lying open, for a passage and that one William Bradford was tenant thereof to the said Geoffrey and that, during Bradford's term, the reversion to the said George, he used at pleasure to pass that way, justifying so doing, and that the said Geoffrey being so seised, made his will, and devised the premises to John, his son, in fee,

[1] *Coote v. Gilbert* (1613), *ut supra*; *Denyson v. Burke* (1596), *ut supra*.

[2] *Griffith v. Johnson* (1617), 1 Rolle, Abr., *Action sur Case*, pl. G, 2, p. 42; *Yerworth v. Pearce* (1647), 1 Rolle, Abr., *Action sur Case*, pl. R, 5, p. 52, also Aleyn 31, 82 E.R. 900; *Bonyon v. Trotter* (1650), 1 Rolle, Abr., *Action sur Case*, pl. R, 8, p. 52.

[3] *Cooper v. Smith* (1617), Croke Jac. 423, 79 E.R. 362, Popham 128, 79 E.R. 1231, also J. Bridgman 60, 123 E.R. 1200; *Painter v. Warn* (1613), 2 Bulstrode 141, 80 E.R. 1017.

and he lays a title in him, and that John, being seised in fee, by an indenture of bargain and sale for a year made between him and George Hall, the defendant, he, the said John, bargained and sold to him, the said George Hall, the premises and all the estate, right, title, and interest of him, the said George Tomblin (which should have been John Tomblin) to the premises, *habendum* to him the said George and his assigns for a year, by virtue of which and of the Statute of Uses,[1] the said George Hall was possessed. And the reversion in fee being to John Tomblin, he, by a release of the next day, conveyed the reversion in fee to George Hall, by virtue whereof, he became seised in fee. And he justified the residue of the trespass.

The plaintiff replies, and maintains her cause of action, and traverses that Geoffrey Tomblin, at the time of his will or afterwards, was seised in fee of the said close called The Yard, as the defendant has alleged.

The defendant maintains his plea that George Tomblin was seised in fee. And, thereupon, issue was joined. And there was a verdict for the defendant.

Dodd moved in arrest of judgment that it appears by the defendant's setting out the title in his plea that, by the conveyance by the bargain and sale, the defendant not having a title, though he has a verdict, ought not to have judgment, because it is said to be conveyed to John Tomblin.

But, that appearing to be a mere mistake of the name and there being enough set forth in the conveyances to entitle the defendant and the traverse being of another thing and found for the defendant, the court gave judgment for the defendant.

[Other copies of this report: Georgetown Univ. Law Sch. MS. B88–10, p. 1074.]

435

Beverton, qui tam v. Goodiere

(Ex. 1713)

Where an informer settles out of court to receive less than the full statutory fine, the crown's share thereof will be likewise reduced.

Lincoln's Inn MS. Misc. 539, f. [122v]

The plaintiff exhibited a personal information for £200 forfeiture grounded upon the Statute 11 & 12 Will. III, ca. 10,[2] for having in his custody against the form of that Statute certain East India goods, by which Statute two-thirds are given to the informer and one-third to the crown. The goods were recovered, and the informer had two-thirds and the crown one. And, the Act giving the penalty

---

1 Stat. 27 Hen. VIII, c. 10 (*SR*, III, 539–542).

2 Stat. 11 Will. III, c. 10 (*SR*, VII, 598–599).

of £200 above that forfeiture and making the like distribution of that forfeiture also, the defendant, by license, compounded with the plaintiff for his two-thirds for £50.

It was considered by all the barons whether the queen ought to have more upon that composition than £25. And by the opinion of all that she ought not, being half as much as the informer had and it amounts to a full third, the fine was rated accordingly.

[Other copies of this report: Georgetown Univ. Law Sch. MS. B88–10, p. 1076.]

436

Darbison, ex dem. Long v. Beaumont

(Ex. 1713)

In this case, a devise in remainder to the heirs male of the body of a person living at the time of the will and also when the remainder should take effect was held to be valid.

1 Peere Williams 229, 24 E.R. 366

John Specot, seised in fee of the manor of Penheal and divers other lands etc. in the counties of Cornwall and Devon, [on] 19 August 1703, makes his will, and, after devising the premisses to trustees for the term of twenty-one years for the payment of debts etc., he settles the same on the first son of his (the testator's) body lawfully begotten and the heirs male of the body of such first son lawfully issuing and, for default of such issue, to the heirs of his (the testator's) body lawfully to be begotten, and for default of such issue, to his cousin John Sparke for 99 years, if he should solely live, remainder to his first etc. son in tail male; and in default of such issue, remainder to the heirs male of the body of the testator's aunt Elizabeth Long lawfully begotten; and for default of such issue, remainder of all his lands to his (the testator's) right heirs.

The said testator also gives a legacy to his said aunt Elizabeth: Long, whereby he takes notice that she was living, and that she had three sons, A., B., and C., to whom he gives a legacy of £500.

He also gives to Dorothy Beaumont (who was his heir at law) an annuity out of the said premisses of £150 *per annum*, and to her children £500 apiece.

Afterwards the testator died without issue, and John Sparke also died without issue upon which the question was, who was entitled to the testator's real estate whether his heir at law, Dorothy Beaumont, or A., the eldest son of the testator's aunt, Elizabeth Long.

For the heir at law it was objected, that, her right was in its nature favorable, and to be supported by the common law of England, and therefore all devises that disinherited the heir were to be construed strictly. That to make this devise good to A. it must be construed either a contingent remainder or the words 'heirs male', be, taken as *descriptio personae*, so as to vest a remainder in him. That as a contingent remainder, it could not be good, because there was no freehold to support it, all the precedent estates, being for years; and if it were good as a contingent remainder in its original creation, yet Elizabeth Long being living a the testator's death, such remainder could not by the rule of law vest, as it ought to have done, at the determination of the particular estate; the heirs male of the bond of the testator's aunt Long, could not be understood by way of *designatio* or *descriptio personae*; for that is such a description as is *vice nominis*; whereas the word 'heirs' did not agree with the person pretended to be described; he was not heir of Elizabeth Long, nor could be, white she was living; and 'heirs' being a legal term, could be understood only in a legal sense, unless some other word or words accompanying it should determine, the sense otherwise, as heir apparent, or heir now living; and the word 'begotten' did not determine the sense otherwise, because heirs begotten (1 Inst. 20b; 2 Vern. 545, 711; Pre. Cha. 491; *post*, Hewit v. Ireland, 427, and Gore v. Gore, *post*, vol. 2, 33[1]) or to be begotten had the same legal constructions and it did not appear that the devisor had any intention to confide that devise to the issue male of Elizabeth Long then living, much less to A. only, who would take as the heir described by this, devise.

But it was adjudged by the whole court of Exchequer (except Baron Bury) that A., the eldest son of the testator's aunt Elizabeth Long was entitled to the premisses, and not the heir at law; which judgment was afterwards reversed by the opinion of the two Chief Justices in the Exchequer chamber; and that reversal at last reversed in the House of Peers (1 Bro. P.C. 489);[2] and the reasons upon which the court of Exchequer gave judgment, and upon which (as it was apprehended) the House of Lords affirmed that judgment, were these:

That A. the eldest son of Elizabeth Long, was the person designed to take by the appellation of the heir male of the body of the testator's aunt Elizabeth Long lawfully begotten.

As to the objection, that Mrs. Long being living, there could not, in a legal sense, be any heir male of her body begotten to take by the will, it was answered that the intent of the testator by the devise (which was the only matter in question) did plainly appear not only from the words of that part of the will but throughout the whole will.

---

[1] E. Coke, *First Institute* (1628), f. 20b; *Cook v. Cook* (1706), 2 Vernon 545, 23 E.R. 952; *Musgrave v. Parry* (1715), 2 Vernon 710, 23 E.R. 1067, also 1 Eq. Cas. Abr. 71, 202, 21 E.R. 884, 990; *Hewet v. Ireland* (1718), Precedents in Chancery 489, 24 E.R. 219, 1 Peere Williams 426, 24 E.R. 456, also Gilbert Rep. 145, 25 E.R. 102, 2 Eq. Cas. Abr. 139, 22 E.R. 119; *Gore v. Gore* (1722), 2 Peere Williams 28, 24 E.R. 629, also W. Kelynge 254, 25 E.R. 599, 9 Modern 4, 88 E.R. 278, 10 Modern 501, 88 E.R. 826, 2 Strange 958, 93 E.R. 967, 2 Barnardiston K.B. 209, 229, 355, 94 E.R. 453, 467, 550, 2 Eq. Cas. Abr. 339, 22 E.R. 289.

[2] *Darbison v. Beaumont* (1714), 3 Brown P.C. 60, 1 E.R. 1177.

That the word 'heir' had in law several significations: in the strictest, it signified one who had succeeded to a dead ancestor; but, in a more general sense, it signified an heir apparent, which supposed he ancestor to, be living;

That in this last sense the word 'heir' was used in statutes, law books, and records (see the writ of ravishment ward, *quare filium et heredem rapuit*, and 2 Inst. 439, and 25 Edw. III,[1] which makes it treason to kill the heir of the king) and since the law had given to this word several senses, it would be hard to expound it in that which was the strictest, and most rigorous, and would destroy great part of the will; at the same time, that by law it might have another sense, which would support the whole will and intent of the party;

That the intent of the party being the principal rule for the exposition of a will, the testator was excused from using the strict and proper terms and phrases of and had liberty to use such expressions as he pleased; for, pleased they were such as sufficiently declared his intent, it was enough; and, his intent should take place, if by any possibility consistent with the rules of law.

Now the testator in his will took notice, that the sons of his aunt Elizabeth Long were living, and gave them legacies:

He also took notice, that Elizabeth Long the ancestor was living at that time, and gave her a legacy; and therefore could not intend that the first son should take strictly as heir, which was impossible if she was living but as, heir apparent he might.

Again, the testator gave his heir, the defendant, an annuity and therefore did not intend that she should have the whole estate; and the limitation to the right heirs was expressly in failure of issue male of his aunt, Elizabeth Long, so that the intent was plain, that the apparent heir male of the body of his aunt Long, who was the lessor of the plaintiff, should take before his heir general, who was the defendant Dorothy, and that she should not take more than an annuity, as long as there should be issue male of his said aunt, Elizabeth Long.

That by this construction, every part of the will would stand and, be consistent, and the word 'heir' would also be taken in a sense that the law be allowed of.

But, if it were to be construed otherwise, several parts, and some whole lines together if a sensible will must be expunged, and the heir at law must take, contrary to the express meaning of the testator.

Lastly, that this case was the same with the case of Burchett v. Durdant, 2 Vent. 311, which had formerly been disputed under the names of James v. Richardson, 1 Vent. 334, 2 Lev. 232, Raym. 330, T. Jones, 99, 457,[2] where a devise, to the heirs male of the body of Robert Durdant then living, was adjudged in

---

[1] E. Coke, *Second Institute* (1642), p. 439; Stat. 25 Edw. III, stat. 5, c. 2 (*SR*, I, 319–320).

[2] *Burchett v. Durdant*, 2 Ventris 311, 86 E.R. 458, also Dodd 60; *James v. Richardson*, 1 Ventris 334, 86 E.R. 216, 2 Levinz 232, 83 E.R. 533, T. Raymond 330, 83 E.R. 172, T. Jones 99, 84 E.R. 1166, Pollexfen 457, 86 E.R. 610, also Dodd 60.

Westminster Hall and twice affirmed in the House of Lords to be a good limitation to George, the eldest son of Robert Durdant, though Robert Durdant was then living, since there could be no great difference between heirs male of the body of the testator's aunt Long lawfully begotten, the words 'then begotten' being tantamount to 'then living'.

Fortescue 18, 92 E.R. 743

By direction of the Court of Exchequer, an ejectment was brought to try the title of several lands in Cornwall of about £600 *per annum*, late the estate of John Speccot, Esq., deceased.

And a special verdict was found, whereby it appears that the said John Speccot, being seised of the said lands, the 19th day of August 1703, made his last will and testament in writing and thereby declares that as to all his estate, both real and personal, of what kind soever, he disposes and limits as therein follows. And first, he directs and appoints that all his debts, legacies, and funerals be paid by his executors, and if his personal estate was not sufficient, then to be paid out of his real estate.

And for that purpose, he devised all his lands unto his loving cousins John Sparke, and Jonathan Sparke, for twenty-one years, in trust to pay his debts, legacies, and funerals, and that when his debts, legacies, and funerals should be discharged, the said term should determine and be void.

And from and after the determination of that estate, then be devises the same lands unto the first son of his body lawfully to be begotten and to the heirs male of the body of such first son, and, in default of such issue, to the heirs of his body lawfully to be begotten, and, for want of such issue, then unto his cousin, John Sparke, for the term of ninety-nine years, if he should so long live, and after his decease, to the first son of the said John Sparke, and to the heirs male of the body of such first son, and to the second and every other son of the body of the said John Sparke to be begotten in tail male. Then to his cousin, Jonathan Sparke, for ninety-nine years, and to his first and every other son to be begotten in tail male. Then comes the limitation, on which the question is made, which immediately follows, and runs thus.

'And for and in default of such issue, I give and devise the remainder of all my said estate, to the heirs male of the body of my aunt, Mrs. Elizabeth Long, wife of Richard Long, clerk, lawfully begotten, and for and in default of such issue, the reversion and remainder of all my said lands and estate to be and remain to my right heirs forever.'

The jury find the will, *in haec verba*, in which he takes notice of his sister and heir Dorothy, the defendant, Dr. Beaumont's wife, and that he had £2450 of hers in his hands, which he directs his trustees to pay; and then gives his said sister an annuity of £150 out of the said lands so limited to the said Long during her life, and then gives £500 apiece to the children of his said sister, Dorothy, the defendant, if she should have more than one, and, if but one, £1000 payable out of the said lands.

Then be takes notice that his aunt Elizabeth Long was living and had children, for he gives her a legacy of £100 and some small matter to the children of his aunt, Elizabeth Long.

The jury further find that the testator John Speccot died the 25th of August 1703, without issue; and that the said John and Jonathan Sparke entered and were possessed, and raised sufficient to pay debts, legacies, and funerals and find that the said term of twenty-one years is ended and determined.

Then they find, that the said John and Jonathan Sparke both died without issue and that the defendant Dorothy Beaumont, wife of the defendant John Beaumont, is sister and heir of the said testator John Speccot, by virtue of which, they in right of Dorothy, entered after the determination of the said term of twenty-one years.

Then it is found that the said Elizabeth Long, aunt of the said testator, had, at the time of making the said will, three sons of her body begotten and no more and that Thomas Long, the lessor of the plaintiff, was then the eldest son of the said Elizabeth Long and that she was alive at the time of the death of the said testator and is still living.

The special verdict was argued twice before the barons of the Exchequer by counsel on both sides, wherein the general question was between the defendant Dorothy, who claimed as heir of the testator, and the lessor of the plaintiff, Thomas Long, who claimed by the will, as being the person designed therein by the limitation to the heirs male of the body of his aunt, Elizabeth Long, lawfully begotten antecedent to the limitation to the testator's right heirs.

The particular question on this special verdict was whether the lessor of the plaintiff Thomas Long, the eldest son and heir apparent of Elizabeth Long, his mother, she being living, could take any estate by the said limitation in the will. It being objected that *nemo est haeres viventis* and that Mrs. Long being living, there could not, in propriety of law, be any heir male of her body begotten to take by this will.

I argued this cause in the Exchequer first of all for the lessor of the plaintiff wherein he obtained judgment, and, after that, I argued it in the House of Lords, where that judgment was affirmed. My argument was to this effect that this limitation to the heirs male of the body of Elizabeth Long, though living, is a good limitation so as to vest a good estate tail in her eldest son by an express designation of the person and by a necessary implication. It is true, according to the general sense and meaning of the word heir and, according to the strictest meaning, the lessor of the plaintiff is not heir as long as his mother lives, but here is so plain a designation of the person and so evident and full a description of him that in a will it is tantamount to a limitation to the first and every other son of Elizabeth Long. In a deed, the law is strict, because it is always supposed to be made by the advice of counsel, and, therefore, legal words and terms of art that have a fixed and settled signification in the law are always made use of and inserted to avoid dispute. But in a will, a man is supposed to be *in articulo mortis*, to have no counsel or friend to advise him, and, therefore, he is excused from using technical words and law phrases, which in deeds are necessary, nor is he tied down to forms of speech but has a liberty to express his last desires in such words as he has learned in the course of his education. And, therefore, Dyer says, in Plowden, Com., 414,[1] that a man has a power in his last will like to an Act of Parliament. This then being the case, I hope to make it out that the expression the testator has used is not even improper in this case. But the objection is *nemo est haeres viventis*, that they say is a maxim. It is more properly called a definition, which makes it one sort of heir, only such, as is in its most strict sense; that is, he that my Lord Hobart calls heir *in concreto*, which means one to whom lands actually descend in right of blood, from a dead ancestor, and so is Co. Litt. 7; Hob. 31.[2] And this definition he has from the civil law, which says *haeredes sunt qui in jus defuncti succedunt*. Calvin's *Lexicon*. Now take it in this strict sense, no person can be heir, unless his ancestor had an estate to descend. Therefore, there is another more extensive meaning of the word, which is, heir *in abstracto*, one who upon the death of his ancestor would inherit his lands, if be left any, *i.e.* one capable of inheriting. And this is the sense this word generally has in deeds and wills, where the limitations are to the heirs of other persons. Again, by the word heir is understood, either *simpliciter*, *i.e.* heir at common law or *per accidens, i.e.* heir by custom, as heir by gavelkind that denotes all the sons, that in borough English denotes the youngest. In the last place, there is another meaning of the word heir, which is nearest our purpose and the most common and vulgar acceptation of the word and that is what my Lord Hobart calls an heir *secundum quid, i.e.* heir apparent or nominal heir, one who would inherit were his ancestor dead, one who stands next the parent and would inherit were his parent dead; and this heir is taken notice of in our law. Littleton, ss. 42, 114; Bracton, lib. 2, c. 33.[3]

Now, among the various meanings of the word heir, I hope to make it appear, that the testator meant it in this last sense of the word heir; that is, such persons as would be heirs to his aunt Elizabeth Long, if she were then dead. But it may be said that no testator should have a meaning against law and, therefore, I will mention some authorities both from statutes and law books, ancient and modern, wherein heir apparent or the first son has been understood by the word heir in the life of the ancestor. Westminster II, cap. 35, 13 Edw. I,[4] which gives the writ of ravishment of ward, says that if any one shall by force take away or

---

1 *Newis v. Lark* (1571), 2 Plowden 403, 413, 75 E.R. 609, 623.

2 E. Coke, *First Institute* (1628), f. 7; *Counden v. Clerke* (1614), Hobart 29, 31, 80 E.R. 180, 181, also Moore K.B. 860, 72 E.R. 955, 1 Eq. Cas. Abr. 213, 22 E.R. 998.

3 T. Littleton, *Tenures*, §§ 42, 114; *Bracton on the Laws and Customs of England* (S. E. Thorne, trans., 1968), vol. 2, pp. 207–208.

4 Stat. 13 Edw. I, Westminster II, c. 35 (*SR*, I, 88–89).

marry the heir of any person, such person may have a writ of ravishment of ward. If the eldest son or only daughter of any man be taken away by force, the writ is *quare filium et haeredem* of such a one *contra voluntatem rapuit.* 2 Inst. 439; 2 Vent. 313.[1] So, in the case of an only daughter of Mr. Eriseys in Cornwall, in the case of The Queen and Killigrew, the indictment was *quare filiam et haeredem,* etc. There is the Statute of Merton, 21 Hen. III, c. 6,[2] concerning wards, begins thus, 'of heirs that are led away or by force married'. So there is [the] Statute of Marlborough, against fraudulent conveyances,[3] [which] begins thus, 'as touching them that use to enfeoff their eldest sons and heirs, being within age, to defraud the lord'. The [Statute] 25 Edw. III, c. 2,[4] is very material; it is the Statute of Treasons. It is there declared high treason to compass or imagine the death of the eldest son and heir of the king or to violate the wife of the king's eldest son and heir; Littleton, s. 103. *The Mirror of Justices*, c. 1, s. 3, says, the heir shall forfeit nothing in prejudice of his ancestor, living the ancestor. *Glanvill*, 45, 6;[5] no one, says he, having a son and heir, can give any of his inheritance to a bastard without the consent of such heir, but. if he have no son and heir nor daughter and heir of his body begotten, he may dispose of all as he pleases. This is exceedingly strong, for here are our very words heirs male of the body. Now since the word heir has so many various significations and is allowed in the law to be used in the sense I contend for, it is unreasonable and a violation of all the rules of exposition to say it must be meant in that sense which is the only one that will set aside the main design and scope of the will. It is hard to say that a man who lies at the point of death and has no adviser shall not be allowed to use that language which is to be found in our law books and allowed in our proceedings at law. But supposing, after all, it should not be a proper term, yet if the testator has a mind to make use of it and his meaning and intent be clear and apparent what person he means in a will, it is sufficient. And why may not this gentleman, in using this term heir, be as well understood as a statute, a writ, or a law book? And why may not a judge understand it as well in a will as a writ?

The intention of the party works strongly in a deed but much more in a will. My Lord Hale says the intention of the testator is the law to expound wills. And the true reason why a man had greater liberty in a will than in a deed was given by the Lord Chief Justice Holt in the case of Idle and Cook, because by the

---

1 E. Coke, *Second Institute* (1642), p. 439; *Burchett v. Durden* (1690), 2 Ventris 311, 86 E.R. 458.

2 Stat. 20 Hen. III, c. 6 (*SR*, I, 3).

3 Stat. 52 Hen. III, c. 6 (*SR*, I, 20).

4 Stat. 25 Edw. III, stat. 5, c. 2 (*SR*, I, 319–320).

5 T. Littleton, *Tenures*, § 103; W. J. Whittaker, ed., *The Mirror of Justices* (1895), 7 Selden Soc. 12; G. D. G. Hall, ed., *Treatise . . . Called Glanvill* (1983), pp. 70–71.

Statute of Wills, 32 Hen. VIII,[1] such a liberty is given; for that Act says a man may dispose of his lands according to his own free will and pleasure, *i.e.* to use such words, terms, and phrases, as he thinks proper. I will mention some cases to that purpose: a devise of land to the Earl of Hertford, Lord Treasurer, though this appellation was not then true, yet it is made good by reputation, though [there was] no such person strictly, Hob. 32,[2] because of the apparent intent of the party. And this vulgar notion of the word heir falls in with the civil law, which calls children *domestici haeredes, et vivo quoque patre, quodammodo domini existimantur.* Calvin's *Lexicon.*

A devise *ecclesiae Sancti Andreae Holborn* is a good devise to the rector of that church and his successors, and yet no person [is] described in the will, but, because it was thought probable, the rector was intended; therefore, his meaning must take place, because the words cannot, which is stronger than our case. There is Fitzherbert, tit. *Devise*, 27; Plowd. 345; 10 Co. 57; Hob. 33.[3] Devise to one and his heirs male, this is a good estate tail, though not said of what body, for the apparent intent of the party, and yet there is no such heir in the law, which would be void if it were in a deed, which is a stronger case than ours, for here the words 'of the body' are supplied and in ours only explained. Besides, he might not mean heirs of his body, but in our case [it is] impossible to mean otherwise than son. 27 Hen. VIII, 27; 1 Vent. 229.[4] Lord Hale, in the case of Pibus v. Mitford, 1 Vent. 381,[5] is of opinion, that even in a covenant to stand seised to the use of the heirs male of the body of J.S. by his second wife, that the son by the second venter should take, though there was a daughter by the first venter, who was strictly heir, because he was a special heir, according to the intent of the party. For, as my Lord Hobart says, though none can be truly heir but he that the law makes so, yet there is an heir by appellation and vulgar acceptation, which imitates the state of a true heir. And, therefore, if by will, I appoint that J.S. shall be heir of

---

1 *Idle v. Cook* (1705), Holt K.B. 164, 90 E.R. 989, 2 Salkeld 620, 91 E.R. 525, 1 Peere Williams 70, 24 E.R. 298, 11 Modern 57, 88 E.R. 883, 2 Lord Raymond 1144, 92 E.R. 257, 2 Eq. Cas. Abr. 299, 22 E.R. 252; Stat. 32 Hen. VIII, c. 1 (*SR*, III, 744–746).

2 *Counden v. Clerke* (1614), *ut supra.*

3 Fitzherbert, Abr., *Devise*, pl. 27; *Brett v. Rigden* (1568), 1 Plowden 340, 345, 75 E.R. 516, 524; *Case of the Chancellor of the University of Oxford* (1613), 10 Coke Rep. 53, 77 E.R. 1006; *Counden v. Clerke* (1614), *ut supra.*

4 YB Mich. 27 Hen. VIII, f. 27, pl. 11 (1535); *King v. Melling* (1672), 1 Ventris 225, 86 E.R. 151, also 1 Ventris 214, 86 E.R. 144, Pollexfen 101, 86 E.R. 526, 3 Keble 42, 52, 95, 84 E.R. 584, 589, 614, 2 Levinz 58, 83 E.R. 448, 3 Salkeld 296, 91 E.R. 835, 1 Eq. Cas. Abr. 181, 21 E.R. 973, Lincoln's Inn MS. Misc. 500, f. 209.

5 *Pibus v. Mitford* (1673–1674), 1 Ventris 372, 86 E.R. 239, also 3 Keble 239, 316, 338, 84 E.R. 697, 741, 754, 3 Salkeld 337, 91 E.R. 859, T. Raymond 228, 83 E.R. 119, 2 Levinz 75, 83 E.R. 456, 1 Modern 98, 121, 159, 86 E.R. 761, 780, 800, 1 Freeman 351, 369, 89 E.R. 262, 275, Lincoln's Inn MS. Misc. 500, ff. 214, 224, 236.

my land, he shall have it in fee, for such estate as his ancestor had, such he is to inherit. Hob. 75.[1]

The next question is whether the testator intended the lessor of the plaintiff to take as heir apparent. And I think here is a plain and manifest intention. He takes notice that his aunt was living, for he mentions her to be the wife of Richard Long, clerk, not only so, but gives her a legacy of £100. From hence it follows necessarily he meant 'apparent' in the vulgar sense, that is, the first son, for he could not mean heirs of a dead ancestor but the heirs of a living one, and that is, heir apparent. Again, the next heir is expressly disinherited, and the defendant had no estate devised to her and had only the expectation of a dry reversion after several estates tail, which is of no consideration in the law.

And there is a further argument why it must be taken to be heir apparent, because the heir general cannot take till failure of issue in his aunt, Elizabeth Long. The words are 'in default of such issue', *i.e.* of Elizabeth Long, the reversion and remainder, of all my said lands and estate to be and remain to his own right heirs. These words infer a strong negative and are as much as if he had said that as long as there is male issue of Elizabeth Long in being, my right heirs shall not inherit, or as if he had said on failure of issue of Elizabeth Long, then, and not till then, my heir shall have it, so that, if the issue of Elizabeth Long cannot take, nobody can. Like the case of 13 Hen. VII, 17:[2] a man devises that, after the decease of his wife, his son and heir should have his house; it was held his son and heir in this case could not have the house during his wife's life; for although it is not expressly devised to her, yet by necessary intendment, the wife must have it, else nobody can; for it cannot descend to the heir, because the testator had broke the descent.

Now, according to their construction, the testator must be *inops mentis*, as well as *inops concilii*, that for three lines together, he should express himself in terms very plain and very significant but should mean nothing by them.

No man is supposed to use any words without some meaning. And so is the rule of law laid down in Plowden, Com., 523, 540,[3] that not one word of a man's will is to be pared off, if it may bear any reasonable sense or meaning. A devise to a man and his issue, if the devisee had issue, it is a joint estate to them all, but, if he have no issue, the devisee shall take an estate tail. But how is that, say the books, since issue cannot take *in praesenti*, there being no issue; rather than that word shall be void, they shall take *in futuro*. 6 Co., Wild's Case, whereas in

---

[1] *Spark v. Purnell* (1614), Hobart 75, 80 E.R. 224, also Moore K.B. 864, 72 E.R. 958.

[2] YB Hil. 13 Hen. VII, f. 17, pl. 22 (1498).

[3] *Welcden v. Elkington* (1578), 2 Plowden 516, 523, 75 E.R. 763, 772; *Paramour v. Yardley* (1579), 2 Plowden 539, 540, 75 E.R. 794, 796.

a deed, the donee has but an estate for life. Co. Litt. 20b; 1 Vent. 382.[1] There is a case of the 26 Eliz. quoted by Lord Hale: a man takes notice in his will that his brother was dead and had a son and he himself had three daughters, who were his right and immediate heirs; he gave them £2000 but gave his land to his heir male; it was held that this was a good devise to his brother's son, though not heir, nor perhaps ever would, yet held a good name of purchase. The next case is Burchet and Durdant, 2 Vent. 312, which is the same case with ours, but not quite so strong; it had formerly been disputed under the name of James and Richardson, 1 Vent. 334; 2 Lev. 232; Raym. 330; 2 Jones 99; Pollexfen 457, where a devise to the heirs male of the body of Robert Durdant then living was adjudged twice in the king's bench, once in the Exchequer chamber, and twice affirmed in the House of Lords. And [it was] held to be a good limitation to George, the eldest son of Robert Durdant, though Robert Durdant was living. Now, there can be no great difference between heirs male of the body of Robert Durdant, now living, and heirs male of the body of my aunt Long, now begotten, these words now begotten being tantamount to now living.

If that case be law, which has been adjudged so often, ours is so too, that the lessor of the plaintiff takes by purchase and that it was a remainder vested in the life of Elizabeth Long and that this is a sufficient designation of the person to take and is as much as if he had said 'to his heirs apparent'. Every circumstance in this case of Burchet and Durdant is in ours, and, in our case, [there] are some strong circumstances not in that. The first reason in our case is that the testator took notice that the ancestor was living and therefore could not intend heir general but a particular heir, *i.e.* heir apparent. Our case is the same, nay stronger, for there it was only found that George was godson and nephew to the devisor, which might be and yet he not know his godson was living. But here, a legacy is given her, and not only so, but by express words also, he calls her the wife of Richard Long, clerk. In the next place, George Durdant was heir apparent, *i.e.* heir in common parlance, and he described him in this manner, because the name perhaps might not occur to the memory of the testator. All this happens in our case, the lessor of the plaintiff is heir apparent. Then, there is another material circumstance in that case and that is now living, which demonstrated who he meant.

So it goes in qualification of the strict notion of heir, and so denoted and explained it to be heir apparent. Now in our case, we have words of the same import and signification, and those are 'lawfully begotten', 'heirs of the body now living', and 'heirs of the body now begotten', being tantamount to now living; and this meaning is greatly enforced by the distinction and opposition the testator himself has made between heirs of the body begotten and heirs of the body to be begot-

[1] *Wild's Case* (1599), 6 Coke Rep. 16, 77 E.R. 277, also Gouldsborough 139, 75 E.R. 1050, 1 Eq. Cas. Abr. 181, 21 E.R. 973, *sub nom. Richardson v. Yardley*, Moore K.B. 397, 72 E.R. 652; E. Coke, *First Institute* (1628), f. 20; *Pibus v. Mitford* (1674), *ut supra*.

ten. Where the limitations in this will are to heirs male of the body where there were none living, he always and in every place says heirs of the body to be begotten. And in the only place where there was issue, he says, heirs of the body begotten. And in no less than five places, he says, to be begotten, where he knew there was no issue. And in the only and last place, where he knew there was issue and had taken notice of them, he varies his phrase, drops the future tense, and puts it in words *de praesenti*, heirs of the body begotten. This could not well happen to be by accident. It is scarcely possible the last of six expressions should vary from the five first, unless it was designed. Now in the former case, such construction was made to support the will, and the intent of the party. But here to construe this to extend to future heirs would be for no other purpose than to make the will void and to defeat the main intent of the devisor. When a man speaks improperly in a will, the law will sometimes suppose he meant properly, as if he say *haeredibus procreatis*, if there be no issue, the law will suppose he meant *procreandis* to support the will. But when a man speaks properly, to suppose and intend he meant improperly, so as to destroy the will, as in this case, is such a construction as I believe was scarcely ever heard of.

Again, in that case it is devised to the heirs male of the body of Robert Long, now living, and for want of such heirs, then over, but our words are 'in default of such issue', which points out to his aunt's three sons only and their issue, which makes our case much stronger, for, thereby, the severe expression of heirs is softened by showing what heirs he meant, such as were issue of the body. And, hereby, an estate tail, by necessary implication, is vested in the three sons by succession one after another. And by this, it appears that the devisor by 'heirs male of the body' meant issue male. Now, issue of the body is of the same import as heirs of the body, as appears by the Statute de Donis, of Westminster II,[1] and many other authorities. And, if this had been a devise to the issue of Elizabeth Long, the words subsequent, and in default of such issue, would have made it an estate tail in the lessor of plaintiff and so in succession to the other sons.

Nor is it any objection to say that it would be uncertain which of the issue should take first, for, if a devise be to the issue and their issue and there be more than one, it must go to the eldest in a course of descent. Otherwise, issue would not be *nomen collectivum*. And this was the opinion of my Lord Hale, in 1 Vent. 229, who explodes the doctrine of the uncertainty of such a devise and says that the case of Sayer and Taylor, which is that way in 3 Cro. 742[2] is too rank to pass for law. There is the case, too, of Lodington and Kime, 3 Lev. 431.[3] [There was a] devise to Evers Armin for life and, in case he shall have issue male, then to such

[1] Stat. 13 Edw. I, c. 1 (*SR*, I, 71–72).

[2] *King v. Melling* (1672), *ut supra*; *Taylor v. Sayer* (1600), Croke Eliz. 742, 78 E.R. 975, also 1 Eq. Cas. Abr. 212, 21 E.R. 997.

[3] *Loddington v. Kime* (1695), 3 Levinz 431, 83 E.R. 766, also 1 Lord Raymond 203, 91 E.R. 1031, 1 Salkeld 224, 91 E.R. 198, 2 Eq. Cas. Abr. 331, 22 E.R. 282.

issue male and his heirs; this was held to be a good devise to the first son and heir male in tail and that he took by purchase. And here it was objected that it was uncertain which of the male issue should take first. But [it was] held by the whole court that the heir shall not be disinherited by probabilities. But here, it is by express terms, for the heir is not to take, as heir, till after the failure of issue male of Elizabeth Long. So is 13 Hen. VII, 17; Bro. *Devise* 52;[1] a man devises his goods to his wife, and, after the death of his wife, that his son and heir should have his house; here, son and heir cannot have the house during his wife's life, for though not expressly devised to his wife, yet, by necessary intendment, the wife must have it, else no body can, for it cannot descend to the heir, because the testator has broke the descent. Vaugh. 263.[2]

So here, if the issue of Elizabeth Long cannot take, nobody can, for the heir cannot inherit, by the express words of the will, till failure of issue male of Elizabeth Long. Now to suppose him to have no meaning in these three lines together is to suppose him *inops mentis*, as well as *concilii*, so that the eldest issue male should take, even though they were twins, he that was the first born should take. So is Dyer 333;[3] a devise to the house or family of such a one [was] held to be a good devise to the chief and eldest person of the family, according to the course of common law. But after all, the words 'now living', might have another sense, but the true reason was that this was the most probable reason and most agreeable to the intent of the party. In the next place, the consequence of this construction they contended for in that case was not so fatal as in ours, for, if in that case they had rejected the words 'now living', that would have cut off but one single branch of that family. It would have set aside only George Durdant, for, if there were other issue born after, as there might be, those would have enjoyed this estate by the subsequent words 'and to such other heirs male and female as he should hereafter happen to have'. But, in our case, not only the lessor of the plaintiff, but all the family of the Longs, root and branch, are to be cut off and set aside, though the heir at law is expressly postponed to all the issue of Elizabeth Long.

But then, it is objected, if the lessor of plaintiff take by purchase and by designation of the person, be can take but an estate for life. I answer he shall take an estate tail. And so it was held in the case of Burchet and Durdant and is there resolved as the third point of that case, for the court held that the words 'heirs of the body now living' would make an estate tail, though the son took by purchase, because heirs is *nomen collectivum* and is sometimes so taken when it is only heir in the singular number, as a devise to one for life, remainder to the heir male of his body, this is an estate tail in the devisee. So is the case of Pawsey and Lother,

---

[1] YB Hil. 17 Hen. VII, f. 17, pl. 22 (1502); 1 Brooke, Abr., *Devise*, pl. 52.

[2] *Gardner v. Sheldon* (1671), Vaughan 259, 124 E.R. 1064, also 1 Freeman 11, 89 E.R. 9, 2 Keble 781, 84 E.R. 494, 1 Eq. Cas. Abr. 197, 21 E.R. 986.

[3] *Chapman's Case* (1574), 3 Dyer 333, 73 E.R. 754.

2 Rolle's Abr., 253.[1] But then, it may be said that the subsequent words in that case helped to make it an estate tail, for the subsequent words, which are 'and to such other heirs male and female as he shall hereafter happen to have of his body', that is, as Robert, the father, should have, give every other son of Robert an estate tail. But they do not at all affect the estate of George, which subsists only on the words 'heirs of the body of Robert now living', for by the other words he is excluded. But this is no new objection, for Mr. Justice Dolben, the only judge against that judgment, made the same objection but was overruled. Nay, it is said in 2 Lev. 232,[2] that after the first judgment in the case of James and Richardson, a new ejectment was brought of other lands in the same will after the death of George Durdant, the son, against his heir to try this point again, and it was adjudged over again, and the judgment [was] affirmed in the House of Lords that George took a fee tail, and not an estate for life only.

In the last place, it is objected and strongly insisted on that, if Thomas, the eldest son, take by purchase, though he should take an estate tail, yet that none of the rest of the children can take. There is a full answer to that. The subsequent words 'in default of such issue' will make it an estate tail by implication to all the issue, for, if 'heirs of the body' are here words equivalent to 'issue of the body', as we contend they are, then, these words 'in default of such issue' plainly make an estate tail. And so is the opinion of my Lord Hale in the case of King and Melling, 1 Vent. 230.[3] [There was a] devise to his son Bernard for life and, after his decease, to the issue of his body and, for want of such issue, then over, which words in a will, says he, make an estate tail by implication and that the remainder over could never take till issue failed. But there is another answer to this, and that is that this very objection has been overruled in that case of Burchet and Durdant, for, if in that case, the estate had vested in George by purchase, and he had the inheritance, the other issue which took by descent from the ancestor could not take at all. And this very argument was used by Mr. Justice Dolben, who was against the judgment. By this construction, says he, the heirs born after are excluded, and yet that did not prevail. 1 Vent. 334.[4]

The sum of the argument is this, this dying man has expressed himself, though not in the strictest terms, yet in such terms as the law allows and owns. The language he uses is to be found in statutes, law books, and records. Here is no estate devised contrary to the rules of law, nor any maxim of law broken; according to our construction, every line of this will is significant and every word has some meaning and all the parts are consistent one with another, but, according to their construction, a man is made to speak for three lines together and to mean nothing and a whole family is set aside against the express words of the testator.

---

1 *Pawsey v. Lowdell* (1651), 2 Rolle, Abr., *Parolls*, pl. H, 4, p. 253.

2 *James v. Richardson* (1678), 2 Levinz 232, 83 E.R. 533.

3 *King v. Melling* (1672), *ut supra*.

4 *James v. Richardson* (1679), 1 Ventris 334, 86 E.R. 216.

After long debate and consideration, the Lord Chief Baron [WARD] and the rest of the barons (except Baron Bury) were of opinion that the lessor of the plaintiff, Thomas Long, the eldest son of Elizabeth Long, had a good title by the said will and so gave judgment for the plaintiff. But a writ of error being brought in the Exchequer chamber; this judgment was, by the opinion of the two chief justices, reversed. But, by the opinion of the House of Lords, *nemine contradicente*, this reversal was reversed, and the judgment of the Exchequer [was] affirmed.[1]

1 Eq. Cas. Abr. 214, 21 E.R. 999

A. devises all his lands to B. and C. and the survivor of them for the term of twenty-one years for the payment of his debts and legacies and after payment the term to cease and, after the end or sooner determination of that estate, he devises the premisses to the first son of his body and to the heirs males of the body of such son lawfully issuing and, for default of such issue, to B. for ninety-nine years, if he so long live, without impeachment of waste, remainder to the first and other sons of B. and the heir's male of their bodies successively, remainder to C. for ninety-nine years, if he so long live, remainder to his first and other sons in tail male successively, remainder to the heirs males of my aunt, Mrs. Elizabeth Long, wife of Richard Long, clerk, lawfully begotten, with remainder to his own right heirs, and by his will gave £150 annuity to Dorothy Beaumont, his sister, the plaintiff in error, for life and £500 to her children, and to his aunt, Elizabeth Long, £100, and to her children £500, and dies without issue.

B. and C. entered by virtue of the devise for twenty-one years. And afterwards, both died without issue. And John Beaumont and Dorothy, his wife, entered in right of Dorothy, as heir at law to the testator, the term of twenty-one years being determined and the debts and legacies paid. Thomas Long, oldest son of Elizabeth (she having, at the time of making the said will, three sons, *viz.* the said Thomas and two others) entered and brought ejectment.

And in the Exchequer, judgment was given by the Lord Chief Baron WARD, PRICE, and LOVELL, against Baron BURY, for the plaintiff, Thomas Long. But, in Trinity Term 1713, this judgment was reversed in the Exchequer chamber. And upon error brought in the House of Lords, it was argued that this reversal should be affirmed:

First, because Dorothy, being heir at law to the testator, her right, as such, was to be favored and all devises to disinherit an heir at law were to be taken strictly.

Secondly, that to make this devise good to Thomas Long, it must be construed either a contingent remainder or the words heirs males be taken as a *descriptio personae* to vest in him as a contingent remainder. It cannot be good for

[1] *Darbison v. Beaumont* (1714), *Lords' Journal*, vol. 19, p. 696, 3 Brown P.C. 60, 1 E.R. 1177.

want of a freehold to support it, all the preceding estates being only for years. Besides, if it were good as a contingent remainder in its creation, yet Elizabeth Long, the mother, being alive when the particular estate determined, it cannot vest, because *non est haeres viventis.*[1] As a *descriptio personae* it cannot vest, for that ought to be such a description as is *vice nominis*, which the words heirs male's (being a legal term and not accompanied with any other words to determine the sense otherwise, as heir apparent or heir now living etc.) cannot amount to, and the word begotten does not determine the sense otherwise, nor does any intent appear to consider the devisee to the issue male of Elizabeth Long, much less to Thomas Long only, as the person described in this devise.

But notwithstanding these reasons, it was adjudged that the judgment should stand and the judgment of reversal be reversed, though ten of the judges were of opinion that the devise was void and only the three judges (Lovell being dead) beforementioned held it good.

[Orders of 23 February 1713 and 3 July 1714: Public Record Office E.126/20, ff. 36v, 155.]

[Connected cases: Long v. Beaumont (Ex. 1709), see above, Case No. 340.]

437

Ludlam v. Moore

(Ex. 1713)

The defense of the statute of frauds must be pleaded specially.

Lincoln's Inn MS. Misc. 539, f. [125]

In the Office of Pleas in the Exchequer by a Hilary term record 10 Queen Anne [1712].

The plaintiff [George Ludlam] declares against the defendant [Zachary Moor] in an action upon the case, for that, whereas the defendant, the 24 January 8 the queen [1710] at London in the parish of St. Mary le Bow, in consideration that the plaintiff, at the request of the defendant, had sold and agreed to deliver to the defendant forty tuns of good merchantable alum yearly and in every year for the space of seven years thence next following, the defendant assumed and promised to pay to the plaintiff £15 of lawful money of Great Britain for every tun of the said alum upon the delivery thereof and the defendant then and there paid to the plaintiff 1s. in part of payment for the said alum and though the plaintiff, the 23 January 1709[/10] at the place aforesaid, *obtulit deliberare* to the plaintiff forty tuns of good and merchantable alum for such a quantity of alum by him to be delivered to the defendant for the first year of the said seven years ac-

[1] E. Coke, *First Institute* (1628), ff. 8b, 22b.

cording to the agreement aforesaid, yet the defendant, not regarding but intending to deceive the plaintiff, refused, and still refuses to receive the said alum so tendered to be delivered or any part thereof or to pay for the same according to the agreement aforesaid to the plaintiff's damage of £1800.

The defendant, after an imparlance, pleads *actio non etc.*, because he says that there is not nor ever was any memorandum or note in writing of the promise and assumption in the declaration above specified signed by him or any other person by him lawfully authorized according to the form of the Statute for Preventing of Frauds and Perjuries[1] in that case made and provided. And he avers his plea, and prays judgment etc.

To this plea, the plaintiff demurs, and shows for cause:

First, that the matter and things in the plea contained in form aforesaid by the defendant amount to the general issue and, thereupon, the defendant ought to have pleaded the general issue and to have given the matter and things in the said plea contained in evidence upon the trial;

Second, and that the plea is uncertain, insufficient, and wants form.

The defendant joins in the demurrer, and now [it is] standing for the opinion of the court after two arguments on each side, *viz. Ward* and *Raymond*, Solicitor General, for the plaintiff, and by *Agar* and *Sir Peter King*, Recorder of London, for the defendant.

The first question is whether the plaintiff can maintain this action as laid or not and, if it be maintainable at all, then, how far the remedy upon it shall extend, whether for the whole alum which was yearly to be delivered during the seven years or whether only for the alum that was to be delivered within the first year or the seven [years] for which this action is brought.

And the second question is, if the action be maintainable at all, then whether the defendant ought not to have pleaded the general issue instead of this plea which he has pleaded. The defendant, by his plea, points out the defect of the plaintiff's case as declared upon in regard there was no note or memorandum given or signed, as the Act against Frauds and Perjuries directs. And so he prays judgment *si actio*.

It is necessary, therefore, to observe the words and meaning of that Act upon which the question turns. The Act was made the 29 Car. II, ca. 3, and the fourth paragraph of the Act, which runs thus, that, after the 24th of June 1679, no action shall be brought whereby to charge any person upon any agreement that is not to be performed within the space of one year from the making thereof unless the agreement upon which such action shall be brought or some memorandum or note thereof shall be in writing and signed by the party to be charged therewith or some other person thereunto by him limited lawfully authorized, and, in this case, before the making of that Act, I [Edward Ward] am of the opinion that

[1] Stat. 29 Car. II, c. 3 (*SR*, V, 839–842).

this action was maintainable and, though the plaintiff in such an action upon the first breach aforesaid could not recover damages for the whole sum in question, as the opinion of Jones and Berkeley was in Peck and Ambler's Case, Cro. Car. 350.[1] Yet there might have been a recovery upon each yearly failure for the sum that became due in each year. And a yearly action would have well lain upon the grounds and authorities urged by the plaintiff's counsel in this cause as being a several cause of action springing and arising from the agreement and promise of delivering a yearly quantity in each year. But I think this Act has put a restraint upon the case in question to maintain an action for the first year's failure in delivering the alum within the first year, much less for the succeeding years. This Act was made to restrain all leases by parol for more than three years from the making and all actions upon any and all contracts and agreements for goods, save where the agreements are to be performed within a year after the making of such agreement, in both which respects, the Act has put a limitation of time, and such time is not to be enlarged.

In this case, there is not seven, but one, agreement, and that was made and to take effect from the 24th January 1709[/10]. And though the alum was yearly during the seven years to be delivered, and so the plaintiff's counsel urge, that each year's failure was a new cause of action, yet, there being but one agreement and there being to be several year's deliveries which might give new causes of action each year, yet the succeeding years after the first could give no cause of action because they were for things which were not to be performed within a year after the making of the agreement and, therefore, plainly restrained by the Act. And the agreement here being but one and that an entire agreement subsisting for seven years and to bind [. . .] party so long, though severable in the execution, I think it will not be good within the words and intention of that Act, even for the first year, for that would be a means to avoid the true intent of the Act, which was to confine all actions upon any agreements which were not to be performed in a year. Now, the agreement, which was but one, going as well to the future as the first year and being entire, if it be not good for the whole, it cannot be good for part, because the entire agreement is not to be performed within a year after the making of it. And, as this agreement cannot be split and made several agreements, no more can any cause of action arising upon it be made several.

If this should be as the plaintiff's counsel seemed most to insist, that this agreement should have its effect for each of the seven years and, at each year's end, there should arise a new cause of action, how would the last six years' actions be within a year, for a cause that was not to be performed within a year after the agreement which was made long before the year and in every action to be brought for any year's alum, the plaintiff must found it upon the agreement which was not to be performed within the year, and, if such agreements should

---

1 *Peck v. Ambler* (1634), Croke Car. 349, 79 E.R. 906.

be good for seven years, they must be as good for twenty or thirty years, and so elude the meaning of the Act, which was to bring parol leases to three years and parol agreements to one year, and not further.

And I [Edward Ward] am the rather induced to be of the opinion that this agreement for seven years should not be good for one year, in regard it has been held that, if a man leases by parol for above three years, it will not be a good lease for three though the enjoyment and payment of the rent was to be annual, because restrained by the Act to three from the making. Nay, if a man, by parol, leases for three years only, yet, if it be to commence from a time to come, it is void by the Act, because it must not exceed three years from the making. Nay, it has been held that, if a man, by parol, leases for any lesser term than three years, as for two or one year only, yet, if it be not to commence from the making in point of interest, that is a void lease likewise. And this was the opinion of the two chief justices Holt and Treby and several other justices at a meeting in Trinity term 1696, which I heard and Liber M, 57.[1] So that, as leases are to commence from the making, so contracts are to have an entire performance within a year after the agreement was made.

And the meaning of all was to confine things to a certainty and to annul leases and contracts not warranted by that Act. And the mischiefs before would still continue if an original agreement being entire and but one, though branching itself into yearly performances, should be good for seven years; why not for twenty years, and yet, upon an action for non-performance in the last years, must be founded upon the original agreement made so many years before, which can neither answer the intent nor the words of the Act in being within a year after the agreement. And it will not be good for the first year, the contract and agreement being an entire one, and not several for every year. And so in the same consideration that a parol lease for four years shall not by construction be good for three, two, or one, though the rent reserved is an annual payment and capable of a several performance and cause of action every year.

The agreement here is the sole foundation of the action, and it is an entire agreement, as I said before, and not several agreements though the execution may be at several times.

The great end of this law was to prevent frauds and perjuries and nothing more [will] conduce to it than that men should trust too long to frail memories in making bargains, therefore, not to trust to memory longer than for a year without a writing.

The defendant's plea is but oddly penned, saying there is no note or memorandum in writing of the defendant's assumption or promise, whereas the words of the Act are of the agreement upon which such an action is brought. The variance between the Act and the plea must be admitted to be so in words, but, in

[1] Note (1696), Lincoln's Inn MS. Misc. 559, f. 57, pl. 1.

substance and to the meaning of the law, they are to the same effect, for it is plain this action appears to be founded on an agreement which was to have a continuance for seven years. So, to some purposes and for the maintaining of this action, the defendant's promise and assumption, which rises by operation of law and not by express contract otherwise than as, by, and upon the agreement is the same as to say there was no note of the promise which there is no note of the agreement upon which that promise is laid to be the cause of action. I think the defendant's plea that hints the want of a note is well enough, and the defendant's demurrer admits it.

Now, this Act being a general law and whereof the court *ex officio* and without pleading is bound to take notice, this action being founded upon an agreement in the declaration mentioned which ought to have a note in writing to support it and none such is set forth, it must be intended to be by parol. And, so, by the express words of the Act, no action is maintainable.

On 27 November 1713, in Ludlam and Moore, the judgment of the court [was given].

Baron Price opens the records *prout*, and he is opinion for the plaintiff. The cause assigned amounts not to the general issue, for here is matter of law, and it may be set out so in a special [plea of] justification. Hobt. 127. Special retainer might have been given in evidence, yet [it was] pleaded. 2 Ventris, Sansan's Case; a party has an election, as debt for rent, entry, and expulsion pleaded or given in evidence.[1] As to the defendant's plea, whether the Statute was well pleaded, he holds not. By the Statute, a note is of an agreement in writing. The plea is no note of the defendant's assumption. There are mutual promises here from the plaintiff and defendant. The defendant's assumption is but of one. So the defendant [did] not well set out. And the general law was not well set out, which is an incurable fault. He compares it to the Statute of Limitations,[2] which must be set out. So, it is not a good plea.

This case is not within the Statute because this agreement is to be performed every year during the seven years. And, therefore, it is good for the first year, though doubtful for the succeeding years. Though 1s. was paid, this case, in that clause, it is the intent of the Act to prevent.

Executory and mutual agreements are to be performed every year. 1 Inst. 293. A debt is not recoverable until the last day. But in [an action of] covenant or case, [they are] several. Before Slade's Case, [there was a] doubt, but, now, it is settled. Dy. 114, Peck and Redman; for a delivery of so many quarters of barley

---

[1] *Warner v. Wainsford* (1615), Hobart 127, 80 E.R. 276, also *sub nom. Wainford v. Warner*, 1 Brownlow & Goldesborough 80, 123 E.R. 679; *Sarsfield v. Witherly* (1689), 2 Ventris 292, 86 E.R. 447, also Carthew 82, 90 E.R. 652, Comberbach 45, 152, 90 E.R. 334, 399, *sub nom. Witherly v. Sarsfield*, Holt K.B. 112, 90 E.R. 960, 1 Shower K.B. 125, 89 E.R. 491.

[2] Stat. 21 Jac. I, c. 16 (*SR*, IV, 1222–1223).

yearly, several causes of action [can be brought]. Br., Accion sur case, 108; Cro. Car., Mills and Mills;[1] the law before the Statute settled the meaning of this law. This law is to prevent perjuries. And this [agreement is] to be performed within the year. Smith and Worthall, Hilary [term] 9 Will., brokers' act, [there was] no contract for transferring stock to be good if not to be performed before 1st May [. . .] in February to deliver before 10 May, but Levinz's Entries, 27, [is the] same case in effect. So, if an agreement is performable, though in consideration of marriage if not performed in a year.

So, he concludes for the plaintiff [who does] not fly in the face of the law.

Baron Bury [held] for the defendant. [There are] two questions: first, whether the demurrer is good for the cause shown; second, where a note is necessary.

As to the cause shown, [it is] not a good cause. This plea is not the general issue, for it admits the promise but avoids it, which the general issue denies. He cited Price's authorities and reasons. Coverture [is not] pleaded, though it may be given in evidence. So, in a case of usury or gaming. Matters of fact which amount only to the general issue are not pleadable, as in trover etc. Impertinent pleading is to be avoided. Here, a matter of law arises whether a note is necessary in law or not, and a demurrer determines it rather than a trial. Hobt. 127 is full as to matter of law. So he concludes.

Objection: [There is a] difference between an agreement and an assumption.

Solution: [They are] all one. And a defendant is not bound if there is no promise signed.

Objection: The Statute is not well pleaded.

Solution: This Statute is not pleaded here, but only referred to. '*Non assumpsit infra sex annos*' here is a sufficient reference and intimation.

To the second point, he holds this case within the Statute. And a note is necessary. The payment of 1s. is nothing [and] not within that clause. He observed the words of the fourth paragraph, and read them. This agreement ought to be by the letter and intent of a [*blank*]. This is an agreement for seven years, and [it is] entire for a time, and [it is] not to be performed in or for the first year. [It is] intended not to trust a memory for seven years.

Objection: There are several agreements.

Solution: Before the Statute, [there could be] several actions. But since, [there can] not; if nothing be done during the seven years, the action lies not. [It is] one agreement only, and not [several] for each year. 2 Sanders 337; an *assumpsit* to perform an award for the payment of several sums [makes] every cause a new cause of action, but not a new agreement. 3 Levins 383, March and Free-

[1] E. Coke, *First Institute* (1628), f. 293; *Slade v. Morley* (1602), 4 Coke Rep. 91, 76 E.R. 1072, Moore K.B. 433, 667, 72 E.R. 677, 827, Yelverton 20, 80 E.R. 15; *Pecke v. Redman* (1556), 2 Dyer 113, 73 E.R. 248; YB Hil. 11 Hen. VI, f. 18, pl. 10, 1 Brooke, Abr., *Action sur le case*, 108 (1433); *Mills v. Mills* (1631), Croke Car. 239, 79 E.R. 809; Stat. 8 & 9 Will. III, c. 32 (*SR*, VII, 285–287).

man; debt; before the end, [an action of] covenant lies upon every breach.[1] And where [there is a] covenant to pay a certain sum, [an action of] debt lies. But it is one agreement.

And he concluded for the defendant.

A promise to pay such a sum at his marriage and [there was] no marriage within the nine years, by Holt, it is doubtful, but other judges thought it was good.

As to the cause of the demurrer [that was] assigned by the plaintiff, the defendant might and ought to have pleaded the general issue and given the special matter in evidence, as I [Edward Ward] cannot say but that the defendant might have done so according to the several cases cited for that purpose by the plaintiff's counsel, yet I think he was not bound to do so, but he might set out the want of a note, which indeed is a matter of law, and brings the things in question to a speedier determination than by going to a trial, *viz.* upon a demurrer. My opinion, therefore, is that this action lies not upon this agreement, that the defendant, by his plea, has well set out the defect of a note, and that the plaintiff, by demurring, has admitted such a defect and that the defendant might by a plea set forth such a defect and is not bound to plead the general issue.

And so judgment ought to be *quod querens nil capit per billam*. And, of that opinion, was Baron Bury, and judgment was entered accordingly, *dissentiente* Price.

[Other copies of this report: Georgetown Univ. Law Sch. MS. B88–10, p. 1084.]

Dodd 232

Upon a demurrer in the Exchequer, [it was] adjudged by the Chief Baron [Ward] and Baron Bury against Baron Price, 27 November 1713. In [this] case, the plaintiff declares that in consideration [that] he had agreed to sell and deliver forty tuns of alum yearly and every year to the defendant for seven years, the defendant promised to pay £15 a tun for the same and then said he was ready and offered to deliver forty tuns in the first year but the defendant refused to accept thereof or pay the £15.

The defendant pleaded there was not any note or memorandum in writing. And thereupon [the] plaintiff demurs, because it amounts to the general issue and *caret formam* and insufficient in law.

And [it was] adjudged after several arguments by the Chief Baron [Ward] and Bury against Price:

[1] *Cooke v. Whorewood* (1671), 2 Williams Saunders 337, 85 E.R. 1135, also 2 Keble 767, 84 E.R. 485, 2 Levinz 6, 83 E.R. 427; *March v. Freeman* (1693), 3 Levinz 383, 83 E.R. 742.

First, that it is well pleaded and [the defendant is] not obligated to plead the general issue. Hob. 127; 3 Levinz 40; 10 Rep. 92; Moo. 600; 2 Ven. 292; 5 Mod. 314;[1]

Second, it is an entire contract for seven years; although yearly to be in part performed, it is not yearly a new agreement but only a breach of the old agreement, so it is within the Act of Frauds and Perjuries. 2 Saunders 337; 3 Lev. 383.

Note: [Baron] PRICE argued that [they were] several agreements and [they were] good at least for the first year, which was denied by the others, and [it was] adjudged as above.

There was also a question upon the words of the pleading that [there was] no note of the promise or assumpsit in the count, but the Statute is 'unless the agreement' etc. But [it was] held good.

Note: A case was cited that A. in consideration of 5s. promised to pay B. £100 upon his marriage; [this was] good if the marriage [is] within one year, otherwise not. Thus to pay in consideration of 5s. £100 at the death of A. [is] good if [A.] die within the year. Levinz, Entries, 27,[2] and Smith and Westerne, Hilary [term] 9 Will. [1697 × 1698] [in] the King's Bench.

438

Note

(Ex. 1713)

A renewable contract must be pleaded as for the total period of the renewable time.

Lincoln's Inn MS. Misc. 539, f. [129]

A lease for three years and, at the end of them, for three years more, and so from three years to three years during the lessor's life is good for twelve years if the testator lives so long. So from three years to three years until nine years, that is a good lease for nine years and a lease for 99 years and so for 99 years to 99 years until 300 years is past is a lease for 300 years. 2 rep. 23, Baldwin's Case etc.; Rolle's, *Estate*, 850.[3]

---

[1] *Warner v. Wainsford* (1615), *ut supra*; *Thomas v. Nichols* (1681), 3 Levinz 40, 83 E.R. 566; *Leyfield v. Hillary* (1611), 10 Coke Rep. 88, 92, 77 E.R. 1057, 1065, also 1 Bulstrode 154, 80 E.R. 846, Croke Jac. 317, 79 E.R. 272; *Sarsfield v. Witherly* (1689), *ut supra*; *Hackshaw v. Clerke* (1696), 5 Modern 314, 87 E.R. 677.

[2] *Causton v. Manvillam* (1697), C. Levinz, *Entries* (1702), p. 27.

[3] *Baldwin v. Marton* (1589), 2 Coke Rep. 18, 76 E.R. 430, also 1 Anderson 223, 123 E.R. 442; *Newberry v. Rathbone* (1616), 1 Rolle, Abr., *Estate*, pl. A, 1, p. [850], also 1 Rolle Rep. 288, 81 E.R. 490.

Now, in these cases, though these estates are from three years to three years for nine years or from 99 to 99 for 300 [years], yet the leases must be declared upon to be for nine years and for 300 years and not for the broken terms of years.

A parson agrees with a parishioner that he may retain his tithes for three years under the yearly payment of such a sum, though a parol retainer for one year is good, yet this, being an entire agreement for three years, is not good for one year. Keddington and Sympson, below, f. [*blank*].[1]

[Other copies of this report: Georgetown Univ. Law Sch. MS. B88–10, p. 1099.]

439

Regina v. Barrington

(Ex. 1714)

A customs officer who wrongfully seizes and disposes of a ship can be found in contempt of court.

Lincoln's Inn MS. Misc. 539, f. [197v]

Hilary term 12 Anne 1713[/14].

The Queen against Thomas Barrington and Robert Morly, Custom House officers at Exeter, against whom a [writ of] attachment was awarded upon a contempt upon which their examinations were read and the case appeared to be this.

In December 1712, the defendants seized a ship at Exeter and French wines in it, and exhibited an information thereupon against the wines as forfeited, being French wines, and against the ship as forfeited for that the wines were imported in it with the privity and consent of [*blank*], the master, contrary to the French Prohibition Act,[2] which was then in force. And, thereupon, a writ of appraisement was awarded for the wines and for the ship, and they were severally appraised, the ship at £80 and the wines at so much. The owners of the ship regularly entered their claim of property to the ship on the back of the indenture of appraisement, as usual and another person [. . .] his claim also to the ship. (But that was supposed to be fictitious.)

The wines were claimed by others, and a writ of delivery was awarded for them, but none for the ship, which continued under seizure until April following. And the seizers took away the ship's sails, and laid them up, and set a sort of guard upon the ship of inferior officers. And, when the writ of delivery was brought for the wines, the defendants and other officers who had the custody of the ship, under a mistake (as is pretended) thinking the ship had been also in the writ, which was not, the defendants, both or, at least, Morly, under color of some

[1] *Keddington v. Simpson* (Ex. 1713), Eq. Cases Exch. 681.

[2] Stat. 3 & 4 Ann., c. 12 (*SR*, VIII, 360).

writing from the superior custom officers at Exeter (called a clearing bill), delivered the ship to the claimers of the wine, who or some[one] else for them, strangers to the claimers of the ship, upon record, took it away, by means whereof, the ship was as to them totally lost. And, upon an affidavit of this matter, a [writ of] attachment was awarded.

Barrington, upon his examination, seemingly denied his being concerned in the delivering of the ship. But Morly confessed he put his hand to the clearing bill.

And now, Mr. Attorney General *Northey* (who ought to have been for the queen) and *Ettrick* and *Stevens* endeavored to defend the defendants from any contempt upon the supposition that what was done was only a mistake and not any willful act and, being delivered pursuant to the clearing bill, as they thought, though a mistake, they hoped they should not be punished, being officers, and the rather because, as was alleged, but without any proofs that the property of the ship was not in the claimers, which they were willing to try.

And, to that, PRICE and BANISTER seemed to incline, and PRICE was for clearing both the defendants from the contempt, as thinking what was done under those circumstances not to be a contempt to the court. But BANISTER, though he cleared Barrington, yet he thought Morly guilty for the delivery of the ship, for which there was no authority from this court, where the cause was depending. But BURY and myself [EDWARD WARD] held both the defendants guilty of the contempt, for, when two men make a joint seizure and exhibit an information thereupon, in judgment of law and the fact both, they both have the custody of the ship and must be answerable for it, both to the crown in the case of a condemnation and to the claimer in the case of an acquittal, and none can nor ought to take it out of their hands but by the authority of this court, which is by a writ of delivery. And it is plain that Barrington was instrumental in laying up the sails and putting under-officers aboard. And, though he did not actually sign the clearing bill, as Morly did, yet, by his seizure, he was bound to have the ship forthcoming and to be dealt withal as the court shall direct. And, in such a case as this, he must answer as well as his co-seizer for the ship. And, if such a practice as this may be tolerated that after a merchant's ship is seized and taken out of his custody and power and put wholly into both the seizers' power, who both claim the moiety of it to their own use and the owner has no other way to have it again but by entry of his claim in this court and the seizers refuse or neglect to carry on the cause to trial and yet detain the ship and suffer it to be taken and carried away by strangers without any authority of this court wherein the whole merits of the cause is judicially depending, the claimer is in a bad condition. And the justice of this court is concerned to see that the claimer be restored to his ship, which must have been recovered to the use of the crown and seizers if this claim of the party had not been put in, and yet, when put in, the seizers either refuse to proceed or, through their means or negligence, the ship is taken or carried away and lost to the claimer.

And, as to the clearing bill, it is no manner of excuse, being wholly without any lawful authority, for neither the commissioners of the customs, much less any inferior officers, ought to do anything about the delivering of the ship while the cause is judicially depending in this court, which is a piece of insolence to attempt, though the Attorney General sought some way to entitle the commissioners, though not the inferior officers, to a power for that purpose, which was wholly denied by the court as a strange and unheard of pretense that those who are inferiors and under no obligation of oath nor have a spark of authority by law should dare to discharge anything seized and whereof the court is possessed and judicially depending therein, which was a presumption not to be borne. And, if it were allowed, it would be a means to transfer from this court a judicial power to them to meddle with and determine matters and properties otherwise than the law allows.

And, as to the pretense of excuse that it was a mistake, if any, through mistake, do an apparent injury, it is fit they should make amends. And as to what was said that the claimer was not the true proprietor and the offer to try that, it was impertinent, for the claimer, as to the court, appears to have the property, and must, in law, be so understood. And there is no way left for the court to try whether he was really so or no, for he must be so understood, especially as to the seizers, the only question being whether it was forfeited or not. And, if such an allegation should prevail to make out property before a claim should be entered, all goods seized would be recovered for want of making out property possible by parties owners living in parts beyond the seas and swearing the property never was insisted upon unless when there is a good ground of suspicion that the claim is by fraud and to put the seizers to a needless and chargeable trial and that the claim has not been put before the proclamation.

And, therefore, the court being divided as to Barrington, he was discharged (which I [Edward Ward] thought hardly). But Morly was adjudged to be in contempt of the court and the justice of it. But what fine the court should impose upon him was to be considered and he to stand upon his recognizance in the meantime, the claimer having lost his ship and the offer to try the property being altogether new and impertinent, so long as the cause depends in the court. If, indeed, the defendants and Mr. Attorney General [Northey] waive and discharge the information and proceedings in this court so that no record remains of them, then the claimer of the ship may be at liberty to bring his action of trespass or trover against the seizers. But, for the contempt to the court, the defendant Morly is to be fined.

But, afterwards, it was prayed on Morly's behalf that he might stand upon his recognizance until next term to see what end he could make with the prosecutors and then the court to set the fine, which was by consent ordered accordingly.

But the parties agreed, and the matter was no more heard of, Mr. Attorney General being of counsel for the defendants, through the contempt was to the queen and the court.

[Other copies of this report: Georgetown Univ. Law Sch. MS. B88–10, p. 1109.]

440

Frampton v. Beverton and Clements

(Ex. 1714)

Seizers of goods forfeited for non-payment of duties must deliver them to the bidder who bought them, regardless of any orders of the commissioners of the customs.

Lincoln's Inn MS. Misc. 539, f. [199]

There were uncustomed and prohibited goods, among which, some were East India goods seized, appraised, and recovered. And, upon the proclamation *siquis plus dare voluerit*, Frampton offered £15 above the appraisement, and he was allowed [to be] the bidder and charged to the crown and the informers. And, though these goods were seized, part by one and part by the other informer, yet they were all put into one information and appraisement. And there was one recovery for both, but the bidder had two distinct writs of delivery, one for the wool and the East India goods, which was last in time, and the other for the other goods and carried that for the uncustomed goods to the defendant Beverton. And he showed it to him, and demanded those goods, and offered to pay him his moiety, having paid the queen's moiety.

But Beverton refused to deliver those goods to him unless Frampton would pay him the moiety of the appraisal value of the wool and the East India goods also, for which there had been a recovery and were included in the appraisement and sale to Frampton, which Frampton paid him accordingly. And then he demanded those goods to be delivered, which Beverton, after he had gotten the whole that was due to the seizers for all the goods, then told Frampton that the East India goods, by order of the Commissioners of the Customs had been removed out of the warehouse to London and thence he must have them. And coming thither, he found that the goods so removed were not the same that were in the appraisement, neither in quantity or species. And, therefore, he moved the court that Beverton, who had received the seizer's moiety for all and had paid the queen's moiety or part for the whole, might deliver to him the wool and the East India goods, there being a great deficiency in quantity of the East India goods.

Beverton insisted that, the goods being removed to London, he could not answer for the deficiency, nor did he demand the whole for both seizures, but he confessed he had received the money for the whole.

And the court, being of the opinion that the buyer, having bought and paid for all, ought to have all and that the seizers, having seized all, are answerable for all, ordered Beverton to deliver all to the bidder. And, if he will suffer the goods to be taken out of his hands by color or pretense of any order or authority from the Commissioners of the Customs, who have nothing to do with goods seized, appraised, recovered, and sold in and by this court in a judicial manner, he must be answerable for them, else the jurisdiction and justice of this court is eluded, the profitable course of bidding (much opposed and discountenanced at the Custom House), though of great advantage to the revenue, discouraged and the right and property of the subject evaded and prejudiced.

[Other copies of this report: Georgetown Univ. Law Sch. MS. B88–10, p. 1117.]

441

Montagu's Case

(Ex. 1714)

In this case, the post fine in issue was payable to the plaintiff.

Lincoln's Inn MS. Misc. 539, f. [210v]

Sir James Montagu, on his behalf, moved that Mr. Montagu, being lord of the liberty of Stepney and entitled to all post fines within that liberty, might have a post fine set over to him which became due upon a fine levied of lands which only lay within the liberty but the persons that levied and were parties to the fine for the greater security mentioned the same to be Stepney and Hackney, whereas it appeared by affidavit and the certificate of the Deputy of the Treasurer's Remembrancer that the lands whereof the fines were levied did all really and truly lie within the liberty of Stepney and none of them in Hackney or elsewhere out of the liberty, but, in regard that Hackney was mentioned in the fine, it not being in the *nomine villarum* of the liberty, the Foreign Opposer refused, as in duty he ought, for what appeared before him to set that post fine over to Mr. Montagu's liberty, the law being clear that, in all cases where any part of the land whereof a fine is levied does really lie out of the liberty, the whole post fine in such a case belongs to the crown or its lessee or grantee. But it was considered that, if the parties to the fine, for caution's sake, will mention other towns or places in the fine wherein really and in truth no part of the lands lies but all be within the liberty, it would be very hard and not agreeable to equity or justice or law that, for such caution's sake only between the parties, the lord of the liberty should lose his post fine, the crown having no loss when, in truth, no lands lie out of the liberty.

And, thereupon, the court, in this case, ordered the post fine to be set over to the liberty, as, in the like case, it was done three or four years ago in the Case of Lord Pelham for his liberties in Sussex.[1]

But Lord Pelham's Case was really that he was seised in fee of one liberty and but the lessee for years of another, and the fine was levied of lands which [. . .] lay in both liberties, but, when his bailiff claimed he could not say in which of the liberties by particulars the lands lay so as to have the post fines set over to either of the liberties in certain, yet, since it appeared that all the lands in the fine lay in both liberties and nothing in the guildable, it was but just he should have the post fine, for the crown had no loss, nothing belonging to it, but all was granted away.

[Other copies of this report: Georgetown Univ. Law Sch. MS. B88–10, p. 1125.]

442

Griffith v. Edwards

(Ex. 1714)

The question in this case was whether an assize judge can order an amendment to a sheriff's return at nisi prius sittings in reference to a verdict of viewers.

Lincoln's Inn MS. Misc. 539, f. [205]

12 February 1713[/14].

Dodd [moved] in arrest of judgment:

First, the Act of Parliament, for amending the law, 4 & 5 Anne, 236,[2] the writ of *distringas* is ill awarded in regard the viewers said not six of the first twelve, as the Act directs;

Second, there was no special return on the *distringas*, as the Act directs; 1 Rolle's, *Error*, 798, 799, *quidam venerunt et alium non venerunt* is bad;[3]

Third, *distringas juratores de Comitatu Salopiae ita quod habeant corpora apud in comitatu tuo*, and yet that Poole which is *Comitatu* Montgomery by a special return upon the same certificate that a view has been had according to the command of the writ and here there is no such special return made to the judge of assize nor the court, but only that *executio istius brevis patet in quod panello hac brevi annexo*, which answers not the Act, which is directory and mandatory and introductive of a new way of proceeding.

---

[1] *Lord Raby v. Lord Pelham* (Ex. 1709), see above, Case Nos. 334, 334a.

[2] Stat. 4 & 5 Ann., c. 3, s. 8 (*SR*, VIII, 459).

[3] *Blodwell v. Edwards* (1596), 1 Rolle, Abr., *Error*, pl. L, 2, p. 799, also Moore K.B. 430, 72 E.R. 675, Croke Eliz. 509, 78 E.R. 758, Noy 35, 74 E.R. 1005.

Jeffreys, pro querente: If it is not a special *distringas*, then it is general. And so as to the return, but it is amendable by 18 Eliz.,[1] being a return, though an imperfect return.

Lechmere, pro querente: Here are right viewers pursuant to the Act. Second, special returns are not necessary. The record [is] not of this court, and it comes hither back, a general return. Third, *comitatu tuo non constat* that Poole may not be *in comitatu*. Surely, the return is amendable. The sheriff is still before the court until judgment. Pery and Johnson, in this court.[2]

[It was] insisted upon after the verdict [by] *Dodd*, first, that it appears by the record that Poole is in Montgomeryshire, second, the return is to be to the judge below, not to the court, third, it is amendable how it comes thither that a view was had. (Query whether 18 Eliz. can extend to this new law.)

Distringas sex juratores in hac brevi primo nominatum. Neither is good, the writ nor the return; [it will] stay until moved by the plaintiff next term.

Amendment of the *distringas* was ordered *nisi causa* this day.

Serjeant *Chesshyre*, against the amendment, mentions Scott and Pygram's Case.[3]

Objection: Here is a mistrial, and the jury was not bound to attend. The Statute 18 Eliz., ca. 12,[4] ties up the trial before the chief baron, and not the justices of assize, and so there was no trial at all. And here is a *tales*, which makes the case stronger against an amendment. There is no instance of a like amendment. 2 Cro. 89, Rolls and Bettonshire; a jury was summoned in the queen's time, and the trial was by a *tales* in the king's time, and it was bad; 2 Cro. 141 confirms that authority; but, it being after *in nullo est erratum* pleaded, no [writ of] *certiorari* [lies], 161, 162, the same book, Comyn and Kyneto, because in the King's Bench. Dyer 97; there was a jury and a trial; afterwards, a return of process, in error, was not amended. Michaelmas term 1699, King's Bench, Laicon Child and Harvey; a distraint was returned [. . .]; 3 Cro. 622, trespass; Moor 681; 1 Brownl. 74; defendants may not amend. These go to the substance, not amendable by reason of dam[ages] to a third person or to attaint the jury. The distraint was before the justices, and no issues are returnable against them. But, if that amendment [be allowed], the jury [was] defective; [they would be] liable to issues being tried. Rolle's [Abr.], *Amendment*, Bull's Case, in [an action of] ejectment; a man and wife, £20 costs; if amended, they pay costs.[5]

---

[1] Stat. 18 Eliz. I, c. 14 (*SR*, IV, 625).

[2] *Perry v. Johnson* (Ex. 1714), Georgetown Univ. Law Sch. MS. B88–10, p. 1129, note also *Perry v. Johnson* (H.L. 1713), Georgetown Univ. Law Sch. MS. B88–10, p. 1017.

[3] *Scott, qui tam v. Pigram* (Ex. 1708), see above, Case No. 302.

[4] Stat. 18 Eliz. I, c. 12 (*SR*, IV, 623–634).

[5] *Knowles v. Beckingshaw* (1605), Croke Jac. 89, 79 E.R. 76; *Read v. Potter* (1606), Croke Jac. 138, 141, 79 E.R. 121, 122; *Comyn v. Kyneto* (1607), Croke Jac. 161, 79 E.R.

Ettrick, on the same side: No amendment [can be] here by the common law or statute. 8 rep. 156b.[1] No clerk's faults are amendable but in the same term. And he observes the order of the Statute of Amendments and the judges' application to Parliament for amendments. 8 rep. [*blank*]. Ten causes at common law are not amendable, of which an insufficient trial is one and a mistrial is the same.

Objection: 32 Hen. VIII, ca. [*blank*],[2] that helps jeofails, is no help of the court.

He relies upon 2 Cro. 89; 2 Cro. 396, distress, between Fowkes and John Child.[3] If this distress as now returned, lords exercise jurisdiction and [allow] amendments or give judgment, as they please; if the court below do not amend, the lords may, and ought not to be foreclosed.

Lechmere, same side: The Statute of Jeofails is out of the case. The record is gone to the lords. As to an amendment, this is not the judgment of this court, but of the Exchequer Chamber. There is no instance of a Common Pleas judgment affirmed in the King's Bench and brought in Parliament that the Common Bench amended it. And this court here cannot, for that reason, amend this. A distress is amendable by the record of a plea roll, but the record itself and not the transcript before the Lords. At the King's Bench, March 1672, in point, and, in judgment of law, a record [was] removed. How does this matter stand in Parliament? [Upon a] *certiorari* at the prayer of the plaintiff in error and, before the defendant in error [responds, there may be an] amendment to make good a diminution. And, when a defendant is in court, he may allege a diminution. 1 Leo. 22, Darrell and Thyn.[4]

This amendment is not to be come at, because the record itself is before the Lords, who, if [it be] amendable, may amend it or, if helped as jeofails, they may give a judgment. The superior court only must amend. [In] practice, the difference is where an error is assigned in the process after the writ of error or in the roll, the Lords must amend before the lower court alters the diminution. Cro. Car. 91, Cole's Case. He observes that case is an error *dehors* the record; two diminutions and *certiorari*s were awarded and credit given to the second *certiorari* must be so in nature, though not in words. The defendant must make himself a party to [the writ of] error before he be entitled to have anything because

141; *Anonymous* (1554), 1 Dyer 97, 73 E.R. 212; *Child v. Harvey* (1700), 12 Modern 274, 306, 88 E.R. 1317, 1339, 1 Salkeld 48, 91 E.R. 48, Carthew 506, 90 E.R. 890, 1 Lord Raymond 511, 91 E.R. 1241; *Clerk v. Clerk* (1598), Croke Eliz. 622, 78 E.R. 863; *Anonymous* (1603), Moore K.B. 681, 72 E.R. 836; *King v. King* (1600), 1 Rolle, Abr., *Amendment*, pl. D, 4, p. 202, also Croke Eliz. 776, 78 E.R. 1006.

[1] *Blackamore's Case* (1610), 8 Coke Rep. 156, 77 E.R. 710.

[2] Stat. 32 Hen. VIII, c. 30 (*SR*, III, 786–787).

[3] *Knowles v. Beckingshaw* (1605), *ut supra*; *Fowks v. Child* (1616), Croke Jac. 396, 79 E.R. 338.

[4] *Dayrel v. Thinn* (1584), 1 Leonard 22, 74 E.R. 20.

he asks nothing of the Lords but an amendment in court. The acts of Parliament direct amendments in error to be by affirming judges. 8 Hen. VI, 12; judges *a quo* [have] no power to amend. The Statute 15 Hen. VI is to the like purpose.[1]

There is no precedent that an amendment [was allowed] under these circumstances, nor [is it] showed that [it is] amendable. Here is a mistrial upon the process.

The Chief Baron [Ward] was the judgment of *Nisi Prius*, but not of Assize; these are different capacities. Yelverton 15; an award of *tales* by a judge where the sheriff was commanded to return was a bad distraint.[2] It gave no authority to the Chief Baron to award a *tales* when there was no judge of Assize. Salkeld [*blank*].

[There are two questions]: first, whether the *distringas* is amendable; second, whether it is amendable in this case.

First, the trial is upon the *distringas*, and [it is the] foundation of the judge's authority, and it is not alterable by the judge. And this is the reason of things not alterable at common law until the Statute. The fault in a writ of error is not amendable. He observes the Statute of *Nisi Prius*, 13 Edw. I. The justices *prius venerit*; the trial was upon the *venire* [*facias*] until 43 Edw. III, ca. 11. After that, the trial was upon the *distringas*. Trials in Middlesex were at the bar [of the court] until the Statute 8 Eliz., ca. 22, and there by qualifications.[3]

And he observes the *distringas* in question, and, as thus, what the sheriff and the judge did was without authority.

And [it was] not a legal amended distringas upon these grounds. First, the judge must have the authority to amend. Child and Harvey, Michaelmas [term] 11 Will. III, in a scire facias in a recognizance distraint a die Sancti Trinitatis in tres septimanas nisi prius venerit, and this was a day after tres septimanas, the plea roll and the day en banc right [was] held per curiam not amendable because [there was] no authority to try the cause. Yelverton 118; the omission of the sheriff's name on the distringas was not to be amended. Littleton 253, Blackmore, distringas apud Castrum, habeas corpus apud the Guildhall of Newcastle, and it was not amendable [because of the] defect of authority in the sheriff or judge.[4] [It is] not amendable for defaulting jurors [or] loose issues. But if it were amended, he is liable to issues.

[There may be] no amendment here after a writ of error brought, but it must be in the superior court, though the practice lately is otherwise. Bro., *Amend-*

---

[1] *Wolfe v. Hole* (1627), Croke Car. 91, 79 E.R. 681, also Hutton 92, 123 E.R. 1123; Stat. 8 Hen. VI, c. 12 (*SR*, II, 248–249); Stat. 15 Hen. VI, c. 5 (*SR*, II, 297–298).

[2] *Corne v. Pastow* (1602), Yelverton 16, 80 E.R. 12, also Croke Eliz. 894, 78 E.R. 1117.

[3] Stat. 13 Edw. I, Westminster II, c. 30 (*SR*, I, 85–86); Stat. 42 Edw. III, c. 11 (*SR*, I, 389–390); Stat. 18 Eliz. I, c. 12 (*SR*, IV, 623–624).

[4] *Child v. Harvey* (1700), *ut supra*; *Holsworth v. Proctor* (1607), Yelverton 110, 80 E.R. 75; *Blackamore v. Clotworthy* (1630), Littleton 253, 124 E.R. 233.

ment, 51; 2 Edw. IV, 46.[1] [There is a] question of practice here on writs of error in Parliament.

Ward, same side: The plea roll and the *nisi prius* roll are right; the [writ of] *distringas* is bad, and neither are amendable at common law or by statute. General words in amendments are restrained to the parties. Godbolt, Tolling's Case.[2]

Objection: 3 Modern[3] reaches not this case.

Solution: [There is] no omission of time or place, but it is a substantial error.

In the case of Cro. Eliz. 466, the want of *distringas* was amended in the same, but not another term. Yelverton, 110; Rowland's Case, 5 rep. *Juratum* the warrant, but not the only warrant, for a *distringas* is one. Cro. Car. 274; the *distringas* here was wrong; there was no warrant to the sheriff, judge, or jury. Cro. Eliz. 622; the *venire* was amended by the *distringas*, but not so as to a *distringas* in another term. Fourteen misprisions were not helped.[4]

Serjeant *Pratt*, for the plaintiff: Objection: The record is in the House of Lords, and this court cannot amend.

Solution: It is the constant course of the Common Pleas.

Objection: It is a new judgment in the Exchequer Chamber.

Solution: *Non prosequi.*

Objection: Two diminutions lie.

Solution: [They do] not to rectify an ill *distringas* because it may be helped by a second [writ of] *certiorari.*

Objection: A superior court may make an amendment.

Solution: The practice is otherwise.

Objection: Whatever issue be altered or jury attainted, [there can be] no amendment.

Solution: He agrees with that, but that is not this case.

He agrees it is an improper expression, but the judge is the same and the jury is the same and the jury is punishable, though *tales*. No reason against that was ever urged. It is a mere slip, and it goes not to the right, and the issues are spared. 3 Mod. 78 is a full authority, both for law or reason.[5] *Juratum* without *distringas* is good.

Serjeant *Pengelly*, for the plaintiff: Objection: It is not amendable because it is after [a writ of] error.

---

1 YB Mich. 37 Hen. VI, f. 12, pl. 2 (1458), 1 Brooke, Abr., *Amendment*, pl. 51.

2 *Tollyn and Taylor's Case* (1627), Godbolt 382, 78 E.R. 225.

3 *Jackson v. Warren* (1685), 3 Modern 78, 87 E.R. 50.

4 *Weare v. Woodliff* (1596), Croke Eliz. 466, 78 E.R. 718; *Holdsworth v. Procter* (1607), Yelverton 110, 80 E.R. 75, also Croke Jac. 188, 79 E.R. 164; *Rowland v. James* (1593), 5 Coke Rep. 41, 77 E.R. 118; *Le Marchant v. Rawson* (1632), Croke Car. 274, 278, 79 E.R. 840, 843, also W. Jones 303, 82 E.R. 160; *Clerk v. Clerk* (1598), Croke Eliz. 622, 78 E.R. 863.

5 *Jackson v. Warren* (1685), *ut supra*.

Solution: The practice is otherwise.

Objection: The judgment was in the Exchequer Chamber.

Solution: That is not so but for costs only, without touching the matter.

He insists that, ever since the Statute 8 Hen. VI, and Blackmore's [Case], 161, 162, amendments [are made] by inferior courts as well as superior [courts]. Dyer 105; Kel. 16; Palmer 198, 258, 262. The doubts are cleared. Hardress 505 is full as to this point.[1] For an amendment after a writ of error at the defendant's desire, costs are added. And he lays stress of Hale's sayings there. So the thing is amendable.

Objection: The [writ of] *distringas* is the authority to try [the case].

Solution: It is not so, but only [authority] to convene the jury, and the *nisi prius* roll is the judge's authority to judge of *nisi prius*, and assizes are the same. And the Statute 8 Eliz. gives the authority, and the chief baron is a judge of assize in the judgment of the law. At most, [it is an] improper expression, and it is amendable, everything else [being] right. [The Statute] 8 & 9 Will. III saves jurors [and] issues; neither are place nor time in a *distringas* amended in this case. Cro. El. 760, 761; 1 Keble 258 agree with 3 Mod. 78. The *jurata* is the warrant to judge; the [writ of] distress [is] amendable. Cro. Car. 32. And these cases answer Child and Harvey.[2] The return *nisi prius*, return awarded on record, and the writ both [. . .], the writ is not amendable because there is nothing to amend it by. Lord Kinsale and Francis Compton, 10 Will. III, King's Bench; the *venire* was *teste* before issue was joined, and, after [a writ of] error was brought, it was amended in the Common Bench, and the *teste* and the return were both amended by a rule of the Common Bench dated 12th June 5 Anne [1706].

Mr. Recorder [*Peter King*], same side: This writ is in the court's possession and never out nor in the House of Lords. It is certainly amendable, and [there can be] no amendment where there is nothing to amend. Yet an original writ [can be] amended from [. . .]. 4 Leo., fo. 12, pl. 47; Cro. Eliz. 119; Hobt. 249; Moor. 5, 1 Anderson 24, Bendlows 33. Original writs [can be] amended without anything to amend by court where law altered, not amended. The nisi prius roll was amended by the plea roll after the trial. 8 rep. 162; nisi prius '100' amended to '£100'. Michaelmas [term] 8 Will., [in an action of] ejectment against seven, all pleaded not guilty; the plea roll was five, the nisi prius roll was seven, and it was so amended. Littleton 349, Hetly 164; a name was transposed, the plea roll

---

[1] Stat. 8 Hen. VI, c. 15 (*SR*, II, 252); *Blackamore's Case* (1610), *ut supra*; *Pinde v. Norton* (1554), 1 Dyer 105, 73 E.R. 231; *Chapelyn v. Alleyn* (1621), Palmer 197, 81 E.R. 1040; *Mason v. Molineux* (1621), Palmer 258, 81 E.R. 1071; *Friend, ex dem. Lady Dacres v. Duke of Richmond* (Ex. 1669), Hardres 505, 145 E.R. 570, also Exch. Repts. *tempore* Car. II, 83.

[2] Stat. 8 & 9 Will. III, c. 10 (*SR*, VII, 201); *Wolley v. Mosely* (1600), Croke Eliz. 760, 78 E.R. 992; *Devereux v. Underhill* (1662), 1 Keble 258, 83 E.R. 932; *Jackson v. Warren* (1685), *ut supra*; *Smith v. Wade* (1626), Croke Car. 32, 79 E.R. 631, also Hutton 81, 123 E.R. 1115; *Child v. Harvey* (1700), *ut supra*.

was right, and the nisi prius roll was amended. 5 rep. 42; [a writ of] distress is amendable by the venire. 2 Cro. 443; 5 rep. 41, Rowland's Case; Hutton 81, Cro. Car. 32; Easter [term] 4 Anne, Palliott and Parson; the distress did not mention what plea or action; it was amended. 3 Mod. 78.[1]

Dodd, same side: He supports the judgment. There is nothing to be amended here. That is in the Lords' House, and what process to return is questionable.

Objection: To amend in the Lords' House.

Solution: It is amendable here, as [is the] practice. There is no error in the record removed. [It is] no judgment in the Exchequer Chamber.

Objection: A judge is not to enlarge his jurisdiction.

Solution: *Nisi prius* is amended by the plea roll. Hobt. 246, amendment;[2] the acts for amendment extend to the inferior court as well as the superior.

Ettrick replies: There is a judgment in the Exchequer Chamber. As to Hardress, [the writ of] error brought was not carried up. [The writ of] distress is the authority to return the jury, not the judge's authority. 18 Eliz., for trials, extends not to justices of assize.

Objection: A clerk's omission is not helped unless by *nescience*, no answer to the jurors' issues, lost rates forfeited, default issues.

Lechmere replies: [There is] no answer to the intermediate judgment of the Exchequer Chamber for costs with *remittitur* and so [there are] two judgments, and that renders the matter not amendable by the court. Error in the Common Bench and non prossed error in Parliament is no precedent that the Common Bench amended the [*blank*]. And he differences Hardress' case that nothing [was] done upon [the writ of] error.

Objection: The process here is in this court and not in the Lords' House.

Solution: If there is no diminution, the court here cannot amend the record.

Objection: The authority of the Chief Baron as *nisi prius* [judge] and justice of assize is the same.

Solution: The Chief Baron is not a *nisi prius* judge. [This is] no answer to the *tales* and issues. 3 Mod. [is] strange, but that was upon a motion; the want of authority in judges.

---

[1] *Anonymous* (C.P. 1585), 4 Leonard 12, 74 E.R. 694; *Rookesby's Case* (1588), Croke Eliz. 119, 78 E.R. 376; *Cuppledick v. Terwhit* (1618), Hobart 249, 80 E.R. 396; *Vaughan v. Lord Burgh* (1549), Moore K.B. 5, 72 E.R. 400, 1 Anderson 24, 123 E.R. 334, Benloe 33, 123 E.R. 28; *Blackamore's Case* (1610), *ut supra*; *Anonymous v. Malin* (1630), Littleton 349, 124 E.R. 279, Hetley 164, 124 E.R. 424; *Churcher v. Wright* (1617), Croke Jac. 443, 79 E.R. 378, also 1 Rolle, Abr., *Amendment*, pl. E, 4, p. 204; *Rowland v. James* (1593), *ut supra*; *Smith v. Wade* (1626), *ut supra*; *Jackson v. Warren* (1685), *ut supra*.

[2] *Harris v. Ap John*, Hobart 246, 80 E.R. 391; *Leese v. Arrowsmith* (1618), Hobart 246, 80 E.R. 392.

Salkeld: [There is] no answer to Child and Harvey's Case. And the Bishop of Worcester's Case[1] is distinguished from that case. This amendment [would] subject the jury to an attaint.

[On] Tuesday 16 June, I [EDWARD WARD] put this point to the two chief justices, Powys, Tracy, and Powys, Jr., at Serjeants' Inn. And the two chief justices and some of the other judges seemed very much to doubt whether it be amendable because the Chief Baron that tried the cause had [not] any authority to try it, for, if he that tried the cause was not a justice of assize, any other judge might have as well tried it as the Chief Baron and the want of the *distringas* is helped, but not where void. And the plea roll and *nisi prius* roll being right helped not. I showed them three [*blank*], and they considered until Thursday.

Distringas for a jury to appear 25 November *nisi Edwardus Ward, miles, Dominus Capitalis Baro huius Scaccarii per formam statuti inde providi die lune 24 Novembris instantis apud Westmonasterium in loco habere ubi curia Scaccarii [. . .] prius venerit.* Judgment [was] in the Exchequer Chamber upon a *non prosequi, quod defendens sit in misericordia* for not prosecuting his writ of error and the defendant in error to go without day and to recover £15 10s. 10d. for damages and costs sustained for delay of execution being allowed to him *iuxta formam statuti* and that the record be remitted into the Court of Exchequer for execution thereupon to be made *iuxta formam statuti.*

[Other copies of this report: Georgetown Univ. Law Sch. MS. B88–10, p. 1127.]

Lincoln's Inn MS. Misc. 539, f. [214v]

7 May [1714].

Jeffreys, pro querente, answers the former objections.

First objection: The word *duodecim* is wanting in the *distringas.*

Solution: Roll's, *Amendment*, 204,[2] helps it, and [it is] amendable and to be intended the first twelve that appeared.

Second objection: The sheriff appointed a view at Poole, which is out of the county.

Solution: It does not appear that Poole is out of the county, for, though there is a Poole in Montgomery, there may be a Poole also in Shropshire, and then it is well and to be so intended.

Third objection: It is the sheriff who is to certify the judges of assize that a view has been had, which is not done nor endorsed as it ought; otherwise, it is not good.

Solution: It is not necessary the certificate should be in writing; it might be by parol. And [it is] intended to be done. If [it be] not done, yet it is helped by 18

[1] *Bishop of Worcester's Case* (1696), 1 Salkeld 48, 91 E.R. 47.

[2] *Churcher v. Wright* (1617), *ut supra.*

Eliz.; where there is no return, but blank, the writ [is] good. 3 Cro. 466; 2 Cro. 188.[1]

Dodd, for the defendant: This is a new law and must be observed. The first six were directed to be taken and ought so to appear and be returned to be so according to the command of the writ.

Second, the *distringas* was to the sheriff of Salop, and he had no power to show in Poole in Montgomeryshire. But this is not said that Poole is in Montgomery.

Third, he ought to have certified to the judge, which must appear on the record by an endorsement on the writ. This is a new law introductive of new proceedings, and no statute of amendment touches this nor helps anything in this case. The *distringas* read was directed to the sheriff of Salop. *Sex vel pluries juratores in brevi primo nominatas videre locum* in question 22 July to meet at Tidder's house situate in Poole *in comitatu tuo*, and two showers were appointed *iuxta formam statuti nuper edit' et provis' et quam litarum hoc praecept' fueris execut' justic' nostris ad assisas constare facias executio brevis patet in quaedam pannello hac brevis annexo.* Since the new Statute, the practice [is] according to the Act.

Jeffreys replies, *ut supra*: If six were first summoned and did not appear, any may have the view *non constat.* But there is a Poole in Shropshire. It is not necessary that it should *constare* to the judge that a view was had [. . .] that subsequent laws [be] expounded *prout* precedent. No exception was taken by the defendant at the trial that a lawful view was not had.

Search for precedents, and move on the first day of next term.

[Other copies of this report: Georgetown Univ. Law Sch. MS. B88–10, p. 1153.]

443

Wilkinson v. Archbishop of York

(Ex. 1714)

A clergyman cannot be deprived of his benefice if he returns to it after serving in the royal navy.

Lincoln's Inn MS. Misc. 539, f. [215], pl. 2

In a [motion for a writ of] prohibition touching Armly Chapel, for that the plaintiff, being duly invested as chaplain of that chapel in Yorkshire, was made a chaplain in the queen's navy and, attending in that service and having provided duly for the service in the donative [chapel], was presented in the Archbishop's Court for non-residence in the donative in order to be deprived of the donative.

[1] Stat. 18 Eliz. I, c. 14 (*SR*, IV, 625); *Weare v. Woodliff* (1596), *ut supra*; *Holdsworth v. Procter* (1607), *ut supra*.

And, upon a suggestion of the Statute 21 Hen. VIII, ca. [*blank*], § 28,[1] that that Statute shall not extend to persons in the king's service beyond the seas and the order of Council *tempore* Car. II, 25 April 1679, whereby the king taking into consideration the encouragement that it was that all persons then or thereafter in Holy Orders that go to sea or any of the plantations or with ambassadors or others shall, during their absence in such employment, hold and enjoy the full profits of their benefices and, at their return, be restored to their benefices and profits.

Curia: The prohibition is granted *nisi causa* first day next term, staying in the meantime.

[Other copies of this report: Georgetown Univ. Law Sch. MS. B88–10, p. 1160.]

444

Owen v. Brett

(Ex. 1714)

Amendments to pleadings should not be allowed after a long delay, especially after setting the case for trial.

Lincoln's Inn MS. Misc. 539, f. [215v], pl. 1

[An action of] *indebitatus assumpsit* and *insimul computasset* [was brought] seven years ago, and no trial was had, but issue was joined, and [there were] notices of trial here and an injunction in Wales.

Serjeant *Lloyd*, for the plaintiff, moves to amend a sum of 154 instead of 172 and the date of a note upon which the action was grounded.

Marriott reports from other courts that [there can be] no such amendment after so long a time and after so many notices of trials and motions of 28 November 1712 [and] 10 May 1714 to amend.

In this case, [it was] denied, [and] no further order for amendment [was given], *non obstante* the case of robbery of a hundred, 3 Levinz, and that *non assumpsit infra sex annos* may be pleaded.

Per curiam, no amendment [was allowed].

[Other copies of this report: Georgetown Univ. Law Sch. MS. B88–10, p. 1161.]

1 Stat. 21 Hen. VIII, c. 13, s. 17 (*SR*, III, 295).

445

Carrington v. Hornby

(Ex. 1714)

The question in this case was what fees are due to a sheriff for money levied by him upon an outlawry.

Lincoln's Inn MS. Misc. 539, f. [213]

A motion was made on the behalf of the sheriff of Cheshire for fees for money levied upon a [writ of] outlawry against Hornby. And [the question was] whether any and what fees [were] due in this case of an outlawry and who shall pay them, whether the pleader of a former title having put in his plea and security and having an order thereupon to restore the money levied upon a [writ of] *levari* [*facias*] presented by the prosecutor of the outlawry on the estate seized and pleaded to, he levied no money, but took a bond as the terre tenant's security or the prosecutor of the outlawry or whether the sheriff shall have any fees without an agreement. [It is] too hard upon the pleader to pay for the unjust seizing of his land.

For the sheriff, [it was argued that] security taken is an ease and favor of the terre tenant and the same reason [goes] with money levied. [See the] precedents 10 December 1709, in an extent, Cackin's Case, a bankrupt, the first precedent assignment pleaded poundage paid by the pleader; Prior's Case; Mason and the Sheriff of Montgomery's Case; Sir Thomas Stanley's Case, 23 January 1709, the sheriff was paid his poundage; Stanley was outlawed at the suit of Jet and lands were seized and [a writ of] *levari* [*facias*] issued and bonds were taken for the profits, and yet the terre tenants were forced to pay fees. 10 December 1709, Cackin's Case, upon a seizure of goods for the debt of a bankrupt to the crown, and a prior title was pleaded to those by the creditors, and, upon that plea, the court ordered restitution, the sheriff deducting fees. Samson's Case; a seizure for a debt to the crown and in aid for him, and he paid poundage.[1]

Per curiam: There is no power to compel a prosecutor, though he be in the nature of a relator, to pay poundage nor any reason to compel the pleader to pay or allow. The sheriff must do his duty at his peril.

[Other copies of this report: Georgetown Univ. Law Sch. MS. B88–10, p. 1163.]

---

1 *Pryor's Case* (Ex. 1711), see above, Case No. 390; *Montgomery Sheriff v. Mason* (Ex. 1711), see above, Case No. 396; *Attorney General v. Pearce* (Ex. 1707), see above, Case No. 277a.

Index of Names

[These references are to case numbers, not page numbers.]

Subject Index

[These references are to case numbers, not page numbers.]